Statistical Record OF Asian Americans

Statistical Record OF Asian Americans

Susan B. Gall and
Timothy L. Gall, Editors

Gale Research Inc. • *DETROIT* • *WASHINGTON, D.C.* • *LONDON*

Statistical Record of Asian Americans was produced by
Eastword Publications Development, Inc., Cleveland, Ohio

Gale Research Inc. Staff

Carol DeKane Nagel, *Developmental Editor*
Lawrence W. Baker, *Senior Developmental Editor*

Mary Beth Trimper, *Production Director*
Evi Seoud, *Assistant Production Manager*
Shanna P. Heilveil, *Production Assistant*

Cynthia Baldwin, *Art Director*
Arthur Chartow, *Technical Design Services Manager*
Bernadette M. Gornie, *Cover Designer*
C. J. Jonik, *Keyliner*

This book is printed on acid-free paper that meets the minimum requirements of American National Standard for Information Sciences--Permanence Paper for Printed Library Materials, ANSI Z39.48-1984.

This book is printed on recycled paper that meets Environmental Protection Agency standards.

ISBN 0-8103-8918-5
Printed in the United States of America

Published simultaneously in the United Kingdom
by Gale Research International Limited
(An affiliated company of Gale Research Inc.)

The trademark **ITP** is used under license.

Table of Contents

Expanded Table of Contents

Chapter 1 – Attitudes and Opinions *(continued)*

Chapter 5 – Education *(continued)*

Chapter 7 – Health (*continued*)

Chapter 12 – Population and Vital Statistics (*continued*)

Preface

The American and Canadian Asian and Pacific Islander population segments have grown dramatically in the last two decades. According to the 1990 census in the United States, the number of persons of Asian and Pacific Islander descent doubled between 1980 and 1990, from 3.7 million to 7.2 million (2.7 percent of the total population). The 1991 Census of Canada shows similar growth: persons reporting Asian origins grew from 3.5 percent to 5.1 percent of the total in 1991. Students, researchers, journalists, government officials, and segments of the general public are increasingly interested in this significant and diverse force in American and Canadian societies, and as the interest grows, so too does demand for data. Although in many published compilations of data Asian/Pacific Islanders continue to be grouped in the "Other" category, a number of organizations that gather statistics are beginning to add a category for this ethnicity group to their survey instruments.

Statistical Record of Asian Americans presents a comprehensive record of the Asian/Pacific Islander population in a single compilation by bringing together data gathered by a wide variety of government, non-government, and Asian/Pacific Islander sources. Much of this data has received only limited dissemination until now.

RANGE OF SOURCES

The data compiled for the *Statistical Record of Asian Americans* have come from a wide variety of sources, including periodical literature, government publications, unpublished government sources, and reports and studies from non-government and Asian/Pacific Islander organizations. In the United States, some government agencies began adding the Asian/Pacific Islander category to their databases during the 1980s, expanding somewhat the pool of available sources. However, there are very few areas in which the diversity of the Asian/Pacific Islander population segment is reflected in further breakdown of data by ethnic group (such as Chinese, Japanese, Korean, Asian Indian, Filipino). In a few subject areas, such as religion and sports and recreation, statistical data on Asian/Pacific Islander participation is extremely limited.

In Canada, ethnicity data are not tracked by as broad a range of government agencies and other organizations as in the United States; for example, data on participation in military service, higher education (including law and medical schools), and health care were not readily available by racial/ethnic group.

Because the Asian and Pacific Islander population segment is projected to continue its rapid growth, accurate, accessible data will be required for those in government and non-government organizations who want to reach Asian/Pacific Islanders, either to assess and meet needs or to provide products and services. *Statistical Record of Asian Americans* augments the profile provided by the U.S. and Canada censuses, to give the interested and concerned public a more complete picture of the impact and diversity of the Asian/Pacific Islander populations in the United States and Canada.

COVERAGE OF ETHNIC NATIONALITY GROUPS

A few government agencies and Asian/Pacific Islander organizations do break the Asian/Pacific Islander category down into nationality groups. The Asian ethnic groups used by the U.S. Bureau of Census—Chinese, Japanese, Filipino, Asian Indian, Hawaiian, Korean, Samoan, Tongan, Guamanian, Vietnamese, Other Asian (specify), and Other Pacific Islander (specify)—are rarely used by other data-gathering organizations. In fact, the category "Asian" is a recent addition to many data-gathering instruments. Although the specific term varies (from simply "Asian" to "Asian/Pacific Islander" to numerous variations), in almost every instance the identification is done by the respondent himself or herself. It is therefore impossible to specify which countries of origin or ancestry are represented in any set of data. If the source from which the data were compiled offered any further information on the use of terms, it is provided in the footnotes.

COMPARATIVE RACE/ETHNICITY AND HISTORICAL DATA

Asian/Pacific Islanders represent one of several racial/ethnic groups profiled when data are reported. Whenever possible, entries in the *Statistical Record of Asian Americans* include data on whites, blacks, Hispanics, and native Americans for comparative purposes. In addition, data are presented broken down by sex whenever feasible, to provide the user with as complete a profile as space allows. Historical data are presented whenever meaningful, notably in "Immigration" and "Population and Vital Statistics."

A NOTE ON TERMINOLOGY AND COUNTRY NAMES

Because it is common to compare data from various U.S. Censuses of Population, it is helpful to know the history of the Asian categories in the decennial census survey. The Census of Population began in the United States in 1790 and included the categories "White," "Slave," and "Other." The first Asian category was "Chinese," added in 1870; in 1890, "Japanese" was added. The next change in the way Asians were counted did not come until 1950, when Filipinos were added to the survey. Also in 1950, the census added a line item "Other Race _____." In 1960, "Hawaiian" and "Part Hawaiian" were added as two separate lines on the form (Hawaii became a state in 1959). In 1970, this practice was discontinued and only "Hawaiian" remained on the survey. Also in 1970, "Korean" was added. In 1980, "Vietnamese," "Asian Indian," "Guamanian," and "Samoan" were added. The 1990 Census listed these nine Asian/Pacific Islander choices as well as an "Other A/PI _____" line where respondents could write in other ethnicity information.

The entries in the *Statistical Record of Asian Americans* present data according to the categories used by the organizations that gathered the data. This means, for example, that for immigration to the United States, data are presented for *Burma* and *Cambodia;* for immigration to Canada from the same geographic areas, for *Myanmar* and *Kampuchea*. After consulting with the Office of the U.S. Geographer and the Immigration and Naturalization Service, it became clear that data have been gathered using specific terminology chosen deliberately. (The U.S. government does not recognize the governments of

Myanmar and Kampuchea and therefore uses the nations' traditional names in documents.) Because the data are often self-reported, to alter terms used to describe countries of origin or ethnicity could change the implications of the data; organizations whose data are reported here concurred, expressing their wish that the terminology used to classify data not be edited.

ARRANGEMENT OF CHAPTERS

Entries are organized into chapters arranged alphabetically according to title. Within each chapter, sub-headings organize the entries under broad categories. To meet the needs of both the user with an interest in a general topic and the user with a specific question to answer, two Tables of Contents and a Comprehensive Index are provided. The first Table of Contents lists chapter titles and subheadings; the second, expanded, lists all entry titles in the book under the appropriate chapter title and subheading. The Comprehensive Index is by subject, nationality, and geographic locations.

BIBLIOGRAPHY

In this section, the editors have listed selected books and journals for further reading. The bibliography is organized by major Asian/Pacific Islander ethnic groups.

EDITORIAL ADVISORS

The editors humbly acknowledge the many and varied contributions of the Editorial Advisors, without whose expertise this volume would not have been possible. In their review of our work, the advisors offered helpful suggestions on sources of data and insights on ways to clarify the presentation of the data. After communicating with each of them over the course of this project, we count them as valued friends and colleagues who have deepened our understanding of the many facets of the diverse population segment known as "Asian American" and "Asian Canadian."

Cel Aguigui, Senior Information Specialist
U.S. Bureau of Census

Valerie Chow Bush, Executive Director
Asian American Journalists Association

Tony Chen, former Director of Asian Affairs
Republican National Committee

Lee S. Dutton, Librarian
Donn Hart Southeast Asia Collection
Founder's Memorial Library
Northern Illinois University

Naomi Engle, Reference Librarian
Asian Pacific Resource Center
Montebello Branch, Los Angeles County Public Library

William Fizet
Multiculturalism and Citizenship Canada

YuAn Kim, Commissioner for Asian/Pacific American Affairs
City of Philadelphia

Marjorie Lee, Director
Asian American Studies Center Reading Room
University of California at Los Angeles

Michael Liu, Executive Director
Asian American Resource Workshop

Wei Chi Poon, Head Librarian
Asian American Studies Library
University of California at Berkeley

Carlton Sagara
Asian American Resource Workshop

K. Scott Wong
Asian Studies Department
Williams College

Victor Wong, President
Vancouver Association of Chinese Canadians

Melinda Yee, National Director
Asian Pacific American Political Affairs
Clinton for President/Clinton Inaugural Committee

Elena Yu, Ph.D., M.P.H., Professor
Graduate School of Public Health
San Diego State University

ACKNOWLEDGMENTS

In addition to the Editorial Advisors, a special note of gratitude goes to Clarissa Tom at the Asian/ Pacific Islander Data Consortium Data Center. We also gratefully acknowledge the contributions of the following individuals, each of whom provided valuable assistance to us as we researched and compiled this volume:

Susan Au Allen, Pan Asian American Chamber of Commerce
Jane Badets, Ethnic Data Specialist, Decennial Census, Statistics Canada
Claudette Bennett, U.S. Bureau of Census, Current Population Studies
Matt Boehmer, Defense Manpower Data Center

Fred Bohme, U.S. Bureau of Census, History Branch

Marlene Daugherty, Office of Asian Congregational Enhancement, Presbyterian Church (USA)

Jennifer Day, U.S. Bureau of Census

Linda Gordon, Chief Statistician, Immigration and Naturalization Service

Dr. Vance Grant, Center for Education Statistics

Col. Douglas Hart, Office of the Assistant Secretary of Defense for Public Affairs

Tom Hester, U.S. Bureau of Justice Statistics

Ed Jimerson, Gallup Organization

Audrey Kobayashi, Ethnic Data Specialist, National Association of Japanese Canadians

Dr. Robert Mayberry, Minority Health Programs, Centers for Disease Control

Viviane Renaud, Ethnic Data Specialist, Decennial Census, Statistics Canada

Charles Smith, Executive Director, Asian American Hotel Owners Association

Merle Surosky, Office of Redress, Department of Justice

Ayala Tamir, Asian American Health Forum

Clarissa Tom, Asian Pacific Islander Data Consortium, Asian American Health Forum

Kevin Vaughan, Executive Director, City of Philadelphia Commission on Human Relations

Dr. Patricia E. White, National Science Foundation

Judy Young, Multiculturalism Canada

The editors acknowledge the following individuals who contributed at various stages of the project: Tony Arroyo, Orange County Public Library; Jane Cramer, Brooklyn College Library; Leonard Kniffel, *American Libraries* magazine; Luke Swindler, University of North Carolina at Chapel Hill; and James Tong, Detroit Public Library, who provided helpful insights at the earliest stages of planning; our staff members Judith Arth, and Brian Rajewski, and research and editorial assistant, Brendan Pham; John Schmittroth and Carol Nagel at Gale Research for support and inspiration; and special thanks to Arthur and Alice Gall, Joan Bevan, Nancy Benacci, and Susan Stern for their unique contributions.

Although every attempt has been made to leave no stone unturned in locating data on Asian/Pacific Islanders, we know there are hundreds of organizations collecting information which would enhance this volume. We welcome suggestions from users of this, the first edition of *Statistical Record of Asian Americans*.

Susan B. Gall

Timothy L. Gall

Editors

Statistical
Record
OF Asian
Americans

Attitudes and Opinions

AIDS and Sexuality

★ 1 ★

AIDS Education

Reported results, in percent, of a national survey asking eighth and tenth grade students the following question: "Since the beginning of the seventh grade, have you received instruction in school on AIDS?" Responses are by race/ethnicity.

Answer	Asian/Pacific Islander, %	White, %	Black, %	Hispanic, %	American Indian/ Alaskan, %	Other, %
Yes	30.2%	33.3%	40.2%	39.4%	50.1%	38.4%
No	39.5%	48.7%	41.9%	32.1%	24.8%	38.8%
Don't remember	30.3%	18.0%	18.0%	28.6%	25.1%	22.8%

Source: D. Michael Anderson and Gregory M. Christenson, "Ethnic Breakdown of AIDS–Related Knowledge and Attitudes from the National Adolescent Student Health Survey," *Journal of Health Education* 22, no. 1 (January/February 1991): 30. The sampling frame consisted of all fifty states and the District of Columbia from which a total of 217 schools were selected, representing approximately equal numbers of urban and rural schools. Over 11,000 students were in the sample; 3,617 completed the AIDS portion of the questionnaire.

★ 2 ★

AIDS Prevention Knowledge

Reported results, in percent, of a national survey asking eighth and tenth grade students a series of questions on their AIDS prevention knowledge. Responses are by race/ethnicity.

Behavior	Asian/ Pacific Islander	White	Black	Hispanic	American Indian/ Alaskan	Other
Does this behavior make infection LESS likely?						
"Using condoms (rubbers) during sex:"						
Yes*	76.4	88.3	84.3	75.0	75.4	74.8
No	14.7	5.6	11.6	14.8	6.4	12.0
Don't Know	8.9	6.1	4.0	10.2	18.2	13.3

[Continued]

★ 2 ★

AIDS Prevention Knowledge (Continued)

Reported results, in percent, of a national survey asking eighth and tenth grade students a series of questions on their AIDS prevention knowledge. Responses are by race/ethnicity.

Behavior	Asian/ Pacific Islander	White	Black	Hispanic	American Indian/ Alaskan	Other
"Not having sex:"						
Yes*	66.8	79.7	66.5	62.4	65.2	75.4
No	24.3	15.0	26.1	28.2	17.6	19.0
Don't Know	8.9	5.4	7.4	9.4	17.3	5.6
"Going to the bathroom after having sex:"						
Yes	11.7	6.4	16.7	9.7	18.9	18.4
No*	52.3	61.8	55.1	57.3	42.9	54.5
Don't Know	36.1	31.8	28.3	33.1	38.4	27.0
"Washing after having sex:"						
Yes	23.1	20.0	41.0	33.5	40.0	20.5
No*	49.5	52.5	41.0	36.4	33.1	46.1
Don't Know	27.4	27.5	18.1	30.1	26.9	33.4

*Indicates correct response
Source: D. Michael Anderson and Gregory M. Christenson, "Ethnic Breakdown of AIDS–Related Knowledge and Attitudes from the National Adolescent Student Health Survey," *Journal of Health Education* 22, no. 1 (January/February 1991): 30. The sampling frame consisted of all fifty states and the District of Columbia from which a total of 217 schools were selected, representing approximately equal numbers of urban and rural schools. Over 11,000 students were in the sample; 3,617 completed the AIDS portion of the questionnaire.

★ 3 ★

AIDS Risk Knowledge

Reported results, in percent, of a national survey asking eighth and tenth grade students a series of questions on AIDS risk knowledge, by race/ethnicity.

Question/answer	Asian/ Pacific Islander	White	Black	Hispanic	American Indian/ Alaskan	Other
"Does this behavior make infection MORE likely?"						
"Having sexual intercourse with someone who has AIDS:"						
Yes*	86.9	96.8	90.3	87.8	92.2	89.4
No	11.3	2.9	7.2	10.4	3.5	8.6
Don't Know	1.8	0.3	2.5	1.8	4.3	2.0

[Continued]

★ 3 ★

AIDS Risk Knowledge (Continued)

Reported results, in percent, of a national survey asking eighth and tenth grade students a series of questions on AIDS risk knowledge, by race/ethnicity.

Question/answer	Asian/ Pacific Islander	White	Black	Hispanic	American Indian/ Alaskan	Other
"Being in same classroom with someone who has AIDS:"						
Yes	3.8	4.3	5.9	5.0	0.0	5.1
No*	84.1	88.2	79.6	75.9	84.2	77.9
Don't Know	12.1	7.6	14.5	19.1	15.8	17.0
"Having more than one sex partner:"						
Yes*	75.0	85.0	74.1	75.8	85.3	82.9
No	17.3	7.2	15.4	11.4	10.4	8.1
Don't Know	7.7	7.7	10.6	12.9	4.3	9.1
"Having sex with someone who has had several sex partners:"						
Yes*	73.7	86.7	74.4	75.8	82.0	81.7
No	14.9	5.0	12.8	10.4	10.8	7.2
Don't Know	11.5	8.3	12.9	13.8	7.2	11.1
"A male having sex with another male:"						
Yes*	74.6	82.4	79.7	73.7	85.9	75.1
No	15.5	7.6	11.4	12.2	8.0	10.3
Don't Know	9.9	10.0	8.8	14.1	6.1	14.6
"Sharing drug needles:"						
Yes*	83.3	93.8	86.8	85.9	79.3	80.2
No	14.0	3.3	8.4	10.7	6.4	11.5
Don't Know	2.7	2.9	4.8	3.4	14.2	8.3
"Donating blood:"						
Yes	45.1	43.0	55.0	54.7	49.7	63.9
No*	44.8	43.3	27.4	31.3	19.0	28.4
Don't Know	10.1	13.7	17.6	14.0	31.3	7.8

* Indicates correct response

Source: D. Michael Anderson and Gregory M. Christenson, "Ethnic Breakdown of AIDS–Related Knowledge and Attitudes from the National Adolescent Student Health Survey," *Journal of Health Education* 22, no. 1 (January/February 1991): 30. The sampling frame consisted of all fifty states and the District of Columbia from which a total of 217 schools were selected, representing approximately equal numbers of urban and rural schools. Over 11,000 students were in the sample; 3,617 completed the AIDS portion of the questionnaire.

★ 4 ★

AIDS Transmission Knowledge

Reported results, in percent, of a national survey asking eighth and tenth grade students a series of questions on their AIDS transmission knowledge. Responses are by race/ethnicity.

Question	Asian/ Pacific Islander	White	Black	Hispanic	American Indian/ Alaskan	Other
"There is no known cure for AIDS:"						
True*	82.3	88.9	84.0	82.5	73.7	75.8
False	8.4	4.1	6.7	9.0	19.8	7.8
Don't Know	9.3	7.0	9.3	8.6	6.6	16.5
"A test to determine whether a person has the AIDS virus is now available:"						
True*	84.4	85.0	73.3	76.2	82.5	78.3
False	2.2	5.1	10.7	7.0	9.6	5.6
Don't Know	13.4	9.9	16.1	16.8	8.0	16.1
"A vaccine that protects people from getting the AIDS virus is available:"						
True	8.6	8.5	17.6	14.2	8.8	13.0
False*	58.1	66.9	47.0	51.3	56.2	56.2
Don't Know	33.4	24.7	35.5	34.5	35.0	30.8
"A pregnant woman who has the AIDS virus can give AIDS to her baby:"						
True*	79.9	80.8	84.3	85.0	62.1	71.7
False	4.4	1.4	2.4	2.5	0.0	1.4
Don't Know	15.8	17.8	13.3	12.5	37.9	26.9

*Indicates correct response

Source: D. Michael Anderson and Gregory M. Christenson, "Ethnic Breakdown of AIDS–Related Knowledge and Attitudes from the National Adolescent Student Health Survey," *Journal of Health Education* 22, no. 1 (January/February 1991): 30. The sampling frame consisted of all fifty states and the District of Columbia from which a total of 217 schools were selected, representing approximately equal numbers of urban and rural schools. Over 11,000 students were in the sample; 3,617 completed the AIDS portion of the questionnaire.

★ 5 ★

Beliefs about Sexuality

Reported results, in percent, of a national survey asking eighth and tenth grade students a series of questions on their beliefs about sexuality.

Belief	Asian/ Pacific Islander	White	Black	Hispanic	American Indian/ Alaskan	Other
"I believe that..."						
"It is OK for people my age to say 'no' to having sex:"						
Definitely Yes	66.4	70.5	64.1	54.1	49.2	65.5
Probably Yes	17.1	16.8	16.8	23.4	33.3	11.2
Not Sure	7.6	5.3	8.2	10.1	10.3	10.1
Probably No	4.3	3.6	4.1	7.8	7.3	7.8
Definitely No	4.5	3.9	6.9	4.5	0.0	5.4
"People my age should use condoms (rubbers) if they have sex:"						
Definitely Yes	61.4	76.9	78.3	70.9	60.9	75.2
Probably Yes	18.3	15.0	13.6	14.4	19.1	14.2
Not sure	10.3	5.2	4.1	9.1	13.2	8.2
Probably No	3.1	1.7	1.1	2.8	6.9	0.9
Definitely No	6.9	1.3	3.0	2.9	0.0	1.6
"My friends believe that..."						
"It is OK for people my age to say 'no' to having sex:"						
Definitely Yes	42.8	37.5	30.7	35.1	41.6	39.6
Probably Yes	22.7	26.5	22.0	27.2	40.6	20.0
Not Sure	10.6	17.4	14.7	15.7	2.9	16.0
Probably No	13.0	10.3	14.2	12.2	15.0	10.5
Definitely No	11.0	8.8	18.3	9.8	0.0	13.9
"People my age should use condoms (rubbers) if they have sex:"						
Definitely Yes	32.7	56.8	62.9	53.9	26.8	59.0
Probably Yes	28.7	23.9	16.2	24.0	52.6	20.1
Not Sure	24.2	14.1	9.1	16.0	13.2	10.7
Probably No	6.7	3.3	6.3	3.0	7.4	2.9
Definitely No	7.7	2.0	5.6	3.1	0.0	7.3

Source: D. Michael Anderson and Gregory M. Christenson, "Ethnic Breakdown of AIDS–Related Knowledge and Attitudes from the National Adolescent Student Health Survey," *Journal of Health Education* 22 no. 1 (January/February 1991): 30. The sampling frame consisted of all fifty states and the District of Columbia from which a total of 217 schools were selected, representing approximately equal numbers of urban and rural schools. Over 11,000 students were in the sample; 3,617 completed the AIDS portion of the questionnaire.

★ 6 ★

Lesbian and Gay Identity

Reported results of a survey of thirty-five gay/lesbian Asian Americans regarding identification as Asian American and lesbian or gay.[a]

Experiences	Number
Participation in social or political events in the following communities:	
Asian American only	0
Lesbian/gay only	26
Both lesbian/gay and Asian American	9
In which community do you feel more comfortable?	
Lesbian/gay	20
Asian-American	10
Neither or both	5
What do you consider to be your identity?	
Asian American lesbian woman or gay man	20
Lesbian or gay Asian American	9
Neither or both	7
Disclosure of lesbian/gay identity to family:	
Yes	27
No	8
Disclosure of lesbian/gay identity to parents:	
Yes	9
No	26
Disclosure of lesbian/gay identity to friends:	
Yes	34
No	1
Easier or harder to "come out" to other Asian Americans?	
Easier	4
Harder	27
No difference	4
Feel acknowledged and accepted in lesbian/gay community?	
Yes	4
No	30
Unsure	1
Experience discrimination because of being Asian?	
Women	17 (of 19)
Men	3 (of 16)
Experience discrimination because of being lesbian/gay?	
Women	5
Men	12
Experience more discrimination because of being both Asian and lesbian/gay?	
Women	17
Men	12

Source: Connie S. Chan, "Issues of Identity Development among Asian American Lesbians and Gay Men," *"Gay, Lesbian, and Bisexual Issues in Counseling,"* *Journal of Counseling and Development* 68, no. 1 (Sept.–Oct., 1989): 16. *Note:* (a) The participants were 19 women and 16 men between the ages of 21 and 36 who identified themselves as being both lesbian/gay and Asian American. Of the respondents 90% were of Chinese, Korean, or Japanese ancestry, with the remaining 10% from Filipino, Bangladesh, and Indian backgrounds.

Attitudes on Integration

★ 7 ★

Acceptance of Intermarriage

Reported results, in percent, of a survey asking people to give their opinion on how they would feel if a close relative married an individual from one of the groups listed below.

Opinion	Asian American	Northern White[a]	Southern White[b]	Black	Hispanic	Jew
Strongly favor	2.9%	6.8%	11.3%	7.0%	4.4%	7.2%
Favor	6.6%	13.7%	17.0%	4.5%	6.9%	12.3%
Neither favor nor oppose	46.4%	65.7%	59.2%	29.9%	46.4%	63.1%
Oppose	27.4%	8.6%	7.7%	25.1%	25.2%	11.3%
Strongly oppose	15.0%	3.7%	3.5%	32.4%	15.3%	5.0%
Don't know	1.8%	1.4%	1.3%	1.1%	1.4%	1.2%

Source: Tom W. Smith, *What Americans Think about Jews* (New York: The American Jewish Committee, 1991), table 16, p. 54. Primary source: General Social Survey, National Opinion Research Center, University of Chicago, 1990. *Notes:* (a)Whites raised in the North; asked of people living in the South. (b)Whites raised in the South; asked of people living outside the South.

★ 8 ★

Acceptance of Residential Integration

Reported results, in percent, of a survey conducted by The Gallup Organization asking people to give their opinion on whether they would (yes) or would not (no) like to have one of the below groups listed below as neighbors.

Ethnic group	Response rate in percent		
	Yes	No	Not sure
Asian American groups			
Koreans	79%	14%	7%
Vietnamese	75%	18%	7%
Pakistani	78%	15%	7%
Other groups			
Blacks	83%	12%	5%
Catholics	94%	3%	3%
Hispanics	78%	16%	6%
Jews	91%	5%	4%
Protestants	92%	5%	3%
Religious sects, cults	31%	62%	7%
Russians	74%	19%	7%

Source: Tom W. Smith, *What Americans Think about Jews* (New York: The American Jewish Committee, 1991), table 15, pp. 52–3. Primary source: The Gallup Organization, Princeton, NJ, January 1989.

★ 9 ★

Acceptance of Residential Integration

Reported results, in percent, of a survey conducted by the National Opinion Research Center asking people to give their opinion on how they would feel living in a neighborhood where half of their neighbors were one of the below groups.

Opinion	Asian Americans	Northern Whites[a]	Southern Whites[b]	Blacks	Hispanics	Jews
Strongly favor	3.4%	5.0%	8.4%	4.9%	3.8%	6.2%
Favor	10.3%	16.1%	20.6%	10.9%	9.6%	17.4%
Neither favor nor oppose	48.7%	59.0%	57.7%	41.7%	42.9%	61.4%
Oppose	26.3%	14.5%	9.3%	28.7%	29.5%	10.9%
Strongly oppose	9.4%	3.6%	1.8%	13.1%	12.3%	2.8%
Don't know	2.0%	1.9%	2.2%	0.7%	1.8%	1.4%

Source: Tom W. Smith, *What Americans Think about Jews* (New York: The American Jewish Committee, 1991), table 15, pp. 52–3. Primary source: General Social Survey, National Opinion Research Center, University of Chicago, 1990. *Notes:* (a) Whites raised in the North; asked of people living in the South. (b) Whites raised in the South; asked of people living outside the South.

★ 10 ★

Attitudes about Race Relations

Reported results, in percent, of a survey asking Asian Americans the following question: "Would you say that race relations in this country will get better, or worse?"

Ethnic group	Percent responses			
	Better	Worse	About the same	Don't know
All Asian Americans	9.9%	41.3%	39.7%	9.1%
Chinese	7.4%	46.3%	38.8%	7.4%
Filipino	30.0%	24.2%	27.5%	18.3%
Japanese	12.0%	43.2%	37.7%	7.1%
Korean	2.5%	35.4%	55.7%	6.3%
Vietnamese	8.2%	34.5%	48.2%	9.1%
Asian Indian	2.5%	50.0%	35.0%	12.5%
Others	7.5%	39.8%	44.1%	8.6%

Source: Republican National Committee, unpublished data. Results of an August 1992 survey of 5,000 Asian American adults in California. Names were selected from membership directories of major Asian ethnic organizations and from an ethnic surname database of registered voters. The response rate was 27.9% or 1,149 completed questionnaires. The ethnic composition of the group responding was: Chinese–42%, Filipino–9%, Japanese–21.5%, Korean–17.5%, Vietnamese–24.4%, Asian Indian–32%, and others–15.5%. The overall sample error is about 3% at 95% confidence level.

★ 11 ★

Attitudes on Integration and Intermarriage

Reported results, in percent, of a survey asking people if they objected to residential integration and intermarriage by members of various groups[a].

Reference group	Out-group	Neighborhood	Relative marrying
Asian Americans	Non-Asians	34.6%	41.7%
Northern Whites	Southern Whites	10.8%	8.2%
Southern Whites	Northern Whites	17.5%	10.9%
Blacks	Non-Blacks	46.8%	65.3%
Hispanics	Non-Hispanics	43.2%	41.2%
Jews	Non-Jews	14.1%	16.8%

Source: Tom W. Smith, *What Americans Think about Jews* (New York: The American Jewish Committee, 1991), table 17, p. 55. Primary source: General Social Survey, National Opinion Research Center, University of Chicago, 1990. *Notes:* (a) Out-group objection to members of reference group, in percent.

★ 12 ★

Attitudes toward Selected Groups

Reported results, in percent, of a survey asking people the following question: "Have you ever had good reason that might have made you dislike any of the groups listed on this card or not?" They were then shown a card listing: Asians, Jews, Catholics, Hispanics or Latins, Blacks, Whites, Political Extremists. The responses were as follows:

Group	% of respondents with reason to dislike
Asians	5%
Jews	4%
Catholics	3%
Hispanics or Latins	7%
Blacks	15%
Whites	4%
Political extremists	29%
None of these	60%

Source: The Gallup Organization, Princeton, NJ, March 1982. The results add up to more than 100% due to multiple responses. Survey included 1,729 adults.

★13★

Ethnic Images of Groups Compared to Whites

Reported results of a survey asking people to rank certain ethnic groups on a scale of one to seven (one being most positive, seven being most negative). The results are presented relative to the perception given to whites.

Question/ranking (compared to whites)	Group	Mean difference[a]
"How are certain groups rated concerning wealth (richer versus poorer)?"		
1st	Jews	+0.58
2nd	Whites	0.00
3rd	Southern whites	-0.56
4th	Asian Americans	-0.77
5th	Blacks	-1.60
6th	Hispanics	-1.64
"How are certain groups rated concerning work ethic (hard-working versus lazy)?"		
1st	Jews	+0.38
2nd	Whites	0.00
3rd	Asian Americans	-0.19
4th	Southern Whites	-0.52
5th	Hispanics	-0.99
6th	Blacks	-1.24
"How are certain groups rated concerning violence (not violence-prone versus violence-prone)?"		
1st	Jews	+0.36
2nd	Whites	0.00
3rd	Asian American	-0.15
4th	Southern Whites	-0.23
5th	Hispanics	-0.75
6th	Blacks	-1.00
"How are certain groups rated concerning intelligence (intelligent versus unintelligent)?"		
1st	Jews	+0.15
2nd	Whites	0.00
3rd	Asian American	-0.36
4th	Southern Whites	-0.53
5th	Blacks	-0.93
6th	Hispanics	-0.96
"How are certain groups rated concerning dependency (self-supporting versus live off welfare)?"		
1st	Jews	+0.40
2nd	Whites	0.00
3rd	Southern White	-0.71
4th	Asian Americans	-0.75
5th	Hispanics	-1.72
6th	Blacks	-2.08

[Continued]

★13★

Ethnic Images of Groups Compared to Whites (Continued)

Reported results of a survey asking people to rank certain ethnic groups on a scale of one to seven (one being most positive, seven being most negative). The results are presented relative to the perception given to whites.

Question/ranking (compared to whites)	Group	Mean difference[a]
"How are certain groups rated concerning patriotism (patriotic verse unpatriotic)?"		
1st	Whites	0.00
2nd	Southern Whites	-0.31
3rd	Jew	-0.57
4th	Blacks	-1.03
5th	Asian Americans	-1.16
6th	Hispanics	-1.34

Source: Tom W. Smith, *Ethnic Images, GSS Topical Report No. 19* (Chicago: NORC, Dec. 1990), table 1, p. 9. The data was compiled from a survey conducted by the National Opinion Research Center in which individuals were asked how they rate certain groups' (whites, blacks, Jews, Asian Americans, Southern whites, and Hispanics) characteristics. The ranking reflects the group's position along a scale ranging from most favorable to least favorable, e.g., richer (1st place) to poorer (6th place). *Notes:* (a)The mean difference is the mean rating (on a scale of 1 to 7) received by each group subtracted from the mean rating received by whites. For example, if whites were rated as 4 on wealth and Jews as 3 and blacks as 5, the mean difference would be calculated as +1 for Jews (4-3=+1) and -1 for Blacks (4-5=-1). The mean difference is not a percentage difference; it is only the relative difference between the ratings given to one group and the ratings given to whites.

★14★

Links to Countries of Origin by Years in United States

Reported results, in percent, of a study of Asians and Latinos and their links to their native countries.

Activity	Years in the U.S.					
	Asians			Hispanics		
	0–7	8–15	16+	0–7	8–15	16+
Keeps in touch with friends and relatives	90%	77%	64%	87%	84%	74%
Sends money to friends and relatives	43%	29%	30%	48%	49%	33%
Number in survey	58	69	50	46	88	89

Source: Bruce E. Cain, D. Roberick Kiewitt, and Carole J. Uhlaner, "Acquisition of Partisanship by Latinos and Asian Americans," *American Journal of Political Science* 35, no. 2 (May 1991): 390–422.

★15★

Perceived Intergroup Relations

Reported results, in percent, of a survey asking people to give their opinion on how they thought one ethnic group felt towards other ethnic groups.

Reference Group	Disliked by . . .						
	Asian Americans	Whites	Blacks	Hispanics	American Indians	Catholics	Jews
Asian Americans	1%	29%	17%	10%	4%	5%	8%
Whites	13%	1%	56%	19%	16%	2%	4%
Blacks	10%	53%	2%	18%	7%	6%	11%
Hispanics	6%	36%	26%	2%	4%	3%	7%
American Indians	4%	24%	8%	4%	1%	3%	4%
Catholics	8%	3%	7%	2%	3%	1%	24%
Jews	9%	14%	7%	8%	4%	16%	2%

Source: Tom W. Smith, *What Americans Think about Jews* (New York: The American Jewish Committee, 1991), table 23, pp. 62–63. Primary source: Princeton Survey Research Associates, May 1990.

★16★

Perceived Power and Influence of Ethnic Groups

Reported results, in percent, of a survey asking people to give their opinion on how much political influence certain groups have.

Group	Response rate in percentage			
	Too much	About right	Too little	Don't know
Asian Americans	6.3%	41.0%	37.3%	15.4%
White	25.2%	64.2%	5.8%	4.8%
Southern Whites	10.4%	61.6%	14.7%	13.3%
Blacks	14.2%	31.4%	46.9%	7.5%
Hispanics	4.7%	36.9%	45.5%	12.9%
Jews	21.2%	54.5%	12.6%	11.7%

Source: Tom W. Smith, *What Americans Think about Jews* (New York: The American Jewish Committee, 1991), table 9, pp. 41–42. Primary source: *General Social Survey,* National Opinion Research Center, University of Chicago, 1990. Also in source: quantified difference between the "too much" and "too little" responses.

★ 17 ★

Public Attitudes about Ethnic Groups in the United States

Reported results, in percent, of a survey asking people if various ethnic groups have been good or bad for the country.

Group	Good For Country	Bad For Country	Mixed Feelings	Don't Know
Asian American groups				
Japanese	47%	18%	26%	9%
Chinese	44%	19%	27%	10%
Koreans	24%	30%	31%	15%
Vietnamese	20%	38%	31%	11%
Other ethnic groups				
English	66%	6%	21%	8%
Irish	62%	7%	22%	9%
Jews	59%	9%	24%	8%
Germans	57%	11%	23%	8%
Italians	56%	10%	25%	9%
Poles	53%	12%	25%	11%
Blacks	46%	16%	31%	7%
Mexicans	25%	34%	32%	10%
Puerto Ricans	17%	43%	29%	11%
Haitians	10%	39%	26%	26%
Cubans	9%	59%	22%	10%

Source: Dinker I. Patel, *Journal of State Government* 61, no. 2 (March–April, 1988): 71(6). Primary source: *Public Opinion* (June/July 1982): 34.

★ 18 ★

Relationship between Whites and Asian Americans

Reported results, in percent, of a national telephone survey asking registered voters the following question: "How would you characterize the relationship between white people and Asian Americans?"

Opinion	1990	1991
Very good	8%	7%
Moderately good	30%	29%
In the middle	31%	32%
Not so good	14%	15%
Poor	7%	7%
Not sure	10%	10%

Source: NBC News/*Wall Street Journal*, July 6, 1990 and May 24, 1991. Results of national telephone survey of 1,555 (1990) and 1508 (1991) registered voters conducted in July 1990 and May 1991 by Hart and Teeter Research Company.

★19★

Violence against Korean Americans

Reported results, in percent, of a survey asking Asian Americans if they agreed with the following statement: "Do you think the violence against Korean Americans in the L.A. riot was a sign of racism against Asians?"[a]

Ethnic Group	Yes, it is racism	Don't know	No, it is not racism
All	71.3%	11.4%	17.3%
Chinese	79.8%	8.7%	11.6%
Filipino	51.7%	16.7%	31.7%
Japanese	62.8%	8.2%	29.0%
Korean	63.3%	3.8%	32.9%
Vietnamese	72.7%	20.9%	6.4%
Asian Indian	66.3%	26.3%	7.5%
Others	78.5%	7.5%	14.0%

Source: Republican National Committee, unpublished data. Results of an August 1992 survey of 5,000 Asian American adults in California. Names were selected from membership directories of major Asian ethnic organizations and from an ethnic surname database of registered voters. The response rate was 27.9% or 1,149 completed questionnaires. The ethnic composition of the response was: Chinese–42%, Filipino–9%, Japanese–21.5%, Korean–17.5%, Vietnamese–24.4%, Asian Indian–32%, and others–15.5%. The overall sample error is about 3% at 95% confidence level. *Note:* (a) This question refers to the riots in Los Angeles which followed the jury acquittal of white police officers accused in the beating of Rodney King, a black motorist.

Government and Politics

★20★

Attitudes on Woman Running for Office

Reported results, in percent, of a survey asking Asian Americans the following question: "What do you think about women running for public office? Would you be more likely to vote for a candidate simply because the candidate was a female?"

Ethnic Group	No response	Much more likely	Somewhat more likely	Makes no difference	Somewhat less likely	Much less likely
All	0.9%	8.8%	9.9%	68.7%	6.0%	5.7%
Chinese	0.2%	8.1%	8.7%	76.2%	4.5%	2.3%
Filipino	–	8.3%	9.2%	75.8%	5.8%	0.8%
Japanese	0.5%	6.6%	9.3%	65.6%	9.3%	8.7%
Korean	–	5.1%	7.6%	48.1%	8.9%	30.4%
Vietnamese	7.3%	11.8%	21.8%	49.1%	7.3%	2.7%
Asian Indian	–	11.3%	11.3%	72.5%	–	5.0%
Others	–	15.1%	5.4%	63.4%	8.6%	7.5%

Source: Republican National Committee, unpublished data. Results of an August 1992 survey of 5,000 Asian American adults in California. Names were selected from membership directories of major Asian ethnic organizations and from an ethnic surname database of registered voters. The response rate was 27.9% or 1,149 completed questionnaires. The ethnic composition of the response was: Chinese–42%, Filipino–9%, Japanese–21.5%, Korean–17.5%, Vietnamese–24.4%, Asian Indian–32%, and others–15.5%. The overall sample error is about 3% at 95% confidence level.

★21★

Attitudes toward Intervention in Child Abuse and Neglect

Reported results of a survey of 150 individuals[a] who were given a choice of intervention methods in response to a situation of potential child abuse or neglect. Findings were that the Chinese were more tolerant of parental conduct than were Hispanics and whites; and Chinese were less likely to ask for investigation by protective agencies in potential cases of child abuse and neglect.

Choices of Intervention[b] Vignettes	Chinese Percent			Hispanics Percent			Whites Percent			Sig.
	A	B	C	A	B	C	A	B	C	Test[c]
Encourages to steal from market	2	34	64	0	46	54	0	38	62	ns
Beating and branding for stealing	8	54	38	4	30	66	0	20	80	CW CH
Girl dressed by parents as boy	6	66	28	2	68	30	4	68	28	ns
Left alone by parents	10	56	34	2	34	64	12	46	42	CH HW
Ignore rashes and sores	12	52	36	6	46	48	8	60	32	ns
Boy sleeping with noisy parents	24	44	32	12	68	20	24	60	16	CH
Using drugs in front of daughter	14	44	42	2	34	64	8	52	40	CH HW
Beating for not doing homework	36	30	34	12	26	62	12	18	70	CW CH
Refuse to take girl to counselor	16	66	18	8	62	30	12	64	24	ns
Asked to sleep with lonely mother	40	46	14	28	54	18	30	58	12	ns
Girl sleeping in parent's bed	52	34	14	46	46	8	36	58	6	CW
Scratched to make feel better	60	24	16	10	26	64	16	30	54	CW CH

Source: George K. Hong and Lawrence K. Hong, "Comparative Perspectives on Child Abuse and Neglect: Chinese versus Hispanics and Whites," *Child Welfare* 70, no. 4 (July–August 1991): 463–75. *Note:* (a) Respondents were fifty each of Chinese, Hispanics, and whites. (b) Choices are: A-Nothing needs to be done about this situation; B-The family should be encouraged to seek professional help; C-The child protective agency should be notified to investigate and help the family. (c) ns—not significant, CW—Significant difference between Chinese and whites, CH—Significant difference between Chinese and Hispanics, HW—Significant difference between Hispanics and whites.

★22★

Attitudes toward Police in the Rodney King Case

Reported results, in percent, of a survey asking Asian Americans the following question: "Based on your knowledge of the Rodney King case[a], the police officers involved in beating King should have been found guilty, or innocent?"

Ethnic Group	Guilty	Don't know	Innocent
All	66.9%	19.5%	13.6%
Chinese	69.0%	21.9%	9.1%
Filipino	54.2%	28.3%	17.5%

[Continued]

★22★

Attitudes toward Police
in the Rodney King Case (Continued)

Reported results, in percent, of a survey asking Asian Americans the following question: "Based on your knowledge of the Rodney King case[a], the police officers involved in beating King should have been found guilty, or innocent?"

Ethnic Group	Guilty	Don't know	Innocent
Japanese	66.7%	19.7%	13.7%
Korean	74.7%	5.1%	20.3%
Vietnamese	86.4%	8.2%	5.5%
Asian Indian	60.0%	25.0%	15.0%
Others	49.5%	16.1%	34.4%

Source: Republican National Committee, unpublished data. Results of an August 1992 survey of 5,000 Asian American adults in California. Names were selected from membership directories of major Asian ethnic organizations and from an ethnic surname database of registered voters. The response rate was 27.9% or 1,149 completed questionnaires. The ethnic composition of the response was: Chinese–42%, Filipino–9%, Japanese–21.5%, Korean–17.5%, Vietnamese–24.4%, Asian Indian–32%, and others–15.5%. The overall sample error is about 3% at 95% confidence level. *Note:* (a) This case involved the videotaped beating of black motorist Rodney King by white police officers in Los Angeles. The trial, which was televised, ended in jury acquittal of the police officers.

★23★

Attitudes toward the U.S. Judicial System

Reported results, in percent, of a survey asking Asian Americans the following question: "The verdict in the Rodney King case[a] indicates that minorities, including Asians, cannot get justice in this country."

Ethnic Group	Strongly agree	Agree	Disagree	Strongly disagree	No opinion
All	22.5%	34.7%	24.1%	5.9%	12.7%
Chinese	16.7%	38.6%	24.8%	4.8%	15.1%
Filipino	22.5%	43.3%	19.2%	9.2%	5.8%
Japanese	17.5%	25.1%	36.1%	5.5%	15.8%
Korean	34.2%	24.1%	21.5%	3.8%	16.5%
Vietnamese	27.3%	48.2%	10.9%	2.7%	10.9%
Asian Indian	51.3%	22.5%	13.8%	10.0%	2.5%
Others	22.6%	25.8%	30.1%	10.8%	10.8%

Source: Republican National Committee, unpublished data. Results of an August 1992 survey of 5,000 Asian American adults in California. Names were selected from membership directories of major Asian ethnic organizations and from an ethnic surname database of registered voters. The response rate was 27.9% or 1,149 completed questionnaires. The ethnic composition of the response was: Chinese–42%, Filipino–9%, Japanese–21.5%, Korean–17.5%, Vietnamese–24.4%, Asian Indian–32%, and others–15.5%. The overall sample error is about 3% at 95% confidence level. *Note:* (a) The Rodney King case involved the videotaped beating of black motorist, Rodney King, by white police officers. The police officers were tried and acquitted, by jury.

★24★

Attitudes toward Welfare Programs

Reported results, in percent, of a survey asking Asian Americans if they agreed with the following statement: "The government welfare programs aimed at helping the urban poor actually do more harm than good to the minorities."

Ethnic Group	Strongly agree	Agree	Disagree	Strongly disagree	No opinion
All	17.2%	36.7%	15.7%	3.7%	26.7%
Chinese	14.9%	41.7%	11.0%	4.5%	27.9%
Filipino	22.5%	35.8%	19.2%	3.3%	19.2%
Japanese	1.9%	37.7%	27.3%	0.5%	17.5%
Korean	17.7%	31.6%	10.1%	1.3%	39.2%
Vietnamese	11.8%	23.6%	20.9%	1.8%	41.8%
Asian Indian	27.5%	42.5%	12.5%	10.0%	7.5%
Others	20.4%	24.7%	14.0%	4.3%	36.6%

Source: Republican National Committee, unpublished data. Results of an August 1992 survey of 5,000 Asian American adults in California. Names were selected from membership directories of major Asian ethnic organizations and from an ethnic surname database of registered voters. The response rate was 27.9% or 1,149 completed questionnaires. The ethnic composition of the response was: Chinese–42%, Filipino–9%, Japanese–21.5%, Korean–17.5%, Vietnamese–24.4%, Asian Indian–32%, and others–15.5%. The overall sample error is about 3% at 95% confidence level.

★25★

Confidence in the U.S. Economy

Reported results, in percent, of a survey asking Asian Americans if they agreed with the following statement: "The U.S. is facing a long-term economic decline."

Ethnic Group	Strongly agree	Agree	Disagree	Strongly disagree	No opinion
All	17.1%	51.2%	12.9%	1.0%	17.8%
Chinese	16.5%	52.5%	16.9%	0.2%	13.8%
Filipino	14.2%	49.2%	15.0%	3.3%	18.3%
Japanese	14.8%	47.5%	13.1%	1.1%	23.5%
Korean	11.4%	41.8%	7.6%	3.8%	35.4%
Vietnamese	12.7%	55.5%	4.5%	1.8%	25.5%
Asian Indian	36.3%	56.3%	2.5%	–	5.0%
Others	22.6%	52.7%	11.8%	–	12.9%

Source: Republican National Committee, unpublished data. Results of an August 1992 survey of 5,000 Asian American adults in California. Names were selected from membership directories of major Asian ethnic organizations and from an ethnic surname database of registered voters. The response rate was 27.9% or 1,149 completed questionnaires. The ethnic composition of the response was: Chinese–42%, Filipino–9%, Japanese–21.5%, Korean–17.5%, Vietnamese–24.4%, Asian Indian–32%, and others–15.5%. The overall sample error is about 3% at 95% confidence level.

★26★

Contributions to Candidates and Political Organizations

Reported results, in percent, of a survey asking Asian Americans the following question: "How much did you contribute to political candidates and/or organization last year?"

Ethnic Group	$0.00	Less than $100	$100 to $500	$500 to $1,000	More than $1,000
All	54.1%	24.4%	13.8%	5.1%	2.6%
Chinese	50.0%	25.4%	16.9%	3.5%	4.1%
Filipino	37.5%	29.2%	17.5%	14.2%	1.7%
Japanese	60.7%	21.9%	9.3%	17.1%	1.1%
Korean	68.4%	21.5%	5.1%	2.5%	2.5%
Vietnamese	59.1%	24.5%	6.4%	8.2%	1.8%
Asian Indian	67.5%	23.8%	7.5%	1.3%	–
Others	54.8%	20.4%	22.6%	–	2.2%

Source: Republican National Committee, unpublished data. Results of an August 1992 survey of 5,000 Asian American adults in California. Names were selected from membership directories of major Asian ethnic organizations and from an ethnic surname database of registered voters. The response rate was 27.9% or 1,149 completed questionnaires. The ethnic composition of the response was: Chinese–42%, Filipino–9%, Japanese–21.5%, Korean–17.5%, Vietnamese–24.4%, Asian Indian–32%, and others–15.5%. The overall sample error is about 3% at 95% confidence level.

★27★

Contributions to Candidates for Public Office

Reported results, in percent, of a survey asking Asian Americans the following question: "Have you ever made a contribution to a candidate for public office?"

Ethnic Group	No	Yes
All	54.2%	45.8%
Chinese	50.4%	49.6%
Filipino	38.3%	61.7%
Japanese	59.6%	40.4%
Korean	68.4%	31.6%
Vietnamese	59.1%	40.9%
Asian Indian	67.5%	32.5%
Others	54.8%	45.2%

Source: Republican National Committee, unpublished data. Results of an August 1992 survey of 5,000 Asian American adults in California. Names were selected from membership directories of major Asian ethnic organizations and from an ethnic surname database of registered voters. The response rate was 27.9% or 1,149 completed questionnaires. The ethnic composition of the response was: Chinese–42%, Filipino–9%, Japanese–21.5%, Korean–17.5%, Vietnamese–24.4%, Asian Indian–32%, and others–15.5%. The overall sample error is about 3% at 95% confidence level.

★28★

Contributions to Candidates for Public Office by Party

Reported results, in percent, of a survey asking Asian Americans the following question: "To which party's candidate did you contribute?"

Ethnic Group	No response	Republican	Democrat	Independent	Both GOP & Democrat
All	54.2%	23.2%	15.5%	2.8%	4.3%
Chinese	50.4%	24.4%	16.7%	4.5%	3.9%
Filipino	38.3%	35.0%	17.5%	5.0%	4.2%
Japanese	59.6%	17.5%	16.4%	1.6%	4.9%
Korean	68.4%	24.1%	6.3%	–	1.3%
Vietnamese	59.1%	27.3%	13.6%	–	–
Asian Indian	67.5%	2.5%	20.0%	1.3%	8.8%
Others	54.8%	25.8%	10.8%	–	8.6%

Source: Republican National Committee, unpublished data. Results of an August 1992 survey of 5,000 Asian American adults in California. Names were selected from membership directories of major Asian ethnic organizations and from an ethnic surname database of registered voters. The response rate was 27.9% or 1,149 completed questionnaires. The ethnic composition of the response was: Chinese–42%, Filipino–9%, Japanese–21.5%, Korean–17.5%, Vietnamese–24.4%, Asian Indian–32%, and others–15.5%. The overall sample error is about 3% at 95% confidence level.

★29★

Government Aid to Minority Groups

Reported results, in percent, of a survey asking Asian Americans if they agreed with the following statement: "Government should not make any special effort to help minorities because they should help themselves."

Ethnic Group	Strongly agree	Agree	Disagree	Strongly disagree	No opinion
All	5.0%	17.0%	39.2%	23.9%	15.0%
Chinese	5.8%	13.2%	45.0%	18.4%	17.6%
Filipino	5.8%	15.8%	15.8%	49.2%	13.3%
Japanese	4.9%	26.2%	43.7%	14.2%	10.9%
Korean	2.5%	24.1%	50.6%	13.9%	8.9%
Vietnamese	0.9%	9.1%	36.4%	41.8%	11.8%
Asian Indian	8.8%	17.5%	36.3%	21.3%	16.3%
Others	3.2%	22.6%	25.8%	29.0%	19.4%

Source: Republican National Committee, unpublished data. Results of an August 1992 survey of 5,000 Asian American adults in California. Names were selected from membership directories of major Asian ethnic organizations and from an ethnic surname database of registered voters. The response rate was 27.9% or 1,149 completed questionnaires. The ethnic composition of the response was: Chinese–42%, Filipino–9%, Japanese–21.5%, Korean–17.5%, Vietnamese–24.4%, Asian Indian–32%, and others–15.5%. The overall sample error is about 3% at 95% confidence level.

★30★

Government Aid to Minority Groups

Reported results, in percent, of a survey asking Asian Americans if they agreed with the following statement: "Government should make every effort to improve the social and economic position of blacks and other minority groups."

Ethnic Group	Strongly agree	Agree	Disagree	Strongly disagree	No opinion
All	26.3%	42.9%	15.8%	2.6%	12.4%
Chinese	17.4%	45.5%	14.7%	3.1%	19.4%
Filipino	44.2%	42.5%	10.8%	0.8%	1.7%
Japanese	27.9%	33.9%	21.3%	3.3%	13.7%
Korean	26.6%	44.3%	24.1%	1.3%	3.8%
Vietnamese	41.8%	41.8%	8.2%	–	8.2%
Asian Indian	20.0%	50.0%	26.3%	–	3.8%
Others	33.3%	41.9%	9.7%	7.5%	7.5%

Source: Republican National Committee, unpublished data. Results of an August 1992 survey of 5,000 Asian American adults in California. Names were selected from membership directories of major Asian ethnic organizations and from an ethnic surname database of registered voters. The response rate was 27.9% or 1,149 completed questionnaires. The ethnic composition of the response was: Chinese–42%, Filipino–9%, Japanese–21.5%, Korean–17.5%, Vietnamese–24.4%, Asian Indian–32%, and others–15.5%. The overall sample error is about 3% at 95% confidence level.

★31★

Importance of Foreign Policy in Gubernatorial Elections

Reported results, in percent, of a survey asking Asian Americans the following question: "How important is the Governor's attitude toward Asian countries in your decision of which party to vote for in governor election?"

Ethnic Group	Very important	Somewhat important	Don't know	Not important	Not impor- tant at all
All	36.6%	42.9%	5.2%	8.6%	6.7%
Chinese	26.9%	51.2%	7.9%	9.7%	4.3%
Filipino	64.2%	24.2%	2.5%	2.5%	6.7%
Japanese	29.0%	44.8%	4.9%	9.8%	11.5%
Korean	45.6%	29.1%	2.5%	8.9%	13.9%
Vietnamese	38.2%	46.4%	4.5%	8.2%	2.7%
Asian Indian	42.5%	32.5%	1.3%	15.0%	8.8%
Others	51.6%	36.6%	2.2%	3.2%	6.5%

Source: Republican National Committee, unpublished data. Results of an August 1992 survey of 5,000 Asian American adults in California. Names were selected from membership directories of major Asian ethnic organizations and from an ethnic surname database of registered voters. The response rate was 27.9% or 1,149 completed questionnaires. The ethnic composition of the response was: Chinese–42%, Filipino–9%, Japanese–21.5%, Korean–17.5%, Vietnamese–24.4%, Asian Indian–32%, and others–15.5%. The overall sample error is about 3% at 95% confidence level.

★32★

Importance of Foreign Policy in Presidential Elections

Reported results, in percent, of a survey asking Asian Americans the following question: "How important is the President's Asian foreign policy in your decision of whom to vote for in presidential elections?"

Ethnic Group	Very important	Somewhat important	Don't know	Not important	Not important at all
All	38.3%	41.9%	7.5%	7.3%	5.0%
Chinese	27.9%	49.8%	10.3%	8.5%	3.5%
Filipino	67.5%	20.8%	4.2%	2.5%	5.0%
Japanese	25.1%	54.1%	5.5%	7.7%	7.7%
Korean	46.8%	30.4%	2.5%	7.6%	12.7%
Vietnamese	33.6%	35.5%	12.7%	15.5%	2.7%
Asian Indian	42.5%	42.5%	2.5%	3.8%	8.8%
Others	75.3%	20.4%	3.2%	–	1.1%

Source: Republican National Committee, unpublished data. Results of an August 1992 survey of 5,000 Asian American adults in California. Names were selected from membership directories of major Asian ethnic organizations and from an ethnic surname database of registered voters. The response rate was 27.9% or 1,149 completed questionnaires. The ethnic composition of the response was: Chinese–42%, Filipino–9%, Japanese–21.5%, Korean–17.5%, Vietnamese–24.4%, Asian Indian–32%, and others–15.5%. The overall sample error is about 3% at 95% confidence level.

★33★

Information Sources on Political Issues

Reported results, in percent, of a survey asking Asian Americans the following question: "What is your major source of information about political issues?"

Ethnic Group	TV	Newspaper	Radio	Magazine	Friends
All	39.3%	49.7%	4.4%	5.8%	0.3%
Chinese	34.1%	53.3%	4.15%	7.6%	0.4%
Filipino	50.8%	40.8%	1.7%	5.8%	–
Japanese	32.2%	59.6%	3.3%	4.9%	–
Korean	41.8%	43.0%	1.3%	13.9%	–
Vietnamese	46.4%	41.8%	8.2%	1.8%	–
Asian Indian	27.5%	61.3%	11.3%	–	–
Others	64.5%	28.0%	4.3%	1.1%	2.2%

Source: Republican National Committee, unpublished data. Results of an August 1992 survey of 5,000 Asian American adults in California. Names were selected from membership directories of major Asian ethnic organizations and from an ethnic surname database of registered voters. The response rate was 27.9% or 1,149 completed questionnaires. The ethnic composition of the response was: Chinese–42%, Filipino–9%, Japanese–21.5%, Korean–17.5%, Vietnamese–24.4%, Asian Indian–32%, and others–15.5%. The overall sample error is about 3% at 95% confidence level.

★ 34 ★

Need for a Federal Tax Cut

Reported results, in percent, of a survey asking Asian Americans if they agreed with the following statement: "In the midst of economic recession, we should have a tax-cut."

Ethnic Group	Strongly agree	Agree	Disagree	Strongly disagree	No opinion
All	11.9%	26.1%	27.1%	8.3%	26.6%
Chinese	7.6%	31.6%	24.2%	8.7%	27.9%
Filipino	17.5%	20.0%	36.7%	8.3%	17.5%
Japanese	7.7%	22.4%	33.3%	3.8%	32.8%
Korean	20.3%	12.7%	38.0%	11.4%	17.7%
Vietnamese	14.5%	31.8%	21.8%	3.6%	28.2%
Asian Indian	11.3%	17.5%	32.5%	12.5%	26.3%
Others	25.8%	24.7%	9.7%	14.0%	25.8%

Source: Republican National Committee, unpublished data. Results of an August 1992 survey of 5,000 Asian American adults in California. Names were selected from membership directories of major Asian ethnic organizations and from an ethnic surname database of registered voters. The response rate was 27.9% or 1,149 completed questionnaires. The ethnic composition of the response was: Chinese–42%, Filipino–9%, Japanese–21.5%, Korean–17.5%, Vietnamese–24.4%, Asian Indian–32%, and others–15.5%. The overall sample error is about 3% at 95% confidence level.

★ 35 ★

Need for a Federal Tax Increase

Reported results, in percent, of a survey asking Asian Americans if they agreed with the following statement: "Considering the growing federal deficit, it is time to raise taxes."

Ethnic Group	Strongly agree	Agree	Disagree	Strongly disagree	No opinion
All	4.7%	20.7%	32.5%	27.5%	14.6%
Chinese	4.3%	20.2%	33.3%	26.0%	16.1%
Filipino	13.3%	14.2%	28.3%	27.5%	16.7%
Japanese	2.2%	34.4%	30.1%	23.0%	10.4%
Korean	2.5%	24.1%	44.3%	22.8%	6.3%
Vietnamese	1.8%	24.5%	35.5%	33.6%	4.5%
Asian Indian	11.3%	13.8%	31.3%	15.0%	28.8%
Others	–	3.2%	25.8%	51.6%	19.4%

Source: Republican National Committee, unpublished data. Results of an August 1992 survey of 5,000 Asian American adults in California. Names were selected from membership directories of major Asian ethnic organizations and from an ethnic surname database of registered voters. The response rate was 27.9% or 1,149 completed questionnaires. The ethnic composition of the response was: Chinese–42%, Filipino–9%, Japanese–21.5%, Korean–17.5%, Vietnamese–24.4%, Asian Indian–32%, and others–15.5%. The overall sample error is about 3% at 95% confidence level.

★ 36 ★

Need for Federal Spending Cuts

Reported results, in percent, of a survey asking Asian Americans if they agreed with the following statement: "Considering the growing federal deficit, government should cut spending."

Ethnic Group	Strongly agree	Agree	Disagree	Strongly disagree	No opinion
All	41.4%	43.8%	3.7%	1.2%	9.8%
Chinese	36.0%	49.6%	2.9%	1.2%	10.3%
Filipino	57.5%	30.0%	3.3%	5.0%	4.2%
Japanese	39.9%	49.7%	2.7%	–	7.7%
Korean	48.1%	32.9%	5.1%	–	13.9%
Vietnamese	26.4%	50.9%	7.3%	0.9%	14.5%
Asian Indian	61.3%	31.3%	1.3%	–	6.3%
Others	47.3%	31.2%	7.5%	1.1%	12.9%

Source: Republican National Committee, unpublished data. Results of an August 1992 survey of 5,000 Asian American adults in California. Names were selected from membership directories of major Asian ethnic organizations and from an ethnic surname database of registered voters. The response rate was 27.9% or 1,149 completed questionnaires. The ethnic composition of the response was: Chinese–42%, Filipino–9%, Japanese–21.5%, Korean–17.5%, Vietnamese–24.4%, Asian Indian–32%, and others–15.5%. The overall sample error is about 3% at 95% confidence level.

★ 37 ★

Participation in Campaign Rallies

Reported results, in percent, of a survey asking Asian Americans if they had personally participated in a campaign rally.

Ethnic Group	No	Yes
All	82.4%	17.6%
Chinese	79.5%	20.5%
Filipino	75.8%	24.2%
Japanese	92.3%	7.7%
Korean	78.5%	21.5%
Vietnamese	87.3%	12.7%
Asian Indian	91.3%	8.8%
Others	76.3%	23.7%

Source: Republican National Committee, unpublished data. Results of an August 1992 survey of 5,000 Asian American adults in California. Names were selected from membership directories of major Asian ethnic organizations and from an ethnic surname database of registered voters. The response rate was 27.9% or 1,149 completed questionnaires. The ethnic composition of the response was: Chinese–42%, Filipino–9%, Japanese–21.5%, Korean–17.5%, Vietnamese–24.4%, Asian Indian–32%, and others–15.5%. The overall sample error is about 3% at 95% confidence level.

★38★

Participation in Labor Unions

Reported results, in percent, of a survey asking Asian Americans the following question: "Does anyone in your family belong to a labor union?"

Ethnic Group	No	Yes	Don't know
All	76.7%	19.1%	4.2%
Chinese	75.0%	23.8%	1.2%
Filipino	83.3%	12.5%	4.2%
Japanese	71.0%	23.5%	5.5%
Korean	69.6%	19.0%	11.4%
Vietnamese	80.9%	14.5%	4.5%
Asian Indian	93.8%	6.3%	–
Others	74.2%	11.8%	14.0%

Source: Republican National Committee, unpublished data. Results of an August 1992 survey of 5,000 Asian American adults in California. Names were selected from membership directories of major Asian ethnic organizations and from an ethnic surname database of registered voters. The response rate was 27.9% or 1,149 completed questionnaires. The ethnic composition of the response was: Chinese–42%, Filipino–9%, Japanese–21.5%, Korean–17.5%, Vietnamese–24.4%, Asian Indian–32%, and others–15.5%. The overall sample error is about 3% at 95% confidence level.

★39★

Participation in Political Fund-Raisers

Reported results, in percent, of a survey asking Asian Americans if they had ever personally participated in a political fund-raiser.

Ethnic Group	No	Yes
All	69.8%	30.2%
Chinese	70.2%	29.8%
Filipino	50.0%	50.0%
Japanese	85.8%	14.2%
Korean	69.6%	30.4%
Vietnamese	78.2%	21.8%
Asian Indian	62.5%	37.5%
Others	58.1%	41.9%

Source: Republican National Committee, unpublished data. Results of an August 1992 survey of 5,000 Asian American adults in California. Names were selected from membership directories of major Asian ethnic organizations and from an ethnic surname database of registered voters. The response rate was 27.9% or 1,149 completed questionnaires. The ethnic composition of the response was: Chinese–42%, Filipino–9%, Japanese–21.5%, Korean–17.5%, Vietnamese–24.4%, Asian Indian–32%, and others–15.5%. The overall sample error is about 3% at 95% confidence level.

★40★

Participation in Town Meetings

Reported results, in percent, of a survey asking Asian Americans if they had personally participated in a town meeting.

Ethnic Group	No	Yes
All	84.3%	15.7%
Chinese	82.4%	17.6%
Filipino	78.3%	21.7%
Japanese	95.6%	4.4%
Korean	94.9%	5.1%
Vietnamese	84.5%	15.5%
Asian Indian	91.3%	8.8%
Others	64.5%	35.3%

Source: Republican National Committee, unpublished data. Results of an August 1992 survey of 5,000 Asian American adults in California. Names were selected from membership directories of major Asian ethnic organizations and from an ethnic surname database of registered voters. The response rate was 27.9% or 1,149 completed questionnaires. The ethnic composition of the response was: Chinese–42%, Filipino–9%, Japanese–21.5%, Korean–17.5%, Vietnamese–24.4%, Asian Indian–32%, and others–15.5%. The overall sample error is about 3% at 95% confidence level.

★41★

Party Affiliation

Reported results, in percent, of a survey asking Asian Americans to state their political party affiliation.

Ethnic Group	Strong Democrat	Democrat	Strong Republican	Republican	Independent	Other
All	3.4%	31.1%	9.4%	28.7%	23.8%	3.6%
Chinese	2.1%	26.9%	9.9%	27.7%	27.7%	5.8%
Filipino	8.3%	35.8%	8.3%	23.3%	22.5%	1.7%
Japanese	7.1%	35.0%	7.7%	25.1%	24.6%	0.5%
Korean	–	30.4%	7.6%	41.8%	19.0%	1.3%
Vietnamese	1.8%	35.5%	19.1%	24.5%	19.1%	–
Asian Indian	3.8%	52.5%	–	23.8%	20.0%	–
Others	1.1%	16.1%	9.7%	46.2%	17.2%	9.7%

Source: Republican National Committee, unpublished data. Results of an August 1992 survey of 5,000 Asian American adults in California. Names were selected from membership directories of major Asian ethnic organizations and from an ethnic surname database of registered voters. The response rate was 27.9% or 1,149 completed questionnaires. The ethnic composition of the response was: Chinese–42%, Filipino–9%, Japanese–21.5%, Korean–17.5%, Vietnamese–24.4%, Asian Indian–32%, and others–15.5%. The overall sample error is about 3% at 95% confidence level.

★42★

Perceptions of Fairness in U.S. Society

Reported results, in percent, of a survey asking Asian Americans if they agree with the following statement: "Generally speaking, Asian-Americans get their fair share in this society."

Ethnic Group	Strongly agree	Agree	Disagree	Strongly disagree	No opinion
All	3.7%	27.9%	42.9%	13.4%	12.0%
Chinese	1.4%	29.8%	43.0%	16.3%	9.5%
Filipino	10.8%	13.3%	45.8%	6.7%	23.3%
Japanese	2.2%	33.3%	48.1%	2.7%	13.7%
Korean	11.4%	16.5%	48.1%	19.0%	5.1%
Vietnamese	6.4%	25.5%	42.7%	12.7%	12.7%
Asian Indian	–	36.3%	40.0%	13.8%	10.0%
Others	3.2%	32.3%	26.9%	23.7%	14.0%

Source: Republican National Committee, unpublished data. Results of an August 1992 survey of 5,000 Asian American adults in California. Names were selected from membership directories of major Asian ethnic organizations and from an ethnic surname database of registered voters. The response rate was 27.9% or 1,149 completed questionnaires. The ethnic composition of the response was: Chinese–42%, Filipino–9%, Japanese–21.5%, Korean–17.5%, Vietnamese–24.4%, Asian Indian–32%, and others–15.5%. The overall sample error is about 3% at 95% confidence level.

★43★

Political Activity

Reported results, in percent, of a survey asking Asian Americans if they agree with the following statement: "Asian-Americans are politically active in this country."

Ethnic Group	Strongly agree	Agree	Disagree	Strongly disagree	No opinion
All	2.8%	17.1%	46.7%	19.2%	14.2%
Chinese	0.8%	13.6%	50.0%	26.4%	9.1%
Filipino	2.5%	32.5%	38.3%	5.0%	21.7%
Japanese	2.7%	22.4%	53.6%	7.7%	13.7%
Korean	11.4%	7.6%	39.2%	26.6%	15.2%
Vietnamese	7.3%	9.1%	42.7%	32.7%	8.2%
Asian Indian	–	17.5%	48.8%	8.8%	25.0%
Others	3.2%	21.5%	36.6%	9.7%	29.0%

Source: Republican National Committee, unpublished data. Results of an August 1992 survey of 5,000 Asian American adults in California. Names were selected from membership directories of major Asian ethnic organizations and from an ethnic surname database of registered voters. The response rate was 27.9% or 1,149 completed questionnaires. The ethnic composition of the response was: Chinese–42%, Filipino–9%, Japanese–21.5%, Korean–17.5%, Vietnamese–24.4%, Asian Indian–32%, and others–15.5%. The overall sample error is about 3% at 95% confidence level.

★44★

Political Awareness

Reported results, in percent, of a survey asking Asian Americans the following question: "Would you say that you follow what's going on in government and politics most of the time or some of the time?"

Ethnic Group	Most of the time	Some of the time	Only now and then	Never
All	49.3%	42.1%	8.1%	0.4%
Chinese	51.7%	37.0%	10.1%	1.0%
Filipino	52.5%	44.2%	3.3%	–
Japanese	54.6%	34.4%	10.9%	–
Korean	26.6%	67.1%	6.3%	–
Vietnamese	50.9%	47.3%	1.8%	–
Asian Indian	62.5%	32.5%	5.0%	–
Others	28.0%	62.4%	9.7%	–

Source: Republican National Committee, unpublished data. Results of an August 1992 survey of 5,000 Asian American adults in California. Names were selected from membership directories of major Asian ethnic organizations and from an ethnic surname database of registered voters. The response rate was 27.9% or 1,149 completed questionnaires. The ethnic composition of the response was: Chinese–42%, Filipino–9%, Japanese–21.5%, Korean–17.5%, Vietnamese–24.4%, Asian Indian–32%, and others–15.5%. The overall sample error is about 3% at 95% confidence level.

★45★

Political Parties: Ability to Organize Asian Americans

Reported results, in percent, of a survey asking Asian Americans the following question: "In your opinion, which party does a better job in coordinating and organizing Asian Americans in your area?"

Ethnic Group	Republican	Democrat	Neither	Both	Don't Know
All	16.3%	21.0%	28.0%	4.8%	29.9%
Chinese	14.3%	18.8%	30.6%	3.3%	33.1%
Filipino	24.2%	26.7%	14.2%	10.8%	24.2%
Japanese	8.2%	24.6%	27.3%	4.9%	35.0%
Korean	25.3%	8.9%	30.4%	5.1%	30.4%
Vietnamese	18.2%	30.9%	26.4%	5.5%	19.1%
Asian Indian	7.5%	31.3%	36.3%	–	25.0%
Others	30.1%	7.5%	26.9%	7.5%	28.0%

Source: Republican National Committee, unpublished data. Results of an August 1992 survey of 5,000 Asian American adults in California. Names were selected from membership directories of major Asian ethnic organizations and from an ethnic surname database of registered voters. The response rate was 27.9% or 1,149 completed questionnaires. The ethnic composition of the response was: Chinese–42%, Filipino–9%, Japanese–21.5%, Korean–17.5%, Vietnamese–24.4%, Asian Indian–32%, and others–15.5%. The overall sample error is about 3% at 95% confidence level.

★46★

Political Parties: Importance of Asian American Constituents

Reported results, in percent, of a survey asking Asian Americans the following question: "Which political party, in your opinion, cares more about Asian Americans?"

Ethnic Group	Republican	Democrat	Neither	Both	Don't Know
All	15.0%	25.2%	34.9%	6.4%	18.5%
Chinese	13.2%	21.9%	39.5%	5.4%	20.0%
Filipino	17.5%	32.5%	16.7%	12.5%	20.8%
Japanese	6.6%	31.7%	37.7%	3.8%	20.2%
Korean	24.1%	8.9%	51.9%	5.1%	10.1%
Vietnamese	17.3%	26.4%	30.9%	4.5%	20.9%
Asian Indian	5.0%	56.3%	27.5%	1.3%	10.0%
Others	35.5%	5.4%	25.8%	17.2%	16.1%

Source: Republican National Committee, unpublished data. Results of an August 1992 survey of 5,000 Asian American adults in California. Names were selected from membership directories of major Asian ethnic organizations and from an ethnic surname database of registered voters. The response rate was 27.9% or 1,149 completed questionnaires. The ethnic composition of the response was: Chinese–42%, Filipino–9%, Japanese–21.5%, Korean–17.5%, Vietnamese–24.4%, Asian Indian–32%, and others–15.5%. The overall sample error is about 3% at 95% confidence level.

★47★

Political Parties: Importance of Winning the Presidential Election

Reported results, in percent, of a survey asking Asian Americans the following question: "Do you personally care which political party wins the presidential election?"

Ethnic Group	No	Yes	Don't Know
All	27.2	67.4	5.3
Chinese	31.0	65.7	3.3
Filipino	17.5	71.7	10.8
Japanese	37.7	57.9	4.4
Korean	21.5	69.6	8.9
Vietnamese	26.4	62.7	10.9
Asian Indian	10.0	88.8	1.3
Others	20.4	75.3	4.3

Source: Republican National Committee, unpublished data. Results of an August 1992 survey of 5,000 Asian American adults in California. Names were selected from membership directories of major Asian ethnic organizations and from an ethnic surname database of registered voters. The response rate was 27.9% or 1,149 completed questionnaires. The ethnic composition of the response was: Chinese–42%, Filipino–9%, Japanese–21.5%, Korean–17.5%, Vietnamese–24.4%, Asian Indian–32%, and others–15.5%. The overall sample error is about 3% at 95% confidence level.

★48★

Political Philosophy

Reported results, in percent, of a survey asking Asian Americans if they considered themselves liberal or conservative.

Ethnic Group	Very conservative	Somewhat conservative	Middle of the road	Somewhat liberal	Very liberal
All	12.0%	30.6%	30.7%	20.6%	5.5%
Chinese	9.5%	35.1%	30.2%	19.0%	5.8%
Filipino	11.7%	20.0%	38.3%	19.2%	10.8%
Japanese	15.3%	35.0%	31.1%	13.1%	3.8%
Korean	36.7%	22.8%	22.8%	17.7%	–
Vietnamese	10.0%	28.2%	23.6%	32.7%	5.5%
Asian Indian	–	20.0%	47.5%	27.5%	5.0%
Others	10.8%	31.2%	23.7%	28.0%	5.4%

Source: Republican National Committee, unpublished data. Results of an August 1992 survey of 5,000 Asian American adults in California. Names were selected from membership directories of major Asian ethnic organizations and from an ethnic surname database of registered voters. The response rate was 27.9% or 1,149 completed questionnaires. The ethnic composition of the response was: Chinese–42%, Filipino–9%, Japanese–21.5%, Korean–17.5%, Vietnamese–24.4%, Asian Indian–32%, and others–15.5%. The overall sample error is about 3% at 95% confidence level.

★49★

Registered Voters

Reported results, in percent, of a survey asking Asian Americans if they were registered voters.

Ethnic Group	No	Yes
All	18.2%	81.8%
Chinese	15.7%	84.3%
Filipino	14.2%	85.8%
Japanese	12.0%	88.0%
Korean	32.9%	67.1%
Vietnamese	21.8%	78.2%
Asian Indian	17.5%	82.5%
Others	32.3%	67.7%

Source: Republican National Committee, unpublished data. Results of an August 1992 survey of 5,000 Asian American adults in California. Names were selected from membership directories of major Asian ethnic organizations and from an ethnic surname database of registered voters. The response rate was 27.9% or 1,149 completed questionnaires. The ethnic composition of the response was: Chinese–42%, Filipino–9%, Japanese–21.5%, Korean–17.5%, Vietnamese–24.4%, Asian Indian–32%, and others–15.5%. The overall sample error is about 3% at 95% confidence level.

★50★

Self-Protection of Property

Reported results, in percent, of a survey asking Asian Americans the following question: "Without police protection, do you approve or disapprove of the action of Korean American merchants who armed themselves to protect their property?"

Ethnic Group	Strongly approve	Approve	No opinion	Dis- approve	Strongly disapprove
All	43.6%	40.9%	5.9%	6.7%	2.9%
Chinese	40.1%	44.8%	4.3%	8.7%	2.1%
Filipino	39.2%	43.3%	10.8%	5.8%	0.8%
Japanese	29.5%	51.4%	6.6%	7.7%	4.9%
Korean	69.6%	20.3%	2.5%	5.1%	2.5%
Vietnamese	37.3%	40.9%	10.0%	2.7%	9.1%
Asian Indian	55.0%	33.8%	5.0%	5.0%	1.3%
Others	71.0%	20.4%	5.4%	3.2%	–

Source: Republican National Committee, unpublished data. Results of an August 1992 survey of 5,000 Asian American adults in California. Names were selected from membership directories of major Asian ethnic organizations and from an ethnic surname database of registered voters. The response rate was 27.9% or 1,149 completed questionnaires. The ethnic composition of the response was: Chinese–42%, Filipino–9%, Japanese–21.5%, Korean–17.5%, Vietnamese–24.4%, Asian Indian–32%, and others–15.5%. The overall sample error is about 3% at 95% confidence level.

★51★

U.S. Involvement in Asia

Reported results, in percent, of a survey asking Asian Americans the following question: "How much do you think the U.S. should be involved in Asia?"

Ethnic Group	More involved	About the same	Less involved	Don't know
All	44.1%	29.9%	17.2%	8.8%
Chinese	34.7%	33.9%	20.9%	10.1%
Filipino	70.8%	14.2%	11.7%	3.3%
Japanese	29.0%	35.0%	23.0%	13.1%
Korean	24.1%	43.0%	21.5%	11.4%
Vietnamese	50.9%	38.2%	9.1%	1.8%
Asian Indian	66.3%	10.0%	12.5%	11.3%
Others	78.5%	15.1%	4.3%	2.2%

Source: Republican National Committee, unpublished data. Results of an August 1992 survey of 5,000 Asian American adults in California. Names were selected from membership directories of major Asian ethnic organizations and from an ethnic surname database of registered voters. The response rate was 27.9% or 1,149 completed questionnaires. The ethnic composition of the response was: Chinese–42%, Filipino–9%, Japanese–21.5%, Korean–17.5%, Vietnamese–24.4%, Asian Indian–32%, and others–15.5%. The overall sample error is about 3% at 95% confidence level.

★52★

Voting Decisions: Influencing Factors

Reported results, in percent, of a survey asking Asian Americans the following question: "Which one of the following factors is the most important in your decision of whom to vote for in the past elections?"

Ethnic Group	No Response	What kind of person he is	Where he stands on issues	His party affiliation	Whether he has a good chance to win
All	2.3%	18.9%	74.3%	3.7%	0.9%
Chinese	3.7%	18.2%	75.2%	2.7%	0.2%
Filipino	1.7%	14.2%	77.5%	1.7%	5.0%
Japanese	2.2%	23.0%	69.9%	4.4%	0.5%
Korean	–	27.8%	68.4%	3.8%	–
Vietnamese	–	24.5%	70.0%	4.5%	0.9%
Asian Indian	1.3%	6.3%	92.5%	–	–
Others	1.1%	17.2%	68.8%	11.8%	1.1%

Source: Republican National Committee, unpublished data. Results of an August 1992 survey of 5,000 Asian American adults in California. Names were selected from membership directories of major Asian ethnic organizations and from an ethnic surname database of registered voters. The response rate was 27.9% or 1,149 completed questionnaires. The ethnic composition of the response was: Chinese–42%, Filipino–9%, Japanese–21.5%, Korean–17.5%, Vietnamese–24.4%, Asian Indian–32%, and others–15.5%. The overall sample error is about 3% at 95% confidence level.

★53★

Voting in the 1988 U.S. Presidential Election

Reported results, in percent, of a survey asking Asian Americans the following question: "Which candidate did you vote for in the 1988 presidential election?"

Ethnic Group	Did not vote	George Bush	Michael Dukakis
All	23.2%	50.7%	26.2%
Chinese	21.1%	52.7%	26.2%
Filipino	15.8%	55.0%	29.2%
Japanese	16.9%	56.3%	26.8%
Korean	38.0%	41.8%	20.3%
Vietnamese	30.0%	47.3%	22.7%
Asian Indian	20.0%	23.8%	56.3%
Others	37.6%	58.1%	4.3%

Source: Republican National Committee, unpublished data. Results of an August 1992 survey of 5,000 Asian American adults in California. Names were selected from membership directories of major Asian ethnic organizations and from an ethnic surname database of registered voters. The response rate was 27.9% or 1,149 completed questionnaires. The ethnic composition of the response was: Chinese–42%, Filipino–9%, Japanese–21.5%, Korean–17.5%, Vietnamese–24.4%, Asian Indian–32%, and others–15.5%. The overall sample error is about 3% at 95% confidence level.

Media Usage

★54★

Magazine Readership

Reported responses of a survey of 104 Asians and 99 Hispanics in the New York metropolitan area on readership of magazines by types, 1989.

Magazines	Asians n=104	Hispanics n=99
Business/Trade		
Business Week	39	26
Economist	11	–
Forbes	12	7
Fortune	23	11
Money	17	–
Others	4	–
Scientific		
Discover	8	26
Omni	12	18
Scientific American	7	5
Men's		
GQ-Gentlemen's Quarterly	21	13
Playboy	14	15
Women's		
Cosmopolitan	14	19
Glamour	7	8
Vogue	18	23
Others	23	22
Sports		
Body Builders	–	12
Car & Driver	13	18
Golf Digest	15	1
Sport	–	16
Sports Illustrated	3	34
Sports Today	–	19
General Interest		
Life	3	8
Newsweek	37	12
People	23	28
Time	39	26
TV Guide	5	4
Others	27	43

[Continued]

★ 54 ★

Magazine Readership (Continued)

Reported responses of a survey of 104 Asians and 99 Hispanics in the New York metropolitan area on readership of magazines by types, 1989.

Magazines	Asians	Hispanics
	n=104	n=99
Ethnic: Chinese/Japanese and Spanish		
Ef	13	–
Elle	28	–
With	11	–
Chromos	–	4
Lo Vanidad	–	18
Ola (Hola)	–	25

Source: Nejdet Delener and James P. Neelankauil, "Information Sources and Media Usage: A Comparison between Asian and Hispanic Subcultures," *Journal of Advertising Research* 30 (June/July 1990): 45. The sample consisted of personal interviews of 104 Asians and 99 Hispanics in the New York metropolitan area. Also in source: data on media preferences of the U.S. adult population.

★ 55 ★

Media Usage

Reported responses, in numbers and percent, of a survey of 104 Asians and 99 Hispanics in the New York metropolitan area on media use, 1989.

Media usage	Asians (n=104)		Hispanics (n=99)	
	Number	Percent	Number	Percent
T.V.	78	75.0%	75	75.8%
Radio	59	56.7%	69	69.7%
Newspaper	60	57.7%	53	53.5%
Magazines	34	32.7%	33	33.4%

Source: Nejdet Delener and James P. Neelankauil, "Information Sources and Media Usage: A Comparison between Asian and Hispanic Subcultures," *Journal of Advertising Research* 30 (June/July 1990): 45. The sample consisted of personal interviews with 104 Asians and 99 Hispanics in the New York Metropolitan area. Also in source: data on media preferences of the U.S. adult population.

Attitudes of School Students

★56★

Attitudes of Students Regarding Crisis Situations

Reported responses, in percent, of a survey of students in grades five to eight asking questions designed to identify educationally at-risk students.

Group	Yes (percent)	Sometimes (percent)	No (percent)
"When I am with my friends I do whatever they want, even if it might be wrong."			
Asians	4.3	12.8	83.0
White	7.4	26.7	65.9
Black	6.4	24.3	69.4
Hispanic	8.2	26.9	64.9
American Indians	14.8	25.9	59.3
"I feel so trapped and hopeless that I don't care what happens to me."			
Asians	8.7	23.8	67.4
White	12.7	26.5	60.8
Black	17.6	23.1	59.4
Hispanic	14.8	29.3	55.9
American Indians	21.3	28.8	50.5
"Whenever I need help, I have an adult who will be there for me."			
Asians	44.4	28.9	26.7
White	33.4	30.3	36.2
Black	37.0	25.1	37.9
Hispanic	27.0	30.0	42.9
American Indians	32.5	26.3	41.3
"When I am with friends they can push me to try new and scary things, even if I don't want to do it."			
Asians	10.6	27.7	61.7
White	11.9	28.4	59.8
Black	10.5	27.3	62.2
Hispanic	11.5	28.3	60.2
American Indians	10.0	31.3	58.8
"I haven't got a chance in school, I have given up hope."			
Asians	4.3	6.4	89.4
White	7.3	9.8	82.9
Black	14.0	9.2	76.8
Hispanic	11.6	13.8	74.6
American Indians	16.3	15.0	68.8

[Continued]

34

★ 56 ★

Attitudes of Students Regarding Crisis Situations (Continued)

Reported responses, in percent, of a survey of students in grades five to eight asking questions designed to identify educationally at-risk students.

Group	Yes (percent)	Sometimes (percent)	No (percent)
"I am good at talking my friends into doing something that is not right, something that might get them into trouble."			
Asians	8.5	14.9	76.6
White	13.4	20.0	66.5
Black	15.6	20.2	64.2
Hispanic	17.1	23.3	59.6
American Indians	19.8	23.5	56.8

Source: Melinda G. Leaseburg, et al., "Inventory of Personal Skills for Achievement: Validity and Reliability Study of an Instrument for Identifying Educationally At-Risk Junior High School Students." This paper was presented at the Rural Education Symposium of the American Council on Rural Special Education and the National Rural and Small Schools Consortium, and published in its proceedings (Tucson: March 18–22, 1990), p. 17–18. Data was taken from a test administered to 4,300 students in grades five to eight from twenty-six schools in eight states. Both rural and urban schools were represented that contained populations of white, black, Hispanic, Asian, and American Indian students.

★ 57 ★

Attributions of Academic Performance

Reported findings of a study comparing attitudes of Chinese, Filipino, Japanese, Korean, Vietnamese, and Southeast Asian students[a] in grades four to eleven relating to whether academic success or failure is attributable to effort or to ability.

In general, these Asian American students attributed success to effort more frequently than to ability.

Overall, Language Arts/Social Studies situations resulted in greater attributions of success to effort than did Math/Science situations.

Success was more significantly attributed to effort than was failure attributed to lack of effort.

Koreans had the highest attribution of success to effort, and Southeast Asians had the lowest.

Students receiving lunch subsidies made significantly more attributions to ability than did those who paid for their lunches.

Overall, Asian American students with fewer economic resources seem to believe that ability has a greater effect in Math/Science failure situations than do those who have more resources.

Source: Selected from Donald T. Mizokawa and David B. Rychman, "Attributions of Academic Success and Failure: A Comparison of Six Asian American Ethnic Groups," *Journal of Cross-Cultural Psychology* 21, no. 4 (Dec. 1990): 434–451. *Note:* (a) The 2,511 subjects were selected from 15,000 students from Seattle Public Schools and represented six Asian nationality groups as follows: Chinese–836, Filipino–562, Japanese–232, Korean–166, Vietnamese–344, Southeast Asian–371. Lunch subsidy status: 1,082 paid for school lunches and 1,429 received free or reduced-price lunches under federal guidelines.

★ 58 ★

Factors Affecting High School Academic Performance

Reported results of a study examining whether attitudinal and cultural differences between families of Asian American and non-Asian American high school students contribute to the former's greater success in school.

Factor	Asian Americans[a]	Non-Asian Americans[b]
Number	29	70
Grade point average, mean	4.05	3.70
SAT-verbal, mean	407.3	431.7
SAT-math, mean	535.5	459.9
Factor examined		
Self-motivated to do well in school	55.2%	42.9%
Career choice influenced by personal interests	62.1%	58.6%
Career choice influenced by money	3.4%	31.4%
Career goal: business professional	44.8%	50.0%
Career goal: professional athlete	0.0%	12.9%
Career goal: famous scientist	37.9%	4.3%
Homework: 6 or more hours per week	62.1%	34.3%
Homework: parents show no interest in	37.9%	2.9%
Dating: had to be over 18 to date unchaperoned	41.4%	1.4%
Had cars	41.4%	67.1%
Watched 8 hours or more TV per week	51.4%	46.4%
Affected by loss of rock music, TV, or athletics	0.0%	15.8%
Affected by loss of leisure time	48.3%	18.6%

Source: Selected from Gary L. Reglin and Dale R. Adams, "Why Asian American High School Students Have Higher Grade Point Averages and SAT Scores than Other High School Students," *High School Journal* 73, no. 3 (Feb–March 1990): 143–49.

★ 59 ★

"Model Minority" Stereotype: Negative Consequences

Researchers studying Asian American adolescent mental health offer opinions on negative consequences of "positive" stereotype.

"Model minority" stereotype characterizes Asian Americans as hard working, uncomplaining role models of diligence and achievement. The negative consequences of this stereotype, according to the researchers cited, are:

(1) Positive stereotype pits Asian Americans against the more powerful minority groups, such as blacks and Hispanic Americans, and indirectly blames these groups, rather than the social system, for their failure to "succeed."

(2) The Asian American becomes a convenient scapegoat for low-income, less-educated white and minority Americans who believe Asians usurped jobs or opportunity for college education.

(3) The social and mental health problems of Asian Americans are trivialized.

(4) The stereotype overlooks the immense diversity of Asian American subgroups.

(5) The stereotype overlooks the problems encountered by Southeast Asian refugees and new immigrants in accessing education and employment.

Source: William T. Liu and Elena S. H. Yu, et al. "The Mental Health of Asian American Teenagers: A Research Challenge," Chap. 4 in Stiffman & Davis, *Ethnic Issues in Adolescent Mental Health* (New York: Sage Publications, 1990), p.93.

Reproductive Health

★60★

Attitudes toward Contraceptive Use by Generation in the U.S.

Reported results of a poll of Asian/Pacific Islanders from California community organizations[a] asking if they supported use of contraceptives, by sex, generation in the United States, and Asian ethnicity, 1992.

Profile	Current contraceptive user	Past contraceptive user	Supports use of contraceptives
Gender			
Male	47%	75%	83%
Female	42%	72%	83%
Generation			
1st generation	40%	62%	71%
2nd generation	40%	70%	90%
3rd generation	54%	86%	96%
Ethnicity			
Chinese	44%	67%	84%
Filipino	41%	67%	67%
Japanese	44%	86%	92%
Korean	40%	67%	81%
Southeast Asian	57%	70%	73%
Pacific Islander	64%	79%	85%
Other Asian	26%	39%	45%

Source: Asian/Pacific Islanders for Choice, *The Asian/Pacific Islander Reproductive Health Survey 1991–1992* (Oakland: Asian/Pacific Islanders for Choice, 1992), p. 4. *Note:* (a) Respondents to the survey were solicited from various health care facilities, social service agencies, church groups, student groups, senior citizens groups, and volunteer organizations. Overall, the 1,215 respondents were highly educated with 65% holding at least a bachelor's degree. Thirty-nine percent had incomes over $50,000; 37% had incomes between $20,000 and $50,000; and 24% had incomes less than $20,000. Forty-four percent were in professional positions, 16% in managerial positions, 11% in sales, clerical, or other positions, and 29% were college students or not employed. Sixty-eight percent were female and 32% male. Forty-eight percent lived in the Los Angeles area, 28% in the Sacramento area, and 24% in the San Francisco area. The sponsors of the survey stress that the results represent the attitudes of the highly educated, professional and managerial English-speaking sector of the Asian/Pacific Islander community polled, and are not generalizable to all Asian/Pacific Islander communities in the United States.

★ 61 ★

Attitudes toward Abortion by Generation in the U.S.

Reported results of a poll of Asian/Pacific Islanders from California community organizations[a] asking if they opposed or supported abortion, by sex, generation in the United States, education level, and Asian ethnicity, 1992

Profile	Oppose	Conditional support	Support "right to choose" (or abortion) during early pregnancy
Gender			
Female	5%	25%	70%
Male	6%	26%	68%
Ethnicity			
Chinese	4%	23%	73%
Filipino	9%	37%	53%
Japanese	2%	18%	79%
Korean	7%	30%	63%
Southeast Asian	15%	40%	45%
Pacific Islanders	14%	27%	59%
Other Asian	14%	27%	59%
Generation			
1st generation	8%	34%	58%
2nd generation	3%	18%	80%
3rd generation	3%	16%	81%
Education level			
Low	8%	34%	57%
Middle	5%	26%	69%
High	2%	18%	80%

Source: Asian/Pacific Islanders for Choice, *The Asian/Pacific Islander Reproductive Health Survey 1991–1992* (Oakland: Asian/Pacific Islanders for Choice, 1992), p. 4. *Note:* (a) Respondents to the survey were solicited from various health care facilities, social service agencies, church groups, student groups, senior citizens groups, and volunteer organizations. Overall, the 1,215 respondents were highly educated with 65% holding at least a bachelor's degree. Thirty-nine percent had incomes over $50,000; 37% had incomes between $20,000 and $50,000; and 24% had incomes less than $20,000. Forty-four percent were in professional positions, 16% in managerial positions, 11% in sales, clerical, or other positions, and 29% were college students or not employed. Sixty-eight percent were female and 32% male. Forty-eight percent lived in the Los Angeles area, 28% in the Sacramento area, and 24% in the San Francisco area. The sponsors of the survey stress that the results represent the attitudes of the highly educated, professional and managerial English-speaking sector of the Asian/Pacific Islander community polled, and are not generalizable to all Asian/Pacific Islander communities in the United States.

Volunteerism and Charitable Giving

★62★

Charitable Giving, San Francisco-Oakland Area Donors

Reported results of a survey[a] of known contributors in the San Francisco-Oakland, California, area to study Asian American charitable giving, 1986.

Profile of survey respondents	
Number	321 of Asian descent
Education	82.8% with bachelor's degree or higher
Median gross person income	$34,279
Median gross household income	$53,638
Average contribution to charitable causes, 1986 (in dollars)	$1,325.15
Percent of household income	2.7%
Percent of income contributed by individuals with incomes less than $10,000.	6.6%
Percent of income contributed by individuals with incomes of $20,000 to $60,000	2.2%
Average contribution to charitable causes by individuals who volunteer time	$1,016
In percent of household income, volunteers	2.8%
Average contribution to charitable causes by non-volunteers	$499
In percent of household income, non-volunteers	2.0%

Source: Rosalyn Miyoko Tonai, *Asian American Charitable Giving* (San Francisco: Institute for Nonprofit Organization Management, University of San Francisco, Working Paper No. 24, 1988), p. 1. *Note:* (a) Data collected from 321 Asian American donors selected from mailing lists of Asian nonprofit organizations. Individuals surveyed were known to be donors.

★63★

Charitable Giving, San Francisco-Oakland Area Volunteers

Reported results of a survey[a] of Asian American individuals who volunteer, to compare Asian American charitable giving by volunteers and non-volunteers, 1986.

Contributions	Volunteers	Non-volunteers
Contributions to Asian nonprofit organizations		
% of household income	1.8%	1.0%
% of personal income	2.1%	1.8%
Contributions to all non-profit organizations		
% of household income	2.8%	2.0%
% of personal income	3.0%	2.8%

Source: Rosalyn Miyoko Tonai, *Asian American Charitable Giving* (San Francisco: Institute for Nonprofit Organization Management, University of San Francisco, Working Paper No. 24, 1988), fig. 1.1, p. 19. *Note:* (a) Data collected from 321 Asian American donors selected from mailing lists of Asian nonprofit organizations. Individuals surveyed were known to be donors.

★ 64 ★

Contribution of Volunteer Time,
San Francisco Bay Area

Reported results of a survey of average hours volunteered per month by individuals in the San Francisco Bay area[a] by race/ethnicity, 1989 and 1991.

Ethnic group	Average volunteer hours per month	
	1991	1989
All individuals	12	11
Ethnic group		
Chinese	8	5
African Americans	14	11
Hispanic	9	7
White	14	11

Source: Bradford Smith, Sylvia Shue, and Joseph Villarveal, *Asian and Hispanic Philanthropy* (San Francisco: Institute for Nonprofit Organization Management, University of San Francisco, 1992), table 9, p. 19. Primary source: Tables 18, Market Opinion Research, 1991. *Note:* (a) Data collected during telephone surveys conducted in Alameda, Contra Costa, Marin, San Francisco, San Mateo, and Santa Clara counties by Market Opinion Research of Farmington Hills, Michigan, for the "Bay Area Strive for Five" project. The 1989 survey was conducted from April 20 through May 25, 1989, with a representative sample of 1,362 adults 18 years of age and older. The 1991 survey was conducted between October 4 and October 21, 1991, with a representative sample of 606 adults 18 years of age and older.

★ 65 ★

Contributions of Money by Household,
San Francisco Bay Area

Reported results of a survey of average charitable contributions per year by household in the San Francisco Bay area[a] by race/ethnicity, 1989 and 1991.

Ethnic group	Average annual contribution	
	1991	1989
All households[b]	$633	$643
Ethnic group		
Chinese	$296	$298
African Americans	$436	$513
Hispanic	$201	$451
White	$804	$715

Source: Bradford Smith, Sylvia Shue, and Joseph Villarveal, *Asian and Hispanic Philanthropy* (San Francisco: Institute for Nonprofit Organization Management, University of San Francisco, 1992), table 8, p. 19. Primary source: Tables 19 and 26, Market Opinion Research, 1991. *Notes:* (a) Data collected during telephone surveys conducted in Alameda, Contra Costa, Marin, San Francisco, San Mateo, and Santa Clara counties by Market Opinion Research of Farmington Hills, Michigan, for the "Bay Area Strive for Five" project. (b) The 1989 survey was conducted from April 20 through May 25, 1989, with a representative sample of 1,362 adults 18 years of age and older. The 1991 survey was conducted between October 4 and October 21, 1991, with a representative sample of 606 adults 18 years of age and older.

★66★

Contributions of Time and Money, San Francisco Area

Reported results, in percent, of a survey of household monetary contributions and individual's volunteering of time in the San Francisco Bay area[a] by race/ethnicity, 1989 and 1991.

Group	San Francisco households contributing money		Individuals volunteering time	
	1991	1989	1991	1989
All households[b]	75%	78%		
All individuals			50%	38%
Ethnic group				
Chinese	75%	40%	36%	27%
African American	76%	82%	39%	37%
Hispanic	59%	74%	45%	35%
White	80%	80%	53%	41%

Source: Bradford Smith, Sylvia Shue, and Joseph Villarveal, *Asian and Hispanic Philanthropy* (San Francisco: Institute for Nonprofit Organization Management, University of San Francisco, 1992), table 7, p. 18. *Notes:* (a) Data collected during telephone surveys conducted in Alameda, Contra Costa, Marin, San Francisco, San Mateo, and Santa Clara counties by Market Opinion Research of Farmington Hills, Michigan, for the "Bay Area Strive for Five" project. (b) The 1989 survey was conducted from April 20 through May 25, 1989, with a representative sample of 1,362 adults 18 years of age and older. The 1991 survey was conducted between October 4 and October 21, 1991, with a representative sample of 606 adults 18 years of age and older.

Business and Economics

General

★67★

Average Receipts per Firm by Industry

Average receipts per Asian/Pacific Islander-owned firm, calculated by dividing the total receipts for all firms in a given industry by the number of firms in that industry, and average Asian/Pacific Islander-owned business receipts as a percentage of average receipts for all firms, 1987.

Industry	Average receipts per firm		Asian/Pacific Islander receipts as a percentage of average receipts for all firms
	Asian/Pacific Islander-owned firms	All firms	
All industries	$93,000	$146,000	63%
Agricultural services, forestry, fishing, and mining	38,000		
Construction	91,000	141,000	65%
Manufacturing	144,000	523,000	28%
Transportation and public utilities	58,000	129,000	45%
Wholesale trade	393,000	679,000	58%
Retail trade	150,000	243,000	62%
Finance, insurance, and real estate	40,000	101,000	40%
Services	60,000	70,000	86%
Industries not classified	50,000	57,000	88%

Source: Calculated from Bureau of the Census, U.S. Department of Commerce, *Survey of Minority-Owned Business Enterprises: Asian Americans, American Indians, and Other Minorities,* 1987 Economic Censuses (Washington, DC: U.S. Government Printing Office, June 1991) table 5, p. 27–35 and table 13, p. 108–109. Included in the universe of the survey is any activity for which an IRS form 1040, Schedule C (individual proprietorship or self-employed person); 1065 (partnership); or 1120S (subchapter S corporation) was filed in 1987.

★ 68 ★

Business Ownership

Numbers of businesses owned by Asian/Pacific Islanders by ethnicity and percent change, 1977 and 1987.

Ethnic group[a]	Businesses owned		
	1977	1987	% increase
Chinese	23,000	90,000	291%
Filipino	10,000	40,000	300%
Indian	7,000	52,000	642%
Japanese	27,000	53,000	96%
Korean	9,000	69,000	667%
Vietnamese	–	26,000	–
Other Asian	7,000	25,000	257%
Total	83,000	355,000	328%

Source: "Asian American Demographics," *The American Enterprise* (November/December 1991): 87–90. Primary source: Bureau of the Census, U.S. Department of Commerce. *Notes:* (a) In 1987, black Americans (who were four times as numerous as Asians) owned 424,000 businesses while Hispanics (who were three times as numerous) owned 422,000.

★ 69 ★

Business Ownership and Receipts

Numbers of businesses owned by Asian/Pacific Islanders and dollar receipts (in millions) by ethnicity and percent change, in 1982 and 1987.

Ethnic group	1982		1987		Percent increase	
	Businesses owned	Receipts ($1,000,000)	Businesses owned	Receipts ($1,000,000)	Businesses owned	Receipts
Asian/Pacific Islanders, total	187,691	$12,654	355,331	$33,125	89%	162%
Asian Indian	23,770	1,660	52,266	6,715	120%	304%
Chinese	48,827	4,309	89,717	9,610	84%	123%
Japanese	43,529	2,116	53,372	3,837	23%	81%
Korean	30,919	2,670	69,304	7,683	124%	187%
Vietnamese	4,989	215	25,671	1,361	414%	532%
Filipino	23,359	747	40,412	1,914	73%	156%
Hawaiian	2,927	85	4,279	221	46%	161%
Other Asian/Pacific Islander	9,371	852	20,310	1,784	116%	109%

Source: Bureau of the Census, U.S. Department of Commerce, *Survey of Minority-Owned Business Enterprises: Asian Americans, American Indians, and Other Minorities,* 1987 Economic Censuses (Washington, DC: Government Printing Office, June 1991), table A, p 3. Included in the universe of the survey is any activity for which an IRS Form 1040, Schedule C (individual proprietorship or self-employed person); 1065 (partnership); or 1120S (subchapter S corporation) was filed in 1987. Dollar values are expressed in current dollars—1987 data are expressed in 1987 dollars and 1982 data in 1982 dollars. Consequently, when making comparisons, the effects of inflation should be considered. The large increase from 1982 to 1987 in minority-owned businesses can be attributed in part to a change in IRS regulations which allowed more businesses to file as subchapter S corporations. Many businesses changed their form of ownership from partnerships and other types of corporations to subchapter S corporation to take advantage of tax benefits.

★70★

Business Ownership and Receipts by Industry

Numbers of businesses owned by Asian/Pacific Islanders and dollar receipts (in thousands) by industry[a] and ethnicity of owner, 1987.

Industry group	Asian Indian	Chinese	Japanese	Korean	Viet- namese	Filipino	Hawaiian	Other Asian/ Pacific Islander	Total
Agricultural services, forestry, and fishing	358	774	4,407	557	2,230	739	247	414	9,726
Sales and receipts (in $1,000)	$19,278	$37,495	$145,348	$27,871	$86,698	$26,900	$8,841	$12,878	$365,309
Manufacturing	878	2,685	1,383	1,905	1,947	643	126	554	10,121
Sales and receipts (in $1,000)	$241,067	$494,044	$165,002	$334,092	$103,274	$56,721	$20,564	$46,632	$1,461,396
Transportation and public utilities	2,812	2,576	1,352	1,582	708	1,432	149	1,329	11,940
Sales and receipts (in $1,000)	$158,605	$175,923	$104,773	$87,446	$19,723	$76,520	$9,928	$58,562	$691,480
Mining	112	100	69	16	6	24	8	25	360
Sales and receipts (in $1,000)	$2,071	$2,809	$2,550	(b)	$68	$3,161	(b)	$495	$11,154
Construction	1,199	3,298	2,128	3,249	823	1,448	384	862	13,391
Sales and receipts (in $1,000)	$177,070	$333,144	$216,294	$218,721	$26,953	$84,540	$43,478	$123,990	$1,224,190
Wholesale trade	1,634	3,510	1,826	1,908	330	793	93	560	10,654
Sales and receipts (in $1,000)	$879,785	$1,429,316	$511,116	$876,122	$95,612	$157,518	$8,741	$230,642	$4,188,852
Retail trade	9,314	25,803	9,051	26,161	6,646	6,099	689	4,998	88,761
Sales and receipts (in $1,000)	$1,935,454	$4,268,139	$1,289,714	$4,064,114	$624,988	$442,980	$38,205	$652,159	$13,315,753
Finance, insurance and real estate	3,537	8,906	4,227	2,736	1,132	5,145	286	1,328	27,297
Sales and receipts (in $1,000)	$182,676	$429,065	$163,631	$116,020	$26,247	$102,119	$16,981	$50,116	$1,086,855
Services	29,787	37,232	26,291	28,604	10,461	21,846	2,077	9,044	165,342
Sales and receipts (in $1,000)	$2,917,588	$2,186,744	$1,138,326	$1,773,886	$330,780	$910,854	$65,409	$557,281	$9,880,868
Industries not classified	2,635	4,833	2,638	2,586	1,388	2,243	220	1,196	17,739
Sales and receipts (in $1,000)	$201,090	$252,913	$100,501	(b)	$46,631	$52,820	(b)	$51,089	$705,044

Source: Adapted from Bureau of the Census, U.S. Department of Commerce, *Survey of Minority-Owned Business Enterprises: Asian Americans, American Indians, and Other Minorities,* 1987 Economic Censuses (Washington, DC: Government Printing Office, June 1991), table 2, p. 12–17. Included in the universe of the survey is any activity for which an IRS Form 1040, Schedule C (Individual proprietorship or self-employed person); 1065 (partnership); or 1120S (subchapter S corporation) was filed in 1987. Also in source: data for subsets of the major industry groups, i.e., business services, personal services, auto repair, etc. However, this data is not broken out by ethnicity. *Notes:* (a) The industry group classifications presented below are based on the 1972 SIC system. (b) Withheld to avoid disclosing data for individual companies.

★71★

Business Ownership by Form of Organization, Employees, and Payroll

Numbers of businesses owned by Asian/Pacific Islanders, dollar receipts (in milions), number employed, and annual payroll by organization structure (individual proprietorships, partnerships, and subchapter S corporations), 1987.

Legal form of organization, and ethnic group	All businesses		Businesses with paid employees			
	Firms (number)	Sales/receipts ($1,000,000)	Businesses (number)	Sales/receipts ($1,000,000)	Employees (number)	Annual payroll ($1,000,000)
All U.S. Businesses	13,695,480	$1,994,808	3,487,454	$1,709,301	19,853,333	$299,176
Subchapter S corporations	911,699	1,074,483	684,925	1,043.467	10,483,879	182,371
Individual proprietorships	12,123,747	606,144	2,459,632	401,447	5,966,615	65,412
Partnerships	660,034	314,182	342,897	264,387	3,402,839	51,392
Asians/Pacific Islanders, total	355,331	$33,124,326	92,718	$24,501,338	351,345	$3,501,917
Subchapter S corporations	16,475	8,402,698	12,656	7,977,348	105,402	1,347,721
Asian Indian	5,169	2,566,035	3,975	2,422,921	29,599	395,871

[Continued]

Business Ownership by Form of Organization, Employees, and Payroll (Continued)

Numbers of businesses owned by Asian/Pacific Islanders, dollar receipts (in milions), number employed, and annual payroll by organization structure (individual proprietorships, partnerships, and subchapter S corporations), 1987.

Legal form of organization, and ethnic group	All businesses		Businesses with paid employees			
	Firms (number)	Sales/receipts ($1,000,000)	Businesses (number)	Sales/receipts ($1,000,000)	Employees (number)	Annual payroll ($1,000,000)
Chinese	5,532	2,801,210	4,356	2,667,976	42,478	487,552
Japanese	1,519	960,027	1,098	929,186	10,744	170,364
Korean	1,878	962,501	1,519	925,210	10,522	128,380
Vietnamese	468	115,682	342	106,214	1,973	20,303
Filipino	808	371,832	558	351,269	3,867	58,600
Hawaiian	140	69,126	84	55,923	654	12,165
Other Asian/Pacific Islander	961	556,285	724	518,649	5,565	74,486
Individual proprietorships	320,161	$20,570,018	69,663	$13,276,736	185,065	$1,677,348
Asian Indian	43,162	3,259,140	10,054	2,088,030	23,397	218,327
Chinese	77,418	5,172,118	18,045	3,445,972	57,916	470,139
Japanese	49,446	2,338,847	7,941	1,447,896	20,942	232,001
Korean	65,268	6,212,263	18,997	4,189,231	53,317	476,724
Vietnamese	24,183	1,114,668	4,989	640,518	9,522	79,136
Filipino	38,449	1,365,888	5,656	770,827	10,589	111,689
Hawaiian	4,022	123,885	516	64,869	923	11,378
Other Asian/Pacific Islander	18,213	983,209	3,465	629,393	8,459	77,954
Partnerships	18,695	$4,151,610	10,399	$3,247,254	60,878	$476,848
Asian Indian	3,935	889,509	2,341	675,631	12,737	89,118
Chinese	6,767	1,636,264	4,130	1,348,870	26,369	197,753
Japanese	2,407	538,381	1,147	407,324	6,703	65,730
Korean	2,158	507,904	1,141	387,565	6,691	56,292
Vietnamese	1,020	130,624	509	90,280	1,862	10,894
Filipino	1,155	176,413	497	131,474	2,366	21,698
Hawaiian	117	28,165	40	20,892	379	3,841
Other Asian/Pacific Islander	1,136	244,350	594	185,218	3,771	31,522

Source: Bureau of the Census, U.S. Department of Commerce, *Survey of Minority-Owned Business Enterprises: Asian Americans, American Indians, and Other Minorities,* 1987 Economic Censuses (Washington, DC: U.S. Government Printing Office, June 1991), table 10, p.104, 110. Included in the universe of the survey is any activity for which an IRS Form 1040, Schedule C (individual proprietorship or self-employed person); 1065 (partnership); or 1120S (subchapter S corporation) was filed in 1987. The large increase from 1982 to 1987 in minority-owned businesses can be attributed in part to a change in IRS regulations which allowed more businesses to file as subchapter S corporations. Many businesses changed their form of ownership from partnerships and other types of corporations to subchapter S corporation to take advantage of tax benefits.

★72★

Business Ownership by Employees, Payroll, and Receipts, by Asian Ethnicity

Numbers of Asian/Pacific Islander-owned businesses by ethnicity and annual sales/receipts (in thousands of dollars), and numbers of Asian/Pacific Islander-owned businesses with employees, numbers of employees, and annual payroll, 1987.

Ethnic group	All businesses		Businesses with paid employees			
	Businesses (number)	Sales/receipts ($1,000)	Businesses (number)	Sales/receipts ($1,000)	Employees (number)	Annual payroll ($1,000)
Asian/Pacific Islander, total	355,331	$33,124,326	92,718	$24,501,338	351,345	$3,501,917
Asian Indian	52,266	6,714,684	16,370	5,186,582	65,733	703,316
Chinese	89,717	9,609,592	26,531	7,462,818	126,763	1,155,444
Japanese	53,372	3,837,255	10,186	2,784,406	38,389	468,095
Korean	69,304	7,682,668	21,657	5,502,006	70,530	661,396
Vietnamese	25,671	1,360,974	5,840	837,012	13,357	110,333
Filipino	40,412	1,914,133	6,711	1,253,570	16,822	191,987
Hawaiian	4,279	221,176	640	141,684	1,956	27,384
Other Asian/Pacific Islander	20,310	1,783,844	4,783	1,333,260	17,795	183,962

Source: Bureau of the Census, U.S. Department of Commerce, *Survey of Minority-Owned Business Enterprises: Asian Americans, American Indians, and Other Minorities,* 1987 Economic Censuses (Washington, DC: U.S. Government Printing Office, June 1991), table 5, p. 27–35. Included in the universe of the survey is any activity for which an IRS Form 1040, Schedule C (individual proprietorship or self-employed person); 1065 (partnership); or 1120S (Subchapter S Corporation) was filed in 1987.

★73★

Business Ownership by State

Numbers of Asian/Pacific Islander-owned businesses and percent of total businesses by state (including District of Columbia), ranked (greatest to least) by number of Asian/Pacific Islander firms owned, 1987.

Rank	State	Asian/Pacific Islander		
		Businesses owned	Percent of total businesses	Percent of total U.S. population
	United States	355,331	2.7%	2.9%
1	California	144,353	8.0	9.6
2	New York	35,812	3.9	3.9
3	Hawaii	31,300	51.4	61.8
4	Texas	21,753	2.1	1.9
5	Illinois	14,679	2.6	2.50
6	New Jersey	12,530	3.1	3.5
7	Florida	8,553	1.2	1.2
8	Virginia	7,973	2.7	2.6
9	Maryland	7,831	3.2	2.9
10	Washington	7,559	2.6	4.3
11	Pennsylvania	7,049	1.2	1.2
12	Michigan	4,424	1.0	1.1
13	Georgia	4,092	1.3	1.2
14	Ohio	3,859	0.7	0.8
15	Massachusetts	3,784	1.1	2.4
16	Colorado	3,192	1.2	1.8
17	Oregon	3,007	1.6	2.4

[Continued]

★73★

Business Ownership by State (Continued)

Numbers of Asian/Pacific Islander-owned businesses and percent of total businesses by state (including District of Columbia), ranked (greatest to least) by number of Asian/Pacific Islander firms owned, 1987.

Rank	State	Asian/Pacific Islander		
		Businesses owned	Percent of total businesses	Percent of total U.S. population
18	Louisiana	2,583	1.3	1.0
19	Arizona	2,526	1.3	1.5
20	North Carolina	2,069	0.6	0.8
21	Missouri	2,056	0.7	0.8
22	Connecticut	1,963	1.0	1.5
23	Indiana	1,718	0.6	0.7
24	Oklahoma	1,700	0.8	1.1
25	Minnesota	1,684	0.6	1.8
26	Tennessee	1,574	0.6	0.7
27	Nevada	1,245	2.1	3.2
28	Wisconsin	1,144	0.5	1.1
29	Kansas	1,135	0.7	1.3
30	Utah	1,129	1.1	1.9
31	Mississippi	1,128	1.0	0.5
32	Alaska	1,028	2.1	3.6
33	South Carolina	918	0.6	0.6
34	Alabama	917	0.5	0.5
35	New Mexico	897	1.1	0.9
36	Kentucky	875	0.5	0.5
37	District of Columbia	779	2.7	1.9
38	Iowa	574	0.3	0.9
39	Arkansas	567	0.4	0.5
40	West Virginia	523	0.7	0.4
41	Delaware	436	1.4	1.4
42	Rhode Island	436	0.8	1.8
43	Idaho	433	0.6	0.9
44	Nebraska	385	0.4	0.8
45	New Hampshire	304	0.4	0.8
46	Montana	207	0.3	0.5
47	Maine	165	0.2	0.5
48	Wyoming	154	0.5	0.6
49	North Dakota	119	0.3	0.5
50	South Dakota	108	0.2	0.5
51	Vermont	102	0.2	0.6

Source: Adapted from *Asians in America, 1990 Census, Classification by States* (San Francisco, CA: *Asian Week,* undated), p. 58. Primary source: Bureau of the Census, U.S. Department of Commerce, *Survey of Minority-Owned Business Enterprises: Asian Americans, American Indians, and Other Minorities,* 1987 Economic Censuses (Washington, DC: U.S. Government Printing Office, June 1991), table 5, p. 27–35.

★74★

Business Ownership by State, Receipts, and Payroll

Numbers of Asian/Pacific Islander-owned businesses, average annual sales/receipts (in thousands of dollars), number of employees and average annual salary of total businesses by state (including District of Columbia), 1987.

State	A/PI owned firms with employees		Average annual sales/ receipts per firm ($1,000)		A/I owned firms with employees		Average annual salary/ wages per employee	
	Number of firms	Sales/ receipts ($1,000)	A/PI-owned firms:	All U.S. firms	Number of employees	Annual payroll ($1,000)	A/PI-owned firms:	All U.S. firms
United States	92,718	$24,501,338	$264	$490	351,345	$3,501,917	$9,967	$15,069
Alabama	417	$107,553	$256	$435	1,691	$14,642	$8,659	$13,124
Alaska	250	52,794	211	390	925	11,238	12,149	18,080
Arizona	736	187,903	255	389	3,988	29,867	7,489	12,785
Arkansas	253	42,134	167	305	1,023	7,030	6,872	11,268
California	38,273	10,907,652	285	454	153,519	1,490,434	9,709	15,363
Colorado	952	161,393	170	357	4,017	29,568	7,361	13,872
Connecticut	650	171,402	264	574	2,123	29,085	13,700	17,951
District of Columbia	337	115,676	343	921	1,354	17,293	12,772	20,828
Delaware	155	30,482	197	471	679	5,266	7,756	13,653
Florida	2,670	769,368	288	444	11,698	112,331	9,603	13,630
Georgia	1,533	363,894	237	500	5,203	43,828	8,424	14,805
Hawaii	4,427	1,109,366	251	505	15,046	178,004	11,831	14,034
Idaho	143	25,006	175	287	771	4,937	6,403	11,833
Illinois	3,904	1,056,952	271	635	14,278	151,404	10,604	16,990
Indiana	699	155,192	222	550	3,514	29,785	8,476	13,696
Iowa	232	46,453	200	340	1,136	7,544	6,641	11,541
Kansas	406	62,750	155	345	1,437	11,146	7,756	12,049
Kentucky	324	78,987	244	402	1,660	13,882	8,363	12,435
Louisiana	717	113,709	159	363	1,942	16,760	8,630	12,138
Maine	56	15,515	277	373	489	4,546	9,297	13,901
Maryland	2,172	495,956	228	647	6,757	78,550	11,625	16,569
Massachusetts	803	201,948	251	693	3,155	39,640	12,564	18,295
Michigan	1,402	314,573	224	544	5,961	57,927	9,718	14,802
Minnesota	509	126,937	249	436	2,842	25,965	9,136	14,048
Mississippi	551	110,700	201	317	2,404	15,069	6,268	11,083
Missouri	824	129,157	157	439	2,757	21,347	7,828	14,357
Montana	72	8,504	118	250	323	1,779	5,508	10,413
Nebraska	125	23,342	187	376	491	3,832	9,146	12,568
Nevada	320	58,251	182	551	1,197	11,264	9,410	13,819
New Hampshire	74	25,957	351	479	234	2,465	10,534	15,557
New Jersey	2,846	804,173	283	771	7,828	103,840	13,265	19,208
New Mexico	330	50,767	154	265	1,258	8,235	6,546	10,628
New York	7,061	2,149,917	304	760	21,227	286,030	13,475	19,638
North Carolina	855	168,937	198	435	3,807	27,024	7,099	13,188
North Dakota	43	3,446	80	277	214	1,483	6,930	10,503
Ohio	1,392	302,162	217	497	5,627	52,562	9,340	14,170
Oklahoma	440	69,191	157	309	1,645	12,007	7,299	12,215
Oregon	1,002	253,356	253	380	4,442	34,595	7,789	13,014
Pennsylvania	2,193	690,247	315	642	7,774	84,672	10,892	15,294
Rhode Island	129	28,247	219	646	680	4,852	7,135	15,487
South Carolina	386	71,316	185	365	1,621	10,653	6,572	12,487
South Dakota	7	1,348	193	306	8	88	11,000	10,931
Tennessee	713	139,739	196	417	3,010	20,064	6,666	13,237
Texas	5,704	1,285,592	225	389	16,425	163,621	9,962	14,997
Utah	270	49,695	184	325	1,174	8,213	6,996	11,864

[Continued]

★74★

Business Ownership by State, Receipts, and Payroll (Continued)

Numbers of Asian/Pacific Islander-owned businesses, average annual sales/receipts (in thousands of dollars), number of employees and average annual salary of total businesses by state (including District of Columbia), 1987.

State	A/PI owned firms with employees		Average annual sales/ receipts per firm ($1,000)		A/I owned firms with employees		Average annual salary/ wages per employee	
	Number of firms	Sales/ receipts ($1,000)	A/PI-owned firms:	All U.S. firms	Number of employees	Annual payroll ($1,000)	A/PI-owned firms:	All U.S. firms
Vermont	42	7,715	184	339	169	1,496	8,852	13,166
Virginia	2,209	452,519	205	418	7,188	80,214	11,159	14,443
Washington	2,322	611,190	263	423	9,455	86,223	9,119	14,934
West Virginia	271	62,000	229	298	942	9,009	9,564	12,052
Wisconsin	417	102,993	247	421	2,138	18,571	8,686	13,352
Wyoming	68	8,231	121	307	292	1,708	5,849	10,520

Source: Adapted from *Asians in America, 1990 Census, Classification by States* (San Francisco,CA: *Asian Week*, undated), p. 58. Primary source: Bureau of the Census, U.S. Department of Commerce, *Survey of Minority Owned Business Enterprises: Asian Americans, American Indians, and Other Minorities,* 1987 Economic Censuses (Washington, DC: U.S. Government Printing Office, June 1991), table 5, p. 27–35.

★75★

Entrepreneurs

Asian/Pacific Islander entrepreneurs by ethnicity in percent, 1982 and 1987.

Ethnic group	Percentage of entrepreneurs	
	1982	1987
Chinese	5%	6.3%
Filipino	2.6%	3.3%
Asian Indian	6.6%	7.6%
Japanese	5.9%	6.6%
Korean	6.8%	10.2%
Vietnamese	1.5%	4.9%

Source: "Asian American Demographics," *The American Enterprise* (November/ December 1991): 87–90. Primary source: Analysis provided by William O'Hare of the University of Louisville. Also in source: data on vital statistics, population growth, and family characteristics.

★76★

Hotel Ownership

Selected characteristics of members of the Asian American Hotel Owners Association (AAHOA), 1993.

Asian American Hotel Owners Association
Number of members:1,300
Number of U.S. hotels/motels owned (estimate) by members:3,000
Number of Asian American-owned hotels/motels (estimate), total (AAHOA members and non-members):6,000–7,000

Characteristics:
95% of AAHOA members are Asian Indian, from Gujarati, India (northwestern India, north of Bombay).
90% (estimate) have at least a bachelor's degree; 25% (estimate) have a master's degree or doctorate.
40–45% own hotel/motel franchises with economy lodging chains (such as Days Inn, Ramada, Hampton Inn, Shoney's, Knight's Inn).
55–60% own small, economy lodgings on major and secondary highways.
50% of AAHOA members have the surname Patel, from the Indian name Patedar.

Source: Asian American Hotel Owners Association, telephone interview with Charles Smith, Executive Director, February 3, 1993.

★77★

Management and Financial Assistance

Hours and percent of total hours of assistance and financial aid (in millions of dollars and percent of total dollars) provided to minority businesses by the Minority Business Development Agency by race/ethnicity, 1990 and 1991[a].

Assistance	1991			1990		
	Asian/ Pacific Islander	Black	Hispanic	Asian/ Pacific Islander	Black	Hispanic
Total clients receiving M&TA[b]	1,016	8,874	4,442	1,051	9,063	3,828
Percent of total	6%	53%	27%	7%	56%	24%
Hours of M&TA (billable and non-billable)	18,675	122,653	73,586	20,881	122,214	70,591
Percent	7%	48%	29%	8%	47%	27%
Total business clients	688	4,865	2,799	686	4,869	2,532
Percent	7%	50%	29%	7%	52%	27%
Number of financial packages	107	717	573	144	721	510
Percent	6%	45%	36%	9%	45%	32%
Dollar value of approved packages (in 1,000,000)	$46.1	$123.6	$160	$56.7	$240.6	2$24.3
Percent	12%	33%	43%	10%	42%	39%
Number of contracts	135	2,004	1,314	211	2,337	1,056
Percent	3%	50%	33%	5%	56%	25%
Dollar value of contracts approved (in 1,000,000)	$62.5	$367.4	$339.2	$54.6	$486.7	$363.0
Percent	7%	41%	38%	5%	45%	34%

Source: Minority Business Development Agency, Annual Report, *National Assistance by Minority Group: Comparison of Fiscal Years 1991 and 1990* (Washington, DC: Minority Business Development Agency, 1992), table 27, p. IV–3. *Notes:* (a) Fiscal years October 1–September 30. (b) Management and Technical Assistance.

Metropolitan Statistical Areas

★ 78 ★

Asian Indian-Owned Businesses: Top Metropolitan Areas

Top twenty-five metropolitan statistical areas ranked by number of businesses whose owners are of Asian Indian descent, 1987.

Rank	Metropolitan area	Asian Indian-owned firms
1	New York, NY PMSA[a]	5,744
2	Los Angeles-Long Beach, CA PMSA	4,037
3	Chicago, IL PMSA	3,049
4	Washington, DC-MD-VA MSA[b]	2,086
5	Houston, TX PMSA	1,662
6	Nassau-Suffolk, NY PMSA	1,342
7	Detroit, MI PMSA	1,310
8	Philadelphia, PA-NJ PMSA	1,227
9	Anaheim-Santa Ana, CA PMSA	1,105
10	Newark, NJ PMSA	959
11	Oakland, CA PMSA	942
12	San Jose, CA PMSA	896
13	Middlesex-Somerset-Hunterdon, NJ PMSA	850
14	Dallas, TX PMSA	830
15	San Francisco, CA PMSA	765
16	Bergen-Passaic, NJ PMSA	710
17	Boston, MA PMSA	648
18	Atlanta, GA MSA	610
19	Riverside-San Bernardino, CA PMSA	543
20	Jersey City, NJ PMSA	492
21	Miami-Hialeah, FL PMSA	465
22	Sacramento, CA MSA	433
23	Baltimore, MD MSA	423
24	Tampa-St. Petersburg-Clearwater, FL MSA	404
25	Cleveland, Ohio PMSA	391

Source: Bureau of the Census, U.S. Department of Commerce, *Survey of Minority-Owned Business Enterprises: Asian Americans, American Indians, and Other Minorities,* 1987 Economic Censuses (Washington, DC: U.S. Government Printing Office, June 1991), table 7, p. 60–91. Included in the universe of the survey is any activity for which an IRS Form 1040, Schedule C (individual proprietorship or self-employed person); 1065 (partnership); or 1120S (subchapter S corporation) was filed in 1987. Also in source: statistics for metropolitan statistical areas with 100 or more minority-owned firms in 1987. *Notes:* (a) Primary Metropolitan Statistical Area. (b) Metropolitan Statistical Area.

★79★

Businesses Owned by Metropolitan Statistical Area

Numbers of Asian/Pacific Islander-owned firms, total receipts, and average receipts (in thousands of dollars) per firm for metropolitan statistical areas. Included are metropolitan areas with 100 or more minority-owned firms, ranked (greatest to least) by number of Asian/Pacific Islander firms owned, 1987.

Rank by number of firms	Metropolitan area	Total number of firms	Total Sales/ receipts ($1,000)	Average Sales/ receipts per firm ($1,000)
1	Los Angeles-Long Beach, CA PMSA[a]	62,343	$6,833,644	$110
2	New York, NY PMSA	29,068	2,428,920	84
3	Honolulu, HI MSA[b]	24,380	1,326,973	54
4	San Francisco, CA PMSA	17,118	1,733,188	101
5	Anaheim-Santa Ana, CA PMSA	15,110	1,408,274	93
6	Chicago, IL PMSA	12,469	1,206,103	97
7	Oakland, CA PMSA	11,803	1,048,113	89
8	Washington, DC-MD-VA MSA	11,516	917,858	79
9	San Jose, CA PMSA	11,393	986,659	87
10	Houston, TX PMSA	8,663	802,498	93
11	San Diego, CA MSA	6,326	427,936	68
12	Philadelphia, PA-NJ PMSA	5,461	654,950	120
13	Dallas, TX PMSA	5,459	388,581	71
14	Seattle, WA PMSA	5,433	570,613	105
15	Sacramento, CA MSA	4,175	470,941	113
16	Riverside-San Bernardino, CA PMSA	4,147	470,453	113
17	Nassau-Suffolk, NY PMSA	3,951	425,527	108
18	Atlanta, GA MSA	2,974	325,211	109
19	Detroit, MI PMSA	2,948	290,991	99
20	Newark, NJ PMSA	2,919	253,373	87
21	Bergen-Passaic, NJ PMSA	2,826	279,852	99
22	Boston, MA PMSA	2,576	185,910	72
23	Baltimore, MD MSA	2,556	266,857	104
24	Denver, CO PMSA	2,355	146,071	62
25	Portland, OR PMSA	2,225	215,459	97
26	Middlesex-Somerset-Hunterdon, NJ PMSA	2,067	213,537	103
27	Fort Worth-Arlington, TX PMSA	2,044	140,759	69
28	Miami-Hialeah, FL PMSA	1,795	119,667	67
29	Oxnard-Ventura, CA PMSA	1,780	190,574	107
30	Phoenix, AZ MSA	1,623	154,215	95
31	Jersey City, NJ PMSA	1,608	181,793	113
32	New Orleans, LA MSA	1,570	102,215	65
33	Minneapolis-St. Paul, MN-WI MSA	1,452	139,695	96
34	Fresno, CA MSA	1,352	162,721	120
35	St. Louis, MO-IL MSA	1,330	102,925	77
36	Tampa-St. Petersburg-Clearwater, FL MSA	1,245	108,768	87
37	Salinas-Seaside-Monterey, CA MSA	1,191	116,144	97
38	Stockton, CA MSA	1,175	132,180	112
39	Vallejo-Fairfield-Napa, CA PMSA	1,166	85,112	73
40	Norfolk-Virginia Beach-Newport News, VA MSA	1,156	107,075	93
41	Cleveland, Ohio PMSA	1,101	87,752	79
42	Orlando, FL MSA	1,090	175,206	161

[Continued]

★79★

Businesses Owned by Metropolitan Statistical Area (Continued)

Numbers of Asian/Pacific Islander-owned firms, total receipts, and average receipts (in thousands of dollars) per firm for metropolitan statistical areas. Included are metropolitan areas with 100 or more minority-owned firms, ranked (greatest to least) by number of Asian/Pacific Islander firms owned, 1987.

Rank by number of firms	Metropolitan area	Total number of firms	Total Sales/ receipts ($1,000)	Average Sales/ receipts per firm ($1,000)
43	Fort Lauderdale-Hollywood-Pompano Beach, FL PMSA	1,083	85,369	79
44	Monmouth-Ocean, NJ PMSA	919	87,370	95
45	San Antonio, TX MSA	917	66,285	72
46	Pittsburgh, PA PMSA	906	86,619	96
47	Salt Lake City-Ogden, UT MSA	872	56,990	65
48	Oklahoma City, OK MSA	839	35,636	42
49	Kansas City, MO-KS MSA	813	55,313	68
50	Santa Barbara-Santa Maria-Lompoc, CA MSA	796	61,222	77
51	Las Vegas, NV MSA	794	57,365	72
52	Tacoma, WA PMSA	760	62,854	83
53	Austin, TX MSA	684	54,587	80
54	Bakersfield, CA MSA	681	83,738	123
55	Richmond-Petersburg, VA MSA	613	62,517	102
56	Milwaukee, WI PMSA	594	70,097	118
57	Jacksonville, FL MSA	554	66,889	121
58	Columbus, OH MSA	552	9,640	17
59	Indianapolis, IN MSA	537	58,468	109
60	Modesto, CA MSA	528	61,919	117
61	Anchorage, AK MSA	514	44,740	87
62	Memphis, TN-AR-MS MSA	512	62,838	123
63	Tucson, AZ MSA	510	45,955	90
64	Trenton, NJ PMSA	505	41,625	82
65	Santa Cruz, CA PMSA	503	42,985	85
66	Beaumont-Port Arthur, TX MSA	498	54,361	109
67	Charlotte-Gastonia-Rock Hill, NC-SC MSA	487	58,745	121
68	Cincinnati, OH-KY-IN PMSA	484	49,782	102
69	Raleigh-Durham, NC MSA	481	32,708	68
70	Kileen-Temple, TX MSA	462	22,080	48
71	West Palm Beach-Boca Raton-Delray Beach, FL MSA	450	50,955	113
72	Santa Rosa-Petaluma, CA PMSA	449	46,996	105
73	Albany-Schenectady-Troy, NY MSA	441	67,245	152
74	Hartford, CT PMSA	437	54,072	124
75	Lake County, IL PMSA	420	39,059	93
76	Nashville, TN MSA	393	38,141	97
77	Wilmington, DE-NJ-MD PMSA	388	40,330	104
78	Dayton-Springfield, OH MSA	386	32,669	85
79	Rochester, NY MSA	385	38,336	100
80	Buffalo, NY PMSA	375	36,934	98
81	Allentown-Bethlehem, PA-NJ MSA	370	39,366	106
82	Albuquerque, NM MSA	361	24,095	67
83	Galveston-Texas City, TX PMSA	361	22,231	62
84	Visalia-Tulare-Porterville, CA MSA	359	59,005	164

[Continued]

★79★

Businesses Owned by Metropolitan Statistical Area (Continued)

Numbers of Asian/Pacific Islander-owned firms, total receipts, and average receipts (in thousands of dollars) per firm for metropolitan statistical areas. Included are metropolitan areas with 100 or more minority-owned firms, ranked (greatest to least) by number of Asian/Pacific Islander firms owned, 1987.

Rank by number of firms	Metropolitan area	Total number of firms	Total Sales/ receipts ($1,000)	Average Sales/ receipts per firm ($1,000)
85	Providence, RI PMSA	335	24,287	72
86	Tulsa, OK MSA	335	24,261	72
87	New Haven-Meriden, CT MSA	334	37,456	112
88	Biloxi-Gulfport, MS MSA	318	16,007	50
89	Reno, NV MSA	318	20,214	64
90	Louisville, KY-IN MSA	317	29,778	94
91	Wichita, KS MSA	301	23,733	79
92	Ann Arbor, MI PMSA	295	17,914	61
93	El Paso, TX MSA	289	32,041	111
94	Colorado Springs, CO MSA	288	20,870	72
95	Harrisburg-Lebanon-Carlisle, PA MSA	284	20,453	72
96	Poughkeepsie, NY MSA	272	22,454	83
97	Augusta, GA-SC MSA	270	22,590	84
98	Gary-Hammond, IN PMSA	260	31,018	119
99	Lawrence-Haverhill, MA-NH PMSA	259	14,673	57
100	Syracuse, NY MSA	257	32,072	125
101	Atlantic City, NJ MSA	253	33,276	132
102	Melbourne-Titusville-Palm Bay, FL MSA	247	29,058	118
103	Scranton-Wilkes-Barre, PA MSA	243	28,007	115
104	Lansing-East Lansing, MI MSA	242	13,351	55
105	Bridgeport-Milford, CT PMSA	236	19,705	83
106	Yuba City, CA MSA	235	22,210	95
107	Daytona Beach, FL MSA	233	39,795	171
108	Joliet, IL PMSA	232	15,567	67
109	Orange County, NY PMSA	227	24,110	106
110	Baton Rouge, LA MSA	222	16,129	73
111	Toledo, OH MSA	220	28,672	130
112	Greensboro-Winston-Salem-High Point, NC MSA	219	29,316	133
113	Mobile, AL MSA	218	18,005	83
114	Pensacola, FL MSA	217	20,802	96
115	Knoxville, TN MSA	213	15,255	72
116	Stamford, CT PMSA	213	28,604	134
117	Amarillo, TX MSA	210	7,455	36
118	Spokane, WA MSA	210	10,797	51
119	Columbia, SC MSA	207	19,060	92
120	Aurora-Elgin, IL PMSA	201	27,578	137
121	Olympia, WA MSA	199	14,709	74
123	Akron, OH PMSA	197	18,856	96
124	Jackson, MS MSA	192	18,002	94
125	Youngstown-Warren, OH MSA	192	21,054	110
126	Omaha, NE-IA MSA	191	11,622	61
127	Worcester, MA MSA	190	11,092	58
128	Charleston, SC MSA	189	9,527	50
129	Bremerton, WA MSA	185	12,928	70

[Continued]

★79★

Businesses Owned by Metropolitan Statistical Area (Continued)

Numbers of Asian/Pacific Islander-owned firms, total receipts, and average receipts (in thousands of dollars) per firm for metropolitan statistical areas. Included are metropolitan areas with 100 or more minority-owned firms, ranked (greatest to least) by number of Asian/Pacific Islander firms owned, 1987.

Rank by number of firms	Metropolitan area	Total number of firms	Total Sales/ receipts ($1,000)	Average Sales/ receipts per firm ($1,000)
130	Grand Rapids, MI MSA	182	21,178	116
131	Danbury, CT PMSA	179	11,719	65
1321	Eugene-Springfield, OR MSA	177	22,606	128
133	Fayetteville, NC MSA	175	7,795	45
134	Lakeland-Winter Haven, FL MSA	175	17,485	100
135	Lubbock, TX MSA	170	14,712	87
136	Des Moines, IA MSA	168	19,266	115
137	Lowell, MA-NH PMSA	167	17,792	107
138	Greenville-Spartanburg, SC MSA	166	12,160	73
139	Corpus Christi, TX MSA	165	13,887	84
140	Merced, CA MSA	165	16,457	100
141	Lancaster, PA MSA	164	6,721	41
142	Panama City, FL MSA	162	11,834	73
143	Springfield, MA MSA	157	10,983	70
144	Huntsville, AL MSA	155	11,792	76
145	Birmingham, AL MSA	154	27,813	181
146	Norwalk, CT PMSA	154	9,206	60
147	Boulder-Longmont, CO PMSA	153	12,231	80
148	Flint, MI MSA	151	17,198	114
149	Vancouver, WA PMSA	151	9,445	63
150	Fort Wayne, IN MSA	148	23,132	156
151	Fort Myers-Cape Coral, FL MSA	146	10,139	69
152	Madison, WI MSA	144	8,090	56
153	Shreveport, LA MSA	143	9,321	65
154	Salem, OR MSA	138	14,475	105
155	Chattanooga, TN-GA MSA	136	22,120	163
156	Peoria, IL MSA	136	6,502	48
157	Provo-Orem, UT MSA	136	4,454	33
158	Fort Pierce, FL MSA	134	15,392	115
159	Little Rock-North Little Rock, AR MSA	134	8,299	62
160	Savannah, GA MSA	132	16,388	124
161	Boise City, ID MSA	131	7,408	57
162	Gainesville, FL MSA	131	11,322	86
163	Binghamton, NY MSA	130	15,705	120
164	Columbus, GA-AL MSA	130	44,582	343
165	Springfield, IL MSA	128	11,975	94
166	Roanoke, VA MSA	124	7,287	59
167	Lawton, OK MSA	123	9,532	77
168	Davenport-Rock Island-Moline, IA-IL MSA	115	8,956	78
169	Chico, CA MSA	112	9,645	86
170	Charleston, WV MSA	111	15,058	136
171	Lexington-Fayette, KY MSA	111	6,882	62
172	Reading, PA MSA	109	6,368	58
173	Brazoria, TX PMSA	106	7,586	72

[Continued]

★79★

Businesses Owned by Metropolitan Statistical Area (Continued)

Numbers of Asian/Pacific Islander-owned firms, total receipts, and average receipts (in thousands of dollars) per firm for metropolitan statistical areas. Included are metropolitan areas with 100 or more minority-owned firms, ranked (greatest to least) by number of Asian/Pacific Islander firms owned, 1987.

Rank by number of firms	Metropolitan area	Total number of firms	Total Sales/ receipts ($1,000)	Average Sales/ receipts per firm ($1,000)
174	Fort Collins-Loveland, CO MSA	106	7,436	70
175	New London-Norwich, CT-RI MSA	106	7,758	73
176	Rockford, IL MSA	103	12,479	121
177	Champaign-Urbana-Rantoul, IL MSA	101	12,334	122
178	Lafayette, LA MSA	101	5,339	53
179	Tallahassee, FL MSA	101	5,661	56
180	Lorain-Elyria, OH PMSA	100	7,825	78
181	Pawtucket-Woonsocket-Attleboro, RI-MA PMSA	96	11,747	122
182	Santa Fe, NM MSA	95	3,185	34
183	Wichita Falls, TX MSA	93	6,721	72
184	Fort Smith, AR-OK MSA	90	5,153	57
185	Houma-Thibodaux, LA MSA	90	5,034	56
186	Fort Walton Beach, FL MSA	83	5,672	68
187	Yakima, WA MSA	76	7,501	99
188	Redding, CA MSA	72	5,605	78
189	Bellingham, WA MSA	58	3,024	52
190	Las Cruces, NM MSA	57	3,123	55

Source: Bureau of the Census, U.S. Department of Commerce, *Survey of Minority-Owned Business Enterprises: Asian Americans, American Indians, and Other Minorities,* 1987 Economic Censuses (Washington, DC: U.S. Government Printing Office, June 1991), table 7, p. 60-91. Included in the universe of the survey is any activity for which an IRS Form 1040, Schedule C (individual proprietorship or self-employed person); 1065 (partnership); or 1120S (subchapter S corporation) was filed in 1987. *Notes:* (a) Primary Metropolitan Statistical Area. (b) Metropolitan Statistical Area.

★80★

Businesses Owned, by Metropolitan Statistical Area and Asian Ethnicity

Numbers of Asian/Pacific Islander-owned firms by ethnicity for metropolitan statistical areas with 100 or more minority-owned firms, 1987. (Listing is alphabetical.)

Metropolitan area	Asian Indian	Chinese	Japanese	Korean	Viet-namese	Filipino	Hawaiian	Other Asian/ Pacific Islander	Total
Akron, OH PMSA[a]	89	40	13	17	9	21	1	7	197
Albany-Schenectady-Troy, NY MSA[b]	210	66	35	42	10	56	0	22	441
Albuquerque, NM MSA	51	83	26	44	73	35	22	27	361
Allentown-Bethlehem, PA-NJ MSA	107	101	11	81	14	29	2	25	370
Amarillo, TX MSA	55	9	13	9	92	13	0	19	210
Anaheim-Santa Ana, CA PMSA	1,105	3,278	2,248	3,925	3,074	801	101	578	15,110
Anchorage, AK MSA	31	57	86	210	10	74	11	35	514

[Continued]

★80★

Businesses Owned, by Metropolitan Statistical Area and Asian Ethnicity (Continued)

Numbers of Asian/Pacific Islander-owned firms by ethnicity for metropolitan statistical areas with 100 or more minority-owned firms, 1987. (Listing is alphabetical.)

Metropolitan area	Asian Indian	Chinese	Japanese	Korean	Viet-namese	Filipino	Hawaiian	Other Asian/ Pacific Islander	Total
Ann Arbor, MI PMSA	69	86	36	56	0	13	2	33	295
Atlanta, GA MSA	610	494	95	1,266	207	99	3	200	2,974
Atlantic City, NJ MSA	91	82	15	29	1	15	6	14	253
Augusta, GA-SC MSA	109	68	4	70	0	4	0	15	270
Aurora-Elgin, IL PMSA	55	52	21	20	6	23	0	24	201
Austin, TX MSA	101	155	58	158	79	39	1	93	684
Bakersfield, CA MSA	130	148	81	148	38	97	0	39	681
Baltimore, MD MSA	423	378	89	1,223	27	271	7	138	2,556
Baton Rouge, LA MSA	45	76	11	18	32	10	8	22	222
Beaumont-Port Arthur, TX MSA	31	60	14	9	362	11	0	11	498
Bellingham, WA MSA	8	16	11	9	3	6	0	5	58
Bergen-Passaic, NJ PMSA	710	626	184	768	31	417	2	88	2826
Biloxi-Gulfport, MS MSA	15	35	5	0	253	8	0	2	318
Binghamton, NY MSA	47	24	6	20	0	12	10	11	130
Birmingham, AL MSA	58	46	7	19	5	10	0	9	154
Boise City, ID MSA	13	31	46	9	2	9	2	19	131
Boston, MA PMSA	648	1,124	190	167	133	143	9	162	2,576
Boulder-Longmont, CO PMSA	14	49	48	17	1	12	0	12	153
Brazoria, TX PMSA	14	27	1	9	20	10	0	25	106
Bremerton, WA MSA	1	26	35	35	1	63	1	23	185
Bridgeport-Milford, CT PMSA	77	67	13	30	6	16	0	27	236
Buffalo, NY PMSA	165	75	12	41	23	32	0	27	375
Champaign-Urbana-Ran-toul, IL MSA	4	51	9	30	0	0	0	7	101
Charleston, SC MSA	20	30	21	33	10	60	12	3	189
Charleston, WV MSA	58	6	0	3	6	30	0	8	111
Charlotte-Gastonia-Rock Hill, NC-SC MSA	166	69	47	154	11	22	0	18	487
Chattanooga, TN-GA MSA	49	24	2	23	6	26	0	6	136
Chicago, IL PMSA	3,049	1,955	888	3,878	223	1,623	14	839	12,469
Chico, CA MSA	15	43	14	13	2	16	0	9	112
Cincinnati, OH-KY-IN PMSA	182	102	41	68	17	40	0	34	484
Cleveland, Ohio PMSA	391	214	86	182	32	155	4	37	1101
Colorado Springs, CO MSA	28	48	59	98	14	21	7	13	288
Columbia, SC MSA	93	37	9	33	4	20	0	11	207
Columbus, GA-AL MSA	23	7	10	74	3	12	0	1	130
Columbus, OH MSA	231	97	56	88	14	27	0	39	552
Corpus Christi, TX MSA	34	39	0	19	10	59	1	3	165

[Continued]

★80★

Businesses Owned, by Metropolitan Statistical Area and Asian Ethnicity (Continued)

Numbers of Asian/Pacific Islander-owned firms by ethnicity for metropolitan statistical areas with 100 or more minority-owned firms, 1987. (Listing is alphabetical.)

Metropolitan area	Asian Indian	Chinese	Japanese	Korean	Viet-namese	Filipino	Hawaiian	Other Asian/ Pacific Islander	Total
Dallas, TX PMSA	830	1,026	133	1,887	978	197	41	367	5,459
Danbury, CT PMSA	74	28	16	13	7	16	0	25	179
Davenport-Rock Island-Moline, IA-IL MSA	32	17	7	12	7	26	0	14	115
Dayton-Springfield, OH MSA	157	46	30	78	11	38	0	26	386
Daytona Beach, FL MSA	94	42	21	33	11	15	0	17	233
Denver, CO PMSA	167	397	592	731	212	88	10	158	2355
Des Moines, IA MSA	43	34	13	39	12	12	0	15	168
Detroit, MI PMSA	1,310	426	141	539	27	398	8	99	2,948
El Paso, TX MSA	61	77	20	68	14	32	8	9	289
Eugene-Springfield, OR MSA	14	62	27	33	4	11	5	21	177
Fayetteville, NC MSA	36	15	28	70	7	8	5	6	175
Flint, MI MSA	32	31	10	22	7	19	7	23	151
Fort Collins-Loveland, CO MSA	14	33	24	12	4	2	0	17	106
Fort Lauderdale-Holly-wood-Pompano Beach, FL PMSA	297	255	48	142	54	133	14	140	1083
Fort Myers-Cape Coral, FL MSA	40	20	29	18	1	17	0	21	146
Fort Pierce, FL MSA	42	12	19	17	12	19	0	13	134
Fort Smith, AR-OK MSA	17	18	2	0	30	9	1	13	90
Fort Walton Beach, FL MSA	15	12	12	16	8	10	0	10	83
Fort Wayne, IN MSA	61	23	5	17	15	16	0	11	148
Fort Worth-Arlington, TX PMSA	375	369	51	306	750	59	1	133	2044
Fresno, CA MSA	101	330	480	149	59	133	1	99	1352
Gainesville, FL MSA	41	49	6	6	7	0	6	16	131
Galveston-Texas City, TX PMSA	47	33	9	37	193	22	0	20	361
Gary-Hammond, IN PMSA	67	42	17	65	5	52	1	11	260
Grand Rapids, MI MSA	32	24	32	46	24	18	0	6	182
Greensboro-Winston-Salem-High Point, NC MSA	61	42	24	67	10	8	0	7	219
Greenville-Spartanburg, SC MSA	87	27	3	12	11	7	0	19	166
Harrisburg-Lebanon-Carl-isle, PA MSA	117	25	32	56	13	21	1	19	284
Hartford, CT PMSA	158	110	16	57	42	16	0	38	437

[Continued]

★80★

Businesses Owned, by Metropolitan Statistical Area and Asian Ethnicity (Continued)

Numbers of Asian/Pacific Islander-owned firms by ethnicity for metropolitan statistical areas with 100 or more minority-owned firms, 1987. (Listing is alphabetical.)

Metropolitan area	Asian Indian	Chinese	Japanese	Korean	Viet- namese	Filipino	Hawaiian	Other Asian/ Pacific Islander	Total
Honolulu, HI MSA	85	4,477	11,851	1,968	518	2,825	1,576	1,080	24,380
Houma-Thibodaux, LA MSA	10	13	1	7	54	4	0	1	90
Houston, TX PMSA	1,662	2,226	212	1,115	2,453	448	29	518	8,663
Huntsville, AL MSA	47	28	12	57	0	6	0	5	155
Indianapolis, IN MSA	149	107	27	134	19	66	2	33	537
Jackson, MS MSA	80	53	1	5	38	4	0	11	192
Jacksonville, FL MSA	134	81	45	89	26	159	1	19	554
Jersey City, NJ PMSA	492	248	28	310	51	391	8	80	1608
Joliet, IL PMSA	110	16	17	33	0	28	0	28	232
Kansas City, MO-KS MSA	192	148	70	169	46	103	20	65	813
Kileen-Temple, TX MSA	66	29	20	281	14	36	0	16	462
Knoxville, TN MSA	75	49	16	37	11	9	6	10	213
Lafayette, LA MSA	28	17	1	14	33	2	0	6	101
Lake County, IL PMSA	84	97	42	132	1	42	0	22	420
Lakeland-Winter Haven, FL MSA	53	35	2	17	16	46	0	6	175
Lancaster, PA MSA	42	30	2	21	30	14	0	25	164
Lansing-East Lansing, MI MSA	83	33	36	19	1	21	0	49	242
Las Cruces, NM MSA	15	9	6	13	0	2	1	11	57
Las Vegas, NV MSA	89	177	135	165	25	138	9	56	794
Lawrence-Haverhill, MA-NH PMSA	68	82	4	64	16	13	0	12	259
Lawton, OK MSA	12	12	16	53	16	8	1	5	123
Lexington-Fayette, KY MSA	35	23	15	7	7	11	1	12	111
Little Rock-North Little Rock, AR MSA	37	45	11	16	7	11	0	7	134
Lorain-Elyria, OH PMSA	36	8	6	9	0	34	0	7	100
Los Angeles-Long Beach, CA PMSA	4,037	16,049	11,086	17,165	3,489	7,059	253	3,205	62,343
Louisville, KY-IN MSA	87	61	12	81	16	44	0	16	317
Lowell, MA-NH PMSA	64	38	5	22	6	0	1	31	167
Lubbock, TX MSA	76	49	7	18	9	2	0	9	170
Madison, WI MSA	22	48	22	8	3	18	3	20	144
Melbourne-Titusville-Palm Bay, FL MSA	145	25	9	15	12	21	0	20	247
Memphis, TN-AR-MS MSA	145	156	22	114	44	19	0	12	512
Merced, CA MSA	25	56	4	13	14	42	0	11	165
Miami-Hialeah, FL PMSA	465	395	87	145	25	525	25	128	1795
Middlesex-Somerset-Hunterdon, NJ PMSA	850	571	52	355	31	283	0	75	2067

[Continued]

★80★

Businesses Owned, by Metropolitan Statistical Area and Asian Ethnicity (Continued)

Numbers of Asian/Pacific Islander-owned firms by ethnicity for metropolitan statistical areas with 100 or more minority-owned firms, 1987. (Listing is alphabetical.)

Metropolitan area	Asian Indian	Chinese	Japanese	Korean	Viet-namese	Filipino	Hawaiian	Other Asian/ Pacific Islander	Total
Milwaukee, WI PMSA	213	142	21	73	23	79	0	43	594
Minneapolis-St. Paul, MN-WI MSA	295	376	148	182	160	125	8	158	1452
Mobile, AL MSA	41	36	4	42	67	6	0	22	218
Modesto, CA MSA	97	112	87	70	57	57	0	48	528
Monmouth-Ocean, NJ PMSA	267	267	34	86	13	187	1	64	919
Nashville, TN MSA	148	63	19	84	22	17	0	40	393
Nassau-Suffolk, NY PMSA	1,342	1,154	137	688	14	406	8	202	3,951
New Haven-Meriden, CT MSA	113	99	25	32	25	16	0	24	334
New London-Norwich, CT-RI MSA	41	26	1	4	2	25	0	7	106
New Orleans, LA MSA	242	194	44	227	741	55	4	63	1570
New York, NY PMSA	5,744	10,864	1,435	6,160	373	2,819	28	1,645	29,068
Newark, NJ PMSA	959	715	60	518	63	518	2	84	2919
Norfolk-Virginia Beach-Newport News, VA MSA	168	160	55	229	84	427	3	30	1156
Norwalk, CT PMSA	62	37	11	23	0	13	0	8	154
Oakland, CA PMSA	942	4,756	1,693	1,082	642	1,962	85	641	11,803
Oklahoma City, OK MSA	168	99	58	209	171	62	6	66	839
Olympia, WA MSA	20	21	39	27	8	69	2	13	199
Omaha, NE-IA MSA	45	17	40	36	12	15	1	25	191
Orange County, NY PMSA	116	49	30	11	2	16	0	3	227
Orlando, FL MSA	334	251	48	161	129	99	1	67	1090
Oxnard-Ventura, CA PMSA	192	436	425	195	75	348	16	93	1780
Panama City, FL MSA	37	6	11	6	81	2	0	19	162
Pawtucket-Woonsocket-Attleboro, RI-MA PMSA	42	19	0	11	7	13	0	4	96
Pensacola, FL MSA	42	33	18	2	62	46	0	14	217
Peoria, IL MSA	52	36	14	21	0	1	0	12	136
Philadelphia, PA-NJ PMSA	1,227	1,101	133	2,069	246	420	13	252	5,461
Phoenix, AZ MSA	262	555	167	228	83	146	22	160	1623
Pittsburgh, PA PMSA	354	207	53	117	68	51	2	54	906
Portland, OR PMSA	143	559	391	561	225	137	42	167	2225
Poughkeepsie, NY MSA	125	77	12	28	2	25	0	3	272
Providence, RI PMSA	75	97	17	51	18	42	1	34	335
Provo-Orem, UT MSA	10	25	64	13	4	2	5	13	136
Raleigh-Durham, NC MSA	103	162	53	81	11	11	0	60	481

[Continued]

★80★

Businesses Owned, by Metropolitan Statistical Area and Asian Ethnicity (Continued)

Numbers of Asian/Pacific Islander-owned firms by ethnicity for metropolitan statistical areas with 100 or more minority-owned firms, 1987. (Listing is alphabetical.)

Metropolitan area	Asian Indian	Chinese	Japanese	Korean	Viet-namese	Filipino	Hawaiian	Other Asian/ Pacific Islander	Total
Reading, PA MSA	36	10	20	8	11	11	0	13	109
Redding, CA MSA	14	26	2	5	0	14	1	10	72
Reno, NV MSA	31	89	42	44	34	64	5	9	318
Richmond-Petersburg, VA MSA	207	85	20	211	36	16	8	30	613
Riverside-San Bernardino, CA PMSA	543	906	481	902	263	626	42	384	4147
Roanoke, VA MSA	28	18	10	40	4	23	0	1	124
Rochester, NY MSA	185	64	5	68	14	36	1	12	385
Rockford, IL MSA	35	12	15	33	0	1	0	7	103
Sacramento, CA MSA	433	1,294	1,113	469	215	465	23	163	4,175
St. Louis, MO-IL MSA	298	306	89	209	127	184	5	112	1330
Salem, OR MSA	14	40	24	6	11	18	3	22	138
Salinas-Seaside-Monterey, CA MSA	36	194	347	238	142	164	15	55	1191
Salt Lake City-Ogden, UT MSA	50	181	390	74	32	42	10	93	872
San Antonio, TX MSA	142	214	69	171	111	124	14	72	917
San Diego, CA MSA	273	1,225	1,168	525	837	1,819	94	385	6,326
San Francisco, CA PMSA	765	9,028	2,382	1,304	697	2,299	96	547	17,118
San Jose, CA PMSA	896	3,431	1,833	1,449	2,026	1,238	23	497	11,393
Santa Barbara-Santa Maria-Lompoc, CA MSA	52	195	212	97	34	160	11	35	796
Santa Cruz, CA PMSA	39	143	147	45	6	102	1	20	503
Santa Fe, NM MSA	11	26	26	13	0	1	3	15	95
Santa Rosa-Petaluma, CA PMSA	28	164	86	31	14	89	14	23	449
Savannah, GA MSA	32	64	3	6	21	5	0	1	132
Scranton-Wilkes-Barre, PA MSA	135	28	13	40	10	11	0	6	243
Seattle, WA PMSA	341	1,365	1,346	1,178	345	581	20	257	5,433
Shreveport, LA MSA	41	32	8	22	8	12	0	20	143
Spokane, WA MSA	12	49	82	17	1	30	6	13	210
Springfield, IL MSA	39	13	20	20	8	22	0	6	128
Springfield, MA MSA	39	37	20	35	8	14	1	3	157
Stamford, CT PMSA	77	64	14	16	7	22	5	8	213
Stockton, CA MSA	151	270	196	54	84	235	47	138	1175
Syracuse, NY MSA	86	77	1	42	10	14	10	17	257
Tacoma, WA PMSA	15	84	102	368	47	57	38	49	760
Tallahassee, FL MSA	35	18	2	8	21	1	0	16	101
Tampa-St. Petersburg-Clearwater, FL MSA	404	223	71	161	89	167	12	118	1245
Toledo, OH MSA	88	47	7	24	7	24	0	23	220

[Continued]

★80★

Businesses Owned, by Metropolitan Statistical Area and Asian Ethnicity (Continued)

Numbers of Asian/Pacific Islander-owned firms by ethnicity for metropolitan statistical areas with 100 or more minority-owned firms, 1987. (Listing is alphabetical.)

Metropolitan area	Asian Indian	Chinese	Japanese	Korean	Viet-namese	Filipino	Hawaiian	Other Asian/ Pacific Islander	Total
Trenton, NJ PMSA	175	156	16	87	0	43	0	28	505
Tucson, AZ MSA	68	236	56	37	21	56	6	30	510
Tulsa, OK MSA	70	57	27	76	62	13	16	14	335
Vallejo-Fairfield-Napa, CA PMSA	73	221	148	91	45	461	27	100	1166
Vancouver, WA PMSA	15	31	17	26	36	18	1	7	151
Visalia-Tulare-Porterville, CA MSA	58	72	49	41	0	116	7	16	359
Washington, DC-MD-VA MSA	2,086	1,808	571	4,416	818	838	20	959	11,516
West Palm Beach-Boca Raton-Delray Beach, FL MSA	128	71	26	57	36	79	5	48	450
Wichita, KS MSA	74	51	24	48	67	26	2	9	301
Wichita Falls, TX MSA	22	11	12	12	31	0	0	5	93
Wilmington, DE-NJ-MD PMSA	119	91	16	89	4	52	1	16	388
Worcester, MA MSA	84	37	11	28	9	14	0	7	190
Yakima, WA MSA	11	22	12	4	2	23	2	0	76
Youngstown-Warren, OH MSA	82	22	1	45	3	22	0	17	192
Yuba City, CA MSA	70	35	71	2	10	4	10	33	235

Source: Bureau of the Census, U.S. Department of Commerce, *Survey of Minority-Owned Business Enterprises: Asian Americans, American Indians, and Other Minorities,* 1987 Economic Censuses (Washington, DC: U.S. Government Printing Office, June 1991), table 7, p. 60–91. Included in the universe of the survey is any activity for which an IRS Form 1040, Schedule C (individual proprietorship or self-employed person); 1065 (partnership); or 1120S (subchapter S corporation) was filed in 1987. *Notes:* (a) Primary Metropolitan Statistical Area (b) Metropolitan Statistical Area.

★81★

Chinese-Owned Businesses: Top Metropolitan Areas

Top twenty-five metropolitan statistical areas ranked by number of businesses whose owners are of Chinese descent, 1987.

Rank	Metropolitan area	Chinese-owned firms
1	Los Angeles-Long Beach, CA PMSA[a]	16,049
2	New York, NY PMSA	10,864
3	San Francisco, CA PMSA	9,028
4	Oakland, CA PMSA	4,756
5	Honolulu, HI MSA[b]	4,477
6	San Jose, CA PMSA	3,431
7	Anaheim-Santa Ana, CA PMSA	3,278

[Continued]

★81★

Chinese-Owned Businesses: Top Metropolitan Areas (Continued)

Top twenty-five metropolitan statistical areas ranked by number of businesses whose owners are of Chinese descent, 1987.

Rank	Metropolitan area	Chinese-owned firms
8	Houston, TX PMSA	2,226
9	Chicago, IL PMSA	1,955
10	Washington, DC-MD-VA MSA	1,808
11	Seattle, WA PMSA	1,365
12	Sacramento, CA MSA	1,294
13	San Diego, CA MSA	1,225
14	Nassau-Suffolk, NY PMSA	1,154
15	Boston, MA PMSA	1,124
16	Philadelphia, PA-NJ PMSA	1,101
17	Dallas, TX PMSA	1,026
18	Riverside-San Bernardino, CA PMSA	906
19	Newark, NJ PMSA	715
20	Bergen-Passaic, NJ PMSA	626
21	Middlesex-Somerset-Hunterdon, NJ PMSA	571
22	Portland, OR PMSA	559
23	Phoenix, AZ MSA	555
24	Atlanta, GA MSA	494
25	Oxnard-Ventura, CA PMSA	436

Source: Bureau of the Census, U.S. Department of Commerce, *Survey of Minority-Owned Business Enterprises: Asian Americans, American Indians, and Other Minorities,* 1987 Economic Censuses (Washington, DC: U.S. Government Printing Office, June 1991), table 7, p. 60-91. Included in the universe of the survey is any activity for which an IRS Form 1040, Schedule C (individual proprietorship or self-employed person); 1065 (partnership); or 1120S (subchapter S corporation) was filed in 1987. Also in source: statistics for metropolitan statistical areas with 100 or more minority-owned firms in 1987. *Notes:* (a) Primary Metropolitan Statistical Area. (b) Metropolitan Statistical Area.

★82★

Filipino-Owned Businesses: Top Metropolitan Areas

Top twenty-five metropolitan statistical areas ranked by number of businesses whose owners are of Filipino descent, 1987.

Rank	Metropolitan area	Filipino owned firms
1	Los Angeles-Long Beach, CA PMSA[a]	7,059
2	Honolulu, HI MSA[b]	2,825
3	New York, NY PMSA	2,819
4	San Francisco, CA PMSA	2,299
5	Oakland, CA PMSA	1,962
6	San Diego, CA MSA	1,819
7	Chicago, IL PMSA	1,623
8	San Jose, CA PMSA	1,238
9	Washington, DC-MD-VA MSA	838
10	Anaheim-Santa Ana, CA PMSA	801
11	Riverside-San Bernardino, CA PMSA	626

[Continued]

★82★

Filipino-Owned Businesses: Top Metropolitan Areas (Continued)

Top twenty-five metropolitan statistical areas ranked by number of businesses whose owners are of Filipino descent, 1987.

Rank	Metropolitan area	Filipino owned firms
12	Seattle, WA PMSA	581
13	Miami-Hialeah, FL PMSA	525
14	Newark, NJ PMSA	518
15	Sacramento, CA MSA	465
16	Vallejo-Fairfield-Napa, CA PMSA	461
17	Houston, TX PMSA	448
18	Norfolk-Virginia Beach-Newport News, VA MSA	427
19	Philadelphia, PA-NJ PMSA	420
20	Bergen-Passaic, NJ PMSA	417
21	Nassau-Suffolk, NY PMSA	406
22	Detroit, MI PMSA	398
23	Jersey City, NJ PMSA	391
24	Oxnard-Ventura, CA PMSA	348
25	Middlesex-Somerset-Hunterdon, NJ PMSA	283

Source: Bureau of the Census, U.S. Department of Commerce, *Survey of Minority-Owned Business Enterprises: Asian Americans, American Indians, and Other Minorities,* 1987 Economic Censuses (Washington, DC: U.S. Government Printing Office, June 1991), table 7, p. 60-91. Included in the universe of the survey is any activity for which an IRS Form 1040, Schedule C (individual proprietorship or self-employed person); 1065 (partnership); or 1120S (subchapter S corporation) was filed in 1987. Also in source: statistics for metropolitan statistical areas with 100 or more minority-owned firms in 1987. *Notes:* (a) Primary Metropolitan Statistical Area. (b) Metropolitan Statistical Area.

★83★

Hawaiian-Owned Businesses: Top Metropolitan Areas

Top twenty-five metropolitan statistical areas ranked by number of businesses whose owners are of native Hawaiian descent, 1987.

Rank	Metropolitan area	Native Hawaiian-owned firms
1	Honolulu, HI MSA[a]	1,576
2	Los Angeles-Long Beach, CA PMSA[b]	253
3	Anaheim-Santa Ana, CA PMSA	101
4	San Francisco, CA PMSA	96
5	San Diego, CA MSA	94
6	Oakland, CA PMSA	85
7	Stockton, CA MSA	47
8	Portland, OR PMSA	42
9	Riverside-San Bernardino, CA PMSA	42
10	Dallas, TX PMSA	41
11	Tacoma, WA PMSA	38
12	Houston, TX PMSA	29
13	New York, NY PMSA	28
14	Vallejo-Fairfield-Napa, CA PMSA	27
15	Miami-Hialeah, FL PMSA	25

[Continued]

★ 83 ★

Hawaiian-Owned Businesses: Top Metropolitan Areas (Continued)

Top twenty-five metropolitan statistical areas ranked by number of businesses whose owners are of native Hawaiian descent, 1987.

Rank	Metropolitan area	Native Hawaiian-owned firms
16	Sacramento, CA MSA	23
17	San Jose, CA PMSA	23
18	Albuquerque, NM MSA	22
19	Phoenix, AZ MSA	22
20	Kansas City, MO-KS MSA	20
21	Seattle, WA PMSA	20
22	Washington, DC-MD-VA MSA	20
23	Oxnard-Ventura, CA PMSA	16
24	Tulsa, OK MSA	16
25	Salinas-Seaside-Monterey, CA MSA	15

Source: Bureau of the Census, U.S. Department of Commerce, *Survey of Minority-Owned Business Enterprises: Asian Americans, American Indians, and Other Minorities,* 1987 Economic Censuses (Washington, DC: U.S. Government Printing Office, June 1991), table 7, p. 60-91. Included in the universe of the survey is any activity for which an IRS Form 1040, Schedule C (individual proprietorship or self-employed person); 1065 (partnership); or 1120S (subchapter S corporation) was filed in 1987. Also in source: statistics for metropolitan statistical areas with 100 or more minority-owned firms in 1987. *Notes:* (a) Metropolitan Statistical Area. (b) Primary Metropolitan Statistical Area.

★ 84 ★

Japanese-Owned Businesses: Top Metropolitan Areas

Top twenty-five metropolitan statistical areas ranked by number of businesses whose owners are of Japanese descent, 1987.

Rank	Metropolitan area	Japanese-owned firms
1	Honolulu, HI MSA[a]	11,851
2	Los Angeles-Long Beach, CA PMSA[b]	11,086
3	San Francisco, CA PMSA	2,382
4	Anaheim-Santa Ana, CA PMSA	2,248
5	San Jose, CA PMSA	1,833
6	Oakland, CA PMSA	1,693
7	New York, NY PMSA	1,435
8	Seattle, WA PMSA	1,346
9	San Diego, CA MSA	1,168
10	Sacramento, CA MSA	1,113
11	Chicago, IL PMSA	888
12	Denver, CO PMSA	592
13	Washington, DC-MD-VA MSA	571
14	Riverside-San Bernardino, CA PMSA	481
15	Fresno, CA MSA	480
16	Oxnard-Ventura, CA PMSA	425
17	Portland, OR PMSA	391
18	Salt Lake City-Ogden, UT MSA	390
19	Salinas-Seaside-Monterey, CA MSA	347
20	Houston, TX PMSA	212

[Continued]

★84★

Japanese-Owned Businesses: Top Metropolitan Areas (Continued)

Top twenty-five metropolitan statistical areas ranked by number of businesses whose owners are of Japanese descent, 1987.

Rank	Metropolitan area	Japanese-owned firms
21	Santa Barbara-Santa Maria-Lompoc, CA MSA	212
22	Stockton, CA MSA	196
23	Boston, MA PMSA	190

Source: Bureau of the Census, U.S. Department of Commerce, *Survey of Minority-Owned Business Enterprises: Asian Americans, American Indians, and Other Minorities,* 1987 Economic Censuses (Washington, DC: U.S. Government Printing Office, June 1991), table 7, p. 60-91. Included in the universe of the survey is any activity for which an IRS Form 1040, Schedule C (individual proprietorship or self-employed person); 1065 (partnership); or 1120S (subchapter S corporation) was filed in 1987. Also in source: statistics for metropolitan statistical areas with 100 or more minority-owned firms in 1987. *Notes:* (a) Metropolitan Statistical Area. (b) Primary Metropolitan Statistical Area.

★85★

Korean-Owned Businesses: Top Metropolitan Areas

Top twenty-five metropolitan statistical areas ranked by number of businesses whose owners are of Korean descent, 1987.

Rank	Metropolitan area	Korean-owned firms
1	Los Angeles-Long Beach, CA PMSA[a]	17,165
2	New York, NY PMSA	6,160
3	Washington, DC-MD-VA MSA[b]	4,416
4	Anaheim-Santa Ana, CA PMSA	3,925
5	Chicago, IL PMSA	3,878
6	Philadelphia, PA-NJ PMSA	2,069
7	Honolulu, HI MSA	1,968
8	Dallas, TX PMSA	1,887
9	San Jose, CA PMSA	1,449
10	San Francisco, CA PMSA	1,304
11	Atlanta, GA MSA	1,266
12	Baltimore, MD MSA	1,223
13	Seattle, WA PMSA	1,178
14	Houston, TX PMSA	1,115
15	Oakland, CA PMSA	1,082
16	Riverside-San Bernardino, CA PMSA	902
17	Bergen-Passaic, NJ PMSA	768
18	Denver, CO PMSA	731
19	Nassau-Suffolk, NY PMSA	688
20	Portland, OR PMSA	561
21	Detroit, MI PMSA	539
22	San Diego, CA MSA	525
23	Newark, NJ PMSA	518

Source: Bureau of the Census, U.S. Department of Commerce, *Survey of Minority-Owned Business Enterprises: Asian Americans, American Indians, and Other Minorities,* 1987 Economic Censuses (Washington, DC: U.S. Government Printing Office, June 1991), table 7, p. 60-91. Included in the universe of the survey is any activity for which an IRS Form 1040, Schedule C (individual proprietorship or self-employed person); 1065 (partnership); or 1120S (subchapter S corporation) was filed in 1987. Also in source: statistics for metropolitan statistical areas with 100 or more minority-owned firms in 1987. *Notes:* (a) Primary Metropolitan Statistical Area. (b) Metropolitan Statistical Area.

★86★

Vietnamese-Owned Businesses: Top Metropolitan Areas

Top twenty-five metropolitan statistical areas ranked by number of businesses whose owners are of Vietnamese descent, 1987.

Rank	Metropolitan area	Vietnamese-owned firms
1	Los Angeles-Long Beach, CA PMSA[a]	3,489
2	Anaheim-Santa Ana, CA PMSA	3,074
3	Houston, TX PMSA	2,453
4	San Jose, CA PMSA	2,026
5	Dallas, TX PMSA	978
6	San Diego, CA MSA[b]	837
7	Washington, DC-MD-VA MSA	818
8	Fort Worth-Arlington, TX PMSA	750
9	New Orleans, LA MSA	741
10	San Francisco, CA PMSA	697
11	Oakland, CA PMSA	642
12	Honolulu, HI MSA	518
13	New York, NY PMSA	373
14	Beaumont-Port Arthur, TX MSA	362
15	Seattle, WA PMSA	345
16	Riverside-San Bernardino, CA PMSA	263
17	Biloxi-Gulfport, MS MSA	253
18	Philadelphia, PA-NJ PMSA	246
19	Portland, OR PMSA	225
20	Chicago, IL PMSA	223
21	Sacramento, CA MSA	215
22	Denver, CO PMSA	212
23	Atlanta, GA MSA	207
24	Galveston-Texas City, TX PMSA	193
25	Oklahoma City, OK MSA	171

Source: Bureau of the Census, U.S. Department of Commerce, *Survey of Minority-Owned Business Enterprises: Asian Americans, American Indians, and Other Minorities,* 1987 Economic Censuses (Washington, DC: U.S. Government Printing Office, June 1991), table 7, p. 60-91. Included in the universe of the survey is any activity for which an IRS Form 1040, Schedule C (individual proprietorship or self-employed person); 1065 (partnership); or 1120S (subchapter S corporation) was filed in 1987. Also in source: statistics for metropolitan statistical areas with 100 or more minority-owned firms in 1987. *Notes:* (a) Primary Metropolitan Statistical Area. (b) Metropolitan Statistical Area.

★87★

Receipts by Metropolitan Statistical Areas and Asian Ethnicity

Total receipts (in thousands of dollars) of Asian/Pacific Islander-owned firms by ethnicity for metropolitan statistical areas with 100 or more minority-owned firms, 1987. (Listing is alphabetical.)

Metropolitan area	Asian Indian ($1,000)	Chinese ($1,000)	Japanese ($1,000)	Korean ($1,000)	Vietnamese ($1,000)	Filipino ($1,000)	Hawaiian ($1,000)	Other A/PI ($1,000)	Total
Akron, OH PMSA[a]	9,923	2,981	(c)	3,355	180	1,230	(c)	1,187	18,856
Albany-Schenectady-Troy, NY MSA[b]	44,729	4,389	1,529	10,429	20	5,697	0	452	67,245
Albuquerque, NM MSA	5,886	8,768	986	2,625	1,986	1,378	(c)	2,466	24,095
Allentown-Bethlehem, PA-NJ MSA	10,180	5,960	240	13,803	173	5,332	(c)	3,678	39,366
Amarillo, TX MSA	2,601	1,506	702	258	1,706	682	0	(c)	7,455
Anaheim-Santa Ana, CA PMSA	131,961	331,330	226,416	449,804	156,820	47,098	7,408	57,437	1,408,274
Anchorage, AK MSA	1,063	4,804	6,599	25,245	553	1,908	153	4,415	44,740
Ann Arbor, MI PMSA	2,825	4,831	1,220	5,941	0	926	(c)	2,171	17,914
Atlanta, GA MSA	84,816	58,550	6,324	127,739	6,509	6,986	(c)	34,287	325,211
Atlantic City, NJ MSA	15,675	6,009	4,588	5,151	(c)	1,799	54	(c)	33,276
Augusta, GA-SC MSA	11,868	4,763	(c)	5,014	0	(c)	0	945	22,590
Aurora-Elgin, IL PMSA	5,121	2,941	3,006	13,448	6	926	0	2,130	27,578
Austin, TX MSA	12,213	20,197	4,382	8,658	5,060	–	–	4,077	54,587
Bakersfield, CA MSA	12,627	25,840	3,519	22,362	3,065	10,085	–	6,240	83,738
Baltimore, MD MSA	41,993	48,545	5,078	135,001	–	23,448	–	12,792	266,857
Baton Rouge, LA MSA	6,461	5,013	172	1,950	1,360	–	28	1,145	16,129
Beaumont-Port Arthur, TX MSA	4,694	12,648	21	(c)	33,910	652	0	2,436	54,361
Bellingham, WA MSA	(c)	2,091	191	691	51	(c)	(c)	0	3,024
Bergen-Passaic, NJ PMSA	58,926	56,285	10,660	124,911	894	21,581	(c)	6,595	279,852
Biloxi-Gulfport, MS MSA	3,368	2,441	(c)	0	9,816	382	0	(c)	16,007
Binghamton, NY MSA	10,715	2,080	(c)	0	1,737	(c)	130	1,043	15,705
Birmingham, AL MSA	23,165	4,118	225	(c)	305	(c)	0	(c)	27,813
Boise City, ID MSA	1,009	4,379	618	–	–	1,284	–	118	7,408
Boston, MA PMSA	52,151	83,937	10,860	12,247	6,348	7,232	348	12,787	185,910
Boulder-Longmont, CO PMSA	1,905	5,453	2,512	2,082	(c)	279	0	(c)	12,231
Brazoria, TX PMSA	719	3,160	(c)	930	1,217	842	0	718	7,586
Bremerton, WA MSA	(c)	3,389	2,828	4,702	(c)	1,506	(c)	503	12,928
Bridgeport-Milford, CT PMSA	9,586	5,056	394	3,171	78	245	0	1,175	19,705
Buffalo, NY PMSA	20,149	6,470	490	5,342	982	2,838	0	663	36,934
Champaign-Urbana-Rantoul, IL MSA	3,608	6,786	(c)	1,940	0	0	0	(c)	12,334
Charleston, SC MSA	3,820	1,365	528	2,663	353	798	(c)	(c)	9,527
Charleston, WV MSA	10,860	441	0	477	422	2,858	0	(c)	15,058
Charlotte-Gastonia-Rock Hill, NC-SC MSA	32,822	6,582	5,561	12,087	573	645	0	475	58,745
Chattanooga, TN-GA MSA	9,410	8,422	(c)	2,597	57	1,634	0	(c)	22,120
Chicago, IL PMSA	320,851	252,516	64,035	346,829	12,917	85,878	110	122,967	1,206,103
Chico, CA MSA	4,372	4,103	(c)	841	(c)	(c)	0	329	9,645
Cincinnati, OH-KY-IN PMSA	32,838	7,941	562	5,450	491	2,500	0	(c)	49,782
Cleveland, Ohio PMSA	32,530	17,770	4,276	15,982	2,316	10,934	(c)	3,944	87,752
Colorado Springs, CO MSA	6,804	3,575	2,363	6,915	1,074	139	(c)	632	20,870
Columbia, SC MSA	12,614	2,994	747	1,760	(c)	70	0	875	19,060
Columbus, GA-AL MSA	4,513	(c)	64	3,763	116	1,184	0	(c)	9,640

[Continued]

★87★

Receipts by Metropolitan Statistical Areas and Asian Ethnicity (Continued)

Total receipts (in thousands of dollars) of Asian/Pacific Islander-owned firms by ethnicity for metropolitan statistical areas with 100 or more minority-owned firms, 1987. (Listing is alphabetical.)

Metropolitan area	Asian Indian ($1,000)	Chinese ($1,000)	Japanese ($1,000)	Korean ($1,000)	Vietnamese ($1,000)	Filipino ($1,000)	Hawaiian ($1,000)	Other A/PI ($1,000)	Total
Columbus, OH MSA	14,275	16,150	3,256	7,998	1,620	1,283	0	5,499	44,582
Corpus Christi, TX MSA	4,502	5,752	0	2,217	55	1,240	(c)	121	13,887
Dallas, TX PMSA	77,885	107,298	9,280	118,907	31,363	14,360	794	28,694	388,581
Danbury, CT PMSA	6,564	1,090	2,316	1,224	69	456	0	(c)	11,719
Davenport-Rock Island-Moline, IA-IL MSA	2,467	2,803	(c)	1,441	42	2,203	0	(c)	8,956
Dayton-Springfield, OH MSA	17,150	4,279	941	9,341	(c)	958	0	(c)	32,669
Daytona Beach, FL MSA	26,545	8,634	757	3,285	574	(c)	0	(c)	39,795
Denver, CO PMSA	12,449	30,704	31,491	50,648	11,031	1,574	–	8,174	146,071
Des Moines, IA MSA	7,442	3,292	324	7,466	–	742	–	–	19,266
Detroit, MI PMSA	129,241	56,544	11,738	59,832	1,397	17,546	–	14,693	290,991
El Paso, TX MSA	4,414	21,023	836	4,186	412	269	392	509	32,041
Eugene-Springfield, OR MSA	436	8,673	2,287	9,689	20	752	241	508	22,606
Fayetteville, NC MSA	3,224	(c)	688	3,709	7	135	32	(c)	7,795
Flint, MI MSA	5,872	3,811	31	4,144	105	1,425	133	1,677	17,198
Fort Collins-Loveland, CO MSA	1,412	2,615	1,620	1,745	44	(c)	0	(c)	7,436
Fort Lauderdale-Hollywood-Pompano Beach, FL PMSA	33,548	19,959	1,937	8,999	3,792	2,517	1,068	13,549	85,369
Fort Myers-Cape Coral, FL MSA	5,840	872	169	(c)	(c)	1,514	0	1,744	10,139
Fort Pierce, FL MSA	9,879	1,487	1,105	1,225	168	1,528	0	(c)	15,392
Fort Smith, AR-OK MSA	1,517	524	(c)	0	2,721	391	(c)	(c)	5,153
Fort Walton Beach, FL MSA	664	1,442	629	1,214	854	20	0	849	5,672
Fort Wayne, IN MSA	7,158	7,103	(c)	4,056	1,508	1,199	0	2,108	23,132
Fort Worth-Arlington, TX PMSA	42,496	28,514	1,860	22,049	30,556	5,714	(c)	9,570	140,759
Fresno, CA MSA	27,252	58,668	36,056	9,954	5,056	12,144	(c)	13,591	162,721
Gainesville, FL MSA	3,082	5,636	(c)	(c)	912	0	870	822	11,322
Galveston-Texas City, TX PMSA	5,172	1,630	811	1,532	11,729	275	0	1,082	22,231
Gary-Hammond, IN PMSA	10,382	4,833	774	7,574	63	7,392	(c)	(c)	31,018
Grand Rapids, MI MSA	6,181	3,954	672	8,824	890	75	0	582	21,178
Greensboro-Winston-Salem-High Point, NC MSA	12,229	5,468	613	8,812	564	706	0	924	29,316
Greenville-Spartanburg, SC MSA	6,709	3,753	(c)	1,266	432	100	0	(c)	12,160
Harrisburg-Lebanon-Carlisle, PA MSA	8,489	2,037	1,185	6,382	457	582	(c)	1,321	20,453
Hartford, CT PMSA	23,788	13,169	425	6,739	4,806	4,083	0	1,062	54,072
Honolulu, HI MSA	5,234	313,929	658,148	139,472	14,646	71,428	68,450	55,666	1,326,973
Houma-Thibodaux, LA MSA	1,188	537	(c)	404	2,905	(c)	0	(c)	5,034
Houston, TX PMSA	237,793	216,146	9,973	117,607	150,484	14,940	735	54,820	802,498
Huntsville, AL MSA	5,969	1,795	51	3,977	0	(c)	0	(c)	11,792
Indianapolis, IN MSA	22,302	13,626	1,504	14,344	464	5,071	(c)	1,157	58,468
Jackson, MS MSA	11,437	5,395	(c)	(c)	1,058	112	0	(c)	18,002
Jacksonville, FL MSA	30,668	11,084	1,403	11,765	2,124	8,237	(c)	1,608	66,889
Jersey City, NJ PMSA	99,342	14,529	1,786	19,452	2,374	36,634	148	7,528	181,793
Joliet, IL PMSA	9,572	1,924	743	1,960	0	718	0	650	15,567

[Continued]

★87★

Receipts by Metropolitan Statistical Areas and Asian Ethnicity (Continued)

Total receipts (in thousands of dollars) of Asian/Pacific Islander-owned firms by ethnicity for metropolitan statistical areas with 100 or more minority-owned firms, 1987. (Listing is alphabetical.)

Metropolitan area	Asian Indian ($1,000)	Chinese ($1,000)	Japanese ($1,000)	Korean ($1,000)	Vietnamese ($1,000)	Filipino ($1,000)	Hawaiian ($1,000)	Other A/PI ($1,000)	Total
Kansas City, MO-KS MSA	17,128	14,917	2,429	9,827	2,208	5,085	937	2,782	55,313
Kileen-Temple, TX MSA	3,958	1,645	434	13,464	266	1,762	0	551	22,080
Knoxville, TN MSA	7,029	4,363	284	2,314	269	439	6	551	15,255
Lafayette, LA MSA	2,239	600	(c)	986	1,514	(c)	0	(c)	5,339
Lake County, IL PMSA	7,457	16,183	1,741	12,163	(c)	1,515	0	(c)	39,059
Lakeland-Winter Haven, FL MSA	6,393	4,224	(c)	534	1,873	4,461	0	(c)	17,485
Lancaster, PA MSA	2,382	2,414	(c)	257	939	729	0	(c)	6,721
Lansing-East Lansing, MI MSA	4,105	3,916	1,091	3,587	(c)	652	0	(c)	13,351
Las Cruces, NM MSA	1,201	1,357	(c)	520	0	(c)	(c)	45	3,123
Las Vegas, NV MSA	5,328	22,347	8,379	10,029	1,364	4,403	305	5,210	57,365
Lawrence-Haverhill, MA-NH PMSA	3,604	4,228	(c)	4,973	1,050	(c)	0	818	14,673
Lawton, OK MSA	977	3,699	169	3,424	908	355	(c)	(c)	9,532
Lexington-Fayette, KY MSA	3,999	742	491	601	535	514	(c)	(c)	6,882
Little Rock-North Little Rock, AR MSA	2,463	3,980	193	807	262	76	–	518	8,299
Lorain-Elyria, OH PMSA	3,034	645	24	1,131	0	1,822	0	1,169	7,825
Los Angeles-Long Beach, CA PMSA	599,579	1,963,424	929,134	2,491,288	215,403	310,021	20,290	304,505	6,833,644
Louisville, KY-IN MSA	13,185	7,489	925	3,293	913	2,456	0	1,517	29,778
Lowell, MA-NH PMSA	8,466	4,046	(c)	2,714	134	0	(c)	2,432	17,792
Lubbock, TX MSA	9,072	3,590	35	1,720	295	(c)	0	(c)	14,712
Madison, WI MSA	(c)	5,353	1,262	(c)	(c)	1,077	(c)	398	8,090
Melbourne-Titusville-Palm Bay, FL MSA	22,758	3,142	(c)	590	451	1,029	0	1,088	29,058
Memphis, TN-AR-MS MSA	22,016	20,648	1,966	15,271	2,235	702	0	(c)	62,838
Merced, CA MSA	4,961	8,857	(c)	1,808	403	428	0	(c)	16,457
Miami-Hialeah, FL PMSA	41,595	47,197	(c)	12,315	3,693	13,995	872	(c)	119,667
Middlesex-Somerset-Hunterdon, NJ PMSA	81,631	67,015	2,480	33,531	637	17,122	0	11,121	213,537
Milwaukee, WI PMSA	35,231	18,752	1,011	5,573	716	6,773	0	2,041	70,097
Minneapolis-St. Paul, MN-WI MSA	28,933	52,647	7,610	13,678	13,389	16,608	602	6,228	139,695
Mobile, AL MSA	2,357	1,635	608	3,133	6,150	342	0	3,780	18,005
Modesto, CA MSA	14,713	34,621	5,618	2,967	2,380	1,620	0	(c)	61,919
Monmouth-Ocean, NJ PMSA	31,598	24,386	2,577	7,779	(c)	15,775	(c)	5,255	87,370
Nashville, TN MSA	16,677	7,707	913	8,560	(c)	1,381	(c)	2,903	38,141
Nassau-Suffolk, NY PMSA	147,188	107,693	15,261	90,028	1,434	26,810	68	37,045	425,527
New Haven-Meriden, CT MSA	18,213	10,427	2,586	4,029	(c)	555	0	1,646	37,456
New London-Norwich, CT-RI MSA	3,514	2,776	(c)	502	(c)	410	0	556	7,758
New Orleans, LA MSA	27,242	20,229	1,850	9,937	33,554	1,942	(c)	7,461	102,215
New York, NY PMSA	720,300	781,947	93,921	548,243	17,959	102,015	5,597	158,938	2,428,920
Newark, NJ PMSA	99,796	61,397	4,621	53,351	2,192	21,793	(c)	10,223	253,373
Norfolk-Virginia Beach-Newport News, VA MSA	34,682	20,151	2,006	28,933	5,741	13,875	(c)	1,687	107,075
Norwalk, CT PMSA	3,287	3,515	409	1,266	0	105	0	624	9,206

[Continued]

★87★

Receipts by Metropolitan Statistical Areas and Asian Ethnicity (Continued)

Total receipts (in thousands of dollars) of Asian/Pacific Islander-owned firms by ethnicity for metropolitan statistical areas with 100 or more minority-owned firms, 1987. (Listing is alphabetical.)

Metropolitan area	Asian Indian ($1,000)	Chinese ($1,000)	Japanese ($1,000)	Korean ($1,000)	Vietnamese ($1,000)	Filipino ($1,000)	Hawaiian ($1,000)	Other A/PI ($1,000)	Total
Oakland, CA PMSA	131,954	462,903	147,929	151,151	39,665	73,283	2,851	38,377	1,048,113
Oklahoma City, OK MSA	10,143	7,902	2,159	6,549	7,284	1,599	(c)	(c)	35,636
Olympia, WA MSA	759	904	2,261	8,960	488	1,337	(c)	(c)	14,709
Omaha, NE-IA MSA	3,087	2,614	1,765	3,763	393	(c)	(c)	(c)	11,622
Orange County, NY PMSA	18,265	2,750	503	1,500	(c)	1,092	0	(c)	24,110
Orlando, FL MSA	109,220	38,439	2,487	14,311	6,058	4,691	–	–	175,206
Oxnard-Ventura, CA PMSA	37,491	49,885	29,722	23,295	2,0212	15,385	1,543	13,041	190,574
Panama City, FL MSA	4,586	1,126	513	1,757	3,852	(c)	0	(c)	11,834
Pawtucket-Woonsocket-Attle-boro, RI-MA PMSA	3,382	6,714	0	645	(c)	1,006	0	(c)	11,747
Pensacola, FL MSA	9,733	2,893	2,293	(c)	2,932	2,316	0	635	20,802
Peoria, IL MSA	3,563	2,146	(c)	703	0	(c)	0	90	6,502
Philadelphia, PA-NJ PMSA	141,160	105,798	(c)	320,194	9,221	54,293	(c)	24,284	654,950
Phoenix, AZ MSA	24,268	72,671	9,499	20,557	4,532	4,825	(c)	17,863	154,215
Pittsburgh, PA PMSA	35,155	19,655	4,014	16,940	2,285	4,157	(c)	4,413	86,619
Portland, OR PMSA	8,329	60,489	66,355	59,560	15,240	5,486	(c)	(c)	215,459
Poughkeepsie, NY MSA	11,274	8,882	978	1,320	(c)	(c)	0	(c)	22,454
Providence, RI PMSA	5,212	11,084	1,778	2,874	885	2,454	(c)	(c)	24,287
Provo-Orem, UT MSA	422	1,299	1,441	322	(c)	(c)	322	648	4,454
Raleigh-Durham, NC MSA	7,093	15,765	2,139	5,133	(c)	(c)	0	2,578	32,708
Reading, PA MSA	3,781	1,154	80	80	117	658	0	498	6,368
Redding, CA MSA	965	4,002	(c)	528	0	110	(c)	(c)	5,605
Reno, NV MSA	2,008	8,201	2,739	3,118	1,669	1,457	194	828	20,214
Richmond-Petersburg, VA MSA	18,803	11,915	498	27,064	1,284	1,649	24	1,280	62,517
Riverside-San Bernardino, CA PMSA	103,997	130,677	39,022	130,061	11,507	23,349	2,242	29,598	470,453
Roanoke, VA MSA	2,370	1,778	30	2,511	88	510	0	(c)	7,287
Rochester, NY MSA	23,440	7,794	(c)	5,313	285	1,504	(c)	(c)	38,336
Rockford, IL MSA	3,232	3,294	697	4,485	0	(c)	0	771	12,479
Sacramento, CA MSA	53,125	274,132	76,903	34,162	16,408	16,211	(c)	(c)	470,941
St. Louis, MO-IL MSA	27,108	25,383	4,688	19,393	6,614	9,197	(c)	10,542	102,925
Salem, OR MSA	1,040	5,767	1,885	897	1,613	2,623	4	646	14,475
Salinas-Seaside-Monterey, CA MSA	9,320	23,623	36,162	31,069	7,789	5,695	103	2,383	116,144
Salt Lake City-Ogden, UT MSA	3,314	14,682	23,323	8,095	2,720	990	–	3,866	56,990
San Antonio, TX MSA	12,433	25,673	4,145	12,674	6,211	3,221	217	1,711	66,285
San Diego, CA MSA	33,324	137,079	76,459	55,645	33,850	69,704	2,615	19,260	427,936
San Francisco, CA PMSA	99,627	1,088,344	180,509	158,043	45,251	97,404	–	64,010	1,733,188
San Jose, CA PMSA	128,751	396,038	111,319	138,797	109,123	65,053	4,071	33,507	986,659
Santa Barbara-Santa Maria - Lompoc, CA MSA	5,555	13,583	18,017	11,967	1,395	6,778	(c)	3,927	61,222
Santa Cruz, CA PMSA	5,589	13,913	9,227	9,873	–	3,525	–	858	42,985
Santa Fe, NM MSA	356	1,268	1,444	117	0	(c)	(c)	(c)	3,185
Santa Rosa-Petaluma, CA PMSA	4,327	16,487	10,184	10,947	812	3,741	498	(c)	46,996
Savannah, GA MSA	5,221	9,251	(c)	499	1,250	167	0	(c)	16,388
Scranton-Wilkes-Barre, PA MSA	12,065	3,110	(c)	6,833	500	4,871	0	628	28,007

[Continued]

★87★

Receipts by Metropolitan Statistical Areas and Asian Ethnicity (Continued)

Total receipts (in thousands of dollars) of Asian/Pacific Islander-owned firms by ethnicity for metropolitan statistical areas with 100 or more minority-owned firms, 1987. (Listing is alphabetical.)

Metropolitan area	Asian Indian ($1,000)	Chinese ($1,000)	Japanese ($1,000)	Korean ($1,000)	Vietnamese ($1,000)	Filipino ($1,000)	Hawaiian ($1,000)	Other A/PI ($1,000)	Total
Seattle, WA PMSA	124,201	124,905	100,133	121,333	13,322	57,935	(c)	28,784	570,613
Shreveport, LA MSA	3,613	1,499	229	1,504	1,287	678	0	511	9,321
Spokane, WA MSA	126	5,167	2,893	1,500	(c)	1,111	(c)	(c)	10,797
Springfield, IL MSA	2,963	1,980	571	2,825	1,688	884	0	72	10,983
Springfield, MA MSA	5,412	2,565	242	2,078	(c)	1,225	(c)	453	11,975
Stamford, CT PMSA	9,736	9,935	1,395	5,704	755	738	13	328	28,604
Stockton, CA MSA	13,772	50,464	33,221	4,923	8,950	10,652	2,212	7,986	132,180
Syracuse, NY MSA	15,760	4,877	(c)	3,700	40	3,081	(c)	4,614	32,072
Tacoma, WA PMSA	760	11,743	8,080	30,417	3,130	1,973	617	6,134	62,854
Tallahassee, FL MSA	4,180	347	(c)	94	574	(c)	0	466	5,661
Tampa-St. Petersburg-Clear-water, FL MSA	42,829	19,874	4,396	14,686	6,767	8,830	1,262	10,124	108,768
Toledo, OH MSA	13,211	8,098	(c)	3,010	979	1,704	0	1,670	28,672
Trenton, NJ PMSA	19,036	9,046	448	12,572	0	523	0	(c)	41,625
Tucson, AZ MSA	2,924	33,020	1,590	5,445	804	1,319	75	778	45,955
Tulsa, OK MSA	9,512	7,234	819	2,596	1,531	1,717	440	412	24,261
Vallejo-Fairfield-Napa, CA PMSA	9,489	32,602	6,061	10,891	874	18,340	2,086	4,769	85,112
Vancouver, WA PMSA	371	4,476	(c)	2,588	697	1,313	(c)	(c)	9,445
Visalia-Tulare-Porterville, CA MSA	12,207	25,903	8,187	2,496	0	8,822	287	1,103	59,005
Washington, DC-MD-VA MSA	227,120	133,382	29,948	406,691	33,937	28,003	(c)	58,777	917,858
West Palm Beach-Boca Raton-Delray Beach, FL MSA	23,621	13,592	2,389	5,260	620	3,735	526	1,212	50,955
Wichita, KS MSA	8,610	4,742	1,357	2,259	2,359	3,084	(c)	1,322	23,733
Wichita Falls, TX MSA	3,662	1,547	413	880	204	0	0	15	6,721
Wilmington, DE-NJ-MD PMSA	18,047	6,445	848	9,714	(c)	3,917	(c)	1,359	40,330
Worcester, MA MSA	6,718	2,149	237	809	841	338	0	(c)	11,092
Yakima, WA MSA	480	4,454	(c)	2,345	(c)	222	(c)	0	7,501
Youngstown-Warren, OH MSA	13,344	1,440	(c)	2,730	175	3,365	0	(c)	21,054
Yuba City, CA MSA	12,343	5,534	2,091	(c)	90	4	70	2,078	22,210

Source: Bureau of the Census, U.S. Department of Commerce, *Survey of Minority-Owned Business Enterprises: Asian Americans, American Indians, and Other Minorities,* 1987 Economic Censuses (Washington, DC: U.S. Government Printing Office, June 1991), table 7, p. 60-91. Included in the universe of the survey is any activity for which an IRS Form 1040, Schedule C (individual proprietorship or self-employed person); 1065 (partnership); or 1120S (subchapter S corporation) was filed in 1987. *Notes:* (a) Primary Metropolitan Statistical Area. (b) Metropolitan Statistical Area. (c) Data withheld to avoid disclosing data for individual companies.

States

★88★

Alabama: Businesses by Asian Ethnicity, Employees, and Sales

Numbers of Alabama businesses owned by Asian/Pacific Islanders by ethnicity and annual sales/receipts (in thousands of dollars), and numbers of Asian/Pacific Islander-owned businesses with employees, numbers of employees, and annual payroll, 1987.

Ethnic group	All businesses		Businesses with paid employees			
	Businesses (number)	Sales/receipts ($1,000)	Businesses (number)	Sales/receipts ($1,000)	Employees (number)	Annual payroll ($1,000)
Asian/Pacific Islander, total	917	125,771	417	107,553	1,691	14,642
Asian Indian	331	66,358	184	58,037	1,060	9,413
Chinese	178	12,929	77	10,676	293	1,810
Japanese	58	2,678	18	2,206	54	385
Korean	176	14,953	84	11,440	155	1,230
Vietnamese	78	6,907	19	4,488	22	322
Filipino	42	4,171	15	3,601	46	569
Hawaiian	3	6	0	0	0	0
Other Asian/Pacific Islander	51	17,769	20	17,105	61	913

Source: Bureau of the Census, U.S. Department of Commerce, *Survey of Minority-Owned Business Enterprises: Asian Americans, American Indians, and Other Minorities,* 1987 Economic Censuses (Washington, DC: U.S. Government Printing Office, June 1991), table 5, p. 27-35. Included in the universe of the survey is any activity for which an IRS Form 1040, Schedule C (individual proprietorship or self-employed person); 1065 (partnership); or 1120S (subchapter S corporation) was filed in 1987.

★89★

Alaska: Businesses by Asian Ethnicity, Employees, and Sales

Numbers of Alaska businesses owned by Asian/Pacific Islanders by ethnicity and annual sales/receipts (in thousands of dollars), and numbers of Asian/Pacific Islander-owned businesses with employees, numbers of employees, and annual payroll, 1987.

Ethnic group	All businesses		Businesses with paid employees			
	Businesses (number)	Sales/receipts ($1,000)	Businesses (number)	Sales/receipts ($1,000)	Employees (number)	Annual payroll ($1,000)
Asian/Pacific Islander, total	1028	78,378	250	52,794	925	11,238
Asian Indian	35	4,033	4	(a)	(a)	(a)
Chinese	95	12,398	40	9,784	238	2,664
Japanese	261	16,498	58	11,430	189	3,110
Korean	319	32,982	98	25,267	411	4,523
Vietnamese	32	1,283	5	481	9	139
Filipino	167	4,526	33	2,370	39	431
Hawaiian	24	322	2	(a)	(a)	(a)
Other Asian/Pacific Islander	95	6,336	10	3,462	39	371

Source: Bureau of the Census, U.S. Department of Commerce, *Survey of Minority-Owned Business Enterprises: Asian Americans, American Indians, and Other Minorities,* 1987 Economic Censuses (Washington, DC: U.S. Government Printing Office, June 1991), table 5, p. 27-35. Included in the universe of the survey is any activity for which an IRS Form 1040, Schedule C (individual proprietorship or self-employed person); 1065 (partnership); or 1120S (subchapter S corporation) was filed in 1987. *Note:* (a) Withheld to avoid disclosing data for individual companies.

★90★

Arizona: Businesses by Asian Ethnicity, Employees, and Sales

Numbers of Arizona businesses owned by Asian/Pacific Islanders by ethnicity and annual sales/receipts (in thousands of dollars), and numbers of Asian/Pacific Islander-owned businesses with employees, numbers of employees, and annual payroll, 1987.

Ethnic group	All businesses		Businesses with paid employees			
	Businesses (number)	Sales/receipts ($1,000)	Businesses (number)	Sales/receipts ($1,000)	Employees (number)	Annual payroll ($1,000)
Asian/Pacific Islander, total	2,526	$233,206	736	$187,903	3,988	$29,867
Asian Indian	408	35,432	114	24,989	513	5,067
Chinese	923	135,843	382	107,601	2,531	16,889
Japanese	279	13,171	47	7,758	172	1,786
Korean	323	32,628	85	21,540	476	3,058
Vietnamese	115	6,322	27	3,824	34	247
Filipino	232	8,407	36	4,811	124	931
Hawaiian	30	1,403	6	306	2	85
Other Asian/Pacific Islander	216	19,903	39	17,074	136	1,804

Source: Bureau of the Census, U.S. Department of Commerce, *Survey of Minority-Owned Business Enterprises: Asian Americans, American Indians, and Other Minorities,* 1987 Economic Censuses (Washington, DC: U.S. Government Printing Office, June 1991), table 5, p. 27-35. Included in the universe of the survey is any activity for which an IRS Form 1040, Schedule C (individual proprietorship or self-employed person); 1065 (partnership); or 1120S (subchapter S corporation) was filed in 1987.

★91★

Arkansas: Businesses by Asian Ethnicity, Employees, and Sales

Numbers of Arkansas businesses owned by Asian/Pacific Islanders by ethnicity and annual sales/receipts (in thousands of dollars), and numbers of Asian/Pacific Islander-owned businesses with employees, numbers of employees, and annual payroll, 1987.

Ethnic group	All businesses		Businesses with paid employees			
	Businesses (number)	Sales/receipts ($1,000)	Businesses (number)	Sales/receipts ($1,000)	Employees (number)	Annual payroll ($1,000)
Asian/Pacific Islander, total	567	$50,488	253	$42,134	1023	$7,030
Asian Indian	156	18,406	71	14,964	460	3,605
Chinese	205	23,644	101	19,174	381	2,351
Japanese	41	1,582	8	935	13	118
Korean	42	2,880	19	1,865	65	307
Vietnamese	48	3,003	19	2,291	45	259
Filipino	38	973	17	778	22	180
Hawaiian	1	(a)	0	0	0	0
Other Asian/Pacific Islander	36	(a)	18	2,127	37	210

Source: Bureau of the Census, U.S. Department of Commerce, *Survey of Minority-Owned Business Enterprises: Asian Americans, American Indians, and Other Minorities,* 1987 Economic Censuses (Washington, DC: U.S. Government Printing Office, June 1991), table 5, p. 27-35. Included in the universe of the survey is any activity for which an IRS Form 1040, Schedule C (individual proprietorship or self-employed person); 1065 (partnership); or 1120S (subchapter S corporation) was filed in 1987. *Note:* (a) Withheld to avoid disclosing data for individual companies.

★92★

California: Businesses by Asian Ethnicity, Employees, and Sales

Numbers of California businesses owned by Asian/Pacific Islanders by ethnicity and annual sales/receipts (in thousands of dollars), and numbers of Asian/Pacific Islander-owned businesses with employees, numbers of employees, and annual payroll, 1987.

Ethnic group	All businesses		Businesses with paid employees			
	Businesses (number)	Sales/receipts ($1,000)	Businesses (number)	Sales/receipts ($1,000)	Employees (number)	Annual payroll ($1,000)
Asian/Pacific Islander, total	144,353	$14,620,377	38,273	$10,907,652	153,519	$1,490,434
Asian Indian	10,248	1,476,288	2,979	1,103,790	12,554	122,994
Chinese	42,828	5,218,497	13,012	4,073,168	61,890	586,292
Japanese	24,711	2,004,461	5,310	1,466,452	20,126	241,542
Korean	28,158	3,766,642	9,369	2,825,610	36,433	329,182
Vietnamese	11,855	665,138	2,781	430,597	7,504	54,864
Filipino	18,471	805,398	2,911	514,578	7,254	81,206
Hawaiian	872	54,002	133	34,458	493	7,410
Other Asian/Pacific Islander	7,210	629,951	1,778	458,999	7,265	66,944

Source: Bureau of the Census, U.S. Department of Commerce, *Survey of Minority-Owned Business Enterprises: Asian Americans, American Indians, and Other Minorities,* 1987 Economic Censuses (Washington, DC: U.S. Government Printing Office, June 1991), table 5, p. 27-35. Included in the universe of the survey is any activity for which an IRS Form 1040, Schedule C (individual proprietorship or self-employed person); 1065 (partnership); or 1120S (subchapter S corporation) was filed in 1987.

★93★

Colorado: Businesses by Asian Ethnicity, Employees, and Sales

Numbers of Colorado businesses owned by Asian/Pacific Islanders by ethnicity and annual sales/receipts (in thousands of dollars), and numbers of Asian/Pacific Islander-owned businesses with employees, numbers of employees, and annual payroll, 1987.

Ethnic group	All businesses		Businesses with paid employees			
	Businesses (number)	Sales/receipts ($1,000)	Businesses (number)	Sales/receipts ($1,000)	Employees (number)	Annual payroll ($1,000)
Asian/Pacific Islander, total	3192	$215,875	952	$161,393	4,017	$29,568
Asian Indian	244	25,254	91	20,135	561	3,067
Chinese	583	52,171	235	45,700	1,384	9,268
Japanese	855	45,373	221	32,389	554	6,174
Korean	886	64,614	281	46,206	1,122	8,437
Vietnamese	243	13,113	49	5,523	139	845
Filipino	137	3,134	20	2,020	39	345
Hawaiian	21	957	2	(a)	(a)	(a)
Other Asian/Pacific Islander	223	11,259	53	9,420	218	1,432

Source: Bureau of the Census, U.S. Department of Commerce, *Survey of Minority-Owned Business Enterprises: Asian Americans, American Indians, and Other Minorities,* 1987 Economic Censuses (Washington, DC: U.S. Government Printing Office, June 1991), table 5, p. 27-35. Included in the universe of the survey is any activity for which an IRS Form 1040, Schedule C (individual proprietorship or self-employed person); 1065 (partnership); or 1120S (subchapter S corporation) was filed in 1987. *Note:* (a) Withheld to avoid disclosing data for individual companies.

★94★

Connecticut: Businesses by Asian Ethnicity, Employees, and Sales

Numbers of Connecticut businesses owned by Asian/Pacific Islanders by ethnicity and annual sales/receipts (in thousands of dollars), and numbers of Asian/Pacific Islander-owned businesses with employees, numbers of employees, and annual payroll, 1987.

Ethnic group	All businesses		Businesses with paid employees			
	Businesses (number)	Sales/receipts ($1,000)	Businesses (number)	Sales/receipts ($1,000)	Employees (number)	Annual payroll ($1,000)
Asian/Pacific Islander, total	1,963	$222,679	650	$171,402	2,123	$29,085
Asian Indian	721	92,719	270	72,627	860	11,505
Chinese	512	51,456	170	40,692	670	8,679
Japanese	115	10,347	19	6,962	114	1,688
Korean	206	28,038	87	19,914	193	2,983
Vietnamese	95	20,594	36	18,918	137	2,603
Filipino	161	10,678	37	7,161	86	889
Hawaiian	5	(a)	0	0	0	0
Other Asian/Pacific Islander	148	8,847	31	5,128	63	738

Source: Bureau of the Census, U.S. Department of Commerce, *Survey of Minority-Owned Business Enterprises: Asian Americans, American Indians, and Other Minorities,* 1987 Economic Censuses (Washington, DC: U.S. Government Printing Office, June 1991), table 5, p. 27-35. Included in the universe of the survey is any activity for which an IRS Form 1040, Schedule C (individual proprietorship or self-employed person); 1065 (partnership); or 1120S (subchapter S corporation) was filed in 1987. *Note:* (a) Withheld to avoid disclosing data for individual companies.

★95★

Delaware: Businesses by Asian Ethnicity, Employees, and Sales

Numbers of Delaware businesses owned by Asian/Pacific Islanders by ethnicity and annual sales/receipts (in thousands of dollars), and numbers of Asian/Pacific Islander-owned businesses with employees, numbers of employees, and annual payroll, 1987.

Ethnic group	All businesses		Businesses with paid employees			
	Businesses (number)	Sales/receipts ($1,000)	Businesses (number)	Sales/receipts ($1,000)	Employees (number)	Annual payroll ($1,000)
Asian/Pacific Islander, total	436	$43,160	155	$30,482	679	$5,266
Asian Indian	143	20,711	59	16,368	374	3,015
Chinese	102	7,683	40	5,946	134	960
Japanese	16	1,202	5	804	15	112
Korean	90	9,043	27	5,092	104	818
Vietnamese	8	(a)	1	(a)	(a)	(a)
Filipino	52	3,221	19	2,272	52	361
Hawaiian	1	(a)	0	0	0	0
Other Asian/Pacific Islander	24	1,300	4	(a)	(a)	(a)

Source: Bureau of the Census, U.S. Department of Commerce, *Survey of Minority-Owned Business Enterprises: Asian Americans, American Indians, and Other Minorities,* 1987 Economic Censuses (Washington, DC: U.S. Government Printing Office, une 1991), table 5, p. 27-35. Included in the universe of the survey is any activity for which an IRS Form 1040, Schedule C (individual proprietorship or self-employed person); 1065 (partnership); or 1120S (subchapter S corporation) was filed in 1987. *Note:* (a) Withheld to avoid disclosing data for individual companies.

★96★

District of Columbia: Businesses by Asian Ethnicity, Employees, and Sales

Numbers of District of Columbia businesses owned by Asian/Pacific Islanders by ethnicity and annual sales/receipts (in thousands of dollars), and numbers of Asian/Pacific Islander-owned businesses with employees, numbers of employees, and annual payroll, 1987.

Ethnic group	All Businesses		Businesses with paid employees			
	Businesses (number)	Sales/receipts ($1,000)	Businesses (number)	Sales/ receipts ($1,000)	Employees (number)	Annual pay-roll ($1,000)
Asian/Pacific Islander, total	779	$132,546	337	$115,676	1,354	$17,293
Asian Indian	131	29,355	34	27,210	196	4,216
Chinese	200	28,465	80	25,688	351	4,431
Japanese	69	8,330	16	7,590	120	2,244
Korean	245	53,782	173	49,787	613	5,474
Vietnamese	22	2,294	10	2,106	40	250
Filipino	54	4,025	9	3,295	34	678
Hawaiian	3	7	0	0	0	0
Other Asian/Pacific Islander	55	6,288	15	(a)	(a)	(a)

Source: Bureau of the Census, U.S. Department of Commerce, *Survey of Minority-Owned Business Enterprises: Asian Americans, American Indians, and Other Minorities,* 1987 Economic Censuses (Washington, DC: U.S. Government Printing Office, June 1991), table 5, p. 27-35. Included in the universe of the survey is any activity for which an IRS Form 1040, Schedule C (individual proprietorship or self-employed person); 1065 (partnership); or 1120S (subchapter S corporation) was filed in 1987. *Note:* (a) Withheld to avoid disclosing data for individual companies.

★97★

Florida: Businesses by Asian Ethnicity, Employees, and Sales

Numbers of Florida businesses owned by Asian/Pacific Islanders by ethnicity and annual sales/receipts (in thousands of dollars), and numbers of Asian/Pacific Islander-owned businesses with employees, numbers of employees, and annual payroll, 1987.

Ethnic group	All Businesses		Businesses with paid employees			
	Businesses (number)	Sales/receipts ($1,000)	Businesses (number)	Sales/receipts ($1,000)	Employees (number)	Annual pay-roll ($1,000)
Asian/Pacific Islander, total	8,553	$978,073	2,670	$769,368	11,698	$112,331
Asian Indian	2,520	432,320	1,012	350,932	4,415	40,989
Chinese	1,673	196,587	655	164,310	3,313	28,028
Japanese	484	84,034	90	73,765	1,258	15,822
Korean	952	81,357	274	54,784	719	6,851
Vietnamese	629	35,656	158	21,706	377	3,812
Filipino	1,482	65,461	272	42,043	622	6,059
Hawaiian	64	(a)	35	(a)	(a)	(a)
Other Asian/Pacific Islander	749	82,658	174	61,828	994	10,770

Source: Bureau of the Census, U.S. Department of Commerce, *Survey of Minority-Owned Business Enterprises: Asian Americans, American Indians, and Other Minorities,* 1987 Economic Censuses (Washington, DC: U.S. Government Printing Office, June 1991), table 5, p. 27-35. Included in the universe of the survey is any activity for which an IRS Form 1040, Schedule C (individual proprietorship or self-employed person); 1065 (partnership); or 1120S (subchapter S corporation) was filed in 1987. *Note:* (a) Withheld to avoid disclosing data for individual companies.

★98★

Georgia: Businesses by Asian Ethnicity, Employees, and Sales

Numbers of Georgia businesses owned by Asian/Pacific Islanders by ethnicity and annual sales/receipts (in thousands of dollars), and numbers of Asian/Pacific Islander-owned businesses with employees, numbers of employees, and annual payroll, 1987.

Ethnic group	All businesses		Businesses with paid employees			
	Businesses (number)	Sales/receipts ($1,000)	Businesses (number)	Sales/receipts ($1,000)	Employees (number)	Annual payroll ($1,000)
Asian/Pacific Islander, total	4,092	$463,354	1,533	$363,894	5,203	$43,828
Asian Indian	1,056	150,690	523	122,100	2,178	16,688
Chinese	715	83,343	270	73,315	1,022	8,342
Japanese	134	9,183	20	3,530	80	787
Korean	1,525	151,767	554	111,096	1,368	11,821
Vietnamese	249	8,880	49	5,381	78	828
Filipino	164	12,022	41	10,435	168	1,562
Hawaiian	4	231	2	(a)	(a)	(a)
Other Asian/Pacific Islander	245	47,238	74	38,037	309	3,800

Source: Bureau of the Census, U.S. Department of Commerce, *Survey of Minority-Owned Business Enterprises: Asian Americans, American Indians, and Other Minorities,* 1987 Economic Censuses (Washington, DC: U.S. Government Printing Office, June 1991), table 5, p. 27-35. Included in the universe of the survey is any activity for which an IRS Form 1040, Schedule C (individual proprietorship or self-employed person); 1065 (partnership); or 1120S (subchapter S corporation) was filed in 1987. *Note:* (a) Withheld to avoid disclosing data for individual companies.

★99★

Hawaii: Businesses by Asian Ethnicity, Employees, and Sales

Numbers of Hawaiian businesses owned by Asian/Pacific Islanders by ethnicity and annual sales/receipts (in thousands of dollars), and numbers of Asian/Pacific Islander-owned businesses with employees, numbers of employees, and annual payroll, 1987.

Ethnic group	All businesses		Businesses with paid employees			
	Businesses (number)	Sales/receipts ($1,000)	Businesses (number)	Sales/receipts ($1,000)	Employees (number)	Annual payroll ($1,000)
Asian/Pacific Islander, total	31,300	$1,656,030	4,427	$1,109,366	15,046	$178,004
Asian Indian	115	9,008	28	7,650	66	740
Chinese	4,962	337,265	763	240,883	3,530	36,878
Japanese	15,751	869,341	2,324	595,908	7,702	98,499
Korean	2,061	148,515	379	87,130	1,172	10,382
Vietnamese	529	14,859	42	5,892	78	584
Filipino	3,891	95,789	381	50,294	801	9,676
Hawaiian	2,550	109,094	359	67,489	1,011	11,851
Other Asian/Pacific Islander	1,441	72,159	151	54,120	686	9,394

Source: Bureau of the Census, U.S. Department of Commerce, *Survey of Minority-Owned Business Enterprises: Asian Americans, American Indians, and Other Minorities,* 1987 Economic Censuses (Washington, DC: U.S. Government Printing Office, June 1991), table 5, p. 27-35. Included in the universe of the survey is any activity for which an IRS Form 1040, Schedule C (individual proprietorship or self-employed person); 1065 (partnership); or 1120S (subchapter S corporation) was filed in 1987.

★ 100 ★

Idaho: Businesses by Asian Ethnicity, Employees, and Sales

Numbers of Idaho businesses owned by Asian/Pacific Islanders by ethnicity and annual sales/receipts (in thousands of dollars), and numbers of Asian/Pacific Islander-owned businesses with employees, numbers of employees, and annual payroll, 1987.

Ethnic group	All businesses		Businesses with paid employees			
	Businesses (number)	Sales/receipts ($1,000)	Businesses (number)	Sales/receipts ($1,000)	Employees (number)	Annual payroll ($1,000)
Asian Pacific/Islander, total	433	$30,671	143	$25,006	771	$4,937
Asian Indian	26	1,651	6	1,157	27	172
Chinese	104	14,561	64	13,923	562	3,273
Japanese	156	8,557	34	5,676	101	861
Korean	37	1,363	12	1,163	21	152
Vietnamese	7	338	3	(a)	(a)	(a)
Filipino	38	2,480	13	2,077	29	320
Hawaiian	19	316	2	(a)	(a)	(a)
Other Asian/Pacific Islander	46	1,405	9	1,010	31	159

Source: Bureau of the Census, U.S. Department of Commerce, *Survey of Minority-Owned Business Enterprises: Asian Americans, American Indians, and Other Minorities,* 1987 Economic Censuses (Washington, DC: U.S. Government Printing Office, June 1991), table 5, p. 27-35. Included in the universe of the survey is any activity for which an IRS Form 1040, Schedule C (individual proprietorship or self-employed person); 1065 (partnership); or 1120S (subchapter S corporation) was filed in 1987. *Note:* (a) Withheld to avoid disclosing data for individual companies.

★ 101 ★

Illinois: Businesses by Asian Ethnicity, Employees, and Sales

Numbers of Illinois businesses owned by Asian/Pacific Islanders by ethnicity and annual sales/receipts (in thousands of dollars), and numbers of Asian/Pacific Islander-owned businesses with employees, numbers of employees, and annual payroll, 1987.

Ethnic group	All businesses		Businesses with paid employees			
	Businesses (number)	Sales/receipts ($1,000)	Businesses (number)	Sales/receipts ($1,000)	Employees (number)	Annual payroll ($1,000)
Asian/Pacific Islander, total	14,679	$1,437,700	3,904	$1,056,952	14,278	$151,404
Asian Indian	3,766	402,048	1,102	289,497	4,317	50,624
Chinese	2,380	306,546	870	249,256	4,000	39,235
Japanese	1,054	73,949	194	48,188	677	8,226
Korean	4,278	394,148	1,165	274,146	3,548	35,572
Vietnamese	272	16,403	52	8,706	90	869
Filipino	1,891	103,074	289	66,637	710	7,487
Hawaiian	14	110	2	(a)	(a)	(a)
Other Asian/Pacific Islander	1,024	141,422	230	120,522	936	9,391

Source: Bureau of the Census, U.S. Department of Commerce, *Survey of Minority-Owned Business Enterprises: Asian Americans, American Indians, and Other Minorities,* 1987 Economic Censuses (Washington, DC: U.S. Government Printing Office, June 1991), table 5, p. 27-35. Included in the universe of the survey is any activity for which an IRS Form 1040, Schedule C (individual proprietorship or self-employed person); 1065 (partnership); or 1120S (subchapter S corporation) was filed in 1987. *Note:* (a) Withheld to avoid disclosing data for individual companies.

★ 102 ★

Indiana: Businesses by Asian Ethnicity, Employees, and Sales

Numbers of Indiana businesses owned by Asian/Pacific Islanders by ethnicity and annual sales/receipts (in thousands of dollars), and numbers of Asian/Pacific Islander-owned businesses with employees, numbers of employees, and annual payroll, 1987.

Ethnic group	All businesses		Businesses with paid employees			
	Businesses (number)	Sales/receipts ($1,000)	Businesses (number)	Sales/receipts ($1,000)	Employees (number)	Annual payroll ($1,000)
Asian/Pacific Islander, total	1,718	$189,720	699	$155,192	3,514	$29,785
Asian Indian	540	80,579	240	64,064	1,301	11,024
Chinese	328	42,148	157	36,680	1,138	7,939
Japanese	124	4,289	28	3,032	119	914
Korean	293	34,860	114	29,766	629	5,430
Vietnamese	69	3,244	22	2,525	61	433
Filipino	240	24,600	94	19,125	266	4,045
Hawaiian	7	(a)	2	(a)	(a)	(a)
Other Asian/Pacific Islander	117	(a)	42	(a)	(a)	(a)

Source: Bureau of the Census, U.S. Department of Commerce, *Survey of Minority-Owned Business Enterprises: Asian Americans, American Indians, and Other Minorities,* 1987 Economic Censuses (Washington, DC: U.S. Government Printing Office, June 1991), table 5, p. 27-35. Included in the universe of the survey is any activity for which an IRS Form 1040, Schedule C (individual proprietorship or self-employed person); 1065 (partnership); or 1120S (subchapter S corporation) was filed in 1987. *Note:* (a) Withheld to avoid disclosing data for individual companies.

★ 103 ★

Iowa: Businesses by Asian Ethnicity, Employees, and Sales

Numbers of Iowa businesses owned by Asian/Pacific Islanders by ethnicity and annual sales/receipts (in thousands of dollars), and numbers of Asian/Pacific Islander-owned businesses with employees, numbers of employees, and annual payroll, 1987.

Ethnic group	All businesses		Businesses with paid employees			
	Businesses (number)	Sales/receipts ($1,000)	Businesses (number)	Sales/receipts ($1,000)	Employees (number)	Annual payroll ($1,000)
Asian/Pacific Islander, total	574	$53,182	232	$46,453	1136	$7,544
Asian Indian	137	16,365	63	14,084	296	1,842
Chinese	132	14,870	71	13,743	407	2,412
Japanese	69	1,015	6	380	6	76
Korean	84	11,807	42	10,179	266	1,961
Vietnamese	41	(a)	3	426	10	34
Filipino	46	3,490	24	3,346	66	632
Hawaiian	1	(a)	(a)	(a)	(a)	(a)
Other Asian/Pacific Islander	64	5,635	23	4,295	85	587

Source: Bureau of the Census, U.S. Department of Commerce, *Survey of Minority-Owned Business Enterprises: Asian Americans, American Indians, and Other Minorities,* 1987 Economic Censuses (Washington, DC: U.S. Government Printing Office, June 1991), table 5, p. 27-35. Included in the universe of the survey is any activity for which an IRS Form 1040, Schedule C (individual proprietorship or self-employed person); 1065 (partnership); or 1120S (subchapter S corporation) was filed in 1987. *Note:* (a) Withheld to avoid disclosing data for individual companies.

★ 104 ★

Kansas: Businesses by Asian Ethnicity, Employees, and Sales

Numbers of Kansas businesses owned by Asian/Pacific Islanders by ethnicity and annual sales/receipts (in thousands of dollars), and numbers of Asian/Pacific Islander-owned businesses with employees, numbers of employees, and annual payroll, 1987.

Ethnic group	All businesses		Businesses with paid employees			
	Businesses (number)	Sales/receipts ($1,000)	Businesses (number)	Sales/receipts ($1,000)	Employees (number)	Annual payroll ($1,000)
Asian/Pacific Islander, total	1,135	$74,700	406	$62,750	1,437	$11,146
Asian Indian	302	28,030	121	23,024	378	3,603
Chinese	233	17,925	89	14,914	569	3,355
Japanese	97	4,468	26	3,341	69	574
Korean	177	9,080	77	7,184	169	1,209
Vietnamese	126	6,315	40	4,551	90	570
Filipino	113	8,837	38	7,480	120	1,295
Hawaiian	15	45	0	0	0	0
Other Asian/Pacific Islander	72	(a)	15	2,256	42	540

Source: Bureau of the Census, U.S. Department of Commerce, *Survey of Minority-Owned Business Enterprises: Asian Americans, American Indians, and Other Minorities,* 1987 Economic Censuses (Washington, DC: U.S. Government Printing Office, June 1991), table 5, p. 27-35. Included in the universe of the survey is any activity for which an IRS Form 1040, Schedule C (individual proprietorship or self-employed person); 1065 (partnership); or 1120S (subchapter S corporation) was filed in 1987. *Note:* (a) Withheld to avoid disclosing data for individual companies.

★ 105 ★

Kentucky: Businesses by Asian Ethnicity, Employees, and Sales

Numbers of Kentucky businesses owned by Asian/Pacific Islanders by ethnicity and annual sales/receipts (in thousands of dollars), and numbers of Asian/Pacific Islander-owned businesses with employees, numbers of employees, and annual payroll, 1987.

Ethnic group	All businesses		Businesses with paid employees			
	Businesses (number)	Sales/receipts ($1,000)	Businesses (number)	Sales/receipts ($1,000)	Employees (number)	Annual payroll ($1,000)
Asian/Pacific Islander, total	875	$88,685	324	$78,987	1,660	$13,882
Asian Indian	321	51,180	152	43,475	752	7,395
Chinese	142	14,851	76	13,826	494	2,655
Japanese	56	2,507	8	1,652	65	338
Korean	148	7,350	20	3,924	74	495
Vietnamese	37	2,108	11	1,086	49	206
Filipino	111	10,689	36	8,998	138	1,988
Hawaiian	1	(a)	0	0	0	0
Other Asian/Pacific Islander	59	(a)	21	6,026	88	805

Source: Bureau of the Census, U.S. Department of Commerce, *Survey of Minority-Owned Business Enterprises: Asian Americans, American Indians, and Other Minorities,* 1987 Economic Censuses (Washington, DC: U.S. Government Printing Office, June 1991), table 5, p. 27-35. Included in the universe of the survey is any activity for which an IRS Form 1040, Schedule C (individual proprietorship or self-employed person); 1065 (partnership); or 1120S (subchapter S corporation) was filed in 1987. *Note:* (a) Withheld to avoid disclosing data for individual companies.

★ 106 ★

Louisiana: Businesses by Asian Ethnicity, Employees, and Sales

Numbers of Louisiana businesses owned by Asian/Pacific Islanders by ethnicity and annual sales/receipts (in thousands of dollars), and numbers of Asian/Pacific Islander-owned businesses with employees, numbers of employees, and annual payroll, 1987.

Ethnic group	All businesses		Businesses with paid employees			
	Businesses (number)	Sales/receipts ($1,000)	Businesses (number)	Sales/receipts ($1,000)	Employees (number)	Annual pay-roll ($1,000)
Asian/Pacific Islander, total	2,583	$170,799	717	$113,709	1,942	$16,760
Asian Indian	448	51,974	151	40,060	599	5,129
Chinese	385	37,139	144	29,280	725	4,958
Japanese	67	2,602	9	(a)	(a)	(a)
Korean	343	16,971	86	9,144	105	1,777
Vietnamese	1,062	47,226	254	23,951	227	2,953
Filipino	109	3,968	17	2,272	45	382
Hawaiian	16	(a)	2	(a)	(a)	(a)
Other Asian/Pacific Islander	153	10,919	54	9,002	241	1,561

Source: Bureau of the Census, U.S. Department of Commerce, *Survey of Minority-Owned Business Enterprises: Asian Americans, American Indians, and Other Minorities,* 1987 Economic Censuses (Washington, DC: U.S. Government Printing Office, June 1991), table 5, p. 27-35. Included in the universe of the survey is any activity for which an IRS Form 1040, Schedule C (individual proprietorship or self-employed person); 1065 (partnership); or 1120S (subchapter S corporation) was filed in 1987. *Note:* (a) Withheld to avoid disclosing data for individual companies.

★ 107 ★

Maine: Businesses by Asian Ethnicity, Employees, and Sales

Numbers of Maine businesses owned by Asian/Pacific Islanders by ethnicity and annual sales/receipts (in thousands of dollars), and numbers of Asian/Pacific Islander-owned businesses with employees, numbers of employees, and annual payroll, 1987.

Ethnic group	All Businesses		Businesses with paid employees			
	Businesses (number)	Sales/receipts ($1,000)	Businesses (number)	Sales/receipts ($1,000)	Employees (number)	Annual payroll ($1,000)
Asian/Pacific Islander, total	165	$18,521	56	$15,515	489	$4,546
Asian Indian	18	(a)	11	1,954	40	348
Chinese	55	12,481	23	11,085	429	3,907
Japanese	26	851	5	396	4	65
Korean	12	538	4	309	6	60
Vietnamese	10	268	2	(a)	(a)	(a)
Filipino	23	2,098	4	(a)	(a)	(a)
Hawaiian	2	(a)	1	(a)	(a)	(a)
Other Asian/Pacific Islander	19	2,285	6	1,771	10	166

Source: Bureau of the Census, U.S. Department of Commerce, *Survey of Minority-Owned Business Enterprises: Asian Americans, American Indians, and Other Minorities,* 1987 Economic Censuses (Washington, DC: U.S. Government Printing Office, June 1991), table 5, p. 27-35. Included in the universe of the survey is any activity for which an IRS Form 1040, Schedule C (individual proprietorship or self-employed person); 1065 (partnership); or 1120S (subchapter S corporation) was filed in 1987. *Note:* (a) Withheld to avoid disclosing data for individual companies.

★ 108 ★

Maryland: Businesses by Asian Ethnicity, Employees, and Sales

Numbers of Maryland businesses owned by Asian/Pacific Islanders by ethnicity and annual sales/receipts (in thousands of dollars), and numbers of Asian/Pacific Islander-owned businesses with employees, numbers of employees, and annual payroll, 1987.

Ethnic group	All businesses		Businesses with paid employees			
	Businesses (number)	Sales/receipts ($1,000)	Businesses (number)	Sales/receipts ($1,000)	Employees (number)	Annual payroll ($1,000)
Asian/Pacific Islander, total	7,831	$701,690	2,172	$495,956	6,757	$78,550
Asian Indian	1,607	193,513	396	155,495	1,934	33,328
Chinese	1,437	109,873	374	80,529	1,537	12,451
Japanese	336	12,756	28	5,663	135	1,422
Korean	3,067	293,423	1,033	187,249	2,322	22,810
Vietnamese	212	7,891	22	(a)	(a)	(a)
Filipino	744	39,666	188	29,042	354	3,780
Hawaiian	10	349	1	(a)	(a)	(a)
Other Asian/Pacific Islander	418	44,219	130	37,978	475	4,759

Source: Bureau of the Census, U.S. Department of Commerce, *Survey of Minority-Owned Business Enterprises: Asian Americans, American Indians, and Other Minorities,* 1987 Economic Censuses (Washington, DC: U.S. Government Printing Office, June 1991), table 5, p. 27-35. Included in the universe of the survey is any activity for which an IRS Form 1040, Schedule C (individual proprietorship or self-employed person); 1065 (partnership); or 1120S (subchapter S corporation) was filed in 1987. *Note:* (a) Withheld to avoid disclosing data for individual companies.

★ 109 ★

Massachusetts: Businesses by Asian Ethnicity, Employees, and Sales

Numbers of Massachusetts businesses owned by Asian/Pacific Islanders by ethnicity and annual sales/receipts (in thousands of dollars), and numbers of Asian/Pacific Islander-owned businesses with employees, numbers of employees, and annual payroll, 1987.

Ethnic group	All businesses		Businesses with paid employees			
	Businesses (number)	Sales/receipts ($1,000)	Businesses (number)	Sales/receipts ($1,000)	Employees (number)	Annual payroll ($1,000)
Asian/Pacific Islander, total	3,784	292,291	803	201,948	3,155	39,640
Asian Indian	1,008	90,394	234	63,271	689	11,012
Chinese	1,456	116,008	313	87,702	1,700	20,417
Japanese	262	13,321	40	7,364	139	1,649
Korean	367	26,342	78	13,851	210	2,261
Vietnamese	195	9,352	34	3,721	63	611
Filipino	239	14,361	43	10,329	117	1,408
Hawaiian	22	516	2	(a)	(a)	(a)
Other Asian/Pacific Islander	235	21,997	59	15,710	237	2,282

Source: Bureau of the Census, U.S. Department of Commerce, *Survey of Minority-Owned Business Enterprises: Asian Americans, American Indians, and Other Minorities,* 1987 Economic Censuses (Washington, DC: U.S. Government Printing Office, June 1991), table 5, P. 27-35. Included in the universe of the survey is any activity for which an IRS form 1040, Schedule C (individual proprietorship or self-employed person); 1065 (partnership); or 1120S (subchapter S corporation) was filed in 1987. *Note:* (a) Withheld to avoid disclosing data for individual companies.

★ 110 ★

Michigan: Businesses by Asian Ethnicity, Employees, and Sales

Numbers of Michigan businesses owned by Asian/Pacific Islanders by ethnicity and annual sales/receipts (in thousands of dollars), and numbers of Asian/Pacific Islander-owned businesses with employees, numbers of employees, and annual payroll, 1987.

Ethnic group	All businesses		Businesses with paid employees			
	Businesses (number)	Sales/receipts ($1,000)	Businesses (number)	Sales/receipts ($1,000)	Employees (number)	Annual payroll ($1,000)
Asian/Pacific Islander, total	4,424	$405,221	1,402	$314,573	5,961	$57,927
Asian Indian	1,713	162,926	489	123,578	2,102	27,400
Chinese	703	81,075	302	68,579	1,934	13,229
Japanese	300	15,723	60	11,834	199	2,568
Korean	803	90,941	350	72,242	1,055	7,660
Vietnamese	80	3,313	17	2,069	42	396
Filipino	534	25,889	106	17,071	269	3,209
Hawaiian	25	(a)	4	(a)	(a)	(a)
Other Asian/Pacific Islander	266	25,354	74	19,200	360	3,465

Source: Bureau of the Census, U.S. Department of Commerce, *Survey of Minority-Owned Business Enterprises: Asian Americans, American Indians, and Other Minorities,* 1987 Economic Censuses (Washington, DC: U.S. Government Printing Office, June 1991), table 5, p. 27-35. Included in the universe of the survey is any activity for which an IRS Form 1040, Schedule C (individual proprietorship or self-employed person); 1065 (partnership); or 1120S (subchapter S corporation) was filed in 1987. *Note:* (a) Withheld to avoid disclosing data for individual companies.

★ 111 ★

Minnesota: Businesses by Asian Ethnicity, Employees, and Sales

Numbers of Minnesota businesses owned by Asian/Pacific Islanders by ethnicity and annual sales/receipts (in thousands of dollars), and numbers of Asian/Pacific Islander-owned businesses with employees, numbers of employees, and annual payroll, 1987.

Ethnic group	All businesses		Businesses with paid employees			
	Businesses (number)	Sales/receipts ($1,000)	Businesses (number)	Sales/receipts ($1,000)	Employees (number)	Annual payroll ($1,000)
Asian/Pacific Islander, total	1,684	$153,953	509	$126,937	2,842	$25,965
Asian Indian	328	31,137	78	22,645	223	2,600
Chinese	425	59,332	189	54,295	1,441	11,703
Japanese	190	8,686	28	6,354	84	958
Korean	202	14,403	50	10,880	216	2,307
Vietnamese	192	14,461	96	12,184	479	2,421
Filipino	162	18,520	33	16,213	287	5,256
Hawaiian	8	602	3	496	12	60
Other Asian/Pacific Islander	177	6,812	32	3,870	100	660

Source: Bureau of the Census, U.S. Department of Commerce, *Survey of Minority-Owned Business Enterprises: Asian Americans, American Indians, and Other Minorities,* 1987 Economic Censuses (Washington, DC: U.S. Government Printing Office, June 1991), table 5, p. 27-35. Included in the universe of the survey is any activity for which an IRS Form 1040, Schedule C (individual proprietorship or self-employed person); 1065 (partnership); or 1120S (subchapter S corporation) was filed in 1987.

★ 112 ★

Mississippi: Businesses by Asian Ethnicity, Employees, and Sales

Numbers of Mississippi businesses owned by Asian/Pacific Islanders by ethnicity and annual sales/receipts (in thousands of dollars), and numbers of Asian/Pacific Islander-owned businesses with employees, numbers of employees, and annual payroll, 1987.

Ethnic group	All businesses		Businesses with paid employees			
	Businesses (number)	Sales/receipts ($1,000)	Businesses (number)	Sales/receipts ($1,000)	Employees (number)	Annual payroll ($1,000)
Asian/Pacific Islander, total	1,128	$133,767	551	$110,700	2,404	$15,069
Asian Indian	343	62,144	250	57,389	1,766	9,574
Chinese	330	51,361	138	36,171	448	2,762
Japanese	18	1,557	4	387	33	97
Korean	20	2,068	8	955	26	124
Vietnamese	372	16,637	131	11,677	19	1,835
Filipino	21	(a)	6	789	10	93
Hawaiian	1	(a)	0	0	0	0
Other Asian/Pacific Islander	23	(a)	14	3,332	102	584

Source: Bureau of the Census, U.S. Department of Commerce, *Survey of Minority-Owned Business Enterprises: Asian Americans, American Indians, and Other Minorities,* 1987 Economic Censuses (Washington, DC: U.S. Government Printing Office, June 1991), table 5, p. 27-35. Included in the universe of the survey is any activity for which an IRS Form 1040, Schedule C (individual proprietorship or self-employed person); 1065 (partnership); or 1120S (subchapter S corporation) was filed in 1987. *Note:* (a) Withheld to avoid disclosing data for individual companies.

★ 113 ★

Missouri: Businesses by Asian Ethnicity, Employees, and Sales

Numbers of Missouri businesses owned by Asian/Pacific Islanders by ethnicity and annual sales/receipts (in thousands of dollars), and numbers of Asian/Pacific Islander-owned businesses with employees, numbers of employees, and annual payroll, 1987.

Ethnic group	All businesses		Businesses with paid employees			
	Businesses (number)	Sales/receipts ($1,000)	Businesses (number)	Sales/receipts ($1,000)	Employees (number)	Annual payroll ($1,000)
Asian/Pacific Islander, total	2,056	$164,617	824	$129,157	2,757	$21,347
Asian Indian	464	42,916	194	34,171	635	5,140
Chinese	400	41,402	206	31,692	786	5,633
Japanese	160	6,205	32	3,957	89	818
Korean	366	31,396	157	25,848	595	4,143
Vietnamese	176	8,659	65	6,416	137	822
Filipino	276	16,076	83	12,321	234	2,483
Hawaiian	31	2,046	6	1,501	18	176
Other Asian/Pacific Islander	183	15,917	81	13,251	263	2,132

Source: Bureau of the Census, U.S. Department of Commerce, *Survey of Minority-Owned Business Enterprises: Asian Americans, American Indians, and Other Minorities,* 1987 Economic Censuses (Washington, DC: U.S. Government Printing Office, June 1991), table 5, p. 27-35. Included in the universe of the survey is any activity for which an IRS Form 1040, Schedule C (individual proprietorship or self-employed person); 1065 (partnership); or 1120S (subchapter S corporation) was filed in 1987.

★ 114 ★

Montana: Businesses by Asian Ethnicity, Employees, and Sales

Numbers of Montana businesses owned by Asian/Pacific Islanders by ethnicity and annual sales/receipts (in thousands of dollars), and numbers of Asian/Pacific Islander-owned businesses with employees, numbers of employees, and annual payroll, 1987.

Ethnic group	All businesses		Businesses with paid employees			
	Businesses (number)	Sales/receipts ($1,000)	Businesses (number)	Sales/receipts ($1,000)	Employees (number)	Annual payroll ($1,000)
Asian/Pacific Islander, total	207	13,317	72	8,504	323	1,779
Asian Indian	10	894	3	698	17	96
Chinese	56	6,401	38	5,861	232	1,285
Japanese	65	1,620	9	987	37	182
Korean	16	552	2	(a)	(a)	(a)
Vietnamese	7	2,263	6	(a)	(a)	(a)
Filipino	36	953	9	530	14	100
Hawaiian	4	17	0	0	0	0
Other Asian/Pacific Islander	13	617	5	428	23	116

Source: Bureau of the Census, U.S. Department of Commerce, *Survey of Minority-Owned Business Enterprises: Asian Americans, American Indians, and Other Minorities,* 1987 Economic Censuses (Washington, DC: U.S. Government Printing Office, June 1991), table 5, p. 27-35. Included in the universe of the survey is any activity for which an IRS Form 1040, Schedule C (individual proprietorship or self-employed person); 1065 (partnership); or 1120S (subchapter S corporation) was filed in 1987. *Note:* (a) Withheld to avoid disclosing data for individual companies.

★ 115 ★

Nebraska: Businesses by Asian Ethnicity, Employees, and Sales

Numbers of Nebraska businesses owned by Asian/Pacific Islanders by ethnicity and annual sales/receipts (in thousands of dollars), and numbers of Asian/Pacific Islander-owned businesses with employees, numbers of employees, and annual payroll, 1987.

Ethnic group	All businesses		Businesses with paid employees			
	Businesses (number)	Sales/receipts ($1,000)	Businesses (number)	Sales/receipts ($1,000)	Employees (number)	Annual payroll ($1,000)
Asian/Pacific Islander, total	385	$28,625	125	$23,342	491	$3,832
Asian Indian	77	7,011	30	5,617	109	741
Chinese	51	7,131	21	6,370	229	1,657
Japanese	84	6,709	29	5,996	62	840
Korean	78	5,925	26	4,519	63	419
Vietnamese	34	1,420	11	840	28	175
Filipino	24	429	3	(a)	(a)	(a)
Hawaiian	2	(a)	0	0	0	0
Other Asian/Pacific Islander	35	(a)	5	(a)	(a)	(a)

Source: Bureau of the Census, U.S. Department of Commerce, *Survey of Minority-Owned Business Enterprises: Asian Americans, American Indians, and Other Minorities,* 1987 Economic Censuses (Washington, DC: U.S. Government Printing Office, June 1991), table 5, p. 27-35. Included in the universe of the survey is any activity for which an IRS Form 1040, Schedule C (individual proprietorship or self-employed person); 1065 (partnership); or 1120S (subchapter S corporation) was filed in 1987. *Note:* (a) Withheld to avoid disclosing data for individual companies.

★ 116 ★

Nevada: Businesses by Asian Ethnicity, Employees, and Sales

Numbers of Nevada businesses owned by Asian/Pacific Islanders by ethnicity and annual sales/receipts (in thousands of dollars), and numbers of Asian/Pacific Islander-owned businesses with employees, numbers of employees, and annual payroll, 1987.

Ethnic group	All businesses		Businesses with paid employees			
	Businesses (number)	Sales/receipts ($1,000)	Businesses (number)	Sales/receipts ($1,000)	Employees (number)	Annual payroll ($1,000)
Asian/Pacific Islander, total	1,245	$83,915	320	$58,251	1,197	$11,264
Asian Indian	127	8,375	19	5,237	70	744
Chinese	296	32,815	129	26,269	650	6,062
Japanese	209	12,432	35	7,871	211	1,858
Korean	220	13,617	56	9,816	115	1,112
Vietnamese	65	3,147	19	1,101	39	245
Filipino	241	6,545	29	3,289	41	628
Hawaiian	17	568	7	418	8	57
Other Asian/Pacific Islander	70	6,416	26	4,250	63	558

Source: Bureau of the Census, U.S. Department of Commerce, *Survey of Minority-Owned Business Enterprises: Asian Americans, American Indians, and Other Minorities,* 1987 Economic Censuses (Washington, DC: U.S. Government Printing Office, June 1991), table 5, p. 27-35. Included in the universe of the survey is any activity for which an IRS Form 1040, Schedule C (individual proprietorship or self-employed person); 1065 (partnership); or 1120S (subchapter S corporation) was filed in 1987.

★ 117 ★

New Hampshire: Businesses by Asian Ethnicity, Employees, and Sales

Numbers of New Hampshire businesses owned by Asian/Pacific Islanders by ethnicity and annual sales/receipts (in thousands of dollars), and numbers of Asian/Pacific Islander-owned businesses with employees, numbers of employees, and annual payroll, 1987.

Ethnic group	All businesses		Businesses with paid employees			
	Businesses (number)	Sales/receipts ($1,000)	Businesses (number)	Sales/receipts ($1,000)	Employees (number)	Annual payroll ($1,000)
Asian/Pacific Islander, total	304	$34,092	74	$25,957	234	$2,465
Asian Indian	93	19,746	23	17,437	98	1,148
Chinese	101	9,312	33	7,069	115	1,133
Japanese	34	(a)	4	(a)	(a)	(a)
Korean	39	3,451	4	1,111	11	144
Vietnamese	2	(a)	0	0	0	0
Filipino	12	964	6	(a)	(a)	(a)
Hawaiian	2	(a)	1	(a)	(a)	(a)
Other Asian/Pacific Islander	21	619	3	340	10	40

Source: Bureau of the Census, U.S. Department of Commerce, *Survey of Minority-Owned Business Enterprises: Asian Americans, American Indians, and Other Minorities,* 1987 Economic Censuses (Washington, DC: U.S. Government Printing Office, June 1991), table 5, p. 27-35. Included in the universe of the survey is any activity for which an IRS Form 1040, Schedule C (individual proprietorship or self-employed person); 1065 (partnership); or 1120S (subchapter S corporation) was filed in 1987. *Note:* (a) Withheld to avoid disclosing data for individual companies.

★ 118 ★

New Jersey: Businesses by Asian Ethnicity, Employees, and Sales

Numbers of New Jersey businesses owned by Asian/Pacific Islanders by ethnicity and annual sales/receipts (in thousands of dollars), and numbers of Asian/Pacific Islander-owned businesses with employees, numbers of employees, and annual payroll, 1987.

Ethnic group	All businesses		Businesses with paid employees			
	Businesses (number)	Sales/receipts ($1,000)	Businesses (number)	Sales/receipts ($1,000)	Employees (number)	Annual payroll ($1,000)
Asian/Pacific Islander, total	12,530	1,201,478	2,846	804,173	7,828	103,840
Asian Indian	3,937	451,068	933	311,905	2,717	33,982
Chinese	2,880	257,444	705	177,006	2,188	30,532
Japanese	453	30,229	84	21,312	385	4,506
Korean	2,480	284,708	669	188,495	1,338	17,290
Vietnamese	237	8,511	37	3,697	74	593
Filipino	2,059	122,320	318	73,247	792	11,465
Hawaiian	19	(a)	0	0	0	0
Other Asian/Pacific Islander	465	47,198	100	28,511	334	5,472

Source: Bureau of the Census, U.S. Department of Commerce, *Survey of Minority-Owned Business Enterprises: Asian Americans, American Indians, and Other Minorities,* 1987 Economic Censuses (Washington, DC: U.S. Government Printing Office, June 1991), table 5, p. 27-35. Included in the universe of the survey is any activity for which an IRS Form 1040, Schedule C (individual proprietorship or self-employed person); 1065 (partnership); or 1120S (subchapter S corporation) was filed in 1987. *Note:* (a) Withheld to avoid disclosing data for individual companies.

★ 119 ★

New Mexico: Businesses by Asian Ethnicity, Employees, and Sales

Numbers of New Mexico businesses owned by Asian/Pacific Islanders by ethnicity and annual sales/receipts (in thousands of dollars), and numbers of Asian/Pacific Islander-owned businesses with employees, numbers of employees, and annual payroll, 1987.

Ethnic group	All businesses		Businesses with paid employees			
	Businesses (number)	Sales/receipts ($1,000)	Businesses (number)	Sales/receipts ($1,000)	Employees (number)	Annual payroll ($1,000)
Asian/Pacific Islander, total	897	$66,611	330	$50,767	1,258	$8,235
Asian Indian	221	26,785	103	20,766	374	2,525
Chinese	214	18,178	97	15,909	523	3,315
Japanese	87	6,842	26	5,780	154	1,074
Korean	94	5,027	28	3,634	114	682
Vietnamese	87	2,874	28	1,790	47	288
Filipino	65	2,040	21	1,755	26	183
Hawaiian	27	1,224	5	1,133	20	168
Other Asian/Pacific Islander	102	3,641	22	(a)	(a)	(a)

Source: Bureau of the Census, U.S. Department of Commerce, *Survey of Minority-Owned Business Enterprises: Asian Americans, American Indians, and Other Minorities,* 1987 Economic Censuses (Washington, DC: U.S. Government Printing Office, June 1991), table 5, p. 27-35. Included in the universe of the survey is any activity for which an IRS Form 1040, Schedule C (individual proprietorship or self-employed person); 1065 (partnership); or 1120S (subchapter S corporation) was filed in 1987. *Note:* (a) Withheld to avoid disclosing data for individual companies.

★ 120 ★

New York: Businesses by Asian Ethnicity, Employees, and Sales

Numbers of New York businesses owned by Asian/Pacific Islanders by ethnicity and annual sales/receipts (in thousands of dollars), and numbers of Asian/Pacific Islander-owned businesses with employees, numbers of employees, and annual payroll, 1987.

Ethnic group	All businesses		Businesses with paid employees			
	Businesses (number)	Sales/receipts ($1,000)	Businesses (number)	Sales/receipts ($1,000)	Employees (number)	Annual payroll ($1,000)
Asian/Pacific Islander, total	35,812	$3,192,830	7,061	$2,149,917	21,227	$286,030
Asian Indian	8,253	1,044,903	2,025	795,442	6,517	99,744
Chinese	12,587	942,205	2,233	637,129	8,148	95,934
Japanese	1,730	120,915	243	83,963	975	16,500
Korean	7,208	682,366	1,641	391,001	3,606	43,732
Vietnamese	462	22,453	85	(a)	(a)	(a)
Filipino	3,502	154,540	444	79,972	794	11,468
Hawaiian	57	6,257	2	(a)	(a)	(a)
Other Asian/Pacific Islander	2,013	219,191	388	162,410	1,187	18,652

Source: Bureau of the Census, U.S. Department of Commerce, *Survey of Minority-Owned Business Enterprises: Asian Americans, American Indians, and Other Minorities,* 1987 Economic Censuses (Washington, DC: U.S. Government Printing Office, June 1991), table 5, p. 27-35. Included in the universe of the survey is any activity for which an IRS Form 1040, Schedule C (individual proprietorship or self-employed person); 1065 (partnership); or 1120S (subchapter S corporation) was filed in 1987. *Note:* (a) Withheld to avoid disclosing data for individual companies.

★ 121 ★

North Carolina: Businesses by Asian Ethnicity, Employees, and Sales

Numbers of North Carolina businesses owned by Asian/Pacific Islanders by ethnicity and annual sales/receipts (in thousands of dollars), and numbers of Asian/Pacific Islander-owned businesses with employees, numbers of employees, and annual payroll, 1987.

Ethnic group	All businesses		Businesses with paid employees			
	Businesses (number)	Sales/receipts ($1,000)	Businesses (number)	Sales/receipts ($1,000)	Employees (number)	Annual payroll ($1,000)
Asian/Pacific Islander, total	2,069	$210,477	855	$168,937	3,807	$27,024
Asian Indian	667	104,700	378	88,369	2,048	13,916
Chinese	419	38,816	176	30,051	889	6,255
Japanese	209	16,269	42	13,529	156	1,428
Korean	475	36,626	198	27,697	531	4,078
Vietnamese	55	2,138	7	1,616	15	139
Filipino	68	3,513	18	2,377	47	550
Hawaiian	7	(a)	0	0	0	0
Other Asian/Pacific Islander	169	8,415	36	5,298	121	658

Source: Bureau of the Census, U.S. Department of Commerce, *Survey of Minority-Owned Business Enterprises: Asian Americans, American Indians, and Other Minorities,* 1987 Economic Censuses (Washington, DC: U.S. Government Printing Office, June 1991), table 5, p. 27-35. Included in the universe of the survey is any activity for which an IRS Form 1040, Schedule C (individual proprietorship or self-employed person); 1065 (partnership); or 1120S (subchapter S corporation) was filed in 1987. *Note:* (a) Withheld to avoid disclosing data for individual companies.

★ 122 ★

North Dakota: Businesses by Asian Ethnicity, Employees, and Sales

Numbers of North Dakota businesses owned by Asian/Pacific Islanders by ethnicity and annual sales/receipts (in thousands of dollars), and numbers of Asian/Pacific Islander-owned businesses with employees, numbers of employees, and annual payroll, 1987.

Ethnic group	All businesses		Businesses with paid employees			
	Businesses (number)	Sales/receipts ($1,000)	Businesses (number)	Sales/receipts ($1,000)	Employees (number)	Annual payroll ($1,000)
Asian/Pacific Islander, total	119	$9,064	43	$7,387	214	$1,483
Asian Indian	36	4,775	19	3,945	60	535
Chinese	27	3,374	16	3,142	148	893
Japanese	9	197	0	0	0	0
Korean	13	114	0	0	0	0
Vietnamese	1	(a)	1	(a)	(a)	(a)
Filipino	20	604	3	300	6	55
Hawaiian	1	(a)	0	0	0	0
Other Asian/Pacific Islander	12	(a)	4	(a)	(a)	(a)

Source: Bureau of the Census, U.S. Department of Commerce, *Survey of Minority-Owned Business Enterprises: Asian Americans, American Indians, and Other Minorities,* 1987 Economic Censuses (Washington, DC: U.S. Government Printing Office, June 1991), table 5, p. 27-35. Included in the universe of the survey is any activity for which an IRS Form 1040, Schedule C (individual proprietorship or self-employed person); 1065 (partnership); or 1120S (subchapter S corporation) was filed in 1987. *Note:* (a) Withheld to avoid disclosing data for individual companies.

★ 123 ★

Ohio: Businesses by Asian Ethnicity, Employees, and Sales

Numbers of Ohio businesses owned by Asian/Pacific Islanders by ethnicity and annual sales/receipts (in thousands of dollars), and numbers of Asian/Pacific Islander-owned businesses with employees, numbers of employees, and annual payroll, 1987.

Ethnic group	All businesses		Businesses with paid employees			
	Businesses (number)	Sales/receipts ($1,000)	Businesses (number)	Sales/receipts ($1,000)	Employees (number)	Annual payroll ($1,000)
Asian/Pacific Islander, total	3,859	$388,173	1392	$302,162	5,627	$52,562
Asian Indian	1,527	188,006	541	153,330	2,485	27,873
Chinese	662	67,531	292	56,022	1,597	10,289
Japanese	267	11,024	45	6,281	118	1,699
Korean	621	62,160	255	44,078	593	6,044
Vietnamese	113	7,342	34	6,054	109	811
Filipino	442	30,449	140	18,982	388	3,067
Hawaiian	6	(a)	2	(a)	(a)	(a)
Other Asian/Pacific Islander	221	21,661	83	17,415	337	2,779

Source: Bureau of the Census, U.S. Department of Commerce, *Survey of Minority-Owned Business Enterprises: Asian Americans, American Indians, and Other Minorities,* 1987 Economic Censuses (Washington, DC: U.S. Government Printing Office, June 1991), table 5, p. 27-35. Included in the universe of the survey is any activity for which an IRS Form 1040, Schedule C (individual proprietorship or self-employed person); 1065 (partnership); or 1120S (subchapter S corporation) was filed in 1987. *Note:* (a) Withheld to avoid disclosing data for individual companies.

★ 124 ★

Oklahoma: Businesses by Asian Ethnicity, Employees, and Sales

Numbers of Oklahoma businesses owned by Asian/Pacific Islanders by ethnicity and annual sales/receipts (in thousands of dollars), and numbers of Asian/Pacific Islander-owned businesses with employees, numbers of employees, and annual payroll, 1987.

Ethnic group	All businesses		Businesses with paid employees			
	Businesses (number)	Sales/receipts ($1,000)	Businesses (number)	Sales/receipts ($1,000)	Employees (number)	Annual payroll ($1,000)
Asian/Pacific Islander, total	1,700	$98,174	440	$69,191	1,645	$12,007
Asian Indian	388	30,656	125	23,997	579	3,942
Chinese	239	24,870	101	19,230	520	3,399
Japanese	133	4,071	32	2,985	70	572
Korean	390	13,751	56	6,331	178	1,545
Vietnamese	292	13,241	64	7,732	128	822
Filipino	111	5,129	34	4,267	78	1,025
Hawaiian	33	984	9	829	40	318
Other Asian/Pacific Islander	114	5,472	19	3,820	52	384

Source: Bureau of the Census, U.S. Department of Commerce, *Survey of Minority-Owned Business Enterprises: Asian Americans, American Indians, and Other Minorities,* 1987 Economic Censuses (Washington, DC: U.S. Government Printing Office, June 1991), table 5, p. 27-35. Included in the universe of the survey is any activity for which an IRS Form 1040, Schedule C (individual proprietorship or self-employed person); 1065 (partnership); or 1120S (subchapter S corporation) was filed in 1987.

★ 125 ★

Oregon: Businesses by Asian Ethnicity, Employees, and Sales

Numbers of Oregon businesses owned by Asian/Pacific Islanders by ethnicity and annual sales/receipts (in thousands of dollars), and numbers of Asian/Pacific Islander-owned businesses with employees, numbers of employees, and annual payroll, 1987.

Ethnic group	All businesses		Businesses with paid employees			
	Businesses (number)	Sales/receipts ($1,000)	Businesses (number)	Sales/receipts ($1,000)	Employees (number)	Annual payroll ($1,000)
Asian/Pacific Islander, total	3,007	$312,231	1,002	$253,356	4,442	$34,595
Asian Indian	208	13,664	61	8,977	163	1,050
Chinese	813	101,752	345	87,639	2,371	17,353
Japanese	565	89,597	160	81,661	662	7,135
Korean	645	74,930	238	51,345	809	5,514
Vietnamese	257	17,687	78	13,318	280	1,890
Filipino	214	14,601	54	10,416	157	1,653
Hawaiian	68	(a)	14	(a)	(a)	(a)
Other Asian/Pacific Islander	237	(a)	52	(a)	(a)	(a)

Source: Bureau of the Census, U.S. Department of Commerce, *Survey of Minority-Owned Business Enterprises: Asian Americans, American Indians, and Other Minorities,* 1987 Economic Censuses (Washington, DC: U.S. Government Printing Office, June 1991), table 5, p. 27-35. Included in the universe of the survey is any activity for which an IRS Form 1040, Schedule C (individual proprietorship or self-employed person); 1065 (partnership); or 1120S (subchapter S corporation) was filed in 1987. *Note:* (a) Withheld to avoid disclosing data for individual companies.

★ 126 ★

Pennsylvania: Businesses by Asian Ethnicity, Employees, and Sales

Numbers of Pennsylvania businesses owned by Asian/Pacific Islanders by ethnicity and annual sales/receipts (in thousands of dollars), and numbers of Asian/Pacific Islander-owned businesses with employees, numbers of employees, and annual payroll, 1987.

Ethnic group	All businesses		Businesses with paid employees			
	Businesses (number)	Sales/receipts ($1,000)	Businesses (number)	Sales/receipts ($1,000)	Employees (number)	Annual payroll ($1,000)
Asian/Pacific Islander, total	7,049	$805,466	2,193	$690,247	7,774	$84,672
Asian Indian	1,910	108,589	582	155,887	2,410	26,674
Chinese	1,424	137,405	509	106,903	2,229	19,128
Japanese	241	85,693	52	81,911	594	9,057
Korean	2,148	344,786	705	257,626	1,801	19,874
Vietnamese	394	15,264	93	(a)	(a)	(a)
Filipino	486	76,848	140	64,624	469	6,467
Hawaiian	20	(a)	1	(a)	(a)	(a)
Other Asian/Pacific Islander	426	36,881	111	23,296	271	3,472

Source: Bureau of the Census, U.S. Department of Commerce, *Survey of Minority-Owned Business Enterprises: Asian Americans, American Indians, and Other Minorities,* 1987 Economic Censuses (Washington, DC: U.S. Government Printing Office, June 1991), table 5, p. 27-35. Included in the universe of the survey is any activity for which an IRS Form 1040, Schedule C (individual proprietorship or self-employed person); 1065 (partnership); or 1120S (subchapter S corporation) was filed in 1987. *Note:* (a) Withheld to avoid disclosing data for individual companies.

★ 127 ★

Rhode Island: Businesses by Asian Ethnicity, Employees, and Sales

Numbers of Rhode Island businesses owned by Asian/Pacific Islanders by ethnicity and annual sales/receipts (in thousands of dollars), and numbers of Asian/Pacific Islander-owned businesses with employees, numbers of employees, and annual payroll, 1987.

Ethnic group	All businesses		Businesses with paid employees			
	Businesses (number)	Sales/receipts ($1,000)	Businesses (number)	Sales/receipts ($1,000)	Employees (number)	Annual payroll ($1,000)
Asian/Pacific Islander, total	436	$39,806	129	$28,247	680	$4,852
Asian Indian	111	7,745	35	5,878	79	747
Chinese	117	18,617	47	16,215	508	3,202
Japanese	20	1,801	7	1,490	6	156
Korean	58	3,474	15	2,432	26	283
Vietnamese	24	1,247	3	(a)	(a)	(a)
Filipino	63	3,689	14	2,232	61	464
Hawaiian	1	(a)	0	0	0	0
Other Asian/Pacific Islander	42	3,233	8	(a)	(a)	(a)

Source: Bureau of the Census, U.S. Department of Commerce, *Survey of Minority-Owned Business Enterprises: Asian Americans, American Indians, and Other Minorities,* 1987 Economic Censuses (Washington, DC: U.S. Government Printing Office, June 1991), table 5, p. 27-35. Included in the universe of the survey is any activity for which an IRS Form 1040, Schedule C (individual proprietorship or self-employed person); 1065 (partnership); or 1120S (subchapter S corporation) was filed in 1987. *Note:* (a) Withheld to avoid disclosing data for individual companies.

★ 128 ★

South Carolina: Businesses by Asian Ethnicity, Employees, and Sales

Numbers of South Carolina businesses owned by Asian/Pacific Islanders by ethnicity and annual sales/receipts (in thousands of dollars), and numbers of Asian/Pacific Islander-owned businesses with employees, numbers of employees, and annual payroll, 1987.

Ethnic group	All businesses		Businesses with paid employees			
	Businesses (number)	Sales/receipts ($1,000)	Businesses (number)	Sales/receipts ($1,000)	Employees (number)	Annual payroll ($1,000)
Asian/Pacific Islander, total	918	$80,056	386	$71,316	1,621	$10,653
Asian Indian	386	51,722	225	46,371	1,015	6,166
Chinese	121	11,889	60	10,894	360	2,269
Japanese	45	2,073	13	1,497	27	285
Korean	143	10,396	41	6,795	92	873
Vietnamese	45	2,174	20	1,838	48	293
Filipino	110	1,802	6	1,102	27	253
Hawaiian	12	(a)	0	0	0	0
Other Asian/Pacific Islander	56	(a)	21	2,819	52	514

Source: Bureau of the Census, U.S. Department of Commerce, *Survey of Minority-Owned Business Enterprises: Asian Americans, American Indians, and Other Minorities,* 1987 Economic Censuses (Washington, DC: U.S. Government Printing Office, June 1991), table 5, p. 27-35. Included in the universe of the survey is any activity for which an IRS Form 1040, Schedule C (individual proprietorship or self-employed person); 1065 (partnership); or 1120S (subchapter S corporation) was filed in 1987. *Note:* (a) Withheld to avoid disclosing data for individual companies.

★ 129 ★

South Dakota: Businesses by Asian Ethnicity, Employees, and Sales

Numbers of South Dakota businesses owned by Asian/Pacific Islanders by ethnicity and annual sales/receipts (in thousands of dollars), and numbers of Asian/Pacific Islander-owned businesses with employees, numbers of employees, and annual payroll, 1987.

Ethnic group	All businesses		Businesses with paid employees			
	Businesses (number)	Sales/receipts ($1,000)	Businesses (number)	Sales/receipts ($1,000)	Employees (number)	Annual payroll ($1,000)
Asian/Pacific Islander, total						
Asian Indian	15	$1,670	7	$1,348	8	$88
Chinese	24	1,811	11	1,629	60	303
Japanese	20	336	5	238	5	54
Korean	13	410	4	(a)	(a)	(a)
Vietnamese	3	(a)	1	(a)	(a)	(a)
Filipino	19	609	4	(a)	(a)	(a)
Hawaiian	1	(a)	0	0	0	0
Other Asian/Pacific Islander	13	773	7	643	18	131

Source: Bureau of the Census, U.S. Department of Commerce, *Survey of Minority-Owned Business Enterprises: Asian Americans, American Indians, and Other Minorities,* 1987 Economic Censuses (Washington, DC: U.S. Government Printing Office, June 1991), table 5, p. 27-35. Included in the universe of the survey is any activity for which an IRS Form 1040, Schedule C (individual proprietorship or self-employed person); 1065 (partnership); or 1120S (subchapter S corporation) was filed in 1987. *Note:* (a) Withheld to avoid disclosing data for individual companies.

★ 130 ★

Tennessee: Businesses by Asian Ethnicity, Employees, and Sales

Numbers of Tennessee businesses owned by Asian/Pacific Islanders by ethnicity and annual sales/receipts (in thousands of dollars), and numbers of Asian/Pacific Islander-owned businesses with employees, numbers of employees, and annual payroll, 1987.

Ethnic group	All businesses		Businesses with paid employees			
	Businesses (number)	Sales/receipts ($1,000)	Businesses (number)	Sales/receipts ($1,000)	Employees (number)	Annual payroll ($1,000)
Asian/Pacific Islander, total	1,574	$171,073	713	$139,739	3,010	$20,064
Asian Indian	592	84,283	317	74,382	1,532	10,939
Chinese	327	43,140	161	36,731	958	5,222
Japanese	80	4,097	12	2,654	38	485
Korean	288	30,545	130	20,001	384	2,539
Vietnamese	92	3,446	22	1,420	35	253
Filipino	100	5,562	39	4,551	63	626
Hawaiian	11	(a)	1	(a)	(a)	(a)
Other Asian/Pacific Islander	84	(a)	31	(a)	(a)	(a)

Source: Bureau of the Census, U.S. Department of Commerce, *Survey of Minority-Owned Business Enterprises: Asian Americans, American Indians, and Other Minorities,* 1987 Economic Censuses (Washington, DC: U.S. Government Printing Office, June 1991), table 5, p. 27-35. Included in the universe of the survey is any activity for which an IRS Form 1040, Schedule C (individual proprietorship or self-employed person); 1065 (partnership); or 1120S (subchapter S corporation) was filed in 1987. *Note:* (a) Withheld to avoid disclosing data for individual companies.

★ 131 ★

Texas: Businesses by Asian Ethnicity, Employees, and Sales

Numbers of Texas businesses owned by Asian/Pacific Islanders by ethnicity and annual sales/receipts (in thousands of dollars), and numbers of Asian/Pacific Islander-owned businesses with employees, numbers of employees, and annual payroll, 1987.

Ethnic group	All businesses		Businesses with paid employees			
	Businesses (number)	Sales/receipts ($1,000)	Businesses (number)	Sales/receipts ($1,000)	Employees (number)	Annual payroll ($1,000)
Asian/Pacific Islander, total	21,753	$1,886,067	5,704	$1,285,592	16,425	$163,621
Asian Indian	4,043	594,943	1,246	378,201	3,342	34,477
Chinese	4,585	473,893	1,478	376,154	5,986	46,450
Japanese	687	36,386	145	26,304	559	6,254
Korean	4,230	318,448	1,144	224,960	3,384	36,463
Vietnamese	5,443	283,886	1,080	155,454	1,668	19,354
Filipino	1,250	56,723	199	36,658	549	6,250
Hawaiian	95	5,190	13	(a)	(a)	(a)
Other Asian/Pacific Islander	1,420	116,598	399	87,861	937	14,373

Source: Bureau of the Census, U.S. Department of Commerce, *Survey of Minority-Owned Business Enterprises: Asian Americans, American Indians, and Other Minorities,* 1987 Economic Censuses (Washington, DC: U.S. Government Printing Office, June 1991), table 5, p. 27-35. Included in the universe of the survey is any activity for which an IRS Form 1040, Schedule C (individual proprietorship or self-employed person); 1065 (partnership); or 1120S (subchapter S corporation) was filed in 1987. *Note:* (a) Withheld to avoid disclosing data for individual companies.

★ 132 ★

Utah: Businesses by Asian Ethnicity, Employees, and Sales

Numbers of Utah businesses owned by Asian/Pacific Islanders by ethnicity and annual sales/receipts (in thousands of dollars), and numbers of Asian/Pacific Islander-owned businesses with employees, numbers of employees, and annual payroll, 1987.

Ethnic group	All businesses		Businesses with paid employees			
	Businesses (number)	Sales/receipts ($1,000)	Businesses (number)	Sales/receipts ($1,000)	Employees (number)	Annual payroll ($1,000)
Asian/Pacific Islander, total	1,129	$66,958	270	$49,695	1,174	$8,213
Asian Indian	63	4,058	23	2,721	81	607
Chinese	237	18,928	91	16,140	643	3,242
Japanese	496	25,840	97	19,268	286	3,038
Korean	87	8,417	14	5,559	34	432
Vietnamese	41	3,336	18	2,607	30	231
Filipino	50	1,057	3	(a)	(a)	(a)
Hawaiian	26	(a)	3	(a)	(a)	(a)
Other Asian/Pacific Islander	129	5,322	21	3,400	100	663

Source: Bureau of the Census, U.S. Department of Commerce, *Survey of Minority-Owned Business Enterprises: Asian Americans, American Indians, and Other Minorities,* 1987 Economic Censuses (Washington, DC: U.S. Government Printing Office, June 1991), table 5, p. 27-35. Included in the universe of the survey is any activity for which an IRS Form 1040, Schedule C (individual proprietorship or self-employed person); 1065 (partnership); or 1120S (subchapter S corporation) was filed in 1987. *Note:* (a) Withheld to avoid disclosing data for individual companies.

★ 133 ★

Vermont: Businesses by Asian Ethnicity, Employees, and Sales

Numbers of Vermont businesses owned by Asian/Pacific Islanders by ethnicity and annual sales/receipts (in thousands of dollars), and numbers of Asian/Pacific Islander-owned businesses with employees, numbers of employees, and annual payroll, 1987.

Ethnic group	All businesses		Businesses with paid employees			
	Businesses (number)	Sales/receipts ($1,000)	Businesses (number)	Sales/receipts ($1,000)	Employees (number)	Annual payroll ($1,000)
Asian/Pacific Islander, total	102	$9,949	42	$7,715	169	$1,496
Asian Indian	30	3,116	16	2,862	64	485
Chinese	32	4,928	14	3,610	87	796
Japanese	16	483	2	(a)	(a)	(a)
Korean	13	1,422	6	1,243	18	215
Vietnamese	1	(a)	0	0	0	0
Filipino	3	(a)	1	(a)	(a)	(a)
Hawaiian	1	(a)	1	(a)	(a)	(a)
Other Asian/Pacific Islander	6	(a)	2	(a)	(a)	(a)

Source: Bureau of the Census, U.S. Department of Commerce, *Survey of Minority-Owned Business Enterprises: Asian Americans, American Indians, and Other Minorities,* 1987 Economic Censuses (Washington, DC: U.S. Government Printing Office, June 1991), table 5, p. 27-35. Included in the universe of the survey is any activity for which an IRS Form 1040, Schedule C (individual proprietorship or self-employed person); 1065 (partnership); or 1120S (subchapter S corporation) was filed in 1987. *Note:* (a) Withheld to avoid disclosing data for individual companies.

★ 134 ★

Virginia: Businesses by Asian Ethnicity, Employees, and Sales

Numbers of Virginia businesses owned by Asian/Pacific Islanders by ethnicity and annual sales/receipts (in thousands of dollars), and numbers of Asian/Pacific Islander-owned businesses with employees, numbers of employees, and annual payroll, 1987.

Ethnic group	All businesses		Businesses with paid employees			
	Businesses (number)	Sales/receipts ($1,000)	Businesses (number)	Sales/receipts ($1,000)	Employees (number)	Annual payroll ($1,000)
Asian Pacific/Islander, total	7,973	$602,166	2,209	$452,519	7,188	$80,214
Asian Indian	1,399	140,970	425	113,790	1,814	18,878
Chinese	916	86,908	310	76,225	1,534	18,593
Japanese	366	18,194	65	11,619	175	1,830
Korean	2,947	263,459	1,020	194,327	2,607	31,319
Vietnamese	749	33,015	151	21,118	381	3,734
Filipino	859	30,497	155	20,051	455	3,383
Hawaiian	28	(a)	3	(a)	(a)	(a)
Other Asian/Pacific Islander	709	29,123	80	15,389	222	2,477

Source: Bureau of the Census, U.S. Department of Commerce, *Survey of Minority-Owned Business Enterprises: Asian Americans, American Indians, and Other Minorities,* 1987 Economic Censuses (Washington, DC: U.S. Government Printing Office, June 1991), table 5, p. 27-35. Included in the universe of the survey is any activity for which an IRS Form 1040, Schedule C (individual proprietorship or self-employed person); 1065 (partnership); or 1120S (subchapter S corporation) was filed in 1987. *Note:* (a) Withheld to avoid disclosing data for individual companies.

★ 135 ★

Washington: Businesses by Asian Ethnicity, Employees, and Sales

Numbers of Washington businesses owned by Asian/Pacific Islanders by ethnicity and annual sales/receipts (in thousands of dollars), and numbers of Asian/Pacific Islander-owned businesses with employees, numbers of employees, and annual payroll, 1987.

Ethnic group	All businesses		Businesses with paid employees			
	Businesses (number)	Sales/receipts ($1,000)	Businesses (number)	Sales/receipts ($1,000)	Employees (number)	Annual payroll ($1,000)
Asian/Pacific Islander, total	7,559	$744,585	2,322	$611,190	9,455	$86,223
Asian Indian	485	132,003	128	124,827	770	13,775
Chinese	1,728	175,526	616	149,730	3,559	29,230
Japanese	1,736	127,118	415	89,472	1,519	17,176
Korean	1,723	177,616	720	140,719	2,440	15,940
Vietnamese	467	19,695	122	11,454	243	1,533
Filipino	927	71,162	166	60,594	369	3,970
Hawaiian	85	2,144	11	1,453	41	305
Other Asian/Pacific Islander	408	39,321	144	32,941	514	4,294

Source: Bureau of the Census, U.S. Department of Commerce, *Survey of Minority-Owned Business Enterprises: Asian Americans, American Indians, and Other Minorities,* 1987 Economic Censuses (Washington, DC: U.S. Government Printing Office, June 1991), table 5, p. 27-35. Included in the universe of the survey is any activity for which an IRS Form 1040, Schedule C (individual proprietorship or self-employed person); 1065 (partnership); or 1120S (subchapter S corporation) was filed in 1987.

★ 136 ★

West Virginia: Businesses by Asian Ethnicity, Employees, and Sales

Numbers of West Virginia businesses owned by Asian/Pacific Islanders by ethnicity and annual sales/receipts (in thousands of dollars), and numbers of Asian/Pacific Islander-owned businesses with employees, numbers of employees, and annual payroll, 1987.

Ethnic group	All businesses		Businesses with paid employees			
	Businesses (number)	Sales/receipts ($1,000)	Businesses (number)	Sales/receipts ($1,000)	Employees (number)	Annual payroll ($1,000)
Asian/Pacific Islander, total	523	$74,821	271	$62,000	942	$9,009
Asian Indian	211	39,360	114	35,096	420	4,474
Chinese	60	7,828	31	7,231	145	1,054
Japanese	12	380	2	(a)	(a)	(a)
Korean	24	2,089	16	1,841	41	197
Vietnamese	10	648	4	574	13	65
Filipino	161	20,047	78	17,258	323	3,219
Hawaiian	0	0	0	0	0	0
Other Asian/Pacific Islander	45	4,469	26	(a)	(a)	(a)

Source: Bureau of the Census, U.S. Department of Commerce, *Survey of Minority-Owned Business Enterprises: Asian Americans, American Indians, and Other Minorities,* 1987 Economic Censuses (Washington, DC: U.S. Government Printing Office, June 1991), table 5, p. 27-35. Included in the universe of the survey is any activity for which an IRS Form 1040, Schedule C (individual proprietorship or self-employed person); 1065 (partnership); or 1120S (subchapter S corporation) was filed in 1987. *Note:* (a) Withheld to avoid disclosing data for individual companies.

★ 137 ★

Wisconsin: Businesses by Asian Ethnicity, Employees, and Sales

Numbers of Wisconsin businesses owned by Asian/Pacific Islanders by ethnicity and annual sales/receipts (in thousands of dollars), and numbers of Asian/Pacific Islander-owned businesses with employees, numbers of employees, and annual payroll, 1987.

Ethnic group	All businesses		Businesses with paid employees			
	Businesses (number)	Sales/receipts ($1,000)	Businesses (number)	Sales/receipts ($1,000)	Employees (number)	Annual payroll ($1,000)
Asian/Pacific Islander, total	1,144	$132,758	417	$102,993	2,138	$18,571
Asian Indian	327	62,936	122	53,681	601	8,708
Chinese	268	32,758	143	25,767	960	5,992
Japanese	87	5,678	18	3,778	105	808
Korean	156	15,529	41	10,614	251	1,495
Vietnamese	31	(a)	6	769	41	170
Filipino	141	10,693	59	8,384	180	1,398
Hawaiian	3	(a)	1	(a)	(a)	(a)
Other Asian/Pacific Islander	131	5,164	27	(a)	(a)	(a)

Source: Bureau of the Census, U.S. Department of Commerce, *Survey of Minority-Owned Business Enterprises: Asian Americans, American Indians, and Other Minorities,* 1987 Economic Censuses (Washington, DC: U.S. Government Printing Office, June 1991), table 5, p. 27-35. Included in the universe of the survey is any activity for which an IRS Form 1040, Schedule C (individual proprietorship or self-employed person); 1065 (partnership); or 1120S (subchapter S corporation) was filed in 1987. *Note:* (a) Withheld to avoid disclosing data for individual companies.

★ 138 ★

Wyoming: Businesses by Asian Ethnicity, Employees, and Sales

Numbers of Wyoming businesses owned by Asian/Pacific Islanders by ethnicity and annual sales/receipts (in thousands of dollars), and numbers of Asian/Pacific Islander-owned businesses with employees, numbers of employees, and annual payroll, 1987.

Ethnic group	All businesses		Businesses with paid employees			
	Businesses (number)	Sales/receipts ($1,000)	Businesses (number)	Sales/receipts ($1,000)	Employees (number)	Annual payroll ($1,000)
Asian/Pacific Islander, total	154	$11,294	68	$8,231	292	$1,708
Asian Indian	21	2,019	14	1,795	38	201
Chinese	47	6,279	33	5,270	217	1,335
Japanese	32	749	6	400	12	89
Korean	15	959	2	(a)	(a)	(a)
Vietnamese	5	217	2	(a)	(a)	(a)
Filipino	11	594	3	398	6	57
Hawaiian	3	(a)	2	(a)	(a)	(a)
Other Asian/Pacific Islander	20	477	6	368	19	26

Source: Bureau of the Census, U.S. Department of Commerce, *Survey of Minority-Owned Business Enterprises: Asian Americans, American Indians, and Other Minorities,* 1987 Economic Censuses (Washington, DC: U.S. Government Printing Office, June 1991), table 5, p. 27-35. Included in the universe of the survey is any activity for which an IRS Form 1040, Schedule C (individual proprietorship or self-employed person); 1065 (partnership); or 1120S (subchapter S corporation) was filed in 1987. Also in source: data on American Indians, Aleuts, and Eskimos together with relative standard error of estimate (percent) for the data in the columns. *Note:* (a) Withheld to avoid disclosing data for individual companies.

Crime, Law Enforcement, and Civil Rights

Civil Rights and Hate Crimes

★ 139 ★

Hate Crime Bias-Motivations Reported in the United States

Reported motivations for hate crimes reported by approximately 3,000 law enforcement agencies in 32 states, 1991.

Bias-Motivation	Number	Percent[a]
Race	2,963	62.3
Anti-Asian/Pacific Islander	287	6.0
Anti-White	888	18.7
Anti-Black	1,689	35.5
Anti-American Indian/Alaskan Native	11	0.2
Anti-Multiracial Group	88	1.9
Ethnicity	450	9.5
Anti-Hispanic	242	5.1
Anti-Other Ethnicity/National Origin	208	4.4
Religion	917	19.3
Anti-Jewish	792	16.7
Anti-Catholic	23	0.5
Anti-Protestant	26	0.5
Anti-Islamic (Moslem)	10	0.2
Anti-Other Religion	51	1.1
Anti-Multireligious Group	11	0.2
Anti-Atheism/Agnosticism/etc.	4	0.1
Sexual Orientation	425	8.9
Anti-Homosexual	421	8.9
Anti-Heterosexual	3	0.1
Anti-Bisexual	1	0.0
Total	4,755	100.0

Source: Press release, January 1993, Federal Bureau of Justice, U.S. Department of Justice, Washington, DC 20535. *Note:* (a) Because of rounding, percentages may not add to totals.

★ 140 ★

Hate Crime Offenders in the United States by Suspected Race

Reported data on the race/ethnicity of suspected hate crime offenders by approximately 3,000 law enforcement agencies in 32 states, 1991.

Suspected Race of Offender	Number of Incidents	Percent[a]
Asian/Pacific Islander	47	1.0
White	1,679	36.8
Black	769	16.9
American Indian/Alaskan Native	12	0.3
Multi-racial group	77	1.7
Unknown	1,974	43.3
Total Incidents	4,558[a]	100.0

Source: Press release, January 1993, Federal Bureau of Justice, U.S. Department of Justice, Washington, DC 20535. *Note:* (a) Because of rounding, percentages may not add to total.

★ 141 ★

Intergroup Tension Events in Philadelphia

Analysis of 525 intergroup tension events reported to Philadelphia's Commission on Human Relations (PCHR) between January 1986 and June 1988. The race or ethnic identity of perpetrators and victims were identified in about 60 percent of the intergroup tension events. In the remaining 40 percent, there was no clear distinction between victim and perpetrator: either the perpetrator or the victim was not identified, or both were members of the same group. Shown here are the percent of events associated with five racial-ethnic groups. Also presented are estimates of the relative size of these groups in the city's population.

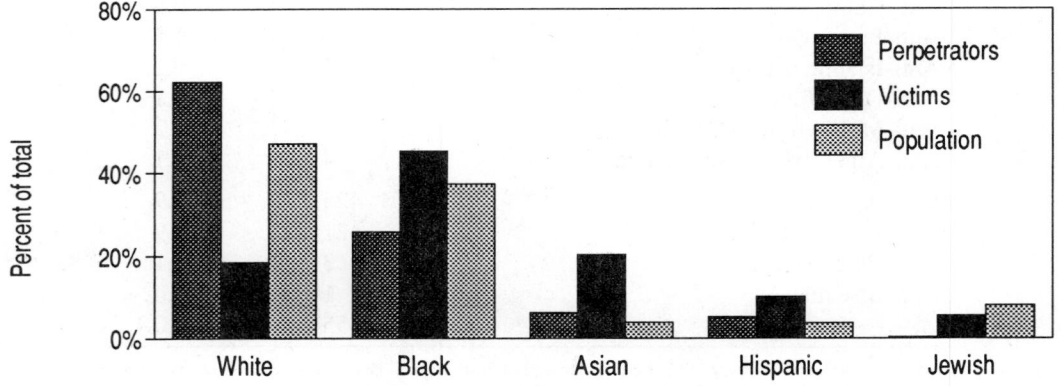

Source: Ira Goldstein and William L. Yancey, "Neighborhood Disputes and Intergroup Tension Events in Philadelphia: 1986-1988," *The State of Intergroup Harmony—1988 (PCHR, 1988).* A report prepared by the Philadelphia Commission on Human Relations, City of Philadelphia. The Commission on Human Relations administers and enforces all statutes and ordinances prohibiting discrimination against persons because of race, color, religion or national origin. The report also relied on data provided by Summary Tape Files 1 and 3, 1980, U.S. Census of Population and Housing.

★ 142 ★

Victims and Offenders in Civil Rights Violations in Boston

Profile of victims and offenders by race/ethnicity and reason for incidents involving civil rights violations, 1983-1987.

Offenders race	Victim's race/ethnicity					
	Asian American	White	Black	Hispanic	Jewish	Total
White	19 (9%)[a]	108 (53%)	19 (9%)	56 (28%)	2 (1%)	24 (100%)
Black	95 (86%)	6 (5%)	4 (4%)	6 (5%)	0 (0%)	111 (100%)
Reasons for incident[b]	Frequency	Percentage				
Passing through the neighborhood	100	30%				
Moving into a neighborhood	45	13%				
Driving through a neighborhood	24	7%				
Want victim to move	11	3%				
Working in a neighborhood	10	3%				
Prejudice	57	17%				
Other	90	27%				
Total	337	100%				

Source: Rhode Island Advisory Committee to the United States Commission on Civil Rights, *Bigotry and Violence in Rhode Island,* 1990, table 1, p. 3. Primary source: Modified from Jack McDevitt's, *The Study of the Implementation of the Massachusetts Civil Rights Act* (Boston: Center for Applied Social Research, Northeastern University, 1989), p. 44 table II. The McDevitt study is based on a random sample of 425 cases consisting of 100 cases per year from each year from 1983 to 1986 and all of the 1987 cases investigated by the Boston Police Department's Community Disorder Unit (CDU) at the time of the study's data collection. The commander of the CDU reviews all reports and determines which of them may be violations of an individual's civil rights. *Note:* (a) Numbers in parentheses are percentages of row total. (b) Reasons for Incident as Recorded in the Investigation by Community Disorder Unit (CDU)

★ 143 ★

Victims and Offenders in Intergroup Tension Events in Philadelphia

Percent of victims and perpetrators of intergroup tension events by race/ethnicity, between 1988 and 1989.

Year	Korean	Cambodian	Other Asian	White	Black	Hispanic	Other
Victims							
1988	8.2	9.1	12.7	25.5	20.0	10.0	14.6
1989	3.8	7.7	11.5	31.7	27.9	8.7	8.7
Perpetrators							
1988	0.9	5.5	5.5	36.4	24.6	0.9	26.4
1989	1.6	1.6	1.6	46.5	23.0	8.7	16.4

Source: Philadelphia Commission on Human Relations (PCHR) and Temple University, Institute for Public Policy Studies, *Race Relations in Philadelphia: A 1989 Perspective—A 1990 Opportunity,* 1990, p.14. This report extends data first reported by Ira Goldstein and William L. Yancey in *The State of Intergroup Harmony—1988* (PCHR, 1988) and reported above. PCHR data reports for 1988 (July through December) and 1989 (January through October). The report shows that among victims, there were declines in the proportion of Hispanic/ Latino, Korean, Cambodian, and other Asian groups (including Vietnamese, Lao, Hmong, Ethnic Chinese, Chinese, and Asian); these declines were offset by rises in the percentage of white and African American. Among perpetrators, there were either stability or declines in the proportion of African Americans, Koreans, Cambodians, and other Asians, with rises among whites, and more strikingly, Hispanics/ Latinos.

Arrests

★ 144 ★

Arrests by Race/Ethnicity: 1980-1985

Arrests by race/ethnicity and percent of total for the year,1980 to 1985.

Race	Year					
	1980	1981	1982	1983	1984	1985
Total (number)	2,195,746	2,291,169	2,138,015	2,145,411	1,831,683	2,118,524
Asian/Pacific	16,715	17,945	18,665	18,284	13,941	18,059
White	1,438,098	1,472,421	1,340,866	1,343,607	1,194,229	1,365,558
Black	720,739	781,983	761,544	766,312	606,443	713,326
American Indian	20,194	18,820	16,940	17,208	17,070	21,581
Total (percent)	100%	100%	100%	100%	100%	100%
Asian/Pacific	0.8%	0.8%	0.9%	0.9%	0.8%	0.9%
White	65.5%	64.3%	62.7%	62.6%	65.2%	64.5%
Black	32.8%	34.1%	35.6%	35.7%	33.1%	33.7%
American Indian	0.9%	0.8%	0.8%	0.8%	0.9%	1.0%
Rate distribution[a]						
Asian/Pacific	1.0	1.0	1.0	1.0	1.0	1.0
White	81.9	80.4	69.7	69.6	81.5	71.7
Black	41.0	42.6	39.6	39.7	41.4	37.4
American Indian	1.1	1.0	0.9	0.9	1.1	1.1

Source: Uniform Crime Reports for the United States, 1980-1985 (Washington DC: Federal Bureau of Investigation, 1986). *Notes:* (a) The rate distribution (Asian/Pacific vs. other racial groups) is calculated by dividing the percentage of non-Asian racial group by that of Asian/Pacific group. Offenses charged for the arrests are violent crimes (murder, forcible rape, robbery, and aggravated assault) and property crimes (burglary, larceny-theft, motor vehicle theft, and arson). Because of rounding, the percent distribution may not add to the total.

★ 145 ★

Arrests by Race/Ethnicity: 1991

Reported data from 10,075 law enforcement agencies on crimes and race/ethnicity of suspect arrested.

Offense charged	Total arrests				
	Total incidents	Asian/Pacific Islander	White	Black	American Indian/Alaskan Native
Total	10,516,399	99,893	7,251,862	3,049,299	115,343
Murder and non–negligent man-slaughter	18,096	168	7,861	9,924	143
Forcible rape	29,767	242	16,306	12,960	259
Robbery	136,176	1,213	51,217	83,146	600
Aggravated assault	364,250	3,031	218,628	139,407	3,184
Burglary	323,670	3,321	222,817	94,688	2,844
Larceny-theft	1,190,037	16,102	792,895	368,053	12,987
Motor vehicle theft	160,103	2,191	93,728	62,918	1,266

[Continued]

★ 145 ★

Arrests by Race/Ethnicity: 1991 (Continued)

Reported data from 10,075 law enforcement agencies on crimes and race/ethnicity of suspect arrested.

Offense charged	Total arrests				
	Total incidents	Asian/Pacific Islander	White	Black	American Indian/Alaskan Native
Arson	14,738	133	11,309	3,164	132
Violent crime[a]	548,289	4,654	294,012	245,437	4,186
Property crime[b]	1,688,548	21,747	1,120,749	528,823	17,229
Crime Index total[c]	2,236,837	26,401	1,414,761	774,260	21,415
Other assaults	772,016	6,713	498,497	257,121	9,685
Forgery and counterfeiting	74,869	652	48,535	25,264	418
Fraud	291,528	1,372	197,643	91,230	1,283
Embezzlement	10,565	94	7,202	3,195	74
Stolen property: buying, receiving, possessing	129,609	994	73,908	54,011	696
Vandalism	249,252	2,303	189,474	55,014	2,461
Weapons: carrying, possessing, etc.	173,490	1,851	98,609	72,137	893
Prostitution and commercialized vice	78,779	864	47,517	29,943	455
Sex offenses (except forcible rape and prostitution)	80,838	840	63,185	15,985	828
Drug abuse violations	763,340	4,108	443,596	312,997	2,639
Gambling	12,464	1,024	5,581	5,843	16
Offenses against family and children	70,945	1,936	47,304	20,942	763
Driving under the influence	1,270,713	10,267	1,129,876	115,724	14,846
Liquor laws	448,880	2,703	391,991	43,576	10,610
Drunkenness	625,127	1,705	507,571	102,307	13,544
Disorderly conduct	558,504	3,140	365,765	182,414	7,185
Vagrancy	30,755	74	15,735	14,341	605
All other offenses (except traffic)	2,428,040	28,325	1,542,890	831,857	24,968
Suspicion	10,184	17	4,150	5,964	53
Curfew and loitering law violations	72,037	1,287	55,389	14,819	542
Runaways	127,627	3,223	102,683	20,355	1,366

Source: U.S. Department of Justice, Federal Bureau of Investigation, *Crime in the United States 1991: Uniform Crime Reports,* released August 30, 1992 (Washington, DC: U.S. Government Printing Office, 1992), table 43, pp. 230-233. *Notes:* (a) Violent crimes are offenses of murder, forcible rape, robbery, and aggravated assault. (b) Property crimes are offenses of burglary, larceny-theft, motor vehicle theft, and arson. (c) Includes arson.

★ 146 ★

Arrests by Race/Ethnicity, in Percent: 1991

Reported data in percent from 10,075 law enforcement agencies on crimes and race/ethnicity of suspect arrested.

Offense charged	Percent distribution[a]		
	Asian/ Pacific Islander	White	Black
Total	0.9	69.0	29.0
Murder and non-negligent manslaughter	0.9	43.4	54.8
Forcible rape	0.8	54.8	43.5
Robbery	0.9	37.6	61.1
Aggravated assault	0.8	60.0	38.3
Burglary	1.0	68.8	29.3
Larceny-theft	1.4	66.6	30.9
Motor vehicle theft	1.4	58.5	39.3
Arson	0.9	76.7	21.5
Violent crime[b]	0.8	53.6	44.8
Property crime[c]	1.3	66.4	31.3
Crime Index total[d]	1.2	63.2	34.6
Other assaults	0.9	64.6	33.3
Forgery and counterfeiting	0.9	64.8	33.7
Fraud	0.5	67.8	31.3
Embezzlement	0.9	68.2	30.2
Stolen property: buying, receiving, possessing	0.8	57.0	41.7
Vandalism	0.9	76.0	22.1
Weapons: carrying, possesing, etc.	1.1	56.8	41.6
Prostitution and commercialized vice	1.1	60.3	38.0
Sex offenses (except forcible rape and prostitution)	1.0	78.2	19.8
Drug abuse violations	0.5	58.1	41.0
Gambling	8.2	44.8	46.9
Offenses against family and children	2.7	66.7	29.5
Driving under the influence	0.8	88.9	9.1
Liquor laws	0.6	87.3	9.7
Drunkenness	0.3	81.2	16.4
Disorderly conduct	0.6	65.5	32.7
Vagrancy	0.2	51.2	46.6
All other offenses (except traffic)	1.2	63.5	34.3
Suspicion	0.2	40.8	58.6
Curfew and loitering law violations	1.8	76.9	20.6
Runaways	2.5	80.5	15.9

Source: U.S. Department of Justice, Federal Bureau of Investigation, *Crime in the United States 1991: Uniform Crime Reports,* released August 30, 1992 (Washington, DC: U.S. Government Printing Office, 1992), table 43, p. 230-233. *Notes:* (a) Because of rounding, percentages may not add to total. (b) Violent crimes are offenses of murder, forcible rape, robbery, and aggravated assault. (c) Property crimes are offenses of burglary, larceny-theft, motor vehicle theft, and arson. (d) Includes arson.

★ 147 ★

Arrests, Eighteen Years and Over: 1991

Reported data from 10,075 law enforcement agencies on crimes and race/ethnicity of suspect arrested.

Offense charged	Total	Asian/Pacific Islander	White	Black	American Indian/Alaskan Native
Total	8,807,080	72,543	6,031,024	2,604,958	98,555
Murder and non-negligent man-slaughter	15,560	136	6,824	8,471	129
Forcible rape	25,066	201	13,707	10,920	238
Robbery	101,373	713	38,090	62,123	447
Aggravated assault	312,337	2,479	189,025	117,997	2,836
Burglary	215,222	1,600	139,926	72,118	1,578
Larceny-theft	827,186	9,421	527,153	281,775	8,837
Motor vehicle theft	90,020	907	52,545	35,989	579
Arson	7,843	51	5,598	2,111	83
Violent crime[a]	454,336	3,529	247,646	199,511	3,650
Property crime[b]	1,140,271	11,979	725,222	391,993	11,077
Crime Index total[c]	1,594,607	15,508	972,868	591,504	14,727
Other assaults	652,408	4,726	423,598	215,443	8,641
Forgery and counterfeiting	68,686	567	43,486	24,257	376
Fraud	280,611	1,174	191,341	86,888	1,208
Embezzlement	9,781	82	6,638	2,998	63
Stolen property: buying, receiving, possessing	94,622	583	53,483	40,097	459
Vandalism	142,654	1,032	102,434	37,517	1,671
Weapons: carrying, possessing, etc.	137,010	1,286	75,997	59,015	712
Prostitution and commercialized vice	77,761	852	46,860	29,608	441
Sex offenses (except forcible rape and prostitution)	66,652	644	52,907	12,378	723
Drug abuse violations	705,083	3,660	415,168	283,825	2,430
Gambling	11,648	1,011	5,417	5,209	11
Offenses against family and children	68,079	1,835	45,202	20,293	749
Driving under the influence	1,257,412	10,172	1,117,463	115,129	14,648
Liquor laws	345,615	2,004	296,659	38,608	8,344
Drunkenness	609,605	1,656	493,706	100,958	13,285
Disorderly conduct	462,260	2,487	300,758	152,475	6,540
Vagrancy	28,515	59	14,005	13,854	597
All other offenses (except traffic)	2,185,778	23,191	1,370,344	769,330	22,913
Suspicion	8,293	14	2,690	5,572	17

Source: U.S. Department of Justice, Federal Bureau of Investigation, *Crime in the United States 1991: Uniform Crime Reports,* released August 30, 1992 (Washington, DC: U.S. Government Printing Office, 1992), table 43, pp. 230-233. *Notes:* (a) Violent crimes are offenses of murder, forcible rape, robbery, and aggravated assault. (b) Property crimes are offenses of burglary, larceny-theft, motor vehicle theft, and arson. (c) Includes arson.

★ 148 ★

Arrests, Eighteen Years and Over, in Percent: 1991

Reported data in percent from 10,075 law enforcement agencies on crimes and race/ethnicity of suspect arrested.

Offense charged	Percent distribution[a]		
	White	Black	Asian/Pacific Islander
Total	68.5	29.6	0.8
Murder and non–negligent manslaughter	43.9	54.4	0.9
Forcible rape	54.7	43.6	0.8
Robbery	57.6	61.3	0.7
Aggravated assault	69.5	37.8	0.8
Burglary	65.0	33.5	0.7
Larceny-theft	63.7	34.1	1.1
Motor vehicle theft	58.4	40.0	1.0
Arson	71.4	26.9	0.7
Violent crime[b]	54.5	43.9	0.8
Property crime[c]	63.6	34.4	1.1
Crime Index total[d]	61.0	37.1	1.0
Other assaults	64.9	33.0	0.7
Forgery and counterfeiting	63.3	35.3	0.8
Fraud	68.2	31.0	0.4
Embezzlement	67.9	30.7	0.8
Stolen property: buying, receiving, possessing	56.5	42.4	0.6
Vandalism	71.8	26.3	0.7
Weapons: carrying, possessing, etc.	55.5	43.1	0.9
Prostitution and commercialized vice	60.3	38.1	1.1
Sex offenses (except forcible rape and prostitution)	79.4	18.6	1.0
Drug abuse violations	58.9	40.3	0.5
Gambling	46.5	44.7	8.7
Offenses against family and children	66.4	29.8	2.7
Driving under the influence	88.9	9.2	0.8
Liquor laws	85.8	11.2	0.6
Drunkenness	81.0	16.6	0.3
Disorderly conduct	65.1	33.0	0.5
Vagrancy	49.1	48.6	0.2
All other offenses (except traffic)	62.7	35.2	1.1
Suspicion	32.4	67.2	0.2

Source: U.S. Department of Justice, Federal Bureau of Investigation, *Crime in the United States 1991: Uniform Crime Reports,* released August 30, 1992 (Washington, DC: U.S. Government Printing Office, 1992), table 43, pp. 230-233. *Notes:* (a) Because of rounding, percentages may not add to total. (b) Violent crimes are offenses of murder, forcible rape, robbery, and aggravated assault. (c) Property crimes are offenses of burglary, larceny-theft, motor vehicle theft, and arson. (d) Includes arson.

★ 149 ★

Arrests, Eighteen Years and Under: 1991

Reported data from 10,075 law enforcement agencies on crimes and race/ethnicity of suspect arrested.

Offense charged	Arrests, Under 18				
	Total	Asian/Pacific Islander	White	Black	American Indian/Alas- kan Native
Total	1,709,319	27,350	1,220,838	444,341	16,790
Murder and non–negligent manslaugh- ter	2,536	32	1,037	1,453	14
Forcible rape	4,701	41	2,599	2,040	21
Robbery	34,803	500	13,127	21,023	153
Aggravated assault	51,913	552	29,603	21,410	348
Burglary	108,448	1,721	82,891	22,570	1,266
Larceny-theft	362,851	6,681	265,742	86,278	4,150
Motor vehicle theft	70,083	1,284	41,183	26,929	687
Arson	6,895	82	5,711	1,053	49
Violent crime[a]	93,953	1,125	46,366	45,926	536
Property crime[b]	548,277	9,768	395,527	136,830	6,152
Crime Index total[c]	642,230	10,893	441,893	182,756	6,688
Other assaults	119,608	1,987	74,899	41,678	1,044
Forgery and counterfeiting	6,183	85	5,049	1,007	42
Fraud	10,917	198	6,302	4,342	75
Embezzlement	784	12	564	197	11
Stolen property: buying, receiving, pos- sessing	34,987	411	20,425	13,914	237
Vandalism	106,598	1,271	87,040	17,497	790
Weapons: carrying, possessing, etc.	36,480	565	22,612	13,122	181
Prostitution and commercialized vice	1,018	12	657	335	14
Sex offenses (except forcible rape and prostitution)	14,186	196	10,278	3,607	105
Drug abuse violations	58,257	448	28,428	29,172	209
Gambling	816	13	164	634	5
Offenses against family and children	2,866	101	2,102	649	14
Driving under the influence	13,301	95	12,413	595	198
Liquor laws	103,265	699	95,332	4,968	2,266
Drunkenness	15,522	49	13,865	1,349	259
Disorderly conduct	96,244	653	65,007	29,939	645
Vagrancy	2,240	15	1,730	487	8
All other offenses (except traffic)	242,262	5,134	172,546	62,527	2,055
Suspicion	1,891	3	1,460	392	36
Curfew and loitering law violations	72,037	1,287	55,389	14,819	542
Runaways	127,627	3,223	102,683	20,355	1,366

Source: U.S. Department of Justice, Federal Bureau of Investigation, *Crime in the United States 1991: Uniform Crime Reports,* released August 30, 1992 (Washington, DC: U.S. Government Printing Office, 1992), table 43, pp. 230-233. *Notes:* (a) Violent crimes are offenses of murder, forcible rape, robbery, and aggravated assault. (b) Property crimes are offenses of burglary, larceny-theft, motor vehicle theft, and arson. (c) Includes arson.

★ 150 ★

Arrests, 18 Years and Under, in Percent: 1991

Reported data in percent from 10,075 law enforcement agencies on crimes and race/ethnicity of suspect arrested.

Offense charged	Percent distribution[a]		
	Asian/Pacific Islander	White	Black
Total	1.6	71.4	26.0
Murder and non-negligent manslaughter	1.3	40.9	57.3
Forcible rape	0.9	55.3	43.4
Robbery	1.4	37.7	60.4
Aggravated assault	1.1	57.0	41.2
Burglary	1.6	76.4	20.8
Larceny-theft	1.8	73.2	23.8
Motor vehicle theft	1.8	58.8	38.4
Arson	1.2	82.8	15.3
Violent crime[b]	1.2	49.4	48.9
Property crime[c]	1.8	72.1	25.0
Crime Index total[d]	1.7	68.8	28.5
Other assaults	1.7	62.6	34.8
Forgery and counterfeiting	1.4	81.7	16.3
Fraud	1.8	57.7	39.8
Embezzlement	1.5	71.9	25.1
Stolen property: buying, receiving, possessing	1.2	58.4	39.8
Vandalism	1.2	81.7	16.4
Weapons: carrying, possessing, etc.	1.5	62.0	36.0
Prostitution and commercialized vice	1.2	64.5	32.9
Sex offenses (except forcible rape and prostitution)	1.4	72.5	25.4
Drug abuse violations	0.8	48.8	50.1
Gambling	1.6	20.1	77.7
Offenses against family and children	3.5	73.3	22.6
Driving under the influence	0.7	93.3	4.5
Liquor laws	0.7	92.3	4.8
Drunkenness	0.3	89.3	8.7
Disorderly conduct	0.7	67.5	31.1
Vagrancy	0.7	77.2	21.7
All other offenses (except traffic)	2.1	71.2	25.8
Suspicion	0.2	77.2	20.7
Curfew and loitering law violations	1.8	76.9	20.6
Runaways	2.5	80.5	15.9

Source: U.S. Department of Justice, Federal Bureau of Investigation, *Crime in the United States 1991: Uniform Crime Reports,* released Sunday, August 30, 1992 (Washington, DC: U.S. Government Printing Office, 1992), table 43, pp. 230-233. *Notes:* (a) Because of rounding, percentages may not add to total. (b) Violent crimes are offenses of murder, forcible rape, robbery, and aggravated assault. (c) Property crimes are offenses of burglary, larceny-theft, motor vehicle theft, and arson. (d) Includes arson.

Prison Inmates

★ 151 ★

Prison Inmates in State and Federal Correctional Facilities: 1990

Number of inmates in state and federal correctional facilities by state within geographic regions and race/ethnicity in the United States.

Region and jurisdiction	Total	Asian/ Pacific Islander	White non-Hispanic	Black non-Hispanic	Hispanic	American Indian/ Alaskan Native
U.S. total	715,649	6,871	274,929	331,880	95,498	6,471
Federal	56,821	461	25,553	15,597	14,346	864
State	658,828	6,410	249,376	316,283	81,152	5,607
Northeast	117,865	270	33,535	57,873	25,705	482
Connecticut	9,577	23	2,571	4,647	2,306	30
Maine	1,503	0	1,439	29	13	22
Massachusetts	8,282	63	4,286	2,367	1,552	14
New Hampshire	1,441	4	1,306	61	67	3
New Jersey	16,721	7	3,673	10,242	2,790	9
New York	56,251	134	9,473	28,473	17,824	383
Pennsylvania	20,822	19	8,541	11,423	824	15
Rhode Island	2,460	20	1,455	653	328	4
Vermont	808	0	791	14	1	2
Midwest	141,726	428	65,857	69,810	4,392	1,239
Illinois	26,712	230	7,993	16,156	2,289	44
Indiana	12,618	8	7,698	4,687	209	16
Iowa	4,522	20	3,466	900	75	61
Kansas	5,500	23	3,301	1,825	268	83
Michigan	31,812	34	12,465	18,711	521	81
Minnesota	3,239	20	1,938	923	95	263
Missouri	14,600	3	7,812	6,708	55	22
Nebraska	2,390	13	1,388	790	108	91
North Dakota	557	1	403	9	12	132
Ohio	31,808	31	14,897	16,476	395	9
South Dakota	1,247	0	909	42	1	295
Wisconsin	6,721	45	3,587	2,583	364	142
South	253,453	506	91,109	146,293	14,359	1,186
Alabama	12,433	19	4,489	7,924	1	0
Arkansas	6,455	0	2,977	3,459	17	2
Delaware	3,449	3	1,268	2,038	138	2
District of Columbia	7,290	12	93	7,012	173	0
Florida	42,306	378	16,004	23,397	2,437	90
Georgia	18,540	4	6,700	11,737	97	2
Kentucky	6,900	1	4,480	2,413	6	0
Louisiana	13,939	2	3,911	9,970	56	0
Maryland	17,057	8	4,291	12,695	60	3
Mississippi	6,852	4	1,824	5,003	14	7
North Carolina	18,346	30	6,819	10,887	163	447

[Continued]

★ 151 ★

Prison Inmates in State and Federal Correctional Facilities: 1990 (Continued)

Number of inmates in state and federal correctional facilities by state within geographic regions and race/ethnicity in the United States.

Region and jurisdiction	Total	Asian/ Pacific Islander	White non-Hispanic	Black non-Hispanic	Hispanic	American Indian/ Alaskan Native
Oklahoma	10,449	7	6,014	3,573	246	609
South Carolina	15,091	2	5,333	9,707	34	15
Tennessee	8,333	2	4,651	3,643	35	2
Texas	49,815	14	15,711	23,266	10,823	1
Virginia	14,649	17	5,227	9,346	54	5
West Virginia	1,549	3	1,317	223	5	1
West	145,784	5,206	58,875	42,307	36,696	2,700
Alaska	2,414	19	1,297	286	53	777
Arizona	13,903	26	7,241	2,228	3,867	541
California	92,604	3,586	28,181	33,542	26,987	308
Colorado	5,593	13	2,717	1,342	1,455	66
Hawaii	2,569	1,350	917	131	167	4
Idaho	1,767	12	1,487	22	186	60
Montana	1,273	0	1,006	21	36	210
Nevada	5,620	65	3,131	1,913	422	89
New Mexico	3,118	10	953	305	1,742	108
Oregon	5,994	21	4,586	840	415	132
Utah	2,799	32	2,020	238	449	60
Washington	7,036	69	4,516	1,388	786	277
Wyoming	1,094	3	823	69	131	68

Source: Louis W. Jankowski, U.S. Department of Justice, Office of Justice Programs, Bureau of Justice Statistics, NCJ-134946, *Correctional Populations in the United States, 1990* (Washington, DC: U.S. Department of Justice, July 1992), table 4.7, p. 50.

★ 152 ★

Prison Inmates under State or Federal Jurisdiction: 1990

Numbers of inmates under state or federal jurisdiction[a] by state within geographic regions and race/ethnicity in the United States.

Region and jurisdiction	Number of prisoners					
	Prisoner population	Asian/ Pacific Islander	White	Black	American Indian/ Alaskan Native	Not known
U.S. total	774,375	2,806	369,485	367,122	6,251	28,711
Federal	67,432	586	44,595	21,146	1,105	0
State	706,943	2,220	324,890	345,976	5,146	28,711
Northeast	123,392	259	56,232	62,098	194	4,609
Connecticut[b,c]	10,500	20	2,819	5,111	7	2,543
Maine	1,523	0	1,484	29	10	0
Massachusetts[c]	8,273	46	4,309	3,011	13	894
New Hampshire	1,342	3	1,283	56	0	0
New Jersey[c]	21,128	1	6,931	13,563	0	633
New York[c]	54,895	140	26,774	27,324	136	521
Pennsylvania	22,290	38	9,988	12,223	23	18
Rhode Island[b]	2,392	11	1,595	781	5	0
Vermont[b,d]	1,049	-	1,049	-	-	-
Midwest	145,791	103	68,213	72,550	1,268	3,657
Illinois[c]	27,516	25	7,958	16,942	38	2,553
Indiana	12,736	3	7,858	4,858	17	0
Iowa	3,967	10	3,002	866	55	34
Kansas[c]	5,775	24	3,371	1,994	80	306
Michigan[c]	34,267	21	13,853	19,651	127	615
Minnesota[c]	3,176	2	1,902	885	256	131
Missouri	14,943	4	8,033	6,881	25	0
Nebraska	2,403	0	1,510	785	96	12
North Dakota[e]	483	1	391	5	85	1
Ohio[d]	31,822	0	15,118	16,704	0	0
South Dakota	1,341	0	972	41	328	0
Wisconsin	7,362	13	4,245	2,938	161	5
South	284,029	235	101,985	167,424	1,193	13,192
Alabama[c]	15,665	2	5,764	9,893	5	1
Arkansas	6,766	1	3,592	3,133	2	38
Delaware[a,b]	3,741	5	1,137	2,268	1	60
District of Columbia[b,c,d]	9,947	0	137	9,801	0	9
Florida[c]	44,387	10	18,206	25,385	7	779
Georgia	22,345	5	7,519	14,808	12	1
Kentucky	9,023	0	6,280	2,741	2	0
Louisiana[e]	18,599	0	5,169	13,427	0	3
Maryland	17,848	0	3,973	13,771	6	98
Mississippi[c]	8,375	6	2,360	5,965	6	38
North Carolina	18,411	9	6,744	11,026	419	213
Oklahoma[c]	12,285	0	6,961	4,258	712	354
South Carolina	17,319	3	5,969	11,301	11	35
Tennessee[e]	10,388	-	5,461	4,562		365

[Continued]

★ 152 ★

Prison Inmates under State or Federal Jurisdiction: 1990 (Continued)

Numbers of inmates under state or federal jurisdiction[a] by state within geographic regions and race/ethnicity in the United States.

Region and jurisdiction	Number of prisoners					
	Prisoner population	Asian/ Pacific Islander	White	Black	American Indian/ Alaskan Native	Not known
Texas[c]	50,042	170	15,071	23,669	5	11,127
Virginia[c]	17,593	23	6,306	11,189	4	71
West Virginia	1,565	1	1,336	227	1	0
West	153,731	1,623	98,460	43,904	2,491	7,253
Alaska[b,d]	2,622	28	1,452	311	831	0
Arizona	14,261	10	11,332	2,461	456	2
California	97,609	-	58,163	34,525	-	4,621
Colorado[d]	7,018	18	5,072	1,671	66	191
Hawaii[b,c,d]	2,533	1,364	590	142	37	400
Idaho[d]	1,961	14	1,824	31	90	2
Montana	1,425	0	1,143	21	261	0
Nevada[c]	5,322	45	3,057	1,673	71	476
New Mexico	3,187	6	2,720	314	108	39
Oregon	6,492	24	4,861	881	146	580
Utah	2,496	38	2,125	221	61	51
Washington[c]	7,995	73	5,245	1,594	305	778
Wyoming[c]	1,110	3	876	59	59	113

Source: Louis W. Jankowski, U.S. Department of Justice, Office of Justice Programs, Bureau of Justice Statistics, NCJ-134946, *Correctional Populations in the United States, 1990* (Washington, DC: U.S. Department of Justice, July 1992), table 5.6, p.83. Inmate population is as of December 31, 1990. *Notes:* (a) Jurisdiction refers to a unit of government or to the legal authority to exercise governmental power. According to the latter meaning, the prisoners under a state's jurisdiction may be in the custody of local jails. To have custody of a prisoner, a state must hold that person in one of its facilities. Early statistical reports gave custody counts that largely have been replaced by jurisdiction counts of state prison populations. A state may have custody of a prisoner over whom another state maintains jurisdiction. All data for Arizona, California, the District of Columbia, Georgia, Illinois, Indiana, Iowa, Massachusetts, Michigan, North Carolina, Texas, West Virginia (men), and Wyoming are custody rather than jurisdiction counts; Florida's counts are based on custody data. A dash (-) indicates not reported. (b) Figures include both jail and prison inmates; jails and prisons are combined in one system. (c) Hispanic prisoners reported under "unknown race." (d) Race was estimated. (e) North Dakota, Louisiana, and Tennessee reported persons whose race was neither black nor white under "other race"; these persons are reported here under "unknown race."

★ 153 ★

State Prisons: Offenders Admitted

Numbers of offenses by category and mean sentence lengths in state prisons (in months) reported to the National Corrections Reporting Program by race/ethnicity, 1989.

Most serious offense	Race					
	Asian/Pacific Islander		White		Black	
	Sentence (mean in months)	Number	Sentence (mean in months)	Number	Sentence (mean in months)	Number
Violent offenses	112.1	215	103.2	23,526	112.2	28,220
Murder	201.2	10	252.0	922	302.7	1,316
Voluntary manslaughter	-	5	120.9	371	159.9	579
Manslaughter	-	7	96.0	1,578	129.5	1,221
Unspecified homicide	-	1	226.4	257	199.2	390
Kidnapping	-	9	121.4	628	149.6	401
Rape	147.2	34	148.6	2,832	150.5	1,687
Sexual assault	84.3	15	93.0	4,422	112.7	1,706
Robbery	109.7	84	100.2	6,246	103.1	13,322
Assault	80.3	42	66.0	5,502	73.4	7,136
Other violence	-	8	56.2	768	74.5	462
Property offenses	68.8	166	58.4	35,573	59.0	31,562
Burglary	83.4	86	677.8	17,078	68.8	13,921
Larceny	60.1	41	48.6	8,074	52.0	8,594
Car theft	46.4	15	37.0	2,799	43.2	2,320
Arson	-	2	89.8	754	89.6	477
Fraud	46.4	15	51.3	4,374	49.1	3,492
Stolen property	-	6	51.1	1,759	52.3	2,188
Other property	-	1	57.6	735	51.7	570
Drug offenses	111.2	94	56.1	20,645	58.1	37,855
Possession	-	8	44.6	4,264	47.0	10,451
Trafficking	70.9	26	61.7	11,794	65.1	20,515
Other drug offense	131.9	60	52.4	4,587	53.9	6,889
Public-order offenses	90.8	30	45.1	8,111	46.5	6,223
Weapons	80.3	16	45.6	1,192	50.8	2,316
Other public order	102.9	14	45.0	6,919	43.9	3,907
Other offenses	-	2	39.0	1,333	47.9	689
Other	-	2	39.0	1,333	47.9	689
All admissions	96.0	510	69.3	89,984	74.2	104,777

Source: Adapted from data generated for the National Corrections Reporting Program, 1989, by Tom Hester, Statistician, Bureau of Justice Statistics, U.S. Department of Justice, December 1992. A dash (–) indicates not known or not applicable.

★ 154 ★

State Prisons: Releases

Numbers of releases by category and mean sentence lengths in state prisons (in months) reported to the National Corrections Reporting Program by race/ethnicity, 1989.

Most serious offense	Asian/Pacific Islander		White		Black	
	Mean	Number	Mean	Number	Mean	Number
Violent offenses	44.8	110	33.2	19,364	38.1	24,016
Murder	-	3	84.0	936	86.2	1,094
Vol manslaughter	-	4	47.3	228	65.4	414
Manslaughter	-	4	24.7	1,215	35.4	847
Unspecified homicide	-	0	52.3	208	52.0	249
Kidnapping	-	4	38.2	579	44.8	364
Rape	42.0	13	44.0	1,996	56.9	1,494
Sex assault	-	6	29.3	3,421	3.3	1,277
Robbery	49.9	52	35.1	5,540	38.8	12,269
Assault	31.3	18	20.9	4,652	22.5	5,651
Other violence	-	6	18.6	589	22.7	357
Property offenses	29.5	99	16.6	31,607	17.7	28,066
Burglary	34.6	39	19.4	15,407	21.1	12,602
Larceny	26.1	37	13.1	7,147	14.8	7,690
Car theft	-	9	11.4	2,018	12.6	1,581
Arson	-	0	24.3	707	26.2	398
Fraud	-	6	13.8	4,169	14.1	3,343
Stolen property	-	4	16.8	1,520	16.7	1,947
Other property	-	4	12.7	639	14.0	505
Drug offenses	30.1	44	13.8	13,967	13.0	18,937
Possession	15.7	10	11.7	3,063	11.0	5,786
Trafficking	38.7	19	15.6	7,288	15.0	9,536
Other drug offense	28.7	15	12.0	3,616	11.1	3,615
Public-order offenses	29.9	16	13.5	6,792	15.7	5,184
Weapons	-	5	15.9	1,066	18.9	1,948
Other public order	30,3	11	13.0	5,726	13.8	3,236
Other offenses	-	1	16.2	1,201	16.8	590
Other	-	1	16.2	1,201	16.8	590

Source: Adapted from data generated for the National Corrections Reporting Program, 1989, by Tom Hester, Statistician, Bureau of Justice Statistics, U.S. Department of Justice, December 1992. A dash (–) indicates not known or not applicable.

Prison Inmates Under Sentence of Death

★ 155 ★

Death Row Prison Inmates in the United States

Inmates under sentence of death at year end, received on death row from court during the year, and executed or otherwise removed from death row in 1990.

Characteristics	Prisoners under sentence of death			
	Present year-end 1990	Received from court in 1990	Removed from death row in 1990	
			Executed	Removed by other means[a]
U.S. total	2,356	244	23	108
Race				
Asian Pacific Islander	14	1	0	1
White	1,375	147	16	64
Black	943	94	7	42
American Indian	24	2	0	1

Source: Louis W. Jankowski, U.S. Department of Justice, Office of Justice Programs, Bureau of Justice Statistics, NCJ-134946, *Correctional Populations in the United States, 1990* (Washington DC: U.S. Department of Justice, July 1992), table 7.1, p. 138. Also in source: Data by sex, Hispanic origin, education, felony history, and age. *Note:* (a) Includes deceased from causes other than execution, commutation of sentence, sentence vacated, and conviction vacated.

★ 156 ★

Death Row Prison Inmates Received from Court: 1990

Characteristics of Asian/Pacific Islander inmates received from court under sentence of death in 1990.

Number received in 1990:	1
State from which sentence received:	California
Age of prisoner:	20 to 24 years
Level of education:	Completed at least 1 year of college
Marital status:	Never married
Legal status at time of capital offense:	Not charged with or sentenced for another crime
Felony history:	No prior felonies

Source: Louis W. Jankowski, U.S. Department of Justice, Office of Justice Programs, Bureau of Justice Statistics, NCJ-134946, *Correctional Populations in the United States, 1990* (Washington, DC: U.S. Department of Justice, July 1992), table 7.11-7.15, pp. 154-63. Table compiled from information extracted from several tables. Also in source: Data on total, black, and white prisoners received from court under sentence of death for 1990.

★ 157 ★

Death Row Prison Inmates Removed: 1990

Characteristics of Asian Pacific/Islander inmates removed from death row in 1990.

Number removed:	1
State from which sentence removed:	Virginia
Status of prisoner:	Awaiting new trial
Means of removal:	Sentence vacated
Time between sentencing and removal:	Less than 12 months
Age of prisoner:	30 to 34 years
Level of education:	Completed 9th to 11th grade level of education
Marital status at time of imprisonment:	Divorced or separated
Legal status at time of capital offense:	Not charged with or sentenced for another crime
Felony history:	No prior felony convictions

Source: Louis W. Jankowski, U.S. Department of Justice, Office of Justice Programs, Bureau of Justice Statistics, NCJ-134946, *Correctional Populations in the United States, 1990* (Washington DC: U.S. Department of Justice, July 1992), table 7.16–7.23, pp. 164-77. Table compiled from information extracted from several tables. Also in source: Data on total, black, and white prisoners removed from death row in 1990.

Parole and Probation

★ 158 ★

Adults on Parole from Federal and State Institutions

Numbers of adults on parole from state and federal institutions by state within geographic regions and race/ethnicity in the United States, 1990.

Region and jurisdiction	Number of adults on parole					
	Parole population 12/31/90	Asian/Pacific Islander	White	Black	American Indian/Alaskan Native	Other, unknown, or not reported
U.S. total	531,407	1,616	238,673	213,970	2,480	74,668
Federal	21,693	131	14,042	7,049	237	234
State	509,714	1,485	224,631	206,921	2,243	74,434
Northeast	128,946	311	59,944	53,916	201	14,574
Connecticut[a]	291	0	137	120	1	33
Maine[b]	0	0	0	0	0	0
Massachusetts[c,d]	4,720	14	2,832	1,133	5	736
New Hampshire[e,f]	522	-	494	-	-	28
New Jersey	23,298	0	10,224	13,046	0	28
New York[a]	42,837	236	8,139	20,990	193	13,279
Pennsylvania	56,657	60	37,548	18,577	2	470
Rhode Island	321	1	270	50	0	0
Vermont	300	0	300	0	0	0

[Continued]

★ 158 ★

Adults on Parole from Federal and State Institutions (Continued)

Numbers of adults on parole from state and federal institutions by state within geographic regions and race/ethnicity in the United States, 1990.

Region and jurisdiction	Number of adults on parole					
	Parole population 12/31/90	Asian/Pacific Islander	White	Black	American Indian/Alaskan Native	Other, unknown, or not reported
Midwest	65,693	49	24,382	24,861	494	15,907
Illinois[a,d]	17,671	10	5,637	10,538	22	1,464
Indiana	3,778	-	-	-	-	3,778
Iowa	2,111	-	-	-	-	2,111
Kansas[a,d]	5,751	26	3,645	1,744	59	277
Michigan	11,901	3	4,854	6,961	46	37
Minnesota[a]	1,873	2	1,190	499	129	53
Missouri[d,g]	9,196	3	5,713	3,437	7	36
Nebraska[a,d]	632	0	391	200	14	27
North Dakota	116	0	104	2	10	0
Ohio	7,945	-	-	-	-	7,945
South Dakota[a]	620	0	477	19	121	3
Wisconsin	4,099	5	2,371	1,461	86	176
South	215,773	17	76,354	100,172	408	38,822
Alabama[f]	5,970	-	2,384	3,586	-	0
Arkansas[a]	3,971	0	2,263	1,698	0	10
Delaware[d,g]	1,283	0	577	706	0	0
District of Colunbia[e,f]	5,346	-	107	5,186	-	53
Florida[a,d,f]	2,064	-	1,325	702	-	37
Georgia[d,f]	22,646	-	9,058	13,588	-	0
Kentucky	3,183	-	-	-	-	3,183
Louisiana[f]	8,877	-	3,153	5,724	-	0
Maryland	11,192	8	3,126	8,030	4	24
Mississippi	3,478	3	1,185	2,286	1	3
North Carolina	9,883	5	3,951	5,635	246	46
Oklahoma[a]	3,236	1	1,947	1,041	157	90
South Carolina[e]	3,543	-	1,528	2,002	-	13
Tennessee	11,327	-	-	-	-	11,327
Texas[a,d,f]	109,726	-	40,959	44,812	-	23,955
Virginia[d,f]	9,048	-	3,936	5,031	-	81
West Virginia	1,000	0	855	145	0	0
West	99,302	1,108	63,951	27,972	1,140	5,131
Alaska[d,g]	568	6	312	74	176	0
Arizona[a,d]	2,711	1	1,361	442	106	801
California[a]	67,562	19	41,455	22,985	5	3,098
Colorado[a,e]	2,396	10	1,869	455	34	28
Hawaii[d,h]	1,425	983	361	81	-	0
Idaho	243	0	200	13	30	0
Montana	811	5	689	16	101	0
Nevada	2,850	8	1,673	936	24	209
New Mexico[d]	1,224	3	1,082	98	41	0
Oregon	8,023	20	6,295	991	177	540
Utah	1,561	9	1,373	141	33	5

[Continued]

★ 158 ★

Adults on Parole from Federal and State Institutions (Continued)

Numbers of adults on parole from state and federal institutions by state within geographic regions and race/ethnicity in the United States, 1990.

Region and jurisdiction	Number of adults on parole					
	Parole population 12/31/90	Asian/Pacific Islander	White	Black	American Indian/Alaskan Native	Other, unknown, or not reported
Washington[e]	9,615	44	7,002	1,725	401	443
Wyoming	313	0	279	15	12	7

Source: Louis W. Jankowski, U.S. Department of Justice, Office of Justice Programs, Bureau of Justice Statistics, NCJ-134946, *Correctional Populations in the United States, 1990* (Washington DC: U.S. Department of Justice, July 1992), table 6.7, p. 122. A dash (–) indicates not known or not applicable. *Notes:* (a) The state reported Hispanic parolees under "unknown" race; however, not all "unknowns" were Hispanic. (b) Maine abolished parole in 1976. (c) Massachusetts reported 708 Hispanics and 28 Cape Verdian parolees under "unknown race." (d) The state estimated the data for race. (e) The state reported American Indian/Alaskan Native, Asian/Pacific Islander, and other race under the "White" or "Black" race categories. (f) See the explanatory notes for details on "unknown race." (g) The state estimated the year end population. (h) Hawaii reported "other" and "unknown" race under "Asian and Pacific Islander."

★ 159 ★

Adults on Probation from Federal and State Institutions

Numbers of adults on probation from federal and state institutions by state within geographic regions and race/ethnicity in the United States, 1990.

Region and jurisdiction	Number of adults on probation					
	Probation population 12/31/90	Asian/ Pacific Islander	White	Black	American Indian/ Alaskan Native	Other, unknown, or not reported
U.S. total	2,670,234	6,237	1,326,695	591,673	14,624	731,005
Federal	58,222	1,160	41,546	13,453	713	1,350
State	2,612,012	5,077	1,285,149	578,220	13,911	729,655
Northeast	466,006	377	209,494	91,774	379	163,982
Connecticut	46,640	-	32,648	13992	-	-
Maine[a]	7,549	-	7,349	200	-	-
Massachusetts	72,459	-	-	-	-	72,459
New Hampshire	3,146	0	3,021	125	0	0
New Jersey	72,341	-	-	-	-	72,341
New York	145,266	266	90,598	50,883	379	3,140
Pennsylvania	97,327	111	69,996	26,544	0	676
Rhode Island	15,366	-	-	-	-	15,366
Vermont	5,912	-	5,882	30	-	-
Midwest	567,839	2,671	287,495	106,036	5,041	166,596
Illinois[a]	95,699	1,244	52,730	34,165	-	7,560
Indiana	68,683	-	-	-	-	68,683
Iowa[b]	13,895	-	-	-	-	13,895
Kansas	22,183	87	17,409	4,345	294	48
Michigan	133,439	1,100	59,902	14,071	971	57,395
Minnesota	59,323	0	50,108	5,761	2,457	997
Missouri[b]	42,322	82	30,977	10,990	41	232

[Continued]

★ 159 ★

Adults on Probation from Federal and State Institutions (Continued)

Numbers of adults on probation from federal and state institutions by state within geographic regions and race/ethnicity in the United States, 1990.

Region and jurisdiction	Number of adults on probation					
	Probation population 12/31/90	Asian/ Pacific Islander	White	Black	American Indian/ Alaskan Native	Other, unknown, or not reported
Nebraska	14,654	0	12,163	1,758	439	294
North Dakota	1,731	9	1,547	17	158	0
Ohio	83,380	59	40,693	28,776	14	13,838
South Dakota	3,160	-	-	-	-	3,160
Wisconsin	29,370	90	21,966	6,153	667	494
South	1,042,012	917	647,896	366,099	3,592	23,508
Alabama[a]	27,686	65	11,695	15,926	-	-
Arkansas[b]	15,983	16	7,495	3,748	19	4,704
Delaware[b]	12,223	6	7,360	4,850	7	-
Dist. of Col.	9,742	-	487	9,255	-	-
Florida[a]	210,781	275	145,920	55,505	120	8,961
Georgia	134,840	4	69,167	65,540	89	40
Kentucky	7,482	-	--	-	-	7,482
Louisiana	30,191	-	13,588	16,603	-	-
Maryland	82,898	268	39,874	41,781	81	894
Mississippi	8,221	11	3,402	4,635	10	163
North Carolina	77,829	80	39,548	35,941	1,657	603
Oklahoma	24,411	27	17,190	5,532	1,608	54
South Carolina	32,287	0	16,024	16,140	0	123
Tennessee	32,719	0	18,871	13,466		382
Texas	308,357	0	240,518	67,839	0	0
Virginia	21,303	164	12,102	8,938	-	99
West Virginia[b]	5,059	1	4,654	400	1	3
West	536,155	1,112	140,264	14,311	4,899	375,569
Alaska	3,599	49	2,320	331	899	0
Arizona	30,397	-	-	-	-	30,397
California	305,700	-	-	-	-	305,700
Colorado	31,111	57	25,625	3,319	110	2,000
Hawaii	11,667	-	--	-	--	11,667
Idaho	4,377	17	4,130	60	170	0
Montana	4,052	4	3,510	44	494	0
Nevada	7,700	24	5,547	1,387	93	649
New Mexico	6,294	9	4,520	290	275	1,200
Oregon	37,631	126	31,452	1,997	679	3,377
Utah	5,830	70	5,255	209	172	124
Washington	84,817	756	55,091	6,602	1,942	20,426
Wyoming	2,980	-	2,814	72	65	29

Source: Louis W. Jankowski, U.S. Department of Justice, Office of Justice Programs, Bureau of Justice Statistics, NCJ-134946, *Correctional Populations in the United States, 1990* (Washington, DC: U.S. Department of Justice, July 1992), table 3.8, p. 31. A dash (–) indicates not reported. *Notes:* (a) The state estimated all numbers in the detailed categories. (b)The state estimated all data.

Wartime Internment

★ 160 ★

U.S. Detention Camps for Japanese Americans, 1942-1946

Location of camps and number of Japanese Americans interned under the terms of Executive Order 9066[a].

Name	Location[b]	Detainees
Central Utah (Topaz), Utah	Millard County, northwest of Delta	8,130
Colorado River (Poston), Arizona	Colorado River Indian Reservation, south of Parker	17,814
Gila River (Rivers), Arizona	Gila River Indian Reservation, west of Sacaton	13,348
Granada (Amache), Colorado	Prowers County between Koen and Granada	7,318
Heart Mountain, Wyoming	Park County between Cody and Ralston	10,767
Jerome (Denson), Arkansas	Chicot and Drew Counties, between Hudspeth and Jerome	8,497
Manzanar, California	Inyo County, between Independence and Lone Pine	10,046
Minidoka (Hunt), Idaho	Jerome County, north of Eden	9,397
Rohwer, Arkansas	Desha County, between Kelso and Rohwer	8,475
Tule Lake (Newell), California	Modoc County, between Stronghold and Newell	18,789

Source: The National Committee for Redress, Japanese American Citizens League, *The Japanese American Incarceration: A Case for Redress,* 4th Ed., (San Francisco: Japanese American Citizens League, 1981), p. 24. Also in source: Data on Japanese Americans serving in World War II and a short history of the expulsion and detention of Japanese Americans during the war. *Notes:* (a) Executive Order 9066, signed on Feb. 19, 1942, by President Franklin D. Roosevelt, authorized the secretary of war to establish military areas and to evacuate civilians from these areas, leading to the removal and relocation of more than 110,000 persons of Japanese ancestry from the West Coast. (b) An additional 26 smaller internment or isolation camps were located in Alaska, Arizona, California, Hawaii, Idaho, Louisiana, Maryland, Massachusetts, Montana, New Mexico, New York, North Carolina, North Dakota, Oklahoma, Tennessee, Texas, Utah, and Wisconsin.

★ 161 ★

U.S. Redress Payments to Japanese Americans Detained During World War II

Numbers of Japanese Americans qualified to receive payments of $20,000 as symbolic redress for detention during World War II[a] under the terms defined by the Civil Liberties Act of 1988.

Status	Number	Redress Allocation
Cases verified as eligible	78,923	$1.58 billion
Cases paid (October 1990-January 1993)	74,962	$1.5 billion
Records paid (includes payments made to heirs of eligible cases)	77,957	
Payments have been made in age-order (oldest qualified detainees paid first).		
The appropriations for redress are limited to $500 million per year (25,000 payments of $20,000 each.)		
Remaining payments will be made after October 1993 (start of fiscal year).		

Source: Office of Redress Administration, Department of Justice, Civil Rights Branch, unpublished data. *Note:* (a) Executive Order 9066, signed on Feb. 19, 1942, by President Franklin D. Roosevelt, authorized the secretary of war to establish military areas and to evacuate civilians from these areas, leading to the removal and relocation of more than 110,000 persons of Japanese ancestry from the West Coast.

★ 162 ★

Relocation of Japanese Canadians during World War II

Location of camp and number of Japanese Canadians involuntarily relocated[a] during 1942.

Relocation destination	Number
Road Construction Camps	945[b]
Blue River–Yellowhead	258
Revelstoke–Sicamous	346
Hope–Princeton	296
Schreiber	32
Black Spur	13
Sugar Beet Projects	3,991
Alberta	2,588
Manitoba	1,053
Ontario (males only)	350
Detention camps in British Columbia	12,029
Greenwood	1,177
Slocan Valley	4,814
Sandon	933
Kaslo	964
Tashme	2,636
New Denver	1,505
Voluntary self-supporting sites in British Columbia	1,161
Special permits to approved employment	1,359
Repatriated to Japan	42
Uprooted prior to March 1942	579
Interned in Ontario	699
In detention in Vancouver	111
Hastings Park Hospital	105
Total	21,460[c]

Source: Audrey Kobayashi, *A Demographic Profile of Japanese Canadians and Social Implications for the Future*, a report prepared for Department of Secretary of State, Canada, September 1989, table 2.1, p. 5. Primary source: British Columbia Security Commission, *Removal of Japanese from Protected Areas*, Vancouver, October 31, 1942. *Notes:* (a) On February 27, 1942, the Canadian government ordered the removal of all persons of Japanese ancestry from the coastal zone of British Columbia. (b) Between March and June 1942, a total of 2,161 Japanese Canadians were placed in road construction camps. Many of them subsequently were allowed to join families in interior detention camps by October 1942. (c) This total represents 90% of the Japanese Canadian population. Ninety-two Japanese Canadians and their children were issued permits on April 11, 1942, exempting them from relocation orders.

★ 163 ★

Relocation of Japanese Canadians during World War II by Province

Results of distribution of Japanese Canadian population by province, 1941-1951.

Province	Year							
	1941	1942	1943	1944	1945	1946	1947	1951
British Columbia	22,096	21,975	16,504	16,103	15,610	14,716	6,776	7,169
Alberta	578	534	3,231	3,469	3,559	3,681	4,180	3,336
Saskatchewan	105	100	129	153	157	164	505	225
Manitoba	42	30	1,084	1,094	1,052	1,052	1,186	1,161
Ontario	234	132	1,650	2,424	2,914	3,742	6,616	8,581
Quebec	48	25	96	344	532	716	1,247	1,137
New Brunswick	3	-	-	-	-	10	10	7
P.E.I.	-	-	-	-	-	-	6	6
Nova Scotia	2	2	1	1	1	1	1	4
Newfoundland	-	-	-	-	-	-	-	2
Yukon & North West Territory	41	39	30	29	29	30	31	35
Total	23,149	22,837	22,725	23,617	23,854	24,112	20,558	21,663
Returned to Japan[a]		42	61	-	-	3,964	-	-

Source: Audrey Kobayashi, *A Demographic Profile of Japanese Canadians and Social Implications for the Future,* a report prepared for Department of Secretary of State, Canada, September 1989, table 2.2, p. 6. A dash (–) indicates not reported. Primary sources: Canada, Department of Labour, *Report on the Re-establishment of Japanese in Canada, 1944-1946* (1947) pp. 11, 15, 25; Canada, Department of Labour, *Report on the Administration of Japanese Affairs in Canada, 1942-1944* (1944), pp. 28-29; Census of Canada. *Note:* (a) Returned to Japan under government–fostered repatriation.

★ 164 ★

Repatriation of Japanese Canadians during World War II by Citizenship Status

Japanese Canadians by citizenship status involved in government-supported repatriation program during World War II, 1945-1947.

Citizenship status	Original Declaration for Repatriation[a]		Requests for Revocation[b]		Number Actually Deported	
	Adults	Dependent Children	Adults	Dependent Children	Adults	Dependent Children
British Columbia						
Japanese Nationals	2,609	16				
Naturalized Canadians	1,297	2				
Canadian born	1,939	3,398				
Total	5,845	3,416	3,908	1,690	1,937	1,726
East of the Rockies						
Japanese Nationals	2,932	17				
Naturalized Canadians	139	0				
Canadian Born	585	323				
Total	1,047	324	619	96	428	228
All Canada						
Japanese Nationals	2,932	17				
Naturalized Canadians	1,436	2				
Canadian Born	2,524	3,740	4,527	1,786	2,365	1,954
Total Adults and Children	10,632		6,313		4,319	

Source: Audrey Kobayashi, *A Demographic Profile of Japanese Canadians and Social Implications for the Future,* a report prepared for Department of Secretary of State, Canada, September 1989, table 2.3, p. 7; and W. Peter Ward, *The Japanese in Canada* (Ottawa: Canadian Historical Society, 1982), pp. 14-15. Primary source: *Report on Re-establishment of Japanese in Canada 1944-1946* (Ottawa: Department of Labor, 1947). *Notes:* (a) Following forced removal of Japanese Canadians from their homes, the Canadian federal government offered them assisted passage to Japan when World War II ended. About one-half of Japanese Canadian evacuees declared their intention to return to Japan. As of March 25, 1946, numbers included in Declarations of Repatriation (from August 31, 1945) were 6,844 adults and 3,503 children, totaling 10,347. (b) Shortly after the war, Japanese Canadians who had accepted the repatriation offer requested relocation indicating a preference to remain in Canada. The federal government fought the relocation request in court and won, but public pressure from Japanese Canadians and whites resulted in the cancellation of repatriation orders in January 1947.

★ 165 ★

Economic Losses of Japanese Canadians after 1941

Reported findings of a study of property losses and loss of income (in hundreds of dollars) due to involuntary relocation[a] of Japanese Canadians during World War II.

Loss category	Loss in 1948 $ Canadian (000)	Loss in 1986 $ Canadian (000)
Income loss	$36,200	$333,040
Fraser Valley farmland	$5,360	$49,314
Other real property	$4,455	$40,986
Fishing assets	$1,125	$10,350
Businesses	$829	$7,627
Other property	$1,124	$10,341
Education fees paid	$150	$1,380
Other losses	$124	$1,141
Less Bird Commission[b] awards	($1,200)	($11,040)
Total	$48,167	$443,139

Source: Price Waterhouse, "The National Association of Japanese Canadians Economic Losses of Japanese Canadians after 1941," 1986, p.1. The study, commissioned by the National Association of Japanese Canadians, was carried out by the public accounting and management consulting firm of Price Waterhouse. *Notes:* (a) On February 27, 1942, the Canadian government ordered the removal of all persons of Japanese ancestry from the coastal zone of British Columbia. (b) The Bird Commission was established in 1947 to inquire into claims made by Japanese Canadians regarding sale of assets under the involuntary relocation program.

Domestic Life

Languages in the United States

★ 166 ★

Home Language by State

Number of persons five years and over who speak only English or who speak a non-English language at home, 1991.

State	Only English	Chinese	Japanese	Korean	Tagalog	Vietnamese	Mon-Khmer	Greek	Italian
Alabama	3,651,936	3,728	2,480	3,232	1,019	2,231	435	1,937	2,853
Alaska	435,260	815	1,450	3,333	5,124	273	57	212	289
Arizona	2,674,519	9,536	3,362	4,829	4,188	4,186	769	2,202	8,892
Arkansas	2,125,884	1,387	1,083	1,112	894	1,701	75	565	1,279
California	18,764,213	575,447	147,451	215,845	464,644	233,074	59,622	32,889	111,133
Colorado	2,722,355	6,261	5,083	8,306	2,769	5,901	807	2,226	5,656
Connecticut	2,593,825	8,234	2,918	2,792	3026	3,378	1,116	10,554	71,309
Delaware	575,393	1,805	424	932	602	382	42	1,177	3,376
Florida	9,996,969	20,839	7,485	9,299	19,618	13,648	1,185	21,396	70,636
Georgia	5,699,642	11,181	6,270	13,433	3,503	6,483	1,659	3,399	4,686
Hawaii	771,485	26,366	69,587	14,636	55,341	4,620	81	177	949
Idaho	867,708	1,029	1,287	550	441	528	50	262	640
Illinois	9,086,726	41,807	13,174	33,973	46,453	7,572	2,565	42,976	66,903
Indiana	4,900,334	6,017	4,722	3,693	2,367	2,112	243	5,287	5,264
Iowa	-	-	-	-	-	-	-	-	-
Kansas	2,158,011	4,272	1,416	3,221	1,375	5,625	576	564	1,402
Kentucky	3,348,473	2,596	2,306	2,676	1,098	1,491	174	664	1,850
Louisiana	3,494,359	4,727	1,385	2,607	2,214	14,352	187	1,391	4,933
Maine	1,036,681	709	553	562	608	6,91	772	1,085	1,814
Maryland	4,030,234	24,508	5,090	23,563	11,329	7,181	1,773	13,146	15,980
Massachusetts	47,53,523	43,248	6,849	7,935	3,800	12,655	1,2178	33,006	81,987
Michigan	8,024,930	15,378	8,478	9,978	8,707	4,817	541	13,431	38,023
Minnesota	3,811,700	6,844	1871	3,368	2,414	8,314	2,699	1,351	2,870
Mississippi	-	-	-	-	-	-	-	-	-
Missouri	-	-	-	-	-	-	-	-	-
Montana	703,198	487	609	283	256	211	6	303	767
Nebraska	-	-	-	-	-	-	-	-	-
Nevada	964,298	5,204	2,322	3,324	8,007	1,739	215	1,313	5,335
New Hampshire	935,825	1,520	465	995	575	187	259	4,086	2,440
New Jersey	5,794,548	47,334	14,272	30,712	38,107	4,892	486	28,080	154,160
New Mexico	896,049	1,686	1,134	1,173	1,017	1,144	37	578	1,880
New York	12,834,328	247,334	29,845	80,394	46,276	11,531	3,169	87,608	400,218
North Carolina	5,931,435	7,252	4,949	6,053	3,019	4,111	1,420	5,354	4,801
North Dakota	543,942	425	171	387	331	212	14	49	106
Ohio	9,517,064	15,475	9,058	8,515	6,328	3,997	1,932	15,391	41,179

[Continued]

127

★ 166 ★

Home Language by State (Continued)

Number of persons five years and over who speak only English or who speak a non-English language at home, 1991.

State	Only English	Chinese	Japanese	Korean	Tagalog	Vietnamese	Mon-Khmer	Greek	Italian
Oklahoma	2,775,957	5,052	2,003	3,471	1,462	5,998	303	662	2,022
Oregon	2,448,772	10,099	6,724	5,574	3,391	7,468	2,036	1,295	3,114
Pennsylvania	10,278,294	24,857	5,570	181,16	7,605	12,843	4,232	17,982	103,844
Rhode Island	776,931	2,640	407	716	1,069	570	3,285	1,853	2,0619
South Carolina	3,118,376	2,343	2,133	2,318	2,976	1,457	227	2,940	2,735
South Dakota	599,232	376	212	392	305	199	140	144	210
Tennessee	44,131,93	5,024	3,393	3,775	1,687	2,058	888	1,598	2,501
Texas	11,635,518	52,220	11,898	26,228	22,256	57,736	5,620	6,422	10,871
Utah	1,432,947	4,483	4,428	2,294	962	2,285	981	1,886	2,446
Vermont	491,112	453	289	144	187	137	12	421	1,289
Virginia	5,327,898	18,037	5,370	25,736	21,018	19,025	3,319	7,453	9,567
Washington	4,098,706	26,378	17,626	23,190	24,574	15,488	9,579	2,959	6,305
West Virginia	1,642,729	1,089	808	586	815	215	16	946	4,691
Wisconsin	4,267,496	5,762	1,884	2,788	1,830	1,899	344	2856	8,661
Wyoming	394,904	401	239	168	198	60	9	321	460
TOTAL	187,346,912	1,302,665	420,533	617,207	835,785	496,677	126,135	382,397	1,292,945

Source: Asian/Pacific Islander Data Consortium (San Francisco: Asian and Pacific Islander Center for Census Information and Services, 1993). Primary source: U.S. Census Bureau, Summary Tape Files 1 and 3. (-) Data unavailable at time of publication.

★ 167 ★

Home Language by Asian Ethnicity

Percent of Asian/Pacific Islanders by ethnic group who speak a language other than English at home, 1989.

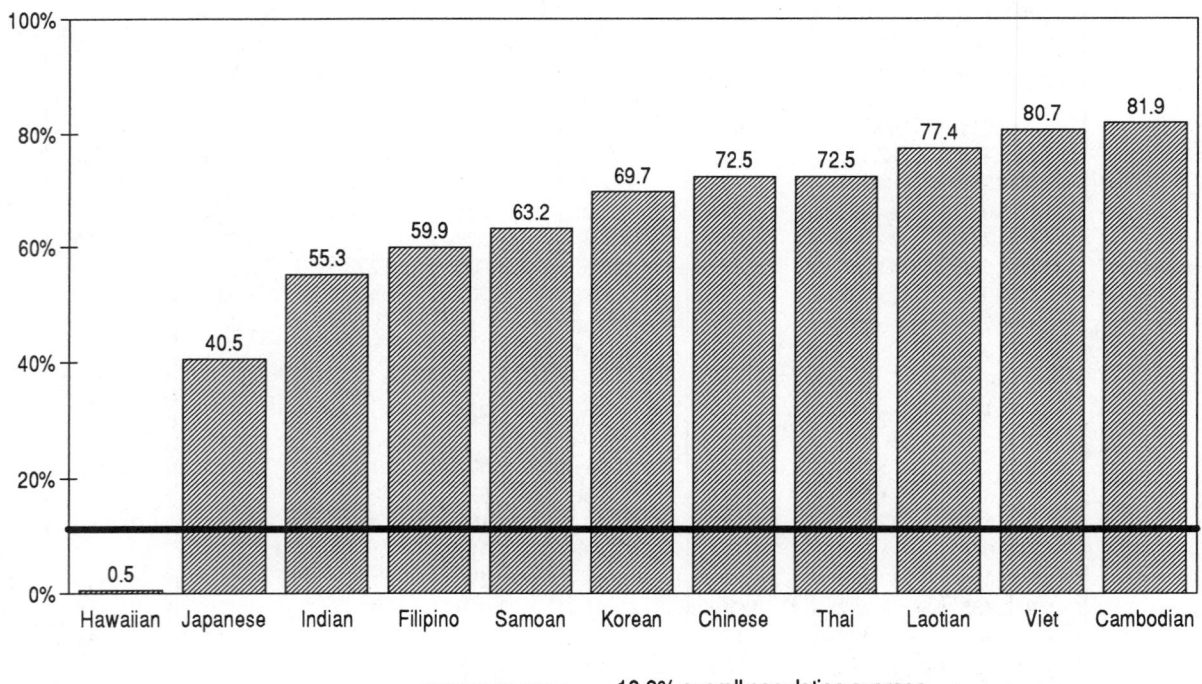

Source: Asian American Health Forum, Inc. (San Francisco, CA, April 1989).

★ 168 ★

Languages Spoken at Home and Work

Percent of Asian/Pacific Islanders by ethnic group who speak a native language at home and English at work, 1990.

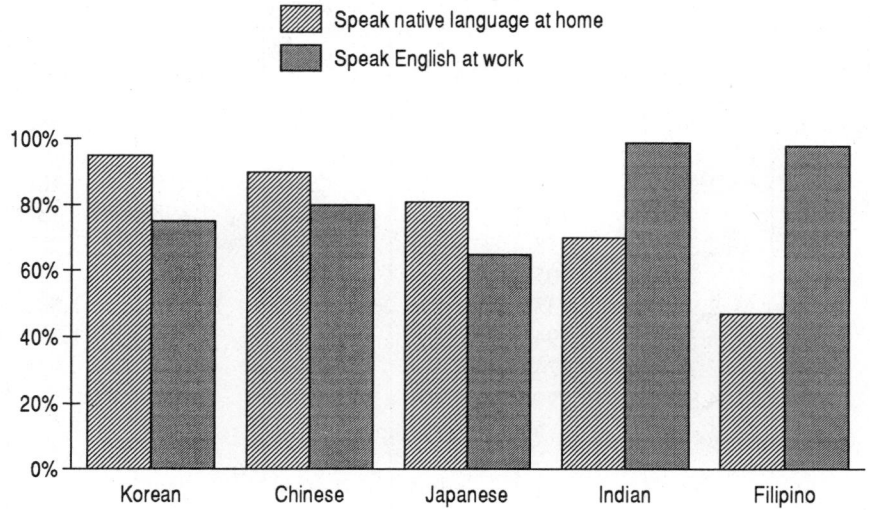

Source: Diane Crispell, "Asian Market Snapshot," *The Numbers News* (Ithaca, NY: Reprint Package #331-A, 1992; reprinted from *The Numbers News,* June 1991): 23. Primary source: Paul Sladkus International, 1990.

★ 169 ★

English Proficiency by Age and U.S. State

Number of persons who speak an Asian or Pacific Islander language at home and report speaking English "very well" to "not well or not at all," by state and age range, 1990.

State	5 to 17 years			18 to 64 years			65 over		
	Speak English			Speak English			Speak English		
	Very well	Well	Not well or not at all	Very well	Well	Not well or not at all	Very well	Well	Not well or not at all
Alabama	1,682	607	466	6,018	4,377	2,091	222	167	212
Alaska	1,391	373	240	4,738	3,363	1900	114	206	365
Arizona	3,026	1178	564	12,058	8,380	4255	687	439	656
Arkansas	1,484	344	227	3,041	1,908	1,538	137	107	186
California	192,323	106,536	66,479	608,057	433,836	328,312	44,086	38,862	87,494
Colorado	3,848	1,691	1,207	11,181	8,709	5,971	761	541	1,258
Connecticut	2,677	1,184	796	10,507	6,362	4,098	395	161	567
Delaware	468	126	62	2,298	1,383	551	84	38	63
Florida	8,696	3,477	1,289	35,168	21,953	10,937	1,665	1,044	1,765
Georgia	5,768	2,579	1,636	16,293	13,916	9,529	444	206	884
Hawaii	1,5934	7,397	3,158	71,775	46,531	26,170	20,430	18,308	16,299
Idaho	558	118	96	2,042	1,179	691	172	118	85
Illinois	1,7276	6,481	3,807	65,849	39,577	22,375	3,223	2,523	5,662

[Continued]

English Proficiency by Age and U.S. State (Continued)

Number of persons who speak an Asian or Pacific Islander language at home and report speaking English "very well" to "not well or not at all," by state and age range, 1990.

State	5 to 17 years			18 to 64 years			65 over		
	Speak English			Speak English			Speak English		
	Very well	Well	Not well or not at all	Very well	Well	Not well or not at all	Very well	Well	Not well or not at all
Indiana	2,101	692	541	9,381	5,957	3,348	395	140	339
Iowa	-	-	-	-	-	-	-	-	-
Kansas	2,517	1,315	734	6,776	5,950	3,570	188	72	284
Kentucky	1,122	457	426	4,899	3,071	1,898	138	83	200
Louisiana	4,081	2,371	958	9,181	6,524	4,932	282	144	544
Maine	457	243	105	1,534	1,091	622	25	22	79
Maryland	9,041	2,976	1,733	31,725	20,693	13,099	1,387	1,056	2,450
Massachusetts	8,636	6,314	4,194	30,559	22,456	19,438	1,226	811	3,072
Michigan	6,687	2,777	1,724	23,572	13,873	8,073	938	586	1,196
Minnesota	5,869	4,849	3,890	11,461	10,967	8,954	283	166	1,337
Mississippi	-	-	-	-	--	-	-	-	-
Missouri	-	-	-	-	-	-	-	-	-
Montana	229	84	44	1,093	594	248	36	35	49
Nebraska	-	-	-	-	-	-	-	-	-
Nevada	2,497	897	400	9,786	6,630	3,298	507	347	708
New Hampshire	490	267	126	2,044	1,341	712	33	40	87
New Jersey	16,893	6,405	3726	61,154	37,838	19,189	2,234	2,001	4,231
New Mexico	822	411	136	3,192	2,013	1,035	183	81	77
New York	42,822	20,635	11,127	133,414	104,370	114,186	5,620	5,259	22,440
North Carolina	3,330	1,477	883	12,512	8,547	5,181	402	213	538
North Dakota	107	36	17	884	582	177	1	8	0
Ohio	5,010	2,522	1,593	21,689	13,650	7,631	888	456	1,156
Oklahoma	2,156	995	580	8,540	6,464	3,034	315	104	387
Oregon	4,750	1,988	825	14,116	10,747	7,051	1,134	610	1,249
Pennsylvania	9,364	4,059	2,958	29,234	20,032	14,800	1,178	865	2,295
Rhode Island	1,465	1141	929	3,888	2,113	2,679	221	68	252
South Carolina	1,250	551	170	5,967	3,510	1,681	345	104	171
South Dakota	177	51	55	923	567	257	16	5	3
Tennessee	2,590	809	633	8,194	5,281	3,263	365	197	304
Texas	25,808	9,701	5,655	71,530	54,959	30,944	2,224	1,409	4,803
Utah	2,928	1,118	434	8,652	5,013	2,996	492	273	440
Vermont	131	52	15	676	421	225	36	14	16
Virginia	11,109	4,137	2,127	39,826	25,966	15,402	1,307	984	2,573
Washington	14,976	6,956	4,060	44,665	30,603	22,333	3,051	2,521	4,651
West Virginia	464	95	81	2,025	1,096	413	115	27	54
Wisconsin	3,548	3,492	2,907	8,976	6,814	6,433	379	240	926
Wyoming	62	12	4	516	373	157	49	35	2

Source: Asian/Pacific Islander Data Consortium (San Francisco: Asian and Pacific Islander Center for Census Information and Services, 1993). Primary source: U.S. Census Bureau, Summary Tape Files 1 and 3. (-) Data unavailable at time of publication.

★ 170 ★

English Proficiency and Linguistic Isolation by State

Numbers of persons five years and over living in non-English speaking households and those who are linguistically isolated[a], by state and ethnic language, 1990. Data also provided for number of persons five years and over living in English-speaking households by state.

State	English	Asian or Pacific Island language		Spanish	
		Linguistically isolated[a]	Not linguistically isolated[a]	Linguistically isolated[a]	Not linguistically isolated[a]
Alabama	1,431,581	1,835	6,382	1,669	29,458
Alaska	159,990	1,217	4,266	516	5,236
Arizona	1,069,239	3,541	11,854	35,265	159,889
Arkansas	849,483	1,050	3,319	1,449	18,023
California	7,271,903	218,169	447,436	500,078	1,300,113
Colorado	1,106,582	4,487	11,299	14,829	92,485
Connecticut	996,661	2,755	7,648	17,317	51,106
Delaware	222,923	437	2,053	907	7,025
Florida	4,170,942	8,591	33,201	175,033	414,081
Georgia	2,199,958	6,226	15,993	7,851	63,031
Hawaii	240,250	22,677	76,585	562	7,277
Idaho	329,060	560	2,337	2,693	14,933
Illinois	3,534,913	17,945	4,6204	66,481	201,276
Indiana	1,918,304	2,675	9,002	4,720	49,825
Iowa	-	-	-	-	-
Kansas	871,344	2,800	6,256	4,782	28,778
Kentucky	1,321,201	1,084	5,184	1,247	20,804
Louisiana	1,257,202	2,995	8,234	4,844	34,688
Maine	398,690	403	1,649	137	4,067
Maryland	1,544,867	8,911	24,462	9,445	53,393
Massachusetts	1,827,335	12,738	21,468	26,003	68,158
Michigan	3,091,527	6,503	19,388	7,690	73,044
Minnesota	1,508,319	6,368	10,366	2,104	25,508
Mississippi	-	-	-	-	-
Missouri	-	-	-	-	-
Montana	284,340	238	1,218	558	5,153
Nebraska	-	-	-	-	-
Nevada	391,166	2,586	9,414	8,882	30,175
New Hampshire	354,823	513	2,005	572	5,112
New Jersey	2,168,366	16,495	4,0978	65,783	169,547
New Mexico	324,298	733	3,185	27,651	147,728
New York	4,906,595	66,651	97,000	206,506	518,918
North Carolina	2,362,918	3,605	12,384	4,975	64,196
North Dakota	210,321	108	901	178	2,634
Ohio	3,755,461	6,819	1,9278	7,677	81,505
Oklahoma	1,120,589	2,719	8,307	4,499	31,998
Oregon	1,002,503	5,463	13,310	6,052	34,359
Pennsylvania	4,029,076	10,021	23,572	16,638	90,649
Rhode Island	298,024	1,530	2,720	4,812	8,519
South Carolina	1,184,459	1,153	6,178	1,827	27,962
South Dakota	234,316	193	818	174	3,436
Tennessee	1,764,836	2,412	8,183	2,433	33,767
Texas	4,545,518	25,118	58,208	307,456	941,700

[Continued]

★ 170 ★

English Proficiency and Linguistic Isolation by State (Continued)

Numbers of persons five years and over living in non-English speaking households and those who are linguistically isolated[a], by state and ethnic language, 1990. Data also provided for number of persons five years and over living in English-speaking households by state.

State	English	Asian or Pacific Island language		Spanish	
		Linguistically isolated[a]	Not linguistically isolated[a]	Linguistically isolated[a]	Not linguistically isolated[a]
Utah	469,812	2,060	8,454	3,130	25,828
Vermont	190,031	177	637	123	1,917
Virginia	2,079,233	9,781	31,350	11,414	66,638
Washington	1,664,430	15,806	41,274	11,251	57,597
West Virginia	656,299	414	2,022	573	9,740
Wisconsin	1,664,800	4,148	7,982	4,452	37,939
Wyoming	153,986	127	627	965	7,409

Source: Asian/Pacific Islander Data Consortium (San Francisco: Asian and Pacific Islander Center for Census Information and Services, 1993). Primary source: U.S. Census Bureau, Summary Tape Files 1 and 3. *Note:* (a) A household in which no person fourteen years and over speaks only English, and no person fourteen years and over speaks English very well. All household members five years and over are classified as "linguistically isolated" even if they speak only English or speak English very well.

Languages in Canada

★ 171 ★

Top Twenty Languages in Canada, 1991

Language history and current use by number and percent of population in Canada, 1991.

Language	Ability to speak		Mother[a] tongue		Home[b] language	
	Number	Percent	Number	Percent	Number	Percent
English	22,505,420	83.4%	16,454,515	61.0%	18,664,635	69.1%
French	8,508,955	31.5%	6,623,235	24.5%	6,369,360	23.6
Non-official languages	4,981,605	18.5%	4,255,960	15.8%	2,463,435	9.1%
Italian	701,910	2.6%	538,690	2.0%	288,290	1.1%
German	684,950	2.5%	490,650	1.8%	134,460	0.5%
Chinese	557,300	2.1%	516,875	1.9%	430,090	1.6%
Spanish	402,435	1.5%	187,615	0.7%	145,045	0.5%
Portuguese	254,465	0.9%	220,630	0.8%	152,530	0.6%
Ukrainian	249,535	0.9%	201,315	0.7%	49,995	0.2%
Polish	239,580	0.9%	200,395	0.7%	117,150	0.4%
Dutch	173,290	0.6%	146,420	0.5%	19,915	0.1%
Punjabi	167,930	0.6%	147,265	0.5%	123,775	0.5%
Arabic	164,380	0.6%	119,255	0.4%	82,450	0.3%
Greek	161,325	0.6%	132,980	0.5%	93,160	0.3%
Tagalog	136,975	0.5%	115,980	0.4%	75,390	0.3%
Vietnamese	113,115	0.4%	83,630	0.3%	79,585	0.3%
Hindi	111,965	0.4%	40,575	0.2%	26,285	0.1%
Hungarian	97,410	0.4%	83,915	0.3%	31,175	0.1%

[Continued]

★ 171 ★

Top Twenty Languages in Canada, 1991 (Continued)

Language history and current use by number and percent of population in Canada, 1991.

Language	Ability to speak		Mother[a] tongue		Home[b] language	
	Number	Percent	Number	Percent	Number	Percent
Cree	93,825	0.3%	82,070	0.3%	60,855	0.2%
Russian	84,055	0.3%	38,030	0.1%	17,165	0.1%
Gujarati	54,210	0.2%	42,175	0.2%	29,030	0.1%

Source: The Daily, (Ottawa: Statistics Canada, January 12, 1993), p. 3. Primary source: Seventeenth (Canada) Census of the Population, 1991. *Notes:* (a)Mother tongue is defined as the first language learned at home in childhood, and still understood at the time of the census. (b) Home language is the language most often spoken at home during the period immediately preceding the census.

★ 172 ★

Top Ten Home Languages, Canada, 1971 and 1991

Number and percent of Canadians who speak a language other than English or French at home, 1971 and 1991.

1971			1991		
Home language	Number	Percent	Home language	Number	Percent
Italian	425,230	2.0%	Chinese	430,090	1.6%
German	213,350	1.0%	Italian	288,290	1.1%
Ukrainian	144,755	0.7%	Portuguese	152,530	0.6%
Greek	86,830	0.4%	Spanish	145,050	0.5%
Chinese	77,895	0.4%	German	134,460	0.5%
Portuguese	74,765	0.3%	Punjabi	123,775	0.5%
Polish	70,960	0.3%	Polish	117,150	0.4%
Magyar (Hungarian)	50,675	0.2%	Greek	93,160	0.3%
Dutch	36,170	0.2%	Arabic	82,450	0.3%
Yiddish	26,330	0.1%	Vietnamese	79,585	0.3%

Source: The Daily, (Ottawa: Statistics Canada, January 12, 1993), p. 3. Primary source: Seventeenth (Canada) Census of the Population, 1991.

★ 173 ★

Mother Tongue by Sex, Canada

Number of respondents in the total population of Canada who report learning an Asian language first in childhood, by sex, 1991.

Mother tongue[a] and sex	Single response[b]	Multiple response[b]
Bengali		
Total	8,480	815
Male	5,025	500
Female	3,460	315
Gujarati		
Total	38,075	4,100
Male	18,530	1,995
Female	19,545	2,105
Hindi		
Total	34,500	6,075
Male	17,235	3,190
Female	17,270	2,890
Punjabi		
Total	136,460	10,805
Male	70,090	5,730
Female	66,370	5,075
Japanese		
Total	29,955	1,295
Male	13,650	625
Female	16,310	665
Korean		
Total	36,185	1,150
Male	13,650	625
Female	18,685	540
Chinese		
Total	498,845	18,030
Male	245,505	9,215
Female	253,340	8,815
Tai languages (includes Lao and Thai)		
Total	14,400	1,810
Male	7,050	905
Female	7,350	905
Lao		
Total	11,625	1,280
Male	6,105	700
Female	5,520	585
Thai		
Total	2,775	525
Male	940	200
Female	1,835	320
Khmer (Cambodian)		
Total	14,435	1,065
Male	7,405	550
Female	7,030	515

[Continued]

★ 173 ★

Mother Tongue by Sex, Canada (Continued)

Number of respondents in the total population of Canada who report learning an Asian language first in childhood, by sex, 1991.

Mother tongue[a] and sex	Single response[b]	Multiple response[b]
Vietnamese		
Total	78,570	5,060
Male	41,920	2,715
Female	36,650	2,345
Indonesian (Malay)		
Total	4,335	640
Male	2,090	335
Female	2,250	305
Tagalog (Pilipino)		
Total	99,715	16,265
Male	36,795	6,495
Female	62,915	9,775

Source: Statistics Canada, *The Nation* (Ottawa: Statistics Canada, 1991 Census of the Population, 93-333, 1992), table 2, pp. 24-49. *Notes:* (a) Mother tongue is the first language learned in childhood. (b) *Single response* indicates that the respondent reported learning only one language in childhood. *Multiple response* indicates that the respondent reported learning more than one language in childhood.

★ 174 ★

Shift in Mother Tongue to Home Language, Canada, 1981 to 1991

Percent of persons with mother tongue[a] other than English or French who shifted to a different home language[b], 1981 to 1991.

Mother tongue	Rate of language shift, percent
Italian	48.0%
Chinese	18.5%
German	72.7%
Portuguese	32.8%
Polish	40.9%
Ukrainian	75.5%
Spanish	26.4%
Dutch	86.8%
Punjabi	17.9%
Greek	31.5%
Arabic	33.8%
Tagalog	41.8%

Source: The Daily, (Ottawa: Statistics Canada), January 12, 1993, p. 3. The rate of language shift varies from one language group to another depending largely on the length of time spent in Canada. Among groups in which immigration has slowed down in recent decades, language shift was often high. (See Dutch, Ukrainian, and German mother tongue.) Conversely, groups experiencing high immigration usually have lower language shift. (See Punjabi, Chinese, and Spanish.) Primary source: Seventeenth (Canada) Census of the Population, 1991. *Notes:* (a) Mother tongue is defined as the first language learned at home in childhood, and still understood at the time of the census. (b) Home language is the language most often spoken at home during the period immediately preceding the census.

★ 175 ★

Shift from Mother Tongue
to English or French, Quebec

Percent of persons who are classified in the top ten mother tongue[a] groups who shift to English or French as their home language[b] in Quebec, 1981 to 1991.

Mother tongue	Shift to English, percent	Shift to French, percent
Italian	73%	27%
Spanish	28%	72%
Arabic	30%	70%
Greek	90%	10%
Portuguese	43%	57%
Chinese	79%	21%
Creole Languages	3%	97%
German	81%	19%
Polish	79%	21%
Vietnamese	12%	88%

Source: The Daily, (Ottawa: Statistics Canada, January 12, 1993), p. 3. Primary source: Seventeenth (Canada) Census of the Population, 1991. *Notes:* (a) Mother tongue is defined as the first language learned at home in childhood, and still understood at the time of the census. (b) Home language is the language most often spoken at home during the period immediately preceding the census.

★ 176 ★

Mother Tongue, Alberta

Number of respondents in Alberta who report learning an Asian language first in childhood, by sex, 1991.

Mother tongue[a] and sex	Single response[b]	Multiple response[b]
Gujarati		
Total	5,500	680
Male	2,695	370
Female	2,800	315
Hindi		
Total	4,310	685
Male	2,155	355
Female	2,155	335
Punjabi		
Total	12,420	955
Male	6,325	535
Female	6,100	420
Japanese		
Total	3,035	150
Male	1,385	75
Female	1,655	75

[Continued]

★ 176 ★

Mother Tongue, Alberta (Continued)

Number of respondents in Alberta who report learning an Asian language first in childhood, by sex, 1991.

Mother tongue[a] and sex	Single response[b]	Multiple response[b]
Korean		
Total	3,150	45
Male	1,480	30
Female	1,665	15
Chinese		
Total	60,265	2,710
Male	29,885	1,360
Female	30,385	1,355
Vietnamese		
Total	12,770	830
Male	6,935	465
Female	5,830	370
Tagalog (Pilipino)		
Total	10,055	1,485
Male	3,600	555
Female	6,460	925

Source: Statistics Canada, *The Nation* (Ottawa: Statistics Canada, 1991 Census of the Population , 93-333, 1992), table 2, pp. 24-49. *Notes:* (a) Mother tongue is the first language learned in childhood. (b) *Single response* indicates that the respondent reported learning only one language in childhood. *Multiple response* indicates that the respondent reported learning more than one language in childhood.

★ 177 ★

Mother Tongue, British Columbia

Number of respondents in British Columbia who report learning an Asian language first in childhood, by sex, 1991.

Mother tongue[a] and sex	Single response[b]	Multiple response[b]
Gujarati		
Total	5,055	750
Male	2,340	365
Female	2,715	385
Hindi		
Total	12,615	1,850
Male	6,055	990
Female	6,560	860
Punjabi		
Total	67,620	4,295
Male	34,175	2,200
Female	33,445	2,095

[Continued]

★ 177 ★

Mother Tongue, British Columbia (Continued)

Number of respondents in British Columbia who report learning an Asian language first in childhood, by sex, 1991.

Mother tongue[a] and sex	Single response[b]	Multiple response[b]
Japanese		
Total	14,520	405
Male	6,480	175
Female	8,045	235
Korean		
Total	7,640	185
Male	3,710	75
Female	3,930	110
Chinese		
Total	153,850	5,470
Male	74,580	2,770
Female	79,265	2,700
Khmer (Cambodian)		
Total	1,020	100
Male	510	45
Female	515	60
Vietnamese		
Total	11,240	750
Male	5,900	420
Female	5,340	325
Indonesian (Malay)		
Total	1,160	185
Male	595	75
Female	565	105
Tagalog (Pilipino)		
Total	17,825	2,845
Male	6,320	1,140
Female	11,510	1,705

Source: Statistics Canada, *The Nation* (Ottawa: Statistics Canada, 1991 Census of the Population, 93-333, 1992), table 2, pp. 24-49. *Notes:* (a) Mother tongue is the first language learned in childhood. (b) *Single response* indicates that the respondent reported learning only one language in childhood. *Multiple response* indicates that the respondent reported learning more than one language in childhood.

★ 178 ★

Mother Tongue, Manitoba

Number of respondents in Manitoba who report learning an Asian language first in childhood, by sex, 1991.

Mother tongue[a] and sex	Single response[b]	Multiple response[b]
Punjabi		
Total	3,265	400
Male	1,595	215
Female	1,675	185
Chinese		
Total	9,825	425
Male	4,880	215
Female	4,945	205
Vietnamese		
Total	2,855	250
Male	1,540	145
Female	1,310	105
Tagalog (Pilipino)		
Total	13,870	2,715
Male	6,195	1,310
Female	7,670	1,405

Source: Statistics Canada, *The Nation* (Ottawa: Statistics Canada, 1991 Census of the Population, 93-333, 1992), table 2, pp. 24-49. *Notes:* (a) Mother tongue is the first language learned in childhood. (b) *Single response* indicates that the respondent reported learning only one language in childhood. *Multiple response* indicates that the respondent reported learning more than one language in childhood.

★ 179 ★

Mother Tongue, Ontario

Number of respondents in Ontario who report learning an Asian language first in childhood, by sex, 1991.

Mother tongue[a] and sex	Single response[b]	Multiple response[b]
Bengali		
Total	4,460	340
Male	2,465	215
Female	1,995	125
Gujarati		
Total	23,390	2,270
Male	11,490	1,075
Female	11,900	1,190
Hindi		
Total	14,625	3,025
Male	7,440	1,585
Female	7,180	1,445
Punjabi		
Total	48,585	4,705
Male	25,390	2,510
Female	23,190	2,185
Japanese		
Total	10,230	585
Male	4,790	285
Female	5,440	295
Korean		
Total	22,060	865
Male	10,640	480
Female	11,425	380
Chinese		
Total	234,175	7,630
Male	115,785	3,925
Female	118,390	3,705
Lao		
Total	4,975	560
Male	2,680	335
Female	2,300	230
Thai		
Total	1,175	190
Male	390	80
Female	780	105
Khmer (Cambodian)		
Total	4,625	255
Male	2,500	135
Female	2,135	120
Vietnamese		
Total	31,735	2,240

[Continued]

★ 179 ★

Mother Tongue, Ontario (Continued)

Number of respondents in Ontario who report learning an Asian language first in childhood, by sex, 1991.

Mother tongue[a] and sex	Single response[b]	Multiple response[b]
Male	16,985	1,190
Female	14,755	1,055
Indonesian (Malay)		
Total	2,200	285
Male	995	165
Female	1,210	115
Tagalog (Pilipino)		
Total	50,980	7,780
Male	18,560	3,025
Female	32,420	4,755

Source: Statistics Canada, *The Nation* (Ottawa: Statistics Canada, 1991 Census of the Population, 93-333, 1992), table 2, pp. 24-49. *Notes:* (a) Mother tongue is the first language learned in childhood. (b) *Single response* indicates that the respondent reported learning only one language in childhood. *Multiple* response indicates that the respondent reported learning more than one language in childhood.

★ 180 ★

Mother Tongue, Quebec

Number of respondents in Quebec who report learning an Asian language first in childhood, by sex, 1991.

Mother tongue[a] and sex	Single response[b]	Multiple response[b]
Bengali		
Total	2,665	290
Male	1,780	205
Female	880	85
Gujarati		
Total	3,045	335
Male	1,485	135
Female	1,560	200
Hindi		
Total	1,445	260
Male	770	135
Female	680	125
Punjabi		
Total	3,475	320
Male	2,020	200
Female	1,455	115

[Continued]

★ 180 ★

Mother Tongue, Quebec (Continued)

Number of respondents in Quebec who report learning an Asian language first in childhood, by sex, 1991.

Mother tongue[a] and sex	Single response[b]	Multiple response[b]
Japanese		
Total	1,310	75
Male	595	35
Female	715	40
Korean		
Total	2,275	35
Male	1,170	10
Female	1,105	20
Chinese		
Total	30,755	1,405
Male	15,145	740
Female	15,615	670
Lao		
Total	3,835	375
Male	1,975	180
Female	1,860	190
Thai		
Total	325	60
Male	80	25
Female	240	35
Khmer (Cambodian)		
Total	6,290	560
Male	3,185	290
Female	3,110	270
Vietnamese		
Total	17,790	900
Male	9,300	450
Female	8,490	445
Indonesian (Malay)		
Total	190	40
Male	100	30
Female	90	15
Tagalog (Pilipino)		
Total	5,470	1,120
Male	1,585	335
Female	3,890	780

Source: Statistics Canada, *The Nation* (Ottawa: Statistics Canada, 1991 Census of the Population, 93-333, 1992), table 2, pp. 24-49. *Notes:* (a) Mother tongue is the first language learned in childhood. (b) *Single response* indicates that the respondent reported learning only one language in childhood. *Multiple response* indicates that the respondent reported learning more than one language in childhood.

★ 181 ★

Mother Tongue, Saskatchewan

Number of respondents in Saskatchewan who report learning an Asian language first in childhood, by sex, 1991.

Mother tongue[a]	Single response[b]	Multiple response[b]
Chinese		
Total	6,510	230
Male	3,300	120
Female	3,210	110
Vietnamese		
Total	1,310	30
Male	770	15
Female	545	15

Source: Statistics Canada, *The Nation* (Ottawa: Statistics Canada, 1991 Census of the Population, 93-333, 1992), table 2, pp. 24-49. *Notes:* (a) Mother tongue is the first language learned in childhood. (b) *Single response* indicates that the respondent reported learning only one language in childhood. *Multiple response* indicates that the respondent reported learning more than one language in childhood.

Marital Status

★ 182 ★

Marital Status by Sex and Race/Ethnicity

Total number of Asian/Pacific Islanders and whites fifteen years and over and marital status, by sex, in percent, 1991.

Group	Total, fifteen years and over (in thousands)	Never married, percent	Married, spouse present	Married, spouse absent	Widowed	Divorced
Total population	193,519	26.5%	55.0%	3.3%	7.1%	8.1%
Male	92,840	30.1%	57.3%	2.8%	2.6%	7.1%
Female	100,680	23.2%	52.9%	3.7%	11.2%	9.1%
Asian/Pacific Islander, total	5,247	31.1%	56.4%	3.4%	5.1%	4.0%
Male	2,484	36.9%	55.2%	3.9%	1.9%	2.1%
Female	2,764	25.9%	57.4%	3.1%	7.9%	5.7%
White, total	164,567	24.3%	58.1%	2.6%	7.0%	8.0%
Male	79,555	28.0%	60.1%	2.3%	2.5%	7.1%
Female	85,012	20.8%	56.1%	2.9%	11.2%	8.9%

Source: Claudette Bennett, Economics and Statistics Administration, Bureau of the Census, U.S. Department of Commerce, The Asian and Pacific Islander Population in the United States: March 1991 and 1990, Current Population Reports, P20-459 (Washington, DC: U.S. Government Printing Office, 1992), table B, p. 5.

★ 183 ★

Outmarriage Rates by Sex

Outmarriage rates of Chinese, Japanese, Korean, Vietnamese men and women in Los Angeles County, 1975, 1977, 1979, and 1985.

Ethnic group	1975	1977	1979	1985
Chinese				
Marriages, total	596	650	716	1,881
Outmarriages, number	250	323	295	564
Outmarriages, percent	44.0%	49.7%	41.2%	30.0%
Men, percent	37.8%	43.7%	43.7%	43.4%
Women, percent	62.2%	56.3%	56.3%	56.6%
Japanese				
Marriages, total	664	756	764	1,404
Outmarriages, number	364	477	463	719
Outmarriages, percent	54.8%	63.1%	60.6%	51.2%
Men, percent	46.4%%	39.4%	47.3%	39.8%
Women, percent	53.6%	60.6%	52.7%	60.2%
Korean				
Marriages, total	250	232	334	543
Outmarriages, number	65	79	92	47
Outmarriages, percent	26.0%	34.1%	27.6%	8.7%
Men, percent	36.9%	26.6%	20.4%	21.4%
Women, percent	63.1%	73.4%	79.6%	78.6%
Vietnamese[a]				
Marriages, total	-	-	-	560
Outmarriages, number	-	-	-	34
Outmarriages, percent	-	-	-	6.0%
Men, percent	-	-	-	25.3%
Women, percent	-	-	-	74.7%

Source: Harry H. L. Kitano and Roger Daniels, *Asian Americans: Emerging Minorities* (Englewood Cliffs, NJ: Prentice Hall, 1988), table 12-15, p. 177. Primary source: Los Angeles County Marriage License Bureau. *Note:* (a) Data for Vietnamese included for 1985 only.

Parental Involvement

★ 184 ★

Parental Involvement in Eighth Graders' Activities

Parental involvement[a] in eighth graders' school-related activities, in percent, by race/ethnicity, 1988.

Parental involvement	Total, all groups	Asian/ Pacific Islander	White, non-Hispanic	Black, non-Hispanic	Hispanic	American Indian/Alaskan Native
Parents who talk with child regularly about:						
Current school experiences	79.4$	59.8%	82.3%	75.0%	67.1%	72.5%
High school plans	47.1%	41.7%	45.0%	57.8%	52.7%	44.6%
Plans after high school	38.3%	36.5%	35.4%	51.4%	44.8%	39.9%
Parents who report family rules about:						
Number of hours of television watched on school days	61.7%	67.1%	58.5%	75.3%	68.7%	62.9%
Doing homework	92.0%	89.3%	91.4%	95.5%	92.3%	95.9%
Maintaining certain grade average	72.7%	74/7%	70.1%	82.3%	79.8%	75.7%
Parents who report that they:						
Never or seldom help with homework	29.4%	42.8%	26.8%	31.4%	44.7%	35.5%
Belong to a parent-teacher organization	31.9%	29.4%	34.3%	30.1%	15.5%	16.6%
Attend the parent-teacher organization meeting	36.2%	41.2%	33.3%	47.8%	43.0%	35.0%
Parents who have contacted school about child's:						
Academic performance	52.5%	36.0%	53.7%	52.1%	48.3%	52.5%
Academic program	34.8%	29.5%	35.1%	34.2%	34.5%	42.5%

Source: U.S. Department of Education, National Center for Education Statistics, *Digest of Education Statistics, 1990* (Washington, DC: U.S. Government Printing Office, 1991), table 22, p. 29. (This table was prepared July 1990.) Primary source: U.S. Department of Education, National Center for Education Statistics, *National Education Longitudinal Study of 1988,* "Base Year Parent Survey," (Washington, DC: U. S. Department of Education, 1989). Also in source: data on parental socioeconomic status, level of education, and family type. *Note:* (a) The respondent was the parent most knowledgeable about the child's education. The responding parent reported on their own and their spouse's activities.

Public Assistance

★ 185 ★

Participation in U.S. Public Assistance Programs

Number of Asian/Americans in selected public assistance programs in the United States and percent of total participants, various years.

Program	Asian American participants (estimated)	Percent of total participants
AFDC[a]	84,675 families	2.3%
	222,023 children	3.1%
SSI[b]	42,100 individuals (65 years or over)[c]	1.8%
Medicaid[d]	447,713 individuals	2.0%
Low-Income Housing[e]	78,923 households	2.0%
Food Stamps[f]	130,000 households	1.8%
WIC[g]	10,243 women	1.4%
	26,319 infants	3.3%
	33,827 children (1 to 4 years)	2.1%
School Lunch[h]		
Free	205,023 children	2.1%
Reduced-price	61,744 children	3.4%
Summer Food[i]	30,000 children	20.0%

Source: U.S. General Accounting Office, *Asian Americans: A Status Report 1990,* (Washington, DC: U.S. Government Printing Office, 1990), table S.1, p. 39. Years for above data vary, as indicated in the footnotes. *Notes:* (a) Department of Health and Human Services (HHS), Family Support Administration, *Characteristics and Financial Circumstances of AFDC Recipients,* 1986. AFDC stands for Aid to Families with Dependent Children. (b) Social Security Administration, "Number and Percent of Persons Aged 65 and Older Receiving Social Security or Supplemental Security Income by Race and Spanish Origin," 1980. (c) Includes participation in other welfare programs, but, according to Social Security Administration officials, responses for people 65 years of age or older reflect primarily Supplemental Security Income. (d) HHS, Health Care Financing Administration, "Medicaid Recipients and Expenditures, by Race and State, Fiscal Year 1986." (e) Department of Housing and Urban Development (HUD), *Annual Housing Survey,* 1987. (f) Department of Agriculture, Food and Nutrition Service, *Characteristics of Food Stamp Households,* 1986. (g) Department of Agriculture, Food and Nutrition Service, *Study of WIC Participant and Program Characteristics,* 1986. Data are from 1984. WIC stands for Special Supplemental Food Program for Women, Infants, and Children. (h) Department of Agriculture, Food and Nutrition Service, *Characteristics of the National School Lunch and School Breakfast Program Participants,* 1988. Data are from 1984. (i) Department of Agriculture, Food and Nutrition Service, *An Evaluation of the Summer Food Service Program,* 1988. Data are from 1986.

Education

Academic Achievement

★ 186 ★

Academic Achievement and Family Values, Indochinese Refugees

Reported results of a study of Lao, Vietnamese, and Chinese-Vietnamese refugees' children's grade point averages relating to family size and family values.

Family activity/value	Grade Point Average of children in family
Parents read aloud	3.14
Parents do not read aloud	2.97
Agree that "Wife should always do as her husband wishes."	2.64
Disagree that "Wife should always do as her husband wishes."	3.16
Husband helps with dishes/laundry	3.21
Husband does not wash dishes/do laundry	2.79
Agree that "College is more important for boys."	2.83
Disagree that "College is more important for boys."	3.14
Family attributes value to "fun and excitement"	2.90
Family attributes less value to "fun and excitement"	3.14
Family attributes value to material possessions	2.66
Family attributes less value to material possessions	3.19
Family agrees "The past is as important as the future."	3.14
Family gives lower rating to preservation of the past	2.66

Source: Nathan Caplan, Marcella H. Choy, and John K. Whitmore, "Indochinese Refugee Families and Academic Achievement," *Scientific American* (February 1992): 36-40. Data from survey conducted by the authors while working together at the Institute for Social Research at the University of Michigan. Study incorporated survey and other data on 6,750 person in five urban areas: Orange County, CA, Seattle, Houston, Chicago, and Boston, and further study of random sample of 200 nuclear families and their 536 school-age children.

★ 187 ★

Academic Achievement Predictors

Reported results of a study of Scholastic Aptitude Test (SAT) scores and high school grade point average as predictors of academic performance for Asian American students in the University of California system[a].

For Asian American students, high school grade point average is the strongest predictor of first-year university grade point average.

For Asian Americans, the SAT-math score contributed 36 percent and the SAT-verbal score contributed only 3 percent to the prediction equation for grade point average. For whites, the situation was reversed: SAT-math and SAT-verbal contributed 3% percent and 32 percent respectively. (These percentages represent contributions to the study author's regression equation, a statistical tool for evaluating interrelationships among factors.)

Filipinos present a notable variation from the generalization. For Filipinos studied, high school grade point average and mathematical skills were less significant than verbal skills in predicting first year university grades.

Findings suggest that high school grades and performance tests have value in predicting future academic performance; however, verbal test scores are less valid as predictors for Asian American students.

Source: Selected from Stanley Sue and Jennifer Abe, *Predictors of Academic Achievement among Asian American and White Students* (New York: College Board Report 88-11, 1988). *Note:* (a) Records of 4,113 Asian American freshman students and 1,000 randomly selected white freshman students from eight University of California campuses in fall 1984 were studied.

★ 188 ★

Academic Credits: High School Graduates

Percent of high school graduates earning credits in selected combinations of academic courses by race/ethnicity, 1982 and 1987.

Year of graduation and academic record[a]	All students	Race/ethnicity			
		Asian	White	Black	Hispanic
1982					
4 Eng., 3 S.S., 3 Sci., 3 Math, 0.5 Comp., 2 F.L.[b]	1.9%	6.0%	2.2%	0.7%	0.5%
4 Eng., 3 S.S., 3 Sci., 3 Math, 0.5 Comp.[c]	2.7%	7.1%	3.1%	1.0%	0.9%
4 Eng., 3 S.S., 3 Sci., 3 Math, 2 F.L.	8.8%	17.0%	10.1%	5.2%	3.5%
4 Eng., 3 S.S., 3 Sci., 3 Math	13.4%	21.0%	14.9%	10.1%	6.3%
4 Eng., 3 S.S., 2 Sci., 2 Math	29.2%	34.5%	30.2%	28.1%	23.5%
1987					
4 Eng., 3 S.S., 3 Sci., 3 Math, 0.5 Comp., 2 F.L.[b]	12.0%	24.3%	12.7%	8.3%	5.5%
4 Eng., 3 S.S., 3 Sci., 3 Math, 0.5 Comp.[c]	16.3%	28.1%	17.2%	11.7%	8.6%
4 Eng., 3 S.S., 3 Sci., 3 Math, 2 F.L.	20.9%	41.9%	21.8%	16.1%	11.8%
4 Eng., 3 S.S., 3 Sci., 3 Math	28.6%	48.3%	29.7%	24.3%	17.9%
4 Eng., 3 S.S., 2 Sci., 2 Math	54.6%	71.8%	53.5%	57.2%	55.1%
Difference—1982 to 1987	**Increase, in percent**				
4 Eng., 3 S.S., 3 Sci., 3 Math, 0.5 Comp., 2 F.L.[b]	10.2%	18.2%	10.5%	7.6%	5.0%
4 Eng., 3 S.S., 3 Sci., 3 Math, 0.5 Comp.[c]	13.6%	21.0%	14.1%	10.7%	7.7%
4 Eng., 3 S.S., 3 Sci., 3 Math, 2 F.L.	12.1%	24.9%	11.7%	10.9%	8.4%
4 Eng., 3 S.S., 3 Sci., 3 Math	15.2%	27.2%	14.8%	14.2%	11.6%
4 Eng., 3 S.S., 2 Sci., 2 Math	25.4%	37.3%	23.4%	29.1%	31.6%

Source: National Center for Education Statistics, U.S. Department of Education, *Digest of Education Statistics 1992* (Washington, DC: U.S. Government Printing Office, October 1992), table 132, p. 133. Primary source: U.S. Department of Education, National Center for Education Statistics, "1987 High School Transcript Study," unpublished tabulations. Calculations are based on unrounded figures. Also in source: data by sex. *Notes:* (a) Eng. = English; S.S. = Social Studies; Sci. = Science; Comp. = Computer Science; and F.L. = Foreign Language. (b) The National Commission for Excellence in Education recommended that all college-bound high school students follow these courses as a minimum. (c) The National Commission for Excellence in Education recommended that all high school students follow these courses as a minimum.

★ 189 ★

Students in Top Schools and Bottom Schools

Percent of students in the top one-third[a] of schools and the bottom one-third of schools for grades four, eight, and twelve by race/ethnicity, 1990.

Grade and School Rank	Percent of students by race/ethnicity				
	Asian/ Pacific Islander	White	Black	Hispanic	American Indian
Grade 4					
Top one-third	36%	42%	7%	20%	24%
Bottom one-third	29%	17%	68%	47%	32%
Grade 8					
Top one-third	43%	34%	13%	14%	22%
Bottom one-third	20%	24%	68%	43%	50%
Grade 12					
Top one-third	46%	40%	13%	23%	23%
Bottom one-third	21%	15%	68%	44%	26%

Source: Ina V. S. Mullis, et al., *The State of Mathematics Achievement: NAEP'S 1990 Assessment of the Nation and the Trial Assessment of the States* (Washington, DC: National Center for Education Statistics, June 1991), table 2.11, p. 100. Also in source: data by community type, region, and parents' education. *Note:* (a) Top one-third and bottom one-third as measured by NAEP. The National Assessment of Educational Progress (NAEP) is referred to as "The Nation's Report Card."

★ 190 ★

Mathematics Proficiency, Grades Four, Eight, and Twelve

Average proficiency and percent of students at or above four anchor levels on the National Assessment of Educational Progress (NAEP)[a] mathematics assessment for grades four, eight, and twelve by race/ethnicity, 1990.

Grade	Percent of Total	Average Proficiency	Percentage of students at or above			
			Level 200	Level 250	Level 300	Level 350
Grade 4						
Asian/Pacific Islander	2	228	85	23	0	0
White	70	223	81	14	0	0
Black	15	194	41	1	0	0
Hispanic	11	201	52	3	0	0
American Indian	2	211	66	3	0	0
Grade 8						
Asian/Pacific Islander	3	285	99	86	32	2
White	71	272	99	77	18	0
Black	15	241	92	36	3	0
Hispanic	10	248	95	47	4	0
American Indian	1	248	97	47	4	0
Grade 12						
Asian/Pacific Islander	3	315	100	97	70	13
White	74	301	100	95	52	6
Black	14	270	100	74	16	0
Hispanic	8	278	100	79	25	1
American Indian	1	290	99	92	39	0

Source: Ina V. S. Mullis, et al., *The State of Mathematics Achievement: NAEP'S 1990 Assessment of the Nation and the Trial Assessment of the States* (Washington, DC: National Center for Education Statistics, June 1991), table 2.1, p. 83. *Note:* (a) The National Assessment of Educational Progress (NAEP) is referred to as "The Nation's Report Card."

★ 191 ★

Math Proficiency in Measurement, Grades Four, Eight and Twelve

Average percent correct for constructed-response[a] measurement questions on the National Assessment of Educational Progress (NAEP)[b] mathematics assessment for grades four, eight, and twelve by race/ethnicity, 1990.

Grade	Total	Asian/ Pacific Islander	White	Black	Hispanic
Grade 4	38%	44%	44%	19%	28%
Grade 8	59%	71%	65%	39%	48%
Grade 12	37%	50%	41%	21%	29%

Source: Ina V. S. Mullis, et al., *The State of Mathematics Achievement: NAEP'S 1990 Assessment of the Nation and the Trial Assessment of the States* (Washington, DC: National Center for Education Statistics, June 1991), table 5.3, p. 140. Also in source: data by sex. *Notes:* (a) Constructed-response questions are questions where the test taker must write in the response. No multiple-choice responses are provided. An example of question for fourth graders is: "60 inches= __ feet." (b) The National Assessment of Educational Progress (NAEP) is referred to as "The Nation's Report Card."

★ 192 ★

Math Proficiency in Numbers and Operations, Grades Four, Eight, and Twelve

Average percent correct for constructed-response[a] numbers and operations questions on the National Assessment of Educational Process (NAEP)[b] mathematics assessment for grades four, eight and twelve by race/ethnicity, 1990.

Grade	Total	Asian/ Pacific Islander	White	Black	Hispanic
Grade 4	61%	70%	65%	50%	53%
Grade 8	52%	64%	56%	41%	42%
Grade 12	61%	72%	64%	46%	48%

Source: Ina V. S. Mullis, et al., *The State of Mathematics Achievement: NAEP'S 1990 Assessment of the Nation and the Trial Assessment of the States* (Washington, DC: National Center for Education Statistics, June 1991), table 5.2, p. 138. Also in source: data by sex. *Notes:* (a) Constructed-response questions are questions where the test taker must write in the response. No multiple-choice responses are provided. (b) The National Assessment of Educational Progress (NAEP) is referred to as "The Nation's Report Card."

★ 193 ★

Math Proficiency in Geometry, Grades Four, Eight, and Twelve

Average percent correct for constructed-response[a] geometry questions on the National Assessment of Educational Process (NAEP)[b] mathematics assessment for grades four, eight, and twelve by race/ethnicity, 1990.

Grade	Total	Asian/ Pacific Islander	White	Black	Hispanic
Grade 4	35%	42%	39%	23%	27%
Grade 8	53%	64%	58%	35%	42%
Grade 12	35%	47%	38%	20%	27%

Source: Ina V.S. Mullis, et al., *The State of Mathematics Achievement: NAEP'S 1990 Assessment of the Nation and the Trial Assessment of the States* (Washington, DC: National Center for Education Statistics, June 1991), table 5.4, p. 142. Also in source: data by sex. *Notes:* (a) Constructed-response questions are questions where the test taker must write in the response. No multiple-choice responses are provided. (b) The National Assessment of Educational Progress (NAEP) is referred to as "The Nation's Report Card."

★ 194 ★

Math Proficiency in Algebra and Functions, Grades Four, Eight, and Twelve

Average percent correct for constructed-response[a] algebra and functions questions on the National Assessment of Educational Process (NAEP)[b] mathematics assessment for grades four, eight and twelve by race/ethnicity, 1990.

Grade	Total	Asian/ Pacific Islander	White	Black	Hispanic
Grade 4	56%	62%	59%	44%	47%
Grade 8	48%	58%	52%	33%	38%
Grade 12	32%	47%	35%	19%	23%

Source: Ina V. S. Mullis, et al., *The State of Mathematics Achievement: NAEP'S 1990 Assessment of the Nation and the Trial Assessment of the States* (Washington, DC: National Center for Education Statistics, June 1991), table 5.6, p. 144. Also in source: data by sex. *Notes:* (a) Constructed-response questions are questions where the test taker must write in the response. No multiple-choice responses are provided. (b) The National Assessment of Educational Progress (NAEP) is referred to as "The Nation's Report Card."

★ 195 ★

Math Proficiency in Problem-Solving, Grades Four, Eight, and Twelve

Average percent correct for constructed-response[a] problem-solving questions on the National Assessment of Educational Process (NAEP)[b] mathematics assessment for grades four, eight, and twelve by race/ethnicity, 1990.

Grade	Total	Asian/ Pacific Islander	White	Black	Hispanic
Grade 4	44%	50%	49%	27%	34%
Grade 8	52%	64%	57%	33%	41%
Grade 12	30%	37%	33%	17%	20%

Source: Ina V. S. Mullis, et al., *The State of Mathematics Achievement: NAEP'S 1990 Assessment of the Nation and the Trial Assessment of the States* (Washington, DC: National Center for Education Statistics, June 1991), table 5.7, p. 145. Also in source: data by sex. *Notes:* (a) Constructed-response questions are questions where the test-taker must write in the response. No multiple-choice responses are provided. (b) The National Assessment of Educational Progress (NAEP) is referred to as "The Nation's Report Card."

★ 196 ★

Math Proficiency: Fourth Graders

Percent of fourth grade students responding correctly to selected test items on the National Assessment of Educational Process (NAEP)[a] mathematics assessment by race/ethnicity, 1990.

Activity	Percent responding correctly			
	Total	Asian	White	Black
Numbers and operations				
Solve story problem (addition)[b]	88.8	89.7	90.6	83.3
Represent place value[b]	67.3	76.2	71.4	56.4
Determine largest number[b]	80.8	84.8	83.5	72.0
Subtract whole numbers[c]	82.0	94.1	85.9	69.1
Subtract whole numbers[c]	61.7	77.8	65.1	49.7
Apply part-whole relationship[c]	18.4	28.2	21.9	7.5
Measurement				
Apply concept of area[b]	31.0	44.8	33.6	20.0
Find greatest monetary value[b]	81.3	86.5	85.2	71.0
Determine greatest metric unit[b]	50.9	57.2	53.4	41.7
Read a ruler[c]	23.5	25.6	28.6	4.9
Convert inches to feet[c]	32.5	43.6	37.0	15.2
Find perimeter of rectangle[c]	33.9	35.1	38.1	20.0
Geometry				
Apply transformational geometry[b]	69.4	74.7	70.6	66.8
Apply properties of a cube[b]	35.6	43.0	37.8	28.8
Identify parallel lines[b]	49.3	39.9	54.6	35.5
Apply properties of a square[c]	56.6	63.0	61.0	43.6
Draw an obtuse angle[c]	5.8	17.7	9.1	6.5
Visualize a geometric figure[c]	62	56.6	67.5	47.3
Data Analysis, Statistics, and Probability				
Read data on bar graph[b]	79.7	83.6	83.5	67.6
Interpret bar graph data[b]	41.6	49.9	26.9	26.6
Interpret pie chart data[b]	43.3	54.4	47.3	31.4
Complete a bar graph[c]	50.7	61.2	58.3	25.6
Algebra and Functions				
Apply concept of equality[b]	30.6	36.1	35.8	16.0
Solve an inequality[b]	17.4	19.1	18.0	13.6
Represent words with symbols[b]	50.1	59.5	53.7	38.5
Solve number sentence (addition)[c]	94.0	98.0	95.3	90.3
Solve number sentence (addition)[c]	69.1	78.1	71.9	60.9
Solve a number sentence[c]	52.1	63.5	57.0	34.4
Estimation				
Estimate length in inches[b]	44.5	57.8	42.5	22.5
Estimate length in centimeters[b]	52.2	49.3	51.8	57.3
Estimate relative height[b]	45.7	38.7	49.5	33.0
Problem solving				
Apply place value[b]	32.1	30.7	35.6	20.4
Visualize geometric shape[c]	71.6	78.2	77.8	49.5
Apply place value[c]	65.9	73.4	72.3	46.1
Apply concept of even number[c]	6.1	9.5	7.9	0.2

Source: Ina V. S. Mullis, et al., *The State of Mathematics Achievement: NAEP's 1990 Assessment of the Nation and the Trial Assessment of the States* (Washington, DC: National Center for Education Statistics, June 1991), table 2.1, p. 83. *Notes:* (a) The National Assessment of Education Progress (NAEP) is referred to as "The Nation's Report Card." (b) Question was multiple choice. (c) Question was "constructed response," i.e., the respondent had to solve the problem and supply the answer.

★ 197 ★

Tenth Graders' Test Achievement, 1990

Mean scores and distribution by quartile of tenth graders on history, mathematics, reading, and science tests by race/ethnicity, 1990.

Achievement test	Total	Race/ethnicity				
		Asian	White	Black	Hispanic	American Indian
Tenth graders' achievement, by standardized score[a]						
History	54.0	55.1	54.6	51.6	53.7	46.0
Mathematics	53.5	57.3	54.5	49.3	52.2	44.9
Reading	53.3	54.3	54.3	49.8	52.2	45.0
Science	53.8	55.7	54.8	49.7	52.6	45.9
Distribution of tenth graders' achievement by score quartile[b]						
History						
Lower quartile	23.9%	22.1%	18.7%	38.9%	38.3%	54.0%
Lower middle quartile	24.6%	23.9%	23.4%	31.3%	26.7%	15.6%
Upper middle quartile	25.7%	23.6%	27.2%	20.4%	23.8%	20.7%
Upper quartile	25.8%	30.4%	30.8%	9.4%	11.2%	9.7%
Mathematics						
Lower quartile	23.6%	14.4%	18.0%	44.0%	36.7%	54.6%
Lower middle quartile	25.3%	20.2%	23.6%	31.1%	31.6%	24.7%
Upper middle quartile	25.3%	26.8%	27.6%	17.2%	19.9%	14.9%
Upper quartile	25.8%	38.6%	30.7%	7.8%	11.9%	5.9%
Reading						
Lower quartile	24.0%	21.7%	19.2%	40.0%	33.6%	52.5%
Lower middle quartile	24.0%	21.7%	19.2%	40.0%	33.6%	52.5%
Upper middle quartile	25.4%	25.6%	27.1%	19.8%	23.1%	14.4%
Upper quartile	25.7%	27.9%	30.6%	11.0%	11.5%	6.7%
Science						
Lower quartile	24.1%	22.0%	17.2%	49.8%	39.2%	42.5%
Lower middle quartile	24.4%	21.0%	22.6%	29.9%	31.0%	35.4%
Upper middle quartile	25.9%	26.8%	29.1%	13.8%	19.8%	10.8%
Upper quartile	25.6%	30.2%	31.1%	6.5%	10.0%	11.4%

Source: National Center for Education Statistics, U.S. Department of Education, *Digest of Education Statistics 1992* (Washington, DC: U.S. Government Printing Office, October 1992), table 120, p. 124. Primary source: U.S. Department of Education, National Center for Education Statistics, *High School and Beyond and National Longitudinal Study* surveys, unpublished tabulations. (This table was prepared May 1992.) Also in source: Data by sex, socioeconomic status, and control of school. *Notes:* (a) Standardized scores with a mean of 50 and standard deviation of 10. (b) Twenty-five percent of all students fall into each one of the quartile groupings.

ACT Test Scores

★ 198 ★

ACT Scores

Scores for ACT (American College Test) sections by academic preparation and race/ethnicity, 1992.

Race/Ethnicity	Core[a] or more					Less than core[a]				
	English	Math	Reading	Science Reasoning	Composite	English	Math	Reading	Science Reasoning	Composite
Asian American/Pacific Islander	21.5	24.0	22.3	21.9	22.5	18.6	21.0	19.3	19.7	19.8
Afro-American/Black	18.0	18.0	18.0	18.0	18.1	15.5	15.9	15.9	16.5	16.1
American Indian/ Alaskan Native	19.0	19.5	20.1	20.0	19.8	16.3	16.6	17.4	17.8	17.1
Caucasian	22.2	22.0	23.2	22.5	22.6	19.4	18.7	20.3	19.9	19.7
Mexican American/ Chicano	19.2	19.9	19.8	19.7	19.8	16.4	16.9	17.1	17.5	17.1
Puerto Rican/Cuban/ Other	20.2	20.7	21.0	20.4	20.7	16.8	17.3	17.7	17.8	17.6

Source: 1992 ACT Assessment Results, Summary Report, National (Iowa City, IA: American College Testing), table 2, p. 4. All average scores are on the scale for the Enhanced ACT Assessment, which was introduced in October 1989. *Notes:* (a) Core curriculum is 4 units of English, 3 units of Mathematics, 3 units of Social Studies, 3 units of Sciences.

★ 199 ★

ACT Scores by Academic Preparation

Average ACT (American College Test) scores of test-takers taking more or less than high school core[a] curriculum, by race/ethnicity, 1992.

Subject	Mean test score					
	Asian/Pacific Islander	Afro-American/ Black	American Indian/Alaskan Native	Caucasian	Mexican American, Chicano	Puerto Rican/ Hispanic
Total Group	(N=22,771)	N=75,356)	(N=9,784)	(N=604,469)	(N=26,163)	(N=13,013)
English	20.5	16.6	17.3	20.9	17.7	18.7
Usage/Mech	10.5	8.0	8.4	10.6	8.7	9.3
Rhetoric Skills	10.4	8.4	8.8	10.7	9.0	9.5
Mathematics	23.0	16.9	17.8	20.4	18.4	19.2
Pre/Elementary Algebra	11.9	8.2	8.8	10.7	9.3	9.8
Alg/Crd-Geometry	11.7	8.6	8.9	10.2	9.2	9.6
Plane Geometry/ Trigonometry	11.8	8.4	9.1	10.4	9.3	9.8
Reading	21.2	16.9	18.4	21.9	18.4	19.5
Social Studies/Science	10.6	8.1	9.0	10.8	8.8	9.4
Arts/Literature	11.0	8.8	9.5	11.6	9.8	10.4

[Continued]

★ 199 ★

ACT Scores by Academic Preparation (Continued)

Average ACT (American College Test) scores of test-takers taking more or less than high school core[a] curriculum, by race/ethnicity, 1992.

Subject	Mean test score					
	Asian/Pacific Islander	Afro-American/ Black	American Indian/Alaskan Native	Caucasian	Mexican American, Chicano	Puerto Rican/ Hispanic
Scientific Reasoning	21.2	17.2	18.6	21.3	18.6	19.2
Composite	21.6	17.0	18.1	21.3	18.4	19.3
Core or more	(N=14,945)	(N=35,166)	(N=4,026)	(N=320,849)	(N=12,787)	(N=7,026)
English	21.5	18.0	19.0	22.2	19.2	20.2
Usage/Mech	11.1	8.8	9.4	11.4	9.6	10.2
Rhetoric Skills	10.9	9.1	9.7	11.4	9.7	10.3
Mathematics	24.0	18.0	19.5	22.0	19.9	20.7
Pre/Elementary-Algebra	12.6	9.1	10.0	11.7	10.4	10.8
Algebra/Geometry	12.2	9.2	9.7	11.0	9.9	10.4
Plane Geometry/ Trigonometry	12.3	8.9	10.0	11.2	10.1	10.5
Reading	22.3	18.0	20.1	23.2	19.8	21.0
Social Studies/Science	11.1	8.6	9.9	11.5	9.4	10.1
Arts/Literature	11.7	9.6	10.5	12.4	10.7	11.4
Scientific Reasoning	21.9	18.0	20.0	22.5	19.7	20.4
Composite	22.5	18.1	19.8	22.6	19.8	20.7
Less than core	(N=7,336)	(N=39,465)	(N=5,255)	(N=277,995)	(N=13,185)	(N=5,608)
English	18.6	15.5	16.3	19.4	16.4	16.8
Usage/Mech	9.3	7.3	7.7	9.7	7.8	8.1
Rhetoric Skills	9.4	7.8	8.2	9.9	8.2	8.5
Mathematics	21.0	15.9	16.6	18.7	16.9	17.3
Pre/Elementary-Algebra	10.7	7.4	8.0	9.5	8.3	8.5
Algebra/Geometry	10.6	8.0	8.3	9.3	8.4	8.7
Plane Geometry/ Trigonometry	10.7	8.0	8.5	9.5	8.6	8.8
Reading	19.3	15.9	17.4	20.3	17.1	17.7
Social Studies/Science	9.7	7.6	8.5	10.0	8.1	8.5
Arts/Literature	9.8	8.1	8.8	10.7	9.0	9.3
Scientific Reasoning	19.7	16.5	17.8	19.9	17.5	17.8
Composite	19.8	16.1	17.1	19.7	17.1	17.6

Source: ACT High School Profile Report, HS Graduating Class 1992 (Iowa City, IA: American College Testing), table 1, p. 3. Data for 1992 are based on the performance of 832,217 students who graduated from high school in the spring of 1992 and who took the ACT Assessment on national test dates during their junior or senior year. *Note:* (a) Core curriculum is 4 units of English, 3 units of Mathematics, 3 units of Social Studies, 3 units of Sciences.

★ 200 ★

ACT Scores by Academic Preparation and Family Income

Numbers of American College Test (ACT) test takers and average scores by family income and race/ethnicity for students taking high school core curriculum[a] and less than core curriculum by race/ethnicity, 1992.

National Reference Group	Annual Family Income					
	Less than $18,000		$18,000-35,999		$36,000 or more	
	N	Composite	N	Composite	N	Composite
All Graduates						
Total group	136,498	18.6	242,076	20.3	357,553	21.7
Core	58,812	20.0	120,604	21.6	207,677	22.9
Less than core	75,456	17.5	118,683	18.9	146,703	20.1
Asian American/Pacific Islander						
Total group	5,191	18.7	6,720	21.0	9,540	23.5
Core	3,075	19.7	4,366	21.8	6,704	24.2
Less than core	1,982	17.3	2,218	19.5	2,660	21.8
Afro-American/Black						
Total group	32,261	16.2	23,603	17.2	14,748	18.5
Core	13,811	17.3	11,428	18.2	7,943	19.5
Less than core	18,172	15.5	11,930	16.3	6,681	17.3
American Indian/Alaskan Native						
Total group	3,402	16.8	3,261	18.4	2,567	19.6
Core	1,110	18.4	1,405	19.7	1,300	21.0
Less than core	2,026	16.2	1,727	17.4	1,198	18.2
Caucasian						
Total group	74,670	19.9	185,396	20.8	307,247	21.9
Core	31,851	21.5	91,905	22.2	178,214	23.0
Less than core	41,925	18.7	91,633	19.4	126,683	20.3
Mexican American/Chicano						
Total group	9,568	17.3	9,040	18.6	6,232	19.9
Core	4,181	18.7	4,490	19.7	3,563	21.0
Less than core	5,321	16.2	4,486	17.4	2,631	18.5
Puerto Rican/Cuban/Other Hispanic						
Total group	3,996	17.4	4,133	19.3	4,029	21.3
Core	1,805	18.9	2,261	20.5	2,569	22.1
Less than core	2,052	16.1	1,778	17.7	1,354	19.6

Source: 1992 ACT Assessment Results, Summary Report, National (Iowa City, IA: American College Testing), table 4, p. 6. All average scores are on the scale for the Enhanced ACT Asessment, which was introduced in October 1989. *Note:* (a) Core curriculum is 4 units of English, 3 units of Mathematics, 3 units of Social Studies, 3 units of Sciences.

★ 201 ★

ACT: Profile of Test takers

Test takers and American College Test (ACT) average composite score by race/ethnicity, 1992.

Race/ethnicity	Number	Composite	Percent
Asian American/Pacific American	22,771	21.6	3%
Afro-American/Black	75,356	17.0	9%
American/Alaskan Native	9,784	18.1	1%
Caucasian American/White	604,469	21.3	73%
Mexican American/Chicano	26,163	18.4	3%
Puerto Rican/Hispanic	13,013	19.3	2%
Other	12,790	19.2	2%
No Response	15,454	21.2	2%
Did Not Respond	52,417	20.4	6%

Source: ACT High School Profile Report, High School Graduating Class 1992 (Iowa City, IA: American College Testing), table 11, p. 11. All average scores are on the scale for the Enhanced ACT Asessment, which was introduced in October 1989.

★ 202 ★

ACT: Trends in Scores, 1988-1992

Number of American College Test (ACT) test takers and average composite score by race/ethnicity, 1988 to 1992.

National Reference Group	Number of students	Composite
Total Graduates		
1988	842,322	20.8
1989	855,171	20.6
1990	817,096	20.6
1991	796,983	20.6
1992	832,217	20.6
Asian American/Pacific Islander		
1988	15,854	21.8
1989	17,751	21.9
1990	19,081	21.7
1991	20,854	21.6
1992	22,771	21.6
Afro-American/Black		
1988	69,509	16.6
1989	74,227	16.6
1990	71,197	17.0
1991	72,681	17.0
1992	75,356	17.0
American Indian/Alaskan Native		
1988	8,096	17.6
1989	9,115	17.5
1990	9,101	18.0
1991	9,358	18.2
1992	9,784	18.1

[Continued]

★ 202 ★

ACT: Trends in Scores, 1988-1992 (Continued)

Number of American College Test (ACT) test takers and average composite score by race/ethnicity, 1988 to 1992.

National Reference Group	Number of students	Composite
Caucasian		
1988	650,999	21.4
1989	661,010	21.3
1990	605,361	21.2
1991	588,060	21.3
1992	604,469	21.3
Mexican American/Chicano		
1988	19,717	18.3
1989	22,685	18.1
1990	22,806	18.3
1991	23,837	18.4
1992	26,163	18.4
Puerto Rican/Cuban/Other Hispanic		
1988	8,622	19.4
1989	9,880	19.3
1990	10,669	19.3
1991	11,135	19.3
1992	13,013	19.3

Source: 1992 ACT Assessment Results, Summary Report, National (Iowa City, IA: American College Testing), table 8, pp. 9-10. All average scores are on the scale for the Enhanced ACT Assessment, which was introduced in October 1989. Averages for 1988 and 1989 are based on scores estimated from a concordance table linking the scale for the original version of the ACT Assessment to that of the Enhanced ACT Assessment.

★ 203 ★

ACT: Trends in Scores by Academic Preparation, 1988-1992

Number of American College Test (ACT) test takers and average composite score by academic preparation and race/ethnicity, 1988 to 1992.

National Reference Group	Core[a] or more		Less than core[a]	
	N	Composite	N	Composite
All graduates				
1988	342,676	22.7	461,726	19.4
1989	380,253	22.5	445,173	19.1
1990	370,379	22.3	394,540	19.1
1991	387,404	22.1	374,976	19.1
1992	419,073	22.0	372,166	19.1
Asian American/Pacific Islander				
1988	8,627	23.1	6,697	20.3
1989	10,437	23.2	6,729	20.1
1990	11,734	22.8	6,714	20.0
1991	13,401	22.6	7,173	19.8
1992	14,945	22.5	7,336	19.8
Afro-American/Black				
1988	25,054	18.2	43,444	15.7
1989	29,549	18.1	43,508	15.6
1990	29,814	18.2	40.127	16.1
1991	32,468	18.2	39,729	16.1
1992	35,166	18.1	39,465	16.1
American Indian/Alaskan Native				
1988	2,366	20.1	5,013	16.8
1989	2,892	19.8	5,453	16.6
1990	3,163	19.9	5,208	17.1
1991	3,727	19.8	5.098	17.2
1992	4,026	19.8	5,255	17.1
Caucasian				
1988	278,582	23.2	364,211	20.0
1989	305,928	23.1	347,334	19.8
1990	290,929	22.8	301,253	19.7
1991	299,557	22.7	282,708	19.7
1992	320,849	22.6	277,995	19.7
Mexican American/Chicano				
1988	7,436	20.2	11,668	17.1
1989	9,030	20.1	12,731	16.8
1990	9,770	19.9	12,349	17.2
1991	11,143	19.9	12,555	17.2
1992	12,787	19.8	13,185	17.1
Puerto Rican/Cuban/Other Hispanic				
1988	3,931	21.4	4,249	17.7
1989	4,763	21.2	4,575	17.5
1990	5,250	20.9	4,886	17.6
1991	5,991	20.7	5006	17.6
1992	7,026	20.7	5,608	17.6

Source: 1992 ACT Assessment Results, Summary Report, National (Iowa City, IA: American College Testing), table 3, p. 5. All average scores are on the scale for the Enhanced ACT Assessment which was introduced in October 1989. Averages for 1988 and 1989 are based on scores estimated from a concordance table linking the scale for the original version of the ACT Assessment to that of the Enhanced ACT Assessment. *Note:* (a) Core curriculum is 4 units of English, 3 units of Mathematics, 3 units of Social Studies, 3 units of Sciences.

Carnegie Units

★ 204 ★

Carnegie Units: Academic and Vocational

Carnegie units[a] completed by high school graduates by curriculum track and race/ethnicity, 1969, 1982, and 1987.

Characteristic	Total Carnegie units			Total academic units			Total vocational units		
	1969	1982	1987	1969	1982	1987	1969	1982	1987
Total	20.5	21.3	22.8	14.9	14.1	15.6	3.7	4.6	4.4
Race/ethnicity									
Asian	22.9	22.1	23.9	15.6	15.8	17.8	3.8	3.1	2.9
White	20.3	21.4	22.9	15.2	14.4	15.7	3.4	4.5	4.5
Black	20.7	21.0	22.1	13.5	13.6	15.0	4.8	4.8	4.5
Hispanic	21.8	21.1	22.5	13.4	12.9	15.1	5.1	5.3	4.3
American Indian	–	21.3	23.2	–	13.3	15.3	–	5.1	4.7

Source: U.S. Department of Education, National Center for Education Statistics, *The Condition of Education, 1992* (Washington, DC: U.S. Government Printing Office, June 1992), table 25-1, p. 246. Primary source: U.S. Department of Education, National Center for Education Statistics, *The 1969 Study of Academic Growth and Prediction: High School and Beyond* (base year study) and 1987 High School Transcript Study; National Assessment of Vocational Education Statistics, The Secondary School Taxonomy, 1989. A dash (–) reflects the fact that the *1969 Study of Academic Growth and Prediction* did not include a category for American Indians. Also in source: Data on "personal use" Carnegie units earned. *Note:* (a) Carnegie units are a standard of measurement that represents one credit for the completion of a one-hour one-year course. Carnegie units are divided among three curricular areas: academic, vocational, and personal use. Within each area, courses are assigned as follows: 1) Academic: Mathematics (basic, general applied, pre-algebra, algebra 1, geometry, advanced/other, advanced calculus); Science (survey, biology, chemistry, physics); English (survey, literature, composition, speech); Social Studies (American history, world history, American government, humanities/other); Fine Arts (fine arts and crafts, music, drama/dance); Foreign Languages (survey, English for speakers of other languages, years 1-4 by language); 2) Vocational: Consumer and Homemaking Education; General Labor Market Preparation (typewriting 1, introductory industrial arts, work experience/career exploration, general labor market skills); Specific Labor Market Preparation (agriculture/renewable resources, business, marketing and distribution, health occupations, occupational home economics, trade and industry, technical and communications); 3) Personal Use: General Skills; Health (physical education); Religion; Military Science.

★ 205 ★

Carnegie Units: Academic by Subject, 1982 and 1987

Average number of Carnegie units[a] earned by high school graduates by race/ethnicity, 1982 and 1987.

Subject	Total, all students	Asian	White	Black	Hispanic
Total, 1987	23.0	24.5	23.1	22.5	22.9
English	4.03	4.31	3.99	4.14	4.23
History/social studies	3.33	3.64	3.30	3.31	3.23
Math	2.97	3.72	2.98	2.90	2.77
Computer science	0.43	0.57	0.45	0.35	0.36
Science	2.59	3.17	2.64	2.39	2.33
Foreign language	1.46	2.17	1.50	1.12	1.27
Arts	1.43	1.12	1.48	1.20	1.35
Physical education	1.97	2.57	1.94	2.01	2.40
Total, 1982	21.2	22.0	21.4	20.5	20.8
English	3.80	3.94	3.78	3.90	3.79
History/social studies	3.10	3.04	3.15	2.97	2.94
Math	2.54	3.11	2.59	2.44	2.22
Computer science	0.11	0.19	0.12	0.10	0.07
Science	2.19	2.56	2.27	1.79	1.79
Foreign language	1.05	1.81	1.13	0.78	0.78
Arts	1.39	1.22	1.45	1.27	1.27
Physical education	1.93	2.21	1.12	2.13	2.13

Source: U.S. Department of Education, National Center for Education Statistics, *Digest of Education Statistics 1992* (Washington, DC: U.S. Government Printing Office, October 1992), table 129, p. 131. Primary source: U.S. Department of Education, National Center for Education Statistics, 1987 High School Transcript Study. (This table was prepared December 1988.) *Note:* (a) Carnegie units are a standard of measurement that represents one credit for the completion of a one-hour one-year course. Carnegie units are divided among three curricular areas: academic, vocational, and personal use. Within each area, courses are assigned as follows: 1) Academic: Mathematics (basic, general applied, pre-algebra, algebra 1, geometry, advanced/other, advanced calculus); Science (survey, biology, chemistry, physics); English (survey, literature, composition, speech); Social Studies (American history, world history, American government, humanities/other); Fine Arts (fine arts and crafts, music, drama/dance); Foreign Languages (survey, English for speakers of other languages, years 1-4 by language); 2) Vocational: Consumer and Homemaking Education; General Labor Market Preparation (typewriting 1, introductory industrial arts, work experience/career exploration, general labor market skills); Specific Labor Market Preparation (agriculture/renewable resources, business, marketing and distribution, health occupations, occupational home economics, trade and industry, technical and communications); 3) Personal Use: General Skills; Health (physical education); Religion; Military Science.

★ 206 ★

Carnegie Units: Trends in Vocational, Earned by Category

Carnegie units[a] completed by high school graduates by vocational education category and race/ethnicity, 1969, 1982, and 1987.

Race	Total			Consumer and home-making education			General labor market preparation			Specific labor market preparation		
	1969	1982	1987	1969	1982	1987	1969	1982	1987	1969	1982	1987
Total	3.7	4.6	4.4	0.5	0.7	0.6	1.1	1.0	0.9	2.1	2.9	2.9
Race/ethnicity												
Asian	3.8	3.1	2.9	0.2	0.3	0.3	1.6	0.9	0.7	2.0	1.9	1.9
White	3.4	4.5	4.5	0.4	0.6	0.6	1.0	1.0	0.9	2.0	2.9	3.0
Black	4.8	4.8	4.5	0.7	0.9	0.7	1.6	1.0	1.0	2.5	2.9	2.8
Hispanic	5.1	5.3	4.3	0.4	0.9	0.6	1.9	1.2	1.0	2.8	3.2	2.7
American Indian	–	5.1	4.7	–	0.5	0.6	–	1.1	0.9	–	3.5	3.2

Source: U.S. Department of Education, National Center for Education Statistics, *The Condition of Education 1992* (Washington, DC: U.S. Government Printing Office, June 1992), table 25-2, p. 24. Primary source: U.S. Department of Education, National Center for Education Statistics, *The 1969 Study of Academic Growth and Prediction: High School and Beyond,* (base year study) and 1987 High School Transcript Study. A dash (–) reflects the fact that *The 1969 Study of Academic Growth and Prediction* did not include a category for American Indians. *Note:* (a) Carnegie units are a standard of measurement that represents one credit for the completion of a one-hour one-year course. Carnegie units are divided among three curricular areas: academic, vocational, and personal use. Courses in the vocational area are assigned as follows: Consumer and Homemaking Education; General Labor Market Preparation (typewriting 1, introductory industrial arts, work experience/career exploration, general labor market skills); Specific Labor Market Preparation (agriculture/renewable resources, business, marketing and distribution, health occupations, occupational home economics, trade and industry, technical and communications).

★ 207 ★

Carnegie Units: Trends in Vocational as Percent of Total

Carnegie units earned as a percentage of total vocational education units by race/ethnicity, 1969, 1982, and 1987.

Race	Consumer and homemaking education			General labor market preparation			Specific labor market preparation		
	1969	1982	1987	1969	1982	1987	1969	1982	1987
Total	12.6%	15.1%	14.1%	37.5%	27.6%	26.0%	49.8%	57.3%	59.9%
Race/ethnicity									
Asian	5.7%	9.4%	11.3%	43.4%	36.4%	28.0%	50.9%	54.2%	60.7%
White	12.9%	14.1%	13.7%	38.1%	28.1%	26.3%	49.0%	57.8%	60.0%
Black	13.3%	20.5%	17.3%	34.3%	25.8%	25.8%	52.5%	53.7%	56.9%
Hispanic	9.0%	17.2%	15.2%	38.4%	25.6%	26.3%	52.6%	57.2%	58.5%
American Indian	–	11.7%	14.3%	–	25.5%	22.8%	–	62.8%	62.9%

Source: U.S. Department of Education, National Center for Education Statistics, *The Condition of Education, 1992* (Washington, DC: U.S. Government Printing Office, June 1992), p. 247. Primary source: U.S. Department of Education, National Center for Education Statistics, *The 1969 Study of Academic Growth and Prediction: High School and Beyond* (base year study) and 1987 High School Transcript Study. The dash (–) reflects the fact that the *1969 Study of Academic Growth and Prediction* did not include a category for American Indians. *Note:* (a) Carnegie units are a standard of measurement that represents one credit for the completion of a one-hour one-year course. Carnegie units are divided among three curricular areas: academic, vocational, and personal use. Courses are assigned in the vocational area as follows: Consumer and Homemaking Education; General Labor Market Preparation (typewriting 1, introductory industrial arts, work experience/career exploration, general labor market skills); Specific Labor Market Preparation (agriculture/renewable resources, business, marketing and distribution, health occupations, occupational home economics trade and industry, technical and communications).

Degrees Conferred

★ 208 ★

Degrees Conferred, Total: 1980-1990

Number of degrees conferred and percent of total (all categories) by race/ethnicity, 1980 to 1990 (1982-83 excluded).

Race/ethnicity	1980-81		1984-85		1986-87		1988-89		1989-90	
	Number	Percent	Number	Percent	Number	Percent	Number	Percent	Number	Percent
Total	1,333,162	100.0	1,781,911	100.0	1,822,550	100.0	1,864,779	100.0	1,926,635	100.0
Asian/Pacific Islander	27,409	2.1	46,013	2.6	56,337	3.1	64,853	3.5	67,749	3.5
White non-Hispanic	1,138,994	85.4	1,492,230	83.7	1,519,632	83.4	1,543,364	82.8	1,589,127	82.5
Black, non-Hispanic	82,002	6.2	111,386	6.3	110,359	6.1	111,096	6.0	116,217	6.0
Hispanic	30,290	2.3	54,706	3.1	56,180	3.1	60,470	3.2	65,863	3.4
American Native/ Alaskan Native	4,949	0.4	8,822	0.5	8,679	0.5	8,724	0.5	9,330	0.5
Nonresident alien	49,518	3.7	68,754	3.9	71,363	3.9	76,272	4.1	78,349	4.1

Source: U.S. Department of Education, National Center for Education Statistics, *Race/Ethnicity Trends in Degrees Conferred by Institutions of Higher Education: 1980-81 through 1989-90* (Washington, DC: U.S. Department of Education, 1992), table 2, p. 8. Primary sources: U.S. Department of Education, National Center for Education Statistics, *Higher Education General Information Survey,* "Degrees and Other Formal Awards Conferred in Institutions of Higher Education," various years; and Integrated Postsecondary Education Data Systems (IPEDS), "Completions" and "Consolidated" surveys, various years. Data for 1980-81 and 1984-85 do not include imputations for race/ethnicity. Data for 1988-89 have been revised from previously published figures.

★ 209 ★

Degrees Conferred by Type: 1979 and 1989

Numbers of bachelor's, master's, and doctoral degrees conferred and percent change for Asian American and total students, 1979 and 1989.

Degree	1979		1989		Percentage increase	
	Total	Asian American	Total	Asian American	Total	Asian American
Bachelor's	919,540	15,407	1,015,239	38,219	11%	148%
Master's	300,255	5,496	308,872	10,714	3%	95%
Doctorate	31,239	428	34,319	624	10%	46%

Source: Eugenia Escueta and Eileen O'Brien, "Asian Americans in Higher Education: Trends and Issues," *Research Briefs* 2, no. 4 (1991): table 3, p. 5. Primary sources: National Center for Education Statistics, "Integrated Postsecondary Education Data System (IPEDS)," unpublished tabulations, 1990; and National Research Council, *Summary Report 1989: Doctorate Recipients from United States Universities,* 1990.

★ 210 ★

Degrees Conferred Relative to White Males by Sex, Degree Level, and Field

Race-sex field concentration ratio[a] by race/ethnicity, sex, and bachelor's and doctoral degrees by field of study for the academic year ending 1990.

Degree conferred	Men			Women			
	Asian	Black	Hispanic	Asian	White	Black	Hispanic
Bachelor's degrees							
Humanities and social/ behavioral sciences	0.77	1.00	1.09	1.10	1.12	0.98	1.30
Natural sciences	1.87	0.77	1.00	1.70	0.70	0.75	0.67
Computer science and engineering	2.12	0.89	1.10	0.65	0.17	0.33	0.23
Education	0.27	1.03	0.87	0.69	3.22	1.71	2.51
Business and management	0.67	0.98	0.87	0.87	0.74	0.90	0.73
Other technical/ professional	0.56	1.30	0.99	1.20	1.69	1.98	1.48
Doctor's degrees							
Humanities and social/ behavioral sciences	0.61	1.19	1.16	0.94	1.13	0.82	1.54
Natural sciences	1.01	0.32	0.93	1.11	0.57	0.19	0.49
Computer science and engineering	2.54	0.41	0.69	0.59	0.23	0.10	0.14
Education	0.28	2.22	1.20	1.02	2.03	3.72	1.57
Business and management[b]	1.92	0.97	0.58	0.65	0.72	0.17	0.19

Source: U.S. Department of Education, National Center for Education Statistics, *The Condition of Education 1992* (Washington, DC: U.S. Government Printing Office, June 1992), p. 70. Primary sources: U.S. Department of Education, National Center for Education Statistics, Integrated Postsecondary Education Data Systems (IPEDS) survey of degrees conferred. *Note:* (a) The race-sex field concentration ratio is calculated as the percentage of a race/ethnicity/sex group earning degrees who majored in a specific field divided by the percentage of white men earning degrees in the same field. (b) Principally composed of health sciences, communications, and communication technologies at the bachelor's degree level and of health sciences, agriculture, and natural resources at the doctor's degree level.

★ 211 ★

First Professional Degrees Conferred: 1980-1990

Number and percent of total professional degrees conferred by race/ethnicity, 1980 to 1990(1982-83 excluded).

Race/ethnicity	1980-81		1984-85		1986-87		1988-89		1989-90	
	Number	Percent	Number	Percent	Number	Percent	Number	Percent	Number	Percent
Total	71,340	100.0%	71,057	100.0%	71,617	100.0%	70,856	100.0%	70,736	100.0%
Asian/Pacific Islander	1,456	2.0%	1,816	2.6%	2,270	3.2%	2,976	4.2%	3,336	4.7%
White non-Hispanic	64,551	90.5%	63,219	89.0%	62,688	87.5%	61,214	86.4%	60,291	85.2%
Black non-Hispanic	2,931	4.1%	3,029	4.3%	3,420	4.8%	3,148	4.4%	3,389	4.8%
Hispanic	1,541	2.2%	1,884	2.7%	2,051	2.9%	2,269	3.2%	2,427	3.4%
American Native/ Alaskan Native	192	0.3%	248	0.3%	304	0.4%	264	0.4%	257	0.4%
Nonresident alien	669	0.9%	861	1.2%	884	1.2%	985	1.4%	1,036	1.5%

Source: U.S. Department of Education, National Center for Education Statistics, *Race/Ethnicity Trends in Degrees Conferred by Institutions of Higher Education: 1980-81 through 1989-90* (Washington, DC: U.S. Department of Education, 1992), table 2, p. 8. Primary sources: U.S. Department of Education, National Center for Education Statistics, *Higher Education General Information Survey,* "Degrees and Other Formal Awards Conferred in Institutions of Higher Education," various years; and Integrated Postsecondary Education Data Systems (IPEDS), "Completions" and "Consolidated" surveys, various years. Data for 1980-81 and 1984-85 do not include imputations for race/ethnicity. Data for 1988-89 have been revised from previously published figures.

★ 212 ★

Doctorates Conferred: 1980-1990

Number and percent of total doctoral degrees conferred by race/ethnicity, 1980 to 1990 (1982-1983 excluded).

Race/ethnicity	1980-81		1984-85		1986-87		1988-89		1989-90	
	Number	Percent	Number	Percent	Number	Percent	Number	Percent	Number	Percent
Total	32,839	100.0	32,307	100.0	34,033	100.0	35,659	100.0	37,980	100.0
Asian/Pacific Islander	877	2.7	1,106	3.4	1,097	3.2	1,324	3.7	1,282	3.4
White non-Hispanic	25,908	78.9	23,934	74.1	24,435	71.8	24,882	69.8	25,793	67.9
Black, non-Hispanic	1,265	3.9	1,154	3.6	1,060	3.1	1,065	3.0	1,145	3.0
Hispanic	456	1.4	677	2.1	750	2.2	628	1.8	783	2.1
American Native/Alaskan Native	130	0.4	119	0.4	104	0.3	85	0.2	102	0.3
Nonresident alien	4,203	12.8	5,317	16.5	6,587	19.4	7,675	21.5	8,875	23.4

Source: U.S. Department of Education, National Center for Education Statistics, *Race/Ethnicity Trends in Degrees Conferred by Institutions of Higher Education: 1980-81 through 1989-90* (Washington, DC: U.S. Department of Education, 1992), table 2, p. 8. Primary sources: U.S. Department of Education, National Center for Education Statistics, *Higher Education General Information Survey,* "Degrees and Other Formal Awards Conferred in Institutions of Higher Education," various years; and Integrated Postsecondary Education Data Systems (IPEDS), "Completions" and "Consolidated" surveys, various years. Data for 1980-81 and 1984-85 do not include imputations for race/ethnicity. Data for 1988-89 have been revised from previously published figures.

★ 213 ★

Master's Degrees Conferred, Total: 1980-1990

Number and percent of total degrees conferred by race/ethnicity, 1980 to 1990 (1982-83 excluded).

Level of degree and race/ethnicity	1980-81		1984-85		1986-87		1988-89		1989-90	
	Number	Percent	Number	Percent	Number	Percent	Number	Percent	Number	Percent
Total	294,183	100.0	280,421	100.0	289,341	100.0	309,770	100.0	321,992	100.0
Asian/Pacific Islander	6,282	2.1	7,782	2.8	8,558	3.0	10,336	3.3	10,646	3.3
White non-Hispanic	241,216	82.0	223,628	79.7	228,870	79.1	242,756	78.4	251,518	78.1
Black, non-Hispanic	17,133	5.8	13,939	5.0	13,867	4.8	14,096	4.6	15,331	4.8
Hispanic	6,461	2.2	6,864	2.4	7,044	2.4	7,282	2.4	7,905	2.5
American Native/ Alaskan Native	1,034	0.4	1,256	0.4	1,104	0.4	1,086	0.4	1,108	0.3
Nonresident alien	22,057	7.5	26,952	9.6	29,898	10.3	34,214	11.0	35,484	11.0

Source: U.S. Department of Education, National Center for Education Statistics, *Race/Ethnicity Trends in Degrees Conferred by Institutions of Higher Education: 1980-81 through 1989-90* (Washington,DC: U.S. Department of Education, 1992), table 2, p. 8. Primary sources: U.S. Department of Education, National Center for Education Statistics, *Higher Education General Information Survey,* "Degrees and Other Formal Awards Conferred in Institutions of Higher Education," various years; and Integrated Postsecondary Education Data Systems (IPEDS), "Completions" and "Consolidated" surveys, various years. Data for 1980-81 and 1984-85 do not include imputations for race/ethnicity. Data for 1988-89 have been revised from previously published figures.

★ 214 ★

Bachelor's Degrees Conferred: 1980-1990

Number and percent of total bachelor's degrees conferred by race/ethnicity, 1980 to 1990 (1982-1983 excluded).

Level of degree and race/ethnicity	1980-81		1984-85		1986-87		1988-89		1989-90	
	Number	Percent	Number	Percent	Number	Percent	Number	Percent	Number	Percent
Total	934,800	100.0	968,311	100.0	991,260	100.0	1,016,350	100.0	1,046,930	100.0
Asian/Pacific Islander	18,794	2.0	25,395	2.6	32,618	3.3	37,686	3.7	39,059	3.7
White non-Hispanic	807,319	86.4	826,106	85.3	841,820	84.9	859,699	84.6	882,996	84.3
Black, non-Hispanic	60,673	6.5	57,473	5.9	56,555	5.7	58.065	5.7	61,074	5.8
Hispanic	21,832	2.3	25,874	2.7	26,990	2.7	29,910	2.9	32,686	3.1
American Native/ Alaskan Native	3,593	0.4	4,246	0.4	3,971	0.4	3,954	0.4	4,338	0.4
Nonresident alien	22,589	2.4	29,217	3.0	29,306	3.0	27,036	2.7	26,777	2.6

Source: U.S. Department of Education, National Center for Education Statistics, *Race/Ethnicity Trends in Degrees Conferred by Institutions of Higher Education: 1980-81 through 1989-90* (Washington, DC: U.S. Department of Education, 1992), table 2, p. 8. Primary sources: U.S. Department of Education, National Center for Education Statistics, *Higher Education General Information Survey,* "Degrees and Other Formal Awards Conferred in Institutions of Higher Education," various years; and Integrated Postsecondary Education Data Systems (IPEDS), "Completions" and "Conslidated" surveys, various years. Date for 1980-81 and 1984-85 do not include imputations for race/ethnicity. Data for 1988-89 have been revised from previously published figures.

★ 215 ★

Associate's Degrees Conferred: 1984-1990

Number and percent of total associate's degrees conferred by race/ethnicity, 1984 to 1990.

Race/ethnicity	1984-85		1986-87		1988-89		1989-90	
	Number	Percent	Number	Percent	Number	Percent	Number	Percent
Total	429,815	100.0	436,299	100.0	432,144	100.0	448,997	100.0
Asian/Pacific Islander	9,914	2.3	11,794	2.7	12,531	2.9	13,426	3.0
White non-Hispanic	355,343	82.7	361,819	82.9	354,813	82.1	368,529	82.1
Black, non-Hispanic	35,791	8.3	35,457	8.1	34,722	8.0	35,278	7.9
Hispanic	19,407	4.5	19,345	4.4	20,381	4.7	22,062	4.9
American Native/Alaskan Native	2,953	0.7	3,196	0.7	3,335	0.8	3,525	0.8
Nonresident alien	6,407	1.5	4,688	1.1	6,362	1.5	6,177	1.4

Source: U.S. Department of Education, National Center for Education Statistics, *Race/Ethnicity Trends in Degrees Conferred by Institutions of Higher Education: 1980-81 through 1989-90* (Washington, DC: U.S. Department of Education,1992), table 2, p. 8. Primary sources: U.S. Department of Education, National Center for Education Statistics, *Higher Education General Information Survey,* "Degrees and Other Formal Awards Conferred in Institutions of Higher Education," various years; and Integrated Postsecondary Education Data Systems (IPEDS), "Completions" and "Consolidated" surveys, various years. Data not available on associate degrees conferred until 1984-85. Data for 1988-89 have been revised from previously published figures.

★ 216 ★

First Professional Degrees Conferred by Field of Study and Sex: 1989-90

Numbers of professional degrees[a] conferred on Asian/Pacific Islander and total students by sex and field of study, 1989-90.

Major field of study	Total	Total — Asian/ Pacific Islander	Men — Total	Men — Asian/ Pacific Islander	Women — Total	Women — Asian/ Pacific Islander
All fields, total[b]	70,736	3,336	43,819	1,966	26,917	1,370
Dentistry (D.D.S. or D.M.D.)	4,093	448	2,830	256	1,263	192
Medicine (M.D.)	15,115	1,351	9,977	867	5,138	484
Optometry (O.D.)	1,072	85	646	39	426	46
Osteopathic Medicine (D.O.)	1,561	63	1,119	44	442	19
Pharmacy (D.Phar.)	1,191	229	482	85	709	144
Podiatry (Pod.D. or D.P.) or Podiatric Medicine (D.P.M.)	675	40	493	27	182	13
Veterinary Medicine (D.V.M.)	2,160	27	901	8	1,259	19
Chiropractic Medicine (D.C. or D.C.M.)	2,581	65	1,906	47	6785	18
Law, general (L.L.B. or J.D.)	36,437	858	21,059	439	15,378	419
Theological professions, general (B.D., M.Div., Rabbi)	5,851	170	4,406	154	1,445	16

Source: National Center for Education Statistics, U.S. Department of Education, *Digest of Education Statistics 1992* (Washington, DC: U.S. Government Printing Office, October 1992), table 259, p. 283. Primary sources: U.S. Department of Education, National Center for Education Statistics, Integrated Postsecondary Education Data System (IPEDS), "Completions" survey. (This table was prepared November 1991.) *Notes:* (a) Preliminary data. (b) Reported racial/ethnic distributions of students by level of degree, field of degree, and sex were used to estimate race/ethnicity for students whose race/ethnicity was not reported. Excludes 183 men and 61 women whose racial/ethnic group and field of study were not available.

★ 217 ★

Doctorates Conferred by Field of Study and Sex: 1989-90

Number of dotorates conferred on Asian/Pacific Islander and total students by sex and field of study, 1989-90.

Major field of study	Total	Asian/ Pacific Islander	Men		Women	
			Total	Asian/ Pacific Islander	Total	Asian/ Pacific Islander
All fields, total	37,980	1,282	24,218	910	13,762	372
Agriculture and natural resources	1,272	33	1,029	22	243	11
Architecture and environmental design	97	3	69	3	28	0
Area and ethnic studies	128	7	68	2	60	5
Business and management	1,142	58	863	51	279	7
Communications	269	5	144	4	125	1
Computer and information sciences	623	29	533	28	90	1
Education	6,922	95	2,931	38	3,991	57
Engineering	4,953	315	4,519	286	434	29
Engineering technologies	12	1	12	1	0	0
Foreign languages	512	8	210	2	302	6
Health sciences	1,543	63	697	37	846	26
Home economics	303	6	89	2	214	4
Law	113	1	90	1	23	0
Letters	1,266	31	566	15	700	16
Liberal/general studies	31	0	13	0	18	0
Library and archival science	41	1	12	0	29	1
Life sciences	3,844	166	2,395	98	1,449	68
Mathematics	915	41	746	30	169	11
Military sciences	0	0	0	0	0	0
Multi-interdisciplinary studies	311	12	203	9	108	3
Parks and recreation	35	1	18	1	17	0
Philosophy and religion	432	10	324	7	108	3
Physical sciences	4,168	157	3,364	123	804	34
Protective services	37	1	24	0	13	1
Psychology	3,353	62	1,414	33	1,939	29
Public affairs	495	16	229	7	266	9
Social sciences	3,023	95	2,037	62	986	33
Theology	1,298	43	1,147	39	151	4
Visual and peforming arts	842	22	472	9	370	13

Source: National Center for Education Statistics, U.S. Department of Education, *Digest of Education Statistics 1991* (Washington, DC: U.S. Government Printing Office, October 1992), table 256, p. 280. Primary source: U.S. Department of Education, National Center for Education Statistics, Integrated Postsecondary Education Data System (IPEDS), "Completions" survey. (This table was prepared November 1991.)

★ 218 ★

Doctorates Conferred, Science and Engineering

Number of doctorates conferred on Asian and total students by major field in science and engineering, biennially 1981 to 1991.

Race/ethnicity and year	1981	1983	1985	1987	1989	1991
Asian U.S. citizens						
All fields, total	465	492	516	542	626	762
Science and Engineering	330	345	373	443	487	577
Physical Sciences, total	46	66	76	67	75	81
Physics and Astronomy	20	27	19	18	33	22
Chemistry	26	39	57	49	42	59
Earth/Atmosphere/Ocean	4	8	8	9	11	7
Math	20	13	14	18	13	23
Computer/Information Science	4	6	2	10	18	32
Agriculture and Biological Science, total	98	116	114	123	127	162
Agricultural Science	8	15	8	17	7	8
Biological Science	90	101	106	106	120	154
Social Science	48	35	35	43	32	44
Psychology	33	35	34	38	38	43
Engineering, total[a]	77	66	90	135	173	185
Chemical Eng.	3	11	20	20	34	25
Electrical Eng.	20	10	13	37	45	59
Mechanical Eng.	13	9	21	25	25	26
All U.S. citizens						
All fields, total	25,061	24,359	23,370	22,983	23,400	24,721
Science and Engineering, total	13,544	13,403	12,947	12,819	13,312	13,923
Physical Science, total	1,956	2,064	2,043	2,080	1,973	2,048
Physics and Astronomy	721	709	698	699	675	737
Chemistry	1,235	1,355	1,345	1,381	1,298	1,311
Earth/Atmosphere/Ocean	472	483	442	425	529	584
Math	482	411	376	345	393	439
Computer/Information Science	168	180	189	243	338	379
Agriculture and Biological Science, total	3,891	3,859	3,831	3,565	3,724	3,799
Agricultural Science	594	649	683	584	607	55
Biological Science	3,297	3,210	3,148	2,981	3,117	3,248
Social Science	2,294	2,199	1,982	1,856	1,807	1,901
Psychology	3,111	3,044	2,805	2,747	2,684	2,796
Engineering, Total	1,170	1,163	1,279	1,558	1,864	1,977
Chemical Eng.	128	162	218	280	352	316
Electrical Eng.	246	218	247	291	394	465
Mechanical Eng.	158	145	193	241	259	279

Source: National Science Foundation, *Science and Engineering Doctorate Awards: 1991* (Washington, DC: National Science Foundation 92-309, 1992), table 3, p. 19. Also in source: Data on blacks, Hispanics, whites, and native Americans. *Note:* (a) Includes doctorate recipients whose engineering fields are not separately shown.

★ 219 ★

Doctorates Conferred on Men, Science and Engineering

Number of doctorates conferred on Asian and total male U.S. citizens by major field in science and engineering, biennially 1981 to 1991.

Field of study	1981	1983	1985	1987	1989	1991
Asian male U.S. citizens						
All fields, total	315	312	329	369	441	469
Science and Engineering, total	246	235	260	320	365	395
Physical Sciences, total,	41	50	53	52	62	62
Physics and astronomy	19	23	16	16	28	17
Chemistry	22	27	37	36	34	45
Earth/Atmosphere/Ocean	3	4	7	8	9	4
Math	14	12	12	14	12	18
Computer/Information Science	3	3	2	6	14	25
Agriculture and Biological Science, total	65	67	74	75	77	94
Agricultural Science	5	9	7	14	4	6
Biological Science	60	58	67	61	73	88
Social Science	33	17	18	27	21	21
Psychology	16	19	18	14	20	12
Engineering, total[a]	71	63	76	124	150	159
Chemical Eng.	2	11	15	18	28	19
Electrical Eng.	19	10	11	35	41	56
Mechanical Eng.	13	8	20	25	24	23
All male U.S. citizens						
All fields,	16,360	15,120	14,223	13,575	13,397	13,885
Science and Engineering, total	10,046	9,457	9,018	8,718	8,751	8,970
Physical Science, total	1,732	1,779	1,720	1,719	1,572	1,648
Physics and Astronomy	676	658	636	634	616	666
Chemistry	1,056	1,121	1,084	1,085	956	982
Earth/Atmosphere/Ocean	425	402	354	342	414	441
Math	402	335	306	280	300	351
Computer/Information Science	148	153	165	193	266	298
Agriculture and Biological Science, total	2,859	2,688	2,679	2,372	2,378	2,414
Agricultural Science	506	549	563	468	451	427
Biological Science	2,353	2,139	2,116	1,904	1,927	1,987
Social Science	1,617	1,444	1,238	1,144	1,060	1,064
Psychology	1,746	1,576	1,396	1,259	1,146	1,044
Engineering , total	1,117	1,080	1,160	1,409	1,615	1,710
Chemical Eng.	120	149	194	239	295	270
Electrical Eng.	238	212	232	278	371	433
Mechanical Eng.	154	139	178	231	240	246

Source: National Science Foundation, *Science and Engineering Doctorate Awards: 1991* (Washington, DC: National Science Foundation 92-309, 1992), table 3, p. 22. Also in source: Data on blacks, Hispanics, whites, and native Americans. *Note:* (a) Includes doctorate recipients whose engineering fields are not separately shown.

★ 220 ★

Doctorates Conferred on Women, Science and Engineering

Number of doctorates conferred on Asian and total female students by major field in science and engineering, biennially 1981 to 1991.

Field of study	1981	1983	1985	1987	1989	1991
Asian female U.S. citizens						
All fields, total	150	180	187	173	185	293
Science and Engineering, total	84	110	113	123	122	182
Physical Sciences, total	5	16	23	15	13	19
Physics and astronomy	1	4	3	2	5	5
Chemistry	4	12	20	13	8	14
Earth/Atmosphere/Ocean	1	4	1	1	2	3
Math	6	1	2	4	1	5
Computer/Information Science	1	3	-	4	4	7
Agriculture and Biological Science, total	33	49	40	48	50	68
Agricultural Science	3	6	1	3	3	2
Biological Science	30	43	39	45	47	66
Social Science	15	18	17	16	11	23
Psychology	17	16	16	24	18	31
Engineering, total[a]	6	3	14	11	23	26
Chemical Eng.	1	-	5	2	6	6
Electrical Eng.	1	-	2	2	4	3
Mechanical Eng.	-	1	1	-	1	3
All female U.S. citizens						
All fields, total, all groups	8,701	9,239	9,147	9,408	10,003	10,836
Science and Engineering, total	3,498	3,946	3,929	4,101	4,561	4,953
Physical Science, total	224	285	323	361	401	400
Physics and Astronomy	45	51	62	65	59	71
Chemistry	179	234	261	296	342	329
Earth/Atmosphere/Ocean	47	81	88	83	115	143
Math	80	76	70	65	93	88
Computer/Information Science	20	27	24	50	72	81
Agriculture and Biological Science, total	1,032	1,171	1,152	1,193	1,346	1,385
Agricultural Science	88	100	120	116	156	124
Biological Science	944	1,071	1,032	1,077	1,190	1,261
Social Science	677	755	744	712	747	837
Psychology	1,365	1,468	1,409	1,488	1,538	1,752
Engineering, total	53	83	119	149	249	267
Chemical Eng.	8	13	24	41	57	46
Electrical Eng.	8	6	15	13	23	32
Mechanical Eng.	4	6	15	10	19	33

Source: National Science Foundation, *Science and Engineering Doctorate Awards: 1991* (Washington, DC: National Science Foundation 92-309, 1992), table 3, p. 19. Also in source: Data on blacks, Hispanics, whites, and native Americans. *Note:* (a) Includes doctorate recipients whose engineering fields are not separately shown.

★ 221 ★

Doctorates Conferred on Non-U.S. Citizens, Science and Engineering

Number of doctorates in science and engineering conferred by Asian country of citizenship, biennially 1981 to 1991.

Country of citizenship, year of doctorate	1981	1983	1985	1987	1989	1991
Sciences, total, all foreign citizens	2,612	2,809	3,223	3,649	4,193	5,650
China, Peoples Republic of	-	8	89	206	454	1,181
China, unspecified	-	-	3	6	6	104
Hong Kong	71	68	66	65	55	87
India	203	205	246	299	285	381
Indonesia, Republic of	35	38	27	29	40	45
Japan	46	72	72	68	86	92
Korea	85	132	190	309	442	655
Pakistan	18	25	28	42	46	58
Philippines	37	38	40	31	36	70
Taiwan	226	327	356	389	427	509
Thailand	60	61	71	75	60	70
Engineering, total, all foreign citizens	1,243	1,489	1,734	1,887	2,306	2,854
China, Peoples Republic of	-	5	48	84	156	415
China, unspecified	1	-	-	3	8	37
Hong Kong	29	30	28	22	38	28
India	176	178	212	204	252	338
Indonesia, Republic of	4	9	15	13	12	17
Japan	31	31	25	15	19	28
Korea	50	104	133	238	308	412
Pakistan	8	13	18	17	15	32
Philippines	3	6	5	4	9	14
Taiwan	218	277	387	398	427	573
Thailand	23	27	25	20	16	18

Source: National Science Foundation, *Science and Engineering Doctorate Awards: 1991* (Washington, DC: National Science Foundation 92-309, 1992), table 5, p. 44-45. A dash (–) indicates lack of data. Also in source: Data on U.S. citizens.

★ 222 ★

Doctorates Conferred on Non-U.S. Citizens with Permanent Visas, Science and Engineering

Number of doctorates in science and engineering conferred on non-citizens with permanent visas by Asian country of citizenship, biennially 1981 to 1991.

Country of citizenship, permanent visas	1981	1983	1985	1987	1989	1991
Sciences, total, non-U.S. citizens with permanent visas	592	579	614	731	756	871
China, Peoples Republic of	-	-	5	13	26	64
China, unspecified	-	-	1	-	1	12
Hong Kong	10	12	13	10	10	9
India	32	40	40	58	59	63
Indonesia, Republic of	2	-	1	3	3	6
Japan	3	7	7	8	12	15
Korea	16	28	28	22	30	51
Pakistan	2	4	1	8	2	9
Philippines	6	3	7	4	4	11
Taiwan	64	73	70	74	75	71
Thailand	3	8	2	12	4	7
Engineering, total non-U.S. citizens with permanent visas	301	319	315	355	365	381
China, Peoples Republic of	-	-	1	7	8	23
China, unspecified	1	-	-	2	2	3
Hong Kong	2	6	4	9	5	7
India	35	35	34	29	35	42
Indonesia, Republic of	1	1	-	2	2	3
Japan	3	4	1	2	1	5
Korea	12	17	19	14	22	36
Pakistan	1	4	5	4	3	2
Philippines	1	-	-	-	1	-
Taiwan	57	68	88	77	67	87
Thailand	3	1	4	1	-	1

Source: National Science Foundation, *Science and Engineering Doctorate Awards: 1991* (Washington, DC: National Science Foundation 92-309, 1992), table 5, pp. 44-45. A dash (–) indicates lack of data. Also in source: Data on U.S. citizens.

★ 223 ★

Doctorates Conferred on Non-U.S. Citizens with Temporary Visas, Science and Engineering

Numbers of doctorates in science and engineering conferred on non-U.S. citizens with temporary visas by Asian country of citizenship, biennially 1981 to 1991.

Country of citizenship, temporary visas	1981	1983	1985	1987	1989	1991
Science, total non-U.S. citizens with temporary visas	2,020	2,230	2,609	2,918	3,437	4,779
China, Peoples Republic of	-	8	84	193	428	1,117
China, unspecified	-	-	2	6	5	92
Hong Kong	61	56	53	55	47	78
India	171	165	206	241	226	318
Indonesia, Republic of	33	38	26	26	37	39
Japan	43	65	65	60	74	77
Korea	69	104	162	287	412	604
Pakistan	16	21	27	34	44	49
Philippines	31	35	33	27	32	59
Taiwan	162	254	286	315	352	438
Thailand	57	53	69	63	56	63
Engineering, total non-U.S. citizens with temporary visas	942	1,170	1,419	1,532	1,941	2,473
China, Peoples Republic of	-	5	47	77	148	392
China, unspecified	-	-	-	1	6	34
Hong Kong	27	24	24	13	33	21
India	141	143	178	175	217	296
Indonesia, Republic of	3	8	15	11	10	14
Japan	28	27	24	13	18	23
Korea	38	87	114	224	286	376
Pakistan	7	9	13	13	12	30
Philippines	2	6	5	4	8	14
Taiwan	161	209	299	321	360	486
Thailand	20	26	21	19	16	17

Source: National Science Foundation, *Science and Engineering Doctorate Awards: 1991* (Washington, DC: National Science Foundation 92-309, 1992), table 5, p. 44-45. A dash (–) indicates lack of data. Also in source: Data on U.S. citizens, and non-citizens with permanent visas.

★ 224 ★

Master's Degrees Conferred on Men by Field of Study: 1989-90

Master's degrees conferred on men by institutions of higher education by race/ethnicity and field of study, 1989-1990.

Field of study	Asian/ Pacific Islander	White non- Hispanic	Black non- Hispanic	Hispanic	American Native/ Alaskan Native	Non- resident alien
Total	6,070	112,976	5,492	3,566	465	24,338
Agriculture/natural resources	30	1,499	36	26	7	647
Architecture/ environmental design	78	1,514	59	70	0	500
Area/ethnic studies	25	489	18	26	4	94
Business/management	1,902	40,334	1,805	1,039	132	5,771
Communications	60	1,300	79	38	4	231
Computer/information sciences	688	3.926	158	105	6	2,085
Education	254	17,315	1,171	699	106	1,289
Engineering/related technologies	1,682	12,170	332	377	33	6,835
Fine/applied arts	90	3,010	129	100	15	405
Foreign languages	12	413	13	53	1	135
Health professions	194	3,542	169	123	21	485
Home economics	6	238	10	4	1	51
Law	14	778	28	22	1	468
Letters	64	2,647	56	88	13	429
Library science	21	819	34	21	3	62
Life sciences	101	1,785	53	49	8	381
Mathematics	112	1,351	39	32	4	667
Military sciences	0	0	0	0	0	0
Physical sciences	150	2,675	64	55	6	1,058
Psychology	44	2,552	139	105	14	138
Public affairs/services	145	5,455	691	258	43	564
Social sciences	214	4,618	220	154	26	1,526
Theology	115	2,362	118	55	11	337
Interdisciplinary studies	69	2,184	71	67	6	180

Source: U.S. Department of Education, National Center for Education Statistics, *Race/Ethnicity Trends in Degrees Conferred by Institutions of Higher Education: 1980-81 through 1989-90* (Washington, DC: U.S. Department of Education, 1992), table 6, p. 19-22. Primary sources: U.S. Department of Education, National Center for Education Statistics, *Higher Education General Information Survey,* "Degrees and Other Formal Awards Conferred in Institutions of Higher Education," various years; and Integrated Postsecondary Education Data Systems (IPEDS), "Completions" and "Consolidated" surveys, various years. Also in source: Data for 1980-81 to 1988-89.

★ 225 ★

Master's Degrees Conferred on Women by Field of Study: 1989-90

Master's degrees conferred on women by institutions of higher education by race/ethnicity and field of study, 1989-1990.

Field of study	Asian/ Pacific Islander	White non- Hispanic	Black non- Hispanic	Hispanic	American Native/ Alaskan Native	Non- resident alien
Total	4,576	138,542	9,839	4,339	643	11,146
Agriculture/natural resources	29	819	14	20	4	242
Architecture/environmental design	50	900	53	33	7	228
Area/ethnic studies	31	374	24	25	5	83
Business/management	1,102	20,661	1,539	592	61	2,265
Communications	95	2,067	156	44	6	289
Computer/information sciences	364	1,511	101	28	2	669
Education	769	56,229	4,414	1,836	299	1,676
Engineering/related technologies	330	2,167	115	72	9	726
Fine/applied arts	174	3,875	117	88	20	523
Foreign languages	30	920	17	130	2	269
Health professions	439	13,605	763	330	62	621
Home economics	44	1,545	95	31	5	123
Law	14	311	14	14	0	205
Letters	120	4,406	123	134	19	450
Library science	72	2,978	138	33	14	154
Life sciences	135	1,883	62	45	6	353
Mathematics	82	944	35	15	2	394
Military sciences	0	0	0	0	0	0
Physical sciences	99	936	27	26	3	348
Psychology	122	5,286	353	201	25	252
Public affairs/services	232	10,145	1,301	416	49	275
Social sciences	158	3,381	227	130	34	731
Theology	44	1,413	64	23	3	141
Interdisciplinary studies	41	2,186	87	73	6	129

Source: U.S. Department of Education, National Center for Education Statistics, *Race/Ethnicity Trends in Degrees Conferred by Institutions of Higher Education: 1980-81 through 1989-90* (Washington, DC: U.S. Department of Education, 1992), table 6, pp. 19-22. Primary sources: U.S. Department of Education, National Center for Education Statistics, *Higher Education General Information Survey,* "Degrees and Other Formal Awards Conferred in Institutions of Higher Education," various years, and Integrated Postsecondary Education Data Systems (IPEDS), "Completions" and "Consolidated" surveys, various years. Also in source: Data for 1980-81 to 1988-89.

★ 226 ★

Bachelor's Degrees Conferred on Men by Field of Study: 1989-90

Bachelor's degrees conferred on men by institutions of higher education by race/ethnicity and field of study, 1989-90.

Field of study	Asian/ Pacific Islander	White non-Hispanic	Black non-Hispanic	Hispanic	American Native/ Alaskan Native	Non-resident alien
Total	19,617	413,469	23,276	14,871	1,828	17,040
Agriculture/natural resources	138	8,119	200	146	49	303
Architecture/environmental design	289	4,554	205	247	16	326
Area/ethnic studies	81	1,403	128	82	13	53
Business/management	3,643	114,068	6,313	3,581	392	4,707
Communications	312	17,836	1,177	480	75	311
Computer/information sciences	1,392	14,564	1,119	548	56	1,499
Education	264	20,438	1,189	643	157	289
Engineering/related technologies	5,647	5,256	2,393	2,205	188	5,118
Fine/applied arts	485	13,221	675	478	68	398
Foreign languages	87	2,468	78	296	6	75
Health professions	403	7,717	515	318	38	244
Home economics	41	1,254	112	43	1	29
Law	11	434	31	25	7	2
Letters	510	18,219	699	536	78	206
Library science	1	13	1	0	0	1
Life sciences	1,613	14,863	672	670	74	433
Mathematics	501	6,406	349	207	24	325
Military Sciences	4	339	19	8	0	14
Physical sciences	607	9,478	304	228	53	421
Psychology	505	13,122	825	607	70	162
Public affairs/services	241	13,947	1,703	658	96	181
Social sciences	2,143	56,153	3,120	2,122	255	1,455
Theology	84	3,469	174	80	5	107
Interdisciplinary studies	615	16,128	1,275	663	107	381

Source: U.S. Department of Education, National Center for Education Statistics, *Race/Ethnicity Trends in Degrees Conferred by Institutions of Higher Education: 1980-81 through 1989-90* (Washington, DC: U.S. Department of Education, 1992), table 5, pp. 15-18. Primary sources: U.S. Department of Education, National Center for Education Statistics, *Higher Education General Information Survey,* "Degrees and Other Formal Awards Conferred in Institutions of Higher Education," various years; and Integrated Postsecondary Education Data Systems (IPEDS), "Completions" and "Consolidated" surveys, various years. Also in source: data for 1980-81 to 1988-89.

★ 227 ★

Bachelor's Degrees Conferred on Women by Field of Study: 1989-90

Bachelor's degrees conferred by institutions of higher education by race/ethnicity and field of study, 1989-90.

Field of study	Asian/ Pacific Islander	White non-Hispanic	Black non-Hispanic	Hispanic	American Native/ Alaskan Native	Non-resident alien
Total	19,442	469,527	37,798	17,815	2,510	9,737
Agriculture/natural resources	110	3,715	122	65	27	76
Architecture/environmental design	183	3,009	106	120	9	197
Area/ethnic studies	220	1,997	199	131	15	77
Business/management	4,683	95,331	9,413	3,601	435	2,914
Communications	623	26,804	2,319	861	102	383
Computer/information sciences	852	5,209	1,236	314	31	614
Education	667	74,829	3,200	2,210	441	388
Engineering/related technologies	1,275	8,208	879	385	29	527
Fine/applied arts	892	21,429	741	581	95	632
Foreign languages	290	6,698	256	835	23	214
Health professions	1,479	42,348	3,677	1,292	225	560
Home economics	369	11,820	823	260	65	170
Law	23	944	73	25	3	4
Letters	872	30,861	1,564	899	148	331
Library science	0	63	2	0	0	3
Life sciences	1,709	14,656	1,365	618	59	438
Mathematics	392	5,641	385	145	23	199
Military Sciences	1	24	5	2	0	1
Physical sciences	353	3,997	368	121	21	180
Psychology	1,173	32,700	2,442	1,461	148	371
Public affairs/services	275	15,085	2,703	828	174	141
Social sciences	2,172	42,265	4,028	1,959	258	995
Theology	38	1,078	68	16	7	36
Interdisciplinary studies	791	20,816	1,824	1,086	172	286

Source: U.S. Department of Education, National Center for Education Statistics, *Race/Ethnicity Trends in Degrees Conferred by Institutions of Higher Education: 1980-81 through 1989-90,* 1992, table 5, p. 15-18. Primary source: U.S. Department of Education, National Center for Education Statistics, *Higher Education General Information Survey,* "Degrees and Other Formal Awards Conferred in Institutions of Higher Education," various years, and Integrated Postsecondary Education Data Systems (IPEDS), "Completions" and "Consolidated" surveys, various years. Also in source: data for 1980-81 to 1988-89.

★ 228 ★

Associate's Degrees Conferred on Men by Field of Study: 1989-90

Associate's degrees conferred on men by institutions of higher learning by race/ethnicity and field of study, 1989-90.

Field of study	Asian/ Pacific Islander	White non-Hispanic	Black non-Hispanic	Hispanic	American Native/ Alaskan Native	Non-resident Alien
Total	6,470	154,301	13,171	9,810	1,436	2,972
Agriculture/natural resources	9	3,045	27	46	33	70
Architecture/environmental design	26	184	13	30	2	13
Area/ethnic studies	0	5	5	0	2	0
Business/management	1,053	26,429	2,958	1,508	212	591
Communications	33	1,809	137	89	7	18
Computer/info sciences	191	2,960	359	198	25	87
Education	19	1,832	269	114	52	25
Engineering/related technologies	2,139	40,491	3,007	2,444	307	582
Fine/applied arts	330	6,837	357	379	76	62
Foreign languages	6	51	2	10	6	3
Health professions	255	6,566	542	442	78	86
Home economics	114	2,343	183	66	12	28
Law	7	451	70	40	9	6
Letters	12	176	30	17	4	5
Library science	0	8	2	0	3	0
Life sciences	40	316	27	32	6	18
Mathematics	55	350	18	47	8	11
Military sciences	1	77	26	10	0	0
Physical sciences	76	1,092	59	61	5	24
Psychology	2	220	34	25	3	1
Public affairs/services	207	10,635	798	656	109	86
Social sciences	56	881	177	120	23	15
Theology	12	332	14	24	0	7
Interdisciplinary studies	1,827	47,211	4,057	3,452	454	1,234

Source: U.S. Department of Education, National Center for Education Statistics, *Race/Ethnicity Trends in Degrees Conferred by Institutions of Higher Education: 1980-81 through 1989-90* (Washington, DC: U.S. Department of Education, 1992), table 4, pp. 11-14. Primary sources: U.S. Department of Education, National Center for Education Statistics, *Higher Education General Information Survey*, "Degrees and Other Formal Awards Conferred in Institutions of Higher Education," various years; and Integrated Postsecondary Education Data Systems (IPEDS), "Completions" and "Consolidated" surveys, various years. Also in source: data for 1980-81 to 1988-89.

★ 229 ★

Associate's Degrees Conferred on Women by Field of Study: 1989-90

Associate's degrees conferred on women by institutions of higher learning by race/ethnicity and field of study, 1989-90.

Field of study	Asian/ Pacific Islander	White non-Hispanic	Black non-Hispanic	Hispanic	American Native/ Alaskan Native	Non-resident alien
Total	6,956	214,228	22,107	12,252	2,089	3,205
Agriculture/natural resources	15	1,503	20	23	13	28
Architecture/environmental design	62	1,490	51	87	5	48
Area/ethnic studies	0	39	5	0	2	10
Business/management	2,265	59,199	7,733	3,587	540	905
Communications	31	1,320	131	54	7	36
Computer/information sciences	174	2,727	572	188	50	73
Education	63	4,702	461	309	124	48
Engineering/related technologies	264	4,079	482	243	34	59
Fine/applied arts	212	5,040	230	217	50	133
Foreign languages	1	202	6	31	5	6
Health professions	1,002	48,463	4,306	1,660	364	364
Home economics	294	5,711	826	456	55	142
Law	47	3,474	273	134	15	21
Letters	15	336	27	19	7	12
Library science	4	85	3	1	5	1
Life sciences	45	432	48	56	7	7
Mathematics	23	211	3	21	6	7
Military sciences	0	14	0	1	0	0
Physical sciences	56	674	48	35	2	13
Psychology	16	635	78	84	6	6
Public affairs/services	78	4,711	874	276	83	24
Social sciences	47	1,219	162	112	39	18
Theology	4	241	9	6	0	4
Interdisciplinary studies	2,248	67,721	5,759	4,652	670	1,239

Source: U.S. Department of Education, National Center for Education Statistics, *Race/Ethnicity Trends in Degrees Conferred by Institutions of Higher Education: 1980-81 through 1989-90* (Washington, DC: U.S. Department of Education, 1992), table 4, p. 11-14. Primary sources: U.S. Department of Education, National Center for Education Statistics, *Higher Education General Information Survey,* "Degrees and Other Formal Awards Conferred in Institutions of Higher Education," various years; and Integrated Postsecondary Education Data Systems (IPEDS), "Completions" and "Consolidated" surveys, various years. Also in source: data for 1980-81 to 1988-89.

Profiles of Doctoral Recipients

★ 230 ★

Profile of Doctoral Recipients by Field of Study: 1989-90

Total number and percent of students who earned doctorate degrees[a] by race/ethnicity and major field of study, 1989-90.

| Race/ethnicity | All fields | Education | Engineering | Humanities | Life sciences | Physical sciences[b] | | | Social sciences/ psychology | Other professional fields |
						Total	Math	Business		
Doctor's degrees conferred (number)	36,027	6,484	4,892	3,820	6,613	5,859	892	1,038	6,076	1,245
Racial/ethnic group (%)										
Asian	4.9	1.7	15.0	2.4	5.5	6.9	6.0	8.8	2.9	3.5
American Indian	0.4	0.6	0.2	0.3	0.2	0.1	0.2	0.3	0.5	0.7
Black	3.8	8.2	1.7	2.3	1.9	0.9	1.0	2.3	4.3	5.7
Mexican-American	0.7	0.9	0.6	0.6	0.8	0.5	0.7	0.6	0.9	0.6
Puerto Rican	0.8	1.0	0.3	0.9	0.7	0.9	0.5	0.2	0.9	0.4
Other Hispanic	1.6	1.4	1.5	2.6	1.2	1.4	1.2	0.8	2.1	1.5
White	86.5	85.4	78.9	89.7	88.3	87.0	88.2	85.7	87.2	86.1
Other/unknown[c]	1.4	0.9	1.9	1.3	1.4	2.3	2.2	1.4	1.2	1.4

Source: National Center for Education Statistics, U.S. Department of Education, *Digest of Education Statistics 1992* (Washington, DC: U.S. Government Printing Office, October 1992), table 283, p. 295. Primary source: National Academy of Sciences, National Research Council, Office of Scientific and Engineering Personnel, *Summary Report 1990: Doctorate Recipients from United States Universities*. (This table was prepared February 1992.) The above classification of degrees by field differs somewhat from that in most publications of the National Center for Education Statistics (NCES). The major differences are that history is included under humanities rather than social sciences and psychology is included under social sciences. The number of degrees also differs slightly from that reported in the NCES "Degrees and Other Formal Awards Conferred" survey. The above tabulation excludes some non-research doctorate degrees such as doctor's degrees in theology. Because of rounding, percents may not add to 100. *Notes:* (a) Includes Ph.D., Ed.D., and comparable degrees at the doctoral level. Excludes first-professional degrees, such as M.D., D.D.S., and D.V.M. (b) Includes mathematics, computer science, physics and astronomy, chemistry, and earth, atmospheric, and marine science. (c) Includes 2,439 individuals who did not report their citizenship at time of doctorate.

★ 231 ★

Profile of Doctorate Recipients in Education: 1979-1990

Total number and percent by race/ethnicity of doctorate recipients[a], 1979-80 to 1989-90.

Race/ethnicity	1979-80	1980-81	1981-82	1982-83	1983-84	1984-85	1985-86	1986-87	1987-88	1988-89	1989-90
Number of doctorates	7,576	7,489	7,266	7,147	6,780	6,717	6,602	6,447	6,349	6,265	6,484
Race/ethnicity (%)											
Asian	1.3	1.8	1.7	1.9	1.5	1.7	1.6	1.7	2.4	1.9	1.7
American Indian	0.8	0.6	0.5	0.7	0.5	0.7	0.5	0.7	0.6	0.4	0.6
Black	8.8	8.8	9.5	8.1	8.5	8.6	8.0	7.3	7.5	8.0	8.2
Mexican American	0.8	1.1	1.2	1.3	1.2	1.2	1.4	1.3	1.2	0.9	0.9
Puerto Rican	0.4	0.6	0.7	0.7	0.6	1.0	0.9	0.9	0.8	1.0	1.0
Other Hispanic	1.1	0.7	1.0	0.9	0.8	1.0	1.3	1.3	0.9	1.2	1.4
White	83.1	83.1	83.6	84.8	85.1	84.5	84.8	85.1	85.3	85.7	85.4
Other/unknown	3.7	3.3	1.8	1.7	1.8	1.4	1.6	1.6	1.2	0.9	0.9

Source: National Center for Education Statistics, U.S. Department of Education, *Digest of Education Statistics 1992* (Washington, DC: U.S. Government Printing Office, October 1992), table 284, p. 296. Primary source: National Academy of Sciences, National Research Council, Office of Scientific and Engineering Personnel, *Doctorate Records File.* (This table was prepared February 1992.) The National Research Council's classification of degrees by field differs somewhat from that in most publications of the National Center for Education Statistics (NCES). The number of degrees also differs slightly from that reported in the NCES "Degrees and Other Formal Awards Conferred" survey. Because of rounding, percents may not add to 100. *Note:* (a) Longitudinal comparisons by race/ethnicity should be done with extreme care, due to periodic changes in the survey.

★ 232 ★

Profile of Doctorate Recipients in Engineering: 1979-1990

Total number and percent by race/ethnicity of doctorate recipients[a] in engineering, 1979-80 to 1989-90.

Race/ethnicity	1979-80	1980-81	1981-82	1982-83	1983-84	1984-85	1985-86	1986-87	1987-88	1988-89	1989-90
Number of doctorates	2,479	2,528	2,644	2,780	2,915	3,165	3,376	3,716	4,190	4,536	4,892
Race/ethnicity (%)											
Asian	17.9	19.2	16.8	16.7	16.5	17.6	15.2	17.1	15.5	16.2	15.0
American Indian	0.2	0.3	0.2	0.1	0.2	0.1	0.3	0.4	0.2	0.3	0.2
Black	1.1	1.3	1.4	1.9	1.0	2.1	1.4	1.3	1.4	1.4	1.7
Mexican American	0.1	0.1	0.3	0.3	0.4	0.4	0.3	0.4	0.5	0.6	0.6
Puerto Rican	0.2	0.3	0.7	0.4	0.5	0.3	0.6	0.2	0.6	0.3	0.3
Other Hispanic	1.5	0.6	1.4	1.3	1.4	0.7	1.1	1.1	1.8	1.2	1.5
White	73.5	74.4	75.2	76.1	76.4	74.5	78.2	76.2	77.0	77.4	78.9
Other/unknown	5.5	3.7	4.0	3.2	3.6	4.3	2.7	3.3	2.9	2.5	1.9

Source: National Center for Education Statistics, U.S. Department of Education, *Digest of Education Statistics 1992* (Washington, DC: U.S. Government Printing Office, October 1992), table 285, p. 296. Primary source: National Academy of Sciences, National Research Council, Office of Scientific and Engineering Personnel, *Doctorate Records File.* (This table was prepared February 1992.) The National Research Council's classification of degrees by field differs somewhat from that in most publications of the National Center for Education Statistics (NCES). The number of degrees also differs slightly from that reported in the NCES "Degrees and Other Formal Awards Conferred" survey. Because of rounding, percents may not add to 100. *Note:* (a) Longitudinal comparisons by race/ethnicity should be done with extreme care, due to periodic changes in the survey.

★ 233 ★

Profile of Doctorate Recipients in Humanities: 1979-1990

Total number and percent by race/ethnicity of doctorate recipients[a] in humanities, 1979-80 to 1989-90.

Race/ethnicity	1979-80	1980-81	1981-82	1982-83	1983-84	1984-85	1985-86	1986-87	1987-88	1988-89	1989-90
Number of doctorates	3,863	3,745	3,560	3,494	3,528	3,428	3,461	3,504	3,553	3,558	3,820
Race/ethnicity (%)[b]											
Asian	1.9	1.7	1.7	1.5	1.8	2.2	1.8	2.1	2.3	2.9	2.4
American Indian	0.3	0.4	0.2	0.2	0.2	0.3	0.2	0.4	0.2	0.2	0.3
Black	2.9	2.8	3.3	2.5	3.3	2.5	2.8	2.8	3.0	2.8	2.3
Mexican American	0.4	0.5	0.8	0.7	0.8	0.8	0.8	0.6	0.8	0.8	0.6
Puerto Rican	0.3	0.7	0.9	0.7	0.7	0.6	0.5	1.1	0.9	0.8	0.9
Other Hispanic	2.2	1.9	2.5	2.2	2.1	2.3	2.1	2.5	2.1	2.1	2.6
White	87.3	88.0	87.8	89.4	88.4	88.9	89.6	88.4	89.1	88.2	89.7
Other/unknown	4.6	4.1	2.8	2.7	2.7	2.4	2.2	2.2	1.6	2.2	1.3

Source: National Center for Education Statistics, U.S. Department of Education, *Digest of Education Statistics 1992* (Washington, DC: U.S. Government Printing Office, October 1992), table 286, p. 297. Primary source: National Academy of Sciences, National Research Council, Office of Scientific and Engineering Personnel, *Doctorate Records File.* (This table was prepared February 1992.) The National Research Council's classification of degrees by field differs somewhat from that in most publications of the National Center for Education Statistics (NCES). The major differences are that history is included under humanities rather than social sciences and that psychology is included under social sciences. The number of degrees also differs slightly from that reported in the NCES "Degrees and Other Formal Awards Conferred" survey. Because of rounding, percents may not add to 100. *Notes:* (a) Includes agricultural, biological, and health sciences. (b) Longitudinal comparisons by race/ethnicity should be done with extreme care, due to periodic changes in the survey.

★ 234 ★

Profile of Doctorate Recipients in Life Sciences: 1979-1990

Total number and percent by race/ethnicity of doctorate recipients[a] in life sciences, 1979-80 to 1989-90.

Race/ethnicity	1979-80	1980-81	1981-82	1982-83	1983-84	1984-85	1985-86	1986-87	1987-88	1988-89	1989-90
Number of doctorates	5,325	5,461	5,565	5,540	5,745	5,748	5,720	5,742	6,143	6,343	6,613
Race/ethnicity (%)[b]											
Asian	5.0	4.6	4.5	5.2	4.6	4.6	4.8	5.6	4.9%	5.2	5.5
American Indian	0.2	0.2	0.3	0.2	0.3	0.4	0.5	0.4	0.4	0.3	0.2
Black	1.5	1.8	1.5	1.6	2.0	2.1	1.9	2.4	2.2	2.1	1.9
Mexican American	0.2	0.3	0.4	0.2	0.3	0.4	0.4	0.4	0.4	0.5	0.8
Puerto Rican	0.1	0.2	0.3	0.3	0.3	0.4	0.4	0.6	0.6	0.6	0.7
Other Hispanic	0.7	0.8	0.8	0.7	0.8	1.1	1.3	1.0	1.3	1.0	1.2
White	86.7	87.6	89.1	89.5	89.1	89.0	88.9	87.3	88.5	88.3	88.3
Other/unknown	5.6	4.5	3.1	2.3	2.6	2.0	1.8	2.3	1.7	2.0	1.4

Source: National Center for Education Statistics, U.S. Department of Education, *Digest of Education Statistics 1992* (Washington, DC: U.S. Government Printing Office, October 1992), table 287, p. 297. Primary source: National Academy of Sciences, National Research Council, Office of Scientific and Engineering Personnel, *Doctorate Records File.* (This table was prepared February 1992.) The National Research Council's classification of degrees by field differs somewhat from that in most publications of the National Center for Education Statistics (NCES). The number of degrees also differs slightly from that reported in the NCES "Degrees and Other Formal Awards Conferred" survey. Because of rounding, percents may not add to 100. *Notes:* (a) Includes agricultural, biological, and health sciences. (b) Longitudinal comparisons by race/ethnicity should be done with extreme care, due to periodic changes in the survey.

★ 235 ★

Profile of Doctorate Recipients in Physical Sciences: 1979-1990

Total number and percent by race/ethnicity of doctorate recipients[a] in physical sciences, 1979-80 to 1989-90.

Race/ethnicity	1979-80	1980-81	1981-82	1982-83	1983-84	1984-85	1985-86	1986-87	1987-88	1988-89	1989-90
Number of doctorates	3,151	3,208	3,348	3,438	3,459	3,531	3,679	3,837	4,046	3,987	4,263
Race/ethnicity (%)[b]											
Asian	7.2	6.5	6.0	6.4	6.4	6.7	6.9	6.8	5.5	6.6	6.4
American Indian	0.2	0.1	0.2	0.3	0.2	0.1	0.2	0.3	0.3	0.6	0.1
Black	0.9	1.2	1.1	1.0	1.3	1.2	1.0	1.0	1.3	1.3	1.0
Mexican American	0.2	0.1	0.2	0.2	0.3	0.5	0.5	0.4	0.6	0.5	0.5
Puerto Rican	0.1	0.4	0.3	0.3	0.4	0.2	0.5	1.0	0.8	0.7	1.0
Other Hispanic	0.7	0.7	0.7	0.8	1.2	0.9	1.0	0.9	1.1	1.3	1.5
White	83.7	85.3	88.5	87.4	87.0	87.0	86.5	86.6	87.3	86.8	87.2
Other/unknown	7.0	5.7	3.0	3.6	3.2	3.2	3.4	3.0	3.1	2.1	2.3

Source: National Center for Education Statistics, U.S. Department of Education, *Digest of Education Statistics 1992* (Washington, DC: U.S. Government Printing Office, October 1992), table 288, p. 298. Primary source: National Academy of Sciences, National Research Council, Office of Scientific and Engineering Personnel, *Doctorate Records File.* (This table was prepared February 1992.) The National Research Council's classification of degrees by field differs somewhat from that in most publications of the National Center for Education Statistics (NCES). The number of degrees also differs slightly from that reported in the NCES "Degrees and Other Formal Awards Conferred" survey. Because of rounding, percents may not add to 100. *Notes:* (a) Includes physics, astronomy, chemistry, and earth, atmospheric, and marine sciences. Excludes mathematics and computer science. (b) Longitudinal comparisons by race/ethnicity should be done with extreme care, due to periodic changes in the survey.

★ 236 ★

Profile of Doctorate Recipients in Social Sciences: 1979-1990

Total number and percent by race/ethnicity of doctorate recipients[a] in social sciences, 1979-80 to 1989-90.

Race/ethnicity	1979-80	1980-81	1981-82	1982-83	1983-84	1984-85	1985-86	1986-87	1987-88	1988-89	1989-90
Number of doctorates	6,253	6,505	6,250	6,055	5,895	5,720	5,841	5,718	5,769	5,955	6,076
Race/ethnicity (%)[b]											
Asian	2.7	2.4	2.4	2.1	2.4	2.5	2.5	3.1	3.2	3.1	2.9
American Indian	0.3	0.2	0.4	0.2	0.2	0.4	0.4	0.5	0.3	0.4	0.5
Black	4.0	3.9	4.6	3.8	4.5	4.3	4.0	3.7	4.3	4.3	4.3
Mexican American	0.4	0.8	0.9	0.9	0.8	0.9	1.0	1.0	1.0	1.0	0.9
Puerto Rican	0.3	0.3	0.6	0.4	0.6	0.5	0.6	0.5	0.7	0.8	0.9
Other Hispanic	1.2	1.1	1.1	1.6	1.3	1.4	1.6	2.0	1.5	1.5	2.1
White	86.5	87.6	87.8	88.2	88.0	87.6	87.9	87.3	87.3	87.5	87.2
Other/unknown	4.5	3.7	2.2	2.8	2.1	2.4	2.0	2.0	1.7	1.6	1.2

Source: National Center for Education Statistics, U.S. Department of Education, *Digest of Education Statistics 1992* (Washington, DC: U.S. Government Printing Office, October 1992), table 289, p. 298. Primary source: National Academy of Sciences, National Research Council, Office of Scientific and Engineering Personnel, *Doctorate Records File.* (This table was prepared February 1992.) The National Research Council's classification of degrees by field differs somewhat from that in most publications of the National Center for Education Statistics (NCES). The main differences are that history is included under humanities rather than social sciences and that psychology is included under social sciences. The number of degrees also differs slightly from that reported in the NCES "Degrees and Other Formal Awards Conferred" survey. Because of rounding, percents may not add to 100. *Notes:* (a) Includes anthropology, area studies, criminology, economics, geography, political science, public policy, psychology, and sociology. (b) Longitudinal comparisons by race/ethnicity should be done with extreme care, due to periodic changes in the survey.

Dropouts

★ 237 ★

Dropout Rates: Foreign-born Youth

Reported results of a study of foreign-born white, Hispanic, and Asian youth to determine what characteristics affect the likelihood of dropping out of high school in the United States, 1980.

Characteristic	Asian	White	Hispanic
Number in study	105	106	197
Age	Percent of group total in sample		
16-17	34	19	72
18-19	31	33	35
20-21	35	38	38
Sex			
Male	40	52	57
Female	60	48	43
	Dropout rate in percent		
Married			
Yes	46	19	72
No	9	14	42
Highest grade attended			
12th & over	3	5	8
9th-11th	30	36	70
0-8th	75	100	100
Non-English language spoken at home			
Yes	16	22	51
No	5	7	21
Ability to speak English			
Poor	20	45	86
Well	12	12	27
Language other than English spoken at home during childhood			
Yes	15	19	50
No	0	6	27
Age of arrival in America			
Age 0-6 years	0	14	22
Age 7-12 years	15	22	41
Age >12 years	16	12	66

Source: Xue Lan Rong and Judith Preissle-Goetz, "High School Droupouts Among Foreign-born Whites, Hispanics, and Asians," paper presented at the Annual Meeting of the American Educational Research Association (Boston: AERA, April 1990).

★ 238 ★

Dropout Rates in Nevada Public Schools

Number and percent of student dropouts in grades nine to twelve in Nevada public schools by race/ethnicity, 1988-89.

Status	Asian/ Pacific Islander	White	Black	Hispanic
Enrollment, number	471	9,391	1,288	1,078
Dropouts, number	14	424	79	99
Percent	2.9%	4.4%	6.0%	8.9%

Source: John Carpenter, "Nevada Public High School Dropouts, School Year 1988-89" (Carson City, NV: Nevada State Department of Education, Planning, Research, and Evaluation Branch, March 1990).

Educational Attainment in Canada

★ 239 ★

Educational Attainment by Immigrant Status and Sex: Chinese Canadians

Numbers of Chinese Canadians by immigrant status and sex who had attained various educational levels, 1986.

Status	Less than 7 years of education	7-11 years of education	12-13 years of education	Some postsecondary education	Postsecondary degree
Immigrant	46,950	54,560	44,880	38,545	81,340
Non-immigrant	1,000	10,700	8,390	12,080	16,560
Male	15,820	32,600	25,125	26,770	54,000
Female	32,130	32,660	28,140	23,850	43,905

Source: Emerald de los Angeles, *Education Chartbook* (Ottawa: Multiculturalism and Citizenship, Policy and Research, Multiculturalism Sector, July 2, 1991), unnumbered. Primary source: 1986 Census of Canada. Also in source: data on Canadians of British, French, European, Arab, Central and South American, Caribbean, black, and aboriginal origins.

★ 240 ★

Educational Attainment by Immigrant Status and Sex: Filipino Canadians

Numbers of Filipino Canadians by immigrant status and sex who had attained various educational levels, 1986.

Status	Less than 7 years of education	7-11 years of education	12-13 years of education	Some postsecondary education	Postsecondary degree
Immigrant	4,245	11,685	7,450	15,700	34,400
Non-immigrant	45	1,285	420	340	280
Male	1,235	5.545	3,240	7,845	13,175
Female	3,045	7,430	4,630	8,200	21,505

Source: Emerald de los Angeles, *Education Chartbook* (Ottawa: Multiculturalism and Citizenship, Policy and Research, Multiculturalism Sector, July 2, 1991), unnumbered. Primary source: 1986 Census of Canada. Also in source: data on Canadians of British, French, European, Arab, Central and South American, Caribbean, black, and aboriginal origins.

★ 241 ★

Educational Attainment by Immigrant Status and Sex: Japanese Canadians

Numbers of Japanese Canadians by immigrant status and sex who had attained various educational levels, 1986.

Status	Less than 7 years of education	7-11 years of education	12-13 years of education	Some postsecondary education	Postsecondary degree
Immigrant	545	1,655	2,345	2,070	5,190
Non-immigrant	515	6,766	5,865	5,785	10,770
Male	500	4,155	3,665	4,080	8,180
Female	560	4,265	4,545	3,785	7,795

Source: Emerald de los Angeles, *Education Chartbook* (Ottawa: Multiculturalism and Citizenship, Policy and Research, Multiculturalism Sector, July 2, 1991), unnumbered. Primary source: 1986 Census of Canada. Also in source: data on Canadians of British, French, European, Arab, Central and South American, Caribbean, black, and aboriginal origins.

★ 242 ★

Educational Attainment by Immigrant Status and Sex: South Asian Canadians

Numbers of South Asian[a] Canadians by immigrant status and sex who had attained various educational levels, 1986.

Status	Less than 7 years of education	7-11 years of education	12-13 years of education	Some postsecondary education	Postsecondary degree
Immigrant	391,905	160,710	229.755	269,375	32.450
Non-immigrant	2,430,590	1,231,300	1,542,610	2,889,925	254,650
Male	1,457,005	668,270	772,865	1,506,650	157.925
Female	1,365,495	723,740	999.500	1,652,655	129,170

Source: Emerald de los Angeles, *Education Chartbook* (Ottawa: Multiculturalism and Citizenship, Policy and Research, Multiculturalism Sector, July 2, 1991), unnumbered. Primary source: 1986 Census of Canada. Also in source: data on Canadians of British, French, European, Arab, Central and South American, Caribbean, black, and aboriginal origins. *Note:* (a) South Asia in this reference includes Bangladesh, Bhutan, India, Nepal, Pakistan, Republic of Maldives, and Sri Lanka.

★ 243 ★

Educational Attainment by Immigrant Status and Sex: Southeast Asian Canadians

Numbers of Southeast Asian[a] Canadians by immigrant status and sex who had attained various educational levels, 1986.

Status	Less than 7 years of education	7-11 years of education	12-13 years of education	Some postsecondary education	Postsecondary degree
Immigrant	10,405	17,960	10,870	9,145	12,020
Non-immigrant	85	585	465	410	735
Male	3,595	10,070	6,180	5,975	7,815
Female	6,890	8,475	5,155	3,585	4,945

Source: Emerald de los Angeles, *Education Chartbook* (Ottawa: Multiculturalism and Citizenship, Policy and Research, Multiculturalism Sector, July 2, 1991), unnumbered. Primary source: 1986 Census of Canada. Also in source: data on Canadians of British, French, European, Arab, Central and South American, Caribbean, black, and aboriginal origins. *Note:* (a) Southeast Asia in this reference includes Brunei, Indonesia, Kampuchea (Cambodia), Laos, Malaysia, Singapore, Thailand, Union of Myanmar (Burma), and Vietnam.

★ 244 ★

Population with Six Years Education or Less: Chinese Canadians

Number and percent of Chinese Canadians with six years of education or less by immigration status and sex, 1986.

Immigration status	Male		Female	
	Number	Percent	Number	Percent
Immigrant	15,320	11.9%	31,640	23.0%
Non-immigrant	505	2.0%	490	2.1%

Source: Emerald de los Angeles, *Education Chartbook* (Ottawa: Multiculturalism and Citizenship, Policy and Research, Multiculturalism Sector, July 2, 1991), unnumbered. Primary source: 1986 Census of Canada. Also in source: data on Canadians of British, French, European, Arab, Central and South American, Caribbean, black, and aboriginal origins.

★ 245 ★

Population with Six Years Education or Less: Filipino Canadians

Number and percent of Filipino Canadians with six years of education or less by immigration status and sex, 1986.

Immigration status	Male		Female	
	Number	Percent	Number	Percent
Immigrant	1,220	4.1%	3,025	6.9%
Non-immigrant	15	1.3%	15	1.3%

Source: Emerald de los Angeles, *Education Chartbook* (Ottawa: Multiculturalism and Citizenship, Policy and Research, Multiculturalism Sector, July 2, 1991), unnumbered. Primary source: 1986 Census of Canada. Also in source: data on Canadians of British, French, European, Arab, Central and South American, Caribbean, black, and aboriginal origins.

★ 246 ★

Population with Six Years Education or Less: Japanese Canadians

Number and percent of Japanese Canadians with six years of education or less by immigration status and sex, 1986.

Immigration status	Male		Female	
	Number	Percent	Number	Percent
Immigrant	205	4.1%	345	5.0%
Non-immigrant	295	1.9%	215	1.5%

Source: Emerald de los Angeles, *Education Chartbook* (Ottawa: Multiculturalism and Citizenship, Policy and Research, Multiculturalism Sector, July 2, 1991), unnumbered. Primary source: 1986 Census of Canada. Also in source: data on Canadians of British, French, European, Arab, Central and South American, Caribbean, black, and aboriginal origins.

★ 247 ★

Population with Six Years Education or Less: South Asian Canadians

Number and percent of South Asian[a] Canadians with six years of education or less by immigration status and sex, 1986.

Immigration status	Male		Female	
	Number	Percent	Number	Percent
Immigrant	5,310	5.0%	13,090	12.8%
Non-immigrant	80	1.2%	140	2.2%

Source: Emerald de los Angeles, *Education Chartbook* (Ottawa: Multiculturalism and Citizenship, Policy and Research, Multiculturalism Sector, July 2, 1991), unnumbered. Primary source: 1986 Census of Canada. Also in source: data on Canadians of British, French, European, Arab, Central and South American, Caribbean, black, and aboriginal origins. *Note:* (a) South Asia in this reference includes Bangladesh, Bhutan, India, Nepal, Pakistan, Republic of Maldives, and Sri Lanka.

★ 248 ★

Population with Six Years Education or Less: Southeast Asian Canadians

Number and percent of Southeast Asian[a] Canadians with six years of education or less by immigration status and sex, 1986.

Immigration status	Male		Female	
	Number	Percent	Number	Percent
Immigrant	3,565	11.0%	6,840	24.5%
Non-immigrant	30	2.6%	55	4.9%

Source: Emerald de los Angeles, *Education Chartbook* (Ottawa: Multiculturalism and Citizenship, Policy and Research, Multiculturalism Sector, July 2, 1991), unnumbered. Primary source: 1986 Census of Canada. Also in source: data on Canadians of British, French, European, Arab, Central and South American, Caribbean, black, and aboriginal origins. *Note:* (a) Southeast Asia in this reference include Brunei, Indonesia, Kampuchea (Cambodia), Laos, Malaysia, Singapore, Thailand, Union of Myanmar (Burma), and Vietnam.

★ 249 ★

Postsecondary School Rate by Immigrant Status and Sex: Chinese Canadians

Number and percent of Chinese Canadians who had at least some postsecondary education in 1986.

Immigration Status	Male		Female	
	Number	Percent	Number	Percent
Immigrant	65,885	51.1%	53,990	39.3%
Non-immigrant	14,895	58.8%	13,755	58.8%

Source: Emerald de los Angeles, *Education Chartbook* (Ottawa: Multiculturalism and Citizenship, Policy and Research, Multiculturalism Sector, July 2, 1991), unnumbered. Primary source: 1986 Census of Canada. Also in source: data on Canadians of British, French, European, Arab, Central and South American, Caribbean, black, and aboriginal origins.

★ 250 ★

Postsecondary School Rate by Immigrant Status and Sex: Filipino Canadians

Number and percent of Filipino Canadians who had at least some postsecondary education in 1986.

Immigration Status	Male		Female	
	Number	Percent	Number	Percent
Immigrant	20,685	69.3%	29,420	67.4%
Non-immigrant	340	28.3%	275	23.7%

Source: Emerald de los Angeles, *Education Chartbook* (Ottawa: Multiculturalism and Citizenship, Policy and Research, Multiculturalism Sector, July 2, 1991), unnumbered. Primary source: 1986 Census of Canada. Also in source: data on Canadians of British, French, European, Arab, Central and South American, Caribbean, black, and aboriginal origins.

★ 251 ★

Postsecondary School Rate by Immigrant Status and Sex: Japanese Canadians

Number and percent of Japanese Canadians who had at least some postsecondary education in 1986.

Immigration Status	Male		Female	
	Number	Percent	Number	Percent
Immigrant	3,245	65.6%	4,025	57.7%
Non-immigrant	9,010	57.7%	7,550	53.6%

Source: Emerald de los Angeles, *Education Chartbook* (Ottawa: Multiculturalism and Citizenship, Policy and Research, Multiculturalism Sector, July 2, 1991), unnumbered. Primary source: 1986 Census of Canada. Also in source: data on Canadians of British, French, European, Arab, Central and South American, Caribbean, black, and aboriginal origins.

★ 252 ★

Postsecondary School Rate by Immigrant Status and Sex: South Asian Canadians

Number and percent of South Asian[a] Canadians who had at least some postsecondary education in 1986.

Immigration Status	Male		Female	
	Number	Percent	Number	Percent
Immigrant	65,065	61.1%	49,855	48.9%
Non-immigrant	2,180	33.7%	2,310	36.5%

Source: Emerald de los Angeles, *Education Chartbook* (Ottawa: Multiculturalism and Citizenship, Policy and Research, Multiculturalism Sector, July 2, 1991), unnumbered. Primary source: 1986 Census of Canada. Also in source: data on Canadians of British, French, European, Arab, Central and South American, Caribbean, black, and aboriginal origins. *Note:* (a) South Asia in this reference includes Bangladesh, Bhutan, India, Nepal, Pakistan, Republic of Maldives, and Sri Lanka.

★ 253 ★

Postsecondary School Rate by Immigrant Status and Sex: Southeast Asian Canadians

Number and percent of Southeast Asian[a] Canadians who had at least some postsecondary education in 1986.

Immigration Status	Male		Female	
	Number	Percent	Number	Percent
Immigrant	13,210	40.7%	7,960	28.5%
Non-immigrant	585	50.0%	580	51.8%

Source: Emerald de los Angeles, *Education Chartbook* (Ottawa: Multiculturalism and Citizenship, Policy and Research, Multiculturalism Sector, July 2, 1991), unnumbered. Primary source: 1986 Census of Canada. Also in source: data on Canadians of British, French, European, Arab, Central and South American, Caribbean, black, and aboriginal origins. *Note:* (a) Southeast Asia in this reference include Brunei, Indonesia, Kampuchea (Cambodia), Laos, Malaysia, Singapore, Thailand, Union of Myanmar (Burma), and Vietnam.

Educational Attainment in the United States

★ 254 ★

Education Levels of Southeast Asian Refugees: 1978-1982

Percent of Southeast Asian refugees[a] age 17 or older who had achieved various educational levels upon entry to the United States between 1978 and 1982.

Level of education[b]	Vietnamese	Chinese[c]	Laotians	Total[d]
No formal education	1.6%[e]	6.5%[e]	21.0%	8.3%
Elementary	34.5%	50.3%	56.6%	44.2%
Secondary	27.4%	24.0%	12.2%	22.2%
High school graduate	22.6%	15.5%	4.9%	15.9%
Some college	13.8%	3.7%[e]	5.1%	9.2%
Total[f]	100.0%	100.0%	100.0%	100.0%

Source: U.S. General Accounting Office, *Asian Americans: A Status Report, 1990,* Washington, DC (U.S. Government Printing Office, 1990) table 3.2, p. 27. Primary source: U.S. Dept. of Health and Human Services, Official Refugee Resettlement, *Southeast Asian Refugee Self-Sufficiency Study* (1985). *Notes:* (a) Includes refugees who arrived in the United States between 1978 and 1982. (b) Source did not indicate what grades were included in elementary, secondary, or high school levels of education. (c) From Vietnam. (d) Percentages based on totals for the three groups combined. (e) This percentage is based on fewer than 50 observations. (f) Detail may not add to 100.0 due to rounding.

★ 255 ★

Educational Attainment by Sex

Total numbers and educational attainment in percent of Asian/Pacific Islander, white, and total population age 25 and older by sex, as of March 1991.

Educational attainment	Total population (in thousands)			Asian/Pacific Islanders (in thousands)		
	Both sexes	Male	Female	Both sexes	Male	Female
Total, 25 years old and over (1,000s)	158,694	75,487	83,207	4,158	1,931	2,227
Percent	100.0%	100.0%	100.0%	100.0%	100.0%	100.0%
Elementary, Total	10.6%	11.0%	10.3%	12.4%	10.2%	14.3%
0 to 4 years	2.4%	2.7%	2.1%	5.3%	4.3%	6.2%
5 to 7 years	3.8%	3.9%	3.7%	4.4%	3.2%	5.4%
8 years	4.4%	4.5%	4.4%	2.7%	2.7%	2.7%
High school, Total	49.6%	46.5%	52.4%	34.4%	32.4%	36.1%
1 to 3 years	11.0%	10.4%	11.4%	5.8%	6.0%	5.7%
4 years	38.6%	36.0%	41.0%	28.5%	26.4%	30.3%
College, Total	39.8%	42.5%	37.4%	53.2%	57.4%	49.6%
1 to 3 years	18.4%	18.2%	18.6%	14.2%	14.2%	14.2%
4 years	12.7%	13.6%	11.9%	23.3%	22.8%	23.7%
5 or more years	8.8%	10.8%	6.9%	15.8%	20.4%	11.8%
Percent 4 years of high school or more	78.4%	78.5%	78.3%	81.8%	83.8%	80.0%

[Continued]

★ 255 ★

Educational Attainment by Sex (Continued)

Total numbers and educational attainment in percent of Asian/Pacific Islander, white, and total population age 25 and older by sex, as of March 1991.

Educational attainment	Total population (in thousands)			Asian/Pacific Islanders (in thousands)		
	Both sexes	Male	Female	Both sexes	Male	Female
Total, 25 to 34 years old (1,000s)	42,905	21,319	21,586	1,213	585	628
Percent	100.0%	100.0%	100.0%	100.0%	100.0%	100.0%
Elementary, Total	4.2%	4.5%	3.8%	4.9%	5.9%	4.0%
0 to 4 years	1.1%	1.3%	0.9%	2.4%	3.0%	1.8%
5 to 7 years	1.6%	1.7%	1.5%	1.2%	1.4%	1.0%
8 years	1.5%	1.6%	1.4%	1.4%	1.5%	1.3%
High school, Total	50.5%	51.1%	49.9%	34.5%	33.3%	35.7%
1 to 3 years	9.7%	9.8%	9.7%	5.9%	7.1%	4.9%
4 years	40.8%	41.3%	40.3%	28.6%	26.2%	30.7%
College, Total	45.3%	44.3%	46.3%	60.6%	60.9%	60.3%
1 to 3 years	21.6%	20.8%	22.4%	20.0%	19.8%	20.1%
4 years	16.3%	15.5%	17.0%	25.1%	23.1%	26.9%
5 or more years	7.4%	8.0%	6.8%	15.5%	17.9%	13.3%
Percent 4 years of high school or more	86.1%	85.7%	86.5%	89.1%	87.1%	91.1%
Total, 35 years old and over (1,000s)	115,789	54,168	61,621	2,945	1,346	1,599
Percent	100.0%	100.0%	100.0%	100.0%	100.0%	100.0%
Elementary, Total	13.0%	13.6%	12.5%	15.5%	12.0%	18.3%
0 to 4 years	2.9%	3.2%	2.6%	6.5%	4.8%	7.9%
5 to 7 years	4.6%	4.7%	4.5%	5.7%	4.0%	7.2%
8 years	5.5%	5.6%	5.4%	3.3%	3.2%	3.3%
High school, Total	49.2%	44.6%	53.2%	34.3%	32.1%	36.2%
1 to 3 years	11.4%	10.7%	12.0%	5.8%	5.5%	6.0%
4 years	37.8%	33.9%	41.2%	28.5%	26.5%	30.2%
College, Total	37.8%	41.8%	34.3%	50.2%	55.9%	45.5%
1 to 3 years	17.2%	17.1%	17.2%	11.8%	11.8%	11.9%
4 years	11.3%	12.8%	10.1%	22.5%	22.6%	22.4%
5 or more years	9.3%	11.9%	7.0%	15.9%	21.5%	11.2%
Percent 4 years of high school or more	75.6%	75.7%	75.5%	78.7%	82.4%	75.6%

Source: Claudette E. Bennett, Economics and Statistics Administration, Bureau of the Census, U.S. Department of Commerce, *The Asian and Pacific Islander Population in the United States: March 1991 and 1990,* Current Population Reports, Population Characteristics, P20-459 (Washington, DC: U.S. Government Printing Office, August 1992), table 3, p. 20. The population universe for the March 1991 and 1990 Current Population Surveys is the estimate of the civilian noninstitutional population of the United States plus members of the Armed Forces in the United States living off post or with their families on post, but excludes all other members of the Armed Forces. Data are estimates based on sample surveys and are subject to sampling variability since they are not based on a complete count of the population. Also in source: data on whites.

★ 256 ★

Asian/Pacific Islander Educational Attainment by State

Numbers of Asian/Pacific Islanders three years and over who have attained various educational levels, by state, 1990.

State	Asian or Pacific Islander						
	Less than 9th grade	9th to 12th grade no deploma	High school gtraduate (includes equivalency)	Some college, no degree	Associate degree	Bachelor's degree	Graduate or professional degree
Alabama	1,384	1,298	1,989	1,774	708	2,452	3,101
Alaska	1,495	1,316	3,112	2,494	668	1,816	522
Arizona	3,271	2,981	5,398	5,682	2,371	6,872	4,973
Arkansas	1,210	1,020	1,564	835	378	843	789
California	234,682	156,293	291,342	289,847	158,082	409,783	175,984
Colorado	4,019	3,329	7,480	5,674	2,551	6,371	4,513
Connecticut	2,766	2,361	3,948	3,153	1,701	6,646	7,729
Delaware	366	390	895	493	258	1,372	1,674
Florida	9,971	10,349	19,624	13,826	7,110	18,523	12,327
Georgia	5,080	4,619	8,992	5,105	2,664	9,569	7,069
Hawaii	61,478	49,881	136,358	71,282	36,081	63,862	21,862
Idaho	481	513	1,309	1,011	339	897	498
Illinois	15,675	11,802	23,911	21,937	12,207	52,212	32,648
Indiana	1,518	1,469	3,558	2,073	1,213	4,688	6,460
Iowa	–	–	–	–	–	–	–
Kansas	2,289	1827	2,534	2,072	667	3,081	3,149
Kentucky	1,051	1,090	1,633	1,173	473	2,062	2,227
Louisiana	3,575	3,296	4,129	2,639	1,140	3,190	3,568
Maine	560	354	942	531	243	535	393
Maryland	6,717	6,086	13,332	10,598	5,222	21,786	20,621
Massachusetts	13,014	7,144	11,302	7,315	4,176	16,210	18,728
Michigan	4,939	4,346	6,953	5,623	3,650	14,286	15,779
Minnesota	7071	2674	5311	3992	2,332	5,576	5,195
Mississippi	–	–	–	–	–	–	–
Missouri	–	–	–	–	–	–	–
Montana	257	222	572	361	101	461	254
Nebraska	–	–	–	–	–	–	–
Nevada	2,936	3,398	6,291	4,853	1,597	3,891	1,464
New Hampshire	505	338	899	508	235	1,226	1,167
New Jersey	11,015	10,902	22,468	15,828	11,062	55,646	39,326
New Mexico	853	778	1,748	1351	489	1,681	1,612
New York	71,882	49,300	77,195	4,5101	25,537	98,288	71,774
North Carolina	3,224	3,116	5,584	3,492	1,969	5,751	5,488
North Dakota	122	154	244	379	157	307	335
Ohio	4,560	4,004	7,517	5,381	2,798	11,876	15,703
Oklahoma	2,080	2,266	3,471	2,992	1,067	3,234	3,073
Oregon	4,334	3,358	7,079	7,254	3,274	7,654	4,417
Pennsylvania	9,825	7,226	12,439	7,175	4,183	15,644	18,079
Rhode Island	2,470	1,049	1,269	836	414	1,325	1,340
South Carolina	1,399	1,411	2,771	1,658	904	2,318	1,946
South Dakota	227	157	379	130	108	273	223
Tennessee	1,895	1,690	3,332	1,981	1,030	3,445	3,935
Texas	19,878	18,436	30,571	25,321	13,157	43,979	31,620
Utah	1,675	1,599	3,896	3,654	1,148	3,006	1,990

[Continued]

★ 256 ★

Asian/Pacific Islander Educational Attainment by State (Continued)

Numbers of Asian/Pacific Islanders three years and over who have attained various educational levels, by state, 1990.

State	Asian or Pacific Islander						
	Less than 9th grade	9th to 12th grade no deploma	High school gtraduate (includes equivalency)	Some college, no degree	Associate degree	Bachelor's degree	Graduate or professional degree
Vermont	90	90	263	153	74	354	374
Virginia	8,638	8,394	18,340	14,621	6,776	23,085	15,111
Washington	15,346	12,036	24,950	22,249	9,602	25,445	10,910
West Virginia	260	200	501	365	180	891	1,708
Wisconsin	4871	1655	2899	2964	1,265	4,251	4,992
Wyoming	136	209	435	221	95	272	166

Source: U.S. Bureau of Census, Summary Tape File 3A. *Note:* A dash (–) indicates data not available at time of publication.

★ 257 ★

Educational Attainment in the Western United States by Sex

Total numbers and educational attainment, in percent, of Asian/Pacific Islander and total population age 25 and older in the western United States[a] by sex, as of March 1991.

Educational attainment	Total population (in thousands)			Asian/Pacific Islander (in thousands)		
	Both sexes	Male	Female	Both sexes	Male	Female
Total, 25 years old and over (1,000s)	32,954	16,099	16,856	2,466	1,158	1,308
Percent	100.0%	100.0%	100.0%	100.0%	100.0%	100.0%
Elementary, Total	10.1%	10.2%	10.1%	11.9%	9.7%	13.8%
0 to 4 years	3.2%	3.4%	3.0	5.8%	5.0%	6.6%
5 to 7 years	3.9%	3.8%	4.0	3.5%	2.0%	4.8%
8 years	3.1%	3.1%	3.1	2.6%	2.6%	2.5%
High school, Total	43.0%	40.0%	45.8%	36.4%	34.8%	37.8%
1 to 3 years	8.9%	8.4%	9.4	6.1%	6.1%	6.1%
4 years	34.0%	31.6%	36.3	30.3%	28.7%	31.7%
College, Total	46.9%	49.7%	44.2%	51.7%	55.6%	48.3%
1 to 3 years	22.6%	22.1%	23.1	16.3%	16.6%	16.0%
4 years	13.6%	14.5%	12.8	23.1%	23.2%	23.0%
5 or more years	10.7%	13.2%	8.3	12.3%	15.7%	9.3%
Percent 4 years of high school or more	80.9%	81.3%	80.5%	82.0%	84.2%	80.0%
Total, 25 to 34 years old (1,000s)	9,398	4,794	4,604	674	324	350
Percent	100.0%	100.0%	100.0%	100.0%	100.0%	100.0%
Elementary, Total	7.0%	7.4%	6.5%	3.8%	5.0%	2.6%
0 to 4 years	2.0%	2.3%	1.6%	2.1%	2.6%	1.7%
5 to 7 years	3.6%	3.6%	3.5%	0.3%	0.2%	0.4%
8 years	1.4%	1.5%	1.3%	1.3%	2.2%	0.5%

[Continued]

Educational Attainment in the Western United States by Sex (Continued)

Total numbers and educational attainment, in percent, of Asian/Pacific Islander and total population age 25 and older in the western United States[a] by sex, as of March 1991.

Educational attainment	Total population (in thousands)			Asian/Pacific Islander (in thousands)		
	Both sexes	Male	Female	Both sexes	Male	Female
High school, Total	46.0%	46.7%	45.3%	40.5%	39.3%	41.6%
1 to 3 years	9.3%	9.4%	9.3%	6.0%	7.5%	4.7%
4 years	36.7%	37.3%	36.1%	34.4%	31.8%	36.9%
College, Total	47.0%	45.9%	48.2%	55.8%	55.7%	55.8%
1 to 3 years	24.0%	23.5%	24.4%	22.9%	23.5%	22.4%
4 years	14.9%	13.8%	16.0%	23.0%	22.1%	23.9%
5 or more years	8.1%	8.5%	7.7%	9.8%	10.2%	9.4%
Percent 4 years of high school or more	83.7%	83.2%	84.2%	90.2%	87.5%	92.7%
Total, 35 years old and over (1,000s)	23,556	11,305	12,251	1,792	834	958
Percent	100.0%	100.0%	100.0%	100.0%	100.0%	100.0%
Elementary, Total	11.4%	11.4%	11.4%	14.9%	11.5%	18.0%
0 to 4 years	3.6%	3.8%	3.5%	7.2%	5.9%	8.4%
5 to 7 years	4.0%	3.9%	4.1%	4.7%	2.7%	6.4%
8 years	3.7%	3.7%	3.8%	3.0%	2.8%	3.2%
High school, Total	41.7%	37.2%	45.9%	34.9%	33.1%	36.4%
1 to 3 years	8.8%	8.0%	9.5%	6.2%	5.6%	6.6%
4 years	32.9%	29.1%	36.4%	28.7%	27.5%	29.8%
College, Total	46.8%	51.4%	42.7%	50.2%	55.5%	45.6%
1 to 3 years	22.0%	21.4%	22.6%	13.8%	14.0%	13.7%
4 years	13.1%	14.8%	11.5%	23.1%	23.6%	22.7%
5 or more years	11.7%	15.2%	8.6%	13.3%	17.9%	9.3%
Percent 4 years of high school or more	79.8%	80.5%	79.1%	78.9%	82.9%	75.4%

Source: Claudette E. Bennett, Economics and Statistics Administration, Bureau of the Census, U.S. Department of Commerce, *The Asian and Pacific Islander Population in the United States: March 1991 and 1990,* Current Population Reports, Population Characteristics, P20-459 (Washington, DC: U.S. Government Printing Office, August 1992), table 3, p. 20. The population universe for the March 1991 and 1990 Current Population Surveys is the estimate of the civilian noninstitutional population to the United States plus members of the Armed Forces in the United States living off post or with their families on post, but excludes all other members of the Armed Forces. Data are estimates based on sample surveys and are subject to sampling variability since they are not based on a complete count of the population. Also in source: data on whites. *Note:* (a) The western region of the United States includes Alaska, Arizona, California, Colorado, Hawaii, Idaho, Montana, Nevada, New Mexico, Oregon, Utah, Washington, and Wyoming.

★ 258 ★

Educational Attainment by Home Language and Sex

Reported results of a survey of 1980 high school seniors (172 males and 172 females). The researchers suggest that Asian American females reach higher levels of educational attainment than Asian American males.

	Males		Females		All	
Variable	License/ certificate or less	2-year degree or more	License/ certificate or less	2-year degree or more	License/ certif. or less	2-year degree or more
	Percent	Percent	Percent	Percent	Percent	Percent
Language spoken at home when a child						
Non-English monolingual/dominant	60%	40%	45%	55%	54%	47%
English monolingual or dominant	70%	30%	63%	38%	66%	34%
Ethnicity						
Chinese	60%	40%	33%	67%	48%	52%
Filipino	79%	21%	56%	44%	66%	34%
Japanese	58%	42%	62%	38%	60%	40%

Source: Paul R. Brandon, "Gender Differences in Educational Attainment among Asian Americans in the 'High-School-and-Beyond' Senior-Cohort Third Follow-Up Survey." Paper presented at the Annual Meeting of the American Educational Research Association, April 16-20, 1990.

★ 259 ★

Educational Attainment:1980 High School Seniors, 1986

Highest level of education attained by 1980 high school seniors, in percent, by race/ethnicity and socioeconomic status[a], spring 1986.

Socioeconomic status	Highest educational attainment of 1980 high school seniors in 1986, percent of total					
	No high school diploma[b]	High school diploma	License[c]	Associate degree	Bachelor's degree	Graduate/ professional degree
Asian	-	49.6%	12.6%	8.7%	27.3%	1.7%
White non-Hispanic	0.8%	60.0%	11.5%	6.6%	20.2%	0.9%
Black non-Hispanic	1.2%	69.4%	13.9%	5.3%	9.9%	0.2%
Hispanic	1.7%	70.2%	13.8%	7.3%	6.8%	0.1%
American Indian	-	61.3%	18.6%	9.3%	10.8%	-
Lower 25%						
Asian	-	53.4%	17.3%	15.7%	12.0%	1.6%
White non-Hispanic	0.9%	75.1%	12.2%	5.0%	6.6%	0.3%
Black non-Hispanic	1.4%	73.0%	12.7%	5.1%	7.7%	0.1%
Hispanic	1.6%	73.9%	11.8%	7.8%	4.9%	-
Middle 50%						
Asian	-	51.1%	11.7%	11.1%	26.1%	-
White non-Hispanic	0.3%	62.0%	13.0%	8.0%	16.3%	0.4%
Black non-Hispanic	0.3%	67.5%	14.7%	6.5%	10.7%	0.3%
Hispanic	1.0%	67.0%	14.7%	6.5%	10.7%	0.2%

[Continued]

★ 259 ★

Educational Attainment:1980 High School Seniors, 1986 (Continued)

Highest level of education attained by 1980 high school seniors, in percent, by race/ethnicity and socioeconomic status[a], spring 1986.

Socioeconomic status	Highest educational attainment of 1980 high school seniors in 1986, percent of total					
	No high school diploma[b]	High school diploma	License[c]	Associate degree	Bachelor's degree	Graduate/ professional degree
Upper 25%						
Asian	-	42.9%	6.5%	4.8%	40.0%	5.9%
White non-Hispanic	-	44.9%	8.6%	6.2%	38.2%	2.2%
Black non-Hispanic	-	56.3%	12.4%	5.4%	25.2%	0.4%
Hispanic	0.3%	60.0%	11.4%	9.6%	18.0%	0.7%

Source: National Center for Education Statistics, U.S. Department of Education, *Digest of Education Statistics 1992* (Washington, DC: U.S. Government Printing Office, October 1992), tables 296 and 298, p. 303-304. Primary source: U. S. Department of Education, National Center for Education Statistics, *High School and Beyond* survey, September 1987. A dash (-) indicates less that 0.05 percent. Because of rounding, percents may not add to 100.0. *Notes:* (a) Socioeconomic status was measured by a composite score of parental education, family income, father's occupation, and household characteristics in 1980. (b) Seniors who dropped out of high school after the spring 1980 survey and had not completed high school by 1986. (c) Includes persons who earned a certificate for completing a program of study.

★ 260 ★

High School Graduates Completing College

Cumulative percentages of 1972, 1980, and 1982 high school graduates completing college, by race/ethnicity and level of degree, 1976 to 1986.

High school seniors	Total	Race/ethnicity				
		Asian	White	Black	Hispanic	American Indian
1972 high school seniors						
1 to 2 year degree[a]						
June 1976	6.4%	8.0%	7.0%	2.1%	3.3%	4.1%
June 1978	7.9%	8.0%	8.5%	3.5%	4.0%	5.5%
June 1980	9.4%	12.8%	9.9%	4.9%	6.6%	11.4%
June 1982	11.8%	21.0%	12.1%	9.4%	9.1%	20.1%
June 1984	14.2%	25.5%	14.7%	11.1%	11.0%	23.5%
June 1986	16.6%	27.7%	17.0%	14.6%	13.7%	26.2%
Bachelor's degree						29.2%
June 1976	14.3%	5.8%	15.6%	7.8%	3.1%	48.5%
June 1978	23.7%	5.8%	25.5%	13.5%	9.1%	53.2%
June 1980	25.1%	5.8%	27.0%	14.7%	9.7%	54.9%
June 1982	26.4%	10.7%	28.1%	18.3%	10.4%	54.9%
June 1984	27.1%	15.3%	28.8%	18.8%	10.8%	56.1%
June 1986	27.7%	18.5%	29.4%	19.2%	10.9%	16.9%
1980 high school seniors						
1 to 2 year degree[a]						
February 1984	8.8%	11.8%	9.0%	6.4%	9.2%	20.4%
February 1986	12.5%	15.7%	12.5%	10.4%	14.7%	9.2%
Bachelor's degree						
February 1986	18.8%	28.7%	20.8%	10.1%	6.8%	9.2%
1982 high school seniors						
1 to 2 year degree[a]						
February 1986	7.9%	5.3%	8.0%	7.1%	9.5%	5.8%

Source: National Center for Education Statistics, U.S. Department of Education, *Digest of Education Statistics 1992* (Washington, DC: U.S. Government Printing Office, October 1992), table 299, p. 305. Primary sources: U.S. Department of Education, National Center for Education Statistics, *High School and Beyond and National Longitudinal Study* surveys, unpublished tabulations. (This table was prepared November 1988.) *Note:* (a) Includes licenses, awards, and associate degree programs of one to two years duration.

Enrollment: Higher Education

★ 261 ★

Higher Education Enrollment by State, 1990

Fall enrollment in institutions of higher education by state (including District of Columbia) and race/ethnicity, 1990.

State	Total	Asian/Pacific Islander	White non-Hispanic	Black non-Hispanic	Hispanic	American Indian/Alaskan Native	Nonresident Alien
Total	13,710,150	554,803	10,674,764	1,223,303	758,054	102,618	396,588
Alabama	247,117	1,699	190,920	48,180	1,138	591	4,589
Alaska	29,833	740	24,264	1,079	634	2,648	468
Arizona	264,735	6,116	205,676	7,585	29,618	8,845	6,895
Arkansas	90,425	740	75,157	12,188	431	438	1,471
California	1,771,746	215,416	1,131,741	114,804	222,749	21,005	66,031
Colorado	231,547	5,417	194,943	6,943	17,319	2,315	4,610
Connecticut	169,480	4,362	144,265	9,952	5,648	433	4,820
Delaware	42,004	710	35,155	4,710	546	99	784
District of Columbia	80,669	3,222	40,977	24,770	2,406	270	9,024
Florida	538,389	10,871	397,880	53,400	58,490	1,616	16,132
Georgia	251,810	4,241	189,189	49,199	2,740	548	5,893
Hawaii	53,772	31,356	16,132	1,457	1,002	162	3,663
Idaho	51,881	706	48,024	310	1,004	485	1,352
Illinois	729,246	32,353	541,347	89,218	48,932	2,245	15,151
Indiana	283,015	3,913	251,389	15,323	4,380	720	7,290
Iowa	170,515	2,430	155,204	4,044	1,587	441	6,809
Kansas	163,478	2,717	143,116	6,798	3,538	1,969	5,340
Kentucky	177,852	1,343	162,549	10,491	738	506	2,225
Louisiana	186,599	2,683	130,361	44,738	3,448	856	4,513
Maine	57,186	418	55,487	296	195	398	392
Maryland	264,862	11,694	195,079	44,582	5,026	852	7,629
Massachusetts	418,874	16,144	349,516	18,376	12,501	1,220	21,117
Michigan	569,803	10,693	475,505	56,786	9,094	3,547	14,178
Minnesota	253,789	4,948	235,231	4,143	1,936	2,002	5,529
Mississippi	122,883	783	85,699	33,699	395	377	1,930
Missouri	289,407	4,487	250,758	23,050	3,434	1,132	6,546
Montana	35,876	120	32,200	114	280	2,427	735
Nebraska	112,831	1,178	104,620	2,723	1,559	729	2,022
Nevada	61,728	2,559	50,910	2,931	3,408	1,043	877
New Hampshire	59,510	760	56,522	669	490	229	840
New Jersey	323,947	14,340	241,666	33,113	21,642	776	12,410
New Mexico	85,596	1,125	52,573	2,176	23,635	4,596	1,491
New York	1,040,484	49,171	753,074	112,173	74,835	3,914	47,317
North Carolina	351,990	5,622	273,874	62,032	2,528	3,082	4,852
North Dakota	37,878	285	34,380	246	195	1,616	1,156
Ohio	555,702	7,356	482,201	45,270	5,467	1,422	13,986
Oklahoma	173,221	2,904	140,865	11,816	2,635	9,609	5,392
Oregon	166,641	6,321	145,797	2,153	2,990	1,694	7,686

[Continued]

★ 261 ★

Higher Education Enrollment by State, 1990 (Continued)

Fall enrollment in institutions of higher education by state (including District of Columbia) and race/ethnicity, 1990.

State	Total	Asian/Pacific Islander	White non-Hispanic	Black non-Hispanic	Hispanic	American Indian/Alaskan Native	Nonresident Alien
Pennsylvania	604,060	13,588	523,157	44,009	7,709	1,011	14,586
Rhode Island	78,273	1,891	69,974	2,558	1,606	222	2,022
South Carolina	159,302	1,494	122,964	31,177	911	334	2,422
South Dakota	34,208	198	31,106	250	94	1,912	648
Tennessee	226,238	2,283	186,541	31,240	1,302	476	4,396
Texas	901,437	27,907	617,626	80,458	148,296	3,006	24,144
Utah	121,303	2,243	110,150	661	2,233	1,322	4,694
Vermont	36,398	569	34,178	375	428	131	717
Virginia	353,442	11,400	280,786	49,566	4,803	860	6,027
Washington	263,278	15,424	225,213	7,361	6,122	3,854	5,304
West Virginia	84,790	688	78,795	3,160	360	139	1,648
Wisconsin	299,774	4,991	271,096	10,667	4,692	2,050	6,278
Wyoming	31,326	184	28,952	284	905	444	557

Source: U.S. Department of Education, National Center for Education Statistics, *Trends in Racial/Ethnic Enrollment in Higher Education: Fall 1980 through Fall 1990* (Washington, DC: U.S. Government Printing Office, 1992), table 6, p. 6. Primary sources: U.S. Department of Education, National Center for Education Statistics, *Higher Education General Information Survey,* "Fall Enrollment in Colleges and Universities" (1978-1984); and Integrated Postsecondary Education Data System (IPEDS) "Fall Enrollment" surveys (1986, 1988, and 1990). Because of underreporting/nonreporting of racial/ethnic data, data prior to 1986 were estimated when possible. Due to rounding, detail may not add to totals.

★ 262 ★

Asian/Pacific Islander
High School Graduates and Undergraduates by Top States

Asian/Pacific Islander high school graduates and undergraduates in two- and four-year institutions in percent of total, by top state, 1988.

State	1988 high school graduates, percent	1988 undergraduates, four-year percent	Two-year
California	11.9	15.8	10.4
Colorado	2.2	2.7	1.6
Hawaii	75.4	54.9	70.3
Illinois	2.5	4.5	3.7
Maryland	3.1	4.9	3.2
Massachusetts	2.0	3.6	2.4
Minnesota	1.9	1.8	1.2
Nevada	3.8	3.4	3.3
New Jersey	2.7	4.2	3.0
New York	3.4	4.8	2.2
Oregon	3.2	4.9	3.1
Texas	2.1	3.1	2.5
Virginia	2.8	2.8	3.2
Washington	5.3	6.8	4.7
U.S., Total	3.0	3.6	4.1

Source: Western Interstate Commission for Higher Education and The College Board, *The Road to College: Educational Progress by Race and Ethnicity* (Boulder, CO: WICHE, 1991), table 9, p. 28. Also in source: data for all 50 states on African Americans, Latinos, American Indians/Alaskan Natives, white non-Latinos.

★ 263 ★

Higher Education Enrollment by Type of Institution in Percent, 1990

Fall enrollment, in percent, in public, private, 2- and 4-year institutions, by race/ethnicity, 1990.

Type and control of institution	Asian/ Pacific Islander	White	Black	Hispanic	American Indian	Nonresident alien
Public	4.1%	77.6%	8.9%	6.0%	0.8%	2.5%
Private	3.7%	78.6%	9.1%	3.7%	0.4%	4.4%
4-year	4.0%	79.2%	8.4%	4.0%	0.6%	3.8%
2-year	4.1%	75.6%	9.8%	8.0%	1.0%	1.4%

Source: U.S. Department of Education, National Center for Education Statistics, *The Condition of Education, 1992* (Washington, DC: U.S. Government Printing Office, June 1992), p. 106. Primary sources: U.S. Department of Education, National Center for Education Statistics, Integrated Postsecondary Education Data System (IPEDS) survey of fall enrollment, various years.

★ 264 ★

Higher Education Enrollment by Type of Institution, 1990

Fall enrollment in institutions of higher education by race/ethnicity[a] and control and level of institution, 1990.

Control and level of institution	All students	Asian/ Pacific Islander	White non-Hispanic	Black non-Hispanic	Hispanic	American Indian/Alas-kan Native	Nonresident alien
Total[b]	13,711,555	544,353	10,436,129	1,206,102	747,863	100,732	396,588
4-year	8,530,276	334,425	6,593,453	703,845	337,525	47,160	322,086
2-year	5,181,279	209,928	3,842,676	502,257	410,338	53,572	74,502
Public total	10,741,588	438,7778	8,183,127	942,501	642,066	89,039	264,767
4-year	5,803,501	233,688	4,507,235	482,658	246,801	37,713	193,708
2 year	4,938,087	205,090	3,675,892	459,843	395,265	51,326	71,059
Private total	2,970,147	105,575	2,253,002	263,601	105,797	11,873	131,821
4-year	2,726,775	100.737	2,086,218	221,187	90,724	9,447	128,378
2 year	243,372	4,838	166,784	42,414	15,073	2,426	3,443

Source: U.S. Department of Education, National Center for Education Statistics, *Trends in Racial/Ethnic Enrollment in Higher Education: Fall 1980 through Fall 1990* (Washington, DC: U.S. Government Printing Office, 1992), table A-1, p. 11. Primary sources: U.S. Department of Education, National Center of Education Statistics, Integrated Postsecondary Education Data System (IPEDS) "Fall Enrollment" survey, 1990. Also in source: data on enrollees whose race/ethnicity is unknown. *Notes:* (a) Represents actual counts reported, or imputed, prior to distribution of "race/ethnicity unknown" category. (b) Total enrollment reflects students counts prior to the distribution of "race/ethnicity unknown" data. After the distribution procedure, total enrollment dropped slightly (to 13,710,150).

★ 265 ★

Higher Education Enrollment by Disability Status

Fall enrollment, in percent, in postsecondary institutions by disability[a] status and race/ethnicity, 1989.

Race/ethnicity	Percent disabled	Percent nondisabled
Asian American	3.2%	4.7%
White non-Hispanic	83.2%	80.6%
Black non-Hispanic	7.7%	7.9%
Hispanic	3.2%	4.7%
American Indian	1.0%	0.6%

Source: National Center for Education Statistics, U.S. Department of Education, *Digest of Education Statistics 1992* (Washington, DC: U.S. Government Printing Office, October 1992), table 197, p. 207. Primary source: U.S. Department of Education, *The 1989-90 National Postsecondary Student Aid Study* (Washington, DC: National Center for Education Statistics, May 1992). Because of rounding, percents may not add to 100. Also in source: data by sex, veteran status, dependency status, housing status, attendance status, and level of study. *Notes:* (a) Disabled students are those who reported they had one or more of the following conditions: a specific learning disability, a visual handicap, hard of hearing, deafness, a speech disability, an orthopedic handicap, or a health impairment.

★ 266 ★

Higher Education Enrollment: Brown University

Numbers of applicants, applicants admitted, and percent admitted of Asian American and total applicants to Brown University, and Asian Americans as percent of total admitted, selected classes, 1979 to 1993.

Applicants	1979	1980	1982	1984	1986	1989	1991	1992	1993
Total freshman class									
Applicants	8,635	9,125	10,565	11,901	11,746	13,707	12,486	12,731	11,720
Admitted	2,856	2,830	2,846	2,559	2,604	2,637	2,788	2,701	2,869
Admit rate (%)	33%	31%	27%	22%	22%	19%	22%	21%	24%
Asian Americans									
Applicants	168	265	307	679	1,006	1,539	1,703	1,564	1,783
Admitted	74	101	141	153	188	256	324	303	424
Admit rate (%)	44%	38%	46%	23%	19%	17%	19%	19%	24%
Asian American admits as % of freshman total	2.6%	3.6%	5.0%	6.0%	7.2%	9.7%	11.6%	11.2%	14.8%

Source: U.S. Commission on Civil Rights, *Civil Rights Issues Facing Asian Americans in the 1990s* (Washington, DC: U.S. Government Printing Office, 1992), table 5.1, p. 110. Primary source: Information for classes 1979 to 1989 was obtained from tables 2a and 2b, *Asian American Students Association at Brown* report (1984). Information for the classes of 1989 to 1993 was provided by the Office of the Dean of Admissions, Brown University. Also in source: summary of three roundtable conferences held by the U.S. Commission on Civil Rights in 1989.

★ 267 ★

Higher Education Enrollment: Harvard University

Numbers of applicants, applicants admitted, and percent admitted of Asian American and total applicants to Harvard University, and Asian Americans as percent of total admitted, classes of 1983-1992.

Applicants	1983	1984	1985	1986	1987	1988	1989	1990	1991	1992
Asian Americans										
Applicants	784	1,015	1,161	1,351	1,391	1,605	1,731	2,054	2,168	2,263
Admitted	118	153	167	180	199	204	220	232	267	291
Admit rate (%)	15.1%	15.1%	14.4%	13.3%	14.3%	12.7%	12.7%	11.3%	12.3%	12.9%
Whites										
Applicants	10,344	10,708	9,849	9,715	8,855	9,219	9,561	9,196	9,270	9,157
Admitted	1,744	1,642	1,609	1,755	1,707	1,629	1,596	1,623	1,474	1,453
Admit rate (%)	16.9%	15.4%	16.3%	18.1%	19.3%	17.7%	16.7%	17.6%	15.9%	15.9%
Asian American admit rate as % of freshman total	5.5%	7.5%	8.5%	8.5%	9.6%	10.4%	10.9%	11.5%	12.9%	14.2%

Source: U.S. Commission on Civil Rights, *Civil Rights Issues Facing Asian Americans in the 1990s* (Washington, DC: U.S. Government Printing Office, 1992), table 5.2, p. 121. Also in source: summary of three roundtable conferences held by the Commission in 1989.

★ 268 ★

Higher Education Enrollment in Percent: 1976-1990

Fall enrollment, in percent, in U.S. colleges and universities by race/ethnicity, 1976 to 1990.

Year	Asian	White	Black	Hispanic	American Indian	Nonresident alien
All institutions						
1976	1.8	82.6	9.4	3.5	0.7	2.0
1978	2.1	81.9	9.4	3.7	0.7	2.2
1980	2.4	81.4	9.2	3.9	0.7	2.5
1982	2.8	80.7	8.9	4.2	0.7	2.7
1984	3.2	80.2	8.8	4.4	0.7	2.7
1986	3.6	79.3	8.7	4.9	0.7	2.8
1988	3.8	78.8	8.7	5.2	0.7	2.8
1990	4.0	77.9	8.9	5.5	0.7	2.9

Source: U.S. Department of Education, National Center for Education Statistics, *The Condition of Education, 1992* (Washington, DC: U.S. Government Printing Office, June 1992), p. 106. Primary source: U.S. Department of Education, National Center for Education Statistics, Integrated Postsecondary Education Data System (IPEDS) survey of fall enrollment, various years.

★ 269 ★

Higher Education Enrollment by Control of Institution in Percent: 1980-1990

Fall enrollment, in percent, by control of institution and race/ethnicity, biennially 1980 to 1990.

Control of institution and race/ethnicity	Percent					
	1980	1982	1984	1986	1988	1990
All institutions						
Total	100.0%	100.0%	100.0%	100.0%	100.0%	100.0%
Asian/Pacific Islander	2.4%	2.8%	3.2%	3.6%	3.8%	4.0%
White non-Hispanic	81.4%	80.7%	80.2%	79.3%	78.8%	77.9%
Black non-Hispanic	9.2%	8.9%	8.8%	8.7%	8.7%	8.9%
Hispanic	3.9%	4.2%	4.4%	4.9%	5.2%	5.5%
Public						
Total	78.2%	788.3%	77.3%	77.7%	77.9%	78.3%
Asian/Pacific Islander	2.0%	2.4%	2.6%	3.0%	3.1%	3.2%
White non-Hispanic	63.3%	62.8%	61.6%	61.2%	61.1%	60.8%
Black non-Hispanic	7.2%	7.0%	6.9%	6.8%	6.8%	6.9%
Hispanic	3.4%	3.6%	3.7%	4.3%	4.5%	4.7%
Private						
Total	21.8%	21.7%	22.7%	22.3%	22.1%	21.7%
Asian/Pacific Islander	0.4%	0.4%	0.5%	0.6%	0.7%	0.8%
White non-Hispanic	18.0%	17.9%	18.6%	18.1%	17.8%	17.0%
Black non-Hispanic	1.9%	1.8%	1.9%	1.8%	1.9%	2.0%
Hispanic	0.5%	0.6%	0.6%	0.7%	0.7%	0.8%

Source: U.S. Department of Education, National Center for Education Statistics, *Trends in Racial/Ethnic Enrollment in Higher Education: Fall 1980 through Fall 1990* (Washington, DC: U.S. Government Printing Office, 1992), table 1, p. 1. Primary sources: U.S. Department of Education, National Center for Education Statistics, *Higher Education General Information Survey,* "Fall Enrollment in Colleges and Universities" (1978-1984); and Integrated Postsecondary Education Data System (IPEDS), "Fall Enrollment" surveys (1986, 1988, and 1990). Because of underreporting/nonreporting of racial/ethnic data, data prior to 1986 were estimated when possible. Due to rounding, detail may not add to totals.

★ 270 ★

Higher Education Enrollment by Control of Institution: 1980-1990

Fall enrollment by control of institution and race/ethnicity, biennially 1980 to 1990.

Control of institution and race/ethnicity	Number in thousands					
	1980	1982	1984	1986	1988	1990
All institutions						
Total	12,087	12,388	12,235	12,504	13,043	13,710
Asian/Pacific Islander	286	351	390	448	497	555
White non-Hispanic	9,833	9,997	9,815	9,921	10,283	10,675
Black non-Hispanic	1,107	1,101	1,076	1,082	1,130	1,223
Hispanic	472	519	535	618	680	758
American Indian/Alaskan Native	84	88	84	90	93	103
Public						
Total	9,456	9,695	9,458	9,714	10,156	10.741
Asian/Pacific Islander	240	296	323	371	406	445
White non-Hispanic	7,656	7,785	7,543	7,654	7,964	8,340
Black non-Hispanic	876	873	844	854	881	952
Hispanic	406	446	456	532	587	648
American Indian/Alaskan Native	74	77	72	79	81	90
Private						
Total	2,630	2,693	2,777	2,790	2,887	2,970
Asian/Pacific Islander	47	55	67	77	91	109
White non-Hispanic	2,177	2,212	2,272	2,267	2,319	2,335
Black non-Hispanic	231	228	232	228	248	271
Hispanic	66	74	79	86	93	110
American Indian/Alaskan Native	10	10	11	11	11	12

Source: U.S. Department of Education, National Center for Education Statistics, *Trends in Racial/Ethnic Enrollment in Higher Education: Fall 1980 through Fall 1990* (Washington, DC: U.S. Government Printing Office, 1992), table 1, p. 1. Primary sources: U.S. Department of Education, National Center for Education Statistics, *Higher Education General Information Survey,* "Fall Enrollment in Colleges and Universitites" (1978-1984) and Integrated Postsecondary Education Data System (IPEDS), "Fall Enrollment" surveys (1986, 1988, and 1990). Because of underreporting/nonreporting of racial/ethnic data, data prior to 1986 were estimated when possible. Due to rounding, detail may not add to totals.

★ 271 ★

Higher Education Enrollment by Sex in Percent: 1980-1990

Fall enrollment, in percent, by race/ethnicity and sex, biennially 1980 to 1990.

Race/ethnicity and sex	Percent					
	1980	1982	1984	1986	1988	1990
All students						
Total	100.0	100.0	100.0	100.0	100.0	100.0
Asian/Pacific Islander	2.4	2.8	3.2	3.6	3.8	4.0
White non-Hispanic	81.4	80.7	80.2	79.3	78.8	77.9
Black non-Hispanic	9.2	8.9	8.8	8.7	8.7	8.9
Hispanic	3.9	4.2	4.4	4.9	5.2	5.5
American Indian/Alaskan Native	0.7	0.7	0.7	0.7	0.7	0.7
Men						
Total	48.5	48.4	47.9	47.1	46.0	45.5
Asian/Pacific Islander	1.3	1.5	1.7	1.9	2.0	2.1
White non-Hispanic	39.5	39.5	38.3	37.2	36.1	35.3
Black non-Hispanic	3.8	3.7	3.6	3.5	3.4	3.5
Hispanic	1.9	2.0	2.1	2.3	2.4	2.5
American Indian/Alaskan Native	0.3	0.3	0.3	0.3	0.3	0.3
Women						
Total	51.5	51.6	52.1	52.9	54.0	54.5
Asian/Pacific Islander	1.1	1.3	1.5	1.7	1.8	2.0
White non-Hispanic	41.9	41.7	41.9	42.2	42.7	42.6
Black non-Hispanic	5.2	5.2	5.2	5.2	5.3	5.4
Hispanic	2.2	2.3	2.3	2.6	2.8	3.0
American Indian/Alaskan Native	0.4	0.4	0.4	0.4	0.4	0.4

Source: U.S. Department of Education, National Center for Education Statistics, *Trends in Racial/Ethnic Enrollment in Higher Education: Fall 1980 through Fall 1990* (Washington, DC: U.S. Government Printing Office, 1992), table 2, p. 2. Primary sources: U.S. Department of Education, National Center for Education Statistics, *Higher Education General Information Survey,* "Fall Enrollment in Colleges and Universities" (1978-1984); and Integrated Postsecondary Education Data System (IPEDS), "Fall Enrollment" surveys (1986, 1988, and 1990). Because of underreporting/nonreporting of racial/ethnic data, data prior to 1986 were estimated when possible. Due to rounding, detail may not add to totals.

★ 272 ★

Higher Education Enrollment by Sex: 1980-1990

Fall enrollment by sex and race/ethnicity, biennially 1980 to 1990.

Race/ethnicity and sex	Number in thousands					
	1980	1982	1984	1986	1988	1990
All students						
Total	12,087	12,388	12,235	12,504	13,043	13,710
Asian/Pacific Islander	286	351	390	448	497	555
White non-Hispanic	9,833	9,997	9,815	9,921	10,283	10,675
Black non-Hispanic	1,107	1,101	1,076	1,082	1,130	1,223
Hispanic	472	519	535	618	680	758
American Indian/Alaskan Native	84	88	84	90	93	103
Nonresident alien	305	331	335	345	361	397
Men						
Total	5,868	5,999	5,859	5,885	5,998	6.239
Asian/Pacific Islander	151	189	210	239	259	287
White non-Hispanic	4,773	4,830	4,690	4,647	4,712	4,841
Black non-Hispanic	464	458	437	436	443	476
Hispanic	232	252	254	290	310	344
American Indian/Alaskan Native	38	40	38	39	39	43
Nonresident alien	211	230	231	233	235	248
Women						
Total	6,219	6,389	6.376	6,619	7,045	7,472
Asian/Pacific Islander	135	162	180	209	237	268
White non-Hispanic	5,060	5,167	5,125	5,273	5,572	5,834
Black non-Hispanic	643	644	639	646	687	747
Hispanic	240	267	281	328	370	414
American Indian/Alaskan Native	46	48	46	51	53	60
Nonresident alien	94	101	104	112	126	149

Source: U.S. Department of Education, National Center for Education Statistics, *Trends in Racial/Ethnic Enrollment in Higher Education: Fall 1980 through Fall 1990* (Washington, DC: U.S. Government Printing Office, 1992), table 2, p. 2. Primary sources:U.S. Department of Education, National Center for Education Statistics, *Higher Education General Information Survey,* "Fall Enrollment in Colleges and Universities" (1978-1984); and Integrated Postsecondary Education Data System (IPEDS), "Fall Enrollment" surveys (1986, 1988, and 1990). Because of underreporting/nonreporting of racial/ethnic data, data prior to 1986 were estimated when possible. Due to rounding, detail may not add to totals.

★ 273 ★

Higher Education Enrollment by Type of Institution in Percent: 1980-1990

Fall enrollment, in percent, by type of institution and race/ethnicity, biennially 1980 to 1990.

Level of institution and race/ethnicity	Percent					
	1980	1982	1984	1986	1988	1990
All institutions						
Total	100.0	100.0	100.0	100.0	100.0	100.0
Asian/Pacific Islander	2.4	2.8	3.2	3.6	3.8	4.0
White non-Hispanic	81.4	80.7	80.2	79.3	78.8	77.9
Black non-Hispanic	9.2	8.9	8.8	8.7	8.7	8.9
Hispanic	3.9	4.2	4.4	4.9	5.2	5.5
American Indian/Alaskan Native	0.7	0.7	0.7	0.7	0.7	0.7
Nonresident Alien	2.5	2.7	2.7	2.8	2.8	2.9
4-year institutions						
Total	62.6	61.7	63.0	62.6	62.7	62.2
White non-Hispanic	51.9	50.9	51.5	50.7	50.5	49.3
Total minority	8.7	8.7	9.2	9.6	9.9	10.6
Asian/Pacific Islander	1.3	1.6	1.8	2.1	2.3	2.5
Black non-Hispanic	5.2	4.9	5.0	4.9	5.0	5.2
Hispanic	1.8	1.8	2.0	2.2	2.3	2.5
American Indian/Alaskan Native	0.3	0.3	0.3	0.3	0.3	0.4
2-year Institutions						
Total	37.4	38.3	37.0	37.4	37.3	37.8
White non-Hispanic	29.4	29.8	28.7	28.7	28.4	28.6
Total minority	7.4	8.0	7.9	8.3	8.5	8.7
Asian/Pacific Islander	1.0	1.3	1.4	1.5	1.5	1.5
Black non-Hispanic	3.9	3.9	3.7	3.7	3.6	3.7
Hispanic	2.1	2.3	2.4	2.7	2.9	3.0
American Indian/Alaskan Native	0.4	0.4	0.4	0.4	0.4	0.4

Source: U.S. Department of Education, National Center for Education Statistics, *Trends in Racial/Ethnic Enrollment in Higher Education: Fall 1980 through Fall 1990* (Washington, DC: U.S. Government Printing Office, 1992), table 3, p. 3. Primary sources: U.S. Department of Education, National Center for Education Statistics, *Higher Education General Information Survey,* "Fall Enrollment in Colleges and Universities" (1978-1984) and Integrated Postsecondary Education Data System (IPEDS), "Fall Enrollment" surveys (1986, 1988, and 1990). Because of underreporting/nonreporting of racial/ethnic data, data prior to 1986 were estimated when possible. Due to rounding, detail may not add to totals.

★ 274 ★

Higher Education Enrollment by Type of Institution: 1980-1990

Fall enrollment by level of institution and race/ethnicity, biennially 1980-1990.

Level of institution and race/ethnicity	Number in thousands					
	1980	1982	1984	1986	1988	1990
All institutions						
Total	12,087	12,388	12,235	12,504	13,043	13,710
Asian/Pacific Islander	286	351	390	448	497	555
White non-Hispanic	9,833	9,997	9,815	9,921	10,283	10,675
Black non-Hispanic	1,107	1,101	1,076	1,082	1,130	1,223
Hispanic	472	519	535	618	680	758
American Indian/Alaskan Native	84	88	84	90	93	103
Nonresident alien	305	331	335	345	361	397
4-year institutions	7,565	7,648	7,708	7,824	8,175	8,529
White non-Hispanic	6,275	6,306	6,301	6,337	6.582	6,757
Total minority	1,050	1,073	1,124	1,195	1,292	1,450
Asian/Pacific Islander	162	193	223	262	297	343
Black non-Hispanic	634	612	617	615	656	715
Hispanic	217	229	246	278	296	344
American Indian/Alaskan Native	37	39	38	40	42	48
Nonresident alien	241	270	282	292	302	322
2-year institutions	4,521	4,740	4,527	4,680	4,868	5,181
White non-Hispanic	3,558	3,692	3,514	3,584	3,702	3,918
Total minority	899	987	961	1,043	1,107	1,189
Asian/Pacific Islander	124	158	167	186	199	212
Black non-Hispanic	472	489	459	467	473	509
Hispanic	255	291	289	340	384	414
American Indian/Alaskan Native	47	49	46	51	50	54
Nonresident alien	64	61	53	53	60	75

Source: U.S. Department of Education, National Center for Education Statistics, *Trends in Racial/Ethnic Enrollment in Higher Education: Fall 1980 through Fall 1990* (Washington, DC: U.S. Government Printing Office, 1992), table 3, p. 3. Primary sources: U.S. Department of Education, National Center for Education Statistics, *Higher Education General Information Survey,* "Fall Enrollment in Colleges and Universities" (1978-1984) and Integrated Postsecondary Education Data System (IPEDS), "Fall Enrollment" surveys (1986, 1988, and 1990). Because of underreporting/nonreporting of racial/ethnic data, data prior to 1986 were estimated when possible. Due to rounding, detail may not add to totals.

★ 275 ★

Community College Enrollment: Illinois

Headcount enrollment (full-and part-time) in public community colleges by percent of total and percent change by race/ethnicity, 1987 and 1991.

Race/ethnicity	1987		1991		Percent change
	Number	Percent	Number	Percent	
Asian/Pacific Islander	11,613	3.6%	14,878	4.1%	11.2
American Indian/Alaskan	1,224	0.4%	1,429	0.4%	7.2
Black	47,552	14.9%	52,226	14.2%	3.0
Hispanic	22,425	7.0%	34,338	9.4%	4.8
White	235,899	73.9%	262,570	71.6%	4.2
Nonresident Alien	574	0.2%	1,179	0.3%	37.3

Source: Illinois Community College Board, *Student Enrollment Data and Trends in the Public Community Colleges of Illinois* (Springfield, IL: Illinois Community College Board, fall 1991), table 5, p. 5. Also in source: data by curriculum area, college, and enrollment status.

Enrollment: Elementary and Secondary Schools

★ 276 ★

Asian/Pacific Islander School Enrollment by State, Preprimary to College

Numbers of Asian/Pacific Islanders age three years and over enrolled in schools in the United States, 1990.

State	Enrolled in:							
	White				Asian or Pacific Islander			
	Preprimary school	Elementary or high school	College	Not enrolled in school	Preprimary school	Elementary or high school	College	Not enrolled in school
Alabama	42,241	480,429	192,902	2,146,889	341	4,708	4,236	11,494
Alaska	9,403	73,864	31,145	279,417	456	3,874	1,434	12,423
Arizona	47,833	460,329	246,642	2,088,322	996	10,110	9,535	30,662
Arkansas	25,537	322,453	99,598	1,422,066	89	3,068	1,436	7,012
California	360,684	3,119,767	1,738,288	14,442,767	46,538	572,418	379,093	1,713,658
Colorado	59,631	475,863	235,374	2,014,312	1,363	12,511	8,767	33,582
Connecticut	60,480	398,993	209,601	2,081,516	1,226	9,369	7,077	28,726
Delaware	9,943	79,552	41,275	382,497	194	1,534	1,451	5,206
Florida	170,393	1,385,232	666,176	8,155,240	2,512	30,252	19,470	92,291
Georgia	81,525	728,099	270,515	3,332,261	1,231	15,503	8,407	45,249
Hawaii	7,540	52,245	26,270	266,904	12,528	124,968	52,165	468,171
Idaho	17,667	196,194	62,928	630,979	137	1,975	1,462	5,121
Illinois	182,292	1,382,046	656,594	6,370,263	5,699	57,544	42,329	166,241
Indiana	86,658	855,850	322,997	3,548,623	814	6,560	8,364	19,021
Iowa	–	–	–	–	–	–	–	–
Kansas	44,648	376,922	164,880	1,552,028	580	7,271	6,362	15,255
Kentucky	46,060	590,792	191,175	2,432,143	416	3,601	2,941	9,478
Louisiana	52,720	496,850	181,998	1,990,471	671	9,478	5,660	22,020
Maine	23,549	202,566	71,536	861,273	162	1,844	867	3,662

[Continued]

★ 276 ★

Asian/Pacific Islander School Enrollment by State, Preprimary to College (Continued)

Numbers of Asian/Pacific Islanders age three years and over enrolled in schools in the United States, 1990.

State	Enrolled in:							
	White				Asian or Pacific Islander			
	Preprimary school	Elementary or high school	College	Not enrolled in school	Preprimary school	Elementary or high school	College	Not enrolled in school
Maryland	67,564	482,046	253,753	2,448,176	2,775	26,132	19,335	83,277
Massachusetts	105,990	742,717	465,580	3,887,330	2,873	27,715	27,865	75,205
Michigan	166,386	1,309,449	594,402	5,361,421	2,759	23,748	18,130	52,555
Minnesota	86,175	692,305	302,553	2,873,744	2,367	23,026	10,484	35,049
Mississippi	–	–	–	–	–	–	–	–
Missouri	–	–	–	–	–	–	–	–
Montana	13,000	135,822	45,793	516,871	99	811	717	2,366
Nebraska	–	–	–	–	–	–	–	–
Nevada	16,079	148,626	61,679	743,262	449	6,538	3,375	26,064
New Hampshire	21,648	173,013	74,316	769,307	257	1,813	1,427	5,020
New Jersey	123,900	864,349	400,518	4,507,590	6,462	54,227	27,807	168,331
New Mexico	17,282	210,445	85,846	784,847	283	2,882	2,029	8,447
New York	246,000	1,931,168	1,028,139	9,681,384	10,697	120,885	89,219	438,734
North Carolina	74,796	737,655	332,248	3,675,751	1,009	9,918	7,795	29,265
North Dakota	10,020	109,333	45,072	415,368	67	606	763	1,562
Ohio	173,677	1,589,567	619,467	6,752,519	1,996	18,107	16,507	48,694
Oklahoma	42,600	431,685	175,661	1,837,775	601	6,652	7,152	16,870
Oregon	48,282	427,003	177,928	1,878,090	1,404	13,434	12,662	36,780
Pennsylvania	185,912	1,568,308	672,314	7,699,031	2,908	28,740	22,669	74,108
Rhode Island	15,111	129,322	80,662	658,774	281	4,119	2,706	9,412
South Carolina	36,171	381,467	156,068	1,739,176	342	4,498	2,933	12,716
South Dakota	11,371	113,911	38,007	447,094	55	753	639	1,649
Tennessee	56,985	640,092	225,467	2,973,176	634	6,415	4,000	18,127
Texas	231,125	2,281,927	906,990	8,797,600	5,813	67,122	48,035	178,888
Utah	41,156	393,353	136,470	952,788	715	7,868	5,539	16,675
Vermont	10,956	92,020	39,494	388,098	119	616	667	1,504
Virginia	88,369	714,414	342,954	3,452,598	2,414	32,546	20,169	96,644
Washington	89,301	689,235	288,014	3,062,836	4,715	44,889	26,778	124,899
West Virginia	20,482	303,566	91,659	1,251,294	172	1,579	1,476	3,980
Wisconsin	87,592	754,335	317,667	3,172,381	1,950	14,236	9,810	22,436
Wyoming	8,422	85,565	31,452	283,014	34	611	525	1,397

Source: U.S. Bureau of Census, Summary Tape File 3A. *Note:* A dash (–) indicates data was unavailable at time of publication.

★ 277 ★

School Enrollment: Trends

Numbers of students enrolled in elementary and secondary public schools and percent by race/ethnicity, 1976, 1984, 1986, and 1988, and change from 1976 to 1988 in percent.

Race/ethnicity	Enrollment in thousands				Percent change 1976 to 1988
	1976	1984	1985	1988	
Total	43,714	39,452	41,156	40,484	-7.4%
White non-Hispanic	33,229	28,106	28,957	28,628	-13.8%
Total minority	10,485	11,346	12,200	11,857	13.1%
Asian/Pacific Islander	535	994	1,158	1,267	136.8%
Black non-Hispanic	6,774	6,389	6,622	6,158	-9.1%
Hispanic	2,807	3,599	4,064	4,071	45.0%
American Indian/Alaskan Native	368	364	356	361	-1.9%
Percent					
Total	100.0%	100.0%	100.0%	100.0%	-
White non-Hispanic	76.0%	71.2%	70.4%	70.7%	-
Total minority	24.0%	28.8%	29.6%	29.3%	-
Asian/Pacific Islander	1.2%	2.5%	2.8%	3.1%	-
Black non-Hispanic	15.5%	16.2%	16.1%	15.2%	-
Hispanic	6.4%	9.1%	9.9%	10.1%	-
American Indian/Alaskan Native	0.8%	0.9%	0.9%	0.9%	-

Source: U.S. Department of Education, National Center for Education Statistics, *The Condition of Education, 1992,* (Washington, DC: U.S. Government Printing Office, June 1992), p. 293. Primary sources: U.S. Department of Education, Office for Civil Rights, *Directory of Elementary and Secondary School Districts and Schools in Selected Districts,* 1976-77, and 1984; 1986 and 1988 Elementary and Secondary School Civil Rights Survey, unpublished tabulations.

★ 278 ★

Asian/Pacific Islander School Enrollees: 1985–1995 (Projected)

Number of Asian/Pacific Islander enrollees in public elementary and secondary schools, 1985-1986 to 1994-1995 (projected).

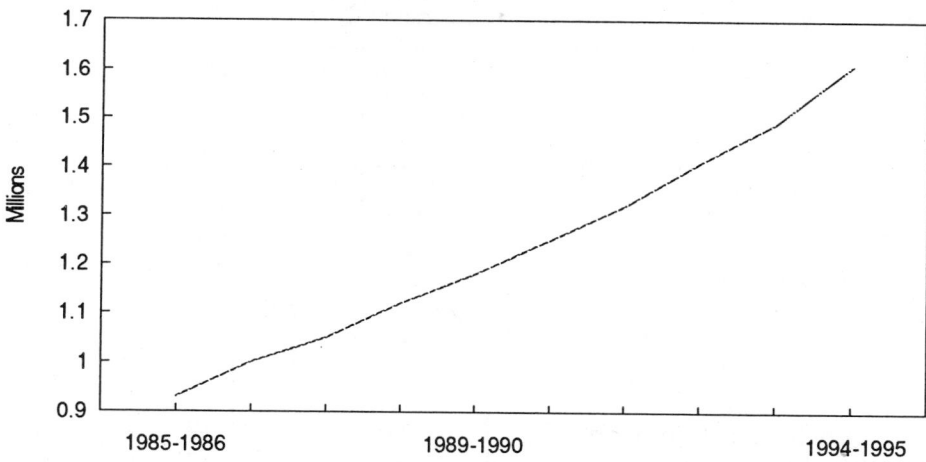

Source: WICHE and The College Board, *The Road to College: Educational Progress by Race and Ethnicity* (Boulder, CO: Western Interstate Commission for Higher Education, 1991), table 17, p. 71-79. Also in source: data for all 50 states on African Americans, Latinos, American Indians/Alaskan Natives, and white non-Latinos. Enrollments are for first through twelfth grade, including enrollments in ungraded and special education programs.

★ 279 ★

Asian/Pacific Islander School Enrollees and High School Graduates: 1985-1995 (Projected)

Number of Asian/Pacific Islander (A/PI) enrollees[a] and high school graduates, 1985-86 to 1989-90 (actual) and 1990-91 to 1994-95 (projected) for total United States.[b]

Year	Total enrollment, A/PI	High school graduates, A/PI
1985-86	938,400	62,090
1986-87	1,005,460	66,990
1987-88	1,055,180	74,540
1988-89	1,122,340	77,680
1989-90	1,181,320	80,950
1990-91	1,252,620	84,020
1991-92	1,324,110	86,840
1992-93	1,405,940	90,960
1993-94	1,490,950	94,890
1994-95	1,599,040	98,090

Source: WICHE and The College Board, *The Road to College: Educational Progress by Race and Ethnicity* (Boulder, CO: Western Interstate Commission for Higher Education, 1991), table 17, p. 71-79. Also in source: data for all 50 states on African Americans, Latinos, American Indians/Alaskan Natives, and white non-Latinos. *Notes:* (a) Enrollments are for first through twelfth grade, including enrollments in ungraded and special education programs. (b) United States total are rounded to the nearest tenth.

★ 280 ★

Asian/Pacific Islander High School Graduates
by State, 1986 and 1995—Projected

Number of Asian/Pacific Islander high school graduates in 1986, projected number of graduates in 1995, and percent change from 1986 to 1995 by state (including District of Columbia).

State	Asian/Pacific Islander		
	1986	1995	Percent change
Alabama	135	242	79.3%
Alaska	146	261	78.8%
Arizona	358	702	96.1%
Arkansas	113	173	53.1%
California	24,011	39,696	65.3%
Colorado	649	836	28.8%
Connecticut	362	635	75.4%
Delaware	73	71	-2.7%
District of Columbia	28	37	32.1%
Florida	1,005	2,237	122.6%
Georgia	379	384	1.3%
Hawaii	7,619	8,069	5.9%
Idaho	131	144	9.9%
Illinois	2,305	3,983	72.8%
Indiana	324	451	39.2%
Iowa	331	304	-8.2%
Kansas	294	452	53.7%
Kentucky	142	305	114.8%
Louisiana	322	435	35.1%
Maine	52	78	50.0%
Maryland	1,439	1,275	-11.4%
Massachusetts	1,023	2,191	114.2%
Michigan	964	899	-6.7%
Minnesota	766	1,755	129.1%
Mississippi	88	87	-1.1%
Missouri	342	336	-1.8%
Montana	67	66	-1.5%
Nebraska	192	188	-2.1%
Nevada	278	438	57.6%
New Hampshire	40	157	292.5%
New Jersey	1,704	4,152	143.7%
New Mexico	143	266	86.0%
New York	4,703	8,201	74.4%
North Carolina	357	733	105.3%
North Dakota	43	43	0.0%
Ohio	664	599	-9.8%
Oklahoma	414	393	-5.1%
Oregon	799	888	11.1%
Pennsylvania	1,115	2,037	82.7%
Rhode Island	127	106	-16.5%
South Carolina	162	342	111.1%
South Dakota	25	26	4.0%

[Continued]

★ 280 ★

Asian/Pacific Islander High School Graduates
by State, 1986 and 1995—Projected (Continued)

Number of Asian/Pacific Islander high school graduates in 1986, projected number of graduates in 1995, and percent change from 1986 to 1995 by state (including District of Columbia).

State	Asian/Pacific Islander		
	1986	1995	Percent change
Tennessee	190	523	175.3%
Texas	3,005	4,683	55.8%
Utah	330	724	119.4%
Vermont	32	126	293.8%
Virginia	1,565	2,954	88.8%
Washington	2,184	3,307	51.4%
West Virginia	51	98	92.2%
Wisconsin	480	978	103.8%
Wyoming	23	23	0.0%
United States	62,094	98,089	58.0%

Source: Western Interstate Commission for Higher Education (WICHE), press release, September 13, 1991. Also in source: data on African Americans, American Indians/Alaskan Natives, Latinos, and white non-Latinos. Primary source: *The Road to College: Educational Progress by Race and Ethnicity* (Boulder, CO: WICHE, 1991). Results of study covering nine years of actual and estimated data are available in the publication. The study was conducted jointly with The College Board, New York.

★ 281 ★

Asian/Pacific Islander School Enrollees and Graduates,
California: 1984-1995 (Projected)

Number of Asian/Pacific Islander (A/PI) enrollees[a] and high school graduates, 1984-85 to 1989-90 (actual) and 1990-91 to 1994-95 (projected) for California.

Year	Total A/PI Enrollment	A/PI High School Graduates
1984-85	326,984	22,381
1985-86	354,319	24,011
1986-87	380,991	25,839
1987-88	407,416	29,711
1988-89	431,133	29,906
1989-90	458,548	31,923
1990-91	493,122	33,244
1991-92	532,023	34,640
1992-93	572,896	36,489
1993-94	618,609	38,293
1994-95	671,300	39,696

Source: Western Interstate Commission for Higher Education (WICHE) and The College Board, *The Road to College: Educational Progress by Race and Ethnicity* (Boulder, CO: WICHE, 1991), table 17, p. 71-79. Also in source: data for all 50 states on African Americans, Latinos, American Indians/Alaskan Natives, white non-Latinos. *Note:* (a) Enrollments are for first through twelfth grade, including enrollments in ungraded and special education programs.

★ 282 ★

Asian/Pacific Islander School Enrollees and Graduates, Florida: 1980-1995 (Projected)

Numbers of Asian/Pacific Islander (A/PI) enrollees[a] and high school graduates, 1980-81 to 1989-90 (actual) and 1990-91 to 1994-95 (projected) for Florida.

Year	Total Enrollment, A/PI	High School Graduates, A/PI
1980-81	10,884	534
1981-82	11,904	617
1982-83	12,983	720
1983-84	13,901	725
1984-85	15,376	888
1985-86	16,615	1,005
1986-87	18,433	1,131
1987-88	19,689	1,337
1988-89	21,437	1,566
1989-90	23,469	1,694
1990-91	25,336	1,839
1991-92	27,435	2,004
1992-93	29,751	2,009
1993-94	32,535	2,126
1994-95	35,801	2,237

Source: Western Interstate Commission for Higher Education (WICHE) and The College Board, *The Road to College: Educational Progress by Race and Ethnicity* (Boulder, CO: WICHE, 1991), table 17, p. 71-79. Also in source: data for all 50 states on African Americans, Latinos, American Indians/Alaskan Natives, white non-Latinos. *Note:* (a) Enrollments are for first through twelfth grade, including enrollments in ungraded and special education programs.

★ 283 ★

Asian/Pacific Islander School Enrollees and Graduates, Hawaii: 1980-1995—Projected

Numbers of Asian/Pacific Islander (A/PI) enrollees[a] and high school graduates, 1980-81 to 1989-90 (actual) and 1990-91 to 1994-95 (projected) for Hawaii.

Years	Total Enrollment, A/PI	High School Graduates, A/PI
1980-81	109,328	9,164
1981-82	107,417	9,005
1982-83	106,904	8,431
1983-84	106,578	8,134
1984-85	106,546	7,847
1985-86	106,548	7,619
1986-87	105,769	7,977
1987-88	108,770	8,101
1988-89	109,327	7,943
1989-90	111,196	7,404

[Continued]

★ 283 ★

Asian/Pacific Islander School Enrollees and Graduates, Hawaii: 1980-1995—Projected (Continued)

Numbers of Asian/Pacific Islander (A/PI) enrollees[a] and high school graduates, 1980-81 to 1989-90 (actual) and 1990-91 to 1994-95 (projected) for Hawaii.

Years	Total Enrollment, A/PI	High School Graduates, A/PI
1990-91	112,933	7,374
1991-92	114,334	7,309
1992-93	115,846	7,473
1993-94	117,303	7,919
1994-95	118,666	8,069

Source: Western Interstate Commission for Higher Education (WICHE) and The College Board, *The Road to College: Educational Progress by Race and Ethnicity* (Boulder, CO: WICHE, 1991), table 17, p. 71-79. Also in source: data for all 50 states on African Americans, Latinos, American Indians/Alaskan Natives, white non-Latinos. *Note:* (a) Enrollments are for first through twelfth grade, including enrollments in ungraded and special education programs.

★ 284 ★

Asian/Pacific Islander School Enrollees and Graduates, Illinois: 1980-1995 (Projected)

Numbers of Asian/Pacific Islander (A/PI) enrollees[a] and high school graduates, 1980-81 to 1989-90 (actual) and 1990-91 to 1994-95 (projected) for Illinois.

Year	Total Enrollment, A/PI	High School Graduates, A/PI
1980-81	26,967	na
1981-82	30,947	na
1982-83	32,744	na
1983-84	33,420	na
1984-85	35,101	na
1985-86	36,821	2,305
1986-87	38,884	2,588
1987-88	40,354	2,945
1988-89	42,024	3,184
1989-90	43,571	3,333
1990-91	44,351	3,546
1991-92	44,651	3,643
1992-93	44,666	3,671
1993-94	46,234	3,819
1994-95	48,116	3,983

Source: Western Interstate Commission for Higher Education (WICHE) and The College Board, *The Road to College: Educational Progress by Race and Ethnicity* (Boulder, CO: WICHE , 1991), table 17, p. 71-79. Also in source: data for all 50 states on African Americans, Latinos, American Indians/Alaskan Natives, white non-Latinos *Note:* (a) Enrollments are for first through twelfth grade, including enrollments in ungraded and special education programs.

★ 285 ★

Asian/Pacific Islander School Enrollees and Graduates, Massachusetts: 1980-1995 (Projected)

Numbers of Asian/Pacific Islander (A/PI) enrollees[a] and high school graduates[b], 1980-81 to 1989-90 (actual) and 1990-91 to 1994-95 (projected) for Massachusetts.

Year	Total Enrollment, A/PI	High School Graduates, A/PI
1980-81	9,612	na
1981-82	10,871	na
1982-83	12,341	na
1983-84	13,211	na
1984-85	14,526	862
1985-86	16,084	1,023
1986-87	17,597	1,096
1987-88	19,531	1,202
1988-89	21,984	1,449
1989-90	23,744	1,600
1990-91	25,994	1,816
1991-92	28,256	1,967
1992-93	30,818	1,863
1993-94	34,298	2,166
1994-95	38,695	2,191

Source: Western Interstate Commission for Higher Education (WICHE) and The College Board, *The Road to College: Educational Progress by Race and Ethnicity* (Boulder, CO: WICHE, 1991), table 17, p. 71-79. Also in source: data for all 50 states on African Americans, Latinos, American Indians/Alaskan Natives, white non-Latinos. *Notes:* (a) Enrollments are for first through twelfth grade, including enrollments in ungraded and special education programs. (b) Historical graduate data are estimates based on Asian/Pacific Islander 12th grade enrollments plus all twelfth grade enrollments multiplied by total graduates for each year.

★ 286 ★

Asian/Pacific Islander School Enrollees and Graduates, New Jersey: 1985-1995 (Projected)

Numbers of Asian/Pacific Islander (A/PI) enrollees[a] and high school graduates[b], 1985-86 to 1989-90 (actual) and 1990-91 to 1994-95 (projected).

Years	Total Enrollment, A/PI[b]	High School Graduates, A/PI
1985-86	17,991	1,704
1986-87	27,254	1,930
1987-88	26,831	2,200
1988-89	37,877	2,451
1989-90	40,869	2,786
1990-91	44,375	2,916
1991-92	48,278	3,276
1992-93	52,379	3,606
1993-94	56,001	3,936
1994-95	61,398	4,152

Source: Western Interstate Commission for Higher Education (WICHE) and The College Board, *The Road to College: Educational Progress by Race and Ethnicity,* (Boulder, CO:W-ICHE, 1991), table 17, p. 71-79. Also in source: data for all 50 states on African Americans, Latinos, American Indians/Alaskan Natives, white non-Latinos. *Notes:* (a) Enrollments are for first through twelfth grade, including enrollments in ungraded and special education programs. (b) Enrollment and graduate data prior to 1988-89 are estimates. Graduate data for 1990 are estimated based on Asian/Pacific Islander twelfth graders plus all twelfth graders multiplied by total graduates for that year.

★ 287 ★

Asian/Pacific Islander School Enrollees and Graduates, New York: 1985-1995 (Projected)

Numbers of Asian/Pacific Islander (A/PI) enrollees[a] and high school graduates, 1980-88 to 1989-90 (actual) and 1990-91 to 1994-95 (projected) .

Years	Total Enrollment, A/PI	High School Graduates, A/PI
1980-81	50,920	na
1981-82	54,698	na
1982-83	59,888	na
1983-84	65,592	na
1984-85	70,885	5,502
1985-86	75,116	4,703
1986-87	80,796	5,240
1987-88	85,582	5,623
1988-89	90,169	6,183
1989-90	94,662	6,515
1990-91	99,873	6,898
1991-92	105,880	6,770
1992-93	112,948	7,497
1993-94	121,706	7,678
1994-95	132,889	8,201

Source: Western Interstate Commission for Higher Education (WICHE) and The College Board, *The Road to College: Educational Progress by Race and Ethnicity,* (Boulder, CO: WICHE, 1991), table 17, p. 71-79. *Note:* (a) Enrollments are for first through twelfth grade, including enrollments in ungraded and special education programs.

★ 288 ★

Asian/Pacific Islander School Enrollees and Graduates, Texas: 1980-1995 (Projected)

Numbers of Asian/Pacific Islander (A/PI) enrollees[a] and high school graduates, 1980-81 to 1989-90 (actual) and 1990-91 to 1994-95 (projected).

Years	Total Enrollments, A/PI	High School Graduates, A/PI
1980-81	27,700	na
1981-82	33,470	na
1982-83	39,809	na
1983-84	43,057	2,384
1984-85	46,105	2,562
1985-86	49,421	3,005
1986-87	52,111	3,194
1987-88	53,359	3,533
1988-89	55,423	3,941
1989-90	57,465	4,077
1990-91	59,562	4,215
1991-92	61,814	4,248
1992-93	64,183	4,510
1993-94	66,322	4,729
1994-95	68,740	4,683

Source: Western Interstate Commission for Higher Education (WICHE) and The College Board, *The Road to College: Educational Progress by Race and Ethnicity* (Boulder, CO: WICHE, 1991), table 17, p. 71-79. *Note:* (a) Enrollments are for first through twelfth grade, including enrollments in ungraded and special education programs.

★ 289 ★

Asian/Pacific Islander School Enrollees and Graduates, Virginia: 1985-1995 (Projected)

Numbers of Asian/Pacific Islander (A/PI) enrollees[a] and high school graduates, 1985-86 to 1989-90 (actual) and 1990-91 to 1994-95 (projected).

Years	Total Enrollment, A/PI[b]	High School Graduates, A/PI[c]
1985-86	23,446	1,565
1986-87	22,970	1,696
1987-88	22,977	1,892
1988-89	26,565	2,073
1989-90	26,608	2,201
1990-91	30,532	2,257
1991-92	31,100	2,399
1992-93	35,497	2,542
1993-94	36,325	2,662
1994-95	41,243	2,954

Source: Western Interstate Commission for Higher Education (WICHE) and The College Board, *The Road to College: Educational Progress by Race and Ethnicity* (Boulder, CO: WICHE, 1991), table 17, p. 71-79. *Notes:* (a) Enrollments are for first through twelfth grade, including enrollments in ungraded and special education programs. (b) Elementary/secondary enrollments by grade level are not available. (c) Projected high school graduate data are based on the actual number of Asian/Pacific Islander graduates divided by total graduates from 1985-86 through 1989-90.

★ 290 ★

Asian/Pacific Islander School Enrollees and Graduates, Washington: 1980-1995 (Projected)

Numbers of Asian/Pacific Islander (A/PI) enrollees[a] and high school graduates, 1980-81 to 1989-90 (actual) and 1990-91 to 1994-95 (projected) for Washington.

Years	Total Enrollment, A/PI	High School Graduates, A/PI
1980-81	25,218	
1981-82	28,806	
1982-83	29,935	
1983-84	30,415	
1984-85	31,534	
1985-86	32,706	2,184
1986-87	34,094	2,219
1987-88	36,033	2,659
1988-89	38,189	2,936
1989-90	40,077	2,891
1990-91	41,630	3,039
1991-92	43,249	3,117
1992-93	44,830	3,184
1993-94	46,534	3,117
1994-95	48,808	3,307

Source: Western Interstate Commission for Higher Education (WICHE) and The College Board, *The Road to College: Educational Progress by Race and Ethnicity,* (Boulder, CO: WICHE, 1991), table 17, p. 71-79. Also in source: data for all 50 states on African Americans, Latinos, American Indians/Alaskan Natives, white non-Latinos. *Note:* (a) Enrollments are for first through twelfth grade, including enrollments in ungraded and special education programs.

★ 291 ★

Independent School Enrollment: 1981-1991

Enrollment in independent schools, in percent, by race/ethnicity and total number of schools reporting, 1981 to 1991 (1983-1985 excluded).

Race/ethnicity	19981-82	1986-87	1988-89	1989-90	1990-91
Racial/ethnic group					
Asian American	3.1%	4.7%	5.1%	5.4%	5.7%
African American	4.2%	4.7%	5.0%	5.2%	5.3%
Latino	1.8%	1.8%	2.0%	2.0%	2.2%
American Indian	0.1%	0.1%	0.1%	0.2%	0.2%
Total minority, all schools	9.1%	11.2%	12.2%	12.7%	13.4%
Number of Schools	785	826	831	821	804

Source: NAIS Statistics 1990-1991: Financial Aid, Financial Operations, Enrollment, Staffing (Boston, MA: National Association of Independent Schools, 1991). Also in source: data on "students of color" as a percentage of total enrollment by school type, school size and region.

★ 292 ★

Independent School Enrollment by School Type and Region: 1991

Enrollment in independent schools by school type, school size, region, and race/ethnicity, 1991.

School type	Asian American	African American	Latino	American Indian	Total	Total Enrollment
School Type[a]						
Boarding (95% or more boarding)	939	431	234		31	935
Boarding-day	1,443	1,659	725	97	3,924	27,009
Day	14,953	13,594	5,335	312	34,194	255,822
Day-boarding	1,784	1,394	671	84	3,933	30,678
Girls'	2,531	2,523	926	42	6,022	35,610
Boys'	1,582	1,274	762	20	3,638	27,524
Coed	14,306	13,281	5,277	462	33,326	257,583
Elementary	2,557	2,412	1,145	55	6,169	56,506
Elementary/secondary	12,091	11,132	4,019	261	27,503	198,534
Secondary	3,771	3,534	1,801	208	9,314	65,677
School Size						
Under 201 students	1,073	1,545	669	78	3,365	28,758
201-300	1,717	2,235	1,068	103	5,123	39,178
301-500	5,244	4,940	2,016	113	12,313	90,474
501-700	3,991	3,099	1,196	65	8,351	56,145
Over 700	6,394	5,259	2,016	165	13,834	106,162
Region[b]						
East	3,150	3,292	1,520	28	7,990	45,809
Middle Atlantic	3,320	4,084	914	46	8,364	61,543
Midwest	2,601	2,522	487	73	5,683	36,534
New England	2,128	2,302	919	139	5,488	52,261
Southeast	2,010	2,061	1,044	52	5,167	60,462
Southwest	1,307	1,342	982	117	3,748	30,116
West	3,903	1,475	1,099	69	6,546	33,992
All Schools	18,419	17,078	6,965	524	42,986	320,717

Source: NAIS Statistics 1990-1991: Financial Aid, Financial Operations, Enrollment, Staffing (Boston, MA: National Association of Independent Schools, 1991). *Note:* (a) School type is defined as follows: Boarding—95% or more boarding; Boarding-day—50 to 94% boarding students; Day—95% or more day students; Day-boarding—51-94% day students. Elementary—any grades preschool through 9; Elementary/secondary—kindergarten through 12, 5 through 12, or 1 through 10; Secondary—7 through 12, 9 through 12, or 7 through post-graduate. (b) Regions are defined as follows: East—New Jersey, New York; Middle Atlantic—Delaware, District of Columbia, Maryland, Pennsylvania, Virginia; Midwest—Illinois, Indiana, Iowa, Kentucky, Michigan, Minnesota, Missouri, Nebraska, North Dakota, Ohio, South Dakota, West Virginia, Wisconsin; New England—Connecticut, Maine, Massachusetts, New Hampshire, Rhode Island, Vermont; Southeast—Alabama, Florida, Georgia, Mississippi, North Carolina, South Carolina, Tennessee; Southwest—Arizona, Arkansas, Colorado, Kansas, Louisiana, New Mexico, Oklahoma, Texas; West—Alaska, California, Hawaii, Idaho, Montana, Nevada, Oregon, Utah, Washington, Wyoming.

★ 293 ★

Asian American Eighth Graders
by Generation in the United States

Asian American eighth graders, in percent by generation in United States, 1988.

Generation	Percent
Total	100.0%
First generation	48.1%
Second generation	30.7%
Third generation or higher	21.2%

Source: U.S. Department of Education, National Center for Education Statistics, *Language Characteristics and Academic Achievement: A Look at Asian and Hispanic Eighth Graders in NELS:88* (Washington, DC: U.S. Department of Education, 1992), table 2.2, p. 18. Primary source: U.S. Department of Education, National Center for Education Statistics, "National Education Longitudinal Study of 1988 (NELS:88), Base-Year Parent" surveys. Also in source: data on Hispanic eighth graders.

★ 294 ★

Asian American Eighth Graders by Place of Birth and Ethnicity

Number of Asian American eighth-graders, and percent by nativity and ethnicity, 1988.

Ethnicity	Number	Percent	Native-born	Foreign-born
Asian, total	1,505	100.0%	52.4%	47.6%
Chinese	309	17.4%	54.3%	45.9%
Filipino	288	20.2%	52.0%	48.2%
Japanese	92	6.0%	69.1%	31.0%
Korean	188	11.0%	35.1%	65.0%
Southeast Asian (Vietnamese, Laotian, Cambodian/Kampuchean, Thai, etc.)	240	12.7%	15.3%	84.9%
Pacific Islander (Samoan, Guamanian, etc.)	99	8.8%	85.6%	14.6%
South Asian (Asian Indian, Pakistani, Bangladeshi, Sri Lankan, etc.)	126	8.7%	45.5%	54.6%
Other Asian[a]/West Asian (Iranian, Afghan, Turkish, etc.)/Middle Eastern (Iraqui, Israeli, Lebanese, etc.)	163	15.3%	67.0%	33.1%

Source: National Center for Education Statistics, *Language Characteristics and Academic Achievement: A Look at Asian and Hispanic Eighth Graders in NELS:88* (Washington, DC: U.S. Department of Education, 1992), table 2.1, p. 17. Primary source: U.S. Department of Education, National Center for Education Statistics, "National Education Longitudinal Study of 1988 (NELS:88), Base-Year Student and Parent" surveys. Also in source: data on Hispanic eighth graders. *Notes:* (a) West Asian and Middle Easterners were included with "Other Asians" in this study because of the small number of students in these categories.

★ 295 ★

Asian American Eighth Graders by Place of Birth, Ethnicity, and Language

Asian American eighth graders, in percent, by nativity, ethnicity, and language proficiency, 1988.

Nativity/ethnicity	Language Minority (LM)[a]	Home language proficiency			English language proficiency		
	Percent	Low	Moderate	High	Low	Moderate	High
Total	72.8%	58.6%	29.7%	11.7%	4.2%	29.3%	66.5%
Student's nativity							
Native-born	59.5%						
Foreign-born	84.1%						
Ethnicity							
Southeast Asian	87.5%	65.0%	27.4%	7.6%	8.8%	34.7%	56.5%
Chinese	85.7%	61.0%	32.2%	6.8%	6.6%	34.2%	59.2%
Filipino	83.4%	53.3%	27.7%	19.0%	1.0%	31.2%	68.0%
South Asian	82.3%	73.8%	22.4%	3.8%	1.4%	20.4%	78.1%
Korean	72.2%	61.9%	28.3%	9.8%	3.0%	21.7%	75.3%
Japanese	63.1%	41.6%	35.3%	23.1%	8.9%	32.6%	58.5%
Other Asian	55.0%	50.7%	33.5%	15.9%	1.9%	25.4%	72.7%
Pacific Islander	39.0%	57.1%	28.8%	14.0%	2.0%	24.8%	73.2%

Source: U.S. Department of Education, National Center for Education Statistics, *Language Characteristics and Academic Achievement: A Look at Asian and Hispanic Eighth Graders in NELS:88* (Washington, DC: U.S. Department of Education, 1992), table 2.5, p. 24, table 2.3, p. 19. Primary source: U.S. Department of Education, National Center for Education Statistics, "National Education Longitudinal Study of 1988 (NELS:88) Base-Year Student and Parent" surveys. Also in source: data on Hispanic eighth graders. *Notes:* (a) Language Minority (LM) is a student in whose home a non-English language is typically spoken.

Financial Aid

★ 296 ★

Financial Aid to Undergraduates

Percentage of undergraduates receiving financial aid and average amount awarded per student by race/ethnicity, 1989-90.

Status	Percent of all undergraduates receiving aid					
	All under-graduates	Asian American	White non-Hispanic	Black non-Hispanic	Hispanic	American Indian
Enrollment in thousands[a]	12,600	575	9,410	1,142	840	83
Any aid, percent						
Total[b]	44.0%	35.5%	41.2%	61.2%	44.2%	51.6%
Federal	30.0%	25.5%	26.3%	50.0%	34.4%	31.8%
Non-federal	32.3%	28.2%	31.2%	40.5%	31.6%	44.1%
Grants, percent						
Total	37.2%	31.2%	34.2%	55.3%	38.7%	46.8%
Federal	21.4%	20.2%	17.5%	42.2%	27.6%	27.5%
Non-federal	28.4%	25.9%	27.2%	37.0%	28.1%	38.4%
Loans, percent						
Total	20.4%	14.7%	19.1%	28.2%	19.9%	16.2%
Federal	19.3%	13.7%	18.0%	27.2%	19.2%	15.5%
Non-federal	2.3%	2.0%	2.4%	2.4%	2.4%	1.5%
Work Study, percent	5.4%	5.7%	5.2%	8.4%	5.3%	6.9%
	Average 1989-90 award for full-time, full-year undergraduates enrolled in fall 1989					
All full-time, full-year undergraduates (thousands)	3,947	174	3,208	301	189	19
Any aid, average award						
Total	$4,732	$5,614	$4,597	$5,116	$5,139	$6,299
Federal	$3,511	$3,650	$3,488	$3,586	$3,502	$4,004
Non-federal	$2,836	$3,304	$2,785	$2,902	$3,002	$3,510
Grants, average award						
Total	$3,095	$3,836	$2,976	$3,433	$3,388	$3,921
Federal	$1,770	$1,886	$1,702	$1,997	$1,867	$2,099
Non-federal	$2,544	$2,874	$2,494	$2,668	$2,698	$2,908
Loans, average award						
Total	$2,764	$2,915	$2,783	$2,543	$2,755	$3,361
Federal	$2,660	$2,840	$2,671	$2,501	$2,632	$3,387
Non-federal	$2,252	$2,541	$2,305	$1,565	$2,047	$1,610
Work Study, average	$1,071	$1,296	$1,033	$1,143	$1,252	$1,182

Source: National Center for Education Statistics, U.S. Department of Education, *Digest of Education Statistics 1992* (Washington, DC: U.S. Government Printing Office, October 1992), table 303, p. 310. Primary source: U.S. Department of Education, National Center for Education Statistics, "The 1989-90 National Postsecondary Student Aid Study." (This table was prepared June 1992.) Also in source: data by age, marital status, attendance, dependency, and housing status. *Notes:* (a) Since these data are based on a sample survey, numbers of undergraduates may not equal totals figures reported elsewhere. (b) Includes students who reported receiving aid but did not specify source or type of aid.

Graduate Record Examinations

★ 297 ★

Asian/Pacific American GRE Test Examinees by Graduate Degree Objective: Trends

Number of Asian/Pacific American[a] examinees, percent of group total, and total examinees by graduate degree objective, 1977-78, 1982-83, 1986-87, and 1987-88.

Degree objective	1977-78		1982-83		1986-87		1987-88	
	Number	Percent[b]	Number	Percent[b]	Number	Percent[b]	Number	Percent[a]
Total	180,447		147,633		187,631		199,395	
Nondegree study	1,866	1%	1.228	<1%	1,263	<1%	1,225	<1%
Master's/Intermed	114,764	64%	90,078	61%	114,447	61%	124,775	63%
Doc/Post-doc	63,817	35%	56,327	38%	71,921	38%	73,395	37%
Asian/Pac Amer	2,678		3,101		5,306		5,993	
Nondegree Study	26	<1%	23	<1%	32	<1%	37	<1%
Master's/Intermed	1,589	59%	1,765	57%	3,122	59%	3,512	59%
Doc/Post-doc	1,063	40%	1,313	42%	2,152	41%	2,444	41%

Source: Diane M. Wah and Dawn S. Robinson, *Examinee and Score Trends for the GRE General Test: 1977-78, 1982-83, 1986-87, and 1987-88* (Princeton, NJ: Educational Testing Service, 1990), table 1.5, p. 29. The number of U.S. citizens taking the GRE General Test each year and the percent who responded to questions in this table follow: 1977-78—189,536 (95%); 1982-83—155,040 (95%); 1986-87—194,568 (96%); 1987-88—221,958 (90%). Also in source: data on American Indian/Aleut, Black/African American, Mexican American, Puerto Rican, Other Hispanic, and white, and on scores. *Note:* (a) U.S. citizens only. (b) Percentages in this table are based on ethnic group.

★ 298 ★

Asian/Pacific American GRE Test Examinees
by Planned Graduate Enrollment Status

Numbers of Asian/Pacific American[a] Graduate Record Examination test takers, percent of group total, and total examinees, by planned graduate enrollment status, 1987-88.

Group	1987-88	
	Number	Percent[b]
Total	202,416	
Full Time	123,425	61
Part Time	52,261	26
Undecided	26,730	13
Asian/Pac Amer	6,078	
Full Time	4,314	71
Part Time	1,052	17
Undecided	712	12

Source: Diane M. Wah and Dawn S. Robinson, *Examinee and Score Trends for the GRE General Test: 1977-78, 1982-83, 1986-87, and 1987-88* (Princeton, NJ: Educational Testing Service, 1990), table 1.6, p. 31. Data for planned enrollment status were collected for the first time during the 1987-88 testing year. Also in source: data on American Indian/Aleut, Black/African American, Mexican American, Puerto Rican, Other Hispanic, and white, and on scores. *Notes:* (a) U. S. citizens only. A total of 221,958 U.S. citizens took the GRE General Test in 1987-88 and 91 percent responded to questions in this table.(b) Percentages in this table are based on ethnic group.

★ 299 ★

Asian/Pacific American GRE Test Examinees by Planned Graduate Field

Numbers of Asian/Pacific Americans[a] and total GRE test takers and percent of total Asian/Pacific Islander testtakers, by planned graduate field of study, 1977-78, 1982-83, 1986-87, and 1987-88.

Planned graduate field	1977-78		1982-83		1986-87		1987-88	
	Number	Percent[b]	Number	Percent[b]	Number	Percent[b]	Number	Percent[b]
Business	6,169		3,423		4,233		5,170	
Asian/Pac Amer	73	1%	61	2%	86	2%	141	3%
Education	35,646		21,947		30,316		29,181	
Asian/Pac Amer	328	<1%	175	<1%	361	1%	330	1%
Engineering	6,671		9,211		13,621		13,759	
Asian/Pac Amer	316	5%	606	7%	1,219	9%	1,372	10%
Humanities/Arts	18,052		13,59		19,399		20,354	
Asian/Pac Amer	195	1%	182	1%	304	2%	344	2%
Life Sciences	32,335		28,265		32,117		31,778	
Asian/Pac Amer	676	2%	600	2%	959	3%	966	3%
Physical Sciences	10,038		15,041		16,702		14,959	
Asian/Pac Amer	211	2%	476	3%	775	5%	745	5%
Social Sciences	24,221		21,289		27,698		31,385	
Asian/Pac Amer	302	1%	369	2%	540	2%	733	2%
Total	180,314		146,680		186,392		189,690	
Asian/Pac Amer	2,671	1%	3,076	2%	5,298	3%	5,728	3%

Source: Diane M. Wah and Dawn S. Robinson, *Examinee and Score Trends for the GRE General Test 1977-78, 1982-83, 1986-87, and 1987-88* (Princeton, NJ : Educational Testing Service, 1990), table 1.9, p. 38-39. *Notes:* (a) U.S. Citizens only. The number of U.S. citizens taking the GRE General Test each year and the percent who responded to questions in this table follow: 1977-78—189,536 (95%); 1982-83—155,040 (95%); 1986-87—194,568 (96%); 1987-88—221,958 (85%). (b) Percent is based on group total.

★ 300 ★

Asian/Pacific American GRE Test Examinees by Undergraduate Field: Trends

Number of Asian/Pacific American[a] examinees and percent of total Asian/Pacific American test takers by undergraduate field of study, 1977-78, 1982-83, 1986-87, and 1987-88.

Undergraduate Field	1977-78		1982-83		1986-87		1987-88	
	Number	Percent	Number	Percent	Number	Percent	Number	Percent
Business, total	5,857		4,450		6,110		7,716	
Asian/Pac Amer	65	1%	66	1%	111	2%	136	2%
Education, total	25,971		16,907		21,030		22,335	
Asian/Pac Amer	158	<1%	107	<1%	207	<1%	190	<1%
Engineering, total	7,763		10,403		16,223		16,355	
Asian/Pac Amer	351	5%	664	6%	1,403	9%	1,590	10%
Humanities/Arts, total	33,125		23,297		31,179		31,826	
Asian/Pac Amer	352	1%	280	1%	482	2%	564	2%
Life Sciences, total	33,383		30,097		35,089		34,768	
Asian/Pac Amer	680	2%	664	2%	1,064	3%	1,042	3%
Physical Sciences, total	14,250		16,524		19,778		18,997	
Asian/Pac Amer	282	2%	501	3%	869	4%	941	5%
Social Sciences, total	39,042		29,733		37,957		39,749	
Asian/Pac Amer	562	1%	542	2%	774	2%	945	2%
Total	180,645		147,378		186,928		188,829	
Asian/Pac Amer	2,681	1%	3,091	2%	5,300	3%	5,739	3%

Source: Diane M. Wah and Dawn S. Robinson, *Examinee and Score Trends for the GRE General Test 1977-78, 1982-83, 1986-87, and 1987-88* (Princeton, NJ : Educational Testing Service, 1990), table 1.3, p. 24-25. The number of U.S. citizens taking the GRE General Test each year and the percent who responded to questions in this table were 1977-78—189,536 (95%); 1982-83—155,040 (95%); 1986-87—194,568 (96%); 1987-88—221,958 (85%). *Note:* (a) U.S. Citizens only. Also in source: data on test scores for all tests and information on the disciplines within each major field.

★ 301 ★

GRE Test Examinees, College Seniors and Graduates: 1987-1990

Graduate Record Examination (GRE) test takers who were college seniors or graduates, in percent of total, by race/ethnicity and test type, 1987-1990.

Test	Asian/ Pacific American	White non-Hispanic	Native American/ Alaskan Native	Black/ African American	Mexican American/ Chicano	Puerto Rican	Other Hispanic/ Latin American	Number of Examinees
General Test	3.5%	80.9%	0.4%	5.5%	1.2%	0.8%	1.2%	353,005
Biology	4.6%	80.7%	0.4%	4.3%	0.9%	1.8%	0.9%	20,332
Chemistry	5.1%	81.3%	0.2%	3.5%	0.7%	1.2%	0.7%	6,689
Computer Science	8.0%	74.4%	0.3%	6.2%	0.4%	0.7%	0.7%	5,972
Economics	5.6%	78.4%	0.3%	3.5%	1.2%	0.5%	1.2%	3,089
Education	0.8%	84.4%	0.4%	8.1%	0.3%	0.5%	0.6%	2,355
Engineering	11.7%	73.6%	0.3%	3.1%	1.3%	1.3%	1.1%	8,240
Geology	1.0%	89.7%	0.2%	0.6%	0.8%	0.7%	0.5%	2,002
History	0.7%	87.1%	0.5%	2.4%	0.8%	0.5%	0.8%	4,905
Literature in English	2.0%	85.4%	0.3%	3.0%	0.8%	0.3%	0.9%	11,969
Mathematics	4.7%	79.6%	0.4%	4.7%	0.7%	0.4%	0.9%	5,008
Physics	5.4%	80.5%	0.3%	1.7%	0.7%	0.4%	0.8%	5,613
Political Science	1.9%	79.3%	0.6%	8.3%	1.0%	0.7%	1.3%	3,738
Psychology	1.9%	83.4%	0.5%	5.2%	1.1%	1.0%	1.3%	28,205
Sociology	1.4%	72.3%	0.8%	16.5%	1.2%	0.7%	0.6%	2,741

Source: Graduate Record Examinations Board, *GRE 1991-92 Guide to the use of the Graduate Record Examinations Program* (Princeton, NJ : Educational Testing Service, 1991), table 6, p. 31. Based on examinees who indicated that they are U.S. citizens and who tested between October 1, 1987, and September 30, 1990. Examinees must have earned their college degrees within two years of the test date to be included. Also in source: explanation of test design and guidelines for interpretation of test scores.

★ 302 ★

GRE Test Examinees by Test Type: 1987-1990

Graduate Record Examination test takers, in percent, by race/ethnicity and test type, 1987 to 1990.

Test	Percent of total examinees						Number of examinees
	Asian/ Pacific American	Black/ African American	Mexican American/ Chicano	Puerto Rican	Other His- panic/Latin American	White (non-Hispanic)	
General Test	2.9%	5.9%	1.4%	0.8%	1.2%	79.1%	711,170
Biology	4.3%	4.2%	0.9%	1.9%	0.9%	78.5%	29,334
Chemistry	5.3%	4.0%	0.7%	1.3%	0.8%	75.8%	8,495
Computer Science	7.8%	4.6%	0.4%	0.6%	0.8%	71.6%	10,127
Economics	5.2%	3.7%	1.1%	0.6%	1.4%	74.0%	4,400
Education	1.0%	9.2%	0.9%	0.5%	0.7%	79.1%	9,113
Engineering	10.8%	3.3%	1.2%	1.2%	1.3%	70.7%	11,756
Geology	0.9%	0.8%	1.0%	0.6%	0.8%	86.9%	2,963
History	0.7%	2.9%	0.8%	0.5%	0.7%	85.3%	7,869
Literature in English	1.6%	2.8%	0.8%	0.2%	0.8%	83.5%	19,834
Mathematics	4.7%	4.6%	0.7%	0.6%	0.9%	74.9%	7,017
Physics	5.6%	1.8%	0.7%	0.6%	0.8%	75.0%	7,580
Political Science	1.9%	7.7%	1.1%	0.8%	1.6%	78.0%	5,240
Psychology	1.9%	5.3%	1.1%	1.0%	1.3%	81.7%	40,878
Sociology	1.4%	12.6%	1.3%	0.9%	0.8%	73.0%	4,963

Source: Graduate Record Examinations, *GRE 1991-92: Guide to the Use of the Graduate Record Examinations Program* (Princeton, NJ : Educational Testing Service, 1991), table 5, p. 31. Based on examinees who indicated that they are U.S. citizens and who tested between October 1, 1987, and September 30, 1990. Also in source: explanation of test design and guidelines for interpretation of test scores.

★ 303 ★

GRE Test Examinees: 1977-78 and 1987-88

Numbers and percent[b] of total Graduate Record Examination (GRE) test takers by race/ethnicity, 1977-78 and 1987-88.

Ethnic group[a]	Examinees			
	1977-78		1987-88	
	Number	Percent[b]	Number	Percent[b]
Total	181,336	100%	203,084	100%
Men	83,428	46%	86,744	43%
Women	97,908	54%	116,340	57%
Asian/Pac Amer	2,686	1%	6,133	3%
Men	1,326	<1%	3,239	2%
Women	1,360	<1%	2,894	1%
White	155,793	86%	173,674	86%
Men	72,075	40%	74,297	37%
Women	83,718	46%	99,377	49%
Black/Afr Amer	12,551	7%	12,592	6%
Men	4,436	2%	4,189	2%
Women	8,115	4%	8,403	4%

[Continued]

★ 303 ★

GRE Test Examinees: 1977-78 and 1987-88 (Continued)

Numbers and percent[b] of total Graduate Record Examination (GRE) test takers by race/ethnicity, 1977-78 and 1987-88.

Ethnic group[a]	Examinees			
	1977-78		1987-88	
	Number	Percent[b]	Number	Percent[b]
Mexican Amer	2,389	1%	2,933	1%
Men	1,219	<1%	1,355	<1%
Women	1,170	<1%	1,578	<1%
Puerto Rican	1,194	<1%	1,890	<1%
Men	567	<1%	833	<1%
Women	627	<1%	1,057	<1%
Other Hispanic	1,223	<1%	2,335	1%
Men	578	<1%	1,050	<1%
Women	645	<1%	1,285	<1%
Amer Indian	917	<1%	1,000	<1%
Men	451	<1%	421	<1%
Women	466	<1%	579	<1%

Source: Diane M. Wah and Dawn S. Robinson, *Examinee and Score Trends for the GRE General Test: 1977-78, 1982-83, 1986-87, and 1987-88* (Princeton, NJ: Educational Testing Service, 1990), table C-2, p. 86. The number of U.S. citizens taking the GRE General Test each year and the percent who responded to questions in this table follow: 1977-78—189,536 (95.7%) and 1987-88—221,958 (91.5%). *Notes:* (a) U.S. citizens only. Ethnic groups are defined as follows: Amer Indian—American Indian, Inuit, or Aleut; Asian/Pac Amer—Asian or Pacific American; Black/Afr Amer—Black or African American; Mexican Amer—Mexican American or Chicano; Puerto Rican—same; Other Hispanic—Other Hispanic or Latin American; White—same; Other—same. (b) Percentages in this table are based on the column total.

★ 304 ★

GRE Test Scores

Numbers and percent[b] of total Graduate Record Examination (GRE) examinees and mean scores by sex and race/ethnicity, 1987-88.

Ethnic group[a]	GRE General Test Score Information				
	Examinees		Verbal	Quantitative	Analytical
	Number	Percent[b]	Mean	Mean	Mean
Total	203,084	100%	508	536	543
Men	86,744	43%	520	582	558
Women	116,340	57%	499	502	532
Asian/Pac Amer	6,133	3%	480	612	539
Men	3,239	2%	472	644	542
Women	2,894	1%	488	575	536
White	173,674	86%	520	546	557
Men	74,297	37%	532	591	571
Women	99,377	49%	512	513	546
Black/Afr Amer	12,592	6%	391	394	406
Men	4,189	2%	401	427	416
Women	8,403	4%	386	378	401

[Continued]

★ 304 ★

GRE Test Scores (Continued)

Numbers and percent[b] of total Graduate Record Examination (GRE) examinees and mean scores by sex and race/ethnicity, 1987-88.

| Ethnic group[a] | GRE General Test Score Information | | Verbal | Quantitative | Analytical |
| | Examinees | | | | |
	Number	Percent[b]	Mean	Mean	Mean
Mexican Amer	2,933	1%	444	461	461
Men	1,355	<1%	457	495	472
Women	1,578	<1%	433	432	451
Puerto Rican	1,890	<1%	396	444	422
Men	833	<1%	407	480	433
Women	1,057	<1%	388	416	414
Other Hispanic	2,335	1%	470	502	494
Men	1,050	<1%	486	552	513
Women	1,285	<1%	456	462	478
Amer Indian	1,000	<1%	464	470	485
Men	421	<1%	480	513	500
Women	579	<1%	452	440	474

Source: Diane M. Wah and Dawn S. Robinson, *Examinee and Score Trends for the GRE General Test: 1977-78, 1982-83, 1986-87, and 1987-88* (Princeton, NJ: Educational Testing Service, 1990), table 2.2, p. 55. A total of 221,958 U.S. citizens took the GRE General Test in 1987-88; 91 percent responded to questions in this table. *Notes:* (a) Ethnic groups are defined as follows: Amer Indian—American Indian, Inuit, or Aleut; Asian/Pac Amer—Asian or Pacific American; Black/Afr Amer—Black or African American; Mexican Amer—Mexican American or Chicano; Puerto Rican—same; Other Hispanic—Other Hispanic or Latin American; White—same; Other—same. (b) Percentages in this table are based on the column total.

Law Schools

★ 305 ★

Applicants to Law Schools: 1984-85 through 1988-89

Numbers of applicants to American Bar Association law schools, mean Law School Admissions Test (LSAT) score, and percent by race/ethnicity, 1984-85 through 1988-89.

| Racial/ethnic group | 1984-85 | | 1985-86 | | 1986-87 | | 1987-88 | | 1988-89 | | 1989-89 Mean |
	Count	%	Count	%	Count	%	Count	%	Count	%	LSAT
Totals	60,338		65,168		68,804		78,930		87,227		
Asian/Pacific Islander	1,270	2.1	1,561	2.4	1,854	2.7	2,284	2.9	2,949	3.4	3,1.8
American Indian	359	0.6	356	0.5	377	0.5	380	0.5	412	0.5	2,8.0
Black/Afro-American	4,406	7.3	4,889,	7.5	5079	7.4	5,758	7.3	6,158	7.1	2,3.2
Caucasian/White	50,241	83.3	53538	82.2	56,027	81.4	61,844	78.4	69,113	79.2	3,3.2
Chicano/Mexican American	739	1.2	839	1.3	843	1.2	783	1.0	906	1.0	2,7.8
Hispanic	1,200	2.0	1,382,	2.1	1,484	2.2	1,838	2.3	2,133	2.4	2,8.4
Puerto Rican	815	1.4	1002	1.5	1,012	1.5	1,034	1.3	1,138	1.3	1,9.6

Source: Law School Admission Services, *Minority Databook, Minority Participation in Legal Education and the Profession* (Newtown, PA: Law School Admission Services, Inc., 1990), table IV-3c, p. 34. Reprinted by permission. Primary source: Law School Admission Services, *National Statistical Report 1984-85 through 1988-89.*

★ 306 ★

Enrollment in J. D. Programs: 1977-1991

Numbers of Asian/Pacific Islanders and total minority students enrolled in juris doctorate (J.D.) programs by year at American Bar Association law schools, 1977 through 1991-92.

Group	No. of Schools Reporting	Academic Year	1st Year	2nd Year	3rd Year	4th Year	Total
Asian/Pacific Islander							
	173	1991-92	2,019	1,621	1,306	82	5,028
	172	1990-91	1,753	1,343	1,134	76	4,306
	172	1989-90	1,501	1,151	946	78	3,676
	171	1988-89	1,282	954	825	72	3,133
	171	1987-88	1,064	804	724	64	2,656
	171	1986-87	929	685	650	39	2,303
	172	1985-86	799	678	622	54	2,153
	171	1984-85	766	610	600	50	2,026
	170	1983-84	711	610	578	63	1,962
	169	1982-83	731	593	562	61	1,947
	169	1981-82	650	579	486	40	1,755
	168	1980-81	641	485	473	42	1,641
	166	1979-80	577	487	452	31	1,547
	164	1978-79	557	435	398	34	1,424
	160	1977-78	509	409	423	41	1,382
Total Minority							
	173	1991-92	7,575	6,155	5,255	425	19,410
	172	1990-91	6,933	5,325	4,676	396	17,330
	172	1989-90	6,172	4,890	4,264	394	15,720
	171	1988-89	5,565	4,408	3,911	411	14,295
	171	1987-88	5,130	3,994	3,717	409	13,250
	171	1986-87	4,740	3,837	3,648	325	12,550
	172	1985-86	4,534	3,806	3,622	384	12,346
	171	1984-85	4,429	3,725	3,432	331	11,917
	170	1983-84	4,393	3,691	3,424	358	11,866
	169	1982-83	4,421	3,624	3,217	349	11,611
	169	1981-82	4,314	3,401	3,118	301	11,134
	168	1980-81	4,124	3,215	2,976	260	10,575
	166	1979-80	3,825	3,150	2,755	283	10,013
	164	1978-79	3,801	2,925	2,902	324	9,952
	160	1977-78	3,574	2,991	2,690	325	9,580

Source: American Bar Association, *A Review of Legal Education in the United States Fall 1991* (Chicago: American Bar Association, 1992), p. 69. Also in source: data by other minority groups.

★ 307 ★

Law School Application Outcome, LSAT Score, and GPA by Race/Ethnicity

Application outcome by average Law School Admission Test (LSAT) score and undergraduate grade point average for Asian/Pacific Islander and all applicants to American Bar Association Law Schools, 1988-89.

Race/ethnic group	Application Outcome				
	Denied	Admit	Admitted, not registered	Registered	Total Applicants
Total Applicants					
Number	29,761	51,665	9,190	42,475	87,227
Avg. LSAT	27.4	35.1	34.5	35.2	31.9
Avg. GPA	2.82	3.16	3.17	3.16	3.03
Asian/Pacific Islander					
Number	1,004	1,777	332	1,445	2,949
Avg. LSAT	26.8	34.9	34.8	35.0	31.8
Avg. GPA	2.87	3.17	3.20	3.17	3.06
American Indian					
Number	145	234	36	198	412
Avg. LSAT	23.7	31.3	32.7	31.1	28.0
Avg. GPA	2.70	3.02	3.13	3.00	2.89
Black/African-American					
Number	2,761	2,800	367	2,433	6,158
Avg. LSAT	19.1	18.0	27.4	28.1	23.2
Avg. GPA	2.55	2.83	2.87	2.82	2.69
Caucasian/White					
Number	22,842	42,848	7,740	35,108	69,113
Avg. LSAT	28.7	35.7	34.9	35.9	33.2
Avg. GPA	2.85	3.19	3.19	3.19	3.07
Chicano/Mexican American					
Number	347	506	62	444	906
Avg. LSAT	22.5	31.6	31.5	31.6	27.8
Avg. GPA	2.70	2.98	2.87	2.99	2.87
Hispanic					
Number	763	1204	174	1030	2,133
Avg. LSAT	23.3	32.2	31.7	32.3	28.4
Avg. GPA	2.72	3.07	3.08	3.06	2.93
Puerto Rican					
Number	214	255	43	212	1,138
Avg. LSAT	21.2	30.9	31.2	30.9	19.6
Avg. GPA	2.73	3.00	3.01	3.00	2.94

Source: Law School Admission Services, *Minority Databook, Minority Participation in Legal Education and the Profession* (Newtown, PA: Law School Admission Services, Inc., 1990), table IV-3c, p.34. Reprinted by permission. Primary source: Law School Admission Services, National Statistical Report 1984-85 through 1988-89.

★ 308 ★

Law School Application Outcome, LSAT Score, and GPA by Race/Ethnicity

Law School Admission Test (LSAT) score and undergraduate grade point average for Asian/Pacific Islander and all applicants to American Bar Association Law Schools, 1988-89.

LSAT	Undergraduate Grade Point Average											
	<2.00	2.00-2.24	2.25-2.49	2.50-2.74	2.75-2.99	3.00-3.24	3.25-3.49	3.50-3.74	_3.75	No GPA	Totals	Mean GPA
Asian/Pacific Islander												
10-13	1	3	8	11	3	6	4	0	1	32	69	2.71
14-17	6	8	7	9	13	9	6	3	2	33	96	2.74
18-21	4	9	20	24	39	20	4	4	4	51	179	2.76
22-25	3	11	35	49	57	48	28	17	6	36	290	2.88
26-20	5	12	38	58	92	62	50	28	23	41	399	2.94
30-33	9	15	39	68	90	99	75	47	23	41	506	3.00
34-37	3	15	34	63	84	134	106	70	26	26	561	3.09
38-41	3	7	13	35	62	80	107	101	45	14	467	3.25
42-45	0	2	2	11	23	46	74	63	32	9	262	3.35
46-48	0	0	1	1	4	8	15	13	10	0	52	3.45
No Score	0	0	0	1	2	2	3	1	2	57	68	3.27
Totals	34	82	197	330	469	514	472	347	164	340	2949	3.06
Mean LSAT	26.4	27.7	28.1	29.6	30.5	32.8	35.2	36.4	36.5	24.7	31.8	
All Applicants												
10-13	101	212	265	243	199	136	63	35	9	601	1864	2.58
14-17	99	278	400	444	363	281	145	68	25	365	2468	2.68
18-21	123	408	721	842	799	592	359	168	57	429	4498	2.75
22-25	143	551	1059	1423	1583	1332	814	385	150	459	7899	2.83
26-29	167	579	1423	2014	2601	2345	1604	885	302	412	12332	2.91
30-33	142	639	1477	2546	3392	3618	2707	1640	680	407	17248	3.00
34-37	95	472	1148	2135	3191	4013	3525	2266	1141	315	18301	3.10
38-41	40	223	563	1143	1861	2842	3014	2511	1360	178	13735	3.22
42-45	12	56	153	339	640	1114	1511	1499	1010	96	6430	3.34
46-48	1	6	20	37	76	159	295	309	260	14	1177	3.44
No Score	10	35	58	83	71	85	58	62	27	786	1275	2.95
Totals	933	3459	7287	11249	14776	16517	14095	9828	5021	4062	87227	3.03
Mean LSAT	24.9	26.8	28.3	29.8	31.1	32.7	34.4	35.8	37.1	23.9	31.9	

Source: Law School Admission Services, *Minority Databook, Minority Participation in Legal Education and the Profession* (Newtown, PA: Law School Admission Services, Inc., 1990), table IV-3c, p. 34. Reprinted by permission. Primary source: Law School Admission Services, *National Statistical Report 1984-85 through 1988-89.*

★ 309 ★

Profile of Asian/Pacific Islander Applicants to Law Schools

Profile of Asian Pacific Islander applicants to Amercian Bar Association law schools by Law School Admissions Test (LSAT) score, grade point average, law school admission, and registration for Asian/Pacific Islander applicants, in percent, 1988-89.

GPA	Average LSAT Score										
	10-13	14-17	18-21	22-25	26-29	30-33	34-37	38-41	42-45	46-48	TOTAL
TOTAL	37	63	128	254	358	465	535	453	253	52	2,598
Admitted	5%	10%	20%	30%	50%	70%	76%	84%	87%	98%	64%
Registered[a]	99%	67%	80%	77%	78%	84%	84%	82%	83%	75%	82%
3.75+	1	2	4	6	13	23	26	45	32	10	162
Admitted	0	50%	75%	67%	62%	91%	92%	89%	97%	99%	88%
Registered	0	99%	99%	50%	87%	90%	75%	85%	81%	80%	82%
3.50-3.74	0	3	4	17	28	47	70	101	63	13	346
Admitted	0	0	0	35%	61%	81%	81%	89%	94%	99%	81%
Registered	0	0	0	83%0	71%	76%	86%	79%	78%	69%	79%
3.25-3.49	4	6	4	28	50	75	106	107	74	15	469
Admitted	25%	0	50%	39%	56%	83%	83%	85%	81%	93%	76%
Registered	99%	0	99%	73%	71%	84%	85%	74%	83%	71%	80%
3.00-3.24	6	9	20	48	62	99	134	80	46	8	512
Admitted	17%	22%	20%	31%	56%	73%	73%	80%	85%	99%	66%
Registered	99%	50%	75%	80%	83%	85%	82%	87%	90%	75%	84%
2.75-2.99	3	13	39	57	92	90	84	62	23	4	467
Admitted	0	15%	18%	30%	54%	67%	74%	89%	83%	99%	59%
Registered	0	50%	71%	76%	82%	82%	85%	89%	84%	75%	83%
2.50-2.74	11	9	24	49	58	68	63	35	11	1	329
Admitted	0	11%	25%	29%	60%	56%	73%	77%	64%	99%	51%
Registered	0	99%	83%	86%	79%	89%	85%	78%	99%	99%	85%
2.25-2.49	8	7	20	35	38	39	34	13	2	1	197
Admitted	0	0	15%	26%	29%	59%	59%	69%	99%	99%	40%
Registered	0	0	67%	78%	73%	83%	85%	89%	50%	99%	81%
2.00-2.24	3	8	9	11	12	15	15	7	2	0	82
Admitted	0	0	0	9%	8%	47%	53%	43%	99%	0	27%
Registered	0	0	0	0	99%	86%	87%	99%	99%	0	86%
Below 2.00	1	6	4	3	5	9	3	3	0	0	34
Admitted	0	0	0	0	20%	56%	33%	67%	0	0	26%
Registered	0	0	0	0	0	80%	0	99%	0	0	67%

Source: National Law School Admission Services, *Minority Databook, Minority Participation in Legal Education and the Professions* (Newtown, PA: Law School Admission Services, 1990) table V-2c, p. 50. Reprinted by permission. Primary source: Law School Admission Services, *National Decision Profiles 1988-89.* Also in source: data on American Indian, Black/Afro-American, Caucasian/White, Hispanic, and Puerto Rican. *Note:* (a) Percent registered is the percent of those admitted who subsequently registered for law school.

★ 310 ★

State of Permanent Residence for Asian/Pacific Islander Applicants to American Bar Association Law Schools

Number and percent of Asian/Pacific Islander applicants to American Bar Association law schools by state of permanent residence and mean Law School Admissions Test (LSAT) score, 1984-85 to through 1988-89

Permanent State	1984-85		1985-86		1986-87		1987-88		1988-89		Mean LSAT
	Count	%	Count	%	Count	%	Count	%	Count	%	
Alabama	1	0.1	0	0.0	5	0.3	4	0.2	3	0.1	-
Alaska	0	0.0	9	0.6	7	0.4	4	0.2	2	0.1	-
Arizona	7	0.6	4	0.3	14	0.8	14	0.6	23	0.8	33.1
Arkansas	2	0.2	4	0.3	3	0.2	2	0.1	2	0.1	-
California	394	31.0	432	27.7	490	26.4	637	27.9	848	28.8	32.3
Colorado	12	0.9	17	1.1	14	0.8	17	0.7	19	0.6	33.9
Connecticut	8	0.6	25	1.6	21	1.1	23	1.0	42	1.4	35.4
Delaware	3	0.2	2	0.1	3	0.2	5	0.2	6	0.2	32.5
District of Columbia	14	1.1	6	0.4	6	0.3	14	0.6	13	0.4	26.2
Florida	24	1.9	25	1.6	37	2.0	44	1.9	56	1.9	30.6
Georgia	5	0.4	9	0.6	27	1.5	21	0.9	23	0.8	30.8
Guam	5	0.4	18	1.2	13	0.7	14	0.6	14	0.5	21.8
Hawaii	139	10.9	166	10.6	176	9.5	194	8.5	212	7.2	31.2
Idaho	0	0.0	2	0.1	3	0.2	1	0.0	2	0.1	-
Illinois	43	3.4	54	3.5	89	4.8	96	4.2	139	4.7	32.4
Indiana	8	0.6	13	0.8	21	1.1	15	0.7	36	1.2	31.0
Iowa	5	0.4	6	0.4	5	0.3	7	0.3	10	0.3	24.9
Kansas	2	0.2	8	0.5	7	0.4	12	0.5	15	0.5	30.6
Kentucky	1	0.1	4	0.3	10	0.5	7	0.3	12	0.4	28.0
Louisiana	7	0.6	7	0.4	2	0.1	19	0.8	17	0.6	31.4
Maine	2	0.2	1	0.1	2	0.1	0	0.0	0	0.0	-
Maryland	31	2.4	35	2.2	48	2.6	76	3.3	91	3.1	32.5
Massachusetts	21	1.7	41	2.6	45	2.4	67	2.9	94	3.2	33.3
Michigan	24	1.9	32	2.0	32	1.7	44	1.9	61	2.1	32.8
Minnesota	15	1.2	8	0.5	10	0.5	13	0.6	27	0.9	30.6
Mississippi	1	0.1	2	0.1	5	0.3	2	0.1	3	0.1	-
Missouri	6	0.5	6	0.4	16	0.9	21	0.9	31	1.1	29.1
Montana	0	0.0	0	0.0	1	0.1	1	0.0	0	0.0	-
Nebraska	2	0.2	4	0.3	5	0.3	6	0.3	7	0.2	23.7
Nevada	2	0.2	0	0.0	4	0.2	4	0.2	7	0.2	28.0
New Hampshire	0	0.0	1	0.1	2	0.1	3	0.1	3	0.1	-
New Jersey	44	3.5	59	3.8	73	3.9	99	4.3	116	3.9	32.5
New Mexico	4	0.3	7	0.4	4	0.2	3	0.1	3	0.1	-
New York	136	10.7	182	11.7	219	11.8	287	12.6	366	12.4	31.5
North Carolina	8	0.6	9	0.6	10	0.5	16	0.7	15	0.5	35.7
North Dakota	2	0.2	2	0.1	0	0.0	2	0.1	1	0.0	-
Ohio	10	0.8	19	1.2	24	1.3	44	1.9	57	1.9	33.0
Oklahoma	9	0.7	10	0.6	14	0.8	7	0.3	15	0.5	25.2
Oregon	9	0.7	14	0.9	11	0.6	17	0.7	16	0.5	28.9
Pennsylvania	29	2.3	32	2.0	40	2.2	51	2.2	60	2.0	31.8
Puerto Rico	2	0.2	5	0.3	6	0.3	2	0.1	1	0.0	-
Rhode Island	1	0.1	3	0.2	3	0.2	6	0.3	6	0.2	22.8
South Carolina	2	0.2	4	0.3	4	0.2	5	0.2	2	0.1	-
South Dakota	6	0.5	6	0.4	5	0.3	2	0.1	1	0.0	-

[Continued]

★ 310 ★

State of Permanent Residence for Asian/Pacific Islander Applicants to American Bar Association Law Schools (Continued)

Number and percent of Asian/Pacific Islander applicants to American Bar Association law schools by state of permanent residence and mean Law School Admissions Test (LSAT) score, 1984-85 to through 1988-89

Permanent State	1984-85		1985-86		1986-87		1987-88		1988-89		Mean LSAT
	Count	%	Count	%	Count	%	Count	%	Count	%	
Tennessee	6	0.5	3	0.2	6	0.3	11	0.5	12	0.4	33.9
Texas	47	3.7	75	4.8	96	5.2	97	4.2	116	3.9	31.6
Utah	7	0.6	9	0.6	5	0.3	12	0.5	12	0.4	30.1
Vermont	0	0.0	1	0.1	0	0.0	1	0.0	1	0.0	-
Virgin Islands	1	0.1	2	0.1	1	0.1	0	0.0	1	0.0	-
Virginia	33	2.6	50	3.2	56	3.0	76	3.3	104	3.5	32.1
Washington	30	2.4	33	2.1	51	2.8	54	2.4	64	2.2	32.3
West Virginia	4	0.3	3	0.2	3	0.2	5	0.2	10	0.3	29.5
Wisconsin	11	0.9	13	0.8	15	0.8	21	0.9	19	0.6	32.1
Wyoming	1	0.1	4	0.3	4	0.2	1	0.0	2	0.1	-
Canadian Provinces	0	0.0	14	0.9	25	1.3	27	1.2	36	1.2	33.4
State Not Indicated	84	6.6	61	3.9	56	3.0	51	2.2	95	3.2	28.2
Totals	1,270		1,561		1,854		2,284		2,949		

Source: Law School Admission Services, *National Statistical Report 1984-85 through 1988-89* (Newtown, PA: LSAS, 1990).

★ 311 ★

Undergraduate Feeder Schools to Law Schools

Top undergraduate feeder schools for Asian/Pacific Islander applicants to American Bar Association law schools, 1984-85 through 1988-89.

Feeder School	1984-85	1985-86	1986-87	1987-88	1988-89
Univ. of Calif-Berkeley	70	76	98	116	157
Univ. of Hawaii-Honolulu	84	96	103	113	126
Univ. of Calif-Los Angeles	64	62	61	89	110
Harvard University MA	26	27	31	46	63
Univ. of Washington	29	27	31	39	51
Univ. of Calif-Irvine	8	10	21	31	48
Univ. of Michigan-Ann Arbor	13	17	20	32	47
Cornell University NY	14	28	32	36	47
Univ. of Pennsylvania	14	15	20	30	46
Univ. of Southern California	35	32	26	35	44
New York Univ Wash Sq & Unv Cl	7	11	11	34	38
Univ. of Calif-Davis	12	18	21	28	33
Univ. of Maryland-College Park	9	9	12	24	31
Univ. of Texas-Austin	5	18	15	14	31
Columbia Univ Columbia Cig NY	10	19	9	18	28
Univ. of Chicago	6	12	9	16	26
Yale University	10	32	26	30	25
Boston University MA	7	5	8	15	25
Stanford University CA	13	13	15	16	24

[Continued]

★311★

Undergraduate Feeder Schools to Law Schools (Continued)

Top undergraduate feeder schools for Asian/Pacific Islander applicants to American Bar Association law schools, 1984-85 through 1988-89.

Feeder School	1984-85	1985-86	1986-87	1987-88	1988-89
Univ. of Illinois-Urbana	13	11	14	20	24
San Francisco State Univ CA	10	14	20	23	23
Northwestern University	13	10	17	12	22
Georgetown University DC	9	9	8	14	22
Princeton University NJ	6	14	19	16	22
Brown University RI	12	11	11	27	20
Wellesley College MA	8	13	10	12	19
Barnard College NY	8	9	14	12	18
SUNY at Buffalo Center NY	4	8	4	7	17
Univ. of Calif-riverside	4	2	4	8	17
SUNY at Stony Brook Center NY	1	1	8	13	17
Univ. of Virginia	3	7	9	15	17
Indiana U Bloomington IN	6	7	4	8	17
Duke University NC	5	11	5	8	16
Rutgers U Rutgr Cl New Brns NJ	4	5	6	11	16
Univ. of Santa Clara	7	5	5	10	16
Univ. of Illinois at Chicago	2	2	9	10	16
Univ. of Wisconsin-Madison	7	9	8	6	15
University of The Philippines	7	8	6	11	15
California St Univ Long Beach	7	5	6	10	15
Univ. of Calif-Santa Barbara	8	11	10	14	15
Univ. of Houston-Central	2	5	6	15	15
Taiwan University	9	9	11	14	15
San Jose State University CA	4	9	10	10	14
George Washington Univ DC	2	5	13	9	14
Univ. of Colorado-Boulder	4	8	7	10	14
Washington University	5	3	10	8	13
Emory University GA	0	2	8	10	13
New York U Business/Public Adm	2	8	9	8	13
Univ. of Minnesota-St Paul	9	4	3	4	13
Dartmouth College NH	6	7	4	5	12
Smith College MA	5	5	5	17	12
Pomona College	5	5	9	4	12
Massachusetts Institute Tech	7	3	4	8	11
Univ. of San Francisco	4	10	7	8	11
Syracuse University NY	0	1	4	9	11
Loyola University of Chicago	2	5	2	2	11
SUNY at Albany Center NY	4	4	8	5	10
Univ. of Calif-Santa Cruz	7	3	6	5	10

Source: Law School Admission Services, *Minority Databook, Minority Participation in Legal Education and the Profession* (Newtown, PA: Law School Admission Services, Inc., 1990), table IV-3c, p.34. Primary source: Law School Admission Services, National Statistical Report 1984-85 through 1988-89.

Medical Schools

★ 312 ★

Asian/Pacific Islander Applications and Acceptances to Medical Schools: 1973-74 to 1991-92

Number of Asian/Pacific Islander[a] applicants, percent of total applicants and number and percent of applicants accepted to medical schools, 1973-74 to 1991-92.

1st Yr. Class	Asian			
	Applicants		Accepted	
	Number	Percent of total applicants	Number	Percent
1973-74	508	1.3%	188	37.0%
1974-75	1,217	2.9%	341	28.0%
1975-76	1,151	2.7%	358	31.1%
1976-77	1,193	2.8%	423	35.5%
1977-78	1,318	3.2%	452	34.3%
1978-79	1,520	4.1%	546	35.9%
1979-80	1,660	4.6%	634	38.2%
1980-81	1,774	4.9%	720	40.6%
1981-82	1,976	5.4%	824	41.7%
1982-83	2,222	6.2%	973	43.8%
1983-84	2,325	6.6%	2,020	43.9%
1984-85	2,775	7.7%	1,203	43.4%
1985-86	2,709	8.2%	1,372	50.6%
1986-87	2,992	9.6%	1,563	52.2%
1987-88	3,189	11.3%	1,895	59.4%
1988-89	3,349	12.5%	2,123	63.4%
1989-90	3,661	14.1%	2,250	61.5%
1990-91	4,345	14.9%	2,583	59.4%
1991-92	5,487	16.5%	2,778	50.6%

Source: Selected from *AAMC Data Book: Statistical Information Related to Medical Education* (Washington, DC: Association of American Medical Colleges, January 1993), table B2, p. 2. Used with permission. Primary source: AAMC Section for Student Services, "Final National Admission Action Summaries." Also in source: data for Commonwealth Puerto Ricans, other Hispanic, and underrepresented minorities (black, American Indian/Alaskan native, Mexican American, Chicano, mainland Puerto Rican). Asian/Pacific Islanders are not classified as "underrepresented" by the Association of American Medical Colleges. *Notes:* (a) The data in this table are limited to United States citizens and aliens with permanent resident visas. Prior to 1981-82, when the definition was clarified, some permanent resident aliens may have been excluded. Percentages may not add due to rounding. "U.S. Citizen" redefined in 1981 to include students with permanent resident visa.

★ 313 ★

Asian/Pacific Islander Medical School Enrollment: 1977-78 to 1991-92

Number of Asian/Pacific Islanders[a] enrolled and percent of total enrolled in U.S. medical schools, 1977-78 to 1991-92.

Year	Asian/Pacific Islander	
	Number enrolled	Percent of total enrollment
1977-78	1,422	2.4%
1978-79	1,592	2.4%
1979-80	1,777	2.7%
1980-81	1,924	2.9%
1981-82	2,518	3.7%
1982-83	2,936	4.4%
1983-84	3,290	4.9%
1984-85	3,763	5.7%
1985-86	4,289	6.5%
1986-87	4,883	7.5%
1987-88	5,738	8.8%
1988-89	6,595	10.1%
1989-90	7,489	11.5%
1990-91	8,436	12.9%
1991-92	9,438	14.4%

Source: Selected from *AAMC Data Book: Statistical Information Related to Medical Education* (Washington, DC: Association of American Medical Colleges, January 1993), table B4, p. 2. Used with permission. Primary source: AAMC Section for Student Services, "Fall Enrollment Questionnaire." Also in source: data for Commonwealth Puerto Ricans, other Hispanic, and underrepresented minorities (black, American Indian/Alaskan native, Mexican American, Chicano, mainland Puerto Rican). Asian/Pacific Islanders are not considered "underrepresented" by the Association of American Medical Colleges. *Note:* (a) The data in this table are limited to United States citizens and aliens with permanent resident visas. Prior to 1981-82, when the definition was clarified, some permanent resident aliens may have been excluded. Percentages may not add due to rounding. "U.S. Citizens" was redefined in 1981 to include students with permanent resident visa.

★ 314 ★

Asian/Pacific Islander Medical School Graduates: 1978-79 to 1990-91

Numbers of Asian/Pacific Islander[a] graduates and percent of total graduates from U.S. medical schools, 1978-79 to 1990-91.

Year	Asian/Pacific Islander	
	Graduates	Percent of total graduates
1978-79	378	2.6%
1979-80	412	2.7%
1980-81	456	2.9%
1981-82	528	3.3%
1982-83	594	3.8%
1983-84	679	4.2%
1984-85	750	4.6%
1985-86	909	5.6%
1986-87	947	6.0%
1987-88	1,119	7.0%
1988-89	1,241	7.9%
1989-90	1,433	9.3%
1990-91	1,687	10.9%

Source: Selected from *AAMC Data Book: Statistical Information Related to Medical Education* (Washington, DC: Association of American Medical Colleges, January 1993), table B5, p.2. Used with permission. Primary source: AAMC Section for Student Services, "Reported Graduates Report." Also in source: data for Commonwealth Puerto Ricans, other Hispanic, and underrepresented minorities (black, American Indian/Alaska native, Mexican American, Chicano, mainland Puerto Rican). *Note:* (a) The data in this table are limited to United States citizens and aliens with permanent resident visas. Prior to 1981-82, when the definition was clarified, some permanent resident aliens may have been excluded. Percentages may not add due to rounding. "U.S. citizens" redefined in 1981 to include students with permanent resident visas.

★ 315 ★

Asian/Pacific Islanders Enrolled in First Year Medical School: 1975-76 to 1991-92

Number of Asian/Pacific Islanders[a] enrolled and percent of total enrolled, 1975-76 to 1991-92.

Year	Asian/Pacific Islander	
	Number enrolled	Percent of total first year class
1975-76	282[a]	1.8%
1976-77	348[a]	2.2%
1977-78	395	2.4%
1978-79	452	2.7%
1979-80	502	3.0%
1980-81	572	3.3%
1981-82	765	4.4%
1982-83	936	5.4%
1983-84	983	5.7%
1984-85	1,124	6.6%
1985-86	1,295	7.6%
1986-87	1,514	9.0%
1987-88	1,827	10.9%
1988-89	2,100	12.4%
1989-90	2,257	13.5%
1990-91	2,527	15.0%
1991-92	2,744	16.1%

Source: Selected from *AAMC Data Book: Statistical Information Related to Medical Education* (Washington, DC: Association of American Medical Colleges, January 1993), table B3, p. 2. Used with permission. Primary source: AAMC Section for Student Services, "Fall Enrollment Questionnaire." Also in source: data for Commonwealth Puerto Ricans, other Hispanic, and underrepresented minorities (black, American Indian/Alaskan native, Mexican American, Chicano, mainland Puerto Rican). Asian/Pacific Islander are not classified as "underrepresented" by the Association of American Medical Colleges. *Notes:* (a) In 1974-75 through 1976-77, ethnic group was called American Oriental. The data in this table are limited to United States citizens and aliens with permanent resident visas. Prior to 1981-82, when the definition was clarified, some permanent resident aliens may have been excluded. Percentages may not add due to rounding. "U.S. Citizen" redefined in 1981 to include students with permanent resident visa.

★ 316 ★

Medical College Female Applicants and Applicants Accepted: 1986-1992

Number of female applicants to U.S. medical colleges, applicants accepted, total and Asian/Pacific Islander, and percent change, 1986–1992.

Women, total	1986	1987	1988	1989	1990	1991	1992	% Change '91 to '92
Applicants	11,267	10,411	10,264	10,546	11,785	13,700	15,619	14.0%
Applicants accepted	5,933	6,205	6,323	6,453	6,656	6,943	7,257	4.5%
Asian/Pacific Islander								
Applicants	1,064	1,155	1,288	1,443	1,757	2,236	2,533	13.3%
Applicants accepted	554	691	784	847	995	1,112	1,085	-2.4%

Source: Association of American Medical Colleges, *Facts: Applicants, Matriculants, and Graduates, 1986-1992* (Washington, DC: AAMC, October 20, 1992), p. 6-7. Also in source: data on white, underrepresented minorities , (including black, American Indian/Alaskan Native, Mexican American/Chicano, Puerto Rican/ mainland), and other minorities (including Commonwealth Puerto Rican, and other Hispanic). Asians or Pacific Islanders are not classified as "underrepresented" by the Association of American Medical Colleges. Data is also included on applicants by state and by MCAT score and grade point average.

★ 317 ★

Medical College Male Applicants and Applicants Accepted: 1986-1992

Number of male applicants to U.S. medical colleges, applicants accepted, total and Asian/Pacific Islander, and percent change, 1986–1992.

Men, total	1986	1987	1988	1989	1990	1991	1992	% Change '91 to '92
Applicants	20,056	17,712	16,457	16,369	17,458	19,601	21,791	11.2%
Applicants accepted	11,159	10,822	10,785	10,522	10,550	10,493	10,207	-2.7%
Asian/Pacific Islander								
Applicants	1,928	2,034	2,061	2,218	2,588	3,251	3,692	13.6%
Applicants accepted	1,009	1,204	1,339	1,403	1,588	1,666	1,634	-1.9%

Source: Association of American Medical Colleges, *Facts: Applicants, Matriculants, and Graduates, 1986-1992* (Washington, DC: AAMC, October 20, 1992), p. 6-7. Also in source: data on white, underrepresented minorities, (including black, American Indian/Alaskan native, Mexican American/Chicano, Puerto Rican/ mainland), and other minorities (including Commonwealth Puerto Rican, and other Hispanic). Asians/Pacific Islanders are not classified as "underrepresented" by the Association of American Medical Colleges. Data is also included on applicants by state and by MCAT score and grade point average.

★ 318 ★

Medical School Enrollments by Sex: 1986-1992

Total and Asian/Pacific Islander number enrolled in U.S. medical schools by sex, 1986-1992, and percent change, 1991 to 1992.

Enrollment	1986	1987	1988	1989	1990	1991	1992	% Change '91 to '92
Enrollment, total	66,125	65,735	65,300	65,016	65,163	65,602	66,142	0.8%
Asian or Pacific Islander, total	4,883	5,738	6,595	7,489	8,436	9,438	9,994	5.9%
Men, total	44,025	43,191	42,315	41,503	40,877	40,640	40,104	-1.3%
Asian/Pacific Islander, men	3,195	3,686	4,205	4,710	5,256	5,804	6,051	4.3%
Women, total	22,100	22,544	22,985	23,513	24,286	24,962	26,038	4.3%
Asian/Pacific Islander, women	1,688	2,052	2,390	2,779	3,180	3,634	3,943	8.5%

Source: Association of American Medical Colleges, *Facts: Applicants, Matriculants, and Graduates, 1986-1992* (Washington, DC: AAMC, October 20, 1992), p. 10. Also in *Source:* data on white, underrepresented minorities , (including black, American Indian/Alaskan native, Mexican American/Chicano, Puerto Rican/ mainland), and other minorities (including Commonwealth Puerto Rican, and other Hispanic). Asians or Pacific Islanders are not classified as "underrepresented." Data is also included on applicants by state and by MCAT score and grade point average.

★ 319 ★

Medical School Graduates by Sex: 1986-1992

Total and Asian/Pacific Islander graduates from U.S. medical schools by sex, 1986 to 1992 and percent change, 1991-1992.

Graduates	1986	1987	1988	1989	1990	1991	1992	% Change '91 to '92
Graduates, total	16,117	15,830	15,919	15,630	15,398	15,427	15,365	-0.4%
Asian/Pacific Islander, total	909	947	1,119	1,241	1,433	1,687	1,920	13.8%
Men, total	11,160	10,723	10,704	10,409	10,167	9,874	9,815	-0.6%
Asian/Pacific Islander, men	613	623	726	805	919	1,064	1,181	11.0%
Women, total	4,957	5,107	5,215	5,221	5,231	5,553	5,550	-0.1%
Asian/Pacific Islander, women	296	324	393	436	514	623	739	18.6%

Source: Association of American Medical Colleges, *Facts: Applicants, Matriculants, and Graduates, 1986-1992* (Washington, DC: AAMC, October 20, 1992), p. 11. Also in source: data on white, underrepresented minorities, (including black, American Indian/Alaskan native, Mexican American/Chicano, Puerto Rican/ mainland), and other minorities (including Commonwealth Puerto Rican, and other Hispanic). Asians or Pacific Islanders are not classified as "underrepresented" by the Association of American Medical Colleges. Data is also included on applicants by state and by MCAT score and grade point average.

★ 320 ★

U.S. Medical School Applicants: 1986-1992

Numbers of U.S. medical school applicants and applicants accepted, total and Asian/Pacific Islander, 1986-1992.

Applicants	1986	1987	1988	1989	1990	1991	1992
Total Applicants	31,323	28,123	26,721	26,915	29,243	33,301	37,410
Total Accepted Applicants	17,092	17,027	17,108	16,975	17,206	17,436	17,464
Asian/Pacific Islander							
Applicants	2,988	3,198	3,349	3,661	4,345	5,487	6,225
Accepted Applicants	1,563	1,895	2,123	2,250	2,583	2,778	2,719

Source: Association of American Medical College, *Facts: Applicants, Matriculants, and Graduates, 1986-1992* (Washington, DC: AAMC, October 20, 1992), p. 6-7. Also in source: data on white, underrepresented minorities, (including black, American Indian/Alaskan native, Mexican American/Chicano, Puerto Rican/ mainland), and other minorities (including Commonwealth Puerto Rican, and other Hispanic). Asians or Pacific Islanders are not classified as "underrepresented." Data is also included on applicants by state and by Medical College Admissions Test (MCAT) MCAT score and grade point average.

Nursing Schools

★ 321 ★

Nursing Enrollments

Number of students and percent of total enrolled in nursing schools by race/ethnicity and type of program, 1991-92.

Race/ethnicity	Undergraduate (Programs reporting)			Graduate (Programs reporting)			Generic[c] (Programs reporting)	
	Generic[a]	RN[b]	Total Bacc.	Master's	Doct	Post Doct	Gen Master's	Gen ND
Race/Ethnicity	(328)	(392)	(431)	(209)	(53)	(3)	(10)	3)
Asian or Pacific Islander	1,970	474	2,815	572	67	0	12	6
Percent	3.1%	1.8%	2.9%	2.5%	2.5%		2.6%	4.5%
Black, non-Hispanic	5,598	1,961	8,448	1,205	112	1	14	9
Percent	8.8%	7.4%	8.8%	5.2%	4.3%	7.1%	3.0%	6.7%
American Indian/Alaskan Native	337	91	434	77	15	0	5	0
Percent	0.5%	0.3%	0.5%	0.3%	0.6%		1.1%	
Hispanic	1,793	692	2,779	387	45	0	5	5
Percent	2.8%	2.6%	2.9%	1.7%	1.7%		0.4%	3.7%
White	52,670	21,804	78,883	19,915	2,184	13	423	114
Percent	83.1%	82.5%	81.9%	86.1%	83.0%	92.9%	92.1%	85.1%

Source: American Association of Colleges of Nursing, *1991-1992 Enrollment and Graduations in Baccalaureate and Graduate Programs in Nursing* (Washington, DC: American Association of Colleges of Nursing, 1992), table 12, p. 15. Also in source: data on enrollment and graduation trends by type of program, geographic region, and gender. Survey forms were mailed to 617 baccalaureate and higher degree programs to compile the source report, which is the eleventh to be published since the establishment of the Data Bank Project in 1978. Institutions that reported estimated data are excluded. *Notes:* (a) Generic baccalaureate programs admit students with no previous nursing education, and require 4-5 years of academic work leading to the baccalaureate nursing degree. (b) RN is Registered Nurse. (c) Generic master's and Doctor of Nursing (ND) are programs which admit students with no previous nursing education (non-nursing baccalaureate graduates).

★ 322 ★

Nursing Enrollments, Undergraduate, 1990-91 and 1991-92

Numbers of students enrolled in baccalaureate Registered Nurse (RN) programs (296 reporting) and percent of total by race/ethnicity, 1990-91 and 1991-92.

Race/ethnicity	1990-91		1991-92	
	Number	Percent	Number	Percent
Asian	311	1.8%	368	2.1%
Black	1,491	8.6%	1,469	8.6%
Native American	144	0.8%	83	0.5%
Hispanic	379	2.2%	377	2.2%
White	14,579	84.5%	14,380	83.8%

Source: American Association of Colleges of Nursing, *1991-1992 Enrollment and Graduations in Baccalaureate and Graduate Programs in Nursing* (Washington, DC: American Association of Colleges of Nursing, 1992), table 15, p. 18. Also in source: data on enrollment and graduation trends by type of program, geographic region, and gender. Survey forms were mailed to 617 baccalaureate and higher degree programs to compile the source report, which is the eleventh to be published since the establishment of the Data Bank Project in 1978. Institutions that reported estimated data are excluded.

★ 323 ★

Nursing Enrollments, Graduate, 1990-91 and 1991-92

Number of students and percent of total enrolled in master's, doctoral, and postdoctoral nursing programs by race/ethnicity, 1990-91 and 1991-92.

Program (Number)	Race/ethnicity	1990–1991 (for Acad. yrs.)		1991–1992 (for Acad. yrs.)	
		Number	Percent	Number	Percent
Master's (182)					
	Asian	507	2.5%	550	2.6%
	Black	1,090	5.5%	1,109	5.3%
	Native American	73	0.4%	73	0.3%
	Hispanic	377	1.9%	348	1.7%
	White	17,813	89.2%	17,981	85.5%
Doctoral (48)					
	Asian	69	2.8%	62	2.5%
	Black	106	4.3%	103	4.2%
	Native American	11	0.4%	13	0.5%
	Hispanic	60	2.4%	40	1.6%
	White	2,130	86.2%	2,049	83.0%
Postdoctoral (3)					
	Asian	0		0	
	Black	0		1	7.1%
	Native American	0		0	
	Hispanic	0		0	
	White	7	87.5%	13	92.9%
Generic Master's (7)					
	Asian	4	1.3%	10	2.3%
	Black	5	1.6%	11	2.4%
	Native Hispanic	2	0.7%	5	1.1%
	Hispanic	2	0.7%	2	0.5%
	White	288	95.4%	407	92.7%
Nursing Doctorate (1)					
	Asian	0		5	7.8%
	Black	0		6	9.4%
	Native American				
	Hispanic	3	7.7%	1	1.6%
	White	36	92.3%	52	81.2%

Source: American Association of Colleges of Nursing, *1991-1992 Enrollment and Graduations in Baccalaureate and Graduate Programs in Nursing* (Washington, DC: American Association of Colleges of Nursing, 1992), table 15, p. 18-19. Also in source: data on enrollment and graduation trends by type of program, geographic region, and gender. Survey forms were mailed to 617 baccalaureate and higher degree programs to compile the source report, which is the eleventh to be published since the establishment of the Data Bank Project in 1978. Institutions that reported estimated data are excluded. *Notes:* (a) Generic baccalaureate programs admit students with no previous nursing education, and require 4-5 years of academic work leading to the baccalaureate nursing degree. (b) RN is Registered Nurse. (c) Generic Master's and Doctor of Nursing (ND) are programs which admit students with no previous nursing education (non-nursing baccalaureate graduates).

Teacher Education

★ 324 ★

Teacher Education Students: Characteristics and Attitudes

Reported results of a survey of teacher education students by race/ethnicity, 1990.

Characteristic	Asian/Pacific Islander	White	Black	Hispanic
"Is English your native language?" (% yes)	38.9%	98.6%	97.0%	48.6%
"What is your academic major?"				
Early Childhood	27.8%	11.9%	21.5%	2.8%
Elementary	50.0	52.3	44.4	58.3
Secondary	11.1	25.3	11.1	13.9
Special	5.6	3.6	14.8	8.3
Bilingual	-	0.7	-	5.6
Racial composition of high school neighborhood:				
More whites than minorities	29.4%	95.0%	18.0%	25.0%
Half minorities/half whites	5.9	4.7	20.3	27.8
More minorities than whites	64.7	0.4	61.7	47.2
Minority students at your high school were predominantly:				
Asian/Pacific Islander	64.7%	9.5%	.8%	2.9%
Black	5.9	63.6	91.6	20.0
Hispanic	17.6	17.4	6.9	77.1
Rate your ability to work as a team:				
Top 10%	17.7%	30.0%	47.8%	37.8%
Above average	27.8	45.8	38.1	37.8
Average	55.6	23.1	11.9	24.3
Below average	-	1.1	2.2	-
Bottom 10%	-	-	-	-
Rate your self-confidence (social):				
Top 10%	22.2%	16.6%	31.9%	16.2%
Above average	33.3	43.3	43.0	40.5
Average	38.9	31.8	22.2	32.4
Below average	-	7.6	3.0	10.8
Bottom 10%	5.6	0.7	-	-
"Was this institution your first choice?" (% yes)	72.2%	70.3%	45.5%	63.9%
"How important was ethnic/racial composition of institution in your decision to attend:"				
Very important	13.3%	1.9%	28.2%	8.8%
Important	26.7	11.9	36.3	26.5
Not very important	38.2	47.6	23.4	38.2
Unimportant	26.7	38.7	12.1	26.5
Racial composition of your teacher education program:				
More whites than minorities	52.9%	92.2%	18.0%	25.7%
Half minorities/half whites	17.6	3.7	10.5	45.7
More minorities than whites	29.4	4.1	71.4	28.6

[Continued]

Teacher Education Students: Characteristics and Attitudes (Continued)

Reported results of a survey of teacher education students by race/ethnicity, 1990.

Characteristic	Asian/Pacific Islander	White	Black	Hispanic
"How important was availability of a minority counselor in your decision to attend?"				
Very important	7.1%	0.4%	13.9%	12.1%
Important	28.6	3.3	34.4	21.2
Not very important	35.7	30.1	36.1	39.4
Unimportant	28.6	66.2	15.6	27.3
"Is your college administration sensitive to minority concerns?" (% yes)	62.5%	88.9%	86.6%	85.7%
"The racial composition of the student body at your institution is:"				
More whites than minorities	52.9%	83.5%	21.9%	25.7%
Half minorities/half whites	23.5	12.5	9.4	42.9
More minorities than whites	23.5	4.0	68.8	31.4
"How much of your free time do you spend with students of a different racial/ethnic background?"				
All of my free time with my own racial/ethnic group	11.1%	18.5%	16.3%	5.6%
Most of my free time with my own racial/ethnic group	16.7	50.6	34.9	41.7
Some of my free time with my own racial/ethnic group	55.6	25.1	41.9	50.0
I do not spend any of my free time with my own racial/ethnic group	16.7	5.9	7.0	2.8
Hours per week talking with/teachers outside of class:				
None	16.7%	14.4%	10.0%	13.9%
1-5 hrs.	55.6	74.2	63.8	66.7
5-10 hrs.	11.1	8.9	16.2	13.9
10-15 hrs.	5.6	1.1	4.6	2.8
15-20 hrs.	5.6	.7	1.5	-
More than 20 hrs.	5.6	.7	3.8	2.8
Hours per week exercising/sports:				
None	16.7%	14.0%	24.2%	33.3%
1-5 hrs.	44.4	45.6	46.0	27.8
5-10 hrs.	5.6	23.5	14.5	25.0
15-20 hrs.	5.6	3.8	6.5	8.3
More than 20 hrs.	27.8	4.8	6.5	5.6
Hours per week in student clubs/groups:				
None	55.6%	56.6%	37.8%	60.0%
1-5 hrs.	33.3	30.7	45.7	31.4
5-10 hrs.	-	8.6	7.9	8.6
10-15 hrs.	-	8.6	7.9	8.6
15-20 hrs.	-	.4	-	-
More than 20	11.1	1.1	3.9	-

[Continued]

★ 324 ★

Teacher Education Students: Characteristics and Attitudes (Continued)

Reported results of a survey of teacher education students by race/ethnicity, 1990.

Characteristic	Asian/Pacific Islander	White	Black	Hispanic
Hours per week watching TV:				
None	22.2%	11.8%	2.3%	16.7%
1-5 hrs.	33.3	44.9	45.7	58.3
5-10 hrs.	22.2	25.0	24.0	11.1
10-15 hrs.	5.6	11.4	12.4	2.8
More than 20 hrs.	16.7	4.0	9.3	5.6
Hours per week at religious service:				
None	22.2%	30.4%	14.1%	25.7%
1-5 hrs.	38.9	53.0	56.3	57.1
5-10 hrs.	11.1	9.6	14.1	8.6
10-15 hrs.	5.6	1.9	7.0	-
15-20 hrs.	5.6	1.9	.8	2.9
More than 20 hrs.	16.7	3.3	7.8	5.7

Source: Selected from American Association of Colleges for Teacher Education, *AACTE/Metropolitan Life Survey of Teacher Education* (Washington, DC: AACTE, 1990). Also in source: responses to questions on ways to increase minority enrollment in teacher education.

Nuclear Engineering

★ 325 ★

Nuclear Engineering: Enrollment and Degrees Conferred by Sex

Numbers enrolled in bachelor's (juniors and seniors), master's, or doctoral degree programs, and degrees conferred in nuclear engineering,by sex and race/ethnicity, 1991.

Race/ethnicity and gender	Enrollment–fall 1991			Degrees granted, July 1990-June 1991		
	Undergraduate	Master's	Doctorate	B.S.	M.S.	Ph.D.
U.S. Citizens						
Asian/Pacific Islander, male	46	11	17	12	5	9
Asian/Pacific Islander, female	3	3	3	1	0	0
White male, not Hispanic	1,185	469	260	314	118	50
White females, not Hispanic	114	60	26	53	16	4
Black male, not Hispanic	33	10	2	9	0	0
Black female, not Hispanic	1	1	0	1	1	0
Hispanic male	25	12	6	8	5	0
Hispanic female	6	0	2	0	0	0
Foreign national						
Male	27	172	302	6	64	51
Female	1	35	30	3	5	4
Totals	758	784	699	407	214	118

Source: Oak Ridge Institute for Science and Education, *Nuclear Engineering Enrollments and Degrees, 1991* (Washington, DC: U.S. Department of Energy and U.S. Nuclear Regulatory Commission, June 1992), table A-6, p. 24. This report was prepared by the Labor and Policy Studies Program, Science and Engineering Education Division, Oak Ridge Institute for Science and Education, Oak Ridge, TN. Also in source: data for American Indians/Alaskan Natives.

SAT Test Scores

★ 326 ★

PSAT/NMSQT Test Takers

Numbers and percent of total high school juniors who took the Preliminary Scholastic Aptitude Test (PSAT) and National Merit Scholarship Qualifying Test (NMSQT) by race/ethnicity, 1991.

Race/ethnicity	Number	Percent
Asian American	67,514	6.2%
White	827,192	76.3%
Black	95,772	8.8%
Mexican American	35,529	3.3%
Puerto Rican	11,674	1.1%
Other Hispanic	26,180	2.4%
American Indian	6,376	0.6%

Source: PSAT/NMSQT Summary Report: National, Regional, and State Data for College-Bound Juniors (New York: The College Board, 1992), table 2, p. 4. Also in source: characteristics and data on high school juniors who took the test. Data by region and state are also available.

★ 327 ★

SAT Test Scores, 1976 and 1992

Mean scores on the Scholastic Aptitude Test (SAT) Verbal and Math tests by race/ethnicity, 1992, and change from 1976[a] to 1992 and from 1991 to 1992.

Race/ethnicity	1992	Change from 1976	Change from 1991
SAT Verbal			
Asian American	413	-1	+2
American Indian	395	+7	+2
Black	352	+20	+1
Mexican American	372	+1	-5
Puerto Rican	366	+2	+5
White	442	-9	+1
All students	423	-8	+1
SAT Math			
Asian American	532	+14	+2
American Indian	442	+22	+5
Black	385	+31	0
Mexican American	425	+15	-2
Puerto Rican	406	+5	0
White	491	-2	+2
All students	476	+4	+2

Source: Press release, "College Board Reports Rise in SAT Scores for Class of 1992" (New York: The College Board, August 27, 1992), table 2, p. 5. The SAT is scored on a scale of 200 to 800 for each of the two sections (verbal and math). Also in source: SAT averages by sex. *Note:* (a) The first year for which SAT scores by ethnic group are available is 1976.

★ 328 ★

SAT Test Scores, 1992

Numbers and percent (of group total) of Asian and total Scholastic Aptitude Test (SAT) test takers by mean verbal and math scores by race/ethnicity, 1992.

Race/ethnicity	Number of SAT Takers	Percent	Percent Male/Female	SAT-V Mean	SAT-M Mean
Asian /Pacific Islander	78,387	8%	50/50	413	532
American Indian/Alaskan Native	7,412	1%	48/52	395	442
Black/African American	99,126	10%	42/58	352	385
Hispanic/Mexican Amer/Chicano	30,336	3%	45/55	372	425
Puerto Rican	12,091	1%	44/56	366	406
Other Hispanic	26,766	3%	45/55	383	433
White	680,806	71%	47/53	442	491

Source: College-Bound Seniors: 1992 Profile of SAT and Achievement Test Takers (New York: The College Board, 1991), p. 6. This table summarizes information for only the 1992 seniors who took SAT or Achievement Tests any time during their high school years through 1992.

★ 329 ★

SAT-Math Scores, Asians by Sex

Numbers of Asian taking the Scholastic Aptitude Test (SAT) and percent (of Asian total) by math score, sex, and mean scores for total and percentiles, 1991.

Score	Asian total		Male		Female	
	Number	Percent	Number	Percent	Number	Percent
750-800	3,427	4%	2,553	7%	874	2%
700-740	6,166	8%	3,960	10%	2,206	6%
650-790	7,544	10%	4,363	11%	3,181	8%
600-640	9,020	12%	4,830	13%	4,190	11%
550-590	9,896	13%	4,984	13%	4,912	13%
500-540	9,792	13%	4,703	12%	5,089	13%
450-490	8,860	12%	3,961	10%	4,899	13%
400-440	8,014	10%	3,483	9%	4,531	12%
350-390	6,334	8%	2,536	7%	3,798	10%
300-340	4,749	6%	1,826	5%	2,923	8%
250-290	2,353	3%	895	2%	1,458	4%
200-240	548	1%	193	1%	355	1%
Number	76,703		38,287		38,416	
Mean	530		553		507	
Standard deviation	133		134		129	
Mean, 25th percentile	430		450		410	
Mean, 50th percentile	530		560		510	
Mean, 75th percentile	630		660		600	

Source: Selected from *College-Bound Seniors National Report: 1991 Profile of SAT and Achievement Test Takers* (New York: The College Board, 1991). This table summarizes information for only the 1991 seniors who took SAT or Achievement Tests any time during their high school years through 1991.

★ 330 ★

SAT-Verbal Scores, Asians by Sex

Numbers of Asians taking the Scholastic Aptitude Test (SAT) and percent (of Asian total) by verbal score, sex, and mean scores for total and percentiles, 1991.

Score	Asian total		Male		Female	
	Number	Percent	Number	Percent	Number	Percent
750-800	178	-	100	-	78	0%
700-740	1,173	2%	652	2%	521	1%
650-690	2,423	3%	1,287	3%	1,136	3%
600-640	3,994	5%	2,138	6%	1,856	5%
550-590	5,491	7%	2,835	7%	2,656	7%
500-540	7,552	10%	3,787	10%	3,765	10%
450-490	9,212	12%	4,591	12%	4,621	12%
400-440	10,219	13%	5,126	13%	5,093	13%
350-390	10,395	14%	5,225	14%	5,170	13%
300-340	9,092	12%	4,433	12%	4,659	12%
250-290	7,732	10%	3,764	10%	3,968	10%
200-240	9,242	12%	4,349	11%	4,893	13%
Number	76,703		38,287		38,416	
Mean	411		416		407	
Standard deviation	132		133		131	
Mean, 25th percentile	310		310		300	
Mean, 50th percentile	410		410		400	
Mean, 75th percentile	500		510		500	

Source: Selected from *College-Bound Seniors National Report: 1991 Profile of SAT and Achievement Test Takers* (New York, The College Board, 1991). A dash (-) represents less than 1%. This table summarizes information for only the 1991 seniors who took SAT or Achievement Tests any time during their high school years through 1991.

★ 331 ★

SAT Reading Comprehension Subscores, Asians by Sex

Numbers of Asians taking the Scholastic Aptitude Test (SAT) and percent (of Asian total) by SAT-Verbal "Reading Comprehension" scores, sex, and mean scores, 1991.

Score	Asian total		Male		Female	
	Number	Percent	Number	Percent	Number	Percent
70-80	1,140	1%	635	2%	505	1%
60-69	5,820	8%	3,124	8%	2,696	7%
50-59	13,155	17%	6,659	17%	6,496	17%
40-49	20,578	27%	10,278	27%	10,300	27%
30-39	20,322	26%	9,977	26%	10,345	27%
20-29	15,688	20%	7,614	20%	8,074	21%
Number	76,703		38,287		38,416	
Mean	41.2		41.6		40.8	
Standard deviation	12.7		12.8		12.6	

Source: Selected from *College-Bound Seniors National Report: 1991 Profile of SAT and Achievement Test Takers* (New York: The College Board, 1991). This table summarizes information for only the 1991 seniors who took SAT or Achievement Tests any time during their high school years through 1991.

★ 332 ★

SAT Vocabulary Subscores, Asians by Sex

Numbers of Asians taking the Scholastic Aptitude Test (SAT) and percent (of Asian total) by SAT-Verbal "Vocabulary" scores, sex, and mean scores, 1991.

Score	Asian Total		Male		Female	
	Number	Percent	Number	Percent	Number	Percent
70-80	1,366	2%	760	2%	606	2%
60-69	6,709	9%	3,578	9%	3,131	8%
50-59	13,359	17%	6,816	18%	6,543	17%
40-49	18,711	24%	9,428	25%	9,283	24%
30-39	19,090	25%	9,476	25%	9,614	25%
20-29	17,468	23%	8,229	21%	9,239	24%
Number	76,703		38,287		38,416	
Mean	41.2		41.7		40.7	
Standard deviation	13.4		13.5		13.4	

Source: Selected from *College-Bound Seniors National Report: 1991 Profile of SAT and Achievement Test Takers* (New York: The College Board, 1991). Note: This table summarizes information for only the 1991 seniors who took SAT or Achievement Tests any time during their high school years through 1991.

★ 333 ★

Advanced Placement Test Scores

Numbers of total and Asian candidates testing for advanced placement[a] credit, with mean score by subject, 1992.

Exam	Total		Asian	
	Number	Mean	Number	Mean
Total exams	566,036	33.04	76,037	3.16
U.S. history	104,749	2.84	11,773	2.97
Art history	4,207	3.16	688	3.15
Art: studio drawing	1,712	3.23	194	3.28
Art: studio general	3,738	3.22	369	3.42
Biology	40,458	3.13	6,749	3.39
Chemistry	25,446	2.83	5,351	3.06
Computer science A	4,917	2.71	930	2.73
Computer science AB	4,474	3.17	958	3.11
Economics, micro	5,528	2.96	1,005	3.09
Economics, macro	6,765	3.12	1,104	3.25
English language and comp.	30,592	2.90	3,269	3.02
English literature and comp.	110,880	3.08	10,028	3.09
European history	27,541	3.11	3,221	3.24
French language	10,776	2.88	1,465	2.79
French literature	1,446	3.11	193	2.99
German language	2,073	3.08	169	2.82
Government and politics, U.S.	23,522	2.95	3,060	2.98
Government and politics, comp.	5,732	2.78	768	2.78
Latin/Virgil	2,193	2.99	324	3.30
Latin/Catullus Horace	974	2.98	121	3.34
Math/Calculus AB	74,919	3.06	12,088	3.29
Math/Calculus BC	15,395	3.61	4,421	3.66

[Continued]

★ 333 ★

Advanced Placement Test Scores (Continued)

Numbers of total and Asian candidates testing for advanced placement[a] credit, with mean score by subject, 1992.

Exam	Total		Asian	
	Number	Mean	Number	Mean
Music theory	1,699	3.08	189	3.54
Physic B	11,725	2.81	2,121	3.03
Physic C mech.	6,960	3.38	1,617	3.47
Physic C, E, and M	3,805	3.32	951	3.41
Psychology	3,814	3.02	387	3.05
Spanish language	26,392	3.62	2,290	3.16
Spanish literature	3,604	3.12	234	3.27
Total number of candidates	378,692		44,865	

Source: The College Board, press release, October 1992. Also in source: data on college and university participation in the Advanced Placement (AP) program and on numbers and characteristics of AP test takers; data for other ethnic groups; and data by Advanced Placement (AP) grade. *Note:* (a) More than 378,000 students in 9,730 secondary schools took college-level AP examinations in May 1992. Qualifying AP grades enable students to receive up to one full year's college credit for high school work.

★ 334 ★

Advanced Placement Examinees, 1982-1992

Number of Advanced Placement[a] test takers who reported race/ethnicity, and percent growth from 1982 to 1992 and from 1987 to 1992.

Category	Number of candidates			Percent growth	
	1982	1987	1992	1982 to 92	1987 to 92
Asian	7,675	21,101	44,865	485%	113%
White	100,499	175,556	260,200	159%	46%
Black	3,217	8,141	15,225	373%	87%
Hispanic	3,362	9,632	26,282	682%	173%
American Indian	336	643	1,655	393%	157%
Total	141,907	259,222	378,692	167%	46%

Source: The College Board, press release, October 1992, table 3. Also in source: data on college and university participation in the Advanced Placement (AP) program and on numbers and characteristics of AP test takers. *Note:* (a) More than 378,000 students in 9,730 secondary schools took college-level AP examinations in May 1992. Qualifying AP grades enable students to receive up to one full year's college credit for high school work.

★ 335 ★

SAT Test of Standard Written English (TSWE) Scores, Asians

Scores of Asian and total students taking the Test of Standard Written English (TSWE), 1991.

Score	Asian test takers		All test takers		Asian test takers			
	Total number	Percent	Total number	Percent	Male, number	Percent	Female, number	Percent
60+	2,480	3%	34,868	3%	1,089	3%	1,391	4%
55-59	8,205	11%	122,223	12%	3,824	10%	4,381	11%
50-54	10,122	13%	156,434	15%	4,779	12%	5,343	14%
45-49	10,319	13%	167,260	16%	5,095	13%	5,224	14%
40-44	9,457	12%	144,433	14%	4,760	12%	4,697	12%
35-39	9,185	12%	136,356	13%	4,620	12%	4,565	12%
30-34	8,492	11%	111,754	11%	4,410	12%	4,082	11%
25-29	6,900	9%	78,282	8%	3,625	9%	3,275	9%
20-24	11,543	15%	81,074	8%	6,085	16%	5,458	14%
Total	76,703		1,032,684		38,287		38,416	
Mean	39.9		42.1		39.4		40.5	
Standard deviation	12.2		11.0		12.1		12.2	

Source: Selected from *College-Bound Seniors National Report: 1991 Profile of SAT and Achievement Test Takers* (New York: The College Board, 1991). This table summarizes information for only the 1991 seniors who took SAT or Achievement Tests any time during their high school years through 1991.

★ 336 ★

SAT Test Takers' Language Proficiency, 1987 and 1992

High school graduates who took the Scholastic Aptitude Test (SAT) in percent by race/ethnicity and language proficiency, 1987 and 1992.

Race/ethnicity	Language spoken					
	English		English and other		Other language	
	1987	1992	1987	1992	1987	1992
All students	86%	84%	8%	8%	5%	8%
Asian American	31%	29%	27%	26%	43%	44%
White	94%	95%	5%	4%	1%	2%
Black	92%	92%	7%	6%	1%	2%
Mexican American	44%	44%	40%	34%	16%	22%
Puerto Rican	23%	30%	45%	37%	32%	34%
Other Hispanic	21%	23%	41%	33%	38%	44%
American Indian	91%	92%	8%	7%	2%	2%
Other	61%	59%	20%	20%	19%	22%

Source: College Board, press release, August 27, 1992, table 4, p. 8. Also in source: data on scores and academic preparation and other characteristics of test takers.

★ 337 ★

SAT Test Takers' Citizenship Characteristics, 1987 and 1992

High school graduates who took the Scholastic Aptitude Test (SAT), in percent by race/ethnicity and citizenship, 1987 and 1992.

Race/ethnicity	Citizenship					
	U.S. citizen		Permanent resident		Citizen of other country	
	1987	1992	1987	1992	1987	1992
All students	95%	92%	3%	5%	2%	3%
Asian American	58%	56%	27%	29%	15%	15%
White	98%	98%	1%	1%	1%	1%
Black	95%	94%	3%	4%	2%	2%
Mexican American	92%	91%	7%	8%	1%	1%
Puerto Rican	99%	99%	-	1%	-	-
Other Hispanic	66%	64%	23%	25%	11%	11%
American Indian	98%	98%	1%	1%	1%	1%
Other	68%	71%	14%	14%	18%	15%

Source: College Board, press release, August 27, 1992, table 4, p. 8. Also in source: data on scores and academic preparation and other characteristics of test takers. A dash (–) indicates less than 0.5 percent.

★ 338 ★

SAT Test Takers' Plans for College, Advanced Placement

Number and percent of Scholastic Aptitude Test (SAT) test takers who report Asian ethnicity, and percent (of Asian total) who intend to pursue advanced placement in college, with mean SAT scores, 1991.

Subject	Asian				
	Number of SAT Takers	Percent	Percen male/female	Verbal Mean	Math Mean
Plans for Advanced Placement					
Art	4,434	6%	45/55	376	497
Biology	11,325	15%	51/49	483	591
Chemistry	9,844	13%	61/39	472	619
Computer Science	4,973	7%	73/27	429	590
English	19,090	26%	43/57	495	578
Foreign Languages	11,575	16%	41/59	475	578
Humanities	1,987	3%	46/54	472	553
Mathematics	27,394	37%	56/44	445	602
Music	2,854	4%	44/56	396	519
Physics	8,790	12%	70/30	472	634
Social Studies	14,181	19%	52/48	505	592

Source: Selected from *College-Bound Seniors National Report: 1991 Profile of SAT and Achievement Test Takers* (New York: The College Board, 1991). This table summarizes information for only the 1991 seniors who took SAT or Achievement Tests any time during their high school years through 1991. Also in source: data for all SAT test takers.

★ 339 ★

SAT: Characteristics of Test Takers' Families

Mean scores of Asian and total Scholastic Aptitude Test (SAT) test takers by level of parental education and family income, 1991.

Characteristic	Number of SAT Takers	All Asians				Number of SAT Takers	All Students			
		Percent	Percent male/female	Verbal Mean	Math Mean		Percent	Percent male/female	Verbal Mean	Math Mean
Highest Level of Parental Education										
No High School Diploma	8,674	12	50/50	324	480	46,206	5	42/58	339	409
High School Diploma	20,100	27	48/52	375	497	354,151	38	45/55	395	443
Associate Degree	3,548	5	48/52	395	492	71,239	8	47/53	407	454
Bachelor's Degree	21,730	29	50/50	421	543	251,386	27	49/51	442	497
Graduate Degree	20,491	27	52/48	480	578	221,408	23	50/50	476	528
Income										
Less than $10,000	7,754	11	52/48	340	485	44,259	5	40/60	353	415
$10,000-$20,000	12,046	17	50/50	353	499	101,434	11	43/57	379	434
$20,000-$30,000	10,895	15	50/50	393	512	133,316	15	46/54	404	452
$30,000-$40,000	11,127	16	49/51	414	523	159,415	18	48/52	418	466
$40,000-$50,000	7,055	10	49/51	435	535	119,401	13	49/51	430	480
$50,000-$60,000	6,012	8	49/51	449	546	97,081	11	49/51	440	491
$60,000-$70,000	4,275	6	50/50	456	556	66,083	7	50/50	449	500
$70,000 or more	11,775	17	53/47	482	590	165,304	19	51/49	469	528

Source: Selected from *College-Bound Seniors National Report: 1991 Profile of SAT and Achievement Test Takers* (New York: The College Board, 1991). This table summarizes information for only the 1991 seniors who took SAT or Achievement Tests any time during their high school years through 1991.

★ 340 ★

SAT Asian Test Takers' Plans for College Financial Aid

Number and percent of Scholastic Aptitude Test (SAT) test takers who report Asian ethnicity, and percent (of Asian total) who intend to apply for financial aid in college, with mean SAT scores, 1991.

Plans to Apply or Financial Aid	Number of SAT Takers	Percent	Percent male/female	Verbal Mean	Math Mean
Yes	54,353	71%	49/51	412	524
No	7,271	10%	53/47	411	558
Don't Know	14,675	19%	52/48	411	535

Source: Selected from *College-Bound Seniors National Report: 1991 Profile of SAT and Achievement Test Takers* (New York: The College Board, 1991). This table summarizes information for only the 1991 seniors who took SAT or Achievement Tests any time during their high school years through 1991. Also in source: data for all SAT test takers.

★ 341 ★

SAT Test Takers' Plans for College, Intended Major

Number and percent of Scholastic Aptitude Test (SAT) test takers who report Asian ethnicity, and percent (of Asian total) who intend to pursue various college majors, with mean SAT scores, 1991.

Intended College Major	Number of SAT Takers	All Asians			
		Percent	Percent male/ female	Vrebal Mean	Math Mean
Agriculture/Natural Resources	272	-	52/48	397	487
Architecture/Environ. Design	2,579	3%	61/39	380	524
Arts:Visual/Performing	3,250	4%	37/63	382	483
Biological Sciences	3,770	5%	45/55	467	571
Business/Commerce	15,581	21%	45/55	379	503
Communications	1,833	2%	25/75	441	498
Computer/Information Sciences	3,320	4%	66/34	373	530
Education	1,935	3%	22/78	380	468
Engineering	12,520	17%	82/18	416	581
Foreign/Classical Languages	437	1%	19/81	387	520
General/Interdisciplinary	263	-	35/65	522	578
Health/Allied Services	14,839	20%	41/59	431	532
Home Economics	150	-	26/74	348	449
Language/Literature	650	1%	27/73	500	560
Library/Archival Sciences	19	-	32/68	395	521
Mathematics	598	1%	50/50	420	630
Military Sciences	309	-	84/16	382	463
Philosophy/Religion/ Theology	170	-	64/36	440	535
Physical Sciences	1,127	2%	65/35	474	620
Public Affairs/Services	739	1%	46/54	374	449
Social Sciences/History	6,237	8%	33/67	460	530
Technical/Vocational	536	1%	64/36	314	419
Undecided	3,504	5%	48/52	416	529

Source: Selected from *College-Bound Seniors National Report: 1991 Profile of SAT and Achievement Test Takers* (New York: The College Board, 1991). This table summarizes information for only the 1991 seniors who took SAT or Achievement Tests any time during their high school years through 1991. A dash (-) indicates less than 1%. Also in source: data for all SAT test takers.

★ 342 ★

SAT Test Takers' Plans for College, Planned Degree

Number and percent of Scholastic Aptitude Test (SAT) test takers who report Asian ethnicity, and percent (of Asian total) who intend to pursue various degrees in college, with mean SAT scores, 1991.

Degree-level goal	Number of Asian SAT Takers	Percent	Percent male/ female	Verbal Mean	Math Mean
Certificate Program	1,090	1%	51/49	309	452
Associate Degree	877	1%	44/56	305	409
Bachelor's Degree	14,725	20%	49/51	353	471
Master's Degree	22,709	30%	52/48	410	536
Doctoral/Related Degree	23,177	31%	50/50	473	585
Other	662	1%	45/55	297	433
Undecided	11,539	15%	47/53	396	513

Source: Selected from *College-Bound Seniors National Report: 1991 Profile of SAT and Achievement Test Takers* (New York: The College Board, 1991). This table summarizes information for only the 1991 seniors who took SAT or Achievement Tests any time during their high school years through 1991. Also in source: data for all SAT test takers.

★ 343 ★

SAT Test Takers' Class Rank and Grade Point Average

High school class rank and grade point average of Asian Scholastic Aptitude Test (SAT) test takers, 1991.

Rank and GPA	Asian, Number of SAT test takers	Percent	Percent male/ female	Verbal Mean	Math Mean
High school class rank					
Top tenth	20,053	29%	51/49	501	627
Second tenth	17,167	25%	50/50	416	548
Second fifth	17,622	25%	52/48	378	497
Third fifth	12,651	18%	49/51	347	440
Fourth fifth	1,810	3%	51/49	325	409
Fifth fifth	454	1%	49/51	312	397
High school GPA					
A+ (97-100)	5,344	7%	52/48	546	656
A (93-96)	12,505	17%	45/55	481	606
A- (90-92)	13,019	17%	47/53	440	569
B (80-89)	34,354	46%	50/50	378	493
C (70-79)	8,991	12%	59/41	334	438
D, E, or F (Below 70)	448	1%	67/33	310	484

Source: Selected from *College-Bound Seniors National Report: 1991 Profile of SAT and Achievement Test Takers* (New York: The College Board, 1991). This table summarizes information for only the 1991 seniors who took SAT or Achievement Tests any time during their high school years through 1991.

★ 344 ★

SAT Test Takers' Academic Study by Subject, 1987 and 1992

Percent of Scholastic Aptitude Test (SAT) test takers by race/ethnicity who report four or more years of study in high school in six academic areas, 1987 and 1992.

Race/ethnicity	Percent who studied four years or more:					
	English	Arts/Music	Social science/ History	Foreign/ Classical languages	Natural sciences	Math
Asian American						
1987	85	13	36	25	45	75
1992	82	14	40	29	49	74
American Indian						
1987	82	14	35	13	29	53
1992	80	17	38	14	34	58
Black						
1987	83	14	32	12	26	54
1992	79	13	36	13	31	57
Mexican American						
1987	87	13	24	11	20	54
1992	83	12	23	12	26	59
Puerto Rican						
1987	84	10	45	31	33	56
1992	82	11	52	30	36	58
Other Hispanic						
1987	84	10	37	27	32	61
1992	80	12	42	27	38	63
White						
1987	89	18	40	22	38	64
1992	85	19	44	24	44	67
All students						
1987	88	17	39	22	37	63
1992	83	18	43	23	42	65

Source: College Board, press release, "College Board Reports Rise in SAT Scores for Class of 1992," August 27, 1992, table 8, p. 11. Also in source: SAT averages by school type and region.

★ 345 ★

SAT Test Takers with Twenty Years
of Academic Study, 1987 and 1992

Percent of Scholastic Aptitude Test (SAT) test takers by race/ethnicity who report twenty or more years of study in six academic areas, 1987 and 1992.

Race/ethnicity	Percent reporting 20 years of study		
	1987	1992	Change in percent, 1987 to 1992
Asian American	38%	46%	+8
American Indian	23%	31%	+8
Black	22%	27%	+5
Mexican American	16%	23%	+7
Puerto Rican	32%	38%	+6
Other Hispanic	32%	38%	+6
White	35%	44%	+9
All students	34%	41%	+7

Source: College Board, press release, "College Board Reports Rise in SAT Scores for Class of 1992," August 27, 1992, table 6, p. 9. Also in source: SAT averages by school type and region.

★ 346 ★

SAT: Characteristics of High Schools

Asian and total students taking the Scholastic Aptitude Test (SAT), by high school type, location, and size of senior class, 1991.

High School Characteristic	Number of Asian SAT Takers	Percent	Percent male/ female	Verbal Mean	Math Mean
Type					
Public	58,190	83%	49/51	406	522
Religiously affiliated	7,564	11%	51/49	434	517
Independent	4,482	6%	52/48	542	583
Location					
Large city	26,750	38%	49/51	392	514
Medium-size city	9,278	13%	49/51	408	517
Small city/town	7,423	11%	50/50	418	517
Suburban	23,569	34%	49/51	437	549
Rural	2,892	4%	47/53	392	481
Size of senior class					
More than 1,000	567	1%	56/44	456	588
750-1,000	1,666	2%	48/52	404	517
500-749	14,806	21%	49/51	405	526
250-499	33,091	48%	49/51	411	524
100-249	13,218	19%	50/50	420	522
Fewer than 100	6,227	9%	48/52	420	531

Source: Selected from *College-Bound Seniors National Report: 1991 Profile of SAT and Achievement Test Takers* (New York: The College Board, 1991). This table summarizes information for only the 1991 seniors who took SAT or Achievement Tests any time during their high school years through 1991.

SAT Scores by Highest Level of Parental Education

Average scores of Scholastic Aptitude Test (SAT) Verbal and Math tests takers by race/ethnicity and educational attainment of parents, 1992.

Race/ethnicity	SAT-Verbal average, parents' educational attainment				
	No high school diploma	High school diploma	Associate degree	Bachelor's degree	Graduate degree
Asian American	332	376	392	422	483
American Indian	327	379	386	413	438
Black	307	336	352	377	403
Mexican American	331	372	389	412	433
Puerto Rican	317	361	364	380	404
Other Hispanic	319	374	390	416	428
White	374	411	421	455	484
All students	338	394	408	444	476
	SAT-Math average, parents' educational attainment				
Asian American	483	498	496	545	583
American Indian	379	425	433	463	484
Black	350	372	383	407	431
Mexican American	394	423	435	460	478
Puerto Rican	354	394	403	430	453
Other Hispanic	375	417	434	467	484
White	420	457	468	506	534
All students	409	443	456	499	530

Source: College Board,press release, "College Board Reports Rise in SAT Scores for Class of 1992," August 27, 1992) table 9, p. 12. Also in source: SAT averages by school type and region.

SAT: University of California Freshmen by Asian Ethnicity

Scholastic Aptitude Test (SAT) scores and high school grade point averages (GPA)s of University of California freshmen by Asian ethnicity, 1984.

Race/ethnicity	High school GPA	SAT-Verbal	SAT-Math
White	3.59	512	577
All Asian American	3.69	456	584
Chinese	3.73	473	612
Filipino	3.56	448	520
Indian/Pakistani	3.80	520	606
Japanese	3.75	510	604
Korean	3.64	418	594
Other Asian Americans	3.72	373	556

Source: Eugenia Escueta and Eileen O'Brien, "Asian Americans in Higher Education: Trends and Issues," *Research Briefs* (Washington: Division of Policy Analysis and Research, American Council on Education, 1991) vol. 2, no. 4, table 2, p. 4. The SAT (Scholastic Aptitude Test) is scored on a scale of 200 to 800 for each of the two sections (verbal and math); the grade point averages are reported based on a 4.0 scale. Primary source: The College Board, *Predictors of Academic Achievement Among Asian American and White Students,* (New York: The College Board), 1988.

Student Attitudes and Behavior

★ 349 ★

Barriers for Female Asian/Pacific Americans to Higher Education

Report of a study of Asian/Pacific American females who are socialized into traditional roles and not academically prepared for higher education. Subjects of this 1987 study were 46 females: Filipino-American (15), Native Hawaiian (15), and Samoan-American (16) in grades 10, 11, and 12 attending an urban public high school in Hawaii.

Grade point average: 1.66 to 2.75.

Over 25% were not enrolled in any mathematics class.

Of those enrolled in mathematics, over 50% were enrolled in mathematics below algebra.

About 50% were not enrolled in any science class.

Only four had plans to pursue higher education.

All but four belonged to families on welfare.

Subjects report being assigned traditional female responsibilities (care for siblings, cooking, cleaning) at home.

Reported conclusion reached by author is that, by enrolling in lower–level mathematics and science classes, females are unknowingly self-selecting themselves from pursuit of higher education.

Source: Rosalind Y. Mau, "Barriers to Higher Education for Asian/Pacific American Females," *The Urban Review* 22, no. 3 (1990): 183-197.

★ 350 ★

Criminal Activities in Schools

Percent of students twelve to nineteen years of age reporting certain criminal activities in their schools within the past six months by race/ethnicity, 1989.

Activity	Total	Race/ethnicity				
		Asian/ Pacific Is.	White	Black	Hispanic	American Indian
Street gangs in school	15.4%	29.2%	11.7%	19.9%	31.8%	11.0%
Something taken directly by force	0.7%	0%	0.6%	0.9%	1.1%	0%
Something stolen from desk/locker/other	12.2%	11.9%	12.2%	12.4%	11.1%	18.5%
Physically attacked	2.9%	1.0%	2.9%	2.7%	3.6%	7.0%
Bring something to school to protect yourself	1.2%	0.6%	1.2%	1.5%	1.2%	3.3%
Teacher attacked or threatened with attack	16.3%	10.2%	16.1%	19.7%	14.2%	14.9%

Source: U.S. Department of Education, National Center for Education Statistics, *The Condition of Education 1992* (Washington, DC: U.S. Government Printing Office, June 1992), p. 116. Primary source: U.S. Department of Justice, Office of Justice Programs, Bureau of Justice Statistics, *National Crime Survey: School Crime Supplement,* 1989.

★ 351 ★

Defensive Behavior against Attacks in Schools

Percent of students twelve to nineteen years of age reporting behavior taken to avoid attacks in the past six months by race/ethnicity, 1989.

Behavior taken to avoid attacks	Total	Race/ethnicity				
		Asian/ Pacific Is.	White	Black	Hispanic	American Indian
Stay home	12%	0.3%	1.1%	1.0%	2.5%	3.2%
Stay away from shortest route to school	1.5%	4.3%	1.0%	2.4%	3.0%	1.0%
Stay away from school entrances	1.3%	3.5%	1.0%	2.1%	1.4%	-
Stay away from halls/stairs	2.1%	3.3%	1.7%	2.9%	3.0%	1.2%
Stay away from cafeteria	1.6%	1.8%	1.3%	3.6%	2.4%	2.3%
Stay away from restrooms	2.7%	2.7%	2.3%	4.0%	3.5%	0.9%
Stay away from other places inside school	1.1%	2.3%	0.8%	1.7%	1.6%	2.0%
Stay away from parking lot	1.3%	2.8%	1.1%	1.6%	2.1%	2.1%
Stay away from other places on grounds	1.7%	2.3%	1.6%	1.8%	2.6%	0.9%
Stay away from extracurricular activities	1.1%	1.9%	0.7%	2.2%	1.0%	4.1%

Source: U.S. Department of Education, National Center for Education Statistics, *The Condition of Education, 1992* (Washington, DC: U.S. Government Printing Office, June 1992), p. 309. Primary source: U.S. Department of Justice, Office of Justice Programs, Bureau of Justice Statistics, *National Crime Survey: School Crime Supplement,* 1989. A dash (–) indicates less than 1 %.

★ 352 ★

Drug and Alcohol Use, Frequent, by High School Seniors

Number and percent of high school seniors by sex and race/ethnicity, who reported using drugs, alcohol, or cigarettes daily (or as specified in table) in a one-year period 1985 to 1989 (data combined).

Type of drug	Percent who used daily in last 30 days											
	Asian American		White		Black		Mexican American		Puerto Rican/Latin American		American Indian	
	Male	Female	Male	Female	Male	Female	Male	Female	Male	Female	Male	Female
Sample size	982	917	28,056	29,808	3,688	4,499	1,518	1,599	680	712	537	531
Marijuana/Hashish	1.7%	0.5%	5.1%	2.1%	2.8%	0.9%	4.2%	1.1%	3.5%	0.5%	8.2%	4.3%
Alcohol												
Daily	2.3%	0.9%	7.0%	2.8%	4.2%	0.7%	8.3%	2.6%	4.0%	0.9%	10.1%	5.4%
Five or more drinks in a row/last 2 weeks	19.4%	10.7%	48.1%	31.3%	24.0%	9.3%	45.3%	23.6%	31.4%	14.5%	48.1%	33.7%
Cigarettes												
Half-pack or more per day	4.4%	4.5%	12.5%	13.3%	3.3%	2.2%	5.2%	2.5%	6.1%	4.2%	18.4%	23.4%

Source: U.S. Department of Education, National Center for Education Statistics, *The Condition of Education, 1992* (Washington, DC: U.S. Government Printing Office, June 1992), p. 313. Primary source: U.S. Department of Health and Human Services; Alcohol, Drug Abuse, and Mental Health Administration; National Institute on Drug Abuse, "Drug Use Among American High School Students, College Students, and Other Young Adults," 1991.

★ 353 ★

Drug and Alcohol Use, Periodic, by High School Seniors

Number and percent of high school seniors by sex and race/ethnicity who reported using drugs or alcohol in a one-year period 1985 to 1989 (data combined).

Type of drug	Percent that have used in the past 12 months									
	Asian American		White		Black		Mexican American		Puerto Rican/Latin American	
	Male	Female	Male	Female	Male	Female	Male	Female	Male	Female
Sample size	982	917	28,056	29,808	3,688	4,499	1,518	1,599	680	712
Marijuana	19.6%	17.1%	40.2%	36.0%	29.8%	18.4%	37.3%	26.0%	30.6%	21.3%
Inhalents[a]	4.8%	3.2%	8.8%	5.2%	2.6%	2.2%	6.0%	4.3%	5.1%	2.9%
Hallucinogens	3.0%	2.2%	8.3%	5.0%	1.9%	0.6%	5.9%	2.2%	6.5%	2.1%
LSD	2.5%	1.9%	7.0%	3.9%	1.3%	0.3%	5.2%	1.6%	3.4%	1.1%
Cocaine	5.8%	5.7%	11.9%	9.3%	6.1%	2.6%	14.7%	7.6%	15.6%	8.2%
Heroin	0.4%	0.2%	0.7%	0.3%	0.7%	0.4%	0.9%	0.4%	1.2%	0.4%
Other opiates[b]	3.1%	2.1%	6.5%	5.3%	1.9%	1.2%	3.2%	2.1%	3.0%	1.6%
Stimulants[b]	5.6%	7.0%	13.6%	14.7%	4.6%	3.1%	11.3%	10.1%	8.0%	5.9%
Sedatives[b]	3.4%	2.6%	5.3%	4.4%	2.2%	1.2%	4.7%	2.7%	4.6%	2.6%
Barbiturates[b]	2.6%	2.3%	4.4%	3.8%	1.9%	1.1%	4.1%	2.4%	4.0%	2.5%
Methaqualone[b]	1.5%	0.9%	2.5%	1.4%	0.9%	0.3%	1.2%	0.5%	2.3%	0.5%
Tranquilizers[b]	3.2%	1.8%	5.8%	5.9%	1.7%	1.4%	2.6%	2.1%	3.1%	4.1%
Alcohol	69.3%	67.5%	88.3%	88.6%	72.5%	63.9%	82.4%	73.6%	80.6%	77.2%

Source: U.S. Department of Education, National Center for Education Statistics, *The Condition of Education, 1992* (Washington, DC: U.S. Government Printing Office, June 1992), p. 312. Primary source: U.S. Department of Health and Human Services, Alcohol, Drug Abuse, and Mental Health Administration, National Institute on Drug Abuse, "Drug Use among American High School Students, College Students, and Other Young Adults," 1991. *Notes:* (a) Respondents represent four-fifths of sample size indicated. (b) Only drug use which was not under a doctor's orders are included here.

★ 354 ★

Drug and Alcohol Use, Occasional, by High School Seniors

Number and percent of high school seniors, by sex and race/ethnicity, who reported using drugs, alcohol, or cigarettes in a one-year period during 1986 to 1989 (data combined).

Type of drug	Percent who used within last 30 days									
	Asian American		White		Black		Mexican American		Puerto Rican/Latin American	
	Male	Female	Male	Female	Male	Female	Male	Female	Male	Female
Sample size	982	917	28,056	29,808	3,688	4,499	1,518	1,599	680	712
Marijuana	9.7%	8.1%	25.0%	19.8%	18.5%	9.9%	22.0%	13.6%	18.9%	9.6%
Inhalents[a]	1.3%	0.8%	3.4%	2.0%	1.4%	1.4%	2.3%	2.1%	2.0%	0.8%
Hallucinogens	1.5%	0.3%	3.5%	1.7%	0.9%	0.3%	2.4%	0.7%	3.0%	0.4%
LSD	1.1%	0.1%	2.8%	1.1%	0.6%	0.2%	1.9%	0.3%	1.6%	0.2%
Cocaine	1.8%	2.6%	5.6%	4.1%	2.6%	1.3%	8.2%	3.0%	8.1%	2.9%
Heroin	0.1%	-	0.3%	0.1%	0.5%	0.3%	0.3%	0.2%	0.9%	0.2%
Other opiates[b]	1.6%	0.7%	2.3%	1.9%	0.9%	0.6%	1.1%	0.7%	1.5%	0.5%
Stimulants[b]	2.1%	3.6%	5.6%	6.0%	1.9%	1.3%	4.9%	4.8%	3.1%	1.2%
Sedatives[b]	1.9%	1.3%	2.2%	1.7%	1.1%	0.5%	2.0%	0.9%	1.8%	1.3%
Barbituates[b]	1.4%	1.0%	1.8%	1.5%	0.9%	0.5%	1.7%	0.8%	1.3%	1.2%
Methaqualone[b]	0.8%	0.6%	0.9%	0.5%	0.5%	0.1%	0.6%	0.2%	0.9%	0.1%
Tranquilizers[b]	1.7%	0.9%	1.9%	2.0%	0.8%	0.5%	0.8%	0.9%	0.6%	1.5%
Alcohol	43.7%	34.2%	72.3%	66.6%	49.2%	32.8%	65.0%	50.5%	55.4%	43.0%
Cigarettes	16.8%	14.3%	29.8%	34.0%	15.6%	13.3%	23.8%	18.7%	22.0%	24.7%

Source: U.S. Department of Education, National Center for Education Statistics, *The Condition of Education, 1992* (Washington, DC: U.S. Government Printing Office, June 1992), p. 312. Primary source: U.S. Department of Health and Human Services, Alcohol, Drug Abuse, and Mental Health Administration, National Institute on Drug Abuse, "Drug Use among American High School Students, College Students, and Other Young Adults," 1991. *Note:* (a) Respondents represent four-fifths of sample size indicated. (b) Only drug use which was not under a doctor's orders are included here.

★ 355 ★

Profile of Asian American Eighth Graders

Asian American eighth-graders by ethnicity and place of birth, in percent, 1988.

Ethnicity	Number	Percent	Native-born	Foreign-born
Asian, total	1,505	100.0%	52.4%	47.6%
Chinese	309	17.4%	54.3%	45.9%
Filipino	288	20.2%	52.0%	48.2%
Japanese	92	6.0%	69.1%	31.0%
Korean	188	11.0%	35.1%	65.0%
Southeast Asian (Vietnamese, Laotian, Cambodian/ Kampuchean, Thai, etc.)	240	12.7%	15.3%	84.9%
Pacific Islander (Samoan, Guamanian, etc.)	99	8.8%	85.6%	14.6%
South Asian (Asian Indian, Pakistani, Bangladeshi, Sri Lankan, etc.)	126	8.7%	45.5%	54.6%
Other Asian[a] West Asian (Iranian, Afghan, Turkish, etc.) Middle Eastern (Iraqui, Israeli, Lebanese, etc.) Other Asian	163	15.3%	67.0%	33.1%

Source: National Center for Education Statistics, *Language Characteristics and Academic Achievement: A Look at Asian and Hispanic Eighth Graders in NELS:88* (Washington, DC: U.S. Department of Education, 1992), table 2.1, p. 17. Primary source: U.S. Department of Education, National Center for Education Statistics, "National Education Longitudinal Study of 1988 (NELS:88), "Base-Year Student and Parent" surveys. Also in source: data on Hispanic eighth graders. *Notes:* (a) West Asian and Middle Easterners were included with "other" Asians in this study because of the small number of students in these categories.

★ 356 ★

Eighth Graders, Asian American by Generation in the United States

Asian American eighth graders by generation in United States, in percent, 1988.

Generation	Percent
Total	100.0%
First generation	48.1%
Second generation	30.7%
Third generation or higher	21.2%

Source: U.S. Department of Education, National Center for Education Statistics, Language Characteristics and Academic Achievement: A Look at Asian and Hispanic Eighth Graders in NELS:88, 1992, table 22, p. 18. Primary source: U.S. Department of Education, National Center for Education Statistics, National Education Longitudinal Study of 1988: "Base-Year Parent" survey. Also in source: data of Hispanic eighth graders.

★ 357 ★

Eighth Graders' Attitudes about Classes

Attitudes of eighth graders about selected class subjects, in percent, by race/ethnicity, 1988.

Class subject and attitude	Percentage who agree with statement					
	All 8th graders	Asian	White	Black	Hispanic	American Indian
Mathematics class						
Look forward to	56.6%	67.6%	52.8%	69.2%	64.2%	63.7%
Afraid to ask questions	20.9%	23.1%	19.3%	22.0%	28.6%	32.5%
Useful in my future	88.0%	90.4%	87.4%	89.3%	89.7%	85.1%
English class						
Look forward to	56.9%	63.6%	52.2%	72.8%	67.5%	66.0%
Afraid to ask questions	15.4%	17.4%	14.2%	16.7%	20.7%	19.6%
Useful in my future	84.1%	88.0%	82.9%	87.9%	88.1%	80.7%
Social studies class						
Look forward to	58.5%	64.0%	56.0%	67.6%	63.3%	60.2%
Afraid to ask questions	15.1%	19.1%	13.7%	16.5%	20.8%	22.2%
Useful in my future	59.1%	64.7%	56.9%	66.7%	63.0%	64.3%
Science class						
Look forward to	61.3%	67.2%	59.0%	68.3%	66.6%	64.3%
Afraid to ask questions	14.9%	16.2%	13.5%	16.0%	20.8%	25.6%
Useful in my future	68.7%	74.5%	67.6%	71.7%	70.4%	67.6%

Source: National Center for Education Statistics, U.S. Department of Education, *Digest of Education Statistics 1992* (Washington, DC: U.S. Government Printing Office, October 1992), table 133, p. 134. Primary source: U.S. Department of Education, National Center for Education Statistics, "National Education Longitudinal Study (NELS) Base Year" survey, 1988. (This table was prepared June 1989).

★ 358 ★

Eighth Graders' Intended High School Program

Percent of Asian eighth graders who indicated their intention to pursue a specific high school program of study, 1988.

Program	Percent of Asian 8th graders who plan to participate:
College prep/academic	37.6%
Vocational, technical, or business	17.4%
General high school	9.8%
Specialized high school	4.1%
Other/unknown	31.1%

Source: National Center for Education Statistics, *Language Characteristics and Academic Achievement: A Look at Asian and Hispanic Eighth Graders in NELS:88* (Washington, DC: U.S. Department of Education, 1992), figure 2.15, p. 40. The National Education Longitudinal Study of 1988 (NELS:88) is a study of a representative national sample of 25,000 students from 1,000 public and private high schools.

★ 359 ★

Eighth Graders' Plans for Further Education

Percent of Asian eighth graders who plan to pursue education after high school graduation, 1988.

Post-high school program	Percent of Asian 8th graders who plan to pursue after high school:
Graduate school	38.7%
College graduation	37.5%
College attendance	11.9%
Postsecondary vocational school	5.0%
No plans after high school graduation	6.9%

Source: National Center for Education Statistics, *Language Characteristics and Academic Achievement: A Look at Asian and Hispanic Eighth Graders in NELS:88* (Washington, DC: U.S. Department of Education, 1992), figure 2.15, p.40. The National Education Longitudinal Study of 1988 (NELS:88) is a study of a representative national sample of 25,000 students from 1,000 public and private high schools.

★ 360 ★

Tenth Graders' Occupation Expectations

Expected occupation at age thirty of tenth graders by race/ethnicity, 1990.

Expected occupation at age 30	Race/ethnicity					
	Total	Asian	White	Black	Hispanic	American Indian
Percent who expect to have occupation at age 30						
Total	100.0%	100.0%	100.0%	100.0%	100.0%	100.0%
Craftsperson or operator	5.6%	2.3%	5.7%	5.7%	5.0%	8.6%
Farmer or farm manager	1.1%	0.2%	1.4%	0.4%	0.6%	1.0%
Housewife/homemaker	2.0%	1.3%	1.9%	1.3%	3.8%	1.5%
Laborer or farm worker	0.8%	0.9%	0.8%	0.8%	0.8%	2.0%
Military, police, or security officer	5.7%	3.2%	5.6%	6.4%	6.6%	8.9%
Professional, business, or managerial	45.7%	56.3%	45.3%	50.3%	40.2%	42.9%
Teacher	4.1%	1.7%	4.7%	2.6%	2.6%	5.0%
Business owner	5.3%	7.1%	5.2%	4.4%	6.8%	4.6%
Technical	4.7%	5.6%	4.2%	5.1%	7.0%	5.5%
Salesperson, clerical, or office worker	4.9%	4.1%	4.6%	6.0%	6.2%	4.3%
Service worker	1.8%	0.4%	1.7%	3.2%	0.9%	1.2%
Other employment	7.7%	4.6%	8.7%	4.4%	6.8%	7.8%
Don't know	10.5%	12.5%	10.3%	9.6%	12.7%	6.8%

Source: National Center for Education Statistics, U.S. Department of Education, *Digest of Education Statistics 1992* (Washington, DC: U.S. Government Printing Office, October 1992), table 134, p. 134. Primary source: U.S. Department of Education, National Center for Education Statistics, "National Education Longitudinal Study (NELS) of 1988, First Follow-up" survey. (This table was prepared June 1989).

Employment and Occupations

Employed Persons

★ 361 ★

School and Work Activities
of Youth Sixteen to Twenty-four

Population sixteen to twenty-four years of age by school and work activities, in percent, 1990.

Activity	Asian/Pacific Islander	White, non-Hispanic.
School only	44%	26%
School and work	22%	28%
Work only	26%	39%
Neither	8%	7%

Source: William P. O'Hare and Judy C. Felt, *Asian Americans: America's Fastest Growing Minority Group, 1991* (Washington, DC: Population Reference Bureau, 1992), figure 5, p. 11. Primary source: Population Reference Bureau analysis of Bureau of the Census Public Use File, March 1990 Supplement, *Current Population Survey.*

★ 362 ★

Workers in the United States by Employment Status and Sex, 1991

Numbers (in thousands) and percent of workers age sixteen and over in the United States by sex and employment status, as of March 1991[a].

Characteristic	Total United States		
	Total population (thousands)	Asian and Pacific Islander (thousands)	White (thousands)
Both sexes, 16 years and over	189,239	5,121	161,163
In civilian labor force	124,074	3,261	106,544
In civilian labor force, percent	65.6%	63.7%	66.1%
Employed	115,187	3,054	99,689
Unemployed	8,887	207	6,855
Unemployed, percent	7.2%	6.3%	6.4%
Not in labor force	65,164	1,860	54,619
Males, 16 years and over	90,269	2,414	77,487
In civilian labor force	67,701	1,742	58,830
In civilian labor force, percent	75.0%	72.1%	75.9%
Employed	62,246	1,631	54,519
Unemployed	5,455	111	4,311
Unemployed, percent	8.1%	6.3%	7.3%
Not in labor force	22,568	673	18,658
Females, 16 years and over	98,970	2,706	83,675
In civilian labor force	56,373	1,519	47,714
In civilian labor force, percent	57.0%	56.1%	57.0%
Employed	52,941	1,423	45,170
Unemployed	3,432	96	2,544
Unemployed, percent	6.1%	6.3%	5.3%
Not in labor force	42,596	1,187	35,961

Source: Claudette E. Bennett, Economics and Statistics Administration, Bureau of the Census, U.S. Department of Commerce, *The Asian and Pacific Islander Population in the United States: March 1991 and 1990,* Current Population Reports, Population Characteristics, P20-459 (Washington, DC: U.S. Government Printing Office, August 1992), table 2, p. 16. The population universe for the March 1991 and 1990 Current Population Surveys is the estimate of the civilian noninstitutional population to the United States plus members of the Armed Forces in the United States living off post or with their families on post, but excludes all other members of the Armed Forces. Data are estimates based on sample surveys and are subject to sampling variability since they are not based on a complete count of the population. *Note:* (a) Data on labor force status, occupation, and class of worker shown in this report reflect characteristics of the population for March 1991 and are not adjusted for seasonal changes. Data released by the Department of Labor, Bureau of Labor Statistics, may not agree entirely with data shown in this report due to differences in methodological procedures and seasonal adjustment of the data.

Workers in the Western United States by Employment Status and Sex, 1991

Numbers (in thousands) and percent of workers age sixteen and over in the western United States by sex and employment status, as of March 1991[a].

Characteristic	Total population (thousands)	Asian/Pacific Islander (thousands)	White (thousands)
Both sexes, 16 years and over	39,375	3,053	34,153
In civilian labor force	25,859	1,926	22,510
In civilian labor force, percent	65.7%	63.1%	65.9%
Employed	24,044	1,792	21,001
Unemployed	1,815	135	1,510
Unemployed, percent	7.0%	7.0%	6.7%
Not in labor force	13,516	1,127	11,643
Males, 16 years and over	19,204	1,429	16,781
In civilian labor force	14,602	1,010	12,827
In civilian labor force, percent	76.0%	70.7%	76.4%
Employed	13,481	938	11,875
Unemployed	1,121	72	952
Unemployed, percent	7.7%	7.1%	7.4%
Not in labor force	4,602	419	3,954
Females, 16 years and over	20,171	1,624	17,372
In civilian labor force	11,257	916	9,683
In civilian labor force, percent	55.8%	56.4%	55.7%
Employed	10,563	853	9,126
Unemployed	694	63	558
Unemployed, percent	6.2%	6.9%	5.8%
Not in labor force	8,914	708	7,688

Source: Claudette E. Bennett, Economics and Statistics Administration, Bureau of the Census, U.S. Department of Commerce, *The Asian and Pacific Islander Population in the United States: March 1991 and 1990,* Current Population Reports, Population Characteristics, P20 - 459 (Washington, DC: U.S. Government Printing Office, August 1992), table 2, p. 16. The population universe for the March 1991 and 1990 Current Population Surveys is the estimate of the civilian noninstitutional population to the United States plus members of the Armed Forces in the United States living off post or with their families on post, but excludes all other members of the Armed Forces. Data are estimates based on sample surveys and are subject to sampling variability since they are not based on a complete count of the population. *Note:* (a) Data on labor force status, occupation, and class of worker shown in this report reflect characteristics of the population for March 1991 and are not adjusted for seasonal changes. Data released by the Department of Labor, Bureau of Labor Statistics, may not agree entirely with data shown in this report due to differences in methodological procedures and seasonal adjustment of the data.

★ 364 ★

Workers in the United States by Job Class

Number (in thousands) and percent of workers age sixteen and over in the United States by job class as of March 1991[a].

Characteristic	Total population	Asian/Pacific Islander	White
Employed persons, 16 years and over (thousands)	115,187	3,054	99,689
Private wage and salary workers, percent	75.5%	76.3%	75.8%
Federal government workers, percent	2.9	4.2	2.5
State government workers, percent	4.1	5.4	3.8
Local government workers, percent	8.6	3.6	8.3
Self-employed workers, percent	8.6	9.8	9.2
Unpaid family workers, percent	0.3	0.7	0.3

Source: Claudette E. Bennett, Economics and Statistics Administration, Bureau of the Census, U.S. Department of Commerce, *The Asian and Pacific Islander Population in the United States: March 1991 and 1990,* Current Population Reports, Population Characteristics, P20-459 (Washington, DC: U.S. Government Printing Office, August 1992), table 2, p. 16. The population universe for the March 1991 and 1990 Current Population Surveys is the estimate of the civilian noninstitutional population to the United States plus members of the Armed Forces in the United States living off post or with their families on post, but excludes all other members of the Armed Forces. Data are estimates based on sample surveys and are subject to sampling variability since they are not based on a complete count of the population. *Notes:* (a) Data on labor force status, occupation and class of worker shown in this report reflect characteristics of the population for March 1991 and are not adjusted for seasonal changes. Data released by the Department of Labor, Bureau of Labor Statistics, may not agree entirely with data shown in this report due to differences in methodological procedures and seasonal adjustment of the data.

★ 365 ★

Workers in the Western United States by Job Class

Number (in thousands) and percent of workers age sixteen and over in the western United States by job class as of March 1991[a].

Characteristic	Total population	Asian/Pacific Islander	White
Employed persons, 16 years and over (thousands)	24,044	1,792	21,001
Private wage and salary workers, percent	73.8%	75.9%	73.9%
Federal government workers, percent	2.8	4.9	2.4
State government workers, percent	4.2	4.8	4.1
Local government workers, percent	8.6	3.4	8.8
Self-employed workers, percent	10.3	10.4	10.5
Unpaid family workers, percent	0.3	0.6	0.3

Source: Claudette E. Bennett, Economics and Statistics Administration, Bureau of the Census, U.S. Department of Commerce, *The Asian and Pacific Islander Population in the United States: March 1991 and 1990,* Current Population Reports, Population Characteristics, P20-459 (Washington, DC: U.S. Government Printing Office, August 1992), table 2, p. 16. The population universe for the March 1991 and 1990 Current Population Surveys is the estimate of the civilian noninstitutional population to the United States plus members of the Armed Forces in the United States living off post or with their families on post, but excludes all other members of the Armed Forces. Data are estimates based on sample surveys and are subject to sampling variability since they are not based on a complete count of the population. *Notes:* (a) Data on labor force status, occupation and class of worker shown in this report reflect characteristics of the population for March 1991 and are not adjusted for seasonal changes. Data released by the Department of Labor, Bureau of Labor Statistics, may not agree entirely with data shown in this report due to differences in methodological procedures and seasonal adjustment of the data.

Occupations

★ 366 ★

Chinese Restaurant Workers in New York

Selected data on conditions for Asian immigrants working as waiters and waitresses in Chinese restaurants in New York City.

Position	Waiters and waitresses
Hours	12 hours a day, six days a week
Pay	Several hundred dollars a month, plus tips
Paid holidays	none
Health insurance	none
Number of restaurants, approximate	1,400
Number of unionized restaurants, approximate	10

Source: Invisible and in Need: Philanthropic Giving to Asian Americans and Pacific Islanders (San Francisco: Asian Americans and Pacific Islanders in Philanthropy [AAPIP], December 1992).

★ 367 ★

Labor Force, Asian/Pacific Islander and White by Occupation

Employed civilian labor force by sex and occupation, in percent March 1991.

Occupation	Male	Female
Asian/Pacific Islander		
Managerial and professional specialty	33.2%	26.4%
Technical, sales, and administrative support	26.3%	42.8%
Service	15.6%	16.7%
Precision production, craft, and repair	9.9%	4.2%
Operators, fabricators, and laborers	12.7%	9.4%
Farming, forestry, and fishing	2.3%	0.5%
White		
Managerial and professional specialty	27.4%	28.5%
Technical, sales, and administrative support	20.8%	44.8%
Service	9.3%	16.2%
Precision production, craft, and repair	19.4%	2.1%
Operators, fabricators, and laborers	18.9%	7.4%
Farming, forestry, and fishing	4.3%	1.1%

Source: Economic and Statistics Administration, Bureau of the Census, Current Population Reports, Population Characteristics Chartbook, *The Asian and Pacific Islander Population in the United States: March 1991 and 1990* (Washington, DC U.S. Printing Office, 1992), p. 20.

★ 368 ★

Labor Force, Asian/Pacific Islander, White, and Total by Occupation

Numbers (in thousands) and percent of employed Asian, white, and total civilians twenty-five years and over by sex and longest job occupation, March 1991.

Occupation of longest job	Asian/Pacific Islander (thousands)		White (thousands)		Total population[b] (thousands)	
	Male	Female	Male	Female	Male	Female
Total[a]	1,247	891	39,093	24,040	44,455	28,656
Executive, administrative, and managerial workers	194	127	7,058	4,099	7,591	4,600
Professional specialty workers	255	147	5,477	4,132	6,064	4,765
Technical and related support workers	82	64	1,288	972	1,486	1,191
Sales workers	148	93	4,860	2,428	5,225	2,724
Administrative support workers, including clerical	113	216	2,031	7,290	2,513	8,613
Private household workers	2	2	6	131	9	160
Protective service workers	16	1	1,112	131	1,326	181
Service workers, except private household	137	105	1,610	2,151	2,199	2,987
Farming, fishing, and forestry workers	18	6	1,443	235	1,547	244
Precision production, craft, and repair workers	138	45	7,602	607	8,521	744
Machine operators, assemblers, and inspectors	86	80	2,761	1,475	3,273	1,925
Transportation and material moving workers	33	1	2,530	131	3,042	161
Handlers, equipment cleaners, helpers, and laborers	26	5	1,313	260	1,661	361
Percent						
Total[a]	100.0	100.0	100.0	100.0	100.0	100.0
Executive, administrative, and managerial workers	15.6	14.3	18.1	17.1	17.1	16.1
Professional specialty workers	20.5	16.5	14.0	17.2	13.6	16.6
Technical and related support workers	6.5	7.1	3.3	4.0	3.3	4.2
Sales workers	11.8	10.4	12.4	10.1	11.8	9.5
Administrative support workers, including clerical	9.1	24.2	5.2	30.3	5.7	30.1
Private household workers	0.1	0.3	0	0.5	0	0.6
Protective service workers	1.3	0.1	2.8	0.5	3.0	0.6
Service workers, except private household	11.0	11.8	4.1	8.9	4.9	10.4
Farming, fishing, and forestry workers	1.5	0.7	3.7	1.0	3.5	0.9
Precision production, craft, and repair workers	11.0	5.0	19.4	2.5	19.2	2.6
Machine operators, assemblers, and inspectors	6.9	9.0	7.1	6.1	7.4	6.7
Transportation and material moving workers	2.7	0.1	6.5	0.5	6.8	0.6
Handlers, equipment cleaners, helpers, and laborers	2.0	0.5	3.4	1.1	3.7	1.3

Source: Claudette E. Bennett, Economics and Statistics Administration, Bureau of the Census, U.S. Department of Commerce, *The Asian and Pacific Islander Population in the United States: March 1991 and 1990,* Current Population Reports, Population Characteristics, P20-459 (Washington, DC: U.S. Government Printing Office, August 1992), table 4, p. 22. Educational attainment is that attained in 1990. *Notes:* (a) Armed forces not included. (b) Total includes persons with no education, not shown separately.

★ 369 ★

Labor Force, Asian/Pacific Islander by Occupation, and Education

Numbers (in thousands) and percent of full-time employed Asian/Pacific Islanders twenty-five years and over by sex, longest job occupation, and educational attainment, March 1991.

Occupation of longest job	Asian /Pacific Islander, total (thousands)		Less than high school (thousands)		Four years of high school (thousands)		One to three years of college (thousands)		Four or more years of college (thousands)	
	Male	Female	Male	Female	Male	Female	Male	Female	Male	Female
Total[a]	1,247	891	116	98	298	241	188	132	629	412
Executive, administrative, and managerial workers	194	127	3	8	16	26	31	13	144	80
Professional specialty workers	255	147	0	0	7	8	11	10	237	128
Technical and related support workers	82	64	5	1	20	4	9	8	48	50
Sales workers	148	93	9	13	30	34	23	13	83	33
Administrative support workers, including clerical	113	216	16	11	33	66	25	53	39	83
Private household workers	2	2	0	0	0	0	2	1	0	1
Protective service workers	16	1	2	0	5	0	3	0	6	1
Service workers, except private household	137	105	24	22	69	41	19	18	23	21
Farming, fishing, and forestry workers	18	6	9	0	9	5	0	1	1	0
Precision production, craft, and repair workers	138	45	17	5	54	27	35	8	28	4
Machine operators, assemblers, and inspectors	86	80	20	35	31	25	17	7	10	11
Transportation and material moving workers	33	1	4	0	15	1	6	0	8	0
Handlers, equipment cleaners, helpers, and laborers	26	5	6	2	9	3	6	0	3	0
Percent										
Total[a]	100.0	100.0	100.0	100.0	100.0	100.0	100.0	100.0	100.0	100.0
Executive, administrative, and managerial workers	15.6	14.3	2.7	8.4	5.5	11.0	16.6	9.8	22.9	19.3
Professional specialty workers	20.5	16.5	0	0	2.4	3.5	6.0	7.4	37.6	31.2
Technical and related support workers	6.5	7.1	4.4	1.5	6.6	1.8	4.5	5.9	7.7	12.1
Sales workers	11.8	10.4	8.0	13.6	10.2	14.0	12.1	9.7	13.2	8.0
Administrative support workers, including clerical	9.1	24.2	13.8	10.9	11.0	27.3	13.5	40.4	6.2	20.2
Private household workers	0.1	0.3	0	0	0	0	0.9	0.7	0	0.3
Protective service workers	1.3	0.1	1.8	0	1.6	0	1.7	0	0.9	0.2
Service workers, except private household	11.0	11.8	21.1	22.7	23.1	17.1	10.0	13.6	3.6	5.0
Farming, fishing, and forestry workers	1.5	0.7	7.4	0	2.9	2.2	0	0.6	0.1	0
Precision production, craft, and repair workers	11.0	5.0	14.4	4.9	18.0	11.1	18.5	6.3	4.4	0.9
Machine operators, assemblers, and inspectors	6.9	9.0	16.8	35.9	10.6	10.4	9.3	5.5	1.6	2.7
Transportation and material moving workers	2.7	0.1	3.8	0	5.1	0.5	3.1	0	1.2	0
Handlers, equipment cleaners, helpers, and laborers	2.0	0.5	5.6	1.9	3.1	1.2	3.4	0	0.5	0

Source: Claudette E. Bennett, Economics and Statistics Administration, Bureau of the Census, U.S. Department of Commerce, *The Asian and Pacific Islander Population in the United States: March 1991 and 1990,* Current Population Reports, Population Characteristics, P20-459 (Washington, DC: U.S. Government Printing Office, August 1992), table 4, p. 22. Educational attainment is that attained in 1990. Also in source: data by education for the United States population as a whole and for white Americans. *Notes:* (a) Armed forces not included. (b) Total includes persons with no education, not shown separately.

★ 370 ★

Likelihood of Entering Management, Asian Men

American-born Chinese, Filipino, Japanese, and white men with a college degree and twenty years experience who became managers, in percent[a].

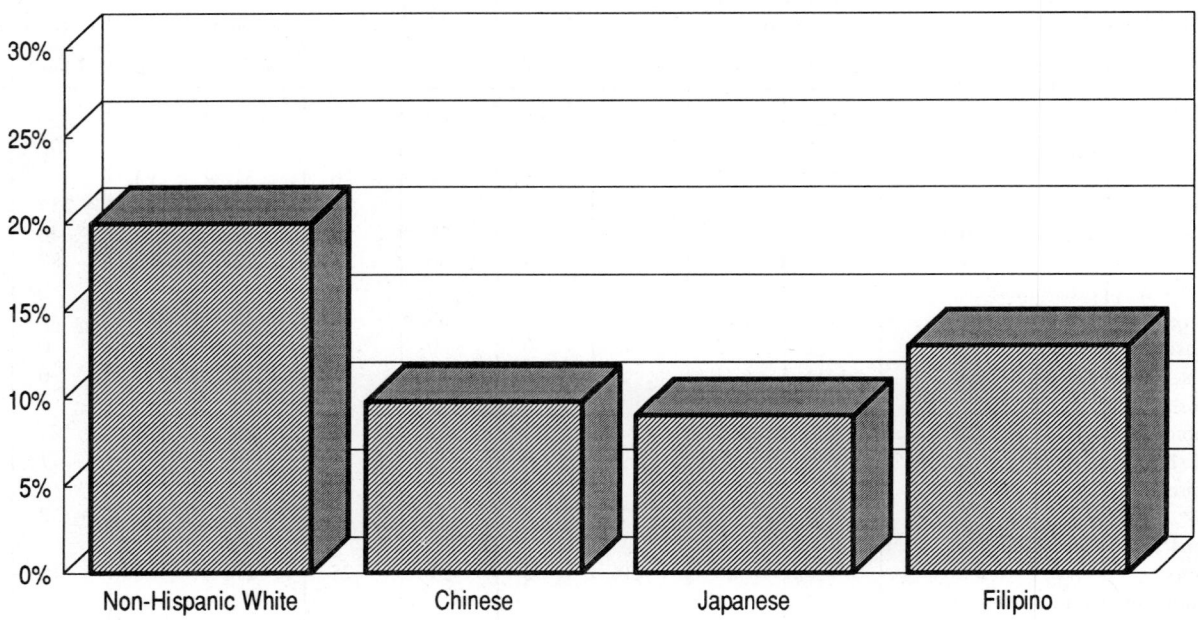

Source: U.S. Commission on Civil Rights, *Voices across America: Roundtable Discussions of Asian Civil Rights Issues,* summary and transcript of roundtable conferences in Houston, New York City, and San Francisco, May-June, 1989 (Washington, DC: U.S. Commission on Civil Rights, not dated), fig. 2, p. 3. Primary source: *The Economic Progress of Americans of Asian Descent: An Exploratory Investigation* (Washington, DC: U.S. Commission on Civil Rights, October 1988). *Note:* (a) Data is adjusted for education, experience, industry, and other relevant factors.

★ 371 ★

Occupational Distribution of the Employed Civilian Labor Force, 1991

A higher proportion of Asian and Pacific Islander men than women were employed in the managerial and professional specialty occupations. However, the proportion of Asian and Pacific Islander women employed in technical, sales, and administrative support jobs was more than one and one-half times the proportion of Asian and Pacific Islander men. Conversely, the proportion of Asian and Pacific Islander men employed in precision production, craft, and repair jobs was twice that of Asian and Pacific Islander women.

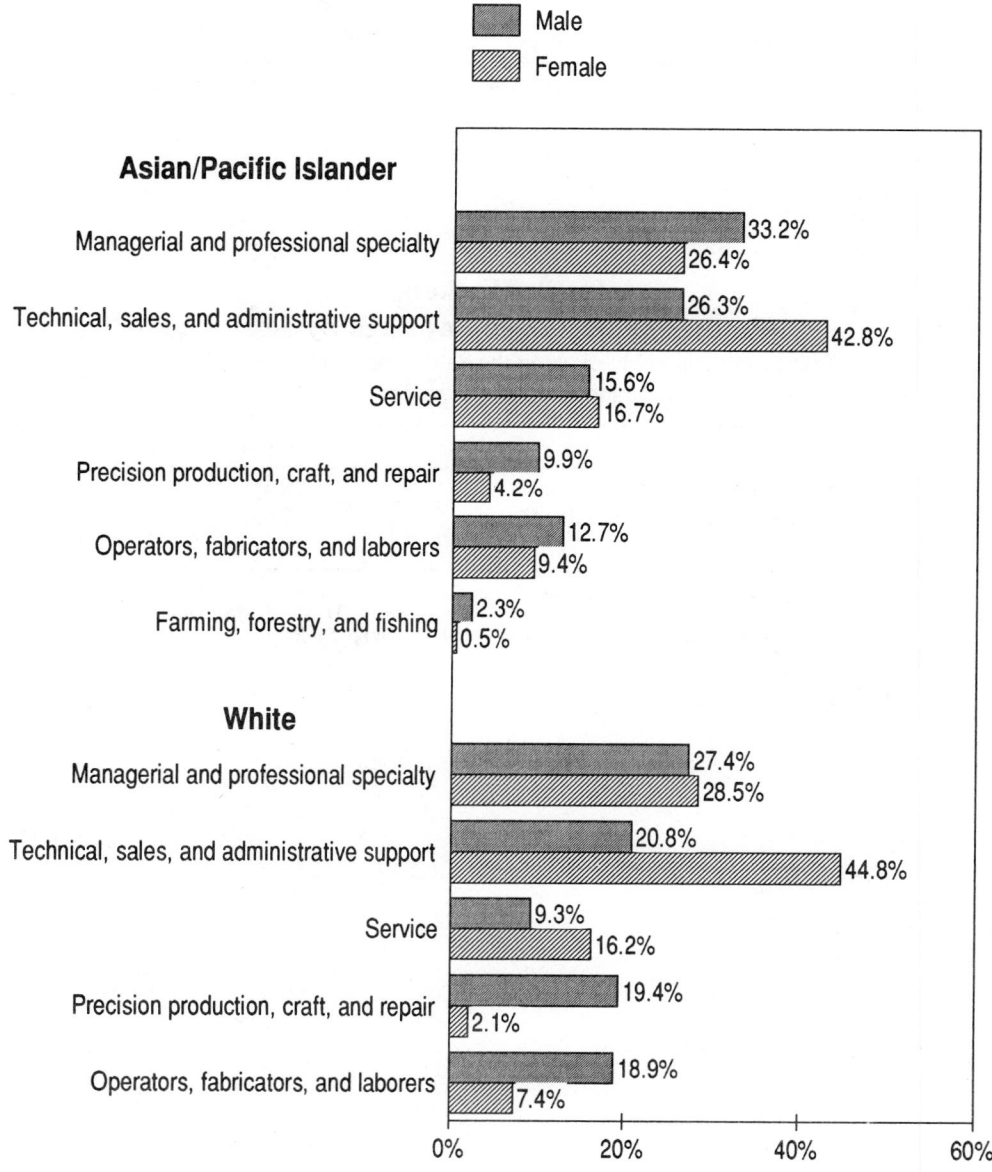

Source: Economic and Statistics Administration, Bureau of the Census, Current Population Reports, Population Characteristics Chartbook, *The Asian and Pacific Islander Population in the United States: March 1991 and 1990* (Washington, DC: U.S. Government Printing Office, 1992).

★ 372 ★

Professional and Managerial Workers

Percentage of Asian Americans holding professional or managerial jobs.

Ethnic group	Percent
Asian Indians	47%
Chinese	30%
Japanese	28%
Koreans	22%
Whites	24%

Source: U.S. Bureau of the Census, data from the 1980 Census.

★ 373 ★

Textile Workers
in the San Francisco Bay Area by Sex

Textile and apparel workers in the San Francisco Bay area who are Asian/Pacific Islander, by sex, in percent.

Sex	Percent
Men, Asian/Pacific Islander	28%
Women, Asian/Pacific Islander	53%
Other race/ethnicity	19%

Source: "Access and Utilization of Health Care," *Fact Sheet* (San Francisco: Asian American Health Form, 1993). Primary source: L. D. Morris, "Minorities, Jobs, and Health," *AAOHN Journal,* 1989, 37 (2): pp. 53-55.

★ 374 ★

Workers in the United States by Occupation

Numbers (in thousands) and percent of workers age sixteen and over in the United States by sex and occupation, 1991[a].

Characteristic	Total population	Asian/ Pacific Islander	White
Males, employed, 16 years and over (thousands)	62,246	1,631	54,519
Managerial and professional specialty, percent	26.3%	33.2%	27.4%
Technical, sales, and administrative support, percent	20.5	26.3	20.8
Service, percent	10.4	15.6	9.3
Farming, forestry, and fishing, percent	4.1	2.3	4.3
Precision production, craft, and repair, percent	18.8	9.9	19.4
Operators, fabricators, and laborers, percent	19.9	12.7	18.9
Females, employed, 16 years and over (thousands)	52,941	1,423	45,170
Managerial and professional specialty, percent	27.2%	26.4%	28.5%
Technical, sales, and administrative support, percent	44.1	42.8	44.8
Service, percent	17.6	16.7	16.2
Farming, forestry, and fishing, percent	0.9	0.5	1.1
Precision production, craft, and repair, percent	2.2	4.2	2.1
Operators, fabricators, and laborers, percent	8.1	9.4	7.4

Source: Claudette E. Bennett, Economics and Statistics Administration, Bureau of the Census, U.S. Department of Commerce, *The Asian and Pacific Islander Population in the United States: March 1991 and 1990,* Current Population Reports, Population Characteristics, P20-459 (Washington, DC: U.S. Government Printing Office, August 1992), table 2, p. 16. The population universe for the March 1991 and 1990 Current Population Surveys is the estimate of the civilian noninstitutional population to the United States plus members of the Armed Forces in the United States living off post or with their families on post, but excludes all other members of the Armed Forces. Data are estimates based on sample surveys and are subject to sampling variability since they are not based on a complete count of the population. *Note:* (a) Data on labor force status, occupation and class of worker shown in this report reflect characteristics of the population for March 1991 and are not adjusted for seasonal changes. Data released by the Department of Labor, Bureau of Labor Statistics, may not agree entirely with data shown in this report due to differences in methodological procedures and seasonal adjustment of the data.

★ 375 ★

Workers in the Western United States by Occupation

Numbers (in thousands) and percent of workers age sixteen and over in the western United States by sex and occupation, 1991[a].

Characteristic	Total population	Asian and Pacific Islander	White
Males, employed, 16 years and over (thousands)	13,481	938	11,875
Percent	100.0	100.0	100.0
Managerial and professional specialty	27.0	29.2	27.2
Technical, sales, and administrative support	22.2	28.5	21.6
Service	10.8	14.7	10.2
Farming, forestry, and fishing	4.7	3.9	4.9
Precision production, craft, and repair	17.7	11.7	18.3
Operators, fabricators, and laborers	17.5	11.8	17.9
Females, employed, 16 years and over (thousands)	10,563	853	9,126
Percent	100.0	100.0	100.0
Managerial and professional specialty	28.7	25.2	29.4
Technical, sales, and administrative support	44.3	47.1	43.9
Service	17.8	14.1	18.0
Farming, forestry, and fishing	1.1	0.9	1.2
Precision production, craft, and repair	2.4	4.9	2.1
Operators, fabricators, and laborers	5.8	7.8	5.4

Source: Claudette E. Bennett, Economics and Statistics Administration, Bureau of the Census, U.S. Department of Commerce, *The Asian and Pacific Islander Population in the United States: March 1991 and 1990,* Current Population Reports, Population Characteristics, P20-459 (Washington, DC: U.S. Government Printing Office, August 1992), table 2, p. 16. The population universe for the March 1991 and 1990 Current Population Surveys is the estimate of the civilian noninstitutional population to the United States plus members of the Armed Forces in the United States living off post or with their families on post, but excludes all other members of the Armed Forces. Data are estimates based on sample surveys and are subject to sampling variability since they are not based on a complete count of the population. *Note:* (a) Data on labor force status, occupation and class of worker shown in this report reflect characteristics of the population for March 1991 and are not adjusted for seasonal changes. Data released by the Department of Labor, Bureau of Labor Statistics, may not agree entirely with data shown in this report due to differences in methodological procedures and seasonal adjustment of the data.

Scientists and Engineers

★ 376 ★

Employed Scientists and Engineers by Field, 1988

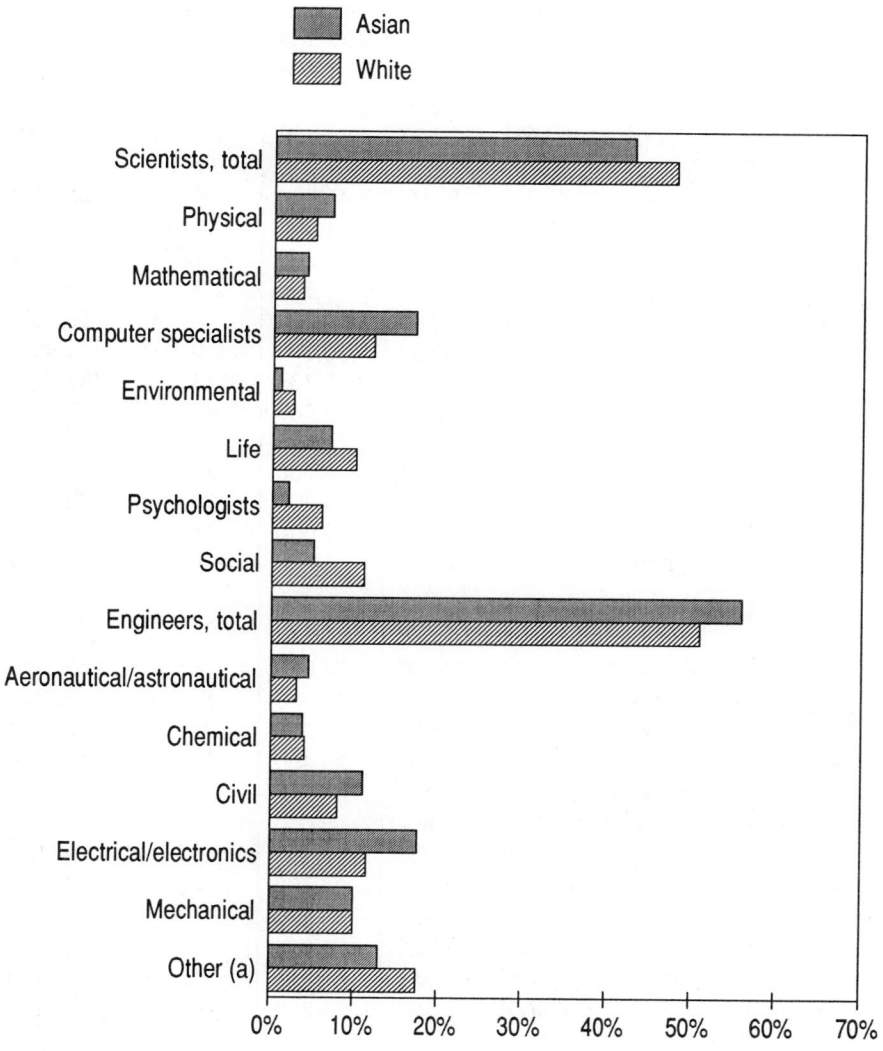

Source: Patricia E. White, *Women and Minorities in Science and Engineering: An Update* (Washington, DC: National Science Foundation 92-303, January 1992), table 1, p. 33, chart 3.3. *Note:* (a) Includes industrial, materials, mining, nuclear, petroleum, and other.

★ 377 ★

Scientists and Engineers by Field and Race/Ethnicity, 1978 and 1988

Employed scientists and engineers, total and by field, by race/ethnicity, 1978 and 1988.

Field	Total employed		Asian		White		Black	
	1978	1988	1978	1988	1978	1988	1978	1988
Total scientists and engineers	2,609,800	5,286,400	108,800	268,100	2,416,500	4,761,900	47,700	139,200
Scientists, total	1,071,000	2,567,800	38,800	117,100	989,800	2,299,400	26,900	94,800
Physical scientists	208,300	312,000	8,700	20,600	194,500	279,500	3,500	6,500
Chemists	143,000	197,000	6,800	15,100	132,600	174,600	2,900	4,800
Physicists and astronomers	46,400	77,800	1,200	4,400	44,300	70,800	500	900
Other	18,800	37,100	600	1,100	17,600	34,200	100	800
Mathematical scientists	53,700	168,600	1,500	9,200	49,400	145,700	2,800	9,500
Mathematicians	46,300	145,100	1,100	7,300	42,700	125,100	2,500	8,900
Statisticians	7,300	23,500	400	1,900	6,600	20,500	300	600
Computer specialists	177,000	708,300	8,400	46,900	164,500	625,300	3,200	26,000
Environmental scientists	68,900	113,400	1,900	1,600	60,400	107,100	700	1,000
Earth scientists	54,000	94,200	1,300	1,200	49,700	89,400	200	700
Oceanographers	7,300	4,600	100	100	3,700	3,800	500	100
Atmospheric scientists	7,600	14,600	600	200	7,000	13,900	-	100
Life scientists	244,100	458,600	6,300	20,100	229,100	413,900	5,700	9,500
Biological scientists	164,000	299,400	4,100	15,200	153,100	267,700	4,500	7,700
Agricultural scientists	49,600	124,000	1,100	2,900	47,500	113,600	800	1,400
Medical scientists	30,500	35,200	1,100	1,900	28,500	32,500	400	400
Psychologists	121,700	275,900	700	4,600	115,300	256,000	3,800	10,100
Social scientists	197,400	531,000	11,300	14,200	176,700	472,000	7,200	32,300
Economists	62,100	219,800	4,500	7,000	56,500	199,300	400	8,400
Sociologists and anthropologists	40,900	93,900	1,600	3,700	35,400	78,400	2,300	8,800
Other	94,400	217,300	5,200	3,500	84,700	194,400	4,500	15,100
Engineers, total	1,538,800	2,718,600	70,000	151,000	1,426,700	2,462,500	20,800	44,400
Aeronautical and astronautical	62,000	119,400	2,000	9,300	57,800	106,900	1,000	1,600
Chemical	84,200	148,500	4,000	8,000	78,300	136,000	300	1,700
Civil	211,700	355,900	14,800	25,400	191,300	316,100	2,700	6,200
Electrical and electronics	341,500	640,900	20,200	44,000	310,700	570,700	5,800	11,000
Industrial	NA	172,300	NA	5,000	NA	160,300	NA	3,100
Materials	NA	65,600	NA	4,400	NA	59,300	NA	600
Mechanical	299,300	497,800	12,800	26,300	280,200	455,700	2,300	7,100
Mining	NA	21,300	NA	500	NA	20,600	NA	-
Nuclear	NA	29,000	NA	2,000	NA	26,400	NA	500
Petroleum	NA	37,400	NA	400	NA	34,500	NA	400
Other	540,100	630,400	16,200	25,800	508,300	575,900	8,800	12,300

Source: Patricia E. White, *Women and Minorities in Science and Engineering: An Update* (Washington, DC: National Science Foundation 92-303, January 1992), table 1, p. 78. "NA" indicates a response rate that is too low to be reported. Primary source: National Science Foundation, Science Resources Studies Division, Scientific and Technical Personnel Data System (STPDS). Also in source: data by sex, and for Hispanics and Native Americans. Racial/ethnic categories will not sum to total because racial and ethnic categories are not mutually exclusive (Hispanics may also be included in one of the racial groups) and because total employed included "other" and "no report" categories.

★ 378 ★

Scientists and Engineers by Field, Sex and Race/Ethnicity

Employed male and female scientists and engineers, total and by field, by race/ethnicity, 1986.

Field and sex	Total employed[a]	Asian	White	Black	Native American	Hispanic[b]
Total, all fields	4,626,500	226,800	4,190,400	114,900	23,600	93,400
Male	3,927,800	190,500	3,581,500	80,500	21,000	73,800
Female	698,600	36,300	608,900	34,500	2,700	19,600
Scientists, total	2,186,300	94,000	1,973,100	73,700	10,300	46,100
Male	1,586,700	65,000	1,448,300	43,600	7,900	29,800
Female	599,600	29,000	524,800	30,100	2,400	16,400
Physical scientists	288,400	15,400	261,800	6,200	1,000	4,800
Male	250,100	11,200	230,100	4,500	1,000	3,900
Female	38,300	4,200	31,700	1,700	-	900
Mathematical scientists	131,000	5,900	115,500	6,800	200	3,100
Male	97,100	5,100	85,200	4,500	100	1,900
Female	33,900	800	30,300	2,300	100	1,200
Computer specialists	562,600	36,100	497,100	18,900	2,200	9,300
Male	400,000	27,300	354,100	11,700	1,800	6,400
Female	162,500	8,800	143,000	7,200	400	2,900
Environmental scientists	111,300	2,100	105,800	1,000	400	1,800
Male	98,400	2,000	93,400	900	400	1,700
Female	12,900	200	12,400	100	100	200
Life scientists	411,800	15,000	377,900	8,800	2,800	9,900
Male	309,000	9,400	288,900	5,500	1,800	5,900
Female	102,800	5,600	89,100	3,300	1,000	4,100
Psychologists	253,500	5,200	234,100	9,100	1,900	5,900
Male	138,400	800	131,700	3,100	1,400	2,700
Female	115,200	4,400	102,500	6,000	500	3,100
Social scientists	427,800	14,200	380,800	22,900	1,700	11,400
Male	293,800	9,200	265,000	13,500	1,300	7,400
Female	134,000	5,000	115,800	9,400	400	4,000
Engineers, total	2,440,100	132,800	2,217,300	41,300	13,300	47,200
Male	2,341,100	125,500	2,133,200	36,900	13,100	44,000
Female	99,000	7,300	84,100	4,400	300	3,200

Source: Patricia E. White, *Women and Minorities in Science and Engineering: An Update* (Washington, DC: National Science Foundation 92-303, January 1992), table 2, p. 79. Primary source: National Science Foundation, Science Resources Studies Division, Scientific and Technical Personnel Data System (STPDS). A dash (–) represents too few cases to estimate. *Notes:* (a) Racial/ethnic categories are not mutually exclusive (Hispanics may also be included in one of the racial groups) and because total employed includes "other" and "no report" categories. (b) Includes members of all racial groups. Detail may not sum to totals because of rounding.

★ 379 ★

Scientists and Engineers by Years of Experience and Race/Ethnicity

Employed scientists and engineers by field, race/ethnicity, and years of professional experience, 1986.

Field and racial/ethnic group	Total employed[a]	Years of professional experience								
		1 or less	2-4	5-9	10-14	15-19	20-24	25-29	30-34	35 and over
Total, scientists and engineers	4,626,500	104,200	584,200	726,700	680,900	625,800	526,500	459,600	359,200	417,400
Asian	226,800	7,500	25,800	38,200	38,400	35,000	32,300	24,500	12,500	7,300
White	4,190,400	91,600	522,800	646,500	607,200	564,900	469,300	419,700	338,100	402,100
Black	114,900	2,600	18,800	21,700	23,400	14,100	12,600	7,600	5,600	3,100
Native American	23,600	300	1,600	2,700	2,400	2,500	5,600	2,900	1,500	3,300
Hispanic[b]	93,400	3,000	18,900	19,500	13,900	13,200	7,800	6,400	3,900	3,800
Scientists, total	2,186,300	73,600	367,700	412,600	354,300	307,400	227,600	155,900	117,200	111,400
Asian	94,000	4,500	15,100	19,800	15,900	12,400	9,800	9,000	3,800	2,100
White	1,973,100	65,600	328,300	366,400	317,600	280,900	205,500	139,700	109,300	107,100
Black	73,700	1,800	14,400	14,900	15,100	8,800	7,000	4,800	3,200	800
Native American	10,300	-	1,200	1,600	600	400	3,200	1,200	700	1,200
Hispanic[b]	46,100	2,000	13,100	10,000	6,400	7,300	2,900	1,500	1,500	600
Physical scientists	288,400	7,400	29,500	33,400	36,700	39,100	40,900	37,500	25,300	31,100
Asian	15,400	300	900	2,200	2,200	3,100	2,800	2,300	700	500
White	261,800	6,800	26,900	29,700	32,400	34,500	36,800	33,700	23,900	30,200
Black	6,200	200	1,200	700	500	1,000	800	900	600	100
Native American	1,000	-	-	100	-	-	400	300	-	200
Hispanic[b]	4,800	-	700	300	700	1,000	600	700	500	200
Mathematical scientists	131,000	2,400	17,100	18,200	17,300	23,100	20,200	13,300	9,000	6,200
Asian	5,900	200	900	400	500	500	1,300	600	1,300	-
White	115,500	2,000	15,400	17,000	14,900	21,200	17,200	10,800	7,000	5,900
Black	6,800	200	300	600	1,300	600	1,300	1,700	600	200
Native American	200	-	100	-	-	-	-	100	-	-
Hispanic[b]	3,100	-	800	500	400	1,200	100	100	-	-
Computer specialists	562,600	13,300	105,400	123,900	115,500	86,500	53,700	29,000	15,800	6,300
Asian	36,100	1,500	7,400	8,100	8,900	4,600	2,900	1,900	200	-
White	497,100	11,100	91,400	109,900	102,000	77,700	47,000	26,100	14,900	6,200
Black	18,900	400	3,600	3,500	3,900	2,900	1,900	500	700	100
Native American	2,200	-	200	200	100	100	1,400	-	-	-
Hispanic[b]	9,300	400	3,000	2,600	1,000	900	900	100	200	-
Environmental scientists	111,300	3,600	16,500	21,500	18,200	10,100	8,200	11,700	8,100	10,300
Asian	2,100	100	100	200	800	300	300	100	200	-
White	105,800	3,400	15,800	20,200	16,600	9,600	7,800	11,300	7,700	10,200
Black	1,000	-	100	100	700	100	-	100	-	-
Native American	400	-	100	100	100	-	-	100	100	100
Hispanic[b]	1,800	100	300	700	100	100	200	200	200	-
Life scientists	411,800	13,800	68,800	81,400	61,400	51,700	38,400	26,800	28,700	28,300
Asian	15,000	1,000	2,400	3,500	2,300	2,400	1,300	1,600	300	200
White	377,900	12,200	63,400	72,000	56,100	47,300	36,400	24,200	27,400	27,300
Black	8,800	100	1,000	2,400	2,300	1,200	500	400	400	200
Native American	2,800	-	200	700	200	-	100	500	500	600
Hispanic[b]	9,900	700	2,900	2,400	1,200	1,200	300	300	500	400
Psychologists	253,500	8,800	38,300	50,100	44,900	39,000	28,500	16,500	12,600	8,200
Asian	5,200	100	200	3,600	300	500	100	100	200	-
White	234,100	8,200	36,100	43,600	40,600	36,900	27,100	15,400	12,200	7,900

[Continued]

★ 379 ★

Scientists and Engineers by Years of Experience and Race/Ethnicity (Continued)

Employed scientists and engineers by field, race/ethnicity, and years of professional experience, 1986.

Field and racial/ethnic group	Total employed[a]	Years of professional experience								
		1 or less	2-4	5-9	10-14	15-19	20-24	25-29	30-34	35 and over
Black	9,100	200	1,200	1,700	3,600	600	500	1,000	200	100
Native American	1,900	-	100	300	300	200	700	100	-	300
Hispanic[b]	5,900	200	2,000	1,600	700	1,100	200	-	-	-
Social scientists	427,800	24,300	92,200	84,100	60,400	58,000	37,600	21,100	17,700	20,900
Asian	14,200	1,400	3,100	1,700	1,000	1,000	1,100	2,400	900	1,300
White	380,800	21,800	79,400	74,000	55,100	53,700	33,300	18,300	16,100	19,400
Black	22,900	700	6,900	5,900	2,800	2,500	2,100	200	600	100
Native American	1,700	-	500	400	100	-	400	100	100	100
Hispanic[b]	11,400	600	3,200	1,900	2,200	1,900	600	100	100	-
Engineers, total	2,440,100	30,600	216,500	314,100	326,600	318,400	298,800	303,700	242,000	306,000
Asian	132,800	3,000	10,700	18,400	22,500	22,600	22,500	15,600	8,700	5,200
White	2,217,300	26,000	194,400	280,100	289,600	284,000	263,800	280,000	228,800	295,000
Black	41,300	800	4,500	6,800	8,300	5,300	5,700	2,800	2,400	2,300
Native American	13,300	200	400	1,100	1,800	2,100	2,500	1,700	800	2,100
Hispanic[b]	47,200	1,100	5,800	9,500	7,500	5,900	4,900	4,900	2,400	3,200

Source: Patricia E. White, *Women and Minorities in Science and Engineering: An Update* (Washington, DC: National Science Foundation 92.303, January 1992), table 6, p. 85-86. Primary source: National Science Foundation, Science Resources Studies Division, Scientific and Personnel Data System (STPDS). A dash (–) represent too few cases to estimate. *Notes:* All figures have been rounded to the nearest 100. Detail may not sum to totals because of rounding. (a) Detail will not add to total employed because racial and ethnic categories are not mutually exclusive (Hispanics may also be included in one of the racial groups) and because total employed included "other" and "no report" categories. (b) Includes members of all racial groups.

★380★

Scientists and Engineers with Bachelor's Degrees by Race/Ethnicity

Total employed scientists and engineers with Bachelor's degrees by field and race/ethnicity, 1990.

Field of degree	Bachelor's recipients[a]					
	Total[b]	Asian	White	Black	Native American	Hispanic[c]
Total, science and engineering	485,500	21,100	396,000	24,100	3,100	17,200
Sciences, total	358,700	13,300	293,300	19,100	2,100	12,100
Physical sciences	16,500	800	13,600	900	-	700
Chemistry	9,200	600	7,300	500	-	400
Physics and astronomy	4,700	100	4,100	100	-	300
Other	2,600	-	2,200	200	-	-
Mathematics and statistics	26,600	1,200	21,900	1,300	200	800
Computer science	62,500	4,500	48,700	3,300	400	2,100
Environmental science	4,700	100	4,300	-	-	100
Agricultural and biological sciences	69,200	1,700	56,600	3,000	400	1,100
Agricultural sciences	24,500	400	21,500	600	-	500
Biology	44,700	1,300	35,200	2,500	400	700
Psychology	63,300	1,000	52,000	3,400	400	2,900
Social sciences	116,000	3,800	96,100	7,200	600	4,300
Economics	38,800	2,000	33,100	1,800	-	1,500

[Continued]

★ 380 ★

Scientists and Engineers with Bachelor's Degrees by Race/Ethnicity (Continued)

Total employed scientists and engineers with Bachelor's degrees by field and race/ethnicity, 1990.

Field of degree	Bachelor's recipients[a]					
	Total[b]	Asian	White	Black	Native American	Hispanic[c]
Sociology and anthropology	26,900	600	21,500	2,600	200	600
Other	50,300	1,200	41,500	3,000	400	2,300
Engineering, total	126,700	7,800	102,700	5,000	900	5,200
Aeronautical and astronautical	5,800	200	5,200	100	-	300
Chemical	6,100	300	4,700	300	-	200
Civil	13,200	600	10,800	200	100	900
Electrical and electronics	47,900	5,200	36,200	2,500	300	1,400
Industrial	11,000	300	9,000	700	-	800
Materials	1,300	-	1,100	-	-	-
Mechanical	25,600	1,000	21,500	800	400	1,200
Mining	800	-	700	-	-	-
Nuclear	700	-	700	-	-	-
Petroleum	900	-	800	-	-	100
Other	13,400	200	12,100	300	-	100

Source: Patricia E. White, *Women and Minorities in Science and Engineering: An Update* (Washington, DC: National Science Foundation 92.303, January 1992), table 5, p. 83. Primary source: National Science Foundation, Science Resources Studies Division, Survey of Science, Social Science and Engineering Graduates (Recent Science and Engineering Graduates) unpublished tabulations. Also in source: data by sex. A dash (–) represents too few cases to estimate; cells with fewer than 20 cases are not reported. *Notes:* All figures have been rounded to the nearest 100. Detail may not sum to totals because of rounding. (a) Graduates who receive their degree in academic years 1988 or 1989. (b) Racial and ethnic categories will not sum to total employed because racial and ethnic categories are not mutually exclusive (Hispanics may also be included in one of the racial groups) and because total employed includes "other" and "no reports" categories. (c) Includes members of all racial groups.

★ 381 ★

Scientists and Engineers with Master's Degrees by Race/Ethnicity

Total employed scientists and engineers with master's degrees by field and race/ethnicity, 1990.

Field of degree	Master's recipients[a]					
	Total[b]	Asian	White	Black	Native American	Hispanic[c]
Total, science and engineering	100,600	10,100	77,000	3,700	500	3,300
Sciences, total	66,700	5,600	51,700	2,700	300	1,900
Physical sciences	5,100	400	4,300	200	-	-
Chemistry	2,100	200	1,600	-	-	-
Physics and astronomy	1,800	200	1,600	-	-	-
Other	1,400	-	1,100	100	-	-
Mathematics and statistics	8,400	700	7,000	200	-	200
Computer science	19,400	3,100	13,700	500	-	500
Environmental science	4,000	100	3,500	-	-	100
Agricultural and biological sciences	11,700	700	9,600	200	-	500
Agricultural sciences	4,500	300	3,600	200	-	200
Biology	7,200	500	6,000	-	-	300
Psychology	4,500	200	3,600	300	-	100
Social sciences	13,400	500	10,000	1,200	300	500

[Continued]

Scientists and Engineers with Master's Degrees by Race/Ethnicity (Continued)

Total employed scientists and engineers with master's degrees by field and race/ethnicity, 1990.

Field of degree	Master's recipients[a]					
	Total[b]	Asian	White	Black	Native American	Hispanic[c]
Economics	3,500	200	2,600	400	-	-
Sociology and anthropology	2,300	-	1,500	400	200	-
Other	7,600	200	6,000	400	-	400
Engineering, total	33,900	4,500	25,200	1,000	200	1,400
Aeronautical and astronautical	1,400	100	1,200	-	-	100
Chemical	1,400	200	1,100	-	-	100
Civil	4,200	800	2,800	200	-	200
Electrical and electronics	10,500	1,800	7,200	400	100	300
Industrial	2,200	200	1,700	100	-	200
Materials	1,000	200	800	-	-	-
Mechanical	6,800	700	5,300	100	-	100
Mining	400	-	400	-	-	-
Nuclear	200	-	200	-	-	-
Petroleum	300	-	300	-	-	-
Other	5,500	400	4,500	100	-	300

Source: Patricia E. White, *Women and Minorities in Science and Engineering: An update* (Washington, DC: National Science Foundation 92.303, January 1992), table 5, p. 84. Primary source: National Science Foundation, Science Resources Studies Division, Survey of Science, Social Science and Engineering Graduates (Recent Science and Engineering Graduates) unpublished tabulations. Also in source: data by sex. A dash (–) represents too few cases to estimate; cells with fewer than 20 cases are not reported. *Notes:* (a) Graduates who receive their degree in academic years 1988 or 1989. (b) Racial and ethnic categories will not sum to total employed because racial and ethnic categories are not mutually exclusive (Hispanics may also be included in one of the racial groups) and because total employed includes "other" and "no reports" categories. (c) Includes members of all racial groups. All figures have been rounded to the nearest 100. Detail may not sum to totals because of rounding.

Scientists and Engineers with Doctorates by Race/Ethnicity

Total employed doctoral scientists and engineers by field and race/ethnicity, 1979 and 1989.

Field	Total [a,b]		Asian		White		Black	
	1979	1989	1979	1989	1979	1989	1979	1989
Total, scientists and engineers	314,257	448,643	22,932	41,239	285,613	397,623	3,235	7,190
Scientists, total	263,915	373,860	15,057	26,618	243,581	338,409	3,133	6,572
Physical scientists	60,222	70,209	4,719	7,217	54,690	61,624	403	831
Chemists	39,659	45,649	3,246	5,119	35,828	39,519	320	657
Physicists and astronomers	20,563	24,560	1,473	2,098	18,862	22,105	83	174
Mathematical scientists	15,250	17,611	1,130	1,676	13,788	15,663	144	198
Mathematicians	12,843	14,867	820	1,171	11,746	13,473	131	163
Statisticians	2,407	2,744	310	505	2,042	2,190	-	35
Computer specialists	6,684	19,797	561	2,422	6,072	17,070	-	191
Environmental scientists	14,575	19,787	539	1,338	13,869	18,178	65	228
Earth scientists	11,083	15,138	394	1,042	10,570	13,839	61	218
Oceanographers	1,662	2,460	57	135	1,570	2,318	-	-
atmospheric scientists	1,830	2,189	88	161	1,729	2,021	-	-
Life scientists	78,857	115,833	5,417	9,298	72,012	104,302	883	1,645

[Continued]

★ 382 ★

Scientists and Engineers with Doctorates by Race/Ethnicity (Continued)

Total employed doctoral scientists and engineers by field and race/ethnicity, 1979 and 1989.

Field	Total [a,b]		Asian		White		Black	
	1979	1989	1979	1989	1979	1989	1979	1989
Biological scientists	45,617	67,250	3,282	5,670	41,477	60,458	564	851
Agricultural scientist	12,789	16,504	759	972	11,876	15,320	68	158
Medical scientists	20,451	32,079	1,376	2,656	18,659	28,524	251	636
Psychologists	37,848	60,596	412	947	36,551	57,961	602	1,364
Social scientists	50,479	70,027	2,279	3,720	46,599	63,611	1,032	2,115
Economists	13,978	18,588	779	1,358	12,811	16,800	265	340
Sociologists and anthropologists	10,198	13,529	316	447	9,535	12,567	207	363
Other	26,303	37,910	1,184	1,915	24,253	34,244	560	1,412
Engineers, total	50,342	74,783	7,875	14,621	42,032	59,214	102	618
Aeronautical and astronautical	2,364	6,367	232	1,395	2,122	4,803	-	165
Chemical	6,166	7,959	1,200	1,899	4,953	6,004	-	39
Civil	5,157	6,951	1,204	1,303	3,875	5,552	-	79
Electrical and electronic	8,597	15,088	1,272	3,248	7,252	11,646	-	118
Materials	5,732	8,280	813	1,936	4,865	6,254	-	46
Mechanical	5,245	7,390	1,165	1,510	4,057	5,814	22	-
Nuclear	2,286	2,437	222	416	1,986	1,995	-	-
Systems design	4,931	3,896	570	364	4,293	3,474	24	42
Other	9,864	16,415	1,197	2,550	8,629	13,672	28	106

Source: Patricia E. White, Ph.D., *Women and Minorities in Science and Engineering: An Update* (Washington, DC: National Science Foundation 92.303, January 1992) table 3, p. 81. Primary source: National Science Foundation, Science Resources Studies Division, Survey of Doctorate Recipients, unpublished tabulations. Also in source: data by sex, and for Hispanics and Native Americans. A dash (–) represents too few cases to estimate; cells with less than 20 cases are not reported. *Notes:* (a) Includes scientists and engineers who received their doctorates between 1946 and 1988 and were employed full-time or part-time or held post-doctoral appointments in February 1989. All holders of doctorates are included regardless of citizenship status (i.e., U.S. citizen; non-U.S. citizen, permanent visa; and non-U.S. citizen, temporary visa). Field categories represent the specialty most closely related to the respondent's principal employment. Individuals who did not report science and engineering employment were assigned the specialty of their doctoral degree. (b) Racial/ethnic categories will not sum to total because racial and ethnic categories are not mutually exclusive (Hispanics may also be included in one of the racial groups) and because total employed includes "other" and "no report" categories.

★ 383 ★

Scientists and Engineers with Doctorates by Sex and Race/Ethnicity

Total employed doctoral scientists and engineers by field, sex, and race/ethnicity, 1989.

Field[a] and sex	Total employed[b,c]	Asian	White	Black	Native American	Hispanic[d]
Total, scientists and engineers[d]	448,643	41,239	397,623	7,190	772	8,094
Male	371,483	35,911	328,542	4,954	589	6,412
Female	77,160	5,328	69,081	2,236	183	1,682
Scientists, total	373,860	26,618	338,409	6,572	690	6,820
Male	299,015	21,772	271,100	4,370	520	5,201
Female	74,845	4,846	67,309	2,202	170	1,619
Physical scientists	70,209	7,217	61,624	831	155	1,158
Male	64,139	6,230	56,680	734	136	963
Female	6,070	987	4,944	97	-	195
Mathematical scientists	17,611	1,676	15,663	198	-	322
Male	15,766	1,422	14,116	160	-	292
Female	1,845	254	1,547	38	-	30
Computer/information specialists	19,797	2,422	17,070	191	-	351
Male	17,493	2,174	15,033	173	-	327
Female	2,304	248	2,037	-	-	24
Environmental scientists	19,787	1,338	18,178	228	23	319
Male	18,123	1,252	16,612	223	21	292
Female	1,664	86	1,566	-	-	27
Life scientists	115,833	9,298	104,302	1,645	181	1,907
Male	89,558	7,069	81,056	993	112	1,465
Female	26,275	2,229	23,246	652	69	442
Psychologists	60,596	947	57,961	1,364	137	1,276
Male	38,754	490	37,470	590	91	746
Female	21,842	457	20,491	774	46	530
Social scientists	70,027	3,720	63,611	2,115	169	1,487
Male	55,182	3,135	50,133	1,497	138	1,116
Female	14,845	585	13,478	618	31	371
Engineers, total	74,783	14,621	59,214	618	82	1,274
Male	72,468	14,139	57,442	584	69	1,211
Female	2,315	482	1,772	34	-	63

Source: Patricia E. White, *Women and Minorities in Science and Engineering: An Update* (Washington, DC: National Science Foundation 92-303, January 1992), table 4, p. 82. Primary source: National Science Foundation, Science Resources Studies Division, Survey of Doctorate Recipients, unpublished tabulations, tables B-67 and B-67A. A dash (–) represents too few cases to estimate; cells with fewer than 20 cases are not reported. *Notes:* (a) Field categories represent the specialty most closely related to the respondent's principal employment. Individuals who did not report science and engineering employment were assigned the specialty of their doctoral degree. (b) Includes scientists and engineers who received their doctorates between 1946 and 1988 and were employed full-time or part-time or held postdoctoral appointments in February 1989. All holders of doctorates are included, regardless of citizenship status (i.e., U.S. citizen; non-U.S. citizen, permanent visa; and non-U.S. citizen, temporary visa). (c) Racial/ethnic categories will not sum to total employed because racial and ethnic categories are not mutually exclusive (Hispanics may also be included in one of the racial groups) and because total employed includes "other" and "no report" categories. (d) Includes members of all racial groups.

★ 384 ★

Unemployment and Underemployment: Scientists and Engineers

Unemployment and underemployment data for science and engineering graduates by degree level and race/ethnicity, 1990.

Characteristics/degree level[a]	Asian	White	Black	Native American	Hispanic[b]
Unemployment rate					
Bachelor's	5.6	3.0	6.4	1.5	4.4
Master's	3.3	1.6	4.6	-	4.3
Doctorate	0.7	0.8	3.7	1.5	0.8
Science and eng. underemployment rate					
Doctorate	0.9	1.3	2.9	1.6	1.4

Source: Patricia E. White, *Women and Minorities in Science and Engineering: An Update* (Washington, DC: National Science Foundation, 92-303, January, 1992), table 3.1, p. 32. Primary source: National Science Foundation, Science Resources Studies Division, Survey of Earned Doctorates, unpublished tabulations. A dash (–) represents too few cases to estimate. *Notes:* (a) Data for bachelor's and master's degrees were reported in 1990 by 1988 and 1989 graduates; data for doctorates were reported in 1989 by recipients who received degrees between 1946 and 1988. (b) Includes members of all racial groups.

Education

★ 385 ★

Faculty, Two-Year Postsecondary Schools

Vocational and non-vocational public two-year postsecondary school faculty, in percent, by race/ethnicity, 1987.

Race-ethnicity	All faculty	Vocational	Non-vocational
Total	100.0%	100.0%	100.0%
Asian	1.7%	1.3%	2.0%
White, non-Hispanic	91.0%	90.7%	91.2%
Black, non-Hispanic	3.1%	3.3%	3.0%
Hispanic	3.5%	3.7%	3.4%
Native American	0.7%	1.0%	0.4%

Source: National Center for Education Statistics, U.S. Department of Education, Office of Educational Research and Improvement, *Vocational Education in the United States: 1969-1990*, NCES 92-669 (Washington, DC: U.S. Government Printing Office, April 1992), table 56, p. 123. Also in source: data by sex and age.

★ 386 ★

Faculty: Tenure Status by Sex

Tenure rates of faculty, in percent, by sex and race/ethnicity, 1989.

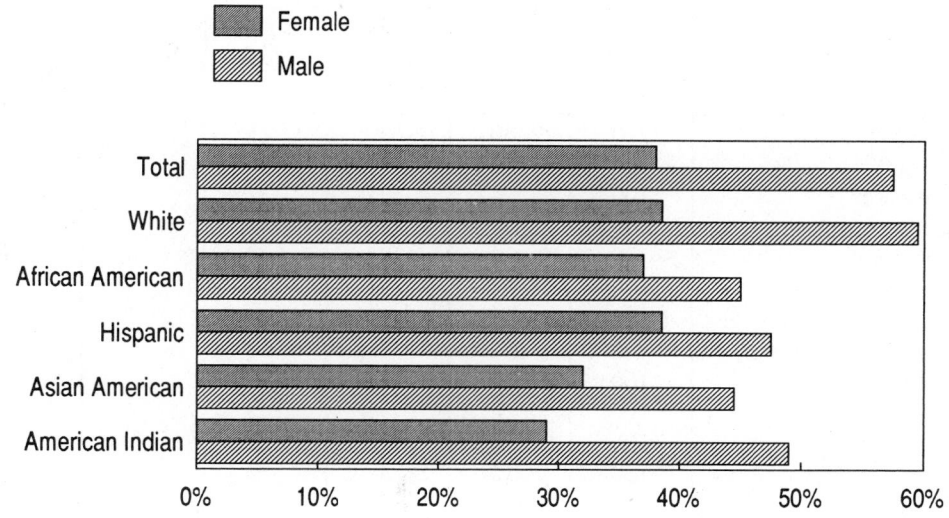

Source: Eugenia Escueta and Eileen O'Brien, "Asian Americans in Higher Education: Trends and Issues," *Research Briefs* 2, no. 4 (Washington, DC: American Council on Education, Division of Policy Analysis and Research, 1991): 8. Primary source: Equal Employment Opportunity Commission, *1989 EEO-6 Detail Summary Report,* U.S. Summary, unpublished data, 1991.

★ 387 ★

Faculty Tenure Rates

Tenure status of full-time faculty, in percent by race/ethnicity, 1989.

Race/ethnicity	Tenure track		Non-tenure track
	Tenured	Not tenured	
Total	52%	21%	27%
Asian American	41%	28%	31%
White	53%	21%	26%
African American	41%	26%	33%
Hispanic	45%	25%	30%
American Indian	42%	21%	37%

Source: Eugenia Escueta and Eileen O'Brien, "Asian Americans in Higher Education: Trends and Issues," *Research Briefs* 2, no. 4 (Washington, DC: American Council on Education, Division of Policy Analysis and Research, 1991): p. 8. Primary source: Equal Employment Opportunity Commission, *1989 EEO-6 Detail Summary Report,* U.S. Summary, unpublished data, 1991.

★ 388 ★

Faculty in Higher Education

Number and percent of regular and temporary instructional faculty by type and control of institution and race/ethnicity, fall 1987.

Institution	Race					
	Total	Asian	White, non-Hispanic	Black, Non-Hispanic	Hispanic	American Indian
Number (thousands)	770	30	690	25	18	6
Percent total	100	4	90	3	2	1
Public research	100	4	91	1	2	1
Private research	100	4	85	7	5	(a)
Public doctoral	100	4	93	2	1	1
Private doctoral	100	4	91	(a)	4	1
Public comprehensive	100	6	88	3	2	1
Private comprehensive	100	6	88	3	2	1
Liberal arts	100	6	88	3	2	1
Public 2-year	100	2	91	3	4	1
Private 2-year	100	2	90	4	2	2
Medical	100	15	82	2	(a)	1
Other	100	4	92	4	1	(a)

Source: National Center for Education Statistics, U.S. Department of Education, *Digest of Education Statistics 1992* (Washington, DC: U.S. U.S. Government Printing Office, October 1992, table 215, p. 227. Primary source: U.S. Department of Education, National Center for Education Statistics, National Survey of Postsecondary Faculty (NSOPF), 1988. (This table was prepared June 1990.) Also in source: data by sex and type of employment. *Notes:* (a) Less than 0.5 percent.

★ 389 ★

Faculty in Higher Education, Part-time

Number and percent of part-time regular instructional faculty by type and control of institution and race/ethnicity, fall 1987.

Selected Characteristics	Race					
	Total	Asian	White, non-Hispanic	Black, non-Hispanic	Hispanic	American Indian
Number in thousands	174	6	156	6	4	2
Percent total	100	3	90	4	3	1
Public research	100	-	98	1	-	1
Private research	100	2	83	12	2	2
Public doctoral	100	-	94	2	2	2
Private doctoral	100	-	91	-	9	-
Public comprehensive	100	9	84	2	2	4
Private comprehensive	100	0	97	-	3	-
Liberal arts	100	-	82	14	2	1
Public 2-year	100	2	92	3	3	0
Private 2-year	100	(a)	(a)	(a)	(a)	(a)
Medical	100	(a)	(a)	(a)	(a)	(a)
Other	100	1	97	1	-	-

Source: National Center for Education Statistics, U.S. Department of Education, *Digest of Education Statistics 1992* (Washington, DC: U.S. Government Printing Office, October 1992), table 216 p. 227. Primary source: U.S. Department of Education, National Center for Education Statistics, National Survey of Postsecondary Faculty (NSOPF), 1988. (This table was prepared June 1990.) Also in source: data by sex and type of employment. *Notes:* (a) Too few cases for reliable estimates. A dash (-) indicates less than 0.5 percent.

★ 390 ★

Faculty in Higher Education by Field

Number and percent of full-time regular instructional faculty by field and race/ethnicity, fall 1987.

Faculty characteristics	Race/ethnicity					
	Total	Asian	White, non-Hispanic	Black, Non-Hispanic	Hispanic	American Indian
Number (thousands)	489	21	438	16	11	4
All fields	100	4	90	3	2	1
Agriculture and home economics	100	2	94	0	3	1
Business	100	6	88	4	1	1
Education	100	1	88	6	4	1
Engineering	100	11	87	-	2	-
Fine arts	100	1	92	3	3	-
Health	100	7	88	2	1	-
Humanities	100	2	90	3	5	1
Natural sciences	100	6	91	2	1	-
Social sciences	100	2	90	5	3	1
Other	100	3	89	5	2	1

Source: National Center for Education Statistics, U.S. Department of Education, *Digest of Education Statistics 1992* (Washington, DC: U.S. Government Printing Office, October 1992), table 214, p. 226. Primary source: U.S. Department of Education, National Center for Education Statistics, National Survey of Postsecondary Faculty (NSOPF), 1988. (This table was prepared June 1990.) Also in source: data by sex, age, degree, and rank. A dash (-) represents less than 0.5 percent.

★ 391 ★

Faculty in Higher Education by Rank and Sex

Number of full-time instructional faculty in institutions of higher education by sex and race/ethnicity, fall 1985.

Academic rank and sex	Race/ethnicity					
	Total	Asian/Pacific Islander	White, non-Hispanic	Black, non-Hispanic	Hispanic	American Indian/Alaskan Native
Men and women, all ranks	464,072	18,370	417,036	19,227	7,704	1,735
Professors	129,269	4,788	119,868	2,859	1,455	299
Associate professors	111,092	4,130	100,630	4,201	1,727	404
Assistant professors	111,308	5,469	97,496	5,895	1,968	480
Instructors	75,411	1,806	66,799	4,572	1,798	436
Lecturers	9,766	360	8,477	631	251	47
Other faculty	27,226	1,817	23,766	1,069	505	69
Men, all ranks	336,009	14,846	303,953	10,456	5,360	1,394
Professors	114,258	4,395	106,335	2,058	1,206	264
Associate professors	85,156	3,451	77,483	2,595	1,280	347
Assistant professors	71,463	4,240	62,582	2,923	1,316	402
Instructors	43,251	1,105	38,592	2,107	1,141	306
Lecturers	5,098	212	4,436	304	117	29
Other faculty	16,783	1,443	14,525	469	300	46

[Continued]

★ 391 ★

Faculty in Higher Education by Rank and Sex (Continued)

Number of full-time instructional faculty in institutions of higher education by sex and race/ethnicity, fall 1985.

Academic rank and sex	Race/ethnicity					
	Total	Asian/Pacific Islander	White, non-Hispanic	Black, non-Hispanic	Hispanic	American Indian/Alaskan Native
Women, all ranks	128,063	3,524	113,083	8,771	2,344	341
Professors	15,011	393	13,533	801	249	35
Associate professors	25,936	679	23,147	1,606	447	57
Assistant professors	39,845	1,229	34,914	2,972	652	78
Instructors	32,160	701	28,207	2,465	657	130
Lecturers	4,668	148	4,041	327	134	18
Other faculty	10,443	374	9,241	600	205	23

Source: National Center for Education Statistics, U.S. Department of Education, *Digest of Education Statistics 1992* (Washington, DC: U.S. Government Printing Office, October 1992), table 212, p. 224. Primary source: U.S. Equal Employment Opportunity Commission, *Higher Education Staff Information Report File,* 1985, unpublished data. (This table was prepared June 1989.) Data exclude faculty employed by system offices. Totals may differ from figures reported on other tables because of varying survey methodologies.

★ 392 ★

Faculty in Higher Education by Type of Institution

Number and percent of full-time regular instructional faculty by type and control of institution and race/ethnicity, fall 1987.

Selected characteristics	Race/ethnicity					
	Total	Asian	White, non-Hispanic	Black, non-Hispanic	Hispanic	American Indian
Number (thousands)	489	21	438	16	11	3
Total, percent	100.0	4.2	89.5	3.2	2.3	0.7
Public research	100.0	4.8	90.4	1.6	2.4	0.7
Private research	100.0	3.5	85.4	6.1	5.0	-
Public doctoral	100.0	4.5	92.0	1.8	1.1	0.6
Private doctoral	100.0	5.9	91.3	0.1	2.2	0.5
Public comprehensive	100.0	5.8	88.0	3.5	2.1	0.6
Private comprehensive	100.0	4.4	91.2	1.7	1.6	1.1
Liberal arts	100.0	2.7	86.9	8.0	1.2	1.2
Public 2-year	100.0	1.6	91.0	3.0	3.5	0.9
Private 2-year	100.0	0.5	94.1	3.1	2.3	-
Medical	100.0	10.3	85.3	3.0	-	1.4
Other	100.0	1.0	95.1	2.3	1.6	-

Source: National Center for Education Statistics, U.S. Department of Education, *Digest of Education Statistics 1992* (Washington, DC: U.S. Government Printing Office, October 1992), table 213, p. 225. Primary source: U.S. Department of Education, National Center for Education Statistics, National Survey of Postsecondary Faculty (NSOPF), 1988. (This table was prepared June 1990.) Also in source: data by sex, age, highest degree, academic rank, and base salary. A dash (-) indicates less than 0.05 percent.

★ 393 ★

Teachers at Independent Schools

Number of teachers at independent schools by school type, school size, region, and teacher's race/ethnicity, 1990 and 1991.

School characteristics	Asian American	African American	Latino	American Indian	Total	Percent teachers of Racial/Ethnic groups
School type (see Notes)						
Boarding (95% or more boarding)	11	19	22	1	53	4.3
Boarding-day (50-94% boarding)	35	59	50	6	150	3.8
Day (95% or more day)	238	557	406	24	1,225	4.3
Day-boarding (51-94% day)	23	52	51	1	127	3.7
Girls'	44	98	61	5	208	4.6
Boys'	20	47	40	1	108	3.4
Coed	243	542	428	26	1,239	4.3
Elementary any grades, (pre-school-9)	46	103	70	5	224	3.5
Elem/secondary (K-12, 5-12 or 1-10)	180	437	316	15	948	4.2
Secondary (7-12, 9-12, 7-PG)	81	147	143	12	383	4.8
School size						
Under 201 students	24	57	51	3	135	3.1
201-300	35	77	87	3	202	4.0
301-500	85	174	141	6	406	4.0
501-700	62	122	86	8	278	4.4
Over 700	101	257	164	12	534	4.9
Region (see Notes)						
East	60	125	86	0	271	4.6
Middle Atlantic	46	211	83	3	343	4.7
Midwest	19	60	41	2	122	2.9
New England	50	98	55	8	211	3.0
Southeast	12	42	87	5	146	2.7
Southwest	17	73	79	8	177	5.7
West	103	78	98	6	285	7.4
All schools	307	687	529	32	1,555	4.2

Source: NAIS Statistics 1990-1991: Financial Aid, Financial Operations, Enrollment, Staffing. Boston, MA: National Association of Independent Schools, 1991. *Notes:* "School Type" is defined as follows: Boarding-95% or more boarding; Boarding-Day-50 to 94% boarding students; Day-95% or more day students; Day-Boarding-51-94% day students; Elementary-any grades preschool through 9; Elem/secondary-kindergarten through 12, 5 through 12, or 1 through 10; Secondary-7 through 12, 9 through 12, or 7 through postgraduate. Regions are defined as follows: East-New Jersey, New York; Middle Atlantic-Delaware, District of Columbia, Maryland, Pennsylvania, Virginia; Midwest-Illinois, Indiana, Iowa, Kentucky, Michigan, Minnesota, Missouri, Nebraska, North Dakota, Ohio, South Dakota, West Virginia, Wisconsin; New England-Connecticut, Maine, Massachusetts, New Hampshire, Rhode Island, Vermont; Southeast-Alabama, Florida, Georgia, Mississippi, North Carolina, South Carolina, Tennessee; Southwest-Arizona, Arkansas, Colorado, Kansas, Louisiana, New Mexico, Oklahoma, Texas; West-Alaska, California, Hawaii, Idaho, Montana, Nevada, Oregon, Utah, Washington, Wyoming; U.S. Territories-Guam, Puerto Rico, U.S. Virgin Islands.

★ 394 ★

Teachers in Elementary and Secondary Schools

Numbers and percent of teachers in public and private elementary and secondary schools by highest degree earned, years of experience, and race/ethnicity, 1987 and 1988.

Selected characteristics	Total[a]	Highest degree earned, percent						Years of full-time teaching experience, percent			
		No degree	Associate	Bachelor's	Master's	Education specialist	Doctor's	Less than 3	3 to 9	10 to 20	Over 20
Public schools											
Asian or Pacific Islander	20,709	-	-	52.8	28.7	13.5	-	11.2	22.1	43.0	23.7
Hispanic	67,084	-	-	84.5	29.9	6.7	-	11.9	33.2	40.9	13.9
Black	187,836	-	-	49.7	42.4	0.6	0.0	6.1	19.4	46.3	28.2
White	1,994,389	0.2	0.4	52.1	40.3	6.2	0.8	8.0	26.6	44.4	21.0
American Indian or Alaskan	23,998	-	-	50.1	40.5	7.5	-	5.7	24.3	49.7	20.2
Private schools											
Asian or Pacific Islander	3,491	-	-	56.2	-	-	-	-	-	-	-
Hispanic	8,569	-	-	60.8	19.7	-	-	22.0	41.4	25.8	-
Black	7,015	-	-	69.1	16.6	-	-	27.0	42.2	21.3	0
White	281,152	2.9	1.3	61.2	30.3	2.7	1.6	18.4	37.7	30.2	13.8
American Indian or Alaskan	2,747	-	-	93.7	-	-	-	-	-	-	-

Source: National Center for Education Statistics, U.S. Department of Education, *Digest of Education Statistics 1992* (Washington, DC: U.S. Government Printing Office, October 1992), table 65, p. 76. Primary source: U.S. Department of Education, National Center for Education Statistics, "Schools and Staffing Survey, 1987-1988." (This table was prepared June 1990.) Also in source: data by sex, age, and level. A dash (-) indicates too few sample cases (fewer than 30) for a reliable estimate. *Notes:* (a) Total differs from data appearing in other tables because of differences in surveys.

Labor Force Projections

★ 395 ★

Labor Force: Composition, 1976, 1988, and 2000

Composition of the labor force age sixteen and over (in thousands), change (in thousands and percent), and growth rate by sex and race/ethnicity, 1976, 1988, and projected to 2000.

Race	Level, thousands			Change, thousands		Change, percent		Growth rate	
	1976	1988	2000	1976-88	1988-2000	1976-88	1988-2000	1976-88	1988-2000
Total, 16 and over	96,158	121,669	141,134	25,511	19,465	26.5	16.0	2.0	1.2
Asian and other, 16 and over[a]	1,826	3,709	5,688	1,883	1,979	103.1	53.4	6.1	3.6
Men	1,036	2,015	3,029	979	1,014	94.5	50.3	5.7	3.5
Women	790	1,694	2,659	904	965	114.4	57.0	6.6	3.8
White, 16 and over	84,767	104,756	118,981	19,989	14,225	23.6	13.6	1.8	1.1
Men	51,033	58,317	63,288	7,284	4,971	14.3	8.5	1.1	0.7
Women	33,735	46,439	55,693	12,704	9,254	37.7	19.9	2.7	1.5
Black, 16 and over	9,565	13,205	16,465	3,640	3,260	38.1	24.7	2.7	1.9
Men	5,105	6,596	8,007	1,491	1,411	29.2	21.4	2.2	1.6
Women	4,460	6,609	8,458	2,149	1,849	48.2	28.0	3.3	2.1
Hispanic, 16 and over[b]	4,279	8,982	14,321	4,703	5,339	109.9	59.4	6.4	4.0
Men	2,625	5,409	8,284	2,784	2,875	106.1	53.2	6.2	3.6
Women	1,654	3,573	6,037	1,919	2,464	116.0	69.0	6.6	4.5

Source: Howard N. Fullerton, Jr., "New Labor Force Projections, Spanning 1988 to 2000," *Monthly Labor Review* (November 1989), table 4, p. 8. Also in source: data by age, sex, and participation rate. Primary source: Office of Employment Projection, Bureau of Labor Statistics. *Notes:* (a) The "Asian and other" group includes American Indians, Alaskan Natives, Asians, and Pacific Islanders. The historic data are derived by subtracting "Black" from the "Black and other" group; projections are made directly. (b) Persons of Hispanic origin may be of any race.

★ 396 ★

Labor Force: Numbers and Growth Rate, 1976, 1988, and 2000

Numbers of the labor force (in thousands) by race/ethnicity and percent change, 1976, 1988, and projected to 2000.

Group	Level			Change		Growth rate	
	1976	1988	2000	1976-88	1988-2000	1976-88	1988-2000
Asian and other, 16 and over[a]	2,910	5,725	8,688	2,815	2,963	5.8	3.5
White, 16 and over	137,106	158,194	171,171	21,088	12,977	1.2	0.7
Black, 16 and over	16,216	20,692	24,754	4,476	4,062	2.1	1.5
Hispanic, 16 and over[b]	7,051	13,325	20,490	6,274	7,165	5.4	0.0

Source: Howard N. Fullerton, Jr., "New Labor Force Projections, Spanning 1988 to 2000," *Monthly Labor Review* (November 1989), table 3, p. 6. Primary source: Office of Employment Projections, Bureau of Labor Statistics. Also in source: data by age and sex. *Note:* (a) The "Asian and other" group includes American Indians, Alaskan Natives, Asians, and Pacific Islanders. The historic data are derived by subtracting "Black" from the "Black and other" group; projections are made directly. (b) Persons of Hispanic origin may be of any race.

★ 397 ★

Labor Force: Participation Rate by Sex and Race, 1976, 1988, and 2000

Labor force participation rate and growth rate for workers age sixteen and over by sex and race/ethnicity, 1976, 1988, and projected to 2000.

Group	Participation rate (%)			Growth rate (%)	
	1976	1988	2000	1976-88	1988-2000
Total, 16 and over[a]	61.6	65.9	69.0	0.6	0.4
Asian and other, 16 and over	62.8	65.0	65.5	0.3	0.1
Men	74.9	74.4	74.6		
Women	51.6	56.5	57.5		
White, 16 and over	61.8	66.2	69.5	0.6	0.4
Men	78.4	76.9	76.6		
Women	46.9	56.4	62.9		
Black, 16 and over	58.9	63.8	66.5	0.7	0.3
Men	69.7	71.0	71.4		
Women	50.0	58.0	62.5		
Hispanic, 16 and over[b]	60.7	67.4	69.9	0.9	0.3
Men	79.6	81.9	80.3		
Women	44.1	53.2	59.4		

Source: Howard N. Fullerton, Jr., "New Labor Force Projections, Spanning 1988 to 2000," *Monthly Labor Review* (November 1989), table 4, p. 8. Primary source: Office of Employment Projections, Bureau of Labor Statistics. Also in source: data by age, sex and other characteristics. *Note:* (a) The "Asian and other" group includes American Indians, Alaskan Natives, Asians, and Pacific Islanders. The historic data are derived by subtracting "Black" from the "Black and other" group; projections are made directly. (b) Persons of Hispanic origin may be of any race.

★ 398 ★

Labor Force: Entrants and Leavers, 1988-2000

Projected number and percent of entrants and leavers and net change to the labor force by sex and race/ethnicity, 1988 to 2000.

Group	Entrants		Leavers		Net change	
	Number	Percent	Number	Percent	Number	Percent
Total	42,832	100.0	23,371	100.0	19,461	100.0
Asian and other	2,364	5.5	504	2.2	1,860	9.6
Men	1,232	2.9	282	1.2	950	4.9
Women	1,132	2.6	222	0.9	910	4.7
White, non-Hispanic	28,597	66.8	19,393	83.0	9,204	47.3
Men	13,522	31.6	11,257	48.2	2,265	11.6
Women	15,075	35.2	8,136	34.8	6,939	35.7
Black	5,385	12.6	2,329	10.0	3,056	15.7
Men	2,423	5.7	1,121	4.8	1,302	6.7
Women	2,962	6.9	1,208	5.2	1,754	9.0
Hispanic	6,486	15.1	1,145	4.9	5,341	27.4
Men	3,558	8.3	681	2.9	2,877	14.8
Women	2,928	6.8	464	2.0	2,464	12.7

Source: Howard N. Fullerton, Jr., "New Labor Force Projections, Spanning 1988 to 2000," *Monthly Labor Review* (November 1989) table 7, p. 11. Primary source: Office of Employment Projections, Bureau of Labor Statistics. Also in source: data by age.

★ 399 ★

Labor Force: Median Age, Historical and Projected

Median age of the labor force by race/ethnicity, for selected historical years and projected years, 1994 and 2000.

Group	Median age in:						
	1962	1970	1976	1980	1988	1994	2000
Total	40.5	39.0	35.3	34.3	35.9	37.5	39.3
Asian and other[a]	0	0	33.6	33.8	36.1	37.3	38.5
White	40.9	39.3	35.6	34.8	36.1	37.8	39.6
Black	38.3	29.3	34.0	33.3	34.3	35.8	37.4
Hispanic[b]	0	0	32.6	30.7	32.9	33.9	35.2

Source: Howard N. Fullerton, Jr., "New Labor Force Projections, Spanning 1988 to 2000," *Monthly Labor Review* (November 1989), table 6, p. 10. Primary source: Office of Employment Projections, Bureau of Labor Statistics. Also in source: data by sex and age. *Notes:* (a) The "Asian and other" group includes American Indians, Alaskan Natives, Asians, and Pacific Islanders. The historic data are derived by subtracting "Black" from the "Black and other" group; projections are made directly. (b) Persons of Hispanic origin may be of any race.

★ 400 ★

Labor Force Participation Projections for 2000

Projections of the civilian labor force age sixteen and over at three levels of participation by race/ethnicity, 2000.

Group	Participation rate (in percent)			Level (in thousands)		
	High	Moderate	Low	High	Moderate	Low
Asian and other[a]	68.3	65.5	63.8	6,304	5,688	5,540
White	71.2	69.5	67.8	123,392	118,981	116,041
Black	68.3	66.5	65.1	17,074	16,465	16,103
Hispanic[b]	71.6	69.9	68.2	14,696	14,321	13,971

Source: Howard N. Fullerton, Jr., "New Labor Force Projections, Spanning 1988 to 2000," *Monthly Labor Review* (November 1989), table 5, p. 9. Primary source: Office of Employment Projections, Bureau of Labor Statistics. Also in source: data by sex and age. *Notes:* (a) The "Asian and other" group includes American Indians, Alaskan Natives, Asians, and Pacific Islanders. The historic data are derived by subtracting "Black" from the "Black and other" group; projections are made directly. (b) Persons of Hispanic origin may be of any race.

Law Enforcement

★ 401 ★

State Law Enforcement Agency Employees, 1990

Number of state law enforcement agency full-time sworn employees (in agencies with 100 or more officers) by state agency, in percent by race/ethnicity, 1990.

Name of agency	Full-time sworn employees, in percent				
	Asian/Pacific Islander	White, non-Hispanic	Black, non-Hispanic	Hispanic, any race	American Indian/Alaskan Native
Alabama Department of Public Safety	0.0	68.5	31.5	0.0	0.0
Alaska State Troopers	0.4	93.7	1.6	2.0	2.4
Arizona Department of Public Safety	0.3	82.9	2.0	12.7	2.1
Arkansas State Police	0.4	88.4	10.5	0.4	0.2
California Highway Patrol	2.6	82.3	3.9	11.1	0.1
Colorado State Patrol	0.6	87.5	2.0	9.3	0.6
Connecticut State Police	0.2	89.2	5.7	4.6	0.3
Delaware State Police	0.0	88.1	9.8	2.1	0.0
Florida Highway Patrol	0.2	81.6	12.2	5.8	0.2
Georgia State Police	0.0	89.2	10.6	0.1	0.1
Idaho State Police	0.0	96.8	0.0	2.6	0.5
Illinois State Police	0.8	82.6	11.6	4.8	0.1
Indiana State Police	0.0	91.3	8.2	0.5	0.0
Iowa State Patrol	0.2	98.1	1.0	0.7	0.0
Kansas Highway Patrol	0.0	97.3	1.0	1.2	0.5
Kentucky State Police	0.1	96.3	3.2	0.3	0.0
Louisiana State Police	0.0	86.9	12.9	0.3	0.0
Maine State Police	0.0	100.0	0.0	0.0	0.0
Maryland State Police	0.2	82.5	16.7	0.2	0.2
Massachusetts State Police	0.0	92.3	5.4	1.8	0.4
Michigan State Police	0.2	87.5	8.7	2.7	0.9
Minnesota State Patrol	0.0	97.5	1.0	0.4	1.2
Mississippi Highway Safety Patrol	0.0	77.5	22.5	0.0	0.0
Missouri State Highway Patrol	0.1	90.7	7.3	0.8	1.0
Montana Highway Patrol	0.0	98.0	0.0	0.0	2.0
Nebraska State Patrol	0.0	97.8	0.6	1.3	0.2
Nevada Highway Patrol	1.5	90.6	2.3	4.5	1.1
New Hampshire State Police	0.0	99.2	0.4	0.0	0.4
New Jersey State Police	0.8	86.5	7.9	4.2	0.5
New Mexico State Police	0.0	70.7	1.1	26.7	1.6
New York State Police	0.1	83.1	10.0	6.6	0.3
North Carolina State Highway Patrol	0.1	86.2	12.5	0.0	1.2
North Dakota Highway Patrol	0.0	96.5	0.0	0.0	3.5
Ohio State Highway Patrol	0.5	90.5	7.9	1.0	0.1
Oklahoma Highway Patrol	0.1	88.8	4.6	0.6	5.9
Oregon State Police	1.0	96.7	0.6	1.1	0.6
Pennsylvania State Police	0.4	89.6	8.3	1.5	0.1

[Continued]

306

★ 401 ★

State Law Enforcement Agency Employees, 1990 (Continued)

Number of state law enforcement agency full-time sworn employees (in agencies with 100 or more officers) by state agency, in percent by race/ethnicity, 1990.

Name of agency	Full-time sworn employees, in percent				
	Asian/Pacific Islander	White, non-Hispanic	Black, non-Hispanic	Hispanic, any race	American Indian/Alaskan Native
Rhode Island State Police	0.0	95.6	2.2	2.2	0.0
South Carolina Highway Patrol	0.0	86.5	13.3	0.2	0.0
South Dakota Highway Patrol	0.0	98.6	0.0	0.0	1.4
Tennessee Department of Safety	0.2	93.0	6.4	0.4	0.0
Texas Department of Public Safety	0.2	76.8	5.9	16.7	0.4
Utah Highway Patrol	0.6	96.3	0.0	2.2	0.9
Vermont Department of Public Safety	0.0	98.0	2.0	0.0	0.0
Virginia State Police	0.0	93.0	6.8	0.1	0.1
Washington State Patrol	1.1	92.6	3.0	1.5	1.7
West Virginia State Police	0.0	98.1	1.7	0.2	0.0
Wisconsin State Patrol	0.4	93.8	2.1	1.7	2.1
Wyoming Highway Patrol	0.0	99.3	0.7	0.0	0.0

Source: Brian A. Reaves, U.S. Department of Justice, Office of Justice Programs, Bureau of Justice Statistics, NCJ-134436, *Law Enforcement Management and Administrative Statistics, 1990: Data for Individual State and Local Agencies with 100 or More Officers* (Washington, DC: U.S. Department of Justice, September 1992), table 4a, p. 37. Percentages are based on employee counts for the pay period that included June 15, 1990. Detail may not add to 100% because of rounding. A dash (–) indicates information on race and ethnicity of sworn employees was not provided by an agency. Pecentages are based on employee counts for the pay period that included June 15, 1990. Detail may not add to 100% because of rounding. Data are from the 1990 Law Enforcement Management and Administrative Statistics (LEMAS) survey questionnaire mailed to all 780 state and local law enforcement agencies that reported employing ten or more sworn officers in the *1986 Directory Survey of Law Enforcement Agencies*. Local law enforcement agencies are included from all states except North Dakota, Vermont, and Wyoming; these States had no local law enforcement agencies that met the criteria of the survey.

★ 402 ★

Law Enforcement Agency Employees by Locality, 1990

Number of state and local law enforcement agency full-time sworn employees (in agencies with 100 or more officers) by locality, in percent by race/ethnicity, 1990.

State\locality	Department	Full-time sworn employees, percent				
		Asian/ Pacific Islander	White, non-Hispanic	Black, non-Hispanic	Hispanic, any race	American Indian/Alaskan Native
Alabama						
Jefferson	Jefferson County Sheriff	0.0	74.9	25.1	0.0	0.0
Jefferson	Birmingham Police	0.3	64.0	35.7	0.0	0.0
Madison	Huntsville Police	0.0	94.0	5.3	0.4	0.4
Mobile	Mobile County Sheriff	0.0	87.9	12.1	0.0	0.0
Mobile	Mobile Police	0.0	80.0	19.7.	0.0	0.3
Montgomery	Montgomery County Sheriff	0.0	50.3	49.7	0.0	0.0
Montgomery	Montgomery Police	0.0	73.2	26.8	0.0	0.0
Tuscaloosa	Tuscaloosa Police	0.0	80.4	18.5	1.2	0.0
Alaska						
Anchorage	Anchorage Police	2.6	89.5	4.1	1.9	1.9
Arizona						
Maricopa	Maricopa County Sheriff	0.2	90.6	1.4	7.0	0.7
Maricopa	Glendale Police	0.0	90.2	1.1	8.7	0.0
Maricopa	Mesa Police	0.3	91.9	1.0	6.0	0.8
Maricopa	Phoenix Police	0.6	84.5	3.6	11.0	0.4
Maricopa	Scottsdale Police	0.6	98.3	0.0	1.2	0.0
Maricopa	Tempe Police	0.4	94.9	1.3	3.4	0.0
Pima	Pima County Sheriff	1.2	76.9	3.3	17.5	1.2
Pima	Tucson Police	0.7	75.6	3.1	20.0	0.7
Pinal	Pinal County Sheriff	0.9	80.6	1.9	16.7	0.0
Arkansas						
Jefferson	Pine Bluff Police	0.0	82.0	18.0	0.0	0.0
Pulaski	Pulaski County Sheriff	0.0	82.0	18.0	0.0	0.0
Pulaski	Little Rock Police	0.0	91.1	8.9	0.0	0.0
Pulaski	North Little Rock Police	0.8	92.7	6.5	0.0	0.0
Sebastian	Fort Smith Police	0.0	95.4	4.6	0.0	0.0
California						
Alameda	Alameda County Sheriff	3.6	74.7	13.8	7.4	0.5
Alameda	Berkeley Police	10.7	60.7	21.3	6.2	1.1
Alameda	Fremont Police	3.2	79.5	3.2	10.9	3.2
Alameda	Hayward Police	3.7	80.7	2.5	12.4	0.6
Alameda	Oakland Police	8.0	55.4	25.3	10.7	0.6
Contra Costa	Contra Costa County Sheriff	0.0	83.2	9.8	5.4	1.6
Contra Costa	Concord Police	1.4	94.5	0.7	2.8	0.7
Contra Costa	Richmond Police	5.0	54.7	27.9	10.1	2.2
El Dorado	El Dorado County Sheriff	0.0	96.2	0.8	2.3	0.8
Fresno	Fresno Police	1.4	69.9	7.7	20.3	0.7
Imperial	Imperial County Sheriff	0.0	44.2	5.4	48.1	2.3
Kern	Kern County Sheriff	1.3	85.9	1.7	10.0	1.1
Kern	Bakersfield Police	0.8	87.3	4.7	6.4	0.8

[Continued]

★ 402 ★

Law Enforcement Agency Employees by Locality, 1990 (Continued)

Number of state and local law enforcement agency full-time sworn employees (in agencies with 100 or more officers) by locality, in percent by race/ethnicity, 1990.

State\locality	Department	Full-time sworn employees, percent				
		Asian/ Pacific Islander	White, non-Hispanic	Black, non-Hispanic	Hispanic, any race	American Indian/Alaskan Native
Los Angeles	Los Angeles County Sheriff	2.1	74.1	9.2	14.4	0.1
Los Angeles	Beverly Hills Police	4.0	86.5	2.4	7.1	0.0
Los Angeles	Burbank Police	2.1	89.0	1.4	6.2	1.4
Los Angeles	Compton Police	3.2	24.6	59.5	12.7	0.0
Los Angeles	El Monte Police	1.8	76.1	1.8	20.4	0.0
Los Angeles	Glendale Police	5.4	78.4	3.9	11.8	0.5
Los Angeles	Inglewood Police	3.9	64.6	19.9	11.2	0.5
Los Angeles	Long Beach Police	1.4	82.7	5.3	10.1	0.5
Los Angeles	Los Angeles Airport Police	5.9	26.5	53.4	14.2	0.0
Los Angeles	Los Angeles Police	2.8	62.5	13.4	21.0	0.3
Los Angeles	Pasadena Police	1.4	57.2	18.9	22.5	0.0
Los Angeles	Pomona Police	1.7	86.0	3.5	8.7	0.0
Los Angeles	Santa Monica Police	1.9	71.4	9.3	16.1	1.2
Los Angeles	Torrance Police	2.1	90.2	1.5	5.7	0.5
Los Angeles	West Covina Police	0.0	85.3	4.6	10.1	0.0
Los Angeles	Downey Police	1.0	84.8	0.0	12.4	1.9
Los Angeles	Los Angeles School Police	1.7	30.4	48.1	19.7	0.0
Marin	Marin County Sheriff	1.1	89.1	4.0	5.1	0.6
Monterey	Monterey County Sheriff	3.5	68.9	11.4	16.3	0.0
Monterey	Salinas Police	5.3	81.1	2.3	11.4	0.0
Orange	Orange County Sheriff	2.4	80.3	3.7	12.5	1.1
Orange	Costa Mesa Police	3.5	90.1	2.1	4.3	0.0
Orange	Fullerton Police	2.0	87.4	0.0	9.9	0.7
Orange	Garden Grove Police	3.6	86.3	1.8	8.3	0.0
Orange	Huntington Beach Police	1.8	93.2	1.8	2.7	0.5
Orange	Newport Beach Police	0.0	96.0	0.7	3.4	0.0
Orange	Orange Police	0.7	90.7	1.3	7.3	0.0
Orange	Santa Ana Police	2.1	70.4	2.4	24.6	0.5
Riverside	Riverside County Sheriff	1.5	75.6	8.0	14.5	0.5
Riverside	Riverside Police	1.0	76.1	7.7	15.2	0.0
Sacramento	Sacramento County Sheriff	4.3	83.3	4.1	7.1	1.2
Sacramento	Sacramento Police	7.5	74.3	6.3	11.9	0.0
San Bernardino	San Bernardino County Sheriff	1.2	80.7	4.1	11.3	2.6
San Bernardino	Ontario Police	0.0	84.0	13.3	2.8	0.0
San Bernardino	San Bernardino Police	1.3	78.2	5.9	14.2	0.4
San Diego	San Diego County Sheriff	3.2	73.2	7.6	14.8	1.2
San Diego	Oceanside Police	2.2	79.9	2.7	13.0	2.2
San Diego	San Diego Police	4.0	76.0	7.7	11.4	0.9
San Francisco	San Francisco Airport Police	10.1	70.3	14.2	5.4	0.0
San Francisco	San Francisco Police	10.5	70.1	8.8	10.1	0.5
San Francisco	Bay Area Rapid Transit Police	8.6	62.6	20.9	6.5	1.4
San Joaquin	San Joaquin County Sheriff	1.2	84.5	3.3	11.0	0.0
San Joaquin	Stockton Police	0.0	89.7	9.1	1.2	0.0
San Luis Obispo	San Luis Obispo County Sheriff	0.0	90.2	0.8	4.9	4.1

[Continued]

★ 402 ★

Law Enforcement Agency Employees by Locality, 1990 (Continued)

Number of state and local law enforcement agency full-time sworn employees (in agencies with 100 or more officers) by locality, in percent by race/ethnicity, 1990.

State\locality	Department	Full-time sworn employees, percent				
		Asian/ Pacific Islander	White, non-Hispanic	Black, non-Hispanic	Hispanic, any race	American Indian/Alaskan Native
San Mateo	San Mateo County Sheriff	1.8	82.6	7.6	8.0	0.0
San Mateo	San Mateo Police	0.0	89.2	3.6	4.5	2.7
Santa Barbara	Santa Barbara County Sheriff	0.0	46.4	26.6	26.9	0.0
Santa Barbara	Santa Barbara Police	3.6	84.8	2.2	9.4	0.0
Santa Clara	Santa Clara County Sheriff	2.6	75.7	3.4	17.6	0.8
Santa Clara	San Jose Police	5.9	70.5	3.8	19.3	0.6
Santa Clara	Santa Clara Police	2.1	91.0	1.4	5.6	0.0
Santa Clara	Sunnyvale Police	1.7	92.2	3.5	2.6	0.0
Santa Cruz	Santa Cruz County Sheriff	2.4	87.2	1.6	8.0	0.8
Shasta	Shasta County Sheriff	0.0	96.8	0.0	3.2	0.0
Solano	Vallejo Police	6.1	67.2	15.3	10.7	0.8
Sonoma	Sonoma County Sheriff	0.0	93.0	0.0	5.0	2.0
Sonoma	Santa Rosa Police	--	--	--	--	--
Stanislaus	Stanislaus County Sheriff	1.1	82.0	5.4	10.3	1.1
Stanislaus	Modesto Police	1.1	88.9	1.6	7.4	1.1
Tulare	Tulare County Sheriff	0.5	77.9	1.3	18.4	1.9
Ventura	Ventura County Sheriff	1.7	85.7	2.0	10.4	0.2
Ventura	Oxnard Police	2.8	74.5	4.8	15.9	2.1
Ventura	Ventura Police	1.7	85.1	2.5	9.9	0.8
Colorado						
Adams	Adams County Sheriff	0.0	88.3	1.3	10.4	0.0
Adams	Westminister Police	1.9	92.4	1.0	4.8	0.0
Arapahoe	Arapahoe County Sheriff	1.3	86.7	6.0	5.4	0.6
Arapahoe	Aurora Police	0.5	92.8	2.3	3.3	1.0
Boulder	Boulder County Sheriff	--	--	--	--	--
Boulder	Boulder Police	0.8	87.5	5.8	5.0	0.8
Denver	Denver Police	0.2	76.3	6.8	16.2	0.5
El Paso	El Paso County Sheriff	0.3	87.6	8.3	3.2	0.6
El Paso	Colorado Springs Police	0.5	85.7	4.9	8.4	0.5
Jefferson	Jefferson County Sheriff	0.6	95.9	1.2	1.8	0.6
Jefferson	Arvada Police	0.0	95.7	0.0	2.6	1.7
Jefferson	Lakewood Police	0.5	95.8	1.0	2.6	0.0
Larimer	Larimer County Sheriff	1.5	96.9	0.0	1.5	0.0
Pueblo	Pueblo Police	0.0	79.6	0.0	19.8	0.6
Connecticut						
Fairfield	Bridgeport Police	0.0	70.2	14.7	15.2	0.0
Fairfield	Danbury Police	0.0	91.9	5.2	3.0	0.0
Fairfield	Norwalk Police	0.6	79.9	12.8	6.1	0.6
Fairfield	Stamford Police	0.0	88.3	4.0	7.4	0.3
Fairfield	Greenwich Police	0.0	94.9	4.4	0.6	0.0
Fairfield	Stratford Police	0.0	92.0	3.0	4.0	1.0
Hartford	Hartford Police	0.0	70.0	16.3	13.8	0.0
Hartford	New Britain Police	0.0	93.7	3.5	2.8	0.0

[Continued]

★ 402 ★

Law Enforcement Agency Employees by Locality, 1990 (Continued)

Number of state and local law enforcement agency full-time sworn employees (in agencies with 100 or more officers) by locality, in percent by race/ethnicity, 1990.

State\locality	Department	Full-time sworn employees, percent				
		Asian/ Pacific Islander	White, non-Hispanic	Black, non-Hispanic	Hispanic, any race	American Indian/Alas-kan Native
Hartford	East Hartford Police	0.0	93.7	2.7	2.7	0.9
Hartford	West Hartford Police	0.0	95.1	3.3	1.6	0.0
New Haven	Meriden Police	0.0	90.6	4.3	5.1	0.0
New Haven	New Haven Police	0.0	79.2	17.4	3.3	0.0
New Haven	Waterbury Police	0.0	81.0	6.0	13.0	0.0
New Haven	Milford Police	0.0	99.1	0.0	0.9	0.0
New Haven	West Haven Police	0.0	94.3	4.7	0.9	0.0
New Haven	Hamden Police	0.0	98.0	2.0	0.0	0.0
Delaware						
New Castle	New Castle County Police	0.0	87.8	9.2	2.9	0.0
New Castle	Wilmington Police	0.4	66.0	28.2	5.0	0.4
District of Columbia						
Washington, DC	Metropolitan Airports Authority	0.0	71.3	14.6	14.0	0.0
Washington, DC	Washington Metropolitan Police	0.8	32.2	64.4	2.6	0.1
Washington, DC	Metro Transit Police	0.4	62.0	36.9	0.8	0.0
Florida						
Alachua	Alachua County Sheriff	1.0	85.4	12.5	0.5	0.5
Alachua	Gainesville Police	1.0	82.7	12.4	3.5	0.5
Brevard	Brevard County Sheriff	0.0	94.4	5.6	0.0	0.0
Broward	Broward County Sheriff	0.1	78.2	16.8	4.9	0.0
Broward	Fort Lauderdale Police	0.2	86.3	8.6	4.6	0.2
Broward	Hollywood Police	0.7	87.7	6.0	5.3	0.4
Broward	Pompano Beach Police	0.0	81.5	12.2	6.3	0.0
Broward	Plantation Police	0.8	95.5	2.3	1.5	0.0
Broward	Coral Springs Police	0.0	98.0	1.3	0.7	0.0
Broward	Sunrise Police	0.8	92.0	3.2	4.0	0.0
Charlotte	Charlotte County Sheriff	0.0	95.2	3.2	1.6	0.0
Citrus	Citrus County Sheriff	0.0	94.3	5.0	0.6	0.0
Collier	Collier County Sheriff	0.2	90.8	2.0	6.5	0.4
Dade	Metro-Dade Police	0.0	59.2	14.9	25.5	0.3
Dade	Coral Gables Police	0.0	80.5	2.3	17.3	0.0
Dade	Hialeah Police	0.0	60.0	1.9	38.1	0.0
Dade	Miami Police	0.3	35.3	19.9	44.5	0.0
Dade	Miami Beach Police	0.0	81.8	1.6	16.6	0.0
Dade	North Miami Police	0.0	82.4	5.9	11.8	0.0
Duval	Jacksonville Sheriff	0.3	81.1	17.5	1.1	0.0
Escambia	Escambia County Sheriff	0.4	91.9	6.5	0.8	0.4
Escambia	Pensacola Police	0.0	89.6	10.4	0.0	0.0
Hillsborough	Hillsborough County Sheriff	0.3	75.0	12.8	11.0	0.9
Hillsborough	Tampa Police	0.2	76.3	11.8	11.3	0.4
Indian River	Indian River County Sheriff	0.0	91.5	8.5	0.0	0.0
Lee	Lee County Sheriff	0.9	92.2	4.0	2.8	0.0

[Continued]

★ 402 ★

Law Enforcement Agency Employees by Locality, 1990 (Continued)

Number of state and local law enforcement agency full-time sworn employees (in agencies with 100 or more officers) by locality, in percent by race/ethnicity, 1990.

State\locality	Department	Full-time sworn employees, percent				
		Asian/ Pacific Islander	White, non-Hispanic	Black, non-Hispanic	Hispanic, any race	American Indian/Alaskan Native
Lee	Fort Myers Police	0.0	94.1	5.1	0.7	0.0
Leon	Tallahassee Police	0.0	78.5	19.8	1.7	0.0
Marion	Marion County Sheriff	0.0	92.6	4.9	2.5	0.0
Marion	Ocala Police	0.0	85.7	14.3	0.0	0.0
Martin	Martin County Sheriff	0.0	93.3	4.2	2.4	0.0
Orange	Orange County Sheriff	0.0	90.1	6.1	3.7	0.0
Orange	Orlando Police	0.8	79.4	14.4	5.1	0.4
Palm Beach	Palm Beach County Sheriff	0.1	77.0	17.5	5.4	0.0
Palm Beach	Boca Raton Police	1.6	87.1	4.8	6.5	0.0
Palm Beach	West Palm Beach Police	0.0	78.5	15.1	6.4	0.0
Pasco	Pasco County Sheriff	0.0	96.6	2.7	0.7	0.0
Pinellas	Pinellas County Sheriff	0.2	90.0	7.1	2.4	0.3
Pinellas	Clearwater Police	0.4	92.0	6.3	1.3	0.0
Pinellas	St. Petersburg Police	0.8	85.8	11.7	1.1	0.6
Polk	Polk County Sheriff	0.0	90.8	7.5	1.7	0.0
Polk	Lakeland Police	1.0	92.4	5.1	1.5	0.0
Sarasota	Sarasota County Sheriff	0.8	97.1	2.1	0.0	0.0
Sarasota	Sarasota Police	0.0	92.1	7.3	0.5	0.0
Seminole	Seminole County Sheriff	1.1	89.8	5.9	3.2	0.0
St. John	St. John County Sheriff	0.5	93.7	4.7	1.0	0.0
St. Lucie	St. Lucie County Sheriff	0.0	84.5	14.1	1.0	0.3
Volusia	Volusia County Sheriff	0.4	93.4	5.8	0.0	0.4
Volusia	Daytona Beach Police	0.0	87.1	10.4	2.5	0.0
Georgia						
Bibb	Bibb County Sheriff	0.6	65.0	34.4	0.0	0.0
Bibb	Macon Police	0.0	68.8	29.6	1.5	0.0
Chatham	Chatham County Police	0.0	69.2	30.8	0.0	0.0
Chatham	Savannah Police	0.9	62.0	35.6	1.5	0.0
Clayton	Clayton County Police	0.5	89.4	8.6	1.0	0.5
Cobb	Cobb County Sheriff	0.0	94.4	4.5	1.1	0.0
Cobb	Cobb County Police	0.3	95.8	3.3	0.6	0.0
De Kalb	De Kalb County Police	0.0	79.3	20.4	0.3	0.0
Dougherty	Albany Police	0.5	58.2	39.2	1.1	1.1
Fulton	Fulton County Police	0.0	81.2	17.9	1.0	0.0
Fulton	Atlanta Police	0.0	45.8	52.5	1.6	0.1
Gwinnett	Gwinnett County Police	0.0	93.9	6.1	0.0	0.0
Muscogee	Columbus Police	0.0	72.1	27.4	0.5	0.0
Richmond	Richmond County Sheriff	0.0	84.0	16.0	0.0	0.0
Richmond	Augusta Police	0.0	62.8	35.8	1.4	0.0
Hawaii						
Hawaii	Hawaii Police	98.1	1.9	0.0	0.0	0.0
Honolulu	Honolulu Police	78.5	19.6	0.8	1.1	0.0
Kauai	Kauai County Police	57.9	35.7	1.4	5.0	0.0
Maui	Maui County Police	52.8	41.1	0.0	6.0	0.0

[Continued]

★ 402 ★

Law Enforcement Agency Employees by Locality, 1990 (Continued)

Number of state and local law enforcement agency full-time sworn employees (in agencies with 100 or more officers) by locality, in percent by race/ethnicity, 1990.

State\locality	Department	Full-time sworn employees, percent				
		Asian/ Pacific Islander	White, non-Hispanic	Black, non-Hispanic	Hispanic, any race	American Indian/Alaskan Native
Idaho						
Ada	Ada County Sheriff	1.6	93.7	0.0	2.4	2.4
Ada	Boise Police	1.9	96.2	0.6	1.3	0.0
Illinois						
Cook	Cook County Sheriff	--	--	--	--	--
Cook	Cook County Police	0.0	78.1	16.8	4.9	0.2
Cook	Chicago Police	0.4	69.6	23.6	6.3	0.1
Cook	Evanston Police	0.6	74.1	22.8	2.5	0.0
Cook	Oak Park Police	0.9	83.2	12.4	3.5	0.0
Cook	Skokie Police	1.0	93.3	1.9	3.8	0.0
Cook	Schaumburg Police	0.0	97.7	0.0	2.3	0.0
Du Page	Du Page County Sheriff	0.0	95.9	1.7	2.5	0.0
Kane	Kane County Sheriff	0.0	86.7	8.3	5.0	0.0
Kane	Aurora Police	0.0	87.0	6.7	6.2	0.0
Kane	Elgin Police	0.0	89.3	7.8	2.9	0.0
Lake	Lake County Sheriff	0.0	91.9	6.5	1.1	0.5
Lake	Waukegan Police	0.0	82.5	13.3	4.2	0.0
Macon	Decatur Police	0.0	96.4	3.6	0.0	0.0
Peoria	Peoria Police	0.0	93.7	4.9	1.0	0.5
Sangamon	Springfield Police	0.0	94.5	5.5	0.0	0.0
Will	Will County Sheriff	0.3	92.8	5.1	1.8	0.0
Will	Joliet Police	0.0	89.2	10.8	0.0	0.0
Winnebago	Rockford Police	0.0	87.9	6.0	5.2	0.8
Indiana						
Allen	Allen County Sheriff	0.0	95.8	2.5	0.8	0.8
Allen	Fort Wayne Police	0.0	78.8	17.6	3.3	0.3
Delaware	Muncie Police	0.0	90.4	9.6	0.0	0.0
Howard	Kokomo Police	0.0	92.0	5.0	1.0	2.0
Lake	Lake County Sheriff	0.0	80.6	14.1	5.3	0.0
Lake	East Chicago Police	0.0	37.3	31.4	31.4	0.0
Lake	Gary Police	0.0	26.0	67.3	6.7	0.0
Lake	Hammond Police	0.0	90.8	2.7	6.0	0.5
Madison	Anderson Police	0.0	93.8	6.2	0.0	0.0
Marion	Indianapolis Police	0.0	83.5	15.8	0.7	0.0
Marion	Marion County Sheriff	0.0	92.1	7.7	0.2	0.0
St. Joseph	St. Joseph County Police	0.0	93.5	4.9	1.6	0.0
St. Joseph	South Bend Police	0.0	84.1	15.0	0.9	0.0
Vanderburgh	Vanderburgh County Sheriff	0.0	93.1	6.9	0.0	0.0
Vanderburgh	Evansville Police	0.0	95.9	4.1	0.0	0.0
Vigo	Terre Haute Police	0.0	98.3	1.7	0.0	0.0
Iowa						
Black Hawk	Waterloo Police	0.0	97.4	2.6	0.0	0.0

[Continued]

★ 402 ★

Law Enforcement Agency Employees by Locality, 1990 (Continued)

Number of state and local law enforcement agency full-time sworn employees (in agencies with 100 or more officers) by locality, in percent by race/ethnicity, 1990.

State\locality	Department	Full-time sworn employees, percent				
		Asian/ Pacific Islander	White, non-Hispanic	Black, non-Hispanic	Hispanic, any race	American Indian/Alaskan Native
Linn	Cedar Rapids Police	0.0	98.0	2.0	0.0	0.0
Polk	Polk County Sheriff	0.0	95.4	3.1	1.5	0.0
Polk	Des Moines Police	0.3	92.6	4.0	2.9	0.3
Scott	Davenport Police	0.0	95.1	2.8	1.4	0.7
Woodbury	Sioux City Police	0.0	97.3	0.0	0.0	2.7
Kansas						
Johnson	Johnson County Sheriff	0.5	96.4	2.7	0.0	0.5
Johnson	Overland Park Police	0.0	92.4	4.6	3.1	0.0
Sedgwick	Sedgwick County Sheriff	0.0	93.0	4.2	2.1	0.7
Sedgwick	Wichita Police	0.0	92.2	4.7	2.8	0.2
Shawnee	Topeka Police	0.4	93.8	2.3	3.5	0.0
Wyandotte	Kansas City Police	0.0	74.7	21.2	3.7	0.3
Kentucky						
Jefferson	Jefferson County Police	0.0	82.3	17.7	0.0	0.0
Jefferson	Louisville Police	0.0	83.5	16.5	0.0	0.0
Lexington	Lexington Police	0.3	89.1	10.6	0.0	0.0
Lousiana						
Ascension	Ascension Parish Sheriff	0.0	83.0	17.0	0.0	0.0
Bossier	Bossier Police	0.8	88.1	9.3	0.8	0.8
Caddo	Caddo Parish Sheriff	0.0	74.0	25.2	0.7	0.0
Caddo	Shreveport Police	0.7	69.1	30.2	0.0	0.0
Calcasieu	Calcasieu Parish Sheriff	0.0	83.5	16.2	0.3	0.0
Calcasieu	Lake Charles Police	0.0	76.0	23.3	0.0	0.8
E. Baton Rouge	E. Baton Rouge Parish Sheriff	0.2	88.3	11.5	0.0	0.0
E. Baton Rouge	Baton Rouge Police	0.0	77.8	21.3	0.7	0.2
Jefferson	Jefferson Parish Sheriff	0.4	85.7	12.9	1.1	0.0
Jefferson	Kenner Police	0.0	89.7	10.3	0.0	0.0
Lafayette	Lafayette Parish Sheriff	0.0	88.4	11.6	0.0	0.0
Lafayette	Lafayette Police	0.0	90.1	9.9	0.0	0.0
Lafourche	Lafourche Parish Sheriff	0.0	81.9	18.1	0.0	0.0
Orleans	New Orleans Police	0.1	59.9	39.4	0.6	0.0
Ouachita	Ouachita Parish Sheriff	0.0	87.5	12.5	0.0	0.0
Ouachita	Monroe Police	0.0	78.4	21.6	0.0	0.0
Plaquemines	Plaquemines Parish Sheriff	0.7	58.9	40.4	0.0	0.0
Rapides	Rapides Parish Sheriff	0.0	80.7	19.3	0.0	0.0
Rapides	Alexandria Police	0.0	84.1	15.9	0.0	0.0
St. John	St. John Parish Sheriff	0.0	71.9	28.1	0.0	0.0
St. Bernard	St. Bernard Parish Sheriff	0.0	99.4	0.6	0.0	0.0
St. Tammany	St. Tammany Parish Sheriff	0.0	90.0	9.6	0.4	0.0
Terrebonne	Terrebonne Parish Sheriff	0.0	75.1	24.9	0.0	0.0

[Continued]

★ 402 ★

Law Enforcement Agency Employees by Locality, 1990 (Continued)

Number of state and local law enforcement agency full-time sworn employees (in agencies with 100 or more officers) by locality, in percent by race/ethnicity, 1990.

State\locality	Department	Full-time sworn employees, percent				
		Asian/ Pacific Islander	White, non-Hispanic	Black, non-Hispanic	Hispanic, any race	American Indian/Alaskan Native
Maine						
Cumberland	Portland Police	0.0	99.3	0.7	0.0	0.0
Maryland						
Anne Arundel	Anne Arundel County Police	0.2	92.3	6.6	0.4	0.6
Baltimore (city)	Baltimore Police	0.3	72.3	26.5	0.5	0.4
Baltimore	Baltimore County Police	0.1	92.7	6.7	0.6	0.0
Charles	Charles County Sheriff	0.7	86.6	11.2	1.5	0.0
Harford	Harford County Sheriff	0.4	88.8	10.8	0.0	0.0
Howard	Howard County Police	0.4	87.5	11.0	1.1	0.0
Montgomery	Montgomery County Police	0.8	86.5	11.1	1.1	0.5
Prince George's	Prince George's County Police	0.5	65.6	32.5	1.3	0.1
Massachusetts						
Bristol	Fall River Police	0.0	97.9	2.1	0.0	0.0
Bristol	New Bedford Police	0.0	81.4	16.9	1.7	0.0
Essex	Lawrence Police	0.0	94.7	1.5	3.8	0.0
Essex	Lynn Police	0.0	89.5	7.2	3.3	0.0
Hampden	Chicopee Police	0.0	95.8	1.7	2.5	0.0
Hampden	Holyoke Police	0.0	80.0	18.0	2.0	0.0
Hampden	Springfield Police	0.0	84.9	10.0	5.1	0.0
Middlesex	Cambridge Police	0..0	82.3	17.0	0.7	0.0
Middlesex	Lowell Police	0.0	93.2	0.6	6.2	0.0
Middlesex	Malden Police	0.0	98.3	1.7	0.0	0.0
Middlesex	Medford Police	0.0	94.1	4.2	1.7	0.0
Middlesex	Newton Police	1.5	94.1	2.9	1.5	0.0
Middlesex	Somerville Police	0.0	96.3	3.0	0.7	0.0
Middlesex	Waltham Police	0.0	94.4	4.2	1.4	0.0
Middlesex	Framingham Police	0.0	93.5	4.6	0.9	0.9
Norfolk	Brookline Police	0.0	96.4	3.6	0.0	0.0
Norfolk	Weymouth Police	0.0	98.0	1.0	1.0	0.0
Plymouth	Brockton Police	0.0	91.5	7.1	1.4	0.0
Suffolk	Boston Police	0.6	74.1	20.5	4.8	0.0
Suffolk	Mass. Bay Transit Authority	1.4	76.6	15.6	6.4	0.0
Worcester	Worcester Police	0.0	92.9	5.1	2.0	0.0
Michigan						
Calhoun	Battle Creek Police	1.8	83.6	12.7	1.8	0.0
Genesee	Flint Police	0.3	69.5	27.3	2.9	0.0
Ingham	Ingham County Sheriff	0.0	84.6	12.0	3.4	0.0
Ingham	Lansing Police	0.4	88.4	5.6	4.0	1.6
Kalamazoo	Kalamazoo County Sheriff	0.0	92.3	7.7	0.0	0.0
Kalamazoo	Kalamazoo Police	0.0	82.1	15.4	2.1	0.4
Kent	Kent County Sheriff	0.4	96.7	1.8	0.7	0.4
Kent	Grand Rapids Police	1.4	88.5	7.2	1.1	1.8
Macomb	Macomb County Sheriff	0.0	98.2	1.8	0.0	0.0

[Continued]

★ 402 ★

Law Enforcement Agency Employees by Locality, 1990 (Continued)

Number of state and local law enforcement agency full-time sworn employees (in agencies with 100 or more officers) by locality, in percent by race/ethnicity, 1990.

State\locality	Department	Full-time sworn employees, percent				
		Asian/ Pacific Islander	White, non-Hispanic	Black, non-Hispanic	Hispanic, any race	American Indian/Alaskan Native
Macomb	Warren Police	0.0	99.6	0.0	0.4	0.0
Macomb	Sterling Heights Police	1.3	98.1	0.0	0.6	0.0
Oakland	Oakland County Sheriff	0.2	88.2	9.2	1.6	0.9
Oakland	Pontiac Police	0.0	70.4	23.3	6.3	0.0
Oakland	Troy Police	0.0	99.2	0.8	0.0	0.0
Oakland	Southfield Police	0.0	97.0	3.0	0.0	0.0
Saginaw	Saginaw Police	0.0	68.9	24.6	5.7	0.8
Washtenaw	Washtenaw County Sheriff	1.1	79.6	17.7	1.6	0.0
Washtenaw	Ann Arbor Police	1.2	89.4	7.6	1.8	0.0
Wayne	Wayne County Sheriff	0.3	57.2	42.1	0.5	0.0
Wayne	Dearborn Police	0.0	97.5	0.5	2.0	0.0
Wayne	Detroit Police	0.2	46.6	51.8	1.3	0.2
Wayne	Highland Park Police	0.0	43.6	56.4	0.0	0.0
Wayne	Livonia Police	0.0	100	0.0	0.0	0.0
Wayne	Taylor Police	0.0	100	0.0	0.0	0.0
Minnesota						
Hennepin	Minneapolis Police	0.5	91.6	3.2	2.1	2.6
Ramsey	Ramsey County Sheriff	0.4	93.0	2.2	3.0	1.3
Ramsey	St. Paul Police	1.1	90.8	4.9	2.3	0.9
St. Louis	Duluth Police	0.0	97.6	0.8	0.0	1.6
Mississippi						
Harrison	Harrison County Sheriff	0.0	85.0	15.0	0.0	0.0
Hinds	Jackson Police	0.0	62.9	37.1	0.0	0.0
Misouri						
Buchanan	St. Joseph Police	1.0	97.0	0.0	2.0	0.0
Greene	Springfield Police	0.0	97.8	1.1	1.1	0.0
Jackson	Independence Police	0.6	98.7	0.6	0.0	0.0
Jackson	Kansas City Police	0.2	84.5	12.9	2.3	0.2
St. Louis (city)	St. Louis Police	0.0	73.2	26.3	0.5	0.0
St. Louis	St. Louis County Police	0.2	93.1	5.6	0.9	0.2
Montana						
Yellowstone	Billings Police	1.0	96.1	1.0	1.9	0.0
Nebraska						
Douglas	Omaha Police	0.0	86.0	10.8	2.7	0.5
Lancaster	Lincoln Police	0.8	95.0	2.5	1.3	0.4
Nevada						
Clark	Las Vegas Metropolitan Police	1.1	86.6	7.5	3.7	1.1
Clark	North Las Vegas Police	0.0	83.5	11.0	5.5	0.0
Washoe	Washoe County Sheriff	0.0	92.8	2.5	3.1	1.6
Washoe	Reno Police	0.7	92.0	2.3	3.3	1.7

[Continued]

★ 402 ★

Law Enforcement Agency Employees by Locality, 1990 (Continued)

Number of state and local law enforcement agency full-time sworn employees (in agencies with 100 or more officers) by locality, in percent by race/ethnicity, 1990.

State\locality	Department	Full-time sworn employees, percent				
		Asian/ Pacific Islander	White, non-Hispanic	Black, non-Hispanic	Hispanic, any race	American Indian/Alaskan Native
New Hampshire						
Hillsborough	Manchester Police	0.0	98.8	0.6	0.0	0.6
Hillsborough	Nashua Police	0.0	98.1	0.6	1.3	0.0
New Jersey						
Bergen	Bergen County Sheriff	0.0	78.4	20.1	1.6	0.0
Bergen	Hackensack Police	0.0	91.7	5.5	2.8	0.0
Camden	Camden County Prosecutor	0.0	80.0	20.0	0.0	0.0
Camden	Camden County Sheriff	0.0	61.5	33.8	4.7	0.0
Camden	Camden Police	0.3	55.3	33.7	10.7	0.0
Camden	Cherry Hill Police	0.0	97.4	2.6	0.0	0.0
Camden	Delaware River Port Authority	0.7	75.7	20.0	3.6	0.0
Cumberland	Vineland Police	0.0	90.7	0.9	7.5	0.9
Essex	ESsex County Sheriff	0.0	74.0	20.0	6.0	0.0
Essex	Essex County Police	0.0	85.9	11.3	2.8	0.0
Essex	East Orange Police	0.0	43.3	54.7	2.0	0.0
Essex	Newark Police	0.0	58.0	31.3	10.7	0.0
Essex	Bloomfield Police	0.0	96.2	2.9	1.0	0.0
Essex	Irvington Police	0.0	80.1	16.8	3.1	0.0
Hudson	Bayonne Police	0.0	96.9	1.8	2.4	0.0
Hudson	Hoboken Police	0.0	77.9	4.6	17.6	0.0
Hudson	Jersey City Police	0.0	86.6	7.2	6.2	0.0
Hudson	Kearny Police	0.0	99.2	0.0	0.8	0.0
Hudson	Union City Police	0.0	76.4	1.9	21.7	0.0
Hudson	West New York Police	0.0	85.0	0.0	15.0	0.0
Mercer	Trenton Police	0.0	83.2	13.4	3.4	0.0
Mercer	Hamilton Township Police	0.0	98.8	0.6	0.6	0.0
Middlesex	New Brunswick Police	1.6	83.1	10.5	4.8	0.0
Middlesex	Perth Amboy Police	0.0	89.7	1.7	8.6	0.0
Middlesex	Edison Police	--	--	--	--	--
Middlesex	Woodbridge Police	0.0	97.7	0.0	2.3	0.0
Morris	Parsippany - Troy Hills Police	0.9	99.1	0.0	0.0	0.0
Ocean	Dover Township Police	0.0	99.3	0.0	0.7	0.0
Passaic	Passaic County Sheriff	0.0	58.0	21.3	20.8	0.0
Passaic	Clifton Police	0.0	98.6	0.0	1.4	0.0
Passaic	Passaic Police	0.0	66.2	18.8	15.0	0.0
Passaic	Paterson Police	0.3	73.0	14.8	11.6	0.3
Passaic	Wayne Police	0.0	99.0	0.0	1.0	0.0
Union	Elizabeth Police	0.0	86.5	5.1	8.4	0.0
Union	Linden Police	0.0	98.4	1.6	0.0	0.0
Union	Plainfield Police	0.8	56.3	34.1	8.7	0.0
Union	Union Township Police	0.0	96.5	2.6	0.0	0.9

[Continued]

★ 402 ★

Law Enforcement Agency Employees by Locality, 1990 (Continued)

Number of state and local law enforcement agency full-time sworn employees (in agencies with 100 or more officers) by locality, in percent by race/ethnicity, 1990.

State\locality	Department	Full-time sworn employees, percent				
		Asian/ Pacific Islander	White, non-Hispanic	Black, non-Hispanic	Hispanic, any race	American Indian/Alas-kan Native
New Mexico						
Bernalillo	Bernalillo County Sheriff	0.0	60.1	4.2	34.3	1.4
Bernalillo	Albuquerque Police	0.4	58.0	2.4	37.9	1.4
Santa Fe	Santa Fe Police	0.0	32.2	0.0	67.0	0.9
New York						
Albany	Albany Police	0.3	93.4	6.0	0.3	0.0
Broome	Binghamton Police	0.0	100.0	0.0	0.0	0.0
Dutchess	Dutchess County Sheriff	0.0	99.1	0.9	0.0	0.0
Erie	Erie County Sheriff	0.0	87.9	9.9	1.9	0.3
Erie	Buffalo Police	0.0	74.3	19.2	6.0	0.5
Erie	Amherst Police	0.0	100.0	0.0	0.0	0.0
Erie	Cheektowaga Police	0.0	100.0	0.0	0.0	0.0
Monroe	Monroe County Sheriff	0.2	91.3	5.2	3.2	0.2
Monroe	Rochester Police	0.8	77.7	13.2	7.3	1.0
Nassau	Nassau County Police	0.2	95.3	2.5	2.0	0.1
New York City	New York City Housing Police	0.8	67.4	20.1	11.7	0.0
New York City	New York City Transit Police	0.8	66.7	18.5	14.0	0.0
New York City	New York City Social Services	--	--	--	--	--
New York City	New York City Fire Department	0.0	80.4	14.0	5.7	0.0
New York City	New York City Police	0.7	76.2	11.2	11.8	0.1
New York City	Port Authority of NY-NJ	1.9	81.1	11.0	5.0	0.9
Niagara	Niagara Falls Police	0.0	96.1	3.2	0.6	0.0
Oneida	Oneida County Sheriff	0.0	98.1	1.4	0.5	0.0
Onondaga	Onondaga County Sheriff	0.2	95.9	3.3	0.0	0.6
Onondaga	Syracuse Police	0.0	93.3	6.7	0.0	0.0
Rensselaer	Troy Police	0.0	99.2	0.8	0.0	0.0
Rockland	Clarkstown Police	0.0	97.8	0.0	2.2	0.0
Schenectady	Schenectady Police	0.0	98.6	1.4	0.0	0.0
Suffolk	Suffolk County Police	0.2	93.5	2.3	4.0	0.1
Westchester	Westchester County Police	0.0	90.4	6.3	3.3	0.0
Westchester	Mt. Vernon Police	0.6	77.8	16.5	5.1	0.0
Westchester	New Rochelle Police	0.0	86.7	10.1	3.2	0.0
Westchester	White Plains Police	0.0	87.5	8.5	4.0	0.0
Westchester	Yonkers Police	0.2	92.6	5.2	2.1	0.0
North Carolina						
Buncombe	Asheville Police	0.0	93.8	6.3	0.0	0.0
Cumberland	Cumberland County Sheriff	0.0	77.3	18.2	2.0	2.5
Cumberland	Fayetteville Police	2.7	70.5	26.8	0.0	0.0
Durham	Durham Police	0.0	66.1	33.2	0.4	0.4
Forsyth	Winston-Salem Police	0.0	91.0	9.0	0.0	0.0
Gaston	Gastonia Police	0.0	93.1	6.3	0.7	0.0
Guilford	Guilford County Sheriff	0.0	81.9	17.6	0.0	0.5
Guilford	Greensboro Police	0.0	86.1	13.4	0.2	0.2

[Continued]

★ 402 ★

Law Enforcement Agency Employees by Locality, 1990 (Continued)

Number of state and local law enforcement agency full-time sworn employees (in agencies with 100 or more officers) by locality, in percent by race/ethnicity, 1990.

State\locality	Department	Full-time sworn employees, percent				
		Asian/ Pacific Islander	White, non-Hispanic	Black, non-Hispanic	Hispanic, any race	American Indian/Alaskan Native
Guilford	High Point Police	0.0	86.0	13.4	0.6	0.0
Mecklenburg	Mecklenburg County Police	0.0	86.3	11.9	1.9	0.0
Mecklenburg	Charlotte Police	0.0	77.9	22.1	0.0	0.0
Nash	Rocky Mount Police	0.0	76.1	23.9	0.0	0.0
New Hanover	New Hanover County Sheriff	0.0	86.7	13.3	0.0	0.0
New Hanover	Wilmington Police	0.0	80.0	20.0	0.0	0.0
Wake	Raleigh Police	0.0	85.7	13.1	0.5	0.7
Ohio						
Butler	Hamilton Police	0.0	92.4	5.7	1.9	0.0
Clark	Springfield Police	0.0	94.1	4.0	2.0	0.0
Cuyahoga	Cuyahoga County Sheriff	0.0	80.9	17.8	0.7	0.7
Cuyahoga	Cleveland Police	0.1	72.1	24.6	3.3	0.0
Franklin	Franklin County Sheriff	0.5	85.2	14.3	0.0	0.0
Franklin	Columbus Police	0.0	85.7	14.3	0.0	0.0
Hamilton	Hamilton County Sheriff	0.1	82.0	17.8	0.	0.0
Hamilton	Cincinnati Police	0.3	82.7	16.5	0.3	0.1
Lucas	Lucas County Sheriff	1.3	53.6	35.8	9.3	0.0
Lucas	Toledo Police	0.0	78.8	17.0	4.1	0.1
Montgomery	Montgomery County Sheriff	0.5	95.1	4.3	0.0	0.0
Montgomery	Dayton Police	0.2	82.6	16.8	0.4	0.0
Stark	Canton Police	0.0	82.4	16.4	0.6	0.6
Summit	Summit County Sheriff	0.0	89.4	10.1	0.0	0.5
Summit	Akron Police	0.2	81.3	18.5	0.0	0.0
Oklahoma						
Cleveland	Norman Police	0.0	96.7	1.7	0.8	0.8
Comanche	Lawton Police	0.7	87.0	6.2	6.2	0.0
Oklahoma	Oklahoma County Sheriff	0.0	92.3	5.4	1.2	1.2
Oklahoma	Oklahoma City Police	0.5	89.0	7.3	1.0	2.2
Tulsa	Tulsa County Sheriff	0.0	89.8	5.1	0.0	5.1
Tulsa	Tulsa Police	0.3	86.2	9.1	0.4	4.0
Oregon						
Clackamas	Clackamas County Sheriff	0.6	99.4	0.0	0.0	0.0
Lane	Lane County Sheriff	0.0	96.8	1.1	0.0	2.1
Lane	Eugene Police	0.7	95.6	3.0	0.0	0.7
Marion	Salem Police	0.0	100.0	0.0	0.0	0.0
Multnomah	Multnomah County Sheriff	0.7	97.9	0.7	0.7	0.0
Multnomah	Portland Police	1.7	92.5	3.1	2.0	0.8
Washington	Washington County Shreiff	0.5	98.1	1.0	0.5	0.0
Pennsylvania						
Allegheny	Allegheny County Sheriff	0.9	88.7	10.4	0.0	0.0
Allegheny	Allegheny County Police	0.0	92.7	7.3	0.0	0.0
Allegheny	Pittsburgh Police	0.1	75.5	24.3	0.2	0.0

[Continued]

★ 402 ★

Law Enforcement Agency Employees by Locality, 1990 (Continued)

Number of state and local law enforcement agency full-time sworn employees (in agencies with 100 or more officers) by locality, in percent by race/ethnicity, 1990.

| State\locality | Department | Full-time sworn employees, percent | | | | |
		Asian/ Pacific Islander	White, non-Hispanic	Black, non-Hispanic	Hispanic, any race	American Indian/Alaskan Native
Berks	Reading Police	0.6	96.2	1.9	1.3	0.0
Dauphin	Harrisburg Police	0.6	70.1	24.7	4.5	0.0
Erie	Erie Police	0.0	94.3	5.2	0.5	0.0
Lackawanna	Scranton Police	0.0	99.3	0.7	0.0	0.0
Lancaster	Lancaster Police	0.0	92.9	4.8	2.4	0.0
Lehigh	Allentown Police	0.0	84.9	5.9	9.1	0.0
Montgomery	Lower Merion Township Police	0.0	98.5	1.5	0.0	0.0
Northampton	Bethlehem Police	0.0	98.4	0.0	1.6	0.0
Philadelphia	Philadelphia Police	0.0	73.5	23.2	2.8	0.5
Philadelphia	S.E. Penn. Transit Authority	0.5	49.5	46.0	4.0	0.0
Rhode Island						
Kent	Warwick Police	0.0	99.4	0.6	0.0	0.0
Providence	Cranston Police	0.0	99.3	0.7	0.0	0.0
Providence	Pawtucket Police	0.0	99.3	0.7	0.0	0.0
Providence	Providence Police	0.0	95.0	5.0	0.0	0.0
South Carolina						
Charleston	Charleston Police	0.4	66.0	30.8	2.8	0.0
Charleston	North Charleston Police	0.0	80.4	17.4	2.2	0.0
Greenville	Greenville County Sheriff	0.0	85.9	14.1	0.0	0.0
Greenville	Greenville Police	0.6	78.9	19.3	0.6	0.6
Lexington	Lexington County Sheriff	0.8	85.2	12.3	0.8	0.8
Richland	Richland County Sheriff	--	--	--	--	--
Richland	Columbia Police	0.4	74.6	24.6	0.4	0.0
Spartanburg	Spartanburg Police	0.0	86.7	13.3	0.0	0.0
South Dakota						
Minnehaha	Sioux Falls Police	0.0	98.5	1.5	0.0	0.0
Tennessee						
Davidson	Nashville Metropolitan Police	0.0	87.0	12.5	0.5	0.0
Hamilton	Chattanooga Police	0.3	82.5	16.7	0.5	0.0
Knox	Knox County Sheriff	0.0	98.3	1.7	0.0	0.0
Knox	Knoxville Police	0.0	95.4	4.6	0.0	0.0
Madison	Jackson Police	0.0	80.9	19.1	0.0	0.0
Shelby	Shelby County Sheriff	0.0	71.8	28.0	0.2	0.0
Shelby	Memphis Police	0.0	67.8	32.1	0.0	0.1
Sullivan	Sullivan County Sheriff	0.0	97.8	2.2	0.0	0.0
Washington	Johnson City Police	0.0	98.2	1.8	0.0	0.0
Texas						
Bell	Kileen Police	2.6	89.5	1.8	6.1	0.0
Bexar	San Antonio Police	0.2	56.0	5.8	37.9	0.0
Cameron	Brownsville Police	0.0	16.7	0.0	83.3	0.0
Collin	Plano Police	0.0	94.7	2.4	2.4	0.6
Dallas	DFW Airport Police	1.1	83.5	9.2	4.4	1.8

[Continued]

★ 402 ★

Law Enforcement Agency Employees by Locality, 1990 (Continued)

Number of state and local law enforcement agency full-time sworn employees (in agencies with 100 or more officers) by locality, in percent by race/ethnicity, 1990.

State\locality	Department	Full-time sworn employees, percent				
		Asian/ Pacific Islander	White, non-Hispanic	Black, non-Hispanic	Hispanic, any race	American Indian/Alas- kan Native
Dallas	Dallas County Sheriff	0.0	83.8	12.2	4.0	0.0
Dallas	Carrollton Police	0.0	94.8	0.9	4.3	0.0
Dallas	Dallas Police	0.0	77.3	15.5	6.2	1.0
Dallas	Garland Police	0.0	93.5	2.3	3.7	0.5
Dallas	Grand Prairie Police	0.0	88.9	5.6	5.6	0.0
Dallas	Irving Police	0.4	92.9	2.5	3.8	0.4
Dallas	Mesquite Police	0.0	92.5	2.5	3.1	1.9
Dallas	Richardson Police	--	--	--	--	--
Ector	Odessa Police	0.0	85.0	3.5	11.6	0.0
El Paso	El Paso County Sheriff	0.0	15.5	5.9	76.5	2.1
El Paso	El Paso Police	0.5	36.2	2.2	60.7	0.4
Fort Bend	Fort Bend County Sheriff	0.0	82.9	7.9	9.2	0.0
Galveston	Galveston Police	1.2	71.2	11.0	16.0	0.6
Gregg	Longview Police	0.0	93.0	7.0	0.0	0.0
Harris	Harris County Sheriff	0.3	70.5	19.0	9.9	0.3
Harris	Houston Airport Police	0.0	63.9	22.4	13.6	0.0
Harris	Houston Police	0.4	73.7	14.4	11.4	0.1
Harris	Pasadena Police	0.0	94.9	1.0	4.1	0.0
Hidalgo	Hidalgo County Sheriff	0.0	9.0	0.8	90.2	0.0
Hidalgo	McAllen Police	0.0	13.0	0.0	87.0	0.0
Jefferson	Beaumont Police	0.0	87.7	10.5	1.8	0.0
Jefferson	Port Arthur Police	0.0	82.4	14.8	2.8	0.0
Lubbock	Lubbock Police	0.0	87.7	1.0	11.3	0.0
McLennan	Waco Police	0.0	78.3	11.1	10.6	0.0
Midland	Midland Police	0.0	84.3	2.6	13.1	0.0
Montgomery	Montgomery County Sheriff	0.0	93.9	3.5	2.6	0.0
Nueces	Corpus Christi Police	0.8	54.0	4.1	41.1	0.0
Potter	Amarillo Police	0.0	92.8	1.6	5.6	0.0
Smith	Tyler Police	0.0	95.7	4.3	0.0	0.0
Tarrant	Tarrant County Sheriff	0.0	87.9	8.0	4.0	0.2
Tarrant	Arlington Police	0.0	87.1	6.7	6.2	0.0
Tarrant	Fort Worth Police	0.4	80.5	10.7	8.1	0.2
Taylor	Abilene Police	0.0	89.9	3.0	6.0	1.2
Tom Green	San Angelo Police	0.0	85.2	2.6	12.3	0.0
Travis	Travis County Sheriff	0.0	80.2	6.6	13.2	0.0
Travis	Austin Police	0.4	75.1	9.8	14.7	0.0
Webb	Laredo Police	0.0	1.6	0.0	98.4	0.0
Wichita	Wichita Falls Police	0.0	96.8	2.5	0.0	0.6
Utah						
Salt Lake	Salt Lake County Sheriff	0.3	97.5	0.3	2.0	0.0
Salt Lake	Salt Lake City Police	0.3	93.1	2.2	2.5	1.9
Weber	Ogden Police	0.9	97.2	0.9	0.9	0.0

[Continued]

★ 402 ★

Law Enforcement Agency Employees by Locality, 1990 (Continued)

Number of state and local law enforcement agency full-time sworn employees (in agencies with 100 or more officers) by locality, in percent by race/ethnicity, 1990.

State\locality	Department	Full-time sworn employees, percent				
		Asian/ Pacific Islander	White, non-Hispanic	Black, non-Hispanic	Hispanic, any race	American Indian/Alaskan Native
Virginia						
Alexandria (city)	Alexandria City Police	1.2	84.4	12.1	1.6	0.8
Arlington	Arlington County Police	0.0	85.7	12.3	1.9	0.0
Chesapeake (city)	Chesapeake Police	0.4	88.5	10.7	0.4	0.0
Chesterfield	Chesterfield County Police	0.0	92.7	5.5	1.0	0.7
Fairfax	Fairfax County Police	0.4	89.6	8.5	1.4	0.1
Hampton (city)	Hampton Police	0.0	83.3	16.7	0.0	0.0
Henrico	Henrico County Police	0.0	89.1	10.4	0.5	0.0
Loudoun	Loudoun County Sheriff	0.6	95.0	2.5	1.3	0.6
Lynchburgh (city)	Lynchburg City Police	0.0	90.6	9.4	0.0	0.0
Newport News (city)	Newport News City Police	0.4	82.9	16.0	0.8	0.0
Norfolk (city)	Norfolk Police	0.4	88.2	10.6	0.7	0.0
Portsmouth (city)	Portsmouth Police	1.0	84.5	14.0	0.5	0.0
Prince William	Prince William County Police	0.3	88.6	8.4	2.0	0.7
Richmond (city)	Richmond City Police	0.0	72.6	26.0	1.4	0.0
Roanoke (city)	Roanoke City Sheriff	0.0	95.5	3.3	1.2	0.0
Roanoke (city)	Roanoke City Police	0.0	94.3	4.4	0.6	0.6
Virginia Beach (city)	Virginia Beach Police	1.2	88.8	8.0	1.5	0.5
Washington						
King	King Co. Dept of Public Safety	4.4	88.8	4.5	1.4	0.9
King	Bellevue Police	6.1	89.3	3.8	0.0	0.8
King	Seattle Police	5.7	83.9	6.5	2.4	1.5
Pierce	Pierce County Sheriff	4.3	91.8	1.7	0.0	2.2
Pierce	Tacoma Police	0.0	90.0	4.6	1.5	4.0
Snohomish	Snohomish County Sheriff	0.0	94.0	2.7	3.4	0.0
Snohomish	Everett Police	3.8	93.1	0.8	0.8	1.5
Spokane	Spokane County Sheriff	--	--	--	--	--
Spokane	Spokane Police	0.4	95.0	2.5	1.3	0.8
West Virginia						
Cabell	Huntington Police	0.0	99.0	1.0	0.0	0.0
Kanawha	Charleston Police	0.0	88.6	11.4	0.0	0.0
Wisconsin						
Brown	Brown County Sheriff	0.0	97.7	0.0	0.0	2.3
Brown	Green Bay Police	0.0	100.0	0.0	0.0	0.0
Dane	Dane County Sheriff	0.0	95.3	2.4	1.4	0.9
Dane	Madison Police	0.0	91.0	6.0	3.0	0.0
Kenosha	Kenosha Police	0.6	95.6	1.3	2.5	0.0
Milwaukee	Milwaukee County Sheriff	0.7	79.2	14.6	2.5	3.0

[Continued]

★ 402 ★

Law Enforcement Agency Employees by Locality, 1990 (Continued)

Number of state and local law enforcement agency full-time sworn employees (in agencies with 100 or more officers) by locality, in percent by race/ethnicity, 1990.

State\locality	Department	Full-time sworn employees, percent				
		Asian/ Pacific Islander	White, non- Hispanic	Black, non- Hispanic	Hispanic, any race	American Indian/Alas- kan Native
Milwaukee	Milwaukee Police	0.0	82.5	11.8	4.4	1.3
Milwaukee	West Allis Police	0.8	98.5	0.0	0.0	0.8
Racine	Racine County Sheriff	0.0	94.4	4.0	1.7	0.0
Racine	Racine Police	0.0	89.6	7.9	2.5	0.0
Waukesha	Waukesha County Sheriff	0.0	90.1	0.7	8.5	0.7

Source: Brian A. Reaves, U.S. Department of Justice, Office of Justice Programs, Bureau of Justice Statistics, NCJ-134436, *Law Enforcement Management and Administrative Statistics, 1990: Data for Individual State and Local Agencies with 100 or More Officers* (Washington, DC: U.S. Department of Justice, September 1992), table 4a, p. 37. A dash (--) indicates information on race and ethnicity of sworn employees was not provided by an agency. Percentages are based on employee counts for the pay period that included June 15, 1990. Detail may not add to 100% because of rounding. Data are from the 1990 Law Enforcement Management and Administrative Statistics (LEMAS) survey questionnaire mailed to all 780 state and local law enforcement agencies that reported employing ten or more sworn officers in the *1986 Directory Survey of Law Enforcement Agencies*. Local law enforcement agencies are included from all states except North Dakota, Vermont, and Wyoming; these States had no local law enforcement agencies that met the criteria of the survey.

Lawyers

★ 403 ★

Lawyers, New Graduates by Type of Practice, 1991

Numbers and percent of graduates from American Bar Association-approved law schools[a] in 1991, by type of employment, sex, and race/ethnicity.

Type of employment	Asian/ Pacific Islander	Caucasian	Black American	Hispanic
Number of graduates, total	622	20,709	1,012	701
Male	333	12,276	455	394
Female	289	8,433	557	307
Academic, percent				
Male	1.5%	0.7%	1.5%	1.0%
Female	1.7%	1.0%	1.3%	0.7%
Business/industry				
Male	7.8%	7.6%	7.5%	5.6%
Female	3.5%	6.3%	4.8%	5.5%
Private practice				
Male	64.3%	64.7%	48.1%	61.4%
Female	59.3%	59.1%	39.9%	52.8%
Government, total				
Male	13.8%	12.1%	22.9%	19.0%
Female	16.6%	13.5%	26.4%	20.9%
Clerkship, Federal				
Male	3.9%	5.5%	7.0%	3.0%
Female	6.2%	6.1%	7.0%	5.5%
Clerkship, State				
Male	5.1%	5.1%	4.8%	4.1%
Female	5.9%	7.4%	7.5%	3.9%
Public Interest				
Male	1.2%	1.3%	5.5%	3.0%
Female	3.5%	2.9%	7.4%	7.2%

Source: National Association for Law Placement, *ERSS (Employment Report and Salary Survey) Sampler, Women and Minorities Class of 1991* (Washington, DC: NALP, 1992), p. 18. *Note:* (a) Ninety-two percent of American Bar Association-approved law schools contributed data for this report.

★ 404 ★

Lawyers, New Graduates Starting Salaries, 1991

Numbers of graduates from American Bar Association-approved law schools[a] in 1991 and median starting salaries (full-time employment only), by race/ethnicity.

Race/ethnicity	Number of employed graduates	Median starting salary
Total	16,443	$40,000
Asian/Pacific Islander	457	$50,600
Caucasian	14,160	$40,000
Black American	618	$35,000
Hispanic	500	$40,000

Source: National Association for Law Placement, *ERSS (Employment Report and Salary Survey) Sampler, Women and Minorities Class of 1991* (Washington, DC: NALP, 1992), p. 19. *Note:* (a) Ninety-two percent of American Bar Association-approved law schools contributed data for this report.

Professional Sports

★ 405 ★

Professional Athletes by Sport

Number of professional athletes by sport and race/ethnicity, 1986.

Sport[a](Pool of professionals)	Asian/ Pacific Islander	White	Black	Hispanic	Total
Football (28 teams; 1400 players)[b]	7[e]	605	770	15	1,400
Baseball (26 teams; 737 players)[c]	1[f]	500	141	95	737
Hockey (21 teams; 525 players)	0	525	0	0	525
Basketball (23 teams; 345 players)	0	103	241	1	345
Golf, men's (top 125 money winners)	2[f]	119	3	1	125
Golf, women's (top 75 money winners)	1[f]	73	0	1	75
Tennis, men's (top 150 men, singles and doubles)	0	136	2	12	150
Tennis, women's (top 100 women, singles and doubles)	0	96	2	2	100
Auto racing (top 125 drivers in CART, USAC, NASCAR, IHRA, and Grand Prix Circuit)[d]	0	102	0	23	125
Total, male	10	2,089	1,157	147	3,406
Total, female	1	170	2	3	176
Total, both sexes, all sports	11	2,259	1,159	150	3,582

Source: Wilbert M. Leonard II and Jonathan E. Reymen, "The Odds of Attaining Professional Athlete Status: Refining the Computation", *Sociology of Sport Journal* 5, no. 2 (1988); table 1, p. 166. *Notes:* (a) Data for team sports came from league offices and standard sport publications for 1986-87; data for individual sports came from lists of top money winners for 1986 (only touring, not teaching, professionals were tabulated). (b) Total figure includes those on injured reserve list during the season. (c) Each team has 24 roster players (624 players), but players on disabled lists, in the minor leagues with major league contracts (e.g., Bill Caudill and Dale Berra), major leaguers released up to 6-1-87, and minor leaguers brought up to the majors as of 6-1-87 are also included in the 737 total. (d) One woman, Shirley Muldowney, is included in the 102 white drivers. (e) Pacific Islanders. (f) Asian.

★ 406 ★

Odds of Attaining Professional Athlete Status, by Sex

Odds of attaining professional athlete status in any sport by sex and race/ethnicity, 1986.

Race/ethnicity (all sports)	Male	Female
Asian/Pacific Islanders vs. all others	2/10,000,000	2/100,000,000
Asian/Pacific Islanders vs. only other Asian/Pacific Islanders	1/100,000	1/100,000
Whites vs. all others	4/100,000	4/1,000,000
Whites vs. only other whites	5/100,000	4/1,000,000
Blacks vs. all others	2/100,000	4/100,000,000
Blacks vs. only other blacks	2/10,000	3/10,000,000
Hispanics vs. all others[a]	3/1,000,000	6/100,000,000
Hispanics vs. only other Hispanics	4/100,000	9/10,000,000
Native Americans vs. all others	6/100,000,000	--
Native Americans vs. only other Native Americans	9/1,000,000	--
Totals, all groups and all sports	7/100,000	4/1,000,000

Source: Wilbert M. Leonard II and Jonathan E. Reymen, "The Odds of Attaining Professional Athlete Status: Refining the Computation," *Sociology of Sport Journal* 5, no. 2 (1988); table 2, p. 167. A dash (--) indicates too few cases to calculate. *Note:* (a) These figures are somewhat misleading because they are based only on the U.S. population although more than half the Hispanic athletes are not U.S. citizens.

★ 407 ★

Odds of Attaining Professional Athlete Status, by Sport

Odds of attaining professional athlete status in football, baseball, basketball, hockey, golf, tennis, or auto racing by age and race/ethnicity.

Sport (age range)	Asian/Pacific Islanders	White	Black	Hispanic	Native American
Football (20-39)					
vs. all groups	2/10,000,000	16/1,000,000	21/1,000,000	4/10,000,000	8/100,000,000
vs. own group	1/100,000	20/1,000,000	20/100,000	6/1,000,000	1/100,000
Baseball (18-39)					
vs. all groups	2/100,000,000	12/1,000,000	3/1,000,000	2/1,000,000	-
vs. own group	1/1,000,000	15/1,000,000	31/1,000,000	34/1,000,000	-
Basketball (20-39)					
vs. all groups	-	28/10,000,000	65/10,000,000	3/100,000,000	-
vs. own group	-	35/10,000,000	62/10,000,000	4/10,000,000	-
Hockey (17-39; all white)	-	15/1,000,000	-	-	-
Golf, men's (20-39)					
vs. all groups	5/100,000,000	32/10,000,000	8/100,000,000	3/100,000,000	-
vs. own group	32/10,000,000	40/10,000,000	8/10,000,000	4/10,000,000	-
Golf, women's (20-39)					
vs. all groups	3/10,000,000	19/10,000,000	-	3/100,000,000	-
vs. own group	14/100,000,000	24/10,000,000	-	4/10,000,000	-
Tennis, men's (16-34)					
vs. all groups	-	35/10,000,000	5/10,000,000	3/10,000,000	-
vs. own group	-	44/10,000,000	4/10,000,000	4/10,000,000	-

[Continued]

★ 407 ★

Odds of Attaining Professional Athlete Status, by Sport (Continued)

Odds of attaining professional athlete status in football, baseball, basketball, hockey, golf, tennis, or auto racing by age and race/ethnicity.

Sport (age range)	Asian/Pacific Islanders	White	Black	Hispanic	Native American
Tennis, women's (15-34)					
vs. all groups	-	23/10,000,000	5/100,000,000	5/100,000,000	-
vs. own group	-	30/10,000,000	4/10,000,000	7/10,000,000	-
Auto racing (16-39)[a]					
Male[b]	-		-		-
vs. all groups	-	1,1,000,000		5/100,000,000	
vs. own group	-	2/1,000,000	-	73/10,000,000	-
Auto racing (16-39)[a]					
Female[b]	-		-		-
vs. all groups	-	1/100,000,000		73/10,000,000	
vs. own group	-	2/100,000,000	-	-	-

Source: Wilbert M. Leonard II and Jonathan E. Reymen, "The Odds of Attaining Professional Athlete Status: Refining the Computation", *Sociology of Sport Journal* 5, no. 2 (1988), table 3, p. 168. A dash (–) indicates too few cases to calculate. *Note:* (a) Auto racers often drive past age 39. However, the researchers were unable to obtain ages for all 125 drivers studied, so the odds are based on population data only to age 39. (b) Technically there is no sex segregation in auto racing. Therefore, male totals have been aggregated to compute the rates.

Medical Professions

★ 408 ★

U.S. Medical School Faculty

Numbers of Asian/Pacific Islander faculty members at U.S. medical schools by department and percent of total faculty, 1991.

Department	Asian	Percent of Total	Dept. Total
Anatomy	106	6.3	1,677
Biochemistry	207	10.0	2,077
Microbiology	145	9.3	1,564
Pathology-Basic	296	11.0	2,699
Pharmacology	143	10.0	1,480
Physiology	127	7.0	1,802
Other Basic Science	61	5.4	1,136
Subtotal Basic Science	1,085	8.7	12,435
Anesthesiology	364	12.2	2,989
Dermatology	26	6.4	409
Family Medicine	41	2.6	1,591
Internal Medicine	1,099	7.4	14,880
Neurology	140	7.4	1,900
OB/GYN	192	7.4	2,582
Ophthalmology	90	7.7	1,164
Orthopedic Surgery	43	4.9	871

[Continued]

★ 408 ★

U.S. Medical School Faculty (Continued)

Numbers of Asian/Pacific Islander faculty members at U.S. medical schools by department and percent of total faculty, 1991.

Department	Asian	Percent of Total	Dept. Total
Otolaryngology	35	5.7	610
Pathology-Clinical	137	10.3	1,325
Pediatrics	496	7.5	6,614
Physical Medicine	65	10.9	595
Psychiatry	275	5.1	5,419
Public Health	71	5.8	1,232
Radiology	471	11.1	4,249
Surgery	320	5.7	5,606
Other Clinical	3	4.9	61
Subtotal Clinical	3,868	7.4	52,097
Vet Sciences	1	2.1	48
Allied Health	5	1.9	257
Dentistry	--	--	81
Social Sciences	1	0.9	113
Administration	7	1.8	383
All Other	31	5.2	600
All Departments	4,998	7.6	66,014

Source: AAMC Section for Operational Studies, Faculty Roster System. *Note:* The data are reported voluntarily by the schools and thus reflect school-to-school differences in timeliness and consistency of reporting. The database contains records of approximately 85 percent of all active full-time U.S. medical school faculty. The 15 percent undercount should be taken into consideration when using the data. A dash (–) indicates too few cases to calculate.

★ 409 ★

Percentage of Clinically Trained Mental Health Personnel

Numbers and percent of clinically trained mental health personnel, by discipline, sex, age, and race, 1982, 1988, and 1989.

Sociodemographic characteristics	Discipline and year			
	Psychiatry 1982	Psychology 1989	Social work 1989	Psychiatric nursing 1988
Total (N)	(30,642)	(56,530)	(81,737)	(10,567)
Male (N)	(25,348)	(35,275)	(23,050)	(444)[a]
American Indian/Alaska Native	0.4 %	0.2%	0.7%	
Hispanic	5.9 %	1.5 %	3.0 %	
Black (not Hispanic)	1.4%	1.3%	4.2 %	
White (non- Hispanic)	83.9%	96.1 %	88.9 %	
Not specified			1.7 %	
Female (N)	(5,294)	(21,255)	(58,687)	(10,123)
American Indian/Alaska Native	0.1%	0.2%	0.6 %	0.6%
Asian/Pacific Islander	22.7 %	1.1%	1.6 %	0.3%
Hispanic	3.7%	1.8%	2.8 %	1.5%
Black (not Hispanic)	3.1%	2.0%	7.3 %	1.6%
White (not Hispanic)	70.5 %	94.9 %	86.5 %	96.0%
Not specified			1.2 %	

Source: R.W. Manderscheid and M.A. Sonnenschein, eds., Mental Health, United States, 1990, National Institute of Mental Health, DHHS Pub. No. (ADM) 90-1708 (*Washington, DC: U.S. Government Printing* Office, 1990, table 4.2, p. 207. *Note:* (a) Because of small sample estimates for the male population, estimates are provided for the total male population only.

Health

AIDS

★ 410 ★

AIDS Cases, Adult/Adolescent by Sex and Race/Ethnicity

AIDS[a] cases in the United States reported by state health departments by age at diagnosis, sex, and race/ethnicity, biennially 1985 to 1991, and total by race/ethnicity, cases, and percent, 1984 to 1991.

Age at diagnosis, sex, race/ethnicity	Number, by year of report					Total, 1984 to 1991[b,c], percent
	1984 to 1991[b,c]	1985	1987	1989[c]	1991[c]	
Total[d]	189,323	8,219	21,120	33,649	33,477	—
Male						
All males, thirteen years and over[d]	167,552	7,566	19,113	29,670	28,941	100.0%
Asian or Pacific Islander[f]	1,079	48	127	212	191	0.6%
White, not Hispanic	99,509	4,805	12,353	17,549	16,066	59.4%
Black, not Hispanic	44,283	1,717	4,326	8,062	8,360	26.4%
Hispanic	22,049	986	2,245	3,723	4,161	13.2%
American Indian[d]	255	7	25	54	51	0.2%
Female						
All females, thirteen years and over[d]	18,646	523	1,686	3,383	4,029	100.0%
Asian or Pacific Islander[f]	96	1	11	18	17	0.5%
White, not Hispanic	5,152	143	547	949	1,038	27.6%
Black, not Hispanic	10,362	284	896	1,900	2,322	55.6%
Hispanic	2,948	92	229	496	627	15.8%
American Indian[e]	42	3	3	9	9	0.2%

Source: Centers for Disease Control, National Center for Infectious Diseases, Division of HIV/AIDS. The AIDS case definition was changed in September 1987 to allow for the presumptive diagnosis of AIDS-associated diseases and conditions and to expand the spectrum of human immunodeficiency virus-associated diseases reportable as AIDS. Excludes residents of U.S. territories. *Notes:* (a) AIDS is an acronym for "Acquired Immuno-Deficiency Syndrome." (b) Includes cases prior to 1984. (c) Data are as of September 30, 1991, and reflect reporting delays. (d) Includes all other races not shown separately. (e) Includes Aleut and Eskimo. (f) Includes Chinese, Japanese, Filipino, Hawaiian (includes part Hawaiian), and other Asian or Pacific Islander.

★411★

AIDS Cases, Pediatric by Race/Ethnicity

AIDS[a] cases in children in the United States reported by state health departments by race/ethnicity, biennially 1985 to 1991, and total by race/ethnicity, cases, and percent, 1984 to 1991.

Race/ethnicity	Total, 1984 to 1991[b,c]	1985	1987	1989[c]	1991[c]	Total, 1984 to 1991[b,c], %
All children, under thirteen years[d]	3,125	130	321	596	507	100.0%
Asian or Pacific Islander[f]	17	-	1	3	4	0.5%
White, not Hispanic	711	25	85	111	114	22.8%
Black, not Hispanic	1,743	85	161	341	306	55.8%
Hispanic	642	20	72	137	81	20.5%
American Indian[e]	7	-	2	1	1	0.2%

Source: Centers for Disease Control, National Center for Infectious Diseases, Division of HIV/AIDS. The AIDS case definition was changed in September 1987 to allow for the presumptive diagnosis of AIDS-associated diseases and conditions and to expand the spectrum of human immunodeficiency virus-associated diseases reportable as AIDS. Excludes residents of U.S. territories. *Notes:* (a) AIDS is an acronym for "Acquired Immuno-Deficiency Syndrome." (b) Includes cases prior to 1984. (c) Data are as of September 30, 1991, and reflect reporting delays. (d) Includes all other races not shown separately. (e) Includes Aleut and Eskimo. (f) Includes Chinese, Japanese, Filipino, Hawaiian (includes part Hawaiian), and other Asian or Pacific Islander.

★412★

AIDS Deaths, Adult/Adolescent by Age at Diagnosis, Sex, and Race/Ethnicity

Deaths per year of persons (fourteen years and over) diagnosed with AIDS[a] in the United States reported by state health departments by age at diagnosis, sex, and race/ethnicity, and percent distribution, all years, 1984 to 1991.

Age at diagnosis, sex, and race/ethnicity	Number, by year of death[b,c]									Total, 1984 to 1991[b,c], %
	Total, 1984 to 1991	1984	1985	1986	1987	1988	1989[c]	1990[c]	1991[c]	
Total[d]	122,203	3,322	6,584	11,329	15,125	19,120	24,847	25,747	13,882	
Male										
All males, 13 years and over[d]	108,984	3,025	6,030	10,282	13,472	16,946	22,057	22,800	12,371	100%
Asian or Pacific Islander[f]	688	17	29	53	74	104	149	155	102	6%
White, not Hispanic	65,114	1,859	3,754	6,446	8,026	9,864	12,822	13,588	7,636	59.7%
Black, not Hispanic	28,616	740	1,473	2,427	3,550	4,650	6,016	6,050	3,125	26.3%
Hispanic	14,243	404	768	1,335	1,788	2,274	2,997	2,931	1,457	13.1%
American Indian[e]	163	3	4	12	22	23	28	38	32	0.1%
Age										
13 to 19 years	306	13	23	38	43	41	59	56	28	0.3%
20 to 29 years	19,795	578	1,158	1,948	2,549	3,185	3,917	3,929	2,128	18.2%
30 to 39 years	49,709	1,386	2,759	4,734	6,146	7,611	10,100	10,426	5,614	45.6%
40 to 49 years	26,126	697	1,328	2,327	3,042	3,944	5,345	5,768	3,218	24.0%
50 to 59 years	9,286	273	564	867	1,142	1,500	1,892	1,885	985	8.5%
60 years and over	3,762	78	198	368	550	665	744	736	398	3.5%

[Continued]

★ 412 ★

AIDS Deaths, Adult/Adolescent by Age at Diagnosis, Sex, and Race/Ethnicity (Continued)

Deaths per year of persons (fourteen years and over) diagnosed with AIDS[a] in the United States reported by state health departments by age at diagnosis, sex, and race/ethnicity, and percent distribution, all years, 1984 to 1991.

Age at diagnosis, sex, and race/ethnicity	Number, by year of death[b,c]									Total, 1984 to 1991[b,c], %
	Total, 1984 to 1991	1984	1985	1986	1987	1988	1989[c]	1990[c]	1991[c]	
Female										
All females, 13 years and over[d]	11,518	247	448	898	1,384	1,893	2,464	2,624	1,371	100%
Asian or Pacific Islander[f]	72	1	-	7	6	16	17	11	12	0.6%
White, not Hispanic	3,187	59	144	256	432	533	635	699	388	27.7%
Black, not Hispanic	6,451	140	218	483	762	1,043	1,398	1,508	795	56.0%
Hispanic	1,766	47	83	148	182	299	403	393	170	15.3
American Indian[e]	22	-	3	1	2	1	5	5	4	0.2%
Age										
13 to 19 years	92	1	5	11	11	11	13	24	12	0.8%
20 to 29 years	2,898	90	132	245	359	459	572	635	343	25.2%
30 to 39 years	5,285	108	203	408	611	885	1,206	1,195	594	45.9%
40 to 49 years	1,760	23	48	105	181	279	402	448	253	15.3%
50 to 59 years	705	9	18	44	91	106	141	174	108	6.1%
60 years and over	778	16	42	85	131	153	130	148	61	6.8%

Source: Centers for Disease Control, National Center for Infectious Diseases, Division of HIV/AIDS. The AIDS case definition was changed in September 1987 to allow for the presumptive diagnosis of AIDS-associated diseases and conditions and to expand the spectrum of human immunodeficiency virus-associated diseases reportable as AIDS. Excludes residents of U.S. territories. *Notes:* (a) AIDS is an acronym for "Acquired Immuno-Deficiency Syndrome." (b) Includes cases prior to 1984. (c) Data are as of September 30, 1991, and reflect reporting delays. (d) Includes all other races not shown separately. (e) Includes Aleut and Eskimo. (f) Includes Chinese, Japanese, Filipino, Hawaiian (includes part Hawaiian), and other Asian or Pacific Islander.

★ 413 ★

AIDS Deaths, Pediatric by Race/Ethnicity

Deaths per year of children (thirteen years and under) diagnosed with AIDS[a] in the United States reported by state health departments by race/ethnicity and percent distribution, all years, 1984 to 1991.

Race/ethnicity	Number, by year of death[b,c]									Total, 1984 to 1991, %
	Total, 1984 to 1991	1984	1985	1986	1987	1988	1989[c]	1990[c]	1991[c]	
All children, under 13 years[d]	1,701	50	106	149	269	281	326	323	140	100.0%
Asian or Pacific Islander[f]	11	-	2	2	1	3	1	1	1	0.6%
White, not Hispanic	402	9	29	35	69	67	88	61	32	23.6%
Black, not Hispanic	929	29	59	82	130	151	164	197	84	54.6%
Hispanic	352	12	16	30	67	60	71	62	23	20.7%
American Indian[e]	5	-	-	-	2	-	1	1	-	0.3%

Source: Centers for Disease Control, National Center for Infectious Diseases, Division of HIV/AIDS. The AIDS case definition was changed in September 1987 to allow for the presumptive diagnosis of AIDS-associated diseases and conditions and to expand the spectrum of human immunodeficiency virus-associated diseases reportable as AIDS. Excludes residents of U.S. territories. *Notes:* (a) AIDS is an acronym for "Acquired Immuno-Deficiency Syndrome." (b) Includes cases prior to 1984. (c) Data are as of September 30, 1991, and reflect reporting delays. (d) Includes all other races not shown separately. (e) Includes Aleut and Eskimo. (f) Includes Chinese, Japanese, Filipino, Hawaiian (includes part Hawaiian), and other Asian or Pacific Islander.

★ 414 ★

AIDS Cases, Adult/Adolescent by Exposure Category and Race/Ethnicity

Persons thirteen years and older in the United States who are reported as diagnosed with AIDS[a] by exposure category and race/ethnicity, as of June 1992.

Adult/adolescent exposure category	Asian/ Pacific Islander	White, not Hispanic	Black, not Hispanic	Hispanic	American Indian/ Alaska Native	Total[d]
Men who have sex with men	1,045	91,390	23,029	14,865	203	130,822
Injecting drug use	61	10,483	25,892	14,864	71	51,477
Men who have sex with men and inject drugs	33	8,295	3,981	2,113	52	14,487
Hemophilia/coagulation disorder	20	1,530	150	157	9	1,875
Heterosexual contact:	52	2,932	8,327	2,692	13	14,045
Sex with injecting drug user	22	1,547	3,935	1,921	10	7,451
Sex with bisexual male	14	388	247	90	2	743
Sex with person with hemophilia	2	91	14	6	-	113
Sex with transfusion recipient with HIV infection	2	158	56	56	-	274
Sex with HIV-infected person, risk not specified	9	682	1,253	590	1	2,537
Receipt of blood transfusion, blood components, or tissue[b]	96	3,189	838	521	7	4,659
Other/undetermined[c]	100	3,133	3,655	1,950	22	8,916
Adult/adolescent total[d]	1,407	120,952	65,872	37,162	377	226,281

Source: Centers for Disease Control, U.S. Department of Health and Human Resources, *HIV/AIDS Surveillance Report,* (Atlanta: Centers for Disease Control, July 1992), pp. 1-18. *Notes:* (a) AIDS is an acronym for "Acquired Immuno-Deficiency Syndrome." (b) Nineteen adults/adolescents and two children developed AIDS after receiving blood screened negative for HIV antibody. Five additional adults developed AIDS after receiving tissue or organs from HIV-infected donors. Two of the five received tissue or organs from a donor who was negative for HIV antibody at the time of donation. (c) "Other" refers to six health-care workers who developed AIDS after occupational exposure to HIV-infected blood, as documented by evidence of seroconversion; and to two patients who developed AIDS after exposure to HIV within the health-care setting, as documented by laboratory studies. "Undetermined" refers to patients whose mode of exposure to HIV is unknown. This includes patients under investigation; patients who died, were lost to follow-up, or refused interview; and patients whose mode of exposure to HIV remains undetermined after investigation. (d) Includes persons whose race/ethnicity is unknown, and whose mode of exposure was related to specific countries of origin. See Source for details.

★ 415 ★

AIDS Cases, Adult/Adolescent by Exposure Category and Race/Ethnicity in Percent

Percent of total persons thirteen years and older in the United States who are reported as diagnosed with AIDS[a] by exposure category and race/ethnicity, as of June 1992.

Adult/adolescent exposure category	Asian/ Pacific Islander	White, not Hispanic	Black, not Hispanic	Hispanic	American Indian/ Alaska Native	Total[d]
	Percent	Percent	Percent	Percent	Percent	Percent
Men who have sex with men	74%	76%	35%	40%	54%	58%
Injecting drug use	4%	9%	39%	40%	19%	23%
Men who have sex with men and inject drugs	2%	7%	6%	6%	14%	6%
Hemophilia/coagulation disorder	1%	1%	-	-	2%	1%
Heterosexual contact:	4%	2%	13%	7%	3%	6%
Receipt of blood transfusion, blood components, or tissue[b]	7%	3%	1%	1%	2%	2%
Other/undetermined[c]	7%	3%	6%	5%	6%	4%
Adult/adolescent total	100%	100%	100%	100%	100%	100%

Source: Centers for Disease Control, U.S. Department of Health and Human Resources, *HIV/AIDS Surveillance Report* (Atlanta: Centers for Disease Control, July 1992), pp. 1-18. *Notes:* (a) AIDS is an acronym for "Acquired Immuno-Deficiency Syndrome. (b) Nineteen adults/adolescents and two children developed AIDS after receiving blood screened negative for HIV antibody. Five additional adults developed AIDS after receiving tissue or organs from HIV-infected donors. Two of the five received tissue or organs from a donor who was negative for HIV antibody at the time of donation. (c) "Other" refers to six health-care workers who developed AIDS after occupational exposure to HIV-infected blood, as documented by evidence of seroconversion; and to two patients who developed AIDS after exposure to HIV within the health-care setting, as documented by laboratory studies. "Undetermined" refers to patients whose mode of exposure to HIV is unknown. This includes patients under investigation; patients who died, were lost to follow-up, or refused interview; and patients whose mode of exposure to HIV remains undetermined after investigation. (d) Includes persons whose race/ethnicity is unknown.

★ 416 ★

AIDS Cases, Pediatric by Exposure Category and Race/Ethnicity

Persons under thirteen years of age in the United States who are reported as diagnosed with AIDS[a] by exposure category and race/ethnicity, as of June 1992.

Pediatric exposure category	Asian/ Pacific Islander	White, not Hispanic	Black, not Hispanic	Hispanic	American Indian/ Alaska Native	Total[b]
Hemophilia/coagulation disorder	3	123	25	28	-	179
Mother with/at risk for HIV infection	9	515	1,944	831	11	3,315
Injecting drug use	3	241	919	393	4	1,561
Sex with injecting drug user	2	101	303	264	1	673
Sex with bisexual male	1	29	27	15	-	72
Sex with person with hemophilia	-	11	4	2	-	17
Sex with transfusion recipient with HIV infection	-	5	5	7	-	17
Sex with HIV-infected person, risk not specified	1	36	85	47	2	172
Receipt of blood transfusion, blood components, or tissue	-	23	31	16	-	70
Has HIV infection, risk not specified	2	68	295	83	4	452

[Continued]

★416★

AIDS Cases, Pediatric by Exposure Category and Race/Ethnicity (Continued)

Persons under thirteen years of age in the United States who are reported as diagnosed with AIDS[a] by exposure category and race/ethnicity, as of June 1992.

Pediatric exposure category	Asian/ Pacific Islander	White, not Hispanic	Black, not Hispanic	Hispanic	American Indian/ Alaska Native	Total[b]
Receipt of blood transfusion, blood components, or tissue[c]	7	157	66	69	-	300
Undetermined[d]	-	15	65	23	-	104
Pediatric total	19	810	2,100	951	11	3,898

Source: Centers for Disease Control, U.S. Department of Health and Human Resources, *HIV/AIDS Surveillance Report* (Atlanta: Centers for Disease Control, July 1992), pp. 1-18. *Notes:* (a) AIDS is an acronym for "Acquired Immuno-Deficiency Syndrome." (b) Includes persons whose race/ethnicity is unknown. (c) Two children developed AIDS after receiving blood screened negative for HIV antibody. (d) Refers to patients whose mode of exposure to HIV is unknown. This includes patients under investigation; patients who died, were lost to follow-up, or refused interview; and patients whose mode of exposure to HIV remains undetermined after investigation.

★417★

AIDS Cases, Pediatric by Exposure Category and Race/Ethnicity in Percent

Percent of total persons under thirteen years of age in the United States who are reported as diagnosed with AIDS[a] by exposure category and race/ethnicity, as of June 1992.

Pediatric exposure category	Asian/ Pacific Islander	White, not Hispanic	Black, not Hispanic	Hispanic	American Indian/ Alaska Native	Total[b]
Hemophilia/coagulation disorder	16%	15%	1%	3%	-	5%
Mother with/at risk for HIV infection	47%	64%	93%	87%	100%	85%
Receipt of blood transfusion, blood components, or tissue[c]	37%	19%	3%	7%		8%
Undetermined[d]		2%	3%	2%		3%
Pediatric total	100%	100%	100%	100%	100%	100%

Source: Centers for Disease Control, U.S. Department of Health and Human Resources, *HIV/AIDS Surveillance Report* (Atlanta: Centers for Disease Control, July 1992), pp. 1-18. *Notes:* (a) AIDS is an acronym for "Acquired Immuno-Deficiency Syndrome." (b) Includes persons whose race/ethnicity is unknown. (c) Two children developed AIDS after receiving blood screened negative for HIV antibody. (d) Refers to patients whose mode of exposure to HIV is unknown. This includes patients under investigation; patients who died, were lost to follow-up, or refused interview; and patients whose mode of exposure to HIV remains undetermined after investigation.

AIDS Cases, Male Adult/Adolescent by Exposure Category and Race/Ethnicity

Males thirteen years and over in the United States who are reported as diagnosed with AIDS[a] by exposure category and race/ethnicity, as of June 1992.

Male exposure category	Asian/ Pacific Islander	White, not Hispanic	Black, not Hispanic	Hispanic	American Indian/ Alaska Native	Total[d]
	Number	Number	Number	Number	Number	Number
Men who have sex with men	1,045	91,390	23,029	14,865	203	130,822
Injecting drug use	44	7,902	18,914	12,386	39	39,364
Men who have sex with men and inject drugs	33	8,295	3,981	2,113	52	14,487
Hemophilia/coagulation disorder	20	1,501	141	154	9	1,834
Heterosexual contact:	11	965	3,838	697	3	5,521
Sex with injecting drug user	7	550	1,304	375	3	2,239
Sex with person with hemophilia	-	7	2	2	-	11
Sex with transfusion recipient with HIV infection	-	46	23	22	-	92
Sex with HIV-infected person, risk not specified	1	312	554	277	-	1,144
Receipt of blood transfusion, blood components, or tissue[b]	56	2,054	449	277	2	2,843
Other/undetermined[c]	81	2,653	2,685	1,603	15	7,087
Male total	1,290	114,760	53,037	32,095	323	201,958

Source: Centers for Disease Control, U.S. Department of Health and Human Resources, *HIV/AIDS Surveillance Report* (Atlanta: Centers for Disease Control, July 1992), pp. 1-18. *Notes:* (a) AIDS is an acronym for "Acquired Immuno-Deficiency Syndrome." (b) Nineteen adults/adolescents and two children developed AIDS after receiving blood screened negative for HIV antibody. Five additional adults developed AIDS after receiving tissue or organs from HIV-infected donors. Two of the five received tissue or organs from a donor who was negative for HIV antibody at the time of donation. (c) "Other" refers to six health-care workers who developed AIDS after occupational exposure to HIV-infected blood, as documented by evidence of seroconversion; and to two patients who developed AIDS after exposure to HIV within the health-care setting, as documented by laboratory studies. "Undetermined" refers to patients whose mode of exposure to HIV is unknown. This includes patients under investigation; patients who died, were lost to follow-up, or refused interview; and patients whose mode of exposure to HIV remains undetermined after investigation. (d) Includes 518 persons whose race/ethnicity is unknown.

★ 419 ★

AIDS Cases, Male Adult/Adolescent by Exposure Category and Race/Ethnicity in Percent

Percent of males thirteen years and over in the United States who are reported as diagnosed with AIDS[a] by exposure category and race/ethnicity, as of June 1992.

Male exposure category	Asian/ Pacific Islander	White, not Hispanic	Black, not Hispanic	Hispanic	American Indian/ Alaska Native	Total[d]
	Percent	Percent	Percent	Percent	Percent	Percent
Men who have sex with men	81%	80%	43%	46%	63%	65%
Injecting drug use	3%	7%	36%	39%	12%	19%
Men who have sex with men and inject drugs	3%	7%	8%	7%	16%	7%
Hemophilia/coagulation disorder	2%	1%	0%	0%	3%	1%
Heterosexual contact:	1%	1%	7%	2%	1%	3%
Receipt of blood transfusion, blood components, or tissue[b]	4%	2%	1%	1%	1%	1%
Other/undetermined[c]	6%	2%	5%	5%	5%	4%
Male total	100%	100%	100%	100%	100%	100%

Source: Centers for Disease Control, U.S. Department of Health and Human Resources, *HIV/AIDS Surveillance Report* (Atlanta: Centers for Disease Control, July 1992), pp. 1-18. *Notes:* (a) AIDS is an acronym for "Acquired Immuno-Deficiency Syndrome." (b) Nineteen adults/adolescents and two children developed AIDS after receiving blood screened negative for HIV antibody. Five additional adults developed AIDS after receiving tissue or organs from HIV-infected donors. Two of the five received tissue or organs from a donor who was negative for HIV antibody at the time of donation. (c) "Other" refers to six health-care workers who developed AIDS after occupational exposure to HIV-infected blood, as documented by evidence of seroconversion; and to two patients who developed AIDS after exposure to HIV within the health-care setting, as documented by laboratory studies. "Undetermined" refers to patients whose mode of exposure to HIV is unknown. This includes patients under investigation; patients who died, were lost to follow-up, or refused interview; and patients whose mode of exposure to HIV remains undetermined after investigation. (d) Includes 518 persons whose race/ethnicity is unknown.

★ 420 ★

AIDS Cases, Female Adult/Adolescent by Exposure Category and Race/Ethnicity

Females thirteen years and older in the United States who are reported as diagnosed with AIDS[a] by exposure category and race/ethnicity, as of June 1992.

Female exposure category	Asian/ Pacific Islander	White, not Hispanic	Black, not Hispanic	Hispanic	American Indian/ Alaska Native	Total[d]
Injecting drug use	17	2,581	6,978	2,478	32	12,113
Hemophilia/coagulation disorder	-	29	9	3	-	41
Heterosexual contact:	41	1,967	4,489	1,995	10	8,524
Sex with injecting drug user	15	997	2,631	1,546	7	5,212
Sex with bisexual male	14	388	247	90	2	743
Sex with person with hemophilia	2	84	12	4	-	102
Sex with transfusion recipient with HIV infection	2	112	33	34	-	182
Sex with HIV-infected person, risk not specified	8	370	699	313	1	1,393
Receipt of blood transfusion, blood components, or tissue[b]	40	1,135	389	244	5	1,816
Other/undetermined[c]	19	480	970	347	7	1,829
Female total	117	6,192	12,835	5,067	54	24,323

Source: Centers for Disease Control, U.S. Department of Health and Human Resources, *HIV/AIDS Surveillance Report* (Atlanta: Centers for Disease Control, July 1992), pp. 1-18. *Notes:* (a) AIDS is an acronym for "Acquired Immuno-Deficiency Syndrome." (b) Nineteen adults/adolescents and two children developed AIDS after receiving blood screened negative for HIV antibody. Five additional adults developed AIDS after receiving tissue or organs from HIV-infected donors. Two of the five received tissue or organs from a donor who was negative for HIV antibody at the time of donation. (c) "Other" refers to six health-care workers who developed AIDS after occupational exposure to HIV-infected blood, as documented by evidence of seroconversion; and to two patients who developed AIDS after exposure to HIV within the health-care setting, as documented by laboratory studies. "Undetermined" refers to patients whose mode of exposure to HIV is unknown. This includes patients under investigation; patients who died, were lost to follow-up, or refused interview; and patients whose mode of exposure to HIV remains undetermined after investigation. (d) Includes 518 persons whose race/ethnicity is unknown.

★ 421 ★

AIDS Cases, Female Adult/Adolescent by Exposure Category and Race/Ethnicity in Percent

Percent females thirteen years and older in the United States who are reported as diagnosed with AIDS[a] by exposure category and race/ethnicity, as of June 1992.

Female exposure category	Asian/ Pacific Islander	Hispanic	Black, not Hispanic	White, not Hispanic	American Indian/ Alaska Native	Total[d]
Injecting drug use	15%	49%	54%	42%	59%	50%
Hemophilia/coagulation disorder	0%	0%	0%	0%		0%
Heterosexual contact	35%	39%	35%	32%	19%	35%
Receipt of blood transfusion, blood components, or tissue[b]	34%	5%	3%	18%	9%	7%
Other/undetermined[c]	16%	7%	8%	8%	13%	8%
Female total	100%	100%	100%	100%	100%	100%

Source: Centers for Disease Control, U.S. Department of Health and Human Resources, *HIV/AIDS Surveillance Report* (Atlanta: Centers for Disease Control, July 1992), pp. 1-18. *Notes:* (a) AIDS is an acronym for "Acquired Immuno-Deficiency Syndrome." (b) Nineteen adults/adolescents and two children developed AIDS after receiving blood screened negative for HIV antibody. Five additional adults developed AIDS after receiving tissue or organs from HIV-infected donors. Two of the five received tissue or organs from a donor who was negative for HIV antibody at the time of donation. (c) "Other" refers to six health-care workers who developed AIDS after occupational exposure to HIV-infected blood, as documented by evidence of seroconversion; and to two patients who developed AIDS after exposure to HIV within the health-care setting, as documented by laboratory studies. "Undetermined" refers to patients whose mode of exposure to HIV is unknown. This includes patients under investigation; patients who died, were lost to follow-up, or refused interview; and patients whose mode of exposure to HIV remains undetermined after investigation. (d) Includes 518 persons whose race/ethnicity is unknown.

★ 422 ★

AIDS Cases, Male Adult/Adolescent by Age at Diagnosis and Race/Ethnicity

Males thirteen years and older in the United States who are reported as diagnosed with AIDS[a] by age at diagnosis and race/ethnicity, as of June 1992.

Males Age at diagnosis	Asian/ Pacific Islander	White, not Hispanic	Black, not Hispanic	Hispanic	American Indian/ Alaska Native	Total[b]
Under 5 years	7	269	922	402	8	1,610
5 to 12 years	6	213	140	111	-	470
13 to 19 years	7	293	190	134	6	630
20 to 24 years	48	3,584	2,257	1,397	16	7,314
25 to 29 years	175	17,074	8,170	5,361	67	30,912
30 to 34 years	257	26,821	13,003	8,117	87	48,381
35 to 39 years	289	25,473	12,612	7,213	64	45,758
40 to 44 years	216	17,937	7,751	4,610	41	30,634
45 to 49 years	139	10,545	4,154	2,439	21	17,344
50 to 54 years	69	5,707	2,322	1,345	8	9,475
55 to 59 years	44	3,488	1,352	809	6	5,716
60 to 64 years	14	2,069	716	393	6	3,203
65 or older	32	1,769	510	277	1	2,591
Male total	1,303	115,242	54,099	32,608	331	204,038

Source: Centers for Disease Control, U.S. Department of Health and Human Resources, *HIV/AIDS Surveillance Report* (Atlanta: Centers for Disease Control, July 1992), pp. 1-18. *Notes:* (a) AIDS is an acronym for "Acquired Immuno-Deficiency Syndrome." (b) Includes 518 persons whose race/ethnicity is unknown.

★ 423 ★

AIDS Cases, Female Adult/Adolescent by Age at Diagnosis and Race/Ethnicity

Females thirteen years and older in the United States who are reported as diagnosed with AIDS[a] by age at diagnosis and race/ethnicity, as of June 1992.

Females/Age at diagnosis	Asian/ Pacific Islander	White, not Hispanic	Black, not Hispanic	Hispanic	American Indian/ Alaska Native	Total[b]
Under 5 years	-	263	904	358	3	1,532
5 to 12 years	6	65	134	80	-	286
13 to 19 years	1	65	135	40	1	242
20 to 24 years	7	391	804	383	5	1,597
25 to 29 years	9	1,145	2,396	1,100	10	4,672
30 to 34 years	22	1,440	3,508	1,332	16	6,332
35 to 39 years	16	1,046	2,923	1,046	7	5,051
40 to 44 years	25	600	1,507	551	7	2,693
45 to 49 years	11	322	645	262	4	1,250
50 to 54 years	7	225	390	157	1	781
55 to 59 years	5	242	226	88	to	562
60 to 64 years	8	198	144	48	2	400
65 or older	6	518	157	60	1	743
Female total	123	6,520	13,873	5,505	57	26,141

Source: Centers for Disease Control, U.S. Department of Health and Human Resources, *HIV/AIDS Surveillance Report* (Atlanta: Centers for Disease Control, July 1992), pp. 1-18. *Notes:* (a) AIDS is an acronym for "Acquired Immuno-Deficiency Syndrome." (b) Includes 518 persons whose race/ethnicity is unknown.

Births

★ 424 ★

Births, Live, 1970, 1980, and 1989

Numbers of live births in the United States by mother's race/ethnicity, 1970, 1980, and 1989.

Race/ethnicity of mother	Numbers of live births[a]		
	1970	1980	1989
Total, all mothers	3,731,386	3,612,258	4,040,958
Asian or Pacific Islander	27,706	74,355	133,075
Chinese	7,044	11,671	20,982
Japanese	7,744	7,482	8,689
Filipino	8,066	13,968	24,585
Other Asian or Pacific Islander[b]	4,852	41,234	78,819
White, total	3,109,956	2,936,351	3,192,355
White, non-Hispanic[c]	-	1,245,221	2,526,367
Black, total	561,992	568,080	673,124
Black, non-Hispanic[c]	-	299,646	611,269
American Indian or Alaskan Native	22,264	29,389	39,478
Hispanic origin[d]	-	307,163	532,249

Source: Health United States, 1991 (Washington, DC: U.S. Government Printing Office, 1992). Primary source: National Center for Health Statistics, Division of Analysis, from data compiled by the Division of Vital Statistics. _Notes:_ (a) Includes live births with unknown birth weight. (b) Includes Hawaiians and part Hawaiians. (c) The race groups "White, total" and "Black, total" include persons of both Hispanic and non-Hispanic origin. Data for "White, non-Hispanic" and "Black, non-Hispanic" shown only for states with an Hispanic origin item on their birth certificates. (d) Persons of Hispanic origin may be of any race.

★ 425 ★

Births by Low Birth Weight, 1970, 1980, and 1989

Percent of babies born in the United States with low birth weight (less than 2,500 grams)[a] and very low birth weight (less than 1,500 grams) by mother's race/ethnicity, 1970, 1980, and 1989.

Race/ethnicity of mothers of:	Percent of live births		
	1970	1980	1990
Low birth weight (less than 2,500 grams) babies			
Total births, all mothers	7.9%	6.8%	7.1%
Asian or Pacific Islander	8.8%	6.7%	6.5%
Chinese	6.7%	5.2%	4.9%
Japanese	9.0%	6.6%	6.7%
Filipino	10.0%	7.4%	7.4%
Other Asian or Pacific Islander[b]	9.4%	6.9%	6.7%
White	6.9%	5.7%	5.7%
White, non-Hispanic[c]	-	5.7%	5.6%

[Continued]

★ 425 ★

Births by Low Birth Weight, 1970, 1980, and 1989 (Continued)

Percent of babies born in the United States with low birth weight (less than 2,500 grams)[a] and very low birth weight (less than 1,500 grams) by mother's race/ethnicity, 1970, 1980, and 1989.

Race/ethnicity of mothers of:	Percent of live births		
	1970	1980	1990
Black	13.9%	12.7%	13.5%
Black, non-Hispanic[c]	-	12.7%	13.6%
American Indian or Alaskan Native	8.0%	6.4%	6.3%
Hispanic origin[c,d]	-	6.1%	6.2%
Very low birth weight (less than 1,500 grams) babies			
Total births, all mothers	1.2%	1.2%	1.3%
Asian or Pacific Islander	1.2%	0.9%	0.9%
Chinese	0.8%	0.7%	0.6%
Japanese	1.5%	0.9%	0.9%
Filipino	1.1%	1.0%	1.1%
Other Asian or Pacific Islander[b]	1.4%	1.0%	0.9%
White	1.0%	0.9%	1.0%
White, non-Hispanic[c]	-	0.9%	0.9%
Black	2.4%	2.5%	3.0%
Black, non-Hispanic[c]	-	2.5%	3.0%
American Indian or Alaskan Native	1.0%	0.9%	1.0%
Hispanic origin[d]	-	1.0%	1.1%

Source: Health United States, 1991 (Washington, DC: U.S. Government Printing Office, 1992). Primary source: National Center for Health Statistics, Division of Analysis, from data compiled by the Division of Vital Statistics. *Notes:* (a) One ounce equals approximately 28 grams; one pound equals approximately 454 grams. (b) Includes Hawaiians and part Hawaiians. (c) The race groups "White, total" and "Black, total" include persons of both Hispanic and non-Hispanic origin. Data for "White, non-Hispanic" and "Black, non-Hispanic" shown only for states with an Hispanic origin item on their birth certificates. (d) Persons of Hispanic origin may be of any race.

★ 426 ★

Births by Low Birth Weight and Race/Ethnicity of Mother

Low birth weight newborns in the United States by race/ethnicity in percent, 1982.

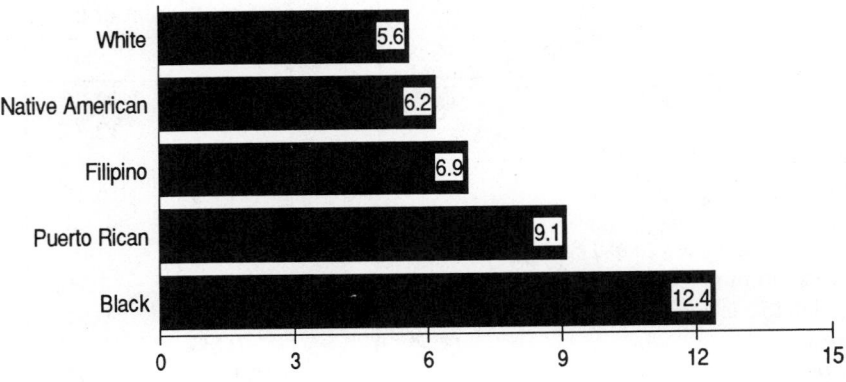

Percent of low birthweight newborn babies

In the United States, 60 percent of babies who die before age one were born underweight. Incidence of low birth weight varies from one minority population to the next; those cited above show serious disparities with the white population in the percentage of underweight newborns.

Source: U.S. Department of Health and Human Service, *Report of the Secretary's Task Force on Black and Minority Health, Vol. VI* (Washington, DC: U.S. Government Printing Office, 1985).

★ 427 ★

Births by Age of Mother, 1970, 1980, and 1989

Live births in the United States in percent by age and race/ethnicity of mother, 1970, 1980, and 1989.

Age and race/ethnicity of mother	Percent of live births		
	1970	1980	1989
Age of mother less than 18 years			
Total, all racial/ethnic groups	6.3	5.8	4.8
Asian or Pacific Islander	3.1	1.5	2.0
Chinese	1.1	0.3	0.3
Japanese	2.0	1.0	0.9
Filipino	3.7	1.6	1.9
Other Asian or Pacific Islander[a]	7.0	1.8	2.6
White	4.8	4.5	3.6
White, non-Hispanic[b]	-	4.0	3.0
Black	14.8	12.5	10.5
Black, non-Hispanic[b]	-	12.7	10.5
American Indian or Alaskan Native	7.5	9.4	7.5
Hispanic origin[c]	-	7.4	6.7

[Continued]

★ 427 ★

Births by Age of Mother, 1970, 1980, and 1989 (Continued)

Live births in the United States in percent by age and race/ethnicity of mother, 1970, 1980, and 1989.

Age and race/ethnicity of mother	Percent of live births		
	1970	1980	1989
Age of mother 18 to 19 years			
Total, all racial/ethnic groups	11.3	9.8	8.1
Asian or Pacific Islander	6.6	3.9	3.7
Chinese	3.9	1.0	0.7
Japanese	4.1	2.3	1.8
Filipino	7.1	4.0	4.0
Other Asian or Pacific Islander[a]	13.8	4.9	4.6
White	10.4	9.0	7.2
White, non-Hispanic[b]	-	8.5	6.5
Black	16.6	14.5	12.9
Black, non-Hispanic[b]	-	14.7	13.0
American Indian or Alaskan Native	12.8	14.6	12.1
Hispanic origin[c]	-	11.6	10.0

Source: Health United States, 1991 (Washington, DC: U.S. Government Printing Office, 1992). Primary source: National Center for Health Statistics, Division of Analysis, from data compiled by the Division of Vital Statistics. *Notes:* (a) Includes Hawaiians and part Hawaiians. (b) The race groups "White, total" and "Black, total" include persons of both Hispanic and non-Hispanic origin. Data for "White, non-Hispanic" and "Black, non-Hispanic" shown only for states with an Hispanic origin item on their birth certificates. (c) Persons of Hispanic origin may be of any race.

★ 428 ★

Births by Age of Mother, 1980-1988

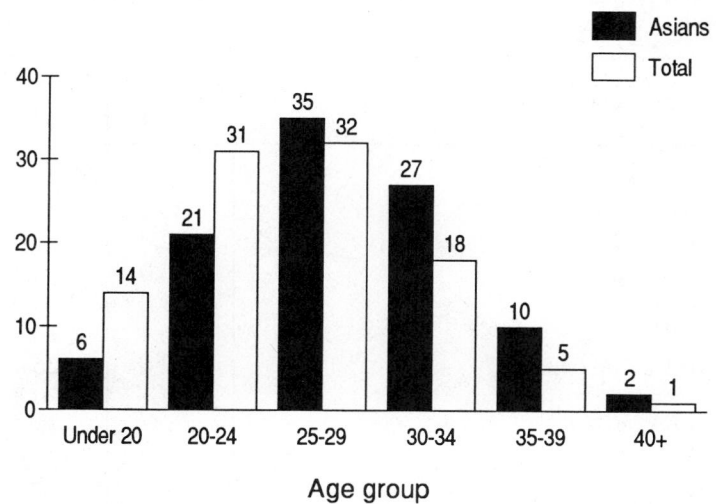

Age group

Source: William P. O'Hare and Judy C. Felt, *Asian Americans: America's Fastest Growing Minority Group, 1991* (Washington, DC: Population Reference Bureau, Inc., 1991), fig. 4, p. 9. Primary source: National Center for Health Statistics, "Advance Report of Final Natality Statistics: 1988," *Monthly Vital Statistics Report 39* (Supplement to August 15, 1990), table 28, and unpublished data from NCHS.

★ 429 ★

Births to Unmarried Mothers by Race/Ethnicity, 1970, 1980, and 1989

Percent of live births to unmarried mothers in the United States by race/ethnicity of mother, 1970, 1980, and 1989.

Race/ethnicity of unmarried mother	Percent of live births		
	1970[a]	1980	1989
Total, all racial/ethnic groups	10.7	18.4	27.1
Asian or Pacific Islander	8.7	7.3	12.4
Chinese	3.0	2.7	4.2
Japanese	4.6	5.2	9.4
Filipino	9.1	8.6	14.8
Other Asian or Pacific Islander[b]	16.5	8.5	14.2
White	5.5	11.2	19.2
White, non-Hispanic[c]	-	9.6	16.1
Black	37.5	56.1	65.7
Black, non-Hispanic[c]	-	57.3	66.0
American Indian or Alaskan Native	22.4	39.2	52.7
Hispanic origin[d]	-	23.6	35.5

Source: Health United States, 1991 (Washington, DC: U.S. Government Printing Office, 1992). Primary source: National Center for Health Statistics, Division of Analysis, from data compiled by the Division of Vital Statistics. *Notes:* (a) Excludes births that occurred in states not reporting marital status. (b) Includes Hawaiians and part Hawaiians. (c) The race groups "White, total" and "Black, total" include persons of both Hispanic and non-Hispanic origin. Data for "White, non-Hispanic" and "Black, non-Hispanic" shown only for states with an Hispanic origin item on their birth certificates. (d) Persons of Hispanic origin may be of any race.

★ 430 ★

Births by Education and Race/Ethnicity of Mother, 1970, 1980, and 1989

Percent of live births the United States by selected years of education and race/ethnicity of mother, 1970, 1980, and 1989.

Education and race/ethnicity of mother	Percent of live births		
	1970	1980	1989
Education less than twelve years			
Total, all racial/ethnic groups	30.8	23.7	23.2
Asian or Pacific Islander	22.0	21.0	19.5
Chinese	23.0	15.2	14.9
Japanese	11.8	5.0	3.3
Filipino	26.4	16.4	10.2
Other Asian or Pacific Islander[a]	28.6	26.4	26.1
White	27.1	20.8	21.6
White, non-Hispanic[b]	-	18.3	15.3
Black	51.2	36.4	30.4
Black, non-Hispanic[b]	-	37.4	29.9
American Indian or Alaskan Native	60.5	44.2	37.2
Hispanic origin[c]	-	51.1	52.8

[Continued]

★ 430 ★

Births by Education and Race/Ethnicity of Mother, 1970, 1980, and 1989 (Continued)

Percent of live births the United States by selected years of education and race/ethnicity of mother, 1970, 1980, and 1989.

Education and race/ethnicity of mother	Percent of live births		
	1970	1980	1989
Education of mother 16 years or more			
Total, all racial/ethnic groups	8.6	14.0%	17.4
Asian or Pacific Islander	20.9	30.8	31.2
Chinese	34.0	41.5	40.5
Japanese	20.7	36.8	43.6
Filipino	28.1	37.1	36.0
Other Asian or Pacific Islander[a]	3.1	25.5	25.3
White	9.6	15.5	19.2
White, non-Hispanic[b]	-	16.4	22.0
Black	2.8	6.2	7.2
Black, non-Hispanic[b]	-	5.7	7.2
American Indian or Alaskan Native	2.7	3.5	4.3
Hispanic origin[c]	-	4.2	5.1

Source: Health United States, 1991 (Washington, DC: U.S. Government Printing Office, 1992). Primary source: National Center for Health Statistics, Division of Analysis, from data compiled by the Division of Vital Statistics. *Notes:* (a) Includes Hawaiians and part Hawaiians. (b) The race groups "White, total" and "Black, total" include persons of both Hispanic and non-Hispanic origin. Data for "White, non-Hispanic" and "Black, non-Hispanic" shown only for states with an Hispanic origin item on their birth certificates. (c) Persons of Hispanic origin may be of any race.

★ 431 ★

Births by Prenatal Care and Race/Ethnicity of Mother, 1970, 1980, and 1989

Percent of live births in the United States by early, late, or no prenatal care[a] and race/ethnicity of mother, 1970, 1980, and 1989.

Prenatal care and race/ethnicity of mother,	Percent of live births		
	1970	1980	1989
Prenatal care began during first trimester			
Total, all racial/ethnic groups	68.0	76.3	75.5
Asian or Pacific Islander	67.3	73.7	74.8
Chinese	71.8	82.6	81.5
Japanese	78.1	86.1	86.2
Filipino	60.6	77.3	77.6
Other Asian or Pacific Islander[b]	54.9	67.6	70.8
White	72.3	79.2	78.9
White, non-Hispanic[c]	-	81.2	82.7
Black	44.2	62.4	60.0
Black, non-Hispanic[c]	-	60.7	59.9
American Indian or Alaskan Native	38.2	55.8	57.9
Hispanic origin[d]	-	60.2	59.5
Prenatal care began during third trimester, or no prenatal care			
Total, all racial/ethnic groups	7.9	5.1	6.4
Asian or Pacific Islander	6.8	6.5	6.1

[Continued]

★ 431 ★

Births by Prenatal Care and Race/Ethnicity of Mother, 1970, 1980, and 1989 (Continued)

Percent of live births in the United States by early, late, or no prenatal care[a] and race/ethnicity of mother, 1970, 1980, and 1989.

Prenatal care and race/ethnicity of mother,	Percent of live births		
	1970	1980	1989
Chinese	6.5	3.7	3.6
Japanese	4.1	2.1	2.7
Filipino	7.2	4.0	4.7
Other Asian or Pacific Islander[a]	10.7	9.0	7.6
White	6.3	4.3	5.2
White, non-Hispanic[c]	-	3.5	3.7
Black	16.6	8.9	11.9
Black, non-Hispanic[c]	-	9.7	12.0
American Indian or Alaskan Native	28.9	15.2	13.4
Hispanic origin[d]	-	12.0	13.0

Source: Health United States, 1991 (Washington, DC: U.S. Government Printing Office, 1992). Excludes births that occurred in states not reporting education and/or prenatal care. Primary source: National Center for Health Statistics, Division of Analysis, from data compiled by the Division of Vital Statistics. *Notes:* (a) Early prenatal care is defined as care that begins during the first trimester of pregnancy; late prenatal care is defined as care that begins during the last trimester of pregnancy. (b) Includes Hawaiians and part Hawaiians. (c) The race groups "White, total" and "Black, total" include persons of both Hispanic and non-Hispanic origin. Data for "White, non-Hispanic" and "Black, non-Hispanic" shown only for states with an Hispanic origin item on their birth certificates. (d) Persons of Hispanic origin may be of any race.

★ 432 ★

Births by Age of Mother and Race/Ethnicity of Child, 1988

Numbers of live births in the United States by age of mother and race/ethnicity of child, 1988.

Age of mother	All races[a]	Race/ethnicity of child						
		Asian or Pacific Islander				White	Black	Other
		Hawaiian	Chinese	Japanese	Filipino			
Total, all ages	3,760,561	7,193	17,880	9,802	21,482	2,991,373	608,193	59,259
Under 15 years	10,220	3	2	3	18	4,101	5,860	77
15 to 19 years	467,485	1,139	196	285	1,235	318,725	134,270	3,380
15 years	25,002	58	5	11	54	13,276	11,001	157
16 years	53,474	109	14	23	117	33,052	18,913	345
17 years	89,313	185	30	51	213	59,714	26,895	610
18 years	129,563	337	59	94	368	89,950	35,399	951
19 years	170,133	450	88	106	483	122,733	42,062	1,317
20 to 24 years	1,141,320	2,578	1,759	1,449	4,406	894,195	207,330	13,414
25 to 29 years	1,201,350	1,990	6,501	3,241	6,972	997,233	152,306	21,238
30 to 34 years	696,354	1,085	6,731	3,421	5,834	580,398	78,129	14,587
35 to 39 years	214,336	335	2,447	1,287	2,597	173,681	26,216	5,442
40 to 44 years	28,334	62	233	112	399	22,264	3,888	981
45 to 49 years	1,162	1	11	4	21	776	194	140

Source: Public Health Service, U.S. Department of Health and Human Services, "Supplements to the Monthly Vital Statistics Report, Series 24: Compilations of Data on Nationality, Mortality, Marriage, Divorce, and Induced Terminations of Pregnancy, No. 1," *Vital and Health Statistics* (Hyattsville, MD: National Center for Health Statistics, May 1989), table 23. *Note:* (a) Includes births of other races not shown separately.

★ 433 ★

Births to Women Nineteen Years and Under

Births to mothers age nineteen years or under[a] in the United States by race/ethnicity, 1982.

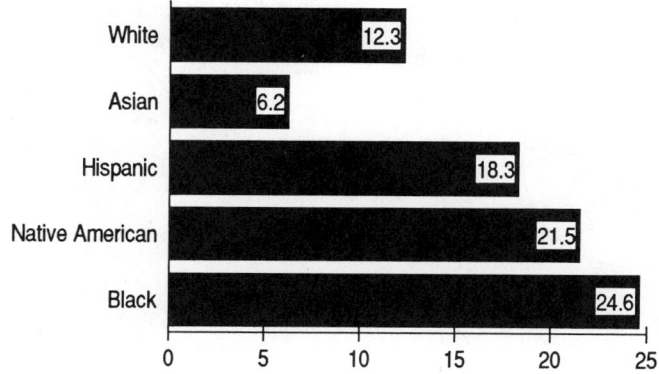

Percentage of live birth to women 19 years old and under

Source: U.S. Department of Health and Human Service, *Report of the Secretary's Task Force on Black and Minority Health, Vol. VI* (Washington, DC: U.S. Government Printing Office, 1985). *Note:* (a) The neonatal mortality rate among teenage mothers is 1.5 times as high as that of mothers age twenty years and over.

★ 434 ★

Births by Birth Weight and Race/Ethnicity of Child, 1985

Numbers of births in the United States by birth weight and race/ethnicity, 1985.

| Birth weight[a] | All races[b] | Asian or Pacific Islander | | | | | | |
		Hawaiian	Chinese	Japanese	Filipino	White	Black	Other
Total	3,760,561	7,193	17,880	9,802	21,482	2,991,373	608,193	59,259
Less than 2,500 grams (considered low birth weight)	253,554	460	900	581	1,492	168,390	75,414	3,625
Less than 500 grams	4,809	5	5	8	16	2,719	1,950	62
500 to 999 grams	17,667	22	40	29	63	10,554	6,608	188
1,000 to 1,499 grams	23,108	49	59	45	102	14,774	7,560	280
1,500 to 1,999 grams	48,394	94	172	96	262	32,054	14,591	630
2,000 to 2,499 grams	159,576	290	624	403	1,049	108,289	44,705	2,465
2,500 to 2,999 grams	595,533	1,332	3,385	1,880	4,666	421,411	143,370	12,690
3,000 to 3,499 grams	1,378,097	2,879	7,943	4,202	8,918	1,079,501	232,928	25,174
3,500 to 3,999 grams	1,110,689	1,890	4,492	2,467	5,102	945,828	123,194	14,025
4,000 to 4,499 grams	345,355	530	992	583	1,089	307,161	27,436	3,060
4,500 to 4,999 grams	64,293	76	138	68	174	58,046	4,374	521
5,000 grams or more	8,328	11	15	11	28	7,390	648	83
Not stated	4,712	15	15	10	13	3,646	829	81

Source: Public Health Service, U.S. Department of Health and Human Services, "Supplements to the Monthly Vital Statistics Report, Series 24: Compilations of Data on Nationality, Mortality, Marriage, Divorce, and Induced Terminations of Pregnancy, No. 1," *Vital and Health Statistics* (Hyattsville, MD: National Center for Health Statistics, May 1989), table 24. *Notes:* (a) One ounce equals approximately 28 grams; one pound equals approximately 454 grams. (b) Includes births of other races not shown separately.

★ 435 ★

Births in Hawaii by Race

Total numbers of births in Hawaii by race/ethnicity, 1987.

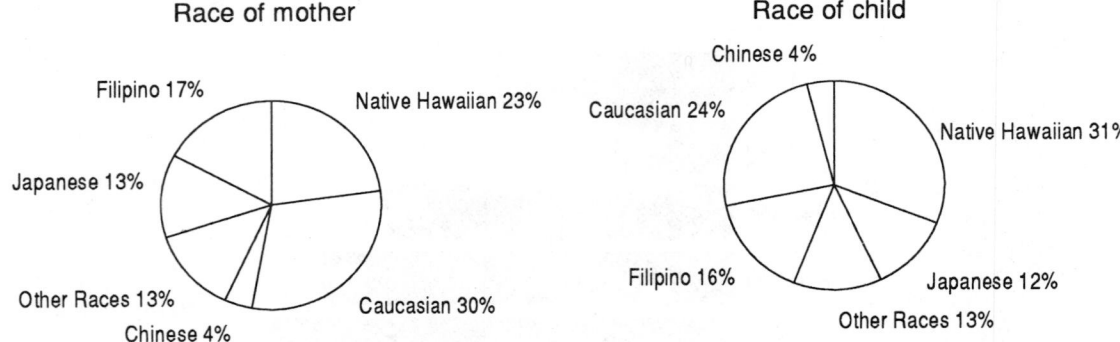

Source: Papa Ola Lokahi, *State of Hawaii Native Hawaiian Health Data Book 1990* (Honolulu: The Office of Hawaiian Affairs, August 1, 1990), p.16. Primary source: Hawaii State Department of Health, Vital Statistics Office. Data files upon which this figure is based are community-oriented and a profile of the community in general.

★ 436 ★

Births, Low Birth Weight in Hawaii by Race/Ethnicity

Rate of low birth weight births per 1,000 live births among residents of Hawaii, 1988.

Type of birth	State, total	Hawaiian	Part-Hawaiian	Chinese	Filipino	Japanese	Caucasian	Other
Total	68.6	101.7	68.4	40.2	96.1	73	56.2	61
Single	60.3	90.9	63.6	35.5	88	62.9	46.1	47.6
Plural	514.4	250	390.8	266.7	636.4	613.6	578.3	521.1

Source: Papa Ola Lokahi, *State of Hawaii Native Hawaiian Health Data Book 1990* (Honolulu: The Office of Hawaiian Affairs, August 1, 1990), p. 22. Primary source: Hawaii State Department of Health, Vital Statistics Office. Data files upon which this figure is based are community oriented and a profile of the community in general.

★ 437 ★

Births to Unmarried Mothers in Hawaii by Race/Ethnicity

Numbers of births in Hawaii to unmarried mothers by race/ethnicity, 1987.

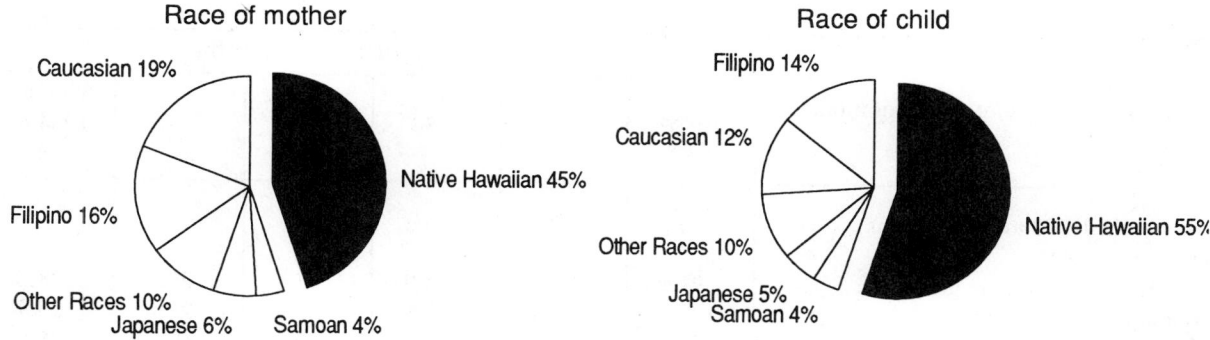

Race of mother

Caucasian 19%
Native Hawaiian 45%
Filipino 16%
Other Races 10%
Japanese 6%   Samoan 4%

Race of child

Filipino 14%
Caucasian 12%
Other Races 10%
Native Hawaiian 55%
Japanese 5%
Samoan 4%

Source: Papa Ola Lokahi, *State of Hawaii Native Hawaiian Health Data Book 1990* (Honolulu: The Office of Hawaiian Affairs, August 1, 1990), p. 18. Primary source: Hawaii State Department of Health, Vital Statistics Office. Data files upon which this figure is based are community-oriented and a profile of the community in general.

★ 438 ★

Infant Mortality by Birth Weight and Race/Ethnicity of Mother

Infant deaths per 1,000 live births in the United States by birth weight[a] and race/ethnicity of mother, 1960 and 1983 to 1986.

Birth weight and race/ethnicity of mother	Infant deaths per 1,000 live births					
	1960[b]	1983	1984	1985	1986	Average, 1984 to 1986
Birth weight less than 1,500 grams (very low birth weight)						
Total, all racial/ethnic groups	752.6	393.6	383.5	381.0	364.8	376.3
Asian or Pacific Islander	-	352.9	363.4	384.4	347.2	364.7
Chinese	-	(f)	(f)	369.6[f]	(f)	331.1
Japanese	-	(f)	(f)	238.8[f]	(f)	290.2
Filipino	-	321.0[f]	287.3[f]	350.9[f]	285.7[f]	307.1
Other Asian or Pacific Islander[c]	-	342.4	408.7	414.9	370.4	397.7
White	769.4	402.4	389.5	385.1	369.8	381.4
White, non-Hispanic[d]	-	398.8	387.4	384.0	369.4	380.2
Black	706.4	378.7	372.5	370.5	353.6	365.2
Black, non-Hispanic[d]	-	372.0	370.6	360.3	345.7	358.4
American Indian or Alaskan Native	-	376.1	356.7	388.9	422.6	389.7
Hispanic origin[e]	-	382.2	381.7	359.8	347.1	362.1

[Continued]

★438★

Infant Mortality by Birth Weight and Race/Ethnicity of Mother (Continued)

Infant deaths per 1,000 live births in the United States by birth weight[a] and race/ethnicity of mother, 1960 and 1983 to 1986.

Birth weight and race/ethnicity of mother	Infant deaths per 1,000 live births					
	1960[b]	1983	1984	1985	1986	Average, 1984 to 1986
Birth weight 1,500 to 2,499 grams						
(low birth weight)						
Total, all racial/ethnic groups	91.9	30.0	28.9	27.8	27.2	28.0
Asian or Pacific Islander	-	25.3	23.8	22.5	25.5	23.9
Chinese	-	(f)	(f)	(f)	(f)	29.9
Japanese	-	(f)	(f)	(f)	(f)	22.2
Filipino	-	(f)	(f)	(f)	(f)	17.9
Other Asian or Pacific Islander[c]	-	25.8	25.5	22.5	27.6	25.3
White	93.8	31.3	30.8	28.9	28.1	29.3
White, non-Hispanic[e]	-	31.7	30.2	28.8	28.6	29.2
Black	85.1	26.6	24.4	25.1	24.2	24.6
Black, non-Hispanic[d]	-	26.7	23.4	26.1	24.5	24.7
American Indian or Alaskan Native	-	44.7[f]	45.8[f]	42.7[f]	51.6[f]	46.7
Hispanic origin[e]	-	26.8	29.1	27.3	25.9	27.4
Birth weight 2,500 grams or more						
Total, all racial/ethnic groups	11.2	4.5	4.3	4.2	4.1	4.2
Asian or Pacific Islander	-	3.8	4.1	3.2	3.4	3.5
Chinese	-	(f)	(f)	2.6[f]	2.5[f]	2.8
Japanese	-	(f)	(f)	(f)	(f)	2.9
Filipino	-	(f)	4.5[f]	3.4[f]	3.6[f]	3.9
Other Asian or Pacific Islander[c]	-	3.7	4.2	3.5	3.6	3.7
White	9.7	4.1	3.9	3.9	3.7	3.8
White, non-Hispanic[d]	-	4.1	3.8	3.8	3.7	3.8
Black	20.2	6.9	6.3	6.2	6.2	6.2
Black, non-Hispanic[d]	-	7.1	6.5	6.2	6.4	6.4
American Indian or Alaskan Native	-	9.1	7.6	7.3	7.5	7.4
Hispanic origin[e]	-	4.2	3.9	3.8	3.5	3.7

Source: Health United States, 1991 (Washington, DC: U.S. Government Printing Office, 1992). Primary source: National Center for Health Statistics, Division of Analysis, from data compiled by the Division of Vital Statistics. *Notes:* (a) One ounce equals approximately 28 grams; one pound equals approximately 454 grams. (b) Data are shown by race of child in 1960. (c) Includes Hawaiians and part Hawaiians. (d) The race groups "White, total" and "Black, total" include persons of both Hispanic and non-Hispanic origin. Data for "White, non-Hispanic" and "Black, non-Hispanic" shown only for states with an Hispanic origin item on their birth certificates. In 1983-86, twenty-three States and the District of Columbia included this item. (e) Persons of Hispanic origin may be of any race. (f) Birth weight–specific infant mortality rates are considered unreliable for groups with fewer than 200 births with birth weight less than 1,500 grams, fewer than 2,000 births with birth weight 1,500 to 2,499 grams, and fewer than 20,000 births with birth weight 2,500 grams or more. Birth weight–specific rates are considered highly unreliable and are not shown for groups with fewer than 150 births with birth weight less than 1,500 grams, fewer than 1,500 births with birth weight 1,500 to 2,499 grams, and fewer than 15,000 births with birth weight 2,500 grams or more.

★ 439 ★

Infant and Neonatal Deaths by Race/Ethnicity of Mother, 1960 and 1983 to 1986

Numbers of infant, neonatal, and post-neonatal deaths per 1,000 live births in the United States by race/ethnicity of the mother, 1960 and 1983 to 1986.

Race/ethnicity of mother	Infant deaths per 1,000 live births					
	1960[a]	1983	1984	1985	1986	1984 to 1986
Total, all racial/ethnic groups	25.1	10.9	10.4	10.4	10.1	10.3
Asian or Pacific Islander	-	8.3	8.9	7.8	7.8	8.1
Chinese	-	9.5	7.2	5.8	5.9	6.3
Japanese	-	(e)	(e)	6.0[e]	7.2[e]	6.5
Filipino	-	8.4	8.5	7.7	7.2	7.8
Other Asian or Pacific Islander[b]	-	8.3	9.7	8.6	8.6	8.9
White	22.2	9.3	8.9	8.9	8.5	8.8
White, non-Hispanic[c]	-	9.2	8.7	8.7	8.4	8.6
Black	42.1	19.2	18.2	18.6	18.2	18.3
Black, non-Hispanic[c]	-	19.1	18.1	18.3	18.0	18.1
American Indian or Alaskan Native	-	15.2	13.4	13.1	13.9	13.5
Hispanic origin[d]	-	9.5	9.3	8.8	8.4	8.8
Neonatal deaths per 1,000 live births						
Total, all racial/ethnic groups	18.4	7.1	6.8	6.8	6.5	6.7
Asian or Pacific Islander	-	5.2	5.7	4.8	4.8	5.1
Chinese	-	5.5	4.4	3.3	3.1	3.6
Japanese	-	(e)	(e)	3.1[e]	4.7[e]	3.8
Filipino	-	5.6	5.3	5.1	4.9	5.1
Other Asian or Pacific Islander[b]	-	5.2	6.5	5.4	5.3	5.7
White	16.9	6.1	5.8	5.8	5.5	5.7
White, non-Hispanic[c]	-	6.0	5.7	5.7	5.4	5.6
Black	27.3	12.5	11.9	12.3	11.9	12.0
American Indian or Alaskan Native	-	7.5	6.4	6.1	6.1	6.2
Hispanic origin[d]	-	6.2	6.2	5.7	5.5	5.7
Post-neonatal deaths per 1,000 live births						
Total, all racial/ethnic groups	6.7	3.8	3.6	3.6	3.6	3.6
Asian or Pacific Islander	-	3.1	3.1	2.9	3.0	3.0
Chinese	-	(e)	(e)	2.5[e]	2.8[e]	2.7
Japanese	-	(e)	(e)	(e)	2.5[e]	2.7
Filipino	-	2.8[e]	3.2[e]	2.7[e]	2.3	2.7
Other Asian or Pacific Islander[b]	-	3.1	3.2	3.1	3.3	3.2
White	5.3	3.2	3.1	3.1	3.0	3.1
White, non-Hispanic[c]	-	3.2	3.0	3.0	3.0	3.0
Black	14.8	6.7	6.3	6.3	6.3	6.3
Black, non-Hispanic[c]	-	7.0	6.6	6.4	6.5	6.5
American Indian or Alaskan Native	-	7.7	7.0	7.0	7.8	7.3
Hispanic origin[d]	-	3.3	3.1	3.2	2.9	3.1

Source: Health United States, 1991 (Washington, DC: U.S. Government Printing Office, 1992). Primary source: National Center for Health Statistics, Division of Analysis, from data compiled by the Division of Vital Statistics. *Notes:* (a) Data are shown by race/ethnicity of child in 1960. (b) Includes Hawaiians and part Hawaiians. (c) The race groups "White, total" and "Black, total" include persons of both Hispanic and non-Hispanic origin. Data for "White, non-Hispanic" and "Black, non-Hispanic" shown only for states with an Hispanic origin item on their birth certificates. In 1983-86, twenty-three States and the District of Columbia included this item. (d) Data shown only for states with an Hispanic-origin item on their birth certificates. In 1983-86, twenty-three States and the District of Columbia included this item. (e) Infant and neonatal mortality rates for groups with fewer than 10,000 births are considered unreliable. Postneonatal mortality rates for groups with fewer than 20,000 births are considered unreliable. Infant and neonatal mortality rates for groups with fewer than 7,500 births are considered highly unreliable and are not shown. Post-neonatal mortality rates for groups with fewer than 15,000 births are considered highly unreliable and are not shown.

★ 440 ★

Fetal Deaths in Hawaii by Race/Ethnicity

Numbers of fetal deaths in Hawaii by mother's race/ethnicity, 1987.

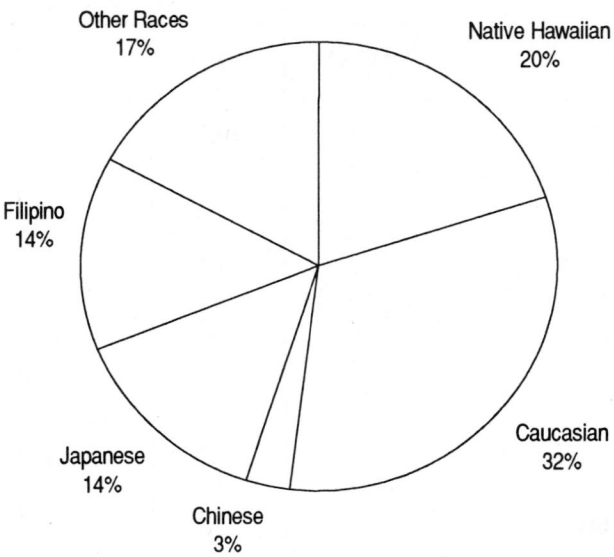

Source: Papa Ola Lokahi, *State of Hawaii Native Hawaiian Health Data Book 1990* (Honolulu: The Office of Hawaiian Affairs, August 1, 1990), p. 46. Primary source: Hawaii State Department of Health, Vital Statistics Office. Data files upon which this figure is based are community-oriented and a profile of the community in general.

★ 441 ★

Infant Deaths in Hawaii by Race/Ethnicity

Numbers of infant deaths in Hawaii by infant's race/ethnicity, 1987.

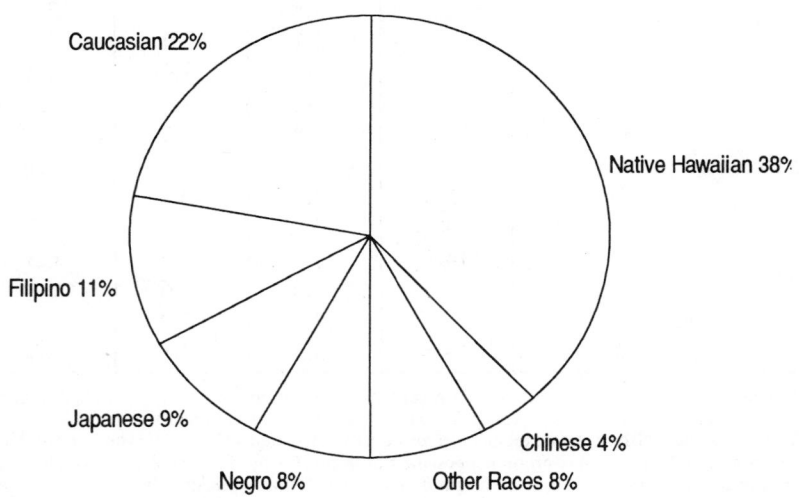

Source: Papa Ola Lokahi, *State of Hawaii Native Hawaiian Health Data Book 1990* (Honolulu: The Office of Hawaiian Affairs, August 1, 1990), p. 48. Primary source: Hawaii State Department of Health, Vital Statistics Office. Data files upon which this figure is based are community-oriented and a profile of the community in general.

★ 442 ★

Infant Mortality Rates

Infant mortality rates for white, black, and Asian Americans, 1986.

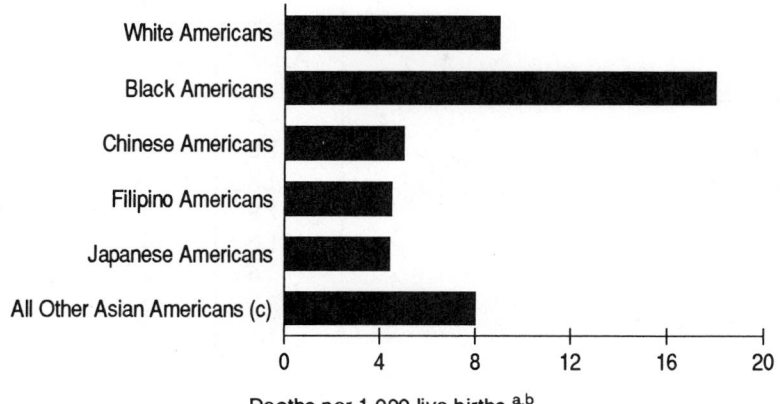

Deaths per 1,000 live births [a,b]

Source: U.S. General Accounting Office, *Asian Americans: A Status Report, 1990* (Washinton DC: U.S. Government Printing Office, 1990), fig. 4.3, p.32. Primary source: HHS, PHS, National Center for Health Statistics, *Vital Statistics of the united States, Vol. II* (1986). Notes: The National Center for Health Statistics notes that infant mortality rates for Asian Americans "should be interpreted with caution because of inconsistencies in reporting race on birth and death certificates." (b) Infant mortality rates from 1982, presented in the PHS report, *The Facts* (1988), showed similar differences among groups. (c) Includes deaths among Hawaiians and part-Hawaiians.

★ 443 ★

Childbearing Patterns by Race/Ethnicity, 1982

Numbers and percent of mothers by selected age range, marital status, and number of children by race/ethnicity, 1982.

Age of mother	Asian	White	Black	Hispanic[a]	American Indian/Alaska Native
Age of mother					
Under 15 years	88	4,153	5,395	1,288	126
15 to 19 years	6,278	357,948	140,534	60,369	8,749
20 to 24 years	23,872	958,509	207,640	115,275	15,364
25 to 29 years	36,303	961,053	143,748	90,393	10,236
30 to 34 years	26,394	503,847	69,781	47,999	4,886
35 to 39 years	8,146	136,664	21,341	18,056	1,627
40 to 44 years	1,351	19,027	3,966	3,809	287
45 to 49 years	131	853	236	201	14
Births, in percent, to mothers under 20 years	6.2%	12.3%	24.6%	18.3%	21.5%
Births, in percent, to mothers over 35 years	9.4%	5.3%	4.3%	6.5%	4.7%
Marital status:					
Out of wedlock births, number	8,642	355,180	335,927	86,488	14,998
Percent	8.4%	12.1%	56.7%	25.6%	36.3%
Parity[b]					
First births, percent	41.8%	43.3%	39.2%	37.0%	36.9%
High parity (4 children or more), percent	10.7%	8.6%	14.2%	16.4%	17.0%

Source: U.S. Department of Health and Human Services, *Report of the Secretary's Task Force on Black and Minority Health, Vol. I: Executive Summary* (Washington, D.C.: U.S. Department of Health and Human Services, August 1985), table 15, p. 176. Primary source: National Center for Health Statistics. Also in source: a general assessment of Asian American health status in the United States. *Note:* (a) Refers to births to residents of twenty-three states reporting Hispanic origins of the mother or birth certificates. These states accounted for an estimated 95 percent of all births of Hispanic origin in the United States in 1982. (b) Condition of having borne previous children.

★ 444 ★

Congenital Malformations by Race/Ethnicity, 1981–1986

Numbers born with various congenital malformations per 10,000 live births in the United States by race/ethnicity, 1981 to 1986.

Malformation[a] (defined below)	Number per 10,000 live births				
	Asian	Black	Hispanic	American Indian	White
Anencephaly	4.4	2.1	4.4	3.6	3.0
Spina bifida without anencephaly	1.8	3.3	5.9	4.1	5.1
Hydrocephalus without spina bifida	4.8	8.1	4.6	10.8	5.4
Microcephalus	1.9	4.8	2.8	2.6	2.1
Ventricular septal defect	21.0	14.4	13.8	19.1	17.4
Atrial septal defect	2.5	2.1	1.2	4.1	2.1
Valve stenosis and atresia	2.8	5.9	1.9	8.2	3.2
Patent ductus arteriosus	25.1	49.9	20.7	33.5	26.5
Pulmonary artery stenosis	1.8	5.4	1.4	0	1.5
Cleft palate without cleft lip	4.6	3.7	3.7	9.8	5.9
Cleft lip with or without cleft palate	12.9	4.4	8.6	17.5	9.7
Clubfoot without central nervous system defects	14.4	19.9	19.1	15.5	27.5
Hip dislocation without central nervous system defects	25.0	13.8	24.0	31.4	32.3
Hypospadias	16.5	24.6	14.9	17.5	32.7
Rectal altresia and stenosis	3.8	2.8	3.0	4.6	3.7
Fetal alcohol syndrome	0.3	6.0	0.8	29.9	0.9
Down syndrome	11.3	6.5	11.6	6.7	8.5
Autosomal abnormalities, excluding Down syndrome	2.9	2.1	2.1	3.1	2.2
Total	157.8	179.9	144.4	222.0	189.8

Definitions of Malformations:

Anencephaly: Absence of top and back of the skull and most of the brain, usually causing still birth or newborn death.

Spina bifida without anencephaly: Longitudinal gap in the spinal column, with serious consequences (e.g. paralysis) when the spinal cord and nerve roots in the gap segment are malformed.

Hydrocephalus without spina bifida: Expansion of the fluid-filled compartments within the brain, often at the expense of the brain tissue.

Microcephalus: Very small brain, usually accompanied by mental retardation.

Ventricular septal defect: Hole in the wall between the two main (lower) pumping chambers of the heart, often compromising heart efficiency.

Atrial septal defect: Hole in the wall between the two auxiliary (upper) pumping chambers of the heart, often compromising heart efficiency.

Valve stenosis and atresia: Absence or narrowing of a heart valve.

Patent ductus arteriosus: Persistence of a heart-lung bypass vessel that is normal in the fetus, but that should begin to close immediately after birth for efficient heart-lung function.

Pulmonary artery stenosis: Complete obstruction of the blood vessel(s) leading from the heart to the lungs.

Cleft palate without cleft lip: Front to back cleft in the hard or soft palate or both (roof of the mouth), usually interfering with feeding and speech development.

Cleft lip with or without cleft palate: Vertical cleft (single or double) in the upper lip.

Clubfoot without central nervous system defects: Deformation of a (usually) fully developed foot and ankle.

Hip dislocation without central nervous system defects: Dislocated or (more often) dislocatable hip joint, usually due to shallow socket.

Hypospadias: Opening of the urethra in the base or shaft of the penis rather than at its tip.

Rectal altresia and stenosis: Narrowing or complete impassability of the rectum.

Fetal alcohol syndrome: A variable combination of mental deficiency, certain abnormal facial features, prenatal and subsequent growth retardation, and various physical malformations in offspring of women drinking heavily during pregnancy.

Down syndrome: A variable pattern of mental retardation and physical abnormalities due to presence of an extra (third) copy of chromosome 21 (or a specific segment thread) in all or, occasionally, some cells of the body.

Autosomal abnormalities, excluding Down syndrome. All other abnormalities in number or structure of any of the 22 nonsex chromosome pairs.

Source: U.S. Department of Health and Human Services, Public Health Service, Health Resources and Services Administrators, *Health Status of Minorities and Low-Income Groups,* 3rd ed. (Washington, DC: U.S. Government Printing Office, 1991), table 8. Primary source: Centers for Disease Control, G. F. Chavez, J. F. Cordero, J. E. Becerra, "Leading Major Congenital Malformations among Minority Groups in the United States, 1981-1986," *Morbidity and Mortality Weekly Report 1988,* 35 (No. SS-3), table 1, p. 19. *Notes:* (a) By organ and/or system.

Deaths

★ 445 ★

Death Rates by Age and Race/Ethnicity

Numbers of deaths per 100,000 population in the United States by age and race/ethnicity, 1987 to 1989.

Age and race/ethnicity	Deaths per 100,000 resident population		
	1987	1988	1989
Asian or Pacific Islander			
Under 1 year	610.6	609.2	659.5
1 to 14 years	23.7	23.9	25.9
15 to 24 years	57.1	57.1	55.6
25 to 44 years	76.2	76.8	80.6
45 to 64 years	398.8	402.3	386.8
65 years and over	2,458.3	2,430.3	2,379.2
White			
Under 1 year	845.1	832.0	815.5
1 to 14 years	30.8	30.4	29.4
15 to 24 years	93.8	95.1	91.5
25 to 44 years	146.3	148.6	150.8
45 to 64 years	810.5	790.4	761.2
65 years and over	5,059.9	5,106.4	4,957.6
Black			
Under 1 year	2,003.7	1,996.6	2,023.7
1 to 14 years	47.9	49.0	48.4
15 to 24 years	135.0	145.2	150.8
25 to 44 years	350.8	367.0	373.6
45 to 64 years	1,375.5	1,379.9	1,355.2
65 years and over	5,592.2	5,649.8	5,585.3
Hispanic[a]			
Under 1 year	919.7	963.9	1,013.5
1 to 14 years	28.8	30.3	32.9
15 to 24 years	113.2	113.3	121.4
25 to 44 years	176.1	184.8	201.4
45 to 64 years	592.6	609.2	611.1
65 years and over	3,523.3	3,481.9	3,516.9

Source: National Center for Health Statistics, *Vital Statistics of the United States, Vol. II, Mortality, Part A, 1985-1989. Public Health Service* (Washington, DC: U.S. Government Printing Office, 1991). Death rates for Hispanics, Asian or Pacific Islanders, and American Indian or Alaskan Natives were computed by the Office of Analysis and Epidemiology, National Center for Health Statistics. *Note:* (a) The race groups include persons of both Hispanic and non-Hispanic origin. Hispanic data shown only for states with an Hispanic-origin item on their death certificates.

★ 446 ★

Death Rates by Accidents/Homicides/Suicides, Age, and Race/Ethnicity

Numbers of deaths per 100,000 population in the United States by selected cause of death, age, and race/ethnicity, 1987 to 1989.

Age and race/ethnicity	Deaths per 100,000 population by:					
	Accidents/adverse effects			Homicide/suicide		
	1987	1988	1989	1987	1988	1989
1 to 14 years						
Total, all racial/ethnic groups	14.6	14.4	13.7	2.0	2.2	2.3
Asian or Pacific Islander	9.4	9.5	9.8	1.5	1.6	2.4
White	13.7	13.3	12.8	1.6	1.7	1.7
Black	19.8	20.4	18.9	4.3	5.0	5.4
Hispanic[a]	11.5	12.2	13.0	1.7	1.8	2.3
American Indian or Alaskan Native	22.2	23.8	23.3	2.4	2.5	3.8
15 to 24 years						
Total, all racial/ethnic groups	48.9	49.5	45.8	26.9	28.6	30.3
Asian or Pacific Islander	26.2	29.1	25.0	15.5	13.2	17.5
White	51.5	52.0	48.1	21.4	21.9	22.3
Black	35.6	36.6	34.9	58.9	67.6	75.2
Hispanic[a]	46.7	49.3	51.3	38.7	38.6	43.4
American Indian or Alaskan Native	86.1	88.8	84.0	41.3	48.4	48.0
25 to 44 years						
Total, all racial/ethnic groups	35.4	35.8	35.4	28.4	28.8	28.7
Asian or Pacific Islander	16.4	15.5	15.8	11.8	14.5	14.6
White	34.0	34.3	33.9	24.0	23.8	23.5
Black	47.3	48.9	47.7	63.6	67.5	68.0
Hispanic[a]	37.1	40.0	42.5	33.9	34.1	37.8
American Indian or Alaskan Native	100.1	97.2	94.2	46.8	46.5	47.3

Source: National Center for Health Statistics, *Vital Statistics of the United States, Vol. II: Mortality, Part A, 1985-1989. Public Health Service* (Washington, DC: U.S. Government Printing Office, 1991). Death rates for Hispanics, Asian or Pacific Islanders, and American Indian or Alaskan Natives were computed by the Office of Analysis and Epidemiology, National Center for Health Statistics. *Note:* (a) The race groups include persons of both Hispanic and non-Hispanic origin. Data shown for Hispanic origina are from states with an Hispanic-origin item on their death certificates.

★ 447 ★

Death Rates by Heart Disease/Malignant Neoplasms, Age, and Race/Ethnicity

Numbers of deaths per 100,000 population in the United States by selected cause of death, age, and race/ethnicity, 1987 to 1989.

Age and race/ethnicity	Deaths per 100,000 population by:					
	Diseases of heart			Malignant neoplasms		
	1987	1988	1989	1987	1988	1989
45 to 64 years						
Total, all racial/ethnic groups	270.9	259.3	241.5	301.7	296.6	290.9
Asian or Pacific Islander	103.6	99.1	94.6	147.5	159.5	147.9
White	257.3	244.2	225.8	293.7	288.7	282.8
Black	425.1	425.9	409.2	410.7	400.6	399.0
Hispanic[a]	161.8	166.2	158.0	148.5	151.9	160.6
American Indian or Alaskan Native	234.1	224.1	241.7	153.5	182.6	182.7
65 years and over						
Total, all racial/ethnic groups	2,074.6	2,066.4	1,949.2	1,059.8	1,067.6	1,085.1
Asian or Pacific Islander	880.9	870.0	831.7	559.5	548.8	561.0
White	2,087.6	2,079.5	1,959.9	1,054.0	1,062.0	1,079.0
Black	2,179.9	2,180.9	2,080.6	1,231.8	1,241.4	1,269.8
Hispanic[a]	1,352.9	1,335.6	1,336.0	693.4	665.4	727.3
American Indian or Alaskan Native	1,144.4	1,128.3	1,211.4	583.8	606.5	684.2

Source: National Center for Health Statistics, *Vital Statistics of the United States, Vol. II: Mortality, Part A, 1985-1989. Public Health Service* (Washington, DC: U.S. Government Printing Office, 1991). Death rates for Hispanics, Asian or Pacific Islanders, and American Indian or Alaskan Natives were computed by the Office of Analysis and Epidemiology, National Center for Health Statistics. *Note:* (a) The race groups include persons of both Hispanic and non-Hispanic origin. Data shown for Hispanic origina are from states with an Hispanic-origin item on their death certificates.

★ 448 ★

Deaths, Asian/Pacific Islander by Selected Causes and Sex

Numbers of Asian/Pacific Islander male and female deaths and total deaths in the United States by selected cause of death, 1985 to 1989.

Cause of death, sex, and race/ethnicity	Number of deaths				
	1985	1986	1987	1988	1989
Total, all races					
Total deaths, all causes	2,086,440	2,105,361	2,123,323	2,167,999	2,150,466
Diseases of heart	771,169	765,490	760,353	765,156	733,867
Cerebrovascular diseases	153,050	149,643	149,835	150,517	145,551
Malignant neoplasms	461,563	469,376	476,927	485,048	496,152
Chronic obstructive pulmonary diseases	74,662	76,559	78,380	82,853	84,344
Pneumonia and influenza	67,615	69,812	69,225	77,662	76,550
Chronic liver disease and cirrhosis	26,767	26,159	26,201	26,409	26,694
Diabetes mellitus	36,969	37,184	38,532	40,368	46,833
Nephritis, nephrotic syndrome, and nephrosis	21,349	21,767	22,052	22,392	21,118
Septicemia	17,182	18,795	19,916	20,925	19,333
Atherosclerosis	23,926	22,706	22,474	22,086	19,357
Human immunodeficiency virus infection[a]	-	-	13,468	16,602	22,082

[Continued]

★ 448 ★

Deaths, Asian/Pacific Islander by Selected Causes and Sex (Continued)

Numbers of Asian/Pacific Islander male and female deaths and total deaths in the United States by selected cause of death, 1985 to 1989.

Cause of death, sex, and race/ethnicity	Number of deaths				
	1985	1986	1987	1988	1989
Accidents and adverse effects	93,457	95,277	95,020	97,100	95,028
Suicide	29,453	30,904	30,796	30,407	30,232
Homicide and legal intervention	19,893	21,731	21,103	22,032	22,909
Asian or Pacific Islander, male					
Total deaths, all causes	9,441	9,795	10,496	11,155	11,688
Diseases of heart	2,837	2,853	3,137	3,225	3,240
Cerebrovascular diseases	658	718	788	791	821
Malignant neoplasms	2,262	2,281	2,454	2,639	2,821
Chronic obstructive pulmonary diseases	276	308	327	353	391
Pneumonia and influenza	315	334	329	376	473
Chronic liver disease and cirrhosis	133	115	133	145	161
Diabetes mellitus	172	186	183	200	217
Nephritis, nephrotic syndrome, and nephrosis	98	101	113	134	134
Septicemia	71	82	79	97	81
Atherosclerosis	40	42	44	40	38
Human immunodeficiency virus infection[a]	-	-	69	99	132
Accidents and adverse effects	734	791	827	864	809
Suicide	230	237	257	255	270
Homicide and legal intervention	164	195	190	221	279
Asian or Pacific Islander, female					
Total deaths, all causes	6,446	6,719	7,193	7,808	8,354
Diseases of heart	1,729	1,834	1,875	2,065	2,186
Cerebrovascular diseases	669	641	719	789	846
Malignant neoplasms	1,649	1,752	1,902	2,115	2,236
Chronic obstructive pulmonary diseases	146	120	159	168	167
Pneumonia and influenza	201	226	253	242	328
Chronic liver disease and cirrhosis	66	78	82	78	79
Diabetes mellitus	132	175	184	188	231
Nephritis, nephrotic syndrome, and nephrosis	68	81	83	80	105
Septicemia	44	62	80	59	68
Atherosclerosis	46	37	43	46	46
Human immunodeficiency virus infection[a]	-	-	10	8	14
Accidents and adverse effects	380	366	407	433	442
Suicide	123	118	126	109	143
Homicide and legal intervention	79	97	79	109	102

Source: National Center for Health Statistics, *Vital Statistics of the United States, Vol. II: Mortality, Part A, 1985-1989, Public Health Service* (Washington, DC: U.S. Government Printing Office, 1991). Data computed by the Division of Analysis from data compiled by the Division of Vital Statistics. *Note:* (a) Categories for the coding and classification of human immunodeficiency virus infection were introduced in the United States beginning with mortality data for 1987.

★ 449 ★

Deaths, Asian/Pacific Islander by Sex, Ranked by Selected Causes

Selected causes of death in the United States ranked for Asian/Pacific Islander males and females, 1985 to 1989.

Cause of death, race/ethnicity and sex	Rank				
	1985	1986	1987	1988	1989
Total, all racial/ethnic groups					
Diseases of heart	1	1	1	1	1
Cerebrovascular diseases	3	3	3	3	3
Malignant neoplasms	2	2	2	2	2
Chronic obstructive pulmonary diseases	5	5	5	5	5
Pneumonia and influenza	6	6	6	6	6
Chronic liver disease and cirrhosis	9	9	9	9	9
Diabetes mellitus	7	7	7	7	7
Nephritis, nephrotic syndrome, and nephrosis	11	11	11	10	12
Septicemia	14	13	13	13	14
Atherosclerosis	10	10	10	11	13
Human immunodeficiency virus infection[a]	-	-	15	15	11
Accidents and adverse effects	4	4	4	4	4
Suicide	8	8	8	8	8
Homicide and legal intervention	12	12	12	12	10
Asian or Pacific Islander, male					
Diseases of heart	1	1	1	1	1
Cerebrovascular diseases	4	4	4	4	3
Malignant neoplasms	2	2	2	2	2
Chronic obstructive pulmonary diseases	6	6	6	6	6
Pneumonia and influenza	5	5	5	5	5
Chronic liver disease and cirrhosis	11	12	11	11	12
Diabetes mellitus	8	9	9	9	9
Nephritis, nephrotic syndrome, and nephrosis	13	13	12	13	13
Septicemia	14	14	14	15	15
Atherosclerosis	16	16	17	19	20
Human immunodeficiency virus infection[a]	-	-	15	14	14
Accidents and adverse effects	3	3	3	3	4
Suicide	7	7	7	7	8
Homicide and legal intervention	9	8	8	8	7
Asian or Pacific Islander female					
Diseases of heart	1	1	2	2	2
Cerebrovascular diseases	3	3	3	3	3
Malignant neoplasms	2	2	1	1	1
Chronic obstructive pulmonary diseases	6	8	7	7	7
Pneumonia and influenza	5	5	5	5	5
Chronic liver disease and cirrhosis	13	13	12	13	13
Diabetes mellitus	7	6	6	6	6
Nephritis, nephrotic syndrome, and nephrosis	12	12	11	12	11
Septicemia	15	14	13	14	14

[Continued]

★ 449 ★

Deaths, Asian/Pacific Islander by Sex, Ranked by Selected Causes (Continued)

Selected causes of death in the United States ranked for Asian/Pacific Islander males and females, 1985 to 1989.

Cause of death, race/ethnicity and sex	Rank				
	1985	1986	1987	1988	1989
Atherosclerosis	14	15	15	15	15
Human immunodeficiency virus infection	-	-	24	27	24
Accidents and adverse effects	4	4	4	4	4
Suicide	9	9	9	10	8
Homicide and legal intervention	11	11	14	10	12

Source: National Center for Health Statistics, *Vital Statistics of the United States, Vol. II: Mortality, Part A, 1985-1989. Public Health Service* (Washington, DC: U.S. Government Printing Office, 1991). *Note:* (a) Categories for the coding and classification of human immunodeficiency virus infection were introduced in the United States beginning with mortality data for 1987.

★ 450 ★

Deaths, Six Leading Causes for Asian/Pacific Islanders

Deaths by six leading causes for Asian/Pacific Islander males and females in the United States, 1991.

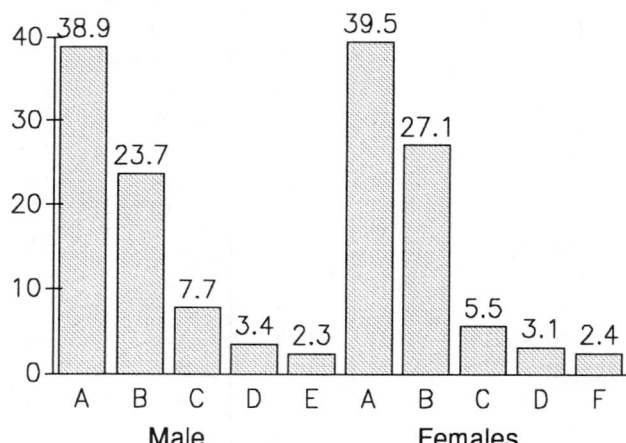

A Total cardiovascular diseases   C Accidents   E Suicide
B Cancer   D Pneumonia/Influenza   F Diabetes

Source: 1993 Heart and Stroke Facts Statistics (Dallas, TX: American Heart Association, 1992), p. 3. Primary source: National Center for Health Statistics and the American Heart Association.

★ 451 ★

Deaths, Ranked by Selected Causes by Sex and Race/Ethnicity

Selected causes of death in the United States ranked by race/ethnicity and sex, 1989.

Cause of death	Causes of death, ranked						
	All persons	Male			Female		
	All races	Asian/ Pacific Islander	White	Black	Asian/ Pacific Islander	White	Black
Diseases of heart	1	1	1	1	2	1	1
Malignant neoplasms	2	2	2	2	1	2	2
Cerebrovascular diseases	3	3	4	5	3	3	3
Accidents and adverse effects	4	4	3	3	4	6	5
Chronic obstructive pulmonary diseases	5	6	5	9	7	5	9
Pneumonia and influenza	6	5	6	7	5	4	6
Diabetes mellitus	7	9	8	10	6	7	4
Suicide	8	8	7	13	8	12	19
Chronic liver disease and cirrhosis	9	12	9	11	13	11	12
Homicide and legal intervention	10	7	11	4	12	18	10
Human immunodeficiency virus infection[a]	11	14	10	6	24	23	13
Nephritis, nephrotic syndrome, and nephrosis	12	13	12	12	11	10	8
Atherosclerosis	13	20	14	17	15	8	16
Septicemia	14	15	13	14	14	9	11

Source: National Center for Health Statistics, Vital Statistics of the United States, Vol. II: Mortality, Part A, 1985-1989, Public Health Service (Washington, DC: U.S. Government Printing Office, 1991). Data computed by the Division of Analysis from data compiled by the Division of Vital Statistics. *Note:* (a) Categories for the coding and classification of human immunodeficiency virus infection were introduced in the United States beginning with mortality data for 1987.

★ 452 ★

Deaths by Disease, Asian/Pacific Islanders by Age Range and Sex

Average number of Asian/Pacific Islander deaths per year (expected, actual, and difference) in the United States by disease category, age range, and sex, 1979 to 1981.

Asian/Pacific Islanders	Results	Average deaths per year								Total Deaths
		CVD[a]	Cancer	Cirrhosis	Infant mortality	Diabetes	Unintentional injuries	Homicide	All other	
Under 45 years										
Males	Observed	148	140	15	300	4	378	108	271	1,364
	Expected[b]	240	195	49	405	14	823	152	483	2,361
	Excess[c]	-92	-55	-34	-105	-10	-445	-44	-212	924
Females	Observed	83	176	3	252	3	152	49	199	924
	Expected[b]	107	221	22	309	13	260	48	271	1,251
	Excess	-24	-45	-19	-57	-10	-101	1	-72	-327
Under 70 years										
Males	Observed	1,083	873	73	300	51	476	142	642	3,640
	Expected[b]	2,142	1,344	190	405	72	999	181	1,208	6,541
	Excess[c]	-1,059	-471	-117	-105	-21	-523	-39	-566	-2,901

[Continued]

★ 452 ★

Deaths by Disease, Asian/Pacific Islanders by Age Range and Sex (Continued)

Average number of Asian/Pacific Islander deaths per year (expected, actual, and difference) in the United States by disease category, age range, and sex, 1979 to 1981.

Asian/Pacific Islanders	Results	Average deaths per year								Total Deaths
		CVD[a]	Cancer	Cirrhosis	Infant mortality	Diabetes	Unintentional injuries	Homicide	All other	
Females	Observed	506	732	31	252	46	216	58	451	2,292
	Expected[b]	914	1,182	96	309	68	335	57	704	3,665
	Excess[c]	-408	-450	-65	-57	-22	-119	1	-253	-1,373

Source: U.S. Department of Health and Human Services, *Report of the Secretary's Task Force on Black and Minority Health, Volume I: Executive Summary* (Washington, DC: U.S. Department of Health and Human Services, August 1985), table 10, p. 82. Primary source: Duke University, analysis commissioned by the Task Force on Black and Minority Health, 1984-1985. Also in source: general assessment of Asian American health status in the United States. *Notes:* (a) Cardiovascular disease (CVD) combines heart disease and stroke. (b) The expected number is calculated from the rate observed in the white population. Asian/Pacific Islander death rates are consistently lower than expected on the basis used here. (c) Percent of total excess was not calculated in this table because excess deaths were virtually all negative.

★ 453 ★

Deaths by Selected Causes by Race/Ethnicity and Sex

Selected causes of deaths in the United States for males and females by race/ethnicity, 1989.

Cause of death and sex	Asian/ Pacific Islander	White	Black
Males			
All causes	11,688	950,852	146,393
Diseases of heart	3,240	325,397	38,321
Cerebrovascular diseases	821	48,563	7,739
Malignant neoplasms	2,821	228,301	31,452
Chronic obstructive pulmonary diseases	391	44,046	3,593
Pneumonia and influenza	473	30,892	4,168
Chronic liver disease and cirrhosis	161	14,414	2,517
Diabetes mellitus	217	16,282	3,072
Nephritis, nephrotic syndrome, and nephrosis	134	8,093	2,047
Septicemia	81	6,728	1,643
Atherosclerosis	38	6,652	547
Human immunodeficiency virus infection[a]	132	14,114	5,475
Accidents and adverse effects	809	52,691	9,503
Suicide	270	21,858	1,771
Homicide and legal intervention	279	8,337	8,888
Females			
All causes	8,354	902,989	121,249
Diseases of heart	2,186	323,469	39,110
Cerebrovascular diseases	846	76,953	10,240
Malignant neoplasms	2,236	205,855	24,112
Chronic obstructive pulmonary diseases	167	33,835	2,078
Pneumonia and influenza	328	36,961	3,417

[Continued]

★ 453 ★

Deaths by Selected Causes by Race/Ethnicity and Sex (Continued)

Selected causes of deaths in the United States for males and females by race/ethnicity, 1989.

Cause of death and sex	Asian/ Pacific Islander	White	Black
Chronic liver disease and cirrhosis	79	7,797	1,334
Diabetes mellitus	231	21,771	4,883
Nephritis, nephrotic syndrome, and nephrosis	105	8,514	2,119
Septicemia	68	8,829	1,912
Atherosclerosis	46	11,139	889
Human immunodeficiency virus infection[a]	14	981	1,320
Accidents and adverse effects	442	26,448	3,901
Suicide	143	5,566	382
Homicide and legal intervention	102	2,971	2,074

Source: National Center for Health Statistics, *Vital Statistics of the United States, Vol. II, Mortality: Part A, 1985-1989. Public Health Service* (Washington, DC: U.S. Government Printing Office, 1991). Data computed by the Division of Analysis from data compiled by the Division of Vital Statistics. *Note:* (a) Categories for the coding and classification of human immunodeficiency virus infection were introduced in the United States beginning with mortality data for 1987.

★ 454 ★

Deaths in Hawaii by Race/Ethnicity, 1987

Number of deaths in Hawaii by race/ethnicity, 1987.

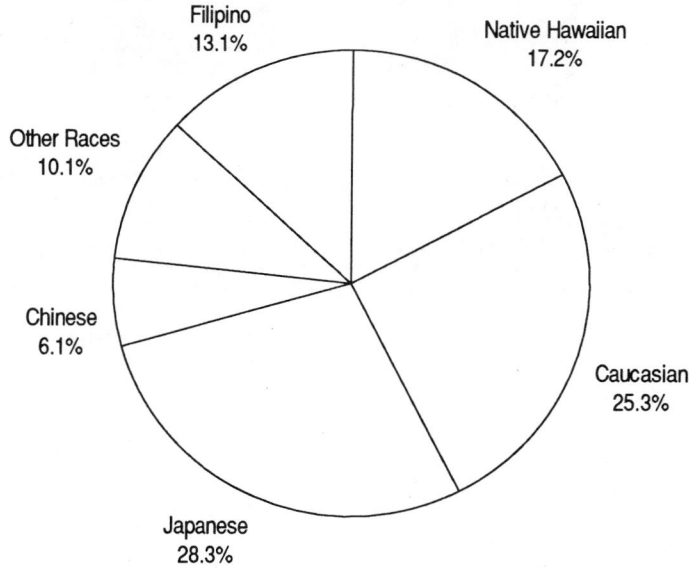

Source: Papa Ola Lokahi, *State of Hawaii Native Hawaiian Health Data Book 1990* (Honolulu: The Office of Hawaiian Affairs, August 1, 1990), p. 40. Primary source: Hawaii State Department of Health, Vital Statistics Office. Data files upon which this figure is based are community-oriented and a profile of the community in general.

★ 455 ★

Life Expectancy

Life expectancy of Asian Americans compared with white Americans in California (1960) and Hawaii (1980).

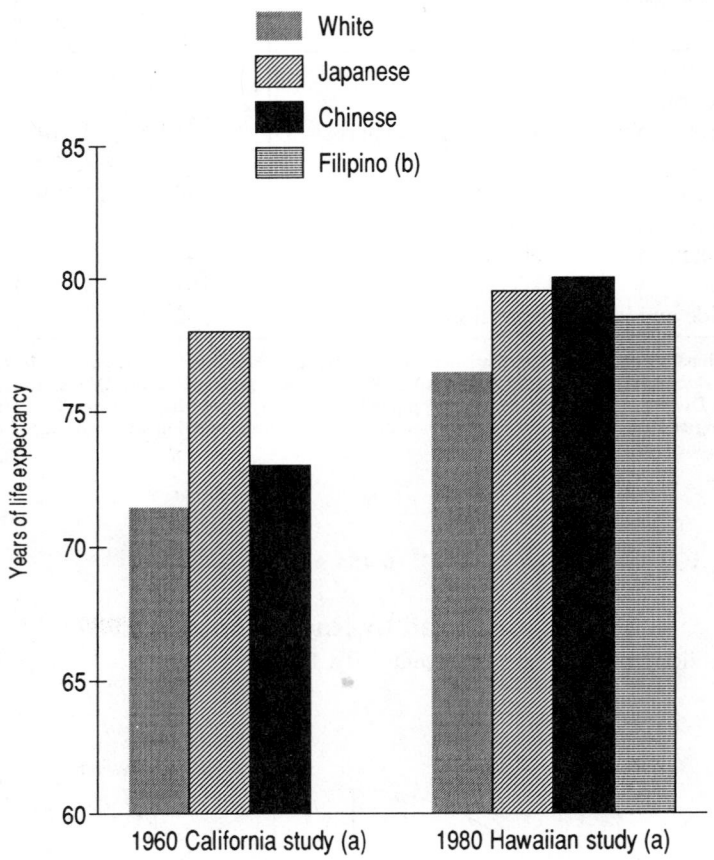

Source: U.S. General Accounting Office, Fact Sheet for the Chairman, Select Committee on Hunger, House of Representatives, *Asian Americans, A Status Report,* (Washington, DC: U.S. Government Printing Office, 1990), p. 30. Primary source: R.W. Gardner, R. Robey, and P.C. Smith, "Asian Americans: Growth, Change, and Diversity," *Population Bulletin* (1985), as presented in the PHS report, *The Facts* (1988), p. 191. *Notes:* (a) Information was gathered only on the Asian American groups shown and includes combined data for both sexes. (b) Filipino Americans were not included in the 1960 California study.

★ 456 ★

Mortality Rates, Males

Mortality rates for white, black, and Asian Americans, 1979-1981.

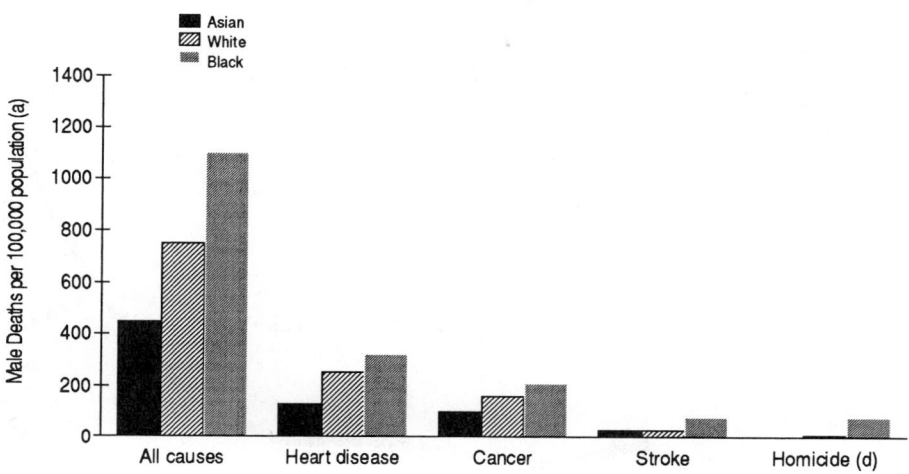

Source: U.S. General Accounting Office, Fact Sheet for the Chairman, Select Committee on Hunger, House of Representatives, *Asian Americans, A Status Report,* (Washington, DC: U.S. Government Printing Office, 1990), p. 30. Primary source: HHS, PHS National Center for Health Statistics; Census Bureau; and the HHS *Report of the Secretary's Task Force on Black and Minority Health,* Vol. 1 (1985), partially presented in the PHS report, *The Facts,* pp. 191-3. *Notes:* (a) Average annual age-adjusted death rates. The PHS report, *The Facts* (1988), notes that "Death rates for Asian/Pacific Americans are probably underestimated due to less frequent reporting of these rates on death certificates as compared with the Census." (b) Under the age of 45.

★ 457 ★

Mortality Rates, Females

Mortality rates for white, black, and Asian Americans, 1979-1981.

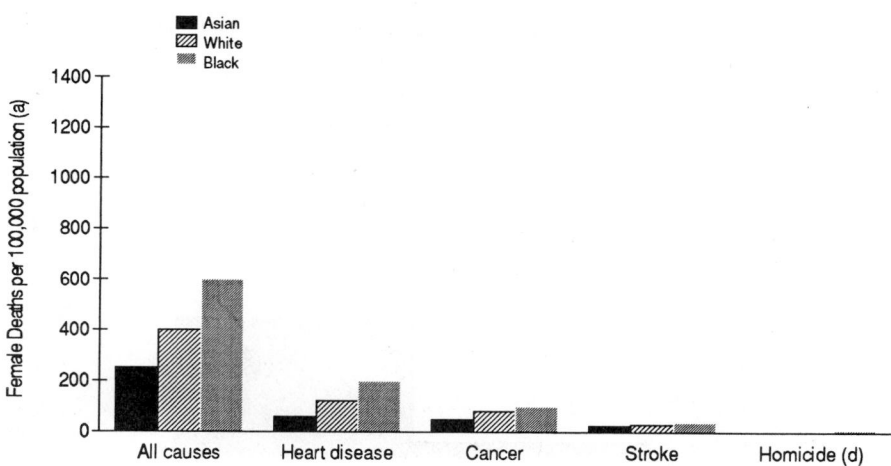

Source: U.S. General Accounting Office, Fact Sheet for the Chairman, Select Committee on Hunger, House of Representatives, *Asian Americans, A Status Report,* (Washington, DC: U.S. Government Printing Office, 1990), p. 30. Primary source: HHS, PHS National Center for Health Statistics; Census Bureau; and the HHS *Report of the Secretary's Task Force on Black and Minority Health,* Vol. 1 (1985), partially presented in the PHS report, *The Facts,* pp. 191-3. *Notes:* (a) Average annual age-adjusted death rates. The PHS report, *The Facts* (1988), notes that "Death rates for Asian/Pacific Americans are probably underestimated due to less frequent reporting of these rates on death certificates as compared with the Census." (b) Under the age of 45.

★ 458 ★

Suicide, Asian Americans

In a study of suicides, the older Asian American population, particularly women, showed a marked contrast to the white population.

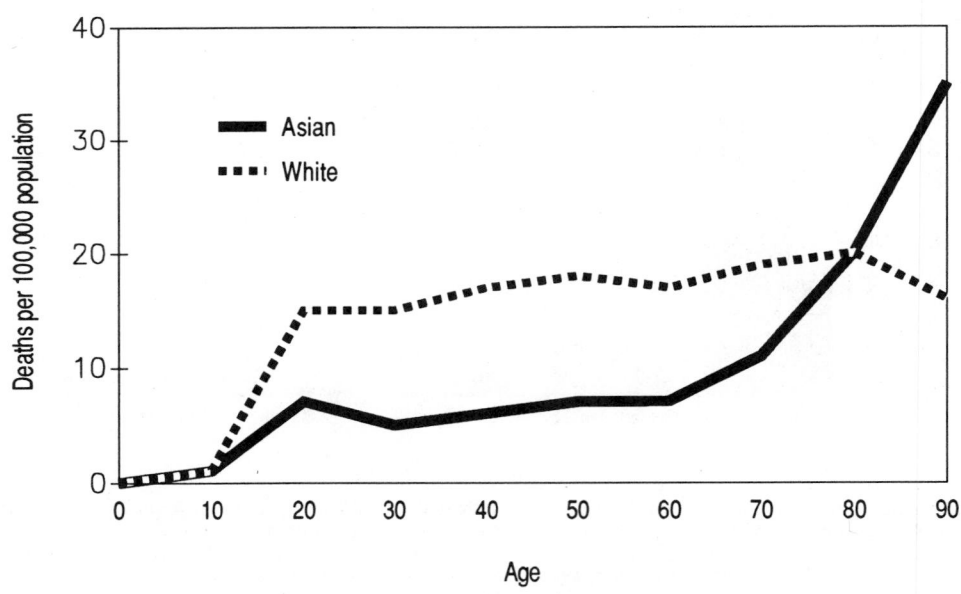

Source: Office of Minority Health Resource Center, U.S. Department of Health and Human Services, Public Health Service, *Closing the Gap: Homicide, Suicide, Unintentional Injuries, and Minorities* (Washington, DC: U.S. Government Printing Office, 1990). Primary source: *Report of the Secretary's Task Force on Black and Minority Health, Vol. V* (Washington, DC: U.S. Government Printing Office, 1985).

★ 459 ★

Suicide, Chinese American Women

Rates of suicide among older Chinese American women and white women surveyed, 1977-1979.

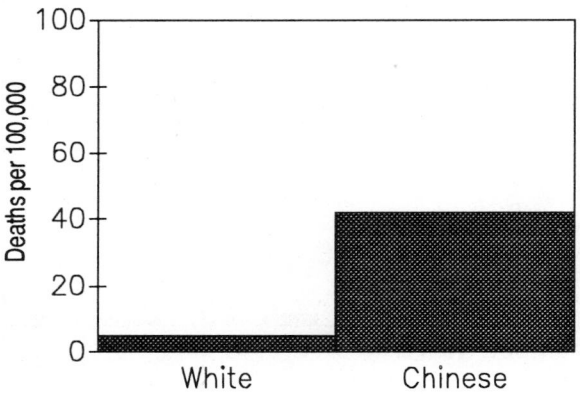

Source: Office of Minority Health Resource Center, U.S. Department of Health and Human Services, Public Health Service, *Closing the Gap: Homicide, Suicide, Unintentional Injuries, and Minorities* (Washington, DC: U.S. Government Printing Office, 1990). Primary source: *Report of the Secretary's Task Force on Black and Minority Health, Vol. V* (Washington, DC, U.S. Government Printing Office, 1985).

Disease and Health Problems

★ 460 ★

Blood Pressure Screening, Hawaii

Profile of Hawaiian population participating in blood pressure screening[a], 1988.

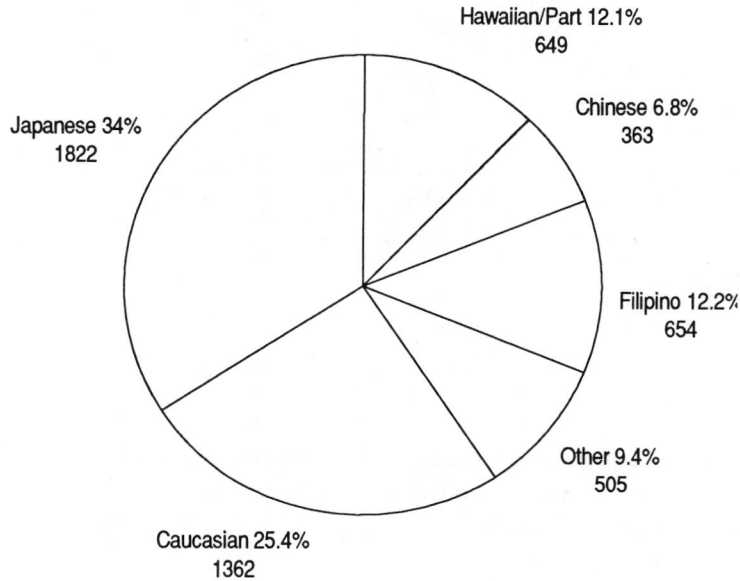

Hawaiian/Part 12.1%
649

Chinese 6.8%
363

Japanese 34%
1822

Filipino 12.2%
654

Other 9.4%
505

Caucasian 25.4%
1362

Source: Papa Ola Lokahi, *State of Hawaii Native Hawaiian Health Data Book 1990* (Honolulu: The Office of Hawaiian Affairs, August 1, 1990), p. 55. Primary source: Hawaii State Department of Health, State Hypertension Screening. Data are from records maintained by this service organization and reflect clients' usage of services. These data are not a reflection of the community in general, but a profile of the characteristics of individuals utilizing a particular service. *Note:* (a) Based on 15,274 persons screened.

★ 461 ★

Children Failing Hearing Screening, Hawaii, 1986 to 1987

Percent of the school age population in Hawaii failing to pass hearing screening tests by race/ethnicity, 1986 to 1987.

Ethnicity	School population, percent	Failing hearing screening, percent
Hawaiian	2%	4%
Part-Hawaiian	20%	28%
Samoan	3%	8%
Japanese	19%	18%
Filipino	19%	18%
Caucasian	20%	15%

Source: Papa Ola Lokahi, *State of Hawaii Native Hawaiian Health Data Book 1990* (Honolulu: The Office of Hawaiian Affairs, August 1, 1990), p. 73. Primary source: Hawaii State Department of Health, Family Health Services Division. Data are from records maintained by this service organization and reflect clients' usage of services. These data are not a reflection of the community in general, but a profile of the characteristics of individuals utilizing a particular service.

★ 462 ★

Cholesterol Screening, Abnormal Levels, Hawaii

Profile of Hawaiian population participating in cholesterol screening who register abnormal cholesterol levels, by race and island of residence, 1988.

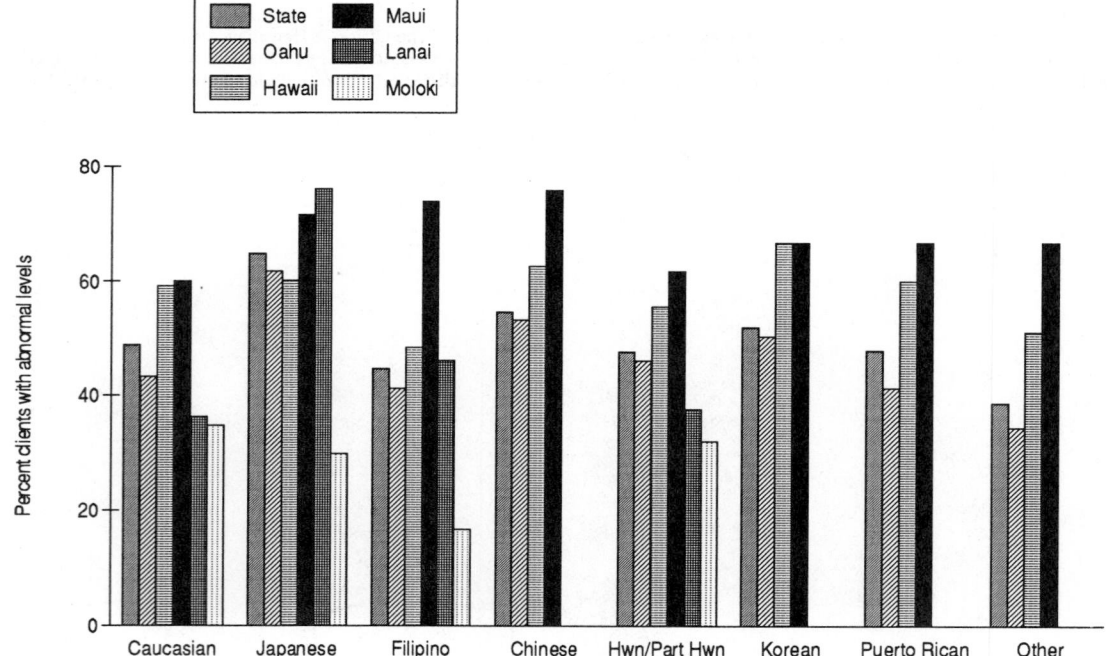

Source: Papa Ola Lokahi, *State of Hawaii Native Hawaiian Health Data Book 1990* (Honolulu: The Office of Hawaiian Affairs, August 1, 1990), p. 53. Primary source: Hawaii State Department of Health, Chronic Disease Branch, FY 1987-1988 (July-June). Data are from records maintained by this service organization and reflect clients' usage of services. These data are not a reflection of the community in general, but a profile of the characteristics of individuals utilizing a particular service. *Note:* (a) Percents based on total screened.

★ 463 ★

Cholesterol Screening Program, Hawaii

Profile of Hawaiian population participating in cholesterol screening program by race/ethnicity, 1988.

Total Screened

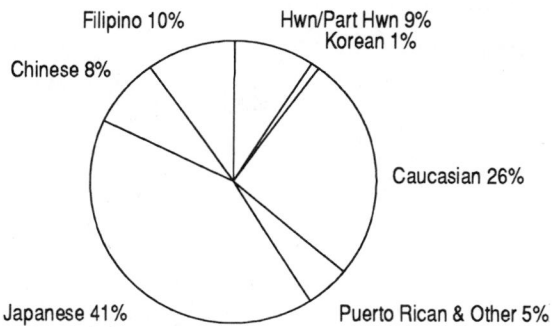

**Number abnormal
>199 mgm/dl**

**Number abnormally high
>239 mgm/dl**

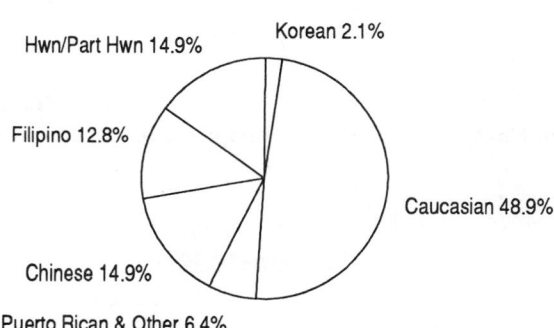

Source: Papa Ola Lokahi, *State of Hawaii Native Hawaiian Health Data Book 1990* (Honolulu: The Office of Hawaiian Affairs, August 1, 1990), p. 52. Primary source: Hawaii State Department of Health, Cholesterol Screening Program. Data are from records maintained by this service organization and reflect clients' usage of services. These data are not a reflection of the community in general, but a profile of the characteristics of individuals utilizing a particular service.

★ 464 ★

Chronic Otitis Media, Hawaii

Diagnosed cases of chronic otitis media, or chronic middle ear infection, in Hawaii, in percent.

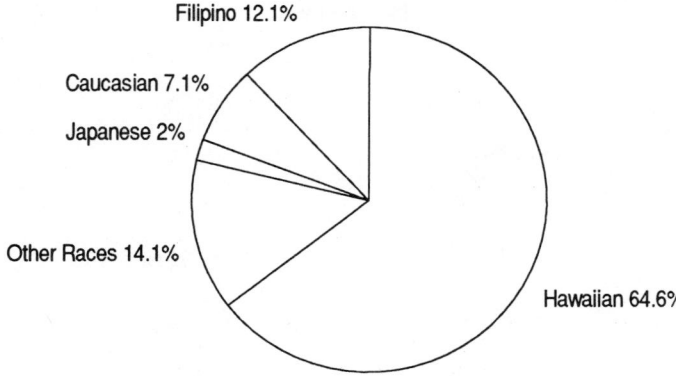

Source: Papa Ola Lokahi, *State of Hawaii Native Hawaiian Health Data Book 1990* (Honolulu: The Office of Hawaiian Affairs, August 1, 1990), p. 73. Primary source: Hawaii State Department of Health, Family Health Services Division. Data are from records maintained by this service organization and reflect clients' usage of services. These data are not a reflection of the community in general, but a profile of the characteristics of individuals utilizing a particular service.

★ 465 ★

Diabetes Screening, Hawaii

Profile of Hawaiian population participating in diabetes screening, 1988.

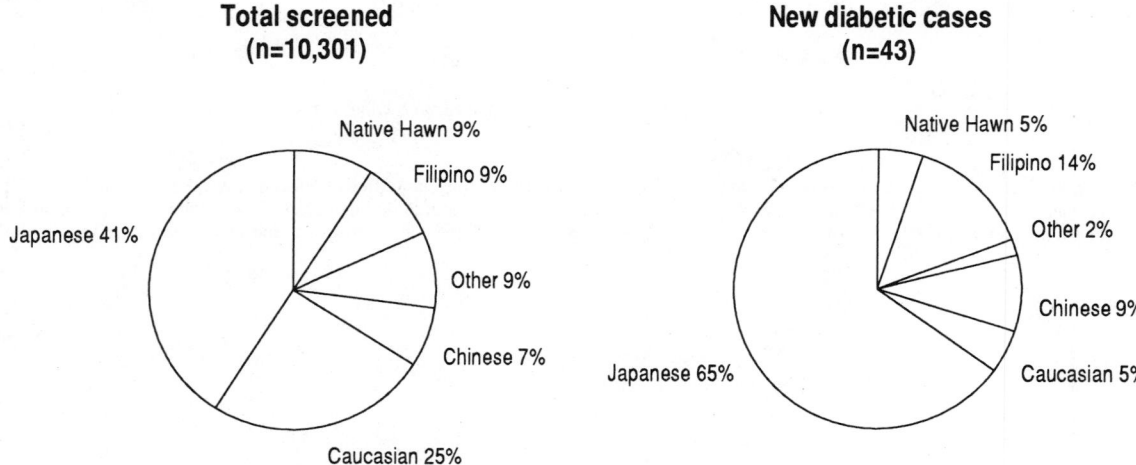

Source: Papa Ola Lokahi, *State of Hawaii Native Hawaiian Health Data Book 1990* (Honolulu: The Office of Hawaiian Affairs, August 1, 1990), p. 54. Primary source: Hawaii State Department of Health, Chronic Disease Branch Diabetes Screening Program. Data are from records maintained by this service organization and reflect clients' usage of services. These data are not a reflection of the community in general, but a profile of the characteristics of individuals utilizing a particular service.

★ 466 ★

Hepatitis B among Asian Americans
Selected data on the Asian/Pacific American population and hepatitis B infection.

Only 1 percent of the general population is chronically infected with hepatitis B in contrast to 5–15 percent among Asian/ Pacific Americans.

Infection rates are highest among refugees from Cambodia, Laos, and Vietnam, followed by immigrants from China, Hong Kong, Taiwan, Korea, the Philippines, and Japan.

Infected individuals are 300 times more likely than noninfected individuals to develop liver cancer and more likely to develop cirrhosis and hepatoma.

90 percent of infants infected perinatally will become chronic carriers.

Source: Invisible and in Need: Philanthropic Giving to Asian Americans and Pacific Islanders (San Francisco: Asian Americans and Pacific Islanders in Philanthropy [AAPIP], December 1992). Primary sources: L. Easterlin, "Health of Asian Immigrants: Hepatitis B, A Major Concern," *Urban Medicine* 3.1 (1988): 10-12; and Steve Chin, "Asian Health: A Special Prescription," *San Francisco Examiner* (July 7, 1991).

★ 467 ★

Hepatitis B Morbidity Rate in the United States
Rate of morbidity per 100,000 population infected with hepatitis B by race/ethnicity, 1987.

Race	Percent
Asian/Pacific Islander	34.9%
Caucasian	10.7%
African American	20.3%
Hispanic	10.6%
Native American	32.5%

Source: "Hepatitis B among Asians and Pacific Islanders" Fact Sheet (San Francisco: Asian American Health Forum, 1993).

★ 468 ★

Hypertension in Males, California

Filipino, African American, and general male populations 18 years and over in California who have been diagnosed with hypertension[a], in percent, 1979.

Males/age	Percent with hypertension
18-49 years	
Filipino	31
African American	25
General population	12
49 years and over	
Filipino	61
African American	67
General Population	47

Source: "Hypertension among Asians and Pacific Islanders," *Fact Sheet* (San Francisco: Asian American Health Forum, Inc., 1993). Primary source: G. R. Starving, et al., "Hypertension and Related Health Issues among Asians and Pacific Islanders in California," *Public Health Reports, 1988,* 103 (1): 28-37. *Note:* (a) Asian/Pacific Islanders are less likely to be aware of their hypertension, to be under treatment with medication, and to be controlling their blood pressure than other ethnic groups. Asian/Pacific Islanders had their blood pressure checked less often and visited physicians less frequently.

★ 469 ★

Hypertension in the Population, California

Selected racial/ethnic groups in California diagnosed with hypertension[a], in percent, 1979.

Race/ethnicity	Hypertension prevalence, in percent
Chinese	16%
Filipino	25%
Japanese	19%
Other Asian/Pacific Islander	20%
African American	26%
Caucasian	20%
Hispanic	16%

Source: "Hypertension among Asians and Pacific Islanders," *Fact Sheet* (San Francisco: Asian American Health Forum, 1993). Primary source: G. R. Starving, et al., "Hypertension and Related Health Issues Among Asians and Pacific Islanders in California," *Public Health Reports, 1988,* 103 (1): 28-37. *Note:* (a) Asian/Pacific Islanders are less likely to be aware of their hypertension, to be under treatment with medication, and to be controlling their blood pressure than other ethnic groups. Asian/Pacific Islanders had their blood pressure checked less often and visited physicians less frequently.

★ 470 ★

Hypertension in Women, California

Filipino, African American, and general female populations 50 years and over in California who have been diagnosed with hypertension[a], in percent, 1979.

Women, 50 years and over	Percent
Filipino	65%
African American	63%
General population, California	47%

Source: "Hypertension Among Asians and Pacific Islanders," *Fact Sheet* (San Francisco: American Health Forum, Inc., 1993). Primary source: G. R. Starving, et al., "Hypertension and Related Health Issues Among Asians and Pacific Islanders in California," *Public Health Reports, 1988*, 103 (1): 28-37. *Note:* (a) Asian Pacific Islanders are less likely to be aware of their hypertension, to be under treatment with medication and to be controlling their blood pressure than other ethnic groups. Asian Pacific Islanders had their blood pressure checked less often and visited physicians less frequently.

★ 471 ★

Malaria in the United States

Number of cases of malaria per 1,000 population by race/ethnicity, 1992.

Race/ethnicity	Cases per 1,000
Asian/Pacific Islander[a]	11.81
White	0.15
Black	0.68
Hispanic	0.33

Source: "Parasitic Diseases among Asians and Pacific Islanders," *Fact Sheet* (San Francisco: American Health Forum, 1993). *Note:* (a) 55 percent of all malaria cases in the United States occur within the Southeast Asian refugee community.

★ 472 ★

Parasitism among Asian Immigrants and Refugees

Selected facts about parasitism among immigrants from Asian countries and refugees.

Up to 50 percent of Asian immigrants and refugees continue to carry some type of parasite long after they have arrived in the United States.

Most parasites carried by Asian immigrants and refugees are intestinal infestations.

The most serious infestations cause considerable discomfort and may pose public health risks.

Source: Invisible and in Need: Philanthropic Giving to Asian Americans and Pacific Islanders (San Francisco: Asian Americans and Pacific Islanders in Philanthropy [AAPIP], December 1992).

★ 473 ★

Southeast Asian Refugees with Mental Health Service Needs, California

Reported results of the California Department of Mental Health Survey of Southeast Asian refugees and the general population requiring mental health services, by percent.

Population Group	Percent requiring mental health services
Southeast Asian refugees	14.5%
General population	3.0%

Source: "Mental Health Among Asians and Pacific Islanders," *Fact Sheet* (San Francisco: Asian American Health Forum, Inc., 1993).

★ 474 ★

Thalassemia Among Asian/Pacific Americans

Selected facts about the Asian/Pacific American population affected by thalassemia, a congenital blood disorder similar to sickle cell anemia.

Thalassemia, a congenital blood disorder similar to sickle cell anemia, disproportionately affects Asian/Pacific Americans.

Approximately 3 to 7 percent of Chinese Americans and up to 36 percent of Southeast Asian immigrants carry the genetic trait in asymptomatic forms.

Although this genetic disorder can affect American-born Asians, thalassemia is most pronounced among immigrants.

Source: Invisible and in Need: Philanthropic Giving to Asian Americans and Pacific Islanders (San Francisco: Asian Americans and Pacific Islanders in Philanthropy [AAPIP], December 1992).

★ 475 ★

Tuberculosis among Asian Americans

Incidence of tuberculosis by race/ethnicity, 1989.

Race/ethnicity	Cases per 100,000
Asian/Pacific Islander[a]	36
Caucasian	4
African American	28
Hispanic	18
Native American	18
General population	9

Source: "Tuberculosis among Asians and Pacific Islanders," *Fact Sheet* (San Francisco: Asian American Health Forum, Inc., 1993). Primary source: "Tuberculosis among Asians/Pacific Islanders-United States, 1985," *MMWR* 1987, 36 (20): 81. *Note:* (a) Among Asian/Pacific Islanders, the tuberculosis incidence rate is four times greater than the general population.

★ 476 ★

Tuberculosis among Asian Immigrants

Percent of Asian immigrants with tuberculosis, by country of origin, 1985.

Country of Origin	Asian immigrants with tuberculosis, percent from:
Cambodia, Laos, and Vietnam	27.3%
Philippines	25.2%
Korea	14.7%
China	9.6%
Other Asian/Pacific Islanders	16.8%
Recent immigrants/refugees	94%

Source: "Tuberculosis among Asians and Pacific Islanders" *Fact Sheet* (San Francisco: Asian American Health Forum, Inc., 1993). Primary source: "Tuberculosis Among Asians/Pacific Islanders-United States, 1985," *MMWR* 1987, 36 (20): 81.

★ 477 ★

Tuberculosis among Asian/Pacific Americans

Selected facts about the Asian/Pacific American population affected by tuberculosis.

Tuberculosis is growing among Asian/Pacific Americans at a rate five times that of the population in general.

The Asian countries with high levels of immigration to the United States—Cambodia, Laos, Vietnam, the Philippines, Korea, India and China are also the countries where tuberculosis rates are highest.

Because immigration from these countries is likely to continue at a significant rate, the high incidence of tuberculosis is likely to remain a problem in Asian/Pacific American immigrant communities.

Source: Invisible and in Need: Philanthropic Giving to Asian Americans and Pacific Islanders (San Francisco: Asian Americans and Pacific Islanders in Philanthropy [AAPIP], December 1992). Primary source: Testimony of Stewart Coulter, communicable disease specialist, State of California Department of Health Services, "TB Control and Refugee Health Program" in *California Asian Health Issues in the 1990s* (Sacramento: California Commission for Economic Development, Asian Pacific Islander Health Coalition, transcripts of a public hearing held April 20, 1990).

Disease Rates

★ 478 ★

Cancer Deaths by Cancer Site and Race/Ethnicity

Number of deaths by cancer site and race/ethnicity, 1988.

Cancer Site	Numbers of deaths during 1988					
	Chinese	Japanese	Hispanic[a]	American Indian	Black	
					Male	Female
All sites	1,388	1,012	9,602	1,151	30,321	23,647
Oral cavity	53	9	167	28	939	303
Esophagus	24	23	164	22	1,580	470
Stomach	98	130	582	48	1,316	802
Colon and rectum	159	153	866	102	2,637	3,014
Liver and other biliary	151	60	565	71	720	564
Pancreas	83	85	585	55	1,355	1,469
Lung (male)	211	127	1,218	197	10,112	-
Lung (female)	102	64	535	111	-	4,019
Breast (female)	99	62	798	66	-	4,467
Cervix uteri	21	8	240	29	-	974
Other uterus	31	32	231	30	-	953
Ovary	16	10	110	11	-	888
Prostate	26	43	482	64	4,582	-
Bladder	18	14	132	13	411	371
Kidney	18	19	241	30	501	319
Brain and central nervous system (CNS)	23	14	248	22	358	311
Lymphomas	49	36	477	35	684	513
Leukemia	38	28	464	49	806	672
Multiple myeloma	15	12	179	20	631	716

Source: American Cancer Society, *Cancer Facts and Figures for Minority Americans*, 1991, p. 8. Primary source: Data gathered from actual death certificates in 1988. *Note:* (a) Hispanic deaths are presented only for those states which record Hispanic origin on death certificates. This is approximately 80 percent of the entire U.S. Hispanic population.

Cancer Incidence by Cancer Site and Race/Ethnicity

Reported incidence of cancer per 100,000 population[a] in the United States by race/ethnicity, 1977 to 1983.

Cancer Site	Cases per 100,000 population							
	Chinese	Japanese	Filipino	Native Hawaiian	White	Black	American Indian	Mexican American
All sites	247.6	242.5	212.4	346.5	345.1	382.8	137.6	245.1
Oral cavity	15.4	4.8	8.9	9.0	11.3	15.0	2.1	6.6
Esophagus	3.3	2.8	3.4	7.3	3.0	11.6	1.0	1.6
Stomach	10.5	26.6	7.8	27.0	7.9	14.5	15.1	15.3
Colon and rectum	40.4	48.8	30.3	31.7	50.1	50.3	9.6	26.2
Liver	9.6	3.6	5.4	5.5	1.8	3.6	2.1	3.1
Gallbladder	1.0	1.5	1.4	1.3	1.3	1.0	10.0	4.6
Pancreas	6.3	7.1	4.9	8.0	9.1	13.8	3.7	11.0
Lung	40.6	27.1	27.3	66.9	51.8	69.8	6.3	23.4
Melanoma (skin)	0.7	1.2	1.0	1.1	9.2	0.8	1.9	1.9
Breast	57.8	55.0	41.3	106.1	88.8	75.2	21.3	52.1
Cervix uteri	10.3	5.9	8.6	15.2	8.7	19.7	19.9	16.1
Corpus uteri	18.0	17.7	11.3	28.2	25.7	15.0	7.2	11.3
Ovary	9.2	8.8	9.7	14.4	13.8	10.2	7.5	11.3
Prostate	29.6	43.8	44.0	56.1	77.9	125.5	31.0	76.3
Urinary bladder	9.0	8.0	4.4	8.5	17.0	9.6	1.4	7.9
Kidney	3.5	3.6	3.1	4.2	7.1	6.8	5.7	6.4
Brain and central nervous system (CNS)	2.4	2.4	1.9	3.0	6.1	3.4	1.2	3.7
Hodgkin's disease	0.6	0.5	1.2	1.0	3.0	1.8	0.2	2.6
Non-Hodgkin's lymphoma	8.5	7.2	8.3	8.4	10.9	7.2	2.8	6.7
Leukemia	4.8	5.7	7.1	8.2	10.6	9.1	4.6	6.9

Source: American Cancer Society, *Cancer Facts and Figures for Minority Americans,* (1991), p. 5. *Note:* (a) Incidence rates reported are based on data from the "Surveillance, Epidemiology and End Results (SEER)" program, provided by the Special Populations Branch of the National Cancer Institute. Numerator data are the number of cases reported to cancer registries; denominator data are the general population counts of the 1980 Census of the Population.

★ 480 ★

Cancer Mortality Rate by Cancer Site and Race/Ethnicity

Mortality rates[a] from cancer per 100,000 population by cancer site and race/ethnicity, 1977 to 1983.

Cancer Site	Mortality rates per 100,000							
	Chinese	Japanese	Filipino	Native Hawaiian	White	Black	American Indian	Mexican American
All sites	125.0	108.0	72.0	207.2	164.2	209.8	89.3	132.0
Oral cavity	5.4	1.7	2.4	3.9	3.3	5.7	1.8	1.9
Esophagus	2.8	2.1	1.8	7.2	2.6	9.1	2.0	1.7
Stomach	7.6	17.9	3.5	21.8	5.2	10.0	5.8	11.8
Colon and rectum	17.9	16.8	7.9	14.6	21.4	22.4	8.9	13.2
Liver	10.1	3.4	3.5	5.2	1.9	3.6	2.0	3.9
Gallbladder	0.7	1.1	0.6	0.5	0.9	0.7	2.6	3.2
Pancreas	6.4	7.0	3.5	10.0	8.4	11.2	4.6	10.2
Lung	31.7	19.8	14.5	56.5	41.6	51.3	18.1	19.5
Melanoma (skin)	0.2	0.2	0.3	0.3	2.2	0.4	0.3	0.4
Breast	12.0	10.2	7.8	37.2	26.8	26.9	9.0	19.4
Cervix uteri	3.3	2.2	1.9	5.6	3.2	8.7	5.5	4.2
Corpus uteri	2.7	2.4	1.7	6.3	3.9	6.5	1.8	2.3
Ovary	3.8	4.4	2.6	8.2	8.1	6.4	3.2	5.9
Prostate	7.4	8.4	8.7	15.8	21.1	43.9	11.7	19.4
Urinary bladder	1.7	1.8	1.4	2.9	3.8	3.8	1.0	2.3
Kidney	1.7	1.6	0.8	2.3	3.2	2.7	2.7	2.6
Brain and central nervous system (CNS)	1.3	1.3	1.1	2.0	4.2	2.4	1.3	3.2
Hodgkin's disease	0.3	0.1	0.3	0.2	0.9	0.6	0.3	1.0
Non-Hodgkin's lymphoma	2.8	3.5	3.4	5.6	5.2	3.3	2.1	3.1
Leukemia	4.1	3.5	4.1	6.8	6.7	5.8	2.9	4.8

Source: American Cancer Society, *Cancer Facts and Figures for Minority Americans,* (1991), p. 6. Primary source: Data is from Division of Vital Statistics, National Center for Health Statistics, Department of Health and Human Services. *Note:* (a) Mortality rates are age-adjusted to the 1970 census population distribution. "Age-adjustment" or "age-standardization" is a method used to make valid comparisons among rates by assuming the same age distribution among different groups being compared.

★ 481 ★

Cancer Survival Rate by Cancer Site and Race/Ethnicity
Five-year survival rates by cancer site and race/ethnicity, in percent, 1975 to 1984.

Cancer Site	Five year survival rate[a] in percent							
	Chinese	Japanese	Filipino	Native Hawaiian	White	Black	American Indian	Mexican American
All sites	47.5	53.1	46.1	43.2	51.9	39.6	35.4	48.4
Oral cavity	55.7	44.4	46.6	42.8	54.0	33.0	38.6	60.7
Esophagus	11.5	5.8	3.4	0.0	6.5	4.2	--	0.0
Stomach	21.6	29.8	18.8	12.9	15.3	17.5	8.9	17.8
Colon and rectum	53.1	61.7	44.8	58.4	53.2	46.7	39.7	45.0
Liver	2.0	1.5	6.7	6.6	3.8	3.1	0.0	0.0
Gallbladder	-	16.2	-	26.2	9.2	8.9	2.8	8.5
Pancreas	0.0	2.6	5.2	0.0	2.7	3.2	0.0	1.2
Lung	15.1	14.3	13.2	13.0	13.2	11.7	0.0	10.8
Melanoma (skin)	-	81.0	-	-	81.2	57.5	-	82.1
Breast	80.8	85.4	73.7	68.0	76.1	63.2	46.2	70.6
Cervix uteri	74.6	70.2	73.0	67.7	68.2	61.6	63.5	70.5
Corpus uteri	86.1	84.1	79.9	74.6	86.0	54.9	82.7	77.0
Ovary	43.3	43.5	44.7	46.8	37.6	40.9	42.9	38.7
Prostate	72.5	80.5	71.7	72.0	72.6	63.4	54.2	72.4
Urinary bladder	78.5	80.8	58.4	51.4	76.6	53.4	-	64.6
Kidney	60.7	63.1	47.0	59.0	51.9	56.3	49.7	51.4
Brain and central nervous system (CNS)	35.9	40.6	29.6	38.9	23.3	28.5	37.6	32.2
Hodgkin's disease	-	-	43.5	74.1	74.7	71.0	--	69.0
Non-Hodgkin's lymphoma	50.3	41.1	33.8	40.2	50.2	47.9	31.1	41.1
Leukemia	19.8	26.0	22.3	21.1	35.5	28.0	21.4	25.7

Source: American Cancer Society, *Cancer Facts and Figures for Minority Americans* (1991), p. 7. Primary source: Data reported by National Cancer Institute Special Populations Branch. *Note:* (a) Survival statistics are usually reported as five-year "relative survival rates," which is the ratio of the observed survival rate for the patient group to the expected survival rate for persons in the general population similar to the patient group with respect to age, sex, minority group, and calendar year of observation.

★ 482 ★

Disease Rates, Southeast Asian Refugees, Whites, and Blacks

Numbers of cases of tuberculosis, hepatitis B, chronic infection, and malaria by race/ethnicity, various years.

Disease	Southeast Asian refugees[a]	Whites	Blacks	Total U.S. population
Tuberculosis	250	4	28	9
Hepatitis B[b]				
Chronic infection	10,000	190	850	300
Overall infection	70,000	3,200	13,700	4,800
Malaria[c]	150	(d)	(d)	4

Source: U.S. General Accounting Office, *Asian Americans: A Status Report, 1990* (Washington, DC: U.S. Government Printing Office, 1990), table 4.2, p. 35. Primary source: Centers for Disease Control (CDC), *Reports* (Atlanta: Centers for Disease Control, July and August 1989). *Notes:* (a) Rates for Southeast Asian refugees are based on disease statistics from 1987 for refugees arriving in 1986. According to CDC, the risk of infection is greatest during the year after immigration. (b) Rate for Southeast Asian refugees is from early 1980s. Rates for whites, blacks, and total U.S. population are from the 1976 to 1980 National Health and Nutrition Examination Surveys. (c) Rates based on Southeast Asian refugees arriving between 1980 and 1988. Rates for total U.S. population based on 1985 population estimates and infections reported between 1983 and 1988. Malaria infections are only acquired abroad, according to CDC. (d) A breakdown for whites versus blacks is not available.

Health Care of Women

★ 483 ★

Reproductive Health Care Practices, Asian Pacific American Women

Selected reproductive health care practices of Asian Pacific American women and all women of color in the United States who participated in "Women of Color Reproductive Health Poll," in percent, 1991.

Percent who report:	Asian/Pacific American	Women of color, total
Having an annual physical	59%	82%
Ever having a pap smear	71%	90%
Ever having a mammogram	40%	52%

Source: Invisible and in Need: Philanthropic Giving to Asian Americans and Pacific Islanders (San Francisco: Asian Americans and Pacific Islanders in Philanthropy [AAPIP], December 1992). Primary source: "Women of Color Reproductive Health Poll" (New York: Communications Consortium and National Council of Negro Women, 1991).

Injuries

★ 484 ★

Injury Deaths in Children, 1980-1985

Death rate[a] by leading injury cause,and numbers of deaths for children (birth to fourteen years of age) by race/ethnicity, 1980 to 1985.

Injury Cause	Deaths per 100,000 population (total numbers of deaths, 1980-1985)				
	Oriental	White	Black	Native American	All Races[b]
All injuries, rate	17.5 (917)	17.5 (44,217)	29.3 (13,634)	33.9 (918)	19.3 (59,711)
Motor vehicle occupant	3.1 (162)	3.3 (8,224)	2.6 (1,217)	6.9 (186)	3.2 (9,796)
Pedestrian, traffic	2.9 (153)	2.2 (5,487)	3.8 (1,748)	3.6 (98)	2.4 (7,489)
Drowning	3.4 (180)	2.6 (6,438)	3.9 (1,814)	4.8 (131)	2.8 (8,568)
House fire	1.0 (51)	1.6 (4,080)	6.0 (2,795)	3.3 (90)	2.3 (7,021)
Fall	0.9 (49)	0.4 (933)	0.7 (333)	0.6 (17)	0.4 (1,332)
Homicide	1.9 (101)	1.3 (3,355)	4.7 (2,191)	2.7 (7)	1.9 (5,722)

Source: U.S. Department of Health and Human Services, Public Health Service, Health Resources and Services Administrators, *Health Status of Minorities and Low-Income Groups,* 3rd ed. (Washington, DC: U.S. Government Printing Office, 1991), table 3. Primary source: A. E. Walter, S. P. Baker and A. Szocka, "Childhood Injury Deaths: National Analysis and Geographic Variations," *American Journal of Public Health* 79, no. 3 (March 1989): table 2, p. 312. *Notes:* (a) Rate is for 100,000deaths per year. Total deaths over the six-year period is in parentheses. (b) Includes cases where race was unknown.

★ 485 ★

Injury Deaths in Children, Ratio to Whites

Ratio of death rate by selected injury causes in children (birth to fourteen years) for minority group members relative to whites in the United States, 1980 to 1985.

Injury Cause	Ratio of death rate for group to death rate for whites		
	Asian Pacific Islander	Black	Native American
All injuries	1.00	1.67	1.94
Motor vehicle occupant	0.94	0.79	2.09
Pedestrian, traffic	1.32	1.73	1.64
Drowning	1.31	1.50	1.85
House fire	0.63	3.75	2.06
Fall	2.25	1.75	1.50
Homicide	1.46	3.62	2.08

Source: U.S. Department of Health and Human Services, Public Health Service, Health Resources and Services Administrators, *Health Status of Minorities and Low-Income Groups,* 3rd ed. (Washington, DC: U.S. Government Printing Office, 1991), table 4. Primary source: A. E. Walter, S. P. Baker and A. Szocka, "Childhood Injury Deaths: National Analysis and Geographic Variations," *American Journal of Public Health* 79, no. 3 (March 1989): table 3, p. 312.

Medical Care

★ 486 ★

Doctor Visits

Reported number of visits to doctors per year per person by race/ethnicity.

Race/ethnicity	Visits per year
Asian/Pacific Islander	4.5
White, non-Hispanic	6.5
Black, non-Hispanic	7
Mexican Americans	5.5

Source: "Access and Utilization of Health Care" fact sheet (San Francisco: Asian American Health Forum, 1993).

★ 487 ★

Developmentally Disabled, Hawaii Community Services

Clients of community services for the developmentally disabled in Hawaii by race/ethnicity, 1989. (n=2,005)

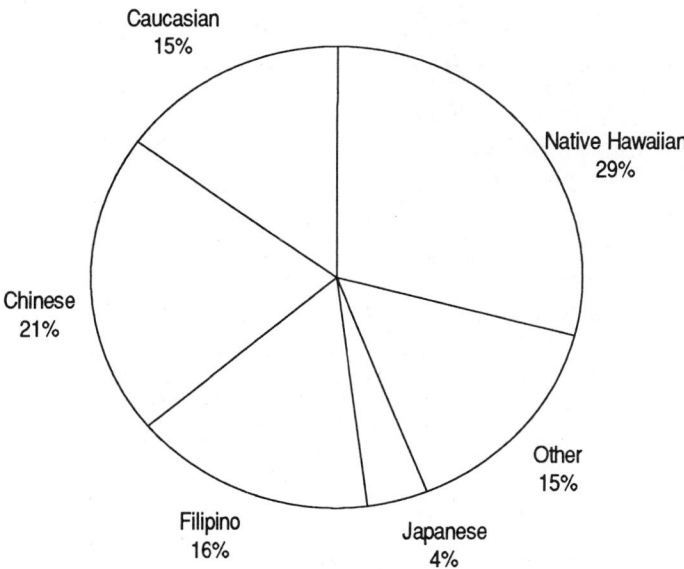

Source: Papa Ola Lokahi, *State of Hawaii Native Hawaiian Health Data Book 1990* (Honolulu: The Office of Hawaiian Affairs, August 1, 1990), p. 61. Primary source: Hawaii State Department of Health, Developmental Disability Division. Data are from records maintained by this service organization and reflect clients' usage of services. These data are not a reflection of the community in general, but a profile of the characteristics of individuals utilizing a particular service.

★ 488 ★

Healthy Start/Family Support Services, Hawaii

Reported profile of a child abuse prevention program in Hawaii by race/ethnicity, January to June 1989.

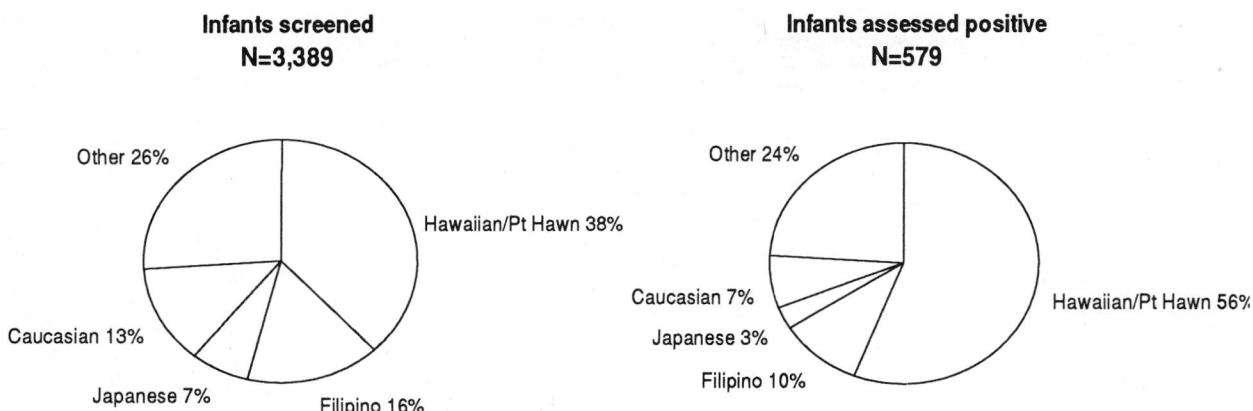

Source: Papa Ola Lokahi, *State of Hawaii Native Hawaiian Health Data Book 1990* (Honolulu: The Office of Hawaiian Affairs, August 1, 1990), p. 66. Primary source: Hawaii State Department of Health, Family Health Services Division. Data are from records maintained by this service organization and reflect clients' usage of services. These data are not a reflection of the community in general, but a profile of the characteristics of individuals utilizing a particular service.

★ 489 ★

Health Benefits, Employer-Provided

Results of a survey, in percent, of population in California and total United States regarding employer-provided health benefits, by race/ethnicity.

Race/ethnicity	Percent covered
In California	
Asian/Pacific Islanders	51%
White, non-Hispanic	65%
Black, non-Hispanic	52%
In United States, total	
Asian/Pacific Islanders	53%
White, non-Hispanic	69%
Black, non-Hispanic	na[a]

Source: "Access and Utilization of Health Care" fact sheet (San Francisco: Asian American Health Forum, 1993). Primary source: E. R. Brown, et al., "Health Insurance Coverage of Californians in 1989," *CPS Report* (California Policy Seminar, University of California). *Note:* (a) Not available.

★ 490 ★

Health Insurance Coverage

Results of a survey, in percent, of population in California and total United States regarding health insurance coverage, by race/ethnicity.

Race/ethnicity	Percent covered
Asian/Pacific Islander	80%
White, non-Hispanic	85%
Black, non-Hispanic	84%
Hispanic	68%

Source: "Access and Utilization of Health Care" fact sheet (San Francisco: Asian American Health Forum, 1993). Primary source: E. R.Brown, et al. "Health Insurance Coverage of Californians in 1989," *CPS Report* (California Policy Seminar, University of California).

★491★

Health Risk Behaviors of Adolescents, Idaho

Reported results of a survey of 7,776 rural Idaho students in grades eight to twelve regarding various health risk behaviors.

Survey Item	Asian	White	Black	Hispanic	American Indian[a]
Seat belt use					
Never	17	664	30	126	64
Rarely	28	1417	13	117	74
Sometimes	43	1710	17	132	81
Most of the time	46	1710	21	80	86
Helmet use: bicycle					
Do not ride	26	1118	32	138	62
Never	89	4798	39	265	213
Sometimes	8	373	6	29	18
Most of the time	4	110	0	6	2
Always	6	95	2	8	9
Helmet use: motorcycle					
Do not ride	66	2577	32	243	117
Never	12	491	15	77	46
Sometimes	14	872	12	54	57
Most of the time	17	906	6	31	31
Always	25	1675	15	47	54
Physical fights in last thirty days					
None	116	6046	48	387	249
One	6	235	8	31	25
Two to three	0	0	0	0	0
Four to five	0	0	0	0	0
Six or more	0	0	0	0	0
Suicidal thoughts in last thirty days					
No	93	4875	41	312	188
Yes	41	1611	35	131	112
Cigarette smoking					
No	66	2741	25	153	83
Yes	63	3579	49	294	212
Chewing tobacco/snuff					
No	81	4213	29	276	160
Yes	51	2288	48	170	138
Occasions of alcohol in last thirty days					
Never	32	1649	13	74	41
None	47	1869	25	129	92
One to five	41	2106	15	156	110
Six to fifteen	9	598	8	43	26
Sixteen or more	5	272	17	48	35
Occasions of five or more drinks in last thirty days					
Never	28	1647	17	78	49

[Continued]

★ 491 ★

Health Risk Behaviors of Adolescents, Idaho (Continued)

Reported results of a survey of 7,776 rural Idaho students in grades eight to twelve regarding various health risk behaviors.

Survey Item	Asian	White	Black	Hispanic	American Indian[a]
None	63	2666	27	172	113
One	18	781	6	52	42
Two to five	14	902	12	85	55
Six or more	9	516	17	63	44

Source: Stephanie A. Salzman and James T. Girvan, "Rural Adolescent Health Risk Behavior: Age, Gender, and Ethnic Differences" (1991), table 3, pp. 21-22. Paper presented at annual meeting of American Educational Research Association, April 3-7, 1991. *Note:* (a) American Indian is the term used by the researchers for Native Americans.

Medical Education

★ 492 ★

Enrollment in Selected Health Occupation Fields of Study by Race/Ethnicity

Numbers and percent of all enrollees (first-year and total) in academic programs in the United States for selected health care occupations by race/ethnicity for academic years 1979–80 and 1989–90.

Field of study and race/ethnicity	First-year enrollment				Total enrollment			
	1979-80[a]	1989-90	1979-80[a]	1989-90	1979-80[a]	1989-90	1979-80[a]	1989-90
	Number	Number	Percent	Percent	Number	Number	Percent	Percent
Allopathic medicine								
All races[b]	16,930	16,756	100.0	100.0	63,800	65,016	100.0	100.0
Asian	502	2,257	3.0	13.5	1,777	7,489	2.8	11.5
White, non-Hispanic	14,259	12,039	84.2	71.8	54,854	48,961	86.0	75.3
Black, non-Hispanic	1,108	1,221	6.5	7.3	3,627	4,145	5.7	6.4
Hispanic	790	964	4.7	5.8	2,514	3,537	3.9	5.4
Mexican American	290	307	1.7	1.8	964	1,087	1.5	1.7
Mainland Puerto Rican	86	139	0.5	0.8	283	452	0.4	0.7
Other Hispanic[c]	414	518	2.4	3.1	1,267	1,998	2.0	3.1
American Indian	63	82	0.4	0.5	212	258	0.3	0.4
Osteopathic medicine								
All races	1,426	1,844	100.0	100.0	4,571	6,615	100.0	100.0
Asian	29	158	2.0	8.6	70	463	1.5	7.0
White, non-Hispanic[b]	1,333	1,524	93.5	82.6	4,330	5,694	94.7	86.1
Black, non-Hispanic	40	68	2.8	3.7	100	173	2.2	2.6
Hispanic	18	79	1.3	4.3	45	246	1.0	3.7
American Indian	6	15	0.4	0.8	26	39	0.6	0.6

[Continued]

★ 492 ★

Enrollment in Selected Health Occupation Fields of Study by Race/Ethnicity (Continued)

Numbers and percent of all enrollees (first-year and total) in academic programs in the United States for selected health care occupations by race/ethnicity for academic years 1979–80 and 1989–90.

Field of study and race/ethnicity	First-year enrollment				Total enrollment			
	1979-80[a]	1989 -90	1979-80[a]	1989-90	1979-80[a]	1989-90	1979-80[a]	1989-90
	Number	Number	Percent	Percent	Number	Number	Percent	Percent
Podiatry								
All races	718	579	100.0	100.0	2,531	2,397	100.0	100.0
Asian	26	41	3.6	7.1	63	156	2.5	6.5
White, non-Hispanic[b]	641	427	89.3	73.7	2,342	1,869	92.5	78.0
Black, non-Hispanic	41	62	5.7	10.7	93	240	3.7	10.0
Hispanic	8	46	1.1	7.9	28	123	1.1	5.1
American Indian	2	3	0.3	0.5	5	6	0.2	0.3
Dentistry[d]								
All races	6,066	3,938	100.0	100.0	22,482	16,198	100.0	100.0
Asian	289	648	4.8	16.5	895	2,393	4.0	14.8
White, non-Hispanic[b]	5,321	2,769	87.7	70.3	20,029	11,701	89.1	72.2
Black, non-Hispanic	274	263	4.5	6.7	1,009	983	4.5	6.1
Hispanic	163	243	2.7	6.2	489	1,064	2.2	6.6
American Indian	19	15	0.3	0.4	60	57	0.3	0.4
Optometry								
All races	1,209	1,258	100.0	100.0	4,500	4,723	100.0	100.0
Asian	-	164	-	13.1	208	534	4.6	11.3
White, non-Hispanic[b]	-	961	-	76.4	4,156	3,748	92.4	79.4
Black, non-Hispanic	-	43	-	3.4	56	132	1.2	2.8
Hispanic	-	87	-	6.9	67	293	1.5	6.2
American Indian	-	3	-	0.2	13	16	0.3	0.3
Pharmacy[e]								
All races	7,905	8,009	100.0	100.0	22,560	22,764	100.0	100.0
Asian	367	-	4.6	-	971	2,130	4.3	9.4
White, non-Hispanic[b]	6,971	-	88.2	-	20,185	18,325	89.5	80.5
Black, non-Hispanic	387	-	4.9	-	958	1,301	4.2	5.7
Hispanic	162	-	2.0	-	410	945	1.8	4.2
American Indian	18	-	0.2	-	36	63	0.2	0.3
Veterinary medicine								
All races[b]	2,255	2,194	100.0	100.0	7,803	8,456	100.0	100.0
Asian	-	37	-	1.7	-	133	-	1.6
White, non-Hispanic[b]	-	2,019	-	92.0	-	7,847	-	92.8
Black, non-Hispanic	-	62	-	2.8	-	219	-	2.6
Hispanic	-	65	-	3.0	-	220	-	2.6
American Indian	-	11	-	0.5	-	37	-	0.4
Registered nurses[f]								
All races[b]	107,476	108,580	100.0	100.0	239,486	201,458	100.0	100.0

[Continued]

389

★ 492 ★

Enrollment in Selected Health Occupation Fields of Study by Race/Ethnicity (Continued)

Numbers and percent of all enrollees (first-year and total) in academic programs in the United States for selected health care occupations by race/ethnicity for academic years 1979–80 and 1989–90.

Field of study and race/ethnicity	First-year enrollment				Total enrollment			
	1979-80[a]	1989-90	1979-80[a]	1989-90	1979-80[a]	1989-90	1979-80[a]	1989-90
	Number	Number	Percent	Percent	Number	Number	Percent	Percent
Asian	-	3,223	-	3.0	-	5,201	-	2.6
White, non-Hispanic[b]	96,406	88,975	89.7	81.9	219,369	168,358	91.6	83.6
Black, non-Hispanic	7,295	12,146	6.8	11.2	12,630	20,789	5.3	10.3
Hispanic	1,664	3,532	1.5	3.3	3,079	6,046	1.3	3.0
American Indian	-	704	-	0.6	-	1,064	-	0.5

Sources: Bureau of Health Professions, *Minorities and Women in the Health Fields* (New York: Association of American Medical Colleges, Section for Student Services, 1990), unpublished data; American Association of Colleges of Osteopathic Medicine, *Annual Statistical Report 1990* (Rockville, MD: AACOM, 1990); National League for Nursing, *Nursing Datasource* (New York: NLN, 1990), *Nursing Data Book, 1980* (New York: NLN, 1981);and *State-Approved Schools of Nursing, RN, 1973* (New York: NLN, 1973); U.S. Department of Health, Education, and Welfare, Division of Nursing, *Source Book, Nursing Personnel, Health Resources Administration* (Washington, DC: U.S. Department of Health, Education and Welfare, Pub. No. HRA 75-43, 1975); American Dental Association, *Annual Report on Dental Education 1989/90* (Chicago: ADA, 1990); Association of Schools and Colleges of Optometry, Washington, DC, unpublished data, 1991; American Association of Colleges of Pharmacy, Alexandria, VA, unpublished data, 1991; Association of American Veterinary Medical Colleges, Washington, DC, unpublished data, 1991; Colleges of Podiatric Medicine, *Annual Report to the American Association of Colleges of Podiatric Medicine 1980-1989*, unpublished data, 1990. *Notes:* (a) First-year and total enrollments for registered nurse students are for 1978-79. (b) Includes race/ethnicity unspecified. (c) Includes Puerto Rican Commonwealth students. (d) Excludes Puerto Rican schools. (e) Pharmacy first-year enrollment data are for students in the first year of the final three years of pharmacy education. Pharmacy total enrollment data are for students in the final three years of pharmacy. (f) Minority distribution based only on programs reporting minority data.

Mental Health

★ 493 ★

Mental Health Services, Hawaii

Numbers of patients receiving mental health services in Hawaii by native Hawaiian ethnicity, 1988.

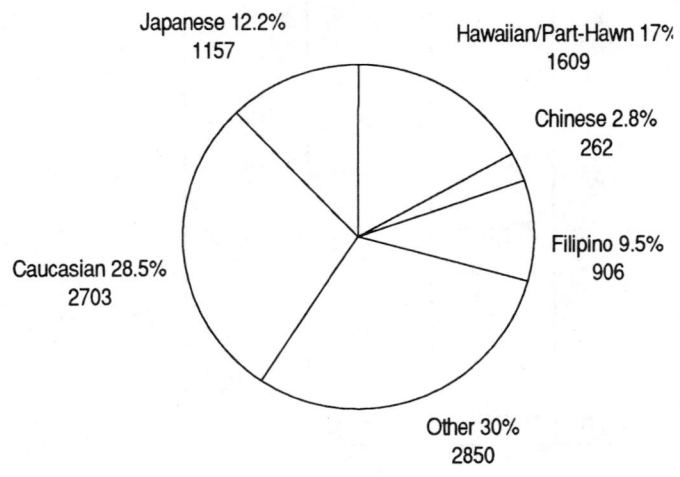

[Continued]

★ 493 ★

Mental Health Services, Hawaii (Continued)

Ethnicity	Carryover[a]	New Admits	Readmits	Total	Discharge
Total, all patients:	5,793	1,917	1,777	9,487	4,143
Total, all Hawaiian	873	364	372	1,609	710
Native Hawaiian	155	69	54	278	188
Part Hawaiian	718	295	318	1,331	522
Total, other races	4,920	1,553	1,405	7,878	3,433

Source: Papa Ola Lokahi, *State of Hawaii Native Hawaiian Health Data Book 1990* (Honolulu: The Office of Hawaiian Affairs, August 1, 1990), p. 56. Primary source: Hawaii State Department of Health, Behavioral Health Services Administration. Data are from records maintained by this service organization and reflect clients' usage of services. These data are not a reflection of the community in general, but a profile of the characteristics of individuals utilizing a particular service. Note: (a) Patients already receiving services as of January 1, 1988.

★ 494 ★

Mental Health Status of Elderly Chinese and Japanese American Women

Elderly Chinese and Japanese American women have the highest suicide rate of all racial and ethnic groups, including European Americans. A 1987 study of 2,800 Southeast Asians conducted by the California State Department of Mental Health revealed that 95 percent of them needed psychological help, compared with 33 percent of the population in general. Recent federal studies reveal as much as a 300 percent increase in the suicide rate among Asian American children.

Source: Invisible and in Need: Philanthropic Giving to Asian Americans and Pacific Islanders (San Francisco: Asian Americans and Pacific Islanders in Philanthropy [AAPIP], December 1992). Primary source: Steve Chin, "Asian Health: A Special Prescription" *San Francisco Examiner* (July 7, 1991).

Prenatal and Infant Care

★495★

Breastfeeding Mothers, Demographic Characteristics

Number and percent of low-income Southeast Asian[a] and non-Southeast Asian mothers whose children were breastfed, by various demographic characteristics.

	Children Breastfed									
	Southeast Asian				Non-Southeast Asian					
Characteristic	U.S. born		Foreign born		White		Black		Other	
	Number	Percent	Number	Percent	Number	Percent	Number	Percent	Number	Percent
Marital status										
Ever married	116	10%	41	93%	223	75%	33	79%	48	75%
Never married	0	-	0	-	14	36%	10	10%	7	-
Household income, percent of poverty level										
Greater than poverty level (<100%)	115	10%	41	93%	133	71%	29	52%	47	64%
Less than poverty level (>100%)	1%	-	0%	--	104	75%	14	86%	8	-
Parental education										
None	66	14%	22	95%	0	-	0	-	0	-
Less than high school	39	5%	13	92%	13	46%	5	-	9	-
High school	7	-	0	-	84	62%	10	30%	9	-
College and above	4	-	6	-	140	82%	28	79%	37	78%
Participation in WIC[b] during pregnancy										
Yes	95	8%	NA[c]	NA	48	60%	20	40%	21	52%
No	21	19%	NA	NA	189	76%	23	83%	34	74%
Sex of child										
Male	60	7%	24	96%	115	75%	24	50%	33	67%
Female	56	14%	17	88%	122	71%	19	79%	22	64%
Children <18 years of age										
One or two	19	11%	6	-	179	74%	28	68%	40	70%
Three or four	44	2%	18	89%	47	79%	15	53%	12	42%
More than five	53	17%	17	100%	11	27%	0	-	3	-
Breastfed only (n)	12		38		173		27		36	
Duration of breastfeeding (months)	9.0±3.4		13.6±0.7		5.8±0.5		4.5±0.9		5.5±1.3	
Age at introduction of breast-milk substitutes (months)	6.0±5.2		12.7±0.9		3.6±0.3		2.9±0.6		3.6±0.4	
All children (n)	116		41		237		43		55	
Introduction of semi-solid/solid (months)	7.9±0.3		8.9±0.8		5.0±0.2		4.3±0.4		5.9±0.7	

Source: Mary K. Serdula, et al., "Correlates of Breastfeeding in a Low-Income Population of Whites, Blacks, and Southeast Asians," *Journal of the American Dietetic Association* 91, no. 1 (Jan. 1991): tables 2 and 4, pp. 40, 43, and 45. *Notes:* (a) Survey respondents were from a low-income urban county in St. Paul, Minnesota. (b) WIC is a supplemental food program for women, infants, and children. (c) NA = not applicable.

★ 496 ★

Prenatal Care, Early

Proportion of mothers in the United States with early[a] prenatal care by race/ethnicity[b] of mother, 1989.

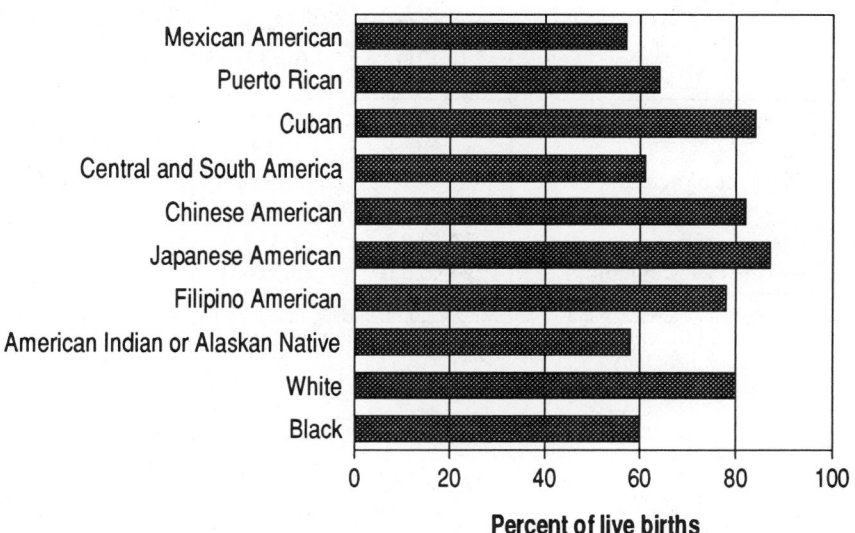

Percent of live births

Source: Health United States, 1991 (Washington, DC: U.S. Government Printing Office, 1992). Primary source: National Center for Health Statistics, National Vital Statistics System. *Note:* (a) Early prenatal care is defined as care beginning in the first trimester of pregnancy. Late prenatal care is defined as care beginning in the third trimester. (b) Data on Hispanic origin of mother are from thirty states and the District of Columbia.

★ 497 ★

Prenatal Care, Late or None

Proportion of mothers in the United States with late[a] or no prenatal care by race/ethnicity[b] of mother, 1989.

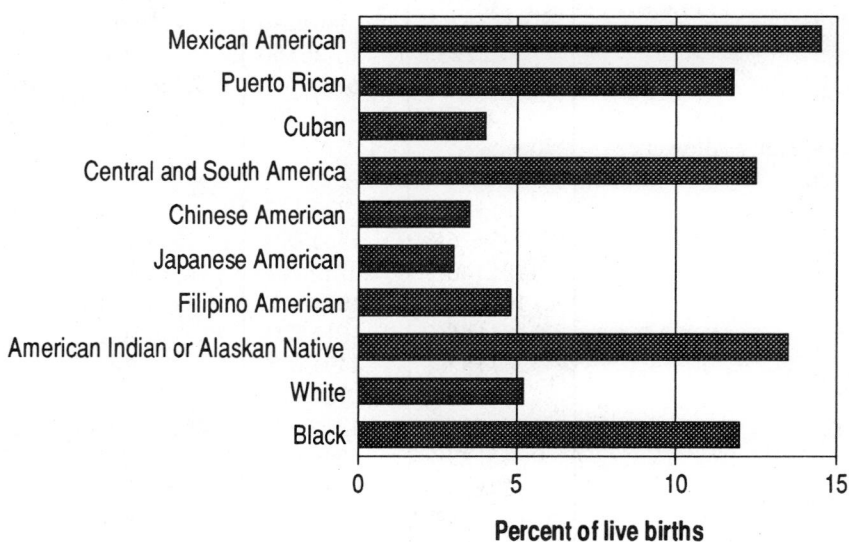

Percent of live births

Source: Health United States, 1991 (Washington, DC: U.S. Government Printing Office, 1992). Primary source: National Center for Health Statistics, National Vital Statistics System. *Note:* (a) Early prenatal care is defined as care beginning in the first trimester of pregnancy. Late prenatal care is defined as care beginning in the third trimester. (b) Data on Hispanic origin of mother are from thirty states and the District of Columbia.

★ 498 ★

Southeast Asians During Pregnancy

Selected health characteristics compiled during a study of Cambodian, Laotian, and Vietnamese and non-Southeast Asian low-income pregnant women conducted from 1978 to 1990.

Characteristic	Cambodian (n=91)	Laotian (n=37)	Vietnamese (n=59)	Non-Southeast Asian (n=165)
Height (cm)	153±5	149±5	152±7	154±3
Weight (kg)	50±8	48±7	47±7	50±3
Desirable weight, percent of actual	98±14	99±13	94±12	97±7
Age (years)	27±6	25±6	26±5	25±3
First medical visit (week of pregnancy)	14.5±6.1	17.3±7.9	17.5±8.0	17.4±6.9
First nutrition visit (week of pregnancy)	24.0±8.6	25.5±8.0	25.9±8.0	25.8±8.1

Source: Vicky Newman, William Norcross, and Roger McDonald, "Nutrient Intake of Low-Income Southeast Asian Pregnant Women," *Journal of the American Dietetic Association* 91, no. 7 (July 1991): table 1, p. 794.

★ 499 ★

Southeast Asians During Pregnancy, Diet

Dietary intake[a] and percent of Recommended Dietary Allowance (RDA) of Cambodian, Laotian, Vietnamese, and non-Southeast Asian pregnant women.

Dietary Constituents	Cambodian (n=91)	Laotian (n=37)	Vietnamese (n=59)	Non-Southeast Asian (n=165)
Energy (kcal)	1,750±755	1,630±576	1,932±753	1,989±712
Protein (g)	87±38	86±38	93±42	84±35
Fat (g)	42±22	42±25	60±32	82±40
Carbohydrate (g)	255±123	227±80	254±102	236±92
Alcohol (g)	0.0±0.0	0.0±0.0	0.0±0.0	0.3±2.2
Fiber (g)	3.9±2.1	3.9±2.2	3.8±2.4	4.5±3.2
Cholesterol (mg)	328±248	346±246	416±266	420±273
Caffeine (mg)	21±58	26±50	25±58	59±115
Sodium (mg)	3,693±2,179	2,862±1,679	3,367±2,107	2,708±1,538
Potassium (mg)	2,441±1,095	2,576±1,289	2,756±1,289	3,055±1,282
Recommended Daily Allowance (RDA), percent				
Energy	81±35%	77±27%	90±35%	91±31%
Protein	173±76%	176±76%	187±86%	166±68%
Ascorbic acid	178±140%	205±201%	168±143%	186±180%
Thiamin	109±42%	107±41%	121±40%	94±37%
Riboflavin	86±45%	101±52%	110±50%	122±53%
Niacin	247±85%	249±88%	242±78%	203±68
Vitamin B-6	81±43%	76±38%	75±41%	75±38%
Vitamin B-12	176±241%	243±284%	262±307%	238±217
Folate	46±29%	54±31%	55±35%	72±48%
Vitamin A	129±88%	199±239%	190±225%	187±215%
Vitamin D	21±26%	28±30%	42±39%	56±52%
Vitamin E	44±36%	59±47%	77±84%	111±113%
Iron	45±23%	46±21%	46±18%	42±22%

[Continued]

★ 499 ★

Southeast Asians During Pregnancy, Diet (Continued)

Dietary intake[a] and percent of Recommended Dietary Allowance (RDA) of Cambodian, Laotian, Vietnamese, and non-Southeast Asian pregnant women.

Dietary Constituents	Cambodian (n=91)	Laotian (n=37)	Vietnamese (n=59)	Non-Southeast Asian (n=165)
Calcium	42±28%	51±31%	67±43%	88±53%
Phosphorus	86±37%	92±38%	106±47%	119±53%
Magnesium	71±36%	70±30%	80±42%	91±48%
Zinc	78±41%	81±50%	82±46%	75±42%
Selenium	203±90%	182±82%	212±84%	138±67%
Mean Adequacy Ratio[a]	65±19%	60±17%	71±17%	74±16%

Source: Vicky Newman, William Norcross, and Roger McDonald, "Nutrient Intake of Low-Income Southeast Asia Pregnant Women," *Journal of the American Dietetic Association* 91, no. 7 (July 1991): table 3, pp. 796-797. *Note:* (a) Southeast Asian pregnant women consumed significantly lower amounts of fat, riboflavin, folate, vitamins D and E, calcium, phosphorus, potassium, and magnesium. They consumed significantly higher amounts of thiamin, niacin, sodium, and selenium.

Smoking, Alcohol, and Drug Use

★ 500 ★

Alcohol and Drug Abuse Service Use, Hawaii

Numbers of clients receiving alcohol and drug abuse services by sex and Hawaiian native status, 1981 to 1983.

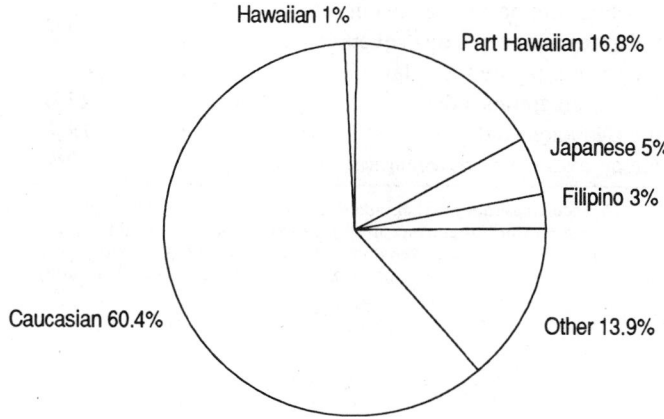

Source: Papa Ola Lokahi, *State of Hawaii Native Hawaiian Health Data Book 1990* (Honolulu: The Office of Hawaiian Affairs, August 1, 1990), p. 52. Primary source: Hawaii State Department of Health, Cholesterol Screening Program. Data are from records maintained by this service organization and reflect clients' usage of services. These data are not a reflection of the community in general, but a profile of the characteristics of individuals utilizing a particular service.

★ 501 ★

Drug Abuse Service Use

Clients receiving drug abuse services by treatment modality in percent by race/ethnicity, 1987.

Race/Ethnicity	Treatment modality, percent			
	Detoxification	Maintenance	Drug Free	Total
Asian	0.2%	0.2%	0.7%	0.6%
White	64.8%	41.1%	62.8%	57.8%
Black	20.3%	28.7%	22.1%	23.6%
Hispanic	13.6%	29.5%	12.7%	16.7%
American Indian/Alaskan Native	1.0%	0.3%	1.3%	1.0%
Total	100.0%	100.0%	100.0%	100.0%

Source: U.S. Department of Health and Human Services, Public Health Service, Health Resources and Services Administrators, *Health Status of Minorities and Low-Income Groups: Third ed.* (Washington, DC: U.S. Government Printing Office, 1991) table 24. Primary source: National Institute on Drug Abuse and National Institute on Alcohol Abuse and Alcoholism, *National Drug and Alcoholism Treatment Unit Survey (NDATUS), 1987 Final Report,* table 25, p. 41.

★ 502 ★

Smoking Habits, Lao Refugees in the United States

Reported results of a survey of 195 Lao male refugees on smoking behavior, 1989.

Habit	Percent
Smoked cigarettes	72%
Had first cigarette in Laos	99%
Started smoking before age twenty	82%
Started smoking before age seventeen	55%
Smoke twenty cigarettes a day	46%
Smoke ten cigarettes a day	27%
Smoke two packs a day	18%
Smoke an average thirty cigarettes a day	9%

Source: "Tobacco Use among Asians and Pacific Islander," *Fact Sheet* (San Francisco: Asian American Health Forum, Inc., 1993). Primary source: Barbra L. Levin, "Cigarette Smoking Habits and Characteristics in the Laotian Refugee: A Perspective Pre- and Post-Resettlement" (Chicago: Cook County Department of Public Health, 1989).

★ 503 ★

Tobacco Use among Asian/Pacific Islanders

Selected published facts regarding tobacco use among the Asian/Pacific Islander population,

While there are no reliable national estimates of smoking prevalence among Asian/Pacific Islanders, preliminary studies indicate that some of the recent Asian/Pacific Islanders immigrant groups have the highest prevalence of smoking in the United States, particularly among men.

A survey of 209 Vietnamese living in the San Francisco Bay area showed that Vietnamese women smoke at about one–third the rate of U.S. women, while Vietnamese men smoke at a rate almost twice that of U.S. men. More than one–quarter of respondents either believed that cigarette smoking did not cause cancer, did not know that it did, or had never heard of cancer[a].

Source: "Tobacco Use among Asians and Pacific Islanders," *Fact Sheet* (San Francisco: Asian American Health Forum, Inc., 1993). *Note:* (a) Christopher Jenkins, et al. "Cancer Risks and Prevention Behaviors Among Vietnamese Refugees," Division of General Internal Medicine (San Francisco: University of California).

Housing

★ 504 ★

Housing Units by Plumbing, by State

Number of occupied housing units that contain complete plumbing and that lack plumbing by state and race/ethnicity, 1990.

State	Asian/Pacific Islander		White		Black	
	Complete	Lacking	Complete	Lacking	Complete	Lacking
Alabama	5,974	19	1,151,527	7,783	320,893	12,903
Alaska	4,558	113	147,092	6,341	6,620	65
Arizona	15,462	123	1,176,063	3,622	35,772	145
Arkansas	2,985	14	752,091	8,214	116,368	4,603
California	765,416	7253	7,859,252	31,647	737,425	4,924
Colorado	16,516	52	1,152,846	3,992	48,213	135
Connecticut	13,023	51	1,095,353	3,054	89,169	647
Delaware	2,320	0	204,785	525	36,418	598
Florida	40,539	229	4,450,320	13,204	540,514	7,639
Georgia	18,985	136	1,751,149	8,169	558,546	14,403
Hawaii	201,100	1765	137,337	1,418	7,292	50
Idaho	2,380	40	343,614	1,969	1,141	13
Illinois	79,457	545	3,436,703	13,528	542,168	5,502
Indiana	10,463	17	1,879,578	10,370	147,504	733
Iowa	–	–	–	–	–	–
Kansas	7,873	51	865,143	3,324	47,283	241
Kentucky	4,291	22	1,246,779	32,221	91,143	1,258
Louisiana	9,645	69	1,065,765	4,490	396,936	9,525
Maine	1,602	18	452,451	7,352	1,465	10
Maryland	37,026	143	1,290,556	4,912	395,250	5,021
Massachusetts	37,271	473	2,057,857	6,614	96,670	1,044
Michigan	27,371	107	2,897,587	10,573	436,620	3,666
Minnesota	16,281	383	1,573,086	8,503	30,231	216
Mississippi	–	–	–	–	–	–
Missouri	–	–	–	–	–	–
Montana	1,050	14	287,659	2,147	655	15
Nebraska	–	–	–	–	–	–
Nevada	10,131	78	407,416	1,457	25,794	115
New Hampshire	2,258	27	402,423	2,291	2,287	24
New Jersey	72,515	330	2,302,796	7,412	328,424	3,407
New Mexico	3,557	70	433,761	3,311	9,956	64
New York	196,052	2,080	5,164,881	27,032	931,726	13,604
North Carolina	12,664	50	1,965,573	14,413	472,293	18,067
North Dakota	833	8	230,503	1,293	1,046	0
Ohio	25,847	173	3,602,841	20,980	409,724	2,966

[Continued]

★ 504 ★

Housing Units by Plumbing, by State (Continued)

Number of occupied housing units that contain complete plumbing and that lack plumbing by state and race/ethnicity, 1990.

State	Asian/Pacific Islander		White		Black	
	Complete	Lacking	Complete	Lacking	Complete	Lacking
Oklahoma	8,955	86	1,023,912	5,133	76,931	997
Oregon	19,135	144	1,037,862	5,765	14,971	144
Pennsylvania	35,875	263	4,026,177	21,673	370,213	3,637
Rhode Island	4,155	67	351,667	1,284	12,377	82
South Carolina	5,189	22	919,151	4,616	311,553	11,904
South Dakota	641	10	243,754	1,390	890	17
Tennessee	8,237	37	1,557,217	19,258	257,239	4,390
Texas	88,092	533	4,774,662	33,556	668,500	11,118
Utah	8,656	88	507,290	1,191	3,645	15
Vermont	668	7	206,526	1,915	555	3
Virginia	40,615	206	1,821,672	19,674	374,375	15,553
Washington	57,903	364	1,701,988	8,610	50,017	304
West Virginia	1,984	54	649,009	15,533	20,213	303
Wisconsin	12,188	476	1,701,872	10,376	74,404	600
Wyoming	762	8	160,066	786	1,053	0

Source: Asian/Pacific Islander Data Consortium (San Francisco: Asian and Pacific Islander Center for Census Information and Services, 1993). Primary source: U.S. Census Bureau, Summary Tape Files 1 and 3. *Note:* A dash (–) indicates data was not available at time of publication.

★ 505 ★

Housing Units, Owner Occupied, by State

Number and total occupancy of owner-occupied housing units by state and race/ethnicity, 1990

State	Occupied housing units			Persons in owner-occupied units		
	Asian/ Pacific Islander	White	Black	Asian/ Pacific Islander	White	Black
Alabama	2,492	864,839	190,029	9,039	2,282,938	589,309
Alaska	1,885	88,644	1,841	6,605	253,929	5,825
Arizona	8,019	781,104	14,726	27,782	2,044,877	47,055
Arkansas	1,678	550,646	64,124	5,952	1,424,583	196,220
California	422,888	4,726,016	269,482	1,578,499	12,672,572	851,675
Colorado	8,506	744,085	18,385	28,690	1,983,741	53,741
Connecticut	6,681	767,282	28,075	25,250	2,110,865	96,675
Delaware	1,445	153,188	17,986	5,180	412,505	56,261
Florida	23,453	3,136,089	257,396	85,410	7,657,976	853,259
Georgia	9,200	1,258,392	263,825	35,654	3,400,779	842,515
Hawaii	128,069	60,863	831	444,078	167,263	2,847
Idaho	1,388	245,347	444	4,364	690,607	1,351
Illinois	41,971	2,404,636	207,749	165,681	6,617,190	733,343
Indiana	4,796	1,369,131	68,233	16,821	3,759,675	207,794
Iowa	–	–	–	–	–	–

[Continued]

★ 505 ★

Housing Units, Owner Occupied, by State (Continued)

Number and total occupancy of owner-occupied housing units by state and race/ethnicity, 1990

State	Occupied housing units			Persons in owner-occupied units		
	Asian/ Pacific Islander	White	Black	Asian/ Pacific Islander	White	Black
Kansas	3,304	607,461	20,509	13,307	1,603,551	58,573
Kentucky	2,089	916,757	39,975	7,710	2,474,713	112,721
Louisiana	4,655	769,790	206,821	19,828	2,113,488	663,823
Maine	845	325,335	517	2,808	890,036	1,527
Maryland	23,885	933,949	172,992	88,768	2,553,267	553,299
Massachusetts	15,051	1,282,659	25,556	56,455	3,650,966	90,081
Michigan	13,868	2,180,229	210,731	52,202	6,068,906	655,965
Minnesota	6,788	1,159,766	9,159	26,988	3,239,744	30,244
Mississippi	–	–	–	–	–	–
Missouri	–	–	–	–	–	–
Montana	492	198,177	245	1,543	526,113	553
Nebraska	5,037	233,501	8,471	17,466	618,364	28,308
Nevada	–	–	–	–	–	–
New Hampshire	1,302	277,681	790	4,296	784,651	2,258
New Jersey	42,551	1,625,427	123,715	166,385	4,616,766	439,672
New Mexico	1,795	300,318	4,275	6,502	817,351	12,680
New York	74,082	3,119,937	232,515	294,250	8,878,364	844,506
North Carolina	6,121	1,442,521	243,438	22,475	3,704,944	737,804
North Dakota	237	154,439	114	858	423,917	363
Ohio	12,535	2,561,119	173,178	45,358	7,032,099	518,987
Oklahoma	3,878	725,480	36,805	14,752	1,865,194	106,049
Oregon	9,167	670,898	5,682	32,370	1,767,182	17,081
Pennsylvania	18,799	2,953,215	190,003	72,682	8,046,636	584,399
Rhode Island	1,704	217,982	3,213	6,540	610,195	11,559
South Carolina	2,975	682,577	190,548	10,555	1,798,823	623,755
South Dakota	276	166,355	145	1,144	450,171	449
Tennessee	3,811	1,130,006	123,862	14,226	2,983,640	390,656
Texas	42,226	3,110,162	307,267	167,160	8,610,821	940,061
Utah	4,291	352,864	1,348	16,382	1,197,714	4,180
Vermont	329	144,398	237	946	398,949	696
Virginia	24,085	1,296,422	191,749	92,800	3,442,780	577,153
Washington	30,534	1,101,393	18,114	107,588	2,936,964	56,420
West Virginia	1,093	497,121	11,215	4,270	1,319,290	28,905
Wisconsin	4,078	1,180,147	22,654	15,187	3,290,774	76,136
Wyoming	405	110,499	385	1,040	304,854	920

Source: Asian/Pacific Islander Data Consortium (San Francisco: Asian and Pacific Islander Center for Census Information and Services, 1993). Primary source: U.S. Census Bureau, Summary Tape Files 1 and 3. *Note:* A dash (–) indicates data was not available at time of publication.

Statistical Record of Asian Americans

★ 506 ★

Housing Units, Renter Occupied, by State

Number and total occupancy of renter-occupied housing units by state and race/ethnicity, 1990.

State	Number of units			Persons in renter-occupied units		
	Asian/ Pacific Islander	White	Black	Asian/ Pacific Islander	White	Black
Alabama	3,501	294,471	143,767	8,614	636,505	399,383
Alaska	2,786	64,789	4,844	8,503	159,026	14,286
Arizona	7,566	398,581	21,191	17,607	874,032	56,091
Arkansas	1,321	209,659	56,847	4,051	478,319	164,105
California	349,781	3,164,883	472,867	1,126,837	7,495,911	1,203,731
Colorado	8,062	412,753	29,963	20,610	865,990	70,065
Connecticut	6,393	331,125	61,741	18,119	675,116	160,262
Delaware	875	52,122	19,030	2,379	108,628	51,409
Florida	17,315	1,327,435	290,757	46,049	2,884,746	825,641
Georgia	9,921	500,926	309,124	28,530	1,107,031	838,880
Hawaii	74,796	77,892	6,511	218,139	196,101	19,907
Idaho	1,032	100,236	710	2,661	242,985	1,892
Illinois	38,031	1,045,595	339,921	100,787	2,135,738	895,180
Indiana	5,684	520,817	80,004	12,722	1,129,149	202,481
Iowa	–	–	–	–	–	–
Kansas	4,620	261,006	27,015	11,978	568,511	72,913
Kentucky	2,224	362,243	52,426	5,948	838,528	133,551
Louisiana	5,059	300,465	199,640	15,652	665,050	589,269
Maine	775	134,468	958	2,095	284,950	2,385
Maryland	13,284	361,519	227,279	38,131	785,697	592,987
Massachusetts	22,693	781,812	72,158	67,939	1,590,944	185,969
Michigan	13,610	727,931	229,555	36,189	1,550,979	582,541
Minnesota	9,876	421,823	21,288	36,503	807,966	54,276
Mississippi	–	–	–	–	–	–
Missouri	–	–	–	–	–	–
Montana	572	91,629	425	1,161	195,830	1,074
Nebraska	–	–	–	–	–	–
Nevada	5,172	175,372	17,438	14,083	380,598	46,141
New Hampshire	983	127,033	1,521	2,618	273,527	4,165
New Jersey	30,294	684,781	208,116	88,910	1,415,705	543,199
New Mexico	1,832	136,754	5,745	4,635	313,614	15,527
New York	124,050	2,071,976	712,815	357,357	4,183,007	1861,160
North Carolina	6,593	537,465	246,922	18,122	1,157,989	657,723
North Dakota	604	77,357	932	1,368	160,127	2,713
Ohio	13,485	1,062,702	239,512	32,783	2,294,207	584,471
Oklahoma	5,163	303,565	41,123	12,215	675,311	111,571
Oregon	10,112	372,729	9,433	25,255	828,010	22,566
Pennsylvania	17,339	1,094,635	183,847	45,933	2,209,142	445,657
Rhode Island	2,518	134,969	9,246	9,044	275,791	23,361
South Carolina	2,236	241,190	132,909	5,445	535,427	379,909
South Dakota	375	78,789	762	1,127	167,197	2,047
Tennessee	4,463	446,469	137,767	11,209	971,575	356,668
Texas	46,399	1,698,056	372,351	122,338	3,899,596	997,148
Utah	4,453	155,617	2,312	12,357	398,508	5,888

[Continued]

★ 506 ★

Housing Units, Renter Occupied, by State (Continued)

Number and total occupancy of renter-occupied housing units by state and race/ethnicity, 1990.

State	Number of units			Persons in renter-occupied units		
	Asian/ Pacific Islander	White	Black	Asian/ Pacific Islander	White	Black
Vermont	346	64,043	321	946	135,831	1,010
Virginia	16,736	544,924	198,179	47,573	1,225,046	524,318
Washington	27,733	609,205	32,207	73,066	1,313,673	77,843
West Virginia	945	167,421	9,301	2,071	375,198	23,460
Wisconsin	8,586	532,101	52,350	31,327	1,116,276	153,946
Wyoming	365	50,353	668	885	114,139	1,638

Source: Asian/Pacific Islander Data Consortium (San Francisco: Asian and Pacific Islander Center for Census Information and Services, 1993). Primary source: U.S. Census Bureau, Summary Tape Files 1 and 3. *Note:* A dash (–) indicates data was not available at time of publication.

★ 507 ★

Housing Units, Renter Occupied, by State and Gross Rent

Number of Asian/Pacific Islander renter-occupied housing units with various gross rent levels by state, 1990.

State	Rent for Asian/Pacific Islander renter–occupied housing units						
	Less than $200	$200 to $299	$300 to $499	$500 to $749	$750 to $999	$1000 or more	No cash rent
Alabama	188	985	1,813	414	28	0	50
Alaska	33	213	991	725	276	273	256
Arizona	302	960	4,103	1,629	210	93	259
Arkansas	103	482	522	104	8	12	90
California	11,884	15,172	74,867	134,839	71,604	31,190	7,938
Colorado	742	1,288	4,059	1,396	306	113	97
Connecticut	86	133	1,139	2,749	1,245	878	89
Delaware	24	6	339	419	33	17	24
Florida	561	1,266	7,064	6,288	1,065	443	593
Georgia	213	539	4,185	3,865	539	363	209
Hawaii	6,622	5,518	17,050	23,347	10,629	5,255	5,658
Idaho	162	249	421	115	2	0	71
Illinois	1,786	2,876	15,288	13,230	2,756	1,440	591
Indiana	192	1,436	2,533	953	336	76	113
Iowa	–	–	–	–	–	–	–
Kansas	519	1,201	2,110	543	65	29	129
Kentucky	100	544	936	323	86	126	104
Louisiana	426	1,124	2,535	622	97	54	164
Maine	14	55	331	308	15	4	46
Maryland	354	283	2,386	6,167	2,523	1,247	294
Massachusetts	1,274	1,019	3,629	8,231	5,593	2,593	289
Michigan	417	1,236	5,758	4,016	1,158	770	167
Minnesota	1,669	1,455	4,424	1,775	379	82	60
Mississippi	–	–	–	–	–	–	–

[Continued]

★ 507 ★

Housing Units, Renter Occupied, by State and Gross Rent (Continued)

Number of Asian/Pacific Islander renter-occupied housing units with various gross rent levels by state, 1990.

State	Rent for Asian/Pacific Islander renter–occupied housing units						
	Less than $200	$200 to $299	$300 to $499	$500 to $749	$750 to $999	$1000 or more	No cash rent
Missouri	–	–	–	–	–	–	–
Montana	102	216	177	22	0	0	49
Nebraska	–	–	–	–	–	–	–
Nevada	84	340	2,657	1,599	221	116	135
New Hampshire	0	32	275	444	157	36	33
New Jersey	426	469	4,095	12,837	6,199	5,617	528
New Mexico	108	324	906	235	89	34	110
New York	4,740	6,483	32,183	43,190	21,405	14,068	1,706
North Carolina	160	650	3,716	1,569	139	116	211
North Dakota	85	224	156	54	2	0	78
Ohio	736	1,748	7,096	2,702	537	343	279
Oklahoma	411	1,582	2,577	368	40	45	129
Oregon	773	1,710	5,326	1,710	234	67	218
Pennsylvania	562	1,280	7,773	5,671	1,222	333	364
Rhode Island	96	88	1,175	885	175	78	21
South Carolina	106	212	1,303	355	103	0	157
South Dakota	63	83	140	53	0	0	36
Tennessee	116	784	2,356	686	157	190	135
Texas	1,523	8,667	25,589	7,148	1,460	866	893
Utah	320	1,348	2,100	448	62	4	118
Vermont	12	10	101	124	53	30	5
Virginia	464	448	3,809	6,971	3,027	1,573	359
Washington	2,946	3,328	11,665	6,950	1,342	547	766
West Virginia	89	376	335	100	0	13	23
Wisconsin	672	1,929	4,231	1,429	185	48	71
Wyoming	83	75	135	44	5	0	17

Source: Asian/Pacific Islander Data Consortium (San Francisco: Asian and Pacific Islander Center for Census Information and Services, 1993). Primary source: U.S. Census Bureau, Summary Tape Files 1 and 3. *Note:* A dash (–) indicates data was not available at time of publication.

★ 508 ★

Housing Units, Total Occupied, by State

Number of occupied housing units by state and race/ethnicity, 1990.

State	Asian/ Pacific Islander	White	Black	American Indian, Eskimo, or Aleut	Other
Alabama	5,993	1,159,310	333,796	6,173	1,518
Alaska	4,671	153,433	6,685	22,373	1,753
Arizona	15,585	1,179,685	35,917	50,245	87,411
Arkansas	2,999	760,305	120,971	5,118	1,786
California	772,669	7,890,899	742,349	81,991	893,298
Colorado	16,568	1,156,838	48,348	9,489	51,246
Connecticut	13,074	1,098,407	89,816	2,453	26,729
Delaware	2,320	205,310	37,016	850	2,001
Florida	40,768	4,463,524	548,153	16,115	66,309
Georgia	19,121	1,759,318	572,949	5,274	9,953
Hawaii	202,865	138,755	7,342	1,624	5,681
Idaho	2,420	345,583	1,154	4,498	7,068
Illinois	80,002	3,450,231	547,670	8,497	115,840
Indiana	10,480	1,889,948	148,237	5,341	11,349
Iowa	–	–	–	–	–
Kansas	7,924	868,467	47,524	7,887	12,924
Kentucky	4,313	1,279,000	92,401	2,617	1,451
Louisiana	9,714	1,070,255	406,461	6,353	6,486
Maine	1,620	459,803	1,475	2,049	365
Maryland	37,169	1,295,468	400,271	4,829	11,254
Massachusetts	37,744	2,064,471	97,714	4,364	42,817
Michigan	27,478	2,908,160	440,286	19,358	24,049
Minnesota	16,664	1,581,589	30,447	13,926	5,227
Mississippi	–	–	–	–	–
Missouri	–	–	–	–	–
Montana	1,064	289,806	670	13,396	1,227
Nebraska	–	–	–	–	–
Nevada	10,209	408,873	25,909	7,002	14,304
New Hampshire	2,285	404,714	2,311	916	960
New Jersey	72,845	2,310,208	331,831	5,166	74,661
New Mexico	3,627	437,072	10,020	33,478	58,512
New York	198,132	5,191,913	945,330	19,634	284,313
North Carolina	12,714	1,979,986	490,360	26,411	7,555
North Dakota	841	231,796	1,046	6,794	401
Ohio	26,020	3,623,821	412,690	8,693	16,322
Oklahoma	9,041	1,029,045	77,928	78,956	11,165
Oregon	19,279	1,043,627	15,115	13,300	11,992
Pennsylvania	36,138	4,047,850	373,850	6,248	31,880
Rhode Island	4,222	352,951	12,459	1,428	6,917
South Carolina	5,211	923,767	323,457	3,179	2,430
South Dakota	651	245,144	907	11,800	532
Tennessee	8,274	1,576,475	261,629	4,878	2,469
Texas	88,625	4,808,218	679,618	25,305	469,171
Utah	8,744	508,481	3,660	6,011	10,377

[Continued]

★ 508 ★

Housing Units, Total Occupied, by State (Continued)

Number of occupied housing units by state and race/ethnicity, 1990.

State	Asian/ Pacific Islander	White	Black	American Indian, Eskimo, or Aleut	Other
Vermont	675	208,441	558	812	164
Virginia	40,821	1,841,346	389,928	5,682	14,053
Washington	58,267	1,710,598	50,321	25,618	27,627
West Virginia	2,038	664,542	20,516	1,094	367
Wisconsin	12,664	1,712,248	75,004	11,742	10,460
Wyoming	770	160,852	1,053	2,814	3,350

Source: Asian/Pacific Islander Data Consortium (San Francisco: Asian and Pacific Islander Center for Census Information and Services, 1993). Primary source: U.S. Census Bureau, Summary Tape Files 1 and 3. *Note:* A dash (–) indicates data was not available at time of publication.

★ 509 ★

Monthly Housing Expenses: Mortgages, by State

Monthly housing expenses for Asian/Pacific Islanders with mortgages on their owner–occupied housing units by state, 1990.

State	With a mortgage					
	Less than $300	$300 to $499	$500 to $699	$700 to $999	$1000 to $1499	$1500 or more
Alabama	69	286	482	560	296	151
Alaska	16	36	94	395	545	218
Arizona	126	525	1,214	2,126	1,781	566
Arkansas	61	329	310	209	61	28
California	7,328	22,136	23,212	46,885	100,055	131,027
Colorado	157	758	1178	2664	1,437	398
Connecticut	20	134	320	768	1,641	2,175
Delaware	22	58	132	285	415	301
Florida	400	1,917	3,977	6,097	3,696	1,966
Georgia	160	502	1238	2,674	1,925	958
Hawaii	3,316	10,332	9,960	13,783	18,447	14,045
Idaho	51	199	333	162	34	0
Illinois	118	1,091	3,220	7,747	10,036	6,942
Indiana	84	567	723	980	667	470
Iowa	–	–	–	–	–	–
Kansas	34	377	514	775	311	280
Kentucky	28	360	345	338	278	209
Louisiana	84	571	950	932	370	185
Maine	2	93	117	160	169	47
Maryland	145	759	1,771	4,119	7,186	6,177
Massachusetts	92	463	795	1,412	3,150	3,659
Michigan	109	991	1,814	2,647	2,688	2,711
Minnesota	62	406	872	2,275	1,218	469
Mississippi	–	–	–	–	–	–

[Continued]

★ 509 ★

Monthly Housing Expenses: Mortgages, by State (Continued)

Monthly housing expenses for Asian/Pacific Islanders with mortgages on their owner–occupied housing units by state, 1990.

State	With a mortgage					
	Less than $300	$300 to $499	$500 to $699	$700 to $999	$1000 to $1499	$1500 or more
Missouri	–	–	–	–	–	–
Montana	8	78	84	84	39	7
Nebraska	–	–	–	–	–	–
Nevada	57	318	718	1,820	814	267
New Hampshire	5	30	97	140	425	258
New Jersey	105	666	1,579	3,983	9,135	17,809
New Mexico	15	195	299	396	232	162
New York	167	1,450	3,556	5,927	9,629	17,888
North Carolina	122	605	889	1,437	1,133	553
North Dakota	6	19	27	70	40	26
Ohio	122	1,061	1,837	2,584	2,458	1,692
Oklahoma	62	516	921	843	456	164
Oregon	103	945	2,005	2,226	873	286
Pennsylvania	184	1567	2,474	3,340	3,432	2,823
Rhode Island	0	142	241	232	368	148
South Carolina	91	340	593	655	362	170
South Dakota	15	12	67	39	40	2
Tennessee	70	356	704	858	695	264
Texas	471	2,464	6,445	11,467	8,296	3,955
Utah	102	542	1094	943	224	93
Vermont	0	19	42	45	41	34
Virginia	120	908	1,733	4,075	7,071	6,281
Washington	499	2,386	4,167	7,935	5,423	1,683
West Virginia	16	81	139	129	177	186
Wisconsin	20	323	501	818	610	500
Wyoming	9	54	84	38	6	14

Source: Asian/Pacific Islander Data Consortium (San Francisco: Asian and Pacific Islander Center for Census Information and Services, 1993). Primary source: U.S. Census Bureau, Summary Tape Files 1 and 3. *Note:* A dash (–) indicates data was not available at time of publication.

★ 510 ★

Monthly Housing Expenses: Not mortgaged, by State

State	Not mortgaged				
	Less than $100	$100 to $199	$200 to $299	$300 to $399	$400 or more
Alabama	8	142	49	15	7
Alaska	2	32	69	38	32
Arizona	28	238	347	180	60
Arkansas	6	160	121	19	15
California	2,936	20,143	11,450	4,847	3,546
Colorado	33	390	419	63	104

[Continued]

★ 510 ★

Monthly Housing Expenses: Not mortgaged, by State (Continued)

State	Not mortgaged				
	Less than $100	$100 to $199	$200 to $299	$300 to $399	$400 or more
Connecticut	0	6	46	124	183
Delaware	0	44	47	9	8
Florida	123	872	720	254	229
Georgia	27	210	198	83	109
Hawaii	3,477	19,178	7,880	1,517	733
Idaho	7	156	81	9	2
Illinois	19	295	1,108	988	730
Indiana	0	241	187	87	86
Iowa	–	–	–	–	–
Kansas	12	164	173	78	24
Kentucky	21	134	60	20	17
Louisiana	44	230	193	54	26
Maine	0	4	47	3	16
Maryland	19	154	554	469	247
Massachusetts	5	6	222	307	285
Michigan	20	312	449	293	411
Minnesota	10	198	200	74	38
Mississippi	–	–	–	–	–
Missouri	–	–	–	–	–
Montana	0	40	31	0	0
Nebraska	–	–	–	–	–
Nevada	29	132	169	36	24
New Hampshire	0	9	0	14	30
New Jersey	13	88	250	548	1,501
New Mexico	3	123	56	7	11
New York	63	219	799	989	2,046
North Carolina	30	253	180	123	14
North Dakota	0	13	19	0	3
Ohio	23	434	466	223	172
Oklahoma	17	255	185	16	62
Oregon	9	313	778	337	135
Pennsylvania	19	727	948	392	379
Rhode Island	0	9	38	43	34
South Carolina	20	84	137	7	10
South Dakota	10	8	22	0	0
Tennessee	35	175	147	60	27
Texas	219	1,134	1,813	905	832
Utah	41	399	154	76	20
Vermont	7	0	7	3	0
Virginia	31	222	306	173	180
Washington	225	1,896	1,803	629	176
West Virginia	13	108	51	30	12
Wisconsin	2	120	189	140	183
Wyoming	12	67	25	7	0

Source: Asian/Pacific Islander Data Consortium (San Francisco: Asian and Pacific Islander Center for Census Information and Services, 1993). Primary source: U.S. Census Bureau, Summary Tape Files 1 and 3. *Note:* A dash (–) indicates data was not available at time of publication.

Immigration

★ 511 ★

Immigration Trends by Race and Decade, 1820-1980

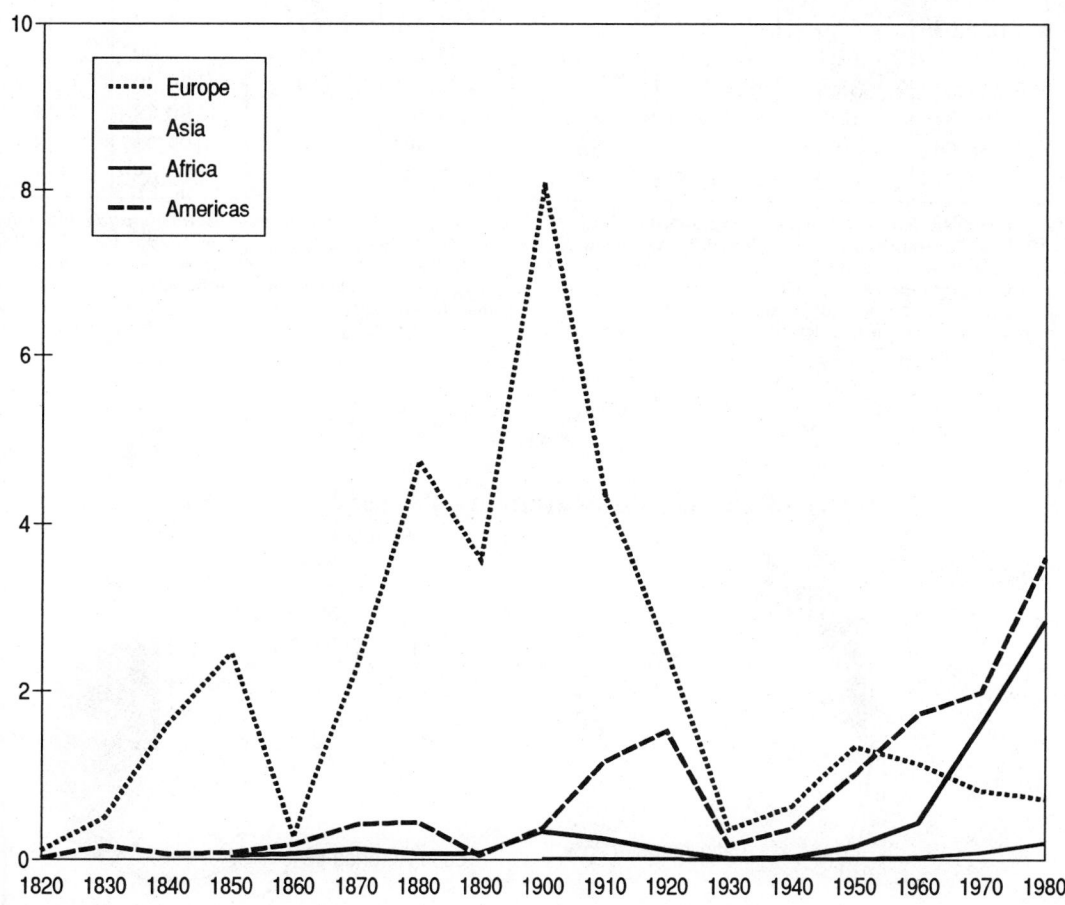

Source: Data for 1981 to 1990 are from U.S. Immigration and Naturalization Service (INS), *Statistical Yearbook of the Immigration and Naturalization Service, 1991* (Washington, DC: U.S. Government Printing Office, 1992), table 3, p. 32. Data for 1820 to 1980 were adapted from Leon F. Bouvier and Robert W. Gardner, "Immigration to the U.S.: The Unfinished Story," *Population Bulletin* 41, no. 4 (November 1986): table 1, p. 8. Primary source: INS, *Statistical Yearbook* (Washington, DC: U.S. Government Printing Office, 1986), table IMM 1.2.

★ 512 ★

Immigration by Region of Last Residence, 1820-1990

Number and percent of total immigrants admitted to the United States per decade by world region, 1820-1990.

Intercensal decade	Total	Europe[a]		Asia[b]		Africa		Americas[c]	
		Percent	Number	Percent	Number	Percent	Number	Percent	Number
1821-1830	151,824	70.1	106,429	-	-	-	-	7.9	11,994
1831-1840	599,125	81.7	489,485	-	-	-	-	25.6	153,376
1841-1850	1,713,251	93.2	1,596,750	-	-	-	-	3.6	61,680
1851-1860	2,598,214	94.4	2,452,714	1.6	4,1571	-	-	2.9	75,348
1861-1870	2,314,824	89.2	2,064,823	2.8	64,815	-	-	7.2	166,667
1871-1880	2,812,191	80.8	2,272,250	4.4	123,736	-	-	14.4	404,956
1881-1890	5,246,613	90.3	4,737,691	1.3	68,206	-	-	8.1	424,976
1891-1900	3,687,564	96.4	3,554,811	2.0	73,751	-	-	1.1	40,563
1901-1910	8,795,386	91.6	8,056,573	3.7	325,430	0.1	8,795	4.1	360,610
1911-1920	5,735,811	75.3	4,319,066	4.3	246,640	0.1	5,736	19.9	1,141,426
1921-1930	4,107,209	60.0	2,464,325	2.7	110,895	0.2	8,214	36.9	1,515,560
1931-1940	528,431	65.8	347,708	3.0	15,853	0.3	1,585	30.3	160,114
1941-1950	1,035,039	60.0	621,023	3.1	32,086	0.7	7,245	34.3	355,019
1951-1960	2,515,479	52.7	1,325,657	6.1	153,444	0.6	15,093	39.6	996,130
1961-1970	3,321,677	33.8	1,122,727	12.9	428,496	0.9	29,895	51.7	1,717,307
1971-1980	4,493,314	17.8	799,810	35.3	1,586,140	1.8	80,880	44.1	1,981,551
1981-1990	7,338,062	9.6	705,630	38.3	2,817,391	2.6	192,212	48.7	3,580,928
TOTALS	56,994,014	65.0	37,037,472	11.7	6,088,454	0.6	349,655	23.0	13,148,205

Source: Data for 1981 to 1990 are from U.S. Immigration and Naturalization Service (INS), *Statistical Yearbook of the Immigration and Naturalization Service, 1991* (Washington, DC: U.S. Government Printing Office, 1992), table 3, p. 32. Data for 1820 to 1980 were adapted from Leon F. Bouvier and Robert W. Gardner, "Immigration to the U.S.: The Unfinished Story," *Population Bulletin* 41, no. 4 (November 1986): table 1, p. 8. Primary source: INS, *Statistical Yearbook* (Washington, DC: U.S. Government Printing Office, 1986), table IMM 1.2. A dash (–) indicates less than 0.05 percent. Numbers may not add to totals due to rounding and the exclusion of data for immigrants from Oceania. *Notes:* (a) Includes all of former USSR except 1931-1950 when USSR is divided into European USSR and Asian USSR. (b) Asia, according to INS definition, includes Southwest Asia, e.g., Iraq, Israel, Syria, Turkey. (c) Includes Canada, Mexico, the Caribbean, Central America, and South America.

★ 513 ★

Source of United States Immigrants, 1950s and 1980s

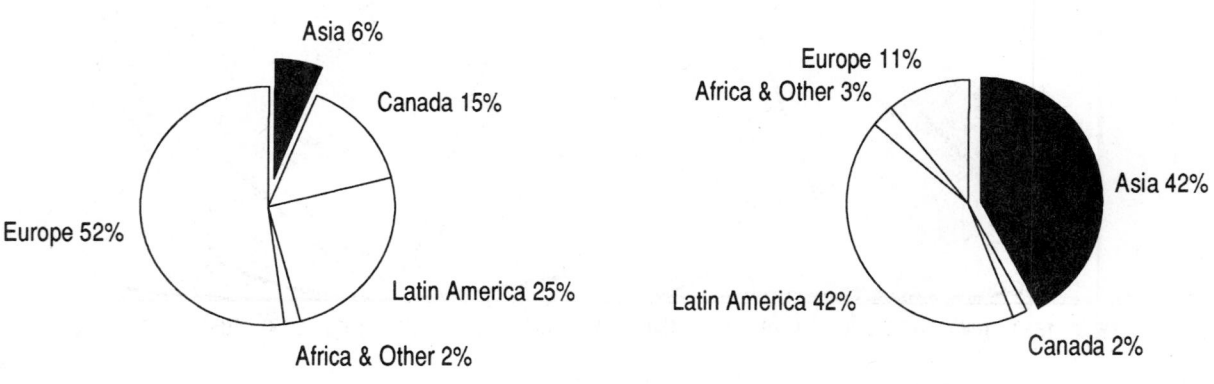

Source: William P. O'Hare and Judy C. Felt, *Asian Americans: America's Fastest Growing Minority Group* (Washington, DC: Population Reference Bureau, Inc., 1991), fig. 3, p. 6.

★ 514 ★

Immigration from Asia and the Pacific Islands, 1950s to 1980s

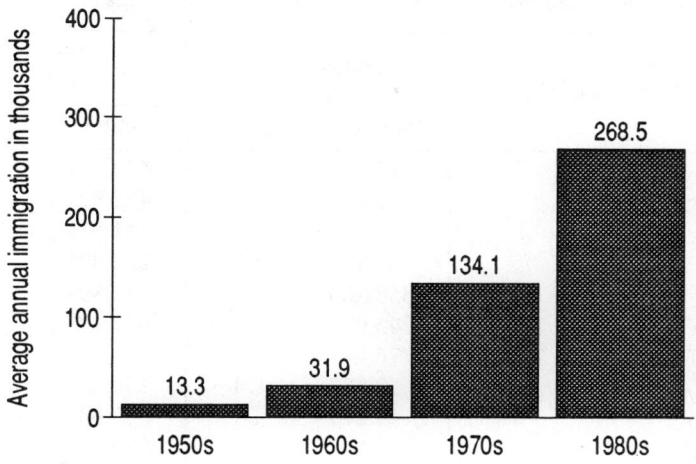

Source: William P. O'Hare and Judy C. Felt, *Asian Americans: America's Fastest Growing Minority Group* (Washington, DC: Population Reference Bureau, Inc., 1991), fig. 2, p. 5

★ 515 ★

Immigration by Country of Origin, 1850-1990

Immigrants admitted to the United States by selected Asian ethnic group by decade, 1850-1990.

Decade	Chinese	Japanese	Asian Indian	Korean	Filipino	Vietnamese
1850-1860	41,397	-	43	-	-	-
1861-1870	64,301	186	69	-	-	-
1871-1880	123,201	149	163	-	-	-
1881-1890	61,711	2,270	269	-	-	-
1891-1900	14,799	25,942	68	-	-	-
1901-1910	20,605	129,797	4,713	7,697	-	-
1911-1920	21,278	83,837	2,082	1,049	869	-
1921-1930	29,907	33,462	1,886	598	54,747	-
1931-1940	4,928	1,948	496	60	6,159	-
1941-1950	16,709	1,555	1,761	-	4,691	-
1951-1960	9,657[a]	46,250	1,973	6,231	19,307	-
1961-1970	34,764	39,98	27,189	34,526	98,376	3,788
1971-1980	12,326	49,775	164,134	271,956	360,216	179,681
1981-1990	366,622[b]	43.248	261,841	338,824	495,271	401,419

Sources: For 1851-1980, U.S. Commission on Civil Rights, *The Economic Status of Americans of Asian Descent: An Exploratory Investigation* (Washington, DC: U.S. Commission on Civil Rights Clearinghouse Publication 95, October 1988), table 2.2, p. 21. For 1981-1990, selected from U.S. Immigration and Naturalization Service (INS), *Statistical Yearbook of the Immigration and Naturalization Service, 1991* (Washington, DC: U.S. Government Printing Office, 1992), table 3, p. 32. Primary source: For 1851-1980, INS, *Statistical Yearbook of the Immigration and Naturalization Service,* various years. Data on Filipino migration to mainland United States for the decades 1911-1940 were derived from the INS *Report of the Commissioner General of Immigration.* A dash (–) represents less than 0.5 percent. *Notes:* (a) Beginning in 1957, Chinese total includes immigration from Taiwan. (b) Beginning in 1982, Taiwan was no longer included in the Chinese total. Immigration from Taiwan to the United States from 1982 to 1990 was 118,105. These immigrants are not included in the total for Chinese which appears in the table.

★ 516 ★

Immigration by Asian Country of Origin, 1980-1989

Asian/Pacific Islander population by ancestry, 1980, and numbers of immigrants admitted to the United States by selected Asian country of origin, 1980 to 1989.

Ancestry/Country of Origin	Population 1980		Immigration[a] 1980 to 1989	
	Number	Percent	Number	Percent
China[b]	812,178	22	433,031	15
Philippines	781,894	21	473,831	17
Japan	716,331	19	41,739	1
India	387,223	10	253,891	9
Korea	358.303	10	338,891	12
Vietnam	245,025	7	679,378	24
Samoa/Tonga/Guam	76,441	2	6,214	-
Laos[c]	52,887	1	256,727	9
Thailand	45,279	1	59,638	2
Cambodia	16,044	-	210,724	7
Pakistan	15,792	-	55,900	2
Other	219,953	6	55,485	2
Total	3,726,440	100	2,865,339	100

Source: William P. O'Hare and Judy C. Felt, *Asian Americans: America's Fastest Growing Minority Group* (Washington, DC: Population Reference Bureau, 1991), table 1, p. 2. Primary sources: Bureau of the Census, *Subject Reports, Asian and Pacific Islander Population in the United States: 1980*, PC80-2-1E (Washington, DC: U.S. Government Printing Office, 1983), table 2; and U.S. Immigration and Naturalization Service, *1989 Statistical Yearbook* (Washington, DC: Government Printing Office, 1990), tables 3 and 27. A dash (–) represents less than 0.5 percent. *Notes:* (a) Includes refugees. (b) Includes Taiwan, Hong Kong, and Macau. (c) Includes Hmong.

★ 517 ★

Immigration by Region and Country of Birth, 1981-1991

Numbers of immigrants admitted to the United States by world region and selected Asian country of birth, 1981-1991.

Region and country of birth	1981	1982	1983	1984	1985	1986	1987	1988	1989	1990	1991
All countries	596,600	594,131	559,763	543,903	570,009	601,708	601,516	643,025	1,090,924	1,536,483	1,827,167
Europe	66,695	69,174	58,867	64,076	63,043	62,512	61,174	64,797	82,891	112,401	135,234
Asia[b]	264,332	313,272	277,697	256,272	264,691	268,248	257,684	264,465	312,149	338,581	358,533
Afghanistan	1,881	1,569	2,566	3,222	2,794	2,831	2,424	2,873	3,232	3,187	2,879
Bangladesh	756	639	787	823	1,146	1,634	1,649	1,325	2,180	4,252	10,676
Burma	1,083	820	723	719	990	863	941	803	1,170	1,120	946
Cambodia	12,749	13,438	18,120	11,856	13,563	13,501	12,460	9,629	6,076	5,179	3,251
China	25,803	(a)	(a)	(a)	(a)	(a)	(a)	(a)	(a)	(a)	(a)
China, Mainland	(a)	27,100	25,777	23,363	24,787	25,106	25,841	28,717	32,272	31,815	33,025
Hong Kong	4,055	4,971	5,948	5,465	5,171	5,021	4,706	8,546	9,740	9,393	10,427
India	21,522	21,738	25,451	24,964	26,026	26,227	27,803	26,268	31,175	30,667	45,064
Indonesia	1,006	1,194	952	1,113	1,269	1,183	1,254	1,342	1,513	3,498	2,223
Iran	11,105	10,314	11,163	13,807	16,071	16,505	14,426	15,246	21,243	24,977	19,569
Iraq	2,535	3,105	2,343	2,930	1,951	1,323	1,072	1,022	1,516	1,756	1,494
Israel	3,542	3,356	3,239	3,066	3,113	3,790	3,699	3,640	4,244	4,664	4,181
Japan	3,896	3,903	4,092	4,043	4,086	3,959	4,174	4,512	4,849	5,734	5,049
Jordan	3,825	2,923	2,718	2,438	2,998	3,081	3,125	3,232	3,921	4,449	4,259

[Continued]

Immigration by Region and Country of Birth, 1981-1991 (Continued)

Numbers of immigrants admitted to the United States by world region and selected Asian country of birth, 1981-1991.

Region and country of birth	1981	1982	1983	1984	1985	1986	1987	1988	1989	1990	1991
Korea	32,663	31,724	33,339	33,042	35,253	35,776	35,849	34,703	34,222	32,301	26,518
Kuwait	317	286	344	437	503	496	507	599	710	691	861
Laos	15,805	36,528	23,662	12,279	9,133	7,842	6,828	10,667	12,524	10,446	9,950
Lebanon	3,955	3,529	2,941	3,203	3,385	3,994	4,367	4,910	5,716	5,634	6,009
Malaysia	1,033	1,046	852	879	939	886	1,016	1,250	1,506	1,867	1,860
Pakistan	5,288	4,536	4,807	5,509	5,744	5,994	6,319	5,438	8,000	9,729	20,355
Philippines	43,772	45,102	41,546	42,768	47,978	52,558	50,060	50,697	57,034	63,756	63,596
Saudi Arabia	159	134	170	208	228	275	294	338	381	518	552
Singapore	408	390	362	377	460	480	469	492	566	620	535
Sri Lanka	448	505	472	554	553	596	630	634	757	976	1,377
Syria	2,127	2,354	1,683	1,724	1,581	1,604	1,669	2,183	2,675	2,972	2,837
Taiwan	(a)	9,884	16,698	12,478	14,895	13,424	11,931	9,670	13,974	15,151	13,274
Thailand	4,799	5,568	5,875	4,885	5,239	6,204	6,733	6,888	9,332	8,914	7,397
Turkey	2,766	2,864	2,263	1,793	1,691	1,753	1,596	1,642	2,007	2,468	2,528
Vietnam	55,631	72,553	37,560	37,236	31,895	29,993	24,231	25,789	37,739	48,792	55,307
Yemen	577	484	507	331	435	480	727	619	966	1,945	1,547
Other Asia	826	715	737	760	814	869	884	791	909	1,110	987
Africa	15,029	14,314	15,084	15,540	17,117	17,463	17,724	18,882	25,166	35,893	36,179
Oceania	4,198	3,852	3,515	3,818	4,054	3,894	3,993	3,839	4,360	6,182	6,236
North America	210,427	158,057	168,487	166,706	182,045	207,714	216,550	250,009	607,398	957,558	1,210,981
Canada	11,191	10,786	11,390	10,791	11,385	11,039	11,876	11,783	12,151	16,812	13,504
Mexico	101,268	56,106	59,079	57,557	61,077	66,533	72,351	95,039	405,172	679,068	946,167
Caribbean	73,301	67,379	73,306	74,265	83,281	101,632	102,899	112,357	88,932	115,351	140,139
Central America	24,509	23,626	24,601	24,088	26,302	28,380	29,296	30,715	101,034	146,202	111,093
Other North America	158	160	111	5	-	130	128	115	109	125	78
South America	35,913	35,448	36,087	37,460	39,058	41,874	44,385	41,007	58,926	85,819	79,934

Source: U.S. Immigration and Naturalization Service (INS), *Statistical Yearbook of the Immigration and Naturalization Service, 1991* (Washington, DC: U.S. Government Printing Office, 1992), table 3, p. 32. A dash (–) represents zero. *Notes:* (a) Prior to fiscal year 1982, data for "China, Mainland" and Taiwan are included in "China." After 1982, "China, Mainland" is the INS designation for immigrants from areas under the control of the government in Beijing. (b) Asia, according to INS definition, includes Southwest Asia, i.e., Iraq, Israel, Syria, and Turkey.

★ 518 ★

Immigration by State of Intended Residence and Country of Birth, 1991

Numbers of immigrants admitted from selected Asian countries of birth intending to reside in each of the fifty states, District of Columbia, or U.S. Territories, 1991.

State of intended residence	All countries	Bangla-desh	China, Mainland[a]	Hong Kong	India	Korea	Pakistan	Philippines	Taiwan	Vietnam
Total	1,827,167	10,676	33,025	10,427	45,064	26,518	20,355	63,596	13,274	55,307
Alabama	2,706	17	56	12	183	106	34	90	39	310
Alaska	1,525	-	21	9	17	150	5	382	12	43
Arizona	40,642	12	210	76	210	168	56	355	71	806
Arkansas	2,559	9	16	4	48	27	5	84	9	132
California	732,735	1,064	12,265	4,468	10,291	7,301	3,084	32,698	5,840	21,542
Colorado	13,782	5	182	35	142	240	35	211	67	723
Connecticut	12,365	118	201	60	703	145	277	370	72	534
Delaware	1,937	5	54	10	96	217	25	60	28	13
District of Columbia	5,510	39	125	14	69	62	42	109	17	779
Florida	141,068	371	495	217	1,224	424	855	1,501	191	1,623
Georgia	23,556	122	238	63	1,175	550	426	274	235	1,396
Hawaii	8,659	6	594	265	28	514	15	4,367	100	498
Idaho	7,088	-	22	6	18	28	3	52	8	60
Illinois	73,388	118	1,164	293	3,827	1,162	1,464	2,924	368	967
Indiana	4,512	7	135	35	253	141	85	232	62	162
Iowa	3,331	2	35	17	89	125	13	89	41	531
Kansas	5,620	18	63	23	131	83	33	127	53	451
Kentucky	1,753	7	55	14	113	86	23	100	24	347
Louisiana	4,917	31	108	39	251	88	44	202	68	708
Maine	1,155	2	43	18	25	31	2	45	1	112
Maryland	17,470	125	499	124	984	1,048	377	791	272	697
Massachusetts	27,020	126	1,150	451	1,061	232	249	411	264	1,961
Michigan	16,090	136	326	96	1,064	482	304	659	229	685
Minnesota	7,461	6	188	50	226	260	41	217	61	732
Mississippi	1,254	6	23	20	88	15	5	83	22	146
Missouri	4,470	19	139	28	218	168	86	263	94	709
Montana	826	-	11	1	10	43	-	46	2	3
Nebraska	3,020	-	12	6	25	84	7	81	21	441
Nevada	10,470	16	140	33	85	118	41	692	74	207
New Hampshire	1,421	4	59	14	86	90	15	40	34	92
New Jersey	56,164	560	1,020	291	4,939	1,434	1,296	2,885	863	886
New Mexico	13,519	3	37	12	76	46	6	88	28	240
New York	188,104	6,854	9,667	2,311	9,133	5,209	7,504	4,045	1,581	2,235
North Carolina	16,772	3	114	51	421	258	122	239	82	626
North Dakota	565	-	6	3	17	6	4	27	-	160
Ohio	8,632	40	279	111	843	335	126	512	206	343
Oklahoma	6,403	36	80	11	211	116	51	132	51	443
Oregon	24,575	10	317	90	124	257	30	305	65	908
Pennsylvania	20,033	78	542	163	1,361	983	251	555	264	1,619
Rhode Island	3,644	2	64	28	73	25	17	86	21	54
South Carolina	3,836	14	63	48	175	90	19	202	47	100
South Dakota	519	3	6	8	9	27	1	30	3	70
Tennessee	3,828	23	80	11	266	107	41	141	61	456
Texas	212,600	340	792	307	2,601	1,104	1,806	1,775	875	5,257
Utah	5,737	3	110	27	58	86	51	106	52	369
Vermont	709	1	15	7	25	9	3	11	11	147
Virginia	24,942	259	382	79	1,194	1,093	1,197	1,352	293	1,896
Washington	33,826	27	555	291	386	811	94	1,563	266	1,889
West Virginia	763	3	24	2	71	31	15	51	13	51

[Continued]

★ 518 ★

Immigration by State of Intended Residence and Country of Birth, 1991 (Continued)

Numbers of immigrants admitted from selected Asian countries of birth intending to reside in each of the fifty states, District of Columbia, or U.S. Territories, 1991.

State of intended residence	All countries	Bangla-desh	China, Mainland[a]	Hong Kong	India	Korea	Pakistan	Philippines	Taiwan	Vietnam
Wisconsin	5,888	13	116	36	282	129	43	145	52	104
Wyoming	566	2	9	6	16	11	2	19	1	8
U.S. territories and possessions										
Guam	2,113	-	31	15	5	141	7	1,666	57	35
Northern Mariana Is.	114	5	5	-	1	4	-	83	-	-
Puerto Rico	10,353	1	81	14	13	6	3	9	1	1
Virgin Islands	2,083	-	1	4	15	-	7	6	1	-
Other or unknown	2,569	5	-	-	9	2	8	8	1	-

Source: U.S. Immigration and Naturalization Service (INS), *Statistical Yearbook of the Immigration and Naturalization Service, 1991* (Washington, DC: U.S. Government Printing Office, 1992), table 16, p 58. A dash (–) represents zero. *Notes:* (a) After 1982, the INS used the designation "China, Mainland" for immigrants from areas under the control of the government in Beijing.

★ 519 ★

Immigrants by Country of Birth and Metropolitan Area of Intended Residence

Numbers of immigrants from selected Asian countries of birth intending to reside in selected U.S. Metropolitan Statistical Areas, 1991.

Metropolitan Statistical Area[a]	All countries	Bangladesh	China, Mainland[a]	Hong Kong	India	Korea	Laos	Pakistan	Philippines	Taiwan	Vietnam
Total	1,827,167	10,676	33,025	10,427	45,064	26,518	9,950	20,355	63,596	13,274	55,307
Los Angeles-Long Beach, CA	257,160	775	3,626	1,302	2,565	4,419	100	1,203	12,147	2,748	5,156
New York, NY	163,006	6,550	8,964	2,131	7,368	4,579	3	6,676	3,421	1,200	786
Chicago, IL	60,590	93	1,023	235	3,409	960	25	1,348	2,546	276	767
San Diego, CA	59,329	17	309	132	193	214	344	55	3,548	181	1,683
Anaheim-Santa Ana, CA	59,015	107	502	183	783	946	84	277	1,526	745	5,366
Miami-Hialeah, FL	58,918	54	152	79	243	97	-	432	267	43	73
Houston, TX	53,690	142	362	170	1,281	269	50	1,089	673	295	2,518
Riverside-San Bernardino, CA	50,608	51	157	70	416	292	96	152	1,324	228	550
Dallas, TX	39,352	116	210	67	699	431	87	379	275	276	1,177
Washington, DC-MD-VA	36,370	363	742	144	1,653	1,441	58	1,432	1,186	416	2,611
Fresno, CA	33,033	-	53	19	449	33	1,621	44	157	19	102
San Francisco, CA	29,989	21	4,068	1,352	431	204	24	157	3,702	351	1,096
San Jose, CA	28,942	34	962	390	1,774	386	52	226	2,463	848	4,640
Oakland, CA	24,416	23	1,667	710	1,391	271	269	317	2,941	432	1,309
Boston-Lawrence-Salem-Lowell-Brockton, MA	21,922	114	1,083	418	839	149	73	208	306	210	1,458
Phoenix, AZ	21,027	11	160	61	144	117	22	35	193	48	623
Visalia-Tulare-Porterville, CA	17,874	1	17	2	71	4	224	22	217	2	4
Oxnard-Ventura, CA	17,144	8	60	9	123	75	6	15	575	52	148
Bakersfield, CA	17,008	3	11	8	201	46	4	35	516	12	33
Newark, NJ	16,909	59	259	60	872	213	2	292	636	227	253
El Paso, TX	16,425	2	12	4	26	45	-	2	36	10	8
Atlanta, GA	15,619	111	175	54	889	384	78	377	126	189	1,275
Philadelphia, PA-NJ	15,009	110	464	142	1,169	822	95	224	528	166	1,367
Salinas-Seaside-Monterey, CA	14,581	-	33	10	30	80	-	8	341	11	95

[Continued]

★ 519 ★

Immigrants by Country of Birth and Metropolitan Area of Intended Residence (Continued)

Numbers of immigrants from selected Asian countries of birth intending to reside in selected U.S. Metropolitan Statistical Areas, 1991.

Metropolitan Statistical Area[a]	All countries	Bangladesh	China, Mainland[a]	Hong Kong	India	Korea	Laos	Pakistan	Philippines	Taiwan	Vietnam
Fort Lauderdale-Hollywood-Pompano Beach, FL	14,520	109	96	44	209	42	-	171	130	38	88
McAllen-Edinburg-Mission, TX	14,496	-	2	-	10	11	-	1	30	3	-
Santa Barbara-Santa Maria-Lompoc, CA	14,269	3	32	2	29	24	94	4	222	35	39
West Palm Beach-Boca Raton-Delray Beach, FL	13,903	147	59	21	125	12	3	47	84	15	44
Stockton, CA	13,458	-	81	62	263	16	378	195	625	16	507
Nassau-Suffolk, NY	13,300	222	370	106	956	256	3	514	325	227	95
Sacramento, CA	13,156	3	390	146	474	128	486	155	628	74	583
Bergen-Passaic, NJ	12,816	272	168	46	893	653	-	144	518	153	29
Portland, OR	12,194	7	213	82	101	190	128	19	197	43	818
Fort Worth-Arlington, TX	11,893	43	56	24	185	52	20	139	103	96	831
Santa Cruz, CA	10,674	-	37	5	31	11	-	3	104	3	13
Tampa-St. Petersburg-Clearwater, FL	10,629	6	41	14	150	92	80	15	200	31	597
Jersey City, NJ	9,922	51	108	43	922	152	1	342	787	42	92
Detroit, MI	8,968	114	173	66	675	216	110	228	431	120	98
Seattle, WA	8,884	15	452	253	281	452	170	79	978	196	1,255
San Antonia, TX	8,883	-	24	4	52	74	5	38	105	31	113
Yakima, WA	8,690	-	16	2	1	4	1	-	25	1	-
Modesto, CA	8,682	-	32	6	190	14	19	64	75	6	19
Merced, CA	8,605	6	2	-	165	5	501	20	53	-	2
San Juan, PR	8,165	1	60	8	8	4	-	3	1	1	1
Yuma, AZ	7,760	-	-	-	7	5	-	2	35	-	-
Denver, CO	7,234	4	125	22	91	134	94	34	128	42	638
Brownsville-Harlingen, TX	7,085	-	2	-	3	5	-	-	37	4	-
Middlesex-Somerset-Hunterdon, NJ	6,935	61	203	63	1,430	130	3	264	374	255	56
Las Vegas, NV	6,686	4	90	25	61	95	7	23	416	58	162
Honolulu, HI	6,579	6	568	258	24	487	54	15	3,022	93	484
Other MSA	243,233	687	3,721	1,139	8,770	4,864	3,887	2,365	8,405	2,215	14,327
Non-MSA	186,213	150	833	234	1,939	1,913	589	466	5,904	491	1,318

Source: U.S. Immigration and Naturalization Service (INS), *Statistical Yearbook of the Immigration and Naturalization Service, 1991* (Washington, DC: U.S. Government Printing Office, 1992), table 18, p 62. A dash (–) represents zero. *Note:* (a) The INS uses the designation "China, Mainland" for immigrants from areas under the control of the government in Beijing.

★ 520 ★

Immigration by Country of Birth, Age, and Sex

Numbers of immigrants admitted to the United States from selected Asian countries of birth by age and sex, and percent and median age for male and female immigrants.

Age and sex	All countries	Bangladesh	China, Mainland[a]	Hong Kong	India	Korea	Pakistan	Philippines	Taiwan	Vietnam
Total	1,827,167	10,676	33,025	10,427	45,064	26,518	20,355	63,596	13,274	55,307
Under 5 years	36,669	402	526	543	1,462	2,520	711	2,545	361	1,761
5-9 years	49,609	347	802	883	1,244	916	533	3,297	667	3,421
10-14 years	66,237	317	1,483	1,219	1,426	1,502	494	4,321	1,188	5,088
15-19 years	109,261	692	2,110	1,270	1,898	1,889	682	5,394	833	9,801
20-24 years	354,747	1,808	2,478	688	4,670	2,141	2,260	5,231	819	9,065
25-29 years	380,682	2,455	4,074	1,399	8,745	3,514	4,383	7,855	1,835	5,045
30-34 years	276,464	2,256	2,944	1,515	7,430	3,274	4,360	8,939	2,611	3,647
35-39 years	182,200	1,242	2,652	1,100	5,192	2,509	2,764	6,151	1,793	3,690
40-44 years	120,980	466	2,692	858	3,321	2,198	1,564	4,520	1,016	3,222
45-49 years	78,393	248	2,057	252	2,193	1,836	845	2,938	476	2,534
50-54 years	57,023	153	1,866	274	1,985	1,322	655	2,880	387	2,187
55-59 years	41,330	120	2,226	182	1,819	944	414	2,817	412	1,880
60-64 years	30,856	78	2,499	121	1,562	770	308	2,699	373	1,629
65-69 years	21,616	60	2,311	65	1,130	543	203	2,026	292	1,103
70-74	11,109	19	1,342	32	584	371	103	1,200	114	694
75-79	5,938	10	676	18	286	185	53	569	68	359
80 years and over	3,680	2	286	8	114	82	20	212	29	177
Male	1,213,767	8,271	15,246	5,211	27,349	13,144	15,463	26,764	6,024	26,581
Under 5 years	18,580	200	256	285	696	1,242	347	1,376	194	899
5-9 years	25,228	185	419	471	626	467	262	1,676	326	1,788
10-14 years	34,112	183	779	624	745	801	268	2,229	662	2,724
15-19 years	64,888	461	1,104	659	932	1,017	373	2,667	293	5,375
20-24 years	263,149	1,331	739	340	1,943	719	1,599	1,669	375	4,694
25-29 years	268,701	2,027	1,638	642	5,583	1,412	3,562	2,734	716	2,544
30-34 years	188,466	1,935	1,485	745	5,602	1,791	3,687	3,418	1,269	1,615
35-39 years	122,263	1,101	1,297	541	3,806	1,393	2,353	2,604	839	1,464
40-44 years	80,507	399	1,301	429	2,298	1,237	1,306	2,024	461	1,184
45-49 years	52,509	193	993	125	1,353	1,126	655	1,277	247	1,036
50-54 years	35,995	94	846	146	1,019	774	434	1,205	163	847
55-59 years	23,893	65	962	84	860	417	231	1,101	127	757
60-64 years	15,741	45	1,080	60	744	295	172	1,100	143	704
65-69 years	10,331	33	1,123	31	589	214	109	832	125	450
70-74 years	5,047	11	728	17	302	146	64	496	51	281
75-79 years	2,611	5	363	9	174	63	28	252	23	151
80 years and over	3,680	2	286	3	74	29	11	103	10	67
Female	613,166	2,404	17,765	5,215	17,706	13,363	4,886	36,825	7,239	28,700
Under 5 years	18,086	202	270	258	766	1,278	364	1,168	167	861
5 -9 years	24,370	162	383	412	618	449	271	1,620	340	1,630
10-14 years	32,112	134	704	595	681	701	226	2,092	525	2,357
15-19 years	44,357	231	1,005	611	966	872	309	2,727	539	4,422
20-24 years	91,576	476	1,739	348	2,726	1,421	661	3,562	444	4,371
25-29 years	111,944	428	2,436	756	3,162	2,100	820	5,119	1,117	2,498
30-34 years	87,968	321	1,458	770	1,827	1,478	672	5,519	1,341	2,030
35-39 years	59,910	141	1,350	559	1,385	1,116	410	3,547	952	2,225
40-44 years	40,452	67	1,391	429	1,023	961	257	2,495	554	2,034
45-49 years	25,870	55	1,064	127	840	710	189	1,661	229	1,498
50-54 years	21,058	59	1,018	128	965	547	220	1,675	224	1,340

[Continued]

417

★ 520 ★

Immigration by Country of Birth, Age, and Sex (Continued)

Numbers of immigrants admitted to the United States from selected Asian countries of birth by age and sex, and percent and median age for male and female immigrants.

Age and sex	All countries	Bangladesh	China, Mainland[a]	Hong Kong	India	Korea	Pakistan	Philippines	Taiwan	Vietnam
55-59 years	17,432	55	1,264	98	958	527	183	1,716	285	1,122
60-64 years	15,109	33	1419	61	817	473	136	1,599	229	925
65-69 years	11,278	27	1,188	34	540	329	94	1,194	166	653
70-74 years	6,053	8	609	15	282	225	39	704	63	413
75-79 years	3,325	5	313	9	110	122	25	317	45	208
80 years and over	2,172	-	154	5	40	53	9	109	19	110
Percent male	66.4%	77.5%	46.2%	50.0%	60.7%	49.6%	76.0%	42.1%	45.4%	48.15
Percent female	33.6%	22.5%	53.8%	50.0%	39.3%	50.4%	24.0%	57.9%	54.5%	51.9%
Median age	28.8	28.4	38.9	27.4	31.9	31.2	31.2	31.7	31.7	23.9
Median age, male	28.6	29.3	39.6	27.1	32.7	32.6	31.8	31.5	31.9	23.9
Median age, female	29.3	25.0	38.3	27.7	29.9	29.6	28.7	31.8	31.6	26.2

Source: U.S. Immigration and Naturalization Service (INS), *Statistical Yearbook of the Immigration and Naturalization Service, 1991* (Washington, DC: U.S. Government Printing Office, 1992), table 12, p. 52. A dash (–) represents zero. *Note:* (a) The INS uses the designation "China, Mainland" for immigrants from areas under the control of the government in Beijing.

★ 521 ★

Immigration by Type of Admission, Region, and Country of Birth, 1991

Numbers of immigrants admitted to the United States by world region and selected Asian country of birth, 1991.

Region and country of birth	Immigrants			New Arrivals			Adjustments		
	Total	Subject to numerical limitations	Exempt from numerical limitations	Total	Subject to numerical limitations	Exempt from numerical limitations	Total	Subject to numerical limitations	Exempt from numerical limitations
All countries	1,827,167	293,846	1,533,321	443,107	271,513	171,594	1,384,060	22,333	1,361,724
Europe	135,234	27,553	107,681	40,082	24,1340	15,952	95,152	3,423	91,729
Asia	358,533	133,298	225,235	204,241	119,257	84,984	154,292	14,041	140,251
Afghanistan	2,879	206	2,673	459	193	266	2,420	13	2,407
Bangladesh	10,676	5,657	5,019	6,025	5,510	515	4,651	147	4,504
Burma	946	642	304	732	594	138	214	48	166
Cambodia	3,251	213	3,038	504	200	304	2,747	13	2,734
China, Mainland[a]	33,025	19,118	13,907	26,169	17,292	8,877	6,856	1,826	5,030
Hong Kong	10,427	8,668	1,759	8,575	7,907	668	1,852	761	1,091
India	45,064	20,894	24,170	23,935	17,056	6,879	21,129	3,838	17,291
Indonesia	2,223	1,657	566	1,672	1,529	143	551	128	423
Iran	19,569	4,182	15,387	5,634	3,528	2,106	13,935	654	13,281
Iraq	1,494	441	1,053	592	323	269	902	118	784
Israel	4,181	1,595	2,586	1,736	1,139	597	2,445	456	1,989
Japan	5,049	1,881	3,168	2,486	1,313	1,173	2,563	568	1,995
Jordan	4,259	1,484	2,775	2,491	1,392	1,099	1,768	92	1,676
Korea	26,518	12,880	13,638	18,351	11,894	6,457	8,167	986	7,181
Kuwait	861	306	555	330	230	100	531	76	455
Laos	9,950	179	9,771	291	156	135	9,659	23	9,636
Lebanon	6,009	2,419	3,590	3,155	2,081	1,074	2,854	338	2516

[Continued]

★ 521 ★

Immigration by Type of Admission, Region, and Country of Birth, 1991 (Continued)

Numbers of immigrants admitted to the United States by world region and selected Asian country of birth, 1991.

Region and country of birth	Immigrants			New Arrivals			Adjustments		
	Total	Subject to numerical limitations	Exempt from numerical limitations	Total	Subject to numerical limitations	Exempt from numerical limitations	Total	Subject to numerical limitations	Exempt from numerical limitations
Malaysia	1,860	853	1,007	780	618	162	1,080	235	845
Pakistan	20,355	5,830	14,525	7,301	5,551	1,750	13,054	279	12,775
Philippines	63,596	20,256	43,340	44,410	19,942	24,468	19,186	314	18,872
Saudi Arabia	552	269	283	325	249	76	227	20	207
Singapore	535	228	307	234	140	94	301	88	213
Sri Lanka	1,377	719	658	712	603	109	665	116	549
Syria	2,837	916	1,921	1,304	832	472	1,533	84	1,449
Taiwan	13,274	9,657	3,617	8,433	7,138	1,295	4,841	2,519	2,322
Thailand	7,397	1,478	5,919	2,302	1,418	884	5,095	60	5,035
Turkey	2,528	670	1,858	1,158	562	596	1,370	108	1,262
Vietnam	55,307	9,008	46,299	32,165	8,957	23,208	23,142	51	23,091
Yemen	1,547	439	1,108	1,325	414	911	222	25	197
Other Asia	987	553	434	655	496	159	332	57	275
Africa	36,179	7,718	28,461	9,959	6,626	3,333	26,220	1,092	25,128
Oceania	6,236	1,485	4,751	2,453	1,250	1,203	3,783	235	3,548
North America	1,210,981	97,194	1,113,787	148,823	94,694	54,129	1,062,158	2,500	1,059,658
Canada	13,504	5,761	7,743	7,899	4,878	3,021	5,605	883	4,722
Mexico	946,167	19,683	926,484	43,927	19,069	24,858	902,240	614	901,626
Caribbean	140,139	49,599	90,540	65,595	49,018	16,577	74,544	581	73,963
Central America	111,093	22,129	88,964	31,367	21,713	9,654	79,726	416	79,310
Other North America	78	22	56	35	16	19	43	6	37
South America	79,934	26,598	53,336	37,549	25,556	11,993	42,385	1,042	41,343

Source: U.S. Immigration and Naturalization Service (INS), *Statistical Yearbook of the Immigration and Naturalization Service, 1991* (Washington, DC: U.S. Government Printing Office, 1992), table 6, p. 40. *Note:* (a) The INS uses the designation "China, Mainland" for immigrants from areas under the control of the government in Beijing.

★ 522 ★

Immigration by Occupation, Region, and Country of Birth, 1991

Immigrants admitted to the United States by major occupational group, world region, and selected country of birth, 1991.

Region and country of birth	Total	Occupation Total	Prof. specialty and technical	Executive, admin., and managerial	Sales	Admin support	Precision production, craft, and repair	Operator, fabricator, and laborer	Farming, forestry, and fishing	Service	No occupation or not reported[a]
All countries	1,827,167	1,319,923	58,921	27,945	19,726	31,435	52,891	100,304	932,606	96,095	507,244
Europe	135,234	54,206	13,832	4,049	1,913	4,704	7,273	7,801	4,323	10,311	81,028
Asia	358,533	156,509	28,317	12,988	7,304	10,474	9,693	13,344	58,338	16,051	202,024
Afghanistan	2,879	749	105	53	86	52	65	97	18	273	2,130
Bangladesh	10,676	6,932	430	138	916	209	36	333	4,590	280	3,744
Burma	946	427	106	37	34	50	67	30	26	77	519
Cambodia	3,251	805	44	13	39	22	101	324	96	166	2,446
China, Mainland[b]	33,025	17,037	3,309	1,506	602	1,493	927	2,830	5,232	1,138	15,988
Hong Kong	10,427	4,469	1,133	1,005	223	956	418	164	128	442	5,958
India	45,064	24,431	5,188	1,758	313	992	281	210	14,678	1,011	20,633
Indonesia	2,223	1,041	293	275	74	139	39	25	77	119	1,182
Iran	19,569	7,109	1,783	1,176	623	666	794	531	463	1,073	12,460
Iraq	1,494	478	142	53	31	30	45	53	43	81	1,016
Israel	4,181	1,683	472	188	115	128	143	71	407	159	2,498
Japan	5,049	1,732	398	376	76	182	66	28	231	375	3,317
Jordan	4,259	1,461	235	131	110	89	102	188	412	194	2,798
Korea	26,518	9,444	1,414	617	288	1,008	213	651	4,661	592	17,074
Kuwait	861	255	73	26	19	24	4	10	65	34	606
Laos	9,950	1,434	57	3	8	25	150	784	111	296	8,516
Lebanon	6,009	2,579	582	323	156	177	248	150	626	317	3,430
Malaysia	1,860	961	282	167	23	108	21	28	180	152	899
Pakistan	20,355	14,454	776	640	181	254	119	149	11,669	666	5,901
Philippines	63,596	27,622	7,578	2,636	755	2,113	1,357	1,191	8,521	3,471	35,974
Saudi Arabia	552	83	18	10	7	5	3	1	31	8	469
Singapore	535	256	82	42	18	35	8	7	27	37	279
Sri Lanka	1,377	833	186	65	32	71	20	21	326	112	544
Syria	2,837	1,110	248	81	65	44	136	76	316	144	1727
Taiwan	13,274	5,628	2,011	1,233	270	984	62	83	678	307	7,646
Thailand	7,397	1,855	286	154	261	209	89	80	469	307	5,542
Turkey	2,528	1,246	220	86	32	62	114	60	476	196	1,282
Vietnam	55,307	19,385	764	131	1,928	294	4,034	4,679	3,596	3,959	35,922
Yemen	1,547	635	12	7	6	7	3	476	111	13	912
Other Asia	987	375	90	58	13	46	28	14	74	52	612
Africa	36,179	22,500	2,816	1,489	1,171	1,405	698	1,684	9,568	3,669	13,679
Oceania	6,236	3,834	562	256	132	316	250	255	1,459	604	2,402
North America	1,210,981	1,035,460	10,201	7,478	7,785	12,242	31,991	70,161	835,484	60,118	175,521
Canada	13,504	6,655	2,080	1,327	510	790	539	507	202	700	6,849
Mexico	946,167	869,097	2,283	2,896	3,933	4,552	21,749	50,628	749,027	34,029	77,070
Caribbean	140,139	82,196	3,996	1,684	1,546	3,883	4,720	6,757	49,147	10,463	57,943
Central America	111,093	77,462	1,830	1,564	1,795	3,012	4,979	12,268	37,097	14,917	33,631
Other North America	78	50	12	7	1	5	4	1	11	9	28
South America	79,934	47,351	3,193	1,682	1,420	2,292	2,986	7,056	23,383	5,339	32,583

Source: U.S. Immigration and Naturalization Service (INS), *Statistical Yearbook of the Immigration and Naturalization Service, 1991* (Washington, DC: U.S. Government Printing Office, 1992), table 20, p. 66. *Note:* (a) Includes homemakers, students, unemployed or retired persons, and others not reporting or with an unknown occupation. (b) The INS uses the designation "China, Mainland" for immigrants from areas under the control of the government in Beijing.

By Ethnic Group

★ 523 ★

Bangladeshi Immigration
by Top 10 States of Intended Residence, 1991

Number of immigrants and percent of total admitted from Bangladesh[a] by top
states of intended residence, 1991.

State	Immigrants from Bangladesh	
	Number	Percent[b]
New York	6,854	64.2%
California	1,064	10.0%
New Jersey	560	5.3%
Florida	371	3.5%
Texas	340	3.2%
Virginia	259	2.4%
Michigan	136	1.3%
Massachusetts	126	1.2%
Maryland	125	1.2%
Georgia	122	1.1%
Total, other states	723	6.8%
Total	10,680	100.0%

Source: Adapted from U.S. Immigration and Naturalization Service, *Statistical Yearbook of the Immigration and Naturalization Service, 1991* (Washington, DC: U.S. Government Printing Office, 1992), table 16, p, 58. *Note:* (a) Total 1991 Bangladeshi immigration to the United States was 10,676.

★ 524 ★

Bangladeshi Immigration
by Top Five Metropolitan Areas of Intended Residence, 1991

Number of immigrants, and percent of total admitted from Bangladesh by top
metropolitan areas of intended residence, 1991.

Metropolitan Area	Immigrants from Bangladesh	
	Number	Percent[a]
New York (NY)	6,550	61.4
Los Angeles (CA)	775	7.3
Washington (DC)	363	3.4
Bergen-Passaic (NJ)	272	2.6
Nassau-Suffolk (NY)	222	2.1

Source: Compiled from data in *Statistical Yearbook of the Immigration and Naturalization Service, 1991* (Washington DC: U.S. Government Printing Office, 1992), tables 12 and 18, pp. 53 and 62. *Note:* (a) Total 1991 Bangladeshi immigration to the United States was 10,676.

★ 525 ★

Chinese Immigration
by Top Five Metropolitan Areas of Intended Residence, 1991

Number of immigrants and percent of total admitted from China[a] by top metropolitan areas of of intended residence, 1991.

Metropolitan Area	Immigrants from China	
	Number	Percent[b]
New York (NY)	8,964	27.1%
San Francisco (CA)	4,068	12.3%
Los Angeles (CA)	3,626	11.0%
Oakland (CA)	1,667	5.1%
Boston (MA)	1,083	3.3%

Source: Compiled from data in *Statistical Yearbook of the Immigration and Naturalization Service, 1991* (Washington, DC: U.S. Government Printing Office, 1992), tables 12 and 18, pp. 53 and 62. *Note:* (a) The INS uses the designation "China, Mainland" for immigrants from areas under the control of the government in Beijing. (b) Total 1991 Chinese immigration to the United States was 33,025.

★ 526 ★

Chinese Immigration
by Top Ten States of Intended Residence, 1991

Number of immigrants and percent of total admitted from China[a] by top states of intended residence, 1991.

State	Immigrants from China	
	Number	Percent[b]
California	12,265	37.1%
New York	9,667	29.3%
Illinois	1,164	3.5%
Massachusetts	1,150	3.5%
New Jersey	1,020	3.1%
Texas	792	2.4%
Hawaii	594	1.8%
Washington	555	1.7%
Pennsylvania	542	1.6%
Maryland	499	1.5%
Total, other states	4,779	14.5%
Total	33,027	100.0%

Source: Adapted from U.S. Immigration and Naturalization Service (INS), *Statistical Yearbook of the Immigration and Naturalization Service, 1991* (Washington, DC: U.S. Government Printing Office, 1992), table 16, p. 58. *Note:* (a) The INS uses the designation "China, Mainland" for immigrants from areas under the control of the government in Beijing. (b) Total 1991 Chinese immigration to the United States was 33,025.

★ 527 ★

Filipino Immigration
by Top Five Metropolitan Areas of Intended Residence, 1991

Number of immigrants and percent of total admitted from thePhilippines[a] by top metropolitan areas of of intended residence, 1991.

Metropolitan Area	Immigrants from Philippines	
	Number	Percent of Total[a]
Los Angeles (CA)	12,147	19.1%
San Francisco (CA)	3,702	5.8%
San Diego (CA)	3,548	5.6%
New York (NY)	3,421	5.4%
Honolulu (HI)	3,022	4.8%

Source: Compiled from data in *Statistical Yearbook of the Immigration and Naturalization Service, 1991* (Washington, DC: U.S. Government Printing Office, 1992), tables 12 and 18, pp. 53 and 62.
Note: (a) Total 1991 Philippines immigration to the United States was 63,596.

★ 528 ★

Filipino Immigration
by Top Ten States of Intended Residence, 1991

Number of immigrants and percent of total admitted from the Philippines[a] by top states of intended residence, 1991.

State	Immigrants from the Philippines	
	Number	Percent[a]
California	32,698	51.4%
Hawaii	4,367	6.9%
New York	4,045	6.4%
Illinois	2,924	4.6%
New Jersey	2,885	4.5%
Texas	1,775	2.8%
Washington	1,563	2.5%6
Florida	1,501	2.4%
Virginia	1,352	2.1%
Maryland	791	1.2%
Total, other states	9,686	15.3%
Total	63,587	100.0%

Source: Adapted from U.S. Immigration and Naturalization Service, *Statistical Yearbook of the Immigration and Naturalization Service, 1991* (Washington, DC: U.S. Government Printing Office, 1992), table 16, p. 58. *Note:* (a) Total 1991 Philippines immigration to the United States was 63,596.

★ 529 ★

Hong Kong Immigration
by Top Five Metropolitan Areas of Intended Residence, 1991

Number of immigrants and percent of total admitted from Hong Kong[a] by top metropolitan areas of of intended residence, 1991.

Metropolitan Area	Immigrants from Hong Kong	
	Number	Percent[a]
New York (NY)	2,131	20.4%
San Francisco (CA)	1,352	13.0%
Los Angeles (CA)	1,302	12.5%
Oakland (CA)	710	6.8%
San Jose (CA)	390	3.7%

Source: Compiled from data in *Statistical Yearbook of the Immigration and Naturalization Service, 1991* (Washington, DC: U.S. Government Printing Office, 1992), tables 12 and 18, pp. 53 and 62. *Note:* (a) Total 1991 Hong Kong immigration to the United States was 10,427.

★ 530 ★

Hong Kong Immigration
by Top Ten States of Intended Residence, 1991

Number of immigrants and percent of total admitted from Hong Kong[a] by top states of intended residence, 1991.

State	Immigrants from Hong Kong	
	Number	Percent[a]
California	4,468	42.9%
New York	2,311	22.2%
Massachusetts	451	4.3%
Texas	307	2.9%
Illinois	293	2.8%
Washington	291	2.8%
New Jersey	291	2.8%
Hawaii	265	2.5%
Florida	217	2.1%
Pennsylvania	163	1.6%
Total, other states	1,369	13.1%
Total	10,426	100.0%

Source: Adapted from U.S. Immigration and Naturalization Service, *Statistical Yearbook of the Immigration and Naturalization Service, 1991* (Washington, DC: U.S. Government Printing Office, 1992), table 16, p. 58. *Note:* (a) Total 1991 Hong Kong immigration to the United States was 10,427.

★ 531 ★

Indian Immigration
by Top Five Metropolitan Areas of Intended Residence, 1991

Number of immigrants and percent of total admitted from India[a] by top metropolitan areas of of intended residence, 1991.

Metropolitan Area	Immigrants from India	
	Number	Percent[a]
New York (NY)	7,368	16.4%
Chicago (IL)	3,409	7.6%
Los Angeles (CA)	2,565	5.7%
San Jose (CA)	1,774	3.9%
Washington (DC)	1,653	3.7%

Source: Compiled from data in *Statistical Yearbook of the Immigration and Naturalization Service, 1991* (Washington, DC: U.S. Government Printing Office, 1992), tables 12 and 18, pp. 53 and 62.
Note: (a) Total 1991 Indian immigration to the United States was 45,064.

★ 532 ★

Indian Immigration
by Top Ten States of Intended Residence, 1991

Number of immigrants and percent of total admitted from India[a] by top states of intended residence, 1991.

State	Immigrants from India	
	Number	Percent[a]
California	10,291	22.8%
New York	9,133	20.3%
New Jersey	4,939	11.0%
Illinois	3,827	8.5%
Texas	2,601	5.8%
Pennsylvania	1,361	3.0%
Florida	1,224	2.7%
Virginia	1,194	2.7%
Georgia	1,175	2.6%
Michigan	1,064	2.6%
Total, other states	8,251	18,3%
Total	45,060	100.0%

Source: Adapted from U.S. Immigration and Naturalization Service, *Statistical Yearbook of the Immigration and Naturalization Service, 1991* (Washington, DC: U.S. Government Printing Office, 1992), table 16, p. 58. *Note:* (a) Total 1991 Indian immigration to the United States was 45,064.

★ 533 ★

Korean Immigration
by Top Five Metropolitan Areas of Intended Residence, 1991

Number of immigrants and percent of total admitted from Korea[a] by top metropolitan areas of of intended residence, 1991.

Metropolitan Area	Immigrants from Korea	
	Number	Percent[a]
New York (NY)	4,579	17.3%
Los Angeles (CA)	4,419	16.7%
Washington (DC)	1,441	5.43%
Chicago (IL)	960	3.6%
Anaheim-Santa Ana (CA)	946	3.6%

Source: Compiled from data in *Statistical Yearbook of the Immigration and Naturalization Service, 1991* (Washington, DC: U.S. Government Printing Office, 1992), tables 12 and 18, pp. 53 and 62.
Note: (a) Total 1991 Korean immigration to the United States was 26,518.

★ 534 ★

Korean Immigration
by Top Ten States of Intended Residence, 1991

Number of immigrants and percent of total admitted from Korea[a] by top states of intended residence, 1991.

State	Immigrants from Korea	
	Number	Percent[a]
California	7,301	27.5%
New York	5,209	19.6%
New Jersey	1,434	5.4%
Illinois	1,162	4.4%
Texas	1,104	4.2%
Virginia	1,093	4.1%
Maryland	1,048	4.0%
Pennsylvania	983	3.7%
Washington	811	3.1%
Georgia	550	2.1%
Total, other states	5,826	22.0%
Total	26,521	100.0%

Source: Adapted from U.S. Immigration and Naturalization Service, *Statistical Yearbook of the Immigration and Naturalization Service, 1991* (Washington, DC: U.S. Government Printing Office, 1992), table 16, p. 58. *Note:* (a) Total 1991 Korean immigration to the United States was 26,518.

★ 535 ★

Pakistani Immigration
by Top Five Metropolitan Areas of Intended Residence, 1991

Number of immigrants and percent of total admitted from Pakistan[a] by top metropolitan areas of of intended residence, 1991.

Metropolitan Area	Immigrants from Pakistan	
	Number	Percent of Total[a]
New York (NY)	6,676	32.8%
Washington (DC)	1,432	7.0%
Chicago (IL)	1,348	6.6%
Los Angeles (CA)	1,203	5.9%
Houston (TX)	1,089	5.4%

Source: Compiled from data in *Statistical Yearbook of the Immigration and Naturalization Service, 1991* (Washington, DC: U.SGovernment Printing Office, 1992), tables 12 and 18, pp. 53 and 62.
Note: (a) Total 1991 Pakistan immigration to the United States was 20,355.

★ 536 ★

Pakistani Immigration
by Top Ten States of Intended Residence, 1991

Number of immigrants and percent of total admitted from Pakistan[a] by top states of intended residence, 1991.

State	Immigrants from Pakistan	
	Number	Percent[a]
New York	7,504	36.9%
California	3,084	15.2%
Texas	1,806	8.9%
Illinois	1,464	7.2%
New Jersey	1,296	6.4%
Virginia	1,197	5.9%
Florida	855	4.20
Georgia	426	2.1%
Maryland	377	1.9%
Michigan	304	1.5%
Total, other states	2,044	10.0%
Total	20,357	100.0%

Source: Adapted from U.S. Immigration and Naturalization Service, *Statistical Yearbook of the Immigration and Naturalization Service, 1991* (Washington, DC: U.S. Government Printing Office, 1992), table 16, p. 58. *Note:* (a) Total 1991 Pakistan immigration to the United States was 20,355.

★ 537 ★

Taiwanese Immigration
by Top Five Metropolitan Areas of Intended Residence, 1991

Number of immigrants and percent of total admitted from Taiwan[a] by top metropolitan areas of of intended residence, 1991.

Metropolitan Area	Immigrants from Taiwan	
	Number	Percent of Total[a]
Los Angeles (CA)	2,748	20.7%
New York (NY)	1,200	9.0%
San Jose (CA)	848	6.4%
Anaheim-Santa Ana (CA)	745	5.6%
Oakland (CA)	432	3.3%

Source: Compiled from data in *Statistical Yearbook of the Immigration and Naturalization Service, 1991* (Washington, DC: U.S. Government Printing Office, 1992), tables 12 and 18, pp. 53 and 62. *Note:* (a) Total 1991 Taiwan immigration to the United States was 13,274.

★ 538 ★

Taiwanese Immigration
by Top Ten States of Intended Residence, 1991

Number of immigrants and percent of total admitted from Taiwan[a] by top states of intended residence, 1991.

State	Immigrants from Taiwan	
	Number	Percent[a]
California	5,840	44.0%
New York	1,581	19.9%
Texas	875	6.6%
New Jersey	863	6.5%
Illinois	368	2.8%
Virginia	293	2.2%
Maryland	272	2.1%5
Washington	266	2.0%
Massachusetts	264	2.0%
Pennsylvania	264	2.0%
Total, other states	1,327	10.0%
Total	12,213	100.0%

Source: Adapted from U.S. Immigration and Naturalization Service, *Statistical Yearbook of the Immigration and Naturalization Service, 1991* (Washington, DC: U.S. Government Printing Office, 1992), table 16, p. 58. *Note:* (a) Total 1991 Taiwan immigration to the United States was 13,274.

★ 539 ★

Vietnamese Immigration
by Top Five Metropolitan Areas of Intended Residence, 1991

Number of immigrants and percent of total admitted from Vietnam[a] by top metropolitan areas of of intended residence, 1991.

Metropolitan Area	Immigrants from Vietnam	
	Number	Percent of Total[a]
Anaheim-Santa Ana (CA)	5,366	9.7%
Los Angeles (CA)	5,156	9.3%
San Jose (CA)	4,640	8.4%
Washington (DC)	2,611	4.7%
San Diego (CA)	1,683	3.0%

Source: Compiled from data in *Statistical Yearbook of the Immigration and Naturalization Service, 1991* (Washington, DC: U.S. Government Printing Office, 1992), tables 12 and 18, pp. 53 and 62. *Note:* (a) Total 1991 Vietnam immigration to the United States was 55,307.

★ 540 ★

Vietnamese Immigration
by Top Ten States of Intended Residence, 1991

Number of immigrants and percent of total admitted from Vietnam[a] by top states of intended residence, 1991.

States	Immigrants from Vietnam	
	Number	Percent[a]
California	21,542	39.0%
Texas	5,257	9.5%
New York	2,235	4.0%
Massachuttes	1,961	3.6%
Virginia	1,896	3.4%
Washington	1,889	3.4%
Florida	1,623	2.9%
Pennsylvania	1,619	2.9%
Georgia	1,396	2.5%
Illinois	967	1.8%
Total, other states	14,916	27.0%
Total	55,301	100.0%

Source: Adapted from U.S. Immigration and Naturalization Service, *Statistical Yearbook of the Immigration and Naturalization Service, 1991* (Washington, DC: U.S. Government Printing Office, 1992), table 16, p. 58. *Note:* (a) Total 1991 Vietnam immigration to the United States was 55,307.

By State

★ 541 ★

Immigration to California by Country of Birth, 1991

Numbers of immigrants to California, total to the United States and percent to California by selected Asian country of birth, 1991.

Country	Total to California	Total to the U.S.	Percent to California
Bangladesh	1,064	10,676	10.0%
China[a]	12,265	33,025	37.1%
Hong Kong	4,468	10,427	42.9%
India	10,291	45,064	22.8%
Korea	7,301	26,518	27.5%
Pakistan	3,084	20,355	15.2%
Philippines	32,698	63,596	51.4%
Taiwan	5,840	13,274	44.0%
Vietnam	21,542	55,307	39.0%

Source: Compiled from data in *Statistical Yearbook of the Immigration and Naturalization Service, 1991* (Washington, DC: U.S. Government Printing Office, 1992), table 16, p. 58. *Note:* (a) The INS uses the designation "China, Mainland" for immigrants from areas under the control of the government in Beijing.

★ 542 ★

Immigration to Florida by Country of Birth, 1991

Numbers of immigrants to Florida, total to U.S. and percent to Florida by selected Asian country of birth, 1991.

Country	Total to Florida	Total to the U.S.	Percent to Florida
Bangladesh	371	10,676	3.5%
China[a]	495	33,025	1.5%
Hong Kong	217	10,427	2.1%
India	1,224	45,064	2.7%
Korea	424	26,518	1.6%
Pakistan	855	20,355	4.2%
Philippines	1,501	63,596	2.4%
Taiwan	191	13,274	1.4%
Vietnam	1,623	55,307	3.0%

Source: Compiled from data in *Statistical Yearbook of the Immigration and Naturalization Service, 1991* (Washington, DC: U.S. Government Printing Office, 1992), table 16, p. 58. *Note:* (a) The INS uses the designation "China, Mainland" for immigrants from areas under the control of the government in Beijing.

★ 543 ★

Immigration to Illinois by Country of Birth, 1991

Numbers of immigrants to Illinois, total to U.S. and percent to Illinois by selected Asian country of birth, 1991.

Country	Total to Illinois	Total to the U.S.	Percent to Illinois
Bangladesh	118	10,676	1.1%
China[a]	1,164	33,025	3.5%
Hong Kong	293	10,427	2.8%
India	3,827	45,064	8.5%
Korea	1,162	26,518	4.4%
Pakistan	1,464	20,355	7.2%
Philippines	2,924	63,596	4.6%
Taiwan	368	13,274	2.8%
Vietnam	967	55,307	1.8%

Source: Compiled from data in *Statistical Yearbook of the Immigration and Naturalization Service, 1991* (Washington, DC: U.S. Government Printing Office, 1992), table 16, p. 58. *Note:* (a) The INS uses the designation "China, Mainland" for immigrants from areas under the control of the government in Beijing.

★ 544 ★

Immigration to Maryland by Country of Birth, 1991

Numbers of immigrants to Maryland, total to U.S. and percent to Maryland by selected Asian country of birth, 1991.

Country	Total to Maryland	Total to the U.S.	Percent to Maryland
Bangladesh	125	10,676	1.2%
China[a]	499	33,025	1.5%
Hong Kong	124	10,427	1.2%
India	984	45,064	2.2%
Korea	1,048	26,518	4.0%
Pakistan	377	20,355	1.9%
Philippines	791	63,596	1.2%
Taiwan	272	13,274	2.1%
Vietnam	697	55,307	1.3%

Source: Compiled from data in *Statistical Yearbook of the Immigration and Naturalization Service, 1991* (Washington, DC: U.S. Government Printing Office, 1992), table 16, p. 58. *Note:* (a) The INS uses the designation "China, Mainland" for immigrants from areas under the control of the government in Beijing.

★ 545 ★

Immigration to Michigan by Country of Birth, 1991

Numbers of immigrants to Michigan, total to U.S. and percent to Michigan by selected Asian country of birth, 1991.

Country	Total to Michigan	Total to the U.S.	Percent to Michigan
Bangladesh	136	10,676	1.3%
China[a]	326	33,025	1.0%
Hong Kong	96	10,427	0.9%
India	1,064	45,064	2.4%
Korea	482	26,518	1.8%
Pakistan	304	20,355	1.5%
Philippines	659	63,596	1.0%
Taiwan	229	13,274	1.7%
Vietnam	685	55,307	1.2%

Source: Compiled from data in *Statistical Yearbook of the Immigration and Naturalization Service, 1991* (Washington, DC: U.S. Government Printing Office, 1992), table 16, p. 58. *Note:* (a) The INS uses the designation "China, Mainland" for immigrants from areas under the control of the government in Beijing.

★ 546 ★

Immigration to Massachusetts by Country of Birth, 1991

Numbers of immigrants to Massachusetts, total to U.S. and percent to Masschusetts by selected Asian country of birth, 1991.

Country	Total to Massachusetts	Total to the U.S.	Percent to Massachusetts
Bangladesh	126	10,676	1.2%
China[a]	1,150	33,025	3.5%
Hong Kong	451	10,427	4.3%
India	1,061	45,064	2.4%
Korea	232	26,518	0.9%
Pakistan	249	20,355	1.2%
Philippines	411	63,596	0.7%
Taiwan	264	13,274	2.0%
Vietnam	1,961	55,307	3.6%

Source: Compiled from data in *Statistical Yearbook of the Immigration and Naturalization Service, 1991* (Washington, DC: U.S. Government Printing Office, 1992), table 16, p. 58. *Note:* (a) The INS uses the designation "China, Mainland" for immigrants from areas under the control of the government in Beijing.

★ 547 ★

Immigration to New Jersey by Country of Birth, 1991

Numbers of immigrants to New Jersey, total to U.S. and percent to New Jersey by selected Asian country of birth, 1991.

Country	Total to New Jersey	Total to the U.S.	Percent to New Jersey
Bangladesh	560	10,676	5.3%
China[a]	1,020	33,025	3.1%
Hong Kong	291	10,427	2.8%
India	4,939	45,064	11.0%
Korea	1,434	26,518	5.4%
Pakistan	1,296	20,355	6.4%
Philippines	2,885	63,596	4.5%
Taiwan	86.3	13,274	6.5%
Vietnam	886	55,307	1.6%

Source: Compiled from data in *Statistical Yearbook of the Immigration and Naturalization Service, 1991* (Washington, DC: U.S. Government Printing Office, 1992), table 16, p. 58. *Note:* (a) The INS uses the designation "China, Mainland" for immigrants from areas under the control of the government in Beijing.

★ 548 ★

Immigration to New York by Country of Birth, 1991

Numbers of immigrants to New York, total to U.S. and percent to New York by selected Asian country of birth, 1991.

Country	Total to New York	Total to the U.S.	Percent to New York
Bangladesh	6,854	10,676	64.2%
China[a]	9,667	33,025	29.3%
Hong Kong	2,311	10,427	22.2%
India	9,133	45,064	20.3%
Korea	5,209	26,518	19.6%
Pakistan	7,504	20,355	36.9%
Philippines	4,045	63,596	6.4%
Taiwan	1,581	13,274	11.9%
Vietnam	2,235	55,307	4.0%

Source: Compiled from data in *Statistical Yearbook of the Immigration and Naturalization Service, 1991* (Washington, DC: U.S. Government Printing Office, 1992), table 16, p. 58. *Note:* (a) The INS uses the designation "China, Mainland" for immigrants from areas under the control of the government in Beijing.

★ 549 ★

Immigration to Pennsylvania by Country of Birth, 1991

Numbers of immigrants to Pennsylvania, total to U.S. and percent to Pennsylvania by selected Asian country of birth, 1991.

Country	Total to Pennsylvania	Total to the U.S.	Percent to Pennsylvania
Bangladesh	78	10,676	0.7%
China[a]	542	33,025	1.6%
Hong Kong	163	10,427	1.6%
India	1,361	45,064	3.0%
Korea	983	26,518	3.7%
Pakistan	251	20,355	1.2%
Philippines	555	63,596	0.9%
Taiwan	264	13,274	2.0%
Vietnam	1,619	55,307	2.9%

Source: Compiled from data in *Statistical Yearbook of the Immigration and Naturalization Service, 1991* (Washington, DC: U.S. Government Printing Office, 1992), table 16, p. 58. *Note:* (a) The INS uses the designation "China, Mainland" for immigrants from areas under the control of the government in Beijing.

★ 550 ★

Immigration to Texas by Country of Birth, 1991

Numbers of immigrants to Texas, total to U.S. and percent to Texas by selected Asian country of birth, 1991.

Country	Total to Texas	Total to the U.S.	Percent to Texas
Bangladesh	340	10,676	3.2%
China[a]	790	33,025	2.4%
Hong Kong	307	10,427	2.9%
India	2,601	45,064	5.8%
Korea	1,104	26,518	4.2%
Pakistan	1,806	20,355	8.9%
Philippines	1,775	63,596	2.8%
Taiwan	875	13,274	6.6%
Vietnam	5,257	55,307	9.5%

Source: Compiled from data in *Statistical Yearbook of the Immigration and Naturalization Service, 1991* (Washington, DC: U.S. Government Printing Office, 1992), table 16, p. 58. *Note:* (a) The INS uses the designation "China, Mainland" for immigrants from areas under the control of the government in Beijing.

★ 551 ★

Immigration to Washington by Country of Birth, 1991

Numbers of immigrants to Washington, total to U.S. and percent to Washington by selected Asian country of birth, 1991.

Country	Total to Washington	Total to the U.S.	Percent to Washington
Bangladesh	27	10,676	0.3%
China[a]	55	33,025	0.2%
Hong Kong	291	10,427	2.8%
India	386	45,064	0.9%
Korea	811	26,518	3.1%
Pakistan	94	20,355	0.5%
Philippines	1,563	63,596	2.5%
Taiwan	266	13,274	2.0%
Vietnam	1,889	55,307	3.4%

Source: Compiled from data in *Statistical Yearbook of the Immigration and Naturalization Service, 1991* (Washington, DC: U.S. Government Printing Office, 1992), table 16, p. 58. *Note:* (a) The INS uses the designation "China, Mainland" for immigrants from areas under the control of the government in Beijing.

By City

★ 552 ★

Immigration to Anaheim-Santa Ana by Country of Birth, 1991

Numbers to Anaheim–Santa Ana, total to California, and percent of total to California by selected Asian country of birth, 1991.

Country	Number to Santa-Ana	Total to California	Percent to Santa Ana
Bangladesh	107	1,064	10.1%
China[a]	502	12,265	4.1%
Hong Kong	183	4,468	4.1%
India	783	10,291	7.6%
Korea	946	7,301	13.0%
Pakistan	277	3,084	9.0%
Philippines	1,526	32,698	4.7%
Taiwan	745	5,840	12.8%
Vietnam	5,366	21,542	24.9%

Source: Compiled from data in *Statistical Yearbook of the Immigration and Naturalization Service, 1991* (Washington, DC: U.S. Government Printing Office, 1992), table 18, p. 62. *Note:* (a) The INS uses the designation "China, Mainland" for immigrants from areas under the control of the government in Beijing.

★ 553 ★

Immigration to Atlanta by Country of Birth, 1991

Numbers to Atlanta, total to Georgia, and percent of total to Georgia by selected Asian country of birth, 1991.

Country	Number to Atlanta	Total to Georgia	Percent to Atlanta
Bangladesh	111	122	91.0%
China[a]	175	238	73.5%
Hong Kong	54	63	85.7%
India	889	1,175	75.7%
Korea	384	550	69.8%
Pakistan	377	426	88.5%
Philippines	126	274	46.0%
Taiwan	189	235	80.4%
Vietnam	1,275	1,396	91.3%

Source: Compiled from data in *Statistical Yearbook of the Immigration and Naturalization Service, 1991* (Washington, DC: U.S. Government Printing Office, 1992), table 18, p. 62. *Note:* (a) The INS uses the designation "China, Mainland" for immigrants from areas under the control of the government in Beijing.

★ 554 ★

Immigration to Boston by Country of Birth, 1991

Numbers to Boston, total to Masachusetts, and percent of total to Massachusetts by selected Asian country of birth, 1991.

Country	Number to Boston	Total to Mas-sachusetts	Percent to Boston
Bangladesh	114	126	90.5%
China[a]	1,083	1,150	94.2%
Hong Kong	418	451	92.7%
India	839	1,061	79.1%
Korea	149	232	64.2%
Pakistan	208	249	83.5%
Philippines	306	411	74.5%
Taiwan	210	264	79.6%
Vietnam	1,458	1,961	74.4%

Source: Compiled from data in *Statistical Yearbook of the Immigration and Naturalization Service, 1991* (Washington, DC: U.S. Government Printing Office, 1992), table 18, p. 62. *Note:* (a) The INS uses the designation "China, Mainland" for immigrants from areas under the control of the government in Beijing.

★ 555 ★

Immigration to Chicago by Country of Birth, 1991

Numbers to Chicago, total to Illinois, and percent of total to Illinois by selected Asian country of birth, 1991.

Country	Number to Chicago	Total to Illinois	Percent to Chicago
Bangladesh	93	118	78.8%
China[a]	1,023	1,164	87.9%
Hong Kong	235	293	80.2%
India	3,409	3,827	89.1%
Korea	960	1,162	82.6%
Pakistan	1,348	1,464	92.1%
Philippines	2,546	2,924	87.1%
Taiwan	276	368	75.0%
Vietnam	767	967	79.3%

Source: Compiled from data in *Statistical Yearbook of the Immigration and Naturalization Service, 1991* (Washington, DC: U.S. Government Printing Office, 1992), table 18, p. 62. *Note:* (a) The INS uses the designation "China, Mainland" for immigrants from areas under the control of the government in Beijing.

★ 556 ★

Immigration to Dallas by Country of Birth, 1991

Numbers to Dallas, total to Texas, and percent of total to Texas by selected Asian country of birth, 1991.

Country	Number to Dallas	Total to Texas	Percent to Dallas
Bangladesh	116	340	34.1%
China[a]	210	792	26.5%
Hong Kong	67	307	21.8%
India	699	2,601	26.9%
Korea	431	1,104	39.0%
Pakistan	379	1,806	21.0%
Philippines	275	1,775	15.5%
Taiwan	276	875	31.5%
Vietnam	1,177	5,257	22.4%

Source: Compiled from data in *Statistical Yearbook of the Immigration and Naturalization Service, 1991* (Washington, DC: U.S. Government Printing Office, 1992), table 18, p. 62. *Note:* (a) The INS uses the designation "China, Mainland" for immigrants from areas under the control of the government in Beijing.

★ 557 ★

Immigration to Detroit by Country of Birth, 1991

Numbers to Detroit, total to Michigan, and percent of total to Michigan by selected Asian country of birth, 1991.

Country	Number to Detroit	Total to Michigan	Percent to Detroit
Bangladesh	114	136	83.8%
China[a]	173	326	53.1%
Hong Kong	66	96	69.5%
India	675	1,064	63.4%
Korea	216	482	44.8%
Pakistan	228	304	75.0%
Philippines	431	659	65.4%
Taiwan	120	229	52.4%
Vietnam	98	685	14.3%

Source: Compiled from data in *Statistical Yearbook of the Immigration and Naturalization Service, 1991* (Washington, DC: U.S. Government Printing Office, 1992), table 18, p. 62. *Note:* (a) The INS uses the designation "China, Mainland" for immigrants from areas under the control of the government in Beijing.

★ 558 ★

Immigration to Houston by Country of Birth, 1991

Numbers to Houston, total to Texas, and percent of total to Texas by selected Asian country of birth.

Country	Number to Houston	Total to Texas	Percent to Houston
Bangladesh	142	340	41.8%
China[a]	362	792	45.7%
Hong Kong	170	307	55.4%
India	1,281	2,601	49.3%
Korea	269	1,104	24.4%
Pakistan	1,089	1,806	60.3%
Philippines	673	1,775	37.9%
Taiwan	295	875	33.7%
Vietnam	2,518	5,257	47.9%

Source: Compiled from data in *Statistical Yearbook of the Immigration and Naturalization Service, 1991* (Washington, DC: U.S. Government Printing Office, 1992), table 18, p. 62. *Note:* (a) The INS uses the designation "China, Mainland" for immigrants from areas under the control of the government in Beijing.

★ 559 ★

Immigration to Los Angeles by Country of Birth, 1991

Numbers to Los Angeles, total to California, and percent of total to California by selected Asian country of birth, 1991.

Country	Number to Los Angeles	Total to California	Percent to Los Angeles
Bangladesh	775	1,064	72.8%
China[a]	3,626	12,265	29.6%
Hong Kong	1,302	4,468	29.1%
India	2,565	10,291	24.9%
Korea	4,419	7,301	60.5%
Pakistan	1,203	3,084	39.0%
Philippines	12,147	32,698	37.2%
Taiwan	2,748	5,840	47.1%
Vietnam	5,156	21,542	23.9%

Source: Compiled from data in *Statistical Yearbook of the Immigration and Naturalization Service, 1991* (Washington, DC: U.S. Government Printing Office, 1992), table 18, p. 62. *Note:* (a) The INS uses the designation "China, Mainland" for immigrants from areas under the control of the government in Beijing.

★ 560 ★

Immigration to Miami by Country of Birth, 1991

Numbers to Miami, total to Florida, and percent of total to Florida by selected Asian country of birth, 1991.

Country	Number to Miami	Total to Florida	Percent to Miami
Bangladesh	54	371	14.6%
China[a]	152	495	30.7%
Hong Kong	79	217	36.4%
India	243	1,224	19.9%
Korea	97	424	22.9%
Pakistan	432	855	50.5%
Philippines	267	1,501	17.8%
Taiwan	43	191	22.5%
Vietnam	73	1,623	4.5%

Source: Compiled from data in *Statistical Yearbook of the Immigration and Naturalization Service, 1991* (Washington, DC: U.S. Government Printing Office, 1992), table 18, p. 62. *Note:* (a) The INS uses the designation "China, Mainland" for immigrants from areas under the control of the government in Beijing.

★ 561 ★

Immigration to New York City by Country of Birth, 1991

Numbers to New York City, total to New York state, and percent of total to New York state by selected Asian country of birth, 1991.

Country	Number to New York City	Total to New York state	Percent to New York City
Bangladesh	6,550	6,854	95.6%
China[a]	8,964	9,667	92.7%
Hong Kong	2,131	2,311	92.2%
India	7,368	9,133	80.7%
Korea	4,579	5,209	87.9%
Pakistan	6,676	7,504	89.0%
Philippines	3,421	4,045	84.6%
Taiwan	1,200	1,581	75.9%
Vietnam	786	2,235	35.2%

Source: Compiled from data in *Statistical Yearbook of the Immigration and Naturalization Service, 1991* (Washington, DC: U.S. Government Printing Office, 1992), table 18, p. 62. *Note:* (a) The INS uses the designation "China, Mainland" for immigrants from areas under the control of the government in Beijing.

★ 562 ★

Immigration to San Francisco by Country of Birth, 1991

Numbers to San Francisco, total to California, and percent of total to California by selected Asian country of birth, 1991.

Country	Number to San Francisco	Total to California	Percent to San Francisco
Bangladesh	21	1,064	2.0%
China[a]	4,068	12,265	33.2%
Hong Kong	1,352	4,468	30.3%
India	431	10,291	4.2%
Korea	204	7,301	2.8%
Pakistan	157	3,084	5.1%
Philippines	3,702	32,698	11.3%
Taiwan	351	5,840	6.0%
Vietnam	1,096	21,542	5.1%

Source: Compiled from data in *Statistical Yearbook of the Immigration and Naturalization Service, 1991* (Washington, DC: U.S. Government Printing Office, 1992), table 18, p. 62. *Note:* (a) The INS uses the designation "China, Mainland" for immigrants from areas under the control of the government in Beijing.

★ 563 ★

Immigration to Seattle by Country of Birth, 1991

Numbers to Seattle, total to Washington, and percent of total to Washington by selected Asian country of birth, 1991.

Country	Number to Seattle	Total to Washington	Percent to Seattle
Bangladesh	15	27	55.6%
China[a]	452	555	81.4%
Hong Kong	253	291	86.9%
India	281	386	72.8%
Korea	452	811	55.7%
Pakistan	79	94	84.0%
Philippines	978	1,563	62.6%
Taiwan	196	266	73.7%
Vietnam	1,255	1,889	66.4%

Source: Compiled from data in *Statistical Yearbook of the Immigration and Naturalization Service, 1991* (Washington, DC: U.S. Government Printing Office, 1992), table 18, p. 62. *Note:* (a) The INS uses the designation "China, Mainland" for immigrants from areas under the control of the government in Beijing.

Refugees: United States

★ 564 ★

Refugee Source Countries, 1991

Top ten source countries for refugees admitted to the United States in 1991.

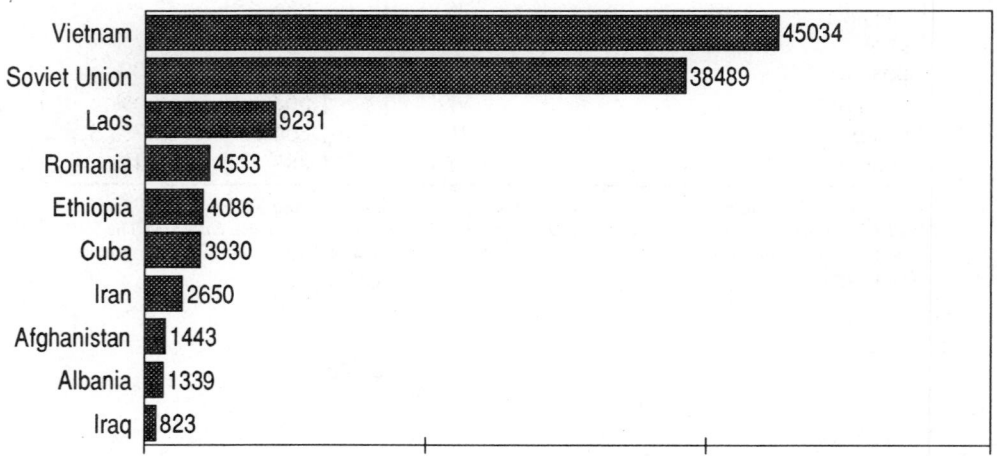

Vietnam	45034
Soviet Union	38489
Laos	9231
Romania	4533
Ethiopia	4086
Cuba	3930
Iran	2650
Afghanistan	1443
Albania	1339
Iraq	823

Source: Administration for Children and Families, Office of Refugee Resettlement, *Refugee Resettlement Program, Report to the Congress* (Washington, DC: U.S. Department of Health and Human Services, January 31, 1992), figure 1, p. 5.

★ 565 ★

Refugee Status Granted by Country of Origin, 1980-1991

Numbers of applications for refugee status approved[a] by the United States Immigration and Naturalization Service (INS) by country, for 1980 to 1988, 1989, 1990, and 1991.

Country	1980-1988	1989	1990	1991	Total
Afghanistan	23,840	1,770	1,593	1,477	8,680
Albania	421	47	98	1,319	1,885
Angola	501	19	60	23	603
Benin	0	0	4	0	4
Bulgaria	1,140	110	327	562	2,134
Cambodia	116,191	2,114	260	102	118,667
Cameroon	0	0	3	0	3
China[b]	1,156	2	6	5	1,169
Cuba	8,597	2,517	1,318	2,168	14,600
Czechoslovakia	8,896	925	341	158	10,320
Egypt	120	0	0	0	120
El Salvador	107	8	15	6	136
Ethiopia	19,663	1,697	3,061	3,978	28,399
Ghana	0	0	7	0	7

[Continued]

★ 565 ★

Refugee Status Granted by Country of Origin, 1980-1991 (Continued)

Numbers of applications for refugee status approved[a] by the United States Immigration and Naturalization Service (INS) by country, for 1980 to 1988, 1989, 1990, and 1991.

Country	1980-1988	1989	1990	1991	Total
Greece	421	0	0	0	421
Hong Kong	1,777	102	208	30	2,117
Hungary	4,916	1,075	274	7	6,272
Iran	24,015	5,132	3,312	2,577	35,036
Iraq	6,654	111	47	728	7,540
Laos	120,544	10,780	9,060	8,425	148,809
Lebanon	448	1	0	0	449
Lesotho	28	2	2	5	37
Liberia	0	.0	4	1	5
Libya	17	1	0	344	362
Macau	81	0	1	0	82
Malawi	49	6	0	0	55
Mozambique	91	4	3	12	110
Namibia	89	0	0	0	89
Nicaragua	200	323	527	89	1,139
Peru	0	0	3	0	3
Philippines	96	0	0	0	96
Poland	32,735	3,585	1,483	312	38,115
Romania	29,087	3,173	3,561	2,779	38,600
Somalia	9	14	33	163	219
South Africa	188	21	34	19	262
Sudan	32	1	7	24	64
Syria	745	1	0	1	747
Tanzania	1	0	0	0	1
Turkey	721	0	0	0	721
Uganda	69	40	27	125	261
USSR	48,191	39,704	52,866	57,445	198,206
Vietnam	258,922	22,198	21,078	24,985	327,183
Yugoslavia	74	1	6	0	81
Zaire	127	18	70	75	290
All Others	341	0	0	15	356
Totals	711,303	95,505	99,697	107,962	1,014,467

Source: Administration for Children and Families, Office of Refugee Resettlement, *Refugee Resettlement Program, Report to the Congress* (Washington, DC: U.S. Department of Health and Human Services, January 31, 1992), pp. 12 and A-10. *Notes:* (a) Refugee status application approvals under P.L. 96-212, section 207, effective April 1, 1980. Numbers approved during a year differ slightly from the numbers actually entering during that year. "Refugee" is an individual who seeks admission to the United States because of persecution in his country of nationality (or a well-founded fear of persecution) on account of race, religion, nationality, membership in a particular social group, or political opinion. (b) The INS uses the designation "China, Mainland" for immigrants from areas under the control of the government in Beijing.

★ 566 ★

Asylum Granted by Country of Origin, 1980-1992

Applications for asylum[a] granted by the United States Immigration and Naturalization Service (INS) by nationality during 1980 to 1988, 1989, 1990, and 1991.

Nationality	1980-1988	1989	1990	1991	Total
Afghanistan	1,293	19	19	28	1,359
Albania	2	0	1	0	3
Angola	8	2	1	1	12
Argentina	30	0	0	0	30
Australia	1	0	0	0	1
Bahrain	0	1	1	0	2
Bangladesh	3	2	1	1	7
Benin	1	0	0	0	1
Bolivia	0	1	0	0	1
Bulgaria	62	14	20	11	107
Burkina Faso	0	1	0	0	1
Burma	2	10	10	6	28
Cambodia	20	4	7	2	33
Cape Verde	1	1	0	0	2
Chad	0	0	1	0	1
Chile	35	9	1	0	45
China[b]	194	98	505	200	997
Colombia	6	10	15	2	33
Costa Rica	6	0	0	0	6
Cuba	285	77	158	75	595
Czechoslovakia	185	47	17	2	251
Egypt	47	3	3	1	54
El Salvador	839	337	226	135	1,537
Ethiopia	2,062	456	349	277	3,144
Fiji	0	0	1	0	1
Germany (East)	25	4	3	0	32
Ghana	75	6	4	5	90
Greece	0	1	0	0	1
Guatemala	44	67	58	34	203
Guinea	2	0	1	0	3
Guyana	9	0	0	0	9
Haiti	62	3	2	1	68
Honduras	19	14	5	4	42
Hungary	287	31	11	2	331
India	4	3	0	7	14
Iran	18,588	602	218	132	19,540
Iraq	233	12	13	12	270
Israel	2	0	3	3	8
Italy	3	0	0	0	3
Jordan	4	1	3	3	11
Kenya	3	1	1	0	5
Kuwait	0	1	0	27	28
Laos	21	7	29	24	81
Lebanon	139	58	67	41	305
Lesotho	0	0	1	0	1
Liberia	22	14	8	13	57

[Continued]

★ 566 ★

Asylum Granted by Country of Origin, 1980-1992 (Continued)

Applications for asylum[a] granted by the United States Immigration and Naturalization Service (INS) by nationalityduring 1980 to 1988, 1989, 1990, and 1991.

Nationality	1980-1988	1989	1990	1991	Total
Libya	339	35	13	5	392
Malawi	8	1	0	0	9
Mauritania	0	0	2	2	4
Mexico	7	0	0	0	7
Morocco	1	0	3	0	4
Mozambique	0	0	1	0	1
Namibia	4	0	0	0	4
Nicaragua	8,076	3,617	1,444	368	13,505
Nigeria	2	2	1	0	5
Pakistan	73	14	8	4	99
Panama	36	183	128	1	338
Peru	4	17	17	0	38
Philippines	119	5	3	1	128
Poland	3,588	285	39	3	3,915
Romania	1,084	575	180	26	1,865
Saudi Arabia	1	0	0	0	1
Seychelles	9	0	0	0	9
Singapore	1	1	1	0	3
Somalia	141	119	199	85	544
South Africa	92	14	8	8	122
Sri Lanka	2	1	6	3	12
Sudan	1	0	8	0	9
Surinam	1	0	19	8	28
Syria	225	21	52	8	306
Taiwan	4	0	2	0	6
Togo	0	0	1	0	1
Turkey	9	0	0	1	10
USSR	255	109	246	79	689
Uganda	155	7	2	4	168
United Arab Emirates	0	0	1	0	1
United Kingdom	1	0	0	0	1
Venezuela	1	1	0	0	2
Vietnam	114	7	9	3	133
Yemen (Aden)	114	7	9	3	133
Yemen (Sanaa)	9	1	0	0	10
Yugoslavia	69	4	9	0	82
Zaire	11	5	5	6	27
Zambia	1	0	0	0	1
Zimbabwe	5	0	2	0	7
Stateless	6	1	1	1	9
All Others	326	0	0	31	357
Total Cases	39,997	6,942	4,173	1,696	52,208

Source: Administration for Children and Families, Office of Refugee Resettlement, *Refugee Resettlement Program, Report to the Congress* (Washington, DC: U.S. Department of Health and Human Services, January 31, 1992), p. A-16. Primary source: U.S. Immigration and Naturalization Service (INS), unpublished tabulations. *Notes:* (a) Asylum application approvals under Pub. L. No. 96-212, section 208. Asylum requests come from individuals who meet the criteria of refugee and who are requesting approval to remain in the United States. (b) The INS uses the designation "China, Mainland" for immigrants from areas under the control of the government in Beijing.

★ 567 ★

Planned Secondary Resettlement (PSR) Program Summary

Outcomes for refugee families who have been assisted with resettlement to communities where they are more likely to achieve self-sufficiency in the United States, since 1983.

Number of PSR participants:	422 families (1,700 individuals) have relocated.
Employment:	All families found full-time employment. Almost 90% work in production jobs in factories.
Wages:	Men earn an average of $6.90 per hour; women, $5.81.
Family Income:	Average monthly income for all participants is $1,952. Monthly income ranged from $1,830 for 1991 participants to $2,300 for participants with several years of experience.
Welfare Dependency:	Welfare dependency decreased from 100% prior to relocation to zero after relocation, with the exception of elderly refugees on Supplemental Security Income (SSI).
Home Ownership	103 PSR families have become homeowners.
Secondary Migration	Approximately 95% of PSR participants have remained in their new communities.
Cost and Benefits:	Average cost per family of resettlement through PSR is $8,000. Average welfare cost savings per family are estimated to be $987 per month. PSR families repay resettlement cost to government in approximately eight months.

Source: Administration for Children and Families, Office of Refugee Resettlement, *Refugee Resettlement Program, Report to the Congress* (Washington, DC: U. S. Department of Health and Human Services, January 31, 1992), pp. 34-35. The Planned Secondary Resettlement (PSR) program provides an opportunity for unemployed refugees and their families to relocate from areas of high welfare dependency to communities offering favorable employment prospects. Eligibility is limited to refugees who have experienced continuing unemployment.

★ 568 ★

Cash Assistance by Refugee Nationality, 1991

Numbers of refugees receiving cash assistance[a] during the first twelve months after arrival in the United States by state, 1991.

States	Cambodia	Laos	Vietnam	USSR	Poland	Cuba	Afghan-istan	Iran	Ethiopia	Total
Alabama	0	6	179	0	0	0	0	1	0	186
Arizona	0	7	242	69	0	1	47	1	28	442
Arkansas	0	0	35	1	0	0	0	0	0	36
California	284	1,717	7,790	1,338	5	41	351	583	136	12,942
Colorado	7	23	261	107	0	0	30	0	35	474
Connecticut[b]	0	0	208	91	4	0	7	2	6	349
Delaware	0	0	7	15	0	0	0	0	0	23
District of Columbia	6	21	157	1	0	0	3	0	34	233
Florida[b]	0	0	810	0	0	837	0	0	0	2,043
Georgia	0	26	396	26	0	0	19	7	46	531
Hawaii	0	32	160	0	0	0	0	0	0	192
Idaho	0	0	21	51	0	7	3	0	0	97
Illinois	11	49	666	430	4	16	10	25	60	1,652
Indiana	0	0	37	6	0	0	5	0	0	53
Iowa	0	33	157	5	0	0	0	0	2	229
Kansas	2	48	274	15	0	0	7	0	24	384
Kentucky	2	1	73	62	0	3	0	0	0	144
Louisiana	2	57	341	7	0	0	0	0	3	418
Maine	4	0	74	45	0	0	10	0	14	171
Maryland	1	10	618	21	0	0	7	6	56	758

[Continued]

★ 568 ★

Cash Assistance by Refugee Nationality, 1991 (Continued)

Numbers of refugees receiving cash assistance[a] during the first twelve months after arrival in the United States by state, 1991.

States	Cambodia	Laos	Vietnam	USSR	Poland	Cuba	Afghan-istan	Iran	Ethiopia	Total
Massachusetts	3	43	1,294	360	0	15	0	7	44	1,972
Michigan	0	79	300	84	10	0	0	5	4	651
Minnesota	23	308	288	97	2	0	4	0	30	785
Mississippi	0	0	76	0	0	0	0	0	0	76
Missouri[b]	0	0	280	116	0	2	0	0	34	432
Montana	0	9	4	42	0	0	0	0	0	110
Nebraska	0	16	387	0	0	0	0	0	0	488
Nevada	0	0	35	0	0	27	1	9	13	102
New Hampshire	0	7	28	0	0	0	0	0	0	90
New Jersey	0	0	275	94	6	48	1	1	7	473
New Mexico[b]	0	0	206	4	0	40	3	0	0	262
New York	18	16	653	8,798	305	2	111	154	16	10,141
North Carolina	0	17	194	26	0	5	0	0	2	262
North Dakota	0	0	51	4	0	0	0	1	0	62
Ohio	2	17	86	71	0	7	0	0	0	227
Oklahoma[b]	0	0	287	16	0	0	0	3	0	307
Oregon	0	50	444	627	2	0	3	0	28	1,314
Pennsylvania	27	47	549	464	3	0	3	0	36	1,218
Rhode Island	41	84	27	97	0	0	0	0	0	260
South Carolina	0	7	10	0	0	0	0	0	0	17
South Dakota	0	1	10	64	0	0	8	0	19	133
Tennessee	0	44	156	11	0	0	7	1	3	247
Texas[b]	0	0	1,794	20	0	20	9	3	21	1,954
Utah	0	0	121	80	0	0	0	0	0	209
Vermont	0	0	96	0	14	10	0	0	0	120
Virginia	7	11	223	6	3	0	45	8	84	404
Washington	27	115	1,319	453	6	6	3	7	92	2,139
West Virginia	0	0	21	0	0	0	0	0	0	21
Wisconsin	0	230	18	0	0	0	0	0	0	304
Wyoming	0	0	0	0	0	0	0	0	0	0
Total[c]	467	3,131	21,738	13,824	364	1,087	697	824	877	46,137
Percent	1.01%	6.79%	47.12%	29.96%	0.79%	2.36%	1.51%	1.79%	1.90%	100.0%

Source: Administration for Children and Families, Office of Refugee Resettlement(ORR), *Refugee Resettlement Program, Report to the Congress* (Washington, DC: U.S. Department of Health and Human Services, January 31, 1992), p. A-18. *Notes:* (a) Includes refugee cash assistance (RCA) for the first twelve months after arrival and aid to families with dependent children (AFDC) and state payments for Supplemental Security Income (SSI) for the first four months after arrival. Some states did not report AFDC and SSI payments on the ORR-10 data collection form because no reimbursement could be made from ORR funds. (b) State reported Southeast Asians as one category; ORR recorded them as Vietnamese. (c) Total includes other European, Iraq, and Other categories.

★ 569 ★

Southeast Asian Refugee and Amerasian Arrivals by Month, 1991

Numbers of refugees[a] and Amerasians[b] arriving in the United States by month from October 1990 through November 1991.

Month	Number of Arrivals			
	Southeast Asian Refugees	Amerasian Immigrants	All Other Refugees[a]	Total
October	2,134	461	2,749	5,344
November	3,569	1,573	4,952	10,094
December	4,523	1,711	5,999	12,233
January	1,696	584	3,486	5,766
February	1,775	1,737	3,864	7,376
March	3,087	1,022	4,592	8,701
April	3,623	1,766	3,764	9,153
May	2,576	1,947	4,580	9,103
June	4,466	892	5,579	10,937
July	3,547	843	4,511	8,901
August	2,036	1,361	6,336	9,733
September	4,926	2,596	8,936	16,458
TOTAL	37,958	16,493	59,348	113,799

Source: Administration for Children and Families, Office of Refugee Resettlement, *Refugee Resettlement Program, Report to the Congress* (Washington, DC: U.S. Department of Health and Human Services, January 31, 1992), p. A-1. The fiscal year is October 1, 1990 to September 30, 1991. *Notes:* (a) This column includes refugees resettled under the Private Sector initiative. (b) In the context of refugee resettlement, Amerasians are children born in Vietnam to Vietnamese mothers and American fathers and are admitted to the United States under the Amerasian Homecoming Act of 1988 (Pub. L. No. 100-202) as immigrants, but are entitled to the same social services and assistance benefits as refugees.

★ 570 ★

Refugee Resettlement Program Grants

Agencies receiving grants in fiscal year 1991 (October 1, 1990 to September 30, 1991) to provide Planned Secondary Resettlement (PSR) services to relocate 716 refugees.

Grantee	Populations Served	Amount
Montana Association for Refugee Services, Billings, Montana	Hmong	$207,582
Asian Community Services, Decatur, Georgia	Hmong, Lao	$181,000
Inter-Religious Council, Syracuse, New York	Hmong	$150,000
Khmer Association, Aurora, Colorado	Cambodian	$175,857
Hmong American Planning and Development Center, Grand Prairie, Texas	Hmong, Lao	$240,000
Lutheran Family Services of North Carolina, Greensboro	Lao, Cambodian	$210,000
Southeast Asian Mutual Assistance Association, Garden City, Kansas	Lao	$165,000
Total		$1,329,439
1990 Grantees[a]		
State of Hawaii	Lao	
Catholic Social Services of Charlotte, North Carolina	Lao	
Lutheran Family Service of Columbia, South Carolina	Lao	

Source: Administration for Children and Families, Office of Refugee Resettlement, *Refugee Resettlement Program, Report to the Congress* (Washington, DC: U.S. Department of Health and Human Services, January 31, 1992), p. 34. The Planned Secondary Resettlement (PSR) program provides an opportunity for unemployed refugees and their families to relocate from areas of high welfare dependency to communities offering favorable employment prospects. Eligibility is limited to refugees who have experienced continuing unemployment. *Note:* (a) These agencies continued to implement PSR project through FY 1991 with FY 1990 funding.

Southeast Asian Refugees: United States

★ 571 ★

Refugee Legislation and Arrivals, 1975-1990

Number of Southeast Asian refugees resettled from 1975 through September 30, 1991 under various acts of legislation in the United States.

Resettled under Special Parole Program (1975)	129,792	
Resettled under Humanitarian Parole Program (1975)	602	
Resettled under Special Lao Program (1976)	3,466	
Resettled under Expanded Parole Program (1976)	11,000	
Resettled under Boat Cases Program as of August 1, 1977	1,883	
Resettled under Indochinese Parole Programs:		
	August 1, 1977-September 30, 1977	680
	October 1, 1977-September 30, 1978	20,397
	October 1, 1978-September 30, 1 979	80,678
	October 1, 1979-September 30, 1 980	166,727
Resettled under Refugee Act of 1980:		
	October 1, 1980-September 30, 1981	132,454
	October 1, 1981-Septemebr 30, 1982	72,155
	October 1, 1982-September 30, 1983	39,167
	October 1, 1983-September 30, 1984	52,000
	October 1, 1984-September 30, 1985	49,853
	October 1, 1985-September 30, 1986	45,391
	October 1, 1986-September 30, 1987	40,164
	October 1, 1987-September 30, 1988	35,083
	October 1, 1988-September 30, 1989	37,066
	October 1, 1989-September 30, 1990	38,758
	October 1, 1990-September 30, 1991	37,958
Total, Southeast Asian Refugees	995,274	
Resettled under the Amerasian Homecoming Act of 1988:		
	October 1, 1987-September 30, 1988	364
	October 1, 1988-September 30, 1989	8,721
	October 1, 1989-September 30, 1990	13,307
	October 1, 1990-September 30, 1991	16,493
Total, Amerasians (includes accompanying family members)	38,885	
Total, Southeast Asian Refugees and Amerasians	1,034,159	

Source: Administration for Children and Families, Office of Refugee Resettlement, *Refugee Resettlement Program, Report to the Congress* (Washington, DC: U.S. Department of Health and Human Services, January 31, 1992), p. A-15. Prior to the passage of the Refugee Act of 1980, most Southeast Asian refugees entered the United States as "parolees" (refugees) under a series of parole authorizations granted by the Attorney General under the Immigration and Nationality Act. These parole authorizations are usually identified by the terms used in this table.

★ 572 ★

Southeast Asian Refugee Arrivals by Nationality, 1975-1991

Numbers of Southeast Asian refugees[a] by nationality and year of arrival in the United States, fiscal years 1975 to 1991.

Fiscal year	Country of nationality			
	Cambodia	Laos	Vietnam[c]	Total
1975	4,600	800	125,000	130,394
1976[b]	1,100	10,200	3,200	14,466
1977	300	400	1,900	2,563
1978	1,300	8,000	11,100	20,397
1979	6,000	30,200	44,500	80,678
1980	16,000	55,500	95,200	166,727
1981	27,100	19,300	86,10	132,454
1982	20,100	9,400	42,600	72,155
1983	13,191	2,946	23,030	39,167
1984	19,849	7,224	24,927	52,000
1985	19,237	5,233	25,383	49,853
1986	10,054	12,894	22,443	45,391
1987	1,949	15,604	22,611	40,164
1988	2,900	14,589	17,958	35,447
1989	2,220	12,762	30,805	45,787
1990	2,325	8,712	41,021	52,065
1991	186	9,231	45,034	54,451

Source: U.S. Commission on Civil Rights, *Recent Activities against Citizens and Residents of Asian Descent, 1988,* Clearinghouse Publication No. 88 (Washington, DC: U.S. Government Printing Office, 1987), table 4, p. 22. Telephone interview with Linda Gordon, chief statistician, Office of Refugee Resettlement, U.S. Department of Health and Human Services, January 26, 1993. Primary source: Linda Gordon, telephone interview, February 19, 1992.
Notes: (a) Figures for fiscal years 1975-1991 are estimates from Linda Gordon. Yearly totals correspond to official records maintained by the Department of Health and Human Services. Totals for nationality groups do not add to overall totals due to rounding. (b) Includes transition quarter. (c) Beginning with 1988, figures for Vietnam include Amerasians and their family members admitted on immigrant visas but eligible for refugee program services.

★ 573 ★

Southeast Asian Refugee and Amerasians
by State of Initial Resettlement, 1991

Numbers of Southeast Asian refugees and Amerasians[a] by state of initial settlement following entry to the United States, 1991.

State	Country of Citizenship				
	Cambodia	Laos	Vietnam	Amer-asians[a]	Total
Alabama	0	8	64	208	280
Alaska	0	0-	4	1	5
Arizona	3	25	607	375	1,010
Arkansas	0	23	74	42	139
California	57	5,217	11,723	3,563	20,560
Colorado	7	137	318	186	648
Connecticut	8	36	249	187	480
Delaware	0	0	9	0	9
District of Columbia	2	43	330	647	1,022
Florida	7	43	702	585	1,337
Georgia	2	84	805	842	1,733
Hawaii	0	13	171	113	297
Idaho	0	3	10	27	40
Illinois	0	132	410	383	925
Indiana	1	0	104	55	160
Iowa	0	175	243	315	733
Kansas	3	66	296	161	526
Kentucky	0	17	261	275	553
Louisiana	0	96	402	263	761
Maine	0	0	19	86	105
Maryland	1	19	365	133	518
Massachusetts	12	95	918	352	1,377
Michigan	1	105	393	282	781
Minnesota	4	901	341	125	1,371
Mississippi	0	0	80	19	99
Missouri	0	30	350	376	756
Montana	0	15	3	0	18
Nebraska	1	18	437	316	772
Nevada	0	0	81	32	113
New Hampshire	0	3	69	11	83
New Jersey	0	5	458	315	778
New Mexica	0	0	153	126	279
New York	2	72	786	1,147	2,007
North Carolina	0	50	321	279	650
North Dakota	0	0	30	141	171
Ohio	15	109	234	84	442
Oklahoma	0	17	314	156	487
Oregon	5	77	362	307	751
Pennsylvania	20	86	582	460	1,148
Rhode Island	0	100	18	13	131
South Carolina	0	7	49	16	72
South Dakota	0	0	24	40	64
Tennessee	6	109	314	300	729

[Continued]

★ 573 ★

Southeast Asian Refugee and Amerasians
by State of Initial Resettlement, 1991 (Continued)

Numbers of Southeast Asian refugees and Amerasians[a] by state of initial settlement following entry to the United States, 1991.

State	Country of Citizenship				
	Cambodia	Laos	Vietnam	Amerasians[a]	Total
Texas	2	185	2,655	1,577	4,419
Utah	15	13	187	182	397
Vermont	0	0	9	112	121
Virginia	7	34	988	350	1,379
Washington	4	245	1,138	863	2,250
West Verginia	0	0	1	38	39
Wisconsin	0	818	74	9	902
Wyoming	0	0	0	0	0
Guam	0	0	4	12	16
Other	0	0	2	6	8

Source: Administration for Children and Families, Office of Refugee Resettlement, *Refugee Resettlement Program, Report to the Congress* (Washington, DC: U.S. Department of Health and Human Services, January 31, 1992), p. A-5. *Notes:* (a) In the context of refugee resettlement, Amerasians are children born in Vietnam to Vietnamese mothers and American fathers and are admitted to the U.S. under the Amerasian Homecoming Act of 1988 (Pub. L. No. 100-202) as immigrants, but are entitled to the same social services and assistance benefits as refugees. This tabulation includes infants born in the Refugee Processing Center in the Philippines who have been granted Amerasian status retroactively by legislation signed November 5, 1990.

★ 574 ★

Southeast Asian Refugees
by State, 1975-1992

Cumulative numbers of Southeast Asian refugees (estimated)[a] who entered the United States between May 1975 and June 1992.

State of Residence	Southeast Asians, Total (est.)
Alabama	3,600
Alaska	100
Arizona	8,900
Arkansas	3,500
California	405,600
Colorado	13,700
Connecticut	9,000
Delaware	400
District of Columbia	2,500
Florida	17,600
Georgia	14,200
Hawaii	8,500
Idaho	1,900
Illinois	30,900

[Continued]

453

★ 574 ★

Southeast Asian Refugees
by State, 1975-1992 (Continued)

Cumulative numbers of Southeast Asian refugees (estimated)[a] who entered the United States between May 1975 and June 1992.

State of Residence	Southeast Asians, Total (est.)
Indiana	4,600
Iowa	11,200
Kansas	11,800
Kentucky	3,800
Louisiana	16,600
Maine	1,800
Maryland	12,000
Massachusetts	32,000
Michigan	14,000
Minnesota	37,400
Mississippi	2,000
Missouri	9,300
Montana	1,100
Nebraska	3,600
Nevada	2,700
New Hampshire	1,200
New Jersey	9,500
New Mexico	2,600
New York	35,800
North Carolina	7,900
North Dakota	1,100
Ohio	13,500
Oklahoma	10,100
Oregon	22,100
Pennsylvania	31,500
Rhode Island	7,900
South Carolina	2,700
South Dakota	1,100
Tennessee	7,500
Texas	76,200
Utah	9,900
Vermont	700
Virginia	25,900
Washington	47,400
West Virginia	400
Wisconsin	18,200
Wyoming	200
Guam	300
Other Territories	(b)
Total	1,018,000

Source: Office of Refugee Resettlement, *Monthly Data Report* (Washington, DC: Department of Health and Human Services, June 1992, and prepared October 30, 1992). *Notes:* (a) Adjusted for secondary migration through September 30, 1991, rounded to the nearest hundred. Not adjusted for deaths in the United States or emigration. These figures do not include Amerasian immigrants. The secondary migration adjustment is limited to refugees who received cash and/or noncash assistance from the state. (b) Fewer than 100.

★ 575 ★

Southeast Asian Refugees, Top 20 States

Estimated geographic location of Southeast Asian refugees by state in numbers and percent of total who arrived between May 1986 and April 1991, as of September 30, 1991.

State	Number	Percent
California	396,200	39.8
Texas	75,000	7.5
Washington	48,600	4.9
Minnesota	36,000	3.6
New York	34,800	35
Massachusetts	31,200	3.1
Pennsylvania	30,900	3.1
Illinois	30,700	3.1
Virginia	25,100	2.5
Oregon	21,600	2.2
Wisconsin	17,100	1.7
Florida	16,800	1.7
Louisiana	16,400	1.6
Colorado	13,400	13
Michigan	13,400	1.3
Georgia	13,400	13
Ohio	13,300	13
Maryland	11,800	1.2
Kansas	11,600	1.2
Iowa	11,200	1.1
Total	868,500	87.3
Other	126,800	12.7
Total	995,300	100.0

Source: Administration for Children and Families, Office of Refugee Resettlement, *Refugee Resettlement Program, Report to the Congress* (Washington, DC: U.S. Department of Health and Human Services, January 31, 1992), p. A-11.

★ 576 ★

Refugee Secondary Migration by State

Secondary migration[a] by refugees from all countries by state, as of June 30, 1991. In 1991, Southeast Asian refugees accounted for 48 percent of the total.

State	Non-movers	Out-migrants	In-migrants	Net migration
Alabama[b]	0	57	33	(24)
Alaska[c]	0	31	0	(31)
Arizona[b]	3,323	346	116	(230)
Arkansas[b]	212	36	94	58
California	12,839	1,031	1,410	379
Colorado[b]	854	161	135	(26)
Conecticut	323	71	25	(46)
Delaware	17	3	6	3
Dist. of Columbia	228	347	5	(342)
Florida	1,681	431	103	(328)
Georgia[b]	1,099	163	144	(19)
Hawaii	186	53	19	(34)
Idaho	119	90	7	(83)
Illinois	4,275	266	357	91
Indiana	50	89	3	(86)
Iowa[b]	544	141	283	142
Kansas	412	143	49	(94)
Kentucky	236	135	2	(133)
Louisiana[b]	1,639	118	233	115
Maine	0	39	0	(39)
Maryland[b]	2,020	158	223	65
Massachusetts	1,911	291	253	(38)
Michigan[b]	1,362	174	72	(102)
Minnesota	955	191	68	(123)
Mississippi	66	24	0	(24)
Missouri	420	247	18	(229)
Montana	54	9	1	(8)
Nebraska	559	157	20	(137)
Nevada[b]	90	30	12	(18)
New Hampshire	100	46	7	(39)
New Jersey	662	317	56	(261)
New Mexico	253	82	8	(74)
New York	9,938	635	203	(432)
North Carolina[b]	792	70	702	632
North Dakota	150	83	12	(71)
Ohio	203	127	20	(107)
Oklahoma[b]	609	97	67	(30)
Oregon	1,154	256	160	(96)
Pennsylvania	1,638	326	138	(188)
Rhode Island[b]	1,543	67	105	38
South Carolina[b]	71	47	50	3
South Dakota	201	52	29	(23)
Tennessee	471	171	13	(158)
Texas[b]	4,920	567	972	405
Utah	381	112	39	(73)
Vermont	133	40	5	(35)

[Continued]

★ 576 ★

Refugee Secondary Migration by State (Continued)

Secondary migration[a] by refugees from all countries by state, as of June 30, 1991. In 1991, Southeast Asian refugees accounted for 48 percent of the total.

State	Non-movers	Out-migrants	In-migrants	Net migration
Virginia[b]	1,135	325	234	(91)
Washington[b]	11,790	147	2,237	2,090
West Virginia	20	16	1	(15)
Wisconsin	298	112	6	(106)
Wyoming[b]	0	7	0	(7)
Total	71,936	8,755	8,755	0

Source: Administration for Children and Families, Office of Refugee Resettlement, *Refugee Resettlement Program, Report to the Congress* (Washington, DC: U.S. Department of Health and Human Services, January 31, 1992), table 11, p. A-20. Examination of the data shows two major migration patterns: a movement into Washington and California from all other parts of the United States and a substantial amount of population exchange between contiguous or geographically close states. The first pattern is consistent with the historical pattern of migration by the refugees from Southeast Asia and the second is predictable from general theories of migration. This table represents a compilation of unadjusted data reports by the states. The population base is refugees receiving state-administered services on June 30, 1991. Persons without Social Security numbers or other information to document state of arrival (a total of 8,531) were dropped from the analysis. *Notes:* (a) Secondary migration is defined as a change of residence across a state line at any time between initial arrival in the United States and the reporting date. With regard to any given state, out-migrants are persons initially placed there who were living elsewhere on the reporting date, and in-migrants are persons living there on the reporting date who were initially placed elsewhere. (b) Reporting base includes refugees receiving social services without cash or medical assistance. (c) Not participating in the refugee program.

★ 577 ★

Characteristics of Southeast Asian Refugees

Selected characteristics of Southeast Asian refugees 16 years and over at the time of their entry into the United States. The sample includes refugees who arrived between May 1986 and April 1991.

Year of Entry	Percent		
	Average Education, in years	Speaking No English	Speaking English Well/ Fluently
1991	8.0	53.7%	4.1%
1990	7.9	43.1%	4.8%
1989	5.2	67.0%	5.2%
1988	4.4	62.9%	1.7%
1987	5.1	65.8%	3.2%
1986	5.5	56.9%	2.7%

Source: Administration for Children and Families, Office of Refugee Resettlement, *Refugee Resettlement Program, Report to the Congress* (Washington, DC: U.S. Department of Health and Human Services, January 31, 1992), p. 57. Data refer to self-reported characteristics of incoming Southeast Asian refugees at time of arrival in the United States and should not be confused with the current characteristics of these refugees. The survey includes only those refugees who have arrived in the United States during a five–year period ending five months before the time of interviewing

★ 578 ★

Southeast Asian Refugees Adjustment Patterns, 1991

Selected characteristics on adjustment patterns in percent, of Southeast Asian refugees sixteen years and over. The sample includes Southeast Asian refugees who arrived in the United States between May 1986 and April 1991.

Characteristic	Length of Residence in Months					
	0-6	7-12	13-18	19-24	24-30	31-60
Labor force participation	17.9%	30.9%	38.2%	31.9%	29.4%	35.9%
Unemployment	(b)	28.6%	25.3%	13.0%	19.2%	17.6%
Weekly wages of employed persons, dollars	(b)	$178.55	$205.75	$200.65	$213.24	$247.82
In English training	43.6%	36.7%	40.5%	29.9%	23.2%	21.1%
In other training or schooling	17.9%	29.1%	21.0%	24.3%	29.1%	21.2%
Speaking English well or fluently	10.3%	28.0%	37.7%	32.6%	31.6%	40.7%
Speaking no English	30.8%	16.9%	16.0%	17.4%	25.4%	22.1%

Source: Administration for Children and Families, Office of Refugee Resettlement, *Refugee Resettlement Program, Report to the Congress*[a].(Washington, DC: U.S. Department of Health and Human Services, January 31, 1992), p. 58. The survey includes only those refugees who have arrived in the United States during a five–year period ending five months before the time of interviewing. *Notes:* (a) In previous reports this table included Southeast Asian refugees living in households receiving cash assistance. Since measured changes in use of assistance over time may result from changes in the sample as well as changes in household composition under the current longitudinal survey design, the item was omitted from this report. A substantial proportion of the individuals covered were not in the same household one year earlier. (b) Base number of persons in this category is less than 10.

★ 579 ★

Southeast Asian Refugee Occupations
in Country of Origin and United States

Occupational data, in percent, of Southeast Asian refugees 16 years and over in country of origin and in the United States. The sample includes Southeast Asian refugees who arrived between May 1986 and April 1991.

Occupation	In Country of Origin	In U.S.
Professional/Managerial	9.4%	14.0%
Sales/Clerical	26.2%	16 2%
Total, White Collar	35.6%	17.6%
Skilled	13.8%	24.4%
Semi-skilled	3.5%	35.4%
Laborers	0.0%	4.3.0%
Total, Blue Collar	17.3%	64.1%
Service Workers	7.7%	17.7%
Farmers/fishers	39.4%	0.6%

Source: Administration for Children and Families, Office of Refugee Resettlement, *Refugee Resettlement Program, Report to the Congress,* (Washington, *DC:* U.S. Department of Health and Human Services, January 31, 1992), p. 56. The survey includes only those refugees who have arrived in the United States during a five–year period ending five months before the time of interviewing.

★ 580 ★

Southeast Asian Refugees Employment Status

Labor force participation and unemployment rate, in percent, of Southeast Asian refugees[a] by year of entry into the United States
The sample includes Southeast Asian refugees who arrived between May 1986 and April 1991.

Year of entry	Labor Force Participation, percent					Unemployment Rate, percent					Response Rate[b], percent
	1987	1988	1989	1990	1991	1987	1988	1989	1990	1991	1991
1991	-	-	-	-	23%	-	-	-	-	14%	92%
1990	-	-	-	21%	35%	-	-	-	31%	28%	89%
1989	-	-	21%	35%	32%	-	-	27%	14%	18%	87%
1988	-	20%	30%	33%	36%	-	21%	24%	5%	12%	80%
1987	22%	30%	35%	30%	31%	32%	24%	5%	2%	9%	72%
1986	32%	33%	38%	37%	37%	11%	7%	7%	5%	5%	72%
Total Sample[c]	39%	37%	37%	36%	36%	12%	8%	11%	8%	14%	81%
U.S. Rates[d]	66%	66%	66%	66%	66%	6%	5%	5%	5.5%	6%	-

Source: Administration for Children and Families, Office of Refugee Resettlement, *Refugee Resettlement Program, Report to the Congress,* (U.S. Department of Health and Human Services, January 31, 1992), p. 54. *Notes:* (a) Household members 16 years of age and older. (b) Proportion of original sample of 747 successfully located and interviewed, by year of entry. The total number interviewed, 608, was 81 percent of the original sample. (c) The figures for "total sample" include members of households whose sampled person arrived during the five–year period preceding the survey. (d) September unadjusted figures from the Bureau of Labor Statistics, Department of Labor.

★ 581 ★

Southeast Asian Refugees, Reasons for Not Seeking Employment

Selected reasons Southeast Asians cite for not seeking employment[a] by age of refugee, 1991. The sample
includes Southeast Asian refugees who arrived in the United States between May 1986 and April 1991.

Age	Percent of Southeast Asian Refugees Citing				
	Limited English	Education	Family Needs	Health	Other[b]
16-24 years	5.9%	82.2%	6.0%	0.7%	5.2%
25-34 years	13.3%	30.2%	34.7%	7.1%	14.7%
35-44 years	11.0%	25.5%	35.7%	15.9%	11.9%
Over 44 years	9.3%	9.7%	13.6%	56.8%	10.6%

Source: Administration for Children and Families, Office of Refugee Resettlement, *Refugee Resettlement Program, Report to the Congress* (Washington, DC: U.S. Department of Health and Human Services, January 31, 1992), p. 56. The survey includes only those refugees who have arrived in the United States during a five–year period ending five months before the time of interviewing. *Note:* (a) The total of those not seeking work for the reasons cited above equals 100 percent for each age group when added across. (b) Includes responses combining reasons for not seeking employment. This table includes all household members 16 years of age and older.

★ 582 ★

Southeast Asian Refugee Adjustment and English Proficiency, 1991

English language proficiency related to labor force participation and unemployment[a] in percent, and average weekly wages in dollars for Southeast Asian refugees. The sample includes Southeast Asian refugees who arrived in the United States between May 1986 and April 1991.

Ability to Speak and Understand English	Labor Force Participation	Unemployment	Average Weekly Wages
Not at all	7.6%	16.0%	$178.61
A little	34.9%	15.4%	$216.86
Well	50.4%	14.7%	$251.43
Fluently	46.1%	8.5%	$241.90

Source: Administration for Children and Families, Office of Refugee Resettlement, *Refugee Resettlement Program, Report to the Congress* (Washington, DC: U.S. Department of Health and Human Services, January 31, 1992), p. 57. The survey includes only those refugees who arrived in the United States during a five–year period ending five months before the time of interviewing. *Note:* (a) Labor force and unemployment figures refer to all household members 16 years of age and older.

★ 583 ★

Characteristics of Southeast Asian Households by Public Cash Assistance Status

Southeast Asian refugee households receiving public cash assistance[a] or having earnings only, or a combination of both by size of household, number of wage earners per household, and households with at least one fluent English speaker. The sample includes Southeast Asian refugees who arrived in the United States between May 1986 and April 1991.

Characteristic	Southeast Asian Refugee Households with:			
	Assistance Only	Assistance and Earnings	Earnings Only	Total sample (N=608)
Average household size	5.7	6.1	4.4	5.3
Average number of wage-earners per household	0.0	1.7	2.1	1.0
Percent of household members:				
Under the age of 6	19.5%	8.0%	5.9%	13.3%
Under the age of 16	45.6%	25.1%	18.0%	33.4%
Households with at least one fluent English speaker	7.5%	21.7%	293%	16.8%
Sampled households, total	52.6%	13.7%	33.8%	

Source: Administration for Children and Families, Office of Refugee Resettlement, *Refugee Resettlement Program, Report to the Congress* (Washington, DC: U.S. Department of Health and Human Services, January 31, 1992), p. 59. The survey includes only those refugees who have arrived in the United States during a five–year period ending five months before the time of interviewing. *Notes:* (a) Federal resettlement assistance to refugees is provided by the Office of Refugee Resettlement primarily through state-administered refugee resettlement program. Refugees who meet Immigration and Naturalization (INS) status requirements and who possess appropriate INS documentation may be eligible.

★ 584 ★

Immigration by Region, Country of Last Residence, and Immigration Class, 1991

Number of immigrants to Canada by world region, selected Asian country of last residence, and immigration class, 1991.

Country	Immigration Class								Total
	Family	Assisted Relative	Refugee	Entrepreneur	Investor	Self-employed	Retired	Other Independent	
Europe	15,736	6,203	1,108	592	91	737	429	11,166	48,056
Africa	3,551	1,254	5,194	602	47	141	83	3,364	16,087
Asia									
Sri Lanka	1,869	535	1,301	16	2	0	5	233	6,826
China, Mainland[a]	4,231	347	448	43	23	36	34	8,375	13,915
Taiwan	475	103	1	1,017	2,068	61	540	218	4,488
Hong Kong	8,332	2,321	16	3,602	2,474	304	2,196	3,052	22,340
India	10,279	1,275	31	137	21	26	9	721	12,848
Israel	356	160	16	62	1	26	15	774	1,426
Japan	191	6	0	54	18	8	41	179	502
Lebanon	2,164	2,797	1,865	263	2	30	96	3,547	11,987
Pakistan	1,781	117	350	89	40	20	11	165	2,883
Syria	357	174	82	210	3	9	81	408	1,389
Bangladesh	255	23	89	3	0	0	0	98	1,063
Indonesia	94	15	1	67	22	0	28	50	280
Iran	729	370	1,963	171	11	13	39	811	6,209
Iraq	136	50	390	11	0	7	7	59	799
Jordan	178	34	15	169	7	14	4	94	532
Kuwait	57	57	128	151	0	25	16	167	636
Philippines	5,662	1,358	14	60	68	39	43	5,058	12,335
Saudi Arabia	37	21	91	236	32	60	14	337	862
Myanmar (Burma)	53	29	14	0	0	0	4	4	107
Malaysia	584	150	8	111	3	7	12	259	1,173
Singapore	190	134	2	101	31	5	51	284	807
Afghanistan	166	4	1,071	0	4	0	0	32	1,353
Brunei	196	106	0	22	5	0	22	189	543
Kampuchea	61	15	0	0	1	0	0	9	424
Korea North	2	0	0	0	0	0	0	0	2
Korea South	602	294	1	1,166	91	34	0	295	2,484
Laos	22	1	11	0	0	0	0	4	1,006
Macao	118	39	0	48	23	0	17	35	288
Nepal	12	8	1	0	0	0	0	11	34
Qatar	1	4	25	48	0	7	6	31	128
Thailand	189	4	1	3	0	0	0	23	262
Viet Nam	4,293	1,489	1,047	0	1	0	0	22	8,963
Arab Emirates	33	30	90	299	29	84	5	177	778
Total, Asia	43,753	12,110	9,095	8,195	4,984	815	3,299	25,885	119,997
Australasia	535	60	0	27	4	19	10	297	953
N. and Central America	5,865	628	2,364	118	27	14	279	2,856	20,001
Caribbean/Antilles	10,258	827	126	19	13	9	59	1,485	12,922
South America	5,711	902	406	343	23	78	52	1,894	10,582

[Continued]

★ 584 ★

Immigration by Region, Country of Last Residence, and Immigration Class, 1991 (Continued)

Number of immigrants to Canada by world region, selected Asian country of last residence, and immigration class, 1991.

Country	Immigration Class								Total
	Family	Assisted Relative	Refugee	Entrepreneur	Investor	Self-employed	Retired	Other Independent	
Oceania									
Fiji	771	191	5	0	0	0	1	448	1,593
Samoa West	2	0	0	0	0	0	0	1	3
Fr. Polynesia	3	0	0	0	0	0	0	4	7
Tonga	3	0	0	0	0	0	0	0	3
Mauritius	174	69	0	5	0	0	0	79	328
Seychelles	4	0	74	0	0	0	0	13	224
Total, Oceania	969	263	81	5	0	0	4	550	2,183
Total, World	86,378	22,247	18,374	9,901	5,189	1,953	4,215	47,497	230,781

Source: Immigration 1991, Quarterly Statistics (Ottawa: Employment and Immigration Canada, December, 1991), p 17. *Note:* (a) Employment and Immigration Canada uses the term "China, Mainland" for immigrants from areas under the control of the government in Beijing.

★ 585 ★

Immigration by Country of Last Residence and Province of Intended Destination, 1991

Numbers of immigrants to Canada by world region and selected country of last residence by province of intended destination, 1991.

Country	Newfoundland	PEI	Nova Scotia	New Brunswick	Quebec	Ontario	Manitoba	Saskatchewan	Alberta	British Columbia	Yukon	Northwest Territories	Total
Europe, total	321	26	269	127	8,069	30,078	1,425	401	3,226	4,041	31	42	48,056
Africa, total	40	9	200	34	5,663	7,961	321	231	865	759	1	3	16,087
Asia													
Sri Lanka	19	0	6	6	1,509	5,040	37	3	91	114	0	1	6,826
China, Mainland[a]	51	12	154	63	2,161	5,910	323	429	1,261	3,544	6	1	13,915
Taiwan	0	7	21	3	546	1,090	44	35	125	2,617	0	0	4,488
Hong Kong	14	4	77	52	2,304	11,220	314	207	1,829	6,301	0	18	22,340
India	31	0	40	11	840	6,752	352	75	1,194	3,542	3	8	12,848
Israel	0	0	2	2	547	787	9	5	38	36	0	0	1,426
Japan	0	1	3	0	39	182	8	0	43	226	0	0	502
Lebanon	2	4	131	10	7,137	3,915	24	9	558	197	0	0	11,987
Pakistan	8	2	5	5	686	1,759	48	25	195	150	0	0	2,883
Syria	0	0	9	1	930	349	3	1	76	17	0	3	1,389
Bangladesh	6	0	1	1	728	286	9	0	14	18	0	0	1,063
Indonesia	5	0	1	0	15	122	3	2	13	119	0	0	280
Iran	11	8	29	18	1,364	3,356	99	58	166	1,100	0	0	6,209
Iraq	1	0	10	4	208	452	7	27	49	41	0	0	799
Jordan	0	0	11	1	218	241	5	1	42	13	0	0	532
Kuwait	1	0	20	3	300	252	4	2	19	35	0	0	636
Philippines	1	2	17	5	1,126	7,022	965	101	1,120	1,950	6	20	12,335
Saudi Arabia	5	0	7	1	579	217	9	2	22	20	0	0	862
Myanmar (Burma)	0	0	0	0	10	58	1	1	16	21	0	0	107
Malaysia	2	1	1	0	58	533	45	4	211	317	0	1	1,173
Singapore	1	0	4	0	31	318	6	8	106	331	0	2	807

[Continued]

★ 585 ★

Immigration by Country of Last Residence and Province of Intended Destination, 1991 (Continued)

Numbers of immigrants to Canada by world region and selected country of last residence by province of intended destination, 1991.

Country	Newfoundland	PEI	Nova Scotia	New Brunswick	Quebec	Ontario	Manitoba	Saskatchewan	Alberta	British Columbia	Yukon	Northwest Territories	Total
Afghanistan	0	0	0	0	135	1,009	15	13	130	51	0	0	1,353
Brunei	0	0	5	0	2	57	1	0	300	178	0	0	543
Kampuchea	0	0	0	0	110	156	24	1	111	22	0	0	424
Korea North	0	0	0	0	1	1	0	0	0	0	0	0	2
Korea South	0	0	23	0	639	1,113	99	1	159	450	0	0	2,484
Laos	0	0	0	0	295	368	171	29	76	67	0	0	1,006
Macao	6	0	3	5	54	145	11	1	32	31	0	0	288
Nepal	0	0	0	0	3	20	1	0	8	2	0	0	34
Thailand	0	0	0	1	66	69	4	2	34	79	6	1	262
Viet Nam	16	0	102	67	1,675	3,953	336	260	1,477	1,058	10	9	8,963
Arab Emirates	0	0	47	0	458	241	2	1	16	13	0	0	778
Total, Asia	180	44	741	259	24,971	57,191	2,980	1,303	9,554	22,679	31	64	119,997
Australasia	4	4	7	5	47	319	28	20	164	352	2	1	953
North & Central America	60	67	246	225	6,215	7,686	558	408	1,857	2,653	14	12	20,001
Caribbean	31	0	21	16	3,501	8,591	169	40	362	189	0	2	12,922
South America	2	0	19	17	2,881	6,591	160	45	406	456	5	0	10,582
Oceania													
Fiji	0	0	0	1	6	189	3	1	527	866	0	0	1,593
Mauritius	3	0	0	0	136	156	1	2	17	13	0	0	328
Seychelles	0	0	0	0	207	8	1	0	6	2	0	0	224
Total, Oceania	3	0	1	1	360	365	5	3	551	894	0	0	2,183
Total, World	614	150	1,504	684	51,707	118,782	5,646	2,451	16,985	32,023	84	124	

Source: Immigration 1991, Quarterly Statistics (Ottawa: Employment and Immigration Canada, December, 1991). *Note:* (a) Employment and Immigration Canada uses the term "China, Mainland" for immigrants from areas under the control of the government in Beijing.

★ 586 ★

Immigration From Top Source Countries, 1990 and 1991

Number and percent of total immigrants per year to Canada and ranking of top Asian source countries, and total numbers of immigrants and percent of total from top twenty source countries and from all countries, 1990 and 1990.

Country	1990			1991		
	Rank	Number	Percent	Rank	Number	Percent
Hong Kong	1	29,261	13.7	1	22,340	9.7
Poland	2	16,579	7.7	2	15,731	6.8
China	8	7,989	3.7	3	13,915	6.0
India	5	10,624	5.0	4	12,848	5.6
Philippines	4	12,042	5.6	5	12,335	5.3
Viet Nam	6	9,081	4.2	7	8,963	3.9
Taiwan	13	3,681	1.7	14	4,488	1.9
Sri Lanka	15	3,106	1.4	--	n/a	--
Top Twenty	--	3,106	1.4	--	157,654	--
Total	--	214,230	--	--	230,781	--

Source: Employment and Immigration Canada, *Immigration Quarterly Statistics, 1991* (Ottawa: Immigration Statistics, 1992), p. 3.

★ 587 ★

Immigration by Top Ten Countries of Birth, Recent and Total

Top ten countries of birth for recent immigrants[a] and all immigrants to Canada.

All Immigrants			Recent Immigrants		
Country	Number	Percent	Country	Number	Percent
Total, all	4,342,890	100.0%	Total, all	1,238,455	100.0%
United Kingdom	717,745	16.5%	**Hong Kong**	96,540	7.8%
Italy	351,620	8.1%	Poland	77,455	6.3%
United States	249,080	5.7%	**China, P.R. of**	75,840	6.1%
Poland	184,695	4.3%	**India**	73,105	5.9%
Germany	180,525	4.2%	United Kingdom	71,365	5.8%
India	173,670	4.0%	**Viet Nam**	69,520	5.6%
Portugal	161,180	3.7%	**Philippines**	64,290	5.2%
China, P.R. of	157,405	3.6%	United States	55,415	4.5%
Hong Kong	152,455	3.5%	Portugal	35,440	2.9%
Netherlands	129,615	3.0%	Lebanon	34,065	2.8%

Source: 1991 Census of Canada (Ottawa: Statistics Canada, unpublished tabulations). *Note:* (a) Includes immigrants who came to Canada between 1981 and 1991.

★ 588 ★

Immigrants by World Region, 1989-1991

Number of immigrants admitted to Canada by world region, percent of total, and percent change from prior year, 1989 to 1991.

Region	1989		1990		% change, 1989-1990	1991		% change, 1990-1991
	Number	Percent	Number	Percent		Number	Percent	
Asia/Pacific	93,261	48.6	111,739	52.2%	19.8	97,578	42.3	-12.7
Africa/Middle East	12,199	6.4	13,440	6.3	10.2	41,642	18.0	--
South and Central Americas	8,685	4.5	8,898	4.2	2.5	36,908	16.0	--
United States.	6,931	3.6	6,084	2.8	-12.2	6,597	2.9	8.4
Europe	52,105	27.1	51,945	24.2	-0.3	40,513	17.6	-22.0
Great Britain	8,420	4.4	5,104	2.4	-39.4	7,543	3.3	47.8
Total, all	192,001	100.0	214,230	100.0	11.6	230,781	100.0	7.7

Source: Employment and Immigration Canada, *Immigration Quarterly Statistics, 1991* (Ottawa: Immigration Statistics, 1992), p. 2. A dash (--) indicates the percent cannot be calculated meaningful due to changes in the category.

By Province

★ 589 ★

Immigrants to Alberta by Top Ten Countries of Birth, Recent and Total

Top ten countries of birth for recent immigrants[a] and all immigrants to Alberta, Canada.

All immigrants			Recent immigrants		
Country	Number	Percent	Country	Number	Percent
Total, all	381,515	100.0%	Total, all	113,095	100.0%
United Kingdom	67,545	59.7%	**Viet Nam**	12,210	10.8%
United States	29,635	26.2%	United Kingdom	8,820	7.8%
Germany	22,825	20.2%	**China, P.R. of**	8,620	7.6%
Poland	21,860	19.3%	Poland	8,195	7.2%
Viet Nam	19,320	17.1%	**Hong Kong**	8,015	7.1%
China, P.R. of	18,865	16.7%	**Philippines**	6,795	6.0%
Netherlands	18,620	16.5%	**India**	6,390	5.7%
Hong Kong	15,460	13.7%	United States	6,295	5.6%
India	15,285	13.5%	El Salvador	3,560	3.1%
Philippines	12,550	11.1%	Lebanon	2,080	1.8%

Source: 1991 Census of Canada (Ottawa: Statistics Canada, unpublished tabulations). *Note:* (a) Includes immigrants who came to Canada between 1981 and 1991.

★ 590 ★

Immigrants to British Columbia by Top Ten Countries of Birth, Recent and Total

Top ten countries of birth for recent immigrants[a] and all immigrants to British Columbia, Canada.

All immigrants			Recent Immigrants[a]		
Country	Number	Percent	Country	Number	Percent
Total, all	723,170	100.0%	Total, all	194,345	100.0%
United Kingdom	158,480	21.9%	**Hong Kong**	29,290	15.1%
United States	54,310	7.5%	**China, P.R. of**	23,860	12.3%
China, P.R. of	53,640	7.4%	**India**	20,790	10.7%
India	52,685	7.3%	U.K.	14,690	7.6%
Hong Kong	47,725	6.6%	**Philippines**	12,160	6.3%
Germany	39,890	5.5%	United States	10,660	5.5%
Netherlands	24,875	3.4%	**Viet Nam**	8,700	4.5%
Philippines	24,060	3.3%	**Taiwan**	5,895	3.0%
Italy	21,845	3.0%	Poland	5,725	2.9%
Poland	16,915	2.3%	Iran	4,690	2.4%

Source: 1991 Census of Canada (Ottawa: Statistics Canada, unpublished tabulations). *Note:* (a) Includes immigrants who came to Canada between 1981 and 1991.

★ 591 ★

Immigrants to Ontario by Top Ten Countries of Birth, Recent and Total

Top ten countries of birth for recent immigrants[a] and all immigrants to Ontario, Canada.

Total immigrants			Recent Immigrants[a]		
Country	Number	Percent	Country	Number	Percent
Total, all	2,369,175	100.0%	Total, all	669,375	100.0%
United Kingdom	408,875	17.3%	**Hong Kong**	53,965	8.1%
Italy	233,905	9.9%	Poland	52,875	7.9%
Portugal	116,295	4.9%	U.K.	39,940	6.0%
Poland	109,480	4.6%	India	39,635	5.9%
United States	98,130	4.1%	**China, P.R. of**	34,805	5.2%
Germany	89,040	3.8%	**Viet Nam**	32,490	4.9%
India	88,450	3.7%	**Philippines**	32,260	4.8%
Jamaica	86,465	3.6%	Portugal	27,720	4.1%
Hong Kong	80,390	3.4%	Jamaica	27,285	4.1%
Netherlands	73,700	3.1%	Guyana	26,185	3.9%

Source: 1991 Census of Canada (Ottawa: Statistics Canada, unpublished tabulations). *Note:* (a) Includes immigrants who came to Canada between 1981 and 1991.

★ 592 ★

Immigrants to Quebec by Top Ten Countries of Birth, Recent and Total

Top ten countries of birth for recent immigrants[a] and all immigrants to Quebec, Canada.

Total immigrants			Recent immigrants[a]		
Country	Number	Percent	Country	Number	Percent
Total, all	591,210	100.0%	Total, all	195,085	100.0%
Italy	78,685	13.3%	Lebanon	18,750	9.6%
France	38,265	6.5%	Haiti	16,755	8.6%
Haiti	37,215	6.3%	**Viet Nam**	11,535	5.9%
United States	27,770	4.7%	France	8,760	4.5%
Lebanon	25,935	4.4%	El Salvador	7,320	3.8%
Greece	25,700	4.3%	United States	6,425	3.3%
United Kingdom	25,605	4.3%	Poland	5,785	3.0%
Portugal	24,155	4.1%	**China, P.R. of**	5,300	2.7%
Viet Nam	20,720	3.5%	Morocco	5,300	2.7%
Poland	19,010	3.2%	**Kampuchea**	5,240	2.7%

Source: 1991 Census of Canada (Ottawa: Statistics Canada, unpublished tabulations). *Note:* (a) Includes immigrants who came to Canada between 1981 and 1991.

By Metropolitan Area

★ 593 ★

Immigrants to Montreal by Top Ten Countries of Birth, Recent and Total

Top ten countries of birth for recent immigrants[a] and all immigrants to Montreal, Quebec, Canada.

All immigrants			Recent immigrants[a]		
Country	Number	Percent	Country	Number	Percent
Total, all	520,535	100.0%	Total, all	173,370	100.0%
Italy	75,925	14.6%	Lebanon	17,565	10.1%
Haiti	34,975	6.7%	Haiti	15,785	9.1%
France	26,995	5.2%	**Viet Nam**	10,390	6.0%
Greece	25,095	4.8%	France	6,590	3.8%
Lebanon	23,860	4.6%	El Salvador	6,495	3.7%
United Kingdom	21,695	4.2%	Poland	5,125	3.0%
Portugal	21,145	4.1%	Morocco	4,910	2.8%
Viet Nam	18,690	3.6%	**China, P.R. of**	4,870	2.8%
Poland	17,420	3.3%	Portugal	4,605	2.7%
United States	15,875	3.0%	**Kampuchea**	4,495	2.6%

Source: 1991 Census of Canada (Ottawa: Statistics Canada, unpublished tabulations). *Note:* (a) Includes immigrants who came to Canada between 1981 and 1991.

★ 594 ★

Immigrants to Ottawa-Hull by Top Ten Countries of Birth, Recent and Total

Top ten countries of birth for recent immigrants[a] and all immigrants to Ottawa-Hull (Ontario-Quebec) metropolitan area, Canada.

All Immigrants			Recent Immigrants[a]		
Country	Number	Percent	Country	Number	Percent
Total, all	134,750	100.0%	Total, all	45,505	100.0%
United Kingdom	23,920	17.8%	Lebanon	5,170	11.4%
Lebanon	8,920	6.6%	United Kingdom	3,060	6.7%
Italy	8,420	6.2%	Poland	2,550	5.6%
United States	7,055	5.2%	**Viet Nam**	2,485	5.5%
Germany	5,435	4.0%	**China, P.R. of**	2,230	4.9%
India	5,215	3.9%	Somalia	2,045	4.5%
Poland	4,610	3.4%	**India**	1,615	3.5%
Viet Nam	4,415	3.3%	**Hong Kong**	1,520	3.3%
Portugal	4,360	3.2%	United States	1,520	3.3%
China, P.R. of	4,215	3.1%	Iran	1,470	3.2%

Source: 1991 Census of Canada (Ottawa: Statistics Canada, unpublished tabulations). *Note:* (a) Includes immigrants who came to Canada between 1981 and 1991.

★ 595 ★

Immigrants to Toronto by Top Ten Countries of Birth, Recent and Total

Top ten countries of birth for recent immigrants[a] and all immigrants to Toronto, Ontario, Canada.

All immigrants			Recent immigrants[a]		
Country	Number	Percent	Country	Number	Percent
Total, all	1,468,620	100.0%	Total, all	487,645	100.0%
United Kingdom	182,770	12.4%	**Hong Kong**	49,755	10.2%
Italy	154,610	10.5%	**India**	33,705	6.9%
Portugal	82,470	5.6%	Poland	32,675	6.7%
Jamaica	75,030	5.1%	**China, P.R. of**	29,155	6.0%
Hong Kong	72,290	4.9%	**Philippines**	28,255	5.8%
India	70,450	4.8%	Jamaica	24,590	5.0%
Poland	62,785	4.3%	Guyana	23,895	4.9%
China, P.R. of	55,475	3.8%	**Viet Nam**	23,380	4.8%
Philippines	52,005	3.5%	Portugal	20,555	4.2%
Guyana	50,695	3.5%	United Kingdom	18,565	3.8%

Source: 1991 Census of Canada (Ottawa: Statistics Canada, unpublished tabulations). *Note:* (a) Includes immigrants who came to Canada between 1981 and 1991.

★ 596 ★

Immigrants to Vancouver by Top Ten Countries of Birth, Recent and Total

Top ten countries of birth for recent immigrants[a] and all immigrants to Vancouver, British Columbia[b], Canada.

All immigrants			Recent immigrants		
Country	Number	Percent	Country	Number	Percent
Total, all	476,530	100.0%	Total, all	159,195	100.0%
United Kingdom	83,585	17.5%	**Hong Kong**	28,585	18.0%
China, P.R. of	48,935	10.3%	**China, P.R. of**	22,405	14.1%
Hong Kong	45,650	9.6%	**India**	14,845	9.3%
India	35,895	7.5%	**Philippines**	10,910	6.9%
United States	22,685	4.8%	United Kingdom	9,295	5.8%
Philippines	21,400	4.5%	**Viet Nam**	7,365	4.6%
Germany	19,095	4.0%	**Taiwan**	5,815	3.7%
Italy	14,310	3.0%	United States	5,525	3.5%
Viet Nam	12,765	2.7%	Poland	4,850	3.0%
Fiji	11,095	2.3%	Iran	4,465	2.8%

Source: 1991 Census of Canada(Ottawa: Statistics Canada, unpublished tabulations). *Notes:* (a) Includes immigrants who came to Canada between 1981 and 1991. (b) Vancouver Census Metropolitan Area.

★ 597 ★

Immigrants to Victoria by Top Ten Countries of Birth, Recent and Total

Top ten countries of birth for recent immigrants[a] and all immigrants to Victoria, British Columbia[b], Canada.

All immigrants			Recent immigrants[a]		
Country	Number	Percent	Country	Number	Percent
Total, all	55,405	100.0%	Total, all	7,855	100.0%
United Kingdom	23,975	43.3%	United Kingdom	1,615	20.6%
United States	5,055	9.1%	**China, P.R. of**	1,005	12.8%
Germany	3,140	5.7%	United States	815	10.4%
China, P.R. of	2,610	4.7%	**India**	675	8.6%
India	2,215	4.0%	Germany	340	4.3%
Netherlands	2,145	3.9%	**Hong Kong**	300	3.8%
Portugal	990	1.8%	**Viet Nam**	280	3.6%
Hong Kong	935	1.7%	**Philippines**	215	2.7%
Poland	795	1.4%	Rep. of South Africa	180	2.3%
Italy	775	1.4%	Poland	175	2.2%

Source: 1991 Census of Canada (Ottawa: Statistics Canada, unpublished tabulations). *Notes:* (a) Includes immigrants who arrived in Canada between 1981 and 1991. (b) Victoria Census Metropolitan Area.

Income, Spending, and Wealth

Affluence

★ 598 ★

Affluent Asian/Pacific Islander Households in the United States

Percent of A/PI and white households with annual income of $50,000 or more, and states with highest number of counties[a] with affluent Asian Americans.

Catagory	Percent/number
Asian-headed	35%
White-headed	26%
States with top 20 counties for affluent Asian Americans	No. of counties
New Jersey	8
New York	5
California	1
Connecticut	1
Illinois	1
Michigan	1
Texas	1
Virginia	1
Wisconsin	1

Source: Judith Waldrop and Linda Jacobsen, "American Affluence," *American Demographics* 14: 12 (December 1992), p. 34. Also in source: data on Hispanics. *Note:* (a) Includes only counties with Asian/Pacific Islander population of 2,000 or more.

★ 599 ★

Asian/Pacific Islander Population in Affluent U.S. Counties

Counties (or county equivalents)[a] ranked by percent of Asian/Pacific Islander households with 1989 incomes of $50,000 or more.

Rank	County (metropolitan area)	All Asian households	Percent affluent
1	Nassau, NY (Nassau-Suffolk)	9,804	66.5
2	Somerset, NJ (Middlesex-Somerset-Hunterdon)	3,244	65.7
3	Rockland, NY (New York)	2,570	65.5
4	Waukesha, WI (Milwaukee)	704	65.5
5	Westchester, NY (New York)	9,396	65.1
6	Morris, NJ (Newark)	4,507	64.0
7	Monmouth, NJ (Monmouth-Ocean)	4,198	61.9
8	Fairfield, CT (Bridgeport-Stamford-Norwalk-Danbury)	4,571	61.3
9	Gloucester, NJ (Philadelphia)	738	61.1
10	Loudoun, VA (Washington)	465	60.9
11	Bergen, NJ (Bergen-Passaic)	15,559	60.2
12	Mercer, NJ (Trenton)	2,517	59.0
13	Dutchess, NY (Poughkeepsie)	1,721	58.2
14	Oakland, MI (Detroit)	7,019	56.8
15	DuPage, IL (Chicago)	10,676	56.7
16	Union, NJ (Newark)	4,094	56.6
17	Suffolk, NY (Nassau-Suffolk)	5,066	56.4
18	Ventura, CA (Oxnard-Ventura)	8,534	56.3
19	Fort Bend, TX (Houston)	3,505	55.9
20	Middlesex, NJ (Middlesex-Somerset-Hunterdon)	12,026	55.9

Source: Judith Waldrop and Linda Jacobsen, "American Affluence," *American Demographics,* 14: 12 (Dec. 1992), p. 40. Also in source: data on Hispanics. *Note:* (a) Includes only counties with Asian/Pacific Islander population of 2,000 or more. Numbers of households are from the 1990 Census.

Consumer Spending

★ 600 ★

Banking Habits

Results of a survey, in percent, of banking habits by race/ethnicity. Survey conducted October 1992 to January 1993.

Percent who have:	Asian American	Hispanic American	African American
Checking account	81%	37%	45%
Savings account	62%	28%	40%
Certificate of deposit or money market account	12%		5%
No bank account or no answer		50%	41%

Source: Christy Fisher, "Poll: Hispanics Stick to Brands," *Advertising Age* (February 15, 1993). Reports results of a survey from October 1992 to January 1993. Personal and telephone interviews were conducted with 2,000 Hispanic Americans, 1,000 African Americans, 500 Asian Americans. Primary source: Market Segment Research, Miami, FL.

★ 601 ★

Consumer Behavior

Reported results of a survey of consumer behavior by race/ethnicity. Survey conducted October 1992–January 1993.

Behavior	Asian American	Hispanic American	African American
Number of times per month respondents shop for food	3.56	3.06	2.42
Percent who used a coupon in the last 30 days	40%	36%	43%
Percent who subscribe to cable TV	40%	36%	47%
Percent who speak:			
native language only	33%	51%	-
English only	14%	3%	-
speak native language and English equally	25%	26%	-
Hours per week spent:			
watching TV (English-language)	8	-	-
listening to radio (English language)	8	-	-
watching TV (Spanish language)	-	14	-
listening to radio (Spanish language)	-	11	-

[Continued]

★ 601 ★

Consumer Behavior (Continued)

Reported results of a survey of consumer behavior by race/ethnicity. Survey conducted October 1992–January 1993.

Behavior	Asian American	Hispanic American	African American
Percent reporting factor influences buying decision:			
brand name	45%	62%	54%
item on sale	45%	35%	41%
quality most important	59%	67%	67%
price most important	30%	26%	21%

Source: Christy Fisher, "Poll: Hispanics Stick to Brands," *Advertising Age* (February 15, 1993). Reports results of a survey from October 1992 to January 1993. Personal and telephone interviews were conducted with 2,000 Hispanic Americans, 1,000 African Americans, 500 Asian Americans. Primary source: Market Segment Research, Miami, FL.

★ 602 ★

Consumer Purchasing Habits

Reported results, in percent, of a survey of consumer product purchases by race/ethnicity. Survey conducted October 1992–January 1993.

Product	Percent purchasing products in a 30-day period		
	Asian Americans	African Americans	Hispanics
Regular coffee	49	54	72
Decaffeinated coffee	13	19	20
Regular carbonated soft drinks	70	71	77
Diet carbonated soft drinks	12	23	20
Powdered drink mix	14	35	35
Fruit juice/nectar	73	68	78
Beer	44	31	38
Wine	16	11	10
Ready-to-eat cereal	44	72	78
Hot cereal	22	42	21
Shampoo	89	76	93
Conditioner	59	52	61
Hair spray	29	15	27
Gel	14	14	16
Mousse	22	6	17
Toothpaste	93	92	95
Denture cleaner	8	4	13
Ready-to-eat frozen entrees	11	18	8
Latin frozen entrees	6	2	3
Chinese frozen entrees	8	3	1
Frozen breakfast foods	6	9	2
Frozen vegetables	17	40	21
Bath soaps	89	95	97

[Continued]

★ 602 ★

Consumer Purchasing Habits (Continued)

Reported results, in percent, of a survey of consumer product purchases by race/ethnicity. Survey conducted October 1992–January 1993.

Product	Percent purchasing products in a 30-day period		
	Asian Americans	African Americans	Hispanics
Deodorants	26	84	89
Dishwashing detergent	79	86	88
Baby food	7	6	11
Powdered soups	13	17	16
Canned soups	36	53	32
Canned vegetables	17	44	42
Canned fruits	28	35	42
Solid air fresheners	13	24	12
Aerosol air fresheners	20	34	35
Powdered cleaners	46	57	53
Fabric softener	51	67	81
Liquid cleaners	43	61	57
Toilet paper	93	95	95
Disposable diapers	9	7	16
Cloth diapers	1	1	1
Chocolate bars	36	33	23
Non-chocolate candy	17	11	9
Chewing gum	39	35	26
Bleach	57	76	73
Artificial sweeteners	17	16	12
Diet frozen desserts	1	1	3
White rice	90	73	89
Packaged cheese	39	53	65
Yogurt	28	23	25
Packaged sliced meats	43	39	55
Potato chips	41	52	36
Microwave popcorn	18	23	16
Insecticide spray	31	28	30
Dried fruit products	17	14	14
Underwear	66	63	66
Non-menthol cigarettes	22	12	14
Menthol cigarettes	4	16	5
Cat food	5	10	7
Dog food	10	14	14
Packaged cookies	44	46	42
Cake mixes	14	24	9
Sunscreen	9	3	5
Analgesics/headache remedies	48	60	80
Antacids	13	20	29
Laxatives	7	14	11
Cough syrup	28	41	50
Cold remedies	42	38	37
Stomach remedies	18	32	35
Condoms	12	16	9

[Continued]

★ 602 ★

Consumer Purchasing Habits (Continued)

Reported results, in percent, of a survey of consumer product purchases by race/ethnicity. Survey conducted October 1992–January 1993.

Product	Percent purchasing products in a 30-day period		
	Asian Americans	African Americans	Hispanics
Jams & jellies	37	28	36
Peanut butter	51	54	31
Ice cream	43	35	43
Ice cream toppings	6	6	4

Source: Christy Fisher, "Poll: Hispanics Stick to Brands," *Advertising Age* (February 15, 1993). Reports results of a survey from October 1992 to January 1993. Personal and telephone interviews were conducted with 2,000 Hispanic Americans, 1,000 African Americans, 500 Asian Americans. Primary source: Market Segment Research, Miami, FL.

★ 603 ★

Ownership of Consumer Electronic Products

Results of a survey in percent, of ownership of electronic products, by race/ethnicity. Survey conducted October 1992 to January, 1993.

Product	Percent of ethnic groups owning products		
	Asian American	African American	Hispanic American
VCR	89.4	73.5	73.1
Camera	89.4	67.6	58.7
Microwave	79.1	66.8	62.3
Answering machine	50.0	47.2	27.5
Videogame system	41.8	42.3	39.8
Dishwasher	46.9	34.6	26.1
Compact Disc player	45.5	31.9	26.7
Personal computer	30.5	19.8	9.6
Beeper	19.5	16.9	14.0
Camcorder	35.6	15.0	17.1
Cellular phone	24.3	10.3	6.7

Source: Christy Fisher, "Poll: Hispanics Stick to Brands," *Advertising Age* (February 15, 1993). Reports results of a survey from October 1992 to January 1993. Personal and telephone interviews were conducted with 2,000 Hispanic Americans, 1,000 African Americans, 500 Asian Americans. Primary source: Market Segment Research, Miami, FL.

★ 604 ★

Vehicles Available by Race of Householder by Occupied Housing Units

State	Asian or Pacific Islander		White		Black	
	None	1 or more	None	1 or more	None	1 or more
Alabama	449	5,544	69,346	1,089,964	85,551	248,245
Alaska	591	4,080	10,011	143,422	671	6,014
Arizona	1,256	14,329	73,275	1,106,410	6,830	29,087
Arkansas	243	2,756	52,677	707,628	33,989	86,982
California	77,583	695,086	570,823	7,320,076	150,326	592,023
Colorado	1,536	15,032	69,023	1,087,815	9,818	38,530
Connecticut	807	12,267	83,712	1,014,695	27,577	62,239
Delaware	84	2,236	12,062	193,248	7,693	29,323
Florida	2,228	38,540	327,037	4,136,487	135,219	412,934
Georgia	781	18,340	93,288	1,666,030	148,168	424,781
Hawaii	21,578	181,287	12,110	126,645	676	6,666
Idaho	149	2,271	15,300	330,283	146	1,008
Illinois	10,831	69,171	346,304	3,103,927	203,603	344,067
Indiana	839	9,641	133,575	1,756,373	38,253	109,984
Kansas	729	7,195	47,838	820,629	9,530	37,994
Kentucky	377	3,936	129,518	1,149,482	28,824	63,577
Louisiana	1,088	8,626	76,034	994,221	129,453	277,008
Maine	100	1,520	39,697	420,106	205	1,270
Maryland	2,456	34,713	100,693	1,194,775	109,998	290,273
Massachusetts	8,199	29,545	257,184	1,807,287	36,098	61,616
Michigan	1,900	25,578	194,644	2,713,516	140,468	299,818
Minnesota	2,928	13,736	123,175	1,458,414	11,095	19,352
Montana	104	960	18,141	271,665	110	560
Nevada	800	9,409	27,912	380,961	5,081	20,828
New Hampshire	117	2,168	25,361	379,353	275	2,036
New Jersey	5,367	67,478	230,798	2,079,410	99,562	232,269
New Mexico	249	3,378	24,682	412,390	1,316	8,704
New York	80,301	117,831	1,187,127	4,004,786	534,052	411,278
North Carolina	786	11,928	122,211	1,857,775	114,622	375,738
North Dakota	50	791	14,379	217,417	78	968
Ohio	2,379	23,641	285,587	3,338,234	123,607	289,083
Oklahoma	828	8,213	64,174	964,871	16,941	60,987
Oregon	2,499	16,780	79,250	964,377	3,888	11,227
Pennsylvania	6,717	29,421	490,791	3,557,059	168,629	205,221
Rhode Island	671	3,551	33,641	319,310	3,627	8,832
South Carolina	330	4,881	52,708	871,059	82,905	240,552
South Dakota	42	609	13,877	231,267	47	860
Tennessee	472	7,802	110,083	1,466,392	70,091	191,538
Texas	5,630	82,995	276,856	4,531,362	145,390	534,228
Utah	689	8,055	25,330	483,151	632	3,028
Vermont	58	617	16,503	191,938	107	451
Virginia	2,176	38,645	112,359	1,728,987	88,454	301,474
Washington	6,472	51,795	117,274	1,593,324	10,415	39,906
West Virginia	207	1,831	86,224	578,318	7,319	13,197
Wisconsin	2,364	10,300	133,248	1,579,000	29,726	45,278
Wyoming	44	726	6,965	153,887	136	917

Source: Asian/Pacific Islander Data Consortium (San Francisco, CA: Asian and Pacific Islander Center for Census Information and Services, 1993). Primary source: U.S. Census Bureau, Summary Tape Files 1 and 3.

Income

★ 605 ★

Earnings in the United States, All Workers by Sex

Male and female[a] Asian/Pacific Islander, white, and total population by income range and median earnings, 1991.

Characteristic	Total population	Asian/ Pacific Islander	White
Males with earnings	72,348	1,848	62,952
Percent	100.0	100.0	100.0
$1 to $9,999 or less	23.9	21.8	22.9
$10,000 to $19,999	21.9	23.8	21.0
$20,000 to $29,999	19.6	19.0	19.8
$30,000 to $39,999	14.6	14.5	15.0
$40,000 to $49,999	8.3	7.0	8.7
$50,000 and over	11.7	13.9	12.5
Median earnings (dollars)	$21,522	$21,583	$22,185
Standard error[b] (dollars)	$102	$628	$108
Male year-round, full-time earners	49,171	1,345	43,127
Median earnings (dollars)	$27,678	$26,764	$28,881
Standard error (dollars)	$207	$735	$229
Females with earnings	61,732	1,640	52,525
Percent	100.0	100.0	100.0
$1 to $9,999 or less	41.5	35.4	41.5
$10,000 to $19,999	28.8	28.3	28.5
$20,000 to $29,999	17.3	17.7	17.4
$30,000 to $39,999	7.4	10.4	7.5
$40,000 to $49,999	2.9	3.4	2.9
$50,000 and over	2.1	4.9	2.1
Median earnings (dollars)	$12,250	$14,368	$12,283
Standard error (dollars)	$80	$775	$88
Female year-round, full-time earners	31,682	946	26,598
Median earnings (dollars)	$19,822	$21,323	$20,048
Standard error (dollars)	$127	$591	$116
Per capita income (dollars)	$14,387	$13,420	$15,265

Source: Claudette E. Bennett, Economics and Statistics Administration, Bureau of the Census, U.S. Department of Commerce, *The Asian and Pacific Islander Population in the United States: March 1991 and 1990,* Current Population Reports, Population Characteristics, P20-459 (Washington, DC: U.S. Government Printing Office, August 1992), table 2, p. 16. The population universe for the March 1991 and 1990 Current Population Surveys is the estimate of the civilian noninstitutional population in the United States plus members of the Armed Forces in the United States living off post or with their families on post, but excludes all other members of the Armed Forces. Data are estimates based on sample surveys and are subject to sampling variability since they are not based on a complete count of the population. *Notes:* (a) For persons age 15 years and older. (b) Standard error is higher for Asians than for other groups because the Asian sample population is smaller.

★ 606 ★

Earnings in the Western United States, All Workers by Sex

Numbers[a] and percent of male and female Asian/Pacific Islander, white, and total population in the western[b] United States by income range and median earnings, 1991.

Characteristic	Total population	Asian/ Pacific Islander	White
Males with earnings	15,685	1,062	13,779
Percent	100.0	100.0	100.0
$1 to $9,999 or less	23.9	22.2	23.7
$10,000 to $19,999	21.8	21.7	21.8
$20,000 to $29,999	17.8	18.7	17.7
$30,000 to $39,999	14.5	16.9	14.3
$40,000 to $49,999	8.8	7.2	9.0
$50,000 and over	13.2	13.3	13.5
Median earnings (dollars)	$21,775	$22,002	$21,879
Standard error[c] (dollars)	$290	$1,068	$315
Male year-round, full-time earners	10,305	772	9,029
Median earnings (dollars)	$29,591	$28,013	$29,911
Standard error[c] (dollars)	$568	$1,949	$507
Females with earnings	12,575	981	10,889
Percent	100.0	100.0	100.0
$1 to $9,999 or less	41.4	33.8	42.4
$10,000 to $19,999	26.3	27.2	26.2
$20,000 to $29,999	17.5	18.8	17.1
$30,000 to $39,999	8.6	12.5	8.2
$40,000 to $49,999	3.4	3.3	3.5
$50,000 and over	2.8	4.4	2.7
Median earnings (dollars)	$12,233	$15,334	$11,940
Standard error[c] (dollars)	$203	$1,101	$216
Female year-round, full-time earners	6,038	559	5,103
Median earnings (dollars)	$21,248	$22,157	$21,080
Standard error[c] (dollars)	$257	$1,018	$285
Per capita income (dollars)	$15,118	$13,774	$15,444

Source: Claudette E. Bennett, Economics and Statistics Administration, Bureau of Census, U.S. Department of Commerce, *The Asian and Pacific Islander Population in the United States: March 1991 and 1990,* Current Population Reports, Population Characteristics, P20-459 (Washington, DC: U.S. Government Printing Office, August 1992), table 2, p. 16. The population universe for the March 1991 and 1990 Current Population Surveys is the estimate of the civilian noninstitutional population to the United States plus members of the Armed Forces in the United States living off post or with their families on post, but excludes all other members of the Armed Forces. Data are estimates based on sample surveys and are subject to sampling variability since they are not based on a complete count of the population. *Notes:* (a) For persons 15 years of age and older. (b) Western U.S. includes Alaska, Arizona, California, Colorado, Hawaii, Idaho, Montana, Nevada, New Mexico, Oregon, Utah, Washington, and Wyoming. (c) Standard error is higher for Asians than for other groups because the Asian sample population is smaller.

★ 607 ★

Earnings, Full-time U.S. Workers

Numbers and percent Asian/Pacific Islander, white, and total full-time workers[a]
by income range and median earnings, 1990.

United States	Total population	Asian/ Pacific Islander	White
Total (thousands)	73,800	2,163	63,652
Total with earnings (thousands)	73,722	2,157	63,579
Percent	100.0%	100.0%	100.0%
$1 to $2,499 or loss	1.1%	0.9%	1.2%
$2,500 to $4,999	0.8	0.4	0.8
$5,000 to $7,499	1.9	1.6	1.8
$7,500 to $9,999	3.2	3.4	2.9
$10,000 to $12,499	6.7	7.8	6.2
$12,500 to $14,999	5.6	6.4	5.3
$15,000 to $17,499	8.1	7.7	7.8
$17,500 to $19,999	6.5	6.5	6.3
$20,000 to $22,499	9.1	8.9	9.1
$22,500 to $24,999	5.3	5.8	5.2
$25,000 to $27,499	8.0	7.0	8.0
$27,500 to $29,999	4.2	3.1	4.2
$30,000 to $32,499	7.3	6.6	7.4
$32,500 to $34,999	3.1	1.9	3.2
$35,000 to $37,499	5.2	6.5	5.4
$37,500 to $39,999	2.3	3.1	2.4
$40,000 to $42,499	4.2	3.8	4.4
$42,500 to $44,999	1.5	0.7	1.6
$45,000 to $49,999	3.7	3.0	3.8
$50,000 to $59,999	5.1	6.0	5.5
$60,000 to $74,999	3.2	4.5	3.4
$75,000 and over	3.9	4.3	4.2
Median earnings (dollars)	$25,511	$25,193	$26,083
Standard[b] error (dollars)	$87	$616	$93

Source: Claudette E. Bennett, Economics and Statistics Administration, Bureau of the Census, U.S. Department of Commerce, *The Asian and Pacific Islander Population in the United States: March 1991 and 1990,* Current Population Reports, Population Characteristics, P20-459 (Washington, DC: U.S. Government Printing Office, August 1992), table 5, p. 24. The population universe for the March 1991 and 1990 Current Population Surveys is the estimate of the civilian noninstitutional population in the United States plus members of the Armed Forces in the United States living off post or with their families on post, but excludes all other members of the Armed Forces. Data are estimates based on sample surveys and are subject to sampling variability since they are not based on a complete count of the population. *Notes:* (a) Data for workers age 25 and over. (b) Standard error is higher for Asians than for other groups because the Asian sample population is smaller.

★ 608 ★

Earnings, Full-time U.S. Workers, Female

Numbers and percent of female Asian/Pacific Islander, white, and total full-time workers[a] by income range, and median earnings, 1990.

Earnings	Total population	Asian/ Pacific Islander	White
Female (thousands)	28,724	895	24,071
Total with earnings (thousands)	28,649	889	24,001
Percent	100.0%	100.0%	100.0%
$1 to $2,499 or loss	1.4%	1.2%	1.4%
$2,500 to $4,999	1.1	0.6	1.1
$5,000 to $7,499	2.7	2.1	2.7
$7,500 to $9,999	4.9	4.9	4.5
$10,000 to $12,499	9.7	10.6	9.2
$12,500 to $14,999	8.1	7.5	8.0
$15,000 to $17,499	11.3	9.5	11.4
$17,500 to $19,999	8.4	6.6	8.4
$20,000 to $22,499	10.8	10.4	11.0
$22,500 to $24,999	6.2	6.1	6.4
$25,000 to $27,499	8.1	6.6	8.0
$27,500 to $29,999	4.4	3.6	4.5
$30,000 to $32,499	6.1	6.9	6.2
$32,500 to $34,999	2.4	2.0	2.5
$35,000 to $37,499	3.7	5.3	3.7
$37,500 to $39,999	1.6	2.1	1.6
$40,000 to $42,499	2.6	2.9	2.7
$42,500 to $44,999	0.9	0.5	0.9
$45,000 to $49,999	1.9	2.5	2.0
$50,000 to $59,999	2.0	3.9	2.0
$60,000 to $74,999	1.0	2.4	1.0
$75,000 and over	0.9%	1.9%	0.9%
Median earnings (dollars)	$20,556	$21,691	$20,759
Standard error[b] (dollars)	$102	$606	$110

Source: Claudette E. Bennett, Economics and Statistics Administration, Bureau of the Census, U.S. Department of Commerce, *The Asian and Pacific Islander Population in the United States: March 1991 and 1990,* Current Population Reports, Population Characteristics, P20-459 (Washington, DC: U.S. Government Printing Office, August 1992), table 5, p. 24. The population universe for the March 1991 and 1990 Current Population Surveys is the estimate of the civilian noninstitutional population in the United States plus members of the Armed Forces in the United States living off post or with their families on post, but excludes all other members of the Armed Forces. Data are estimates based on sample surveys and are subject to sampling variability since they are not based on a complete count of the population. *Notes:* (a) Data for workers age 25 and over. (b) Standard error is higher for Asians than for other groups because the Asian sample population is smaller.

★ 609 ★

Earnings, Full-time U.S. Workers, Male

Numbers and percent of male Asian/Pacific Islander, white, and total full-time workers[a] by income range and median earnings, 1990.

Earnings	Total population	Asian Pacific Islander	White
Male (thousands)	45,076	1,268	39,581
Total with earnings (thousands)	45,074	1,268	39,578
Percent	100.0%	100.0%	100.0%
$1 to $2,499 or loss	1.0%	0.7%	1.0%
$2,500 to $4,999	0.6	0.2	0.6
$5,000 to $7,499	1.4	1.3	1.3
$7,500 to $9,999	2.1	2.3	1.9
$10,000 to $12,499	4.9	5.8	4.4
$12,500 to $14,999	3.9	5.6	3.6
$15,000 to $17,499	6.1	6.5	5.6
$17,500 to $19,999	5.3	6.4	5.0
$20,000 to $22,499	8.0	7.9	8.0
$22,500 to $24,999	4.6	5.7	4.5
$25,000 to $27,499	7.9	7.3	8.0
$27,500 to $29,999	4.1	2.7	4.1
$30,000 to $32,499	8.0	6.3	8.1
$32,500 to $34,999	3.5	1.8	3.6
$35,000 to $37,499	6.2	7.4	6.4
$37,500 to $39,999	2.8	3.9	2.8
$40,000 to $42,499	5.3	4.5	5.5
$42,500 to $44,999	1.8	0.8	1.9
$45,000 to $49,999	4.8	3.3	5.0
$50,000 to $59,999	7.2	7.5	7.6
$60,000 to $74,999	4.6	6.0	4.8
$75,000 and over	5.8%	6.0%	6.3%
Median earnings (dollars)	$29,987	$27,741	$30,598
Standard error[b] (dollars)	$166	$1,396	$117

Source: Claudette E. Bennett, Economics and Statistics Administration, Bureau of the Census, U.S. Department of Commerce, *The Asian and Pacific Islander Population in the United States: March 1991 and 1990,* Current Population Reports, Population Characteristics, P20-459 (Washington, DC:U.S. Government Printing Office, August 1992), table 5, p. 24. The population universe for the March 1991 and 1990 Current Population Surveys is the estimate of the civilian noninstitutional population to the United States plus members of the Armed Forces in the United States living off post or with their families on post, but excludes all other members of the Armed Forces. Data are estimates based on sample surveys and are subject to sampling variability since they are not based on a complete count of the population. *Notes:* (a) Data for workers age 25 and over. (b) Standard error is higher for Asians than for other groups because the Asian sample population is smaller.

★ 610 ★

Earnings, Full-time U.S. Workers by Occupation and Sex

Numbers and median earnings of Asian/Pacific Islanders, white, and total full-time workers[a] by sex and occupation, 1990.

Occupation of longest job	1990 Earnings in U.S. dollars					
	Total population		Asian/Pacific Islander		White	
	Male	Female	Male	Female	Male	Female
Executive, administrative, and managerial workers	41,305	26,307	37,980	30,237	41,706	26,257
Professional speciality workers	41,369	29,645	45,450	36,891	41,446	29,831
Technical and related support workers	31,505	24,495	30,971	26,985	31,750	24,419
Sales workers	30,753	18,359	23,434	16,992	31,168	18,898
Administrative support workers, including clerical	27,628	19,242	23,320	21,562	28,994	19,010
Private household workers	13,966	7,860	(S)	(S)	13,422	7,339
Protective service workers	30,097	23,176	30,135	(S)	31,367	22,709
Service workers, except private household	16,511	12,284	17,842	13,553	17,020	12,187
Farming, fishing, and forestry workers	15,259	9,913	18,879	50,886	15,608	9,673
Precision production, craft, and repair workers	27,742	19,152	25,009	19,494	28,291	19,067
Machine operators, assemblers, and inspectors	23,892	14,984	20,985	12,538	25,103	15,308
Transportation and material moving workers	25,457	16,381	25,305	(S)	25,905	16,088
Handlers, equipment cleaners, helpers, and laborers	19,979	14,165	18,475	(S)	20,756	14,818

Source: Claudette E. Bennett, Economics and Statistics Administration, Bureau of the Census, U.S. Department of Commerce, Economics and Statistics Administration, Bureau of the Census, U.S. Department of Commerce, *The Asian and Pacific Islander Population in the United States: March 1991 and March 1990,* Current Population Reports, Population Characteristics, P20-459 (Washington, DC: U.S. Government Printing Office, August 1992), table 9, p. 41. Data are estimates based on sample surveys and are subject to sampling variability since they are not based on a complete count of the population. An (S) means that median earnings are not shown when the base is less than or equal to 5,000 persons. *Note:* (a) Data are for full-time workers age 25 years old and older.

★ 611 ★

Earnings, Full-time U.S. Asian/Pacific Islander Workers by Occupation, Sex, and Education

Median earnings, Asian/Pacific Islander full-time workers[a] by occupation, sex, and education 1990.

Occupation of longest job	1990 Earnings in U.S. Dollars									
	Total[b]		Less than high school		4 years of high school		1 to 3 years of college		4 or more years of college	
	Male	Female	Male	Female	Male	Female	Male	Female	Male	Female
Executive, administrative, and managerial workers	37,980	30,237	(S)	19,905	21,711	25,198	36,099	24,568	41,998	34,194
Professional speciality workers	45,450	36,891	-	-	45,771	31,813	39,532	41,019	46,605	36,430
Technical and related support workers	30,971	26,985	(S)	(S)	31,301	(S)	19,592	24,397	31,620	28,931
Sales workers	23,434	16,992	16,708	8,928	20,165	14,892	21,511	12,911	27,454	23,173
Administrative support workers, including clerical	23,320	21,562	24,255	32,514	19,311	17,832	26,858	22,106	24,266	22,542
Private household workers	(S)	(S)	-	-	-	-	(S)	(S)	-	(S)
Protective service workers	30,135	(S)	(S)	-	(S)	-	(S)	-	35,220	(S)
Service workers, except private household	17,842	13,553	13,941	11,974	20,485	13,774	18,621	14,019	14,563	16,888
Farming, fishing, and forestry workers	18,879	50,886	30,465	-	18,271	(S)	-	(S)	(S)	-
Precision production, craft, and repair workers	25,009	19,494	15,463	(S)	22,768	18,772	27,044	22,095	41,142	(S)
Machine operators, assemblers, and inspectors	20,985	12,538	15,491	11,281	21,387	15,474	25,230	19,578	30,246	10,636
Transportation and material moving workers	25,305	(S)	(S)	-	28,050	(S)	26,249	(S)	13,621	-
Handlers, equipment cleaners, helpers, and laborers	18,475	(S)	14,034	(S)	18,117	(S)	27,557	(S)	(S)	-

Source: Claudette E. Bennett, Economics and Statistics Administration, Bureau of the Census, U.S. Department of Commerce, *The Asian and Pacific Islander Population in the United States: March 1991 and 1990,* Current Population Reports, Population Characteristics, P20-459 (Washington, DC: U.S. Government Printing Office, August 1992), table 9, p. 41. The population universe for the March 1991 and 1990 Current Population Surveys is the estimate of the civilian non-institutional population of the United States plus members of the Armed Forces in the United States living off post or with their families on post, but excludes all other members of the Armed Forces. Data are estimates based on sample surveys and are subject to sampling variability since they are not based on a complete count of the population. Data where base is less than 75,000 may not meet statistical standards for reliability of derived figures. A dash (-) represents zero or round to zero. An "S" means that the median earnings are not shown when the base is less than or equal to 5,000 persons. Also in source: the standard error in dollars for median earnings, and data for whites. *Notes:* (a) Data are for full-time workers age 25 years and older. (b) Total includes persons with no education, not shown separately.

★ 612 ★

Earnings, Unemployment, and Poverty

Median family income, averge number of earners per family, unemployment rate, and poverty rate by race/ethnicity[a].

Race	Median family income	Average number of earners per family	Unemployment rate, percent	Poverty rate, percent
Asian Americans	$35,900	1.8	3.5%	14%
Whites, non-Hispanic	35,000	1.7	4.2%	8%
Hispanics	23,400	1.7	10.3%	26%
Blacks	20,200	1.5	12.3%	31%
All U.S.	$34,200	1.7	6.8%	13%

Source: "Asian-American Demographics," *The American Enterprise* (November/December, 1991): 87-90. Primary source: U.S. Bureau of Labor Statistics, Bureau of the Census. *Note:* (a) Data is for 1989 (cols. 1, 2, and 4) and 1990 (col. 3).

Earnings by Educational Attainment

★ 613 ★

Earnings and Educational Attainment

Relative earnings of American-born Asian men as a percent of the earnings of non-Hispanic white men with comparable characteristics, 1988.

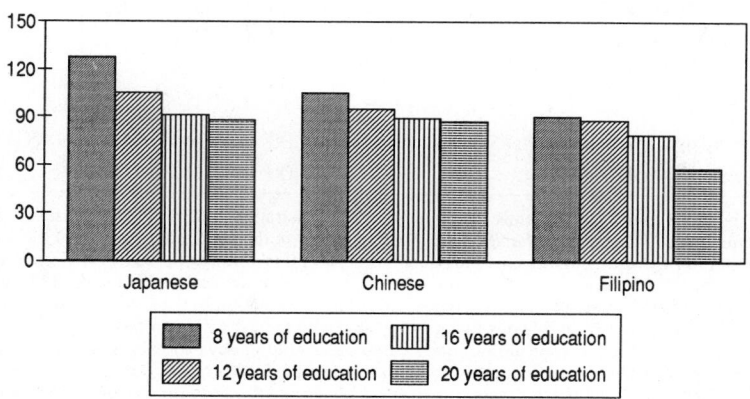

Source: U.S. Commission on Civil Rights, *Voices across America: Roundtable Discussions of Asian Civil Rights Issues* (Washington, DC: U.S. Commission on Civil Rights, not dated), fig. 1, p. 2 (summary and transcript of roundtable conferences in Houston, New York City, and San Francisco, May-July 1989). Primary source: *The Economic Progress of Americans of Asian Descent: An Exploratory Investigation* (Washington, DC: U.S. Commission on Civil Rights, October 1988).

★ 614 ★

Earnings, U.S. Workers
with Less than High School Education

Numbers and percent Asian/Pacific Islander, white, and total full-time workers[a] with less than a high school education by income range and median earnings, 1990.

All workers	Total population	Asian/Pacific Islander	White
Both sexes (thousands)	8,093	213	6,583
Total with earnings (thousands)	8,080	213	6,571
Percent	100.0	100.0	100.0
$1 to $2,499 or loss	1.7	3.9	1.7
$2,500 to $4,999	1.8	1.4	1.7
$5,000 to $7,499	5.4	4.0	5.3
$7,500 to $9,999	8.8	12.1	8.3
$10,000 to $12,499	14.7	14.3	14.0
$12,500 to $14,999	9.7	15.0	9.1
$15,000 to $17,499	11.7	10.1	12.1
$17,500 to $19,999	7.9	8.1	7.5
$20,000 to $22,499	8.9	5.1	9.2
$22,500 to $24,999	4.7	3.3	4.8
$25,000 to $27,499	5.5	5.8	6.0
$27,500 to $29,999	2.8	1.8	3.1
$30,000 to $32,499	5.0	4.1	5.4
$32,500 to $34,999	1.9	1.6	1.9
$35,000 to $37,499	2.8	4.6	2.8
$37,500 to $39,999	1.0	1.4	1.0
$40,000 to $42,499	1.6	0.4	1.6
$42,500 to $44,999	0.5	0.3	0.6
$45,000 to $49,999	1.3	0.5	1.4
$50,000 to $59,999	1.4	2.2	1.3
$60,000 to $74,999	0.6	-	0.7
$75,000 and over	0.4	-	0.4
Median earnings (dollars)	$16,698.00	$14,876.00	$17,054
Standard error[b] (dollars)	$179.00	$1,035.00	$191

Source: Claudette E. Bennett, Economics and Statistics Administration, Bureau of the Census, U.S. Department of Commerce, *The Asian and Pacific Islander Population in the United States: March 1991 and 1990,* Current Population Reports, Population Characteristics, P20-459 (Washington, DC: U.S. Government Printing Office, August 1992), table 5, p. 24. The population universe for the March 1991 and 1990 Current Population Surveys is the estimate of the civilian noninstitutional population in the United States plus members of the Armed Forces in the United States living off post or with their families on post, but excludes all other members of the Armed Forces. Data are estimates based on sample surveys and are subject to sampling variability since they are not based on a complete count of the population. *Notes:* (a) Data for workers age 25 and over. (b) Standard error is higher for Asians than for other groups because the Asian sample population is smaller.

★ 615 ★

Earnings, U.S. Workers
with Less than High School Education, Female

Numbers and percent female Asian/Pacific Islander, white, and total full-time workers[a] with less than a high school education by income range and median earnings, 1990.

Female workers	Total population	Asian/Pacific Islander	White
Female (thousands)	2,653	98	2,036
Total with earnings (thousands)	2,641	98	2,023
Percent	100.0	100.0	100.0
$1 to $2,499 or loss	1.7	4.3	1.5
$2,500 to $4,999	3.1	1.7	2.8
$5,000 to $7,499	8.6	8.7	9.2
$7,500 to $9,999	13.9	18.5	13.1
$10,000 to $12,499	19.4	19.7	19.0
$12,500 to $14,999	13.3	10.2	13.5
$15,000 to $17,499	13.0	7.5	13.7
$17,500 to $19,999	7.4	6.1	6.8
$20,000 to $22,499	6.9	5.6	7.2
$22,500 to $24,999	3.0	2.2	3.0
$25,000 to $27,499	3.3	8.0	3.5
$27,500 to $29,999	1.2	2.5	1.2
$30,000 to $32,499	2.1	2.5	2.2
$32,500 to $34,999	0.5	-	0.6
$35,000 to $37,499	0.8	2.4	0.9
$37,500 to $39,999	0.2	-	0.2
$40,000 to $42,499	0.3	-	0.4
$42,500 to $44,999	0.4	-	0.4
$45,000 to $49,999	0.5	-	0.5
$50,000 to $59,999	0.3	-	0.2
$60,000 to $74,999	0.1	-	0.1
$75,000 and over	0.2	-	0.1
Median earnings (dollars)	$13,148	$12,133	$13,325
Standard error[b] (dollars)	$274	$1,242	$309

Source: Claudette E. Bennett, Economics and Statistics Administration, Bureau of the Census, U.S. Department of Commerce, *The Asian and Pacific Islander Population in the United States: March 1991 and 1990,* Current Population Reports, Population Characteristics, P20-459 (Washington, DC: Government Printing Office, August 1992), table 5, p. 24. The population universe for the March 1991 and 1990 Current Population Surveys is the estimate of the civilian noninstitutional population in the United States plus members of the Armed Forces in the United States living off post or with their families on post, but excludes all other members of the Armed Forces. Data are estimates based on sample surveys and are subject to sampling variability since they are not based on a complete count of the population. *Notes:* (a) Data for workers age 25 and over. (b) Standard error is higher for Asians than for other groups because the Asian sample population is smaller.

★616★

Earnings, U.S. Workers
with Less than High School Education, Male

Numbers and percent of male Asian/Pacific Islander, white, and total full-time workers[a] with less than a high school education by income range and median earnings, 1990.

Male workers	Total population	Asian/Pacific Islander	White
Male (thousands)	5,440	116	4,547
Total with earnings (thousands)	5,440	116	4,547
Percent	100.0	100.0	100.0
$1 to $2,499 or loss	1.7	3.6	1.7
$2,500 to $4,999	1.2	1.1	1.2
$5,000 to $7,499	3.8	-	3.5
$7,500 to $9,999	6.4	6.7	6.2
$10,000 to $12,499	12.4	9.8	11.7
$12,500 to $14,999	7.9	19.1	7.2
$15,000 to $17,499	11.0	12.2	11.4
$17,500 to $19,999	8.1	9.8	7.8
$20,000 to $22,499	9.9	4.7	10.2
$22,500 to $24,999	5.5	4.3	5.6
$25,000 to $27,499	6.5	3.9	7.1
$27,500 to $29,999	3.6	1.3	4..0
$30,000 to $32,499	6.4	5.4	6.8
$32,500 to $34,999	2.6	2.9	2.5
$35,000 to $37,499	3.7	6.5	3.7
$37,500 to $39,999	1.5	2.5	1.4
$40,000 to $42,499	2.2	0.7	2.2
$42,500 to $44,999	0.6	0.5	0.6
$45,000 to $49,999	1.6	1.0	1.9
$50,000 to $59,999	2.0	4.1	1.9
$60,000 to $74,999	0.8	-	0.9
$75,000 and over	0.4	-	0.5
Median earnings (dollars)	$19,199	$16,983	$19,741
Standard error[b] (dollars)	$313	$1,542	$344

Source: Claudette E. Bennett, Economics and Statistics Administration, Bureau of the Census, U.S. Department of Commerce, *The Asian and Pacific Islander Population in the United States: March 1991 and 1990,* Current Population Reports, Population Characteristics, P20-459 (Washington, DC: Government Printing Office, August 1992), table 5, p. 24. The population universe for the March 1991 and 1990 Current Population Surveys is the estimate of the civilian noninstitutional population in the United States plus members of the Armed Forces in the United States living off post or with their families on post, but excludes all other members of the Armed Forces. Data are estimates based on sample surveys and are subject to sampling variability since they are not based on a complete count of the population. *Notes:* (a) Data for workers age 25 and over. (b) Standard error is higher for Asians than for other groups because the Asian sample population is smaller.

★ 617 ★

Earnings, U.S. Workers
with Less than High School Education by Occupation and Sex

Median earnings of Asian/Pacific Islander, white, and total full-time workers[a] with less than a high school education by sex and occupation, 1990.

Occupation of longest job	1990 Earnings in U.S. Dollars					
	Total population		Asian/Pacific Islander		White	
	Male	Female	Male	Female	Male	Female
Executive, administrative, and managerial workers	$28,501	$21,622	(S)	$19,905	$30,166	$20,875
Professional specialty workers	26,797	16,233	-	-	26,411	14,906
Technical and related support workers	27,317	19,835	(S)	(S)	26,383	19,393
Sales workers	18,889	12,759	16,708	8,928	19,199	13,136
Administrative support workers, including clerical	21,341	15,861	24,255	32,514	20,398	15,592
Private household workers	-	7,031	-	-	-	6,540
Protective service workers	15,125	15,281	(S)	-	15,636	15,069
Service workers, except private household	13,409	11,349	13,941	11,974	13,477	11,131
Farming, fishing, and forestry workers	11,568	10,784	30,465	-	11,833	10,784
Precision production, craft, and repair workers	21,874	15,018	15,463	(S)	22,282	15,713
Machine operators, assemblers, and inspectors	19,630	13,359	15,491	11,281	20,018	13,624
Transportation and material moving workers	21,868	12,089	(S)	-	22,174	11,846
Handlers, equipment cleaners, helpers, and laborers	$15,648	$11,673	$14,034	(S)	$16,430	$11,217

Source: Claudette E. Bennett, Economics and Statistics Administration, Bureau of the Census, U.S. Department of Commerce, *The Asian and Pacific Islander Population in the United States: March 1991 and March 1990,* Current Population Reports, Population Characteristics, P20-459 (Washington, DC: U.S. Government Printing Office, August 1992), table 9, p. 41. Data are estimates based on sample surveys and are subject to sampling variability since they are not based on a complete count of the population. A dash represents zero or round to zero. An (S) means that median earnings are not shown when the base is less than or equal to 5,000 persons. *Note:* (a) Data for workers age 25 and over.

★ 618 ★

Earnings, U.S. Workers
with Four Years of High School

Numbers and percent of Asian/Pacific Islander, white, and total full-time workers[a] with four years of high school by income range and median earnings, 1990.

All workers	Total population	Asian/Pacific Islanders	White
Both sexes (thousands)	28,499	554	24,540
Total with earnings (thousands)	28,460	551	24,503
Percent	100.0	100.0	100.0
$1 to $2,499 or loss	1.3	-	1.4
$2,500 to $4,999	0.9	0.2	0.9
$5,000 to $7,499	2.2	2.2	2.1
$7,500 to $9,999	3.9	4.4	3.5
$10,000 to $12,499	8.7	10.5	8.1
$12,500 to $14,999	7.3	11.1	7.1
$15,000 to $17,499	10.7	13.3	10.3
$17,500 to $19,999	7.9	11.4	7.7
$20,000 to $22,499	10.9	12.5	11.0
$22,500 to $24,999	5.6	7.0	5.7
$25,000 to $27,499	8.6	5.2	8.7
$27,500 to $29,999	4.0	2.2	4.2
$30,000 to $32,499	6.8	6.0	6.9
$32,500 to $34,999	2.8	0.9	2.9
$35,000 to $37,499	4.4	3.0	4.6
$37,500 to $39,999	1.9	1.6	2.1
$40,000 to $42,499	3.4	0.7	3.7
$42,500 to $44,999	1.1	-	1.2
$45,000 to $49,999	2.5	1.1	2.7
$50,000 to $59,999	2.8	3.3	3.0
$60,000 to $74,999	1.2	2.1	1.3
$75,000 and over	0.9	1.2	1.0
Median earnings (dollars)	$21,615	$19,288	$22,053
Standard error[b] (dollars)	$102	$700	$109

Source: Claudette E. Bennett, Economics and Statistics Administration, Bureau of the Census, U.S. Department of Commerce, *The Asian and Pacific Islander Population in the United States: March 1991 and 1990,* Current Population Reports, Population Characteristics, P20-459 (Washington, DC: U.S. Government Printing Office, August 1992), table 5, p. 24. The population universe for the March 1991 and 1990 Current Population Surveys is the estimate of the civilian noninstitutional population in the United States plus members of the Armed Forces in the United States living off post or with their families on post, but excludes all other members of the Armed Forces. Data are estimates based on sample surveys and are subject to sampling variability since they are not based on a complete count of the population. *Notes:* (a) Data for workers age 25 and over. (b) Standard error is higher for Asians than for other groups because the Asian sample population is smaller.

★ 619 ★

Earnings, U.S. Workers
with Four Years of High School, Female

Numbers and percent of female Asian/Pacific Islander, white, and total full-time work-ers[a] with four years of high school by income range and median earnings, 1990.

Female workers	Total population	Asian/Pacific Islander	White
Female (thousands)	11,838	241	10,037
Total with earnings (thousands)	11,801	239	10,003
Percent	100.0	100.0	100.0
$1 to $2,499 or loss	1.7	-	1.9
$2,500 to $4,999	1.2	0.5	1.3
$5,000 to $7,499	3.3	2.3	3.1
$7,500 to $9,999	6.1	7.4	5.6
$10,000 to $12,499	13.1	14.1	12.6
$12,500 to $14,999	10.7	15.2	10.6
$15,000 to $17,499	14.5	13.7	14.8
$17,500 to $19,999	9.8	12.1	9.7
$20,000 to $22,499	11.5	10.5	11.8
$22,500 to $24,999	5.8	2.5	6.1
$25,000 to $27,499	7.3	3.7	7.2
$27,500 to $29,999	3.4	3.6	3.4
$30,000 to $32,499	4.3	6.1	4.4
$32,500 to $34,999	1.2	0.3	1.2
$35,000 to $37,499	1.8	1.8	1.8
$37,500 to $39,999	0.9	-	1.0
$40,000 to $42,499	1.1	-	1.1
$42,500 to $44,999	0.4	-	0.4
$45,000 to $49,999	0.8	0.9	0.9
$50,000 to $59,999	0.7	3.0	0.7
$60,000 to $74,999	0.4	2.3	0.4
$75,000 and over	0.2	-	0.2
Median earnings (dollars)	$17,412	$16,918	$17,552
Standard error[b] (dollars)	$127	$906	$169

Source: Claudette E. Bennett, Economics and Statistics Administration, Bureau of the Census, U.S. Depart-ment of Commerce, *The Asian and Pacific Islander Population in the United States: March 1991 and 1990,* Current Population Reports, Population Characteristics, P20-459 (Washington, DC: U.S. Government Print-ing Office, August 1992), table 5, p. 24. The population universe for the March 1991 and 1990 Current Pop-ulation Surveys is the estimate of the civilian noninstitutional population in the United States plus members of the Armed Forces in the United States living off post or with their families on post, but excludes all other members of the Armed Forces. Data are estimates based on sample surveys and are subject to sampling vari-ability since they are not based on a complete count of the population. *Notes:* (a) Data for workers age 25 and over. (b) Standard error is higher for Asians than for other groups because the Asian sample population is smaller.

★ 620 ★

Earnings, U.S. Workers
with Four Years of High School, Male

Numbers and percent of male Asian/Pacific Islander, white, and total full-time work-ers[a] with four years of high school by income range and median earnings, 1990.

Male workers	Total population	Asian/Pacific Islander	White
Male (thousands)	16,661	312	14,503
Total with earnings (thousands)	16,658	312	14,500
Percent	100.0	100.0	100.0
$1 to $2,499 or loss	1.0	-	1.1
$2,500 to $4,999	0.7	-	0.6
$5,000 to $7,499	1.5	2.2	1.4
$7,500 to $9,999	2.4	2.2	2.1
$10,000 to $12,499	5.6	7.7	5.0
$12,500 to $14,999	4.9	8.0	4.6
$15,000 to $17,499	8.1	13.0	7.1
$17,500 to $19,999	6.5	10.9	6.3
$20,000 to $22,499	10.5	14.1	10.5
$22,500 to $24,999	5.5	10.4	5.4
$25,000 to $27,499	9.4	6.3	9.8
$27,500 to $29,999	4.5	1.2	4.7
$30,000 to $32,499	8.5	5.9	8.6
$32,500 to $34,999	3.9	1.3	4.1
$35,000 to $37,499	6.3	3.9	6.6
$37,500 to $39,999	2.6	2.8	2.8
$40,000 to $42,499	5.1	1.2	5.5
$42,500 to $44,999	1.7	-	1.8
$45,000 to $49,999	3.7	1.3	3.9
$50,000 to $59,999	4.3	3.6	4.6
$60,000 to $74,999	1.8	1.9	2.0
$75,000 and over	1.4	2.1	1.6
Median earnings (dollars)	$25,872	$21,063	$26,526
Standard error[b](dollars)	$154	$755	$159

Source: Claudette E. Bennett, Economics and Statistics Administration, Bureau of the Census, U.S. Depart-ment of Commerce,*The Asian and Pacific Islander Population in the United States: March 1991 and 1990,* Current Population Reports, Population Characteristics, P20-459 (Washington, DC: U.S. Government Print-ing Office, August 1992), table 5, p. 24. The population universe for the March 1991 and 1990 Current Pop-ulation Surveys is the estimate of the civilian noninstitutional population in the United States plus members of the Armed Forces in the United States living off post or with their families on post, but excludes all other members of the Armed Forces. Data are estimates based on sample surveys and are subject to sampling vari-ability since they are not based on a complete count of the population. *Notes:* (a) Data for workers age 25 and over. (b) Standard error is higher for Asians than for other groups because the Asian sample population is smaller.

★ 621 ★

Earnings, U.S. Workers
with Four Years of High School by Occupation

Median earnings of Asian/Pacific Islander, white, and total full-time workers with four years of high school by sex and occupation, 1990.

Occupation of longest job	1990 Earnings in U.S. Dollars					
	Total population		Asian/Pacific Islander		White	
	Male	Female	Male	Female	Male	Female
Executive, administrative, and managerial workers	$32,448	$22,058	$21,711	$25,198	$33,074	22,015
Professional specialty workers	33,330	20,543	45,771	31,813	34,640	21,112
Technical and related support workers	30,898	21,250	31,301	(S)	31,299	21,511
Sales workers	26,437	15,553	20,165	14,892	26,669	16,106
Administrative support workers, including clerical	26,682	18,681	19,311	17,832	27,533	18,514
Private household workers	(S)	7.740	-	-	(S)	7,212
Protective service workers	26,086	22,293	(S)	-	27,610	21,375
Service workers, except private household	17,211	1`2,168	20,485	13,774	18,200	12,054
Farming, fishing, and forestry workers	16,395	8,480	18,271	(S)	16,784	7,284
Precision production, craft, and repair workers	27,329	19,348	22,768	18,772	27,601	19,369
Machine operators, assemblers, and inspectors	25,124	15,818	21,387	15,474	26,122	16,007
Transportation and material moving workers	25,916	16,355	28,050	(S)	26,429	16,042
Handlers, equipment cleaners, helpers, and laborers	$21,124	$14,943	$18,117	(S)	$22,189	$15,092

Source: Claudette E. Bennett, Economics and Statistics Administration, Bureau of Census, U.S. Department of Commerce, *The Asian and Pacific Islander Population in the United States: March 1991 and March 1990,* Current Population Reports, Population Characteristics, P20-459 (Washington, DC: U.S. Government Printing Office, August 1992), table 9, p. 41. Data are estimates based on sample surveys and are subject to sampling variability since they are not based on a complete count of the population. A dash (-) represents zero or round to zero. An (S) means that median earnings are not shown when the base is less than or equal to 5,000 persons. *Note:* (a) Data for workers age 25 and over.

★ 622 ★

Earnings, U.S. Workers
with One to Three Years of College

Numbers and percent Asian/Pacific Islander, white, and total full-time workers[a]
with one to three years of college by income range and median earnings, 1990.

All workers	Total population	Asian/ Pacific Islanders	White
Total (thousands)	15,813	325	13,659
Total with earnings (thousands)	15,799	324	13,647
Percent	100.0	100.0	100.0
$1 to $2,499 or loss	0.9	1.7	1.0
$2,500 to $4,999	0.6	0.5	0.6
$5,000 to $7,499	1.3	1.4	1.3
$7,500 to $9,999	1.8	1.7	1.7
$10,000 to $12,499	5.1	6.8	4.7
$12,500 to $14,999	5.0	5.3	4.8
$15,000 to $17,499	7.8	8.5	7.5
$17,500 to $19,999	7.0	7.2	6.5
$20,000 to $22,499	10.0	11.9	9.9
$22,500 to $24,999	5.8	7.3	5.7
$25,000 to $27,499	9.5	10.8	9.3
$27,500 to $29,999	4.8	3.6	4.8
$30,000 to $32,499	8.7	5.3	8.9
$32,500 to $34,999	3.3	2.8	3.4
$35,000 to $37,499	6.2	8.3	6.5
$37,500 to $39,999	2.5	2.7	2.6
$40,000 to $42,499	4.4	5.0	4.7
$42,500 to $44,999	1.6	0.4	1.6
$45,000 to $49,999	3.9	1.8	4.1
$50,000 to $59,999	4.8	4.4	5.2
$60,000 to $74,999	2.7	2.2	2.8
$75,000 and over	2.3	0.3	2.6
Median earnings (dollars)	$26,216	$24,211	$26,737
Standard error[b] (dollars)	$157	$1,320	$173

Source: Claudette E. Bennett, Economics and Statistics Administration, Bureau of the Census, U.S. Department of Commerce, *The Asian and Pacific Islander Population in the United States: March 1991 and 1990,* Current Population Reports, Population Characteristics, P20-459 (Washington, DC: U.S. Government Printing Office, August 1992), table 5, p. 24. The population universe for the March 1991 and 1990 Current Population Surveys is the estimate of the civilian noninstitutional population in the United States plus members of the Armed Forces in the United States living off post or with their families on post, but excludes all other members of the Armed Forces. Data are estimates based on sample surveys and are subject to sampling variability since they are not based on a complete count of the population. *Notes:* (a) Data for workers age 25 and over. (b) Standard error is higher for Asians than for other groups because the Asian sample population is smaller.

★ 623 ★

Earnings, U.S. Workers
with One to Three Years of College, Female

Numbers and percent Asian/Pacific Islander, white, and total full-time workers[a] with one to three years of college by income range and median earnings, 1990.

Female workers	Total population	Asian/Pacific Islander	White
Female (thousands)	6,488	132	5,399
Total with earnings (thousands)	6,474	130	5,387
Percent	100.0	100.0	100.0
$1 to $2,499 or loss	1.1	1.6	1.2
$2,500 to $4,999	0.8	0.6	0.7
$5,000 to $7,499	1.9	0.7	1.9
$7,500 to $9,999	3.0	0.4	3.0
$10,000 to $12,499	7.7	9.4	7.1
$12,500 to $14,999	7.5	6.1	7.4
$15,000 to $17,499	11.8	9.6	11.6
$17,500 to $19,999	9.4	5.6	9.2
$20,000 to $22,499	12.7	18.1	12.6
$22,500 to $24,999	7.2	12.7	7.3
$25,000 to $27,499	10.2	9.0	10.2
$27,500 to $29,999	5.0	3.7	5.0
$30,000 to $32,499	7.2	1.4	7.6
$32,500 to $34,999	2.5	4.0	2.6
$35,000 to $37,499	4.0	5.9	4.2
$37,500 to $39,999	1.1	2.0	1.1
$40,000 to $42,499	2.4	0.8	2.7
$42,500 to $44,999	0.7	-	0.7
$45,000 to $49,999	1.4	1.5	1.4
$50,000 to $59,999	1.2	5.5	1.3
$60,000 to $74,999	0.6	0.7	0.6
$75,000 and over	0.4	0.5	0.3
Median earnings (dollars)	$21,324	$22,198	$21,547
Standard error[b] (dollars)	$183	$1,036	$203

Source: Claudette E. Bennett, Economics and Statistics Administration, Bureau of the Census, U.S. Department of Commerce, *The Asian and Pacific Islander Population in the United States: March 1991 and 1990,* Current Population Reports, Population Characteristics, P20-459 (Washington, DC: U.S. Government Printing Office, August 1992), table 5, p. 24. The population universe for the March 1991 and 1990 Current Population Surveys is the estimate of the civilian noninstitutional population in the United States plus members of the Armed Forces in the United States living off post or with their families on post, but excludes all other members of the Armed Forces. Data are estimates based on sample surveys and are subject to sampling variability since they are not based on a complete count of the population. *Notes:* (a) Data for workers age 25 and over. (b) Standard error is higher for Asians than for other groups because the Asian sample population is smaller.

★ 624 ★

Earnings, U.S. Workers
with One to Three Years of College, Male

Numbers and percent Asian/Pacific Islander, white, and total full-time workers[a] with one to three years of college by income range and median earnings, 1990.

Male workers	Total population	Asian Pacific Islander	White
Male (thousands)	9,324	193	8,260
Total with earnings (thousands)	9,324	193	8,260
Percent	100.0	100.0	100.0
$1 to $2,499 or loss	0.8	1.8	0.9
$2,500 to $4,999	0.4	0.4	0.5
$5,000 to $7,499	0.9	1.9	0.9
$7,500 to $9,999	1.0	2.5	0.9
$10,000 to $12,499	3.3	5.1	3.1
$12,500 to $14,999	3.2	4.7	3.1
$15,000 to $17,499	5.1	7.7	4.8
$17,500 to $19,999	5.3	8.2	4.6
$20,000 to $22,499	8.1	7.8	8.1
$22,500 to $24,999	4.8	3.7	4.6
$25,000 to $27,499	9.0	12.0	8.7
$27,500 to $29,999	4.6	3.6	4.7
$30,000 to $32,499	9.7	8.0	9.7
$32,500 to $34,999	3.8	2.0	3.9
$35,000 to $37,499	7.7	9.9	8.0
$37,500 to $39,999	3.4	3.1	3.5
$40,000 to $42,499	5.8	7.9	5.9
$42,500 to $44,999	2.2	0.6	2.2
$45,000 to $49,999	5.6	2.0	5.9
$50,000 to $59,999	7.3	3.6	7.7
$60,000 to $74,999	4.1	3.3	4.3
$75,000 and over	3.7	0.1	4.1
Median earnings (dollars)	$30,865	$26,292	$31,336
Standard error[b] (dollars)	$200	$1,128	$213

Source: Claudette E. Bennett, Economics and Statistics Administration, Bureau of the Census, U.S. Department of Commerce, *The Asian and Pacific Islander Population in the United States: March 1991 and 1990,* Current Population Reports, Population Characteristics, P20-459 (Washington, DC: U.S. Government Printing Office, August 1992), table 5, p. 24. The population universe for the March 1991 and 1990 Current Population Surveys is the estimate of the civilian noninstitutional population in the United States plus members of the Armed Forces in the United States living off post or with their families on post, but excludes all other members of the Armed Forces. Data are estimates based on sample surveys and are subject to sampling variability since they are not based on a complete count of the population. *Notes:* (a) Data for workers age 25 and over. (b) Standard error is higher for Asians than for other groups because the Asian sample population is smaller.

★ 625 ★

Earnings, U.S. Workers
with Four or More Years of College

Numbers and percent Asian/Pacific Islander, white, and total full-time workers[a] with four or more years of college by income range and median earnings, 1990.

All workers	Total population	Asian/Pacific Islander	White
Total (thousands)	21,188	1,046	18,723
Total with earnings (thousands)	21,177	1,044	18,714
Percent	100.0	100.0	100.0
$1 to $2,499 or loss	0.8	0.6	0.9
$2,500 to $4,999	0.4	0.2	0.5
$5,000 to $7,499	0.6	0.9	0.5
$7,500 to $9,999	1.0	1.4	1.0
$10,000 to $12,499	2.2	4.9	2.0
$12,500 to $14,999	2.0	2.3	2.0
$15,000 to $17,499	3.4	3.9	3.3
$17,500 to $19,999	3.7	3.0	3.8
$20,000 to $22,499	6.2	6.8	6.0
$22,500 to $24,999	4.6	5.3	4.3
$25,000 to $27,499	7.0	7.2	6.9
$27,500 to $29,999	4.6	3.7	4.4
$30,000 to $32,499	7.8	7.9	7.7
$32,500 to $34,999	3.8	2.3	3.9
$35,000 to $37,499	6.6	8.4	6.4
$37,500 to $39,999	3.2	4.5	3.1
$40,000 to $42,499	6.2	5.9	6.3
$42,500 to $44,999	2.2	1.2	2.3
$45,000 to $49,999	6.0	4.9	6.0
$50,000 to $59,999	10.0	8.8	10.4
$60,000 to $74,999	7.2	7.6	7.4
$75,000 and over	10.4	8.2%	11.1
Median earnings (dollars)	$35,646	$34,469	$36,134
Standard error[b] (dollars)	$195	$1,612	$214

Source: Claudette E. Bennett, Economics and Statistics Administration, Bureau of the Census, U.S. Department of Commerce, *The Asian and Pacific Islander Population in the United States: March 1991 and 1990,* Current Population Reports, Population Characteristics, P20-459 (Washington, DC: U.S. Government Printing Office, August 1992), table 5, p. 24. The population universe for the March 1991 and 1990 Current Population Surveys is the estimate of the civilian noninstitutional population in the United States plus members of the Armed Forces in the United States living off post or with their families on post, but excludes all other members of the Armed Forces. Data are estimates based on sample surveys and are subject to sampling variability since they are not based on a complete count of the population. *Notes:* (a) Data for workers age 25 and over. (b) Standard error is higher for Asians than for other groups because the Asian sample population is smaller.

★ 626 ★

Earnings, U.S. Workers
with Four or More Years of College, Female

Numbers and percent of female Asian/Pacific Islander, white, and total full-time workers[a] with four or more years of college by income range and median earnings, 1990.

Worker	Total population	Asian/ Pacific Islander	White
Female (thousands)	7,672	415	6,547
Total with earnings (thousands)	7,662	414	6,538
Percent	100.0	100.0	100.0
$1 to $2,499 or loss	0.8	1.1	0.9
$2,500 to $4,999	0.5	0.3	0.5
$5,000 to $7,499	0.5	0.9	0.5
$7,500 to $9,999	1.4	1.3	1.4
$10,000 to $12,499	2.7	6.8	2.6
$12,500 to $14,999	2.9	2.2	2.9
$15,000 to $17,499	5.5	7.1	5.4
$17,500 to $19,999	5.8	3.9	6.1
$20,000 to $22,499	9.6	9.2	9.5
$22,500 to $24,999	7.2	7.0	7.1
$25,000 to $27,499	9.1	7.4	8.9
$27,500 to $29,999	6.6	3.9	6.6
$30,000 to $32,499	9.4	10.3	9.1
$32,500 to $34,999	4.7	2.9	4.9
$35,000 to $37,499	7.3	8.0	7.1
$37,500 to $39,999	3.4	3.8	3.3
$40,000 to $42,499	5.8	5.9	6.0
$42,500 to $44,999	1.9	1.0	2.0
$45,000 to $49,999	4.4	4.3	4.5
$50,000 to $59,999	5.3	5.0	5.4
$60,000 to $74,999	2.6	3.5	2.6
$75,000 and over	2.6	3.9	2.7
Median earnings (dollars)	$28,992	$29,149	$29,109
Standard error[b] (dollars)	$323	$1,720	$352

Source: Claudette E. Bennett, Economics and Statistics Administration, Bureau of the Census, U.S. Department of Commerce, *The Asian and Pacific Islander Population in the United States: March 1991 and 1990,* Current Population Reports, Population Characteristics, P20-459 (Washington, DC: U.S. Government Printing Office, August 1992), table 5, p. 24. The population universe for the March 1991 and 1990 Current Population Surveys is the estimate of the civilian noninstitutional population in the United States plus members of the Armed Forces in the United States living off post or with their families on post, but excludes all other members of the Armed Forces. Data are estimates based on sample surveys and are subject to sampling variability since they are not based on a complete count of the population. *Notes:* (a) Data for workers age 25 and over. (b) Standard error is higher for Asians than for other groups because the Asian sample population is smaller.

★ 627 ★

Earnings, U.S. Workers
with Four or More Years of College, Male

Numbers and percent of male Asian/Pacific Islander, white, and total full-time work-ers[a] with four or more years of college by income range and median earnings, 1990.

Male workers	Total population	Asian Pacific Islander	White
Male (thousands)	13,516	630	12,176
Total with earnings (thousands)	13,516	630	12,176
Percent	100.0	100.0	100.0
$1 to $2,499 or loss	0.8	0.3	0.9
$2,500 to $4,999	0.4	0.1	0.4
$5,000 to $7,499	0.7	0.9	0.6
$7,500 to $9,999	0.8	1.5	0.8
$10,000 to $12,499	1.9	3.6	1.7
$12,500 to $14,999	1.6	2.4	1.5
$15,000 to $17,499	2.2	1.7	2.2
$17,500 to $19,999	2.5	2.5	2.5
$20,000 to $22,499	4.2	5.1	4.1
$22,500 to $24,999	3.1	4.2	2.9
$25,000 to $27,499	5.9	7.1	5.8
$27,500 to $29,999	3.4	3.6	3.2
$30,000 to $32,499	7.0	6.3	6.9
$32,500 to $34,999	3.3	1.8	3.4
$35,000 to $37,499	6.3	8.7	6.0
$37,500 to $39,999	3.0	5.0	2.9
$40,000 to $42,499	6.4	5.9	6.4
$42,500 to $44,999	2.3	1.4	2.4
$45,000 to $49,999	6.9	5.3	6.8
$50,000 to $59,999	12.7	11.4	13.1
$60,000 to $74,999	9.8	10.2	9.9
$75,000 and over	14.8	10.9	15.5
Median earnings (dollars)	$41,131	$37,547	$41,661
Standard error[b] (dollars)	$252	$1,189	$265

Source: Claudette E. Bennett, Economics and Statistics Administration, Bureau of the Census, U.S. Depart-ment of Commerce, *The Asian and Pacific Islander Population in the United States: March 1991 and 1990,* Current Population Reports, Population Characteristics, P20-459 (Washington, DC: U.S. Government Print-ing Office, August 1992), table 5, p. 24. The population universe for the March 1991 and 1990 Current Pop-ulation Surveys is the estimate of the civilian noninstitutional population in the United States plus members of the Armed Forces in the United States living off post or with their families on post, but excludes all other members of the Armed Forces. Data are estimates based on sample surveys and are subject to sampling vari-ability since they are not based on a complete count of the population. *Notes:* (a) Data for workers age 25 and over. (b) Standard error is higher for Asians than for other groups because the Asian sample population is smaller.

★ 628 ★

Earnings, Asian/Pacific Islander Full-time Workers by Years of School Completed
Numbers and percent Asian/Pacific Islander full-time workers[a] by years of school completed by income range and median earnings, 1990.

United States	Years of school completed				
	Total	Less than high school	4 years of high school	1 to 3 years of college	4 or more years of college
Total (thousands)	2,163	213	554	325	1,046
Total with earnings (thousands)	2,157	213	551	324	1,044
Percent	100.0	100.0	100.0	100.0	100.0
$1 to $2,499 or loss	0.9	3.9	-	1.7	0.6
$2,500 to $4,999	0.4	1.4	0.2	0.5	0.2
$5,000 to $7,499	1.6	4.0	2.2	1.4	0.9
$7,500 to $9,999	3.4	12.1	4.4	1.7	1.4
$10,000 to $12,499	7.8	14.3	10.5	6.8	4.9
$12,500 to $14,999	6.4	15.0	11.1	5.3	2.3
$15,000 to $17,499	7.7	10.1	13.3	8.5	3.9
$17,500 to $19,999	6.5	8.1	11.4	7.2	3.0
$20,000 to $22,499	8.9	5.1	12.5	11.9	6.8
$22,500 to $24,999	5.8	3.3	7.0	7.3	5.3
$25,000 to $27,499	7.0	5.8	5.2	10.8	7.2
$27,500 to $29,999	3.1	1.8	2.2	3.6	3.7
$30,000 to $32,499	6.6	4.1	6.0	5.3	7.9
$32,500 to $34,999	1.9	1.6	0.9	2.8	2.3
$35,000 to $37,499	6.5	4.6	3.0	8.3	8.4
$37,500 to $39,999	3.1	1.4	1.6	2.7	4.5
$40,000 to $42,499	3.8	0.4	0.7	5.0	5.9
$42,500 to $44,999	0.7	0.3	-	0.4	1.2
$45,000 to $49,999	3.0	0.5	1.1	1.8	4.9
$50,000 to $59,999	6.0	2.2	3.3	4.4	8.8
$60,000 to $74,999	4.5	-	2.1	2.2	7.6
$75,000 and over	4.3	-	1.2	0.3	8.2
Median earnings (dollars)	$25,193	$14,876	$19,288	$24,211	$34,469
Standard error[b] (dollars)	$616	$1,035	$700	$1,320	$1,612

Source: Claudette E. Bennett, Economics and Statistics Administration, Bureau of the Census, U.S. Department of Commerce, *The Asian and Pacific Islander Population in the United States: March 1991 and 1990,* Current Population Reports, Population Characteristics, P20-459 (Washington, DC: U.S. Government Printing Office, August 1992), table 5, p. 24. The population universe for the March 1991 and 1990 Current Population Surveys is the estimate of the civilian noninstitutional population in the United States plus members of the Armed Forces in the United States living off post or with their families on post, but excludes all other members of the Armed Forces. Data are estimates based on sample surveys and are subject to sampling variability since they are not based on a complete count of the population. *Notes:* (a) Data for workers age 25 and over. (b) Standard error is higher for Asians than for other groups because the Asian sample population is smaller.

★ 629 ★

Earnings, Asian/Pacific Islander Full-time Workers by Years of School Completed, Female

Percent of female Asian/Pacific Islander full-time workers[a] by years of school completed by income range and median earnings, 1990.

Female workers	Years of school completed				
	Total	Less than high school	4 years of high schol	1 to 3 years of college	4 or more years of college
Female (thousands)	895	98	241	132	415
Total with earnings (thousands)	889	98	239	130	414
Percent	100.0	100.0	100.0	100.0	100.0
$1 to $2,499 or loss	1.2	4.3	-	1.6	1.1
$2,500 to $4,999	0.6	1.7	0.5	0.6	0.3
$5,000 to $7,499	2.1	8.7	2.3	0.7	0.9
$7,500 to $9,999	4.9	18.5	7.4	0.4	1.3
$10,000 to $12,499	10.6	19.7	14.1	9.4	6.8
$12,500 to $14,999	7.5	10.2	15.2	6.1	2.2
$15,000 to $17,499	9.5	7.5	13.7	9.6	7.1
$17,500 to $19,999	6.6	6.1	12.1	5.6	3.9
$20,000 to $22,499	10.4	5.6	10.5	18.1	9.2
$22,500 to $24,999	6.1	2.2	2.5	12.7	7.0
$25,000 to $27,499	6.6	8.0	3.7	9.0	7.4
$27,500 to $29,999	3.6	2.5	3.6	3.7	3.9
$30,000 to $32,499	6.9	2.5	6.1	1.4	10.3
$32,500 to $34,999	2.0	-	0.3	4.0	2.9
$35,000 to $37,499	5.3	2.4	1.8	5.9	8.0
$37,500 to $39,999	2.1	-	-	2.0	3.8
$40,000 to $42,499	2.9	-	-	0.8	5.9
$42,500 to $44,999	0.5	-	-	-	1.0
$45,000 to $49,999	2.5	-	0.9	1.5	4.3
$50,000 to $59,999	3.9	-	3.0	5.5	5.0
$60,000 to $74,999	2.4	-	2.3	0.7	3.5
$75,000 and over	1.9	-	-	0.5	3.9
Median earnings (dollars)	$21,691	$12,133	$16,918	$22,198	$29,149
Standard error[b] (dollars)	$606	$1,242	$906	$1,036	$1,720

Source: Claudette E. Bennett, Economics and Statistics Administration, Bureau of the Census, U.S. Department of Commerce, *The Asian and Pacific Islander Population in the United States: March 1991 and 1990,* Current Population Reports, Population Characteristics, P20-459 (Washington, DC: U.S. Government Printing Office, August 1992), table 5, p. 24. The population universe for the March 1991 and 1990 Current Population Surveys is the estimate of the civilian noninstitutional population in the United States plus members of the Armed Forces in the United States living off post or with their families on post, but excludes all other members of the Armed Forces. Data are estimates based on sample surveys and are subject to sampling variability since they are not based on a complete count of the population. *Notes:* (a) Data for workers age 25 and over. (b) Standard error is higher for Asians than for other groups because the Asian sample population is smaller.

★ 630 ★

Earnings, Asian/Pacific Islander full-time Workers by Years of School Completed, Male

Percent of male Asian/Pacific Islander full-time workers[a] by years of school completed by income range and median earnings, 1990.

Male workers	Years of school completed				
	Total	Less than high school	4 years of high school	1 to 3 years of college	4 or more years of college
Male (thousands)	1,268	116	312	193	630
Total with earnings (thousands)	1,268	116	312	193	630
Percent	100.0	100.0	100.0	100.0	100.0
$1 to $2,499 or loss	0.7	3.6%	-	1.8	0.3
$2,500 to $4,999	0.2	1.1	-	0.4	0.1
$5,000 to $7,499	1.3	-	2.2	1.9	0.9
$7,500 to $9,999	2.3	6.7	2.2	2.5	1.5
$10,000 to $12,499	5.8	9.8	7.7	5.1	3.6
$12,500 to $14,999	5.6	19.1	8.0	4.7	2.4
$15,000 to $17,499	6.5	12.2	13.0	7.7	1.7
$17,500 to $19,999	6.4	9.8	10.9	8.2	2.5
$20,000 to $22,499	7.9	4.7	14.1	7.8	5.1
$22,500 to $24,999	5.7	4.3	10.4	3.7	4.2
$25,000 to $27,499	7.3	3.9	6.3	12.0	7.1
$27,500 to $29,999	2.7	1.3	1.2	3.6	3.6
$30,000 to $32,499	6.3	5.4	5.9	8.0	6.3
$32,500 to $34,999	1.8	2.9	1.3	2.0	1.8
$35,000 to $37,499	7.4	6.5	3.9	9.9	8.7
$37,500 to $39,999	3.9	2.5	2.8	3.1	5.0
$40,000 to $42,499	4.5	0.7	1.2	7.9	5.9
$42,500 to $44,999	0.8	0.5	-	0.6	1.4
$45,000 to $49,999	3.3	1.0	1.3	2.0	5.3
$50,000 to $59,999	7.5	4.1	3.6	3.6	11.4
$60,000 to $74,999	6.0	-	1.9	3.3	10.2
$75,000 and over	6.0	-	2.1	0.1	10.9
Median earnings (dollars)	$27,741	$16,983	$21,063	$26,292	$37,547
Standard error[b] (dollars)	$1,396	$1,542	$755	$1,128	$1,189

Source: Claudette E. Bennett, Economics and Statistics Administration, Bureau of the Census, U.S. Department of Commerce, *The Asian and Pacific Islander Population in the United States: March 1991 and 1990,* Current Population Reports, Population Characteristics, P20-459 (Washington, DC: U.S. Government Printing Office, August 1992), table 5, p. 24. The population universe for the March 1991 and 1990 Current Population Surveys is the estimate of the civilian noninstitutional population in the United States plus members of the Armed Forces in the United States living off post or with their families on post, but excludes all other members of the Armed Forces. Data are estimates based on sample surveys and are subject to sampling variability since they are not based on a complete count of the population. *Notes:* (a) Data for workers age 25 and over. (b) Standard error is higher for Asians than for other groups because the Asian sample population is smaller.

★ 631 ★

Median Earnings, U.S. Workers by Education and Sex

Median earnings in U.S. dollars for Asian/Pacific Islander, white, and total workers[a] by education and sex 1990.

Gender/education level achieved	Median Earnings		
	Tota population	Asian/Pacific Islander	White
All	$25,511	$25,193	$26,083
Male	29,987	27,741	30,598
Female	20,556	21,691	20,759
Less than high school education			
All	$16,698	$14,876	$17,054
Male	19,199	16,983	19,741
Female	13,148	12,133	13,325
4 years of high school			
All	$21,615	$19,288	$22,053
Male	25,872	21,063	26,526
Female	17,412	16,918	17,552
1 to 3 years of college			
All	$26,216	$24,211	$26,737
Male	30,865	26,292	31,336
Female	21,324	22,198	21,547
4 or more years of college			
All	$35,646	$34,469	$36,134
Male	41,131	37,547	41,661
Female	28,992	29,149	29,109

Source: Claudette E. Bennett, Economics and Statistics Administration, Bureau of the Census, U.S. Department of Commerce, *The Asian and Pacific Islander Population in the United States: March 1991 and 1990,* Current Population Reports, Population Characteristics, P20-459 (Washington, DC: U.S. Government Printing Office, August 1992), table 5, p. 24. The population universe for the March 1991 and 1990 Current Population Surveys is the estimate of the civilian noninstitutional population in the United States plus members of the Armed Forces in the United States living off post or with their families on post, but excludes all other members of the Armed Forces. Data are estimates based on sample surveys and are subject to sampling variability since they are not based on a complete count of the population. *Note:* (a) Data for workers age 25 and over.

★ 632 ★

Household Income

Numbers and percent of Asian/Pacific Islander, white, and total families[a] by income range and median income, March 1991.

Total United States	All families		
	Total population	Asian/Pacific Islander	White
Total United States			
Total (thousands)	66,322	1,536	56,803
Percent	100.0	100.0	100.0
Under $5,000	3.6	3.9	2.5
$5,000 to $9,999	5.8	4.6	4.7
$10,000 to $14,999	7.5	5.7	7.0
$15,000 to $19,999	7.9	7.0	7.6
$20,000 to $24,999	8.5	5.5	8.4
$25,000 to $34,999	16.2	12.8	16.5
$35,000 to $49,999	20.1	19.7	20.8
$50,000 to $59,999	9.3	9.1	9.8
$60,000 to $74,999	8.9	12.5	9.5
$75,000 and over	12.3	19.2	13.2
Median income (dollars)	$35,353	$42,245	$36,915
Standard error[b] (dollars)	$168	$1,571	$178
Total, Western United States			
Total (thousands)	13,474	917	11,806
Percent	100.0	100.0	100.0
Under $5,000	2.6	4.3	2.3
$5,000 to $9,999	5.5	4.1	5.1
$10,000 to $14,999	7.3	5.7	7.1
$15,000 to $19,999	7.5	6.3	7.4
$20,000 to $24,999	8.2	5.4	8.5
$25,000 to $34,999	16.2	12.5	16.5
$35,000 to $49,000	19.7	19.0	20.1
$50,000 to $59,999	9.1	8.3	9.4
$60,000 to $74,999	9.5	13.7	9.2
$75,000 and over	14.4	20.8	14.2
Median income (dollars)	$36,687	$43,538	$36,837
Standard error (dollars)	$397	$2,443	$427

Source: Claudette E. Bennett, Economics and Statistics Administration, Bureau of the Census, U.S. Department of Commerce, *The Asian and Pacific Islander Population in the United States: March 1991 and 1990,* Current Population Reports, Population Characteristics, P20-459 (Washington, DC: U.S. Government Printing Office, August 1992), table 9, p. 41. *Notes:* (a) Data for workers age 25 and over. (b) Standard error is higher for Asians than for other groups because the Asian sample population is smaller.

★ 633 ★

Income, Married Couple Families, Total and Western United States

Numbers and percent of Asian/Pacific Islander, white, and total married couple families[a] by income range and median income, March 1991.

Total money income and region	Total population	Asian/Pacific Islander	White
Total United States			
Total (thousands)	52,147	1,230	47,014
Percent	100.0	100.0	100.0
Under $5,000	1.3	3.2	1.2
$5,000 to $9,999	3.3	2.4	3.0
$10,000 to $14,999	6.0	5.1	5.8
$15,000 to $19,999	7.0	7.1	6.9
$20,000 to $24,999	8.1	4.5	8.0
$25,000 to $34,999	16.4	11.5	16.6
$35,000 to $49,999	22.0	20.4	22.0
$50,000 to $59,999	10.7	10.2	10.8
$60,000 to $74,999	10.5	14.1	10.6
$75,000 and over	14.8	21.4	15.2
Median income (dollars)	$39,895	$46,495	$40,331
Standard error[b] (dollars)	$208	$1,753	$211
Western U.S.			
Total (thousands)	10,645	716	9,545
Percent	100.0	100.0	100.0
Under $5,000	1.5	2.9	1.4
$5,000 to $9,999	2.9	2.5	2.9
$10,000 to $14,999	5.8	5.4	5.8
$15,000 to $19,999	7.0	7.0	6.9
$20,000 to $24,999	7.7	4.1	8.1
$25,000 to $34,999	15.9	10.0	16.4
$35,000 to $49,000	21.0	19.7	21.2
$50,000 to $59,999	10.4	9.5	10.4
$60,000 to $74,999	10.7	15.3	10.3
$75,000 and over	17.1	23.6	16.6
Median income (dollars)	$41,051	$48,539	$40,618
Standard error (dollars)	$548	$3,034	$583

Source: Claudette E. Bennett, Economics and Statistics Administration, Bureau of the Census, U.S. Department of Commerce, *The Asian and Pacific Islander Population in the United States: March 1991 and 1990,* Current Population Reports, Population Characteristics, P20-459 (Washington, DC: U.S. Government Printing Office, August 1992), table 9, p. 41. *Notes:* (a) Data for workers age 25 and over. (b) Standard error is higher for Asians than for other groups because the Asian sample population is smaller.

★ 634 ★

Income, Single Householder Families, Total and Western United States

Numbers and percent of Asian/Pacific Islander, white, and total single householder families[a] by income range and median income, March 1991.

Total money income and region	Total population		Asian/ Pacific Islander		White	
	Female householder, no spouse present	Male householder, no spouse present	Female householder, no spouse present	Male householder, no spouse present	Female householder, no spouse present	Male householder, no spouse present
Total, United States						
Total (thousands)	11,268	2,907	194	112	7,512	2,276
Percent	100.0	100.0	100.0	100.0	100.0	100.0
Under $5,000	13.9	4.3	4.9	10.2	10.5	3.4
$5,000 to $9,999	17.1	7.9	17.4	5.7	14.8	6.9
$10,000 to $14,999	14.0	9.6	11.1	2.8	13.8	9.3
$15,000 to $19,999	11.4	10.3	8.5	3.4	11.8	10.1
$20,000 to $24,999	10.0	9.9	11.7	5.8	10.5	10.0
$25,000 to $34,999	14.5	18.4	20.7	13.9	15.8	18.0
$35,000 to $49,999	11.2	20.1	12.0	25.4	13.0	20.7
$50,000 to $59,999	3.2	7.1	1.6	9.2	4.0	8.1
$60,000 to $74,999	2.6	6.1	5.7	6.6	3.2	6.8
$75,000 and over	2.2	6.4	6.6	17.0	2.6%	6.8
Median income (dollars)	$16,932	$29,046	$22,587	$41,742	$19,528	$30,570
Standard error[b](dollars)	$257	$791	$2,394	$5,466	$399	$769
Total, Western U.S.						
Total (thousands)	2,084	745	126	76	1,644	618
Percent	100.0	100.0	100.0	100.0	100.0	100.0
Under $5,000	8.1	3.9	7.0	12.9	7.7	2.3
$5,000 to $9,999	17.4	9.1	13.4	3.5	16.5	9.1
$10,000 to $14,999	14.4	8.0	8.2	4.1	14.6	8.1
$15,000 to $19,999	9.9	8.6	6.0	-	9.8	9.8
$20,000 to $24,999	10.2	9.6	11.0	8.0	10.6	10.0
$25,000 to $34,999	15.5	21.8	23.6	17.5	15.2	22.1
$35,000 to $49,000	14.3	17.0	14.4	20.0	14.7	17.2
$50,000 to $59,999	4.0	5.8	2.5	6.6	4.5	6.2
$60,000 to $74,999	3.5	8.3	7.0	9.8	3.6	7.8
$75,000 and over	2.8	8.1	6.9	17.7%	2.7	7.5
Median income (dollars)	$20,087	$30.139	$26,294	$39,524	$20,527	$29,813
Standard error (dollars)	$800	$1,550	$4,030	$7,236	$862	$1,594

Source: Claudette E. Bennett, Economics and Statistics Administration, Bureau of the Census, U.S. Department of Commerce, *The Asian and Pacific Islander Population in the United States: March 1991 and 1990,* Current Population Reports, Population Characteristics, P20-459 (Washington, DC: U.S. Government Printing Office, August 1992), table 9, p. 41. *Notes:* (a) Data for workers age 25 and over. (b) Standard error is higher for Asians than for other groups because the Asian sample population is smaller.

★ 635 ★

Income: Asian/Pacific Islander Families, Total and Western United States

Numbers and percent of Asian/Pacific Islander families[a] by type by income range and median income, 1991.

Total money income and region	Asian/ Pacific Islander			
	All families	Married couple families	Female householder, no spouse present	Male householder, no spouse present
Total, United States				
Total (thousands)	1,536	1,230	194	112
Percent	100.0	100.0	100.0	100.0
Under $5,000	3.9	3.2	4.9	10.2
$5,000 to $9,999	4.6	2.4	17.4	5.7
$10,000 to $14,999	5.7	5.1	11.1	2.8
$15,000 to $19,999	7.0	7.1	8.5	3.4
$20,000 to $24,999	5.5	4.5	11.7	5.8
$25,000 to $34,999	12.8	11.5	20.7	13.9
$35,000 to $49,999	19.7	20.4	12.0	25.4
$50,000 to $59,999	9.1	10.2	1.6	9.2
$60,000 to $74,999	12.5	14.1	5.7	6.6
$75,000 and over	19.2	21.4	6.6	17.0
Median income (dollars)	$42,245	$46,495	$22,587	$41,742
Standard[b] error (dollars)	$1,571	$1,753	$2,394	$5,466
Total, Western U.S.				
Total (thousands)	917	716	126	76
Percent	100.0	100.0	100.0	100.0
Under $5,000	4.3	2.9	7.0	12.9
$5,000 to $9,999	4.1	2.5	13.4	3.5
$10,000 to $14,999	5.7	5.4	8.2	4.1
$15,000 to $19,999	6.3	7.0	6.0	-
$20,000 to $24,999	5.4	4.1	11.0	8.0
$25,000 to $34,999	12.5	10.0	23.6	17.5
$35,000 to $49,000	19.0	19.7	14.4	20.0
$50,000 to $59,999	8.3	9.5	2.5	6.6
$60,000 to $74,999	13.7	15.3	7.0	9.8
$75,000 and over	20.8	23.6	6.9	17.7
Median income (dollars)	$43,538	$48,539	$26,294	$39,524
Standard error (dollars)	$2,443	$3,034	$4,030	$7,236

Source: Claudette E. Bennett, Economics and Statistics Administration, Bureau of the Census, U.S. Department of Commerce, *The Asian and Pacific Islander Population in the United States: March 1991 and 1990,* Current Population Reports, Population Characteristics, P20-459 (Washington, DC: U.S. Government Printing Office, August 1992), table 9, p. 41. *Notes:* (a) Data for workers age 25 and over. (b) Standard error is higher for Asians than for other groups because the Asian sample population is smaller.

★ 636 ★

Aggregate Household Income in 1989 by Race

State	Asian or Pacific Islander	White	Black	American Indian, Eskimo, or Aleut	Other race
Alabama	218,371,076	39,059,383,730	6,436,245,484	152,338,892	42,155,591
Alaska	209,509,632	8,118,722,569	268,024,690	735,246,665	75,134,789
Arizona	591,090,668	43,874,321,730	999,747,565	951,252,601	2,183,907,074
Arkansas	106,477,451	22,094,202,081	2,049,982,861	118,274,452	42,831,818
California	37,582,328,962	386,859,100,036	24,629,824,287	2,924,325,513	28,958,254,648
Colorado	595,637,793	44,728,577,466	1,349,421,242	236,029,627	1,287,498,243
Connecticut	851,504,339	60,792,615,290	3,078,437,012	90,383,262	713,803,386
Delaware	133,018,055	9,109,912,851	1,066,201,694	31,945,296	56,990,472
Florida	1,733,734,664	170,779,656,281	12,793,695,592	458,567,746	1,874,374,732
Georgia	870,837,634	72,144,590,362	13,616,540,450	170,185,192	312,261,856
Hawaii	9,867,544,539	6,761,105,474	236,483,529	60,974,350	187,911,354
Idaho	82,873,611	11,030,646,222	30,682,763	100,951,425	159,492,632
Illinois	4,066,754,274	149,052,604,725	14,704,864,025	282,887,548	3,517,616,020
Indiana	547,107,133	67,289,012,596	3,658,884,325	142,683,204	329,572,682
Kansas	301,038,746	30,371,035,873	1,130,938,842	198,030,561	345,412,817
Kentucky	221,652,896	38,300,713,564	1,883,166,852	56,693,568	34,719,864
Louisiana	335,156,537	36,381,857,302	7,186,658,988	143,060,350	173,737,662
Maine	58,464,622	15,484,622,886	46,966,529	50,727,146	9,962,821
Maryland	2,159,684,295	66,604,843,497	14,412,303,324	195,039,602	430,124,035
Massachusetts	1,685,083,076	96,122,679,051	3,101,335,020	137,772,885	1,010,963,635
Michigan	1,467,975,409	115,999,469,168	11,658,522,240	527,835,653	681,507,771
Minnesota	578,881,713	60,360,890,526	790,615,739	315,465,984	145,144,673
Montana	28,090,807	8,513,251,353	14,333,033	252,777,777	22,518,167
Nevada	403,626,180	16,290,996,054	720,778,895	193,558,719	442,014,806
New Hampshire	114,038,333	17,224,651,961	87,330,806	29,521,161	29,352,325
New Jersey	4,716,045,074	124,213,991,642	11,624,578,798	199,313,974	2,430,848,727
New Mexico	135,173,434	14,436,694,107	248,102,898	676,933,931	1,364,907,427
New York	9,549,481,968	246,396,060,966	29,093,790,228	568,809,009	7,110,701,721
North Carolina	506,363,657	71,203,365,458	11,119,364,261	654,325,856	190,767,071
North Dakota	26,177,320	6,742,599,138	24,350,239	116,393,656	9,406,710
Ohio	1,425,971,834	132,589,668,720	9,821,291,618	219,344,475	431,398,863
Oklahoma	307,565,143	32,812,372,995	1,653,615,797	1,836,492,640	257,721,564
Oregon	659,287,426	35,985,915,914	361,967,982	344,777,756	298,737,569
Pennsylvania	1,693,800,939	152,662,536,142	9,619,644,490	174,358,895	667,493,221
Rhode Island	149,554,668	14,090,700,043	323,781,121	35,952,101	171,869,737
South Carolina	191,967,571	33,346,452,199	6,851,540,398	92,643,421	67,804,343
South Dakota	19,038,797	7,055,384,322	23,055,687	190,987,620	10,830,806
Tennessee	347,440,659	52,891,759,502	5,628,633,998	125,100,602	66,842,919
Texas	3,604,511,878	185,260,044,524	15,922,042,948	784,187,305	10,963,697,788
Utah	262,556,378	18,094,594,168	92,663,860	122,350,432	267,785,991
Vermont	26,157,373	7,405,122,714	20,484,063	19,398,352	4,904,745
Virginia	2,098,424,109	82,147,367,506	10,586,660,875	219,732,851	552,640,689
Washington	2,221,117,664	66,468,035,242	1,458,585,797	687,021,706	729,208,756
West Virginia	168,653,154	18,079,861,859	398,409,214	19,727,484	8,195,658
Wisconsin	404,401,384	61,569,296,601	1,676,653,873	264,578,705	263,056,956
Wyoming	17,169,055	5,345,064,048	23,639,645	54,456,557	84,721,279

Source: Asian/Pacific Islander Data Consortium (San Francisco, CA: Asian and Pacific Islander Center for Census Information and Services, 1993). Primary source: U.S. Census Bureau, Summary Tape Files 1 and 3.

★ 637 ★

Per Capita Income[a] in 1989 by Race

State	Asian Pacific Islander	White	Black	American Indian, Eskimo, or Aleut	Other race
Alabama	10,814	13,235	6,473	8,390	8,285
Alaska	13,113	19,903	12,816	9,140	12,601
Arizona	11,713	14,964	9,688	4,878	6,789
Arkansas	9,875	11,472	5,729	8,643	6,587
California	13,733	19,028	11,578	11,809	7,594
Colorado	10,826	15,544	10,704	9,111	7,791
Connecticut	18,174	21,466	11,695	13,657	7,726
Delaware	16,379	17,263	9,683	14,404	7,624
Florida	12,514	16,052	7,550	11,090	8,102
Georgia	12,758	15,832	7,997	11,745	8,479
Hawaii	14,616	18,598	10,607	12,415	10,667
Idaho	9,809	11,723	8,785	6,843	5,826
Illinois	14,710	16,817	8,922	11,495	7,508
Indiana	15,948	13,553	8,739	9,898	8,498
Kansas	10,528	13,817	8,445	8,767	7,501
Kentucky	13,652	11,439	7,460	8,212	6,853
Louisiana	8,899	12,956	5,687	7,073	9,415
Maine	10,414	13,019	10,089	7,840	7,643
Maryland	16,264	19,789	12,343	13,987	10,174
Massachusetts	12,665	18,003	10,867	11,176	6,797
Michigan	14,950	15,071	9,195	9,252	8,078
Minnesota	8,057	14,765	8,714	6,732	7,171
Montana	8,443	11,634	7,657	5,422	6,629
Nevada	11,973	16,241	9,366	9,818	8,526
New Hampshire	13,881	16,028	12,577	11,887	9,079
New Jersey	17,913	20,406	11,542	14,423	8,956
New Mexico	10,655	12,678	8,579	5,141	7,320
New York	14,247	18,584	10,566	10,202	7,342
North Carolina	11,127	14,450	7,926	8,097	7,974
North Dakota	9,281	11,359	7,875	4,755	5,356
Ohio	16,703	14,049	8,702	10,053	7,878
Oklahoma	10,435	12,859	7,356	7,227	6,466
Oregon	10,734	13,778	8,240	8,890	6,506
Pennsylvania	13,210	14,688	9,140	10,546	5,772
Rhode Island	9,325	15,573	9,031	9,015	7,129
South Carolina	11,391	14,115	6,800	10,288	10,187
South Dakota	7,040	11,230	8,124	4,040	6,211
Tennessee	11,918	13,201	7,414	10,231	8,630
Texas	12,029	14,629	8,102	11,086	6,239
Utah	8,284	11,274	8,385	5,125	7,415
Vermont	9,667	13,597	8,991	8,077	7,235
Virginia	14,022	17,361	9,439	14,049	10,249
Washington	11,584	15,564	10,440	8,862	6,891
West Virginia	23,658	10,574	7,416	6,508	5,425
Wisconsin	8,128	13,793	7,021	6,878	6,449
Wyoming	8,057	12,629	8,490	5,439	8,118

Source: Asian/Pacific Islander Data Consortium (San Francisco, CA: Asian and Pacific Islander Center for Census Information and Services, 1993). Primary source: U.S. Census Bureau, Summary Tape Files 1 and 3. *Note:* (a) Calculated by dividing the aggregate household income by the total population.

★ 638 ★

Income, Household by State

Median household income by race/ethnicity, by state, 1989.

State	Total	Asian	White	Black
United States	$30,056	$36,784	$31,435	$19,758
Alabama	23,597	27,610	26,792	13,997
Alaska	41,408	35,056	44,998	31,474
Arizona	27,540	28,204	29,245	20,564
Arkansas	21,147	24,609	22,550	12,128
California	35,798	39,769	37,724	26,079
Colorado	30,140	28,125	31,024	21,676
Connecticut	41,721	48,560	43,407	28,011
Delaware	34,875	41,526	36,660	24,286
District of Columbia	30,727	30,141	45,991	24,576
Florida	27,483	30,465	28,981	18,055
Georgia	29,021	33,743	32,445	18,689
Hawaii	38,829	40,951	37,406	27,215
Idaho	25,257	26,326	25,567	21,900
Illinois	32,252	38,442	34,358	20,990
Indiana	28,797	31,436	29,588	19,101
Iowa	26,229	20,307	26,427	16,010
Kansas	27,291	23,320	28,036	18,422
Kentucky	22,534	30,712	23,202	14,871
Louisiana	21,949	22,567	26,436	12,029
Maine	27,854	27,823	27,901	26,250
Maryland	39,386	45,446	41,964	30,746
Massachusetts	36,952	34,706	38,083	25,402
Michigan	31,020	38,327	32,463	18,851
Minnesota	30,909	22,685	31,322	18,878
Mississippi	20,136	16,975	24,940	11,625
Missouri	26,362	27,059	27,179	18,374
Montana	22,988	20,649	23,524	20,364
Nebraska	26,016	23,109	26,435	17,038
Nevada	31,011	30,396	31,813	22,528
New Hampshire	36,329	42,963	36,379	31,657
New Jersey	40,927	52,846	42,740	29,145
New Mexico	24,087	28,223	25,872	19,561
New York	32,965	35,439	35,811	24,089
North Carolina	26,647	28,520	29,300	17,979
North Dakota	23,213	15,585	23,634	21,066
Ohio	28,706	34,243	30,026	17,716
Oklahoma	23,577	22,283	24,851	15,725
Oregon	27,250	25,120	27,574	18,432
Pennsylvania	29,069	31,361	30,065	20,064
Rhode Island	32,181	25,394	33,103	20,377
South Carolina	26,256	30,454	30,118	16,555
South Dakota	22,503	19,119	23,220	20,890
Tennessee	24,807	29,092	26,244	16,432
Texas	27,016	30,792	29,728	17,853
Utah	29,470	25,071	29,999	19,878

[Continued]

★ 638

Income, Household by State (Continued)

Median household income by race/ethnicity, by state, 1989.

State	Total	Asian	White	Black
Vermont	29,792	27,824	29,852	28,625
Virginia	33,328	41,488	36,039	21,987
Washington	31,183	31,424	31,685	24,066
West Virginia	20,795	37,031	21,034	13,174
Wisconsin	29,442	18,490	30,216	16,189
Wyoming	27,096	20,130	27,600	16,708

Source: Felicity Barringer, "White-Black Disparity in Income Narrowed in 80's , Census Shows," *New York Times,* Friday, July 24, 1992, pp. A1, A9. Primary source: U.S. Census Bureau. Also in source: Data for American Indians and Hispanics.

★ 639 ★

Income, Household by Five Highest and Five Lowest States

Median household income by race/ethnicity, ranked by highest and lowest Asian/Pacific Islander household income, 1989.

State	Total	Asian	White	Black
The five states with **highest** Asian/ Pacific Islander incomes				
New Jersey	$40,927	$52,846	$42,740	$29,145
Connecticut	41,721	48,560	43,407	28,011
Maryland	39,386	45,446	41,964	30,746
New Hampshire	36,329	42,963	36,379	31,657
Delaware	34,875	41,526	36,660	24,286
The five states with **lowest** Asian Pacific Islander incomes				
Wyoming	$27,096	$20,130	$27,600	416,708
South Dakota	22,503	19,119	23,220	20,890
Wisconsin	29,442	18,490	30,216	16,189
Mississippi	20,136	16,975	24,940	11,625
North Dakota	23,213	15,585	23,634	21,066

Source: Felicity Barringer, "White-Black Disparity in Income Narrowed in 80's , Census Shows," *New York Times,* Friday, July 24, 1992, pp. A1, A9. Primary source: U.S. Census Bureau. Also in source: Data for American Indians and Hispanics.

★ 640 ★

Income, Number of Earners per U.S. Family

Percent of Asian/Pacific Islander, white, and total families with 0 to 6 wage earners, March 1991.

Number of Earners in Family	Total Population	Asian/Pacific Islander	White
Percent	100.0%	100.0%	100.0%
No earners	14.4%	10.4%	13.9%
One earner	27.5%	26.5%	26.5%
Two earners	44.5%	44.2%	45.8%
Three earners	9.9%	11.3%	10.2%
Four earners	3.0%	5.5%	3.1%
Five earners	0.5%	1.1%	0.5%
Six earners	0.1%	0.3%	0.1%
Seven or more earners	-	0.7%	-

Source: Claudette E. Bennett, Economics and Statistics Administration, Bureau of the Census, U.S. Department of Commerce, *The Asian and Pacific Islander Population in the United States: March 1991 and 1990,* Current Population Reports, Population Characteristics, P20-459 (Washington, DC: Government Printing Office, Issued August 1992), table 8, p. 38. The population universe for the March 1991 and 1990 Current Population Surveys is the estimate of the civilian noninstitutional population in the United States plus members of the Armed Forces in the United States living off post or with their families on post, but excludes all other members of the Armed Forces. Data are estimates based on sample surveys and are subject to sampling variability since they are not based on a complete count of the population. A dash (-) represents too few cases to estimate; medians were not calculated for cells with fewer than 20 cases.

★ 641 ★

Income, Household, with Earners per U.S. Household

Percent of Asian/Pacific Islander, white, and total families by household income range, and percent of households with 0 to 6 wage earners, March 1991.

Household Income in 1990	Total Population	Asian/Pacific Islander	White
Percent	100.0	100.0	100.0
Under $5,000	5.2	4.9	4.0
$5,000 to $9,999	9.7	6.4	8.8
$10,000 to $14,999	9.5	7.0	9.2
$15,000 to $19,999	8.8	7.3	8.7
$20,000 to $24,999	8.9	5.6	9.0
$25,000 to $34,999	15.8	13.2	16.1
$35,000 to $49,999	17.5	19.9	18.0
$50,000 to $59,000	7.8	8.1	8.2
$60,000 to $74,999	7.2	11.0	7.6
$75,000 and over	9.7	16.6	10.4
Median income (dollars)	$29,943	$38,449	$31,231
Standard error[a] (dollars)	$153	$1,139	$143
Number of Earners			
Percent	100.0	100.0	100.0
No earners	21.1	14.2	20.8
One earner	33.3	31.5	32.5
Two earners	35.0	37.6	35.9
Three earners	7.7	9.8	7.9
Four earners	2.	5.2	2.3
Five earners	0.4%	0.9	0.4
Six earners	0.1	0.3	0.1
Seven or more earners	-	0.6	-

Source: Claudette E. Bennett, Economics and Statistics Administration, Bureau of the Census, U.S. Department of Commerce, *The Asian and Pacific Islander Population in the United States: March 1991 and 1990,* Current Population Reports, Population Characteristics, P20-459 (Washington, DC: Government Printing Office, Issued August 1992), table 7, p. 35. The population universe for the March 1991 and 1990 Current Population Surveys is the estimate of the civilian noninstitutional population in the United States plus members of the Armed Forces in the United States living off post or with their families on post, but excludes all other members of the Armed Forces. Data are estimates based on sample surveys and are subject to sampling variability since they are not based on a complete count of the population. *Notes:* (a) Standard error is higher for Asians than for other groups because the Asian sample population is smaller. A dash (-) represents too few cases to estimate; medians were not calculated for cells with fewer than 20 cases.

Poverty

★ 642 ★

Distribution of Poor in the United States

Numbers and percent of poor in the United States, by race/ethnicity, 1990. Asian Pacific Islanders represent 2.6 percent of the Nation's poor.

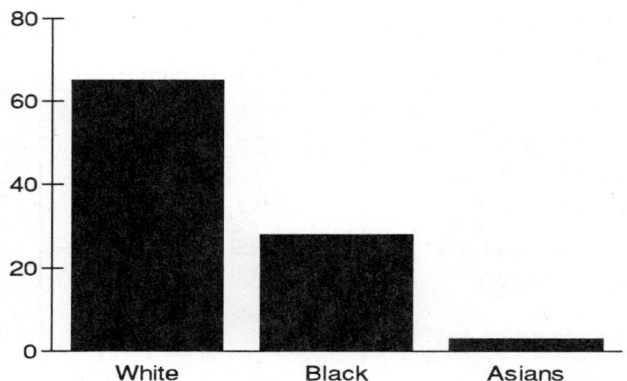

Source: U.S. Bureau of the Census, Current Population Reports, Series P-60, No. 179, *Income, Poverty, and Wealth in the United States: A Chartbook* (Washington, DC: Government Printing Office, 1992).

★ 643 ★

Poverty Rates for Recent Immigrant Families

Numbers and percent of recent Asian/Pacific Islander immigrant and white families in poverty[a], 1988.

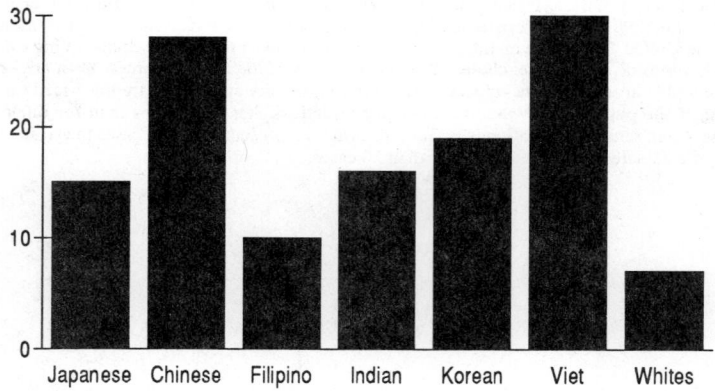

Source: U.S. Commission on Civil Rights, *Voices across America: Roundtable Discussions of Asian Civil Rights Issues* (Washington, DC: U.S. Commission on Civil Rights, not dated), fig. 3, p. 5. (summary and transcript of roundtable conferences in Houston, New York City, and San Francisco, May-July 1989). Primary source: *The Economic Progress of Americans of Asian Descent: An Exploratory Investigation* (Washington, DC: U.S. Commission on Civil Rights, October 1988). *Note:* (a) The poverty threshold varies by size of family, number of children, and age of the head of household. For this data, poverty threshold for a one-person family was annual income of $3,774; for a family of 6, the annual poverty threshold income was approximately $10,000.

★ 644 ★

Poverty Status in the United States, of Families

Numbers (in thousands) and percent of Asian/Pacific Islander, whites, and total families below the poverty level by family characteristics, March 1991.

Characteristic	Total population (thousands)	Asian/Pacific Islander (thousands)	White
All income levels in 1990			
Families	66,322	1,536	56,803
Family householder—			
65 years old and over	10,900	135	9,797
Not a high school graduate[a]	14,351	225	11,493
Below Poverty Level in 1990			
Family householder—			
65 years old and over—			
Number	686	11	443
Percent	6.3	8.4	4.5
Not a high school graduate[a]			
Number	3,406	59	2,218
Percent	23.7	26.1	19.3
Poverty Status of Families by Type of Family			
All families below poverty level			
Number	7,098	169	4,622
Percent	10.7	11.0	8.1
Married couple families below poverty level			
Number	2,981	108	2,386
Percent	5.7	8.7	5.1
Female householder, no spouse present below poverty level—			
Number	3,768	43	2,010
Percent	33.4	22.3	26.8
Male householder, no spouse present below poverty level-			
Number	349	18	226
Percent	12.0	15.9	9.9
Related Children under 18 Years in Families			
All related children under 18 years in families	63,908	2,001	51,312
Number below poverty level	12,715	363	7,736
Percent below poverty level	19.9	18.1	15.1
Married-couple families	47,962	1,693	41,755
Number below poverty level	4,907	258	3,836
Percent below poverty level	10.2	15.2	9.2
Female householder, no husband present	13,794	244	7,957
Number below poverty level	7,363	89	3,629
Percent below poverty level	53.4	36.4	45.6
Male householder, no wife present	2,153	64	1,600
Number below poverty level	444	16	271
Percent below poverty level	20.6	24.7	16.9

Source: Claudette E. Bennett, Economics and Statistics Administration, Bureau of the Census, U.S. Department of Commerce, *The Asian and Pacific Islander Population in the United States: March 1991 and 1990,* Current Population Reports, Population Characteristics, P20-459 (Washington, DC: Government Printing Office, August 1992), table 8, p. 38. The population universe for the March 1991 and 1990 Current Population Surveys is the estimate of the civilian noninstitutional population in the United States plus members of the Armed Forces in the United States living off post or with their families on post, but excludes all other members of the Armed Forces. Data are estimates based on sample surveys and are subject to sampling variability since they are not based on a complete count of the population. *Note:* (a) Householder, all ages.

★ 645 ★

Poverty Status in the United States, by Age

Numbers (in thousands) and percent of Asian/Pacific Islander, white, and total persons below the poverty level by age range, 1990.

Characteristic	Total population	Asian/ Pacific Islander	White
All income levels in 1990			
Total persons[a]	248,644	7,014	208,611
Less than 18 years	65,049	2,126	51,929
18 to 64 years	153,503	4,375	129,784
65 years and over	30,093	514	26,898
Below poverty level in 1990			
Total persons[a]	33,585	858	22,326
Percent below poverty level[b]	13.5	12.2	10.7
Less than 18 years	20.6	17.6	15.9
18 to 64 years	10.7	9.6	8.8
65 years and over	12.2	12.1	10.1
Percent[c]	100.0	100.0	100.0
Less than 18 years	40.0	43.6	36.9
18 to 64 years	49.1	49.2	51.0
65 years and over	10.9	7.2	12.1

Source: Claudette E. Bennett, Economics and Statistics Administration, Bureau of the Census, U.S. Department of Commerce, *The Asian and Pacific Islander Population in the United States: March 1991 and 1990,* Current Population Reports, Population Characteristics, P20-459 (Washington, DC: Government Printing Office, August 1992), table 2, p. 16. The population universe for the March 1991 and 1990 Current Population Surveys is the estimate of the civilian noninstitutional population to the United States plus members of the Armed Forces in the United States living off post or with their families on post, but excludes all other members of the Armed Forces. Data are estimates based on sample surveys and are subject to sampling variability since they are not based on a complete count of the population. *Notes:* (a) Excludes unrelated individuals less than 15 years of age. (b) Percentages based on persons from all income levels. (c) Percentages based on all persons below the poverty level in 1990.

★ 646 ★

Persons Below the Poverty Level in the Western[a] United States

Numbers (in thousands) and percent of Asian/Pacific Islander, whites, and total persons below the poverty level in the western United States, 1990.

Characteristic	Total population	Asian/Pacific Islander	White
All income levels in 1990			
Total persons[b]	52,835	4,107	45,622
Less than 18 years	14,530	1,194	12,345
18 to 64 years	32,605	2,538	28,138
65 years and over	5,700	375	5,139
Below poverty level in 1990			
Total persons[b]	6,877	522	5,584
Percent below poverty level[c]	13.0	12.7	12.2
Less than 18 years	19.8	19.1	18.5
18 to 64 years	10.8	9.8	10.3
65 years and over	8.5	11.8	7.9
Percent[d]	100.0	100.0	100.0
Less than 18 years	41.7	43.7	41.0
18 to 64 years	51.2	47.9	51.7
65 years and over	7.1	8.5	7.3

Source: Claudette E. Bennett, Economics and Statistics Administration, Bureau of the Census, U.S. Department of Commerce, *The Asian and Pacific Islander Population in the United States: March 1991 and 1990,* Current Population Reports, Population Characteristics, P20-459 (Washington, DC: Government Printing Office, Issued August 1992), table 2, p. 18. The population universe for the March 1991 and 1990 Current Population Surveys is the estimate of the civilian noninstitutional population to the United States plus members of the Armed Forces in the United States living off post or with their families on post, but excludes all other members of the Armed Forces. Data are estimates based on sample surveys and are subject to sampling variability since they are not based on a complete count of the population. *Notes:* (a) Western United States includes Alaska, Arizona, California, Colorado, Hawaii, Idaho, Montana, Nevada, New Mexico, Oregon, Utah, Washington, and Wyoming. (b) Excludes unrelated individuals less than 15 years of age. (c) Percentages based on persons from all income levels. (d) Percentages based on all persons below the poverty level in 1990.

★ 647 ★

Asian/Pacific Islanders Below the Poverty Level by Age, 1989

State	Asian Pacific Islander						
	Under 5	5	6 to 11	12 to 17	18 to 64	65 to 74	75 and over
Alabama	282	54	420	410	2,857	74	71
Alaska	217	41	124	118	835	55	0
Arizona	756	173	540	735	6,094	194	78
Arkansas	173	31	201	243	1,254	49	21
California	41,448	9,502	56,064	48,479	226,847	12,951	6,870
Colorado	1,019	182	879	1,050	5,674	334	119
Connecticut	363	44	215	295	2,733	112	41
Delaware	52	3	25	69	642	25	11
Florida	1,397	286	1,789	1,722	13,182	558	254
Georgia	670	148	784	863	5,700	138	46
Hawaii	6,629	1,359	7,129	6,210	27,416	3,641	3,200
Idaho	147	14	247	159	1,033	9	25
Illinois	2,333	494	2,484	2,329	20,398	1,643	968
Indiana	563	33	263	265	3,835	97	47
Kansas	718	131	630	724	4,178	99	63
Kentucky	205	76	250	336	1,780	30	10
Louisiana	1,115	291	1,641	1,367	6,181	184	121
Maine	50	14	104	158	441	6	0
Maryland	719	125	934	1,042	7,410	511	208
Massachusetts	2,978	662	3,461	2,229	15,358	820	395
Michigan	1,487	266	1,677	1,461	9,899	281	137
Minnesota	4,392	966	4,229	3,051	10,601	403	141
Montana	57	36	79	52	579	16	0
Nevada	289	67	294	390	2,613	150	40
New Hampshire	88	10	114	158	569	8	2
New Jersey	1,266	265	1,445	1,646	11,924	599	486
New Mexico	266	56	190	285	1,608	5	12
New York	6,854	1,274	8,292	8,601	65,501	4,413	2,783
North Carolina	799	108	689	748	4,694	133	42
North Dakota	54	8	24	62	576	1	2
Ohio	1,190	242	1,142	983	9,791	292	163
Oklahoma	461	92	407	467	5,074	124	76
Oregon	1,112	188	1,228	1,224	8,623	413	130
Pennsylvania	2,386	524	2,755	2,689	15,046	632	192
Rhode Island	708	213	719	403	2,384	84	35
South Carolina	198	15	335	167	1,562	39	20
South Dakota	87	13	49	46	359	6	4
Tennessee	385	73	579	401	2,954	91	40
Texas	3,570	756	4,715	5,477	32,244	1,228	595
Utah	837	125	626	693	4,297	144	39
Vermont	16	4	41	9	311	18	3
Virginia	807	176	1,064	1,330	9,269	439	294
Washington	3,636	783	4,251	3,924	18,971	1,158	776
West Virginia	65	11	24	93	834	38	2
Wisconsin	4,302	873	3,589	2,055	9,676	364	149
Wyoming	22	4	24	34	327	9	0

Source: Asian/Pacific Islander Data Consortium (San Francisco, CA: Asian and Pacific Islander Center for Census Information and Services, 1993). Primary source: U.S. Census Bureau, Summary Tape Files 1 and 3.

Scientists and Engineers

★ 648 ★

Salaries, Scientists and Engineers by Field and Sex

Median annual salaries in U.S. dollars of scientists and engineers by field of degree, sex, and race/ethnicity, 1986.

Field and sex	Total Employed[a]	Asian	White	Black	Native American	Hispanic[b]
Total, all fields	$38,400	$39,100	$38,700	$31,500	$41,000	$34,600
Male	39,800	40,700	40,000	33,500	42,600	36,600
Female	29,900	30,100	30,200	26,200	29,800	25,200
Scientists, total	35,700	37,000	35,900	29,000	40,500	30,600
Male	38,000	40,500	38,100	31,400	44,100	33,900
Female	29,000	28,800	29,400	25,400	29,100	22,900
Physical scientists	40,700	39,300	40,900	35,600	63,400	41,300
Male	42,000	42,200	42,000	39,300	63,400	43,100
Female	31,300	31,400	31,800	24,300	-	33,900
Mathematical scientists	39,800	38,500	40,000	37,000	22,500	38,700
Male	42,500	39,300	42,800	38,400	19,900	42,100
Female	31,000	30,600	31,000	32,900	25,000	31,000
Computer specialists	37,300	37,400	37,500	32,200	39,300	31,500
Male	38,900	39,600	39,000	34,200	42,400	33,800
Female	33,200	30,800	33,700	29,300	20,500	25,800
Environmental scientists	37,500	40,600	37,600	31,800	27,000	40,500
Male	38,400	41,100	38,500	29,600	26,700	42,400
Female	30,100	35,100	30,100	36,100	28,000	21,200
Life scientists	33,100	35,700	33,200	29,300	40,600	29,700
Male	35,400	40,500	35,400	33,300	46,500	35,200
Female	25,200	28,400	25,100	21,600	32,500	18,700
Psychologists	33,400	22,500	33,900	26,800	41,200	25,400
Male	36,500	39,600	36,600	27,400	41,900	26,400
Female	29,000	19,300	29,700	26,600	37,400	24,000
Social scientists	31,800	38,700	32,200	22,800	34,300	25,600
Male	34,700	41,900	35,100	23,800	39,100	28,500
Female	25,000	31,700	25,200	21,400	21,500	18,700
Engineers, total	40,800	40,500	41,000	35,700	41,300	38,000
Male	41,100	40,800	41,200	35,900	41,500	38,300
Female	34,300	35,000	34,300	32,900	34,700	33,900

Source: Patricia E. White, *Women and Minorities in Science and Engineering: An Update* (Washington, DC: National Science Foundation, 92-303, January 1992), table 24, p. 121. Primary source: National Science Foundation, Science Resources Studies Division, Scientific and Technical Personnel Data System (STPDS). Salaries are for individuals employed full-time. A dash (-) represents too few cases to estimate. *Notes:* (a) Detail will not average to total because racial and ethnic categories are not mutually exclusive (Hispanics may also be included in one of the racial groups) and because the total employed includes "other" and "no report" categories. (b) Includes members of all racial groups.

★ 649 ★

Salaries, Scientists and Engineers by Degrees Earned

Median annual salaries in U.S. dollars of scientists and engineers by race/ethnicity, 1990.

Median annual salary[a]	Asian	White	Black	Native American	Hispanic[b]
Bachelor's	$30,000	$26,100	$24,000	$21,900	$25,100
Master's	35,900	37,500	35,000	-	36,100
Doctorate	55,000	54,800	48,500	50,100	50,000

Source: Patricia E. White, *Women and Minorities in Science and Engineering: An Update,* (Washington, DC: National Science Foundation, 92-303, January 1992), table 31, p. 32. Primary source: National Science Foundation, Science Resources Studies Division, unpublished tabulations. A dash (-) represents too few cases to estimate. *Notes:* (a) Data for bachelor's and master's degrees were reported in 1990 by 1988 and 1989 graduates; data for doctorates were reported in 1989 by recipients who received degrees between 1946 and 1988. (b) Includes members of all racial groups.

★ 650 ★

Salaries, Scientists and Engineers with Bachelor's Degrees by Field

Median annual salaries in U.S. dollars of recent science and engineering graduates[a] by field of degree and race/ethnicity, 1990.

Field of degree	Total[b]	Asian	White	Black	Native American	Hispanic[c]
Total, sciences and engineering	$26,000	$30,000	$26,100	$24,000	$21,900	$25,100
Sciences, total	$23,000	$27,900	$23,000	$22,200	-	$21,100
Physical sciences	25,100	-	25,000	-	-	24,000
Mathematics and statistics	23,600	-	24,000	-	-	-
Computer science	30,100	33,200	30,100	28,000	-	30,000
Environmental science	23,700	-	23,600	-	-	-
Life sciences	21,000	-	21,000	20,100	-	-
Psychology	18,600	-	18,600	-	-	-
Social sciences	21,900	-	21,500	21,900	-	-
Engineering, total	$33,000	$32,800	$33,300	$32,500	-	$32,200

Source: Patricia E. White, *Women and Minorities in Science and Engineering: An Update* (Washington, DC: National Science Foundation, 92-303, January 1992), table 26, p. 123. Primary source: National Science Foundation, Science Resources Studies Division, Survey of Science, Social Science, and Engineering Graduates (Recent Science and Engineering Graduates), Characteristics of Science and Engineering Graduates. Also in source: Data by sex. All figures have been rounded to the nearest 100. Median salaries are for full-time employed civilians only. A dash (-) represents too few cases to estimate; medians were not calculated for cells with fewer than 20 cases. *Notes:* (a) Includes graduates who received their degrees in academic year 1988 or 1989. (b) Racial/ethnic categories will not average to total because racial and ethnic categories are not mutually exclusive (Hispanics' salaries may also be included in the salaries of one of the racial groups) and because total median salaries include salaries for "other" and "no report" categories. (c) Includes members of all racial groups.

★ 651 ★

Salaries, Scientists and Engineers with Master's Degrees by Field

Median annual salaries in U.S. dollars of recent science and engineering graduates[a] by field of degree and race/ethnicity, 1990.

Field of degree	Total[b]	Asian	White	Black	Native American	Hispanic[c]
Total, sciences and engineering	$37,000	$35,900	$37,500	$35,000	-	$36,100
Sciences, total	33,800	33,000	34,000	$30,100	-	29,000
Physical sciences	34,900	32,100	35,900	-	-	-
Mathematics and statistics	32,800	-	32,800	-	-	-
Computer science	42,100	36,000	43,900	-	-	-
Environmental science	33,800	-	34,300	-	-	-
Life sciences	26,900	-	26,900	-	-	-
Psychology	32,000	-	32,100	-	-	-
Social sciences	31,000	-	31,100	-	-	-
Engineers, total	$41,400	$39,100	$42,100	$41,900	-	$40,100

Source: Patricia E. White, *Women and Minorities in Science and Engineering: An Update* (Washington, DC: National Science Foundation, 92-303, January 1992), table 26, p. 123. Primary source: National Science Foundation, Science Resources Studies Division, Survey of Science, Social Science, and Engineering Graduates (Recent Science and Engineering Graduates), Characteristics of Science and Engineering Graduates. Also in source: Data by sex. All figures have been rounded to the nearest 100. Median salaries are for full-time employed civilians only. A dash (-) represents too few cases to estimate; medians were not calculated for cells with fewer than 20 cases. *Notes:* (a) Includes graduates who received their degrees in academic year 1988 or 1989. (b) Racial/ethnic categories will not average to total because racial and ethnic categories are not mutually exclusive (Hispanics' salaries may also be included in the salaries of one of the racial groups) and because total median salaries include salaries for "other" and "no report" categories. (c) Includes members of all racial groups.

★ 652 ★

Salaries, Scientists and Engineers with Doctorates by Field and Sex

Median annual salaries in U.S. dollars of doctoral scientists and engineers by field of degree, sex, and race/ethnicity, 1989.

Field and sex	Total[a,b]	Asian	White	Black	Native American	Hispanic[c]
Total, scientists and engineers	$54,600	$55,000	$54,800	$48,500	$50,100	$50,000
Male	56,000	55,700	56,300	51,200	51,500	50,900
Female	44,800	45,800	44,700	44,400	43,500	42,700
Scientists, total	$52,200	$51,700	$52,400	$47,200	$48,700	$48,300
Male	54,500	53,000	54,800	50,500	51,000	50,300
Female	44,400	45,100	44,400	44,300	40,900	42,400
Physical scientists	56,000	52,500	56,700	50,100	51,300	54,300
Male	57,100	53,300	57,800	50,300	51,300	55,900
Female	47,500	48,500	47,100	45,200	-	43,000
Mathematical scientists	51,600	47,900	51,900	44,500	-	44,000
Male	52,200	48,000	52,700	44,500	-	44,300
Female	45,200	47,000	44,800	-	-	-
Computer specialists	58,500	60,100	58,300	-	-	56,900
Female	50,000	52,200	48,900	-	-	-
Environmental scientists	55,100	55,900	54,800	63,400	-	49,300
Male	55,600	56,900	55,400	63,400	-	49,300
Female	43,600	48,300	43,400	-	-	-

[Continued]

★ 652 ★

Salaries, Scientists and Engineers with Doctorates by Field and Sex (Continued)

Median annual salaries in U.S. dollars of doctoral scientists and engineers by field of degree, sex, and race/ethnicity, 1989.

Field and sex	Total[a,b]	Asian	White	Black	Native American	Hispanic[c]
Life scientists	50,700	50,400	50,800	46,300	51,100	50,100
Male	53,200	52,600	53,300	47,100	-	50,600
Female	43,100	43,700	42,900	44,500	37,200	39,700
Psychologists	50,100	44,200	50,200	44,400	48,500	45,700
Male	51,300	48,600	51,500	46,900	-	49,700
Female	44,300	42,200	44,400	42,900	-	43,700
Social scientists	50,400	48,200	50,600	47,200	48,000	44,300
Male	52,000	50,200	52,500	47,900	-	44,800
Female	44,200	42,500	44,300	45,000	-	43,300
Engineers, total	$62,500	$58,400	$64,300	$55,700	-	55,400
Male	62,800	58,600	65,000	55,500	-	55,600
Female	53,400	54,000	53,200	-	-	50,100

Source: Patricia E. White, *Women and Minorities in Science and Engineering: An Update* (Washington, DC: National Science Foundation, 92-303, January 1992), table 25, p. 122. Primary source: National Science Foundation, Science Resources Studies Division, Survey of Doctorate Recipients, unpublished tabulations. All figures have been rounded to the nearest 100. Median salaries are for full-time employed civilians only. A dash (-) represents too few cases to estimate; medians were not calculated for cells with fewer than 20 cases. *Notes:* (a) Includes civilian scientists and engineers who received their doctorates between 1946 and 1988 and were employed full-time in February 1989. All holders of doctorates are included, regardless of citizenship status (i.e., U.S. citizen; non-U.S. citizen, permanent visa; and non-U.S. citizen, temporary visa). (b) Median salaries of racial/ethnic categories will not average to total because racial and ethnic categories are not mutually exclusive (Hispanics' salaries may also be included in the salaries of one of the racial groups) and because the total median salary includes salaries for "other" and "no report" categories. (c) Includes members of all racial groups.

THE MILITARY

Military Academies

★ 653 ★

U.S. Air Force Academy

Numbers of Asian Americans and total cadets who entered and who graduated, with percent attrition, classes of 1959–1996.

Year	Asian American			Total Graduates		
	No. admitted	No. graduating	% attrition	No. admitted	No. graduating	% attrition
1959	1	0	100.0	289	207	28.4
1960	1	1	0.0	309	227	26.5
1961	2	2	0.0	302	217	28.1
1962	0	0	0.0	458	298	34.9
1963	2	2	0.0	727	499	31.4
1964	4	4	0.0	780	499	36.0
1965	2	2	0.0	801	517	35.5
1966	2	2	0.0	761	470	38.2
1967	5	4	20.0	853	524	38.6
1968	3	2	33.3	1,011	613	39.4
1969	4	2	50.0	1,053	683	35.1
1970	7	7	0.0	1,034	745	27.9
1971	9	4	55.6	1,036	692	33.2
1972	5	2	60.0	1,247	754	39.5
1973	8	5	37.5	1,404	844	39.9
1974	9	5	44.4	1,444	813	43.7
1975	14	7	50.0	1,406	756	46.2
1976	19	12	36.8	1,507	928	38.4
1977	19	13	31.6	1,462	867	40.7
1978	29	13	55.2	1,630	981	39.6
1979	44	24	45.5	1,468	900	38.7
1980	47	26	44.7	1,597	899	43.7
1981	43	26	39.5	1,502	876	41.7
1982	40	22	45.0	1,460	842	42.3
1983	49	34	30.6	1,508	956	36.6
1984	35	25	28.6	1,581	1,027	35.0
1985	52	37	28.8	1,507	945	37.3
1986	37	25	32.4	1,490	961	35.5
1987	59	47	20.3	1,456	969	32.1
1988	39	32	17.9	1,512	1,074	29.0
1989	36	27	25.0	1,397	1,022	26.8

(Continued)

★ 653 ★

U.S. Air Force Academy (Continued)

Numbers of Asian Americans and total cadets who entered and who graduated, with percent attrition, classes of 1959–1996.

Year	Asian American			Total Graduates		
	No. admitted	No. graduating	% attrition	No. admitted	No. graduating	% attrition
1990	32	27	15.6	1,348	993	26.3
1991	39	32	17.9	1,377	977	29.0
1992	44	34	22.7			
Graduate Totals	740	506	31.6			
Cadet Wing[a]						
1993	49	33	32.7			
1994	44	37	15.9			
1995	43	34	20.9			
1996	39	37	5.1			
Wing Totals	175	141	19.4			
Overall Totals	915	647	29.3			

Source: Unpublished data obtained from the U.S. Air Force Academy Public Relations Office, Colorado Springs, CO, January 1993. *Note:* (a) Current enrollment.

★ 654 ★

U.S. Military Academy at West Point

Numbers of Asian males, females, and total graduates, with percent Asian, classes of 1982–1996.

Class Year	Male	Female	Total Asian	Total Graduates	% Asian
1982	23	2	25	898	2.8%
1983	24	2	26	893	2.9%
1984	31	4	35	986	3.5%
1985	20	2	22	1,063	2.1%
1986	22	4	26	1,006	2.6%
1987	21	1	22	1,042	2.1%
1988	29	4	33	981	3.4%
1989	37	4	41	1,066	3.8%
1990	30	1	31	931	3.3%
1991	32	4	36	965	3.7%
1992	47	8	55	943	5.8%
Current Enrollment					
1993	60	15	75	1,032	7.3%
1994	66	15	81	1,080	7.5%
1995	53	13	66	1,085	6.1%
1996	33	4	37	1,067	3.5%

Source: Unpublished data obtained from the Department of the Army, U.S. Military Academy Public Affairs Office, West Point, NY, January 1993.

★ 655 ★

U.S. Naval Academy
Numbers of Asian males, females, and total graduates, classes of 1982–1996

Year	Asian American graduates			Total graduates
	Asian	Male	Female	
1982	33			1050
1983	43			1077
1984	33			1004
1985	41			1044
1986	49			1028
1987	37			1036
1988	37			1060
1989	50			1082
1990	54			108
1991	44			955
1992	46			1031
Current enrollment[a]				
1993	64	50	14	
1994	46	42	4	
1995	46	39	7	
1996	49	40	9	

Source: Unpublished data obtained from the U.S. Naval Academy Public Affairs Office, Annapolis, MD, January 27, 1993. Enrollees at the U.S. Naval Academy are known as Midshipmen. *Note:* (a) Totals are as of December 31, 1992.

Air Force

★ 656 ★

Active Duty U.S. Air Force Personnel by Age
Asian American service in the U.S. Air Force by age and ethnicity (self-reported), as of June 1992.

Age	Chinese	Japanese	Korean	Filipino	Vietnamese	Other Asian	Total Asian	Total, all active duty
17	0	0	1	1	0	2	4	369
18	0	5	5	23	0	27	60	4,803
19	7	8	23	75	0	64	177	14,700
20	10	8	19	116	0	109	262	20,304
21	6	16	28	176	0	112	338	25,104
22	14	18	34	190	0	101	357	24,771
23	19	20	27	198	0	124	388	22,955
24	15	29	22	207	0	118	391	23,141
25	7	23	23	207	0	119	379	23,195
26-30	90	203	110	1,101	2	619	2,125	118,227

(Continued)

★ 656 ★

Active Duty U.S. Air Force Personnel by Age (Continued)

Asian American service in the U.S. Air Force by age and ethnicity (self-reported), as of June 1992.

Age	Chinese	Japanese	Korean	Filipino	Vietnamese	Other Asian	Total Asian	Total, all active duty
31-35	104	231	86	930	0	534	1,885	96,575
36-40	78	185	47	651	0	374	1,335	71,252
41 and above	69	91	15	413	0	151	739	40,551
Total	419	837	440	4,288	2	2,454	8,440	485,947

Source: Extract from Service Personnel Records, Defense Manpower Data Center, Arlington, VA, June 1992, unpublished data. Ethnicity is self-reported by individuals at the time of their enlistment and may be updated upon reenlistment.

★ 657 ★

Active Duty U.S. Air Force Personnel by Rank

Asian American service in the U.S. Air Force by rank and ethnicity (self-reported), as of June 1992.

Rank	Title	Chinese	Japanese	Korean	Filipino	Viet-namese	Other Asian	Total Asian	Total, all active duty
E1	Airman Basic	2	5	20	89	0	56	172	13,017
E2	Airman	6	12	20	95	0	94	227	17,791
E3	Airman 1st Class	30	22	65	427	0	256	800	51,886
E4	Senior Airman	37	112	99	1,147	1	498	1,894	106,395
E5	Staff Sergeant	49	154	68	1,038	0	500	1,809	96,300
E6	Technical Sergeant	45	141	36	649	0	306	1,177	55,505
E7	Master Sergeant	43	97	15	389	0	190	734	38,023
E8	Senior Master Sergeant	7	22	4	41	0	31	105	8,170
E9	Chief Master Sergeant	4	9	0	12	0	21	46	4,094
O1	2nd Lieutenant	16	16	7	32	0	51	122	7,167
O2	1st Lieutenant	20	24	17	52	0	53	166	9,678
O3	Captain	81	119	66	191	1	238	696	41,931
O4	Major	43	52	16	55	0	107	273	18,266
O5	Lieutenant Colonel	24	38	6	44	0	40	152	12,183
O6	Colonel	11	14	1	27	0	13	66	5,226
O7	Brigadier General	0	0	0	0	0	0	0	161
O8	Major General	1	0	0	0	0	0	1	111
O9	Lieutenant General	0	0	0	0	0	0	0	36
O10	General	0	0	0	0	0	0	0	12
Total		419	837	440	4,288	2	2,454	8,440	485,952

Source: Extract from Service Personnel Records, Defense Manpower Data Center, Arlington, VA, June 1992, unpublished data. Ethnicity is self-reported by individuals at the time of their enlistment and may be updated upon reenlistment.

★ 658 ★

Active Duty U.S. Air Force Personnel by Sex

Asian American service in the U.S. Air Force by sex and ethnicity (self-reported), as of June 1992.

Sex	Chinese	Japanese	Korean	Filipino	Viet-namese	Other Asian	Total Asian	Total, all active duty
Male	350	729	328	3,712	2	2,034	7,155	415,606
Female	69	108	112	576	0	420	1,285	70,346
Total	419	837	440	4,288	2	2,454	8,440	485,952

Source: Extract from Service Personnel Records, Defense Manpower Data Center, Arlington, VA, June 1992, unpublished data. Ethnicity is self-reported by individuals at the time of their enlistment.

★ 659 ★

Active DutyU.S. Air Force Personnel by Source of Commission

Asian American officers in the U.S. Air Force by source of commission and ethnicity (self-reported), as of June 1992.

Commission	Chinese	Japanese	Korean	Filipino	Viet-namese	Other Asian	Total Asian	Total, all active duty
Academy, Army	0	1	0	0	0	0	1	127
Academy, Navy	0	0	0	1	0	0	1	80
Academy, Air Force	20	42	13	24	0	102	201	14,316
ROTC/NROTC Scholarship	41	61	34	51	0	107	294	16,544
ROTC/NROTC Non-scholarship	39	74	24	95	0	106	338	22,920
OCS/AOCS/OTS/PLC[a]	43	57	26	114	0	99	339	26,015
Direct Appointment, Professional	38	13	9	78	1	55	194	6,617
Direct Appointment, Non-professional	14	15	7	38	0	33	107	8,047
Total	195	263	113	401	1	502	1,475	94,666

Source: Extract from Service Personnel Records, Defense Manpower Data Center, Arlington, VA, June 1992, unpublished data. Ethnicity is self-reported by individuals at the time of their enlistment and may be updated upon reenlistment. *Note:* (a) Officer Candidate School, Aviation Officer Candidate School, Officer Training School, Platoon Leaders' Course.

★ 660 ★

Active Duty U.S. Air Force Personnel by Years of Service

Asian American service in the U.S. Air Force by years of service and ethnicity (self-reported), as of June 1992.

Years of Service	Chinese	Japanese	Korean	Filipino	Viet-namese	Other Asian	Total Asian	Total, all active duty
1	17	25	54	243	0	185	524	34,143
2	30	23	27	236	1	160	477	30,150
3	23	26	53	264	0	165	531	34,922
4	25	45	42	341	1	176	630	32,599

(Continued)

★ 660 ★

Active Duty U.S. Air Force Personnel by Years of Service (Continued)

Asian American service in the U.S. Air Force by years of service and ethnicity (self-reported), as of June 1992.

Years of Service	Chinese	Japanese	Korean	Filipino	Viet-namese	Other Asian	Total Asian	Total, all active duty
5	20	34	26	223	0	141	444	24,724
6	20	37	26	258	0	124	465	25,982
7	13	33	30	251	0	124	451	26,863
8	20	42	18	220	0	121	421	24,318
9	11	24	15	215	0	85	350	22,522
10	14	50	18	218	0	101	401	21,771
11-15	107	224	90	918	0	566	1,905	98,491
16-20	85	192	35	740	0	388	1,440	75,900
21-25	29	61	6	140	0	103	339	26,071
26 and above	5	21	0	17	0	12	55	6,357
Total	419	837	440	4,284	2	2,451	8,433	484,813

Source: Extract from Service Personnel Records, Defense Manpower Data Center, Arlington, VA, June 1992, unpublished data. Ethnicity is self-reported by individuals at the time of their enlistment and may be updated upon reenlistment.

★ 661 ★

Enlisted Personnel in the U.S. Air Force by Years of Service

Asian American enlistment in the U.S. Air Force by years of service and ethnicity (self-reported), as of June 1992.

Years of Service	Chinese	Japanese	Korean	Filipino	Viet-namese	Other Asian	Total Asian	Total, all enlisted
5	9	19	15	205	0	104	352	19,898
6	13	23	15	233	0	102	386	21,286
7	5	21	21	224	0	96	367	22,022
8	6	19	14	198	0	91	328	19,533
9	5	13	12	199	0	63	292	18,227
10	3	40	13	205	0	78	339	17,817
11-15	61	164	63	817	0	443	1,548	79,813
16-20	54	151	22	676	0	308	1,211	58,592
21-25	19	43	4	117	0	87	270	16,651
26 and above	2	8	0	12	0	11	33	2,831
Total	177	501	179	2,886	0	1,383	5,126	390,083

Source: Extract from Service Personnel Records, Defense Manpower Data Center, Arlington, VA, June 1992, unpublished data. Ethnicity is self-reported by individuals at the time of their enlistment and may be updated upon reenlistment.

★ 662 ★

Service in the U.S. Air Force Guard by Age

Asian American service in the U.S. Air Force Guard by age and ethnicity (self-reported), as of June 1992.

Age	Chinese	Japanese	Korean	Filipino	Viet-namese	Other Asian	Total Asian	Total Guard
17	0	2	0	0	0	1	3	189
18	0	3	1	6	1	3	14	808
19	1	7	2	8	1	2	21	1,462
20	1	7	1	8	0	9	26	2,066
21	2	10	2	18	1	5	38	2,850
22	3	7	3	25	2	10	50	3,267
23	3	6	3	23	0	11	46	3,782
24	5	15	2	35	1	19	77	4,252
25	8	22	3	18	4	12	67	4,510
26-30	26	118	15	145	3	59	366	22,406
31-35	20	102	13	117	3	51	306	18,819
36-40	23	95	9	85	0	33	245	16,163
41 and above	86	357	8	163	1	72	687	37,798
Total	178	751	62	651	17	287	1,946	118,372

Source: Extract from Service Personnel Records, Defense Manpower Data Center, Arlington, VA, June 1992, unpublished data. Ethnicity is self-reported by individuals at the time of their enlistment and may be updated upon reenlistment.

★ 663 ★

Service in the U.S. Air Force Guard by Rank

Asian American service in the U.S. Air Force Guard by rank and ethnicity (self-reported), as of June 1992.

Rank	Title	Chinese	Japanese	Korean	Filipino	Viet-namese	Other Asian	Total Asian	Total Guard
E1	Airman Basic	0	4	2	9	2	6	23	2,179
E2	Airman	1	9	1	12	0	7	30	2,023
E3	Airman 1st Class	6	27	7	32	4	19	95	5,712
E4	Senior Airman	32	101	13	183	6	64	399	18,856
E5	Staff Sergeant	38	189	21	197	3	70	518	31,625
E6	Technical Sergeant	45	179	8	128	1	49	410	24,629
E7	Master Sergeant	22	118	2	39	0	28	209	13,742
E8	Senior Master Sergeant	9	33	0	9	0	5	56	3,888
E9	Chief Master Sergeant	3	14	0	1	0	1	19	1,482
O1	2nd Lieutenant	2	7	2	4	1	7	23	1,152
O2	1st Lieutenant	1	3	1	9	0	3	17	1,254
O3	Captain	4	16	1	4	0	8	33	4,106
O4	Major	9	24	3	7	0	11	54	3,933
O5	Lieutenant Colonel	6	27	0	13	0	7	53	3,048
O6	Colonel	0	0	1	4	0	2	7	623
O7	Brigadier General	0	0	0	0	0	0	0	92
O8	Major General	0	0	0	0	0	0	0	28
O9	Lieutenant General	0	0	0	0	0	0	0	1
Total	General	178	751	62	651	17	287	1946	118,373

Source: Extract from Service Personnel Records, Defense Manpower Data Center, Arlington, VA, June 1992, unpublished data. Ethnicity is self-reported by individuals at the time of their enlistment and may be updated upon reenlistment. The U.S. Air Force does not have a rank of Warrant Officer.

★ 664 ★

Service in the U.S. Air Force Guard by Sex

Asian American service in the U.S. Air Force Guard by sex and ethnicity (self-reported), as of June 1992.

Sex	Chinese	Japanese	Korean	Filipino	Viet-namese	Other Asian	Total Asian	Total Guard
Male	170	702	48	576	13	242	1,751	102,552
Female	8	49	14	75	4	45	195	15,821
Total	178	751	62	651	17	287	1,946	118,373

Source: Extract from Service Personnel Records, Defense Manpower Data Center, Arlington, VA, June 1992, unpublished data. Ethnicity is self-reported by individuals at the time of their enlistment and may be updated upon reenlistment.

★ 665 ★

Service in the U.S. Air Force Guard by Years of Service

Asian American service in the U.S. Air Force Guard by years of service and ethnicity (self-reported), as of June 1992.

Years of Service	Chinese	Japanese	Korean	Filipino	Viet-namese	Other Asian	Total Asian	Total Guard
0	2	11	4	12	5	6	40	2,994
1	4	10	3	17	1	11	46	2,458
2	3	15	2	23	1	16	60	3,493
3	6	13	2	32	2	13	68	3,806
4	2	9	3	25	0	12	51	4,178
5	4	25	4	34	1	16	84	6,095
6	11	27	4	51	1	14	108	5,854
7	14	35	6	42	1	16	114	5,469
8	0	19	5	32	0	14	74	5,585
9	6	27	2	26	1	14	76	5,270
10	4	27	3	34	0	13	81	5,174
11-15	26	135	11	131	1	56	360	22,190
16-20	26	96	8	103	0	32	265	19,023
21-25	28	146	0	42	0	29	245	14,965
26-30	20	66	0	9	0	11	106	5,006
31 and above	17	82	1	20	0	5	125	3,110
99	1	8	4	18	3	9	43	3,703
Total	176	740	58	639	12	281	1906	118,373

Source: Extract from Service Personnel Records, Defense Manpower Data Center, Arlington, VA, June 1992, unpublished data. Ethnicity is self-reported by individuals at the time of their enlistment and may be updated upon reenlistment.

★ 666 ★

Service in the U.S. Air Force Reserve by Age

Asian American service in the U.S. Air Force Reserve by age and ethnicity (self-reported), as of June 1992.

Age	Chinese	Japanese	Korean	Filipino	Viet-namese	Other Asian	Total Asian	Total Reserve
17	1	0	0	0	0	0	1	31
18	1	0	0	1	0	0	2	177
19	0	1	1	3	1	3	9	502
20	1	0	2	11	1	5	20	1,195
21	1	1	1	10	1	9	23	2,521
22	3	3	6	22	1	17	52	5,595
23	4	12	8	48	0	38	110	10,233
24	8	16	7	82	0	45	158	13,735
25	10	17	18	105	1	51	202	15,025
26-30	68	76	49	470	2	206	871	52,692
31-35	47	68	20	262	0	164	561	29,930
36-40	36	59	13	181	0	85	374	21,171
41 and above	105	129	20	259	0	173	686	44,956
Total	285	382	145	1,454	7	796	3,069	197,763

Source: Extract from Service Personnel Records, Defense Manpower Data Center, Arlington, VA, June 1992, unpublished data. Ethnicity is self-reported by individuals at the time of their enlistment and may be updated upon reenlistment.

★ 667 ★

Service in the U.S. Air Force Reserve by Rank

Asian American service in the U.S. Air Force Reserve by rank and ethnicity (self-reported), as of June 1992.

Rank		Chinese	Japanese	Korean	Filipino	Viet-namese	Other Asian	Total Asian	Total Reserve
E1	Airman Basic	0	1	1	1	1	6	10	880
E2	Airman	0	6	4	12	1	10	33	3,739
E3	Airman 1st Class	10	11	17	46	2	35	121	10,804
E4	Senior Airman	44	73	47	492	2	237	895	64,419
E5	Staff Sergeant	58	78	32	531	0	145	844	39,340
E6	Technical Sergeant	38	74	12	155	0	93	372	21,792
E7	Master Sergeant	24	50	5	63	0	56	198	17,455
E8	Senior Master Sergeant	7	7	1	8	0	10	33	4,307
E9	Chief Master Sergeant	1	7	0	8	0	12	28	2,153
O0	2nd Lieutenant	0	0	0	0	0	0	0	0
O1	1st Lieutenant	2	3	1	3	0	9	18	3,377
O2	Captain	11	18	3	24	1	32	89	5,668
O3	Major	52	58	13	69	0	120	312	19,852
O4	Lieutenant Colonel	34	36	8	60	0	43	181	11,293
O5	Colonel	29	42	5	41	0	36	153	10,282
O6	Brigadier General	6	11	1	9	0	7	34	2,624
O7	Major General	0	0	1	0	0	0	1	142
O8	Lieutenant General	0	0	0	0	0	0	0	48
O9	General	0	0	0	0	0	0	0	0

Source: Extract from Service Personnel Records, Defense Manpower Data Center, Arlington, VA, June 1992, unpublished data. Ethnicity is self-reported by individuals at the time of their enlistment and may be updated upon reenlistment.

★ 668 ★

Service in the U.S. Air Force Reserve by Sex

Asian American service in the U.S. Air Force Reserve by sex and ethnicity (self-reported), as of June 1992.

Sex	Chinese	Japanese	Korean	Filipino	Viet-namese	Other Asian	Total Asian	Total Reserve
Male	271	406	102	1245	6	641	2671	178,511
Female	45	69	49	277	1	210	651	39,664
Total	178	751	62	651	17	287	1946	218,176

Source: Extract from Service Personnel Records, Defense Manpower Data Center, Arlington, VA, June 1992, unpublished data. Ethnicity is self-reported by individuals at the time of their enlistment and may be updated upon reenlistment.

★ 669 ★

Service in the U.S. Air Force Reserve by Years of Service

Asian American service in the U.S. Air Force Reserve by years of service and ethnicity (self-reported), as of June 1992.

Years of Service	Chinese	Japanese	Korean	Filipino	Viet-namese	Other Asian	Total Asian	Total Reserve
0	3	1	4	8	1	9	26	2,385
1	2	4	2	15	1	10	34	2,645
2	3	5	5	24	1	18	56	4,122
3	10	4	2	42	1	20	79	6,842
4	18	18	16	101	0	65	218	16,670
5	21	31	17	170	0	95	334	20,626
6	19	29	20	219	1	104	392	25,243
7	14	34	19	152	1	62	282	19,960
8	19	14	5	72	0	34	144	6,982
9	9	12	6	77	0	23	127	7,570
10	10	14	6	79	0	34	143	8,517
11-15	53	70	22	249	0	148	542	34,407
16-20	49	49	10	172	0	86	366	24,790
21-25	35	83	7	84	0	78	287	20,611
26-30	21	47	3	24	0	32	127	11,174
31 and above	30	70	7	34	0	33	165	14,149
Total	316	485	151	1,522	6	851	3,322	226,693

Source: Extract from Service Personnel Records, Defense Manpower Data Center, Arlington, VA, June 1992, unpublished data. Ethnicity is self-reported by individuals at the time of their enlistment and may be updated upon reenlistment.

Army

★ 670 ★

Active Duty U.S. Army Personnel by Age

Asian American service in the U.S. Army by age and ethnicity (self-reported), as of June 1992.

Age	Chinese	Japanese	Korean	Filipino	Viet-namese	Other Asian	Total Asian	Total, all active duty
17	1	0	0	1	1	4	7	762
18	8	6	12	41	12	22	101	9,862
19	18	11	36	101	42	77	285	29,521
20	27	19	64	167	46	95	418	44,857
21	26	27	72	201	28	95	449	51,326
22	23	16	74	152	40	81	386	43,934
23	20	21	64	139	31	75	350	36,068
24	28	15	51	143	28	44	309	32,889
25	17	20	52	131	19	53	292	30,866
26-30	67	97	203	559	77	224	1227	134,984
31-35	46	86	198	539	29	279	1177	104,334
36-40	37	102	138	492	5	279	1053	73,513
41 and above	66	81	175	499	6	174	1001	46,656
Total	384	501	1139	3165	364	1502	7055	639,584

Source: Extract from Service Personnel Records, Defense Manpower Data Center, Arlington, VA, June 1992, unpublished data. Ethnicity is self-reported by individuals at the time of their enlistment and may be updated upon reenlistment.

★ 671 ★

Active Duty U.S. Army Personnel by Rank

Asian American service in the U.S. Army by rank and ethnicity (self-reported), as of June 1992.

Rank	Title	Chinese	Japanese	Korean	Filipino	Viet-namese	Other Asian	Total Asian	Total, all active duty
0									53
E1	Private	15	13	73	170	35	78	384	24,476
E2	Private E2	28	10	64	125	46	84	357	36,611
E3	Private 1st Class	43	30	110	258	65	140	646	67,607
E4	Specialist	72	69	263	737	118	313	1572	166,394
E5	Sergeant	36	38	140	517	28	166	925	99,581
E6	Staff Sergeant	31	49	168	539	16	202	1005	78,597
E7	Sergeant 1st Class	17	46	101	428	5	207	804	50,330
E8	Master Sergeant or 1st Sergeant	8	20	23	78	0	74	203	13,193
E9		4	9	3	19	0	32	67	3,833
W1	Warrant Officer	0	3	6	7	0	5	21	1,987
W2	Chief Warrant Officer 2	2	7	12	27	0	18	66	6,263

(Continued)

★ 671 ★

Active Duty U.S. Army Personnel by Rank (Continued)

Asian American service in the U.S. Army by rank and ethnicity (self-reported), as of June 1992.

Rank	Title	Chinese	Japanese	Korean	Filipino	Viet-namese	Other Asian	Total Asian	Total, all active duty
W3	Chief Warrant Officer 3	1	5	3	8	1	10	28	3,847
W4	Chief Warrant Officer 4	0	5	1	3	0	2	11	2,000
O0									15
O1	2nd Lieutenant	17	20	33	46	17	21	154	8,532
O2	1st Lieutenant	25	24	47	63	15	33	207	12,584
O3	Captain	25	59	60	71	15	52	282	31,751
O4	Major	28	51	15	34	0	39	167	17,808
O5	Lieutenant Colonel	15	28	14	32	2	19	110	10,808
O6	Colonel	16	14	9	16	1	10	66	4,836
O7	Brigadier General	0	2	0	0	0	0	2	194
O8	Major General	2	0	0	0	0	0	2	138
O9	Lieutenant General	0	0	0	0	0	0	0	42
O10	General	0	0	0	0	0	0	0	12
Total		385	502	1,145	3,178	364	1,505	7,079	641,492

Source: Extract from Service Personnel Records, Defense Manpower Data Center, Arlington, VA, June 1992, unpublished data. Ethnicity is self-reported by individuals at the time of their enlistment and may be updated upon reenlistment.

★ 672 ★

Active Duty U.S. Army Personnel by Sex

Asian American service in the U.S. Army by sex and ethnicity (self-reported), as of June 1992.

Sex	Chinese	Japanese	Korean	Filipino	Viet-namese	Other Asian	Total Asian	Total, all active duty
Male	336	440	994	2,787	333	1,336	6,226	564,268
Female	49	62	149	378	31	165	834	75,633
Total	385	502	1,143	3,165	364	1,501	7,060	639,901

Source: Extract from Service Personnel Records, Defense Manpower Data Center, Arlington, VA, June 1992, unpublished data. Ethnicity is self-reported by individuals at the time of their enlistment and may be updated upon reenlistment.

★ 673 ★

Active Duty U.S. Army Personnel by Source of Commission

Asian American officers in the U.S. Army by source of commission and ethnicity (self-reported), as of June 1992.

Commission	Chinese	Japanese	Korean	Filipino	Viet-namese	Other Asian	Total Asian	Total, all active duty
Academy, Army	7	21	16	19	5	33	101	12,455
Academy, Air Force	0	1	0	0	0	0	1	41
Academy, Merchant Marine	0	0	0	0	0	0	0	14
ROTC/NROTC Scholarship	19	47	39	36	11	20	172	12,725

(Continued)

★ 673 ★

Active Duty U.S. Army Personnel by Source of Commission (Continued)

Asian American officers in the U.S. Army by source of commission and ethnicity (self-reported), as of June 1992.

Commission	Chinese	Japanese	Korean	Filipino	Viet-namese	Other Asian	Total Asian	Total, all active duty
ROTC/NROTC Non-scholarship	50	78	64	101	20	66	379	37,039
OCS/AOCS/OTS/PLC[a]	7	14	12	14	2	9	58	8,822
Direct Appointment, Professional	33	27	39	59	12	31	201	7,782
Direct Appointment, Non-professional	12	10	8	32	0	15	77	6,729
Total	128	198	178	261	50	174	989	85,607

Source: Extract from Service Personnel Records, Defense Manpower Data Center, Arlington, VA, June 1992, unpublished data. Ethnicity is self-reported by individuals at the time of their enlistment and may be updated upon reenlistment. *Note:* (a) Officer Candidate chool, Aviation Officer Candidate School, Officer Training School, Platoon Leaders' School

★ 674 ★

Active Duty U.S. Army Personnel by Years of Service

Asian American service in the U.S. Army by years of service and ethnicity (self-reported), as of June 1992.

Years of Service	Chinese	Japanese	Korean	Filipino	Viet-namese	Other Asian	Total Asian	Total, all active duty
1	54	35	175	370	98	177	909	67,453
2	54	45	134	291	84	192	800	73,187
3	51	35	119	281	55	143	684	69,358
4	36	37	94	278	48	127	620	56,427
5	11	24	70	117	16	41	279	34,029
6	13	25	58	133	13	48	290	32,517
7	12	23	40	116	12	34	237	29,404
8	13	20	29	106	9	30	207	26,428
9	11	10	32	101	4	37	195	25,436
10	6	7	43	92	3	26	177	23,202
11-15	46	81	174	565	17	230	1,113	94,127
16-20	48	101	158	617	4	301	1,229	80,306
21-25	22	44	17	106	1	94	284	23,133
26 and above	8	15	2	5	0	25	55	6,265
Total	385	502	1,145	3,178	364	1,505	7,079	641,272

Source: Extract from Service Personnel Records, Defense Manpower Data Center, Arlington, VA, June 1992, unpublished data. Ethnicity is self-reported by individuals at the time of their enlistment and may be updated upon reenlistment.

★ 675 ★

Enlisted U.S. Army Personnel by Years of Service

Asian American enlistment in the U.S. Army by years of service and ethnicity (self-reported), as of June 1992.

Years of service	Chinese	Japanese	Korean	Filipino	Viet-namese	Other Asian	Total Asian	Total, all enlisted
5	5	15	48	100	12	34	214	29,476
6	11	13	49	124	11	37	245	28,068
7	6	10	33	109	8	26	192	24,605
8	6	12	24	101	9	26	178	21,499
9	9	8	31	93	3	28	172	20,991
10	3	5	39	84	2	22	155	19,138
11-15	28	36	144	506	14	192	920	74,106
16-20	23	60	134	560	4	262	1,043	62,299
21-25	13	15	10	88	0	74	200	13,264
26 and above	0	6	1	5	0	20	32	2,200
Total	104	180	513	1,770	63	721	3,351	540,478

Source: Extract from Service Personnel Records, Defense Manpower Data Center, Arlington, VA, June 1992, unpublished data. Ethnicity is self-reported by individuals at the time of their enlistment and may be updated upon reenlistment.

★ 676 ★

Service in the U.S. Army Guard by Age

Asian American service in the U.S. Army Guard by age and ethnicity (self-reported), as of June 1992.

Age	Chinese	Japanese	Korean	Filipino	Viet-namese	Other Asian	Total Asian	Total Guard
16	0	0	0	0	0	0	0	2
17	2	2	6	13	8	6	37	5,267
18	8	12	14	31	7	23	95	10,727
19	12	16	15	48	8	28	127	15,425
20	11	23	21	57	8	36	156	19,955
21	13	25	23	74	17	52	204	22,652
22	10	20	28	101	18	42	219	23,090
23	10	26	24	94	15	35	204	23,199
24	20	26	19	92	11	37	205	21,579
25	14	32	10	93	22	42	213	19,430
26-30	40	110	43	410	33	108	744	81,390
31-35	40	75	29	268	8	54	474	56,548
36-40	27	106	16	204	2	35	390	43,480
41 and above	76	264	17	243	7	33	640	94,118
Total	283	737	265	1,728	164	531	3,708	436,862

Source: Extract from Service Personnel Records, Defense Manpower Data Center, Arlington, VA, June 1992, unpublished data. Ethnicity is self-reported by individuals at the time of their enlistment and may be updated upon reenlistment.

★ 677 ★

Service in the U.S. Army Guard by Sex

Asian American service in the U.S. Army Guard by sex and ethnicity (self-reported), as of June 1992.

Sex	Chinese	Japanese	Korean	Filipino	Viet-namese	Other Asian	Total Asian	Total Guard
Male	262	705	237	1,622	156	478	3,460	404,432
Female	21	32	28	106	8	53	248	32,454
Total	283	737	265	1,728	164	531	3,708	436,886

Source: Extract from Service Personnel Records, Defense Manpower Data Center, Arlington, VA, June 1992, unpublished data. Ethnicity is self-reported by individuals at the time of their enlistment and may be updated upon reenlistment.

★ 678 ★

Service in the U.S. Army Guard by Years of Service

Asian American service in the U.S. Army Guard by years of service and ethnicity (self-reported), as of June 1992.

Years of Service	Chinese	Japanese	Korean	Filipino	Viet-namese	Other Asian	Total Asian	Total Guard
0	13	11	19	58	18	29	148	20,550
1	9	6	24	62	15	52	168	19,916
2	22	30	24	86	28	56	246	26,230
3	14	29	31	99	18	74	265	26,812
4	18	35	26	116	20	50	265	26,580
5	21	32	18	142	19	42	274	28,110
6	16	32	22	83	8	34	195	22,101
7	12	32	8	104	7	33	196	21,573
8	11	27	6	107	2	21	174	17,940
9	12	21	5	101	2	15	156	16,340
10	6	17	11	89	2	10	135	15,889
11-15	36	97	27	310	4	42	516	68,577
16-20	30	125	13	161	3	14	346	50,179
21-25	29	128	4	64	2	12	239	36,504
26-30	10	40	1	31	0	2	84	9,248
31 and above	9	38	1	15	0	1	64	5,898
99	15	37	25	100	16	44	237	24,439
Total	270	726	246	1,670	146	502	3,560	436,886

Source: Extract from Service Personnel Records, Defense Manpower Data Center, Arlington, VA, June 1992, unpublished data. Ethnicity is self-reported by individuals at the time of their enlistment and may be updated upon reenlistment.

★ 679 ★

Service in the U.S. Army Reserve by Age

Asian American service in the U.S. Army Reserve by age and ethnicity (self-reported), as of June 1992.

Age	Chinese	Japanese	Korean	Filipino	Viet-namese	Other Asian	Total Asian	Total Reserve
17	18	8	12	30	14	23	105	5,305
18	40	14	46	96	23	59	278	12,404
19	45	13	48	114	32	80	332	14,422
20	30	27	46	123	36	76	338	18,783
21	41	18	58	138	38	75	368	28,975
22	63	43	73	183	53	112	527	41,078
23	49	50	88	228	54	120	589	53,040
24	49	57	100	253	48	129	636	62,365
25	53	54	85	246	51	109	598	60,129
26-30	170	193	307	702	135	334	1,841	169,398
31-35	93	108	168	376	35	160	940	77,681
36-40	90	111	84	309	18	111	723	53,994
41 and above	261	344	139	634	16	259	1,653	143,021
Total	1,002	1,040	1,254	3,432	553	1,647	8,928	740,595

Source: Extract from Service Personnel Records, Defense Manpower Data Center, Arlington, VA, June 1992, unpublished data. Ethnicity is self-reported by individuals at the time of their enlistment and may be updated upon reenlistment.

★ 680 ★

Service in the U.S. Army Reserve by Rank

Asian American service in the U.S. Army Reserve by rank and ethnicity (self-reported), as of June 1992.

Rank		Chinese	Japanese	Korean	Filipino	Viet-namese	Other Asian	Total Asian	Total Reserve
E1	Private	85	35	97	212	64	125	618	32,582
E2	Private E2	53	36	98	241	68	198	694	80,750
E3	Private 1st Class	91	65	154	356	67	203	936	76,585
E4	Specialist	190	228	486	1,146	239	534	2,823	234,917
E5	Sergeant	91	96	107	494	39	159	986	84,522
E6	Staff Sergeant	35	69	42	210	7	62	425	46,437
E7	Sergeant 1st Class	31	64	13	135	0	56	299	37,438
E8	Master Sergeant or 1st Sergeant	20	33	6	72	0	30	161	17,847
E9		9	24	1	9	0	11	54	4,462
W1	Warrant Office	1	1	1	3	0	1	7	476
W2	Chief Warrant Officer 2	6	5	0	6	1	0	18	3,395
W3	Chief Warrant Officer 3	5	5	0	8	1	3	22	3,520
W4	Chief Warrant Officer 4	1	5	0	3	0	3	12	2,449
O0		0	0	0	0	0	0	0	9
O1	2nd Lieutenant	27	24	39	49	19	29	187	13,027
O2	1st Lieutenant	73	51	64	97	22	48	355	23,139
O3	Captain	92	71	61	134	15	63	436	33,188
O4	Major	105	97	40	126	8	52	428	24,631
O5	Lieutenant Colonel	65	84	37	105	4	48	343	19,646

(Continued)

★ 680 ★

Service in the U.S. Army Reserve by Rank (Continued)

Asian American service in the U.S. Army Reserve by rank and ethnicity (self-reported), as of June 1992.

Rank		Chinese	Japanese	Korean	Filipino	Viet-namese	Other Asian	Total Asian	Total Reserve
O6	Colonel	24	46	10	31	0	23	134	7,199
O7	Brigadier General	1	2	0	0	0	0	3	205
O8	Major General	0	1	0	0	0	0	1	74
O9	Lieutenant General	0	0	0	0	0	0	0	0
O10	General	0	0	0	0	0	0	0	0
Total		1,005	1,042	1,256	3,437	554	1,648	8,942	745,498

Source: Extract from Service Personnel Records, Defense Manpower Data Center, Arlington, VA, June 1992, unpublished data. Ethnicity is self-reported by individuals at the time of their enlistment and may be updated upon reenlistment.

★ 681 ★

Service in the U.S. Army Reserve by Sex

Asian American service in the U.S. Army Reserve by sex and ethnicity (self-reported), as of June 1992.

Sex	Chinese	Japanese	Korean	Filipino	Viet-namese	Other Asian	Total Asian	Total Reserve
Male	837	893	1,043	2,759	478	1,350	7,360	620,776
Female	168	149	213	678	76	298	1,582	125,652
Total	1,005	1,042	1,256	3,437	554	1,648	8,942	746,498

Source: Extract from Service Personnel Records, Defense Manpower Data Center, Arlington, VA, June 1992, unpublished data. Ethnicity is self-reported by individuals at the time of their enlistment and may be updated upon reenlistment.

★ 682 ★

Service in the U.S. Army Reserve by Years of Service

Asian American service in the U.S. Army Reserve by years of service and ethnicity (self-reported), as of June 1992.

Years of Service	Chinese	Japanese	Korean	Filipino	Viet-namese	Other Asian	Total Asian	Total Reserve
0	99	35	102	224	64	138	662	28,715
1	46	24	62	142	35	122	431	23,136
2	49	36	68	199	49	126	527	34,138
3	70	51	101	265	71	171	729	49,094
4	76	51	133	320	80	124	784	66,192
5	97	93	188	362	69	181	990	83,323
6	82	76	192	346	74	148	918	84,877
7	68	75	132	358	51	144	828	83,709
8	39	42	35	157	16	49	338	25,040
9	38	30	26	125	8	35	262	19,415
10	17	21	26	101	5	23	193	18,137
11-15	100	104	87	370	12	121	794	72,019

(Continued)

★ 682 ★

Service in the U.S. Army Reserve by Years of Service (Continued)

Asian American service in the U.S. Army Reserve by years of service and ethnicity (self-reported), as of June 1992.

Years of Service	Chinese	Japanese	Korean	Filipino	Viet-namese	Other Asian	Total Asian	Total Reserve
16-20	96	131	73	232	7	88	627	49,893
21-25	80	138	13	145	0	62	438	55,687
26-30	25	61	5	42	0	31	164	23,857
31 and above	17	67	1	29	0	60	174	23,992
99	6	7	12	20	13	25	83	5,274
Total	906	1,007	1,154	3,213	490	1,510	8,280	746,498

Source: Extract from Service Personnel Records, Defense Manpower Data Center, Arlington, VA, June 1992, unpublished data. Ethnicity is self-reported by individuals at the time of their enlistment and may be updated upon reenlistment.

Coast Guard

★ 683 ★

Active Duty U.S. Coast Guard Personnel by Age

Asian American service in the U.S. Coast Guard by age and ethnicity (self-reported), as of June 1992.

Age	Total Asian	Total, all active duty
17	1	8
18	9	315
19	35	1,170
20	37	1,798
21	29	2,134
22	47	2,330
23	41	2,188
24	29	1,877
25	28	1,750
26-30	138	9,087
31-35	91	7,822
36-40	64	4,672
41 and above	157	3,199
Total	706	38,350

Source: Extract from Service Personnel Records, Defense Manpower Data Center, Arlington, VA, June 1992, unpublished data. Ethnicity is self-reported by individuals at the time of their enlistment and may be updated upon reenlistment. The U.S. Coast Guard does not further classify Asian Americans by ethnicity.

★ 684 ★

Active Duty U.S. Coast Guard Personnel by Rank

Asian American service in the U.S. Coast Guard by rank, as of June 1992.

Rank		Total Asian	Total, all active duty
E1	Seaman Recruit	6	212
E2	Seaman Apprentice	75	3,375
E3	Seaman	82	4,080
E4	Petty Officer 3rd Class	104	7,882
E5	Petty Officer 2nd Class	73	5,911
E6	Petty Officer 1st Class	78	5,791
E7	Chief Petty Officer	62	2,797
E8	Senior Chief Petty Officer	35	573
E9	Master Chief Petty Officer	22	0
W1	Warrant Officer 1	0	303
W2	Warrant Officer 2	15	824
W3	Warrant Officer 3	16	320
W4	Warrant Officer 4	18	422
O1	Ensign	21	694
O2	Lieutenant Junior Grade	39	1,178
O3	Lieutenant	42	1,873
O4	Lieutenant Commander	12	1,039
O5	Commander	5	695
O6	Captain	1	362
O7	Rear Admiral Lower Half	0	13
O8	Rear Admiral Upper Half	0	13
O9	Vice Admiral	0	5
O10	Admiral	0	1
Total		706	38,364

Source: Extract from Service Personnel Records, Defense Manpower Data Center, Arlington, VA, June 1992, unpublished data. Ethnicity is self-reported by individuals at the time of their enlistment and may be updated upon reenlistment. The U.S. Coast Guard does not further classify Asian Americans by ethnicity.

★ 685 ★

Active Duty U.S. Coast Guard Personnel
by Years of Service

Asian American service in the U.S. Coast Guard by years of service as of June 1992.

Years of Service	Total Asian	Total, all active duty
1	78	3,627
2	92	3,612
3	42	2,484
4	54	2,845
5	35	2,353
6	32	2,013
7	19	1,307
8	15	1,320
9	13	1,567

(Continued)

★ 685 ★

Active Duty U.S. Coast Guard Personnel
by Years of Service (Continued)

Asian American service in the U.S. Coast Guard by years of service
as of June 1992.

Years of Service	Total Asian	Total, all active duty
10	24	1,611
11-15	80	7,424
16-20	62	5,295
21-25	114	2,211
26 and above	45	676
Total	705	38,345

Source: Extract from Service Personnel Records, Defense Manpower Data Center,
Arlington, VA, June 1992, unpublished data. Ethnicity is self-reported by individuals
at the time of their enlistment and may be updated upon reenlistment.

★ 686 ★

Service in the U.S.
Coast Guard Reserve by Age

Asian American service in the U.S. Coast Guard Reserve by age and
ethnicity (self-reported), as of June 1992.

Age	Asian American/ Pacific Islander	Total Reserve
18	3	68
19	2	109
20	4	253
21	7	413
22	7	648
23	8	851
24	15	1,041
25	18	1,041
26	12	866
27	9	760
28	16	692
29	13	678
30	13	666
31-35	22	2,759
36-40	10	2,439
41-45	5	2,619
46 and above	4	4,317

Source: Extract from Service Personnel Records, Defense Manpower Data Center,
Arlington, VA, June 1992, unpublished data. Ethnicity is self-reported by individuals
at the time of their enlistment and may be updated upon reenlistment.

★ 687 ★

Service in the U.S. Coast Guard Reserve by Rank

Asian American service in the U.S. Coast Guard by rank and ethnicity (self-reported), as of June 1992.

Rank	Title	Total Asians	Total, all Reserve
E1	Seaman Recruit	4	86
E2	Seaman Apprentice	15	998
E3	Seaman	29	1,949
E4	Petty Officer 3rd Class	79	6,287
E5	Petty Officer 2nd Class	30	3,508
E6	Petty Officer 1st Class	5	2,462
E7	Chief Petty Officer	2	1,247
E8	Senior Chief Petty Officer	0	317
E9	Master Chief Petty Officer	0	244
W1	Warrant Officer 1	0	0
W2	Warrant Officer 2	0	203
W3	Warrant Officer 3	0	93
W4	Warrant Officer 4	0	158
O1	Ensign	1	39
O2	Lieutenant Junior Grade	1	181
O3	Lieutenant	1	773
O4	Lieutenant Commander	0	761
O5	Commander	0	629
O6	Captain	0	295
O7	Rear Admiral Lower Half	0	2
O8	Rear Admiral Upper Half	0	0
O9	Vice Admiral	0	0
O10	Admiral	0	0
Total		167	20,232

Source: Extract from Service Personnel Records, Defense Manpower Data Center, Arlington, VA, June 1992, unpublished data. Ethnicity is self-reported by individuals at the time of their enlistment.

★ 688 ★

Service in the U.S. Coast Guard Reserve by Sex

Asian American service in the U.S. Coast Guard Reserve by sex, as of June 1992.

Sex	Total Asian	Total Reserve
Male	134	17,959
Female	33	2,273
Total	167	20,232

Source: Extract from Service Personnel Records, Defense Manpower Data Center, Arlington, VA, June 1992, unpublished data. Ethnicity is self-reported by individuals at the time of their enlistment and may be updated upon reenlistment.

★ 689 ★

Service in the U.S. Coast Guard Reserve
by Years of Service

Asian American service in the U.S. Coast Guard Reserve by years of service, as of June 1992.

Years of service	Asian Americans	Total Reserve
1	8	3,627
2	11	3,612
3	7	2,484
4	10	2,845
5	21	2,353
6	30	2,013
7	27	1,307
8	9	1,320
9	8	1,567
10	3	1,611
11 and above	14	15,606

Source: Extract from Service Personnel Records, Defense Manpower Data Center, Arlington, VA, June 1992, unpublished data. Ethnicity is self-reported by individuals at the time of their enlistment and may be updated upon reenlistment.

Marine Corps

★ 690 ★

Active Duty U.S. Marine Corps Personnel by Age

Asian American service in the U.S. Marine Corps by age and ethnicity (self-reported), as of June 1992.

Age	Chinese	Japanese	Korean	Filipino	Viet-namese	Other Asian	Total Asian	Total, all active duty
17	0	0	2	2	2	1	7	323
18	4	1	6	25	3	8	47	5,679
19	5	6	20	54	23	26	134	16,036
20	12	11	29	91	18	46	207	20,775
21	9	14	30	116	27	39	235	23,397
22	17	11	11	145	32	30	246	19,989
23	8	8	18	91	23	17	165	13,608
24	9	5	22	53	8	14	111	10,022
25	7	2	10	53	11	13	96	7,796
26-30	19	45	26	168	22	49	329	31,463
31-35	7	32	11	114	0	34	198	20,896
36-40	7	13	6	76	0	40	142	12,353
41 and above	6	5	2	44	0	19	76	6,638
Total	110	153	193	1,032	169	336	1,993	188,975

Source: Extract from Service Personnel Records, Defense Manpower Data Center, Arlington, VA, June 1992, unpublished data. Ethnicity is self-reported by individuals at the time of their enlistment and may be updated upon reenlistment.

★ 691 ★

Active Duty U.S. Marine Corps Personnel by Rank

Asian American service in the U.S. Marine Corps by rank and ethnicity (self-reported), as of June 1992.

Rank	Title	Chinese	Japanese	Korean	Filipino	Viet-namese	Other Asian	Total Asian	Total, all active duty
E1	Private	5	3	12	38	12	19	89	8,644
E2	Private 1st Class	10	8	23	74	35	27	177	18,636
E3	Lance Corporal	27	32	71	312	63	103	608	56,082
E4	Corporal	24	14	29	225	40	43	375	32,171
E5	Sergeant	8	25	19	149	11	36	248	24,764
E6	Staff Sergeant	6	10	5	93	1	20	135	14,631
E7	Gunnery Sergeant	6	8	9	68	0	35	126	9,458
E8	1st Sergeant or Master Sergeant	0	5	0	20	0	10	35	3,651
E9	Sergeant Major Gun-nery or Sergeant Major	2	3	0	1	0	6	12	1,504
W1	Warrant Officer 1	0	2	0	1	0	0	3	336
W2	Warrant Officer 2	0	0	0	1	0	0	1	867
W3	Warrant Officer 3	0	0	0	3	0	0	3	444
W4	Warrant Officer 4	0	0	0	0	0	1	1	248
O1	2nd Lieutenant	3	2	6	6	2	5	24	2,373
O2	1st Lieutenant	6	11	9	20	4	11	61	3,603
O3	Captain	9	26	5	16	1	11	68	6,166
O4	Major	3	3	4	4	0	8	22	3,095
O5	Lieutenant Colonel	1	1	1	1	0	1	5	1,598
O6	Colonel	0	0	0	0	0	0	0	640
O7	Brigadier General	0	0	0	0	0	0	0	33
O8	Major General	0	0	0	0	0	0	0	21
O9	Lieutenant General	0	0	0	0	0	0	0	8
O10	General	0	0	0	0	0	0	0	3
Total		110	153	193	1,032	169	336	1,993	188,976

Source: Extract from Service Personnel Records, Defense Manpower Data Center, Arlington, VA, June 1992, unpublished data. Ethnicity is self-reported by individuals at the time of their enlistment and may be updated upon reenlistment.

★ 692 ★

Active Duty U.S. Marine Corps Personnel by Sex

Asian American service in the U.S. Marine Corps by sex and ethnicity (self-reported), as of June 1992.

Sex	Chinese	Japanese	Korean	Filipino	Viet-namese	Other Asian	Total Asian	Total, all active duty
Male	108	144	175	996	162	322	1,907	180,371
Female	2	9	18	36	7	14	86	8,603
Total	110	153	193	1,032	169	336	1,993	188,974

Source: Extract from Service Personnel Records, Defense Manpower Data Center, Arlington, VA, June 1992, unpublished data. Ethnicity is self-reported by individuals at the time of their enlistment and may be updated upon reenlistment.

★ 693 ★

Active Duty U.S. Marine Corps Personnel by Source of Commission

Asian American officers in the U.S. Marine Corps by source of commission and ethnicity (self-reported), as of June 1992.

Commission	Chinese	Japanese	Korean	Filipino	Viet-namese	Other Asian	Total Asian	Total, all active duty
Academy, Navy	3	4	5	7	1	8	28	1,754
ROTC/NROTC Scholarship	4	7	4	10	0	8	33	3,319
OCS/AOCS/OTS/PLC	14	29	14	26	5	17	105	10,483
Other Asian	1	5	2	9	1	4	22	3,684
Total	22	45	25	52	7	37	188	19,240

Source: Extract from Service Personnel Records, Defense Manpower Data Center, Arlington, VA, June 1992, unpublished data. Ethnicity is self-reported by individuals at the time of their enlistment and may be updated upon reenlistment.

★ 694 ★

Active Duty U.S. Marine Corps Personnel by Years of Service

Asian American service in the U.S. Marine Corps by years of service and ethnicity (self-reported), as of June 1992.

Years of service	Chinese	Japanese	Korean	Filipino	Viet-namese	Other Asian	Total Asian	Total, all active duty
1	13	17	38	121	50	52	291	27,153
2	12	12	35	120	27	57	263	25,900
3	20	16	33	160	37	45	311	25,345
4	15	14	28	166	26	32	281	24,165
5	12	13	15	63	10	11	124	10,633
6	5	9	8	39	7	12	80	9,357
7	4	6	7	37	3	16	73	6,307
8	2	4	3	36	3	6	54	5,968
9	2	11	4	40	1	4	62	5,921
10	2	7	3	19	2	6	39	5,148
11-15	10	24	7	110	3	27	181	21,055
16-20	11	13	9	105	0	52	190	15,719
21-25	1	6	3	16	0	13	39	4,950
26 and above	1	1	0	0	0	3	5	1,353
Total	110	153	193	1,032	169	336	1,993	188,974

Source: Extract from Service Personnel Records, Defense Manpower Data Center, Arlington, VA, June 1992, unpublished data. Ethnicity is self-reported by individuals at the time of their enlistment and may be updated upon reenlistment.

★ 695 ★

Enlisted Personnel in the U.S. Marine Corp by Years of Service

Asian American enlistment in the U.S. Marine Corp by years of service and ethnicity (self-reported), as of June 1992.

Years of service	Chinese	Japanese	Korean	Filipino	Viet-namese	Other Asian	Total Asian	Total, all enlisted
5	9	7	14	61	7	7	105	9,611
6	4	4	7	36	6	12	69	8,419
7	2	1	5	35	3	14	60	5,483
8	2	1	2	33	3	6	47	5,257
9	1	5	3	35	1	4	49	5,190
10	2	6	3	17	2	4	34	4,403
11-15	6	17	6	103	2	21	155	17,560
16-20	7	11	8	98	0	42	166	11,724
21-25	1	4	0	13	0	12	30	3,052
26 and above	1	1	0	0	0	3	5	517
Total	35	57	48	431	24	125	720	169,541

Source: Extract from Service Personnel Records, Defense Manpower Data Center, Arlington, VA, June 1992, unpublished data. Ethnicity is self-reported by individuals at the time of their enlistment and may be updated upon reenlistment.

★ 696 ★

Service in the U.S. Marine Corps Reserve by Age

Asian American service in the U.S. Marine Corps Reserve by age and ethnicity (self-reported), as of June 1992.

Age	Chinese	Japanese	Korean	Filipino	Viet-namese	Other Asian	Total Asian	Total Reserve
17	1	1	0	0	1	0	3	111
18	5	1	5	19	5	2	37	1,234
19	16	5	8	44	10	16	99	3,375
20	24	1	17	46	11	22	121	4,789
21	34	4	18	60	14	15	145	5,835
22	26	7	20	89	29	19	190	8,558
23	24	14	29	103	25	17	212	13,556
24	23	12	24	84	29	24	196	15,555
25	21	15	14	75	21	20	166	14,425
26-30	38	19	39	166	28	39	329	24,202
31-35	13	10	2	41	7		85	7,253
36-40	4	5	1	12	0	3	25	3,519
41 and above	12	4	0	8	0	5	29	7,594
Total	241	98	177	747	180	194	1,637	110,006

Source: Extract from Service Personnel Records, Defense Manpower Data Center, Arlington, VA, June 1992, unpublished data. Ethnicity is self-reported by individuals at the time of their enlistment and may be updated upon reenlistment.

★ 697 ★

Service in the U.S. Marine Corps Reserve by Rank

Asian American service in the U.S. Marine Reserve by rank and ethnicity (self-reported), as of June 1992.

Rank	Title	Chinese	Japanese	Korean	Filipino	Viet-namese	Other Asian	Total Asian	Total Reserve
E1	Private	10	2	12	31	8	10	73	3,302
E2	Private 1st Class	23	4	22	59	19	15	142	6,264
E3	Lance Corporal	84	15	55	231	61	57	503	28,694
E4	Corporal	64	43	60	281	72	68	588	41,060
E5	Sergeant	34	16	20	90	13	21	194	12,623
E6	Staff Sergeant	2	1	2	22	2	2	31	3,531
E7	Gunnery Sergeant	3	4	0	8	0	2	17	2,026
E8	1st Sergeant or Master Sergeant	2	0	0	1	0	2	5	1,265
E9	Sergeant Major Gunnery or Sergeant Major	2	0	0	3	0	0	5	592
W1	Warrant Officer 1	0	0	0	1	1	0	2	104
W2	Warrant Officer 2	0	1	0	0	0	0	1	148
W3	Warrant Officer 3	1	0	0	0	0	1	2	215
W4	Warrant Officer 4	4	1	0	0	0	0	5	443
O1	2nd Lieutenant	0	0	0	0	0	0	0	75
O2	1st Lieutenant	3	0	3	3	1	3	13	584
O3	Captain	5	7	3	15	3	10	43	4,096
O4	Major	4	2	0	2	0	1	9	2,170
O5	Lieutenant Colonel	0	1	0	0	0	1	2	1,886
O6	Colonel	0	1	0	0	0	1	2	928
O7	Brigadier General	0	0	0	0	0	0	0	7
O8	Major General	0	0	0	0	0	0	0	7
O9	Lieutenant General	0	0	0	0	0	0	0	0
O10	General	0	0	0	0	0	0	0	0
Total		241	98	177	747	180	194	1,637	110,020

Source: Extract from Service Personnel Records, Defense Manpower Data Center, Arlington, VA, June 1992, unpublished data. Ethnicity is self-reported by individuals at the time of their enlistment and may be updated upon reenlistment.

★ 698 ★

Service in the U.S. Marine Corps Reserve by Sex

Asian American service in the U.S. Marine Corps Reserve by sex and ethnicity (self-reported), as of June 1992.

Sex	Chinese	Japanese	Korean	Filipino	Viet-namese	Other Asian	Total Asian	Total Reserve
Male	233	93	168	724	177	189	1584	104,631
Female	8	5	9	23	3	5	53	5,388
Total	241	98	177	747	180	194	1637	110,020

Source: Extract from Service Personnel Records, Defense Manpower Data Center, Arlington, VA, June 1992, unpublished data. Ethnicity is self-reported by individuals at the time of their enlistment and may be updated upon reenlistment.

★ 699 ★

Service in the U.S. Marine Corps Reserve by Years of Service

Asian American service in the U.S. Marine Corps Reserve by years of service and ethnicity (self-reported), as of June 1992.

Years of Service	Chinese	Japanese	Korean	Filipino	Viet-namese	Other Asian	Total Asian	Total Reserve
0	22	6	19	62	14	16	139	4,801
1	30	4	14	48	19	23	138	5,509
2	34	2	16	65	17	16	150	5,031
3	15	5	21	49	17	12	119	5,900
4	32	15	25	141	41	30	284	17,843
5	25	16	32	104	25	30	232	17,424
6	24	14	15	104	22	21	200	15,221
7	22	15	22	79	15	22	175	15,344
8	4	3	4	24	3	2	40	2,229
9	4	2	2	12	0	2	22	2,007
10	2	2	2	12	0	4	22	2,014
11-15	9	6	3	24	4	5	51	6,499
16-20	5	4	1	13	0	5	28	3,479
21-25	5	2	0	2	0	3	12	2,585
26-30	4	1	0	1	0	2	8	1,335
31 and above	2	1	0	1	0	0	4	2,351
99	2	0	1	6	3	1	13	448
Total	219	92	158	685	166	178	1,498	110,020

Source: Extract from Service Personnel Records, Defense Manpower Data Center, Arlington, VA, June 1992, unpublished data. Ethnicity is self-reported by individuals at the time of their enlistment and may be updated upon reenlistment.

<hr>

Navy

<hr>

★ 700 ★

Active Duty U.S. Navy Personnel by Age

Asian American service in the U.S. Navy by age and ethnicity (self-reported), as of June 1992.

Age	Chinese	Japanese	Korean	Filipino	Viet-namese	Other Asian	Total Asian	Total, all active duty
17	2	0	4	18	1	2	27	1,320
18	6	8	24	136	18	29	221	11,517
19	26	23	63	302	49	64	527	28,487
20	26	51	63	330	67	89	626	39,479
21	32	35	75	509	77	125	853	45,569
22	30	41	69	495	102	103	840	40,963
23	34	33	63	518	81	66	795	33,898
24	35	35	36	618	51	62	837	29,052
25	25	32	39	711	47	57	911	25,998
26-30	107	174	114	3,900	126	170	4,591	111,098
31-35	47	150	63	3,563	24	99	3,946	81,970
36-40	43	84	28	5,002	8	94	5,259	55,361
41 and above	41	39	12	2,787	2	70	2,951	33,440
Total	454	705	653	18,889	653	1,030	22,384	538,190

Source: Extract from Service Personnel Records, Defense Manpower Data Center, Arlington, VA, June 1992, unpublished data. Ethnicity is self-reported by individuals at the time of their enlistment and may be updated upon reenlistment.

★ 701 ★

Active Duty U.S. Navy Personnel by Rank

Asian American service in the U.S. Navy by rank and ethnicity (self-reported), as of June 1992.

Rank	Title	Chinese	Japanese	Korean	Filipino	Viet-namese	Other Asian	Total Asian	Total, all active duty
E1	Seaman Recruit	17	13	46	499	39	61	675	22,974
E2	Seaman Apprentice	22	32	59	699	75	95	982	39,067
E3	Seaman	50	64	120	1,505	178	193	2,110	69,112
E4	Petty Officer 3rd Class	86	100	148	2,644	189	205	3,372	101,044
E5	Petty Officer 2nd Class	61	130	97	3,986	75	137	4,486	102,649
E6	Petty Officer 1st Class	33	111	37	4,715	14	81	4,991	84,281
E7	Chief Petty Officer	13	43	16	2,726	1	53	2,852	34,128
E8	Senior Chief Petty Officer	6	16	1	1,055	1	23	1,102	10,219
E9	Master Chief Petty Officer	0	2	2	403	0	16	423	4,842
W1	Warrant Officer 1	0	0	0	0	0	0	0	53
W2	Warrant Officer 2	0	1	0	43	0	2	46	1,534

[Continued]

★ 701 ★

Active Duty U.S. Navy Personnel by Rank (Continued)

Asian American service in the U.S. Navy by rank and ethnicity (self-reported), as of June 1992.

Rank	Title	Chinese	Japanese	Korean	Filipino	Viet-namese	Other Asian	Total Asian	Total, all active duty
W3	Warrant Officer 3	0	0	0	34	0	0	34	813
W4	Warrant Officer 4	1	0	0	17	0	0	18	533
O1	Ensign	23	19	32	101	27	41	243	7,753
O2	Lieutenant Junior Grade	36	31	27	100	24	32	250	9,870
O3	Lieutenant	58	80	48	213	28	47	474	24,382
O4	Lieutenant Commander	22	44	13	89	2	23	193	13,368
O5	Commander	16	15	5	46	0	13	95	7,847
O6	Captain	10	4	2	14	0	6	36	3,612
O7	Rear Admiral Lower Half	0	0	0	0	0	1	1	124
O8	Rear Admiral Upper Half	0	0	0	0	0	0	0	80
O9	Vice Admiral	0	0	0	0	0	1	1	29
O10	Admiral	0	0	0	0	0	0	0	9
Total		454	705	653	18,889	653	1,030	22,384	538,323

Source: Extract from Service Personnel Records, Defense Manpower Data Center, Arlington, VA, June 1992, unpublished data. Ethnicity is self-reported by individuals at the time of their enlistment and may be updated upon reenlistment.

★ 702 ★

Active Duty U.S. Navy Personnel by Sex

Asian American service in the U.S. Navy by sex and ethnicity (self-reported), as of June 1992.

Sex	Chinese	Japanese	Korean	Filipino	Viet-namese	Other Asian	Total Asian	Total, all active duty
Male	401	627	557	18,242	600	916	21,343	483,411
Female	53	78	96	647	53	114	1,041	54,912
Total	454	705	653	18,889	653	1030	22,384	538,323

Source: Extract from Service Personnel Records, Defense Manpower Data Center, Arlington, VA, June 1992, unpublished data. Ethnicity is self-reported by individuals at the time of their enlistment and may updated upon reenlistment.

★ 703 ★

Active Duty U.S. Navy Personnel by Source of Commission

Asian American officers in the U.S. Navy by source of commission and ethnicity (self-reported), as of June 1992.

Commission	Chinese	Japanese	Korean	Filipino	Viet-namese	Other Asian	Total Asian	Total, all active duty
Academy, Navy	35	55	25	128	12	33	288	11,782
ROTC/NROTC Scholarship	25	34	29	87	13	57	245	12,838

[Continued]

★ 703 ★

Active Duty U.S. Navy Personnel by Source of Commission (Continued)

Asian American officers in the U.S. Navy by source of commission and ethnicity (self-reported), as of June 1992.

Commission	Chinese	Japanese	Korean	Filipino	Viet-namese	Other Asian	Total Asian	Total, all active duty
ROTC/NROTC Non-scholarship	0	2	3	11	1	7	24	1,825
OCS/AOCS/OTS/PLC[a]	33	43	28	111	26	22	263	15,893
Aviation Cadet	0	0	0	3	1	0	4	383
Direct Appointment, Professional	23	16	14	29	10	8	100	5,305
Direct Appointment, Non-professional	49	43	27	181	17	36	353	18,006
Aviation Training Program	0	0	1	2	1	0	4	404
Direct Appointment, Warrant Officer	1	1	0	105	0	3	110	3,519
Total	166	194	127	657	81	166	1,391	69,970

Source: Extract from Service Personnel Records, Defense Manpower Data Center, Arlington, VA, June 1992, unpublished data. Ethnicity is self-reported by individuals at the time of their enlistment and may be updated upon reenlistment. *Note:* (a) Officer Candidate School, Aviation Officer Candidate School, Officer Training School, Platoon Leader's Course.

★ 704 ★

Active Duty U.S. Navy Personnel by Years of Service

Asian American service in the U.S. Navy by years of service and ethnicity (self-reported), as of June 1992.

Years of service	Chinese	Japanese	Korean	Filipino	Viet-namese	Other Asian	Total Asian	Total, all active duty
1	55	66	116	932	99	142	1,410	49,687
2	56	54	117	1,194	151	174	1,746	61,077
3	61	63	81	1,156	128	161	1,650	55,966
4	49	56	88	1,308	112	112	1,725	51,406
5	42	35	51	1,062	44	56	1,290	35,173
6	27	51	40	1,069	46	25	1,258	31,132
7	18	40	25	911	24	42	1,060	25,085
8	17	39	24	792	10	29	911	22,330
9	11	32	10	722	1	23	799	20,446
10	14	31	10	652	4	29	740	19,757
11-15	45	126	51	2,978	11	64	3,275	78,801
16-20	36	81	22	4,566	0	101	4,806	57,049
21-25	14	22	5	1,053	0	43	1,138	18,593
26 and above	3	5	1	398	0	13	438	5,495
Total	448	701	641	18,793	631	1,014	22,228	531,997

Source: Extract from Service Personnel Records, Defense Manpower Data Center, Arlington, VA, June 1992, unpublished data. Ethnicity is self-reported by individuals at the time of their enlistment and may be updated upon reenlistment.

★ 705 ★

Enlisted Personnel in the U.S. Navy by Years of Service

Asian American enlistment in the U.S. Navy by years of service and ethnicity (self-reported), as of June 1992.

Years of Service	Chinese	Japanese	Korean	Filipino	Viet-namese	Other Asian	Total Asian	Total, all enlisted
5	33	22	36	1,035	36	36	1,198	31,195
6	17	38	31	1,048	39	23	1,196	27,149
7	8	24	15	887	19	33	986	21,220
8	9	24	15	774	8	23	853	18,981
9	4	26	6	705	1	19	761	17,845
10	6	17	8	641	4	23	699	17,204
11-15	27	85	38	2,905	9	47	3,111	67,599
16-20	20	62	15	4,397	0	83	4,577	45,217
21-25	6	13	4	991	1	31	1,046	11,314
26 and above	0	2	1	346	0	8	357	2,187
Total	130	313	169	13,729	117	326	14,784	462,086

Source: Extract from Service Personnel Records, Defense Manpower Data Center, Arlington, VA, June 1992, unpublished data. Ethnicity is self-reported by individuals at the time of their enlistment and may be updated upon reenlistment.

★ 706 ★

Service in the U.S. Navy Reserves by Age

Asian American service in the U.S. Navy Reserves by age and ethnicity (self-reported), as of June 1992.

Age	Chinese	Japanese	Korean	Filipino	Viet-namese	Other Asian	Total Asian	Total Reserves
17	0	0	0	1	0	0	1	20
18	1	0	0	7	1	1	10	561
19	1	3	2	15	5	2	28	1,949
20	4	5	5	40	9	13	76	3,639
21	10	2	13	32	12	7	76	6,271
22	16	6	9	99	27	13	170	12,250
23	27	16	21	149	32	19	264	19,827
24	31	18	19	187	40	33	328	23,496
25	19	17	23	195	38	37	329	24,231
26-30	70	70	62	625	114	139	1,080	66,470
31-35	59	67	34	442	36	46	684	41,124
36-40	46	55	17	541	8	57	724	32,085
41 and above	84	52	15	511	3	50	715	73,777
Total	368	311	220	2,844	325	417	4,485	305,700

Source: Extract from Service Personnel Records, Defense Manpower Data Center, Arlington, VA, June 1992, unpublished data. Ethnicity is self-reported by individuals at the time of their enlistment and may be updated upon reenlistment.

★ 707 ★

Service in the U.S. Navy Reserves by Rank

Asian American service in the U.S. Navy Reserves by rank and ethnicity (self-reported), as of June 1992.

Rank	Title	Chinese	Japanese	Korean	Filipino	Viet-namese	Other Asian	Total Asian	Total Reserves
E1	Seaman Recruit	2	4	3	36	9	5	59	3,900
E2	Seaman Apprentice	10	8	10	105	18	17	168	10,357
E3	Seaman	55	32	39	384	76	65	651	40,116
E4	Petty Officer 3rd Class	76	57	60	859	138	140	1,330	75,245
E5	Petty Officer 2nd Class	62	54	39	621	47	76	899	59,723
E6	Petty Officer 1st Class	23	28	8	398	4	29	490	33,622
E7	Chief Petty Officer	11	12	1	170	0	9	203	14,074
E8	Senior Chief Petty Officer	1	1	0	30	0	4	36	3,167
E9	Master Chief Petty Officer	2	1	0	13	0	2	18	1,482
W1	Warrant Officer 1	0	0	0	0	0	0	0	0
W2	Warrant Officer 2	0	0	0	1	0	0	1	179
W3	Warrant Officer 3	0	0	0	0	0	0	0	195
W4	Warrant Officer 4	0	0	0	0	0	0	0	508
O0		0	0	0	0	0	0	0	363
O1	Ensign	2	0	1	5	5	0	13	2,377
O2	Lieutenant Junior Grade	6	4	8	15	7	8	48	3,176
O3	Lieutenant	43	53	30	90	18	34	268	19,738
O4	Lieutenant Commander	39	28	12	64	2	20	165	18,741
O5	Commander	22	17	5	28	0	5	77	14,440
O6	Captain	14	13	4	30	1	3	65	8,246
O7	Rear Admiral Lower Half	0	0	0	0	0	0	0	33
O8	Rear Admiral Upper Half	0	0	0	0	0	0	0	54
O9	Vice Admiral	0	0	0	0	0	0	0	0
O10	Admiral								
Total		368	312	220	2,849	325	417	4,491	309,736

Source: Extract from Service Personnel Records, Defense Manpower Data Center, Arlington, VA, June 1992, unpublished data. Ethnicity is self-reported by individuals at the time of their enlistment and may be updated upon reenlistment.

★ 708 ★

Service in the U.S. Navy Reserves by Sex

Asian American service in the U.S. Navy Reserves by sex and ethnicity (self-reported), as of June 1992.

Sex	Chinese	Japanese	Korean	Filipino	Viet-namese	Other Asian	Total Asian	Total Reserves
Male	321	262	183	2,545	305	361	3,977	268,729
Female	47	50	37	304	20	56	514	40,765
Total	368	312	220	2,849	325	417	4,491	309,747

Source: Extract from Service Personnel Records, Defense Manpower Data Center, Arlington, VA, June 1992, unpublished data. Ethnicity is self-reported by individuals at the time of their enlistment and may be updated upon reenlistment.

★ 709 ★

Service in the U.S. Navy Reserves by Years of Service

Asian American service in the U.S. Navy Reserves by years of service and ethnicity (self-reported), as of June 1992.

Years of Service	Chinese	Japanese	Korean	Filipino	Viet-namese	Other Asian	Total Asian	Total Reserves
0	9	4	4	37	6	9	69	3,458
1	6	7	5	64	16	7	105	6,683
2	13	7	15	85	18	22	160	9,304
3	17	7	15	115	31	26	211	12,772
4	36	23	32	256	64	36	447	25,996
5	49	40	38	374	89	48	638	36,873
6	39	33	34	361	46	49	562	34,747
7	31	26	24	345	31	72	529	30,643
8	12	20	8	116	12	27	195	13,442
9	13	12	10	75	2	16	128	9,676
10	14	17	3	71	3	9	117	9,603
11-15	43	47	16	389	5	47	547	38,154
16-20	39	32	12	359	0	35	477	24,424
21-25	33	21	4	126	0	10	194	21,275
26-30	7	11	0	44	1	4	67	13,929
31 and above	5	4	0	28	0	0	37	17,537
99	2	1	0	4	1	0	8	1,231
Total	359	308	216	2,812	319	408	4,422	309,747

Source: Extract from Service Personnel Records, Defense Manpower Data Center, Arlington, VA, June 1992, unpublished data. Ethnicity is self-reported by individuals at the time of their enlistment and may be updated upon reenlistment.

All Services

★ 710 ★

Service in the U.S. Military by Service and Ethnicity

Service	Vietnamese	Korean	Filipino	Japanese	Chinese	Other Asian
Air Force	2	440	4,288	837	419	2,454
Air Force Guard	17	62	651	751	178	287
Air Force Reserve	7	151	1.522	475	316	851
Army	364	1,143	3,165	502	385	1,501
Army Guard	164	265	1,728	737	283	531
Army Reserve	554	1,256	3,437	1,042	1,005	1,648
Marine	169	193	1,032	153	110	336
Marine Reserve	180	177	747	98	241	194
Navy	653	653	18,889	705	454	1,030
Naval Reserve	325	220	2,849	312	368	417
Total	2,435	4,560	38,308	5,612	3,759	9,249

Source: Extract from Service Personnel Records, Defense Manpower Data Center, Arlington, VA, June 1992, unpublished data. Ethnicity is self-reported by individuals at the time of their enlistment and may be updated upon reenlistment. Note: The U.S. Coast Guard does not further classify Asian Americans by ethnicity.

★ 711 ★

Chinese Americans in the U.S. Military by Service and Sex

Service	Male	Female	Total
Air Force	350	69	419
Air Force Guard	170	8	178
Air Force Reserve	271	45	316
Army	336	49	385
Army Guard	262	21	283
Army Reserve	837	168	1,005
Marine	108	2	110
Marine Reserve	233	8	241
Navy	401	53	454
Naval Reserve	321	47	368
Total	3,289	470	3,759

Source: Extract from Service Personnel Records, Defense Manpower Data Center, Arlington, VA, June 1992, unpublished data. Ethnicity is self-reported by individuals at the time of their enlistment and may be updated upon reenlistment.

★ 712 ★

Filipino Americans in the U.S. Military by Service and Sex

Service	Male	Female	Total
Air Force	3,712	576	4,288
Air Force Guard	576	75	651
Air Force Reserve	1,245	277	1,522
Army	2,787	378	3,165
Army Guard	1,622	106	1,728
Army Reserve	2,759	678	3,437
Marine	996	36	1,032
Marine Reserve	724	23	747
Navy	18,242	647	18,889
Naval Reserve	2,545	304	2,849
Total	35,208	3,100	38,308

Source: Extract from Service Personnel Records, Defense Manpower Data Center, Arlington, VA, June 1992, unpublished data. Ethnicity is self-reported by individuals at the time of their enlistment and may be updated upon reenlistment.

★ 713 ★

Japanese Americans in the U.S. Military by Service and Sex

Service	Male	Female	Total
Air Force	729	108	837
Air Force Guard	702	49	751
Air Force Reserve	406	69	475
Army	440	62	502
Army Guard	705	32	737

[Continued]

★ 713 ★

Japanese Americans in the U.S. Military
by Service and Sex (Continued)

Service	Male	Female	Total
Army Reserve	893	149	1,042
Marine	144	9	153
Marine Reserve	93	5	98
Navy	627	78	705
Naval Reserve	262	50	312
Total	5,001	611	5,612

Source: Extract from Service Personnel Records, Defense Manpower Data Center, Arlington, VA, June 1992, unpublished data. Ethnicity is self-reported by individuals at the time of their enlistment and may be updated upon reenlistment.

★ 714 ★

Korean Americans in the U.S. Military by Service and Sex

Service	Male	Female	Total
Air Force	328	112	440
Air Force Guard	48	14	62
Air Force Reserve	102	49	151
Army	994	149	1,143
Army Guard	237	28	265
Army Reserve	1,043	213	1,256
Marine	175	18	193
Marine Reserve	168	9	177
Navy	557	96	653
Naval Reserve	183	37	220
Total	3,835	725	4,560

Source: Extract from Service Personnel Records, Defense Manpower Data Center, Arlington, VA, June 1992, unpublished data. Ethnicity is self-reported by individuals at the time of their enlistment and may be updated upon reenlistment.

★ 715 ★

Vietnamese Americans in the U.S. Military
by Service and Sex

Service	Male	Female	Total
Air Force	2	0	2
Air Force Guard	13	4	17
Air Force Reserve	6	1	7
Army	333	31	364
Army Guard	156	8	164
Army Reserve	478	76	554
Marine	162	7	169

[Continued]

★ 715 ★

Vietnamese Americans in the U.S. Military
by Service and Sex (Continued)

Service	Male	Female	Total
Marine Reserve	177	3	180
Navy	600	53	653
Naval Reserve	305	20	325
Total	2,232	203	2,435

Source: Extract from Service Personnel Records, Defense Manpower Data Center, Arlington, VA, June 1992, unpublished data. Ethnicity is self-reported by individuals at the time of their enlistment and may be updated upon reenlistment.

★ 716 ★

Active Duty U.S. Military Personnel by Age

Asian American service in the U.S. military by age and ethnicity (self-reported), as of June 1992.

Age	Chinese	Japanese	Korean	Filipino	Viet-namese	Other Asian	Total Asian	Total, all active duty
17	3	0	7	22	4	9	45	2,782
18	18	20	47	225	33	86	429	32,176
19	56	48	142	532	114	231	1,123	89,914
20	75	89	175	704	131	339	1,513	127,213
21	73	92	205	1,002	132	371	1,875	147,530
22	84	86	188	982	174	315	1,829	131,987
23	81	82	172	946	135	282	1,698	108,717
24	87	84	131	1,021	87	238	1,648	96,981
25	56	77	124	1,102	77	242	1,678	89,605
26-30	283	519	453	5,728	227	1,062	8,272	404,859
31-35	204	499	358	5,146	53	946	7,206	311,597
36-40	165	384	219	6,221	13	787	7,789	217,151
41 and above	182	216	204	3,743	8	414	4,767	130,534
Total	1,367	2,196	2,425	27,374	1,188	5,322	39,872	1,891,046

Source: Extract from Service Personnel Records, Defense Manpower Data Center, Arlington, VA, June 1992, unpublished data. Ethnicity is self-reported by individuals at the time of their enlistment and may be updated upon reenlistment.

★ 717 ★

Active Duty U.S. Military Personnel by Rank of Brigadier General or Higher

Asian American high-ranking officers in the U.S. military as of December 1992.

Name	Rank	Position	Birthplace
Navy			
Robert K. U. Kihune	Vice Admiral (O9)	Director of Training and Doctrine	Hawaii
Air Force			
Dr. Vernon Chong	Major General (O8)	Command Surgeon, Headquarters Air Training Command, and Commander, Joint Military Medical Command	California
Army			
William Shao Chang Chem	Major General (O8)	Program Executive Officer, Global Protection Against Limited Strikes, Office of the Assistant Secretary of the Army for Research Development and Acquisition, Washington, DC, since July 1992	China
John Liu Fugh	Major General (O8)	The Judge Advocate General, United States Army, Washington, DC, since July 1991	China
Eric Ken Shinseki	Brigadier General (O7)	Assistant Division Commander, 3d Infantry Division (Mechanized), United States Army Europe and Seventh Army, since July 1992	Hawaii
Paul Yukio Chinen	Brigadier General (O7)	Commanding General, United States Army Engineer Division, North Atlantic, New York, NY, since September 1992	Hawaii
David Earl Kaleokaika Cooper	Brigadier General (O7)	Chief of Staff, First United States Army, Fort George G. Meade, MD, since October 1991	Hawaii
Frederick Gamchoon Wong	Brigadier General (O7)	Deputy Director for Plans, J-5, United States Pacific Command, Camp H. M. Smith, HI, since February 1990	Hawaii

Source: Data provided by the public affairs offices of the U.S. Air Force, Navy, and Army, January, 1993.

★ 718 ★

Active Duty U.S. Military Personnel by Rank

Asian American service in the U.S. military (all services) by rank and ethnicity (self-reported), as of June 1992.

Rank	Chinese	Japanese	Korean	Filipino	Viet-namese	Other Asian	Total Asian	Total, all active duty
Enlisted Personnel								
E0								54
E1	39	34	151	796	86	214	1,320	69,323
E2	66	62	166	993	156	300	1,743	115,480
E3	150	148	366	2,502	306	692	4,164	248,767
E4	219	295	539	4,753	348	1,059	7,213	413,886
E5	154	347	324	5,690	114	839	7,468	329,205
E6	115	311	246	5,996	31	609	7,308	238,805
E7	79	194	141	3,611	6	485	4,516	134,736
E8	21	63	28	1,194	1	138	1,445	35,806
E9	10	23	5	435	0	75	548	14,576
Warrant Officers								
W1	0	5	6	8	0	5	24	2,376
W2	2	8	12	71	0	20	113	9,488
W3	1	5	3	45	1	10	65	5,424
W4	1	5	1	20	0	3	30	3,203
Officers								
O0								15
O1	59	57	78	185	46	118	543	26,519
O2	87	90	100	235	43	129	684	36,913
O3	173	284	179	491	45	348	1,520	106,103
O4	96	150	48	182	2	177	655	53,576
O5	56	82	26	123	2	73	362	33,131
O6	37	32	12	57	1	29	168	14,676
O7	0	2	0	0	0	1	3	525
O8	3	0	0	0	0	0	3	363
O9	0	0	0	0	0	1	1	120
O10	0	0	0	0	0	0	0	37
Total	1,368	2,197	2,431	27,387	1,188	5,325	39,896	1,893,107

Source: Extract from Service Personnel Records, Defense Manpower Data Center, Arlington, VA, June 1992, unpublished data. Ethnicity is self-reported by individuals at the time of their enlistment and may be updated upon reenlistment.

★ 719 ★

Active Duty U.S. Military Personnel by Sex

Asian American service in the U.S. military (all services) by sex and ethnicity (self-reported), as of June 1992.

Sex	Chinese	Japanese	Korean	Filipino	Viet-namese	Other Asian	Total Asian	Total, all active duty
Male	1,195	1,940	2,054	25,737	1,097	4,608	36,631	1,679,229
Female	173	257	375	1,637	91	713	3,246	212,285
Total	1,368	2,197	2,429	27,374	1,188	5,321	39,877	1,891,514

Source: Extract from Service Personnel Records, Defense Manpower Data Center, Arlington, VA, June 1992, unpublished data. Ethnicity is self-reported by individuals at the time of their enlistment and may be updated upon reenlistment.

★ 720 ★

Active Duty U.S. Military Personnel by Source of Commission

Asian American officers in the U.S. military (all services) by source of commission and ethnicity (self-reported), as of June 1992.

Commission	Chinese	Japanese	Korean	Filipino	Viet-namese	Other Asian	Total Asian	Total, all active duty
Academy, Army	7	22	16	19	5	33	102	12,606
Academy, Navy	38	59	30	136	13	41	317	13,622
Academy, Air Force	20	43	13	24	0	102	202	14,425
Academy, Coast Guard	0	0	0	0	0	0	0	3,053
Academy, Merchant Marine	0	0	0	0	0	0	0	29
ROTC/NROTC Scholarship	89	149	106	184	24	192	744	45,426
ROTC/NROTC Non-scholarship	89	154	91	207	21	179	741	61,784
OCS/AOCS/OTS/PLC	97	143	80	265	33	147	765	63,186
Aviation Cadet	0	0	0	3	1	0	4	427
Direct Appointment, Professional	94	56	62	166	23	94	495	19,708
Direct Appointment, Non-professional	75	68	42	251	17	84	537	32,795
Aviation Training Program	0	0	1	2	1	0	4	404
Direct Appointment Warrant Officer	1	1	0	105	0	3	110	5,109
Other Asian	1	5	2	9	1	4	22	3,684
Total	511	700	443	1,371	139	879	4,043	276,258

Source: Extract from Service Personnel Records, Defense Manpower Data Center, Arlington, VA, June 1992, unpublished data. Ethnicity is self-reported by individuals at the time of their enlistment and may be updated upon reenlistment.

★721★

Active Duty U.S. Military Personnel by Years of Service

Asian American service in the U.S. military (all branches) by years of service and ethnicity (self-reported), as of June 1992.

Years of Service	Chinese	Japanese	Korean	Filipino	Viet-namese	Other Asian	Total Asian	Total, all active duty
1	139	143	383	1,666	247	556	3,134	182,063
2	152	134	313	1,841	263	583	3,286	193,926
3	155	140	286	1,861	220	514	3,176	188,075
4	125	152	252	2,093	187	447	3,256	167,442
5	85	106	162	1,465	70	249	2,137	106,912
6	65	122	132	1,499	66	209	2,093	101,001
7	47	102	102	1,315	39	216	1,821	88,966
8	52	105	74	1,154	22	186	1,593	80,364
9	35	77	61	1,078	6	149	1,406	75,892
10	36	95	74	981	9	162	1,357	71,489
11-15	208	455	322	4,571	31	887	6,474	299,898
16-20	180	387	224	6,028	4	842	7,665	234,269
21-25	66	133	31	1,315	2	253	1,800	74,958
26 and above	17	42	3	420	0	53	535	20,146
Total	1,362	2,193	2,419	27,287	1,166	5,306	39,733	1,885,401

Source: Extract from Service Personnel Records, Defense Manpower Data Center, Arlington, VA, June 1992, unpublished data. Ethnicity is self-reported by individuals at the time of their enlistment and may be updated upon reenlistment.

★722★

Enlisted Personnel in the U.S. Military by Years of Service

Asian American enlisted personnel by years of service and ethnicity (self-reported), as of June 1992.

Years of Service	Chinese	Japanese	Korean	Filipino	Viet-namese	Other Asian	Total Asian	Total all enlisted
5	56	63	113	1,401	55	181	1,869	92,284
6	45	78	102	1,441	56	174	1,896	86,711
7	21	56	74	1,255	30	169	1,605	74,456
8	23	56	55	1,106	20	146	1,406	66,365
9	19	52	52	1,032	5	114	1,274	63,547
10	14	68	63	947	8	127	1,227	59,933
11-15	122	302	251	4,331	25	703	5,734	245,162
16-20	104	284	179	5,731	4	695	6,997	181,287
21-25	39	75	18	1,209	1	204	1,546	45,190
26 and above	3	17	2	363	0	42	427	8,109
Total	446	1,051	909	18,816	204	2,555	23,981	1,593,100

Source: Extract from Service Personnel Records, Defense Manpower Data Center, Arlington, VA, June 1992, unpublished data. Ethnicity is self-reported by individuals at the time of their enlistment and may be updated upon reenlistment.

★ 723 ★

Service in the U.S. Military Reserves by Age

Asian American service in the U.S. Military Reserves (all branches) by age and ethnicity (self-reported), as of June 1992.

Age	Chinese	Japanese	Korean	Filipino	Viet-namese	Other Asian	Total Asian	Total Reserves
17	22	13	18	44	23	30	150	10,933
18	55	30	66	160	37	88	436	25,979
19	75	45	76	232	57	131	616	37,244
20	71	63	92	285	65	161	737	50,680
21	101	60	115	332	83	163	854	69,517
22	121	86	139	519	130	213	1,208	94,486
23	117	124	173	645	126	240	1,425	124,488
24	136	144	171	733	129	287	1,600	142,023
25	125	157	153	732	137	271	1,575	138,791
26-30	412	586	515	2,518	315	885	5,231	420,220
31-35	272	430	266	1,506	89	487	3,050	234,114
36-40	226	431	140	1,332	28	324	2,481	172,851
41 and above	624	1,150	199	1,818	27	592	4,410	408,200
Total	2,357	3,319	2,123	10,856	1,246	3,872	23,773	1,929,528

Source: Extract from Service Personnel Records, Defense Manpower Data Center, Arlington, VA, June 1992, unpublished data. Ethnicity is self-reported by individuals at the time of their enlistment and may be updated upon reenlistment.

★ 724 ★

Service in the U.S. Military Reserves by Rank

Asian American service in the U.S. Military Reserves (all branches) by rank and ethnicity (self-reported), as of June 1992.

Rank	Chinese	Japanese	Korean	Filipino	Viet-namese	Other Asian	Total Asian	Total Reserves
E1	108	63	141	368	98	177	955	64,056
E2	96	74	145	475	120	277	1,187	118,940
E3	266	185	305	1,159	237	454	2,606	202,511
E4	480	640	755	3,619	521	1,241	7,256	563,723
E5	328	582	259	2,388	123	562	4,242	329,606
E6	175	462	96	1,089	17	273	2,112	192,324
E7	105	317	27	496	0	158	1,103	109,611
E8	44	101	8	132	1	53	339	38,241
E9	19	54	1	36	0	26	136	12,239
W1	2	6	2	5	1	3	19	1,221
W2	8	21	0	12	2	2	45	7,194
W3	8	17	0	10	2	4	41	6,923
W4	8	13	0	4	0	3	28	5,947
O0	0	0	0	0	0	0	0	372
O1	42	53	55	82	33	72	337	27,858
O2	106	99	87	180	35	106	613	42,707
O3	210	234	118	335	40	248	1,185	92,821
O4	206	219	65	273	11	134	908	68,100
O5	132	194	49	192	5	99	671	53,338

[Continued]

★ 724 ★

Service in the U.S. Military Reserves by Rank (Continued)

Asian American service in the U.S. Military Reserves (all branches) by rank and ethnicity (self-reported), as of June 1992.

Rank	Chinese	Japanese	Korean	Filipino	Viet-namese	Other Asian	Total Asian	Total Reserves
O6	47	77	17	79	1	36	257	21,318
O7	1	3	1	0	0	0	5	615
O8	0	1	0	0	0	0	1	255
O9	0	0	0	0	0	0	0	1
Total	2,391	3,415	2,131	10,934	1,247	3,928	24,046	1,959,921

Source: Extract from Service Personnel Records, Defense Manpower Data Center, Arlington, VA, June 1992, unpublished data. Ethnicity is self-reported by individuals at the time of their enlistment and may be updated upon reenlistment.

★ 725 ★

Service in the U.S. Military Reserves by Sex

Asian American service in the U.S. Military Reserves (all branches) by sex and ethnicity (self-reported) as of June 1992.

Sex	Chinese	Japanese	Korean	Filipino	Viet-namese	Other Asian	Total Asian	Total Reserves
Male	2,094	3,061	1,781	9,471	1,135	3,261	20,803	1,697,590
Female	297	354	350	1,463	112	667	3,243	262,017
Total	2,391	3,415	2,131	10,934	1,247	3,928	24,046	1,959,932

Source: Extract from Service Personnel Records, Defense Manpower Data Center, Arlington, VA, June 1992, unpublished data. Ethnicity is self-reported by individuals at the time of their enlistment and may be updated upon reenlistment.

★ 726 ★

Service in the U.S. Military Reserves by Years of Service

Asian American service in the U.S. Military Reserves (all branches) by years of service and ethnicity (self-reported), as of June 1992.

Years of Service	Chinese	Japanese	Korean	Filipino	Viet-namese	Other Asian	Total Asian American	Total Reserves
0	148	68	152	401	108	207	1,084	63,347
1	95	51	108	333	86	215	888	60,794
2	121	90	125	458	113	236	1,143	82,968
3	122	105	170	560	139	296	1,392	106,021
4	164	133	219	858	205	252	1,831	159,076
5	196	206	280	1,016	203	317	2,218	194,521
6	172	182	267	945	151	266	1,983	189,640
7	147	183	192	928	105	287	1,842	177,969
8	70	111	58	436	33	113	821	71,861
9	73	92	45	339	13	82	644	60,826
10	43	84	45	307	10	59	548	59,875

[Continued]

★ 726 ★

Service in the U.S. Military Reserves by Years of Service (Continued)

Asian American service in the U.S. Military Reserves (all branches) by years of service and ethnicity (self-reported), as of June 1992.

Years of Service	Chinese	Japanese	Korean	Filipino	Viet-namese	Other Asian	Total Asian American	Total Reserves
11-15	214	389	144	1,224	26	271	2,268	241,086
16-20	196	388	107	868	10	174	1,743	169,119
21-25	175	435	21	379	2	116	1,128	153,958
26-30	66	179	6	127	1	50	429	65,548
31 and above	50	192	3	93	0	66	404	67,916
99	26	53	42	148	36	79	384	35,407
Total	1,930	2,873	1,832	9,019	1,133	2,879	19,666	1,959,932

Source: Extract from Service Personnel Records, Defense Manpower Data Center, Arlington, VA, June 1992, unpublished data. Ethnicity is self-reported by individuals at the time of their enlistment and may be updated upon reenlistment.

★ 727 ★

Service in Operation Desert Storm

Percent by race/ethnicity of military personnel who served in Operation Desert Storm, January–April, 1991.

Service	Asian Pacific Islander	African Americans	Hispanic	Native Americans
Army				
% in service	1.7	28.8	4.1	0.5
% in Desert Storm	1.4	30.4	4.2	0.6
Navy				
% in service	4.3	16.0	5.7	0.5
% in Desert Storm	5.2	19.3	6.4	0.6
Marine Corps				
% in service	1.4	18.9	6.9	0.8
% in Desert Storm	1.5	18.1	7.3	0.9
Air Force				
% in service	1.7	15.2	3.5	0.7
% in Desert Storm	1.2	13.0	3.2	0.6

Source: Extract from Service Personnel Records, Defense Manpower Data Center, Arlington, VA, November, 1992, unpublished data.

Casualties

★ 728 ★

U.S. Military Deaths

Deaths, worldwide, of active duty personnel by pay grade and race/ethnicity, October 1979–December 1991.

Rank/Grade	Asian	White	Black	Other	Total
Officers					
General of the Army—Fleet Admiral	0	1	0	0	1
General—Admiral	0	2	0	0	2
Lieutenant. General—Vice Admiral	0	4	0	0	4
Major General—Rear Admiral (Upper Half)	0	7	0	0	7
Brigadier General—Rear Adm (Lower Half)/ Commodore	0	8	0	0	8
Colonel—Captain	0	190	3	0	193
Lieutenant Colonel—Commander	2	331	11	4	348
Major—Lieutenant Commander	2	525	20	7	554
Captain—Lieutenant	4	930	51	6	991
1st Lieutenant—Lieutenant (Junior Grade)	2	487	24	6	519
2nd Lieutenant—Ensign	2	273	25	3	303
W4—Chief Warrant Officer	0	75	1	1	77
W3—Chief Warrant Officer	1	82	8	0	91
W2—Chief Warrant Officer	0	123	9	2	134
W1—Warrant Officer	0	56	0	1	57
Total Officers	13	3,094	152	30	3,289
Enlisted Personnel					
E-9	4	226	36	7	273
E-8	9	390	98	8	505
E-7	21	1,237	239	28	1,525
E-6	56	1,826	533	66	2,481
E-5	39	2,708	845	103	3,695
E-4	40	4,004	1,168	147	5,359
E-3	39	3,391	846	141	4,417
E-2	15	1,696	346	67	2,124
E-1	10	1,005	285	41	1,341
Total Enlisted	233	16,483	4,396	608	21,720
Total Cadets	0	27	4	0	31
Unknown	0	28	1	1	30
Total Deaths for all Grades	246	19,632	4,553	639	25,070

Source: Worldwide U.S. Active Duty Military Personnel Casualties (Washington, DC: Department of Defense, 1992), table 5, p. 23. This report is prepared annually by Washington Headquarters Services, Directorate for Information, Operations, and Reports, and is available each fiscal year from National Technical Information Service, Springfield, VA. Total deaths include cadets and unknown, which were both zero for Asian.

Population and Vital Statistics

United States Population: Historical Perspective

★ 729 ★

U.S. Census: Asian/Pacific Islander Categories, 1790–1990

History of Asian/Pacific Islander categories in the U.S. Census of Population, 1790 to 1990.

Censal Year	Asian/Pacific Islander Category
1790	First Census includes whites, slaves, other.
1870	Chinese category added.
1890	Japanese category added.
1950	Filipino category added
	Other Race (specify) _____. added.
1960	Hawaiian category added.
	Part Hawaiian category added.
1970	Hawaiian and Part Hawaiian categories combined.
	Korean added.
1980	Vietnamese added.
	Asian Indian added.
	Guamanian added.
	Samoan added.
1990	Other A/PI (specify)_____. added.

Source: Interview with Fred Bohme, U.S. Bureau of Census, History Division, March 9, 1993.

★ 730 ★

Historical and Projected Population

Historical and projected population of the Asian and Pacific Islander population in the United States, 1900-2050.

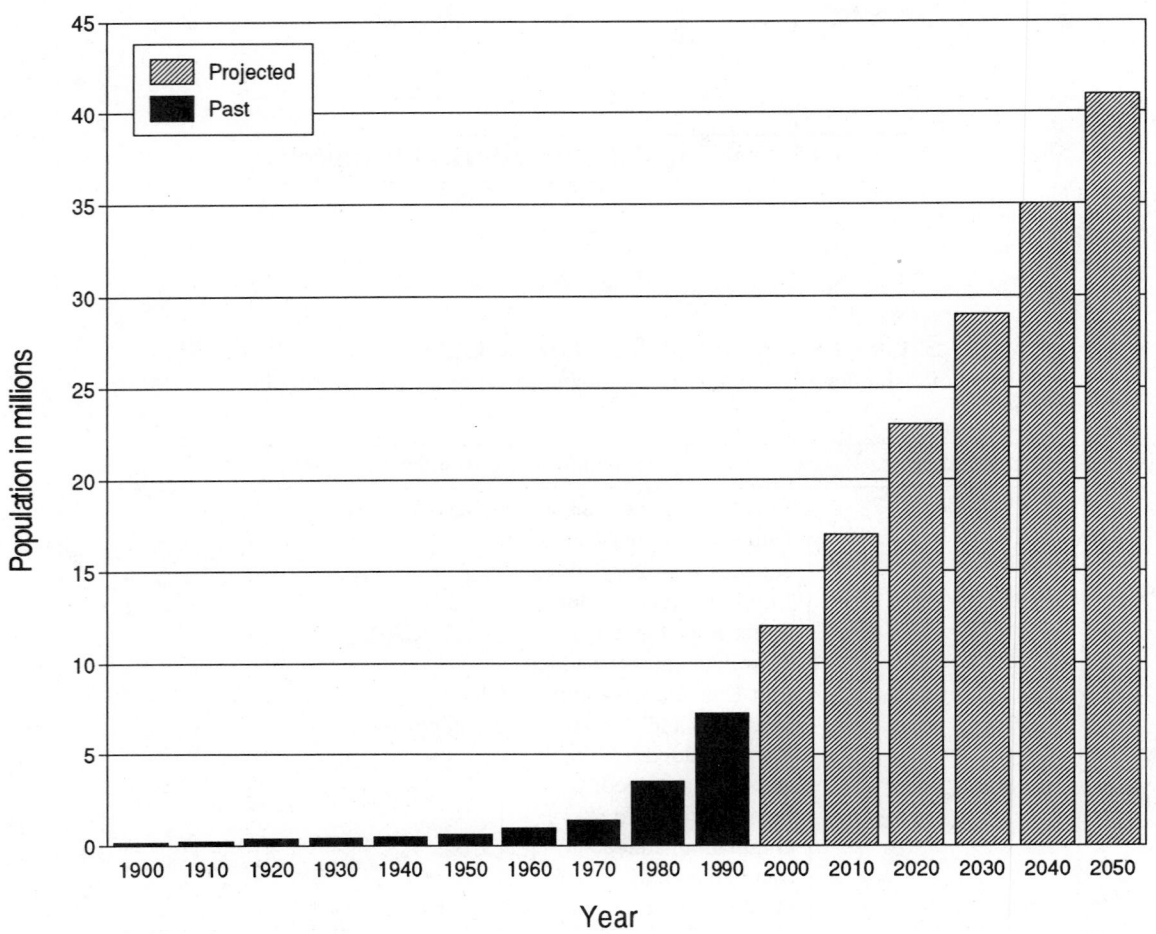

Source: United States Department of Commerce, Economics and Statistics Administration, Bureau of the Census, Press Release, December 4, 1992, "Nation's Population Projected to Grow by 50 Percent During Next 60 Years, Census Bureau Reports" (Washington, DC: U.S. Department of Commerce, 1992) and "Asian American Demographics," *Recognizing Poverty in Boston's Asian American Community* (Boston, MA: The Boston Foundation, 1992).

★ 731 ★

Population, in Percent, in the United States by Race/Ethnicity, 1980–1990

Numbers and percent increase in population by race/ethnicity, 1980 to 1990.

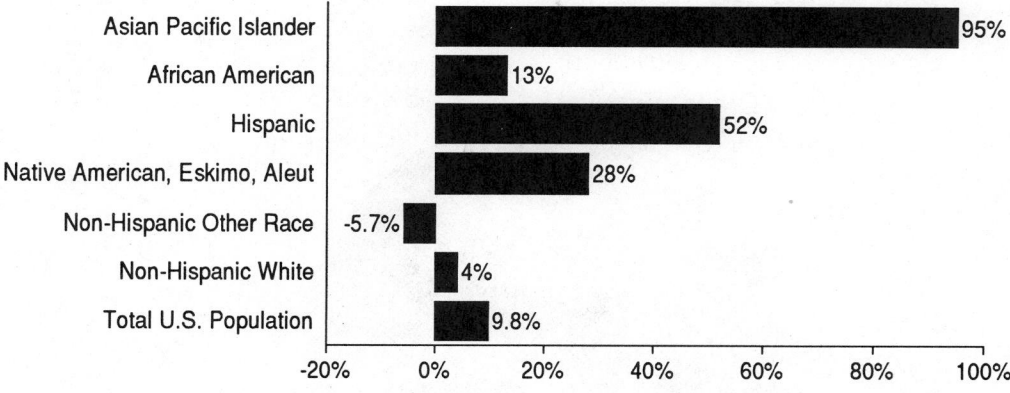

Percent increase in population by race, 1980 to 1990

Source: Asians and Pacific Islander Center for Census Information and Services, San Francisco, CA, 1993. Primary source: U.S. Census Bureau, Summary Tape File 1A.

★ 732 ★

Population in the United States by Race/Ethnicity, 1980–1990

Race/ethnicity	U.S. population, total		Increase, 1980 to 1990	
	1990	1980	Number	Percent
Total U.S. Population	248,709,873	226,545,805	22,164,068	9.8%
Asian/Pacific Islander American	7,273,662	3,726,440	3,547,222	95.2%
Chinese	1,645,472	812,178	833,294	102.6%
Filipino	1,406,770	781,894	624,876	79.9%
Japanese	847,562	716,331	131,231	18.3%
Asian Indian	815,447	387,223	428,224	110.6%
Korean	798,849	357,393	441,456	123.5%
Vietnamese	614,547	245,025	369,522	150.8%
Cambodian	147,411	16,044	131,367	818.8%
Hmong	90,082	5,204	84,878	1,631.0%
Laotian	149,014	47,683	101,331	212.5%
Thai	91,275	45,279	45,996	101.6%
Hawaiian	211,014	172,346	38,668	22.4%
Guamanian	62,964	39,520	23,444	59.3%
Samoan	49,345	30,695	18,650	60.8%
Other Asian/Pacific Islander	343,910	69,625	274,285	393.9%
White, non-Hispanic	188,128,296	180,602,838	7,525,458	4.2%
African American	29,986,060	26,482,349	3,503,711	13.2%
Native American Indian, Eskimo, Aleut	1,959,234	1,534,336	424,898	27.7%
Hispanic	21,113,528	13,935,827	7,177,701	51.5%
Other Race, non-Hispanic	249,093	264,015	(14,922)	-5.7

[Continued]

★ 732 ★

Population in the United States by Race/Ethnicity, 1980–1990 (Continued)

Population of the Asian/Pacific Islander population by ethnicity in percent of Asian total, 1990.

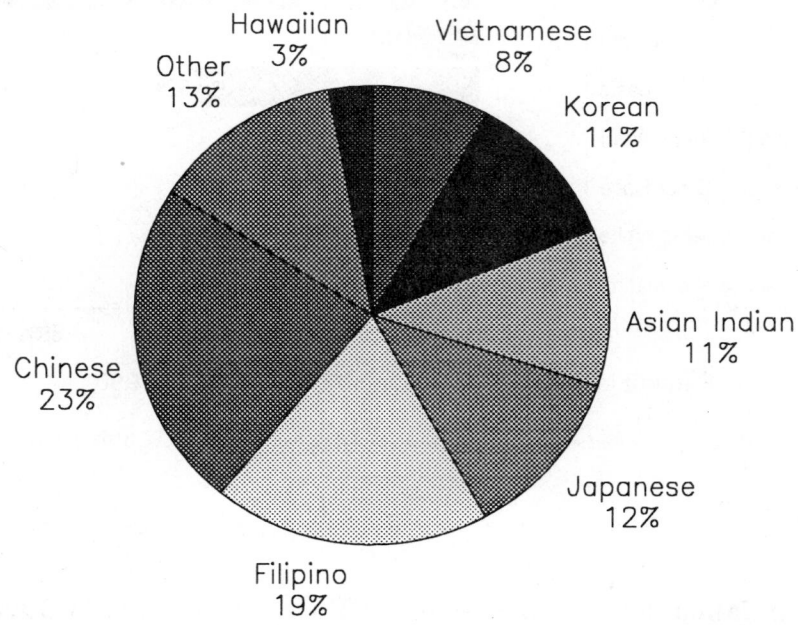

Source: Asians and Pacific Islander Center for Census Information and Services, San Francisco, CA, 1993. Primary source: U.S. Census Bureau, Summary Tape File 1A.

★ 733 ★

Population Growth in the United States by Asian Ethnicity, 1980–1990

Percent increase in population by ethnicity, 1980 to 1990.

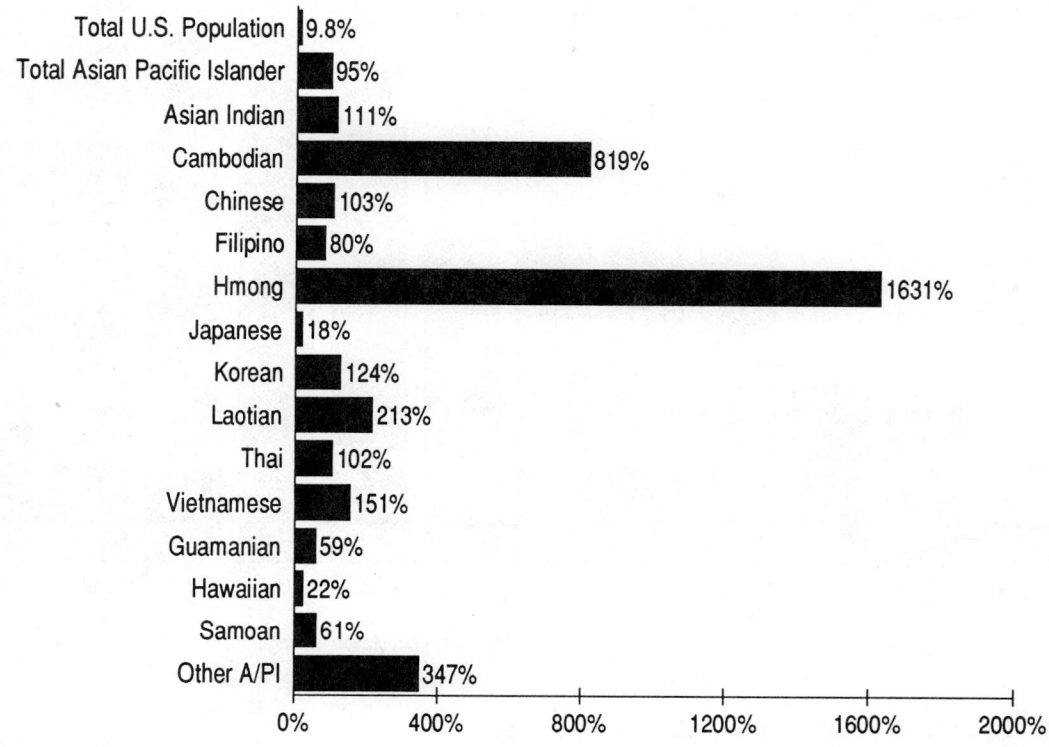

Source: Asians and Pacific Islander Center for Census Information and Services, San Francisco, CA, 1993. Primary source: U.S. Census Bureau, Summary Tape File 1A.

★ 734 ★

Asian/Pacific Islander Population in Percent, Foreign Born

The foreign-born Asian/Pacific Islander population in the United States, in percent, 1989.

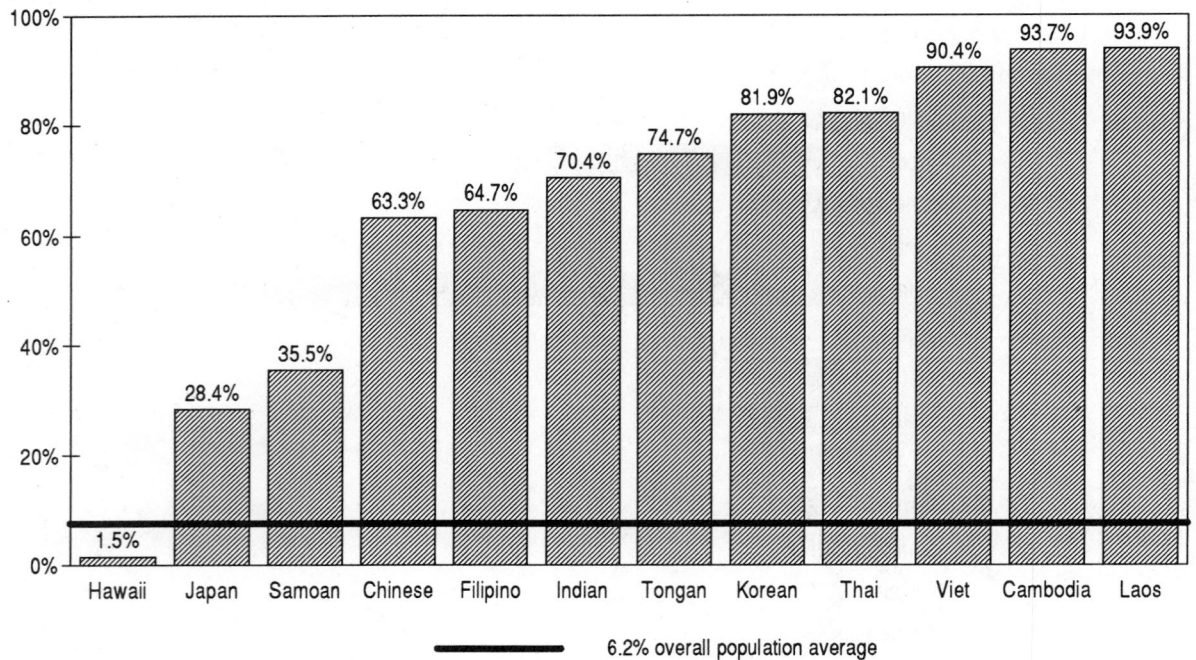

Source: Asian American Health Forum, Inc., San Francisco, CA, April 1989.

★ 735 ★

Population of the United States by Asian Ethnicity by Decade, 1900 to 1990

U.S. population by Asian ethnic group by census year, 1900 to 1990.

Year	Total, U.S.	Total Asian[b]	Chinese	Filipino[a]	Asian Indian	Japanese	Korean	Viet- namese
1900	76,212,168	204,462	118,746	-	-	85,716	-	-
1910	92,228,531	249,926	94,414	2,767	-	152,745	5,008	-
1920	106,021,568	332,432	85,202	26,634	-	220,596	6,181	-
1930	123,202,660	489,326	102,159	108,424	-	278,743	8,332	-
1940	132,165,129	489,984	106,334	98,535	-	285,115	8,568	-
1950	151,325,798	599,091	150,005	122,707	-	326,379	7,030[c]	-
1960	179,323,175	877,934	237,292	176,310	-	464,332	-	-
1970	203,211,926	1,429,562	436,062	343,060	-	591,290	69,150[d]	-
1980	226,545,805	3,466,421	812,178	781,894	387,223	716,331	357,393	245,025
1990	248,709,873	7,273,662[e]	1,645,472	1,406,770	815,447	847,562	798,849	614,547

Source: Robert W. Gardner, Bryant Robey, and Peter C. Smith, "Asian Americans: Growth, Change, and Diversity," *Population Bulletin 40*, no. 4 (October 1985): table 2, p. 8, and Asian/Pacific Islander Data Consortium (San Francisco, CA: ACCIS, 1992). Primary source: U.S. Bureau of Census, Decennial Censuses of Population. A dash (–) indicates that no data was available for the ethnic category in that census year. *Notes:* (a) Included with "other race" for the United States in 1900 and for Alaska in 1920 and 1950. (b) Total only of Asian groups listed for the specific year. In 1980, includes 166,377 Asian Americans not listed in the table, as follows: Cambodian, 16,044; Hmong, 5,204; Laotian, 47,682; Thai, 45, 279; Hawaiian, 172,346; Guamanian, 39,520; Samoan, 30,695; Other A/PI, 69,625. (c) Data for Hawaii only. (d) Excludes Koreans in Alaska. (e) Includes 1,145,015 Asians not listed in the table, as follows: Cambodian, 147,411; Hmong, 90,082; Laotian, 149,014; Thai, 91,275; Hawaiian, 211,014; Guamanian, 62,964; Samoan, 49,345; and Other A/PI, 343,910.

★ 736 ★

Population in Metropolitan Areas

Distribution of the population, by metropolitan and nonmetropolitan residence, region, and race, 1991

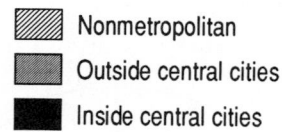

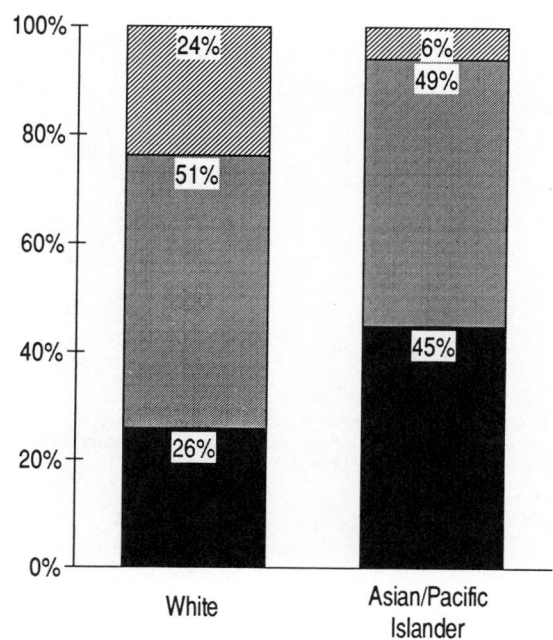

Ninety-four percent of all Asians and Pacific Islanders lived in metropolitan areas in 1991. Almost half (49 percent) of all Asians and Pacific Islanders lived in the suburbs of metropolitan areas; a little less than half (45 percent) lived inside the central cities of metropolitan areas.

Source: Claudette E. Bennett, U.S. Department of Commerce, Bureau of the Census, Current Population Reports, P-20-459, *The Asian Pacific Islander Population in the United States: March 1991 and 1990* (Washington, DC: U.S. Government Printing Office, 1992).

★ 737 ★

Population by Region, 1991

The Asian and Pacific Islander population is highly concentrated in the west region of the United States. In 1991, 4.1 million or about 6 out of every 10 Asians and Pacific Islanders lived in the west (59 percent), where they represented 8 percent of the total population. About 17 percent of Asians and Pacific Islanders lived in the northeast, 14 percent in the south, and 10 percent in the midwest. In comparison, about 19 percent of non-Hispanic whites live in the west.

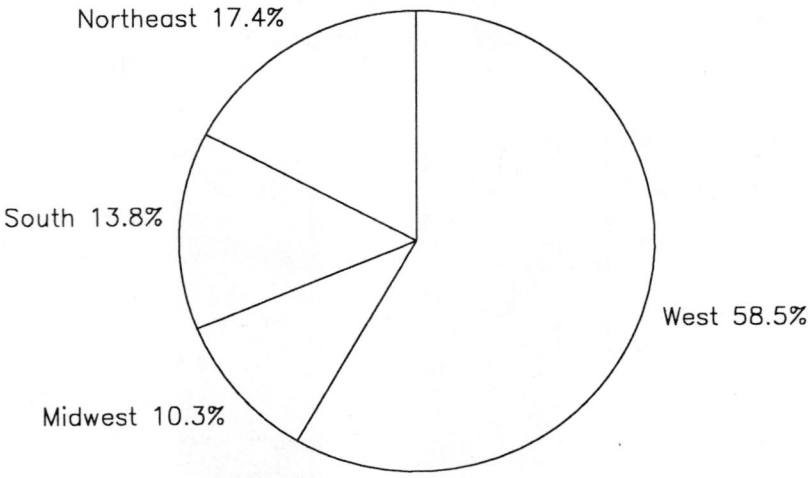

Source: Claudette E. Bennett, U.S. Department of Commerce, Bureau of the Census, Current Population Reports, P-20-459, *The Asian Pacific Islander Population in the United States: March 1991 and 1990* (Washington, DC: U.S. Government Printing Office, 1992).

United States Population: Overview

★ 738 ★

Population by Age, Asian/Pacific Islander and White

Illustration of age distribution of Asian/Pacific Islander and white population, 1991.

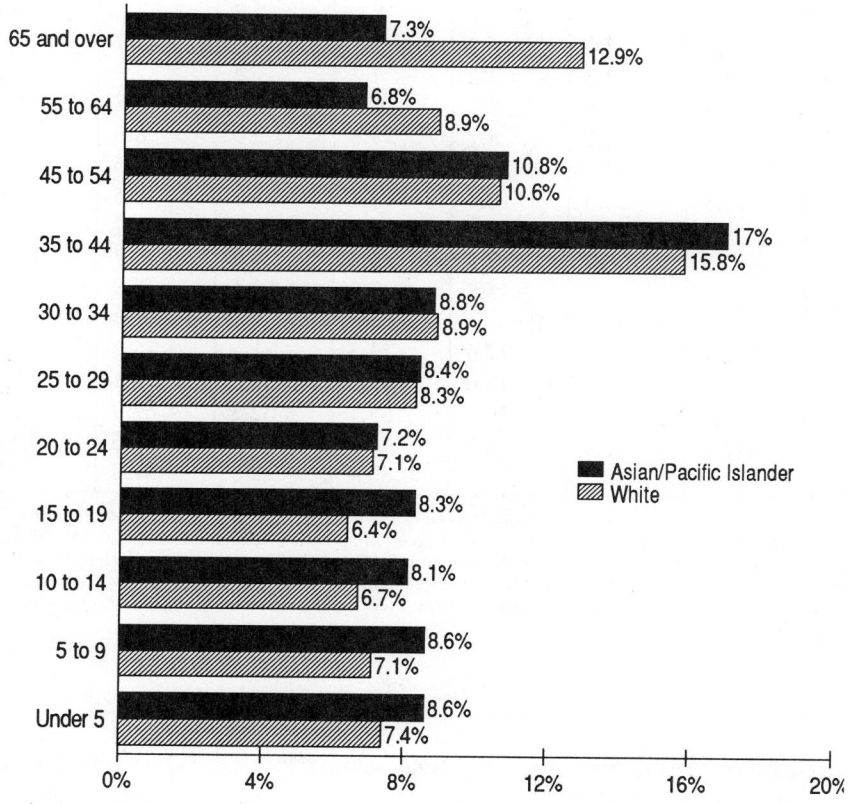

In 1991, the median age of the Asian and Pacific Islander population was 30.4 years, compared with 33.9 years for the white population. A larger proportion of Asians and Pacific Islanders (86 percent) than whites (78 percent) were less than 55 years of age in 1991. Conversely, the proportion of Asians and Pacific Islanders 55 years and over (14 percent) is smaller than that for the white population (22 percent).

Source: Bureau of the Census, U.S. Department of Commerce, *The Asian and Pacific Islander Population in the United States: March 1991 and 1990,* Current Population Reports, Population Characteristics Chartbook (Washington, DC: U.S. Government Printing Office, 1991), figure 4.

★ 739 ★

Population by Age and Sex, Asian/Pacific Islander and White

Asian/Pacific Islander and White populations by age range and sex, in percent, March 1991.

Characteristic	Total population			Asian and Pacific Islander			White		
	Both sexes	Male	Female	Both sexes	Male	Female	Both sexes	Male	Female
Total, all ages (in thousands)	248,886	121,191	127,695	7,023	3,420	3,603	208,754	102,217	106,537
Age	Percent	Percent	Percent	Percent	Percent	Percent	Percent	Percent	Percent
Under 5 years	7.8	8.1	7.4	8.6	9.6	7.7	7.4	7.7	7.0
5 to 9 years	7.4	7.8	7.0	8.6	9.1	8.0	7.1	7.4	6.8
10 to 14 years	7.1	7.4	6.7	8.1	8.7	7.6	6.7	7.0	6.4
15 to 19 years	6.8	7.0	6.5	8.3	9.0	7.7	6.4	6.7	6.2
20 to 24 years	7.2	7.3	7.2	7.2	7.2	7.2	7.1	7.2	7.0
25 to 29 years	8.3	8.5	8.2	8.4	8.1	8.8	8.3	8.5	8.0
30 to 34 years	8.9	9.1	8.7	8.8	9.0	8.6	8.9	9.2	8.7
35 to 44 years	15.5	15.7	15.4	17.0	15.2	18.6	15.8	16.1	15.5
45 to 54 years	10.3	10.3	10.4	10.8	11.3	10.5	10.6	10.5	10.6
55 to 64 years	8.6	8.4	8.8	6.8	5.9	7.7	8.9	8.7	9.0
65 to 74 years	7.3	6.7	7.9	5.3	4.9	5.7	7.8	7.1	8.4
75 years and over	4.8	3.6	5.8	2.0	2.1	1.9	5.1	3.9	6.3
	Percent	Percent	Percent	Percent	Percent	Percent	Percent	Percent	Percent
16 years and over	76.4	75.2	77.6	73.3	71.2	75.2	77.6	76.5	78.6
18 years and over	73.8	72.4	75.0	69.6	67.0	72.1	75.1	73.9	76.2
21 years and over	69.6	68.2	70.9	65.1	62.2	67.9	71.0	69.8	72.2
65 years and over	12.1	10.4	13.7	7.3	7.0	7.6	12.9	11.0	14.7
Median age (years)	33.0	32.1	34.0	30.4	29.0	31.8	33.9	33.0	34.9

Source: Claudette E. Bennett, Economics and Statistics Administration, Bureau of the Census, U.S. Department of Commerce, *The Asian and Pacific Islander Population in the United States: March 1991 and 1990,* Current Population Reports, Population Characteristics, P20-459 (Washington, DC: U.S. Government Printing Office, August 1992), table A, p. 3. The population universe for the March 1991 and 1990 Current Population Surveys are the estimate of the civilian noninstitutional population to the United States plus members of the Armed Forces in the United States living off post or with their families on post, but excludes all other members of the Armed Forces. Data are estimates based on sample surveys and are subject to sampling variability since they are not based on a complete count of the population.

★ 740 ★

Population by Marital Status and Sex, Asian/Pacific Islander and White

Asian/Pacific Islander and white populations by marital status, age range, and sex, in percent, March 1991.

Characteristic	Total population			Asian and Pacific Islander			White		
	Both sexes	Male	Female	Both sexes	Male	Female	Both sexes	Male	Female
Total, 15 years and over (thousands)	193,519	92,840	100,680	5,247	2,484	2,764	164,567	79,555	85,012
Marital Status									
Never married	26.5%	30.1%	23.2%	31.1%	36.9%	25.9%	24.3%	28.0%	20.8%
Married, spouse present	55.0%	57.3%	52.9%	56.4%	55.2%	57.4%	58.1%	60.1%	56.1%
Married, spouse absent	3.3%	2.8%	3.7%	3.4%	3.9%	3.1%	2.6%	2.3%	2.9%
Widowed	7.1%	2.6%	11.2%	5.1%	1.9%	7.9%	7.0%	2.5%	11.2%
Divorced	8.1%	7.1%	9.1%	4.0%	2.1%	5.7%	8.0%	7.1%	8.9%

Source: Claudette E. Bennett, Economics and Statistics Administration, Bureau of the Census, U.S. Department of Commerce, *The Asian and Pacific Islander Population in the United States: March 1991 and 1990,* Current Population Reports, Population Characteristics, P20-459 (Washington, DC: U.S. Government Printing Office, August 1992), table B, p. 5. The population universe for the March 1991 and 1990 Current Population Surveys are the estimate of the civilian noninstitutional population to the United States plus members of the Armed Forces in the United States living off post or with their families on post, but excludes all other members of the Armed Forces. Data are estimates based on sample surveys and are subject to sampling variability since they are not based on a complete count of the population.

★ 741 ★

Population by Marital Status and Sex, Fifteen Years and Older
Asian/Pacific Islander population fifteen years and over by marital status, March 1991.

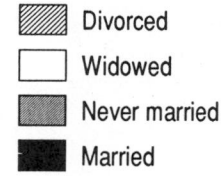

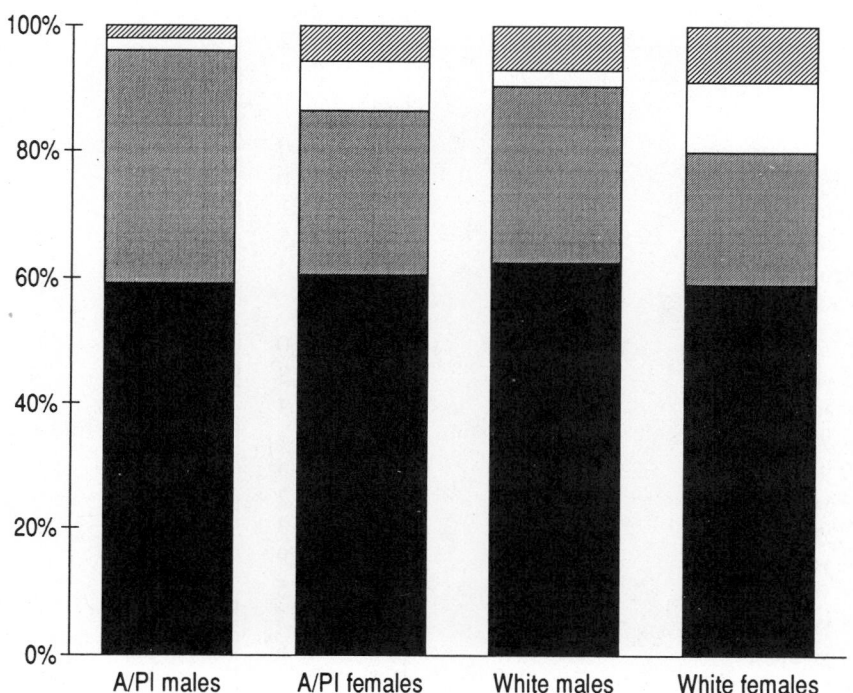

In 1991, there were 5.2 million Asian and Pacific Islander persons fifteen years old and over in the United States; 3.1 million were married and 1.6 million were never married. About one out of three Asian and Pacific Islander men and one out of four Asian and Pacific Islander women were never married. About three times as many woman as men were divorced. About one out of thirteen Asian and Pacific Islander females and 1 out of 54 Asian and Pacific Islander males were widowed. Asians and Pacific Islanders were more likely than whites to be single.

Source: Bureau of the Census, U.S. Department of Commerce, *The Asian and Pacific Islander Population in the United States: March 1991 and 1990,* Current Population Reports, Population Characteristics Chartbook (Washington, DC: U.S. Government Printing Office, 1991), figure 5.

★ 742 ★

Population by Region, Age, Marital Status, and Educational Attainment

Total numbers and percent of Asian/Pacific Islander and white populations by region, age distribution, marital status, and educational attainment, March 1991.

Characteristic	Total population	Asian and Pacific Islander	White
Region			
Total (thousands)	248,886	7,023	208,754
Percent	100.0	100.0	100.0
Northeast	20.4	17.3	21.0
Midwest	24.1	10.3	25.3
South	34.2	13.8	31.9
West	21.2	58.5	21.9
Residence			
Percent	100.0	100.0	100.0
All metropolitan areas	77.6	94.4	76.4
Inside central cities	30.1	45.0	25.7
Outside central cities	47.5	49.4	50.7
Nonmetropolitan areas	22.4	5.6	23.6
Age			
Percent	100.0	100.0	100.0
Under 5 years	7.8	8.6	7.4
5 to 9 years	7.4	8.6	7.1
10 to 14 years	7.1	8.1	6.7
15 to 19 years	6.8	8.3	6.4
20 to 24 years	7.2	7.2	7.1
25 to 29 years	8.3	8.4	8.3
30 to 34 years	8.9	8.8	8.9
35 to 44 years	15.5	17.0	15.8
45 to 54 years	10.3	10.8	10.6
55 to 64 years	8.6	6.8	8.9
65 to 74 years	7.3	5.3	7.8
75 years and over	4.8	2.0	5.1
16 years and over	76.4	73.3	77.6
18 years and over	73.8	69.6	75.1
21 years and over	69.6	65.1	71.0
65 years and over	12.1	7.3	12.9
Median age (years)	33.0	30.4	33.9
Sex			
Percent	100.0	100.0	100.0
Male	48.7	48.7	49.0
Female	51.3	51.3	51.0
Marital Status			
Total, 15 years and over (thousands)	193,519	5,247	164,567
Percent	100.0	100.0	100.0
Never married	26.5	31.1	24.3
Married, spouse present	55.0	56.4	58.1
Married, spouse absent	3.3	3.4	2.6

[Continued]

★ 742 ★

Population by Region, Age, Marital Status, and Educational Attainment (Continued)

Total numbers and percent of Asian/Pacific Islander and white populations by region, age distribution, marital status, and educational attainment, March 1991.

Characteristic	Total population	Asian and Pacific Islander	White
Widowed	7.1	5.1	7.0
Divorced	8.2	4.0	8.0
Educational Attainment			
Total, 25 years and over (thousands)	158,694	4,158	136,299
Percent completed-			
Less than 5 years of school	2.4	5.3	2.0
4 years of high school or more	78.4	81.8	79.9
1 or more years of college	39.8	53.2	40.8
4 or more years of college	21.4	39.0	22.2
5 or more years of college	8.8	15.8	9.2
Median school years completed	12.7	13.7	12.8
Total, 25 to 34 years (thousands)	42,905	1,213	35,902
Percent completed-			
Less than 5 years of school	1.1	2.4	1.1
4 years of high school or more	86.1	89.1	86.7
1 or more years of college	45.3	60.6	46.3
4 or more years of college	23.7	40.6	24.9
5 or more years of college	7.4	15.5	7.8
Median school years completed	12.9	14.6	12.9

Source: Claudette E. Bennett, Economics and Statistics Administration, Bureau of the Census, U.S. Department of Commerce, *The Asian and Pacific Islander Population in the United States: March 1991 and 1990,* Current Population Reports, Population Characteristics, P20-459 (Washington, DC: U.S. Government Printing Office, August 1992), table 1, p. 14. The population universe for the March 1991 and 1990 Current Population Surveys are the estimate of the civilian noninstitutional population to the United States plus members of the Armed Forces in the United States living off post or with their families on post, but excludes all other members of the Armed Forces. Data are estimates based on sample surveys and are subject to sampling variability since they are not based on a complete count of the population.

★ 743 ★

Population by Age, Marital Status and Educational Attainment, Western United States

Total numbers and percent of Asian/Pacific Islander and white populations by area of residence, age distribution, marital status, and educational attainment in the western United States[a], March 1991.

Characteristic	Total population	Asian and Pacific Islander	White
Residence			
Total (thousands)	52,881	4,112	45,661
Percent	100.0	100.0	100.0
All metropolitan areas	84.6	94.2	83.6
Inside central cities	34.8	44.9	33.0
Outside central cities	49.8	49.3	50.6
Nonmetropolitan areas	15.4	5.8	16.4
Age			
Percent	100.0	100.0	100.0
Under 5 years	8.4	9.1	8.2
5 to 9 years	8.0	8.3	8.0
10 to 14 years	7.2	6.7	7.2
15 to 19 years	6.7	8.4	6.4
20 to 24 years	7.4	7.5	7.4
25 to 29 years	8.5	7.9	8.4
30 to 34 years	9.3	8.4	9.4
35 to 44 years	15.9	16.0	15.9
45 to 54 years	10.2	11.1	10.1
55 to 64 years	7.7	7.3	7.8
65 to 74 years	6.8	6.7	7.0
75 years and over	4.0	2.4	4.3
16 years and over	75.1	74.6	75.4
18 years and over	72.4	70.8	72.9
21 years and over	68.3	66.2	68.9
65 years and over	10.8	9.1	11.3
Median age (years)	32.1	31.2	32.4
Sex			
Percent	100.0	100.0	100.0
Male	49.6	48.5	49.9
Female	50.4	51.5	50.1
Marital Status			
Total, 15 years and over (thousands)	40,414	3,122	35,006
Percent	100.0	100.0	100.0
Never married	26.8	32.1	25.4
Married, spouse present	54.5	54.5	55.8
Married, spouse absent	3.6	3.1	3.3
Widowed	5.7	5.8	5.7
Divorced	9.5	4.6	9.7

[Continued]

★ 743 ★

Population by Age, Marital Status and Educational Attainment, Western United States (Continued)

Total numbers and percent of Asian/Pacific Islander and white populations by area of residence, age distribution, marital status, and educational attainment in the western United States[a], March 1991.

Characteristic	Total population	Asian and Pacific Islander	White
Educational Attainment			
Total, 25 years and over (thousands)	32,954	2,466	28.737
Percent completed-			
Less than 5 years of school	3.2	5.8	2.9
4 years of high school or more	80.9	82.0	80.9
1 or more years of college	46.9	51.7	46.8
4 or more years of college	24.3	35.4	24.0
5 or more years of college	10.7	12.3	10.9
Median school years completed	12.9	13.3	12.9
Total, 25 to 34 years (thousands)	9,398	674	8,165
Percent completed-			
Less than 5 years of school	2.0	2.1	2.0
4 years of high school or more	83.7	90.2	82.7
1 or more years of college	47.0	55.8	46.3
4 or more years of college	23.0	32.8	23.0
5 or more years of college	8.1	9.8	8.2
Median school years completed	12.9	13.8	12.9

Source: Claudette E. Bennett, Economics and Statistics Administration, Bureau of the Census, U.S. Department of Commerce, *The Asian and Pacific Islander Population in the United States: March 1991 and 1990,* Current Population Reports, Population Characteristics, P20-459 (Washington, DC: U.S. Government Printing Office, August 1992), table 1, p. 14. The population universe for the March 1991 and 1990 Current Population Surveys are the estimate of the civilian noninstitutional population to the United States plus members of the Armed Forces in the United States living off post or with their families on post, but excludes all other members of the Armed Forces. Data are estimates based on sample surveys and are subject to sampling variability since they are not based on a complete count of the population. *Note:* (a) The western region of the United States includes Alaska, Arizona, California, Colorado, Hawaii, Idaho, Montana, Nevada, New Mexico, Oregon, Utah, Washington, and Wyoming.

Social Aspects of the Population

★ 744 ★

Families by Number of Earners

Asian/Pacific Islander and white families by number of earners per family, in percent, 1991.

Number of earners in family	Total population	Asian and Pacific Islander	White
Percent	100.0	100.0	100.0
No earners	14.4	10.4	13.9
One earner	27.5	26.5	26.5
Two earners	44.5	44.2	45.8
Three earners	9.9	11.3	10.2
Four earners	3.0	5.5	3.1
Five earners	0.5	1.1	0.5
Six earners	0.1	0.3	0.1
Seven or more earners	-	0.7	-

Source: Claudette E. Bennett, Economics and Statistics Administration, Bureau of the Census, U.S. Department of Commerce, *The Asian and Pacific Islander Population in the United States: March 1991 and 1990,* Current Population Reports, Population Characteristics, P20-459 (Washington, DC: U.S. Government Printing Office, August 1992), table 8, p. 38. The population universe for the March 1991 and 1990 Current Population Surveys are the estimate of the civilian noninstitutional population to the United States plus members of the Armed Forces in the United States living off post or with their families on post, but excludes all other members of the Armed Forces. Data are estimates based on sample surveys and are subject to sampling variability since they are not based on a complete count of the population.

★ 745 ★

Households by Income and Number of Earners

Households by income range, median income (in dollars), and percent of households by number of earners for Asian/Pacific Islander and white populations, 1990.

Household Income in 1990	Total population	Asian and Pacific Islander	White
Percent	100.0	100.0	100.0
Under $5,000	5.2	4.9	4.0
$5,000 to $9,999	9.7	6.4	8.8
$10,000 to $14,999	9.5	7.0	9.2
$15,000 to $19,999	8.8	7.3	8.7
$20,000 to $24,999	8.9	5.6	9.0
$25,000 to $34,999	15.8	13.2	16.1
$35,000 to $49,999	17.5	19.9	18.0
$50,000 to $59,000	7.8	8.1	8.2
$60,000 to $74,999	7.2	11.0	7.6

[Continued]

★ 745 ★

Households by Income and Number of Earners (Continued)

Households by income range, median income (in dollars), and percent of households by number of earners for Asian/Pacific Islander and white populations, 1990.

Household Income in 1990	Total population	Asian and Pacific Islander	White
$75,000 and over	9.7	16.6	10.4
Median income (dollars)	$29,943	$38,449	$31,231
Standard error (dollars)	$153	$1,139	$143
Number of Earners			
Percent	100.0	100.0	100.0
No earners	21.1	14.2	20.8
One earner	33.3	31.5	32.5
Two earners	35.0	37.6	35.9
Three earners	7.7	9.8	7.9
Four earners	2.3	5.2	2.3
Five earners	0.4	0.9	0.4
Six earners	0.1	0.3	0.1
Seven or more earners	-	0.6	-

Source: Claudette E. Bennett, Economics and Statistics Administration, Bureau of the Census, U.S. Department of Commerce, *The Asian and Pacific Islander Population in the United States: March 1991 and 1990,* Current Population Reports, Population Characteristics, P20-459 (Washington, DC: U.S. Government Printing Office, August 1992), table 7, p. 35. The population universe for the March 1991 and 1990 Current Population Surveys are the estimate of the civilian noninstitutional population to the United States plus members of the Armed Forces in the United States living off post or with their families on post, but excludes all other members of the Armed Forces. Data are estimates based on sample surveys and are subject to sampling variability since they are not based on a complete count of the population.

★ 746 ★

Families by Poverty Status

Total numbers (in thousands) and percent of Asian/Pacific Islander and white families and percent by poverty status, March 1991.

Characteristic	Total population	Asian and Pacific Islander	White
All income levels in 1990			
Families (thousands)	66,322	1,536	56,803
Family householder-			
65 years old and over	10,900	135	9,797
Not a high school graduate[a]	14,351	225	11,493
Below poverty level in 1990			
Family householder-			
65 years old and over-			
Number (thousands)	686	11	443
Percent	6.3	8.4	4.5
Not a high school graduate[a]-			
Number (thousands)	3,406	59	2,218
Percent	23.7	26.1	19.3
Poverty status by type of family			
All families below poverty level-			
Number (thousands)	7,098	169	4,622
Percent	5.7	8.7	5.1
Female householder, no spouse present below poverty level-			
Number (thousands)	3,768	43	2,010
Percent	33.4	22.3	26.8
Male householder, no spouse present below poverty level-			
Number (thousands)	349	18	226
Percent	12.0	15.9	9.9
Related children under 18 years in families			
All related children under 18 years in families (thousands)	63,908	2,001	51,312
Number below poverty level (thousands)	12,715	363	7,736
Percent below poverty level	19.9	18.1	15.1
Married-couple families	47,962	1,693	41,755
Number below poverty level (thousands)	4,907	258	3,836
Percent below poverty level	10.2	15.2	9.2
Female householder, no husband present	13,794	244	7,957
Number below poverty level (thousands)	7,363	89	3,629
Percent below poverty level	53.4	36.4	45.6
Male householder, no wife present	2,153	64	1,600
Number below poverty level (thousands)	444	16	271
Percent below poverty level	20.6	24.7	16.9

Source: Claudette E. Bennett, Economics and Statistics Administration, Bureau of the Census, U.S. Department of Commerce, *The Asian and Pacific Islander Population in the United States: March 1991 and 1990,* Current Population Reports, Population Characteristics, P20-459 (Washington, DC: U.S. Government Printing Office, August 1992), table 8, p. 38. The population universe for the March 1991 and 1990 Current Population Surveys are the estimate of the civilian noninstitutional population to the United States plus members of the Armed Forces in the United States living off post or with their families on post, but excludes all other members of the Armed Forces. Data are estimates based on sample surveys and are subject to sampling variability since they are not based on a complete count of the population. *Note:* (a) Householders, all ages.

★ 747 ★

Households by Area and Type of Residence

Total number of Asian/Pacific Islander and white households and percent by type of metropolitan area and residence, 1991.

Characteristic	Total population	Asian and Pacific Islander	White
Total (thousands)	94,312	1,958	80,968
Percent	100.0	100.0	100.0
Own or buying home	64.0	50.8	67.3
Renting	34.2	48.4	30.8
Occupier paid no cash rent	1.8	0.8	1.8
All metropolitan areas (thousands)	73,135	1,860	61,842
Percent	100.0	100.0	100.0
Own or buying home	61.4	50.6	65.0
Renting	37.3	49.0	33.6
Occupier paid no cash rent	1.3	0.5	1.3
Central cities (thousands)	29,897	978	22,435
Percent	100.0	100.0	100.0
Own or buying home	48.3	38.9	52.4
Renting	50.6	60.9	46.5
Occupier paid no cash rent	1.1	0.3	1.2
Metropolitan, not in central cities (thousands)	43,238	882	39,407
Percent	100.0	100.0	100.0
Own or buying home	70.4	63.6	72.2
Renting	28.1	35.8	26.3
Occupier paid no cash rent	1.5	0.6	1.4
Outside metropolitan areas (thousands)	21,177	97	19,127
Percent	100.0	100.0	100.0
Own or buying home	73.2	55.7	74.8
Renting	23.3	37.4	21.8
Occupier paid no cash rent	3.5	6.9	3.3

Source: Claudette E. Bennett, Economics and Statistics Administration, Bureau of the Census, U.S. Department of Commerce, *The Asian and Pacific Islander Population in the United States: March 1991 and 1990,* Current Population Reports, Population Characteristics, P20-459 (Washington, DC: U.S. Government Printing Office, August 1992), table 7, p. 35. The population universe for the March 1991 and 1990 Current Population Surveys are the estimate of the civilian noninstitutional population to the United States plus members of the Armed Forces in the United States living off post or with their families on post, but excludes all other members of the Armed Forces. Data are estimates based on sample surveys and are subject to sampling variability since they are not based on a complete count of the population.

★ 748 ★

Households by Family Type and Size

Total number of Asian/Pacific Islander and white households and percent by family type and number of persons per household, 1991.

Characteristic	Total population	Asian and Pacific Islander	White
Type of household			
All households (thousands)	94,312	1,958	80,968
Percent	100.0	100.0	100.0
Family households	70.3	78.4	70.2
Married-couple families	55.3	62.8	58.1
Female householder, no spouse present	11.9	9.9	9.3
Male householder, no spouse present	3.1	5.7	2.8
Nonfamily households	29.7	21.6	29.8
Female householder	16.8	11.3	17.1
Male householder	12.9	10.3	12.7
Size of Household			
Percent	100.0	100.0	100.0
One person	25.0	16.5	25.1
Two persons	32.0	22.4	33.2
Three persons	17.1	18.1	16.8
Four persons	15.4	22.5	15.2
Five persons	6.6	10.0	6.4
Six persons	2.4	5.4	2.1
Seven or more persons	1.5	5.1	1.2

Source: Claudette E. Bennett, Economics and Statistics Administration, Bureau of the Census, U.S. Department of Commerce, *The Asian and Pacific Islander Population in the United States: March 1991 and 1990,* Current Population Reports, Population Characteristics, P20-459 (Washington, DC: U.S. Government Printing Office, August 1992), table 7, p. 35. The population universe for the March 1991 and 1990 Current Population Surveys are the estimate of the civilian noninstitutional population to the United States plus members of the Armed Forces in the United States living off post or with their families on post, but excludes all other members of the Armed Forces. Data are estimates based on sample surveys and are subject to sampling variability since they are not based on a complete count of the population.

★ 749 ★

Families by Type and Size

Total number of Asian/Pacific Islander and white families and percent by family type and size, 1991.

Characteristic	Total population	Asian and Pacific Islander	White
Type of family			
All families (thousands)	66,322	1,536	56,803
Percent	100.0	100.0	100.0
Married-couple families	78.6	80.1	82.8
Female householder, no spouse present	17.0	12.7	13.2
Male householder, no spouse present	4.4	7.3	4.0
Size of family			
Percent	100.0	100.0	100.0
Two persons	41.6	25.5	43.2
Three persons	23.1	21.4	22.8
Four persons	21.3	27.8	21.0
Five persons	9.0	12.9	8.7
Six persons	3.1	6.6	2.8
Seven or more persons	1.9	5.7	1.5

Source: Claudette E. Bennett, Economics and Statistics Administration, Bureau of the Census, U.S. Department of Commerce, *The Asian and Pacific Islander Population in the United States: March 1991 and 1990,* Current Population Reports, Population Characteristics, P20-459 (Washington, DC: U.S. Government Printing Office, August 1992), table 8, p. 38. The population universe for the March 1991 and 1990 Current Population Surveys are the estimate of the civilian noninstitutional population to the United States plus members of the Armed Forces in the United States living off post or with their families on post, but excludes all other members of the Armed Forces. Data are estimates based on sample surveys and are subject to sampling variability since they are not based on a complete count of the population.

★ 750 ★

Households by Size, Asian American and Total United States

Number of Asian/Pacific Islanders households in the United States by size, and total, 1985.

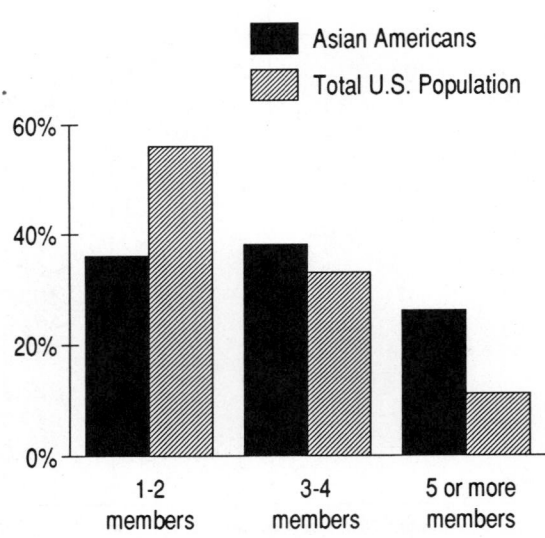

Source: U.S. General Accounting Office, *Asian Americans: A Status Report,* Fact Sheet for the Chairman, Select Committee on Hunger, House of Representatives (Washington, DC: U.S. Government Printing Office, 1990), figure 2.2, p. 21.

★ 751 ★

Population Living in Married Couple Families

Percent of U.S. population living in married couple families, by race/ethnicity, 1990.

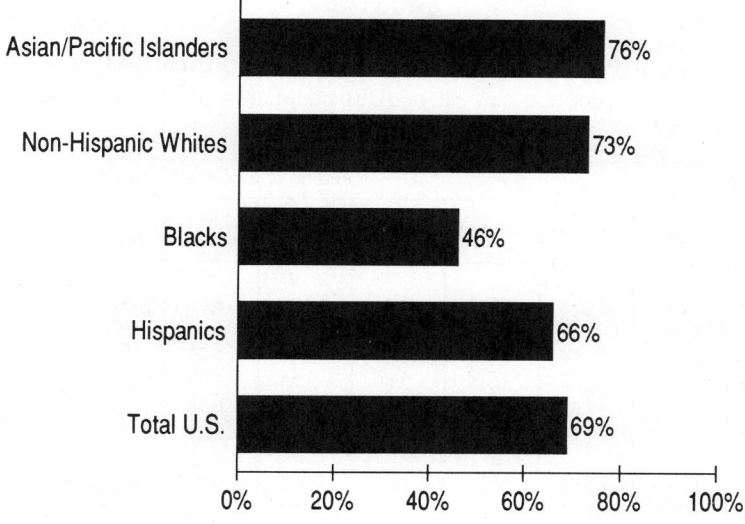

Source: U.S. National Center for Health Statistics, U.S. Bureau of the Census, 1990.

★ 752 ★

Population under Eighteen by Living Arrangements with Parents

Total number (in thousands) of Asian/Pacific Islander and white children under eighteen years and percent by living arrangements with parents, 1991.

Living arrangements of related children under 18 years	Total population	Asian and Pacific Islander	White
Related children under 18 years[a] (thousands)	63,822	2,001	51,258
Percent	100.0	100.0	100.0
Living with-			
Two parents	73.0	84.3	79.6
One parent	24.8	14.2	18.8
Mother only	21.7	12.2	15.8
Father only	3.1	2.0	3.0
Neither parent	2.2	1.5	1.6

Source: Claudette E. Bennett, Economics and Statistics Administration, Bureau of the Census, U.S. Department of Commerce, *The Asian and Pacific Islander Population in the United States: March 1991 and 1990,* Current Population Reports, Population Characteristics, P20-459 (Washington, DC: U.S. Government Printing Office, August 1992), table 8, p. 38. The population universe for the March 1991 and 1990 Current Population Surveys are the estimate of the civilian noninstitutional population to the United States plus members of the Armed Forces in the United States living off post or with their families on post, but excludes all other members of the Armed Forces. Data are estimates based on sample surveys and are subject to sampling variability since they are not based on a complete count of the population. *Note:* (a) The total number of related children under eighteen years in families, by living arrangements, will not match the comparable poverty distribution due to differences in the universe.

United States Population by Ethnicity

★ 753 ★

Asian/Pacific Islander Population by U.S. Metropolitan Area and Ethnicity

Asian/Pacific Islander population in numbers and percent of A/PI population of U.S. Metropolitan Statistical Areas (MSAs), ranked by metropolitan area, 1990.

Metropolitan area[a]	Total Asian	Percent of total Asian population										
		Chinese	Filipino	Japanese	Asian Indian	Korean	Viet-namese	Cam-bodian	Hmong	Laotian	Thai	Other Asian
Los Angeles–Long Beach, CA PMSA	925,561	26.47	23.73	14.02	4.74	15.71	6.76	3.01	0.04	0.40	2.05	3.06
New York, NY PMSA	553,443	44.60	8.88	4.77	19.20	13.49	1.63	0.49	0.00	0.08	0.85	6.00
Honolulu, HI MSA	413,349	15.31	29.04	47.21	0.21	5.48	1.27	0.03	0.00	0.40	0.26	0.81
San Francisco, CA PMSA	316,751	51.35	27.96	7.48	2.69	3.29	3.93	0.52	0.00	0.35	0.44	1.99
Oakland, CA PMSA	259,002	35.02	29.81	8.29	8.35	5.20	6.46	1.46	0.01	2.30	0.46	2.63
San Jose, CA PMSA	254,786	25.52	24.14	10.41	7.91	6.11	21.28	1.55	0.02	0.64	0.35	2.07
Anaheim–Santa Ana, CA PMSA	240,703	17.20	12.61	12.34	6.32	14.92	29.84	1.65	0.24	1.20	0.93	2.75
Chicago, IL PMSA	227,742	17.65	23.89	7.60	23.58	14.69	3.21	1.08	0.09	0.78	1.74	5.69
Washington, DC–MD–VA MSA	200,113	19.51	13.39	4.90	17.76	19.91	11.70	1.94	0.00	1.30	2.19	7.41
San Diego, CA MSA	184,596	10.66	51.98	9.68	2.73	3.64	11.44	2.27	0.86	3.81	0.60	2.34
Seattle, WA PMSA	128,656	21.37	21.69	17.75	4.60	12.68	9.81	4.51	0.35	3.32	1.03	2.91
Houston, TX PMSA	125,529	23.38	10.68	2.94	20.49	5.63	26.32	1.83	0.00	1.16	1.02	6.56
Sacramento, CA MSA	109,242	27.06	18.64	15.62	6.68	5.01	9.57	0.83	5.19	7.20	0.75	3.45
Philadelphia, PA–NJ PMSA	103,537	21.55	11.82	4.16	19.95	21.28	10.06	4.47	0.07	1.22	0.77	4.66
Boston, MA PMSA	94,362	46.79	4.23	6.92	13.04	7.42	9.96	5.26	0.00	0.93	1.00	4.44
Riverside–San Bernardino, CA PMSA	93,473	14.09	30.94	9.59	8.01	10.88	12.11	2.61	0.63	2.09	2.65	6.40
Bergen–Passaic, NJ PMSA	66,540	15.62	15.07	15.75	22.69	25.58	0.69	0.02	0.00	0.11	0.71	3.77
Dallas, TX PMSA	66,250	20.45	8.32	4.56	19.93	13.53	17.39	3.34	0.14	4.04	2.15	6.15
Minneapolis–St. Paul, MN–WI MSA	64,484	11.59	5.05	4.37	11.24	13.52	12.13	4.12	25.49	7.81	0.62	4.06
Nassau–Suffolk, NY PMSA	62,050	29.42	11.85	6.51	28.24	14.54	2.01	0.09	0.00	0.17	1.14	6.01
Stockton, CA MSA	58,374	9.46	28.39	6.45	5.82	1.12	11.92	17.73	7.93	7.26	0.23	3.71
Detroit, MI PMSA	57,141	16.77	17.06	10.58	28.52	12.24	3.07	0.48	2.63	1.54	1.00	6.10
Middlesex–Somerset–Hunterdon, NJ PMSA	56,669	26.26	14.36	2.18	40.54	9.03	2.34	0.04	0.04	0.09	0.38	4.74
Fresno, CA MSA	56,517	8.48	7.63	11.89	9.23	1.74	3.55	6.74	32.42	14.46	0.68	3.16
Newark, NJ PMSA	52,539	26.68	20.76	3.80	30.15	10.01	2.91	0.14	0.00	0.11	0.67	4.75
Atlanta, GA MSA	50,872	18.77	5.04	7.67	19.57	19.89	11.26	4.02	0.59	5.70	1.94	5.55
Portland, OR PMSA	43,768	20.89	11.08	15.61	5.27	13.41	17.26	3.67	0.87	6.63	1.04	4.26
Vallejo–Fairfield–Napa, CA PMSA	43,289	8.65	68.75	7.10	4.64	3.45	2.25	0.08	0.18	1.39	0.93	2.58
Baltimore, MD MSA	42,017	18.81	14.43	4.81	18.41	30.86	4.11	0.44	0.00	0.37	1.79	5.97
Jersey City, NJ PMSA	36,564	13.68	36.16	1.45	31.59	7.67	3.03	0.01	0.00	0.08	0.52	5.80
Denver, CO PMSA	36,013	14.73	8.32	18.85	7.04	17.58	16.30	2.59	2.59	4.76	2.01	5.24
Phoenix, AZ MSA	34,104	28.23	14.88	11.28	11.90	10.27	10.90	2.13	0.03	1.58	2.44	6.37
Norfolk–Virginia Beach–Newport News, VA MSA	34,004	8.60	58.40	5.52	5.58	9.50	5.83	1.25	0.00	0.42	1.43	3.47
Oxnard–Ventura, CA PMSA	32,699	15.25	38.81	15.18	7.20	8.93	7.60	0.54	0.10	0.54	1.45	4.40

[Continued]

★ 753 ★

Asian/Pacific Islander Population by U.S. Metropolitan Area and Ethnicity (Continued)

Asian/Pacific Islander population in numbers and percent of A/PI population of U.S. Metropolitan Statistical Areas (MSAs), ranked by metropolitan area, 1990.

Metropolitan area[a]	Total Asian	Percent of total Asian population										
		Chinese	Filipino	Japanese	Asian Indian	Korean	Viet-namese	Cam-bodian	Hmong	Laotian	Thai	Other Asian
Fort Worth–Arlington, TX PMSA	29,040	15.12	6.97	3.89	15.94	7.16	29.65	1.75	0.27	10.23	2.38	6.64
Miami–Hialeah, FL PMSA	25,869	34.20	14.87	5.06	23.76	5.42	3.92	0.27	0.00	0.42	2.29	9.78
Salinas–Seaside– Monterey, CA MSA	25,369	8.53	45.02	16.54	3.11	14.72	8.09	0.02	0.00	0.08	0.93	2.96
Tacoma, WA PMSA	25,231	5.16	18.88	15.72	1.89	30.08	7.46	13.51	0.04	1.49	1.65	4.12
Las Vegas, NV MSA	24,296	17.23	32.89	11.45	4.40	13.90	5.30	0.88	0.10	3.10	6.31	4.46
St. Louis, MO–IL MSA	23,238	23.53	14.52	8.77	17.90	13.43	9.49	0.37	0.00	1.81	2.76	7.43
Tampa–St. Petersburg– Clearwater, FL MSA	22,424	14.79	16.10	6.15	17.86	11.59	17.57	1.62	0.00	5.29	4.12	4.91
New Orleans, LA MSA	21,112	12.07	9.90	3.11	11.04	4.14	54.09	0.55	0.00	0.63	0.85	3.60
Columbus, OH MSA	20,825	23.70	6.55	15.37	17.82	11.48	5.52	5.95	0.05	5.54	2.12	5.91
Cleveland, OH PMSA	20,289	23.86	14.05	8.36	28.84	10.12	5.65	1.79	0.05	0.81	0.86	5.59
Orlando, FL MSA	19,786	16.91	18.20	5.04	24.80	8.60	16.80	0.54	0.00	1.50	2.04	5.59
Salt Lake City–Ogden, UT MSA	19,588	19.56	7.70	24.84	5.98	9.40	12.25	3.84	0.37	7.91	2.51	5.63
Monmouth–Ocean, NJ PMSA	18,917	32.46	19.40	3.34	23.39	11.87	2.99	0.13	0.00	0.06	0.63	5.74
Milwaukee, WI PMSA	18,445	15.71	9.19	5.16	17.60	9.31	6.13	0.51	18.45	11.02	0.99	5.92
Austin, TX MSA	18,405	28.56	6.49	6.09	15.66	13.50	17.67	1.36	0.00	0.62	2.54	7.50
Modesto, CA MSA	18,072	9.14	13.15	4.54	21.12	2.81	6.80	20.42	5.31	13.36	0.42	2.95
Oklahoma City, OK MSA	17,228	15.92	7.62	6.70	14.32	10.58	30.61	1.07	0.00	3.58	2.97	6.64
Fort Lauderdale–Holly- wood–Pompano Beach, FL PMSA	16,757	28.28	10.66	3.84	34.24	6.36	7.10	0.19	0.00	0.14	2.03	7.16
Kansas City, MO–KS MSA	16,182	16.44	13.63	7.43	15.02	14.99	12.58	1.93	3.60	5.67	2.34	6.37
Bakersfield, CA MSA	15,807	11.97	51.84	5.70	8.94	7.31	3.97	2.05	0.04	2.01	1.47	4.69
Santa Barbara–Santa Maria–Lompoc, CA MSA	15,785	16.06	34.74	18.67	4.64	8.60	5.71	0.28	4.12	2.72	1.19	3.27
Pittsburgh, PA PMSA	15,557	26.52	8.06	7.96	29.27	13.39	5.61	0.58	0.10	0.25	1.59	6.67
San Antonio, TX MSA	15,302	17.08	21.02	10.68	10.42	15.96	11.48	0.96	0.03	1.54	4.29	6.55
Jacksonville, FL MSA	14,925	8.01	57.05	4.27	8.82	5.73	5.81	4.21	0.03	0.89	1.17	4.00
Merced, CA MSA	14,759	3.45	9.56	4.95	15.85	1.99	1.80	0.60	43.76	13.90	1.65	2.49
Providence, RI PMSA	14,331	18.02	7.79	4.05	11.07	7.35	3.47	24.70	6.13	11.86	0.68	4.88
Lowell, MA–NH PMSA	14,205	12.54	1.58	1.18	13.57	3.54	6.20	45.87	0.00	11.28	0.44	3.78
Rochester, NY MSA	13,838	22.97	4.68	5.43	21.53	16.22	10.98	2.62	0.01	9.49	0.81	5.25
Raleigh–Durham, NC MSA	13,705	31.60	5.22	9.45	24.28	12.97	7.87	0.47	0.04	1.40	1.02	5.67
Visalia–Tulare–Porterville, CA MSA	13,013	7.84	32.00	7.99	6.71	2.23	1.26	0.49	14.40	23.31	0.41	3.36
Lake County, IL PMSA	12,363	15.70	32.78	8.96	18.26	15.55	2.12	1.13	0.01	0.19	1.23	4.07
Hartford, CT PMSA	12,073	19.53	7.09	4.37	27.28	10.86	13.01	2.10	0.36	5.94	0.80	8.66
Ann Arbor, MI PMSA	11,645	33.95	5.39	12.28	18.99	18.90	2.98	0.06	0.02	0.52	1.04	5.88
Richmond–Petersburg, VA MSA	11,641	17.47	9.23	5.04	16.26	19.64	14.56	9.85	0.00	1.21	1.17	5.56
Cincinnati, OH–KY–IN PMSA	11,432	22.26	11.36	11.56	24.26	10.50	8.50	3.11	0.01	0.37	1.40	6.67
Tucson, AZ MSA	11,417	30.41	12.71	12.79	9.12	10.91	10.65	0.48	0.00	2.60	3.17	7.16
Charlotte–Gastonia–Rock Hill, NC–SC MSA	11,134	16.00	5.17	6.59	22.75	10.61	20.50	5.38	0.98	5.85	1.20	4.97
Yuba City, CA MSA	10,705	3.94	8.33	7.89	43.04	2.51	0.79	0.13	21.48	6.56	1.19	4.14
Albany–Schenectady– Troy, NY MSA	10,669	29.03	8.10	5.49	26.25	17.37	4.78	0.43	0.00	0.13	0.86	7.55

[Continued]

591

★ 753 ★

Asian/Pacific Islander Population by U.S. Metropolitan Area and Ethnicity (Continued)

Asian/Pacific Islander population in numbers and percent of A/PI population of U.S. Metropolitan Statistical Areas (MSAs), ranked by metropolitan area, 1990.

Metropolitan area[a]	Total Asian	Percent of total Asian population										
		Chinese	Filipino	Japanese	Asian Indian	Korean	Viet-namese	Cam-bodian	Hmong	Laotian	Thai	Other Asian
Buffalo, NY PMSA	10,134	25.81	6.11	6.02	27.09	16.39	6.91	1.00	0.01	3.11	0.78	6.78
Santa Rosa–Petaluma, CA PMSA	9,931	21.84	18.52	17.21	6.57	7.45	7.57	5.61	0.53	8.40	0.82	5.49
Indianapolis, IN MSA	9,865	17.05	14.57	13.44	20.23	15.86	7.58	1.07	0.38	1.00	1.42	7.39
Trenton, NJ PMSA	9,862	30.67	8.27	4.72	32.92	13.58	1.43	0.37	0.00	0.07	0.41	7.56
Nashville, TN MSA	9,843	12.16	6.45	11.48	17.23	11.68	4.71	3.37	0.11	23.74	2.21	6.84
Anchorage, AK MSA	9,713	8.06	32.94	13.92	2.73	31.55	2.63	0.39	0.00	2.06	2.52	3.21
Dayton–Springfield, OH MSA	9,068	15.41	13.26	13.86	22.24	14.57	9.01	1.49	0.00	0.63	2.58	6.96
Wichita, KS MSA	8,947	12.54	7.14	4.74	8.98	5.33	41.59	3.24	0.31	7.86	1.86	6.42
Reno, NV MSA	8,937	23.73	36.88	10.57	6.78	8.52	6.28	0.34	0.00	0.07	2.73	4.11
West Palm Beach–Boca Raton–Delray Beach, FL MSA	8,808	27.23	12.18	4.13	27.19	5.01	11.57	0.10	0.00	1.25	3.58	7.77
Colorado Springs, CO MSA	8,783	8.76	16.93	16.43	3.60	37.21	5.93	0.96	0.00	0.60	3.11	6.48
Madison, WI MSA	8,587	33.06	4.62	7.69	13.63	16.87	4.08	2.35	6.53	3.14	1.23	6.79
New Haven–Meriden, CT MSA	8,342	29.92	8.56	7.41	21.25	12.98	5.26	1.63	0.00	1.41	1.19	10.38
Santa Cruz, CA PMSA	8,163	20.00	29.38	28.30	5.11	7.18	3.03	1.03	0.10	0.18	0.74	4.96
Lansing–East Lansing, MI MSA	8,158	24.31	6.47	6.78	15.19	17.39	10.98	0.31	5.88	3.43	1.37	7.88
Champaign–Urbana–Rantoul, IL MSA	7,973	31.86	7.27	8.34	15.29	19.24	4.63	0.26	0.00	1.92	1.54	9.65
Memphis, TN–AR–MS MSA	7,966	25.16	11.72	7.72	14.54	12.48	11.72	5.37	0.67	3.70	1.72	5.20
Worcester, MA MSA	7,898	18.09	3.36	4.56	21.21	8.13	32.92	2.32	0.15	3.70	1.47	4.10
Grand Rapids, MI MSA	7,692	11.51	5.19	4.63	7.67	22.97	28.09	5.66	0.10	6.63	0.92	6.63
Wilmington, DE–NJ–MD PMSA	7,639	27.27	12.93	7.19	26.47	14.45	3.93	0.08	0.00	0.94	0.79	5.96
Syracuse, NY MSA	7,611	22.95	8.99	5.43	21.72	16.77	9.92	1.92	1.97	2.08	1.06	7.20
Allentown–Bethlehem–Easton, PA–NJ MSA	7,220	24.92	7.30	4.50	26.86	15.35	13.75	0.83	0.00	0.40	0.98	5.11
Albuquerque, NM MSA	7,068	20.94	12.01	13.30	12.00	10.63	16.65	0.68	0.00	4.40	1.94	7.46
Bremerton, WA MSA	6,850	6.09	61.01	14.67	1.11	8.57	4.28	0.35	0.01	0.10	0.73	3.08
Bridgeport–Milford, CT PMSA	6,529	17.72	6.03	3.49	23.40	8.07	10.66	6.79	0.02	14.34	1.67	7.81
Tulsa, OK MSA	6,334	18.44	8.37	6.95	17.16	12.30	19.69	1.01	3.14	2.60	1.82	8.53
Greensboro–Winston-Salem–High Point, NC MSA	6,277	14.34	5.34	9.11	18.64	12.84	15.15	10.10	0.00	5.53	2.26	6.69
Harrisburg–Lebanon–Carlisle, PA MSA	6,160	11.01	7.13	5.19	19.06	16.23	24.89	7.47	0.00	1.92	1.12	5.99
Des Moines, IA MSA	6,134	8.95	5.87	3.34	12.67	11.04	14.51	4.96	2.23	25.35	6.70	4.39
Akron, OH PMSA	6,097	23.42	8.92	7.50	22.88	12.91	3.79	0.71	3.41	7.63	1.80	7.04
Toledo, OH MSA	6,094	27.50	10.53	6.02	22.07	12.47	4.45	0.15	0.31	4.20	1.94	10.35
Killeen–Temple, TX MSA	6,089	5.03	17.97	8.51	4.86	49.58	4.93	0.02	0.00	0.07	3.27	5.78
Spokane, WA MSA	6,087	13.54	12.32	28.65	4.34	13.32	11.42	0.90	4.14	3.19	3.04	5.14
Omaha, NE–IA MSA	6,072	13.22	17.16	15.37	9.95	17.90	10.67	0.92	1.27	1.96	3.61	7.97
El Paso, TX MSA	5,999	13.64	18.27	17.37	8.08	28.39	3.77	0.18	0.00	0.12	1.37	8.82
Charleston, SC MSA	5,835	9.31	60.00	7.16	6.86	5.84	5.23	0.10	0.00	0.02	1.83	3.65
Poughkeepsie, NY MSA	5,793	32.59	5.63	5.83	34.27	9.48	5.96	0.21	0.00	0.41	0.57	5.06
Pensacola, FL MSA	5,752	8.07	45.83	7.51	3.79	4.61	24.27	1.55	0.00	0.40	1.37	2.61
Beaumont–Port Arthur, TX MSA	5,638	8.71	6.86	2.00	7.72	2.57	66.12	0.30	0.00	0.66	1.35	3.71

[Continued]

★ 753 ★

Asian/Pacific Islander Population by U.S. Metropolitan Area and Ethnicity (Continued)

Asian/Pacific Islander population in numbers and percent of A/PI population of U.S. Metropolitan Statistical Areas (MSAs), ranked by metropolitan area, 1990.

Metropolitan area[a]	Total Asian	Percent of total Asian population										
		Chinese	Filipino	Japanese	Asian Indian	Korean	Viet-namese	Cam-bodian	Hmong	Laotian	Thai	Other Asian
Baton Rouge, LA MSA	5,602	23.38	5.27	4.41	22.30	7.00	26.58	0.20	0.00	2.48	1.29	7.10
Olympia, WA MSA	5,545	7.18	16.93	12.19	3.52	24.13	17.69	10.93	0.00	1.97	1.19	4.27
Stamford, CT PMSA	5,500	25.27	10.55	27.47	19.38	6.80	4.16	0.02	0.00	0.16	0.33	5.85
Louisville, KY–IN MSA	5,455	16.30	14.35	9.37	17.40	16.61	14.83	2.14	0.00	1.69	2.00	5.32
Boulder–Longmont, CO PMSA	5,389	24.46	4.94	20.32	8.74	13.79	7.52	4.19	4.97	3.32	1.24	6.51
Atlantic City, NJ MSA	5,316	24.23	19.00	3.31	15.71	12.43	14.32	0.51	0.00	2.50	1.32	6.68
Springfield, MA MSA	5,306	21.67	6.82	7.27	17.45	14.44	13.51	7.56	0.38	2.54	1.04	7.31
Melbourne–Titusville–Palm Bay, FL MSA	5,187	15.96	20.40	9.50	20.42	11.59	9.14	0.64	0.00	0.21	5.24	6.90
Augusta, GA–SC MSA	5,173	13.90	10.67	8.08	22.68	27.88	6.32	0.37	0.00	0.87	2.55	6.69
Lawrence–Haverhill, MA–NH PMSA	5,091	27.20	3.46	5.54	18.33	18.03	14.12	6.62	0.00	0.77	0.73	5.21
Eugene–Springfield, OR MSA	5,049	26.86	9.94	25.83	6.00	14.97	3.98	0.87	0.00	1.92	1.88	7.74
Vancouver, WA PMSA	5,048	14.24	16.01	13.51	4.99	17.89	15.69	8.18	0.00	3.17	1.53	4.79
Fayetteville, NC MSA	4,973	5.39	16.81	11.80	6.29	38.25	6.54	0.08	0.00	0.34	6.31	8.18
Chico, CA MSA	4,927	14.27	8.10	9.66	12.26	3.55	3.06	1.06	26.26	13.72	0.61	7.45
Joliet, IL PMSA	4,848	11.06	29.56	4.58	26.53	8.42	3.03	3.49	0.10	5.45	1.49	6.31
Lafayette–West Lafayette, IN MSA	4,776	36.91	4.52	17.02	17.69	13.55	3.60	0.04	0.02	0.31	0.54	5.78
Aurora–Elgin, IL PMSA	4,636	8.33	9.88	4.55	17.43	9.86	7.42	1.75	1.01	30.52	1.29	7.96
Gainesville, FL MSA	4,603	32.89	10.28	5.04	20.16	13.69	8.78	0.39	0.00	0.26	1.65	6.87
Lancaster, PA MSA	4,594	16.11	4.27	3.74	9.29	10.38	32.24	7.75	5.81	6.20	0.70	3.50
Columbia, SC MSA	4,554	21.74	11.44	8.52	19.04	21.37	7.18	0.46	0.35	0.31	2.81	6.79
Greenville–Spartanburg, SC MSA	4,531	15.85	7.92	7.15	31.32	7.42	9.84	3.58	1.30	9.95	0.88	4.79
Knoxville, TN MSA	4,464	27.35	8.62	12.75	26.14	11.87	4.66	0.47	0.11	0.16	1.34	6.52
Biloxi–Gulfport, MS MSA	4,405	3.56	16.78	3.72	3.65	5.45	63.16	0.14	0.00	0.05	1.50	2.00
Danbury, CT PMSA	4,319	16.93	9.17	3.38	28.25	7.55	8.17	13.80	0.00	6.88	1.13	4.75
Bryan–College Station, TX MSA	4,263	35.05	4.55	2.81	20.27	19.35	6.26	0.07	0.00	0.09	1.60	9.95
Salem, OR MSA	4,180	15.22	15.89	19.95	4.31	10.24	16.60	5.33	1.39	4.38	1.10	5.60
Huntsville, AL MSA	4,100	22.02	6.29	8.05	27.61	23.02	4.98	0.68	0.00	1.29	1.76	4.29
Lexington-Fayette, KY MSA	3,974	28.43	5.71	21.36	20.41	8.78	4.40	0.08	0.00	0.13	1.64	9.06
Binghamton, NY MSA	3,973	27.46	7.70	3.90	19.71	12.81	7.75	0.08	0.00	12.66	1.36	6.57
Birmingham, AL MSA	3,940	27.56	7.51	6.62	24.72	14.26	7.56	0.74	0.00	0.05	2.16	8.81
Pawtucket–Woonsocket–Attleboro, RI–MA PMSA	3,919	12.45	6.61	2.37	16.82	6.20	8.98	15.87	0.15	22.35	1.25	6.94
Iowa City, IA MSA	3,815	38.51	3.67	7.21	13.11	21.31	6.03	0.50	0.00	1.49	1.47	6.71
State College, PA MSA	3,807	39.24	4.89	6.72	19.78	19.25	2.86	0.13	0.00	0.11	0.89	6.12
Appleton–Oshkosh–Neenah, WI MSA	3,772	5.22	2.94	2.78	10.68	6.79	2.39	0.03	57.18	6.84	0.77	4.37
Scranton–Wilkes-Barre, PA MSA	3,747	16.89	10.01	6.81	28.56	17.53	7.53	0.24	0.00	4.80	1.09	6.54
Fort Smith, AR–OK MSA	3,706	3.97	4.13	2.46	3.02	2.08	37.40	0.03	0.11	41.93	0.67	4.21
Gary–Hammond, IN PMSA	3,646	10.83	26.14	7.76	23.64	15.06	4.06	0.25	0.05	1.23	3.59	7.38
Mobile, AL MSA	3,551	11.46	8.59	5.91	10.73	4.70	34.38	9.18	0.00	6.62	1.18	7.24
Galveston–Texas City, TX PMSA	3,495	13.71	16.88	5.29	18.08	6.09	33.51	0.31	0.00	0.23	0.74	5.15
Orange County, NY PMSA	3,489	23.50	14.45	6.56	25.51	16.88	3.61	0.20	0.03	0.63	1.40	7.22

[Continued]

★ 753 ★

Asian/Pacific Islander Population by U.S. Metropolitan Area and Ethnicity (Continued)

Asian/Pacific Islander population in numbers and percent of A/PI population of U.S. Metropolitan Statistical Areas (MSAs), ranked by metropolitan area, 1990.

Metropolitan area[a]	Total Asian	Percent of total Asian population										
		Chinese	Filipino	Japanese	Asian Indian	Korean	Viet-namese	Cam-bodian	Hmong	Laotian	Thai	Other Asian
Fort Walton Beach, FL MSA	3,452	6.58	28.53	10.37	3.16	18.74	7.59	0.03	0.00	0.38	15.56	9.07
New London–Norwich, CT–RI MSA	3,425	20.93	38.51	7.39	14.39	6.60	3.47	1.66	0.00	2.42	1.02	3.59
Lincoln, NE MSA	3,282	23.64	3.75	6.37	12.95	14.59	27.33	1.10	0.00	0.85	1.19	8.23
Little Rock–North Little Rock, AR MSA	3,242	16.47	24.21	10.33	15.02	10.76	8.27	0.40	0.56	4.10	3.64	6.23
Rochester, MN MSA	3,220	15.12	4.75	6.30	8.91	8.48	13.76	27.11	3.70	8.11	0.56	3.20
Amarillo, TX MSA	3,190	5.77	2.60	2.48	9.15	2.26	30.91	0.03	0.00	38.62	2.01	6.18
Kalamazoo, MI MSA	3,129	19.05	6.97	10.90	23.27	16.33	6.94	0.80	0.03	1.12	3.20	11.41
Columbia, MO MSA	3,104	36.50	6.60	6.06	15.79	15.21	3.64	6.77	0.03	0.19	2.64	6.57
Rockford, IL MSA	3,100	12.84	9.81	5.84	15.61	14.16	6.23	0.13	0.58	27.19	2.48	5.13
Richland–Kennewick–Pasco, WA MSA	3,004	14.01	12.28	11.88	9.45	10.52	9.95	1.63	0.87	22.17	1.93	5.29
Flint, MI MSA	2,849	16.60	15.80	5.93	25.80	20.85	6.00	0.32	0.00	0.49	1.47	6.74
Provo–Orem, UT MSA	2,804	29.21	7.67	26.78	4.28	14.12	5.56	1.78	0.29	4.39	1.43	4.49
Chattanooga, TN–GA MSA	2,771	18.08	11.84	6.53	28.11	13.32	6.28	5.99	0.00	3.03	1.88	4.94
Tallahassee, FL MSA	2,726	29.27	11.92	6.38	21.83	12.18	8.22	0.22	0.00	0.04	1.69	8.25
Peoria, IL MSA	2,712	20.10	10.44	7.37	20.69	14.45	15.56	0.48	0.00	2.06	1.44	7.41
Reading, PA MSA	2,711	14.24	21.43	5.61	18.07	12.17	19.96	0.44	0.04	2.84	1.18	4.02
Fort Wayne, IN MSA	2,689	12.76	9.74	5.76	23.88	10.26	14.21	1.82	0.37	10.04	1.86	9.30
Bloomington, IN MSA	2,683	33.10	6.26	11.22	12.64	19.16	2.27	0.22	0.00	0.11	1.71	13.31
Fort Collins–Loveland, CO MSA	2,677	24.99	6.87	18.42	11.54	14.68	8.22	1.23	0.07	0.52	1.27	12.18
Columbus, GA–AL MSA	2,670	7.12	17.49	12.43	5.99	42.73	4.79	1.05	0.00	0.04	2.02	6.33
Lubbock, TX MSA	2,658	25.47	10.16	5.94	22.23	12.00	10.42	0.19	0.00	0.08	2.37	11.14
Boise City, ID MSA	2,646	17.99	10.24	24.38	5.67	13.00	14.17	0.38	0.00	6.12	1.85	6.20
La Crosse, WI MSA	2,638	3.45	1.59	1.55	4.85	5.31	1.29	0.27	73.28	3.22	0.34	4.85
Daytona Beach, FL MSA	2,633	18.57	16.52	7.52	25.41	10.37	10.03	0.42	0.00	2.51	2.54	6.11
Lawton, OK MSA	2,614	4.90	16.64	11.09	3.48	49.01	5.16	1.95	0.31	0.11	3.18	4.17
Hamilton–Middletown, OH PMSA	2,597	23.45	13.52	9.93	30.34	11.47	4.54	1.08	0.00	0.08	0.85	4.74
Charlottesville, VA MSA	2,587	27.87	9.24	8.62	19.98	16.58	7.65	0.19	0.00	0.19	1.08	8.58
Jacksonville, NC MSA	2,562	5.31	47.03	22.60	3.01	9.13	3.12	0.04	0.00	0.12	3.79	5.85
Redding, CA MSA	2,552	8.62	7.88	8.03	4.39	4.08	1.57	3.17	6.54	49.96	1.68	4.08
Lawrence, KS MSA	2,545	39.49	4.79	10.22	13.36	13.36	3.77	0.20	0.12	1.89	2.59	10.22
Corpus Christi, TX MSA	2,537	10.80	41.78	6.42	16.20	7.02	5.56	0.63	0.00	1.14	1.73	8.71
Green Bay, WI MSA	2,490	4.78	3.13	3.01	7.87	4.54	3.05	0.04	56.63	11.85	1.08	4.02
Wausau, WI MSA	2,489	2.41	1.49	0.80	3.90	3.98	1.21	0.60	79.07	4.62	0.32	1.61
Saginaw–Bay City–Midland, MI MSA	2,467	18.61	11.88	6.77	23.02	17.47	2.88	0.28	8.39	4.01	1.34	5.35
Davenport–Rock Island–Moline, IA–IL MSA	2,450	12.65	10.65	6.94	12.82	16.90	25.88	1.47	0.69	4.41	2.73	4.86
South Bend–Mishawaka, IN MSA	2,435	24.11	9.61	10.14	21.97	12.73	8.25	4.52	0.04	1.93	1.31	5.38
Nashua, NH PMSA	2,430	27.20	7.41	6.83	29.59	11.85	8.56	1.19	0.00	0.74	1.60	5.02
Lakeland–Winter Haven, FL MSA	2,429	13.30	15.23	6.05	23.30	7.74	16.14	1.65	0.00	6.67	2.88	7.04
York, PA MSA	2,402	10.32	10.45	6.74	18.11	23.02	15.28	4.54	0.00	3.96	1.25	6.33
Eau Claire, WI MSA	2,376	5.35	3.28	3.58	5.98	5.26	1.98	0.04	67.38	2.15	0.51	4.50
Athens, GA MSA	2,327	33.22	9.24	7.48	16.59	22.91	1.59	0.47	0.04	1.50	1.25	5.72
Savannah, GA MSA	2,296	17.81	13.24	5.75	13.59	16.03	25.78	0.04	0.00	1.61	1.22	4.92
Clarksville–Hopkinsville, TN–KY MSA	2,294	3.88	14.86	9.55	5.45	51.70	3.62	0.17	0.00	0.39	2.18	8.20

[Continued]

★ 753 ★

Asian/Pacific Islander Population by U.S. Metropolitan Area and Ethnicity (Continued)

Asian/Pacific Islander population in numbers and percent of A/PI population of U.S. Metropolitan Statistical Areas (MSAs), ranked by metropolitan area, 1990.

Metropolitan area[a]	Total Asian	Percent of total Asian population										
		Chinese	Filipino	Japanese	Asian Indian	Korean	Viet- namese	Cam- bodian	Hmong	Laotian	Thai	Other Asian
Salem–Gloucester, MA PMSA	2,281	27.49	9.25	12.19	14.51	16.26	10.39	2.81	0.00	0.92	1.80	4.38
Utica–Rome, NY MSA	2,234	14.32	11.68	7.21	17.28	14.28	17.37	1.92	0.13	3.04	4.66	8.10
Bellingham, WA MSA	2,214	14.45	13.69	18.88	7.95	14.09	18.34	6.41	0.00	0.27	1.13	4.79
Panama City, FL MSA	2,156	7.10	19.76	8.77	6.63	11.41	30.57	0.00	0.00	0.00	8.58	7.19
Brockton, MA PMSA	2,126	26.53	14.02	2.82	15.85	9.08	10.87	3.53	2.26	5.03	1.36	8.65
Portsmouth–Dover–Roch- ester, NH–ME MSA	2,055	19.32	13.28	8.32	9.64	13.38	5.55	5.26	0.00	13.33	5.01	6.91
Sheboygan, WI MSA	2,039	1.81	4.95	0.78	15.35	3.43	1.52	1.32	61.55	5.35	0.05	3.87
Norwalk, CT PMSA	2,038	29.05	11.48	7.41	30.81	8.98	2.40	0.00	0.00	0.88	1.91	7.07
Shreveport, LA MSA	1,925	15.06	17.04	8.62	13.35	13.82	11.90	2.65	0.00	1.45	9.40	6.70
Brazoria, TX PMSA	1,919	13.55	17.98	6.04	12.87	7.30	26.37	7.45	0.00	0.16	1.93	6.36
Youngstown–Warren, OH MSA	1,908	16.09	13.26	8.18	30.14	16.82	3.51	0.00	0.00	0.05	2.88	9.07
New Britain, CT PMSA	1,901	16.83	5.00	3.89	21.99	8.21	10.84	4.37	0.05	21.62	0.68	6.52
Macon–Warner Robins, GA MSA	1,900	11.26	19.16	18.11	15.11	14.16	9.47	0.37	0.05	1.16	5.47	5.68
Lafayette, LA MSA	1,884	18.63	3.29	2.76	17.04	6.21	34.61	0.27	0.00	2.12	2.81	12.26
Portland, ME MSA	1,841	15.97	15.43	6.90	8.31	11.62	13.09	19.61	0.00	3.26	0.92	4.89
Yakima, WA MSA	1,825	13.21	39.78	18.08	2.52	10.74	5.10	0.82	0.00	3.29	1.32	5.15
Fort Myers–Cape CoraL, Fl MSA	1,820	19.34	20.16	7.09	20.99	9.40	5.99	0.27	0.00	6.15	3.90	6.70
Wichita Falls, TX MSA	1,772	9.88	15.12	6.83	7.05	11.91	40.91	0.06	0.00	0.06	3.10	5.08
Fitchburg–Leominster, MA MSA	1,754	9.01	3.53	4.39	10.09	15.74	11.46	0.57	9.35	27.08	1.94	6.84
Montgomery, AL MSA	1,735	13.08	14.18	11.18	17.41	14.81	4.61	0.00	0.00	11.93	6.97	5.82
Jackson, MS MSA	1,727	23.62	6.25	5.33	34.68	8.74	11.75	0.00	0.35	0.17	1.97	7.12
Hickory–Morganton, NC MSA	1,638	9.16	3.42	2.38	17.09	5.56	9.34	0.18	26.43	21.67	0.37	4.40
Sioux City, IA–NE MSA	1,613	7.56	5.08	3.10	5.02	7.32	26.78	7.63	1.12	29.57	1.49	5.33
Bloomington–Normal, IL MSA	1,586	23.46	8.89	22.19	19.42	10.72	4.67	0.06	0.00	1.20	3.78	5.61
Roanoke, VA MSA	1,579	16.66	16.09	8.30	16.15	13.30	15.64	1.08	0.00	6.08	1.71	5.00
Waterbury, CT MSA	1,562	19.65	13.96	3.78	29.51	8.77	11.52	2.18	0.00	2.50	0.77	7.36
Fall River, MA–RI PMSA	1,525	16.98	8.46	4.39	4.00	5.51	3.15	48.72	0.00	3.41	0.46	4.92
Springfield, MO MSA	1,525	21.18	12.79	8.13	7.54	19.87	20.26	2.56	0.00	2.36	1.11	4.20
Canton, OH MSA	1,511	18.40	16.15	9.00	26.47	18.00	1.99	0.07	0.07	0.86	2.05	6.95
Fort Pierce, FL MSA	1,451	20.06	21.71	6.62	31.15	9.10	2.21	1.65	0.00	0.07	1.59	5.86
Burlington, VT MSA	1,448	22.86	5.39	10.08	21.41	15.88	11.74	2.28	0.14	2.49	1.86	5.87
Lorain–Elyria, OH PMSA	1,447	16.86	24.53	12.30	20.04	16.10	2.28	0.14	0.00	0.00	1.04	6.70
Benton Harbor, MI MSA	1,446	13.97	18.53	9.61	18.74	24.00	2.77	0.48	0.00	2.56	1.73	7.61
Charleston, WV MSA	1,425	14.74	21.26	4.91	35.30	10.74	2.88	0.00	0.00	1.82	2.88	5.47
Manchester, NH MSA	1,400	28.21	10.29	6.57	15.57	20.07	3.36	2.00	0.00	1.64	2.50	9.79
Sarasota, FL MSA	1,386	19.55	14.79	8.01	13.28	10.97	16.88	2.45	0.00	4.04	4.18	5.84
Abilene, TX MSA	1,383	10.92	31.02	9.26	6.94	12.80	7.95	5.35	0.00	1.08	8.53	6.15
Fargo–Moorhead, ND– MN MSA	1,377	22.22	6.03	5.45	16.92	15.76	17.21	1.96	0.00	1.82	2.03	10.60
Cedar Rapids, IA MSA	1,375	12.22	7.64	9.16	12.07	19.49	21.45	0.73	0.00	8.07	2.69	6.47
Erie, PA MSA	1,375	14.98	10.84	5.38	24.73	12.95	16.36	0.07	0.07	2.47	2.18	9.96
Springfield, IL MSA	1,371	17.58	10.58	5.40	35.81	12.62	6.49	0.80	0.00	1.39	2.63	6.71
Houma–Thibodaux, LA MSA	1,348	8.31	5.27	0.89	4.82	2.15	76.56	0.30	0.00	0.00	0.67	1.04
Waco, TX MSA	1,341	22.00	14.54	8.20	17.00	13.94	15.29	0.00	0.00	0.07	1.49	7.46
Duluth, MN–WI MSA	1,308	16.06	8.26	8.26	9.40	24.39	12.46	0.23	10.78	5.12	0.76	4.28
Medford, OR MSA	1,277	18.79	19.26	24.59	5.48	16.44	3.99	0.55	0.00	0.16	4.15	6.58

[Continued]

595

★ 753 ★

Asian/Pacific Islander Population by U.S. Metropolitan Area and Ethnicity (Continued)

Asian/Pacific Islander population in numbers and percent of A/PI population of U.S. Metropolitan Statistical Areas (MSAs), ranked by metropolitan area, 1990.

Metropolitan area[a]	Total Asian	Percent of total Asian population										
		Chinese	Filipino	Japanese	Asian Indian	Korean	Viet-namese	Cam-bodian	Hmong	Laotian	Thai	Other Asian
Yuma, AZ MSA	1,256	14.81	42.68	17.99	5.25	7.32	3.34	0.00	0.00	0.48	2.31	5.81
Tuscaloosa, AL MSA	1,252	25.40	7.35	13.26	25.08	15.34	2.08	0.00	0.00	0.00	1.04	10.46
Johnson City–Kingsport–Bristol, TN–VA MSA	1,216	24.18	12.99	8.72	23.19	12.17	6.41	0.00	0.00	2.22	2.14	7.98
Evansville, IN–KY MSA	1,190	19.75	11.43	6.81	16.72	16.64	13.45	0.00	0.00	0.00	2.61	12.61
Bradenton, FL MSA	1,165	22.58	13.13	7.64	15.36	7.81	12.27	9.61	0.00	2.75	1.97	6.87
Terre Haute, IN MSA	1,159	26.06	11.04	8.97	20.53	10.53	4.23	0.26	0.00	0.00	1.38	17.00
St. Cloud, MN MSA	1,152	10.42	11.63	4.69	8.33	22.22	13.72	3.99	1.82	11.72	2.17	9.29
Middletown, CT PMSA	1,145	24.10	7.51	6.55	24.72	13.80	4.54	5.68	0.00	3.67	0.96	8.47
Topeka, KS MSA	1,135	24.32	14.63	9.34	18.68	15.59	6.70	0.00	0.00	0.00	2.73	8.02
Vineland–Millville–Bridgeton, NJ PMSA	1,110	10.45	19.82	29.82	17.48	8.74	2.25	0.00	0.00	0.36	0.81	10.27
Waterloo–Cedar Falls, IA MSA	1,108	19.49	6.68	13.36	17.96	22.20	7.04	0.27	0.00	5.23	0.54	7.22
Dothan, AL MSA	1,101	6.09	10.90	19.26	5.36	27.34	18.17	0.54	0.00	0.09	3.27	8.99
Las Cruces, NM MSA	1,089	23.69	12.76	14.33	14.23	11.85	2.57	0.00	0.00	0.09	2.85	17.63
Pascagoula, MS MSA	1,080	7.04	10.93	4.81	5.56	11.11	53.89	0.00	0.00	0.00	2.22	4.44
Mcallen–Edinburg–Mission, TX MSA	1,050	19.43	16.00	11.14	20.19	14.29	2.19	0.10	0.00	0.48	1.05	15.14
Greeley, CO MSA	1,043	12.66	6.14	49.38	3.16	15.15	2.11	1.34	0.00	2.01	3.45	4.60
Battle Creek, MI MSA	1,039	10.11	11.65	36.96	15.78	15.69	1.44	0.00	0.00	0.67	0.96	6.74
Fayetteville–Springdale, AR MSA	1,000	22.40	6.00	7.80	15.90	10.80	9.40	0.00	0.00	16.10	1.20	10.40
Racine, WI PMSA	986	14.40	9.33	6.59	25.76	20.99	8.42	0.20	0.00	4.16	1.12	9.03
Elkhart–Goshen, IN MSA	972	16.56	5.25	9.26	20.99	14.51	7.30	7.72	0.00	8.64	1.34	8.44
Janesville–Beloit, WI MSA	963	11.84	12.25	8.00	9.45	11.53	17.86	15.47	0.52	5.92	2.18	4.98
San Angelo, TX MSA	955	10.68	19.27	6.81	9.01	21.05	12.36	0.00	0.00	7.12	6.81	6.91
Ocala, FL MSA	919	13.82	14.80	6.53	34.60	16.21	7.73	0.00	0.00	0.00	2.18	4.13
Huntington–Ashland, WV–KY–OH MSA	900	13.44	20.33	7.22	30.22	14.56	2.78	0.00	0.00	2.33	1.67	7.44
Santa Fe, NM MSA	886	34.31	9.14	23.25	9.82	10.27	4.29	0.56	0.00	0.11	1.02	7.22
Alexandria, LA MSA	872	8.94	23.17	8.49	11.81	14.68	13.76	4.13	0.00	2.64	4.70	7.68
Rapid City, SD MSA	862	11.83	28.31	10.90	7.77	18.10	5.34	0.00	0.00	0.58	9.16	8.00
Midland, TX MSA	860	23.37	9.77	3.60	26.28	10.23	10.58	4.19	0.00	0.93	1.28	9.77
Grand Forks, ND MSA	840	23.10	28.10	7.74	8.69	16.90	3.21	0.60	0.24	0.12	4.40	6.90
New Bedford, MA MSA	810	36.54	9.38	8.52	8.64	14.57	10.25	0.37	0.12	0.99	3.58	7.04
Niagara Falls, NY PMSA	775	11.87	14.06	6.32	27.23	23.74	5.42	0.00	0.00	1.16	1.94	8.26
Anniston, AL MSA	766	6.40	9.53	11.10	8.09	43.34	5.35	0.65	0.00	0.13	6.01	9.40
Bangor, ME MSA	762	31.89	9.19	10.89	15.22	11.94	10.24	0.13	0.00	0.13	1.05	9.32
Hagerstown, MD MSA	749	11.62	20.69	6.54	12.02	18.02	12.82	0.67	0.00	0.67	3.07	13.89
Asheville, NC MSA	743	19.25	11.17	14.54	16.69	19.11	3.50	4.17	0.00	0.13	3.63	7.81
Cheyenne, WY MSA	741	10.26	27.80	23.08	4.32	19.16	3.51	0.00	0.00	0.00	7.83	4.05
Lima, OH MSA	736	9.92	13.18	14.27	21.47	18.75	3.40	1.22	0.54	12.77	0.82	3.67
Great Falls, MT MSA	734	7.49	38.01	15.12	2.04	19.35	2.18	0.00	0.00	1.23	6.81	7.77
Monroe, LA MSA	722	29.22	8.03	3.74	15.24	4.16	30.47	0.14	0.00	0.00	1.94	7.06
Brownsville–Harlingen, TX MSA	717	16.88	28.45	15.20	10.88	10.18	4.04	0.14	0.00	1.26	0.84	12.13
Lynchburg, VA MSA	712	20.79	14.61	8.01	15.59	16.15	13.62	0.00	0.00	0.42	2.39	8.43
Pueblo, CO MSA	678	18.29	16.08	24.48	11.36	11.50	2.80	0.00	0.15	0.15	1.03	14.16
Elmira, NY MSA	673	19.02	7.43	16.34	23.48	8.92	2.53	0.15	0.00	1.93	1.19	19.02
Sioux Falls, SD MSA	673	14.41	8.62	9.21	6.24	17.24	15.01	7.73	3.57	14.26	1.19	2.53
Kenosha, WI PMSA	645	10.54	23.57	11.16	20.31	23.26	2.17	0.16	1.09	1.09	0.78	5.89
Odessa, TX MSA	644	13.82	21.89	3.88	21.58	5.43	16.46	2.02	0.00	0.00	3.11	11.80
Joplin, MO MSA	641	9.83	11.54	9.05	16.38	9.20	35.26	0.00	0.00	0.00	3.28	5.46

[Continued]

★753★

Asian/Pacific Islander Population by U.S. Metropolitan Area and Ethnicity (Continued)

Asian/Pacific Islander population in numbers and percent of A/PI population of U.S. Metropolitan Statistical Areas (MSAs), ranked by metropolitan area, 1990.

Metropolitan area[a]	Total Asian	Percent of total Asian population										
		Chinese	Filipino	Japanese	Asian Indian	Korean	Viet-namese	Cam-bodian	Hmong	Laotian	Thai	Other Asian
Kankakee, IL MSA	639	13.77	18.00	6.57	32.39	13.30	5.01	0.16	0.47	0.16	0.78	9.39
Jackson, MI MSA	635	9.45	11.34	24.41	17.64	17.95	7.56	0.79	0.00	0.00	1.10	9.76
Muncie, IN MSA	615	26.83	12.03	7.48	16.42	16.59	5.20	0.16	0.16	0.49	3.41	11.22
Tyler, TX MSA	609	20.20	24.79	7.22	18.39	9.20	9.69	2.79	0.00	0.16	1.48	6.08
Longview–Marshall, TX MSA	605	17.52	11.74	6.94	21.32	11.40	19.83	0.50	0.00	0.99	3.80	5.95
Wilmington, NC MSA	571	21.37	15.24	12.96	23.47	10.86	5.08	0.00	0.00	0.53	2.80	7.71
Billings, MT MSA	568	21.83	9.86	27.82	5.81	17.78	3.70	0.35	3.17	7.04	0.88	1.76
Lake Charles, LA MSA	566	20.14	18.20	5.65	20.32	9.01	9.89	0.88	0.00	4.59	3.53	7.77
Mansfield, OH MSA	549	7.65	10.02	14.03	23.32	31.69	7.65	0.00	0.00	0.00	1.46	4.19
Muskegon, MI MSA	544	9.74	13.42	8.64	12.32	31.43	12.32	0.00	0.00	1.29	2.94	7.90
Bristol, CT PMSA	539	24.30	14.84	4.45	23.38	9.65	5.01	8.53	0.00	2.97	0.74	6.12
Pittsfield, MA MSA	537	26.63	4.28	6.89	24.21	15.46	7.82	5.03	0.00	0.00	2.61	7.08
Naples, FL MSA	533	33.77	14.26	6.00	17.82	6.75	8.07	0.00	0.00	0.00	5.07	8.26
Wheeling, WV–OH MSA	524	12.02	26.72	13.55	26.53	9.16	3.63	0.00	0.00	0.00	1.53	6.87
Jamestown–Dunkirk, NY	522	10.92	10.73	4.21	25.67	25.10	4.21	3.64	0.00	5.75	1.34	8.43
Parkersburg–Marietta, WV–OH MSA	506	18.77	15.42	14.43	23.72	16.60	2.96	0.00	0.00	0.00	1.38	6.72
Johnstown, PA MSA	505	10.10	13.47	8.51	33.07	16.83	8.12	0.00	0.00	0.00	1.19	8.71
Lewiston–Auburn, ME MSA	498	25.70	18.67	8.03	11.85	9.84	14.86	0.40	0.00	4.22	2.21	4.22
Decatur, IL MSA	496	13.10	14.52	25.20	16.13	13.51	7.46	0.00	0.00	0.40	2.42	7.26
Enid, OK MSA	495	17.37	12.93	9.49	14.75	12.93	9.90	0.00	0.00	4.04	8.69	9.90
Kokomo, IN MSA	480	20.21	15.21	9.79	19.38	20.83	5.00	0.00	0.00	0.00	2.71	6.88
Albany, GA MSA	475	18.74	18.74	12.63	23.58	11.16	4.63	0.00	0.00	1.47	2.53	6.53
Burlington, NC MSA	475	10.95	8.63	8.21	26.32	15.58	7.79	0.21	0.00	9.89	2.74	9.68
Laredo, TX MSA	473	17.97	6.34	7.82	32.14	18.60	3.38	0.00	0.00	0.00	1.06	12.68
Williamsport, PA MSA	462	12.12	19.91	4.98	22.08	28.79	3.90	0.00	0.00	0.00	0.43	7.79
Steubenville–Weirton, OH–WV MSA	432	10.19	39.12	9.72	16.20	12.04	4.17	0.00	0.00	0.00	4.40	4.17
Dubuque, IA MSA	426	16.20	13.85	19.72	10.09	15.73	13.85	1.17	0.00	0.23	1.41	7.75
Gadsden, AL MSA	415	14.70	6.99	46.02	8.67	5.54	5.06	0.00	0.00	0.00	4.10	8.92
Anderson, IN MSA	399	19.55	15.29	13.03	18.55	22.81	4.26	0.00	0.00	0.50	1.25	4.76
Texarkana, TX–Texarkana, AR MSA	387	8.53	12.40	10.34	19.12	12.14	25.06	0.00	0.00	0.00	0.78	11.63
Cumberland, MD-WV MSA	386	13.21	26.68	5.44	21.50	16.58	1.04	0.00	0.00	0.00	1.04	14.51
Decatur, AL MSA	386	11.92	15.28	10.88	38.60	9.59	4.92	0.52	0.00	1.30	2.85	4.15
Sherman-Denison, TX MSA	385	18.44	15.84	9.09	24.68	12.21	8.05	0.26	0.00	1.56	2.08	7.79
Glens Falls, NY MSA	381	16.80	13.65	7.87	18.37	31.23	3.15	0.00	0.00	0.00	1.05	7.87
Sharon, PA MSA	380	19.47	13.42	11.32	21.58	20.26	4.47	0.26	0.00	0.53	0.79	7.89
Altoona, PA MSA	371	14.56	10.78	8.63	26.15	22.91	4.85	0.00	0.00	0.00	2.43	9.70
Beaver County, PA PMSA	355	19.72	16.34	6.48	18.31	23.66	3.38	0.00	0.00	0.00	2.25	9.86
Pine Bluff, AR MSA	342	25.15	9.65	16.37	21.93	12.57	2.92	0.00	0.00	0.00	2.92	8.48
Anderson, SC MSA	332	19.88	6.33	9.04	30.42	18.07	7.83	0.00	0.00	0.00	4.82	3.61
Danville, VA MSA	321	15.26	28.04	8.10	25.23	8.10	3.12	0.00	0.00	0.00	0.62	11.53
Florence, SC MSA	295	24.07	12.54	5.76	24.41	15.25	1.02	0.00	0.00	1.69	5.08	10.17
Florence, AL MSA	275	23.27	6.18	9.45	33.09	14.55	6.18	0.00	0.00	0.00	1.45	5.82
Bismarck, ND MSA	264	11.74	17.05	6.82	19.70	15.53	11.74	1.89	0.00	5.68	1.89	7.95
Casper, WY MSA	262	18.32	14.50	12.98	8.40	9.54	14.50	1.91	0.00	5.73	3.44	10.69
Victoria, TX MSA	253	13.83	17.00	7.11	28.46	6.72	15.02	0.00	0.00	0.00	1.58	10.28
Jackson, TN MSA	250	20.40	11.60	15.20	20.80	9.20	12.00	0.80	0.00	0.00	0.80	9.20
St. Joseph, MO MSA	247	17.81	19.84	10.53	25.51	16.19	2.43	0.40	0.00	0.00	1.62	5.67
Owensboro, KY MSA	224	16.52	11.16	9.38	35.71	16.52	6.25	0.00	0.00	0.00	0.45	4.02

Source: Asian/Pacific Islander Data Consortium (San Francisco, CA: Asian and Pacific Islander Center for Census Information and Services, 1993). Primary source: U.S. Census Bureau, Summary Tape Files 1 and 3. *Note:* (a) The U.S. Bureau of Census designates the following: PMSA=primary metropolitan statistical area; MSA=metropolitan statistical area. See *Appendix* for detailed definitions.

★ 754 ★

Asian Indian Population by Significant U.S. Metropolitan Areas

Asian Indian population in numbers, percent of the total area population, and percent of Asian/Pacific Islander area population, ranked by metropolitan area[a], 1990.

Metropolitan area[b]	Total population	Total A/PI population	Asian Indian		
			Number	Percent of total	Percent of A/PI
New York, NY PMSA	8,546,846	553,443	106,270	1.2%	19%
Chicago, IL PMSA	6,069,974	227,742	53,702	0.9%	24%
Los Angeles–Long Beach, CA PMSA	8,863,164	925,561	43,829	0.5%	5%
Washington, DC–MD–VA MSA	3,923,574	200,113	35,533	0.9%	18%
Houston, TX PMSA	3,301,937	125,529	25,720	0.8%	20%
Middlesex–Somerset–Hunterdon, NJ PMSA	1,019,835	56,669	22,972	2.3%	41%
Oakland, CA PMSA	2,082,914	259,002	21,633	1.0%	8%
Philadelphia, PA–NJ PMSA	4,856,881	103,537	20,657	0.4%	20%
San Jose, CA PMSA	1,497,577	254,786	20,164	1.4%	8%
Nassau–Suffolk, NY PMSA	2,609,212	62,050	17,523	0.7%	28%
Detroit, MI PMSA	4,382,299	57,141	16,298	0.4%	29%
Newark, NJ PMSA	1,824,321	52,539	15,842	0.9%	30%
Anaheim–Santa Ana, CA PMSA	2,410,556	240,703	15,212	0.6%	6%
Bergen–Passaic, NJ PMSA	1,278,440	66,540	15,095	1.2%	23%
Dallas, TX PMSA	2,553,362	66,250	13,201	0.5%	20%
Boston, MA PMSA	2,870,669	94,362	12,301	0.4%	13%
Jersey City, NJ PMSA	553,099	36,564	11,552	2.1%	32%

Source: Asian/Pacific Islander Data Consortium (San Francisco, CA: Asian and Pacific Islander Center for Census Information and Services, 1993). Primary source: U.S. Census Bureau, Summary Tape Files 1 and 3. *Notes:* (a) Includes metropolitan areas with Asian Indian population greater than 11,000. (b) The U.S. Census Bureau designates the following: PMSA=primary metropolitan statistical area; MSA=metropolitan statistical area. See *Appendix* for detailed definitions.

★ 755 ★

Cambodian Population by Significant U.S. Metropolitan Areas

Cambodian population in numbers, percent of the total area population, and percent of Asian/Pacific Islander area population, ranked by metropolitan area[a], 1990.

Metropolitan area[b]	Total population	Total A/PI population	Cambodian		
			Number	Percent of total	Percent of A/PI
Los Angeles–Long Beach, CA PMSA	8,863,164	925,561	27,819	0.3%	3%
Stockton, CA MSA	480,628	58,374	10,350	2.2%	18%
Lowell, MA–NH PMSA	273,067	14,205	6,516	2.4%	46%
Seattle, WA PMSA	1,972,961	128,656	5,800	0.3%	5%
Boston, MA PMSA	2,870,669	94,362	4,967	0.2%	5%
Philadelphia, PA–NJ PMSA	4,856,881	103,537	4,633	0.1%	4%
San Diego, CA MSA	2,498,016	184,596	4,185	0.2%	2%

Source: Asian/Pacific Islander Data Consortium (San Francisco, CA: Asian and Pacific Islander Center for Census Information and Services, 1993). Primary source: U.S. Census Bureau, Summary Tape Files 1 and 3. *Notes:* (a) Includes metropolitan areas with Cambodian population greater than 4,000. (b) The U.S. Census Bureau designates the following: PMSA=primary metropolitan statistical area; MSA=metropolitan statistical area. See *Appendix* for detailed definitions.

★ 756 ★

Chinese Population by Significant U.S. Metropolitan Areas

Chinese population in numbers, percent of the total area population, and percent of Asian/Pacific Islander area population, ranked by metropolitan area[a], 1990.

Metropolitan area[b]	Total population	Total A/PI population	Chinese		
			Number	Percent of total	Percent of A/PI
New York, NY PMSA	8,546,846	553,443	246,817	2.9%	45%
Los Angeles–Long Beach, CA PMSA	8,863,164	925,561	245,033	2.8%	26%
San Francisco, CA PMSA	1,603,678	316,751	162,636	10.1%	51%
Oakland, CA PMSA	2,082,914	259,002	90,691	4.4%	35%
San Jose, CA PMSA	1,497,577	254,786	65,027	4.3%	26%
Honolulu, HI MSA	836,231	413,349	63,265	7.6%	15%
Boston, MA PMSA	2,870,669	94,362	44,155	1.5%	47%
Anaheim–Santa Ana, CA PMSA	2,410,556	240,703	41,403	1.7%	17%
Chicago, IL PMSA	6,069,974	227,742	40,189	0.7%	18%
Washington, DC–MD–VA MSA	3,923,574	200,113	39,034	1.9%	20%
Sacramento, CA MSA	1,481,102	109,242	29,558	2.0%	27%
Houston, TX PMSA	3,301,937	125,529	29,345	0.9%	23%
Seattle, WA PMSA	1,972,961	128,656	27,490	1.4%	21%
Philadelphia, PA–NJ PMSA	4,856,881	103,537	22,311	0.5%	22%
San Diego, CA MSA	2,498,016	184,596	19,686	0.8%	11%
Nassau–Suffolk, NY PMSA	2,609,212	62,050	18,257	0.7%	29%
Middlesex–Somerset–Hunterdon, NJ PMSA	1,019,835	56,669	14,883	1.5%	26%
Newark, NJ PMSA	1,824,321	52,539	14,020	0.8%	27%
Dallas, TX PMSA	2,553,362	66,250	13,546	0.5%	20%
Riverside–San Bernardino, CA PMSA	2,588,793	93,473	13,166	0.5%	14%
Bergen–Passaic, NJ PMSA	1,278,440	66,540	10,391	0.8%	16%

Source: Asian/Pacific Islander Data Consortium (San Francisco, CA: Asian and Pacific Islander Center for Census Information and Services, 1993). Primary source: U.S. Census Bureau, Summary Tape Files 1 and 3. *Notes:* (a) Includes metropolitan areas with Chinese population greater than 10,000. (b) The U.S. Census Bureau designates the following: PMSA=primary metropolitan statistical area; MSA=metropolitan statistical area. See *Appendix* for detailed definitions.

★ 757 ★

Filipino Population by Significant U.S. Metropolitan Areas

Filipino population in numbers, percent of the total area population, and percent of Asian/Pacific Islander area population, ranked by metropolitan area[a], 1990.

Metropolitan area[b]	Total population	Total A/PI population	Filipino		
			Number	Percent of total	Percent of A/PI
Los Angeles–Long Beach, CA PMSA	8,863,164	925,561	219,653	2.5%	24%
Honolulu, HI MSA	836,231	413,349	120,029	14.4%	29%
San Diego, CA MSA	2,498,016	184,596	95,945	3.8%	52%
San Francisco, CA PMSA	1,603,678	316,751	88,560	5.5%	28%
Oakland, CA PMSA	2,082,914	259,002	77,198	3.7%	30%
San Jose, CA PMSA	1,497,577	254,786	61,518	4.1%	24%
Chicago, IL PMSA	6,069,974	227,742	54,411	0.9%	24%
New York, NY PMSA	8,546,846	553,443	49,156	0.6%	9%
Anaheim–Santa Ana, CA PMSA	2,410,556	240,703	30,356	1.3%	13%
Vallejo–Fairfield–Napa, CA PMSA	451,186	43,289	29,760	6.6%	69%
Riverside–San Bernardino, CA PMSA	2,588,793	93,473	28,919	1.1%	31%
Seattle, WA PMSA	1,972,961	128,656	27,900	1.4%	22%
Washington, DC–MD–VA MSA	3,923,574	200,113	26,793	0.7%	13%
Sacramento, CA MSA	1,481,102	109,242	20,359	1.4%	19%
Norfolk–Virginia Beach–Newport News, VA MSA	1,396,107	34,004	19,858	1.4%	58%
Stockton, CA MSA	480,628	58,374	16,570	3.5%	28%
Houston, TX PMSA	3,301,937	125,529	13,404	0.4%	11%
Jersey City, NJ PMSA	553,099	36,564	13,222	2.4%	36%
Oxnard–Ventura, CA PMSA	669,016	32,699	12,690	1.9%	39%
Philadelphia, PA–NJ PMSA	4,856,881	103,537	12,233	0.3%	12%
Salinas–Seaside–Monterey, CA MSA	355,660	25,369	11,421	3.2%	45%
Newark, NJ PMSA	1,824,321	52,539	10,907	0.6%	21%
Bergen–Passaic, NJ PMSA	1,278,440	66,540	10,027	0.8%	15%

Source: Asian/Pacific Islander Data Consortium (San Francisco, CA: Asian and Pacific Islander Center for Census Information and Services, 1993). Primary source: U.S. Census Bureau, Summary Tape Files 1 and 3. *Notes:* (a) Includes metropolitan areas with Filipino population greater than 10,000. (b) The U.S. Census Bureau designates the following: PMSA=primary metropolitan statistical area; MSA=metropolitan statistical area. See *Appendix* for detailed definitions.

★ 758 ★

Hmong Population by Significant U.S. Metropolitan Areas

Hmong population in numbers, percent of the total area population, and percent of Asian/Pacific Islander area population, ranked by metropolitan area[a], 1990.

Metropolitan area[b]	Total population	Total A/PI population	Hmong		
			Number	Percent of total	Percent of A/PI
Fresno, CA MSA	667,490	56,517	18,321	2.7%	32%
Minneapolis–St. Paul, MN–WI MSA	2,464,124	64,484	16,435	0.7%	25%
Merced, CA MSA	178,403	14,759	6,458	3.6%	44%
Sacramento, CA MSA	1,481,102	109,242	5,673	0.4%	5%
Stockton, CA MSA	480,628	58,374	4,628	1.6%	8%
Milwaukee, WI PMSA	1,432,149	18,445	3,404	0.2%	18%
Yuba City, CA MSA	122,643	10,705	2,299	1.9%	21%
Appleton–Oshkosh–Neenah, WI MSA	315,121	3,772	2,157	0.7%	57%
Wausau, WI MSA	115,400	2,489	1,968	1.7%	79%
La Crosse, WI MSA	97,904	2,638	1,933	2.0%	73%
Visalia–Tulare–Porterville, CA MSA	311,921	13,013	1,874	0.6%	14%
Eau Claire, WI MSA	137,543	2,376	1,601	1.2%	67%
San Diego, CA MSA	2,498,016	184,596	1,585	0.1%	1%
Detroit, MI PMSA	4,382,299	57,141	1,503	0.0%	3%
Green Bay, WI MSA	194,594	2,490	1,410	0.7%	57%
Chico, CA MSA	182,120	4,927	1,294	0.7%	26%
Sheboygan, WI MSA	103,877	2,039	1,255	1.2%	62%

Source: Asian/Pacific Islander Data Consortium (San Francisco, CA: Asian and Pacific Islander Center for Census Information and Services, 1993). Primary source: U.S. Census Bureau, Summary Tape Files 1 and 3. *Notes:* (a) Includes metropolitan areas with Hmong population greater than 1,000. (b) The U.S. Census Bureau designates the following: PMSA=primary metropolitan statistical area; MSA=metropolitan statistical area. See *Appendix* for detailed definitions.

★ 759 ★

Japanese Population by Significant U.S. Metropolitan Areas

Japanese population in numbers, percent of the total area population, and percent of Asian/Pacific Islander area population, ranked by metropolitan area[a], 1990.

Metropolitan area[b]	Total population	Total A/PI population	Japanese		
			Number	Percent of total	Percent of A/PI
Honolulu, HI MSA	836,231	413,349	195,149	23.3%	47%
Los Angeles–Long Beach, CA PMSA	8,863,164	925,561	129,736	1.5%	14%
Anaheim–Santa Ana, CA PMSA	2,410,556	240,703	29,704	1.2%	12%
San Jose, CA PMSA	1,497,577	254,786	26,516	1.8%	10%
New York, NY PMSA	8,546,846	553,443	26,422	0.3%	5%
San Francisco, CA PMSA	1,603,678	316,751	23,682	1.5%	7%
Seattle, WA PMSA	1,972,961	128,656	22,835	1.2%	18%
Oakland, CA PMSA	2,082,914	259,002	21,477	1.0%	8%
San Diego, CA MSA	2,498,016	184,596	17,869	0.7%	16%
Chicago, IL PMSA	6,069,974	227,742	17,310	0.3%	8%
Sacramento, CA MSA	1,481,102	109,242	17,067	1.2%	16%
Bergen–Passaic, NJ PMSA	1,278,440	66,540	10,482	0.8%	16%

Source: Asian/Pacific Islander Data Consortium (San Francisco, CA: Asian and Pacific Islander Center for Census Information and Services, 1993). Primary source: U.S. Census Bureau, Summary Tape Files 1 and 3. *Notes:* (a) Includes metropolitan areas with Japanese population greater than 10,000. (b) The U.S. Census Bureau designates the following: PMSA=primary metropolitan statistical area; MSA=metropolitan statistical area. See *Appendix* for detailed definitions.

★ 760 ★

Korean Population by Significant U.S. Metropolitan Areas

Korean population in numbers, percent of the total area population, and percent of Asian/Pacific Islander area population, ranked by metropolitan area[a], 1990.

Metropolitan area[b]	Total population	Total A/PI population	Korean		
			Number	Percent of total	Percent of A/PI
Los Angeles–Long Beach, CA PMSA	8,863,164	925,561	145,431	1.6%	16%
New York, NY PMSA	8,546,846	553,443	74,632	0.9%	13%
Washington, DC–MD–VA MSA	3,923,574	200,113	39,850	1.0%	20%
Anaheim–Santa Ana, CA PMSA	2,410,556	240,703	35,919	1.5%	15%
Chicago, IL PMSA	6,069,974	227,742	33,465	0.6%	15%
Honolulu, HI MSA	836,231	413,349	22,646	2.7%	5%
Philadelphia, PA–NJ PMSA	4,856,881	103,537	22,028	0.5%	21%
Bergen–Passaic, NJ PMSA	1,278,440	66,540	17,018	1.3%	26%
Seattle, WA PMSA	1,972,961	128,656	16,311	0.8%	13%
San Jose, CA PMSA	1,497,577	254,786	15,565	1.0%	6%
Oakland, CA PMSA	2,082,914	259,002	13,478	0.7%	5%
Baltimore, MD MSA	2,382,172	42,017	12,967	0.5%	31%
San Francisco, CA PMSA	1,603,678	316,751	10,416	0.7%	3%
Riverside–San Bernardino, CA PMSA	2,588,793	93,473	10,166	0.4%	11%
Atlanta, GA MSA	2,833,511	50,872	10,120	0.4%	20%

Source: Asian/Pacific Islander Data Consortium (San Francisco, CA: Asian and Pacific Islander Center for Census Information and Services, 1993). Primary source: U.S. Census Bureau, Summary Tape Files 1 and 3. *Notes:* (a) Includes metropolitan areas with Korean population greater than 10,000. (b) The U.S. Census Bureau designates the following: PMSA=primary metropolitan statistical area; MSA=metropolitan statistical area. See *Appendix* for detailed definitions.

★ 761 ★

Laotian Population by Significant U.S. Metropolitan Areas

Laotian population in numbers, percent of the total area population, and percent of Asian/Pacific Islander area population, ranked by metropolitan area[a], 1990.

Metropolitan area[b]	Total population	Total A/PI population	Laotian		
			Number	Percent of total	Percent of A/PI
Fresno, CA MSA	667,490	56,517	8,174	1.2%	14%
Sacramento, CA MSA	1,481,102	109,242	7,861	0.5%	7%
San Diego, CA MSA	2,498,016	184,596	7,025	0.3%	4%
Oakland, CA PMSA	2,082,914	259,002	5,964	0.3%	2%
Minneapolis–St. Paul, MN–WI MSA	2,464,124	64,484	5,039	0.2%	8%
Seattle, WA PMSA	1,972,961	128,656	4,270	0.2%	3%
Stockton, CA MSA	480,628	58,374	4,236	0.9%	7%
Los Angeles–Long Beach, CA PMSA	8,863,164	925,561	3,742	<0.1%	<1%
Visalia–Tulare–Porterville, CA MSA	311,921	13,013	3,033	1.7%	23%
Fort Worth–Arlington, TX PMSA	1,332,053	29,040	2,971	0.2%	10%
Portland, OR PMSA	1,239,842	43,768	2,901	0.2%	7%
Atlanta, GA MSA	2,833,511	50,872	2,898	0.1%	6%
Anaheim–Santa Ana, CA PMSA	2,410,556	240,703	2,893	0.1%	1%

[Continued]

★ 761 ★

Laotian Population by Significant U.S. Metropolitan Areas (Continued)

Laotian population in numbers, percent of the total area population, and percent of Asian/Pacific Islander area population, ranked by metropolitan area[a], 1990.

Metropolitan area[b]	Total population	Total A/PI population	Laotian		
			Number	Percent of total	Percent of A/PI
Dallas, TX PMSA	2,553,362	66,250	2,678	0.1%	4%
Washington, DC–MD–VA MSA	3,923,574	200,113	2,603	0.1%	1%
Modesto, CA MSA	370,522	18,072	2,415	0.7%	13%
Nashville, TN MSA	985,026	9,843	2,337	0.2%	24%
Merced, CA MSA	178,403	14,759	2,052	1.2%	14%
Milwaukee, WI PMSA	1,432,149	18,445	2,033	0.1%	11%

Source: Asian/Pacific Islander Data Consortium (San Francisco, CA: Asian and Pacific Islander Center for Census Information and Services, 1993). Primary source: U.S. Census Bureau, Summary Tape Files 1 and 3. *Notes:* (a) Includes metropolitan areas with Laotian population greater than 2,000. (b) The U.S. Census Bureau designates the following: PMSA=primary metropolitan statistical area; MSA=metropolitan statistical area. See *Appendix* for detailed definitions.

★ 762 ★

Thai Population by Significant U.S. Metropolitan Areas

Thai population in numbers, percent of the total area population, and percent of Asian/Pacific Islander area population, ranked by metropolitan area[a], 1990.

Metropolitan area[b]	Total population	Total A/PI population	Thai		
			Number	Percent of total	Percent of A/PI
Los Angeles–Long Beach, CA PMSA	8,863,164	925,561	19,016	0.2%	2.1%
New York, NY PMSA	8,546,846	553,443	4,684	0.1%	0.8%
Washington, DC–MD–VA MSA	3,923,574	200,113	4,381	0.1%	2.2%
Chicago, IL PMSA	6,069,974	227,742	3,955	0.1%	1.7%
Riverside–San Bernardino, CA PMSA	2,588,793	93,473	2,474	0.1%	2.6%
Anaheim–Santa Ana, CA PMSA	2,410,556	240,703	2,227	0.1%	0.9%
Las Vegas, NV MSA	741,459	24,296	1,533	0.2%	6.3%
Dallas, TX PMSA	2,553,362	66,250	1,424	0.1%	2.1%
San Francisco, CA PMSA	1,603,678	316,751	1,394	0.1%	0.4%
Seattle, WA PMSA	1,972,961	128,656	1,323	0.1%	1.0%
Houston, TX PMSA	3,301,937	125,529	1,281	0.0%	1.0%
Oakland, CA PMSA	2,082,914	259,002	1,183	0.1%	0.5%
San Diego, CA MSA	2,498,016	184,596	1,109	<0.1%	0.6%
Honolulu, HI MSA	836,231	413,349	1,065	0.1%	0.3%

Source: Asian/Pacific Islander Data Consortium (San Francisco, CA: Asian and Pacific Islander Center for Census Information and Services, 1993). Primary source: U.S. Census Bureau, Summary Tape Files 1 and 3. *Notes:* (a) Includes metropolitan areas with Thai population greater than 1,000. (b) The U.S. Census Bureau designates the following: PMSA=primary metropolitan statistical area; MSA=metropolitan statistical area. See *Appendix* for detailed definitions.

★ 763 ★

Vietnamese Population by Significant U.S. Metropolitan Areas

Vietnamese population in numbers, percent of the total area population, and percent of Asian/Pacific Islander area population, ranked by metropolitan area[a], 1990.

Metropolitan area[b]	Total population	Total A/PI population	Vietnamese		
			Number	Percent of total	Percent of A/PI
Anaheim–Santa Ana, CA PMSA	2,410,556	240,703	71,822	3.0%	30%
Los Angeles–Long Beach, CA PMSA	8,863,164	925,561	62,594	0.7%	7%
San Jose, CA PMSA	1,497,577	254,786	54,212	3.6%	21%
Houston, TX PMSA	3,301,937	125,529	33,035	1.0%	26%
Washington, DC–MD–VA MSA	3,923,574	200,113	23,408	0.6%	12%
San Diego, CA MSA	2,498,016	184,596	21,118	0.9%	11%
Oakland, CA PMSA	2,082,914	259,002	16,732	0.8%	6%
Seattle, WA PMSA	1,972,961	128,656	12,617	0.6%	18%
San Francisco, CA PMSA	1,603,678	316,751	12,451	0.8%	4%
Dallas, TX PMSA	2,553,362	66,250	11,522	0.5%	17%
New Orleans, LA MSA	1,238,816	21,112	11,419	0.9%	54%
Riverside–San Bernardino, CA PMSA	2,588,793	93,473	11,315	0.4%	12%
Sacramento, CA MSA	1,481,102	109,242	10,454	0.7%	15%
Philadelphia, PA–NJ PMSA	4,856,881	103,537	10,418	0.2%	10%

Source: Asian/Pacific Islander Data Consortium (San Francisco, CA: Asian and Pacific Islander Center for Census Information and Services, 1993). Primary source: U.S. Census Bureau, Summary Tape Files 1 and 3. *Notes:* (a) Includes metropolitan areas with Asian Indian population greater than 10,000. (b) The U.S. Census Bureau designates the following: PMSA=primary metropolitan statistical area; MSA=metropolitan statistical area. See *Appendix* for detailed definitions.

Selected United States Cities and Places

★ 764 ★

Arizona Cities and Places Ranked by Asian/Pacific Islander Population

Asian/Pacific Islander population and percent of total population in cities in Arizona, 1990.

City or place	Total population	Asian/Pacific Islander	
		Population	Percent of total
Phoenix	983,403	16,303	1.7%
Tucson	405,390	8,901	2.2%
Tempe	141,865	5,748	4.1%
Mesa	288,091	4,355	1.5%
Glendale	148,134	3,150	2.1%
Chandler	90,533	2,153	2.4%
Sierra Vista	32,983	1,722	5.2%
Scottsdale	130,069	1,600	1.2%

Sources: Adapted from Asian Week, *Asians in America, 1990 Census* (San Francisco, CA: *Asian Week,* 1991), p. 29, and Asian/Pacific Islander Data Consortium (San Francisco, CA: Asian and Pacific Islander Center for Census Information and Services, 1993). Primary source: U.S. Census Bureau, Summary Tape File 1A.

★ 765 ★

California Cities and Places
Ranked by Asian/Pacific Islander Population

Asian/Pacific Islander population and percent of total population in cities in California, 1990.

City or place	Total population	Asian/Pacific Islander	
		Population	Percent of total
Los Angeles	3,485,398	341,807	9.8%
San Francisco	723,959	210,876	29.1%
San Jose	782,248	152,815	19.5%
San Diego	1,110,549	130,945	11.8%
Long Beach	429,433	58,266	13.6%
Sacramento	369,365	55,426	15.0%
Oakland	372,242	54,931	14.8%
Stockton	210,943	48,087	22.8%
Fresno	354,202	44,358	12.5%
Daly City	92,311	40,466	43.8%
Monterey Park	60,738	34,898	57.5%
Fremont	173,339	33,671	19.4%
Alhambra	82,106	31,313	38.1%
Garden Grove	143,050	29,337	20.5%
Torrance	133,107	29,097	21.9%
Santa Ana	293,742	28,585	9.7%

[Continued]

★ 765 ★

California Cities and Places
Ranked by Asian/Pacific Islander Population (Continued)

Asian/Pacific Islander population and percent of total population in cities in California, 1990.

City or place	Total population	Asian/Pacific Islander	
		Population	Percent of total
Glendale	180,038	25,453	14.1%
Vallejo	109,199	25,063	23.0%
Anaheim	266,406	25,018	9.4%
Cerritos	53,240	24,057	45.2%
Sunnyvale	117,229	22,655	19.3%
Carson	83,995	20,972	25.0%
Irvine	110,330	19,970	18.1%
Union City	53,762	17,978	33.4%
Rosemead	51,638	17,725	34.3%

Sources: Adapted from Asian Week, *Asians in America, 1990 Census* (San Francisco, CA: Asian Week, 1991), p. 29, and Asian/Pacific Islander Data Consortium (San Francisco: Asian and Pacific Islander Center for Census Information and Services, 1993). Primary source: U.S. Census Bureau, Summary Tape File 1A.

★ 766 ★

Colorado Cities and Places Ranked by Asian/Pacific Islander Population

Asian/Pacific Islander population and percent of total population in cities in Colorado, 1990.

City or Place	Total population	Asian/Pacific Islander	
		Population	Percent of total
Denver	467,610	11,005	2.4%
Aurora	222,103	8,376	3.8%
Colorado Springs	281,140	6,845	2.4%
Boulder	83,312	3,208	3.9%
Westminister	76,625	2,755	3.7%
Lakewood	126,481	2,435	1.9%
Fort Collins	87,758	2,098	2.4%
Arvada	89,235	1,768	2.0%

Sources: Adapted from Asian Week, *Asians in America, 1990 Census* (San Francisco, CA: Asian Week, 1991), p. 29, and Asian/Pacific Islander Data Consortium (San Francisco: Asian and Pacific Islander Center for Census Information and Services, 1993). Primary source: U.S. Census Bureau, Summary Tape File 1A.

★ 767 ★

Connecticut Cities and Places Ranked by Asian/Pacific Islander Population

Asian/Pacific Islander population and percent of total population in cities in Colorado, 1990.

City or place	Total population	Asian/Pacific Islander	
		population	Percent of total
Bridgeport	141,686	3,288	2.3%
New Haven	130,474	3,141	2.4%
Stamford	108,056	2,811	2.6%
Danbury	65,585	2,582	3.9%
Hartford	139,739	2,024	1.4%
West Hartford CDP[a]	60,110	1,710	2.8%
New Britain	75,491	1,348	1.8%
Norwalk	78,331	1,290	1.6%
East Hartford CDP[a]	50,452	1,120	2.2%
West Haven	54,021	1,098	2.0%
Storrs CDP[a]	12,198	1,059	8.7%

Sources: Adapted from Asian Week, *Asians in America, 1990 Census* (San Francisco, CA: Asian Week, 1991), p. 29, and Asian/Pacific Islander Data Consortium (San Francisco: Asian and Pacific Islander Center for Census Information and Services, 1993). Primary source: U.S. Census Bureau, Summary Tape File 1A. *Note:* (a) The U.S. Census Bureau uses the designation CDP for Census Designated Place. See *Appendix* for detailed definition.

★ 768 ★

Florida Cities and Places
Ranked by Asian/Pacific Islander Population

Asian/Pacific Islander population and percent of total population in cities in Florida, 1990.

City or place	Total population	Asian/Pacific Islander	
		Population	Percent of total
Jacksonville[a]	672,971	12,940	1.9%
St. Petersburg	238,629	3,967	1.7%
Tampa	280,015	3,794	1.4%
Gainesville	84,770	3,343	3.9%
Kendall CDP[b]	87,271	2,596	3.0%
Orlando	164,693	2,564	1.6%
Miami	358,548	2,272	0.6%
Tallahassee	124,773	2,189	1.8%
Coral Springs	79,443	1,684	2.1%
Hollywood	121,697	1,611	1.3%
Pembroke Pines	65,452	1,304	2.0%
Fort Lauderdale	149,377	1,297	0.9%
Town 'n' Country CDP[b]	60,946	1,290	2.1%
Sunrise	64,407	1,247	1.9%
Melbourne	59,646	1,224	2.1%
Plantation	66,692	1,219	1.8%
North Miami Beach	35,359	1,207	3.4%
North Miami	49,998	1,206	2.4%
Boca Raton	61,492	1,167	1.9%
Kendale Lakes CDP[b]	48,524	1,141	2.4%
Miami Beach	92,639	1,124	1.2%

[Continued]

★ 768 ★

Florida Cities and Places
Ranked by Asian/Pacific Islander Population (Continued)

Asian/Pacific Islander population and percent of total population in cities in Florida, 1990.

City or place	Total population	Asian/Pacific Islander	
		Population	Percent of total
Palm Bay	62,632	1,104	1.8%
Clearwater	98,784	1,019	1.0%
Hialeah	188,004	1,013	0.5%

Sources: Adapted from Asian Week, *Asians in America, 1990 Census* (San Francisco, CA: Asian Week, 1991), p. 29, and Asian/Pacific Islander Data Consortium (San Francisco: Asian and Pacific Islander Center for Census Information and Services, 1993). Primary source: U.S. Census Bureau, Summary Tape File 1A. *Notes:* (a) Consolidated city (coextensive with Duval County). (b) The U.S. Census Bureau uses CDP for Census Designated Place. See *Appendix* for detailed definition.

★ 769 ★

Georgia Cities and Places Ranked by Asian/Pacific Islander Population

Asian/Pacific Islander population and percent of total population in cities in Georgia, 1990.

City or place	Total population	Asian/Pacific Islander	
		Population	Percent of total
Atlanta	394,017	3,498	0.9%
Columbus CC[a]	179,278	2,510	1.4%
Savannah	137,560	1,581	1.1%
North Atlanta CDP[b]	27,812	1,562	5.6%
Athens	45,734	1,528	3.3%
Martinez CDP[b]	33,731	1,235	3.7%
Tucker CDP[b]	25,781	1,192	4.6%
Sandy Springs CDP[b]	67,842	1,106	1.6%
South Augusta CDP[b]	55,998	1,047	1.9%

Sources: Adapted from Asian Week, *Asians in America, 1990 Census* (San Francisco, CA: Asian Week, 1991), p. 29, and Asian/Pacific Islander Data Consortium (San Francisco: Asian and Pacific Islander Center for Census Information and Services, 1993). Primary source: U.S. Census Bureau, Summary Tape File 1A. *Notes:* (a) Consolidated city (coextensive with Muscogee County). (b) The U.S. Census Bureau uses CDP for Census Designated Place. See *Appendix* for detailed definition.

★ 770 ★

Hawaii Cities and Places Ranked by Asian/Pacific Islander Population

Asian/Pacific Islander population and percent of total population in cities in Hawaii, 1990.

City or place	Total population	Asian/Pacific Islander	
		Population	Percent of total
Honolulu	365,272	257,552	70.5%
Hilo	37,808	26,533	70.2%
Waipahu	31,435	26,340	83.8%
Kaneohe	35,448	23,261	65.6%
Pearl City	30,993	22,968	74.1%
Waimalu	29,967	20,317	67.8%
Mililani	29,359	17,973	61.2%
Kailua	36,818	14,395	39.1%
Kahului	16,889	13,809	81.8%
Wahiawa	17,386	12,013	69.1%
Ewa Beach	14,315	10,389	72.6%
Halawa	13,408	9,602	71.6%
Walluku	10,688	7,942	74.3%
Waipio	11,812	7,847	66.4%
Nanakuli	9,575	7,675	80.2%
Alea	8,906	6,538	73.4%
Waianae	8,758	6,502	74.2%
Lahaina	9,073	6,002	66.2%
Village Park	7,407	5,506	74.3%
Kapaa	8,149	5,064	62.1%

Sources: Adapted from Asian Week, *Asians in America, 1990 Census* (San Francisco, CA: Asian Week, 1991), p. 29, and Asian/Pacific Islander Data Consortium (San Francisco: Asian and Pacific Islander Center for Census Information and Services, 1993). Primary source: U.S. Census Bureau, Summary Tape File 1A.

★ 771 ★

Maryland Cities and Places Ranked by Asian/Pacific Islander Population

Asian/Pacific Islander population and percent of total population in cities in Maryland, 1990.

City or place	Total population	Asian/Pacific	
		Population	Percent of total
Baltimore	736,014	7,942	1.1%
Wheaton-Glenmont CDP[a]	53,720	5,961	11.1%
Potomac CDP[a]	45,634	5,085	11.1%
Rockville	44,835	4,394	9.8%
Aspen Hill CDP[a]	76,046	4,202	5.5%
Bethesda CDP[a]	62,936	4,177	6.6%
Gaithersburg	39,542	4,022	10.2%
Columbia CDP[a]	75,883	3,625	4.8%
North Potomac CDP[a]	18,456	2,972	16.1%
Colesville CDP[a]	18,819	2,634	14.0%
Fort Washington CDP[a]	24,032	2,625	10.9%
Ellicott City CDP[a]	41,396	2,576	6.2%
North Bethesda CDP[a]	29,656	2,432	8.2%

[Continued]

★ 771 ★

Maryland Cities and Places Ranked by Asian/Pacific Islander Population (Continued)

Asian/Pacific Islander population and percent of total population in cities in Maryland, 1990.

City or place	Total population	Asian/Pacific	
		Population	Percent of total
Germantown CDP[a]	41,145	2,287	5.6%
Montgomery Village CDP	32,315	2,119	6.6%
Redland CDP[a]	16,145	1,993	12.3%
Greenbelt	21,096	1,901	9.0%
Fairland CDP[a]	19,828	1,897	9.6%
Woodlawn CDP[a]	32,907	1,602	4.9%
Adelphi CDP[a]	13,524	1,585	11.7%
White Oak CDP[a]	18,671	1,575	8.4%
Langley Park CDP[a]	17,474	1,562	8.9%
Calverton CDP[a]	12,046	1,559	12.9%
College Park	21,927	1,442	6.6%

Sources: Adapted from Asian Week, *Asians in America, 1990 Census* (San Francisco, CA: Asian Week, 1991), p. 29, and Asian/Pacific Islander Data Consortium (San Francisco: Asian and Pacific Islander Center for Census Information and Services, 1993). Primary source: U.S. Census Bureau, Summary Tape File 1A. *Note:* (a) The U. S.Census Bureau uses CDP for Census Designated Place. See *Appendix* for detailed explanantion.

★ 772 ★

Massachusetts Cities and Places Ranked by Asian/Pacific Islander Population

Asian/Pacific Islander population and percent of total population in cities in Maryland, 1990.

City or place	Total population	Asian/Pacific Islander	
		Population	Percent of total
Boston	574,283	30,388	5.3%
Lowell	103,439	11,493	11.1%
Cambridge	95,802	8,081	8.4%
Quincy	84,985	5,577	6.6%
Worcester	169,759	4,770	2.8%
Brookline CDP[a]	54,718	4,585	8.4%
Newton	82,585	3,760	4.6%
Lynn	81,245	3,003	3.7%
Somerville	76,210	2,824	3.7%
Malden	53,884	2,815	5.2%
Waltham	57,878	2,055	3.6%
Framingham CDP[a]	64,994	1,904	2.9%
Lexington CDP[a]	28,974	1,876	6.5%
Randolph CDP[a]	30,093	1,675	5.6%
Springfield	156,983	1,636	1.0%
Brockton	92,788	1,589	1.7%
Revere	42,786	1,571	3.7%
Chelsea	28,710	1,435	5.0%
Lawrence	70,207	1,358	1.9%
Arlington CDP[a]	44,630	1,351	3.0%
Fall River	92,703	1,230	1.3%

[Continued]

★ 772 ★

Massachusetts Cities and Places
Ranked by Asian/Pacific Islander Population (Continued)

Asian/Pacific Islander population and percent of total population in cities in Maryland, 1990.

City or place	Total population	Asian/Pacific Islander	
		Population	Percent of total
Medford	57,407	1,152	2.0%
Amherst CDP[a]	17,824	1,138	6.4%
Fitchburg	41,194	1,057	2.6%
Wellesley CDP[a]	26,615	1,045	3.9%

Sources: Adapted from Asian Week, *Asians in America, 1990 Census* (San Francisco, CA: Asian Week, 1991), p. 29, and Asian/Pacific Islander Data Consortium (San Francisco: Asian and Pacific Islander Center for Census Information and Services, 1993). Primary source: U.S. Census Bureau, Summary Tape File 1A. *Note:* (a) Census designated place.

★ 773 ★

Michigan Cities and Places Ranked by Asian/Pacific Islander Population

Asian/Pacific Islander population and percent of total population in cities in Michigan, 1990.

City or place	Total population	Asian/Pacific Islander	
		Population	Percent of total
Detroit	1,027,974	8,461	0.8%
Ann Arbor	109,592	8,424	7.7%
Troy	72,884	4,943	6.8%
East Lansing	50,677	3,542	7.0%
Sterling Heights	117,810	3,369	2.9%
Farmington Hills	74,652	2,870	3.8%
West Bloomfield Township	54,843	2,842	5.2%
Canton CDP[a]	57,047	2,562	4.5%
Bloomfield Township CDP[a]	42,137	2,362	5.6%
Lansing	127,321	2,263	1.8%
Grand Rapids	189,126	2,164	1.1%
Rochester Hills	61,766	1,959	3.2%
Warren	144,864	1,942	1.3%
Southfield	75,728	1,801	2.4%
Kalamazoo	80,277	1,505	1.9%
Livonia	100,850	1,352	1.3%
Ypsilanti	24,846	1,074	4.3%

Sources: Adapted from Asian Week, *Asians in America, 1990 Census* (San Francisco, CA: Asian Week, 1991), p. 29, and Asian/Pacific Islander Data Consortium (San Francisco: Asian and Pacific Islander Center for Census Information and Services, 1993). Primary source: U.S. Census Bureau, Summary Tape File 1A. *Note:* (a) The U.S. Census Bureau uses CDP for Census Designated Place. See *Appendix* for detailed definition.

★ 774 ★

Minnesota Cities and Places Ranked by Asian/Pacific Islander Population

Asian/Pacific Islander population and percent of total population in cities in Minnesota, 1990.

City or place	Total population	Asian/Pacific Islander	
		Population	Percent of total
St. Paul	272,235	19,197	7.1%
Minneapolis	368,383	15,723	4.3%
Rochester	70,745	2,926	4.1%
Bloomington	86,335	2,669	3.1%
Brooklyn Park	56,381	1,916	3.4%
Eagan	47,409	1,492	3.1%
Burnsville	51,288	1,169	2.3%
Plymouth	50,889	1,040	2.0%
Richfield	35,710	1,002	2.8%

Sources: Adapted from Asian Week, *Asians in America, 1990 Census* (San Francisco, CA: Asian Week, 1991), p. 29, and Asian/Pacific Islander Data Consortium (San Francisco: Asian and Pacific Islander Center for Census Information and Services, 1993). Primary source: U.S. Census Bureau, Summary Tape File 1A.

★ 775 ★

Nevada Cities and Places Ranked by Asian/Pacific Islander Population

Asian/Pacific Islander population and percent of total population in cities in Nevada, 1990.

City or place	Total population	Asian/Pacific Islander	
		Population	Percent of total
Las Vegas	258,295	9,325	3.6%
Reno	133,850	6,505	4.9%
Paradise	124,682	4,987	4.0%
Sunrise Manor	95,362	3987	4.2%
Spring Valley	51,726	2,631	5.1%
Sparks	53,367	2,395	4.5%
Henderson	64,942	1,316	2.0%
North Las Vegas	47,707	1,127	2.4%
Winchester	23,365	1,087	4.7%

Sources: Adapted from Asian Week, *Asians in America, 1990 Census* (San Francisco, CA: Asian Week, 1991), p. 29, and Asian/Pacific Islander Data Consortium (San Francisco: Asian and Pacific Islander Center for Census Information and Services, 1993). Primary source: U.S. Census Bureau, Summary Tape File 1A.

★ 776 ★

New Jersey Cities and Places Ranked by Asian/Pacific Islander Population

Asian/Pacific Islander population and percent of total population in cities in New Jersey, 1990.

City or place	Total population	Asian/Pacific Islander	
		Population	Percent of total
Jersey City	228,537	25,959	11.4%
Edison	88,680	12,166	13.7%
Fort Lee Borough	31,997	6,505	20.3%
Parsippany–Troy Hill	48,478	4,917	10.1%
Cherry Hill	69,319	4,261	6.1%
Passaic	58,041	4,094	7.1%
East Brunswick	43,548	3,945	9.1%
Newark	275,221	3,281	1.2%
Elizabeth	110,002	3,002	2.7%
Palisades Park Borough	14,536	2,910	20.0%
Paramus Borough	25,067	2,626	10.5%
Clifton	71,742	2,513	3.5%
Livingston	26,609	2,479	9.3%
North Bergen	48,414	2,308	4.8%
Bloomfield	45,061	2,251	5.0%
Bergenfield Borough	24,458	2,224	9.1%
West Orange	39,103	2,183	5.6%
North Brunswick	31,287	2,132	6.8%
Teaneck	37,825	2,127	5.6%
Belleville	34,213	2,055	6.0%
Paterson	140,891	2,024	1.4%
Tenafly Borough	13,326	1,855	13.9%
Ridgewood Village	24,152	1,747	7.2%
Union	50,024	1,675	3.3%
New Brunswick	41,711	1,651	4.0%

Sources: Adapted from Asian Week, *Asians in America, 1990 Census* (San Francisco, CA: Asian Week, 1991), p. 29, and Asian/Pacific Islander Data Consortium (San Francisco: Asian and Pacific Islander Center for Census Information and Services, 1993). Primary source: U.S. Census Bureau, Summary Tape File 1A.

★ 777 ★

New York Cities and Places Ranked by Asian/Pacific Islander Population

Asian/Pacific Islander population and percent of total population in cities in New York, 1990.

City or place	Total population	Asian/Pacific Islander	
		Population	Percent of total
New York	7,322,564	512,719	7.0%
Yonkers	188,082	5,637	3.0%
Rochester	163,860	3,559	2.2%
Syracuse	163,860	3,559	2.2%
Buffalo	328,123	3,261	1.0%
Ithaca	29,541	2,958	10.0%
Albany	101,082	2,326	2.3%
Scarsdale village	16,987	2,319	13.7%
Elmont CDP[a]	28,612	2,108	7.4%
New Rochelle	67,265	1,967	2.9%
Greenville CDP[a]	9,528	1,897	19.9%
Hicksville CDP[a]	40,174	1,754	4.4%
Troy	54,269	1,638	3.0%
White Plains	48,718	1,495	3.1%
Syosset CDP[a]	18,967	1,468	7.7%
Brighton CDP[a]	34,455	1,466	4.3%
New City CDP[a]	33,673	1,399	4.2%
Dix Hills CDP[a]	25,849	1,336	5.2%
East Meadow CDP[a]	36,909	1,302	3.5%
Eastchester CDP[a]	18,537	1,281	6.9%
Mount Vernon	67,153	1,238	1.8%
Valley Stream village	33,946	1,224	3.6%
North Valley Stream CDP[a]	14,574	1,156	7.9%
Spring Valley village	21,802	1,134	5.2%
Binghamton	53,008	1,088	2.1%

Sources: Adapted from Asian Week, *Asians in America, 1990 Census* (San Francisco, CA: Asian Week, 1991), p. 29, and Asian/Pacific Islander Data Consortium (San Francisco: Asian and Pacific Islander Center for Census Information and Services, 1993). Primary source: U.S. Census Bureau, Summary Tape File 1A. *Note:* (a) U.S. Census Bureau uses CDP for Census Designated Place. See *Appendix* for detailed definition.

★ 778 ★

North Carolina Cities and Places Ranked by Asian/Pacific Islander Population

Asian/Pacific Islander population and percent of total population in cities in North Carolina, 1990.

City or place	Total population	Asian/Pacific Islander	
		Population	Percent of total
Charlotte	395,934	7,211	1.8%
Raleigh	207,951	5,127	2.5%
Durham	136,611	2,672	2.0%
Greensboro	183,521	2,633	1.4%
Cary Town	43,858	1,684	3.8%
Chapel Hill Town	38,719	1,684	4.3%
Fayetteville	75,695	1,151	1.5%
Winston-Salem	143,485	1,097	0.8%

Sources: Adapted from Asian Week, *Asians in America, 1990 Census* (San Francisco, CA: Asian Week, 1991), p. 29, and Asian/Pacific Islander Data Consortium (San Francisco: Asian and Pacific Islander Center for Census Information and Services, 1993). Primary source: U.S. Census Bureau, Summary Tape File 1A.

★ 779 ★

Ohio Cities and Places Ranked by Asian/Pacific Islander Population

Asian/Pacific Islander population and percent of total population in cities in Ohio, 1990.

City or place	Total population	Asian/Pacific Islander	
		Population	Percent of total
Columbus	632,910	14,993	2.4%
Cleveland	505,616	5,115	1.0%
Cincinnati	364,040	4,030	1.1%
Toledo	332,943	3,487	1.0%
Akron	223,019	2,701	1.2%
Athens	21,265	1,241	5.8%
Dayton	182,044	1,157	0.6%
Cleveland Heights	54,052	1,138	2.1%

Sources: Adapted from Asian Week, *Asians in America, 1990 Census* (San Francisco, CA: Asian Week, 1991), p. 29, and Asian/Pacific Islander Data Consortium (San Francisco: Asian and Pacific Islander Center for Census Information and Services, 1993). Primary source: U.S. Census Bureau, Summary Tape File 1A.

★ 780 ★

Oregon Cities and Places Ranked by Asian/Pacific Islander Population

Asian/Pacific Islander population and percent of total population in cities in Oregon, 1990.

City or place	Total population	Asian/Pacific Islander	
		Population	Percent of total
Portland	437,319	23,185	5.3%
Beaverton	53,310	4,085	7.7%
Eugene	112,669	3,896	3.5%
Corvallis	44,757	3,610	8.0%
Salem	107,786	2,577	2.4%
Aloha CDP[a]	34,284	2,205	6.4%
Gresham	68,235	1,875	2.7%
Tigard	29,344	1,006	3.4%

Sources: Adapted from Asian Week, *Asians in America, 1990 Census* (San Francisco, CA: Asian Week, 1991), p. 29, and Asian/Pacific Islander Data Consortium (San Francisco: Asian and Pacific Islander Center for Census Information and Services, 1993). Primary source: U.S. Census Bureau, Summary Tape File 1A. *Note:* (a) U.S. Census Bureau uses CDP for Census Designated Place. See *Appendix* for detailed definition.

★ 781 ★

Pennsylvania Cities and Places Ranked by Asian/Pacific Isander Population

Asian/Pacific Islander population and percent of total population in cities in Pennsylvania, 1990.

City or Place	Total population	Asian/Pacific Islander	
		Population	Percent of total
Philadelphia	1,585,577	43,522	2.7%
Pittsburgh	369,879	5,937	1.6%
State College borough	38,923	2,836	7.3%
Allentown	105,090	1,414	1.3%
Bethlehem	71,428	1,228	1.7%
Reading	78,380	1,114	1.4%
Lancaster	55,551	1,091	2.0%
Radnor Township CDP[a]	28,705	1,030	3.6%

Sources: Adapted from Asian Week, *Asians in America, 1990 Census* (San Francisco, CA: Asian Week, 1991), p. 29, and Asian/Pacific Islander Data Consortium (San Francisco: Asian and Pacific Islander Center for Census Information and Services, 1993). Primary source: U.S. Census Bureau, Summary Tape File 1A. *Note:* (a) U.S. Census Bureau uses CDP for Census Designated Place. See *Appendix* for detailed definition.

★ 782 ★

Washington Cities and Places Ranked by Asian/Pacific Islander Population

Asian/Pacific Islander population and percent of total population in cities in Washington, 1990.

City or place	Total population	Asian/Pacific Islander	
		Population	Percent of total
Seattle	516,259	60,819	11.8%
Tacoma	176,664	12,216	6.9%
Bellevue	86,874	8,642	9.9%
Lakewood CDP[a]	58,412	5,577	9.5%
Federal Way CDP[a]	67,554	4,877	7.2%
Spokane	177,196	3,686	2.1%
Renton	41,688	3,277	7.7%
White Center-Shorewood CDP[a]	20,531	3,014	14.7%
East Hill-Meridian CDP[a]	42,696	2,830	6.6%
Everett	69,961	2,738	3.9%
Richmond Highlands CDP[a]	26,037	2,661	10.2%
Cascade-Fairwood CDP[a]	30,107	2,461	8.2%
Redmond	35,800	2,250	6.3%
Lynwood	28,695	2,172	7.6%
Bremerton	38,142	2,012	5.3%
Pullman	23,478	1,994	8.5%
Kirkland	40,052	1,741	4.3%
Mercer Island	20,816	1,674	8.0%
Kent	37,960	1,668	4.4%
Olympia	33,840	1,622	4.8%
Bryn Mawr-Skyway CDP[a]	12,514	1,596	12.8%
Vancouver	46,380	1,473	3.2%
Oak Harbor	17,176	1,455	8.5%
Bellingham	52,179	1,453	2.8%
Spanawy CDP[a]	15,001	1,409	9.4%

Sources: Adapted from Asian Week, *Asians in America, 1990 Census* (San Francisco, CA: Asian Week, 1991), p. 29, and Asian/Pacific Islander Data Consortium (San Francisco: Asian and Pacific Islander Center for Census Information and Services, 1993). Primary source: U.S. Census Bureau, Summary Tape File 1A. *Note:* (a) U.S. Census Bureau uses CDP for Census Designated Place.

★ 783 ★

Wisconsin Cities and Places Ranked by Asian/Pacific Islander Population

Asian/Pacific Islander population and percent of total population in cities in Wisconsin, 1990.

City or place	Total population	Asian/Pacific Islander	
		Population	Percent of total
Milwaukee	628,088	11,817	1.9%
Madison	191,262	7,471	3.9%
La Crosse	51,003	2,474	4.9%
Green Bay	96,466	2,234	2.3%
Wausau	37,060	2,216	6.0%
Eau Claire	56,856	2,150	3.8%
Sheboygan	49,676	1,927	3.9%
Appleton	65,695	1,582	2.4%
Oshkosh	55,006	1,201	2.2%

Sources: Adapted from Asian Week, *Asians in America, 1990 Census* (San Francisco, CA: Asian Week, 1991), p. 29, and Asian/Pacific Islander Data Consortium (San Francisco: Asian and Pacific Islander Center for Census Information and Services, 1993). Primary source: U.S. Census Bureau, Summary Tape File 1A.

United States Metropolitan Statistical Areas

★ 784 ★

Population of Metropolitan Statistical Areas by Race/Ethnicity

Population of U.S. Metropolitan Statistical Areas (MSAs) including Primary Metropolitan Statistical Areas (PMSAs)[a], by race/ethnicity, 1990.

Metropolitan Statistical Area	Total persons	Asian or Pacific Islander	White	Black	American Indian, Eskimo, or Aleut	Other race
Abilene, TX MSA	119,655	1,449	100,237	7,547	450	9,972
Akron, OH PMSA	657,575	6,180	583,900	65,091	1,357	1,047
Albany, GA MSA	112,561	498	60,041	51,522	281	219
Albany–Schenectady–Troy, NY MSA	874,304	10,789	815,315	41,112	1,560	5,528
Albuquerque, NM MSA	480,577	7,386	369,445	13,199	16,296	74,251
Alexandria, LA MSA	131,556	908	92,989	36,805	564	290
Allentown–Bethlehem–Easton, PA–NJ MSA	686,688	7,293	649,890	13,466	688	15,351
Altoona, PA MSA	130,542	380	128,840	1,073	118	131
Amarillo, TX MSA	187,547	3,216	158,517	9,788	1,355	14,671
Anaheim–Santa Ana, CA PMSA	2,410,556	249,192	1,894,593	42,681	12,165	211,925
Anchorage, AK MSA	226,338	10,910	182,736	14,544	14,569	3,579
Anderson, IN MSA	130,669	415	119,734	9,870	299	351
Anderson, SC MSA	145,196	340	120,384	24,151	173	148
Ann Arbor, MI PMSA	282,937	11,724	236,390	31,720	1,076	2,027
Anniston, AL MSA	116,034	869	92,873	21,578	296	418
Appleton–Oshkosh–Neenah, WI MSA	315,121	3,805	306,775	932	2,796	813
Asheville, NC MSA	174,821	765	158,979	14,336	486	255
Athens, GA MSA	156,267	2,352	124,076	29,003	257	579
Atlanta, GA MSA	2,833,511	51,486	2,020,017	736,153	5,532	20,323
Atlantic City, NJ MSA	319,416	5,389	260,185	44,398	778	8,666
Augusta, GA–SC MSA	396,809	5,438	264,801	123,482	941	2,147
Aurora–Elgin, IL PMSA	356,884	4,698	307,694	19,216	693	24,583
Austin, TX MSA	781,572	18,770	600,023	72,254	2,827	87,698
Bakersfield, CA MSA	543,477	16,541	378,479	30,131	7,026	111,300
Baltimore, MD MSA	2,382,172	42,634	1,709,309	616,065	6,444	7,720
Bangor, ME MSA	88,745	798	86,328	467	1,008	144
Baton Rouge, LA MSA	528,264	5,657	363,692	156,509	902	1,504
Battle Creek, MI MSA	135,982	1,068	118,737	14,383	696	1,098
Beaumont–Port Arthur, TX MSA	361,226	5,687	264,365	84,665	890	5,619
Beaver County, PA PMSA	186,093	377	174,759	10,475	203	279
Bellingham, WA MSA	127,780	2,363	119,229	650	4,014	1,524
Benton Harbor, MI MSA	161,378	1,487	133,259	24,872	685	1,075
Bergen–Passaic, NJ PMSA	1,278,440	66,743	1,043,437	106,108	2,221	59,931
Billings, MT MSA	113,419	612	107,921	511	3,235	1,140
Biloxi–Gulfport, MS MSA	197,125	4,495	156,255	35,055	595	725

[Continued]

★ 784 ★

Population of Metropolitan Statistical Areas by Race/Ethnicity (Continued)

Population of U.S. Metropolitan Statistical Areas (MSAs) including Primary Metropolitan Statistical Areas (PMSAs)[a], by race/ethnicity, 1990.

Metropolitan Statistical Area	Total persons	Asian or Pacific Islander	White	Black	American Indian, Eskimo, or Aleut	Other race
Binghamton, NY MSA	264,497	3,990	254,447	4,647	450	963
Birmingham, AL MSA	907,810	4,014	655,609	245,726	1,506	955
Bismarck, ND MSA	83,831	286	81,306	79	2,016	144
Bloomington, IN MSA	108,978	2,713	102,752	2,835	216	462
Bloomington–Normal, IL MSA	129,180	1,624	121,057	5,563	203	733
Boise City, ID MSA	205,775	2,887	198,888	958	1,382	1,660
Boston, MA PMSA	2,870,669	95,044	2,499,859	209,970	5,250	60,546
Boulder–Longmont, CO PMSA	225,339	5,508	210,190	1,959	1,313	6,369
Bradenton, FL MSA	211,707	1,227	190,328	16,400	501	3,251
Brazoria, TX PMSA	191,707	1,961	154,875	15,981	812	18,078
Bremerton, WA MSA	189,731	8,282	171,063	5,107	3,211	2,068
Bridgeport–Milford, CT PMSA	443,722	6,577	371,493	45,826	806	19,020
Bristol, CT PMSA	79,488	544	76,875	1,347	128	594
Brockton, MA PMSA	189,478	2,158	168,133	13,770	445	4,972
Brownsville–Harlingen, TX MSA	260,120	750	214,424	825	413	43,708
Bryan–College Station, TX MSA	121,862	4,313	94,866	13,672	274	8,737
Buffalo, NY PMSA	968,532	10,220	831,903	109,852	5,600	10,957
Burlington, NC MSA	108,213	487	86,373	20,822	303	228
Burlington, VT MSA	131,439	1,465	128,580	814	299	281
Canton, OH MSA	394,106	1,558	365,675	25,187	1,015	671
Casper, WY MSA	61,226	280	59,323	458	404	761
Cedar Rapids, IA MSA	168,767	1,401	163,164	3,334	363	505
Champaign–Urbana–Rantoul, IL MSA	173,025	8,033	146,506	16,559	331	1,596
Charleston, SC MSA	506,875	6,113	343,776	153,227	1,613	2,146
Charleston, WV MSA	250,454	1,450	234,518	13,919	292	275
Charlotte–Gastonia–Rock Hill, NC– SC MSA	1,162,093	11,304	911,904	231,654	4,107	3,124
Charlottesville, VA MSA	131,107	2,623	109,049	18,895	148	392
Chattanooga, TN–GA MSA	433,210	2,825	370,586	58,218	891	690
Cheyenne, WY MSA	73,142	821	66,280	2,218	528	3,295
Chicago, IL PMSA	6,069,974	229,492	4,098,747	1,332,919	11,550	397,266
Chico, CA MSA	182,120	5,170	165,200	2,361	3,241	6,148
Cincinnati, OH–KY–IN PMSA	1,452,645	11,601	1,246,169	190,473	2,078	2,324
Clarksville–Hopkinsville, TN–KY MSA	169,439	2,712	128,583	34,801	688	2,655
Cleveland, OH PMSA	1,831,122	20,528	1,435,768	355,619	3,038	16,169
Colorado Springs, CO MSA	397,014	9,841	341,400	28,593	3,242	13,938
Columbia, MO MSA	112,379	3,129	100,055	8,377	394	424
Columbia, SC MSA	453,331	4,820	307,454	137,906	1,013	2,138
Columbus, GA–AL MSA	243,072	3,107	144,326	91,484	765	3,390
Columbus, OH MSA	1,377,419	21,059	1,184,770	164,602	2,880	4,108
Corpus Christi, TX MSA	349,894	2,646	265,002	13,659	1,394	67,193
Cumberland, MD–WV MSA	101,643	391	98,821	2,270	71	90

[Continued]

★ 784 ★

Population of Metropolitan Statistical Areas by Race/Ethnicity (Continued)

Population of U.S. Metropolitan Statistical Areas (MSAs) including Primary Metropolitan Statistical Areas (PMSAs)[a], by race/ethnicity, 1990.

Metropolitan Statistical Area	Total persons	Asian or Pacific Islander	White	Black	American Indian, Eskimo, or Aleut	Other race
Dallas, TX PMSA	2,553,362	67,195	1,854,577	410,766	12,635	208,189
Danbury, CT PMSA	187,867	4,355	175,780	5,398	301	2,033
Danville, VA MSA	108,711	325	73,817	34,350	117	102
Davenport–Rock Island–Moline, IA–IL MSA	350,861	2,502	322,805	19,115	902	5,537
Dayton–Springfield, OH MSA	951,270	9,278	811,393	126,238	1,915	2,446
Daytona Beach, FL MSA	370,712	2,739	328,530	33,455	915	5,073
Decatur, AL MSA	131,556	389	113,685	14,879	2,434	169
Decatur, IL MSA	117,206	506	102,197	14,135	157	211
Denver, CO PMSA	1,622,980	37,134	1,389,544	95,796	12,571	87,935
Des Moines, IA MSA	392,928	6,218	368,386	14,952	1,015	2,357
Detroit, MI PMSA	4,382,299	57,730	3,332,697	943,479	16,885	31,508
Dothan, AL MSA	130,964	1,201	100,878	27,801	526	558
Dubuque, IA MSA	86,403	437	85,367	354	77	168
Duluth, MN–WI MSA	239,971	1,342	232,507	1,276	4,487	359
Eau Claire, WI MSA	137,543	2,400	134,056	269	617	201
El Paso, TX MSA	591,610	6,485	452,512	22,110	2,590	107,913
Elkhart–Goshen, IN MSA	156,198	997	146,505	7,106	453	1,137
Elmira, NY MSA	95,195	690	88,370	5,245	211	679
Enid, OK MSA	56,735	587	52,403	2,020	1,234	491
Erie, PA MSA	275,572	1,411	257,879	14,304	438	1,540
Eugene–Springfield, OR MSA	282,912	5,557	269,798	2,107	3,207	2,243
Evansville, IN–KY MSA	278,990	1,237	260,832	16,115	477	329
Fall River, MA–RI PMSA	157,272	1,541	154,022	1,086	168	455
Fargo–Moorhead, ND–MN MSA	153,296	1,396	149,004	446	1,497	953
Fayetteville, NC MSA	274,566	5,769	170,069	87,496	4,425	6,807
Fayetteville–Springdale, AR MSA	113,409	1,043	108,743	1,676	1,486	461
Fitchburg–Leominster, MA MSA	102,797	1,789	95,540	2,356	196	2,916
Flint, MI MSA	430,459	2,902	336,651	84,257	3,132	3,517
Florence, AL MSA	131,327	289	114,380	16,263	302	93
Florence, SC MSA	114,344	307	69,501	44,276	145	115
Fort Collins–Loveland, CO MSA	186,136	2,777	175,971	1,114	1,063	5,211
Fort Lauderdale–Hollywood–Pompano Beach, FL PMSA	1,255,488	17,130	1,025,583	193,447	2,634	16,694
Fort Myers–Cape CoraL, Fl MSA	335,113	1,894	306,200	22,184	672	4,163
Fort Pierce, FL MSA	251,071	1,565	214,278	30,709	526	3,993
Fort Smith, AR–OK MSA	175,911	3,755	155,580	6,831	9,054	691
Fort Walton Beach, FL MSA	143,776	3,658	125,191	13,007	776	1,144
Fort Wayne, IN MSA	363,811	2,769	326,568	30,380	1,056	3,038
Fort Worth–Arlington, TX PMSA	1,332,053	30,383	1,070,096	143,850	6,337	81,387
Fresno, CA MSA	667,490	57,239	422,839	33,423	7,119	146,870
Gadsden, AL MSA	99,840	419	85,274	13,799	250	98
Gainesville, FL MSA	204,111	4,656	158,479	38,982	443	1,551
Galveston–Texas City, TX PMSA	217,399	3,569	164,210	38,154	752	10,714

[Continued]

★ 784 ★

Population of Metropolitan Statistical Areas by Race/Ethnicity (Continued)

Population of U.S. Metropolitan Statistical Areas (MSAs) including Primary Metropolitan Statistical Areas (PMSAs)[a], by race/ethnicity, 1990.

Metropolitan Statistical Area	Total persons	Asian or Pacific Islander	White	Black	American Indian, Eskimo, or Aleut	Other race
Gary–Hammond, IN PMSA	604,526	3,716	460,532	117,142	1,108	22,028
Glens Falls, NY MSA	118,539	392	115,157	2,352	214	424
Grand Forks, ND MSA	70,683	881	66,766	1,446	1,244	346
Grand Rapids, MI MSA	688,399	7,831	623,787	41,311	3,394	12,076
Great Falls, MT MSA	77,691	792	72,345	1,061	3,072	421
Greeley, CO MSA	131,821	1,133	117,247	567	785	12,089
Green Bay, WI MSA	194,594	2,522	186,621	1,012	3,869	570
Greensboro–Winston-Salem–High Point, NC MSA	942,091	6,381	747,835	182,284	3,196	2,395
Greenville–Spartanburg, SC MSA	640,861	4,617	522,632	111,334	959	1,319
Hagerstown, MD MSA	121,393	793	112,828	7,245	241	286
Hamilton–Middletown, OH PMSA	291,479	2,659	274,892	13,134	379	415
Harrisburg–Lebanon–Carlisle, PA MSA	587,986	6,251	536,738	39,472	737	4,788
Hartford, CT PMSA	767,841	12,201	641,345	81,550	1,365	31,380
Hickory–Morganton, NC MSA	221,700	1,673	201,558	17,540	417	512
Honolulu, HI MSA	836,231	526,459	264,372	25,875	3,532	15,993
Houma–Thibodaux, LA MSA	182,842	1,370	147,453	26,735	6,814	470
Houston, TX PMSA	3,301,937	126,601	2,188,370	611,243	9,465	366,258
Huntington–Ashland, WV–KY–OH MSA	312,529	937	304,244	6,751	372	225
Huntsville, AL MSA	238,912	4,232	184,197	48,116	1,601	766
Indianapolis, IN MSA	1,249,822	10,081	1,061,142	172,326	2,510	3,763
Iowa City, IA MSA	96,119	3,837	89,649	1,979	176	478
Jackson, MI MSA	149,756	653	135,557	11,983	655	908
Jackson, MS MSA	395,396	1,754	224,999	167,899	346	398
Jackson, TN MSA	77,982	253	53,423	24,170	66	70
Jacksonville, FL MSA	906,727	15,362	701,911	181,265	2,587	5,602
Jacksonville, NC MSA	149,838	2,994	111,939	29,808	939	4,158
Jamestown–Dunkirk, NY	141,895	545	136,311	2,405	558	2,076
Janesville–Beloit, WI MSA	139,510	985	130,803	6,638	369	715
Jersey City, NJ PMSA	553,099	36,777	380,612	79,770	1,460	54,480
Johnson City–Kingsport–Bristol, TN–VA MSA	436,047	1,247	424,751	8,925	766	358
Johnstown, PA MSA	241,247	527	236,459	3,836	152	273
Joliet, IL PMSA	389,650	4,887	335,284	38,382	737	10,360
Joplin, MO MSA	134,910	751	130,093	1,327	2,452	287
Kalamazoo, MI MSA	223,411	3,168	197,427	19,879	1,017	1,920
Kankakee, IL MSA	96,255	644	80,194	14,399	150	868
Kansas City, MO–KS MSA	1,566,280	17,444	1,320,564	200,508	7,631	20,133
Kenosha, WI PMSA	128,181	669	119,187	5,295	472	2,558
Killeen–Temple, TX MSA	255,301	7,201	181,144	49,687	1,405	15,864
Knoxville, TN MSA	604,816	4,540	561,535	36,400	1,505	836
Kokomo, IN MSA	96,946	508	91,410	4,408	246	374

[Continued]

★ 784 ★

Population of Metropolitan Statistical Areas by Race/Ethnicity (Continued)

Population of U.S. Metropolitan Statistical Areas (MSAs) including Primary Metropolitan Statistical Areas (PMSAs)[a], by race/ethnicity, 1990.

Metropolitan Statistical Area	Total persons	Asian or Pacific Islander	White	Black	American Indian, Eskimo, or Aleut	Other race
La Crosse, WI MSA	97,904	2,667	94,319	438	340	140
Lafayette, LA MSA	208,740	1,915	154,146	51,378	440	861
Lafayette–West Lafayette, IN MSA	130,598	4,821	122,013	2,660	320	784
Lake Charles, LA MSA	168,134	590	128,181	38,445	387	531
Lake County, IL PMSA	516,418	12,588	450,666	34,771	1,198	17,195
Lakeland–Winter Haven, FL MSA	405,382	2,486	341,952	54,385	1,158	5,401
Lancaster, PA MSA	422,822	4,652	397,815	10,038	484	9,833
Lansing–East Lansing, MI MSA	432,674	8,320	381,371	31,365	2,655	8,963
Laredo, TX MSA	133,239	484	93,657	156	201	38,741
Las Cruces, NM MSA	135,510	1,164	123,434	2,172	1,009	7,731
Las Vegas, NV MSA	741,459	26,043	602,658	70,738	6,416	35,604
Lawrence, KS MSA	81,798	2,581	72,885	3,324	2,161	847
Lawrence–Haverhill, MA–NH PMSA	393,516	5,146	359,052	7,363	857	21,098
Lawton, OK MSA	111,486	3,065	79,666	19,908	5,153	3,694
Lewiston–Auburn, ME MSA	88,141	514	86,799	443	197	188
Lexington-Fayette, KY MSA	348,428	4,037	305,725	37,212	561	893
Lima, OH MSA	154,340	749	140,402	12,379	252	558
Lincoln, NE MSA	213,641	3,367	202,663	4,659	1,207	1,745
Little Rock–North Little Rock, AR MSA	513,117	3,347	404,808	101,862	1,870	1,230
Longview–Marshall, TX MSA	162,431	635	122,270	35,975	670	2,881
Lorain–Elyria, OH PMSA	271,126	1,479	241,549	21,230	738	6,130
Los Angeles–Long Beach, CA PMSA	8,863,164	954,485	5,035,103	992,974	45,508	1,835,094
Louisville, KY–IN MSA	952,662	5,640	818,898	124,761	1,576	1,787
Lowell, MA–NH PMSA	273,067	14,251	248,937	3,598	388	5,893
Lubbock, TX MSA	222,636	2,722	176,037	17,154	686	26,037
Lynchburg, VA MSA	142,199	743	110,847	30,079	277	253
Macon–Warner Robins, GA MSA	281,103	1,941	180,383	97,294	571	914
Madison, WI MSA	367,085	8,666	344,617	10,511	1,201	2,090
Manchester, NH MSA	147,809	1,442	144,159	1,133	278	797
Mansfield, OH MSA	126,137	578	115,078	9,981	223	277
Mcallen–Edinburg–Mission, TX MSA	383,545	1,088	286,858	806	668	94,125
Medford, OR MSA	146,389	1,429	140,188	340	1,863	2,569
Melbourne–Titusville–Palm Bay, FL MSA	398,978	5,379	358,391	31,417	1,369	2,422
Memphis, TN–AR–MS MSA	981,747	8,178	570,511	399,011	1,791	2,256
Merced, CA MSA	178,403	15,128	120,280	8,523	1,516	32,956
Miami–Hialeah, FL PMSA	1,937,094	26,307	1,413,015	397,993	3,066	96,713
Middlesex–Somerset–Hunterdon, NJ PMSA	1,019,835	56,804	865,158	70,670	1,420	25,783
Middletown, CT PMSA	90,320	1,163	82,829	5,454	143	731
Midland, TX MSA	106,611	888	86,977	8,281	414	10,051
Milwaukee, WI PMSA	1,432,149	18,782	1,183,372	197,183	8,001	24,811

[Continued]

★ 784 ★

Population of Metropolitan Statistical Areas by Race/Ethnicity (Continued)

Population of U.S. Metropolitan Statistical Areas (MSAs) including Primary Metropolitan Statistical Areas (PMSAs)[a], by race/ethnicity, 1990.

Metropolitan Statistical Area	Total persons	Asian or Pacific Islander	White	Black	American Indian, Eskimo, or Aleut	Other race
Minneapolis–St. Paul, MN–WI MSA	2,464,124	65,204	2,270,360	89,710	23,956	14,894
Mobile, AL MSA	476,923	3,619	339,418	130,512	2,570	804
Modesto, CA MSA	370,522	19,223	297,315	6,450	4,039	43,495
Monmouth–Ocean, NJ PMSA	986,327	19,098	895,986	59,264	1,327	10,652
Monroe, LA MSA	142,191	740	96,870	44,096	239	246
Montgomery, AL MSA	292,517	1,782	184,414	105,196	622	503
Muncie, IN MSA	119,659	641	111,232	7,167	274	345
Muskegon, MI MSA	158,983	555	133,931	21,617	1,338	1,542
Naples, FL MSA	152,099	584	139,073	6,986	428	5,028
Nashua, NH PMSA	180,557	2,459	174,851	1,910	297	1,040
Nashville, TN MSA	985,026	10,012	818,424	152,349	2,121	2,120
Nassau–Suffolk, NY PMSA	2,609,212	62,399	2,305,434	193,967	4,636	42,776
New Bedford, MA MSA	175,641	841	161,018	4,623	504	8,655
New Britain, CT PMSA	148,188	1,937	132,519	6,574	190	6,968
New Haven–Meriden, CT MSA	530,180	8,430	441,831	64,220	947	14,752
New London–Norwich, CT–RI MSA	266,819	3,549	245,933	12,077	1,433	3,827
New Orleans, LA MSA	1,238,816	21,380	770,406	430,470	3,615	12,945
New York, NY PMSA	8,546,846	556,399	4,826,081	2,250,026	29,711	884,629
Newark, NJ PMSA	1,824,321	52,898	1,279,952	422,802	3,144	65,525
Niagara Falls, NY PMSA	220,756	806	205,308	12,104	2,011	527
Norfolk–Virginia Beach–Newport News, VA MSA	1,396,107	35,205	947,160	398,093	4,679	10,970
Norwalk, CT PMSA	127,378	2,044	109,752	12,644	138	2,800
Oakland, CA PMSA	2,082,914	269,566	1,372,818	303,826	14,230	122,474
Ocala, FL MSA	194,833	945	167,094	24,844	638	1,312
Odessa, TX MSA	118,934	662	91,309	5,557	647	20,759
Oklahoma City, OK MSA	958,839	17,742	777,589	101,082	45,720	16,706
Olympia, WA MSA	161,238	6,101	148,221	2,864	2,498	1,554
Omaha, NE–IA MSA	618,262	6,374	550,758	51,426	3,159	6,545
Orange County, NY PMSA	307,647	3,549	273,600	22,223	824	7,451
Orlando, FL MSA	1,072,748	20,474	888,913	133,308	3,199	26,854
Owensboro, KY MSA	87,189	229	83,168	3,619	101	72
Oxnard–Ventura, CA PMSA	669,016	34,579	529,166	15,629	4,909	84,733
Panama City, FL MSA	126,994	2,229	109,570	13,713	949	533
Parkersburg–Marietta, WV–OH MSA	149,169	520	146,698	1,567	242	142
Pascagoula, MS MSA	115,243	1,115	90,114	23,581	254	179
Pawtucket–Woonsocket–Attleboro, RI–MA PMSA	329,384	3,987	310,677	5,494	535	8,691
Pensacola, FL MSA	344,406	6,021	277,620	55,893	3,347	1,525
Peoria, IL MSA	339,172	2,759	309,325	25,142	587	1,359
Philadelphia, PA–NJ PMSA	4,856,881	104,595	3,717,175	929,907	8,335	96,869
Phoenix, AZ MSA	2,122,101	36,294	1,799,420	74,257	38,017	174,113
Pine Bluff, AR MSA	85,487	352	47,878	36,877	227	153
Pittsburgh, PA PMSA	2,056,705	15,797	1,867,138	168,382	2,054	3,334

[Continued]

★ 784 ★

Population of Metropolitan Statistical Areas by Race/Ethnicity (Continued)

Population of U.S. Metropolitan Statistical Areas (MSAs) including Primary Metropolitan Statistical Areas (PMSAs)[a], by race/ethnicity, 1990.

Metropolitan Statistical Area	Total persons	Asian or Pacific Islander	White	Black	American Indian, Eskimo, or Aleut	Other race
Pittsfield, MA MSA	79,250	548	76,597	1,702	142	261
Portland, ME MSA	215,281	1,867	211,376	1,188	562	288
Portland, OR PMSA	1,239,842	46,360	1,124,963	38,695	11,307	18,517
Portsmouth–Dover–Rochester, NH– ME MSA	223,578	2,136	218,216	2,285	414	527
Poughkeepsie, NY MSA	259,462	5,826	229,194	21,788	374	2,280
Providence, RI PMSA	654,854	14,522	590,671	30,526	3,079	16,056
Provo–Orem, UT MSA	263,590	3,958	253,596	374	1,913	3,749
Pueblo, CO MSA	123,051	729	104,304	2,253	991	14,774
Racine, WI PMSA	175,034	1,004	152,098	16,999	521	4,412
Raleigh–Durham, NC MSA	735,480	13,834	533,056	183,447	1,933	3,210
Rapid City, SD MSA	81,343	933	72,769	1,288	5,835	518
Reading, PA MSA	336,523	2,746	314,561	10,003	333	8,880
Redding, CA MSA	147,036	2,684	137,977	1,081	3,954	1,340
Reno, NV MSA	254,667	9,824	225,095	5,680	4,921	9,147
Richland–Kennewick–Pasco, WA MSA	150,033	3,115	129,749	2,395	1,124	13,650
Richmond–Petersburg, VA MSA	865,640	11,864	595,714	252,340	2,705	3,017
Riverside–San Bernardino, CA PMSA	2,588,793	100,792	1,930,095	178,525	24,905	354,476
Roanoke, VA MSA	224,477	1,602	194,645	27,602	281	347
Rochester, MN MSA	106,470	3,237	101,880	788	295	270
Rochester, NY MSA	1,002,410	13,978	875,886	93,819	2,870	15,857
Rockford, IL MSA	283,719	3,136	251,783	23,383	697	4,720
Sacramento, CA MSA	1,481,102	114,520	1,170,505	101,940	17,021	77,116
Saginaw–Bay City–Midland, MI MSA	399,320	2,504	346,643	38,810	1,975	9,388
Salem, OR MSA	278,024	4,746	255,212	2,332	4,041	11,693
Salem–Gloucester, MA PMSA	264,356	2,347	257,396	2,448	305	1,860
Salinas–Seaside–Monterey, CA MSA	355,660	27,856	227,008	22,849	3,017	74,930
Salt Lake City–Ogden, UT MSA	1,072,227	25,598	1,000,082	10,464	8,337	27,746
San Angelo, TX MSA	98,458	998	79,533	4,136	373	13,418
San Antonio, TX MSA	1,302,099	16,058	978,505	88,778	4,648	214,110
San Diego, CA MSA	2,498,016	198,311	1,872,256	159,306	20,066	248,077
San Francisco, CA PMSA	1,603,678	329,599	1,058,796	122,494	7,232	85,557
San Jose, CA PMSA	1,497,577	261,466	1,032,190	56,211	9,269	138,441
Santa Barbara–Santa Maria–Lom- poc, CA MSA	369,608	16,429	285,461	10,402	3,351	53,965
Santa Cruz, CA PMSA	229,734	8,512	192,849	2,632	1,821	23,920
Santa Fe, NM MSA	117,043	941	96,454	711	2,948	15,989
Santa Rosa–Petaluma, CA PMSA	388,222	10,774	351,650	5,547	4,397	15,854
Sarasota, FL MSA	277,776	1,430	262,836	12,073	483	954
Savannah, GA MSA	242,622	2,412	152,513	86,228	515	954
Scranton–Wilkes-Barre, PA MSA	734,175	3,827	720,692	7,660	580	1,416

[Continued]

★ 784 ★

Population of Metropolitan Statistical Areas by Race/Ethnicity (Continued)

Population of U.S. Metropolitan Statistical Areas (MSAs) including Primary Metropolitan Statistical Areas (PMSAs)[a], by race/ethnicity, 1990.

Metropolitan Statistical Area	Total persons	Asian or Pacific Islander	White	Black	American Indian, Eskimo, or Aleut	Other race
Seattle, WA PMSA	1,972,961	135,251	1,713,068	81,056	23,727	19,859
Sharon, PA MSA	121,003	393	114,479	5,882	115	134
Sheboygan, WI MSA	103,877	2,061	100,389	430	357	640
Sherman–Denison, TX MSA	95,021	412	85,553	6,565	1,046	1,445
Shreveport, LA MSA	334,341	2,023	213,610	116,892	865	951
Sioux City, IA–NE MSA	115,018	1,624	107,579	1,953	1,999	1,863
Sioux Falls, SD MSA	123,809	714	120,454	754	1,680	207
South Bend–Mishawaka, IN MSA	247,052	2,507	216,984	24,190	846	2,525
Spokane, WA MSA	361,364	6,569	341,874	5,105	5,539	2,277
Springfield, IL MSA	189,550	1,391	173,114	14,373	319	353
Springfield, MA MSA	529,519	5,397	457,749	35,081	864	30,428
Springfield, MO MSA	240,593	1,600	233,186	3,784	1,471	552
St. Cloud, MN MSA	190,921	1,171	188,080	738	637	295
St. Joseph, MO MSA	83,083	266	79,378	2,635	273	531
St. Louis, MO–IL MSA	2,444,099	23,686	1,985,500	423,182	4,947	6,784
Stamford, CT PMSA	202,557	5,570	171,834	20,767	203	4,183
State College, PA MSA	123,786	3,841	116,552	2,801	179	413
Steubenville–Weirton, OH–WV MSA	142,523	439	136,078	5,591	237	178
Stockton, CA MSA	480,628	59,690	353,169	27,094	5,085	35,590
Syracuse, NY MSA	659,864	7,740	605,924	39,095	3,948	3,157
Tacoma, WA PMSA	586,203	29,035	498,642	42,210	8,344	7,972
Tallahassee, FL MSA	233,598	2,788	158,398	70,227	568	1,617
Tampa–St. Petersburg–Clearwater, FL MSA	2,067,959	23,055	1,827,492	185,503	5,467	26,442
Terre Haute, IN MSA	130,812	1,176	122,933	6,029	338	336
Texarkana, TX–Texarkana, AR MSA	120,132	405	92,342	26,423	560	402
Toledo, OH MSA	614,128	6,146	526,555	69,717	1,423	10,287
Topeka, KS MSA	160,976	1,179	141,189	13,365	1,836	3,407
Trenton, NJ PMSA	325,824	9,992	244,656	61,481	533	9,162
Tucson, AZ MSA	666,880	11,964	524,976	20,795	20,330	88,815
Tulsa, OK MSA	708,954	6,563	590,612	58,186	48,196	5,397
Tuscaloosa, AL MSA	150,522	1,264	109,398	39,377	253	230
Tyler, TX MSA	151,309	638	113,676	31,572	520	4,903
Utica–Rome, NY MSA	316,633	2,314	297,746	13,849	613	2,111
Vallejo–Fairfield–Napa, CA PMSA	451,186	47,044	325,761	47,043	3,898	27,440
Vancouver, WA PMSA	238,053	5,670	225,192	2,976	2,296	1,919
Victoria, TX MSA	74,361	257	59,251	4,906	208	9,739
Vineland–Millville–Bridgeton, NJ PMSA	138,053	1,134	101,467	23,318	1,311	10,823
Visalia–Tulare–Porterville, CA MSA	311,921	13,319	204,835	4,618	3,992	85,157
Waco, TX MSA	189,123	1,384	146,100	29,520	563	11,556
Washington, DC–MD–VA MSA	3,923,574	202,437	2,577,933	1,041,934	11,036	90,234
Waterbury, CT MSA	221,629	1,576	196,680	15,414	538	7,421
Waterloo–Cedar Falls, IA MSA	146,611	1,137	136,236	8,584	237	417

[Continued]

★ 784 ★

Population of Metropolitan Statistical Areas by Race/Ethnicity (Continued)

Population of U.S. Metropolitan Statistical Areas (MSAs) including Primary Metropolitan Statistical Areas (PMSAs)[a], by race/ethnicity, 1990.

Metropolitan Statistical Area	Total persons	Asian or Pacific Islander	White	Black	American Indian, Eskimo, or Aleut	Other race
Wausau, WI MSA	115,400	2,499	112,189	89	490	133
West Palm Beach–Boca Raton–Delray Beach, FL MSA	863,518	9,020	732,231	107,705	1,211	13,351
Wheeling, WV–OH MSA	159,301	546	155,313	3,196	145	101
Wichita Falls, TX MSA	122,378	1,851	102,427	11,221	903	5,976
Wichita, KS MSA	485,270	9,109	423,784	36,979	5,160	10,238
Williamsport, PA MSA	118,710	469	115,040	2,816	219	166
Wilmington, DE–NJ–MD PMSA	578,587	7,737	477,243	85,641	1,128	6,838
Wilmington, NC MSA	120,284	616	94,895	24,097	435	241
Worcester, MA MSA	436,905	7,967	408,123	9,553	891	10,371
Yakima, WA MSA	188,823	1,922	139,514	1,938	8,405	37,044
York, PA MSA	417,848	2,471	399,694	11,911	501	3,271
Youngstown–Warren, OH MSA	492,619	1,958	432,024	54,902	785	2,950
Yuba City, CA MSA	122,643	10,996	95,062	3,478	2,616	10,491
Yuma, AZ MSA	106,895	1,393	80,702	3,056	1,429	20,315

Source: Asian/Pacific Islander Data Consortium (San Francisco, CA: Asian and Pacific Islander Center for Census Information and Services, 1993). Primary source: U.S. Census Bureau, Summary Tape Files 1 and 3. *Note:* (a) The U.S. Census Bureau designates the following: CMSA=Consolidated Metropolitan Statistical Area; PMSA=Primary Metropolitan Statistical Area; MSA=Metropolitan Statistical Area. See *Appendix* for detailed definitions.

Population of Metropolitan Statistical Areas by Race/Ethnicity, in Percent

Population of U.S. Metropolitan Statistical Areas (CMSAs) including Primary Metropolitan Statistical Areas (PMSAs)[a], in percent, by race/ethnicity, 1990.

Metropolitan area	Total persons	Population in percent				
		Asian Pacific Islander	White	Black	American Indian, Eskimo, Aleut	Other race
Abilene, TX MSA	119,655	1.2	84	6	0.4	8.3
Akron, OH PMSA	657,575	0.9	89	10	0.2	0.2
Albany, GA MSA	112,561	0.4	53	46	0.3	0.2
Albany–Schenectady–Troy, NY MSA	874,304	1.2	93	5	0.2	0.6
Albuquerque, NM MSA	480,577	1.5	77	3	3.4	15.5
Alexandria, LA MSA	131,556	0.7	71	28	0.4	0.2
Allentown–Bethlehem–Easton, PA– NJ MSA	686,688	1.1	95	2	0.1	2.2
Altoona, PA MSA	130,542	0.3	99	1	0.1	0.1
Amarillo, TX MSA	187,547	1.7	85	5	0.7	7.8
Anaheim–Santa Ana, CA PMSA	2,410,556	10.3	79	2	0.5	8.8
Anchorage, AK MSA	226,338	4.8	81	6	6.4	1.6
Anderson, IN MSA	130,669	0.3	92	8	0.2	0.3
Anderson, SC MSA	145,196	0.2	83	17	0.1	0.1
Ann Arbor, MI PMSA	282,937	4.1	84	11	0.4	0.7
Anniston, AL MSA	116,034	0.8	80	19	0.3	0.4
Appleton–Oshkosh–Neenah, WI MSA	315,121	1.2	97	0	0.9	0.3
Asheville, NC MSA	174,821	0.4	91	8	0.3	0.2
Athens, GA MSA	156,267	1.5	79	19	0.2	0.4
Atlanta, GA MSA	2,833,511	1.8	71	26	0.2	0.7
Atlantic City, NJ MSA	319,416	1.7	81	14	0.2	2.7
Augusta, GA–SC MSA	396,809	1.4	67	31	0.2	0.5
Aurora–Elgin, IL PMSA	356,884	1.3	86	5	0.2	6.9
Austin, TX MSA	781,572	2.4	77	9	0.4	11.2
Bakersfield, CA MSA	543,477	3.0	70	6	1.3	20.5
Baltimore, MD MSA	2,382,172	1.8	72	26	0.3	0.3
Bangor, ME MSA	88,745	0.9	97	1	1.1	0.2
Baton Rouge, LA MSA	528,264	1.1	69	30	0.2	0.3
Battle Creek, MI MSA	135,982	0.8	87	11	0.5	0.8
Beaumont–Port Arthur, TX MSA	361,226	1.6	73	23	0.3	1.6
Beaver County, PA PMSA	186,093	0.2	94	6	0.1	0.2
Bellingham, WA MSA	127,780	1.9	93	1	3.1	1.2
Benton Harbor, MI MSA	161,378	0.9	83	15	0.4	0.7
Bergen–Passaic, NJ PMSA	1,278,440	5.2	82	8	0.2	4.7
Billings, MT MSA	113,419	0.5	95	0	2.9	1.0
Biloxi–Gulfport, MS MSA	197,125	2.3	79	18	0.3	0.4
Binghamton, NY MSA	264,497	1.5	96	2	0.2	0.4
Birmingham, AL MSA	907,810	0.4	72	27	0.2	0.1
Bismarck, ND MSA	83,831	0.3	97	0	2.4	0.2
Bloomington, IN MSA	108,978	2.5	94	3	0.2	0.4
Bloomington–Normal, IL MSA	129,180	1.3	94	4	0.2	0.6
Boise City, ID MSA	205,775	1.4	97	0	0.7	0.8

[Continued]

628

★ 785 ★

Population of Metropolitan Statistical Areas by Race/Ethnicity, in Percent (Continued)

Population of U.S. Metropolitan Statistical Areas (CMSAs) including Primary Metropolitan Statistical Areas (PMSAs)[a], in percent, by race/ethnicity, 1990.

Metropolitan area	Total persons	Population in percent				
		Asian Pacific Islander	White	Black	American Indian, Eskimo, Aleut	Other race
Boston, MA PMSA	2,870,669	3.3	87	7	0.2	2.1
Boulder–Longmont, CO PMSA	225,339	2.4	93	1	0.6	2.8
Bradenton, FL MSA	211,707	0.6	90	8	0.2	1.5
Brazoria, TX PMSA	191,707	1.0	81	8	0.4	9.4
Bremerton, WA MSA	189,731	4.4	90	3	1.7	1.1
Bridgeport–Milford, CT PMSA	443,722	1.5	84	10	0.2	4.3
Bristol, CT PMSA	79,488	0.7	97	2	0.2	0.8
Brockton, MA PMSA	189,478	1.1	89	7	0.2	2.6
Brownsville–Harlingen, TX MSA	260,120	0.3	82	0	0.2	16.8
Bryan–College Station, TX MSA	121,862	3.5	78	11	0.2	7.2
Buffalo, NY PMSA	968,532	1.1	86	11	0.6	1.1
Burlington, NC MSA	108,213	0.5	80	19	0.3	0.2
Burlington, VT MSA	131,439	1.1	98	1	0.2	0.2
Canton, OH MSA	394,106	0.4	93	6	0.3	0.2
Casper, WY MSA	61,226	0.5	97	1	0.7	1.2
Cedar Rapids, IA MSA	168,767	0.8	97	2	0.2	0.3
Champaign–Urbana–Rantoul, IL MSA	173,025	4.6	85	10	0.2	0.9
Charleston, SC MSA	506,875	1.2	68	30	0.3	0.4
Charleston, WV MSA	250,454	0.6	94	6	0.1	0.1
Charlotte–Gastonia–Rock Hill, NC–SC MSA	1,162,093	1.7	78	20	0.4	0.3
Charlottesville, VA MSA	131,107	2.0	83	14	0.1	0.3
Chattanooga, TN–GA MSA	433,210	0.7	86	13	0.2	0.2
Cheyenne, WY MSA	73,142	1.1	91	3	0.7	4.5
Chicago, IL PMSA	6,069,974	3.8	68	22	0.2	6.5
Chico, CA MSA	182,120	2.8	91	1	1.8	3.4
Cincinnati, OH–KY–IN PMSA	1,452,645	0.8	86	13	0.1	0.2
Clarksville–Hopkinsville, TN–KY MSA	169,439	1.6	76	21	0.4	1.6
Cleveland, OH PMSA	1,831,122	1.1	78	19	0.2	0.9
Colorado Springs, CO MSA	397,014	2.5	86	7	0.8	3.5
Columbia, MO MSA	112,379	2.8	89	7	0.4	0.4
Columbia, SC MSA	453,331	1.1	68	30	0.2	0.5
Columbus, GA–AL MSA	243,072	1.3	59	38	0.3	1.4
Columbus, OH MSA	1,377,419	1.5	86	12	0.2	0.3
Corpus Christi, TX MSA	349,894	0.8	76	4	0.4	19.2
Cumberland, MD–WV MSA	101,643	0.4	97	2	0.1	0.1
Dallas, TX PMSA	2,553,362	2.6	73	16	0.5	8.2
Danbury, CT PMSA	187,867	2.3	94	3	0.2	1.1
Danville, VA MSA	108,711	0.3	68	32	0.1	0.1
Davenport–Rock Island–Moline, IA–IL MSA	350,861	0.7	92	5	0.3	1.6
Dayton–Springfield, OH MSA	951,270	1.8	85	13	0.2	0.3

[Continued]

★ 785 ★

Population of Metropolitan Statistical Areas by Race/Ethnicity, in Percent (Continued)

Population of U.S. Metropolitan Statistical Areas (CMSAs) including Primary Metropolitan Statistical Areas (PMSAs)[a], in percent, by race/ethnicity, 1990.

Metropolitan area	Total persons	Population in percent				
		Asian Pacific Islander	White	Black	American Indian, Eskimo, Aleut	Other race
Daytona Beach, FL MSA	370,712	0.7	89	9	0.3	1.4
Decatur, AL MSA	131,556	0.3	86	11	1.9	0.1
Decatur, IL MSA	117,206	0.4	87	12	0.1	0.2
Denver, CO PMSA	1,622,980	2.3	86	6	0.8	5.4
Des Moines, IA MSA	392,928	1.6	94	4	0.3	0.6
Detroit, MI PMSA	4,382,299	1.3	76	22	0.4	0.7
Dothan, AL MSA	130,964	0.9	77	21	0.4	0.4
Dubuque, IA MSA	86,403	0.5	99	0	0.1	0.2
Duluth, MN–WI MSA	239,971	0.6	97	1	1.9	0.2
Eau Claire, WI MSA	137,543	1.7	97	0	0.5	0.2
El Paso, TX MSA	591,610	1.1	76	4	0.4	18.2
Elkhart–Goshen, IN MSA	156,198	0.6	94	5	0.3	0.7
Elmira, NY MSA	95,195	0.7	93	6	0.2	0.7
Enid, OK MSA	56,735	1.0	92	4	2.2	0.9
Erie, PA MSA	275,572	0.5	94	5	0.2	0.6
Eugene–Springfield, OR MSA	282,912	2.0	95	1	1.1	0.8
Evansville, IN–KY MSA	278,990	0.4	93	6	0.2	0.1
Fall River, MA–RI PMSA	157,272	1.8	98	1	0.1	0.3
Fargo–Moorhead, ND–MN MSA	153,296	0.9	97	0	1.8	0.6
Fayetteville, NC MSA	274,566	2.1	62	32	1.6	2.5
Fayetteville–Springdale, AR MSA	113,409	0.9	96	1	1.3	0.4
Fitchburg–Leominster, MA MSA	102,797	1.7	93	2	0.2	2.8
Flint, MI MSA	430,459	0.7	78	20	0.7	0.8
Florence, AL MSA	131,327	0.2	87	12	0.2	0.1
Florence, SC MSA	114,344	0.3	61	39	0.1	0.1
Fort Collins–Loveland, CO MSA	186,136	1.5	95	1	0.6	2.8
Fort Lauderdale–Hollywood–Pompano Beach, FL PMSA	1,255,488	1.4	82	15	0.2	1.3
Fort Myers–Cape CoraL, Fl MSA	335,113	0.6	91	7	0.2	1.2
Fort Pierce, FL MSA	251,071	0.6	85	12	0.2	1.6
Fort Smith, AR–OK MSA	175,911	2.1	88	4	5.2	0.4
Fort Walton Beach, FL MSA	143,776	2.5	87	9	0.5	0.8
Fort Wayne, IN MSA	363,811	0.8	90	8	0.3	0.8
Fort Worth–Arlington, TX PMSA	1,332,053	2.3	80	11	0.5	6.1
Fresno, CA MSA	667,490	8.6	63	5	1.1	22.0
Gadsden, AL MSA	99,840	0.4	85	14	0.3	0.1
Gainesville, FL MSA	204,111	2.3	78	19	0.2	0.8
Galveston–Texas City, TX PMSA	217,399	1.6	76	18	0.4	4.9
Gary–Hammond, IN PMSA	604,526	0.6	76	19	0.2	3.6
Glens Falls, NY MSA	118,539	0.3	97	2	0.2	0.4
Grand Forks, ND MSA	70,683	1.3	94	2	1.8	0.5
Grand Rapids, MI MSA	688,399	1.1	91	6	0.5	1.8
Great Falls, MT MSA	77,691	1.0	93	1	4.0	0.5
Greeley, CO MSA	131,821	0.9	89	0	0.6	9.2

[Continued]

★ 785 ★

Population of Metropolitan Statistical Areas by Race/Ethnicity, in Percent (Continued)

Population of U.S. Metropolitan Statistical Areas (CMSAs) including Primary Metropolitan Statistical Areas (PMSAs)[a], in percent, by race/ethnicity, 1990.

Metropolitan area	Total persons	Population in percent				
		Asian Pacific Islander	White	Black	American Indian, Eskimo, Aleut	Other race
Green Bay, WI MSA	194,594	1.3	96	1	2.0	0.3
Greensboro–Winston-Salem–High Point, NC MSA	942,091	0.7	79	19	0.3	0.3
Greenville–Spartanburg, SC MSA	640,861	0.7	82	17	0.2	0.2
Hagerstown, MD MSA	121,393	0.7	93	6	0.2	0.2
Hamilton–Middletown, OH PMSA	291,479	0.9	94	5	0.1	0.1
Harrisburg–Lebanon–Carlisle, PA MSA	587,986	1.1	91	7	0.1	0.8
Hartford, CT PMSA	767,841	1.6	84	11	0.2	4.1
Hickory–Morganton, NC MSA	221,700	0.8	91	8	0.2	0.2
Honolulu, HI MSA	836,231	63.0	32	3	0.4	1.9
Houma–Thibodaux, LA MSA	182,842	0.8	81	15	3.7	0.3
Houston, TX PMSA	3,301,937	3.8	66	19	0.3	11.1
Huntington–Ashland, WV–KY–OH MSA	312,529	0.3	97	2	0.1	0.1
Huntsville, AL MSA	238,912	1.8	77	20	0.7	0.3
Indianapolis, IN MSA	1,249,822	0.8	85	14	0.2	0.3
Iowa City, IA MSA	96,119	4.0	93	2	0.2	0.5
Jackson, MI MSA	149,756	0.4	91	8	0.4	0.6
Jackson, MS MSA	395,396	0.4	57	42	0.1	0.1
Jackson, TN MSA	77,982	0.3	69	31	0.1	0.1
Jacksonville, FL MSA	906,727	1.7	77	20	0.3	0.6
Jacksonville, NC MSA	149,838	2.0	75	20	0.6	2.8
Jamestown–Dunkirk, NY	141,895	0.4	96	2	0.4	1.5
Janesville–Beloit, WI MSA	139,510	0.7	94	5	0.3	0.5
Jersey City, NJ PMSA	553,099	6.7	69	14	0.3	9.9
Johnson City–Kingsport–Bristol, TN–VA MSA	436,047	0.3	97	2	0.2	0.1
Johnstown, PA MSA	241,247	0.2	98	2	0.1	0.1
Joliet, IL PMSA	389,650	1.3	86	10	0.2	2.7
Joplin, MO MSA	134,910	0.6	96	1	1.8	0.2
Kalamazoo, MI MSA	223,411	1.4	88	9	0.5	0.9
Kankakee, IL MSA	96,255	0.7	83	15	0.2	0.9
Kansas City, MO–KS MSA	1,566,280	1.1	84	13	0.5	1.3
Kenosha, WI PMSA	128,181	0.5	93	4	0.4	2.0
Killeen–Temple, TX MSA	255,301	2.8	71	19	0.6	6.2
Knoxville, TN MSA	604,816	0.8	93	6	0.3	0.1
Kokomo, IN MSA	96,946	0.5	94	5	0.3	0.4
La Crosse, WI MSA	97,904	2.7	96	0	0.4	0.1
Lafayette, LA MSA	208,740	0.9	74	25	0.2	0.4
Lafayette–West Lafayette, IN MSA	130,598	3.7	93	2	0.3	0.6
Lake Charles, LA MSA	168,134	0.4	76	23	0.2	0.3
Lake County, IL PMSA	516,418	2.4	87	7	0.2	3.3
Lakeland–Winter Haven, FL MSA	405,382	0.6	84	13	0.3	1.3

[Continued]

★ 785 ★

Population of Metropolitan Statistical Areas by Race/Ethnicity, in Percent (Continued)

Population of U.S. Metropolitan Statistical Areas (CMSAs) including Primary Metropolitan Statistical Areas (PMSAs)[a], in percent, by race/ethnicity, 1990.

Metropolitan area	Total persons	Population in percent				
		Asian Pacific Islander	White	Black	American Indian, Eskimo, Aleut	Other race
Lancaster, PA MSA	422,822	1.1	94	2	0.1	2.3
Lansing–East Lansing, MI MSA	432,674	1.9	88	7	0.6	2.1
Laredo, TX MSA	133,239	0.4	70	0	0.2	29.1
Las Cruces, NM MSA	135,510	0.9	91	2	0.7	5.7
Las Vegas, NV MSA	741,459	3.5	81	10	0.9	4.8
Lawrence, KS MSA	81,798	3.2	89	4	2.6	1.0
Lawrence–Haverhill, MA–NH PMSA	393,516	1.3	91	2	0.2	5.4
Lawton, OK MSA	111,486	2.8	71	18	4.6	3.3
Lewiston–Auburn, ME MSA	88,141	0.6	98	1	0.2	0.2
Lexington-Fayette, KY MSA	348,428	1.2	88	11	0.2	0.3
Lima, OH MSA	154,340	0.5	91	8	0.2	0.4
Lincoln, NE MSA	213,641	1.6	95	2	0.6	0.8
Little Rock–North Little Rock, AR MSA	513,117	0.7	79	20	0.4	0.2
Longview–Marshall, TX MSA	162,431	0.4	75	22	0.4	1.8
Lorain–Elyria, OH PMSA	271,126	0.6	89	8	0.3	2.3
Los Angeles–Long Beach, CA PMSA	8,863,164	10.8	57	11	0.5	20.7
Louisville, KY–IN MSA	952,662	0.6	86	13	0.2	0.2
Lowell, MA–NH PMSA	273,067	5.2	91	1	0.1	2.2
Lubbock, TX MSA	222,636	1.2	79	8	0.3	11.7
Lynchburg, VA MSA	142,199	0.5	78	21	0.2	0.2
Macon–Warner Robins, GA MSA	281,103	0.7	64	35	0.2	0.3
Madison, WI MSA	367,085	2.4	94	3	0.3	0.6
Manchester, NH MSA	147,809	1.8	98	1	0.2	0.5
Mansfield, OH MSA	126,137	0.5	91	8	0.2	0.2
Mcallen–Edinburg–Mission, TX MSA	383,545	0.3	75	0	0.2	24.5
Medford, OR MSA	146,389	1.8	96	0	1.3	1.8
Melbourne–Titusville–Palm Bay, FL MSA	398,978	1.4	90	8	0.3	0.6
Memphis, TN–AR–MS MSA	981,747	0.8	58	41	0.2	0.2
Merced, CA MSA	178,403	8.5	67	5	0.9	18.5
Miami–Hialeah, FL PMSA	1,937,094	1.4	73	21	0.2	5.0
Middlesex–Somerset–Hunterdon, NJ PMSA	1,019,835	5.6	85	7	0.1	2.5
Middletown, CT PMSA	90,320	1.3	92	6	0.2	0.8
Midland, TX MSA	106,611	0.8	82	8	0.4	9.4
Milwaukee, WI PMSA	1,432,149	1.3	83	14	0.6	1.7
Minneapolis–St. Paul, MN–WI MSA	2,464,124	2.7	92	4	1.7	0.6
Mobile, AL MSA	476,923	0.8	71	27	0.5	0.2
Modesto, CA MSA	370,522	5.2	80	2	1.1	11.7
Monmouth–Ocean, NJ PMSA	986,327	1.9	91	6	0.1	1.1
Monroe, LA MSA	142,191	0.5	68	31	0.2	0.2
Montgomery, AL MSA	292,517	0.6	63	36	0.2	0.2

[Continued]

★ 785 ★

Population of Metropolitan Statistical Areas by Race/Ethnicity, in Percent (Continued)

Population of U.S. Metropolitan Statistical Areas (CMSAs) including Primary Metropolitan Statistical Areas (PMSAs)[a], in percent, by race/ethnicity, 1990.

Metropolitan area	Total persons	Population in percent				
		Asian Pacific Islander	White	Black	American Indian, Eskimo, Aleut	Other race
Muncie, IN MSA	119,659	0.5	93	6	0.2	0.3
Muskegon, MI MSA	158,983	0.4	84	14	0.8	1.7
Naples, FL MSA	152,099	0.4	91	5	0.3	3.3
Nashua, NH PMSA	180,557	1.4	97	1	0.2	0.6
Nashville, TN MSA	985,026	1.0	83	15	0.2	0.2
Nassau–Suffolk, NY PMSA	2,609,212	2.4	88	7	0.2	1.6
New Bedford, MA MSA	175,641	0.5	92	3	0.3	4.9
New Britain, CT PMSA	148,188	1.3	89	4	0.1	4.7
New Haven–Meriden, CT MSA	530,180	1.6	83	12	0.2	2.8
New London–Norwich, CT–RI MSA	266,819	1.3	92	5	0.5	1.4
New Orleans, LA MSA	1,238,816	1.7	62	35	0.3	1.0
New York, NY PMSA	8,546,846	6.5	56	26	0.4	10.4
Newark, NJ PMSA	1,824,321	2.9	70	23	0.2	3.6
Niagara Falls, NY PMSA	220,756	0.4	93	5	0.9	0.2
Norfolk–Virginia Beach–Newport News, VA MSA	1,396,107	2.5	68	29	0.3	0.8
Norwalk, CT PMSA	127,378	1.6	86	10	0.1	2.2
Oakland, CA PMSA	2,082,914	12.9	66	15	0.7	5.9
Ocala, FL MSA	194,833	0.5	86	13	0.3	0.7
Odessa, TX MSA	118,934	0.6	77	5	0.5	17.5
Oklahoma City, OK MSA	958,839	1.9	81	11	4.8	1.7
Olympia, WA MSA	161,238	3.8	92	2	1.6	1.6
Omaha, NE–IA MSA	618,262	1.0	89	8	0.5	1.1
Orange County, NY PMSA	307,647	1.2	89	7	0.3	2.4
Orlando, FL MSA	1,072,748	1.9	83	12	0.3	2.5
Owensboro, KY MSA	87,189	0.3	95	4	0.1	0.1
Oxnard–Ventura, CA PMSA	669,016	5.2	79	2	0.7	12.7
Panama City, FL MSA	126,994	1.8	86	11	0.8	0.4
Parkersburg–Marietta, WV–OH MSA	149,169	0.4	98	1	0.2	0.1
Pascagoula, MS MSA	115,243	1.7	78	20	0.2	0.2
Pawtucket–Woonsocket–Attleboro, RI–MA PMSA	329,384	1.2	94	2	0.2	2.6
Pensacola, FL MSA	344,406	1.8	81	16	1.7	0.4
Peoria, IL MSA	339,172	0.8	91	7	0.2	0.4
Philadelphia, PA–NJ PMSA	4,856,881	2.2	77	19	0.2	2.0
Phoenix, AZ MSA	2,122,101	1.7	85	3	1.8	8.2
Pine Bluff, AR MSA	85,487	0.4	56	43	0.3	0.2
Pittsburgh, PA PMSA	2,056,705	0.8	91	8	0.1	0.2
Pittsfield, MA MSA	79,250	0.7	97	2	0.2	0.3
Portland, ME MSA	215,281	0.9	98	1	0.3	0.1
Portland, OR PMSA	1,239,842	3.7	91	3	0.9	1.5
Portsmouth–Dover–Rochester, NH–ME MSA	223,578	1.6	98	1	0.2	0.2
Poughkeepsie, NY MSA	259,462	2.3	88	8	0.1	0.9

[Continued]

★ 785 ★

Population of Metropolitan Statistical Areas by Race/Ethnicity, in Percent (Continued)

Population of U.S. Metropolitan Statistical Areas (CMSAs) including Primary Metropolitan Statistical Areas (PMSAs)[a], in percent, by race/ethnicity, 1990.

Metropolitan area	Total persons	Population in percent				
		Asian Pacific Islander	White	Black	American Indian, Eskimo, Aleut	Other race
Providence, RI PMSA	654,854	2.2	90	5	0.5	2.5
Provo–Orem, UT MSA	263,590	1.5	96	0	0.7	1.4
Pueblo, CO MSA	123,051	0.6	85	2	0.8	12.0
Racine, WI PMSA	175,034	0.6	87	10	0.3	2.5
Raleigh–Durham, NC MSA	735,480	1.9	72	25	0.3	0.4
Rapid City, SD MSA	81,343	1.2	89	2	7.2	0.6
Reading, PA MSA	336,523	0.8	93	3	0.1	2.6
Redding, CA MSA	147,036	1.8	94	1	2.7	0.9
Reno, NV MSA	254,667	3.9	88	2	1.9	3.6
Richland–Kennewick–Pasco, WA MSA	150,033	2.1	86	2	0.8	9.1
Richmond–Petersburg, VA MSA	865,640	1.4	69	29	0.3	0.4
Riverside–San Bernardino, CA PMSA	2,588,793	3.9	75	7	1.6	13.7
Roanoke, VA MSA	224,477	0.7	87	12	0.1	0.2
Rochester, MN MSA	106,470	3.0	96	1	0.3	0.3
Rochester, NY MSA	1,002,410	1.4	87	9	0.3	1.6
Rockford, IL MSA	283,719	1.1	89	8	0.3	1.7
Sacramento, CA MSA	1,481,102	7.7	79	7	1.2	5.2
Saginaw–Bay City–Midland, MI MSA	399,320	0.6	87	10	0.5	2.4
Salem, OR MSA	278,024	1.7	92	1	1.5	4.2
Salem–Gloucester, MA PMSA	264,356	0.9	97	1	0.1	0.7
Salinas–Seaside–Monterey, CA MSA	355,660	7.8	64	6	0.9	21.1
Salt Lake City–Ogden, UT MSA	1,072,227	2.4	93	1	0.8	2.6
San Angelo, TX MSA	98,458	1.0	81	4	0.4	13.6
San Antonio, TX MSA	1,302,099	1.2	75	7	0.4	16.4
San Diego, CA MSA	2,498,016	7.9	75	6	0.8	9.9
San Francisco, CA PMSA	1,603,678	20.6	66	8	0.5	5.3
San Jose, CA PMSA	1,497,577	17.5	69	4	0.6	9.2
Santa Barbara–Santa Maria–Lompoc, CA MSA	369,608	4.4	77	3	0.9	14.6
Santa Cruz, CA PMSA	229,734	3.7	84	1	0.8	10.4
Santa Fe, NM MSA	117,043	0.8	82	1	2.5	13.7
Santa Rosa–Petaluma, CA PMSA	388,222	2.8	91	1	1.1	4.1
Sarasota, FL MSA	277,776	0.5	95	4	0.2	0.3
Savannah, GA MSA	242,622	1.9	63	36	0.2	0.4
Scranton–Wilkes-Barre, PA MSA	734,175	0.5	98	1	0.1	0.2
Seattle, WA PMSA	1,972,961	6.9	87	4	1.2	1.0
Sharon, PA MSA	121,003	0.3	95	5	0.1	0.1
Sheboygan, WI MSA	103,877	2.0	97	0	0.3	0.6
Sherman–Denison, TX MSA	95,021	0.4	90	7	1.1	1.5
Shreveport, LA MSA	334,341	0.6	64	35	0.3	0.3
Sioux City, IA–NE MSA	115,018	1.4	94	2	1.7	1.6

[Continued]

★ 785 ★

Population of Metropolitan Statistical Areas by Race/Ethnicity, in Percent (Continued)

Population of U.S. Metropolitan Statistical Areas (CMSAs) including Primary Metropolitan Statistical Areas (PMSAs)[a], in percent, by race/ethnicity, 1990.

Metropolitan area	Total persons	Population in percent				
		Asian Pacific Islander	White	Black	American Indian, Eskimo, Aleut	Other race
Sioux Falls, SD MSA	123,809	0.6	97	1	1.4	0.2
South Bend–Mishawaka, IN MSA	247,052	1.0	88	10	0.3	1.0
Spokane, WA MSA	361,364	1.8	95	1	1.5	0.6
Springfield, IL MSA	189,550	0.7	91	8	0.2	0.2
Springfield, MA MSA	529,519	1.0	86	7	0.2	5.8
Springfield, MO MSA	240,593	0.7	97	2	0.6	0.2
St. Cloud, MN MSA	190,921	0.6	99	0	0.3	0.2
St. Joseph, MO MSA	83,083	0.3	96	3	0.3	0.6
St. Louis, MO–IL MSA	2,444,099	1.7	81	17	0.2	0.3
Stamford, CT PMSA	202,557	2.8	85	10	0.1	2.1
State College, PA MSA	123,786	3.1	94	2	0.1	0.3
Steubenville–Weirton, OH–WV MSA	142,523	0.3	95	4	0.2	0.1
Stockton, CA MSA	480,628	12.4	73	6	1.1	7.4
Syracuse, NY MSA	659,864	1.2	92	6	0.6	0.5
Tacoma, WA PMSA	586,203	5.0	85	7	1.4	1.4
Tallahassee, FL MSA	233,598	1.2	68	30	0.2	0.7
Tampa–St. Petersburg–Clearwater, FL MSA	2,067,959	1.1	88	9	0.3	1.3
Terre Haute, IN MSA	130,812	0.9	94	5	0.3	0.3
Texarkana, TX–Texarkana, AR MSA	120,132	0.3	77	22	0.5	0.3
Toledo, OH MSA	614,128	1.0	86	11	0.2	1.7
Topeka, KS MSA	160,976	0.7	88	8	1.1	2.1
Trenton, NJ PMSA	325,824	3.1	75	19	0.2	2.8
Tucson, AZ MSA	666,880	1.8	79	3	3.1	13.3
Tulsa, OK MSA	708,954	0.9	83	8	6.8	0.8
Tuscaloosa, AL MSA	150,522	0.8	73	26	0.2	0.2
Tyler, TX MSA	151,309	0.4	75	21	0.3	3.2
Utica–Rome, NY MSA	316,633	0.7	94	4	0.2	0.7
Vallejo–Fairfield–Napa, CA PMSA	451,186	10.4	72	10	0.9	6.1
Vancouver, WA PMSA	238,053	2.4	95	1	1.6	0.8
Victoria, TX MSA	74,361	0.4	80	7	0.3	13.1
Vineland–Millville–Bridgeton, NJ PMSA	138,053	0.8	73	17	1.5	7.8
Visalia–Tulare–Porterville, CA MSA	311,921	4.3	66	1	1.3	27.3
Waco, TX MSA	189,123	0.7	77	16	0.3	6.1
Washington, DC–MD–VA MSA	3,923,574	5.2	66	27	0.3	2.3
Waterbury, CT MSA	221,629	0.7	89	7	0.2	3.4
Waterloo–Cedar Falls, IA MSA	146,611	0.8	93	6	0.2	0.3
Wausau, WI MSA	115,400	2.2	97	0	0.4	0.1
West Palm Beach–Boca Raton–Delray Beach, FL MSA	863,518	1.0	85	12	0.1	1.6
Wheeling, WV–OH MSA	159,301	0.3	97	2	0.1	0.1
Wichita Falls, TX MSA	122,378	1.5	84	9	0.7	4.9
Wichita, KS MSA	485,270	1.9	87	8	1.1	2.1

[Continued]

★ 785 ★

Population of Metropolitan Statistical Areas by Race/Ethnicity, in Percent (Continued)

Population of U.S. Metropolitan Statistical Areas (CMSAs) including Primary Metropolitan Statistical Areas (PMSAs)[a], in percent, by race/ethnicity, 1990.

Metropolitan area	Total persons	Population in percent				
		Asian Pacific Islander	White	Black	American Indian, Eskimo, Aleut	Other race
Williamsport, PA MSA	118,710	0.4	97	2	0.2	0.1
Wilmington, DE–NJ–MD PMSA	578,587	1.3	82	15	0.2	1.2
Wilmington, NC MSA	120,284	0.5	79	20	0.4	0.2
Worcester, MA MSA	436,905	1.8	93	2	0.2	2.4
Yakima, WA MSA	188,823	1.0	74	1	4.5	19.6
York, PA MSA	417,848	0.6	96	3	0.1	0.8
Youngstown–Warren, OH MSA	492,619	0.4	88	11	0.2	0.6
Yuba City, CA MSA	122,643	9.0	78	3	2.1	8.6
Yuma, AZ MSA	106,895	1.3	75	3	1.3	19.0

Source: Asian/Pacific Islander Data Consortium (San Francisco, CA: Asian and Pacific Islander Center for Census Information and Services, 1993). Primary source: U.S. Census Bureau, Summary Tape Files 1 and 3. *Note:* (a) The U.S. Census Bureau designates the following: CMSA=Consolidated Metropolitan Statistical Area; PMSA=Primary Metropolitan Statistical Area; MSA=Metropolitan Statistical Area. See *Appendix* for detailed definitions.

★ 786 ★

Metropolitan Statistical Areas Ranked by Asian/Pacific Islander Population

Population of U.S. Metropolitan Statistical Areas (MSAs) including Primary Metropolitan Statistical Areas (PMSAs)[a] with Asian/Pacific Islander populations of 50,000, by race/ethnicity, 1990.

Metropolitan area	Total persons	Asian or Pacific Islander	White	Black	American Indian, Eskimo, or Aleut	Other race
Los Angeles–Long Beach, CA PMSA	8,863,164	954,485	5,035,103	992,974	45,508	1,835,094
New York, NY PMSA	8,546,846	556,399	4,826,081	2,250,026	29,711	884,629
Honolulu, HI MSA	836,231	526,459	264,372	25,875	3,532	15,993
San Francisco, CA PMSA	1,603,678	329,599	1,058,796	122,494	7,232	85,557
Oakland, CA PMSA	2,082,914	269,566	1,372,818	303,826	14,230	122,474
San Jose, CA PMSA	1,497,577	261,466	1,032,190	56,211	9,269	138,441
Anaheim–Santa Ana, CA PMSA	2,410,556	249,192	1,894,593	42,681	12,165	211,925
Chicago, IL PMSA	6,069,974	229,492	4,098,747	1,332,919	11,550	397,266
Washington, DC–MD–VA MSA	3,923,574	202,437	2,577,933	1,041,934	11,036	90,234
San Diego, CA MSA	2,498,016	198,311	1,872,256	159,306	20,066	248,077
Seattle, WA PMSA	1,972,961	135,251	1,713,068	81,056	23,727	19,859
Houston, TX PMSA	3,301,937	126,601	2,188,370	611,243	9,465	366,258
Sacramento, CA MSA	1,481,102	114,520	1,170,505	101,940	17,021	77,116
Philadelphia, PA–NJ PMSA	4,856,881	104,595	3,717,175	929,907	8,335	96,869
Riverside–San Bernardino, CA PMSA	2,588,793	100,792	1,930,095	178,525	24,905	354,476
Boston, MA PMSA	2,870,669	95,044	2,499,859	209,970	5,250	60,546
Dallas, TX PMSA	2,553,362	67,195	1,854,577	410,766	12,635	208,189
Bergen–Passaic, NJ PMSA	1,278,440	66,743	1,043,437	106,108	2,221	59,931
Minneapolis–St. Paul, MN–WI MSA	2,464,124	65,204	2,270,360	89,710	23,956	14,894
Nassau–Suffolk, NY PMSA	2,609,212	62,399	2,305,434	193,967	4,636	42,776
Stockton, CA MSA	480,628	59,690	353,169	27,094	5,085	35,590
Detroit, MI PMSA	4,382,299	57,730	3,332,697	943,479	16,885	31,508
Fresno, CA MSA	667,490	57,239	422,839	33,423	7,119	146,870
Middlesex–Somerset–Hunterdon, NJ PMSA	1,019,835	56,804	865,158	70,670	1,420	25,783
Newark, NJ PMSA	1,824,321	52,898	1,279,952	422,802	3,144	65,525
Atlanta, GA MSA	2,833,511	51,486	2,020,017	736,153	5,532	20,323

Source: Asian/Pacific Islander Data Consortium (San Francisco, CA: Asian and Pacific Islander Center for Census Information and Services, 1993). Primary source: U.S. Census Bureau, Summary Tape Files 1 and 3. *Note:* (a) The U.S. Census Bureau designates the following: CMSA=Consolidated Metropolitan Statistical Area; PMSA=Primary Metropolitan Statistical Area; MSA=Metropolitan Statistical Area. See *Appendix* for detailed definitions.

★ 787 ★

Metropolitan Statistical Areas Ranked by Asian/Pacific Islander Population, in Prcent

Population of U.S. Metropolitan Statistical Areas (MSAs) including Primary Metropolitan Statistical Areas (PMSAs)[a], with Asian/Pacific Islander population of 5 percent of total, in percent, by race/ethnicity 1990.

Metropolitan area	Total persons	Population in percent				
		Asian Pacific Islander	White	Black	American Indian, Eskimo, Aleut	Other race
Honolulu, HI MSA	836,231	63.0	32	3	0.4	1.9
San Francisco, CA PMSA	1,603,678	20.6	66	8	0.5	5.3
San Jose, CA PMSA	1,497,577	17.5	69	4	0.6	9.2
Oakland, CA PMSA	2,082,914	12.9	66	15	0.7	5.9
Stockton, CA MSA	480,628	12.4	73	6	1.1	7.4
Los Angeles–Long Beach, CA PMSA	8,863,164	10.8	57	11	0.5	20.7
Vallejo–Fairfield–Napa, CA PMSA	451,186	10.4	72	10	0.9	6.1
Anaheim–Santa Ana, CA PMSA	2,410,556	10.3	79	2	0.5	8.8
Yuba City, CA MSA	122,643	9.0	78	3	2.1	8.6
Fresno, CA MSA	667,490	8.6	63	5	1.1	22.0
Merced, CA MSA	178,403	8.5	67	5	0.9	18.5
San Diego, CA MSA	2,498,016	7.9	75	6	0.8	9.9
Salinas–Seaside–Monterey, CA MSA	355,660	7.8	64	6	0.9	21.1
Sacramento, CA MSA	1,481,102	7.7	79	7	1.2	5.2
Seattle, WA PMSA	1,972,961	6.9	87	4	1.2	1.0
Jersey City, NJ PMSA	553,099	6.7	69	14	0.3	9.9
New York, NY PMSA	8,546,846	6.5	56	26	0.4	10.4
Middlesex–Somerset–Hunterdon, NJ PMSA	1,019,835	5.6	85	7	0.1	2.5
Bergen–Passaic, NJ PMSA	1,278,440	5.2	82	8	0.2	4.7
Lowell, MA–NH PMSA	273,067	5.2	91	1	0.1	2.2
Modesto, CA MSA	370,522	5.2	80	2	1.1	11.7
Oxnard–Ventura, CA PMSA	669,016	5.2	79	2	0.7	12.7
Washington, DC–MD–VA MSA	3,923,574	5.2	66	27	0.3	2.3

Source: Asian/Pacific Islander Data Consortium (San Francisco, CA: Asian and Pacific Islander Center for Census Information and Services, 1993). Primary source: U.S. Census Bureau, Summary Tape Files 1 and 3. *Note:* (a) The U.S. Census Bureau designates the following: CMSA=Consolidated Metropolitan Statistical Area; PMSA=Primary Metropolitan Statistical Area; MSA=Metropolitan Statistical Area. See *Appendix* for detailed definitions.

★ 788 ★

Population of Metropolitan Statistical Areas by Hispanic Origin

Population of U.S. Metropolitan Statistical Areas (MSAs) including Primary Metropolitan Statistical Areas (PMSAs)[a], by race/ethnicity and Hispanic origin[b], 1990.

Metropolitan area	Not of Hispanic Origin					Hispanic Origin				
	Asian or Pacific Islander	White	Black	American Indian, Eskimo,	Other Race	White	Black	American Indian, Eskimo	Asian or Pacific Islander	Other race
Abilene, TX MSA	1,342	92,955	7,336	366	145	7,282	211	84	107	9,827
Akron, OH PMSA	6,081	581,228	64,713	1,302	436	2,672	378	55	99	611
Albany, GA MSA	463	59,556	51,328	265	21	485	194	16	35	198
Albany–Schenectady–Troy, NY MSA	10,541	805,925	39,676	1,470	852	9,390	1,436	90	248	4,676
Albuquerque, NM MSA	6,692	267,965	11,862	14,191	1,557	101,480	1,337	2,105	694	72,694
Alexandria, LA MSA	879	91,932	36,667	528	24	1,057	138	36	29	266
Allentown–Bethlehem–Easton, PA–NJ MSA	7,116	637,155	12,428	594	510	12,735	1,038	94	177	14,841
Altoona, PA MSA	372	128,525	1,056	115	43	315	17	3	8	88
Amarillo, TX MSA	3,057	148,241	9,542	1,123	194	10,276	246	232	159	14,477
Anaheim–Santa Ana, CA PMSA	240,756	1,554,501	39,159	8,584	2,728	340,092	3,522	3,581	8,436	209,197
Anchorage, AK MSA	10,427	178,168	14,126	14,126	233	4,568	418	443	483	3,346
Anderson, IN MSA	407	119,207	9,823	286	61	527	47	13	8	290
Anderson, SC MSA	334	120,013	24,097	163	30	371	54	10	6	118
Ann Arbor, MI PMSA	11,598	232,938	31,334	987	349	3,452	386	89	126	1,678
Anniston, AL MSA	814	92,154	21,476	291	17	719	102	5	55	401
Appleton–Oshkosh–Neenah, WI MSA	3,725	305,397	909	2,747	63	1,378	23	49	80	750
Asheville, NC MSA	745	158,117	14,279	479	28	862	57	7	20	227
Athens, GA MSA	2,289	122,770	28,904	237	56	1,306	99	20	63	523
Atlanta, GA MSA	50,543	1,987,685	731,655	5,202	1,257	32,332	4,498	330	943	19,066
Atlantic City, NJ MSA	5,132	252,425	42,957	685	245	7,760	1,441	93	257	8,421
Augusta, GA–SC MSA	5,260	261,942	122,943	892	152	2,859	539	49	178	1,995
Aurora–Elgin, IL PMSA	4,437	287,685	18,558	543	321	20,009	658	150	261	24,262
Austin, TX MSA	18,039	530,664	69,626	2,148	1,153	69,359	2,628	679	731	86,545
Bakersfield, CA MSA	14,879	340,892	28,851	5,620	1,240	37,587	1,280	1,406	1,662	110,060
Baltimore, MD MSA	41,717	1,691,039	611,990	6,121	1,145	18,270	4,075	323	917	6,575
Bangor, ME MSA	786	85,969	453	998	30	359	14	10	12	114
Baton Rouge, LA MSA	5,533	358,156	155,946	853	244	5,536	563	49	124	1,260
Battle Creek, MI MSA	1,044	117,299	14,258	659	139	1,438	125	37	24	959
Beaumont–Port Arthur, TX MSA	5,469	255,481	83,972	824	239	8,884	693	66	218	5,380
Beaver County, PA PMSA	370	173,870	10,411	193	125	889	64	10	7	154
Bellingham, WA MSA	2,319	117,213	623	3,839	68	2,016	27	175	44	1,456
Benton Harbor, MI MSA	1,432	131,798	24,688	651	126	1,461	184	34	55	949
Bergen–Passaic, NJ PMSA	64,984	966,486	95,783	1,675	1,644	76,951	10,325	546	1,759	58,287
Billings, MT MSA	604	106,068	465	3,086	38	1,853	46	149	8	1,102
Biloxi–Gulfport, MS MSA	4,355	153,807	34,841	554	80	2,448	214	41	140	645
Binghamton, NY MSA	3,945	252,641	4,430	429	207	1,806	217	21	45	756
Birmingham, AL MSA	3,929	652,926	245,350	1,473	143	2,683	376	33	85	812
Bismarck, ND MSA	261	81,087	78	1,951	19	219	1	65	25	125
Bloomington, IN MSA	2,672	101,814	2,789	202	134	938	46	14	41	328
Bloomington–Normal, IL MSA	1,609	120,156	5,485	180	79	901	78	23	15	654
Boise City, ID MSA	2,829	195,120	924	1,247	99	3,768	34	135	58	1,561
Boston, MA PMSA	93,340	2,439,321	195,393	4,503	9,229	60,538	14,577	747	1,704	51,317
Boulder–Longmont, CO PMSA	5,359	201,617	1,879	1,092	197	8,573	80	221	149	6,172
Bradenton, FL MSA	1,192	184,568	15,971	439	113	5,760	429	62	35	3,138
Brazoria, TX PMSA	1,837	139,683	15,425	687	278	15,192	556	125	124	17,800
Bremerton, WA MSA	7,598	167,850	4,973	2,991	150	3,213	134	220	684	1,918
Bridgeport–Milford, CT PMSA	6,319	347,771	43,567	679	645	23,722	2,259	127	258	18,375
Bristol, CT PMSA	538	75,720	1,255	112	44	1,155	92	16	6	550

[Continued]

★ 788 ★

Population of Metropolitan Statistical Areas by Hispanic Origin (Continued)

Population of U.S. Metropolitan Statistical Areas (MSAs) including Primary Metropolitan Statistical Areas (PMSAs)[a], by race/ethnicity and Hispanic origin[b], 1990.

Metropolitan area	Not of Hispanic Origin					Hispanic Origin				
	Asian or Pacific Islander	White	Black	American Indian, Eskimo,	Other Race	White	Black	American Indian, Eskimo	Asian or Pacific Islander	Other race
Brockton, MA PMSA	2,108	164,922	12,418	380	2,606	3,211	1,352	65	50	2,366
Brownsville–Harlingen, TX MSA	602	45,354	567	184	418	169,070	258	229	148	43,290
Bryan–College Station, TX MSA	4,248	87,139	13,409	223	130	7,727	263	51	65	8,607
Buffalo, NY PMSA	10,025	822,166	108,240	5,357	495	9,737	1,612	243	195	10,462
Burlington, NC MSA	482	85,913	20,763	296	23	460	59	7	5	205
Burlington, VT MSA	1,444	127,673	779	286	86	907	35	13	21	195
Canton, OH MSA	1,536	363,402	25,029	985	300	2,273	158	30	22	371
Casper, WY MSA	268	57,888	438	362	18	1,435	20	42	12	743
Cedar Rapids, IA MSA	1,373	162,087	3,288	333	95	1,077	46	30	28	410
Champaign–Urbana–Rantoul, IL MSA	7,896	144,760	16,415	299	170	1,746	144	32	137	1,426
Charleston, SC MSA	5,666	339,487	152,457	1,558	195	4,289	770	55	447	1,951
Charleston, WV MSA	1,407	233,756	13,863	283	103	762	56	9	43	172
Charlotte–Gastonia–Rock Hill, NC–SC MSA	11,022	905,336	230,739	3,984	341	6,568	915	123	282	2,783
Charlottesville, VA MSA	2,594	108,056	18,824	144	105	993	71	4	29	287
Chattanooga, TN–GA MSA	2,752	368,947	58,030	869	73	1,639	188	22	73	617
Cheyenne, WY MSA	748	62,410	2,113	470	91	3,870	105	58	73	3,204
Chicago, IL PMSA	221,462	3,782,766	1,316,602	8,868	5,449	315,981	16,317	2,682	8,030	391,817
Chico, CA MSA	4,961	158,242	2,238	2,946	127	6,958	123	295	209	6,021
Cincinnati, OH–KY–IN PMSA	11,299	1,240,802	189,790	1,975	870	5,367	683	103	302	1,454
Clarksville–Hopkinsville, TN–KY MSA	2,550	126,264	34,284	638	136	2,319	517	50	162	2,519
Cleveland, OH PMSA	20,131	1,419,629	353,517	2,795	1,129	16,139	2,102	243	397	15,040
Colorado Springs, CO MSA	9,273	322,461	27,599	2,641	567	18,939	994	601	568	13,371
Columbia, MO MSA	3,093	99,275	8,306	374	105	780	71	20	36	319
Columbia, SC MSA	4,677	304,504	137,079	978	144	2,950	827	35	143	1,994
Columbus, GA–AL MSA	2,922	141,128	90,710	713	211	3,198	774	52	185	3,179
Columbus, OH MSA	20,542	1,177,950	163,555	2,731	1,278	6,820	1,047	149	517	2,830
Corpus Christi, TX MSA	2,172	151,385	12,809	956	712	113,617	850	438	474	66,481
Cumberland, MD–WV MSA	368	98,510	2,243	69	33	311	27	2	23	57
Dallas, TX PMSA	64,573	1,703,736	402,662	10,558	2,949	150,841	8,104	2,077	2,622	205,240
Danbury, CT PMSA	4,255	170,881	5,049	269	277	4,899	349	32	100	1,756
Danville, VA MSA	313	73,549	34,212	109	13	268	138	8	12	89
Davenport–Rock Island–Moline, IA–IL MSA	2,420	315,455	18,796	794	262	7,350	319	108	82	5,275
Dayton–Springfield, OH MSA	9,085	806,678	125,660	1,815	778	4,715	578	100	193	1,668
Daytona Beach, FL MSA	2,637	319,259	32,985	856	135	9,271	470	59	102	4,938
Decatur, AL MSA	385	113,209	14,832	2,425	19	476	47	9	4	150
Decatur, IL MSA	502	101,838	14,095	150	81	359	40	7	4	130
Denver, CO PMSA	35,296	1,272,389	92,296	9,631	2,363	117,155	3,500	2,940	1,838	85,572
Des Moines, IA MSA	6,075	364,360	14,769	917	193	4,026	183	98	143	2,164
Detroit, MI PMSA	56,350	3,283,490	938,829	15,739	2,675	49,207	4,650	1,146	1,380	28,833
Dothan, AL MSA	1,152	99,923	27,667	518	25	955	134	8	49	533
Dubuque, IA MSA	436	85,077	351	68	34	290	3	9	1	134
Duluth, MN–WI MSA	1,326	231,764	1,252	4,408	68	743	24	79	16	291
Eau Claire, WI MSA	2,372	133,679	261	593	27	377	8	24	28	174
El Paso, TX MSA	5,820	151,313	20,525	1,634	699	301,199	1,585	956	665	107,214
Elkhart–Goshen, IN MSA	981	144,701	7,046	424	114	1,804	60	29	16	1,023
Elmira, NY MSA	649	87,800	4,913	189	203	570	332	22	41	476
Enid, OK MSA	554	51,906	2,002	1,171	16	497	18	63	33	475
Erie, PA MSA	1,374	256,177	14,008	417	232	1,702	296	21	37	1,308

[Continued]

★ 788 ★

Population of Metropolitan Statistical Areas by Hispanic Origin (Continued)

Population of U.S. Metropolitan Statistical Areas (MSAs) including Primary Metropolitan Statistical Areas (PMSAs)[a], by race/ethnicity and Hispanic origin[b], 1990.

Metropolitan area	Not of Hispanic Origin					Hispanic Origin				
	Asian or Pacific Islander	White	Black	American Indian, Eskimo,	Other Race	White	Black	American Indian, Eskimo	Asian or Pacific Islander	Other race
Eugene–Springfield, OR MSA	5,419	265,391	2,040	3,017	193	4,407	67	190	138	2,050
Evansville, IN–KY MSA	1,201	259,873	16,045	461	89	959	70	16	36	240
Fall River, MA–RI PMSA	1,515	152,314	1,026	156	196	1,708	60	12	26	259
Fargo–Moorhead, ND–MN MSA	1,367	148,097	438	1,455	60	907	8	42	29	893
Fayetteville, NC MSA	5,488	165,057	86,216	4,208	299	5,012	1,280	217	281	6,508
Fayetteville–Springdale, AR MSA	1,027	107,724	1,656	1,452	24	1,019	20	34	16	437
Fitchburg–Leominster, MA MSA	1,731	91,456	2,044	175	79	4,084	312	21	58	2,837
Flint, MI MSA	2,824	331,833	83,707	2,918	300	4,818	550	214	78	3,217
Florence, AL MSA	286	114,011	16,222	298	10	369	41	4	3	83
Florence, SC MSA	280	69,252	44,136	141	27	249	140	4	27	88
Fort Collins–Loveland, CO MSA	2,679	169,213	1,043	844	130	6,758	71	219	98	5,081
Fort Lauderdale–Hollywood–Pompano Beach, FL PMSA	16,395	940,345	186,670	2,391	1,248	85,238	6,777	243	735	15,446
Fort Myers–Cape CoraL, Fl MSA	1,776	296,005	21,515	603	120	10,195	669	69	118	4,043
Fort Pierce, FL MSA	1,490	208,242	30,087	444	128	6,036	622	82	753,865	
Fort Smith, AR–OK MSA	3,661	154,363	6,760	8,955	52	1,217	71	99	94	639
Fort Walton Beach, FL MSA	3,471	122,233	12,835	737	73	2,958	172	39	187	1,071
Fort Wayne, IN MSA	2,655	323,422	30,110	995	361	3,146	270	61	114	2,677
Fort Worth–Arlington, TX PMSA	29,292	1,004,656	141,321	5,637	1,114	65,440	2,529	700	1,091	80,273
Fresno, CA MSA	54,110	338,595	31,311	5,070	1,770	84,244	2,112	2,049	3,129	145,100
Gadsden, AL MSA	401	85,078	13,782	242	6	196	17	8	18	92
Gainesville, FL MSA	4,563	153,096	38,621	407	219	5,383	361	36	93	1,332
Galveston–Texas City, TX PMSA	3,357	144,852	37,414	632	182	19,358	740	120	212	10,532
Gary–Hammond, IN PMSA	3,550	435,557	115,786	926	323	24,975	1,356	182	166	21,705
Glens Falls, NY MSA	376	114,156	2,011	192	15	1,001	341	22	16	409
Grand Forks, ND MSA	849	66,128	1,413	1,198	42	638	33	46	32	304
Grand Rapids, MI MSA	7,622	614,151	40,369	3,070	556	9,636	942	324	209	11,520
Great Falls, MT MSA	751	71,569	1,018	2,921	34	776	43	151	41	387
Greeley, CO MSA	1,063	101,977	509	593	177	15,270	58	192	70	11,912
Green Bay, WI MSA	2,493	185,869	992	3,676	39	752	20	193	29	531
Greensboro–Winston-Salem–High Point, NC MSA	6,228	743,804	181,595	3,112	256	4,031	689	84	153	2,139
Greenville–Spartanburg, SC MSA	4,471	519,242	111,015	905	108	3,390	319	54	146	1,211
Hagerstown, MD MSA	772	112,325	7,124	216	51	503	121	25	21	235
Hamilton–Middletown, OH PMSA	2,611	273,854	13,069	363	115	1,038	65	16	48	300
Harrisburg–Lebanon–Carlisle, PA MSA	6,099	532,070	38,532	669	377	4,668	940	68	152	4,411
Hartford, CT PMSA	11,813	618,775	76,697	1,176	1,018	22,570	4,853	189	388	30,362
Hickory–Morganton, NC MSA	1,646	200,698	17,470	407	30	860	70	10	27	482
Honolulu, HI MSA	500,041	249,616	24,717	2,800	2,173	14,756	1,158	732	26,418	13,820
Houma–Thibodaux, LA MSA	1,311	145,554	26,607	6,675	70	1,899	128	139	59	400
Houston, TX PMSA	121,630	1,863,449	596,860	7,364	5,098	324,921	14,383	2,101	4,971	361,160
Huntington–Ashland, WV–KY–OH MSA	901	303,253	6,678	358	65	991	73	14	36	160
Huntsville, AL MSA	4,140	182,334	47,826	1,564	64	1,863	290	37	92	702

[Continued]

★ 788 ★

Population of Metropolitan Statistical Areas by Hispanic Origin (Continued)

Population of U.S. Metropolitan Statistical Areas (MSAs) including Primary Metropolitan Statistical Areas (PMSAs)[a], by race/ethnicity and Hispanic origin[b], 1990.

Metropolitan area	Not of Hispanic Origin					Hispanic Origin				
	Asian or Pacific Islander	White	Black	American Indian, Eskimo,	Other Race	White	Black	American Indian, Eskimo	Asian or Pacific Islander	Other race
Indianapolis, IN MSA	9,817	1,054,263	171,488	2,382	788	6,879	838	128	264	2,975
Iowa City, IA MSA	3,808	88,705	1,941	161	69	944	38	15	29	409
Jackson, MI MSA	641	134,283	11,822	627	80	1,274	161	28	12	828
Jackson, MS MSA	1,702	223,932	167,445	322	51	1,067	454	24	52	347
Jackson, TN MSA	245	53,219	24,065	64	13	204	105	2	8	57
Jacksonville, FL MSA	14,369	687,464	179,595	2,423	397	14,447	1,670	164	993	5,205
Jacksonville, NC MSA	2,740	108,890	29,137	867	169	3,049	671	72	254	3,989
Jamestown–Dunkirk, NY	506	134,436	2,297	534	67	1,875	108	24	39	2,009
Janesville–Beloit, WI MSA	932	129,788	6,593	356	87	1,015	45	13	53	628
Jersey City, NJ PMSA	35,046	262,077	69,856	960	1,695	118,535	9,914	500	1,731	52,785
Johnson City–Kingsport–Bristol, TN–VA MSA	1,210	423,458	8,899	740	50	1,293	26	26	37	308
Johnstown, PA MSA	511	235,501	3,783	144	92	958	53	8	16	181
Joliet, IL PMSA	4,713	325,536	37,767	652	261	9,748	615	85	174	10,099
Joplin, MO MSA	718	129,287	1,320	2,408	27	806	7	44	33	260
Kalamazoo, MI MSA	3,124	195,481	19,668	953	235	1,946	211	64	44	1,685
Kankakee, IL MSA	618	79,208	14,293	140	50	986	106	10	26	818
Kansas City, MO–KS MSA	16,810	1,297,227	198,909	7,070	1,037	23,337	1,599	561	634	19,096
Kenosha, WI PMSA	652	116,223	5,190	443	93	2,964	105	29	17	2,465
Killeen–Temple, TX MSA	6,685	167,589	48,270	1,189	330	13,555	1,417	216	516	15,534
Knoxville, TN MSA	4,451	559,221	36,262	1,469	181	2,314	138	36	89	655
Kokomo, IN MSA	493	90,618	4,375	233	49	792	33	13	15	325
La Crosse, WI MSA	2,545	93,954	405	332	28	365	33	8	122	112
Lafayette, LA MSA	1,873	151,896	51,095	418	343	2,250	283	22	42	518
Lafayette–West Lafayette, IN MSA	4,784	120,724	2,636	302	74	1,289	24	18	37	710
Lake Charles, LA MSA	568	126,922	38,265	362	170	1,259	180	25	22	361
Lake County, IL PMSA	12,135	430,566	33,736	1,009	402	20,100	1,035	189	453	16,793
Lakeland–Winter Haven, FL MSA	2,338	331,732	53,500	1,079	133	10,220	885	79	148	5,268
Lancaster, PA MSA	4,533	392,898	9,147	441	164	4,917	891	43	119	9,669
Lansing–East Lansing, MI MSA	8,155	373,823	30,801	2,435	497	7,548	564	220	165	8,466
Laredo, TX MSA	397	7,427	68	44	234	86,230	88	157	87	38,507
Las Cruces, NM MSA	1,013	55,158	1,968	805	118	68,276	204	204	151	7,613
Las Vegas, NV MSA	24,483	558,875	68,858	5,514	825	43,783	1,880	902	1,560	34,779
Lawrence, KS MSA	2,541	71,747	3,274	2,020	78	1,138	50	141	40	769
Lawrence–Haverhill, MA–NH PMSA	4,827	347,963	3,553	546	327	11,089	3,810	311	319	20,771
Lawton, OK MSA	2,879	77,187	19,547	4,812	138	2,479	361	341	186	3,556
Lewiston–Auburn, ME MSA	499	86,412	422	193	56	387	21	4	15	132
Lexington-Fayette, KY MSA	3,990	303,641	36,950	528	202	2,084	262	33	47	691
Lima, OH MSA	711	139,500	12,301	220	125	902	78	32	38	433
Lincoln, NE MSA	3,335	200,521	4,583	1,090	174	2,142	76	117	32	1,571
Little Rock–North Little Rock, AR MSA	3,262	402,107	101,622	1,809	153	2,701	240	61	85	1,077
Longview–Marshall, TX MSA	615	120,265	35,795	640	63	2,005	180	30	20	2,818
Lorain–Elyria, OH PMSA	1,435	232,874	20,696	680	180	8,675	534	58	44	5,950
Los Angeles–Long Beach, CA PMSA	907,810	3,618,850	934,776	29,159	21,327	1,416,253	58,198	16,349	46,675	1,813,767
Louisville, KY–IN MSA	5,468	815,167	124,220	1,531	511	3,731	541	45	172	1,276
Lowell, MA–NH PMSA	13,986	243,035	3,187	341	325	5,902	411	47	265	5,568
Lubbock, TX MSA	2,616	151,414	16,646	593	356	24,623	508	93	106	25,681
Lynchburg, VA MSA	722	110,302	29,948	268	36	545	131	9	21	217

[Continued]

★ 788 ★

Population of Metropolitan Statistical Areas by Hispanic Origin (Continued)

Population of U.S. Metropolitan Statistical Areas (MSAs) including Primary Metropolitan Statistical Areas (PMSAs)[a], by race/ethnicity and Hispanic origin[b], 1990.

Metropolitan area	Not of Hispanic Origin					Hispanic Origin				
	Asian or Pacific Islander	White	Black	American Indian, Eskimo,	Other Race	White	Black	American Indian, Eskimo	Asian or Pacific Islander	Other race
Macon–Warner Robins, GA MSA	1,878	178,832	96,934	550	77	1,551	360	21	63	837
Madison, WI MSA	8,546	341,057	10,303	1,122	313	3,560	208	79	120	1,777
Manchester, NH MSA	1,411	142,602	1,055	262	64	1,557	78	16	31	733
Mansfield, OH MSA	572	114,444	9,914	217	87	634	67	6	6	190
Mcallen–Edinburg–Mission, TX MSA	847	54,259	518	229	720	232,599	288	439	241	93,405
Medford, OR MSA	1,386	136,957	319	1,722	56	3,231	21	141	43	2,513
Melbourne–Titusville–Palm Bay, FL MSA	5,194	349,276	30,824	1,273	150	9,115	593	96	185	2,272
Memphis, TN–AR–MS MSA	7,931	566,163	397,630	1,735	302	4,348	1,381	56	247	1,954
Merced, CA MSA	14,109	96,701	7,889	1,135	462	23,579	634	381	1,019	32,494
Miami–Hialeah, FL PMSA	24,054	585,607	369,621	2,002	2,403	827,408	28,372	1,064	2,253	94,310
Middlesex–Somerset–Hunterdon, NJ PMSA	55,579	824,182	66,255	1,139	985	40,976	4,415	281	1,225	24,798
Middletown, CT PMSA	1,137	81,607	5,322	136	59	1,222	132	7	26	672
Midland, TX MSA	837	74,499	8,016	347	132	12,478	265	67	51	9,919
Milwaukee, WI PMSA	18,302	1,158,995	195,247	7,237	1,062	24,377	1,936	764	480	23,749
Minneapolis–St. Paul, MN–WI MSA	63,822	2,250,103	87,992	22,733	2,026	20,257	1,718	1,223	1,382	12,868
Mobile, AL MSA	3,535	336,460	130,101	2,516	125	2,958	411	54	84	679
Modesto, CA MSA	18,146	261,323	6,109	3,474	573	35,992	341	565	1,077	42,922
Monmouth–Ocean, NJ PMSA	18,571	872,480	57,088	1,220	611	23,506	2,176	107	527	10,041
Monroe, LA MSA	726	96,045	43,996	217	13	825	100	22	14	233
Montgomery, AL MSA	1,720	183,164	104,851	602	56	1,250	345	20	62	447
Muncie, IN MSA	617	110,733	7,113	253	90	499	54	21	24	255
Muskegon, MI MSA	536	132,045	21,444	1,236	99	1,886	173	102	19	1,443
Naples, FL MSA	496	124,700	5,770	353	46	14,373	1,216	75	88	4,982
Nashua, NH PMSA	2,443	172,725	1,715	279	122	2,126	195	18	16	918
Nashville, TN MSA	9,762	813,503	151,730	1,997	369	4,921	619	124	250	1,751
Nassau–Suffolk, NY PMSA	60,849	2,194,597	182,618	3,854	2,056	110,837	11,349	782	1,550	40,720
New Bedford, MA MSA	824	157,327	4,016	461	5,666	3,691	607	43	17	2,989
New Britain, CT PMSA	1,872	126,507	6,074	177	171	6,012	500	13	65	6,797
New Haven–Meriden, CT MSA	8,217	425,487	62,145	858	566	16,344	2,075	89	213	14,186
New London–Norwich, CT–RI MSA	3,302	241,788	11,540	1,344	328	4,145	537	89	247	3,499
New Orleans, LA MSA	20,265	734,347	426,712	3,331	935	36,059	3,758	284	1,115	12,010
New York, NY PMSA	532,716	4,095,765	1,986,472	19,544	22,687	730,316	263,554	10,167	23,683	861,942
Newark, NJ PMSA	51,280	1,171,053	408,130	2,619	2,940	108,899	14,672	525	1,618	62,585
Niagara Falls, NY PMSA	779	203,818	11,973	1,969	119	1,490	131	42	27	408
Norfolk–Virginia Beach–Newport News, VA MSA	32,993	931,178	394,269	4,342	996	15,982	3,824	337	2,212	9,974
Norwalk, CT PMSA	2,009	104,696	12,172	120	158	5,056	472	18	35	2,642
Oakland, CA PMSA	258,623	1,240,163	295,672	11,204	4,165	132,655	8,154	3,026	10,943	118,309
Ocala, FL MSA	896	162,861	24,542	616	58	4,233	302	22	49	1,254
Odessa, TX MSA	598	74,822	5,391	542	266	16,487	166	105	64	20,493
Oklahoma City, OK MSA	17,115	763,127	100,082	43,834	529	14,462	1,000	1,886	627	16,177
Olympia, WA MSA	5,799	145,367	2,761	2,314	124	2,854	103	184	302	1,430
Omaha, NE–IA MSA	6,107	541,533	50,875	2,914	462	9,225	551	245	267	6,083
Orange County, NY PMSA	3,448	260,968	20,731	702	263	12,632	1,492	122	101	7,188
Orlando, FL MSA	19,459	823,595	129,438	2,926	912	65,318	3,870	273	1,015	25,942
Owensboro, KY MSA	218	82,917	3,606	97	39	251	13	4	11	33
Oxnard–Ventura, CA PMSA	32,665	440,555	14,559	3,430	855	88,611	1,070	1,479	1,914	83,878
Panama City, FL MSA	2,165	108,004	13,612	903	54	1,566	101	46	64	479

[Continued]

★ 788 ★

Population of Metropolitan Statistical Areas by Hispanic Origin (Continued)

Population of U.S. Metropolitan Statistical Areas (MSAs) including Primary Metropolitan Statistical Areas (PMSAs)[a], by race/ethnicity and Hispanic origin[b], 1990.

Metropolitan area	Not of Hispanic Origin					Hispanic Origin				
	Asian or Pacific Islander	White	Black	American Indian, Eskimo,	Other Race	White	Black	American Indian, Eskimo	Asian or Pacific Islander	Other race
Parkersburg–Marietta, WV–OH MSA	517	146,309	1,559	238	67	389	8	4	3	75
Pascagoula, MS MSA	1,087	89,315	23,512	249	20	799	69	5	28	159
Pawtucket–Woonsocket–Attleboro, RI–MA PMSA	3,893	303,034	4,891	449	3,168	7,643	603	86	94	5,523
Pensacola, FL MSA	5,654	273,602	55,564	3,254	96	4,018	329	93	367	1,429
Peoria, IL MSA	2,711	307,065	24,990	563	201	2,260	152	24	48	1,158
Philadelphia, PA–NJ PMSA	101,933	3,656,130	913,437	7,544	3,857	61,045	16,470	791	2,662	93,012
Phoenix, AZ MSA	33,996	1,637,076	70,843	32,270	2,418	162,344	3,414	5,747	2,298	171,695
Pine Bluff, AR MSA	347	47,706	36,771	220	16	172	106	7	5	137
Pittsburgh, PA PMSA	15,616	1,858,577	167,284	1,895	1,605	8,561	1,098	159	181	1,729
Pittsfield, MA MSA	525	76,091	1,650	118	96	506	52	24	23	165
Portland, ME MSA	1,818	210,418	1,126	544	118	958	62	18	49	170
Portland, OR PMSA	45,299	1,101,442	37,852	10,277	923	23,521	843	1,030	1,061	17,594
Portsmouth–Dover–Rochester, NH–ME MSA	2,088	216,766	2,231	388	111	1,450	54	26	48	416
Poughkeepsie, NY MSA	5,761	222,791	20,558	337	250	6,403	1,230	37	65	2,030
Providence, RI PMSA	13,930	577,185	26,652	2,749	2,885	13,486	3,874	330	592	13,171
Provo–Orem, UT MSA	3,864	249,056	359	1,758	65	4,540	15	155	94	3,684
Pueblo, CO MSA	605	75,382	2,029	614	331	28,922	224	377	124	14,443
Racine, WI PMSA	964	147,745	16,693	456	142	4,353	306	65	40	4,270
Raleigh–Durham, NC MSA	13,671	527,982	182,588	1,866	354	5,074	859	67	163	2,856
Rapid City, SD MSA	884	71,882	1,249	5,518	33	887	39	317	49	485
Reading, PA MSA	2,334	307,387	9,214	265	149	7,174	789	68	412	8,731
Redding, CA MSA	2,610	134,001	1,045	3,646	82	3,976	36	308	74	1,258
Reno, NV MSA	9,270	212,416	5,414	4,380	228	12,679	266	541	554	8,919
Richland–Kennewick–Pasco, WA MSA	3,001	123,562	2,305	1,009	216	6,187	90	115	114	13,434
Richmond–Petersburg, VA MSA	11,566	590,648	251,055	2,630	414	5,066	1,285	75	298	2,603
Riverside–San Bernardino, CA PMSA	93,736	1,616,253	169,128	18,411	5,169	313,842	9,397	6,494	7,056	349,307
Roanoke, VA MSA	1,556	193,748	27,452	270	92	897	150	11	46	255
Rochester, MN MSA	3,157	101,255	767	280	41	625	21	15	80	229
Rochester, NY MSA	13,690	862,857	91,161	2,731	733	13,029	2,658	139	288	15,124
Rockford, IL MSA	3,046	246,824	23,174	649	190	4,959	209	48	90	4,530
Sacramento, CA MSA	109,539	1,084,411	98,511	14,029	2,238	86,094	3,429	2,992	4,981	74,878
Saginaw–Bay City–Midland, MI MSA	2,413	339,028	38,207	1,733	224	7,615	603	242	91	9,164
Salem, OR MSA	4,527	246,363	2,231	3,674	202	8,849	101	367	219	11,491
Salem–Gloucester, MA PMSA	2,304	254,346	1,782	249	169	3,050	666	56	43	1,691
Salinas–Seaside–Monterey, CA MSA	25,365	186,166	21,506	2,124	929	40,842	1,343	893	2,491	74,001
Salt Lake City–Ogden, UT MSA	24,919	967,447	9,801	7,408	688	32,635	663	929	679	27,058
San Angelo, TX MSA	951	67,642	3,955	280	129	11,891	181	93	47	13,289
San Antonio, TX MSA	14,380	576,836	85,228	2,785	2,580	401,669	3,550	1,863	1,678	211,530
San Diego, CA MSA	185,144	1,633,281	149,898	15,050	3,862	238,975	9,408	5,016	13,167	244,215
San Francisco, CA PMSA	320,309	923,914	117,872	5,645	2,664	134,882	4,622	1,587	9,290	82,893
San Jose, CA PMSA	251,496	869,874	52,583	6,694	2,366	162,316	3,628	2,575	9,970	136,075
Santa Barbara–Santa Maria–Lompoc, CA MSA	15,050	244,309	9,379	2,126	545	41,152	1,023	1,225	1,379	53,420
Santa Cruz, CA PMSA	7,690	171,203	2,330	1,310	404	21,646	302	511	822	23,516
Santa Fe, NM MSA	860	61,917	593	2,396	330	34,537	118	552	81	15,659

[Continued]

★ 788 ★

Population of Metropolitan Statistical Areas by Hispanic Origin (Continued)

Population of U.S. Metropolitan Statistical Areas (MSAs) including Primary Metropolitan Statistical Areas (PMSAs)[a], by race/ethnicity and Hispanic origin[b], 1990.

Metropolitan area	Not of Hispanic Origin					Hispanic Origin				
	Asian or Pacific Islander	White	Black	American Indian, Eskimo,	Other Race	White	Black	American Indian, Eskimo	Asian or Pacific Islander	Other race
Santa Rosa–Petaluma, CA PMSA	10,234	327,429	5,268	3,663	405	24,221	279	734	540	15,449
Sarasota, FL MSA	1,394	258,095	11,855	471	79	4,741	218	12	36	875
Savannah, GA MSA	2,332	150,939	85,780	491	129	1,574	448	24	80	825
Scranton–Wilkes-Barre, PA MSA	3,741	716,567	7,392	539	296	4,125	268	41	86	1,120
Seattle, WA PMSA	131,551	1,683,246	79,309	22,021	1,841	29,822	1,747	1,706	3,700	18,018
Sharon, PA MSA	381	114,086	5,858	108	64	393	24	7	12	70
Sheboygan, WI MSA	1,999	99,447	412	324	27	942	18	33	62	613
Sherman–Denison, TX MSA	391	84,271	6,511	1,012	41	1,282	54	34	21	1,404
Shreveport, LA MSA	1,962	210,697	116,402	790	96	2,913	490	75	61	855
Sioux City, IA–NE MSA	1,572	105,939	1,910	1,772	97	1,640	43	227	52	1,766
Sioux Falls, SD MSA	689	120,047	739	1,645	41	407	15	35	25	166
South Bend–Mishawaka, IN MSA	2,470	214,455	23,953	817	156	2,529	237	29	37	2,369
Spokane, WA MSA	6,352	337,561	4,972	5,216	269	4,313	133	323	217	2,008
Springfield, IL MSA	1,370	172,135	14,306	310	118	979	67	9	21	235
Springfield, MA MSA	5,173	442,444	32,852	741	674	15,305	2,229	123	224	29,754
Springfield, MO MSA	1,559	231,765	3,747	1,428	103	1,421	37	43	41	449
St. Cloud, MN MSA	1,140	187,486	731	610	44	594	7	27	31	251
St. Joseph, MO MSA	252	78,233	2,615	233	41	1,145	20	40	14	490
St. Louis, MO–IL MSA	23,141	1,967,424	421,594	4,625	1,301	18,076	1,588	322	545	5,483
Stamford, CT PMSA	5,406	163,347	19,701	151	220	8,487	1,066	52	164	3,963
State College, PA MSA	3,817	115,655	2,726	171	67	897	75	8	24	346
Steubenville–Weirton, OH–WV MSA	424	135,521	5,584	225	59	557	7	12	15	119
Stockton, CA MSA	55,774	282,766	24,791	3,807	817	70,403	2,303	1,278	3,916	34,773
Syracuse, NY MSA	7,565	600,795	38,206	3,829	543	5,129	889	119	175	2,614
Tacoma, WA PMSA	27,769	488,396	41,105	7,725	646	10,246	1,105	619	1,266	7,326
Tallahassee, FL MSA	2,710	154,753	69,811	535	110	3,645	416	33	78	1,507
Tampa–St. Petersburg–Clearwater, FL MSA	22,193	1,719,277	181,272	5,023	946	108,215	4,231	444	862	25,496
Terre Haute, IN MSA	1,170	122,286	5,905	317	71	647	124	21	6	265
Texarkana, TX–Texarkana, AR MSA	393	91,229	26,299	545	22	1,113	124	15	12	380
Toledo, OH MSA	6,018	516,853	69,090	1,268	517	9,702	627	155	128	9,770
Topeka, KS MSA	1,103	137,250	13,058	1,660	120	3,939	307	176	76	3,287
Trenton, NJ PMSA	9,736	236,143	59,449	467	364	8,513	2,032	66	256	8,798
Tucson, AZ MSA	11,228	454,919	19,455	17,005	1,011	70,057	1,340	3,325	736	87,804
Tulsa, OK MSA	6,375	582,825	57,651	47,275	294	7,787	535	921	188	5,103
Tuscaloosa, AL MSA	1,228	108,801	39,272	241	32	597	105	12	36	198
Tyler, TX MSA	623	109,853	31,289	478	80	3,823	283	42	15	4,823
Utica–Rome, NY MSA	2,227	294,607	12,820	568	237	3,139	1,029	45	87	1,874
Vallejo–Fairfield–Napa, CA PMSA	43,885	296,929	45,025	3,156	733	28,832	2,018	742	3,159	26,707
Vancouver, WA PMSA	5,478	221,552	2,873	2,129	149	3,640	103	167	192	1,770
Victoria, TX MSA	225	43,835	4,638	141	150	15,416	268	67	32	9,589
Vineland–Millville–Bridgeton, NJ PMSA	1,063	95,129	22,167	1,203	143	6,338	1,151	108	71	10,680
Visalia–Tulare–Porterville, CA MSA	12,468	170,283	4,305	3,228	744	34,552	313	764	851	84,413
Waco, TX MSA	1,323	134,507	29,036	472	142	11,593	484	91	61	11,414
Washington, DC–MD–VA MSA	197,871	2,459,133	1,027,022	9,994	4,768	118,800	14,912	1,042	4,566	85,466

[Continued]

★ 788 ★

Population of Metropolitan Statistical Areas by Hispanic Origin (Continued)

Population of U.S. Metropolitan Statistical Areas (MSAs) including Primary Metropolitan Statistical Areas (PMSAs)[a], by race/ethnicity and Hispanic origin[b], 1990.

Metropolitan area	Not of Hispanic Origin					Hispanic Origin				
	Asian or Pacific Islander	White	Black	American Indian, Eskimo,	Other Race	White	Black	American Indian, Eskimo	Asian or Pacific Islander	Other race
Waterbury, CT MSA	1,515	188,445	14,486	493	306	8,235	928	45	61	7,115
Waterloo–Cedar Falls, IA MSA	1,110	135,633	8,557	224	103	603	27	13	27	314
Wausau, WI MSA	2,429	111,927	87	477	10	262	2	13	70	123
West Palm Beach–Boca Raton– Delray Beach, FL MSA	8,692	683,402	103,309	1,028	474	48,829	4,396	183	328	12,877
Wheeling, WV–OH MSA	538	154,822	3,176	138	58	491	20	7	8	43
Wichita Falls, TX MSA	1,778	98,127	10,986	813	119	4,300	235	90	73	5,857
Wichita, KS MSA	8,881	415,165	36,401	4,773	257	8,619	578	387	228	9,981
Williamsport, PA MSA	454	114,593	2,779	211	32	447	37	8	15	134
Wilmington, DE–NJ–MD PMSA	7,602	471,204	84,479	1,052	375	6,039	1,162	76	135	6,463
Wilmington, NC MSA	612	94,288	23,983	426	51	607	114	9	4	190
Worcester, MA MSA	7,775	399,467	8,478	752	424	8,656	1,075	139	192	9,947
Yakima, WA MSA	1,667	132,147	1,785	7,695	415	7,367	153	710	255	36,629
York, PA MSA	2,416	396,984	11,419	466	182	2,710	492	35	55	3,089
Youngstown–Warren, OH MSA	1,922	427,941	54,349	737	270	4,083	553	48	36	2,680
Yuba City, CA MSA	10,373	89,064	3,328	2,356	202	5,998	150	260	623	10,289
Yuma, AZ MSA	1,188	58,151	2,776	1,178	214	22,551	280	251	205	20,101

Source: Asian/Pacific Islander Data Consortium (San Francisco, CA: Asian and Pacific Islander Center for Census Information and Services, 1993). Primary source: U.S. Census Bureau, Summary Tape Files 1 and 3. *Notes:* (a) The U.S. Census Bureau designates the following: CMSA=Consolidated Metropolitan Statistical Area; PMSA=Primary Metropolitan Statistical Area; MSA=Metropolitan Statistical Area. See *Appendix* for detailed definitions. (b) Hispanics may be of any race.

★789★

Population of Metropolitan Statistical Areas by Asian Ethnicity

Population of U.S. Metropolitan Statistical Areas (MSAs) including Primary Metropolitan Statistical Areas (PMSAs)[a], by Asian ethnicity, 1990.

Metropolitan area	Total, all racial/ ethnic groups	Chinese	Filipino	Japa-nese	Asian Indian	Korean	Viet- namese	Cam- bodian	Hmong	Laotian	Thai	Other Asian
Abilene, TX MSA	119,655	151	429	128	96	177	110	74	0	15	118	85
Akron, OH PMSA	657,575	1,428	544	457	1,395	787	231	43	208	465	110	429
Albany, GA MSA	112,561	89	89	60	112	53	22	0	0	7	12	31
Albany–Schenectady–Troy, NY MSA	874,304	3,097	864	586	2,801	1,853	510	46	0	14	92	806
Albuquerque, NM MSA	480,577	1,480	849	940	848	751	1,177	48	0	311	137	527
Alexandria, LA MSA	131,556	78	202	74	103	128	120	36	0	23	41	67
Allentown–Bethlehem–Easton, PA–NJ MSA	686,688	1,799	527	325	1,939	1,108	993	60	0	29	71	369
Altoona, PA MSA	130,542	54	40	32	97	85	18	0	0	0	9	36
Amarillo, TX MSA	187,547	184	83	79	292	72	986	1	0	1,232	64	197
Anaheim–Santa Ana, CA PMSA	2,410,556	41,403	30,356	29,704	15,212	35,919	71,822	3,979	575	2,893	2,227	6,613
Anchorage, AK MSA	226,338	783	3,199	1,352	265	3,064	255	38	0	200	245	312
Anderson, IN MSA	130,669	78	61	52	74	91	17	0	0	2	5	19
Anderson, SC MSA	145,196	66	21	30	101	60	26	0	0	0	16	12
Ann Arbor, MI PMSA	282,937	3,953	628	1,430	2,211	2,201	347	7	2	60	121	685
Anniston, AL MSA	116,034	49	73	85	62	332	41	5	0	1	46	72
Appleton–Oshkosh–Neenah, WI MSA	315,121	197	111	105	403	256	90	1	2,157	258	29	165
Asheville, NC MSA	174,821	143	83	108	124	142	26	31	0	1	27	58
Athens, GA MSA	156,267	773	215	174	386	533	37	11	1	35	29	133
Atlanta, GA MSA	2,833,511	9,549	2,566	3,901	9,955	10,120	5,729	2,043	299	2,898	987	2,825
Atlantic City, NJ MSA	319,416	1,288	1,010	176	835	661	761	27	0	133	70	355
Augusta, GA–SC MSA	396,809	719	552	418	1,173	1,442	327	19	0	45	132	346
Aurora–Elgin, IL PMSA	356,884	386	458	211	808	457	344	81	47	1,415	60	369
Austin, TX MSA	781,572	5,257	1,194	1,121	2,883	2,485	3,253	250	0	115	467	1,380
Bakersfield, CA MSA	543,477	1,892	8,194	901	1,413	1,156	628	324	7	317	233	742
Baltimore, MD MSA	2,382,172	7,904	6,061	2,020	7,737	12,967	1,725	186	1	157	752	2,507
Bangor, ME MSA	88,745	243	70	83	116	91	78	1	0	1	8	71
Baton Rouge, LA MSA	528,264	1,310	295	247	1,249	392	1,489	11	0	139	72	398
Battle Creek, MI MSA	135,982	105	121	384	164	163	15	0	0	7	10	70
Beaumont–Port Arthur, TX MSA	361,226	491	387	113	435	145	3,728	17	0	37	76	209
Beaver County, PA PMSA	186,093	70	58	23	65	84	12	0	0	0	8	35
Bellingham, WA MSA	127,780	320	303	418	176	312	406	142	0	6	25	106
Benton Harbor, MI MSA	161,378	202	268	139	271	347	40	7	0	37	25	110
Bergen–Passaic, NJ PMSA	1,278,440	10,391	10,027	10,482	15,095	17,018	458	16	0	72	473	2,508
Billings, MT MSA	113,419	124	56	158	33	101	21	2	18	40	5	10
Biloxi–Gulfport, MS MSA	197,125	157	739	164	161	240	2,782	6	0	2	66	88
Binghamton, NY MSA	264,497	1,091	306	155	783	509	308	3	0	503	54	261
Birmingham, AL MSA	907,810	1,086	296	261	974	562	298	29	0	2	85	347
Bismarck, ND MSA	83,831	31	45	18	52	41	31	5	0	15	5	21
Bloomington, IN MSA	108,978	888	168	301	339	514	61	6	0	3	46	357
Bloomington–Normal, IL MSA	129,180	372	141	352	308	170	74	1	0	19	60	89
Boise City, ID MSA	205,775	476	271	645	150	344	375	10	0	162	49	164
Boston, MA PMSA	2,870,669	44,155	3,987	6,530	12,301	7,001	9,403	4,967	3	882	948	4,185
Boulder–Longmont, CO PMSA	225,339	1,318	266	1,095	471	743	405	226	268	179	67	351
Bradenton, FL MSA	211,707	263	153	89	179	91	143	112	0	32	23	80
Brazoria, TX PMSA	191,707	260	345	116	247	140	506	143	0	3	37	122
Bremerton, WA MSA	189,731	417	4,179	1,005	76	587	293	24	1	7	50	211
Bridgeport–Milford, CT PMSA	443,722	1,157	394	228	1,528	527	696	443	1	936	109	510
Bristol, CT PMSA	79,488	131	80	24	126	52	27	46	0	16	4	33
Brockton, MA PMSA	189,478	564	298	60	337	193	231	75	48	107	29	184
Brownsville–Harlingen, TX MSA	260,120	121	204	109	78	73	29	1	0	9	6	87
Bryan–College Station, TX MSA	121,862	1,494	194	120	864	825	267	3	0	4	68	424
Buffalo, NY PMSA	968,532	2,616	619	610	2,745	1,661	700	101	1	315	79	687

[Continued]

Population of Metropolitan Statistical Areas by Asian Ethnicity (Continued)

Population of U.S. Metropolitan Statistical Areas (MSAs) including Primary Metropolitan Statistical Areas (PMSAs)[a], by Asian ethnicity, 1990.

Metropolitan area	Total, all racial/ ethnic groups	Chinese	Filipino	Japa-nese	Asian Indian	Korean	Viet-namese	Cam-bodian	Hmong	Laotian	Thai	Other Asian
Burlington, NC MSA	108,213	52	41	39	125	74	37	1	0	47	13	46
Burlington, VT MSA	131,439	331	78	146	310	230	170	33	2	36	27	85
Canton, OH MSA	394,106	278	244	136	400	272	30	1	1	13	31	105
Casper, WY MSA	61,226	48	38	34	22	25	38	5	0	15	9	28
Cedar Rapids, IA MSA	168,767	168	105	126	166	268	295	10	0	111	37	89
Champaign–Urbana–Rantoul, IL MSA	173,025	2,540	580	665	1,219	1,534	369	21	0	153	123	769
Charleston, SC MSA	506,875	543	3,501	418	400	341	305	6	0	1	107	213
Charleston, WV MSA	250,454	210	303	70	503	153	41	0	0	26	41	78
Charlotte–Gastonia–Rock Hill, NC–SC MSA	1,162,093	1,781	576	734	2,533	1,181	2,283	599	109	651	134	553
Charlottesville, VA MSA	131,107	721	239	223	517	429	198	5	0	5	28	222
Chattanooga, TN–GA MSA	433,210	501	328	181	779	369	174	166	0	84	52	137
Cheyenne, WY MSA	73,142	76	206	171	32	142	26	0	0	0	58	30
Chicago, IL PMSA	6,069,974	40,189	54,411	17,310	53,702	33,465	7,313	2,456	212	1,781	3,955	12,948
Chico, CA MSA	182,120	703	399	476	604	175	151	52	1,294	676	30	367
Cincinnati, OH–KY–IN PMSA	1,452,645	2,545	1,299	1,322	2,773	1,200	972	356	1	42	160	762
Clarksville–Hopkinsville, TN–KY MSA	169,439	89	341	219	125	1,186	83	4	0	9	50	188
Cleveland, OH PMSA	1,831,122	4,841	2,851	1,696	5,852	2,053	1,147	364	10	165	175	1,135
Colorado Springs, CO MSA	397,014	769	1,487	1,443	316	3,268	521	84	0	53	273	569
Columbia, MO MSA	112,379	1,133	205	188	490	472	113	210	1	6	82	204
Columbia, SC MSA	453,331	990	521	388	867	973	327	21	16	14	128	309
Columbus, GA–AL MSA	243,072	190	467	332	160	1,141	128	28	0	1	54	169
Columbus, OH MSA	1,377,419	4,936	1,363	3,201	3,710	2,391	1,149	1,239	10	1,154	442	1,230
Corpus Christi, TX MSA	349,894	274	1,060	163	411	178	141	16	0	29	44	221
Cumberland, MD–WV MSA	101,643	51	103	21	83	64	4	0	0	0	4	56
Dallas, TX PMSA	2,553,362	13,546	5,512	3,019	13,201	8,963	11,522	2,216	93	2,678	1,424	4,076
Danbury, CT PMSA	187,867	731	396	146	1,220	326	353	596	0	297	49	205
Danville, VA MSA	108,711	49	90	26	81	26	10	0	0	0	2	37
Davenport–Rock Island–Moline, IA–IL MSA	350,861	310	261	170	314	414	634	36	17	108	67	119
Dayton–Springfield, OH MSA	951,270	1,397	1,202	1,257	2,017	1,321	817	135	0	57	234	631
Daytona Beach, FL MSA	370,712	489	435	198	669	273	264	11	0	66	67	161
Decatur, AL MSA	131,556	46	59	42	149	37	19	2	0	5	11	16
Decatur, IL MSA	117,206	65	72	125	80	67	37	0	0	2	12	36
Denver, CO PMSA	1,622,980	5,304	2,998	6,790	2,534	6,330	5,870	933	931	1,713	724	1,886
Des Moines, IA MSA	392,928	549	360	205	777	677	890	304	137	1,555	411	269
Detroit, MI PMSA	4,382,299	9,580	9,747	6,048	16,298	6,992	1,757	274	1,503	882	572	3,488
Dothan, AL MSA	130,964	67	120	212	59	301	200	6	0	1	36	99
Dubuque, IA MSA	86,403	69	59	84	43	67	59	5	0	1	6	33
Duluth, MN–WI MSA	239,971	210	108	108	123	319	163	3	141	67	10	56
Eau Claire, WI MSA	137,543	127	78	85	142	125	47	1	1,601	51	12	107
El Paso, TX MSA	591,610	818	1,096	1,042	485	1,703	226	11	0	7	82	529
Elkhart–Goshen, IN MSA	156,198	161	51	90	204	141	71	75	0	84	13	82
Elmira, NY MSA	95,195	128	50	110	158	60	17	1	0	13	8	128
Enid, OK MSA	56,735	86	64	47	73	64	49	0	0	20	43	49
Erie, PA MSA	275,572	206	149	74	340	178	225	1	1	34	30	137
Eugene–Springfield, OR MSA	282,912	1,356	502	1,304	303	756	201	44	0	97	95	391
Evansville, IN–KY MSA	278,990	235	136	81	199	198	160	0	0	0	31	150
Fall River, MA–RI PMSA	157,272	259	129	67	61	84	48	743	0	52	7	75
Fargo–Moorhead, ND–MN MSA	153,296	306	83	75	233	217	237	27	0	25	28	146
Fayetteville, NC MSA	274,566	268	836	587	313	1,902	325	4	0	17	314	407
Fayetteville–Springdale, AR MSA	113,409	224	60	78	159	108	94	0	0	161	12	104
Fitchburg–Leominster, MA MSA	102,797	158	62	77	177	276	201	10	164	475	34	120

[Continued]

★ 789 ★

Population of Metropolitan Statistical Areas by Asian Ethnicity (Continued)

Population of U.S. Metropolitan Statistical Areas (MSAs) including Primary Metropolitan Statistical Areas (PMSAs)[a], by Asian ethnicity, 1990.

Metropolitan area	Total, all racial/ ethnic groups	Chinese	Filipino	Japa-nese	Asian Indian	Korean	Viet-namese	Cam-bodian	Hmong	Laotian	Thai	Other Asian
Flint, MI MSA	430,459	473	450	169	735	594	171	9	0	14	42	192
Florence, AL MSA	131,327	64	17	26	91	40	17	0	0	0	4	16
Florence, SC MSA	114,344	71	37	17	72	45	3	0	0	5	15	30
Fort Collins–Loveland, CO MSA	186,136	669	184	493	309	393	220	33	2	14	34	326
Fort Lauderdale–Hollywood– Pompano Beach, FL PMSA	1,255,488	4,739	1,787	643	5,737	1,065	1,190	32	0	24	340	1,200
Fort Myers–Cape CoraL, Fl MSA	335,113	352	367	129	382	171	109	5	0	112	71	122
Fort Pierce, FL MSA	251,071	291	315	96	452	132	32	24	0	1	23	85
Fort Smith, AR–OK MSA	175,911	147	153	91	112	77	1,386	1	4	1,554	25	156
Fort Walton Beach, FL MSA	143,776	227	985	358	109	647	262	1	0	13	537	313
Fort Wayne, IN MSA	363,811	343	262	155	642	276	382	49	10	270	50	250
Fort Worth–Arlington, TX PMSA	1,332,053	4,391	2,025	1,131	4,630	2,078	8,611	507	77	2,971	690	1,929
Fresno, CA MSA	667,490	4,793	4,312	6,722	5,216	986	2,008	3,812	18,321	8,174	387	1,786
Gadsden, AL MSA	99,840	61	29	191	36	23	21	0	0	0	17	37
Gainesville, FL MSA	204,111	1,514	473	232	928	630	404	18	0	12	76	316
Galveston–Texas City, TX PMSA	217,399	479	590	185	632	213	1,171	11	0	8	26	180
Gary–Hammond, IN PMSA	604,526	395	953	283	862	549	148	9	2	45	131	269
Glens Falls, NY MSA	118,539	64	52	30	70	119	12	0	0	0	4	30
Grand Forks, ND MSA	70,683	194	236	65	73	142	27	5	2	1	37	58
Grand Rapids, MI MSA	688,399	885	399	356	590	1,767	2,161	435	8	510	71	510
Great Falls, MT MSA	77,691	55	279	111	15	142	16	0	0	9	50	57
Greeley, CO MSA	131,821	132	64	515	33	158	22	14	0	21	36	48
Green Bay, WI MSA	194,594	119	78	75	196	113	76	1	1,410	295	27	100
Greensboro–Winston-Salem– High Point, NC MSA	942,091	900	335	572	1,170	806	951	634	0	347	142	420
Greenville–Spartanburg, SC MSA	640,861	718	359	324	1,419	336	446	162	59	451	40	217
Hagerstown, MD MSA	121,393	87	155	49	90	135	96	5	0	5	23	104
Hamilton–Middletown, OH PMSA	291,479	609	351	258	788	298	118	28	0	2	22	123
Harrisburg–Lebanon–Carlisle, PA MSA	587,986	678	439	320	1,174	1,000	1,533	460	0	118	69	369
Hartford, CT PMSA	767,841	2,358	856	527	3,294	1,311	1,571	254	43	717	97	1,045
Hickory–Morganton, NC MSA	221,700	150	56	39	280	91	153	3	433	355	6	72
Honolulu, HI MSA	836,231	63,265	120,029	195,149	864	22,646	5,231	113	4	1,638	1,065	3,345
Houma–Thibodaux, LA MSA	182,842	112	71	12	65	29	1,032	4	0	0	9	14
Houston, TX PMSA	3,301,937	29,345	13,404	3,690	25,720	7,070	33,035	2,294	1	1,451	1,281	8,238
Huntington–Ashland, WV–KY– OH MSA	312,529	121	183	65	272	131	25	0	0	21	15	67
Huntsville, AL MSA	238,912	903	258	330	1,132	944	204	28	0	53	72	176
Indianapolis, IN MSA	1,249,822	1,682	1,437	1,326	1,996	1,565	748	106	37	99	140	729
Iowa City, IA MSA	96,119	1,469	140	275	500	813	230	19	0	57	56	256
Jackson, MI MSA	149,756	60	72	155	112	114	48	5	0	0	7	62
Jackson, MS MSA	395,396	408	108	92	599	151	203	0	6	3	34	123
Jackson, TN MSA	77,982	51	29	38	52	23	30	2	0	0	2	23
Jacksonville, FL MSA	906,727	1,195	8,515	638	1,317	855	867	628	5	133	175	597
Jacksonville, NC MSA	149,838	136	1,205	579	77	234	80	1	0	3	97	150
Jamestown–Dunkirk, NY	141,895	57	56	22	134	131	22	19	0	30	7	44
Janesville–Beloit, WI MSA	139,510	114	118	77	91	111	172	149	5	57	21	48
Jersey City, NJ PMSA	553,099	5,002	13,222	532	11,552	2,803	1,107	4	0	30	190	2,122
Johnson City–Kingsport–Bristol, TN–VA MSA	436,047	294	158	106	282	148	78	0	0	27	26	97
Johnstown, PA MSA	241,247	51	68	43	167	85	41	0	0	0	6	44
Joliet, IL PMSA	389,650	536	1,433	222	1,286	408	147	169	5	264	72	306
Joplin, MO MSA	134,910	63	74	58	105	59	226	0	0	0	21	35
Kalamazoo, MI MSA	223,411	596	218	341	728	511	217	25	1	35	100	357

[Continued]

Population of Metropolitan Statistical Areas by Asian Ethnicity (Continued)

Population of U.S. Metropolitan Statistical Areas (MSAs) including Primary Metropolitan Statistical Areas (PMSAs)[a], by Asian ethnicity, 1990.

Metropolitan area	Total, all racial/ ethnic groups	Chinese	Filipino	Japa-nese	Asian Indian	Korean	Viet-namese	Cam-bodian	Hmong	Laotian	Thai	Other Asian
Kankakee, IL MSA	96,255	88	115	42	207	85	32	1	3	1	5	60
Kansas City, MO–KS MSA	1,566,280	2,661	2,205	1,202	2,431	2,426	2,035	313	583	918	378	1,030
Kenosha, WI PMSA	128,181	68	152	72	131	150	14	1	7	7	5	38
Killeen–Temple, TX MSA	255,301	306	1,094	518	296	3,019	300	1	0	4	199	352
Knoxville, TN MSA	604,816	1,221	385	569	1,167	530	208	21	5	7	60	291
Kokomo, IN MSA	96,946	97	73	47	93	100	24	0	0	0	13	33
La Crosse, WI MSA	97,904	91	42	41	128	140	34	7	1,933	85	9	128
Lafayette, LA MSA	208,740	351	62	52	321	117	652	5	0	40	53	231
Lafayette–West Lafayette, IN MSA	130,598	1,763	216	813	845	647	172	2	1	15	26	276
Lake Charles, LA MSA	168,134	114	103	32	115	51	56	5	0	26	20	44
Lake County, IL PMSA	516,418	1,941	4,053	1,108	2,257	1,923	262	140	1	23	152	503
Lakeland–Winter Haven, FL MSA	405,382	323	370	147	566	188	392	40	0	162	70	171
Lancaster, PA MSA	422,822	740	196	172	427	477	1,481	356	267	285	32	161
Lansing–East Lansing, MI MSA	432,674	1,983	528	553	1,239	1,419	896	25	480	280	112	643
Laredo, TX MSA	133,239	85	30	37	152	88	16	0	0	0	5	60
Las Cruces, NM MSA	135,510	258	139	156	155	129	28	0	0	1	31	192
Las Vegas, NV MSA	741,459	4,185	7,991	2,782	1,068	3,376	1,288	214	24	752	1,533	1,083
Lawrence, KS MSA	81,798	1,005	122	260	340	340	96	5	3	48	66	260
Lawrence–Haverhill, MA–NH PMSA	393,516	1,385	176	282	933	918	719	337	0	39	37	265
Lawton, OK MSA	111,486	128	435	290	91	1,281	135	51	8	3	83	109
Lewiston–Auburn, ME MSA	88,141	128	93	40	59	49	74	2	0	21	11	21
Lexington-Fayette, KY MSA	348,428	1,130	227	849	811	349	175	3	0	5	65	360
Lima, OH MSA	154,340	73	97	105	158	138	25	9	4	94	6	27
Lincoln, NE MSA	213,641	776	123	209	425	479	897	36	0	28	39	270
Little Rock–North Little Rock, AR MSA	513,117	534	785	335	487	349	268	13	18	133	118	202
Longview–Marshall, TX MSA	162,431	106	71	42	129	69	120	3	0	6	23	36
Lorain–Elyria, OH PMSA	271,126	244	355	178	290	233	33	2	0	0	15	97
Los Angeles–Long Beach, CA PMSA	8,863,164	245,033	219,653	129,736	43,829	145,431	62,594	27,819	359	3,742	19,016	28,349
Louisville, KY–IN MSA	952,662	889	783	511	949	906	809	117	0	92	109	290
Lowell, MA–NH PMSA	273,067	1,782	225	167	1,928	503	881	6,516	0	1,603	63	537
Lubbock, TX MSA	222,636	677	270	158	591	319	277	5	0	2	63	296
Lynchburg, VA MSA	142,199	148	104	57	111	115	97	0	0	3	17	60
Macon–Warner Robins, GA MSA	281,103	214	364	344	287	269	180	7	1	22	104	108
Madison, WI MSA	367,085	2,839	397	660	1,170	1,449	350	202	561	270	106	583
Manchester, NH MSA	147,809	395	144	92	218	281	47	28	0	23	35	137
Mansfield, OH MSA	126,137	42	55	77	128	174	42	0	0	0	8	23
Mcallen–Edinburg–Mission, TX MSA	383,545	204	168	117	212	150	23	1	0	5	11	159
Medford, OR MSA	146,389	240	246	314	70	210	51	7	0	2	53	84
Melbourne–Titusville–Palm Bay, FL MSA	398,978	828	1,058	493	1,059	601	474	33	0	11	272	358
Memphis, TN–AR–MS MSA	981,747	2,004	934	615	1,158	994	934	428	53	295	137	414
Merced, CA MSA	178,403	509	1,411	730	2,339	294	265	89	6,458	2,052	244	368
Miami–Hialeah, FL PMSA	1,937,094	8,847	3,846	1,310	6,147	1,403	1,014	70	1	108	593	2,530
Middlesex–Somerset–Hunter-don, NJ PMSA	1,019,835	14,883	8,137	1,235	22,972	5,117	1,326	25	25	52	213	2,684
Middletown, CT PMSA	90,320	276	86	75	283	158	52	65	0	42	11	97
Midland, TX MSA	106,611	201	84	31	226	88	91	36	0	8	11	84
Milwaukee, WI PMSA	1,432,149	2,897	1,695	951	3,247	1,718	1,131	94	3,404	2,033	183	1,092
Minneapolis–St. Paul, MN–WI MSA	2,464,124	7,475	3,259	2,816	7,249	8,721	7,819	2,657	16,435	5,039	398	2,616

[Continued]

★789★

Population of Metropolitan Statistical Areas by Asian Ethnicity (Continued)

Population of U.S. Metropolitan Statistical Areas (MSAs) including Primary Metropolitan Statistical Areas (PMSAs)[a], by Asian ethnicity, 1990.

Metropolitan area	Total, all racial/ ethnic groups	Chinese	Filipino	Japa-nese	Asian Indian	Korean	Viet-namese	Cam-bodian	Hmong	Laotian	Thai	Other Asian
Mobile, AL MSA	476,923	407	305	210	381	167	1,221	326	0	235	42	257
Modesto, CA MSA	370,522	1,651	2,376	820	3,817	507	1,228	3,691	959	2,415	75	533
Monmouth–Ocean, NJ PMSA	986,327	6,141	3,669	631	4,424	2,245	566	25	0	11	119	1,086
Monroe, LA MSA	142,191	211	58	27	110	30	220	1	0	0	14	51
Montgomery, AL MSA	292,517	227	246	194	302	257	80	0	0	207	121	101
Muncie, IN MSA	119,659	165	74	46	101	102	32	1	1	3	21	69
Muskegon, MI MSA	158,983	53	73	47	67	171	67	0	0	7	16	43
Naples, FL MSA	152,099	180	76	32	95	36	43	0	0	0	27	44
Nashua, NH PMSA	180,557	661	180	166	719	288	208	29	0	18	39	122
Nashville, TN MSA	985,026	1,197	635	1,130	1,696	1,150	464	332	11	2,337	218	673
Nassau–Suffolk, NY PMSA	2,609,212	18,257	7,356	4,042	17,523	9,024	1,245	58	0	106	708	3,731
New Bedford, MA MSA	175,641	296	76	69	70	118	83	3	1	8	29	57
New Britain, CT PMSA	148,188	320	95	74	418	156	206	83	1	411	13	124
New Haven–Meriden, CT MSA	530,180	2,496	714	618	1,773	1,083	439	136	0	118	99	866
New London–Norwich, CT–RI MSA	266,819	717	1,319	253	493	226	119	57	0	83	35	123
New Orleans, LA MSA	1,238,816	2,549	2,090	657	2,331	875	11,419	116	1	134	180	760
New York, NY PMSA	8,546,846	246,817	49,156	26,422	106,270	74,632	9,044	2,727	8	454	4,684	33,229
Newark, NJ PMSA	1,824,321	14,020	10,907	1,999	15,842	5,258	1,529	76	0	57	354	2,497
Niagara Falls, NY PMSA	220,756	92	109	49	211	184	42	0	0	9	15	64
Norfolk–Virginia Beach–Newport News, VA MSA	1,396,107	2,924	19,858	1,876	1,899	3,231	1,984	424	1	142	486	1,179
Norwalk, CT PMSA	127,378	592	234	151	628	183	49	0	0	18	39	144
Oakland, CA PMSA	2,082,914	90,691	77,198	21,477	21,633	13,478	16,732	3,791	38	5,964	1,183	6,817
Ocala, FL MSA	194,833	127	136	60	318	149	71	0	0	0	20	38
Odessa, TX MSA	118,934	89	141	25	139	35	106	13	0	0	20	76
Oklahoma City, OK MSA	958,839	2,742	1,313	1,154	2,467	1,823	5,273	184	0	616	512	1,144
Olympia, WA MSA	161,238	398	939	676	195	1,338	981	606	0	109	66	237
Omaha, NE–IA MSA	618,262	803	1,042	933	604	1,087	648	56	77	119	219	484
Orange County, NY PMSA	307,647	820	504	229	890	589	126	7	1	22	49	252
Orlando, FL MSA	1,072,748	3,345	3,602	997	4,906	1,701	3,324	106	0	296	403	1,106
Owensboro, KY MSA	87,189	37	25	21	80	37	14	0	0	0	1	9
Oxnard–Ventura, CA PMSA	669,016	4,986	12,690	4,964	2,355	2,921	2,486	175	32	178	474	1,438
Panama City, FL MSA	126,994	153	426	189	143	246	659	0	0	0	185	155
Parkersburg–Marietta, WV–OH MSA	149,169	95	78	73	120	84	15	0	0	0	7	34
Pascagoula, MS MSA	115,243	76	118	52	60	120	582	0	0	0	24	48
Pawtucket–Woonsocket–Attleboro, RI–MA PMSA	329,384	488	259	93	659	243	352	622	6	876	49	272
Pensacola, FL MSA	344,406	464	2,636	432	218	265	1,396	89	0	23	79	150
Peoria, IL MSA	339,172	545	283	200	561	392	422	13	0	56	39	201
Philadelphia, PA–NJ PMSA	4,856,881	22,311	12,233	4,304	20,657	22,028	10,418	4,633	71	1,268	793	4,821
Phoenix, AZ MSA	2,122,101	9,626	5,074	3,848	4,058	3,501	3,717	728	9	538	831	2,174
Pine Bluff, AR MSA	85,487	86	33	56	75	43	10	0	0	0	10	29
Pittsburgh, PA PMSA	2,056,705	4,126	1,254	1,238	4,553	2,083	872	91	16	39	248	1,037
Pittsfield, MA MSA	79,250	143	23	37	130	83	42	27	0	0	14	38
Portland, ME MSA	215,281	294	284	127	153	214	241	361	0	60	17	90
Portland, OR PMSA	1,239,842	9,143	4,849	6,832	2,307	5,871	7,555	1,608	379	2,901	457	1,866
Portsmouth–Dover–Rochester, NH–ME MSA	223,578	397	273	171	198	275	114	108	0	274	103	142
Poughkeepsie, NY MSA	259,462	1,888	326	338	1,985	549	345	12	0	24	33	293
Providence, RI PMSA	654,854	2,582	1,117	581	1,586	1,053	497	3,540	878	1,700	97	700
Provo–Orem, UT MSA	263,590	819	215	751	120	396	156	50	8	123	40	126
Pueblo, CO MSA	123,051	124	109	166	77	78	19	0	1	1	7	96
Racine, WI PMSA	175,034	142	92	65	254	207	83	2	0	41	11	89
Raleigh–Durham, NC MSA	735,480	4,331	716	1,295	3,327	1,778	1,078	65	6	192	140	777

[Continued]

Population of Metropolitan Statistical Areas by Asian Ethnicity (Continued)

Population of U.S. Metropolitan Statistical Areas (MSAs) including Primary Metropolitan Statistical Areas (PMSAs)[a], by Asian ethnicity, 1990.

Metropolitan area	Total, all racial/ ethnic groups	Chinese	Filipino	Japa-nese	Asian Indian	Korean	Viet-namese	Cam-bodian	Hmong	Laotian	Thai	Other Asian
Rapid City, SD MSA	81,343	102	244	94	67	156	46	0	0	5	79	69
Reading, PA MSA	336,523	386	581	152	490	330	541	12	1	77	32	109
Redding, CA MSA	147,036	220	201	205	112	104	40	81	167	1,275	43	104
Reno, NV MSA	254,667	2,121	3,296	945	606	761	561	30	0	6	244	367
Richland–Kennewick–Pasco, WA MSA	150,033	421	369	357	284	316	299	49	26	666	58	159
Richmond–Petersburg, VA MSA	865,640	2,034	1,075	587	1,893	2,286	1,695	1,147	0	141	136	647
Riverside–San Bernardino, CA PMSA	2,588,793	13,166	28,919	8,966	7,491	10,166	11,315	2,444	591	1,956	2,474	5,985
Roanoke, VA MSA	224,477	263	254	131	255	210	247	17	0	96	27	79
Rochester, MN MSA	106,470	487	153	203	287	273	443	873	119	261	18	103
Rochester, NY MSA	1,002,410	3,179	648	751	2,980	2,245	1,520	362	1	1,313	112	727
Rockford, IL MSA	283,719	398	304	181	484	439	193	4	18	843	77	159
Sacramento, CA MSA	1,481,102	29,558	20,359	17,067	7,296	5,468	10,454	908	5,673	7,861	824	3,774
Saginaw–Bay City–Midland, MI MSA	399,320	459	293	167	568	431	71	7	207	99	33	132
Salem, OR MSA	278,024	636	664	834	180	428	694	223	58	183	46	234
Salem–Gloucester, MA PMSA	264,356	627	211	278	331	371	237	64	0	21	41	100
Salinas–Seaside–Monterey, CA MSA	355,660	2,165	11,421	4,196	788	3,734	2,052	6	0	20	235	752
Salt Lake City–Ogden, UT MSA	1,072,227	3,831	1,509	4,865	1,172	1,841	2,400	753	73	1,550	492	1,102
San Angelo, TX MSA	98,458	102	184	65	86	201	118	0	0	68	65	66
San Antonio, TX MSA	1,302,099	2,613	3,216	1,634	1,594	2,442	1,757	147	5	236	656	1,002
San Diego, CA MSA	2,498,016	19,686	95,945	17,869	5,039	6,722	21,118	4,185	1,585	7,025	1,109	4,313
San Francisco, CA PMSA	1,603,678	162,636	88,560	23,682	8,531	10,416	12,451	1,639	8	1,118	1,394	6,316
San Jose, CA PMSA	1,497,577	65,027	61,518	26,516	20,164	15,565	54,212	3,948	47	1,625	885	5,279
Santa Barbara–Santa Maria– Lompoc, CA MSA	369,608	2,535	5,483	2,947	732	1,358	902	44	651	429	188	516
Santa Cruz, CA PMSA	229,734	1,633	2,398	2,310	417	586	247	84	8	15	60	405
Santa Fe, NM MSA	117,043	304	81	206	87	91	38	5	0	1	9	64
Santa Rosa–Petaluma, CA PMSA	388,222	2,169	1,839	1,709	652	740	752	557	53	834	81	545
Sarasota, FL MSA	277,776	271	205	111	184	152	234	34	0	56	58	81
Savannah, GA MSA	242,622	409	304	132	312	368	592	1	0	37	28	113
Scranton–Wilkes-Barre, PA MSA	734,175	633	375	255	1,070	657	282	9	0	180	41	245
Seattle, WA PMSA	1,972,961	27,490	27,900	22,835	5,914	16,311	12,617	5,800	447	4,270	1,323	3,749
Sharon, PA MSA	121,003	74	51	43	82	77	17	1	0	2	3	30
Sheboygan, WI MSA	103,877	37	101	16	313	70	31	27	1,255	109	1	79
Sherman–Denison, TX MSA	95,021	71	61	35	95	47	31	1	0	6	8	30
Shreveport, LA MSA	334,341	290	328	166	257	266	229	51	0	28	181	129
Sioux City, IA–NE MSA	115,018	122	82	50	81	118	432	123	18	477	24	86
Sioux Falls, SD MSA	123,809	97	58	62	42	116	101	52	24	96	8	17
South Bend–Mishawaka, IN MSA	247,052	587	234	247	535	310	201	110	1	47	32	131
Spokane, WA MSA	361,364	824	750	1,744	264	811	695	55	252	194	185	313
Springfield, IL MSA	189,550	241	145	74	491	173	89	11	0	19	36	92
Springfield, MA MSA	529,519	1,150	362	386	926	766	717	401	20	135	55	388
Springfield, MO MSA	240,593	323	195	124	115	303	309	39	0	36	17	64
St. Cloud, MN MSA	190,921	120	134	54	96	256	158	46	21	135	25	107
St. Joseph, MO MSA	83,083	44	49	26	63	40	6	1	0	0	4	14
St. Louis, MO–IL MSA	2,444,099	5,467	3,373	2,037	4,160	3,120	2,206	85	1	421	641	1,727
Stamford, CT PMSA	202,557	1,390	580	1,511	1,066	374	229	1	0	9	18	322
State College, PA MSA	123,786	1,494	186	256	753	733	109	5	0	4	34	233
Steubenville–Weirton, OH–WV MSA	142,523	44	169	42	70	52	18	0	0	0	19	18
Stockton, CA MSA	480,628	5,523	16,570	3,763	3,395	653	6,958	10,350	4,628	4,236	133	2,165
Syracuse, NY MSA	659,864	1,747	684	413	1,653	1,276	755	146	150	158	81	548

[Continued]

★789★

Population of Metropolitan Statistical Areas by Asian Ethnicity (Continued)

Population of U.S. Metropolitan Statistical Areas (MSAs) including Primary Metropolitan Statistical Areas (PMSAs)[a], by Asian ethnicity, 1990.

Metropolitan area	Total, all racial/ ethnic groups	Chinese	Filipino	Japa-nese	Asian Indian	Korean	Viet- namese	Cam- bodian	Hmong	Laotian	Thai	Other Asian
Tacoma, WA PMSA	586,203	1,301	4,763	3,966	476	7,590	1,883	3,408	11	377	416	1,040
Tallahassee, FL MSA	233,598	798	325	174	595	332	224	6	0	1	46	225
Tampa–St. Petersburg–Clearwa- ter, FL MSA	2,067,959	3,317	3,610	1,379	4,004	2,600	3,939	364	0	1,187	923	1,101
Terre Haute, IN MSA	130,812	302	128	104	238	122	49	3	0	0	16	197
Texarkana, TX–Texarkana, AR MSA	120,132	33	48	40	74	47	97	0	0	0	3	45
Toledo, OH MSA	614,128	1,676	642	367	1,345	760	271	9	19	256	118	631
Topeka, KS MSA	160,976	276	166	106	212	177	76	0	0	0	31	91
Trenton, NJ PMSA	325,824	3,025	816	465	3,247	1,339	141	36	0	7	40	746
Tucson, AZ MSA	666,880	3,472	1,451	1,460	1,041	1,246	1,216	55	0	297	362	817
Tulsa, OK MSA	708,954	1,168	530	440	1,087	779	1,247	64	199	165	115	540
Tuscaloosa, AL MSA	150,522	318	92	166	314	192	26	0	0	0	13	131
Tyler, TX MSA	151,309	123	151	44	112	56	59	17	0	1	9	37
Utica–Rome, NY MSA	316,633	320	261	161	386	319	388	43	3	68	104	181
Vallejo–Fairfield–Napa, CA PMSA	451,186	3,743	29,760	3,075	2,007	1,492	976	35	78	601	403	1,119
Vancouver, WA PMSA	238,053	719	808	682	252	903	792	413	0	160	77	242
Victoria, TX MSA	74,361	35	43	18	72	17	38	0	0	0	4	26
Vineland–Millville–Bridgeton, NJ PMSA	138,053	116	220	331	194	97	25	0	0	4	9	114
Visalia–Tulare–Porterville, CA MSA	311,921	1,020	4,164	1,040	873	290	164	64	1,874	3,033	54	437
Waco, TX MSA	189,123	295	195	110	228	187	205	0	0	1	20	100
Washington, DC–MD–VA MSA	3,923,574	39,034	26,793	9,796	35,533	39,850	23,408	3,882	6	2,603	4,381	14,827
Waterbury, CT MSA	221,629	307	218	59	461	137	180	34	0	39	12	115
Waterloo–Cedar Falls, IA MSA	146,611	216	74	148	199	246	78	3	0	58	6	80
Wausau, WI MSA	115,400	60	37	20	97	99	30	15	1,968	115	8	40
West Palm Beach–Boca Raton– Delray Beach, FL MSA	863,518	2,398	1,073	364	2,395	441	1,019	9	0	110	315	684
Wheeling, WV–OH MSA	159,301	63	140	71	139	48	19	0	0	0	8	36
Wichita Falls, TX MSA	122,378	175	268	121	125	211	725	1	0	1	55	90
Wichita, KS MSA	485,270	1,122	639	424	803	477	3,721	290	28	703	166	574
Williamsport, PA MSA	118,710	56	92	23	102	133	18	0	0	0	2	36
Wilmington, DE–NJ–MD PMSA	578,587	2,083	988	549	2,022	1,104	300	6	0	72	60	455
Wilmington, NC MSA	120,284	122	87	74	134	62	29	0	0	3	16	44
Worcester, MA MSA	436,905	1,429	265	360	1,675	642	2,600	183	12	292	116	324
Yakima, WA MSA	188,823	241	726	330	46	196	93	15	0	60	24	94
York, PA MSA	417,848	248	251	162	435	553	367	109	0	95	30	152
Youngstown–Warren, OH MSA	492,619	307	253	156	575	321	67	0	0	1	55	173
Yuba City, CA MSA	122,643	422	892	845	4,607	269	85	14	2,299	702	127	443
Yuma, AZ MSA	106,895	186	536	226	66	92	42	0	0	6	29	73

Source: Asian/Pacific Islander Data Consortium (San Francisco, CA: Asian and Pacific Islander Center for Census Information and Services, 1993). Primary source: U.S. Census Bureau, Summary Tape Files 1 and 3. *Note:* (a) The U.S. Census Bureau designates the following: CMSA=Consolidated Metropolitan Statistical Area; PMSA=Primary Metropolitan Statistical Area; MSA=Metropolitan Statistical Area. See *Appendix* for detailed definitions.

★ 790 ★

Population of Metropolitan Statistical Areas by Asian Ethnicity, in Percent

Population in U.S. Metropolitan Statistical Areas (MSAs) including Primary Metropolitan Statistical Areas (PMSAs)[a], in percent, by Asian ethnicity, 1990.

Metropolitan area	Population		Percent										
	Total, all groups	Total Asian	Chinese	Filipino	Japanese	Asian Indian	Korean	Viet-namese	Cam-bodian	Hmong	Laotian	Thai	Other Asian
Abilene, TX MSA	119,655	1,383	0.13	0.36	0.11	0.08	0.15	0.09	0.06	0.00	0.01	0.10	0.07
Akron, OH PMSA	657,575	6,097	0.22	0.08	0.07	0.21	0.12	0.04	0.01	0.03	0.07	0.02	0.07
Albany, GA MSA	112,561	475	0.08	0.08	0.05	0.10	0.05	0.02	0.00	0.00	0.01	0.01	0.03
Albany–Schenectady– Troy, NY MSA	874,304	10,669	0.35	0.10	0.07	0.32	0.21	0.06	0.01	0.00	0.00	0.01	0.09
Albuquerque, NM MSA	480,577	7,068	0.31	0.18	0.20	0.18	0.16	0.24	0.01	0.00	0.06	0.03	0.11
Alexandria, LA MSA	131,556	872	0.06	0.15	0.06	0.08	0.10	0.09	0.03	0.00	0.02	0.03	0.05
Allentown–Bethlehem– Easton, PA–NJ MSA	686,688	7,220	0.26	0.08	0.05	0.28	0.16	0.14	0.01	0.00	0.00	0.01	0.05
Altoona, PA MSA	130,542	371	0.04	0.03	0.02	0.07	0.07	0.01	0.00	0.00	0.00	0.01	0.03
Amarillo, TX MSA	187,547	3,190	0.10	0.04	0.04	0.16	0.04	0.53	0.00	0.00	0.66	0.03	0.11
Anaheim–Santa Ana, CA PMSA	2,410,556	240,703	1.72	1.26	1.23	0.63	1.49	2.98	0.17	0.02	0.12	0.09	0.27
Anchorage, AK MSA	226,338	9,713	0.35	1.41	0.60	0.12	1.35	0.11	0.02	0.00	0.09	0.11	0.14
Anderson, IN MSA	130,669	399	0.06	0.05	0.04	0.06	0.07	0.01	0.00	0.00	0.00	0.00	0.01
Anderson, SC MSA	145,196	332	0.05	0.01	0.02	0.07	0.04	0.02	0.00	0.00	0.00	0.01	0.01
Ann Arbor, MI PMSA	282,937	11,645	1.40	0.22	0.51	0.78	0.78	0.12	0.00	0.00	0.02	0.04	0.24
Anniston, AL MSA	116,034	766	0.04	0.06	0.07	0.05	0.29	0.04	0.00	0.00	0.00	0.04	0.06
Appleton–Oshkosh– Neenah, WI MSA	315,121	3,772	0.06	0.04	0.03	0.13	0.08	0.03	0.00	0.68	0.08	0.01	0.05
Asheville, NC MSA	174,821	743	0.08	0.05	0.06	0.07	0.08	0.01	0.02	0.00	0.00	0.02	0.03
Athens, GA MSA	156,267	2,327	0.49	0.14	0.11	0.25	0.34	0.02	0.01	0.00	0.02	0.02	0.09
Atlanta, GA MSA	2,833,511	50,872	0.34	0.09	0.14	0.35	0.36	0.20	0.07	0.01	0.10	0.03	0.10
Atlantic City, NJ MSA	319,416	5,316	0.40	0.32	0.06	0.26	0.21	0.24	0.01	0.00	0.04	0.02	0.11
Augusta, GA–SC MSA	396,809	5,173	0.18	0.14	0.11	0.30	0.36	0.08	0.00	0.00	0.01	0.03	0.09
Aurora–Elgin, IL PMSA	356,884	4,636	0.11	0.13	0.06	0.23	0.13	0.10	0.02	0.01	0.40	0.02	0.10
Austin, TX MSA	781,572	18,405	0.67	0.15	0.14	0.37	0.32	0.42	0.03	0.00	0.01	0.06	0.18
Bakersfield, CA MSA	543,477	15,807	0.35	1.51	0.17	0.26	0.21	0.12	0.06	0.00	0.06	0.04	0.14
Baltimore, MD MSA	2,382,172	42,017	0.33	0.25	0.08	0.32	0.54	0.07	0.01	0.00	0.01	0.03	0.11
Bangor, ME MSA	88,745	762	0.27	0.08	0.09	0.13	0.10	0.09	0.00	0.00	0.00	0.01	0.08
Baton Rouge, LA MSA	528,264	5,602	0.25	0.06	0.05	0.24	0.07	0.28	0.00	0.00	0.03	0.01	0.08
Battle Creek, MI MSA	135,982	1,039	0.08	0.09	0.28	0.12	0.12	0.01	0.00	0.00	0.01	0.01	0.05
Beaumont–Port Arthur, TX MSA	361,226	5,638	0.14	0.11	0.03	0.12	0.04	1.03	0.00	0.00	0.01	0.02	0.06
Beaver County, PA PMSA	186,093	355	0.04	0.03	0.01	0.03	0.05	0.01	0.00	0.00	0.00	0.00	0.02
Bellingham, WA MSA	127,780	2,214	0.25	0.24	0.33	0.14	0.24	0.32	0.11	0.00	0.00	0.02	0.08
Benton Harbor, MI MSA	161,378	1,446	0.13	0.17	0.09	0.17	0.22	0.02	0.00	0.00	0.02	0.02	0.07
Bergen–Passaic, NJ PMSA	1,278,440	66,540	0.81	0.78	0.82	1.18	1.33	0.04	0.00	0.00	0.01	0.04	0.20
Billings, MT MSA	113,419	568	0.11	0.05	0.14	0.03	0.09	0.02	0.00	0.02	0.04	0.00	0.01
Biloxi–Gulfport, MS MSA	197,125	4,405	0.08	0.37	0.08	0.08	0.12	1.41	0.00	0.00	0.00	0.03	0.04
Binghamton, NY MSA	264,497	3,973	0.41	0.12	0.06	0.30	0.19	0.12	0.00	0.00	0.19	0.02	0.10
Birmingham, AL MSA	907,810	3,940	0.12	0.03	0.03	0.11	0.06	0.03	0.00	0.00	0.00	0.01	0.04
Bismarck, ND MSA	83,831	264	0.04	0.05	0.02	0.06	0.05	0.04	0.01	0.00	0.02	0.01	0.03
Bloomington, IN MSA	108,978	2,683	0.81	0.15	0.28	0.31	0.47	0.06	0.01	0.00	0.00	0.04	0.33
Bloomington–Normal, IL MSA	129,180	1,586	0.29	0.11	0.27	0.24	0.13	0.06	0.00	0.00	0.01	0.05	0.07
Boise City, ID MSA	205,775	2,646	0.23	0.13	0.31	0.07	0.17	0.18	0.00	0.00	0.08	0.02	0.08
Boston, MA PMSA	2,870,669	94,362	1.54	0.14	0.23	0.43	0.24	0.33	0.17	0.00	0.03	0.03	0.15
Boulder–Longmont, CO PMSA	225,339	5,389	0.58	0.12	0.49	0.21	0.33	0.18	0.10	0.12	0.08	0.03	0.16
Bradenton, FL MSA	211,707	1,165	0.12	0.07	0.04	0.08	0.04	0.07	0.05	0.00	0.02	0.01	0.04
Brazoria, TX PMSA	191,707	1,919	0.14	0.18	0.06	0.13	0.07	0.26	0.07	0.00	0.00	0.02	0.06

[Continued]

★ 790 ★

Population of Metropolitan Statistical Areas by Asian Ethnicity, in Percent (Continued)

Population in U.S. Metropolitan Statistical Areas (MSAs) including Primary Metropolitan Statistical Areas (PMSAs)[a], in percent, by Asian ethnicity, 1990.

Metropolitan area	Population		Percent										
	Total, all groups	Total Asian	Chinese	Filipino	Japanese	Asian Indian	Korean	Viet-namese	Cam-bodian	Hmong	Laotian	Thai	Other Asian
Bremerton, WA MSA	189,731	6,850	0.22	2.20	0.53	0.04	0.31	0.15	0.01	0.00	0.00	0.03	0.11
Bridgeport–Milford, CT PMSA	443,722	6,529	0.26	0.09	0.05	0.34	0.12	0.16	0.10	0.00	0.21	0.02	0.11
Bristol, CT PMSA	79,488	539	0.16	0.10	0.03	0.16	0.07	0.03	0.06	0.00	0.02	0.01	0.04
Brockton, MA PMSA	189,478	2,126	0.30	0.16	0.03	0.18	0.10	0.12	0.04	0.03	0.06	0.02	0.10
Brownsville–Harlingen, TX MSA	260,120	717	0.05	0.08	0.04	0.03	0.03	0.01	0.00	0.00	0.00	0.00	0.03
Bryan–College Station, TX MSA	121,862	4,263	1.23	0.16	0.10	0.71	0.68	0.22	0.00	0.00	0.00	0.06	0.35
Buffalo, NY PMSA	968,532	10,134	0.27	0.06	0.06	0.28	0.17	0.07	0.01	0.00	0.03	0.01	0.07
Burlington, NC MSA	108,213	475	0.05	0.04	0.04	0.12	0.07	0.03	0.00	0.00	0.04	0.01	0.04
Burlington, VT MSA	131,439	1,448	0.25	0.06	0.11	0.24	0.17	0.13	0.03	0.00	0.03	0.02	0.06
Canton, OH MSA	394,106	1,511	0.07	0.06	0.03	0.10	0.07	0.01	0.00	0.00	0.00	0.01	0.03
Casper, WY MSA	61,226	262	0.08	0.06	0.06	0.04	0.04	0.06	0.01	0.00	0.02	0.01	0.05
Cedar Rapids, IA MSA	168,767	1,375	0.10	0.06	0.07	0.10	0.16	0.17	0.01	0.00	0.07	0.02	0.05
Champaign–Urbana–Rantoul, IL MSA	173,025	7,973	1.47	0.34	0.38	0.70	0.89	0.21	0.01	0.00	0.09	0.07	0.44
Charleston, SC MSA	506,875	5,835	0.11	0.69	0.08	0.08	0.07	0.06	0.00	0.00	0.00	0.02	0.04
Charleston, WV MSA	250,454	1,425	0.08	0.12	0.03	0.20	0.06	0.02	0.00	0.00	0.01	0.02	0.03
Charlotte–Gastonia–Rock Hill, NC–SC MSA	1,162,093	11,134	0.15	0.05	0.06	0.22	0.10	0.20	0.05	0.01	0.06	0.01	0.05
Charlottesville, VA MSA	131,107	2,587	0.55	0.18	0.17	0.39	0.33	0.15	0.00	0.00	0.00	0.02	0.17
Chattanooga, TN–GA MSA	433,210	2,771	0.12	0.08	0.04	0.18	0.09	0.04	0.04	0.00	0.02	0.01	0.03
Cheyenne, WY MSA	73,142	741	0.10	0.28	0.23	0.04	0.19	0.04	0.00	0.00	0.00	0.08	0.04
Chicago, IL PMSA	6,069,974	227,742	0.66	0.90	0.29	0.88	0.55	0.12	0.04	0.00	0.03	0.07	0.21
Chico, CA MSA	182,120	4,927	0.39	0.22	0.26	0.33	0.10	0.08	0.03	0.71	0.37	0.02	0.20
Cincinnati, OH–KY–IN PMSA	1,452,645	11,432	0.18	0.09	0.09	0.19	0.08	0.07	0.02	0.00	0.00	0.01	0.05
Clarksville–Hopkins-ville, TN–KY MSA	169,439	2,294	0.05	0.20	0.13	0.07	0.70	0.05	0.00	0.00	0.01	0.03	0.11
Cleveland, OH PMSA	1,831,122	20,289	0.26	0.16	0.09	0.32	0.11	0.06	0.02	0.00	0.01	0.01	0.06
Colorado Springs, CO MSA	397,014	8,783	0.19	0.37	0.36	0.08	0.82	0.13	0.02	0.00	0.01	0.07	0.14
Columbia, MO MSA	112,379	3,104	1.01	0.18	0.17	0.44	0.42	0.10	0.19	0.00	0.01	0.07	0.18
Columbia, SC MSA	453,331	4,554	0.22	0.11	0.09	0.19	0.21	0.07	0.00	0.00	0.00	0.03	0.07
Columbus, GA–AL MSA	243,072	2,670	0.08	0.19	0.14	0.07	0.47	0.05	0.01	0.00	0.00	0.02	0.07
Columbus, OH MSA	1,377,419	20,825	0.36	0.10	0.23	0.27	0.17	0.08	0.09	0.00	0.08	0.03	0.09
Corpus Christi, TX MSA	349,894	2,537	0.08	0.30	0.05	0.12	0.05	0.04	0.00	0.00	0.01	0.01	0.06
Cumberland, MD–WV MSA	101,643	386	0.05	0.10	0.02	0.08	0.06	0.00	0.00	0.00	0.00	0.00	0.06
Dallas, TX PMSA	2,553,362	66,250	0.53	0.22	0.12	0.52	0.35	0.45	0.09	0.00	0.10	0.06	0.16
Danbury, CT PMSA	187,867	4,319	0.39	0.21	0.08	0.65	0.17	0.19	0.32	0.00	0.16	0.03	0.11
Danville, VA MSA	108,711	321	0.05	0.08	0.02	0.07	0.02	0.01	0.00	0.00	0.00	0.00	0.03
Davenport–Rock Island–Moline, IA–IL MSA	350,861	2,450	0.09	0.07	0.05	0.09	0.12	0.18	0.01	0.00	0.03	0.02	0.03
Dayton–Springfield, OH MSA	951,270	9,068	0.15	0.13	0.13	0.21	0.14	0.09	0.01	0.00	0.01	0.02	0.07
Daytona Beach, FL MSA	370,712	2,633	0.13	0.12	0.05	0.18	0.07	0.07	0.00	0.00	0.02	0.02	0.04
Decatur, AL MSA	131,556	386	0.03	0.04	0.03	0.11	0.03	0.01	0.00	0.00	0.00	0.01	0.01
Decatur, IL MSA	117,206	496	0.06	0.06	0.11	0.07	0.06	0.03	0.00	0.00	0.00	0.01	0.03
Denver, CO PMSA	1,622,980	36,013	0.33	0.18	0.42	0.16	0.39	0.36	0.06	0.06	0.11	0.04	0.12
Des Moines, IA MSA	392,928	6,134	0.14	0.09	0.05	0.20	0.17	0.23	0.08	0.03	0.40	0.10	0.07
Detroit, MI PMSA	4,382,299	57,141	0.22	0.22	0.14	0.37	0.16	0.04	0.01	0.03	0.02	0.01	0.08

[Continued]

655

★ 790 ★

Population of Metropolitan Statistical Areas by Asian Ethnicity, in Percent (Continued)

Population in U.S. Metropolitan Statistical Areas (MSAs) including Primary Metropolitan Statistical Areas (PMSAs)[a], in percent, by Asian ethnicity, 1990.

Metropolitan area	Population		Percent										
	Total, all groups	Total Asian	Chinese	Filipino	Japanese	Asian Indian	Korean	Viet-namese	Cam-bodian	Hmong	Laotian	Thai	Other Asian
Dothan, AL MSA	130,964	1,101	0.05	0.09	0.16	0.05	0.23	0.15	0.00	0.00	0.00	0.03	0.08
Dubuque, IA MSA	86,403	426	0.08	0.07	0.10	0.05	0.08	0.07	0.01	0.00	0.00	0.01	0.04
Duluth, MN–WI MSA	239,971	1,308	0.09	0.05	0.05	0.05	0.13	0.07	0.00	0.06	0.03	0.00	0.02
Eau Claire, WI MSA	137,543	2,376	0.09	0.06	0.06	0.10	0.09	0.03	0.00	1.16	0.04	0.01	0.08
El Paso, TX MSA	591,610	5,999	0.14	0.19	0.18	0.08	0.29	0.04	0.00	0.00	0.00	0.01	0.09
Elkhart–Goshen, IN MSA	156,198	972	0.10	0.03	0.06	0.13	0.09	0.05	0.05	0.00	0.05	0.01	0.05
Elmira, NY MSA	95,195	673	0.13	0.05	0.12	0.17	0.06	0.02	0.00	0.00	0.01	0.01	0.13
Enid, OK MSA	56,735	495	0.15	0.11	0.08	0.13	0.11	0.09	0.00	0.00	0.04	0.08	0.09
Erie, PA MSA	275,572	1,375	0.07	0.05	0.03	0.12	0.06	0.08	0.00	0.00	0.01	0.01	0.05
Eugene–Springfield, OR MSA	282,912	5,049	0.48	0.18	0.46	0.11	0.27	0.07	0.02	0.00	0.03	0.03	0.14
Evansville, IN–KY MSA	278,990	1,190	0.08	0.05	0.03	0.07	0.07	0.06	0.00	0.00	0.00	0.01	0.05
Fall River, MA–RI PMSA	157,272	1,525	0.16	0.08	0.04	0.04	0.05	0.03	0.47	0.00	0.03	0.00	0.05
Fargo–Moorhead, ND–MN MSA	153,296	1,377	0.20	0.05	0.05	0.15	0.14	0.15	0.02	0.00	0.02	0.02	0.10
Fayetteville, NC MSA	274,566	4,973	0.10	0.30	0.21	0.11	0.69	0.12	0.00	0.00	0.01	0.11	0.15
Fayetteville–Springdale, AR MSA	113,409	1,000	0.20	0.05	0.07	0.14	0.10	0.08	0.00	0.00	0.14	0.01	0.09
Fitchburg–Leominster, MA MSA	102,797	1,754	0.15	0.06	0.07	0.17	0.27	0.20	0.01	0.16	0.46	0.03	0.12
Flint, MI MSA	430,459	2,849	0.11	0.10	0.04	0.17	0.14	0.04	0.00	0.00	0.00	0.01	0.04
Florence, AL MSA	131,327	275	0.05	0.01	0.02	0.07	0.03	0.01	0.00	0.00	0.00	0.00	0.01
Florence, SC MSA	114,344	295	0.06	0.03	0.01	0.06	0.04	0.00	0.00	0.00	0.00	0.01	0.03
Fort Collins–Loveland, CO MSA	186,136	2,677	0.36	0.10	0.26	0.17	0.21	0.12	0.02	0.00	0.01	0.02	0.18
Fort Lauderdale–Holly-wood–Pompano Beach, FL PMSA	1,255,488	16,757	0.38	0.14	0.05	0.46	0.08	0.09	0.00	0.00	0.00	0.03	0.10
Fort Myers–Cape CoraL, Fl MSA	335,113	1,820	0.11	0.11	0.04	0.11	0.05	0.03	0.00	0.00	0.03	0.02	0.04
Fort Pierce, FL MSA	251,071	1,451	0.12	0.13	0.04	0.18	0.05	0.01	0.01	0.00	0.00	0.01	0.03
Fort Smith, AR–OK MSA	175,911	3,706	0.08	0.09	0.05	0.06	0.04	0.79	0.00	0.00	0.88	0.01	0.09
Fort Walton Beach, FL MSA	143,776	3,452	0.16	0.69	0.25	0.08	0.45	0.18	0.00	0.00	0.01	0.37	0.22
Fort Wayne, IN MSA	363,811	2,689	0.09	0.07	0.04	0.18	0.08	0.10	0.01	0.00	0.07	0.01	0.07
Fort Worth–Arlington, TX PMSA	1,332,053	29,040	0.33	0.15	0.08	0.35	0.16	0.65	0.04	0.01	0.22	0.05	0.14
Fresno, CA MSA	667,490	56,517	0.72	0.65	1.01	0.78	0.15	0.30	0.57	2.74	1.22	0.06	0.27
Gadsden, AL MSA	99,840	415	0.06	0.03	0.19	0.04	0.02	0.02	0.00	0.00	0.00	0.02	0.04
Gainesville, FL MSA	204,111	4,603	0.74	0.23	0.11	0.45	0.31	0.20	0.01	0.00	0.01	0.04	0.15
Galveston–Texas City, TX PMSA	217,399	3,495	0.22	0.27	0.09	0.29	0.10	0.54	0.01	0.00	0.00	0.01	0.08
Gary–Hammond, IN PMSA	604,526	3,646	0.07	0.16	0.05	0.14	0.09	0.02	0.00	0.00	0.01	0.02	0.04
Glens Falls, NY MSA	118,539	381	0.05	0.04	0.03	0.06	0.10	0.01	0.00	0.00	0.00	0.00	0.03
Grand Forks, ND MSA	70,683	840	0.27	0.33	0.09	0.10	0.20	0.04	0.01	0.00	0.00	0.05	0.08
Grand Rapids, MI MSA	688,399	7,692	0.13	0.06	0.05	0.09	0.26	0.31	0.06	0.00	0.07	0.01	0.07
Great Falls, MT MSA	77,691	734	0.07	0.36	0.14	0.02	0.18	0.02	0.00	0.00	0.01	0.06	0.07
Greeley, CO MSA	131,821	1,043	0.10	0.05	0.39	0.03	0.12	0.02	0.01	0.00	0.02	0.03	0.04
Green Bay, WI MSA	194,594	2,490	0.06	0.04	0.04	0.10	0.06	0.04	0.00	0.72	0.15	0.01	0.05

[Continued]

★ 790 ★

Population of Metropolitan Statistical Areas by Asian Ethnicity, in Percent (Continued)

Population in U.S. Metropolitan Statistical Areas (MSAs) including Primary Metropolitan Statistical Areas (PMSAs)[a], in percent, by Asian ethnicity, 1990.

Metropolitan area	Population		Percent										
	Total, all groups	Total Asian	Chinese	Filipino	Japanese	Asian Indian	Korean	Viet-namese	Cam-bodian	Hmong	Laotian	Thai	Other Asian
Greensboro–Winston–Salem–High Point, NC MSA	942,091	6,277	0.10	0.04	0.06	0.12	0.09	0.10	0.07	0.00	0.04	0.02	0.04
Greenville–Spartanburg, SC MSA	640,861	4,531	0.11	0.06	0.05	0.22	0.05	0.07	0.03	0.01	0.07	0.01	0.03
Hagerstown, MD MSA	121,393	749	0.07	0.13	0.04	0.07	0.11	0.08	0.00	0.00	0.00	0.02	0.09
Hamilton–Middletown, OH PMSA	291,479	2,597	0.21	0.12	0.09	0.27	0.10	0.04	0.01	0.00	0.00	0.01	0.04
Harrisburg–Lebanon–Carlisle, PA MSA	587,986	6,160	0.12	0.07	0.05	0.20	0.17	0.26	0.08	0.00	0.02	0.01	0.06
Hartford, CT PMSA	767,841	12,073	0.31	0.11	0.07	0.43	0.17	0.20	0.03	0.01	0.09	0.01	0.14
Hickory–Morganton, NC MSA	221,700	1,638	0.07	0.03	0.02	0.13	0.04	0.07	0.00	0.20	0.16	0.00	0.03
Honolulu, HI MSA	836,231	413,349	7.57	14.35	23.34	0.10	2.71	0.63	0.01	0.00	0.20	0.13	0.40
Houma–Thibodaux, LA MSA	182,842	1,348	0.06	0.04	0.01	0.04	0.02	0.56	0.00	0.00	0.00	0.00	0.01
Houston, TX PMSA	3,301,937	125,529	0.89	0.41	0.11	0.78	0.21	1.00	0.07	0.00	0.04	0.04	0.25
Huntington–Ashland, WV–KY–OH MSA	312,529	900	0.04	0.06	0.02	0.09	0.04	0.01	0.00	0.00	0.01	0.00	0.02
Huntsville, AL MSA	238,912	4,100	0.38	0.11	0.14	0.47	0.40	0.09	0.01	0.00	0.02	0.03	0.07
Indianapolis, IN MSA	1,249,822	9,865	0.13	0.11	0.11	0.16	0.13	0.06	0.01	0.00	0.01	0.01	0.06
Iowa City, IA MSA	96,119	3,815	1.53	0.15	0.29	0.52	0.85	0.24	0.02	0.00	0.06	0.06	0.27
Jackson, MI MSA	149,756	635	0.04	0.05	0.10	0.07	0.08	0.03	0.00	0.00	0.00	0.00	0.04
Jackson, MS MSA	395,396	1,727	0.10	0.03	0.02	0.15	0.04	0.05	0.00	0.00	0.00	0.01	0.03
Jackson, TN MSA	77,982	250	0.07	0.04	0.05	0.07	0.03	0.04	0.00	0.00	0.00	0.00	0.03
Jacksonville, FL MSA	906,727	14,925	0.13	0.94	0.07	0.15	0.09	0.10	0.07	0.00	0.01	0.02	0.07
Jacksonville, NC MSA	149,838	2,562	0.09	0.80	0.39	0.05	0.16	0.05	0.00	0.00	0.00	0.06	0.10
Jamestown–Dunkirk, NY	141,895	522	0.04	0.04	0.02	0.09	0.09	0.02	0.01	0.00	0.02	0.00	0.03
Janesville–Beloit, WI MSA	139,510	963	0.08	0.08	0.06	0.07	0.08	0.12	0.11	0.00	0.04	0.02	0.03
Jersey City, NJ PMSA	553,099	36,564	0.90	2.39	0.10	2.09	0.51	0.20	0.00	0.00	0.01	0.03	0.38
Johnson City–Kingsport–Bristol, TN–VA MSA	436,047	1,216	0.07	0.04	0.02	0.06	0.03	0.02	0.00	0.00	0.01	0.01	0.02
Johnstown, PA MSA	241,247	505	0.02	0.03	0.02	0.07	0.04	0.02	0.00	0.00	0.00	0.00	0.02
Joliet, IL PMSA	389,650	4,848	0.14	0.37	0.06	0.33	0.10	0.04	0.04	0.00	0.07	0.02	0.08
Joplin, MO MSA	134,910	641	0.05	0.05	0.04	0.08	0.04	0.17	0.00	0.00	0.00	0.02	0.03
Kalamazoo, MI MSA	223,411	3,129	0.27	0.10	0.15	0.33	0.23	0.10	0.01	0.00	0.02	0.04	0.16
Kankakee, IL MSA	96,255	639	0.09	0.12	0.04	0.22	0.09	0.03	0.00	0.00	0.00	0.01	0.06
Kansas City, MO–KS MSA	1,566,280	16,182	0.17	0.14	0.08	0.16	0.15	0.13	0.02	0.04	0.06	0.02	0.07
Kenosha, WI PMSA	128,181	645	0.05	0.12	0.06	0.10	0.12	0.01	0.00	0.01	0.01	0.00	0.03
Killeen–Temple, TX MSA	255,301	6,089	0.12	0.43	0.20	0.12	1.18	0.12	0.00	0.00	0.00	0.08	0.14
Knoxville, TN MSA	604,816	4,464	0.20	0.06	0.09	0.19	0.09	0.03	0.00	0.00	0.00	0.01	0.05
Kokomo, IN MSA	96,946	480	0.10	0.08	0.05	0.10	0.10	0.02	0.00	0.00	0.00	0.01	0.03
La Crosse, WI MSA	97,904	2,638	0.09	0.04	0.04	0.13	0.14	0.03	0.01	1.97	0.09	0.01	0.13
Lafayette, LA MSA	208,740	1,884	0.17	0.03	0.02	0.15	0.06	0.31	0.00	0.00	0.02	0.03	0.11
Lafayette–West Lafayette, IN MSA	130,598	4,776	1.35	0.17	0.62	0.65	0.50	0.13	0.00	0.00	0.01	0.02	0.21
Lake Charles, LA MSA	168,134	566	0.07	0.06	0.02	0.07	0.03	0.03	0.00	0.00	0.02	0.01	0.03
Lake County, IL PMSA	516,418	12,363	0.38	0.78	0.21	0.44	0.37	0.05	0.03	0.00	0.00	0.03	0.10
Lakeland–Winter Haven, FL MSA	405,382	2,429	0.08	0.09	0.04	0.14	0.05	0.10	0.01	0.00	0.04	0.02	0.04
Lancaster, PA MSA	422,822	4,594	0.18	0.05	0.04	0.10	0.11	0.35	0.08	0.06	0.07	0.01	0.04

[Continued]

★ 790 ★

Population of Metropolitan Statistical Areas by Asian Ethnicity, in Percent (Continued)

Population in U.S. Metropolitan Statistical Areas (MSAs) including Primary Metropolitan Statistical Areas (PMSAs)[a], in percent, by Asian ethnicity, 1990.

Metropolitan area	Population		Percent										
	Total, all groups	Total Asian	Chinese	Filipino	Japanese	Asian Indian	Korean	Viet-namese	Cam-bodian	Hmong	Laotian	Thai	Other Asian
Lansing–East Lansing, MI MSA	432,674	8,158	0.46	0.12	0.13	0.29	0.33	0.21	0.01	0.11	0.06	0.03	0.15
Laredo, TX MSA	133,239	473	0.06	0.02	0.03	0.11	0.07	0.01	0.00	0.00	0.00	0.00	0.05
Las Cruces, NM MSA	135,510	1,089	0.19	0.10	0.12	0.11	0.10	0.02	0.00	0.00	0.00	0.02	0.14
Las Vegas, NV MSA	741,459	24,296	0.56	1.08	0.38	0.14	0.46	0.17	0.03	0.00	0.10	0.21	0.15
Lawrence, KS MSA	81,798	2,545	1.23	0.15	0.32	0.42	0.42	0.12	0.01	0.00	0.06	0.08	0.32
Lawrence–Haverhill, MA–NH PMSA	393,516	5,091	0.35	0.04	0.07	0.24	0.23	0.18	0.09	0.00	0.01	0.01	0.07
Lawton, OK MSA	111,486	2,614	0.11	0.39	0.26	0.08	1.15	0.12	0.05	0.01	0.00	0.07	0.10
Lewiston–Auburn, ME MSA	88,141	498	0.15	0.11	0.05	0.07	0.06	0.08	0.00	0.00	0.02	0.01	0.02
Lexington-Fayette, KY MSA	348,428	3,974	0.32	0.07	0.24	0.23	0.10	0.05	0.00	0.00	0.00	0.02	0.10
Lima, OH MSA	154,340	736	0.05	0.06	0.07	0.10	0.09	0.02	0.01	0.00	0.06	0.00	0.02
Lincoln, NE MSA	213,641	3,282	0.36	0.06	0.10	0.20	0.22	0.42	0.02	0.00	0.01	0.02	0.13
Little Rock–North Little Rock, AR MSA	513,117	3,242	0.10	0.15	0.07	0.09	0.07	0.05	0.00	0.00	0.03	0.02	0.04
Longview–Marshall, TX MSA	162,431	605	0.07	0.04	0.03	0.08	0.04	0.07	0.00	0.00	0.00	0.01	0.02
Lorain–Elyria, OH PMSA	271,126	1,447	0.09	0.13	0.07	0.11	0.09	0.01	0.00	0.00	0.00	0.01	0.04
Los Angeles–Long Beach, CA PMSA	8,863,164	925,561	2.76	2.48	1.46	0.49	1.64	0.71	0.31	0.00	0.04	0.21	0.32
Louisville, KY–IN MSA	952,662	5,455	0.09	0.08	0.05	0.10	0.10	0.08	0.01	0.00	0.01	0.01	0.03
Lowell, MA–NH PMSA	273,067	14,205	0.65	0.08	0.06	0.71	0.18	0.32	2.39	0.00	0.59	0.02	0.20
Lubbock, TX MSA	222,636	2,658	0.30	0.12	0.07	0.27	0.14	0.12	0.00	0.00	0.00	0.03	0.13
Lynchburg, VA MSA	142,199	712	0.10	0.07	0.04	0.08	0.08	0.07	0.00	0.00	0.00	0.01	0.04
Macon–Warner Robins, GA MSA	281,103	1,900	0.08	0.13	0.12	0.10	0.10	0.06	0.00	0.00	0.01	0.04	0.04
Madison, WI MSA	367,085	8,587	0.77	0.11	0.18	0.32	0.39	0.10	0.06	0.15	0.07	0.03	0.16
Manchester, NH MSA	147,809	1,400	0.27	0.10	0.06	0.15	0.19	0.03	0.02	0.00	0.02	0.02	0.09
Mansfield, OH MSA	126,137	549	0.03	0.04	0.06	0.10	0.14	0.03	0.00	0.00	0.00	0.01	0.02
Mcallen–Edinburg–Mission, TX MSA	383,545	1,050	0.05	0.04	0.03	0.06	0.04	0.01	0.00	0.00	0.00	0.00	0.04
Medford, OR MSA	146,389	1,277	0.16	0.17	0.21	0.05	0.14	0.03	0.00	0.00	0.00	0.04	0.06
Melbourne–Titusville–Palm Bay, FL MSA	398,978	5,187	0.21	0.27	0.12	0.27	0.15	0.12	0.01	0.00	0.00	0.07	0.09
Memphis, TN–AR–MS MSA	981,747	7,966	0.20	0.10	0.06	0.12	0.10	0.10	0.04	0.01	0.03	0.01	0.04
Merced, CA MSA	178,403	14,759	0.29	0.79	0.41	1.31	0.16	0.15	0.05	3.62	1.15	0.14	0.21
Miami–Hialeah, FL PMSA	1,937,094	25,869	0.46	0.20	0.07	0.32	0.07	0.05	0.00	0.00	0.01	0.03	0.13
Middlesex–Somerset–Hunterdon, NJ PMSA	1,019,835	56,669	1.46	0.80	0.12	2.25	0.50	0.13	0.00	0.00	0.01	0.02	0.26
Middletown, CT PMSA	90,320	1,145	0.31	0.10	0.08	0.31	0.17	0.06	0.07	0.00	0.05	0.01	0.11
Midland, TX MSA	106,611	860	0.19	0.08	0.03	0.21	0.08	0.09	0.03	0.00	0.01	0.01	0.08
Milwaukee, WI PMSA	1,432,149	18,445	0.20	0.12	0.07	0.23	0.12	0.08	0.01	0.24	0.14	0.01	0.08
Minneapolis–St. Paul, MN–WI MSA	2,464,124	64,484	0.30	0.13	0.11	0.29	0.35	0.32	0.11	0.67	0.20	0.02	0.11
Mobile, AL MSA	476,923	3,551	0.09	0.06	0.04	0.08	0.04	0.26	0.07	0.00	0.05	0.01	0.05
Modesto, CA MSA	370,522	18,072	0.45	0.64	0.22	1.03	0.14	0.33	1.00	0.26	0.65	0.02	0.14
Monmouth–Ocean, NJ PMSA	986,327	18,917	0.62	0.37	0.06	0.45	0.23	0.06	0.00	0.00	0.00	0.01	0.11
Monroe, LA MSA	142,191	722	0.15	0.04	0.02	0.08	0.02	0.15	0.00	0.00	0.00	0.01	0.04
Montgomery, AL MSA	292,517	1,735	0.08	0.08	0.07	0.10	0.09	0.03	0.00	0.00	0.07	0.04	0.03

[Continued]

★ 790 ★

Population of Metropolitan Statistical Areas by Asian Ethnicity, in Percent (Continued)

Population in U.S. Metropolitan Statistical Areas (MSAs) including Primary Metropolitan Statistical Areas (PMSAs)[a], in percent, by Asian ethnicity, 1990.

Metropolitan area	Population		Percent										
	Total, all groups	Total Asian	Chinese	Filipino	Japanese	Asian Indian	Korean	Viet-namese	Cam-bodian	Hmong	Laotian	Thai	Other Asian
Muncie, IN MSA	119,659	615	0.14	0.06	0.04	0.08	0.09	0.03	0.00	0.00	0.00	0.02	0.06
Muskegon, MI MSA	158,983	544	0.03	0.05	0.03	0.04	0.11	0.04	0.00	0.00	0.00	0.01	0.03
Naples, FL MSA	152,099	533	0.12	0.05	0.02	0.06	0.02	0.03	0.00	0.00	0.00	0.02	0.03
Nashua, NH PMSA	180,557	2,430	0.37	0.10	0.09	0.40	0.16	0.12	0.02	0.00	0.01	0.02	0.07
Nashville, TN MSA	985,026	9,843	0.12	0.06	0.11	0.17	0.12	0.05	0.03	0.00	0.24	0.02	0.07
Nassau–Suffolk, NY PMSA	2,609,212	62,050	0.70	0.28	0.15	0.67	0.35	0.05	0.00	0.00	0.00	0.03	0.14
New Bedford, MA MSA	175,641	810	0.17	0.04	0.04	0.04	0.07	0.05	0.00	0.00	0.00	0.02	0.03
New Britain, CT PMSA	148,188	1,901	0.22	0.06	0.05	0.28	0.11	0.14	0.06	0.00	0.28	0.01	0.08
New Haven–Meriden, CT MSA	530,180	8,342	0.47	0.13	0.12	0.33	0.20	0.08	0.03	0.00	0.02	0.02	0.16
New London–Norwich, CT–RI MSA	266,819	3,425	0.27	0.49	0.09	0.18	0.08	0.04	0.02	0.00	0.03	0.01	0.05
New Orleans, LA MSA	1,238,816	21,112	0.21	0.17	0.05	0.19	0.07	0.92	0.01	0.00	0.01	0.01	0.06
New York, NY PMSA	8,546,846	553,443	2.89	0.58	0.31	1.24	0.87	0.11	0.03	0.00	0.01	0.05	0.39
Newark, NJ PMSA	1,824,321	52,539	0.77	0.60	0.11	0.87	0.29	0.08	0.00	0.00	0.00	0.02	0.14
Niagara Falls, NY PMSA	220,756	775	0.04	0.05	0.02	0.10	0.08	0.02	0.00	0.00	0.00	0.01	0.03
Norfolk–Virginia Beach–Newport News, VA MSA	1,396,107	34,004	0.21	1.42	0.13	0.14	0.23	0.14	0.03	0.00	0.01	0.03	0.08
Norwalk, CT PMSA	127,378	2,038	0.46	0.18	0.12	0.49	0.14	0.04	0.00	0.00	0.01	0.03	0.11
Oakland, CA PMSA	2,082,914	259,002	4.35	3.71	1.03	1.04	0.65	0.80	0.18	0.00	0.29	0.06	0.33
Ocala, FL MSA	194,833	919	0.07	0.07	0.03	0.16	0.08	0.04	0.00	0.00	0.00	0.01	0.02
Odessa, TX MSA	118,934	644	0.07	0.12	0.02	0.12	0.03	0.09	0.01	0.00	0.00	0.02	0.06
Oklahoma City, OK MSA	958,839	17,228	0.29	0.14	0.12	0.26	0.19	0.55	0.02	0.00	0.06	0.05	0.12
Olympia, WA MSA	161,238	5,545	0.25	0.58	0.42	0.12	0.83	0.61	0.38	0.00	0.07	0.04	0.15
Omaha, NE–IA MSA	618,262	6,072	0.13	0.17	0.15	0.10	0.18	0.10	0.01	0.01	0.02	0.04	0.08
Orange County, NY PMSA	307,647	3,489	0.27	0.16	0.07	0.29	0.19	0.04	0.00	0.00	0.01	0.02	0.08
Orlando, FL MSA	1,072,748	19,786	0.31	0.34	0.09	0.46	0.16	0.31	0.01	0.00	0.03	0.04	0.10
Owensboro, KY MSA	87,189	224	0.04	0.03	0.02	0.09	0.04	0.02	0.00	0.00	0.00	0.00	0.01
Oxnard–Ventura, CA PMSA	669,016	32,699	0.75	1.90	0.74	0.35	0.44	0.37	0.03	0.00	0.03	0.07	0.21
Panama City, FL MSA	126,994	2,156	0.12	0.34	0.15	0.11	0.19	0.52	0.00	0.00	0.00	0.15	0.12
Parkersburg–Marietta, WV–OH MSA	149,169	506	0.06	0.05	0.05	0.08	0.06	0.01	0.00	0.00	0.00	0.00	0.02
Pascagoula, MS MSA	115,243	1,080	0.07	0.10	0.05	0.05	0.10	0.51	0.00	0.00	0.00	0.02	0.04
Pawtucket–Woonsocket–Attleboro, RI–MA PMSA	329,384	3,919	0.15	0.08	0.03	0.20	0.07	0.11	0.19	0.00	0.27	0.01	0.08
Pensacola, FL MSA	344,406	5,752	0.13	0.77	0.13	0.06	0.08	0.41	0.03	0.00	0.01	0.02	0.04
Peoria, IL MSA	339,172	2,712	0.16	0.08	0.06	0.17	0.12	0.12	0.00	0.00	0.02	0.01	0.06
Philadelphia, PA–NJ PMSA	4,856,881	103,537	0.46	0.25	0.09	0.43	0.45	0.21	0.10	0.00	0.03	0.02	0.10
Phoenix, AZ MSA	2,122,101	34,104	0.45	0.24	0.18	0.19	0.16	0.18	0.03	0.00	0.03	0.04	0.10
Pine Bluff, AR MSA	85,487	342	0.10	0.04	0.07	0.09	0.05	0.01	0.00	0.00	0.00	0.01	0.03
Pittsburgh, PA PMSA	2,056,705	15,557	0.20	0.06	0.06	0.22	0.10	0.04	0.00	0.00	0.00	0.01	0.05
Pittsfield, MA MSA	79,250	537	0.18	0.03	0.05	0.16	0.10	0.05	0.03	0.00	0.00	0.02	0.05
Portland, ME MSA	215,281	1,841	0.14	0.13	0.06	0.07	0.10	0.11	0.17	0.00	0.03	0.01	0.04
Portland, OR PMSA	1,239,842	43,768	0.74	0.39	0.55	0.19	0.47	0.61	0.13	0.03	0.23	0.04	0.15
Portsmouth–Dover–Rochester, NH–ME MSA	223,578	2,055	0.18	0.12	0.08	0.09	0.12	0.05	0.05	0.00	0.12	0.05	0.06
Poughkeepsie, NY MSA	259,462	5,793	0.73	0.13	0.13	0.77	0.21	0.13	0.00	0.00	0.01	0.01	0.11

[Continued]

★ 790 ★

Population of Metropolitan Statistical Areas by Asian Ethnicity, in Percent (Continued)

Population in U.S. Metropolitan Statistical Areas (MSAs) including Primary Metropolitan Statistical Areas (PMSAs)[a], in percent, by Asian ethnicity, 1990.

Metropolitan area	Population		Percent										
	Total, all groups	Total Asian	Chinese	Filipino	Japanese	Asian Indian	Korean	Viet-namese	Cam-bodian	Hmong	Laotian	Thai	Other Asian
Providence, RI PMSA	654,854	14,331	0.39	0.17	0.09	0.24	0.16	0.08	0.54	0.13	0.26	0.01	0.11
Provo–Orem, UT MSA	263,590	2,804	0.31	0.08	0.28	0.05	0.15	0.06	0.02	0.00	0.05	0.02	0.05
Pueblo, CO MSA	123,051	678	0.10	0.09	0.13	0.06	0.06	0.02	0.00	0.00	0.00	0.01	0.08
Racine, WI PMSA	175,034	986	0.08	0.05	0.04	0.15	0.12	0.05	0.00	0.00	0.02	0.01	0.05
Raleigh–Durham, NC MSA	735,480	13,705	0.59	0.10	0.18	0.45	0.24	0.15	0.01	0.00	0.03	0.02	0.11
Rapid City, SD MSA	81,343	862	0.13	0.30	0.12	0.08	0.19	0.06	0.00	0.00	0.01	0.10	0.08
Reading, PA MSA	336,523	2,711	0.11	0.17	0.05	0.15	0.10	0.16	0.00	0.00	0.02	0.01	0.03
Redding, CA MSA	147,036	2,552	0.15	0.14	0.14	0.08	0.07	0.03	0.06	0.11	0.87	0.03	0.07
Reno, NV MSA	254,667	8,937	0.83	1.29	0.37	0.24	0.30	0.22	0.01	0.00	0.00	0.10	0.14
Richland–Kennewick–Pasco, WA MSA	150,033	3,004	0.28	0.25	0.24	0.19	0.21	0.20	0.03	0.02	0.44	0.04	0.11
Richmond–Petersburg, VA MSA	865,640	11,641	0.23	0.12	0.07	0.22	0.26	0.20	0.13	0.00	0.02	0.02	0.07
Riverside–San Bernar-dino, CA PMSA	2,588,793	93,473	0.51	1.12	0.35	0.29	0.39	0.44	0.09	0.02	0.08	0.10	0.23
Roanoke, VA MSA	224,477	1,579	0.12	0.11	0.06	0.11	0.09	0.11	0.01	0.00	0.04	0.01	0.04
Rochester, MN MSA	106,470	3,220	0.46	0.14	0.19	0.27	0.26	0.42	0.82	0.11	0.25	0.02	0.10
Rochester, NY MSA	1,002,410	13,838	0.32	0.06	0.07	0.30	0.22	0.15	0.04	0.00	0.13	0.01	0.07
Rockford, IL MSA	283,719	3,100	0.14	0.11	0.06	0.17	0.15	0.07	0.00	0.01	0.30	0.03	0.06
Sacramento, CA MSA	1,481,102	109,242	2.00	1.37	1.15	0.49	0.37	0.71	0.06	0.38	0.53	0.06	0.25
Saginaw–Bay City–Mid-land, MI MSA	399,320	2,467	0.11	0.07	0.04	0.14	0.11	0.02	0.00	0.05	0.02	0.01	0.03
Salem, OR MSA	278,024	4,180	0.23	0.24	0.30	0.06	0.15	0.25	0.08	0.02	0.07	0.02	0.08
Salem–Gloucester, MA PMSA	264,356	2,281	0.24	0.08	0.11	0.13	0.14	0.09	0.02	0.00	0.01	0.02	0.04
Salinas–Seaside–Monterey, CA MSA	355,660	25,369	0.61	3.21	1.18	0.22	1.05	0.58	0.00	0.00	0.01	0.07	0.21
Salt Lake City–Ogden, UT MSA	1,072,227	19,588	0.36	0.14	0.45	0.11	0.17	0.22	0.07	0.01	0.14	0.05	0.10
San Angelo, TX MSA	98,458	955	0.10	0.19	0.07	0.09	0.20	0.12	0.00	0.00	0.07	0.07	0.07
San Antonio, TX MSA	1,302,099	15,302	0.20	0.25	0.13	0.12	0.19	0.13	0.01	0.00	0.02	0.05	0.08
San Diego, CA MSA	2,498,016	184,596	0.79	3.84	0.72	0.20	0.27	0.85	0.17	0.06	0.28	0.04	0.17
San Francisco, CA PMSA	1,603,678	316,751	10.14	5.52	1.48	0.53	0.65	0.78	0.10	0.00	0.07	0.09	0.39
San Jose, CA PMSA	1,497,577	254,786	4.34	4.11	1.77	1.35	1.04	3.62	0.26	0.00	0.11	0.06	0.35
Santa Barbara–Santa Maria–Lompoc, CA MSA	369,608	15,785	0.69	1.48	0.80	0.20	0.37	0.24	0.01	0.18	0.12	0.05	0.14
Santa Cruz, CA PMSA	229,734	8,163	0.71	1.04	1.01	0.18	0.26	0.11	0.04	0.00	0.01	0.03	0.18
Santa Fe, NM MSA	117,043	886	0.26	0.07	0.18	0.07	0.08	0.03	0.00	0.00	0.00	0.01	0.05
Santa Rosa–Petaluma, CA PMSA	388,222	9,931	0.56	0.47	0.44	0.17	0.19	0.19	0.14	0.01	0.21	0.02	0.14
Sarasota, FL MSA	277,776	1,386	0.10	0.07	0.04	0.07	0.05	0.08	0.01	0.00	0.02	0.02	0.03
Savannah, GA MSA	242,622	2,296	0.17	0.13	0.05	0.13	0.15	0.24	0.00	0.00	0.02	0.01	0.05
Scranton–Wilkes-Barre, PA MSA	734,175	3,747	0.09	0.05	0.03	0.15	0.09	0.04	0.00	0.00	0.02	0.01	0.03
Seattle, WA PMSA	1,972,961	128,656	1.39	1.41	1.16	0.30	0.83	0.64	0.29	0.02	0.22	0.07	0.19
Sharon, PA MSA	121,003	380	0.06	0.04	0.04	0.07	0.06	0.01	0.00	0.00	0.00	0.00	0.02
Sheboygan, WI MSA	103,877	2,039	0.04	0.10	0.02	0.30	0.07	0.03	0.03	1.21	0.10	0.00	0.08
Sherman–Denison, TX MSA	95,021	385	0.07	0.06	0.04	0.10	0.05	0.03	0.00	0.00	0.01	0.01	0.03
Shreveport, LA MSA	334,341	1,925	0.09	0.10	0.05	0.08	0.08	0.07	0.02	0.00	0.01	0.05	0.04
Sioux City, IA–NE MSA	115,018	1,613	0.11	0.07	0.04	0.07	0.10	0.38	0.11	0.02	0.41	0.02	0.07
Sioux Falls, SD MSA	123,809	673	0.08	0.05	0.05	0.03	0.09	0.08	0.04	0.02	0.08	0.01	0.01

[Continued]

★790★

Population of Metropolitan Statistical Areas by Asian Ethnicity, in Percent (Continued)

Population in U.S. Metropolitan Statistical Areas (MSAs) including Primary Metropolitan Statistical Areas (PMSAs)[a], in percent, by Asian ethnicity, 1990.

Metropolitan area	Population		Percent										
	Total, all groups	Total Asian	Chinese	Filipino	Japanese	Asian Indian	Korean	Viet-namese	Cam-bodian	Hmong	Laotian	Thai	Other Asian
South Bend–Mishawaka, IN MSA	247,052	2,435	0.24	0.09	0.10	0.22	0.13	0.08	0.04	0.00	0.02	0.01	0.05
Spokane, WA MSA	361,364	6,087	0.23	0.21	0.48	0.07	0.22	0.19	0.02	0.07	0.05	0.05	0.09
Springfield, IL MSA	189,550	1,371	0.13	0.08	0.04	0.26	0.09	0.05	0.01	0.00	0.01	0.02	0.05
Springfield, MA MSA	529,519	5,306	0.22	0.07	0.07	0.17	0.14	0.14	0.08	0.00	0.03	0.01	0.07
Springfield, MO MSA	240,593	1,525	0.13	0.08	0.05	0.05	0.13	0.13	0.02	0.00	0.01	0.01	0.03
St. Cloud, MN MSA	190,921	1,152	0.06	0.07	0.03	0.05	0.13	0.08	0.02	0.01	0.07	0.01	0.06
St. Joseph, MO MSA	83,083	247	0.05	0.06	0.03	0.08	0.05	0.01	0.00	0.00	0.00	0.00	0.02
St. Louis, MO–IL MSA	2,444,099	23,238	0.22	0.14	0.08	0.17	0.13	0.09	0.00	0.00	0.02	0.03	0.07
Stamford, CT PMSA	202,557	5,500	0.69	0.29	0.75	0.53	0.18	0.11	0.00	0.00	0.00	0.01	0.16
State College, PA MSA	123,786	3,807	1.21	0.15	0.21	0.61	0.59	0.09	0.00	0.00	0.00	0.03	0.19
Steubenville–Weirton, OH–WV MSA	142,523	432	0.03	0.12	0.03	0.05	0.04	0.01	0.00	0.00	0.00	0.01	0.01
Stockton, CA MSA	480,628	58,374	1.15	3.45	0.78	0.71	0.14	1.45	2.15	0.96	0.88	0.03	0.45
Syracuse, NY MSA	659,864	7,611	0.26	0.10	0.06	0.25	0.19	0.11	0.02	0.02	0.02	0.01	0.08
Tacoma, WA PMSA	586,203	25,231	0.22	0.81	0.68	0.08	1.29	0.32	0.58	0.00	0.06	0.07	0.18
Tallahassee, FL MSA	233,598	2,726	0.34	0.14	0.07	0.25	0.14	0.10	0.00	0.00	0.00	0.02	0.10
Tampa–St. Petersburg–Clearwater, FL MSA	2,067,959	22,424	0.16	0.17	0.07	0.19	0.13	0.19	0.02	0.00	0.06	0.04	0.05
Terre Haute, IN MSA	130,812	1,159	0.23	0.10	0.08	0.18	0.09	0.04	0.00	0.00	0.00	0.01	0.15
Texarkana, TX–Texarkana, AR MSA	120,132	387	0.03	0.04	0.03	0.06	0.04	0.08	0.00	0.00	0.00	0.00	0.04
Toledo, OH MSA	614,128	6,094	0.27	0.10	0.06	0.22	0.12	0.04	0.00	0.00	0.04	0.02	0.10
Topeka, KS MSA	160,976	1,135	0.17	0.10	0.07	0.13	0.11	0.05	0.00	0.00	0.00	0.02	0.06
Trenton, NJ PMSA	325,824	9,862	0.93	0.25	0.14	1.00	0.41	0.04	0.01	0.00	0.00	0.01	0.23
Tucson, AZ MSA	666,880	11,417	0.52	0.22	0.22	0.16	0.19	0.18	0.01	0.00	0.04	0.05	0.12
Tulsa, OK MSA	708,954	6,334	0.16	0.07	0.06	0.15	0.11	0.18	0.01	0.03	0.02	0.02	0.08
Tuscaloosa, AL MSA	150,522	1,252	0.21	0.06	0.11	0.21	0.13	0.02	0.00	0.00	0.00	0.01	0.09
Tyler, TX MSA	151,309	609	0.08	0.10	0.03	0.07	0.04	0.04	0.01	0.00	0.00	0.01	0.02
Utica–Rome, NY MSA	316,633	2,234	0.10	0.08	0.05	0.12	0.10	0.12	0.01	0.00	0.02	0.03	0.06
Vallejo–Fairfield–Napa, CA PMSA	451,186	43,289	0.83	6.60	0.68	0.44	0.33	0.22	0.01	0.02	0.13	0.09	0.25
Vancouver, WA PMSA	238,053	5,048	0.30	0.34	0.29	0.11	0.38	0.33	0.17	0.00	0.07	0.03	0.10
Victoria, TX MSA	74,361	253	0.05	0.06	0.02	0.10	0.02	0.05	0.00	0.00	0.00	0.01	0.03
Vineland–Millville–Bridgeton, NJ PMSA	138,053	1,110	0.08	0.16	0.24	0.14	0.07	0.02	0.00	0.00	0.00	0.01	0.08
Visalia–Tulare–Porterville, CA MSA	311,921	13,013	0.33	1.33	0.33	0.28	0.09	0.05	0.02	0.60	0.97	0.02	0.14
Waco, TX MSA	189,123	1,341	0.16	0.10	0.06	0.12	0.10	0.11	0.00	0.00	0.00	0.01	0.05
Washington, DC–MD–VA MSA	3,923,574	200,113	0.99	0.68	0.25	0.91	1.02	0.60	0.10	0.00	0.07	0.11	0.38
Waterbury, CT MSA	221,629	1,562	0.14	0.10	0.03	0.21	0.06	0.08	0.02	0.00	0.02	0.01	0.05
Waterloo–Cedar Falls, IA MSA	146,611	1,108	0.15	0.05	0.10	0.14	0.17	0.05	0.00	0.00	0.04	0.00	0.05
Wausau, WI MSA	115,400	2,489	0.05	0.03	0.02	0.08	0.09	0.03	0.01	1.71	0.10	0.01	0.03
West Palm Beach–Boca Raton–Delray Beach, FL MSA	863,518	8,808	0.28	0.12	0.04	0.28	0.05	0.12	0.00	0.00	0.01	0.04	0.08
Wheeling, WV–OH MSA	159,301	524	0.04	0.09	0.04	0.09	0.03	0.01	0.00	0.00	0.00	0.01	0.02
Wichita Falls, TX MSA	122,378	1,772	0.14	0.22	0.10	0.10	0.17	0.59	0.00	0.00	0.00	0.04	0.07
Wichita, KS MSA	485,270	8,947	0.23	0.13	0.09	0.17	0.10	0.77	0.06	0.01	0.14	0.03	0.12
Williamsport, PA MSA	118,710	462	0.05	0.08	0.02	0.09	0.11	0.02	0.00	0.00	0.00	0.00	0.03
Wilmington, DE–NJ–MD PMSA	578,587	7,639	0.36	0.17	0.09	0.35	0.19	0.05	0.00	0.00	0.01	0.01	0.08

[Continued]

★ 790 ★

Population of Metropolitan Statistical Areas by Asian Ethnicity, in Percent (Continued)

Population in U.S. Metropolitan Statistical Areas (MSAs) including Primary Metropolitan Statistical Areas (PMSAs)[a], in percent, by Asian ethnicity, 1990.

Metropolitan area	Population		Percent										
	Total, all groups	Total Asian	Chinese	Filipino	Japanese	Asian Indian	Korean	Viet-namese	Cam-bodian	Hmong	Laotian	Thai	Other Asian
Wilmington, NC MSA	120,284	571	0.10	0.07	0.06	0.11	0.05	0.02	0.00	0.00	0.00	0.01	0.04
Worcester, MA MSA	436,905	7,898	0.33	0.06	0.08	0.38	0.15	0.60	0.04	0.00	0.07	0.03	0.07
Yakima, WA MSA	188,823	1,825	0.13	0.38	0.17	0.02	0.10	0.05	0.01	0.00	0.03	0.01	0.05
York, PA MSA	417,848	2,402	0.06	0.06	0.04	0.10	0.13	0.09	0.03	0.00	0.02	0.01	0.04
Youngstown–Warren, OH MSA	492,619	1,908	0.06	0.05	0.03	0.12	0.07	0.01	0.00	0.00	0.00	0.01	0.04
Yuba City, CA MSA	122,643	10,705	0.34	0.73	0.69	3.76	0.22	0.07	0.01	1.87	0.57	0.10	0.36
Yuma, AZ MSA	106,895	1,256	0.17	0.50	0.21	0.06	0.09	0.04	0.00	0.00	0.01	0.03	0.07

Source: Asian/Pacific Islander Data Consortium (San Francisco, CA: Asian and Pacific Islander Center for Census Information and Services, 1993). Primary source: U.S. Census Bureau, Summary Tape Files 1 and 3. *Note:* (a) The U.S. Census Bureau designates the following: CMSA=Consolidated Metropolitan Statistical Area; PMSA=Primary Metropolitan Statistical Area; MSA=Metropolitan Statistical Area. See *Appendix* for detailed definitions.

★ 791 ★

Population of Metropolitan Statistical Areas by Pacific Islander Ethnicity

Population in U.S. Metropolitan Statistical Areas (MSAs) including Primary Metropolitan Statistical Areas (PMSAs)[a], by Pacific Islander ethnicity, 1990.

Metropolitan area	Total persons	Hawaiian	Samoan	Tongan	Other Polynesian	Guamanian	Other Micronesian	Melanesian	Pacific Islander not specified
Abilene, TX MSA	119,655	40	5	0	0	21	0	0	0
Akron, OH PMSA	657,575	42	9	1	0	28	0	0	3
Albany, GA MSA	112,561	9	6	1	1	6	0	0	0
Albany–Schenectady–Troy, NY MSA	874,304	62	18	1	8	16	7	1	7
Albuquerque, NM MSA	480,577	178	38	8	5	74	10	2	3
Alexandria, LA MSA	131,556	16	· 8	0	0	10	2	0	0
Allentown–Bethlehem–Easton, PA–NJ MSA	686,688	34	23	0	2	9	2	0	3
Altoona, PA MSA	130,542	2	0	0	0	7	0	0	0
Amarillo, TX MSA	187,547	24	0	0	0	2	0	0	0
Anaheim–Santa Ana, CA PMSA	2,410,556	3,166	2,979	345	148	1,406	247	79	119
Anchorage, AK MSA	226,338	491	391	140	16	130	8	2	19
Anderson, IN MSA	130,669	8	1	0	0	7	0	0	0
Anderson, SC MSA	145,196	5	0	0	0	3	0	0	0
Ann Arbor, MI PMSA	282,937	44	9	0	2	8	9	1	6
Anniston, AL MSA	116,034	13	19	1	0	66	4	0	0
Appleton–Oshkosh–Neenah, WI MSA	315,121	19	3	1	0	9	0	1	0
Asheville, NC MSA	174,821	14	2	0	0	6	0	0	0
Athens, GA MSA	156,267	11	7	0	1	6	0	0	0
Atlanta, GA MSA	2,833,511	296	110	1	18	126	14	23	26
Atlantic City, NJ MSA	319,416	30	25	0	5	10	2	0	1
Augusta, GA–SC MSA	396,809	95	· 35	0	1	125	2	1	6
Aurora–Elgin, IL PMSA	356,884	30	6	0	0	22	4	0	0
Austin, TX MSA	781,572	184	43	1	4	106	12	4	11
Bakersfield, CA MSA	543,477	351	105	3	9	236	9	6	15
Baltimore, MD MSA	2,382,172	292	61	1	5	211	11	3	33
Bangor, ME MSA	88,745	16	14	0	0	4	2	0	0

[Continued]

★791★

Population of Metropolitan Statistical Areas by Pacific Islander Ethnicity (Continued)

Population in U.S. Metropolitan Statistical Areas (MSAs) including Primary Metropolitan Statistical Areas (PMSAs)[a], by Pacific Islander ethnicity, 1990.

Metropolitan area	Total persons	Hawaiian	Samoan	Tongan	Other Polynesian	Guamanian	Other Micronesian	Melanesian	Pacific Islander not specified
Baton Rouge, LA MSA	528,264	37	9	0	0	7	0	0	2
Battle Creek, MI MSA	135,982	20	0	0	0	5	4	0	0
Beaumont–Port Arthur, TX MSA	361,226	23	3	0	3	9	11	0	0
Beaver County, PA PMSA	186,093	8	3	0	0	8	1	1	1
Bellingham, WA MSA	127,780	85	12	1	0	32	6	0	13
Benton Harbor, MI MSA	161,378	17	8	3	0	13	0	0	0
Bergen–Passaic, NJ PMSA	1,278,440	79	26	0	5	61	0	6	26
Billings, MT MSA	113,419	31	11	1	0	0	1	0	0
Biloxi–Gulfport, MS MSA	197,125	41	17	0	0	23	4	0	5
Binghamton, NY MSA	264,497	9	2	0	1	5	0	0	0
Birmingham, AL MSA	907,810	42	9	0	0	14	1	2	6
Bismarck, ND MSA	83,831	7	0	1	0	12	1	0	1
Bloomington, IN MSA	108,978	21	4	0	1	3	0	1	0
Bloomington–Normal, IL MSA	129,180	13	9	0	1	3	0	4	8
Boise City, ID MSA	205,775	122	54	7	7	21	29	1	0
Boston, MA PMSA	2,870,669	242	114	6	13	240	15	14	38
Boulder–Longmont, CO PMSA	225,339	70	12	4	1	27	1	2	2
Bradenton, FL MSA	211,707	32	2	3	18	4	1	0	2
Brazoria, TX PMSA	191,707	23	6	2	0	5	5	0	1
Bremerton, WA MSA	189,731	367	168	3	0	852	25	1	16
Bridgeport–Milford, CT PMSA	443,722	31	6	2	0	8	0	1	0
Bristol, CT PMSA	79,488	3	1	0	0	1	0	0	0
Brockton, MA PMSA	189,478	16	2	0	0	9	1	0	4
Brownsville–Harlingen, TX MSA	260,120	9	1	5	0	11	0	6	1
Bryan–College Station, TX MSA	121,862	22	9	0	1	14	4	0	0
Buffalo, NY PMSA	968,532	38	8	4	1	33	0	0	2
Burlington, NC MSA	108,213	8	0	0	0	1	2	0	1
Burlington, VT MSA	131,439	4	6	0	0	4	2	0	1
Canton, OH MSA	394,106	32	2	1	0	11	0	1	0
Casper, WY MSA	61,226	9	2	0	1	4	2	0	0
Cedar Rapids, IA MSA	168,767	14	3	4	0	5	0	0	0
Champaign–Urbana–Rantoul, IL MSA	173,025	24	14	0	2	16	0	3	1
Charleston, SC MSA	506,875	139	29	0	2	95	6	0	7
Charleston, WV MSA	250,454	11	6	0	0	7	0	0	1
Charlotte–Gastonia–Rock Hill, NC–SC MSA	1,162,093	83	21	7	3	42	4	0	10
Charlottesville, VA MSA	131,107	19	4	2	0	4	5	0	2
Chattanooga, TN–GA MSA	433,210	35	6	0	1	6	6	0	0
Cheyenne, WY MSA	73,142	47	11	0	0	17	2	0	3
Chicago, IL PMSA	6,069,974	514	212	9	21	859	16	7	112
Chico, CA MSA	182,120	139	34	1	3	23	24	6	13
Cincinnati, OH–KY–IN PMSA	1,452,645	95	20	0	3	31	5	0	15
Clarksville–Hopkinsville, TN–KY MSA	169,439	144	112	0	3	140	16	1	2
Cleveland, OH PMSA	1,831,122	134	26	3	7	43	6	2	18
Colorado Springs, CO MSA	397,014	432	176	3	11	399	22	0	15
Columbia, MO MSA	112,379	17	4	0	0	2	0	1	1
Columbia, SC MSA	453,331	82	55	14	1	104	5	0	5
Columbus, GA–AL MSA	243,072	146	122	3	3	150	8	0	5
Columbus, OH MSA	1,377,419	133	18	3	1	62	1	0	16
Corpus Christi, TX MSA	349,894	60	5	0	3	32	4	0	5
Cumberland, MD–WV MSA	101,643	3	1	0	0	1	0	0	0
Dallas, TX PMSA	2,553,362	442	119	36	24	248	35	3	38
Danbury, CT PMSA	187,867	22	2	0	0	9	0	1	2

[Continued]

★791★

Population of Metropolitan Statistical Areas by Pacific Islander Ethnicity (Continued)

Population in U.S. Metropolitan Statistical Areas (MSAs) including Primary Metropolitan Statistical Areas (PMSAs)[a], by Pacific Islander ethnicity, 1990.

Metropolitan area	Total persons	Hawaiian	Samoan	Tongan	Other Polynesian	Guamanian	Other Micronesian	Melanesian	Pacific Islander not specified
Danville, VA MSA	108,711	1	0	0	0	3	0	0	0
Davenport–Rock Island–Moline, IA–IL MSA	350,861	29	17	0	1	4	0	1	0
Dayton–Springfield, OH MSA	951,270	116	27	0	1	55	5	2	4
Daytona Beach, FL MSA	370,712	55	17	0	3	31	0	0	0
Decatur, AL MSA	131,556	1	0	0	0	2	0	0	0
Decatur, IL MSA	117,206	1	4	0	0	3	1	0	1
Denver, CO PMSA	1,622,980	574	112	37	18	292	51	5	32
Des Moines, IA MSA	392,928	53	6	0	0	17	1	0	7
Detroit, MI PMSA	4,382,299	323	95	4	7	108	18	4	30
Dothan, AL MSA	130,964	49	23	0	1	26	0	1	0
Dubuque, IA MSA	86,403	5	1	0	0	1	4	0	0
Duluth, MN–WI MSA	239,971	19	1	1	0	4	7	0	2
Eau Claire, WI MSA	137,543	12	4	0	0	5	1	0	2
El Paso, TX MSA	591,610	182	65	0	6	210	16	0	7
Elkhart–Goshen, IN MSA	156,198	16	2	0	5	2	0	0	0
Elmira, NY MSA	95,195	8	5	0	0	3	1	0	0
Enid, OK MSA	56,735	7	0	0	0	0	80	0	5
Erie, PA MSA	275,572	15	1	8	0	11	0	0	1
Eugene–Springfield, OR MSA	282,912	255	39	4	13	83	47	48	19
Evansville, IN–KY MSA	278,990	24	9	0	0	9	4	0	1
Fall River, MA–RI PMSA	157,272	7	2	0	0	7	0	0	0
Fargo–Moorhead, ND–MN MSA	153,296	12	5	0	0	2	0	0	0
Fayetteville, NC MSA	274,566	290	144	3	5	316	20	2	16
Fayetteville–Springdale, AR MSA	113,409	21	4	0	0	7	10	0	1
Fitchburg–Leominster, MA MSA	102,797	17	11	0	3	4	0	0	0
Flint, MI MSA	430,459	33	6	0	0	13	0	0	1
Florence, AL MSA	131,327	9	0	0	0	2	0	2	1
Florence, SC MSA	114,344	5	2	0	0	0	0	0	5
Fort Collins–Loveland, CO MSA	186,136	79	8	0	0	10	1	1	1
Fort Lauderdale–Hollywood–Pompano Beach, FL PMSA	1,255,488	159	33	13	20	120	2	1	25
Fort Myers–Cape CoraL, Fl MSA	335,113	31	4	1	6	31	0	0	1
Fort Pierce, FL MSA	251,071	45	13	0	1	40	7	5	3
Fort Smith, AR–OK MSA	175,911	23	1	0	0	20	0	4	1
Fort Walton Beach, FL MSA	143,776	100	11	0	3	84	6	0	2
Fort Wayne, IN MSA	363,811	48	14	0	0	16	1	0	1
Fort Worth–Arlington, TX PMSA	1,332,053	403	99	565	105	123	22	10	16
Fresno, CA MSA	667,490	348	120	9	4	127	23	33	58
Gadsden, AL MSA	99,840	4	0	0	0	0	0	0	0
Gainesville, FL MSA	204,111	31	8	0	1	9	0	0	4
Galveston–Texas City, TX PMSA	217,399	30	7	0	0	17	3	10	7
Gary–Hammond, IN PMSA	604,526	37	16	0	1	14	1	0	1
Glens Falls, NY MSA	118,539	6	1	0	0	4	0	0	0
Grand Forks, ND MSA	70,683	25	2	0	0	7	5	0	2
Grand Rapids, MI MSA	688,399	80	12	1	0	25	10	11	0
Great Falls, MT MSA	77,691	28	4	0	0	26	0	0	0
Greeley, CO MSA	131,821	66	7	0	1	13	2	0	1
Green Bay, WI MSA	194,594	10	4	1	0	8	2	0	7
Greensboro–Winston-Salem–High Point, NC MSA	942,091	66	13	0	1	7	0	0	17
Greenville–Spartanburg, SC MSA	640,861	46	17	0	0	19	2	0	2
Hagerstown, MD MSA	121,393	10	5	0	0	27	0	0	2
Hamilton–Middletown, OH PMSA	291,479	31	11	0	0	5	0	0	15

[Continued]

★ 791 ★

Population of Metropolitan Statistical Areas by Pacific Islander Ethnicity (Continued)

Population in U.S. Metropolitan Statistical Areas (MSAs) including Primary Metropolitan Statistical Areas (PMSAs)[a], by Pacific Islander ethnicity, 1990.

Metropolitan area	Total persons	Hawaiian	Samoan	Tongan	Other Polynesian	Guamanian	Other Micronesian	Melanesian	Pacific Islander not specified
Harrisburg–Lebanon–Carlisle, PA MSA	587,986	56	15	0	1	13	3	0	3
Hartford, CT PMSA	767,841	62	14	0	5	39	2	2	4
Hickory–Morganton, NC MSA	221,700	18	6	0	0	8	3	0	0
Honolulu, HI MSA	836,231	91,967	14,364	2,222	784	1,903	1,424	236	210
Houma–Thibodaux, LA MSA	182,842	18	0	0	2	2	0	0	0
Houston, TX PMSA	3,301,937	422	139	11	37	361	4	12	86
Huntington–Ashland, WV–KY–OH MSA	312,529	20	0	1	0	12	4	0	0
Huntsville, AL MSA	238,912	76	3	0	2	45	1	0	5
Indianapolis, IN MSA	1,249,822	119	27	2	3	62	1	0	2
Iowa City, IA MSA	96,119	17	2	0	1	1	0	0	1
Jackson, MI MSA	149,756	12	0	0	0	3	0	0	3
Jackson, MS MSA	395,396	13	6	0	0	2	0	0	6
Jackson, TN MSA	77,982	3	0	0	0	0	0	0	0
Jacksonville, FL MSA	906,727	184	50	2	2	163	17	4	15
Jacksonville, NC MSA	149,838	175	111	0	16	121	7	1	1
Jamestown–Dunkirk, NY	141,895	1	5	0	0	16	0	1	0
Janesville–Beloit, WI MSA	139,510	6	8	0	0	7	0	0	1
Jersey City, NJ PMSA	553,099	45	22	0	2	128	1	0	15
Johnson City–Kingsport–Bristol, TN–VA MSA	436,047	11	2	0	0	13	5	0	0
Johnstown, PA MSA	241,247	10	3	0	0	4	1	0	4
Joliet, IL PMSA	389,650	24	3	0	0	2	0	0	10
Joplin, MO MSA	134,910	21	3	0	5	7	64	0	10
Kalamazoo, MI MSA	223,411	16	8	0	1	11	1	1	1
Kankakee, IL MSA	96,255	0	1	0	0	1	3	0	0
Kansas City, MO–KS MSA	1,566,280	347	601	40	30	103	88	3	50
Kenosha, WI PMSA	128,181	13	2	0	0	9	0	0	0
Killeen–Temple, TX MSA	255,301	290	220	4	8	562	17	5	6
Knoxville, TN MSA	604,816	43	16	0	2	14	0	1	0
Kokomo, IN MSA	96,946	18	4	0	0	3	2	0	1
La Crosse, WI MSA	97,904	6	2	0	0	8	0	0	13
Lafayette, LA MSA	208,740	22	3	0	1	1	0	0	4
Lafayette–West Lafayette, IN MSA	130,598	28	7	0	1	9	0	0	0
Lake Charles, LA MSA	168,134	15	1	0	0	4	4	0	0
Lake County, IL PMSA	516,418	104	39	0	7	65	3	2	5
Lakeland–Winter Haven, FL MSA	405,382	27	4	1	2	22	1	0	0
Lancaster, PA MSA	422,822	36	9	0	0	11	1	1	0
Lansing–East Lansing, MI MSA	432,674	72	18	0	2	11	8	0	51
Laredo, TX MSA	133,239	8	1	0	0	2	0	0	0
Las Cruces, NM MSA	135,510	35	14	0	1	16	9	0	0
Las Vegas, NV MSA	741,459	1,051	188	20	42	368	37	10	31
Lawrence, KS MSA	81,798	20	5	0	0	9	0	1	1
Lawrence–Haverhill, MA–NH PMSA	393,516	17	6	1	0	31	0	0	0
Lawton, OK MSA	111,486	126	104	0	4	207	6	1	3
Lewiston–Auburn, ME MSA	88,141	6	1	0	0	9	0	0	0
Lexington-Fayette, KY MSA	348,428	23	16	0	3	14	1	2	4
Lima, OH MSA	154,340	9	0	0	0	1	2	0	1
Lincoln, NE MSA	213,641	45	4	1	1	17	10	0	7
Little Rock–North Little Rock, AR MSA	513,117	61	20	1	4	18	1	0	0
Longview–Marshall, TX MSA	162,431	21	3	0	0	5	1	0	0
Lorain–Elyria, OH PMSA	271,126	18	5	3	0	4	0	0	2

[Continued]

665

★ 791 ★

Population of Metropolitan Statistical Areas by Pacific Islander Ethnicity (Continued)

Population in U.S. Metropolitan Statistical Areas (MSAs) including Primary Metropolitan Statistical Areas (PMSAs)[a], by Pacific Islander ethnicity, 1990.

Metropolitan area	Total persons	Hawaiian	Samoan	Tongan	Other Polynesian	Guamanian	Other Micronesian	Melanesian	Pacific Islander not specified
Los Angeles–Long Beach, CA PMSA	8,863,164	8,009	11,934	1,546	537	5,632	201	578	487
Louisville, KY–IN MSA	952,662	118	31	1	1	28	2	0	4
Lowell, MA–NH PMSA	273,067	13	12	0	0	8	2	5	6
Lubbock, TX MSA	222,636	34	5	5	1	14	2	1	2
Lynchburg, VA MSA	142,199	12	5	1	3	1	3	1	5
Macon–Warner Robins, GA MSA	281,103	26	2	0	2	10	0	0	1
Madison, WI MSA	367,085	42	11	0	1	18	5	0	2
Manchester, NH MSA	147,809	32	1	1	0	8	0	0	0
Mansfield, OH MSA	126,137	8	2	0	4	13	0	0	2
Mcallen–Edinburg–Mission, TX MSA	383,545	10	10	0	0	15	2	1	0
Medford, OR MSA	146,389	92	24	0	1	22	8	1	4
Melbourne–Titusville–Palm Bay, FL MSA	398,978	103	23	0	6	47	8	3	2
Memphis, TN–AR–MS MSA	981,747	128	26	0	2	46	1	0	9
Merced, CA MSA	178,403	153	24	10	3	143	13	1	22
Miami–Hialeah, FL PMSA	1,937,094	179	57	8	12	148	3	0	31
Middlesex–Somerset–Hunterdon, NJ PMSA	1,019,835	54	20	0	1	41	5	4	10
Middletown, CT PMSA	90,320	12	2	0	3	0	0	0	1
Midland, TX MSA	106,611	16	0	0	0	1	11	0	0
Milwaukee, WI PMSA	1,432,149	152	38	0	4	115	4	7	17
Minneapolis–St. Paul, MN–WI MSA	2,464,124	297	86	26	4	114	36	9	148
Mobile, AL MSA	476,923	47	2	1	0	9	3	0	6
Modesto, CA MSA	370,522	331	58	0	13	165	9	530	45
Monmouth–Ocean, NJ PMSA	986,327	90	19	6	0	45	4	2	15
Monroe, LA MSA	142,191	6	8	0	0	4	0	0	0
Montgomery, AL MSA	292,517	29	4	0	0	14	0	0	0
Muncie, IN MSA	119,659	19	4	0	0	2	0	1	0
Muskegon, MI MSA	158,983	5	1	0	0	5	0	0	0
Naples, FL MSA	152,099	10	5	0	1	35	0	0	0
Nashua, NH PMSA	180,557	16	5	0	1	7	0	0	0
Nashville, TN MSA	985,026	119	10	0	1	29	1	2	7
Nassau–Suffolk, NY PMSA	2,609,212	138	45	3	3	108	10	3	39
New Bedford, MA MSA	175,641	25	2	0	1	2	1	0	0
New Britain, CT PMSA	148,188	7	7	0	0	16	5	0	1
New Haven–Meriden, CT MSA	530,180	35	16	0	3	31	0	0	3
New London–Norwich, CT–RI MSA	266,819	51	12	1	0	41	7	2	10
New Orleans, LA MSA	1,238,816	110	49	1	5	95	3	2	3
New York, NY PMSA	8,546,846	859	319	12	27	1,432	13	50	244
Newark, NJ PMSA	1,824,321	113	55	1	2	152	6	2	28
Niagara Falls, NY PMSA	220,756	18	0	0	0	13	0	0	0
Norfolk–Virginia Beach–Newport News, VA MSA	1,396,107	550	213	2	22	354	46	4	10
Norwalk, CT PMSA	127,378	3	2	0	0	1	0	0	0
Oakland, CA PMSA	2,082,914	3,892	1,501	971	187	2,432	162	1,144	275
Ocala, FL MSA	194,833	13	5	0	1	7	0	0	0
Odessa, TX MSA	118,934	10	4	0	0	2	0	2	0
Oklahoma City, OK MSA	958,839	260	53	3	5	153	27	1	12
Olympia, WA MSA	161,238	226	63	1	1	230	6	4	25
Omaha, NE–IA MSA	618,262	167	28	3	5	85	13	0	1
Orange County, NY PMSA	307,647	14	17	0	0	18	4	0	7

[Continued]

Population of Metropolitan Statistical Areas by Pacific Islander Ethnicity (Continued)

Population in U.S. Metropolitan Statistical Areas (MSAs) including Primary Metropolitan Statistical Areas (PMSAs)[a], by Pacific Islander ethnicity, 1990.

Metropolitan area	Total persons	Hawaiian	Samoan	Tongan	Other Polynesian	Guamanian	Other Micronesian	Melanesian	Pacific Islander not specified
Orlando, FL MSA	1,072,748	333	141	30	39	98	14	4	29
Owensboro, KY MSA	87,189	1	1	0	0	2	1	0	0
Oxnard–Ventura, CA PMSA	669,016	773	567	61	35	391	17	12	24
Panama City, FL MSA	126,994	32	2	0	0	31	8	0	0
Parkersburg–Marietta, WV–OH MSA	149,169	9	5	0	0	0	0	0	0
Pascagoula, MS MSA	115,243	29	1	0	2	3	0	0	0
Pawtucket–Woonsocket–Attleboro, RI–MA PMSA	329,384	18	6	0	0	26	0	10	8
Pensacola, FL MSA	344,406	124	36	0	5	96	4	0	4
Peoria, IL MSA	339,172	26	5	1	0	15	0	0	0
Philadelphia, PA–NJ PMSA	4,856,881	550	171	9	19	259	18	3	29
Phoenix, AZ MSA	2,122,101	1,024	248	354	77	382	49	12	44
Pine Bluff, AR MSA	85,487	2	0	0	0	8	0	0	0
Pittsburgh, PA PMSA	2,056,705	129	46	8	2	29	3	0	23
Pittsfield, MA MSA	79,250	5	0	0	1	1	0	4	0
Portland, ME MSA	215,281	8	4	0	2	12	0	0	0
Portland, OR PMSA	1,239,842	1,170	281	142	74	406	242	176	101
Portsmouth–Dover–Rochester, NH–ME MSA	223,578	26	9	0	3	43	0	0	0
Poughkeepsie, NY MSA	259,462	15	2	2	1	4	4	0	5
Providence, RI PMSA	654,854	64	15	0	2	91	1	16	2
Provo–Orem, UT MSA	263,590	428	249	351	84	19	13	4	6
Pueblo, CO MSA	123,051	30	4	0	5	4	6	0	2
Racine, WI PMSA	175,034	9	2	0	1	6	0	0	0
Raleigh–Durham, NC MSA	735,480	73	30	0	2	18	1	0	5
Rapid City, SD MSA	81,343	21	1	21	5	22	0	0	1
Reading, PA MSA	336,523	22	4	0	2	5	1	0	1
Redding, CA MSA	147,036	77	19	1	7	28	0	0	0
Reno, NV MSA	254,667	351	121	276	24	52	31	10	22
Richland–Kennewick–Pasco, WA MSA	150,033	68	20	2	1	13	2	0	5
Richmond–Petersburg, VA MSA	865,640	87	41	0	1	78	8	2	6
Riverside–San Bernardino, CA PMSA	2,588,793	2,597	1,851	915	133	1,506	99	88	130
Roanoke, VA MSA	224,477	8	5	0	0	9	0	0	1
Rochester, MN MSA	106,470	4	3	0	0	1	5	0	4
Rochester, NY MSA	1,002,410	70	13	0	10	26	10	1	10
Rockford, IL MSA	283,719	19	3	0	1	8	0	0	5
Sacramento, CA MSA	1,481,102	1,618	730	666	48	991	61	980	184
Saginaw–Bay City–Midland, MI MSA	399,320	17	6	3	0	10	0	0	1
Salem, OR MSA	278,024	179	60	1	8	77	211	3	27
Salem–Gloucester, MA PMSA	264,356	18	21	1	3	18	0	2	3
Salinas–Seaside–Monterey, CA MSA	355,660	676	542	74	15	948	57	143	32
Salt Lake City–Ogden, UT MSA	1,072,227	801	1,193	3,412	348	100	49	42	65
San Angelo, TX MSA	98,458	9	9	0	1	22	2	0	0
San Antonio, TX MSA	1,302,099	352	81	0	3	263	17	3	37
San Diego, CA MSA	2,498,016	3,778	3,929	116	140	5,306	273	34	139
San Francisco, CA PMSA	1,603,678	2,505	4,649	2,775	253	883	77	1,435	271
San Jose, CA PMSA	1,497,577	2,306	1,804	233	66	1,726	99	358	88
Santa Barbara–Santa Maria–Lompoc, CA MSA	369,608	340	73	1	8	199	13	2	8
Santa Cruz, CA PMSA	229,734	225	43	1	4	42	11	13	10

[Continued]

667

★ 791 ★

Population of Metropolitan Statistical Areas by Pacific Islander Ethnicity (Continued)

Population in U.S. Metropolitan Statistical Areas (MSAs) including Primary Metropolitan Statistical Areas (PMSAs)[a], by Pacific Islander ethnicity, 1990.

Metropolitan area	Total persons	Hawaiian	Samoan	Tongan	Other Polynesian	Guamanian	Other Micronesian	Melanesian	Pacific Islander not specified
Santa Fe, NM MSA	117,043	33	3	0	3	12	4	0	0
Santa Rosa–Petaluma, CA PMSA	388,222	467	139	34	15	108	17	50	13
Sarasota, FL MSA	277,776	31	2	0	1	7	1	0	2
Savannah, GA MSA	242,622	58	22	0	0	16	15	0	5
Scranton–Wilkes-Barre, PA MSA	734,175	47	5	1	0	12	14	0	1
Seattle, WA PMSA	1,972,961	2,340	2,347	352	121	863	199	258	115
Sharon, PA MSA	121,003	5	7	0	0	0	1	0	0
Sheboygan, WI MSA	103,877	5	0	0	0	4	1	0	12
Sherman–Denison, TX MSA	95,021	21	4	0	0	1	0	0	1
Shreveport, LA MSA	334,341	34	12	0	0	51	0	0	1
Sioux City, IA–NE MSA	115,018	10	0	0	0	1	0	0	0
Sioux Falls, SD MSA	123,809	26	4	1	0	8	0	2	0
South Bend–Mishawaka, IN MSA	247,052	33	16	10	0	11	1	0	1
Spokane, WA MSA	361,364	251	38	18	5	143	21	1	5
Springfield, IL MSA	189,550	6	5	0	0	6	0	3	0
Springfield, MA MSA	529,519	38	12	5	9	11	3	1	12
Springfield, MO MSA	240,593	26	18	0	2	13	14	0	2
St. Cloud, MN MSA	190,921	4	6	0	0	9	0	0	0
St. Joseph, MO MSA	83,083	10	1	0	0	8	0	0	0
St. Louis, MO–IL MSA	2,444,099	246	70	7	8	89	5	9	14
Stamford, CT PMSA	202,557	14	3	0	0	50	0	1	2
State College, PA MSA	123,786	6	9	0	0	6	0	1	12
Steubenville–Weirton, OH–WV MSA	142,523	5	1	0	0	1	0	0	0
Stockton, CA MSA	480,628	539	150	44	16	324	32	125	86
Syracuse, NY MSA	659,864	70	13	4	5	18	3	4	12
Tacoma, WA PMSA	586,203	1,198	1,195	33	35	1,163	90	5	85
Tallahassee, FL MSA	233,598	38	14	0	0	8	1	0	1
Tampa–St. Petersburg–Clearwater, FL MSA	2,067,959	291	87	63	9	106	15	17	43
Terre Haute, IN MSA	130,812	10	1	0	0	5	0	1	0
Texarkana, TX–Texarkana, AR MSA	120,132	9	2	0	0	1	2	1	3
Toledo, OH MSA	614,128	31	10	1	0	8	0	1	1
Topeka, KS MSA	160,976	18	8	2	0	9	7	0	0
Trenton, NJ PMSA	325,824	22	8	0	6	91	0	0	3
Tucson, AZ MSA	666,880	270	49	29	10	153	24	1	11
Tulsa, OK MSA	708,954	149	18	0	10	36	6	5	5
Tuscaloosa, AL MSA	150,522	7	3	0	0	2	0	0	0
Tyler, TX MSA	151,309	24	2	0	1	1	0	0	1
Utica–Rome, NY MSA	316,633	30	28	1	0	18	1	0	2
Vallejo–Fairfield–Napa, CA PMSA	451,186	1,066	359	75	11	2,000	24	92	128
Vancouver, WA PMSA	238,053	315	53	19	21	155	30	18	11
Victoria, TX MSA	74,361	2	1	0	0	1	0	0	0
Vineland–Millville–Bridgeton, NJ PMSA	138,053	16	4	0	0	4	0	0	0
Visalia–Tulare–Porterville, CA MSA	311,921	150	29	17	0	53	24	0	33
Waco, TX MSA	189,123	32	1	0	0	6	3	0	1
Washington, DC–MD–VA MSA	3,923,574	941	234	3	37	824	143	33	109
Waterbury, CT MSA	221,629	7	3	0	0	4	0	0	0
Waterloo–Cedar Falls, IA MSA	146,611	15	3	0	0	9	0	1	1
Wausau, WI MSA	115,400	3	4	0	0	2	0	0	1
West Palm Beach–Boca Raton–Delray Beach, FL MSA	863,518	96	23	0	3	77	3	0	10

[Continued]

★ 791 ★

Population of Metropolitan Statistical Areas by Pacific Islander Ethnicity (Continued)

Population in U.S. Metropolitan Statistical Areas (MSAs) including Primary Metropolitan Statistical Areas (PMSAs)[a], by Pacific Islander ethnicity, 1990.

Metropolitan area	Total persons	Hawaiian	Samoan	Tongan	Other Polynesian	Guamanian	Other Micronesian	Melanesian	Pacific Islander not specified
Wheeling, WV–OH MSA	159,301	13	2	0	0	1	5	0	1
Wichita Falls, TX MSA	122,378	45	3	0	0	27	1	2	1
Wichita, KS MSA	485,270	75	26	1	5	46	8	0	1
Williamsport, PA MSA	118,710	6	0	0	0	1	0	0	0
Wilmington, DE–NJ–MD PMSA	578,587	43	17	0	0	32	4	0	2
Wilmington, NC MSA	120,284	17	21	0	1	6	0	0	0
Worcester, MA MSA	436,905	46	4	2	0	12	1	1	3
Yakima, WA MSA	188,823	48	18	5	6	14	1	1	4
York, PA MSA	417,848	35	11	0	0	18	2	0	3
Youngstown–Warren, OH MSA	492,619	27	4	2	0	17	0	0	0
Yuba City, CA MSA	122,643	113	45	1	0	107	3	9	13
Yuma, AZ MSA	106,895	76	16	0	2	36	5	2	0

Source: Asian/Pacific Islander Data Consortium (San Francisco, CA: Asian and Pacific Islander Center for Census Information and Services, 1993). Primary source: U.S. Census Bureau, Summary Tape Files 1 and 3. *Note:* (a) The U.S. Census Bureau designates the following: CMSA=Consolidated Metropolitan Statistical Area; PMSA=Primary Metropolitan Statistical Area; MSA=Metropolitan Statistical Area. See *Appendix* for detailed definitions.

United States Consolidated Metropolitan Statistical Areas

★ 792 ★

Population of Consolidated Metropolitan Statistical Areas by Race/Ethnicity

Population of U.S. Consolidated Metropolitan Statistical Areas (CMSAs) and the Primary Metropolitan Statistical Areas (PMSAs) that make up the CMSAs[a], by race/ethnicity, 1990.

Metropolitan area	Total population	Asian or Pacific Islander	White	Black	American Indian, Eskimo, or Aleut	Other race
Boston–Lawrence–Salem, MA–NH CMSA	4,171,643	121,405	3,708,228	239,059	7,542	95,409
Boston, MA PMSA	2,870,669	95,044	2,499,859	209,970	5,250	60,546
Brockton, MA PMSA	189,478	2,158	168,133	13,770	445	4,972
Lawrence–Haverhill, MA–NH PMSA	393,516	5,146	359,052	7,363	857	21,098
Lowell, MA–NH PMSA	273,067	14,251	248,937	3,598	388	5,893
Nashua, NH PMSA	180,557	2,459	174,851	1,910	297	1,040
Salem–Gloucester, MA PMSA	264,356	2,347	257,396	2,448	305	1,860
Buffalo–Niagara Falls, NY CMSA	1,189,288	11,026	1,037,211	121,956	7,611	11,484
Buffalo, NY PMSA	968,532	10,220	831,903	109,852	5,600	10,957
Niagara Falls, NY PMSA	220,756	806	205,308	12,104	2,011	527
Chicago–Gary–Lake County, IL–IN–WI CMSA	8,065,633	256,050	5,772,110	1,547,725	15,758	473,990
Aurora–Elgin, IL PMSA	356,884	4,698	307,694	19,216	693	24,583
Chicago, IL PMSA	6,069,974	229,492	4,098,747	1,332,919	11,550	397,266
Gary–Hammond, IN PMSA	604,526	3,716	460,532	117,142	1,108	22,028
Joliet, IL PMSA	389,650	4,887	335,284	38,382	737	10,360
Kenosha, WI PMSA	128,181	669	119,187	5,295	472	2,558
Lake County, IL PMSA	516,418	12,588	450,666	34,771	1,198	17,195
Cincinnati–Hamilton, OH–KY–IN CMSA	1,744,124	14,260	1,521,061	203,607	2,457	2,739
Cincinnati, OH–KY–IN PMSA	1,452,645	11,601	1,246,169	190,473	2,078	2,324
Hamilton–Middletown, OH PMSA	291,479	2,659	274,892	13,134	379	415
Cleveland–Akron–Lorain, OH CMSA	2,759,823	28,187	2,261,217	441,940	5,133	23,346
Akron, OH PMSA	657,575	6,180	583,900	65,091	1,357	1,047
Cleveland, OH PMSA	1,831,122	20,528	1,435,768	355,619	3,038	16,169
Lorain–Elyria, OH PMSA	271,126	1,479	241,549	21,230	738	6,130
Dallas–Fort Worth, TX CMSA	3,885,415	97,578	2,924,673	554,616	18,972	289,576
Dallas, TX PMSA	2,553,362	67,195	1,854,577	410,766	12,635	208,189
Fort Worth–Arlington, TX PMSA	1,332,053	30,383	1,070,096	143,850	6,337	81,387
Denver–Boulder, CO CMSA	1,848,319	42,642	1,599,734	97,755	13,884	94,304
Boulder–Longmont, CO PMSA	225,339	5,508	210,190	1,959	1,313	6,369
Denver, CO PMSA	1,622,980	37,134	1,389,544	95,796	12,571	87,935
Detroit–Ann Arbor, MI CMSA	4,665,236	69,454	3,569,087	975,199	17,961	33,535
Ann Arbor, MI PMSA	282,937	11,724	236,390	31,720	1,076	2,027
Detroit, MI PMSA	4,382,299	57,730	3,332,697	943,479	16,885	31,508
Hartford–New Britain–Middletown, CT CMSA	1,085,837	15,845	933,568	94,925	1,826	39,673
Bristol, CT PMSA	79,488	544	76,875	1,347	128	594
Hartford, CT PMSA	767,841	12,201	641,345	81,550	1,365	31,380

[Continued]

★ 792 ★

Population of Consolidated Metropolitan Statistical Areas by Race/Ethnicity (Continued)

Population of U.S. Consolidated Metropolitan Statistical Areas (CMSAs) and the Primary Metropolitan Statistical Areas (PMSAs) that make up the CMSAs[a], by race/ethnicity, 1990.

Metropolitan area	Total population	Asian or Pacific Islander	White	Black	American Indian, Eskimo, or Aleut	Other race
Middletown, CT PMSA	90,320	1,163	82,829	5,454	143	731
New Britain, CT PMSA	148,188	1,937	132,519	6,574	190	6,968
Houston–Galveston–Brazoria, TX CMSA	3,711,043	132,131	2,507,455	665,378	11,029	395,050
Brazoria, TX PMSA	191,707	1,961	154,875	15,981	812	18,078
Galveston–Texas City, TX PMSA	217,399	3,569	164,210	38,154	752	10,714
Houston, TX PMSA	3,301,937	126,601	2,188,370	611,243	9,465	366,258
Los Angeles–Anaheim–Riverside, CA CMSA	14,531,529	1,339,048	9,388,957	1,229,809	87,487	2,486,228
Anaheim–Santa Ana, CA PMSA	2,410,556	249,192	1,894,593	42,681	12,165	211,925
Los Angeles–Long Beach, CA PMSA	8,863,164	954,485	5,035,103	992,974	45,508	1,835,094
Oxnard–Ventura, CA PMSA	669,016	34,579	529,166	15,629	4,909	84,733
Riverside–San Bernardino, CA PMSA	2,588,793	100,792	1,930,095	178,525	24,905	354,476
Miami–Fort Lauderdale, FL CMSA	3,192,582	43,437	2,438,598	591,440	5,700	113,407
Fort Lauderdale–Hollywood–Pompano Beach, FL PMSA	1,255,488	17,130	1,025,583	193,447	2,634	16,694
Miami–Hialeah, FL PMSA	1,937,094	26,307	1,413,015	397,993	3,066	96,713
Milwaukee–Racine, WI CMSA	1,607,183	19,786	1,335,470	214,182	8,522	29,223
Milwaukee, WI PMSA	1,432,149	18,782	1,183,372	197,183	8,001	24,811
Racine, WI PMSA	175,034	1,004	152,098	16,999	521	4,412
New York–Northern New Jersey–Long Island, NY–NJ–CT CMSA	18,087,251	873,213	12,699,119	3,289,465	46,191	1,179,263
Bergen–Passaic, NJ PMSA	1,278,440	66,743	1,043,437	106,108	2,221	59,931
Bridgeport–Milford, CT PMSA	443,722	6,577	371,493	45,826	806	19,020
Danbury, CT PMSA	187,867	4,355	175,780	5,398	301	2,033
Jersey City, NJ PMSA	553,099	36,777	380,612	79,770	1,460	54,480
Middlesex–Somerset–Hunterdon, NJ PMSA	1,019,835	56,804	865,158	70,670	1,420	25,783
Monmouth–Ocean, NJ PMSA	986,327	19,098	895,986	59,264	1,327	10,652
Nassau–Suffolk, NY PMSA	2,609,212	62,399	2,305,434	193,967	4,636	42,776
New York, NY PMSA	8,546,846	556,399	4,826,081	2,250,026	29,711	884,629
Newark, NJ PMSA	1,824,321	52,898	1,279,952	422,802	3,144	65,525
Norwalk, CT PMSA	127,378	2,044	109,752	12,644	138	2,800
Orange County, NY PMSA	307,647	3,549	273,600	22,223	824	7,451
Stamford, CT PMSA	202,557	5,570	171,834	20,767	203	4,183
Philadelphia–Wilmington–Trenton, PA–NJ–DE–MD CMSA	5,899,345	123,458	4,540,541	1,100,347	11,307	123,692
Philadelphia, PA–NJ PMSA	4,856,881	104,595	3,717,175	929,907	8,335	96,869
Trenton, NJ PMSA	325,824	9,992	244,656	61,481	533	9,162
Vineland–Millville–Bridgeton, NJ PMSA	138,053	1,134	101,467	23,318	1,311	10,823
Wilmington, DE–NJ–MD PMSA	578,587	7,737	477,243	85,641	1,128	6,838
Pittsburgh–Beaver Valley, PA CMSA	2,242,798	16,174	2,041,897	178,857	2,257	3,613
Beaver County, PA PMSA	186,093	377	174,759	10,475	203	279
Pittsburgh, PA PMSA	2,056,705	15,797	1,867,138	168,382	2,054	3,334
Portland–Vancouver, OR–WA CMSA	1,477,895	52,030	1,350,155	41,671	13,603	20,436
Portland, OR PMSA	1,239,842	46,360	1,124,963	38,695	11,307	18,517
Vancouver, WA PMSA	238,053	5,670	225,192	2,976	2,296	1,919
Providence–Pawtucket–Fall River, RI–MA CMSA	1,141,510	20,050	1,055,370	37,106	3,782	25,202
Fall River, MA–RI PMSA	157,272	1,541	154,022	1,086	168	455

[Continued]

★ 792 ★

Population of Consolidated Metropolitan Statistical Areas by Race/Ethnicity (Continued)

Population of U.S. Consolidated Metropolitan Statistical Areas (CMSAs) and the Primary Metropolitan Statistical Areas (PMSAs) that make up the CMSAs[a], by race/ethnicity, 1990.

Metropolitan area	Total population	Asian or Pacific Islander	White	Black	American Indian, Eskimo, or Aleut	Other race
Pawtucket–Woonsocket–Attleboro, RI–MA PMSA	329,384	3,987	310,677	5,494	535	8,691
Providence, RI PMSA	654,854	14,522	590,671	30,526	3,079	16,056
San Francisco–Oakland–San Jose, CA CMSA	6,253,311	926,961	4,334,064	537,753	40,847	413,686
Oakland, CA PMSA	2,082,914	269,566	1,372,818	303,826	14,230	122,474
San Francisco, CA PMSA	1,603,678	329,599	1,058,796	122,494	7,232	85,557
San Jose, CA PMSA	1,497,577	261,466	1,032,190	56,211	9,269	138,441
Santa Cruz, CA PMSA	229,734	8,512	192,849	2,632	1,821	23,920
Santa Rosa–Petaluma, CA PMSA	388,222	10,774	351,650	5,547	4,397	15,854
Vallejo–Fairfield–Napa, CA PMSA	451,186	47,044	325,761	47,043	3,898	27,440
Seattle–Tacoma, WA CMSA	2,559,164	164,286	2,211,710	123,266	32,071	27,831
Seattle, WA PMSA	1,972,961	135,251	1,713,068	81,056	23,727	19,859
Tacoma, WA PMSA	586,203	29,035	498,642	42,210	8,344	7,972

Source: Asian/Pacific Islander Data Consortium (San Francisco, CA: Asian and Pacific Islander Center for Census Information and Services, 1993). Primary source: U.S. Census Bureau, Summary Tape Files 1 and 3. *Note:* (a) The U.S. Census Bureau designates the following: CMSA=Consolidated Metropolitan Statistical Area; PMSA=Primary Metropolitan Statistical Area; MSA=Metropolitan Statistical Area. See *Appendix* for detailed definitions.

★ 793 ★

Population of Consolidated Metropolitan Statistical Areas by Race/Ethnicity, in Percent

Population of U.S. Consolidated Metropolitan Statistical Areas (CMSAs) and the Primary Metropolitan Statistical Areas (PMSAs) that make up the CMSAs[a], in percent, by race/ethnicity, 1990.

Metropolitan area	Total population	Percent of total				
		Asian Pacific Islander	White	Black	American Indian, Eskimo,	Other race
Boston–Lawrence–Salem, MA–NH CMSA	4,171,643	2.9	89	6	0.2	2.3
Boston, MA PMSA	2,870,669	3.3	87	7	0.2	2.1
Brockton, MA PMSA	189,478	1.1	89	7	0.2	2.6
Lawrence–Haverhill, MA–NH PMSA	393,516	1.3	91	2	0.2	5.4
Lowell, MA–NH PMSA	273,067	5.2	91	1	0.1	2.2
Nashua, NH PMSA	180,557	1.4	97	1	0.2	0.6
Salem–Gloucester, MA PMSA	264,356	0.9	97	1	0.1	0.7
Buffalo–Niagara Falls, NY CMSA	1,189,288	0.9	87	10	0.6	1.7
Buffalo, NY PMSA	968,532	1.1	86	11	0.6	1.1
Niagara Falls, NY PMSA	220,756	0.4	93	5	0.9	0.2
Chicago–Gary–Lake County, IL–IN–WI CMSA	8,065,633	3.2	72	19	0.2	5.9
Aurora–Elgin, IL PMSA	356,884	1.3	86	5	0.2	6.9
Chicago, IL PMSA	6,069,974	3.8	68	22	0.2	6.5
Gary–Hammond, IN PMSA	604,526	0.6	76	19	0.2	3.6

[Continued]

★ 793 ★

Population of Consolidated Metropolitan Statistical Areas by Race/Ethnicity, in Percent (Continued)

Population of U.S. Consolidated Metropolitan Statistical Areas (CMSAs) and the Primary Metropolitan Statistical Areas (PMSAs) that make up the CMSAs[a], in percent, by race/ethnicity, 1990.

Metropolitan area	Total population	Percent of total				
		Asian Pacific Islander	White	Black	American Indian, Eskimo,	Other race
Joliet, IL PMSA	389,650	1.3	86	10	0.2	2.7
Kenosha, WI PMSA	128,181	0.5	93	4	0.4	2.0
Lake County, IL PMSA	516,418	2.4	87	7	0.2	3.3
Cincinnati–Hamilton, OH–KY–IN CMSA	1,744,124	0.8	87	12	0.1	0.2
Cincinnati, OH–KY–IN PMSA	1,452,645	0.8	86	13	0.1	0.2
Hamilton–Middletown, OH PMSA	291,479	0.9	94	5	0.1	0.1
Cleveland–Akron–Lorain, OH CMSA	2,759,823	1.0	82	16	0.2	0.9
Akron, OH PMSA	657,575	0.9	89	10	0.2	0.2
Cleveland, OH PMSA	1,831,122	1.1	78	19	0.2	0.9
Lorain–Elyria, OH PMSA	271,126	0.6	89	8	0.3	2.3
Dallas–Fort Worth, TX CMSA	3,885,415	2.5	75	14	0.5	7.5
Dallas, TX PMSA	2,553,362	2.6	73	16	0.5	8.2
Fort Worth–Arlington, TX PMSA	1,332,053	2.3	80	11	0.5	6.1
Denver–Boulder, CO CMSA	1,848,319	2.3	87	5	0.8	5.1
Boulder–Longmont, CO PMSA	225,339	2.4	93	1	0.6	2.8
Denver, CO PMSA	1,622,980	2.3	86	6	0.8	5.4
Detroit–Ann Arbor, MI CMSA	4,665,236	1.5	77	21	0.4	0.7
Ann Arbor, MI PMSA	282,937	4.1	84	11	0.4	0.7
Detroit, MI PMSA	4,382,299	1.3	76	22	0.4	0.7
Hartford–New Britain–Middletown, CT CMSA	1,085,837	1.5	86	9	0.2	3.7
Bristol, CT PMSA	79,488	0.7	97	2	0.2	0.8
Hartford, CT PMSA	767,841	1.6	84	11	0.2	4.1
Middletown, CT PMSA	90,320	1.3	92	6	0.2	0.8
New Britain, CT PMSA	148,188	1.3	89	4	0.1	4.7
Houston–Galveston–Brazoria, TX CMSA	3,711,043	3.6	68	18	0.3	10.7
Brazoria, TX PMSA	191,707	1.0	81	8	0.4	9.4
Galveston–Texas City, TX PMSA	217,399	1.6	76	18	0.4	4.9
Houston, TX PMSA	3,301,937	3.8	66	19	0.3	11.1
Los Angeles–Anaheim–Riverside, CA CMSA	14,531,529	9.2	65	8	0.6	17.1
Anaheim–Santa Ana, CA PMSA	2,410,556	10.3	79	2	0.5	8.8
Los Angeles–Long Beach, CA PMSA	8,863,164	10.8	57	11	0.5	20.7
Oxnard–Ventura, CA PMSA	669,016	5.2	79	2	0.7	12.7
Riverside–San Bernardino, CA PMSA	2,588,793	3.9	75	7	1.6	13.7
Miami–Fort Lauderdale, FL CMSA	3,192,582	1.4	76	19	0.2	3.6
Fort Lauderdale–Hollywood–Pompano Beach, FL PMSA	1,255,488	1.4	82	15	0.2	1.3
Miami–Hialeah, FL PMSA	1,937,094	1.4	73	21	0.2	5.0
Milwaukee–Racine, WI CMSA	1,607,183	1.2	83	13	0.5	1.8
Milwaukee, WI PMSA	1,432,149	1.3	83	14	0.6	1.7
Racine, WI PMSA	175,034	0.6	87	10	0.3	2.5

[Continued]

★ 793 ★

Population of Consolidated Metropolitan Statistical Areas by Race/Ethnicity, in Percent (Continued)

Population of U.S. Consolidated Metropolitan Statistical Areas (CMSAs) and the Primary Metropolitan Statistical Areas (PMSAs) that make up the CMSAs[a], in percent, by race/ethnicity, 1990.

Metropolitan area	Total population	Percent of total				
		Asian Pacific Islander	White	Black	American Indian, Eskimo,	Other race
New York–Northern New Jersey–Long Island, NY–NJ–CT CMSA	18,087,251	4.8	70	18	0.3	6.5
Bergen–Passaic, NJ PMSA	1,278,440	5.2	82	8	0.2	4.7
Bridgeport–Milford, CT PMSA	443,722	1.5	84	10	0.2	4.3
Danbury, CT PMSA	187,867	2.3	94	3	0.2	1.1
Jersey City, NJ PMSA	553,099	6.7	69	14	0.3	9.9
Middlesex–Somerset–Hunterdon, NJ PMSA	1,019,835	5.6	85	7	0.1	2.5
Monmouth–Ocean, NJ PMSA	986,327	1.9	91	6	0.1	1.1
Nassau–Suffolk, NY PMSA	2,609,212	2.4	88	7	0.2	1.6
New York, NY PMSA	8,546,846	6.5	56	26	0.4	10.4
Newark, NJ PMSA	1,824,321	2.9	70	23	0.2	3.6
Norwalk, CT PMSA	127,378	1.6	86	10	0.1	2.2
Orange County, NY PMSA	307,647	1.2	89	7	0.3	2.4
Stamford, CT PMSA	202,557	2.8	85	10	0.1	2.1
Philadelphia–Wilmington–Trenton, PA–NJ–DE–MD CMSA	5,899,345	2.1	77	19	0.2	2.1
Philadelphia, PA–NJ PMSA	4,856,881	2.2	77	19	0.2	2.0
Trenton, NJ PMSA	325,824	3.1	75	19	0.2	2.8
Vineland–Millville–Bridgeton, NJ PMSA	138,053	0.8	73	17	1.5	7.8
Wilmington, DE–NJ–MD PMSA	578,587	1.3	82	15	0.2	1.2
Pittsburgh–Beaver Valley, PA CMSA	2,242,798	0.7	91	8	0.1	0.2
Beaver County, PA PMSA	186,093	0.2	94	6	0.1	0.2
Pittsburgh, PA PMSA	2,056,705	0.8	91	8	0.1	0.2
Portland–Vancouver, OR–WA CMSA	1,477,895	3.5	91	3	0.9	1.4
Portland, OR PMSA	1,239,842	3.7	91	3	0.9	1.5
Vancouver, WA PMSA	238,053	2.4	95	1	1.6	0.8
Providence–Pawtucket–Fall River, RI–MA CMSA	1,141,510	1.8	92	3	0.3	2.2
Fall River, MA–RI PMSA	157,272	1.8	98	1	0.1	0.3
Pawtucket–Woonsocket–Attleboro, RI–MA PMSA	329,384	1.2	94	2	0.2	2.6
Providence, RI PMSA	654,854	2.2	90	5	0.5	2.5
San Francisco–Oakland–San Jose, CA CMSA	6,253,311	14.8	69	9	0.7	6.6
Oakland, CA PMSA	2,082,914	12.9	66	15	0.7	5.9
San Francisco, CA PMSA	1,603,678	20.6	66	8	0.5	5.3
San Jose, CA PMSA	1,497,577	17.5	69	4	0.6	9.2
Santa Cruz, CA PMSA	229,734	3.7	84	1	0.8	10.4
Santa Rosa–Petaluma, CA PMSA	388,222	2.8	91	1	1.1	4.1
Vallejo–Fairfield–Napa, CA PMSA	451,186	10.4	72	10	0.9	6.1

[Continued]

★ 793 ★

Population of Consolidated Metropolitan Statistical Areas by Race/Ethnicity, in Percent (Continued)

Population of U.S. Consolidated Metropolitan Statistical Areas (CMSAs) and the Primary Metropolitan Statistical Areas (PMSAs) that make up the CMSAs[a], in percent, by race/ethnicity, 1990.

Metropolitan area	Total population	Percent of total				
		Asian Pacific Islander	White	Black	American Indian, Eskimo,	Other race
Seattle–Tacoma, WA CMSA	2,559,164	6.4	86	5	1.3	1.1
Seattle, WA PMSA	1,972,961	6.9	87	4	1.2	1.0
Tacoma, WA PMSA	586,203	5.0	85	7	1.4	1.4

Source: Asian/Pacific Islander Data Consortium (San Francisco, CA: Asian and Pacific Islander Center for Census Information and Services, 1993). Primary source: U.S. Census Bureau, Summary Tape Files 1 and 3. *Note:* (a) U.S. Census Burea designates the following: CMSA=Consolidated Metropolitan Statistical Area; PMSA=Primary Metropolitan Statistical Area; MSA=Metropolitan Statistical Area. See *Appendix* for detailed definitions.

★ 794 ★

Population of Consolidated Metropolitan Statistical Areas by Hispanic Origin

Population of U.S. Consolidated Metropolitan Statistical Areas (CMSAs) and the Primary Metropolitan Statistical Areas (PMSAs) that make up the CMSAs[a], by race and Hispanic origin[b], 1990.

Metropolitan statistical area	Not of Hispanic Origin					Hispanic Origin				
	Asian or Pacific Islander	White	Black	American Indian, Eskimo, Aleut	Other Race	Asian or Pacific Islander	White	Black	American Indian, Aleut	Other race
Boston–Lawrence–Salem, MA–NH CMSA	119,008	3,622,312	218,048	6,298	12,778	2,397	85,916	21,011	1,244	82,631
Boston, MA PMSA	93,340	2,439,321	195,393	4,503	9,229	1,704	60,538	14,577	747	51,317
Brockton, MA PMSA	2,108	164,922	12,418	380	2,606	50	3,211	1,352	65	2,366
Lawrence–Haverhill, MA–NH PMSA	4,827	347,963	3,553	546	327	319	11,089	3,810	311	20,771
Lowell, MA–NH PMSA	13,986	243,035	3,187	341	325	265	5,902	411	47	5,568
Nashua, NH PMSA	2,443	172,725	1,715	279	122	16	2,126	195	18	918
Salem–Gloucester, MA PMSA	2,304	254,346	1,782	249	169	43	3,050	666	56	1,691
Buffalo–Niagara Falls, NY CMSA	10,804	1,025,984	120,213	7,326	614	222	11,227	1,743	285	10,870
Buffalo, NY PMSA	10,025	822,166	108,240	5,357	495	195	9,737	1,612	243	10,462
Niagara Falls, NY PMSA	779	203,818	11,973	1,969	119	27	1,490	131	42	408
Chicago–Gary–Lake County, IL–IN–WI CMSA	246,949	5,378,333	1,527,639	12,441	6,849	9,101	393,777	20,086	3,317	467,141
Aurora–Elgin, IL PMSA	4,437	287,685	18,558	543	321	261	20,009	658	150	24,262
Chicago, IL PMSA	221,462	3,782,766	1,316,602	8,868	5,449	8,030	315,981	16,317	2,682	391,817
Gary–Hammond, IN PMSA	3,550	435,557	115,786	926	323	166	24,975	1,356	182	21,705
Joliet, IL PMSA	4,713	325,536	37,767	652	261	174	9,748	615	85	10,099
Kenosha, WI PMSA	652	116,223	5,190	443	93	17	2,964	105	29	2,465
Lake County, IL PMSA	12,135	430,566	33,736	1,009	402	453	20,100	1,035	189	16,793
Cincinnati–Hamilton, OH–KY–IN CMSA	13,910	1,514,656	202,859	2,338	985	350	6,405	748	119	1,754
Cincinnati, OH–KY–IN PMSA	11,299	1,240,802	189,790	1,975	870	302	5,367	683	103	1,454

[Continued]

★ 794 ★

Population of Consolidated Metropolitan Statistical Areas by Hispanic Origin (Continued)

Population of U.S. Consolidated Metropolitan Statistical Areas (CMSAs) and the Primary Metropolitan Statistical Areas (PMSAs) that make up the CMSAs[a], by race and Hispanic origin[b], 1990.

Metropolitan statistical area	Not of Hispanic Origin					Hispanic Origin				
	Asian or Pacific Islander	White	Black	American Indian, Eskimo, Aleut	Other Race	Asian or Pacific Islander	White	Black	American Indian, Aleut	Other race
Hamilton–Middletown, OH PMSA	2,611	273,854	13,069	363	115	48	1,038	65	16	300
Cleveland–Akron–Lorain, OH CMSA	27,647	2,233,731	438,926	4,777	1,745	540	27,486	3,014	356	21,601
Akron, OH PMSA	6,081	581,228	64,713	1,302	436	99	2,672	378	55	611
Cleveland, OH PMSA	20,131	1,419,629	353,517	2,795	1,129	397	16,139	2,102	243	15,040
Lorain–Elyria, OH PMSA	1,435	232,874	20,696	680	180	44	8,675	534	58	5,950
Dallas–Fort Worth, TX CMSA	93,865	2,708,392	543,983	16,195	4,063	3,713	216,281	10,633	2,777	285,513
Dallas, TX PMSA	64,573	1,703,736	402,662	10,558	2,949	2,622	150,841	8,104	2,077	205,240
Fort Worth–Arlington, TX PMSA	29,292	1,004,656	141,321	5,637	1,114	1,091	65,440	2,529	700	80,273
Denver–Boulder, CO CMSA	40,655	1,474,006	94,175	10,723	2,560	1,987	125,728	3,580	3,161	91,744
Boulder–Longmont, CO PMSA	5,359	201,617	1,879	1,092	197	149	8,573	80	221	6,172
Denver, CO PMSA	35,296	1,272,389	92,296	9,631	2,363	1,838	117,155	3,500	2,940	85,572
Detroit–Ann Arbor, MI CMSA	67,948	3,516,428	970,163	16,726	3,024	1,506	52,659	5,036	1,235	30,511
Ann Arbor, MI PMSA	11,598	232,938	31,334	987	349	126	3,452	386	89	1,678
Detroit, MI PMSA	56,350	3,283,490	938,829	15,739	2,675	1,380	49,207	4,650	1,146	28,833
Hartford–New Britain–Middletown, CT CMSA	15,360	902,609	89,348	1,601	1,292	485	30,959	5,577	225	38,381
Bristol, CT PMSA	538	75,720	1,255	112	44	6	1,155	92	16	550
Hartford, CT PMSA	11,813	618,775	76,697	1,176	1,018	388	22,570	4,853	189	30,362
Middletown, CT PMSA	1,137	81,607	5,322	136	59	26	1,222	132	7	672
New Britain, CT PMSA	1,872	126,507	6,074	177	171	65	6,012	500	13	6,797
Houston–Galveston–Brazoria, TX CMSA	126,824	2,147,984	649,699	8,683	5,558	5,307	359,471	15,679	2,346	389,492
Brazoria, TX PMSA	1,837	139,683	15,425	687	278	124	15,192	556	125	17,800
Galveston–Texas City, TX PMSA	3,357	144,852	37,414	632	182	212	19,358	740	120	10,532
Houston, TX PMSA	121,630	1,863,449	596,860	7,364	5,098	4,971	324,921	14,383	2,101	361,160
Los Angeles–Anaheim–Riverside, CA CMSA	1,274,967	7,230,159	1,157,622	59,584	30,079	64,081	2,158,798	72,187	27,903	2,456,149
Anaheim–Santa Ana, CA PMSA	240,756	1,554,501	39,159	8,584	2,728	8,436	340,092	3,522	3,581	209,197
Los Angeles–Long Beach, CA PMSA	907,810	3,618,850	934,776	29,159	21,327	46,675	1,416,253	58,198	16,349	1,813,767
Oxnard–Ventura, CA PMSA	32,665	440,555	14,559	3,430	855	1,914	88,611	1,070	1,479	83,878
Riverside–San Bernardino, CA PMSA	93,736	1,616,253	169,128	18,411	5,169	7,056	313,842	9,397	6,494	349,307
Miami–Fort Lauderdale, FL CMSA	40,449	1,525,952	556,291	4,393	3,651	2,988	912,646	35,149	1,307	109,756
Fort Lauderdale–Hollywood–Pompano Beach, FL PMSA	16,395	940,345	186,670	2,391	1,248	735	85,238	6,777	243	15,446
Miami–Hialeah, FL PMSA	24,054	585,607	369,621	2,002	2,403	2,253	827,408	28,372	1,064	94,310
Milwaukee–Racine, WI CMSA	19,266	1,306,740	211,940	7,693	1,204	520	28,730	2,242	829	28,019
Milwaukee, WI PMSA	18,302	1,158,995	195,247	7,237	1,062	480	24,377	1,936	764	23,749
Racine, WI PMSA	964	147,745	16,693	456	142	40	4,353	306	65	4,270

[Continued]

★ 794 ★

Population of Consolidated Metropolitan Statistical Areas by Hispanic Origin (Continued)

Population of U.S. Consolidated Metropolitan Statistical Areas (CMSAs) and the Primary Metropolitan Statistical Areas (PMSAs) that make up the CMSAs[a], by race and Hispanic origin[b], 1990.

Metropolitan statistical area	Not of Hispanic Origin					Hispanic Origin				
	Asian or Pacific Islander	White	Black	American Indian, Eskimo, Aleut	Other Race	Asian or Pacific Islander	White	Black	American Indian, Aleut	Other race
New York–Northern New Jersey–Long Island, NY–NJ–CT CMSA	840,462	11,434,303	2,967,422	32,932	34,181	32,751	1,264,816	322,043	13,259	1,145,082
Bergen–Passaic, NJ PMSA	64,984	966,486	95,783	1,675	1,644	1,759	76,951	10,325	546	58,287
Bridgeport–Milford, CT PMSA	6,319	347,771	43,567	679	645	258	23,722	2,259	127	18,375
Danbury, CT PMSA	4,255	170,881	5,049	269	277	100	4,899	349	32	1,756
Jersey City, NJ PMSA	35,046	262,077	69,856	960	1,695	1,731	118,535	9,914	500	52,785
Middlesex–Somerset–Hunterdon, NJ PMSA	55,579	824,182	66,255	1,139	985	1,225	40,976	4,415	281	24,798
Monmouth–Ocean, NJ PMSA	18,571	872,480	57,088	1,220	611	527	23,506	2,176	107	10,041
Nassau–Suffolk, NY PMSA	60,849	2,194,597	182,618	3,854	2,056	1,550	110,837	11,349	782	40,720
New York, NY PMSA	532,716	4,095,765	1,986,472	19,544	22,687	23,683	730,316	263,554	10,167	861,942
Newark, NJ PMSA	51,280	1,171,053	408,130	2,619	2,940	1,618	108,899	14,672	525	62,585
Norwalk, CT PMSA	2,009	104,696	12,172	120	158	35	5,056	472	18	2,642
Orange County, NY PMSA	3,448	260,968	20,731	702	263	101	12,632	1,492	122	7,188
Stamford, CT PMSA	5,406	163,347	19,701	151	220	164	8,487	1,066	52	3,963
Philadelphia–Wilmington–Trenton, PA–NJ–DE–MD CMSA	120,334	4,458,606	1,079,532	10,266	4,739	3,124	81,935	20,815	1,041	118,953
Philadelphia, PA–NJ PMSA	101,933	3,656,130	913,437	7,544	3,857	2,662	61,045	16,470	791	93,012
Trenton, NJ PMSA	9,736	236,143	59,449	467	364	256	8,513	2,032	66	8,798
Vineland–Millville–Bridgeton, NJ PMSA	1,063	95,129	22,167	1,203	143	71	6,338	1,151	108	10,680
Wilmington, DE–NJ–MD PMSA	7,602	471,204	84,479	1,052	375	135	6,039	1,162	76	6,463
Pittsburgh–Beaver Valley, PA CMSA	15,986	2,032,447	177,695	2,088	1,730	188	9,450	1,162	169	1,883
Beaver County, PA PMSA	370	173,870	10,411	193	125	7	889	64	10	154
Pittsburgh, PA PMSA	15,616	1,858,577	167,284	1,895	1,605	181	8,561	1,098	159	1,729
Portland–Vancouver, OR–WA CMSA	50,777	1,322,994	40,725	12,406	1,072	1,253	27,161	946	1,197	19,364
Portland, OR PMSA	45,299	1,101,442	37,852	10,277	923	1,061	23,521	843	1,030	17,594
Vancouver, WA PMSA	5,478	221,552	2,873	2,129	149	192	3,640	103	167	1,770
Providence–Pawtucket–Fall River, RI–MA CMSA	19,338	1,032,533	32,569	3,354	6,249	712	22,837	4,537	428	18,953
Fall River, MA–RI PMSA	1,515	152,314	1,026	156	196	26	1,708	60	12	259
Pawtucket–Woonsocket–Attleboro, RI–MA PMSA	3,893	303,034	4,891	449	3,168	94	7,643	603	86	5,523
Providence, RI PMSA	13,930	577,185	26,652	2,749	2,885	592	13,486	3,874	330	13,171
San Francisco–Oakland–San Jose, CA CMSA	892,237	3,829,512	518,750	31,672	10,737	34,724	504,552	19,003	9,175	402,949
Oakland, CA PMSA	258,623	1,240,163	295,672	11,204	4,165	10,943	132,655	8,154	3,026	118,309
San Francisco, CA PMSA	320,309	923,914	117,872	5,645	2,664	9,290	134,882	4,622	1,587	82,893
San Jose, CA PMSA	251,496	869,874	52,583	6,694	2,366	9,970	162,316	3,628	2,575	136,075
Santa Cruz, CA PMSA	7,690	171,203	2,330	1,310	404	822	21,646	302	511	23,516
Santa Rosa–Petaluma, CA PMSA	10,234	327,429	5,268	3,663	405	540	24,221	279	734	15,449

[Continued]

677

★ 794 ★

Population of Consolidated Metropolitan Statistical Areas by Hispanic Origin (Continued)

Population of U.S. Consolidated Metropolitan Statistical Areas (CMSAs) and the Primary Metropolitan Statistical Areas (PMSAs) that make up the CMSAs[a], by race and Hispanic origin[b], 1990.

Metropolitan statistical area	Not of Hispanic Origin					Hispanic Origin				
	Asian or Pacific Islander	White	Black	American Indian, Eskimo, Aleut	Other Race	Asian or Pacific Islander	White	Black	American Indian, Aleut	Other race
Vallejo–Fairfield–Napa, CA PMSA	43,885	296,929	45,025	3,156	733	3,159	28,832	2,018	742	26,707
Seattle–Tacoma, WA CMSA	159,320	2,171,642	120,414	29,746	2,487	4,966	40,068	2,852	2,325	25,344
Seattle, WA PMSA	131,551	1,683,246	79,309	22,021	1,841	3,700	29,822	1,747	1,706	18,018
Tacoma, WA PMSA	27,769	488,396	41,105	7,725	646	1,266	10,246	1,105	619	7,326

Source: Asian/Pacific Islander Data Consortium (San Francisco, CA: Asian and Pacific Islander Center for Census Information and Services, 1993). Primary source: U.S. Census Bureau, Summary Tape Files 1 and 3. *Notes:* (a) The U.S. Census Bureau designates the following: CMSA=Consolidated Metropolitan Statistical Area; PMSA=Primary Metropolitan Statistical Area; MSA=Metropolitan Statistical Area. See *Appendix* for detailed definition. (b) Persons of Hispanic origin may be of any race.

★ 795 ★

Population of Consolidated Metropolitan Statistical Areas by Asian Ethnicity

Population of U.S. Consolidated Metropolitan Statistical Areas (CMSAs) and the Primary Metropolitan Statistical Areas (PMSAs) that make up the CMSAs[a], by Asian ethnicity, 1990.

Metropolitan area	Total persons	Chinese	Filipino	Japanese	Asian Indian	Korean	Vietnamese	Cambodian	Hmong	Loation	Thai	Other Asian
Boston–Lawrence–Salem, MA–NH CMSA	4,171,643	49,174	5,077	7,483	16,549	9,274	11,679	11,988	51	2,670	1,157	5,393
Boston, MA PMSA	2,870,669	44,155	3,987	6,530	12,301	7,001	9,403	4,967	3	882	948	4,185
Brockton, MA PMSA	189,478	564	298	60	337	193	231	75	48	107	29	184
Lawrence–Haverhill, MA–NH PMSA	393,516	1,385	176	282	933	918	719	337	0	39	37	265
Lowell, MA–NH PMSA	273,067	1,782	225	167	1,928	503	881	6,516	0	1,603	63	537
Nashua, NH PMSA	180,557	661	180	166	719	288	208	29	0	18	39	122
Salem–Gloucester, MA PMSA	264,356	627	211	278	331	371	237	64	0	21	41	100
Buffalo–Niagara Falls, NY CMSA	1,189,288	2,708	728	659	2,956	1,845	742	101	1	324	94	751
Buffalo, NY PMSA	968,532	2,616	619	610	2,745	1,661	700	101	1	315	79	687
Niagara Falls, NY PMSA	220,756	92	109	49	211	184	42	0	0	9	15	64
Chicago–Gary–Lake County, IL–IN–WI CMSA	8,065,633	43,515	61,460	19,206	59,046	36,952	8,228	2,856	274	3,535	4,375	14,433
Aurora–Elgin, IL PMSA	356,884	386	458	211	808	457	344	81	47	1,415	60	369
Chicago, IL PMSA	6,069,974	40,189	54,411	17,310	53,702	33,465	7,313	2,456	212	1,781	3,955	12,948
Gary–Hammond, IN PMSA	604,526	395	953	283	862	549	148	9	2	45	131	269
Joliet, IL PMSA	389,650	536	1,433	222	1,286	408	147	169	5	264	72	306
Kenosha, WI PMSA	128,181	68	152	72	131	150	14	1	7	7	5	38
Lake County, IL PMSA	516,418	1,941	4,053	1,108	2,257	1,923	262	140	1	23	152	503
Cincinnati–Hamilton, OH–KY–IN CMSA	1,744,124	3,154	1,650	1,580	3,561	1,498	1,090	384	1	44	182	885
Cincinnati, OH–KY–IN PMSA	1,452,645	2,545	1,299	1,322	2,773	1,200	972	356	1	42	160	762
Hamilton–Middletown, OH PMSA	291,479	609	351	258	788	298	118	28	0	2	22	123

[Continued]

★ 795 ★

Population of Consolidated Metropolitan Statistical Areas by Asian Ethnicity (Continued)

Population of U.S. Consolidated Metropolitan Statistical Areas (CMSAs) and the Primary Metropolitan Statistical Areas (PMSAs) that make up the CMSAs[a], by Asian ethnicity, 1990.

Metropolitan area	Total persons	Chinese	Filipino	Jap-anese	Asian Indian	Korean	Vietnam ese	Cam-bodian	Hmong	Loation	Thai	Other Asian
Cleveland–Akron–Lorain, OH CMSA	2,759,823	6,513	3,750	2,331	7,537	3,073	1,411	409	218	630	300	1,661
Akron, OH PMSA	657,575	1,428	544	457	1,395	787	231	43	208	465	110	429
Cleveland, OH PMSA	1,831,122	4,841	2,851	1,696	5,852	2,053	1,147	364	10	165	175	1,135
Lorain–Elyria, OH PMSA	271,126	244	355	178	290	233	33	2	0	0	15	97
Dallas–Fort Worth, TX CMSA	3,885,415	17,937	7,537	4,150	17,831	11,041	20,133	2,723	170	5,649	2,114	6,005
Dallas, TX PMSA	2,553,362	13,546	5,512	3,019	13,201	8,963	11,522	2,216	93	2,678	1,424	4,076
Fort Worth–Arlington, TX PMSA	1,332,053	4,391	2,025	1,131	4,630	2,078	8,611	507	77	2,971	690	1,929
Denver–Boulder, CO CMSA	1,848,319	6,622	3,264	7,885	3,005	7,073	6,275	1,159	1,199	1,892	791	2,237
Boulder–Longmont, CO PMSA	225,339	1,318	266	1,095	471	743	405	226	268	179	67	351
Denver, CO PMSA	1,622,980	5,304	2,998	6,790	2,534	6,330	5,870	933	931	1,713	724	1,886
Detroit–Ann Arbor, MI CMSA	4,665,236	13,533	10,375	7,478	18,509	9,193	2,104	281	1,505	942	693	4,173
Ann Arbor, MI PMSA	282,937	3,953	628	1,430	2,211	2,201	347	7	2	60	121	685
Detroit, MI PMSA	4,382,299	9,580	9,747	6,048	16,298	6,992	1,757	274	1,503	882	572	3,488
Hartford–New Britain–Middletown, CT CMSA	1,085,837	3,085	1,117	700	4,121	1,677	1,856	448	44	1,186	125	1,299
Bristol, CT PMSA	79,488	131	80	24	126	52	27	46	0	16	4	33
Hartford, CT PMSA	767,841	2,358	856	527	3,294	1,311	1,571	254	43	717	97	1,045
Middletown, CT PMSA	90,320	276	86	75	283	158	52	65	0	42	11	97
New Britain, CT PMSA	148,188	320	95	74	418	156	206	83	1	411	13	124
Houston–Galveston–Brazoria, TX CMSA	3,711,043	30,084	14,339	3,991	26,599	7,423	34,712	2,448	1	1,462	1,344	8,540
Brazoria, TX PMSA	191,707	260	345	116	247	140	506	143	0	3	37	122
Galveston–Texas City, TX PMSA	217,399	479	590	185	632	213	1,171	11	0	8	26	180
Houston, TX PMSA	3,301,937	29,345	13,404	3,690	25,720	7,070	33,035	2,294	1	1,451	1,281	8,238
Los Angeles–Anaheim–Riverside, CA CMSA	14,531,529	304,588	291,618	173,370	68,887	194,437	148,217	34,417	1,557	8,769	24,191	42,385
Anaheim–Santa Ana, CA PMSA	2,410,556	41,403	30,356	29,704	15,212	35,919	71,822	3,979	575	2,893	2,227	6,613
Los Angeles–Long Beach, CA PMSA	8,863,164	245,033	219,653	129,736	43,829	145,431	62,594	27,819	359	3,742	19,016	28,349
Oxnard–Ventura, CA PMSA	669,016	4,986	12,690	4,964	2,355	2,921	2,486	175	32	178	474	1,438
Riverside–San Bernardino, CA PMSA	2,588,793	13,166	28,919	8,966	7,491	10,166	11,315	2,444	591	1,956	2,474	5,985
Miami–Fort Lauderdale, FL CMSA	3,192,582	13,586	5,633	1,953	11,884	2,468	2,204	102	1	132	933	3,730
Fort Lauderdale–Hollywood–Pompano Beach, FL PMSA	1,255,488	4,739	1,787	643	5,737	1,065	1,190	32	0	24	340	1,200
Miami–Hialeah, FL PMSA	1,937,094	8,847	3,846	1,310	6,147	1,403	1,014	70	1	108	593	2,530
Milwaukee–Racine, WI CMSA	1,607,183	3,039	1,787	1,016	3,501	1,925	1,214	96	3,404	2,074	194	1,181
Milwaukee, WI PMSA	1,432,149	2,897	1,695	951	3,247	1,718	1,131	94	3,404	2,033	183	1,092
Racine, WI PMSA	175,034	142	92	65	254	207	83	2	0	41	11	89
New York–Northern New Jersey–Long Island, NY–NJ–CT CMSA	18,087,251	320,201	104,582	47,608	199,010	118,096	16,728	3,978	35	2,064	7,005	49,290
Bergen–Passaic, NJ PMSA	1,278,440	10,391	10,027	10,482	15,095	17,018	458	16	0	72	473	2,508
Bridgeport–Milford, CT PMSA	443,722	1,157	394	228	1,528	527	696	443	1	936	109	510
Danbury, CT PMSA	187,867	731	396	146	1,220	326	353	596	0	297	49	205
Jersey City, NJ PMSA	553,099	5,002	13,222	532	11,552	2,803	1,107	4	0	30	190	2,122
Middlesex–Somerset–Hunterdon, NJ PMSA	1,019,835	14,883	8,137	1,235	22,972	5,117	1,326	25	25	52	213	2,684
Monmouth–Ocean, NJ PMSA	986,327	6,141	3,669	631	4,424	2,245	566	25	0	11	119	1,086
Nassau–Suffolk, NY PMSA	2,609,212	18,257	7,356	4,042	17,523	9,024	1,245	58	0	106	708	3,731
New York, NY PMSA	8,546,846	246,817	49,156	26,422	106,270	74,632	9,044	2,727	8	454	4,684	33,229
Newark, NJ PMSA	1,824,321	14,020	10,907	1,999	15,842	5,258	1,529	76	0	57	354	2,497
Norwalk, CT PMSA	127,378	592	234	151	628	183	49	0	0	18	39	144
Orange County, NY PMSA	307,647	820	504	229	890	589	126	7	1	22	49	252
Stamford, CT PMSA	202,557	1,390	580	1,511	1,066	374	229	1	0	9	18	322

[Continued]

★ 795 ★

Population of Consolidated Metropolitan Statistical Areas by Asian Ethnicity (Continued)

Population of U.S. Consolidated Metropolitan Statistical Areas (CMSAs) and the Primary Metropolitan Statistical Areas (PMSAs) that make up the CMSAs[a], by Asian ethnicity, 1990.

Metropolitan area	Total persons	Chinese	Filipino	Jap-anese	Asian Indian	Korean	Vietnam ese	Cam-bodian	Hmong	Loation	Thai	Other Asian
Philadelphia–Wilmington–Trenton, PA–NJ–DE–MD CMSA	5,899,345	27,535	14,257	5,649	26,120	24,568	10,884	4,675	71	1,351	902	6,136
Philadelphia, PA–NJ PMSA	4,856,881	22,311	12,233	4,304	20,657	22,028	10,418	4,633	71	1,268	793	4,821
Trenton, NJ PMSA	325,824	3,025	816	465	3,247	1,339	141	36	0	7	40	746
Vineland–Millville–Bridgeton, NJ PMSA	138,053	116	220	331	194	97	25	0	0	4	9	114
Wilmington, DE–NJ–MD PMSA	578,587	2,083	988	549	2,022	1,104	300	6	0	72	60	455
Pittsburgh–Beaver Valley, PA CMSA	2,242,798	4,196	1,312	1,261	4,618	2,167	884	91	16	39	256	1,072
Beaver County, PA PMSA	186,093	70	58	23	65	84	12	0	0	0	8	35
Pittsburgh, PA PMSA	2,056,705	4,126	1,254	1,238	4,553	2,083	872	91	16	39	248	1,037
Portland–Vancouver, OR–WA CMSA	1,477,895	9,862	5,657	7,514	2,559	6,774	8,347	2,021	379	3,061	534	2,108
Portland, OR PMSA	1,239,842	9,143	4,849	6,832	2,307	5,871	7,555	1,608	379	2,901	457	1,866
Vancouver, WA PMSA	238,053	719	808	682	252	903	792	413	0	160	77	242
Providence–Pawtucket–Fall River, RI–MA CMSA	1,141,510	3,329	1,505	741	2,306	1,380	897	4,905	884	2,628	153	1,047
Fall River, MA–RI PMSA	157,272	259	129	67	61	84	48	743	0	52	7	75
Pawtucket–Woonsocket–Attleboro, RI–MA PMSA	329,384	488	259	93	659	243	352	622	6	876	49	272
Providence, RI PMSA	654,854	2,582	1,117	581	1,586	1,053	497	3,540	878	1,700	97	700
San Francisco–Oakland–San Jose, CA CMSA	6,253,311	325,899	261,273	78,769	53,404	42,277	85,370	10,054	232	10,157	4,006	20,481
Oakland, CA PMSA	2,082,914	90,691	77,198	21,477	21,633	13,478	16,732	3,791	38	5,964	1,183	6,817
San Francisco, CA PMSA	1,603,678	162,636	88,560	23,682	8,531	10,416	12,451	1,639	8	1,118	1,394	6,316
San Jose, CA PMSA	1,497,577	65,027	61,518	26,516	20,164	15,565	54,212	3,948	47	1,625	885	5,279
Santa Cruz, CA PMSA	229,734	1,633	2,398	2,310	417	586	247	84	8	15	60	405
Santa Rosa–Petaluma, CA PMSA	388,222	2,169	1,839	1,709	652	740	752	557	53	834	81	545
Vallejo–Fairfield–Napa, CA PMSA	451,186	3,743	29,760	3,075	2,007	1,492	976	35	78	601	403	1,119
Seattle–Tacoma, WA CMSA	2,559,164	28,791	32,663	26,801	6,390	23,901	14,500	9,208	458	4,647	1,739	4,789
Seattle, WA PMSA	1,972,961	27,490	27,900	22,835	5,914	16,311	12,617	5,800	447	4,270	1,323	3,749
Tacoma, WA PMSA	586,203	1,301	4,763	3,966	476	7,590	1,883	3,408	11	377	416	1,040

Source: Asian/Pacific Islander Data Consortium (San Francisco, CA: Asian and Pacific Islander Center for Census Information and Services, 1993). Primary source: U.S. Census Bureau, Summary Tape Files 1 and 3. *Note:* (a) The U.S. Bureau of Census designates the following: CMSA=Consolidated Metropolitan Statistical Area; PMSA=Primary Metropolitan Statistical Area; MSA=Metropolitan Statistical Area. See *Appendix* for detailed definition.

★ 796 ★

Population of Consolidated Metropolitan Statistical Areas by Pacific Islander Ethnicity

Population in U.S. Consolidated Metropolitan Statistical Areas (CMSAs) and the Primary Metropolitan Statistical Areas (PMSAs) that make up the CMSAs[a], by Pacific Islander ethnicity, 1990.

Metropolitan area	Total persons	Hawaiian	Samoan	Tongan	Other Polynesian	Guamanian	Other Micro-nesian	Malanesian	Pacific Islander, not specified
Boston–Lawrence–Salem, MA–NH CMSA	4,171,643	322	160	8	17	313	18	21	51
Boston, MA PMSA	2,870,669	242	114	6	13	240	15	14	38
Brockton, MA PMSA	189,478	16	2	0	0	9	1	0	4
Lawrence–Haverhill, MA–NH PMSA	393,516	17	6	1	0	31	0	0	0
Lowell, MA–NH PMSA	273,067	13	12	0	0	8	2	5	6
Nashua, NH PMSA	180,557	16	5	0	1	7	0	0	0
Salem–Gloucester, MA PMSA	264,356	18	21	1	3	18	0	2	3
Buffalo–Niagara Falls, NY CMSA	1,189,288	56	8	4	1	46	0	0	2
Buffalo, NY PMSA	968,532	38	8	4	1	33	0	0	2
Niagara Falls, NY PMSA	220,756	18	0	0	0	13	0	0	0
Chicago–Gary–Lake County, IL–IN–WI CMSA	8,065,633	722	278	9	29	971	24	9	128
Aurora–Elgin, IL PMSA	356,884	30	6	0	0	22	4	0	0
Chicago, IL PMSA	6,069,974	514	212	9	21	859	16	7	112
Gary–Hammond, IN PMSA	604,526	37	16	0	1	14	1	0	1
Joliet, IL PMSA	389,650	24	3	0	0	2	0	0	10
Kenosha, WI PMSA	128,181	13	2	0	0	9	0	0	0
Lake County, IL PMSA	516,418	104	39	0	7	65	3	2	5
Cincinnati–Hamilton, OH–KY–IN CMSA	1,744,124	126	31	0	3	36	5	0	30
Cincinnati, OH–KY–IN PMSA	1,452,645	95	20	0	3	31	5	0	15
Hamilton–Middletown, OH PMSA	291,479	31	11	0	0	5	0	0	15
Cleveland–Akron–Lorain, OH CMSA	2,759,823	194	40	7	7	75	6	2	23
Akron, OH PMSA	657,575	42	9	1	0	28	0	0	3
Cleveland, OH PMSA	1,831,122	134	26	3	7	43	6	2	18
Lorain–Elyria, OH PMSA	271,126	18	5	3	0	4	0	0	2
Dallas–Fort Worth, TX CMSA	3,885,415	845	218	601	129	371	57	13	54
Dallas, TX PMSA	2,553,362	442	119	36	24	248	35	3	38
Fort Worth–Arlington, TX PMSA	1,332,053	403	99	565	105	123	22	10	16
Denver–Boulder, CO CMSA	1,848,319	644	124	41	19	319	52	7	34
Boulder–Longmont, CO PMSA	225,339	70	12	4	1	27	1	2	2
Denver, CO PMSA	1,622,980	574	112	37	18	292	51	5	32
Detroit–Ann Arbor, MI CMSA	4,665,236	367	104	4	9	116	27	5	36
Ann Arbor, MI PMSA	282,937	44	9	0	2	8	9	1	6
Detroit, MI PMSA	4,382,299	323	95	4	7	108	18	4	30
Hartford–New Britain–Middletown, CT CMSA	1,085,837	84	24	0	8	56	7	2	6

[Continued]

681

★ 796 ★

Population of Consolidated Metropolitan Statistical Areas by Pacific Islander Ethnicity (Continued)

Population in U.S. Consolidated Metropolitan Statistical Areas (CMSAs) and the Primary Metropolitan Statistical Areas (PMSAs) that make up the CMSAs[a], by Pacific Islander ethnicity, 1990.

Metropolitan area	Total persons	Hawaiian	Samoan	Tongan	Other Polynesian	Guamanian	Other Micro- nesian	Malanesian	Pacific Islander, not specified
Bristol, CT PMSA	79,488	3	1	0	0	1	0	0	0
Hartford, CT PMSA	767,841	62	14	0	5	39	2	2	4
Middletown, CT PMSA	90,320	12	2	0	3	0	0	0	1
New Britain, CT PMSA	148,188	7	7	0	0	16	5	0	1
Houston–Galveston–Brazoria, TX CMSA	3,711,043	475	152	13	37	383	12	22	94
Brazoria, TX PMSA	191,707	23	6	2	0	5	5	0	1
Galveston–Texas City, TX PMSA	217,399	30	7	0	0	17	3	10	7
Houston, TX PMSA	3,301,937	422	139	11	37	361	4	12	86
Los Angeles–Anaheim–River- side, CA CMSA	14,531,529	14,545	17,331	2,867	853	8,935	564	757	760
Anaheim–Santa Ana, CA PMSA	2,410,556	3,166	2,979	345	148	1,406	247	79	119
Los Angeles–Long Beach, CA PMSA	8,863,164	8,009	11,934	1,546	537	5,632	201	578	487
Oxnard–Ventura, CA PMSA	669,016	773	567	61	35	391	17	12	24
Riverside–San Bernardino, CA PMSA	2,588,793	2,597	1,851	915	133	1,506	99	88	130
Miami–Fort Lauderdale, FL CMSA	3,192,582	338	90	21	32	268	5	1	56
Fort Lauderdale–Holly- wood–Pompano Beach, FL PMSA	1,255,488	159	33	13	20	120	2	1	25
Miami–Hialeah, FL PMSA	1,937,094	179	57	8	12	148	3	0	31
Milwaukee–Racine, WI CMSA	1,607,183	161	40	0	5	121	4	7	17
Milwaukee, WI PMSA	1,432,149	152	38	0	4	115	4	7	17
Racine, WI PMSA	175,034	9	2	0	1	6	0	0	0
New York–Northern New Jer- sey–Long Island, NY–NJ–CT CMSA	18,087,251	1,462	536	24	40	2,053	43	70	388
Bergen–Passaic, NJ PMSA	1,278,440	79	26	0	5	61	0	6	26
Bridgeport–Milford, CT PMSA	443,722	31	6	2	0	8	0	1	0
Danbury, CT PMSA	187,867	22	2	0	0	9	0	1	2
Jersey City, NJ PMSA	553,099	45	22	0	2	128	1	0	15
Middlesex–Somerset–Hunt- erdon, NJ PMSA	1,019,835	54	20	0	1	41	5	4	10
Monmouth–Ocean, NJ PMSA	986,327	90	19	6	0	45	4	2	15
Nassau–Suffolk, NY PMSA	2,609,212	138	45	3	3	108	10	3	39
New York, NY PMSA	8,546,846	859	319	12	27	1,432	13	50	244
Newark, NJ PMSA	1,824,321	113	55	1	2	152	6	2	28
Norwalk, CT PMSA	127,378	3	2	0	0	1	0	0	0
Orange County, NY PMSA	307,647	14	17	0	0	18	4	0	7
Stamford, CT PMSA	202,557	14	3	0	0	50	0	1	2

[Continued]

★ 796 ★

Population of Consolidated Metropolitan Statistical Areas by Pacific Islander Ethnicity (Continued)

Population in U.S. Consolidated Metropolitan Statistical Areas (CMSAs) and the Primary Metropolitan Statistical Areas (PMSAs) that make up the CMSAs[a], by Pacific Islander ethnicity, 1990.

Metropolitan area	Total persons	Hawaiian	Samoan	Tongan	Other Polynesian	Guamanian	Other Micro-nesian	Malanesian	Pacific Islander, not specified
Philadelphia–Wilmington–Trenton, PA–NJ–DE–MD CMSA	5,899,345	631	200	9	25	386	22	3	34
Philadelphia, PA–NJ PMSA	4,856,881	550	171	9	19	259	18	3	29
Trenton, NJ PMSA	325,824	22	8	0	6	91	0	0	3
Vineland–Millville–Bridge-ton, NJ PMSA	138,053	16	4	0	0	4	0	0	0
Wilmington, DE–NJ–MD PMSA	578,587	43	17	0	0	32	4	0	2
Pittsburgh–Beaver Valley, PA CMSA	2,242,798	137	49	8	2	37	4	1	24
Beaver County, PA PMSA	186,093	8	3	0	0	8	1	1	1
Pittsburgh, PA PMSA	2,056,705	129	46	8	2	29	3	0	23
Portland–Vancouver, OR–WA CMSA	1,477,895	1,485	334	161	95	561	272	194	112
Portland, OR PMSA	1,239,842	1,170	281	142	74	406	242	176	101
Vancouver, WA PMSA	238,053	315	53	19	21	155	30	18	11
Providence–Pawtucket–Fall River, RI–MA CMSA	1,141,510	89	23	0	2	124	1	26	10
Fall River, MA–RI PMSA	157,272	7	2	0	0	7	0	0	0
Pawtucket–Woonsocket–Attleboro, RI–MA PMSA	329,384	18	6	0	0	26	0	10	8
Providence, RI PMSA	654,854	64	15	0	2	91	1	16	2
San Francisco–Oakland–San Jose, CA CMSA	6,253,311	10,461	8,495	4,089	536	7,191	390	3,092	785
Oakland, CA PMSA	2,082,914	3,892	1,501	971	187	2,432	162	1,144	275
San Francisco, CA PMSA	1,603,678	2,505	4,649	2,775	253	883	77	1,435	271
San Jose, CA PMSA	1,497,577	2,306	1,804	233	66	1,726	99	358	88
Santa Cruz, CA PMSA	229,734	225	43	1	4	42	11	13	10
Santa Rosa–Petaluma, CA PMSA	388,222	467	139	34	15	108	17	50	13
Vallejo–Fairfield–Napa, CA PMSA	451,186	1,066	359	75	11	2,000	24	92	128
Seattle–Tacoma, WA CMSA	2,559,164	3,538	3,542	385	156	2,026	289	263	200
Seattle, WA PMSA	1,972,961	2,340	2,347	352	121	863	199	258	115
Tacoma, WA PMSA	586,203	1,198	1,195	33	35	1,163	90	5	85

Source: Asian/Pacific Islander Data Consortium (San Francisco, CA: Asian and Pacific Islander Center for Census Information and Services, 1993). Primary source: U.S. Census Bureau, Summary Tape Files 1 and 3. *Note:* (a) U.S. Bureau of Census designates the following: CMSA=Consolidated Metropolitan Statistical Area; PMSA=Primary Metropolitan Statistical Area; MSA=Metropolitan Statistical Area. See *Appendix* for detailed definition.

United States by State

★ 797 ★

Asian/Pacific Islander Population, Ranked by State, 1980 and 1990

Asian/Pacific Islander population of the fifty states and District of Columbia, percent of total state population, and percent change from 1980 to 1990 by state. States are ranked by Asian/Pacific Islander population in 1990.

State	1990		1980		Percent change, 1980 to 1990
	Population	Percent of state total	Population[a]	Percent of state total	
California	2,845,659	9.6	1,253,818	5.3	127.0
New York	693,760	3.9	310,526	1.8	123.4
Hawaii	685,236	61.8	583,252	60.5	17.5
Texas	319,459	1.9	120,313	0.8	165.5
Illinois	285,311	2.5	159,653	1.4	78.7
New Jersey	272,521	3.5	103,848	1.4	162.4
Washington	210,958	4.3	102,537	2.5	105.7
Virginia	159,053	2.6	66,209	1.2	140.2
Florida	154,302	1.2	56,740	0.6	171.9
Massachusetts	143,392	2.4	49,501	0.9	189.7
Maryland	139,719	2.9	64,278	1.5	117.4
Pennsylvania	137,438	1.2	64,379	0.5	113.5
Michigan	104,983	1.1	56,790	0.6	84.9
Ohio	91,179	0.8	47,820	0.4	90.7
Minnesota	77,886	1.8	26,536	0.7	193.5
Georgia	75,781	1.2	24,457	0.4	208.6
Oregon	69,269	2.4	34,775	1.3	99.2
Colorado	59,862	1.8	29,916	1.0	100.1
Arizona	55,206	1.5	22,032	0.8	150.6
Wisconsin	53,583	1.1	18,164	0.4	195.0
North Carolina	52,166	0.8	21,176	0.4	146.3
Connecticut	50,698	1.5	18,970	0.6	167.3
Missouri	41,277	0.8	23,096	0.5	78.7
Louisiana	41,099	1.0	23,779	0.6	72.8
Nevada	38,127	3.2	14,164	1.8	169.2
Indiana	37,617	0.7	20,557	0.4	83.0
Oklahoma	33,563	1.1	17,275	0.6	94.3
Utah	33,371	1.9	15,076	1.0	121.4
Tennessee	31,839	0.7	13,963	0.3	128.0
Kansas	31,750	1.3	15,078	0.6	110.6
Iowa	25,476	0.9	11,577	0.4	120.1
South Carolina	22,382	0.6	11,834	0.4	89.1
Alabama	21,797	0.5	9,734	0.2	123.9
Alaska	19,728	3.6	8.054	2.0	144.9
Rhode Island	18,325	1.8	5,303	0.6	245.6
Kentucky	17,812	0.5	9,970	0.3	78.7
New Mexico	14,124	0.9	6,825	0.5	106.9

[Continued]

684

★ 797 ★

Asian/Pacific Islander Population, Ranked by State, 1980 and 1990 (Continued)

Asian/Pacific Islander population of the fifty states and District of Columbia, percent of total state population, and percent change from 1980 to 1990 by state. States are ranked by Asian/Pacific Islander population in 1990.

State	1990		1980		Percent change, 1980 to 1990
	Population	Percent of state total	Population[a]	Percent of state total	
Mississippi	13,016	0.5	7,412	0.3	75.6
Arkansas	12,530	0.5	6,740	0.3	85.9
Nebraska	12,422	0.8	7,002	0.4	77.4
District of Columbia	11,214	1.8	6,636	1.0	120.3
Idaho	9,365	0.9	5,948	0.6	57.4
New Hampshire	9,343	0.8	2,929	0.3	219.0
Delaware	9,057	1.4	4,112	0.7	120.3
West Virginia	7,459	0.4	5,194	0.3	43.6
Maine	6,683	0.5	2,947	0.3	126.8
Montana	4,259	0.5	2,503	0.3	70.2
North Dakota	3,462	0.5	1,979	0.3	74.9
Vermont	3,215	0.6	1,355	0.3	137.3
South Dakota	3,123	0.4	1,738	0.3	79.7
Wyoming	2,806	0.6	1,969	0.4	42.5

Source: Asian Week, *Asians in America, 1990 Census, Classification by States,* (San Francisco, CA: *Asian Week,* 1993), p. 4. Primary source: U.S. Census Bureau. *Note:* (a) The 1980 numbers for Asian/Pacific Islanders shown in this table are not entirely comparable with the 1990 counts. The 1980 count of 3,500,439 Asian/Pacific Islanders based on 100 percent tabulations includes only the nine specific Asian/Pacific Islander groups listed separately in the 1980 race item on the Decennial Census survey. The 1980 total Asian/Pacific Islander population of 3,726,440 from sample tabulations is comparable to the 1990 count; these figures include groups not listed separately in the race item on the 1980 census form.

★ 798 ★

Asian/Pacific Islander Population by State and Age

Asian/Pacific Islander population of the fifty states and District of Columbia by age range, 1990.

State	Asian/Pacific Islander Population							
	Age							
	0 to 9	10 to 19	20 to 29	30 to 39	40 to 49	50 to 59	60 and over	Total
Alabama	3,476	3,611	4,626	4,485	3,100	1,497	1,002	21,797
Alaska	3,774	2,983	3,265	4,303	2,722	1,321	1,360	19,728
Arizona	8,885	8,738	11,737	11,280	6,898	3,828	3,840	55,206
Arkansas	2,155	2,369	2,513	2,377	1,627	796	693	12,530
California	465,919	441,467	501,226	542,937	372,431	225,814	295,865	2,845,659
Colorado	10,567	9,974	11,335	11,624	7,278	4,059	5,025	59,862
Connecticut	8,537	8,321	10,794	10,169	6,858	3,438	2,581	50,698
Delaware	1,497	1,437	1,635	1,784	1,399	804	501	9,057
District of Columbia	943	1,188	3,048	2,490	1,431	933	1,181	11,214
Florida	23,142	25,747	28,045	31,510	23,508	12,180	10,170	154,302
Georgia	12,816	12,544	14,843	16,457	10,679	4,935	3,507	75,781
Hawaii	99,271	98,096	102,764	111,523	86,113	63,105	124,364	685,236
Idaho	1,673	1,742	1,792	1,715	1,059	506	878	9,365

[Continued]

685

★ 798 ★

Asian/Pacific Islander Population by State and Age (Continued)

Asian/Pacific Islander population of the fifty states and District of Columbia by age range, 1990.

State	Asian/Pacific Islander Population							
	Age							
	0 to 9	10 to 19	20 to 29	30 to 39	40 to 49	50 to 59	60 and over	Total
Illinois	45,340	46,496	50,531	54,197	43,639	22,603	22,505	285,311
Indiana	5,632	6,339	8,812	7,212	5,157	2,575	1,890	37,617
Iowa	5,107	4,876	6,695	4,199	2,400	1,223	976	25,476
Kansas	5,704	5,891	7,423	5,813	3,731	1,783	1,405	31,750
Kentucky	3,037	2,992	3,644	3,499	2,516	1,275	849	17,812
Louisiana	7,759	8,106	7,474	7,875	5,050	2,592	2,243	41,099
Maine	1,334	1,241	1,337	1,239	793	411	328	6,683
Maryland	21,550	21,693	24,976	27,332	21,473	12,576	10,119	139,719
Massachusetts	25,279	23,180	33,126	28,622	15,690	8,646	8,849	143,392
Michigan	20,136	18,713	19,881	19,158	14,508	6,865	5,722	104,983
Minnesota	21,768	16,564	14,139	11,596	6,955	3,493	3,371	77,886
Mississippi	2,409	2,388	2,594	2,446	1,524	855	800	13,016
Missouri	6,513	7,122	9,193	7,766	5,511	2,889	2,283	41,277
Montana	939	692	834	763	467	274	290	4,259
Nebraska	2,371	2,165	2,859	2,414	1,326	668	619	12,422
Nevada	5,426	5,653	6,691	7,591	5,847	3,653	3,266	38,127
New Hampshire	1,647	1,481	2,112	2,058	1,115	520	410	9,343
New Jersey	45,643	42,467	43,567	58,454	44,496	20,657	17,237	272,521
New Mexico	2,480	2,414	2,530	3,019	1,844	974	863	14,124
New York	96,107	100,042	131,964	144,765	101,187	59,376	60,319	693,760
North Carolina	8,795	8,651	11,059	10,990	6,997	3,472	2,202	52,166
North Dakota	587	642	874	665	400	170	124	3,462
Ohio	14,523	15,259	18,968	17,368	13,245	6,581	5,235	91,179
Oklahoma	5,412	5,741	8,205	6,484	4,121	2,059	1,541	33,563
Oregon	11,523	12,343	14,573	12,877	7,950	4,484	5,519	69,269
Pennsylvania	23,470	24,768	26,768	25,018	18,924	10,061	8,429	137,438
Rhode Island	3,810	3,581	4,025	3,075	1,857	1,062	915	18,325
South Carolina	3,552	3,953	4,363	4,402	3,273	1,716	1,123	22,382
South Dakota	639	609	737	587	287	149	115	3,123
Tennessee	5,305	5,560	6,343	6,451	4,557	2,142	1,481	31,839
Texas	54,326	53,441	61,340	68,662	45,236	19,911	16,543	319,459
Utah	6,886	6,402	6,938	5,848	3,250	1,733	2,314	33,371
Vermont	646	617	814	525	332	161	120	3,215
Virginia	24,314	26,895	29,906	31,828	24,136	12,346	9,628	159,053
Washington	36,705	36,069	37,855	38,912	26,520	15,532	19,365	210,958
West Virginia	1,103	1,464	1,435	1,195	1,241	665	356	7,459
Wisconsin	15,072	10,143	10,574	7,850	4,810	2,700	2,434	53,583
Wyoming	474	443	545	592	316	216	220	2,806

Source: Asian/Pacific Islander Data Consortium (San Francisco, CA: Asian and Pacific Islander Center for Census Information and Services, 1993). Primary source: U.S. Census Bureau, Summary Tape Files 1 and 3.

★ 799 ★

Population by State and Race/Ethnicity

Population of the fifty states and District of Columbia in number and percent by race/ethnicity, 1990.

State	Total population	Asian/Pacific Islander		White		Black		American Indian, Eskimo, or Aleut		Other race	
		Population	Percent	Population	Percent	Population	Percent	Population	Percent	Population	Percent
Alabama	4,040,587	21,797	0.5%	2,975,797	74%	1,020,705	25%	16,506	0.4%	5,782	0.1%
Alaska	550,043	19,728	3.6%	415,492	76%	22,451	4%	85,698	15.6%	6,674	1.2%
Arizona	3,665,228	55,206	1.5%	2,963,186	81%	110,524	3%	203,527	5.6%	332,785	9.1%
Arkansas	2,350,725	12,530	0.5%	1,944,744	83%	373,912	16%	12,773	0.5%	6,766	0.3%
California	29,760,021	2,845,659	9.6%	20,524,327	69%	2,208,801	7%	242,164	0.8%	3,939,070	13.2%
Colorado	3,294,394	59,862	1.8%	2,905,474	88%	133,146	4%	27,776	0.8%	168,136	5.1%
Connecticut	3,287,116	50,698	1.5%	2,859,353	87%	274,269	8%	6,654	0.2%	96,142	2.9%
Delaware	666,168	9,057	1.4%	535,094	80%	112,460	17%	2,019	0.3%	7,538	1.1%
District of Columbia	606,900	11,214	1.9%	179,667	30%	399,604	66%	1,466	0.2%	14,949	2.5%
Florida	12,937,926	154,302	1.2%	10,749,285	83%	1,759,534	14%	36,335	0.3%	238,470	1.8%
Georgia	6,478,216	75,781	1.2%	4,600,148	71%	1,746,565	27%	13,348	0.2%	42,374	0.7%
Hawaii	1,108,229	685,236	61.8%	369,616	33%	27,195	2%	5,099	0.5%	21,083	1.9%
Idaho	1,006,749	9,365	0.9%	950,451	94%	3,370	0%	13,780	1.4%	29,783	3.0%
Illinois	11,430,602	285,311	2.5%	8,952,978	78%	1,694,273	15%	21,836	0.2%	476,204	4.2%
Indiana	5,544,159	37,617	0.7%	5,020,700	91%	432,092	8%	12,720	0.2%	41,030	0.7%
Iowa	2,776,755	25,476	0.9%	2,683,090	97%	48,090	2%	7,349	0.3%	12,750	0.5%
Kansas	2,477,574	31,750	1.3%	2,231,986	90%	143,076	6%	21,965	0.9%	48,797	2.0%
Kentucky	3,685,296	17,812	0.5%	3,391,832	92%	262,907	7%	5,769	0.2%	6,976	0.2%
Louisiana	4,219,973	41,099	1.7%	2,839,138	67%	1,299,281	31%	18,541	0.4%	21,914	0.5%
Maine	1,227,928	6,683	0.5%	1,208,360	98%	5,138	0%	5,998	0.5%	1,749	0.1%
Maryland	4,781,468	139,719	2.9%	3,393,964	71%	1,189,899	25%	12,972	0.3%	44,914	0.9%
Massachusetts	6,016,425	143,392	2.4%	5,405,374	90%	300,130	5%	12,241	0.2%	155,288	2.6%
Michigan	9,295,297	104,983	1.1%	7,756,086	83%	1,291,706	14%	55,638	0.6%	86,884	0.9%
Minnesota	4,375,099	77,886	1.8%	4,130,395	94%	94,944	2%	49,909	1.1%	21,965	0.5%
Mississippi	2,573,216	13,016	0.5%	1,633,461	63%	915,057	36%	8,525	0.3%	3,157	0.1%
Missouri	5,117,073	41,277	0.8%	4,486,228	88%	548,208	11%	19,835	0.4%	21,525	0.4%
Montana	799,065	4,259	0.5%	741,111	93%	2,381	0%	47,679	6.0%	3,635	0.5%
Nebraska	1,578,385	12,422	0.8%	1,480,558	94%	57,404	4%	12,410	0.8%	15,591	1.8%
Nevada	1,201,833	38,127	3.2%	1,012,695	84%	78,771	7%	19,637	1.6%	52,603	4.4%
New Hampshire	1,109,252	9,343	0.8%	1,087,433	98%	7,198	1%	2,134	0.2%	3,144	0.3%
New Jersey	7,730,188	272,521	3.5%	6,130,465	79%	1,036,825	13%	14,970	0.2%	275,407	3.6%
New Mexico	1,515,069	14,124	0.9%	1,146,028	76%	30,210	2%	134,355	8.9%	190,352	12.6%
New York	17,990,455	693,760	3.9%	13,385,255	74%	2,859,055	16%	62,651	0.4%	989,734	5.5%
North Carolina	6,628,637	52,166	0.8%	5,008,491	76%	1,456,323	22%	80,155	1.2%	31,502	0.5%
North Dakota	638,800	3,462	0.5%	604,142	95%	3,524	1%	25,917	4.1%	1,755	0.3%
Ohio	10,847,115	91,179	0.8%	9,521,756	88%	1,154,826	11%	20,358	0.2%	58,996	0.5%
Oklahoma	3,145,585	33,563	1.1%	2,583,512	82%	233,801	7%	252,420	8.0%	42,289	1.3%
Oregon	2,842,321	69,269	2.4%	2,636,787	93%	46,178	2%	38,496	1.4%	51,591	1.8%
Pennsylvania	11,881,643	137,438	1.2%	10,520,201	89%	1,089,795	9%	14,733	0.1%	119,476	1.0%
Rhode Island	1,003,464	18,325	1.8%	917,375	91%	38,861	4%	4,071	0.4%	24,832	2.5%
South Carolina	3,486,703	22,382	0.6%	2,406,974	69%	1,039,884	30%	8,246	0.2%	9,217	0.3%
South Dakota	696,004	3,123	0.5%	637,515	92%	3,258	0%	50,575	7.3%	1,533	0.2%
Tennessee	4,877,185	31,839	0.7%	4,048,068	83%	778,035	16%	10,039	0.2%	9,204	0.2%
Texas	16,986,510	319,459	1.9%	12,774,762	75%	2,021,632	12%	65,877	0.4%	1,804,780	10.6%
Utah	1,722,850	33,371	1.9%	1,615,845	94%	11,576	1%	24,283	1.4%	37,775	2.2%
Vermont	562,758	3,215	0.6%	555,088	99%	1,951	0%	1,696	0.3%	808	0.1%
Virginia	6,187,358	159,053	2.6%	4,791,739	77%	1,162,994	19%	15,282	0.3%	58,290	0.9%
Washington	4,866,692	210,958	4.3%	4,308,937	89%	149,801	3%	81,483	1.7%	115,513	2.4%
West Virginia	1,793,477	7,459	0.4%	1,725,523	96%	56,295	3%	2,458	0.1%	1,742	0.1%
Wisconsin	4,891,769	53,583	1.1%	4,512,523	92%	244,539	5%	39,387	0.8%	41,737	0.9%
Wyoming	453,588	2,806	0.6%	427,061	94%	3,606	1%	9,479	2.1%	10,636	2.3%
Totals	248,709,873	7,273,662	2.9%	199,686,070	80%	29,986,060	12%	1,959,234	0.8%	9,804,847	3.9%

Source: Asian/Pacific Islander Data Consortium (San Francisco, CA: Asian and Pacific Islander Center for Census Information and Services, 1993). Primary source: U.S. Census Bureau, Summary Tape Files 1 and 3.

★ 800 ★

Population by State, Race/Ethnicity, and Hispanic Origin

Population of the fifty states and District of Columbia by race/ethnicity and Hispanic origin, 1990.

State	Non-Hispanic origin					Hispanic origin				
	Asian/ Pacific Islander	White	Black	American Indian, Eskimo, or Aleut	Other race	Asian or Pacific Islander	White	Black	American Indian, Eskimo, or Aleut	Other race
Alabama	21,217	2,960,167	1,017,713	16,221	640	580	15,630	2,992	285	5,142
Alaska	18,730	406,722	21,799	84,594	395	998	8,770	652	1,104	6,279
Arizona	51,530	2,626,185	104,809	190,091	4,275	3,676	337,001	5,715	13,436	328,510
Arkansas	12,144	1,933,082	372,762	12,393	468	386	11,662	1,150	380	6,298
California	2,710,353	17,029,126	2,092,446	184,065	56,093	135,306	3,495,201	116,355	58,099	3,882,977
Colorado	56,773	2,658,945	128,057	22,068	4,249	3,089	246,529	5,089	5,708	163,887
Connecticut	49,114	2,754,184	260,840	5,950	3,912	1,584	105,169	13,429	704	92,230
Delaware	8,854	528,092	111,011	1,938	453	203	7,002	1,449	81	7,085
District of Columbia	10,734	166,131	395,213	1,252	860	480	13,536	4,391	214	14,089
Florida	146,159	9,475,326	1,701,103	32,910	8,285	8,143	1,273,959	58,431	3,425	230,185
Georgia	73,725	4,543,425	1,737,165	12,621	2,358	2,056	56,723	9,400	727	40,016
Hawaii	646,404	347,644	25,916	4,001	2,874	38,832	21,972	1,279	1,098	18,209
Idaho	9,053	928,661	3,211	12,418	479	312	21,790	159	1,362	29,304
Illinois	275,568	8,550,208	1,673,703	18,213	8,464	9,743	402,770	20,570	3,623	467,740
Indiana	36,618	4,965,242	428,612	11,999	2,900	999	55,458	3,480	721	38,130
Iowa	24,926	2,663,840	47,493	6,765	1,084	550	19,250	597	584	11,666
Kansas	30,814	2,190,524	140,761	20,363	1,442	936	41,462	2,315	1,602	47,355
Kentucky	17,201	3,378,022	261,360	5,518	1,211	611	13,810	1,547	251	5,765
Louisiana	39,302	2,776,022	1,291,470	17,539	2,596	1,797	63,116	7,811	1,002	19,318
Maine	6,505	1,203,357	4,937	5,898	402	178	5,003	201	100	1,347
Maryland	136,619	3,326,109	1,177,823	12,143	3,672	3,100	67,855	12,076	829	41,242
Massachusetts	140,338	5,280,292	274,464	10,545	23,237	3,054	125,082	25,666	1,696	132,051
Michigan	102,506	7,649,951	1,282,744	52,571	5,929	2,477	106,135	8,962	3,067	80,955
Minnesota	76,229	4,101,266	93,040	48,251	2,429	1,657	29,129	1,904	1,658	19,536
Mississippi	12,543	1,624,198	911,891	8,316	337	473	9,263	3,166	209	2,820
Missouri	40,087	4,448,465	545,527	18,873	2,419	1,190	37,763	2,681	962	19,106
Montana	4,123	733,878	2,242	46,475	173	136	7,233	139	1,204	3,462
Nebraska	12,026	1,460,095	56,711	11,719	865	396	20,463	693	691	14,726
Nevada	35,897	946,357	76,503	17,480	1,177	2,230	66,338	2,268	2,157	51,426
New Hampshire	9,197	1,079,484	6,749	2,042	447	146	7,949	449	92	2,697
New Jersey	264,341	5,718,966	984,845	12,490	9,685	8,180	411,499	51,980	2,480	265,722
New Mexico	12,587	764,164	27,642	128,068	3,384	1,537	381,864	2,568	6,287	186,968
New York	666,843	12,460,189	2,569,126	50,540	29,731	26,917	925,066	289,929	12,111	960,003
North Carolina	50,593	4,971,127	1,449,142	78,930	2,119	1,573	37,364	7,181	1,225	29,383
North Dakota	3,345	601,592	3,451	25,590	157	117	2,550	73	327	1,598
Ohio	89,195	9,444,622	1,147,440	19,137	7,025	1,984	77,134	7,386	1,221	51,971
Oklahoma	32,366	2,547,588	231,462	246,631	1,378	1,197	35,924	2,339	5,789	40,911
Oregon	67,422	2,579,732	44,982	35,749	1,729	1,847	57,055	1,196	2,747	49,862
Pennsylvania	134,056	10,422,058	1,072,459	13,505	7,303	3,382	98,143	17,336	1,228	112,173
Rhode Island	17,584	896,109	34,283	3,629	6,107	741	21,266	4,578	442	18,725
South Carolina	21,304	2,390,056	1,035,947	8,004	841	1,078	16,918	3,937	242	8,376
South Dakota	3,013	634,788	3,176	49,648	127	110	2,727	82	927	1,406
Tennessee	30,938	4,027,631	774,925	9,685	1,265	901	20,437	3,110	354	7,939
Texas	303,825	10,291,680	1,976,360	52,803	21,937	15,634	2,483,082	45,272	13,074	1,782,843
Utah	32,490	1,571,254	10,868	22,748	893	881	44,591	708	1,535	36,882
Vermont	3,159	552,184	1,868	1,651	235	56	2,904	83	45	573
Virginia	154,183	4,701,650	1,153,133	14,347	3,757	4,870	90,089	9,861	935	54,533
Washington	203,668	4,221,622	146,000	76,397	4,435	7,290	87,315	3,801	5,086	111,078
West Virginia	7,252	1,718,896	55,986	2,363	491	207	6,627	309	95	1,251
Wisconsin	52,284	4,464,677	241,697	37,769	2,148	1,299	47,846	2,842	1,618	39,589
Wyoming	2,622	412,711	3,426	8,857	221	184	14,350	180	622	10,415

Source: Asian/Pacific Islander Data Consortium (San Francisco, CA: Asian and Pacific Islander Center for Census Information and Services, 1993). Primary source: U.S. Census Bureau, Summary Tape Files 1 and 3.

★ 801 ★

Population by Asian Ethnicity and State

Population of the fifty states and District of Columbia by Asian ethnic group, 1990.

State	Chinese	Filipino	Japanese	Asian Indian	Korean	Viet-namese	Cam-bodian	Hmong	Laotian	Thai	Other Asian
Alabama	3,929	1,816	2,028	4,348	3,454	2,274	427	8	799	526	1,479
Alaska	1,342	7,976	2,066	472	4,163	582	50	1	226	369	567
Arizona	14,136	7,904	6,302	5,663	5,863	5,239	787	9	855	1,381	3,560
Arkansas	1,726	1,569	957	1,329	1,037	2,348	28	23	1,982	248	878
California	704,850	731,685	312,989	159,973	259,941	280,223	68,190	46,892	58,058	32,064	80,195
Colorado	8,695	5,426	11,402	3,836	11,339	7,210	1,320	1,202	1,996	1,184	3,512
Connecticut	11,082	5,160	3,811	11,755	5,126	4,085	1,754	46	2,989	529	3,741
Delaware	2,301	1,321	690	2,183	1,229	348	23	0	107	142	544
District of Columbia	3,144	2,082	1,029	1,601	814	747	55	0	51	212	1,188
Florida	30,737	31,945	8,505	31,457	12,404	16,346	1,617	7	2,423	4,457	9,958
Georgia	12,657	5,848	6,372	13,926	15,275	7,801	2,140	320	3,511	1,608	4,306
Hawaii	68,804	168,682	247,486	1,015	24,454	5,468	119	6	1,677	1,220	4,036
Idaho	1,420	1,083	2,719	473	935	600	66	0	482	188	526
Illinois	49,936	64,224	21,831	64,200	41,506	10,309	3,026	433	4,985	5,180	16,939
Indiana	7,371	4,754	4,715	7,095	5,475	2,467	412	57	674	654	2,986
Iowa	4,442	1,607	1,619	3,021	4,618	2,882	611	227	3,374	921	1,715
Kansas	5,330	2,548	2,037	3,956	4,016	6,577	550	613	2,315	675	2,091
Kentucky	2,736	2,193	2,513	2,922	2,972	1,506	231	1	260	403	1,246
Louisiana	5,430	3,731	1,526	5,083	2,750	17,598	308	1	1,024	704	2,018
Maine	1,262	1,058	590	607	858	642	767	0	101	113	452
Maryland	30,868	19,376	6,617	28,330	30,320	8,862	1,768	1	767	2,578	8,661
Massachusetts	53,792	6,212	8,784	19,719	11,744	15,449	14,050	248	3,985	1,424	6,730
Michigan	19,145	13,786	10,681	23,845	16,316	6,117	874	2,257	2,190	1,284	7,006
Minnesota	8,980	4,237	3,581	8,234	11,576	9,387	3,858	16,833	6,381	576	3,309
Mississippi	2,518	1,565	700	1,872	1,123	3,815	24	7	59	239	757
Missouri	8,614	5,624	3,391	6,111	5,731	4,380	628	13	654	1,088	3,037
Montana	655	735	829	248	668	159	4	146	185	107	222
Nebraska	1,775	1,377	1,574	1,218	1,943	1,806	98	78	810	343	923
Nevada	6,618	12,048	4,024	1,825	4,315	1,934	244	24	804	1,823	1,573
New Hampshire	2,314	874	747	1,697	1,501	553	276	2	380	233	544
New Jersey	59,084	53,146	17,253	79,440	38,540	7,330	475	25	478	1,758	13,310
New Mexico	2,607	2,018	1,895	1,593	1,464	1,485	55	0	522	440	1,284
New York	284,144	62,259	35,281	140,985	95,648	15,555	3,646	165	3,253	6,230	42,137
North Carolina	8,859	5,332	5,040	9,847	7,267	5,211	1,367	708	2,048	1,183	3,108
North Dakota	557	708	245	482	526	281	54	2	54	114	294
Ohio	19,447	10,268	10,485	20,848	11,237	4,964	2,213	253	2,578	1,515	5,915
Oklahoma	5,193	3,024	2,385	4,546	4,717	7,320	307	207	902	942	2,459
Oregon	13,652	7,411	11,796	3,508	8,668	9,088	2,101	438	3,262	876	3,432
Pennsylvania	29,562	12,160	6,613	28,396	26,787	15,887	5,495	358	2,048	1,293	7,185
Rhode Island	3,170	1,836	750	1,975	1,294	772	3,655	884	2,579	141	963
South Carolina	3,039	5,521	1,885	3,900	2,577	1,752	239	76	598	565	1,247
South Dakota	385	531	286	287	525	268	76	27	138	129	286
Tennessee	5,653	3,032	3,440	5,911	4,508	2,062	942	79	2,772	586	1,959
Texas	63,232	34,350	14,795	55,795	31,775	69,634	5,887	176	9,332	5,816	21,126
Utah	5,322	1,905	6,500	1,557	2,629	2,797	997	105	1,774	617	1,493
Vermont	679	253	373	529	563	236	58	3	115	80	245
Virginia	21,238	35,067	7,931	20,494	30,164	20,693	3,889	7	2,589	3,312	10,652
Washington	33,962	43,799	34,366	8,205	29,697	18,696	11,096	741	6,191	2,386	6,779
West Virginia	1,170	1,606	780	1,981	777	184	27	0	38	226	494
Wisconsin	7,354	3,690	2,765	6,914	5,618	2,494	521	16,373	3,622	502	2,929
Wyoming	554	408	583	240	402	124	6	0	17	91	213

Source: Asian/Pacific Islander Data Consortium (San Francisco, CA: Asian and Pacific Islander Center for Census Information and Services, 1993). Primary source: U.S. Census Bureau, Summary Tape Files 1 and 3.

★ 802 ★

Population by Pacific Islander Ethnicity and State

Population of the fifty states and District of Columbia by Pacific Islander and Micronesian ethnicity, 1990.

State	Hawaiian	Samoan	Tongan	Other Polynesian	Guamanian	Other Micronesian	Melanesian	Pacific Islander, not specified
Alabama	343	77	2	3	247	13	5	19
Alaska	934	522	158	30	208	30	2	30
Arizona	1,690	416	388	100	709	103	25	76
Arkansas	226	55	1	5	95	14	4	5
California	34,447	31,917	7,919	1,675	25,059	1,566	5,778	2,238
Colorado	1,368	345	45	47	778	89	9	59
Connecticut	269	85	3	16	202	14	8	23
Delaware	65	23	1	2	63	10	0	5
District of Columbia	101	34	1	1	108	10	13	23
Florida	2,049	577	122	139	1,241	102	35	181
Georgia	847	412	5	28	594	53	26	52
Hawaii	138,742	15,034	3,088	885	2,120	1,848	291	261
Idaho	476	145	51	47	95	49	6	4
Illinois	1,000	367	15	36	1,105	48	21	150
Indiana	528	151	15	15	217	15	3	13
Iowa	244	59	10	8	81	15	1	21
Kansas	422	218	9	17	268	67	2	39
Kentucky	338	194	2	12	220	34	3	26
Louisiana	411	169	2	9	291	29	2	13
Maine	115	39	2	9	58	5	2	3
Maryland	636	154	2	14	581	76	24	84
Massachusetts	505	204	15	35	364	27	28	77
Michigan	787	191	12	16	283	73	20	100
Minnesota	383	120	33	5	165	58	9	161
Mississippi	166	78	0	2	70	5	0	16
Missouri	621	775	45	43	272	174	25	51
Montana	179	49	4	5	43	5	6	10
Nebraska	243	54	5	8	117	36	3	11
Nevada	1,534	326	331	77	472	80	20	55
New Hampshire	116	23	1	3	67	11	0	1
New Jersey	638	217	9	26	644	27	15	106
New Mexico	408	119	13	25	149	39	3	5
New York	1,496	586	30	62	1,803	72	65	343
North Carolina	963	416	12	37	636	77	6	49
North Dakota	76	9	1	1	30	13	2	13
Ohio	785	180	14	15	333	42	7	80
Oklahoma	712	203	6	23	451	129	8	29
Oregon	2,415	565	169	126	701	631	242	188
Pennsylvania	859	311	30	21	307	42	5	79
Rhode Island	112	20	0	2	134	3	25	10
South Carolina	426	159	15	9	317	28	0	29
South Dakota	74	13	22	8	50	6	2	10
Tennessee	503	120	1	8	209	31	3	20
Texas	2,979	916	630	200	2,209	307	61	239
Utah	1,396	1,570	3,904	443	148	83	52	79
Vermont	25	18	0	0	24	8	3	3

[Continued]

★ 802 ★

Population by Pacific Islander Ethnicity and State (Continued)

Population of the fifty states and District of Columbia by Pacific Islander and Micronesian ethnicity, 1990.

State	Hawaiian	Samoan	Tongan	Other Polynesian	Guamanian	Other Micronesian	Melanesian	Pacific Islander, not specified
Virginia	1,384	440	6	53	923	135	11	65
Washington	5,423	4,130	448	198	3,779	452	303	307
West Virginia	91	28	5	1	41	2	2	6
Wisconsin	371	106	2	6	229	18	9	60
Wyoming	93	25	2	5	35	4	0	4

Source: Asian/Pacific Islander Data Consortium (San Francisco, CA: Asian and Pacific Islander Center for Census Information and Services, 1993). Primary source: U.S. Census Bureau, Summary Tape Files 1 and 3.

United States Population Projections

★ 803 ★

Population Projected by Race and Hispanic Origin, 1995–2050

Population projections (in thousands) by race/ethnicity and Hispanic origin[c], 1995 to 2050.

Year	Total	Race				Hispanic origin[c]	Not of Hispanic origin, by race			
		Asian[b]	White	Black	American Indian[a]		Asian[b]	White	Black	American Indian[a]
1995	2,058	2,326	1,956	2,459	2,866	2,650	2,300	1,850	2,450	2,900
2000	2,072	2,324	1,968	2,460	2,865	2,650	2,300	1,850	2,450	2,900
2010	2,091	2,275	1,981	2,459	2,854	2,591	2,252	1,850	2,450	2,900
2030	2,114	2,174	2,004	2,452	2,845	2,472	2,152	1,850	2,450	2,900
2050	2,119	2,078	2,009	2,444	2,840	2,358	2,057	1,850	2,450	2,900

Source: Jennifer Cheeseman Day, U.S. Department of Commerce, Economics and Statistics Administration, Bureau of the Census, Current Population Reports, P25-1092, *Population Projections of the United States, by Age, Sex, Race, and Hispanic Origin: 1992-2050* (Washington, DC: U.S. Government Printing Office, 1993), table J, p. xxii. *Notes:* (a) American Indian represents American Indian, Eskimo, and Aleut. (b) Asian represents Asian and Pacific Islander. (c) Persons of Hispanic origin may be of any race.

★ 804 ★

Population Projections by Race and Hispanic Origin, in Percent, 1990 to 2050

Population by race/ethnicity and Hispanic origin in 1990, in percent, and five-year projections in percent, for 1995 to 2050.

In percent	Total	Race				Hispanic origin	Not of Hispanic origin, by race			
		Asian[b]	White	Black	American Indian[a]		Asian[b]	White	Black	American Indian[a]
1990	100.0	3.0	83.9	12.3	0.8	9.0	2.8	75.7	11.8	0.7
Projections										
1995	100.0	3.7	82.8	12.6	0.9	10.1	3.5	73.6	12.1	0.7
2000	100.0	4.5	81.7	12.9	0.9	11.1	4.2	71.6	12.3	0.8
2005	100.0	5.2	80.7	13.2	0.9	12.2	4.9	69.6	12.6	0.8
2010	100.0	5.9	79.6	13.6	0.9	13.2	5.5	67.6	12.8	0.8
2020	100.0	7.2	77.7	14.2	1.0	15.2	6.8	63.9	13.3	0.9
2030	100.0	8.4	75.8	14.8	1.0	17.2	7.9	60.2	13.8	0.9
2040	100.0	9.6	73.8	15.5	1.1	19.2	9.1	56.4	14.4	1.0
2050	100.0	10.7	71.8	16.2	1.2	21.1	10.1	52.7	15.0	1.1

Source: Jennifer Cheeseman Day, U.S. Department of Commerce, Economics and Statistics Administration, Bureau of the Census, Current Population Reports, P25-1092, *Population Projections of the United States, by Age, Sex, Race, and Hispanic Origin: 1992-2050* (Washington, DC: U.S. Government Printing Office, 1993), table I, p. xviii. Also in source: Projections based on higher and lower assumptions of fertility, life expectancy, and net immigration rates. *Notes:* (a) American Indian represents American Indian, Eskimo, and Aleut. (b) Asian represents Asian and Pacific Islander. (c) Persons of Hispanic origin may be of any race.

★ 805 ★

Population Projections by Race, 1990–2050

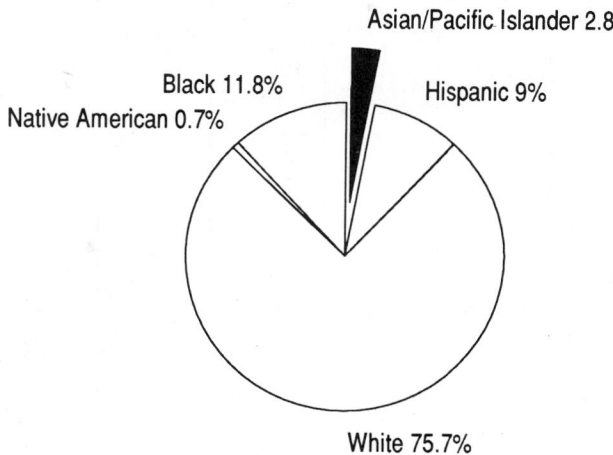

1990

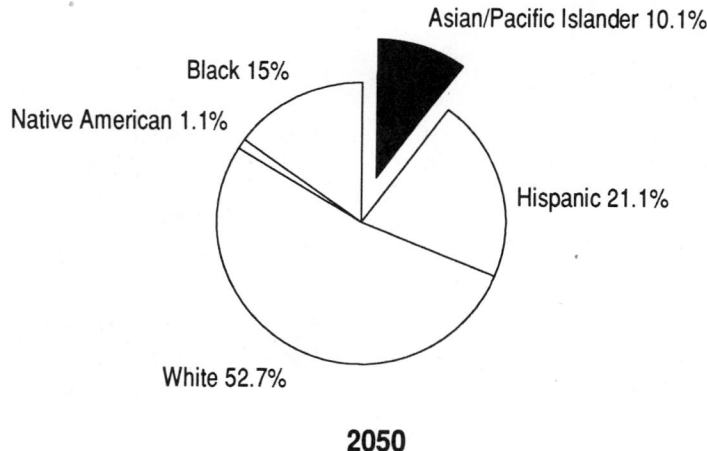

2050

Source: Jennifer Cheeseman Day, U.S. Department of Commerce, Economics and Statistics Administration, Bureau of the Census, Current Population Reports, P25-1092, *Population Projections of the United States, by Age, Sex, Race, and Hispanic Origin: 1992-2050* (Washington, DC: U.S. Government Printing Office, 1993), table I, p. xviii.

★ 806 ★

Population Projections by Age, Race/Ethnicity and Hispanic Origin, 1992–2050

Population by age, race/ethnicity, and Hispanic origin in 1992, and projected in five-year intervals for 1995 to 2050.

Date and age	Total	Race				Hispanic origin	Not of Hispanic origin, by race			
		White	Black	American Indian, Eskimo, and Aleut	Asian and Pacific Islander		White	Black	American Indian, Eskimo, and Aleut	Asian and Pacific Islander
July 1, 1992										
All ages	254,922	212,648	31,673	2,150	8,451	24,136	190,604	30,372	1,873	7,937
Under 5 years	19,497	15,407	3,139	224	727	2,647	12,991	2,993	193	673
5 to 9 years	18,354	14,681	2,783	216	674	2,329	12,561	2,656	184	624
10 to 14 years	18,100	14,426	2,783	215	675	2,170	12,448	2,669	185	627
15 to 19 years	17,080	13,615	2,638	186	641	2,078	11,713	2,530	161	598
20 to 24 years	19,073	15,447	2,689	186	751	2,367	13,290	2,561	158	697
25 to 29 years	20,146	16,484	2,704	182	776	2,453	14,248	2,568	154	722
30 to 34 years	22,236	18,436	2,787	186	828	2,259	16,369	2,661	160	773
35 to 39 years	21,077	17,578	2,562	167	770	1,867	15,881	2,455	146	728
40 to 44 years	18,790	15,837	2,138	142	672	1,460	14,509	2,056	126	639
45 to 49 years	15,353	13,211	1,542	110	489	1,084	12,221	1,484	99	466
50 to 54 years	12,051	10,343	1,258	85	366	824	9,588	1,213	77	348
55 to 59 years	10,485	9,064	1,063	67	291	683	8,436	1,028	61	278
60 to 64 years	10,439	9,149	983	55	252	596	8,598	953	51	241
65 to 69 years	9,988	8,852	882	45	208	480	8,405	860	41	200
70 to 74 years	8,464	7,601	681	34	149	336	7,288	665	31	143
75 to 79 years	6,388	5,773	496	23	95	231	5,557	486	22	92
80 to 84 years	4,129	3,762	301	14	52	149	3,623	295	13	49
85 to 89 years	2,154	1,970	154	7	23	76	1,898	151	7	22
90 to 94 years	848	771	64	3	9	29	744	98	3	9
95 to 99 years	225	204	18	1	2	7	197	18	1	2
100 years and over	45	37	7	0	1	2	36	7	0	1
16 years and over	195,522	165,394	22,424	1,456	6,248	16,582	150,236	21,532	1,277	5,895
18 years and over	188,759	156,995	21,390	1,381	5,994	15,762	145,587	20,540	1,212	5,657
15 to 44 years	118,402	97,397	15,518	1,050	4,438	12,494	86,010	14,831	905	4,168
65 years and over	32,241	28,970	2,603	128	539	1,309	27,751	2,545	118	517
85 years and over	3,272	2,983	243	12	35	114	2,875	239	11	33
Median age	33.4	34.4	28.4	26.3	29.9	26.0	35.5	28.5	26.8	30.2
July 1, 1995										
All ages	262,754	217,511	33,147	2,247	9,849	26,522	193,307	31,702	1,956	9,266
Under 5 years	19,553	15,321	3,177	220	836	2,804	12,753	3,024	193	778
5 to 9 years	19,225	15,190	3,038	226	771	2,621	12,810	2,888	192	713
10 to 14 years	18,895	14,975	2,872	232	816	2,385	12,809	2,743	199	760
15 to 19 years	18,024	14,278	2,804	199	743	2,234	12,240	2,684	172	694
20 to 24 years	17,885	14,281	2,622	183	799	2,336	12,147	2,499	158	746
25 to 29 years	18,994	15,361	2,572	178	882	2,517	13,073	2,432	150	821
30 to 34 years	21,850	17,935	2,800	184	931	2,529	15,630	2,661	157	873
35 to 39 years	22,267	18,429	2,770	177	891	2,162	16,482	2,647	153	843
40 to 44 years	20,233	16,907	2,384	155	787	1,725	15,338	2,286	136	748
45 to 49 years	17,440	14,834	1,853	125	628	1,308	13,641	1,781	111	599
50 to 54 years	13,642	11,714	1,384	94	451	962	10,834	1,332	85	430
55 to 59 years	11,089	9,523	1,140	73	353	768	8,819	1,099	66	337
60 to 64 years	10,.064	8,719	990	59	296	640	8,130	957	54	283
65 to 69 years	9,948	8,733	919	47	249	548	8,227	891	43	239
70 to 74 years	8,852	7,919	706	38	190	407	7,540	688	35	182

[Continued]

694

★806★

Population Projections by Age, Race/Ethnicity and Hispanic Origin, 1992–2050 (Continued)

Population by age, race/ethnicity, and Hispanic origin in 1992, and projected in five-year intervals for 1995 to 2050.

Date and age	Total	Race				Hispanic origin	Not of Hispanic origin, by race			
		White	Black	American Indian, Eskimo, and Aleut	Asian and Pacific Islander		White	Black	American Indian, Eskimo, and Aleut	Asian and Pacific Islander
75 to 79 years	6,693	6,035	516	25	118	262	5,792	503	24	113
80 to 84 years	4,461	4,058	321	17	66	175	3,893	314	16	63
85 to 89 years	2,320	2,118	165	9	28	88	2,034	161	8	27
90 to 94 years	1,002	902	83	5	12	39	866	82	4	12
95 to 99 years	263	235	23	1	4	9	226	22	1	4
100 years and over	54	44	8	0	1	2	42	8	0	1
16 years and over	201,294	169,043	23,461	1,523	7,267	18,252	152,371	22,472	1,334	6,865
18 years and over	194,075	163,327	22,338	1,442	6,969	17,366	147,462	21,397	1,263	6,587
15 to 44 years	119,253	97,191	15,953	1,076	5,032	13,504	84,890	15,209	926	4,724
65 years and over	33,594	30,044	2,740	142	687	1,531	28,621	2,670	131	641
85 years and over	3,638	3,299	278	15	46	138	3,169	273	14	44
Median age	34.3	35.4	29.1	26.7	30.4	26.8	36.6	29.2	27.1	30.7
July 1, 2000										
All ages	274,815	224,594	35,525	2,409	12,287	30,602	196,701	33,834	2,096	11,582
Under 5 years	18,908	14,496	3,183	224	1,006	3,055	11,706	3,014	196	938
5 to 9 years	19,901	15,476	3,234	226	965	2,945	12,787	3,070	199	900
10 to 14 years	20,081	15,642	3,202	249	989	2,817	13,096	3,036	212	920
15 to 19 years	19,758	15,514	3,027	231	986	2,617	13,139	2,881	197	924
20 to 24 years	18,161	14,346	2,707	190	918	2,490	12,076	2,571	164	860
25 to 29 years	17,836	14,100	2,541	182	1,014	2,518	11,808	2,404	156	950
30 to 34 years	19,580	15,725	2,590	174	1,090	2,682	13,287	2,442	147	1,021
35 to 39 years	22,168	18,093	2,826	179	1,070	2,608	15,717	2,682	153	1,009
40 to 44 years	22,494	18,567	2,760	173	994	2,213	16,553	2,634	149	944
45 to 49 years	19,824	16,553	2,304	145	622	1,715	14,992	2,206	127	784
50 to 54 years	17,230	14,650	1,806	117	657	1,314	13,450	1,734	104	628
55 to 59 years	13,319	11,420	1,333	86	479	965	10,536	1,281	78	458
60 to 64 years	10,669	9,134	1,080	67	388	764	8,434	1,039	61	372
65 to 69 years	9,469	8,163	936	52	317	627	7,588	902	47	304
70 to 74 years	8,789	7,743	754	41	251	508	7,274	729	37	241
75 to 79 years	7,447	6,672	569	32	175	365	6,333	553	29	168
80 to 84 years	4,892	4,439	340	19	94	213	4,241	331	18	90
85 to 89 years	2,671	2,430	185	12	44	118	2,319	181	11	43
90 to 94 years	1,170	1,049	97	6	18	50	1,001	95	6	17
95 to 99 years	371	321	40	3	7	17	305	39	3	7
100 years and over	77	63	11	1	2	3	59	11	1	2
16 years and over	211,976	175,894	25,295	1,661	9,127	21,264	156,498	24,131	1,447	8,636
18 years and over	204,123	169,735	24,096	1,565	8,726	20,223	151,283	22,991	1,366	8,260
15 to 44 years	119,997	96,344	16,451	1,129	6,073	15,128	82,581	15,613	967	5,709
65 years and over	34,886	30,880	2,933	165	908	1,900	29,121	2,841	152	873
85 years and over	4,289	3,862	333	22	72	188	3,685	326	20	69
Median age	35.7	37.0	29.8	27.4	31.2	27.8	38.4	29.9	27.6	31.4
July 1, 2005										
All ages	286,324	230,993	37,907	2,583	14,840	34,842	199,274	35,957	2,245	14,005
Under 5 years	18,959	14,254	3,299	242	1,163	3,338	11,214	3,111	212	1,084
5 to 9 years	19,282	14,665	3,240	231	1,145	3,196	11,754	3,060	202	1,070
10 to 14 years	20,804	15,942	3,404	250	1,207	3,147	13,081	3,225	219	1,131
15 to 19 years	20,982	16,204	3,367	249	1,162	3,058	13,441	3,184	211	1,087

[Continued]

Population Projections by Age, Race/Ethnicity and Hispanic Origin, 1992–2050 (Continued)

Population by age, race/ethnicity, and Hispanic origin in 1992, and projected in five-year intervals for 1995 to 2050.

Date and age	Total	Race				Hispanic origin	Not of Hispanic origin, by race			
		White	Black	American Indian, Eskimo, and Aleut	Asian and Pacific Islander		White	Black	American Indian, Eskimo, and Aleut	Asian and Pacific Islander
20 to 24 years	19,845	15,557	2,910	222	1,156	2,865	12,957	2,750	190	1,085
25 to 29 years	18,072	14,139	2,607	189	1,136	2,662	11,721	2,459	163	1,067
30 to 34 years	18,423	14,464	2,556	178	1,225	2,682	12,024	2,411	153	1,152
35 to 39 years	19,894	15,881	2,612	170	1,231	2,756	13,377	2,459	143	1,159
40 to 44 years	23,390	18,229	2,810	175	1,175	2,654	15,810	2,663	149	1,112
45 to 49 years	22,041	18,191	2,666	162	1,022	2,188	16,198	2,542	140	973
50 to 54 years	19,569	16,345	2,244	136	844	1,714	14,783	2,147	119	806
55 to 59 years	16,814	14,286	1,748	107	673	1,310	13,090	1,675	96	645
60 to 64 years	12,833	10,979	1,267	79	508	956	10,105	1,214	71	487
65 to 69 years	10,097	8,606	1,029	59	403	747	7,924	986	54	387
70 to 74 years	8,426	7,293	775	45	314	580	6,759	744	41	302
75 to 79 years	7,463	6,585	614	34	229	455	6,165	591	31	221
80 to 84 years	5,492	4,953	376	24	139	295	4,677	363	22	134
85 to 89 years	2,975	2,697	199	14	65	143	2,563	193	13	62
90 to 94 years	1,391	1,240	113	8	29	68	1,175	111	8	28
95 to 99 years	453	390	49	4	10	22	369	48	4	10
100 years and over	118	92	20	2	4	6	86	20	2	4
16 years and over	222,934	182,807	27,241	1,806	11,080	24,533	160,472	25,875	1,565	10,490
18 years and over	214,564	176,368	25,883	1,703	10,610	23,297	155,144	24,592	1,479	10,052
15 to 44 years	119,606	94,475	16,864	1,183	7,085	16,677	79,330	15,927	1,010	6,662
65 years and over	36,414	31,856	3,175	191	1,193	2,317	29,719	3,056	175	1,148
85 years and over	4,937	4,419	382	28	108	240	4,194	372	26	105
Median age	36.7	38.3	30.3	27.4	31.9	28.4	40.0	30.4	27.6	32.2
July 1, 2010										
All ages	298,109	237,412	40,429	2,772	17,496	39,312	201,668	38,201	2,407	16,522
Under 5 years	19,730	14,617	3,529	264	1,320	3,683	11,270	3,316	230	1,230
5 to 9 years	19,346	14,426	3,358	251	1,311	3,480	11,265	3,158	219	1,224
10 to 14 years	20,196	15,119	3,411	256	1,410	3,404	12,032	3,215	224	1,321
15 to 19 years	21,736	16,526	3,578	249	1,382	3,399	13,440	3,379	219	1,299
20 to 24 years	21,061	16,254	3,239	240	1,329	3,303	13,267	3,042	203	1,245
25 to 29 years	19,709	15,311	2,802	221	1,375	3,023	12,575	2,631	188	1,292
30 to 34 years	18,658	14,502	2,624	186	1,347	2,828	11,934	2,467	160	1,269
35 to 39 years	18,735	14,619	2,577	174	1,366	2,757	12,112	2,427	149*	1,290
40 to 44 years	20,118	16,015	2,598	167	1,338	2,803	13,468	2,443	140	1,264
45 to 49 years	21,961	17,877	2,720	165	1,199	2,619	15,488	2,575	141	1,138
50 to 54 years	21,776	17,983	2,603	153	1,037	2,181	15,995	2,480	132	989
55 to 59 years	19,133	15,981	2,175	126	850	1,702	14,429	2,077	110	814
60 to 64 years	16,245	13,791	1,663	99	692	1,291	12,612	1,590	88	664
65 to 69 years	12,189	10,392	1,212	71	514	933	9,542	1,158	64	494
70 to 74 years	9,046	7,744	858	52	393	692	7,110	819	47	378
75 to 79 years	7,217	6,257	637	38	285	521	5,778	609	35	275
80 to 84 years	5,550	4,934	407	26	183	368	4,592	389	24	176
85 to 89 years	3,388	3,051	223	17	97	200	2,863	215	16	94
90 to 94 years	1,591	1,411	127	10	44	84	1,332	123	9	43
95 to 99 years	563	480	60	5	17	31	451	59	5	17
100 years and over	160	122	29	3	6	9	114	29	3	6
16 years and over	234,650	190,105	29,428	1,950	13,168	28,072	164,564	27,849	1,689	12,477

[Continued]

★ 806 ★

Population Projections by Age, Race/Ethnicity and Hispanic Origin, 1992–2050 (Continued)

Population by age, race/ethnicity, and Hispanic origin in 1992, and projected in five-year intervals for 1995 to 2050.

Date and age	Total	Race				Hispanic origin	Not of Hispanic origin, by race			
		White	Black	American Indian, Eskimo, and Aleut	Asian and Pacific Islander		White	Black	American Indian, Eskimo, and Aleut	Asian and Pacific Islander
18 years and over	226,047	183,576	28,015	1,849	12,606	26,718	159,265	26,514	1,601	11,949
15 to 44 years	120,017	93,227	17,417	1,236	8,137	18,112	76,795	16,389	1,060	7,660
65 years and over	39,705	34,391	3,552	222	1,539	2,838	31,782	3,401	203	1,481
85 years and over	5,702	5,064	439	35	165	324	4,761	425	33	159
Median age	37.4	39.2	30.5	27.8	32.3	29.0	41.1	30.7	27.8	32.5
July 1, 2015										
All ages	310,370	244,073	43,074	2,971	20,252	44,030	204,080	40,551	2,579	19,130
Under 5 years	20,744	15,207	3,770	281	1,486	4,066	11,514	3,531	246	1,386
5 to 9 years	20,134	14,793	3,590	273	1,477	3,827	11,325	3,365	238	1,379
10 to 14 years	20,290	14,882	3,534	278	1,598	3,697	11,539	3,317	242	1,496
15 to 19 years	21,112	15,686	3,582	255	1,588	3,663	12,367	3,366	223	1,492
20 to 24 years	21,764	16,551	3,426	241	1,546	3,637	13,248	3,215	211	1,455
25 to 29 years	20,875	15,981	3,106	238	1,550	3,442	12,875	2,900	202	1,455
30 to 34 years	20,302	15,683	2,816	217	1,585	3,190	12,796	2,636	185	1,494
35 to 39 years	18,963	14,652	2,641	181	1,489	2,903	12,017	2,480	156	1,408
40 to 44 years	18,959	14,752	2,584	170	1,473	2,806	12,200	2,411	146	1,396
45 to 49 years	19,768	15,733	2,522	157	1,357	2,767	13,216	2,368	132	1,285
50 to 54 years	21,721	17,696	2,663	155	1,208	2,608	15,315	2,518	132	1,149
55 to 59 years	21,321	17,618	2,528	141	1,034	2,162	15,645	2,405	122	988
60 to 64 years	18,512	15,456	2,078	117	861	1,673	13,931	1,981	102	825
65 to 69 years	15,473	13,096	1,603	89	685	1,257	11,951	1,527	79	659
70 to 74 years	10,988	9,412	1,018	62	495	865	8,622	969	56	476
75 to 79 years	7,812	6,702	711	44	355	623	6,131	676	40	342
80 to 84 years	5,411	4,730	424	30	228	423	4,339	402	27	220
85 to 89 years	3,473	3,081	244	19	130	251	2,846	233	17	125
90 to 94 years	1,861	1,635	147	12	67	119	1,523	142	12	65
95 to 99 years	670	568	70	6	26	39	531	68	6	25
100 years and over	215	160	40	4	11	12	149	39	4	11
16 years and over	245,077	196,167	31,464	2,085	15,362	31,713	167,334	29,664	1,805	14,562
18 years and over	236,683	189,948	30,036	1,981	14,749	30,252	162,438	28,321	1,714	13,957
15 to 44 years	121,975	93,306	18,134	1,303	9,233	19,640	75,503	17,009	1,123	8,700
65 years and over	45,903	39,383	4,256	267	1,998	3,590	36,092	4,057	241	1,923
85 years and over	6,219	5,443	500	42	234	422	5,049	482	39	226
Median age	37.5	39.5	30.9	28.2	32.8	29.5	41.9	31.1	28.1	33.0
July 1, 2020										
All ages	322,602	250,587	45,743	3,175	23,096	48,952	206,162	42,911	2,756	21,821
Under 5 years	21,388	15,501	3,938	293	1,656	4,422	11,486	3,678	258	1,544
5 to 9 years	21,150	15,376	3,831	291	1,652	4,209	11,564	3,580	255	1,542
10 to 14 years	21,108	15,250	3,772	303	1,784	4,051	11,596	3,529	263	1,669
15 to 19 years	21,193	15,434	3,704	277	1,778	3,962	11,854	3,467	242	1,669
20 to 24 years	21,148	15,726	3,427	247	1,749	3,897	12,192	3,199	215	1,644
25 to 29 years	21,572	16,278	3,266	240	1,769	3,762	12,867	3,067	209	1,666
30 to 34 years	21,452	16,345	3,112	234	1,761	3,608	13,089	2,899	198	1,657
35 to 39 years	20,590	15,824	2,829	211	1,726	3,263	12,871	2,645	180	1,632
40 to 44 years	19,196	14,791	2,628	178	1,599	2,953	12,109	2,465	153	1,516
45 to 49 years	18,646	14,505	2,490	161	1,490	2,773	11,981	2,340	138	1,414
50 to 54 years	19,574	15,592	2,472	148	1,362	2,755	13,083	2,319	125	1,292

[Continued]

★ 806 ★

Population Projections by Age, Race/Ethnicity and Hispanic Origin, 1992–2050 (Continued)
Population by age, race/ethnicity, and Hispanic origin in 1992, and projected in five-year intervals for 1995 to 2050.

Date and age	Total	Race				Hispanic origin	Not of Hispanic origin, by race			
		White	Black	American Indian, Eskimo, and Aleut	Asian and Pacific Islander		White	Black	American Indian, Eskimo, and Aleut	Asian and Pacific Islander
55 to 59 years	21,296	17,365	2,590	144	1,197	2,583	15,005	2,446	122	1,140
60 to 64 years	20,663	17,072	2,424	131	1,036	2,121	15,137	2,300	113	991
65 to 69 years	17,669	14,721	2,001	105	843	1,627	13,242	1,901	91	808
70 to 74 years	14,011	11,925	1,354	78	653	1,166	10,861	1,286	69	629
75 to 79 years	9,554	8,203	851	53	447	780	7,490	806	48	431
80 to 84 years	5,913	5,118	476	34	284	507	4,651	449	31	274
85 to 89 years	3,431	2,990	256	21	163	291	2,721	243	20	157
90 to 94 years	1,959	1,689	166	14	91	151	1,548	159	13	88
95 to 99 years	813	680	84	8	40	56	628	82	8	39
100 years and over	278	203	51	6	18	17	188	51	5	17
16 years and over	254,755	201,434	33,453	2,229	17,639	35,481	169,201	31,422	1,928	16,722
18 years and over	246,299	195,290	31,974	2,116	16,919	33,900	164,485	30,038	1,830	16,047
15 to 44 years	125,150	94,397	18,986	1,386	10,381	21,444	74,983	17,742	1,197	9,784
65 years and over	53,627	46,529	5,240	319	2,539	4,594	41,328	4,977	285	2,443
85 years and over	6,480	5,563	558	48	311	515	5,084	534	45	302
Median age	38.0	39.9	31.4	28.7	33.3	30.2	42.2	31.5	28.5	33.6
July 1, 2030										
All ages	344,951	261,318	51,031	3,610	28,993	59,197	207,674	47,552	3,141	27,388
Under 5 years	21,961	15,371	4,274	329	1,986	5,066	10,779	3,971	292	1,852
5 to 9 years	22,108	15,629	4,153	319	2,007	4,888	11,205	3,859	282	1,874
10 to 14 years	22,847	16,134	4,197	336	2,179	4,802	11,805	3,905	296	2,039
15 to 19 years	23,098	16,409	4,201	322	2,165	4,721	12,155	3,910	282	2,031
20 to 24 years	22,039	15,859	3,767	292	2,121	4,548	11,752	3,494	254	1,991
25 to 29 years	21,072	15,255	3,388	267	2,162	4,293	11,380	3,134	232	2,033
30 to 34 years	21,557	15,844	3,288	241	2,183	4,178	12,064	3,046	210	2,059
35 to 39 years	22,412	16,768	3,298	229	2,117	3,998	13,145	3,066	200	2,003
40 to 44 years	21,952	16,614	3,102	224	2,011	3,728	13,249	2,882	189	1,903
45 to 49 years	20,468	15,696	2,736	196	1,839	3,269	12,734	2,553	167	1,748
50 to 54 years	18,735	14,451	2,516	159	1,609	2,910	11,803	2,355	136	1,531
55 to 59 years	18,157	14,158	2,391	141	1,467	2,740	11,659	2,241	121	1,396
60 to 64 years	18,709	14,918	2,329	128	1,333	2,678	12,478	2,176	107	1,269
65 to 69 years	19,827	16,143	2,411	121	1,153	2,459	13,901	2,263	102	1,101
70 to 74 years	18,038	14,980	2,003	104	951	1,914	13,234	1,888	90	912
75 to 79 years	14,154	11,909	1,447	80	719	1,365	10,664	1,364	70	691
80 to 84 years	9,438	8,141	772	53	473	861	7,350	724	47	456
85 to 89 years	4,750	4,107	354	30	259	443	3,698	331	27	250
90 to 94 years	2,258	1,885	209	18	145	216	1,685	198	17	141
95 to 99 years	938	747	110	10	71	87	666	106	10	70
100 years and over	435	300	85	9	41	33	269	83	8	41
16 years and over	273,428	210,941	37,556	2,557	22,373	43,498	171,490	35,025	2,210	21,205
18 years and over	264,174	204,378	35,875	2,426	21,496	41,610	166,628	33,459	2,095	20,382
15 to 44 years	132,129	96,750	21,043	1,577	12,759	25,465	73,745	19,532	1,367	12,020
65 years and over	69,839	58,211	7,391	424	3,812	7,379	51,468	6,959	371	3,661
85 years and over	8,381	7,039	758	67	517	779	6,318	719	62	502
Median age	39.0	41.0	32.3	28.8	34.3	31.5	43.6	32.5	28.5	34.6

[Continued]

★ 806 ★

Population Projections by Age, Race/Ethnicity and Hispanic Origin, 1992–2050 (Continued)

Population by age, race/ethnicity, and Hispanic origin in 1992, and projected in five-year intervals for 1995 to 2050.

Date and age	Total	Race				Hispanic origin	Not of Hispanic origin, by race			
		White	Black	American Indian, Eskimo, and Aleut	Asian and Pacific Islander		White	Black	American Indian, Eskimo, and Aleut	Asian and Pacific Islander
July 1, 2040										
All ages	364,349	268,778	56,445	4,099	35,027	69,827	205,587	52,285	3,581	33,070
Under 5 years	23,192	15,797	4,732	375	2,289	5,753	10,590	4,382	335	2,131
5 to 9 years	22,947	15,669	4,575	366	2,337	5,548	10,658	4,236	325	2,180
10 to 14 years	23,528	16,021	4,561	378	2,567	5,464	11,104	4,224	336	2,400
15 to 19 years	24,165	16,694	4,550	354	2,567	5,435	11,800	4,212	313	2,405
20 to 24 years	23,788	16,773	4,175	326	2,514	5,310	11,981	3,851	286	2,359
25 to 29 years	22,890	16,204	3,829	311	2,546	5,014	11,687	3,526	271	2,392
30 to 34 years	22,439	15,984	3,610	287	2,559	4,804	11,653	3,324	249	2,409
35 to 39 years	21,914	15,747	3,405	256	2,506	4,529	11,658	3,138	222	2,367
40 to 44 years	22,063	16,121	3,281	231	2,430	4,299	12,230	3,032	201	2,302
45 to 49 years	22,290	16,658	3,201	214	2,218	3,995	13,033	2,970	186	2,105
50 to 54 years	21,467	16,280	2,992	201	1,993	3,669	12,961	2,775	170	1,892
55 to 59 years	20,040	15,414	2,661	174	1,790	3,236	12,475	2,478	147	1,704
60 to 64 years	18,039	13,940	2,399	138	1,562	2,842	11,352	2,237	118	1,489
65 to 69 years	17,094	13,321	2,256	119	1,398	2,624	10,933	2,102	102	1,334
70 to 74 years	16,584	13,303	1,966	103	1,212	2,430	11,088	1,823	86	1,157
75 to 79 years	16,236	13,364	1,798	93	980	2,083	11,460	1,675	79	939
80 to 84 years	12,453	10,526	1,164	71	691	1,427	9,217	1,083	62	665
85 to 89 years	7,300	6,213	619	46	423	788	5,488	576	40	408
90 to 94 years	3,853	3,209	365	29	250	382	2,857	345	26	243
95 to 99 years	1,449	1,144	172	15	119	141	1,013	165	14	116
100 years and over	620	399	133	12	75	54	349	131	12	74
16 years and over	289,907	218,040	41,657	2,905	27,305	51,983	170,952	38,591	2,518	25,863
18 years and over	280,259	211,394	39,840	2,761	26,265	49,813	166,259	36,908	2,390	24,888
15 to 44 years	137,259	97,523	22,850	1,765	15,121	29,391	71,010	21,082	1,542	14,234
65 years and over	75,588	61,477	8,473	489	5,149	9,929	52,403	7,899	422	4,935
85 years and over	13,221	10,964	1,289	102	867	1,365	9,706	1,217	93	841
Median age	39.4	41.7	32.5	29.1	35.3	32.5	44.8	32.5	28.6	35.5
July 1, 2050										
All ages	382,674	274,761	62,181	4,641	41,091	80,675	201,841	57,316	4,078	38,765
Under 5 years	24,411	16,239	5,171	419	2,581	6,417	10,438	4,776	378	2,401
5 to 9 years	24,349	16,263	5,028	410	2,647	6,239	10,634	4,642	368	2,466
10 to 14 years	24,847	16,458	5,036	431	2,921	6,169	10,915	4,650	385	2,727
15 to 19 years	25,071	16,740	4,985	406	2,940	6,128	11,233	4,598	361	2,751
20 to 24 years	24,436	16,667	4,502	367	2,899	5,980	11,279	4,135	325	2,717
25 to 29 years	23,891	16,484	4,121	342	2,943	5,691	11,360	3,774	302	2,763
30 to 34 years	24,129	16,871	3,985	320	2,954	5,538	11,880	3,652	280	2,779
35 to 39 years	23,703	16,689	3,831	298	2,886	5,250	11,958	3,515	259	2,721
40 to 44 years	22,923	16,256	3,591	274	2,801	4,927	11,814	3,297	237	2,648
45 to 49 years	21,811	15,672	3,308	238	2,593	4,522	11,584	3,043	206	2,457
50 to 54 years	21,607	15,838	3,177	208	2,384	4,233	11,999	2,931	180	2,263
55 to 59 years	21,872	16,416	3,127	189	2,140	3,957	12,819	2,897	164	2,035
60 to 64 years	20,748	15,787	2,873	176	1,913	3,586	12,540	2,655	148	1,820
65 to 69 years	19,014	14,637	2,538	148	1,691	3,113	11,815	2,348	125	1,613
70 to 74 years	16,203	12,610	2,062	113	1,418	2,603	10,239	1,910	96	1,355
75 to 79 years	14,264	11,252	1,725	94	1,193	2,250	9,197	1,595	80	1,141

[Continued]

★ 806 ★

Population Projections by Age, Race/Ethnicity and Hispanic Origin, 1992–2050 (Continued)

Population by age, race/ethnicity, and Hispanic origin in 1992, and projected in five-year intervals for 1995 to 2050.

Date and age	Total	Race				Hispanic origin	Not of Hispanic origin, by race			
		White	Black	American Indian, Eskimo, and Aleut	Asian and Pacific Islander		White	Black	American Indian, Eskimo, and Aleut	Asian and Pacific Islander
80 to 84 years	11,744	9,619	1,164	72	889	1,834	7,938	1,061	60	851
85 to 89 years	8,635	7,213	784	54	584	1,219	6,088	720	46	561
90 to 94 years	5,393	4,398	582	39	373	652	3,797	547	35	362
95 to 99 years	2,454	1,898	331	23	202	266	1,654	317	21	197
100 years and over	1,170	755	258	20	138	103	660	252	19	136
16 years and over	304,073	222,508	45,933	3,294	32,337	60,632	167,654	42,312	2,870	30,604
18 years and over	294,044	215,831	43,938	3,128	31,146	58,185	163,175	40,471	2,723	29,490
15 to 44 years	144,153	99,707	25,016	2,007	17,422	33,514	69,523	22,971	1,764	16,380
65 years and over	78,876	62,381	9,445	562	6,489	12,039	51,389	8,750	483	6,215
85 years and over	17,652	14,264	1,955	136	1,297	2,239	12,199	1,836	122	1,256
Median age	39.3	41.5	32.8	29.2	36.1	33.3	44.8	32.8	28.7	36.4

Source: Jennifer Cheeseman Day, U.S. Department of Commerce, Economics and Statistics Administration, Bureau of the Census, Current Population Report, P25-1092, *Population Projections of the United States, by Age, Sex, Race, and Hispanic Origin: 1992-2050* (Washington, DC: U.S. Government Printing Office, 1993), table 2, p. 12. Also in source: data broken down by sex and in more detail by age. Projections are available in one–year increments for the time period 1992 to 2005, in five–year increments for the years 2005 to 2020, and in ten– year increments for the years 2020 to 2050. *Note:* (a) Persons of Hispanic origin may be of any race; accordingly, Asian/Pacific Islanders may be of Hispanic Origin.

★ 807 ★

Population Projections and Annual Rate of Change, Asian/Pacific Islander, 1992–2050

Asian/Pacific Islander population (in thousands) (at mid-year) 1992 and projected to mid-year 2050, and projected annual rate of change, birth rate, death rate, and net immigration.

Calendar year	July 1 population	Rate per 1,000 mid-year population				
		Net change	Natural increase	Births	Deaths	Net Immigration
1992	8,451	54.2	14.3	17.0	2.7	39.8
1993	8,911	52.0	14.2	17.0	2.8	37.8
1994	9,377	50.0	14.1	16.9	2.8	35.9
1995	9,840	48.2	14.0	16.9	2.9	34.2
1996	10,326	46.5	13.9	16.8	2.9	32.6
1997	10,809	44.9	13.7	16.7	3.0	31.1
1998	11,297	43.4	13.6	16.6	3.0	29.8
1999	11,790	42.0	13.5	16.5	3.1	28.6
2000	12,287	40.7	13.3	16.4	3.1	27.4
2001	12,790	39.4	13.1	16.3	3.2	26.3
2002	13,296	38.3	12.9	16.2	3.3	25.3
2003	13,807	37.1	12.8	16.1	3.3	24.4
2004	14,321	36.1	12.6	16.0	3.4	23.5
2005	14,840	35.1	12.4	15.9	3.4	22.7
2006	15,363	34.2	12.3	15.8	3.5	21.9
2007	15,890	33.3	12.1	15.7	3.6	21.2
2008	16,421	32.5	12.0	15.6	3.6	20.5

[Continued]

★ 807 ★

Population Projections and Annual Rate of Change, Asian/Pacific Islander, 1992–2050 (Continued)

Asian/Pacific Islander population (in thousands) (at mid-year) 1992 and projected to mid-year 2050, and projected annual rate of change, birth rate, death rate, and net immigration.

Calendar year	July 1 population	Rate per 1,000 mid-year population				
		Net change	Natural increase	Births	Deaths	Net Immigration
2009	16,957	31.7	11.8	15.5	3.7	19.9
2010	17,496	30.9	11.7	15.5	3.7	19.2
2011	18,039	30.2	11.6	15.4	3.8	18.7
2012	18,587	29.6	11.4	15.3	3.9	18.1
2013	19,138	28.9	11.3	15.2	3.9	17.6
2014	19,693	28.3	11.2	15.2	4.0	17.1
2015	20,252	27.7	11.0	15.1	4.1	16.6
2016	20,814	27.1	10.9	15.1	4.1	16.2
2017	21,379	26.5	10.8	15.0	4.2	15.7
2018	21,948	26.0	10.7	14.9	4.3	15.3
2019	22,521	25.5	10.5	14.9	4.3	14.9
2020	23,096	25.0	10.4	14.8	4.4	14.6
2021	23,675	24.5	10.3	14.8	4.5	14.2
2022	24,257	24.0	10.2	14.7	4.5	13.9
2023	24,841	23.6	10.0	14.6	4.6	13.6
2024	25,428	23.1	9.9	14.6	4.7	13.2
2025	26,017	22.7	9.8	14.5	4.7	12.9
2026	26,608	22.3	9.6	14.4	4.8	12.7
2027	27,202	21.9	9.5	14.4	4.9	12.4
2028	27,797	21.4	9.3	14.3	5.0	12.1
2029	28,394	21.1	9.2	14.2	5.0	11.9
2030	28,993	20.7	9.1	14.1	5.1	11.6
2031	29,592	20.3	8.9	14.1	5.2	11.4
2032	30,193	19.9	8.8	14.0	5.2	11.1
2033	30,795	19.6	8.6	13.9	5.3	10.9
2034	31,398	19.2	8.5	13.9	5.4	10.7
2035	32,002	18.9	8.4	13.8	5.4	10.5
2036	32,606	18.5	8.2	13.7	5.5	10.3
2037	33,210	18.2	8.1	13.7	5.6	10.1
2038	33,816	17.9	7.9	13.6	5.7	10.0
2039	34,421	17.6	7.8	13.6	5.7	9.8
2040	35,027	17.3	7.7	13.5	5.8	9.6
2041	35,633	17.0	7.6	13.4	5.9	9.4
2042	36,239	16.7	7.4	13.4	5.9	9.3
2043	36,846	16.5	7.3	13.3	6.0	9.1
2044	37,452	16.2	7.2	13.3	6.1	9.0
2045	38,059	15.9	7.1	13.2	6.1	8.8
2046	38,665	15.7	7.0	13.2	6.2	8.7
2047	39,272	15.4	6.9	13.1	6.2	8.6
2048	39,879	15.2	6.8	13.1	6.3	8.4
2049	40,485	15.0	6.7	13.0	6.4	8.3
2050	41,091	14.8	6.6	13.0	6.4	8.2

Source: Jennifer Cheeseman Day, U.S. Department of Commerce, Economics and Statistics Administration, Bureau of the Census, Current Population Reports, P25-1092, *Population Projections of the United States, by Age, Sex, Race, and Hispanic Origin: 1992-2050* (Washington, DC: U.S. Government Printing Office, 1993), table 1, p.5.

★ 808 ★

Population Projections and Annual Change, Asian/Pacific Islander, 1992–2050

Asian/Pacific Islander population (in thousands) in 1992 and projected change in population by 2050, and projected annual population change, births, deaths, and net immigration.

Calendar year	January 1 population (in thousands)	Population change during calendar year				
		Net change	Natural Increase	Births	Deaths	Net Immigration
1992	8,223	458	121	144	23	337
1993	8,681	463	127	151	25	337
1994	9,144	469	132	159	26	337
1995	9,613	475	138	166	28	337
1996	10,088	480	143	173	30	337
1997	10,568	485	149	181	32	337
1998	11,053	490	154	188	34	337
1999	11,543	495	159	195	36	337
2000	12,038	500	163	202	39	337
2001	12,538	504	168	209	41	337
2002	13,043	509	172	215	43	337
2003	13,551	513	176	222	46	337
2004	14,064	517	180	229	48	337
2005	14,581	521	184	235	51	337
2006	15,102	525	188	242	54	337
2007	15,627	529	192	249	57	337
2008	16,156	533	197	256	59	337
2009	16,689	537	201	263	62	337
2010	17,226	541	205	270	66	337
2011	17,768	545	209	277	69	337
2012	18,313	549	213	285	72	337
2013	18,862	553	216	292	75	337
2014	19,415	557	220	299	79	337
2015	19,972	560	224	306	82	337
2016	20,533	564	227	313	86	337
2017	21,097	567	231	321	90	337
2018	21,664	571	234	328	94	337
2019	22,235	574	237	335	98	337
2020	22,809	577	240	342	102	337
2021	23,386	580	243	349	106	337
2022	23,966	583	246	356	110	337
2023	24,549	586	249	363	114	337
2024	25,134	588	251	370	119	337
2025	25,722	590	254	377	123	337
2026	26,313	592	256	384	128	337
2027	26,905	594	258	391	133	337
2028	27,500	596	260	397	138	337
2029	28,096	598	261	404	143	337
2030	28,693	599	262	410	148	337
2031	29,292	600	264	417	153	337
2032	29,893	601	265	423	158	337
2033	30,494	602	266	429	163	337
2034	31,097	603	267	435	169	337
2035	31,700	604	267	442	174	337
2036	32,304	604	268	448	180	337

[Continued]

★ 808 ★

Population Projections and Annual Change, Asian/Pacific Islander, 1992–2050 (Continued)

Asian/Pacific Islander population (in thousands) in 1992 and projected change in population by 2050, and projected annual population change, births, deaths, and net immigration.

Calendar year	January 1 population (in thousands)	Population change during calendar year				
		Net change	Natural Increase	Births	Deaths	Net Immigration
2037	32,908	605	268	454	186	337
2038	33,513	605	269	460	192	337
2039	34,118	606	269	466	197	337
2040	34,724	606	269	473	203	337
2041	35,330	606	270	479	209	337
2042	35,936	606	270	485	215	337
2043	36,542	606	270	491	221	337
2044	37,149	607	270	497	227	337
2045	37,756	607	270	503	233	337
2046	38,362	607	270	509	239	337
2047	38,969	607	270	515	245	337
2048	39,575	606	270	521	251	337
2049	40,182	606	270	527	257	337
2050	40,788	606	270	533	263	337

Source: Jennifer Cheeseman Day, U.S. Department of Commerce, Economics and Statistics Administration, Bureau of the Census, Current Population Reports, P25-1092, *Population Projections of the United States, by Age, Sex, Race, and Hispanic Origin: 1992-2050* (Washington, DC: U.S. Government Printing Office, 1993), table 1, p.5.

★ 809 ★

Population Projections, Non-Hispanic Asian/Pacific Islander, 1992–2050

Non-Hispanic Asian/Pacific Islander Population (in thousands) at mid-year 1992, and projected to mid-year 2050, projected annual rate of change, birth rate, death rate, and net immigration for each year included.

Calendar year	July 1 population (in thousands)	Rate per 1,000 mid-year population				
		Net change	Natural increase	Births	Deaths	Net immigration
1992	7,937	54.8	14.2	16.8	2.7	40.7
1993	8,374	52.6	14.0	16.8	2.7	38.6
1994	8,818	50.6	13.9	16.7	2.8	36.6
1995	9,266	48.7	13.8	16.7	2.8	34.8
1996	9,720	46.9	13.7	16.6	2.9	33.2
1997	10,178	45.3	13.6	16.5	2.9	31.7
1998	10,642	43.8	13.4	16.4	3.0	30.3
1999	11,110	42.3	13.3	16.3	3.1	29.1
2000	11,582	41.0	13.1	16.2	3.1	27.9
2001	12,059	39.7	12.9	16.1	3.2	26.8
2002	12,540	38.5	12.7	16.0	3.2	25.7
2003	13,025	37.3	12.6	15.8	3.3	24.8
2004	13,513	36.3	12.4	15.7	3.4	23.9
2005	14,005	35.3	12.2	15.6	3.4	23.1
2006	14,501	34.3	12.1	15.5	3.5	22.3
2007	15,000	33.4	11.9	15.4	3.5	21.5

[Continued]

★ 809 ★

Population Projections, Non-Hispanic Asian/Pacific Islander, 1992–2050 (Continued)

Non-Hispanic Asian/Pacific Islander Population (in thousands) at mid-year 1992, and projected to mid-year 2050, projected annual rate of change, birth rate, death rate, and net immigration for each year included.

Calendar year	July 1 population (in thousands)	Rate per 1,000 mid-year population				
		Net change	Natural increase	Births	Deaths	Net immigration
2008	15,504	32.6	11.8	15.4	3.6	20.8
2009	16,011	31.8	11.6	15.3	3.7	20.2
2010	16,522	31.0	11.5	15.2	3.7	19.5
2011	17,036	30.3	11.4	15.2	3.8	19.0
2012	17,555	29.6	11.2	15.1	3.9	18.4
2013	18,076	29.0	11.1	15.0	3.9	17.9
2014	18,602	28.3	11.0	15.0	4.0	17.4
2015	19,130	27.7	10.8	14.9	4.1	16.9
2016	19,662	27.1	10.7	14.8	4.1	16.4
2017	20,197	26.6	10.6	14.8	4.2	16.0
2018	20,735	26.0	10.5	14.7	4.3	15.6
2019	21,277	25.5	10.3	14.7	4.3	15.2
2020	21,821	25.0	10.2	14.6	4.4	14.8
2021	22,368	24.5	10.1	14.5	4.5	14.4
2022	22,917	24.0	9.9	14.5	4.5	14.1
2023	23,469	23.6	9.8	14.4	4.6	13.8
2024	24,024	23.1	9.7	14.3	4.7	13.4
2025	24,580	22.7	9.5	14.3	4.7	13.1
2026	25,138	22.2	9.4	14.2	4.8	12.8
2027	25,699	21.8	9.3	14.1	4.9	12.6
2028	26,250	21.4	9.1	14.1	5.0	12.3
2029	26,823	21.0	9.0	14.0	5.0	12.0
2030	27,388	20.6	8.8	13.9	5.1	11.8
2031	27,953	20.2	8.7	13.9	5.2	11.6
2032	28,520	19.9	8.6	13.8	5.2	11.3
2033	29,087	19.5	8.4	13.7	5.3	11.1
2034	29,655	19.2	8.3	13.7	5.4	10.9
2035	30,223	18.8	8.1	13.6	5.5	10.7
2036	30,792	18.5	8.0	13.5	5.5	10.5
2037	31,361	18.2	7.9	13.5	5.6	10.3
2038	31,930	17.8	7.7	13.4	5.7	10.1
2039	32,500	17.5	7.6	13.3	5.7	9.9
2040	33,070	17.2	7.5	13.3	5.8	9.8
2041	33,639	16.9	7.3	13.2	5.9	9.6
2042	34,209	16.7	7.2	13.2	5.9	9.4
2043	34,779	16.4	7.1	13.1	6.0	9.3
2044	35,349	16.1	7.0	13.1	6.1	9.1
2045	35,919	15.9	6.9	13.0	6.1	9.0
2046	36,488	15.6	6.8	13.0	6.2	8.8
2047	37,058	15.4	6.7	12.9	6.3	8.7
2048	37,627	15.1	6.5	12.9	6.3	8.6
2049	38,196	14.9	6.4	12.8	6.4	8.5
2050	38,765	14.7	6.3	12.8	6.4	8.3

Source: Jennifer Cheeseman Day, U.S. Department of Commerce, Economics, and Statistics Administration, Bureau of the Census, Current Population Reports, P25-1092, *Population Projections of the United States, by Age, Sex, Race, and Hispanic Origin: 1992-2050* (Washington DC: U.S. Government Printing Office, 1993), table 1, p. 10.

★810★

Population Projections and Annual Change, Non-Hispanic Asian/Pacific Islander, 1992 to 2050

Non-Hispanic Asian/Pacific Islander population (in thousands) in 1992, and projected change in population 2050, and projected annual population change, births, deaths, and net immigration.

Calendar year	Population change during calendar year					
	July 1 population	Net change	Natural increase	Births	Deaths	Net immigration
1992	7,720	435	112	134	21	323
1993	8,165	440	118	140	23	323
1994	8,596	446	123	147	25	323
1995	9,042	451	128	154	26	323
1996	9,493	456	133	161	28	323
1997	9,949	461	138	168	30	323
1998	10,410	466	143	175	32	323
1999	10,876	470	148	181	34	323
2000	11,346	475	152	188	36	323
2001	11,821	479	156	194	38	323
2002	12,300	483	160	200	41	323
2003	12,782	486	164	206	43	323
2004	13,269	490	167	213	45	323
2005	13,759	494	171	219	48	323
2006	14,253	498	175	225	50	323
2007	14,751	501	179	232	53	323
2008	15,252	505	182	238	56	323
2009	15,757	509	186	245	59	323
2010	16,266	513	190	251	62	323
2011	16,779	516	194	258	65	323
2012	17,295	520	197	265	68	323
2013	17,815	524	201	272	71	323
2014	18,339	527	204	278	74	323
2015	18,866	530	207	285	78	323
2016	19,396	534	211	292	81	323
2017	19,930	537	214	298	85	323
2018	20,466	540	217	305	88	323
2019	21,006	543	220	312	92	323
2020	21,549	546	223	318	96	323
2021	22,094	548	225	325	100	323
2022	22,643	551	228	332	104	323
2023	23,193	553	230	338	108	323
2024	23,747	555	232	345	112	323
2025	24,302	557	234	351	117	323
2026	24,859	559	236	357	121	323
2027	25,418	561	238	363	125	323
2028	25,979	562	240	370	130	323
2029	26,542	564	241	376	135	323
2030	27,106	565	242	382	140	323
2031	27,670	566	243	388	144	323
2032	28,236	567	244	393	149	323
2033	28,803	568	245	399	155	323
2034	29,371	568	245	405	160	323
2035	29,939	569	246	411	165	323

[Continued]

★810★

Population Projections and Annual Change,
Non-Hispanic Asian/Pacific Islander, 1992 to 2050 (Continued)

Non-Hispanic Asian/Pacific Islander population (in thousands) in 1992, and projected change in population 2050, and projected annual population change, births, deaths, and net immigration.

Calendar year	Population change during calendar year					
	July 1 population	Net change	Natural increase	Births	Deaths	Net immigration
2036	30,507	569	246	416	170	323
2037	31,076	569	246	422	176	323
2038	31,646	569	247	428	181	323
2039	32,215	570	247	433	187	323
2040	32,785	570	247	439	192	323
2041	33,354	570	247	445	198	323
2042	33,924	570	247	450	204	323
2043	34,494	570	247	456	209	323
2044	35,064	570	247	462	215	323
2045	35,634	570	247	467	221	323
2046	36,204	570	247	473	226	323
2047	36.773	569	246	478	232	323
2048	37,342	569	246	484	238	323
2049	37,911	569	246	489	243	323
2050	38,480	569	246	495	249	323

Source: Jennifer Cheeseman Day, U.S. Department of Commerce, Economics, and Statistics Administration, Bureau of the Census, Current Population Reports, P25-1092, *Population Projections of the United States, by Age, Sex, Race, and Hispanic Origin: 1992-2050* (Washington, DC: U.S. Government Printing Office, 1993), table 1, p. 10.

Canadian Population

★ 811 ★

Population by Ethnic Origin, Canada

Numbers and percent of total of the top ten single-origin ethnic groups[a] in Canada, 1986 and 1991.

1986			1991		
Group	Number	Percent	Group	Number	Percent
Total	25,022,005	100.0%	Total	26,994,045	100.0%
Total single origins (ranked by number)	18,035,665	72.1%	Total single origins (ranked by number)	19,199,795	71.1%
1. British	6,332,725	25.3%	1. French	6,146,605	22.8%
2. French	6,093,160	24.4%	2. British	5,611,050	20.8%
3. German	896,720	3.6%	3. German	911,560	3.4%
4. Italian	709,590	2.8%	4. Canadian	765,095	2.8%
5. Ukrainian	420,210	1.7%	5. Italian	750,055	2.8%
6. Aboriginal	373,265	1.5%	**6. Chinese**	586,645	2.2%
7. Chinese	360,320	1.4%	7. Aboriginal	470,615	1.7%
8. Dutch (Netherlands)	351,765	1.4%	8. Ukrainian	406,645	1.5%
9. South Asian[b]	266,800	1.1%	9. Dutch (Netherlands)	358,185	1.3%
10. Jewish	245,855	1.0%	10. East Indian	324,840	1.2%

Sources: Pamela M. White, *Ethnic Diversity in Canada* (Ottawa: Minister of Supply and Services Canada, 1990), table 1, p. 20 (for 1986); *The Daily* (Ottawa: Statistics Canada, February 26, 1993; for 1991). Primary source: Statistics Canada, December 3, 1987. *Notes:* (a) The Census of Population in Canada is conducted every five years. Ethnic origins data is based on a 20 percent sample. Respondents may report a single origin or multiple ethnic origins. (b) Includes the single origins of Bengali, Gujarati, Punjabi, Singhalese, Tamil, Bangladeshi (not included elsewhere), East Indian (not included elsewhere), Pakistani (not included elsewhere), and Sri Lankan (not included elsewhere).

★ 812 ★

Population by Ethnic Origin, Alberta

Numbers and percent of total of the top ten single-origin ethnic groups[a] in Alberta, 1986 and 1991.

1986			1991		
Group (ranked by number)	Number	Percent	Group	Number	Percent
Total	2,340,265	100.0%	Total	2,519,185	100.0%
Total single origins	1,389,930	59.4%	Total single origins	1,451,000	57.6%
1. British	592,345	25.3%	1. British	493,195	19.6%
2. German	182,870	7.8%	2. German	185,630	7.4%
3. Ukrainian	106,760	4.6%	3. Ukrainian	104,350	4.1%
4. French	77,585	3.3%	4. Canadian	92,490	3.7%
5. Dutch (Netherlands)	55,920	2.4%	5. French	74,615	3.0%
6. Aboriginal	51,670	2.2%	**6. Chinese**	71,635	2.8%
7. Chinese	49,210	2.1%	7. Aboriginal	68,445	2.7%
8. Scandinavian	46,525	2.0%	8. Dutch (Netherlands)	54,750	2.2%
9. South Asianb	30,090	1.3%	9. Polish	32,840	1.3%
10. Polish	28,500	1.2%	10. East Indian	32,240	1.3%

Sources: Pamela M. White, *Ethnic Diversity in Canada* (Ottawa: Minister of Supply and Services Canada, 1990), table 1, p. 20 (for 1986); *The Daily* (Ottawa: Statistics Canada, February 26, 1993; for 1991). Primary source: Statistics Canada, December 3, 1987. *Notes:* (a) The Census of Population in Canada is conducted every five years. Ethnic origins data is based on a 20 percent sample. Respondents may report a single origin or multiple ethnic origins. (b) Includes the single origins of Bengali, Gujarati, Punjabi, Singhalese, Tamil, Bangladeshi (not included elsewhere), East Indian (not included elsewhere), Pakistani (not included elsewhere), and Sri Lankan (not included elsewhere).

★ 813 ★

Population by Ethnic Origin, British Columbia

Numbers and percent of total of the top ten single-origin ethnic groups[a] in British Columbia, 1986 and 1991.

1986			1991		
Group (ranked by number)	Number	Percent	Group	Number	Percent
Total	2,849,585	100.0%	Total	3,247,505	100.0%
Total single origins	1,759,810	61.8%	Total single origins	1,952,850	60.1%
1. British	871,070	30.6%	1. British	812,470	25.0%
2. German	148,280	5.2%	**2. Chinese**	181,185	5.6%
3. Chinese	112,605	4.0%	3. German	156,635	4.8%
4. South Asian[b]	69,250	2.4%	4. East Indian	89,265	2.7%
5. French	68,965	2.4%	5. Aboriginal	74,420	2.3%
6. Dutch (Netherlands)	62,945	2.2%	6. French	68,795	2.1%
7. Aboriginal	61,130	2.1%	7. Dutch (Netherlands)	66,525	2.0%
8. Scandinavian	52,560	1.8%	8. Canadian	60,320	1.9%
9. Ukrainian	48,200	1.7%	9. Ukrainian	52,760	1.6%
10. Italian	46,755	1.6%	10. Italian	49,265	1.5%

Sources: Pamela M. White, *Ethnic Diversity in Canada* (Ottawa: Minister of Supply and Services Canada, 1990), table 1, p. 20 (for 1986); *The Daily* (Ottawa: Statistics Canada, February 26, 1993; for 1991). Primary source: Statistics Canada, December 3, 1987. *Notes:* (a) The Census of Population in Canada is conducted every five years. Ethnic origins data is based on a 20 percent sample. Respondents may report a single origin or multiple ethnic origins. (b) Includes the single origins of Bengali, Gujarati, Punjabi, Singhalese, Tamil, Bangladeshi (not included elsewhere), East Indian (not included elsewhere), Pakistani (not included elsewhere), and Sri Lankan (not included elsewhere).

★ 814 ★

Population by Ethnic Origin, Manitoba

Top ten single-origin ethnic groups[a] in Manitoba, 1986 and 1991.

1986			1991		
Group (ranked by number)	Number	Percent	Group	Number	Percent
Total	1,049,320	100.0%	Total	1,079,395	100.0%
Total single origins	681,580	65.0%	Total single origins	669,405	62.0%
1. British	224,375	21.4%	1. British	183,490	17.0%
2. German	96,160	9.2%	2. German	93,995	8.7%
3. Ukrainian	79,940	7.6%	3. Aboriginal	74,340	6.9%
4. French	55,720	5.3%	4. Ukrainian	74,285	6.9%
5. Aboriginal	55,410	5.3%	5. French	53,580	5.0%
6. Dutch (Netherlands)	27,875	2.7%	6. Dutch (Netherlands)	24,465	2.3%
7. Polish	22,015	2.1%	**7. Filipino**	22,045	2.0%
8. Filipino	15,815	1.5%	8. Polish	21,600	2.0%
9. Scandinavian	14,835	1.4%	9. Canadian	15,375	1.4%
10. Jewish	13,870	1.3%	10. Jewish	12,265	1.1%

Sources: Pamela M. White, *Ethnic Diversity in Canada* (Ottawa: Minister of Supply and Services Canada, 1990), table 1, p. 20 (for 1986); *The Daily* (Ottawa: Statistics Canada, February 26, 1993; for 1991). Primary source: Statistics Canada, December 3, 1987. *Notes:* (a) The Census of Population in Canada is conducted every five years. Ethnic origins data is based on a 20 percent sample. Respondents may report a single origin or multiple ethnic origins.

★ 815 ★

Population by Ethnic Origin, New Brunswick

Numbers and percent of total of the top ten single-origin ethnic groups[a] in New Brunswick, 1986 and 1991 Census.

1986			1991		
Group (ranked by number)	Number	Percent	Group	Number	Percent
Total			Total	716,495	100.0%
Total single origins			Total single origins	503,820	70.3%
1. British	251,315	35.8%	1. British	236,385	33.0%
2. French	232,570	33.1%	2. French	235,010	32.8%
3. Aboriginal	3,885	0.6%	3. Canadian	9,325	1.3%
4. German	3,760	0.5%	4. German	4,480	0.6%
5. Dutch (Netherlands)	2,900	0.4%	5. Aboriginal	4,270	0.6%
6. Scandinavian	1,215	0.2%	6. Dutch (Netherlands)	3,045	0.4%
7. Black	935	0.1%	7. Italian	1,320	0.2%
8. Italian	865	0.1%	**8. Chinese**	1,255	0.2%
9. Chinese	765	0.1%	9. Black	1,050	0.1%
10. South Asian[b]	735	0.1%	10. Danish	850	0.1%

Sources: Pamela M. White, *Ethnic Diversity in Canada* (Ottawa: Minister of Supply and Services Canada, 1990), table 1, p. 20 (for 1986); *The Daily* (Ottawa: Statistics Canada, February 26, 1993; for 1991). Primary source: Statistics Canada, December 3, 1987. *Notes:* (a) The Census of Population in Canada is conducted every five years. Ethnic origins data is based on a 20 percent sample. Respondents may report a single origin or multiple ethnic origins. (b) Includes the single origins of Bengali, Gujarati, Punjabi, Singhalese, Tamil, Bangladeshi (not included elsewhere), East Indian (not included elsewhere), Pakistani (not included elsewhere), and Sri Lankan (not included elsewhere).

★ 816 ★

Population by Ethnic Origin, Newfoundland

Numbers and percent of total of the top ten single-origin ethnic groups[a], Newfoundland, 1986 and 1991.

1986			1991		
Group	Number	Percent	Group	Number	Percent
Total	564,000	100.0%	Total	563,940	100.0%
Total single origins	470,280	83.4%	Total single origins	465,645	82.6%
1. British	449,760	79.7%	1. British	442,810	78.5%
2. French	11,315	2.0%	2. French	9,700	1.7%
3.Aboriginal	3,825	0.7%	3.Aboriginal	5,345	0.9%
4. German	1,155	0.2%	4. German	1,315	0.2%
5. South Asian[b]	680	0.1%	5. Canadian	1,225	0.2%
6. Chinese	610	0.1%	**6. Chinese**	740	0.1%
7. Dutch (Netherlands)	395	0.1%	7. East Indian	710	0.1%
8. Filipino	285	0.1%	8. Dutch (Netherlands)	440	0.1%
9. Scandinavian	265	0.0%	9. Italian	295	0.1%

Sources: Pamela M. White, *Ethnic Diversity in Canada* (Ottawa: Minister of Supply and Services Canada, 1990), table 1, p. 20 (for 1986); *The Daily* (Ottawa: Statistics Canada, February 26, 1993; for 1991). Primary source: Statistics Canada, December 3, 1987. *Notes:* (a) The Census of Population in Canada is conducted every five years. Ethnic origins data is based on a 20 percent sample. Respondents may report a single origin or multiple ethnic origins. (b) Includes the single origins of Bengali, Gujarati, Punjabi, Singhalese, Tamil, Bangladeshi (not included elsewhere), East Indian (not included elsewhere), Pakistani (not included elsewhere), and Sri Lankan (not included elsewhere).

★ 817 ★

Population by Ethnic Origin, Northwest Territories

Numbers and percent of total of the top ten single-origin ethnic groups[a] in the Northwest Territories, 1986 and 1991.

1986			1991		
Group (ranked by number)	Number	Percent	Group	Number	Percent
Total	52,020	100.0%	Total	57,435	100.0%
Total single origins	39,980	76.9%	Total single origins	41,545	72.3%
1. Aboriginal	27,175	52.2%	1. Aboriginal	29,415	51.2%
2. British	7,015	13.5%	2. British	5,885	10.2%
3. French	1,510	2.9%	3. French	1,395	2.4%
4. German	1,085	2.1%	4. Canadian	1,035	1.8%
5. Ukrainian	400	0.8%	5. German	885	1.5%
6. Scandinavian	305	0.6%	6. Ukrainian	445	0.8%
7. Italian	255	0.5%	7. Dutch (Netherlands)	305	0.5%
8. Dutch (Netherlands)	240	0.5%	**8. Chinese**	270	0.5%
9. Chinese	240	0.5%	**9. Filipino**	210	0.4%
10. Filipino	155	0.3%	10. Italian	160	0.3%

Sources: Pamela M. White, *Ethnic Diversity in Canada* (Ottawa: Minister of Supply and Services Canada, 1990), table 1, p. 20 (for 1986); *The Daily* (Ottawa: Statistics Canada, February 26, 1993; for 1991). Primary source: Statistics Canada, December 3, 1987. *Note:* (a) The Census of Population in Canada is conducted every five years. Ethnic origins data is based on a 20 percent sample. Respondents may report a single origin or multiple ethnic origins.

★ 818 ★

Population by Ethnic Origin, Nova Scotia

Numbers and percent of total of the top ten single-origin ethnic groups[a] in Nova Scotia, 1986 and 1991.

1986			1991		
Group (ranked by number)	Number	Percent	Group	Number	Percent
Total	864,150	100.0%	Total	890,950	100.0%
Total Single Origins	535,905	62.0%	Total Single Origins	532,845	59.8%
1. British	417,690	48.3%	1. British	391,805	44.0%
2. French	52,900	6.1%	2. French	55,310	6.2%
3. German	21,205	2.5%	3. German	24,825	2.8%
4. Dutch (Netherlands)	9,320	1.1%	4. Black	10,825	1.2%
5. Black	7,915	0.9%	5. Canadian	9,675	1.1%
6. Aboriginal	5,960	0.7%	6. Dutch (Netherlands)	8,960	1.0%
7. Italian	2,260	0.3%	7. Aboriginal	7,530	0.8%
8. Lebanese	2,135	0.2%	8. Italian	2,715	0.3%
9. South Asian[b]	1,950	0.2%	9. Polish	2,360	0.3%
10. Polish	1,840	0.2%	10. Lebanese	2,335	0.3%

Sources: Pamela M. White, *Ethnic Diversity in Canada* (Ottawa: Minister of Supply and Services Canada, 1990), table 1, p. 20 (for 1986); *The Daily* (Ottawa: Statistics Canada, February 26, 1993; for 1991). Primary source: Statistics Canada, December 3, 1987. *Notes:* (a) The Census of Population in Canada is conducted every five years. Ethnic origins data is based on a 20 percent sample. Respondents may report a single origin or multiple ethnic origins. (b) Includes the single origins of Bengali, Gujarati, Punjabi, Singhalese, Tamil, Bangladeshi (not included elsewhere), East Indian (not included elsewhere), Pakistani (not included elsewhere), and Sri Lankan (not included elsewhere).

★ 819 ★

Population by Ethnic Origin, Ontario

Numbers and percent of total of the top single-origin ethnic groups[a] in Ontario, 1986 and 1991.

1986			1991		
Group	Number	Percent	Group	Number	Percent
Total	9,001,170	100.0%	Total	9,977,050	100.0%
Total single origins	9,952,105	66.1%	Total single origins	6,698,995	67.1%
1. British	2,912,830	32.4%	1. British	2,536,515	25.4%
2. French	531,580	5.9%	2. French	527,580	5.3%
3. Italian	461,375	5.1%	3. Canadian	525,240	5.3%
4. German	285,155	3.2%	4. Italian	486,760	4.9%
5. Dutch (Netherlands)	171,150	1.9%	5. German	289,420	2.9%
6. Chinese	156,170	1.7%	**6. Chinese**	273,870	2.7%
7. Portuguese	139,220	1.5%	7. Dutch (Netherlands)	179,760	1.8%
8. South Asian[b]	135,135	1.5%	8. Portuguese	176,300	1.8%

Sources: Pamela M. White, *Ethnic Diversity in Canada* (Ottawa: Minister of Supply and Services Canada, 1990), table 1, p. 20 (for 1986); *The Daily* (Ottawa: Statistics Canada, February 26, 1993; for 1991). Primary source: Statistics Canada, December 3, 1987. *Notes:* (a) The Census of Population in Canada is conducted every five years. Ethnic origins data is based on a 20 percent sample. Respondents may report a single origin or multiple ethnic origins. (b) Includes the single origins of Bengali, Gujarati, Punjabi, Singhalese, Tamil, Bangladeshi (not included elsewhere), East Indian (not included elsewhere), Pakistani (not included elsewhere), and Sri Lankan (not included elsewhere).

★ 820 ★

Population by Ethnic Origin, Prince Edward Island

Numbers and percent of total of the top ten single-origin ethnic groups[a] in Prince Edward Island, 1986 and 1991.

1986			1991		
Group	Number	Percent	Group	Number	Percent
Total	125,090	100.0%	Total	128,100	100.0%
Total single origins	74,105	59.2%	Total single origins	72,930	56.9%
1. British	59,275	47.4%	1. British	56,405	44.0%
2. French	11,130	8.9%	2. French	11,845	9.2%
3. Dutch (Netherlands)	1,280	1.0%	3. Dutch (Netherlands)	1,250	1.0%
4. German	535	0.4%	4. Canadian	795	0.6%
5. Aboriginal	410	0.3%	5. German	645	0.5%
6. Lebanese	230	0.2%	6. Aboriginal	400	0.3%
7. South Asian[b]	205	0.2%	7. Lebanese	255	0.2%
8. Scandinavian	135	0.1%	8. Polish	145	0.1%
9. Chinese	130	0.1%	9. Danish	120	0.1%
10. Polish	100	0.1%	10. East Indian	95	0.1%

Sources: Pamela M. White, *Ethnic Diversity in Canada* (Ottawa: Minister of Supply and Services Canada, 1990), table 1, p. 20 (for 1986); *The Daily* (Ottawa: Statistics Canada, February 26, 1993; for 1991). Primary source: Statistics Canada, December 3, 1987. *Notes:* (a) The Census of Population in Canada is conducted every five years. Ethnic origins data is based on a 20 percent sample. Respondents may report a single origin or multiple ethnic origins. (b) Includes the single origins of Bengali, Gujarati, Punjabi, Singhalese, Tamil, Bangladeshi (not included elsewhere), East Indian (not included elsewhere), Pakistani (not included elsewhere), and Sri Lankan (not included elsewhere).

★ 821 ★

Population by Ethnic Origin, Quebec

Numbers and percent of total of the top ten single-origin ethnic groups[a] in Quebec, 1986 and 1991,

1986			1991		
Group(ranked by number)	Number	Percent	Group	Number	Percent
Total	6,454,490	100.0%	Total	6,810,300	100.0%
Total single origins	6,010,010	93.1%	Total single origins	6,237,905	91.6%
1. French	5,015,565	77.7%	1. French	5,077,825	74.6%
2. British	319,550	5.0%	2. British	286,075	4.2%
3. Italian	163,880	2.5%	3. Italian	174,525	2.6%
4. Jewish	81,190	1.3%	4. Jewish	77,600	1.1%
5. Aboriginal	49,320	0.8%	5. Aboriginal	65,405	1.0%
6. Greek	47,450	0.7%	6. Greek	49,890	0.7%
7. Black	37,425	0.6%	7. Black	41,165	0.6%
8. Portuguese	29,700	0.5%	8. Portuguese	37,165	0.5%
9. German	26,780	0.4%	9. Chinese	36,815	0.5%
10. Chinese	23,205	0.4%	10. Lebanese	31,580	0.5%

Sources: Pamela M. White, *Ethnic Diversity in Canada* (Ottawa: Minister of Supply and Services Canada, 1990), table 1, p. 20 (for 1986); *The Daily* (Ottawa: Statistics Canada, February 26, 1993; for 1991). Primary source: Statistics Canada, December 3, 1987. *Note:* (a) The Census of Population in Canada is conducted every five years. Ethnic origins data is based on a 20 percent sample. Respondents may report a single origin or multiple ethnic origins.

★ 822 ★

Population by Ethnic Origin, Saskatchewan

Numbers and percent of total of the top ten single-origin ethnic groups[a] in Saskatchewan, 1986 and 1991.

1986			1991		
Group (ranked by number)	Number	Percent	Group	Number	Percent
Total	996,695	100.0%	Total	976,035	100.0%
Total single origins	604,750	60.7%	Total single origins	558,675	57.2%
1. British	222,115	22.3%	1. British	160,725	16.5%
2. German	128,850	12.9%	2. German	121,305	12.4%
3. Ukrainian	60,550	6.1%	3. Aboriginal	66,270	6.8%
4. Aboriginal	55,645	5.6%	4. Ukrainian	55,955	5.7%
5. French	33,535	3.4%	5. French	30,075	3.1%
6. Scandinavian	24,895	2.5%	6. Canadian	28,850	3.0%
7. Polish	13,325	1.3%	7. Norwegian	13,105	1.3%
8. Dutch (Netherlands)	13,025	1.3%	8. Polish	11,770	1.2%
9. Hungarian	8,115	0.8%	9. Dutch (Netherlands)	11,285	1.2%
10. Chinese	7,210	0.7%	10. Hungarian	7,920	0.8%

Sources: Pamela M. White, *Ethnic Diversity in Canada* (Ottawa: Minister of Supply and Services Canada, 1990), table 1, p. 20 (for 1986); *The Daily* (Ottawa: Statistics Canada, February 26, 1993; for 1991). Primary source: Statistics Canada, December 3, 1987. *Note:* (a) The Census of Population in Canada is conducted every five years. Ethnic origins data is based on a 20 percent sample. Respondents may report a single origin or multiple ethnic origins.

★ 823 ★

Population by Ethnic Origin, Yukon

Top single-origin ethnic groups[a] in the Yukon, 1986 and 1991.

1986			1991		
Group (ranked by number)	Number	Percent	Group	Number	Percent
Total	23,360	100.0%	Total	27,660	100.0%
Total single origins	12,855	55.0%	Total single origins	14,160	51.2%
1. British	5,370	23.0%	1. British	5,300	19.2%
2. Aboriginal	3,280	14.0%	2. Aboriginal	3,780	13.7%
3. German	880	3.8%	3. German	1,060	3.8%
4. French	775	3.3%	4. French	875	3.2%
5. Scandinavian	445	1.9%	5. Canadian	735	2.7%
6. Dutch (Netherlands)	350	1.5%	6. Ukrainian	390	1.4%
7. Ukrainian	340	1.5%	7. Dutch (Netherlands)	295	1.1%
8. Chinese	105	0.4%	8. Norwegian	180	0.7%
9. Hungarian	95	0.4%	9. Hungarian (Magyar)	140	0.5%
10. Polish	75	0.3%	10. Italian	135	0.5%
11. Italian	75	0.3%			

Sources: Pamela M. White, *Ethnic Diversity in Canada* (Ottawa: Minister of Supply and Services Canada, 1990), table 1, p. 20 (for 1986); *The Daily* (Ottawa: Statistics Canada, February 26, 1993; for 1991). Primary source: Statistics Canada, December 3, 1987. *Note:* (a) The Census of Population in Canada is conducted every five years. Ethnic origins data is based on a 20 percent sample. Respondents may report a single origin or multiple ethnic origins.

Public Life

Foundations and Philanthropic Organizations

★ 824 ★

Foundation Dollars to Organizations by Asian Ethnicity, 1983–1990

Foundation grants in dollars and percent of total awarded to Asian Pacific American organizations by year and by race/ethnicity, 1983 to 1990.

Population Group	Grants to Asian Pacific American organizations	
	In dollars	In percent of total foundation dollars
Mixed Asian	$8,410,886	24.3%
Chinese	8,687,256	25.1%
Japanese	3,102,399	9.0%
Korean	2,062,602	6.0%
Filipino	285,482	.8%
Mixed Southeast Asian	7,304,144	21.1%
Vietnamese	399,137	1.2%
Cambodian	1,205,397	3.4%
Laotian	1,306,436	3.8%
Hmong	1,429,362	4.1%
Pacific Islander	142,000	.4%
Samoan	17,000	0.0%
Hawaiian	292,939	.8%
Indian	15,000	0.0%
Total	$34,660,040	100.0%

Source: Invisible and in Need: Philanthropic Giving to Asian Americans and Pacific Islanders (San Francisco: Asian Americans and Pacific Islanders in Philanthropy [AAPIP], December 1992). Primary source: The Foundation Center in New York, which classifies every grant over $5,000 reported to the Center.

★ 825 ★

Foundation Grants to Asian Pacific American Organizations by Year, 1983-1990

Foundation grants awarded to Asian Pacific American organizations by year, 1983 to 1990.

| Year | Asian Pacific American Organizations | | |
	Total Dollars	Grants received (in dollars)	Grants received (in percent of total)
1983	$1,649,802,914	$3,304,868	0.2%
1984	1,849,262,981	3,967,695	0.2%
1985	2,089,997,956	4,213,710	0.2%
1986	2,556,418,549	4,051,610	0.16%
1987	2,619,089,688	5,434,677	0.2%
1988	2,834,844,663	5,210,571	0.18%
1989	3,676,692,835	4,371,982	0.12%
1990	2,157,232,662	4,104,926	0.19%
Total	19,433,342,253	34,660,040	0.18%

Source: Invisible and in Need: Philanthropic Giving to Asian Americans and Pacific Islanders (San Francisco: Asian Americans and Pacific Islanders in Philanthropy [AAPIP], December 1992). Primary source: The Foundation Center in New York, which classifies every grant over $5,000 reported to the Center. Note: In the period from 1983 to 1990, Asian/Pacific Americans represented the fastest growing population segment in the United States. In 1990, Asian/Pacific Americans represented 2.9 percent of the total U.S. population.

★ 826 ★

Foundation Grants to Asian Pacific American Organizations by Category, 1983-1990

Foundation grants of dollars (in millions) and percent of total grants to Asian Pacific American organizations by category of service, 1983-1990.

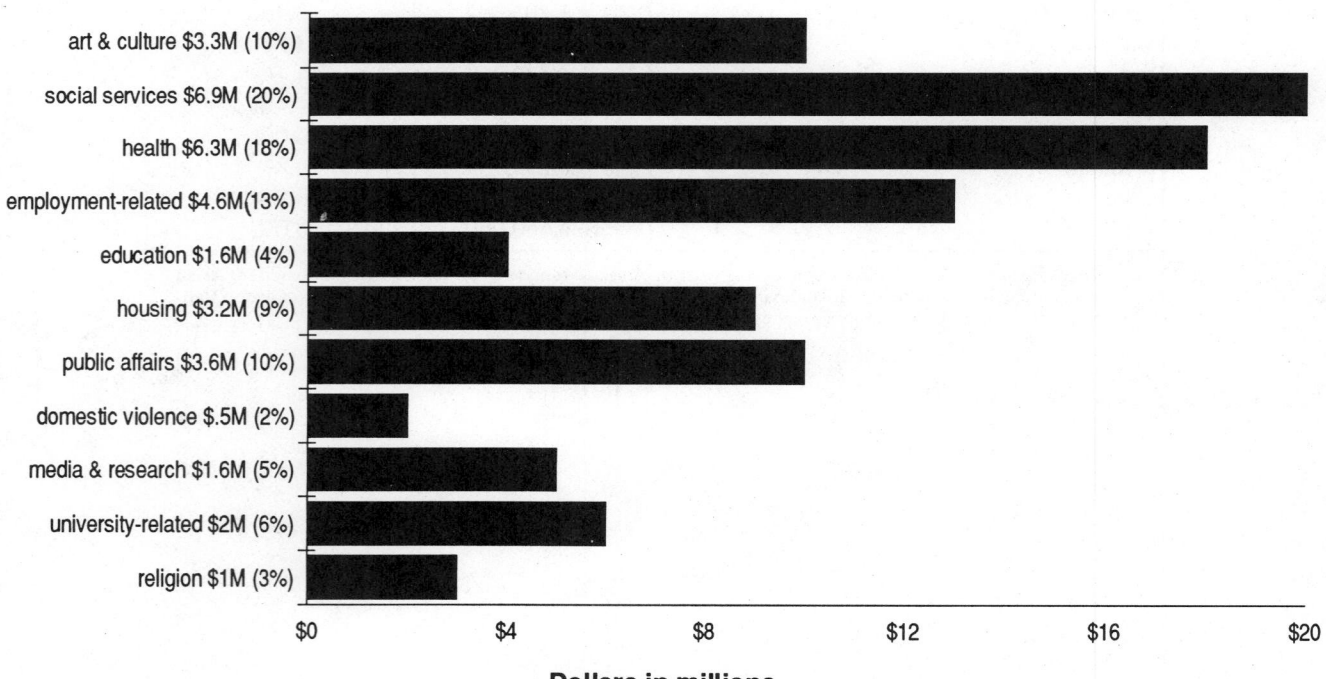

Dollars in millions

Source: Invisible and in Need: Philanthropic Giving to Asian Americans and Pacific Islanders (San Francisco: Asian Americans and Pacific Islanders in Philanthropy [AAPIP], December 1992). Primary source: The Foundation Center in New York, which classifies every grant over $5,000 reported to the Center.

★ 827 ★

Philanthropic Organizations, Asian Pacific American Trustees

Selected data on Asian Pacific Americans as members of boards of trustees and staff of philanthropic organizations, as of 1991.

Asian Pacific Americans in the United States represent:

Less than 1 percent of the trustees for twenty-five top private, community, and corporate foundations.

Almost 3 percent of the total population.

Source: Invisible and in Need: Philanthropic Giving to Asian Americans and Pacific Islanders (San Francisco: Asian Americans and Pacific Islanders in Philanthropy [AAPIP], December 1992).

★ 828 ★

Voluntary Organizations, Young Adults' Participation

Participation of young adults[a] in voluntary organizations, in percent, by race/ethnicity, 1984 to 1986.

Organization	Total	Asian	White, non-Hispanic	Black, non-Hispanic	Hispanic	American Indian
Sports teams of clubs	36.0%	41.4%	36.5%	31.9%	34.6%	41.1%
Church activities	32.2%	31.0%	30.6%	44.2%	32.4%	30.0%
Social or hobby clubs	21.8%	28.7%	22.3%	21.5%	17.1%	27.9%
Union, trade, farm, or other professional associates	17.7%	27/3%	18.2%	14.9%	15.8%	19.7%
Literary, art discussion or study group	10.6%	23.2%	10.2%	13.1%	11.6%	8.9%
Community groups[b]	9.4%	10.5%	8.5%	16.2%	8.5%	13.0%
Youth organizations	9.2%	10.8%	8.7%	12.0%	9.5%	11.6%
PTA or other academic group	7.0%	9.1%	6.4%	12.0%	5.6%	6.5%
Political clubs	6.2%	5.9%	5.9%	8.2%	6.9%	9.6%
Organized volunteer work[c]	5.8%	14.1%	5.5%	6.8%	4.3%	4.2%
Service organizations[d]	4.0%	5.9%	3.9%	4.0%	4.7%	7.2%
Other voluntary group	9.6%	10.3%	9.7%	10.3%	7.1%	7.8%

Source: U.S. Department of Education, National Center for Education Statistics, *Digest of Education Statistics, 1990* (Washington, DC: U.S. Government Printing Office, 1991), table 354, p. 372. (This table was prepared October 1987). Some young adults participated in more than one organization. Primary source; U.S. Department of Education, National Center for Education Statistics, *High School and Beyond* survey. Also in source: data on young adults by socioeconomic status, high school curriculum, sex, and level of participation in high school extracurricular activities. *Notes:* (a) Sample survey in 1986 based on high school seniors in spring 1980. Respondents to the survey were asked about their voluntary participation in selected organizations over the previous twenty-four month period. (b) Includes participation in community centers, neighborhood improvement, or social action associations or groups. (c) Hospital volunteer, for example. (d) Includes organizations such as Rotary, Junior Chamber of Commerce, etc.

Government Service

★ 829 ★

Clinton Administration Appointees

Appointments of Asian/Pacific Islanders to Executive Branch staff positions as of March 1993.

Position	Appointee
The White House	
Deputy Assistant to the President, Office of Public Liaison	Doris Matsui
Deputy Director for White House Personnel	Marie Haley
Special Assistant to the President for Congressional Affairs	Barbara Chow
Special Assistant to the President for Domestic Policy	Shirley Sagara
Special Assistant to the President, Office of the Secretary	Brant Lee
Department of Transportation	
Assistant Secretary, Congressional Affairs	Neil Dhillon

Source: Vida Benavides, Director of Constituencies, Democratic National Committee, telephone conversation with editor, March 10, 1993.

★ 830 ★

Bush Administration Appointees, Boards and Commissions

Asian American federal government officeholders appointed by President George Bush as of November 15, 1992.

Agency	Office	Appointee
Advanced Building Technology Council, Dept. of Housing and Urban Development	Member	I-Kuang Liang, A.I.A.
Advisory Committee on Structure Safety for Veterans Affairs	Member	Peter Chang
Advisory Council on Trade Policy and Negotiations	Member	David Sen Lin Lee
Architectural and Transportation Barriers Compliance Board		Perry Diaz
Board of Regents of the Uniformed Medical University and Health Sciences	Member	Gopal Pal, D.D.S., M.S.
Christopher Columbus Quincentenary Jubilee Commission	Member	John Tsu, Ph.D.
Citizen Advisory Committee on Equal Opportunity, U.S. Dept. of Agriculture	Member	Mae Takahasahi
Citizen Advisory Committee on Equal Opportunity, U.S. Dept. of Agriculture	Member	Cherry Kinoshita
Commission on Civil Liberties and Public Education Fund	Member	George Oki
Commission on Civil Liberties and Public Education Fund	Member	Sadao Nakashima
Commission on Civil Liberties and Public Education Fund	Member	Edwin Chikashi Hiroto
Commission on Civil Liberties and Public Education Fund	Member	Grant Ujifusa
Commission on Civil Liberties and Public Education Fund	Member	Tomio Moriguchi
Commission on Civil Liberties and Public Education Fund	Member	William Marumoto
Commission on Civil Liberties and Public Education Fund	Member	Bruce T. Kaji
Commission on National and Community Service	Member	Shirley Sagawa
Commission on National and Community Service	Member	Karen Young
Credit Standards Advisory Committee		Henry Yee

[Continued]

★ 830 ★

Bush Administration Appointees, Boards and Commissions (Continued)

Asian American federal government officeholders appointed by President George Bush as of November 15, 1992.

Agency	Office	Appointee
Defense Advisory Committee on Women in Service, Dept. of Defense	Member	Jane Hu, Ph.D.
East West Center, Board of Governors, University of Hawaii	Member	Ko-Yung Tung, J.D.
Federal Committee on Apprenticeship, Dept. of Labor	Member	Charles Ku, D.D.S.
Goldwater Scholarship and Excellence in Education Foundation, Board of Trustees	Member	Timothy Tong, Ph.D.
Goldwater Scholarship and Excellence in Education Foundation, Board of Trustees	Member	Charles Szu
J. William Fulbright Foreign Scholarship Board	Member	Shu-Park Chan, Ph.D.
J. William Fulbright Foreign Scholarship Board	Member	Esther Yao, Ph.D.
Minority Business Resource Center Advisory Committee, Dept. of Transportation	Member	Jerry Chang
Minority Enterprise Development Advisory Council, Dept. of Commerce	Member	Alba Bachelde
Minority Enterprise Development Advisory Council, Dept. of Commerce	Member	Ben Maynigo
National Advisory Council on Education Statistics	Member	Helen Chang
National Advisory Council on Educational Research and Improvement		Eunice Sato
National Advisory Council on the Public Service	Member	Samuel Mok
National Advisory Dental Research Council, National Institutes of Health	Member	Roger S. C. Eng, D.D.S.
National Cancer Advisory Board	Member	Kenneth Chan, Ph.D.
National Commission on Library and Information Science	Member	Ben-Chieh Liu, Ph.D.
National Commission on Library and Information Science	Member and Executive Director	Peter Young, Ph.D.
National Commission on Library and Information Science	Member	Julie Wu, Ph.D.
National Council on the Arts	Member	Catherine Woo, Ph.D.
National Council on the Humanities	Member	Mikiso Hane
National Heart, Lung and Blood Advisory Council, National Institutes of Health	Member	Zachariah Zachariah, M.D.
National Institute for Building Science	Member	Peter S. Chan (a)
National Museum Service Board	Member	Ruth Watanabe
National Park System Advisory Board, Dept. of Interior	Member	Sarah Kim
National Science Board, National Science Foundation	Member	Benjeman S. Shen, Ph.D.
National Small Business Advisory Council, Dept. of Commerce	Member	Florence Fang
National Small Business Advisory Council, Dept. of Commerce	Member	Elizabeth Szu
National Small Business Advisory Council, Dept. of Commerce	Member	Theresa Chang
National Women's Business Council	Member	Patricia Saiki
National Nutrition Monitoring Council	Member	Helen Lee
President's Administrative Conference	Member	Susan Allen, J.D.
President's Advisory Committee on the Arts, John F. Kennedy Center for the Performing Arts	Member	Sidney Chan, C.P.A.
President's Commission on Broadcasting to the People's Republic of China	Member	Nien Cheng
President's Committee on the National Medal of Science	Member	Yuan Tseh Lee, Ph.D.
President's Committee on the National Medal of Science	Member	Yuet Wai Kan
President's Export Council	Member	Donna Fujimoto Cole
President's Export Council	Member	Jonathan Kaji

[Continued]

★830★

Bush Administration Appointees, Boards and Commissions (Continued)

Asian American federal government officeholders appointed by President George Bush as of November 15, 1992.

Agency	Office	Appointee
Presidential Commission on Minority Business Development	Member	David Lam, Ph.D.
Presidential Commission on Minority Business Development	Member	Hernando Caampued
Presidential Committee on the Arts and Humanities	Member	Oscar Tang
Presidential Committee on the Arts and Humanities	Member	Dominic Lam, Ph.D.
Presidential Council on Physical Fitness and Sports	Member	Samuel Lee
Presidential Council on Physical Fitness and Sports	Member	Cory S. Servaas
Presidential Meritorious Award Commission, Office of Personnel Management		Virender Bisla, Ph.D.
Public Health Service Corporation Council, Dept. of Health and Human Services	Member	Grace Shu, Ph.D.
Review Board for the Distinguish Presidential Rank Award Program, Office of Personnel Management		Hobih Chen
Sallie Mae–Student Loan Marketing Association	Board of Directors	Gloria Hom, Ph.D.
Services Policy Advisory Committee, Office of U.S. Trade Representative	Member	Yong S. Kim
Take Pride In America,	Member, Advisory Board	Charles Kim
Take Pride In America, Dept. of Interior	Member, Advisory Board	Anna Chennault
U.S. Army Corps of Engineer	Member	Gen. Paul Chinen (Ret.)
U.S. Civil Rights Commission	Vice Chairman	Charles Pei Wang
U.S.-Japan Culture and Education Interchange Commission	Member	John Tsu, Ph.D.
U.S.-Japan Friendship Exchange Commission	Member	John Tsu, Ph.D.
United Services Organization (USO)	Board of Governors	Johnny Yune
Veterans Appeals Board, Dept. of Veteran's Affairs	Member	Un Hun Ang, M.D.
Western Interstate Nuclear Board		Jack Vlcek
White House Commission on Presidential Scholars	Member	Jun Hatoyama, M.D.
White House Commission on Presidential Scholars	Member	Jan Gabay
White House Commission on Presidential Scholars	Member	Anna Chennault

Source: Tony Chen, Director of Asian Affairs, Political Coalitions, Republican National Committee, Letter to editor, November 19, 1992. Because appointed officials serve at the pleasure of the President, these officeholders are subject to change following the inauguration of Bill Clinton, a Democrat, as President in January 1993. *Note:* (a) Pending Senate confirmation as of November 1992.

★ 831 ★

Bush Administration Appointees, Executive Branch

Asian American federal government officeholders appointed by President George Bush as of November 15, 1992.

Agency	Office	Appointee
The White House	Deputy Assistant to the President for Public Liaison	Clayton Fong
	Associate Director, Industrial Policy, Office of Science and Technology	Eugene Wong, Ph.D.
	West Wing Receptionist, The White House	Nancy Huang
	State Director, Farmers Home Administration, Hawaii	Michael Liu
	Director, Atlantic and Pacific Issue, International Security Affairs	Kien Duc Trung Pham
	Special Assistant, Under Secretary, Dept. of Navy	Eddie Serrano
	Confidential Assistant to the Assistant Secretary Office for Civil Rights	Andy Sun
	Deputy Regional Representative of the Secretary for Region Ten	Naomi K. Iwata Sanchez
	Special Assistant to Assistant Secretary Defense Program D	Catherine M. Kaliniak
	Confidential Assistant to the Director of Congressional and Legislative Affairs	Santanu K. Baruah
	Special Assistant to the Director of U.S. Fish and Wildlife Services	Clare J. Erekson
	Director, Office of Coordinated Care, Health Care Financial Administration	Edmund C. Moy
	Deputy Assistant Secretary for Legislative Affairs	Jack Chow, M.D.
	Deputy Director, Office of Refugee Resettlement	Nguyen Van Hahn, Ph.D.
	Special Assistant to the Director, Region IX	Walter Liang
	Director, Office of International Trade	Aileen Kishaba
	Deputy Assistant Secretary for South Asian Affairs	Sichan Siv
	Alternate Representative, Special Political Affairs Office United Nations	Tahir-Kheli Shirin
	U.S. Marshal–District of Northern Marianas	Jose Mariano
Department of Agriculture	Executive Director, Agriculture Stabilization and Conservation Service Office, Hawaii	Ralph K. Ajieu
Department of Commerce	Associate Director, Office of Operations, Minority Business Development Agency	Bharat Bhargava
Department of Defense	Assistant Secretary for Program Analysis and Evaluation	David Chu, Ph.D.
Department of Education	Deputy Director, Office of BiLingual Education and Minority	Ngoc Bich Nguyen
Department of Energy	Staff Assistant to the Administrative Assistant to the Secretary	Alberto D. Leyson
Department of Health and Human Services	Executive Director, President's Committee on Mental Retardation	Sambu N. Banik, Ph.D.
Department of Interior	Deputy Assistant Secretary for International and Territorial Affairs	William Houston

[Continued]

★ 831 ★

Bush Administration Appointees, Executive Branch (Continued)

Asian American federal government officeholders appointed by President George Bush as of November 15, 1992.

Agency	Office	Appointee
Department of Justice	Director, Asylum, Policy and Review Unit	Jan C. Ting, J.D.
Department of Labor	Staff Assistant, Office of the Secretary	June Stadheim
Department of State	U.S. Ambassador to Nepal	Julia Chang Bloch
Department of Transportation	Attorney-Adviser, Federal Transit Administration	Robert Wong, J.D.
Department of Veterans Administration	Executive Assistant to the Secretary	Kyo Jhin, Ph.D.
Small Business Administration	Administrator, Small Business Administration	Patricia Saiki

Source: Tony Chen, Director of Asian Affairs, Political Coalitions, Republican National Committee, Letter to editor, November 19, 1992. Because appointed officials serve at the pleasure of the President, these officeholders are subject to change following the inauguration of Bill Clinton, a Democrat, as President in January 1993.

★ 832 ★

Bush Administration Appointees, Independent Agencies

Asian American federal government officeholders appointed by President George Bush as of November 15, 1992.

Agency	Office	Appointee
Commodity Future Trading Commission	Chairman	Wendy Lee Gramm, Ph.D.
U.S. Peace Corps	Director	Elaine Chao
Commission on Copyright Royalty Tribunal	Chair	Cindy Daub
Federal Maritime Commission	Commissioner	Ming Hsu
U.S. Office of Personnel Management	Director	Dinah Lin Cheng
International Boundary and Water Commission	U.S. Commissioner	Narendra N. Gunaji, Ph.D.
Federal Trade Commission	Commissioner	Dennis Yao, Ph.D.
General Service Administration	Deputy Director, Region VI	Stanford Fong
Equal Employment Opportunity Commission	Member	Joy Cherian, J.D.
International Development Cooperation Agency	Office of Science and Technology Population Bureau, U.S.	Brij Sirvastav
U.S. International Development Cooperation Agency		Michael Theiman
U.S. International Development Cooperation Agency		Mohamed Cassam

Source: Tony Chen, Director of Asian Affairs, Political Coalitions, Republican National Committee, Letter to editor, November 19, 1992. Because appointed officials serve at the pleasure of the President, these officeholders are subject to change following the inauguration of Bill Clinton, a Democrat, as President in January 1993.

★ 833 ★

Bush Administration Appointees, Summary

Number of Asian American federal government officeholders appointed by President George Bush as of November 15, 1992.

Agency	Number of Appointees
Total, all agencies listed	124
The White House	3
Department of Agriculture	4
Department of Commerce	1
Department of Defense	3
Department of Education	3
Department of Energy	2
Department of Health and Human Services	4
Department of Interior	3
Department of Justice	2
Department of Labor	1
Department of State	3
Department of Transportation	1
Department of Veterans Affairs	1
Small Business Administration	3
Independent Agencies	12
Boards and Commissions	78

Source: Tony Chen, Director of Asian Affairs, Political Coalitions, Republican National Committee, Letter to editor, November 19, 1992. Because appointed officials serve at the pleasure of the President, these officeholders are subject to change following the inauguration of Bill Clinton, a Democrat, as President in January 1993.

★ 834 ★

U.S. Congress Members, 1956–1992

Asian American members of the House of Representatives and Senate of the U.S. Congress, by state, 1956 to 1992.

Year elected	Name	House/Senate	State
1956 to 1960	Dalip Singh Saund	House	California
1959	Hiram Fong	Senate	Hawaii (became a state in 1959)
	Daniel K. Inouye	House	Hawaii
1962	Daniel K. Inouye	Senate	
	Sparks Matsunaga	House	Hawaii (replaced Inouye)
1964	Patsy Takemoto Mink	House	Hawaii (newly created 2nd seat)
1974	Norman Mineta	House	California
1976	S. I. Hayakawa	Senate	California
1976	Sparks Matsunaga	Senate	Hawaii
1978	Robert Matsui	House	California
1992	Jay Kim	House	California
1992	Mark Takano	House	California

Source: *Asian Week*, November 6, 1992, pp. 4–5.

★ 835 ★

Asian Americans in Politics by State

Numbers of Asian/Pacific Americans holding elected or appointed positions in state, county, and municipal governments in the United States, by state.

State	Positions held by Asian/Pacific Islanders	
	Level of government	Number of positions held
Arizona	Total, all levels	4
	State, total	3
	County and Municipal, total	1
Arkansas	Total, all levels	2
	State, total	1
	County and Municipal, total	1
California	Total, all levels	308
	State, total	125
	County and Municipal, total	122
	—Mayors	11
	—Vice Mayors	2
	—City Managers	4
	—Council members	23
	Boards of Education	61
Colorado	Total, all levels	1
	County and Municipal, total	1
	—Council member	
Hawaii	Total, all levels	299
	State, total	204
	—State legislature	34
	County and Municipal, total	32
	Boards of Education	19
	Office of Hawaiian Affairs	10
Idaho	Total, all levels	3
	State, total	2
	County and Municipal, total	1
Illinois	Total, all levels	23
	State, total	15
	—State Commissions, total	14
	County and Municipal, total	6
	Boards of Education	2
Kansas	Total, all levels	1
	County and Municipal, total	1
Maryland	Total, all levels	9
	State, total	7
	County and Municipal, total	1
	Boards of Education	1
Massachusetts	Total, all levels	4
	State, total	3
	County and Municipal, total	1
	—Mayor	

[Continued]

★ 835 ★

Asian Americans in Politics by State (Continued)

Numbers of Asian/Pacific Americans holding elected or appointed positions in state, county, and municipal governments in the United States, by state.

State	Positions held by Asian/Pacific Islanders	
	Level of government	Number of positions held
Michigan	Total, all levels	3
	State, total	2
	County and Municipal, total	1
Minnesota	Total, all levels	1
	—Mayor	
Mississippi	Total, all levels	2
	—Mayors	
Missouri	Total, all levels	1
Nebraska	Total, all levels	1
New Hampshire	Total, all levels	2
New York	Total, all levels	7
	County and Municipal, total	2
	School Boards	5
North Dakota	Total, all levels	1
Oregon	Total, all levels	14
	State, total	8
	County and Municipal, total	6
Texas	Total, all levels	11
	State, total	2
	County and Municipal, total	9
	—Mayor	1
	—City Manager	1
	—Aldermen	2
	—Council members	2
Utah	Total, all levels	1
Washington	Total, all levels	33
	State, total,	10
	County and Municipal, total	23
	—Mayors	3
	—City Manager	1
	Boards of Education	5

Source: Selected from Asian Pacific American Municipal Officials (APAMO), *National Directory of Asian/Pacific American Elected and Appointed Officials* (Washington, DC: APAMO and National League of Cities, 1990).

★ 836 ★

Candidates for State Offices

Asian American candidates who ran for state offices in 1992, by party affiliation and election outcome.

Office	Candidate	Party	Results	Percent of vote
Arizona				
State Legislature	Manny Wong	I	Lost	(5 of 6)
Oregon				
State Treasurer	David Chen	R	Lost	46%
Washington				
State Legislature-District 11	Velma Veloria	D	Won	71%
State Legislature-District 21	Paul Shin	D	Won	58%
California				
State Legislature-District 3: Northern Sierra	Lon Hatamiya	D	Lost	41.8%
State Legislature-District 37: Oxnard	Nao Takasugi	R	Won	50.2%
State Legislature-District 49: Alhambra	Sophie Wong	R	Lost	39.75%

Source: Asian Week, November 6, 1992, pp. 4-5.

★ 837 ★

Candidates for U.S. House of Representative

Asian American candidates who ran for seats in the U.S. House of Representatives in 1992 by party affiliation and election outcome.

Office	Candidate	Party	Results	
U.S. House of Representatives			Outcome	Percent of vote
California				
District 5: Sacramento	Robert Matsui	D	Re-elected	68.9%
District 14: San Mateo County	Bill Quraishi	R	Lost	8.8%
District 15: Santa Clara/Saratoga	Norman Mineta	D	Re-elected	63.6%
District 16: San Jose to Gilroy	Amani Kuumba	P and F	Lost	6.1%
District 22: San Luis Obispo/Santa Barbara	Gloria Ochoa	D	Lost	35.4%
District 24: Thousand Oaks	San Korman	R	Lost in primary	23.7%
District 31: Alhambra	Nisar Hai	R	Lost in primary	34%
District 41: Yorba Linda/Chino	Jay Kim	R	Won	59.0%
District 43: Riverside	Mark Takano	D	Won	47.4%
Delaware				
District 1	S. B. Woo	D	Lost	43%
New York				
District 6: Queens	Dayanand Bhagvandin	R	Lost	19%
Texas				
District 25	Esther Yao, Ph.D.	R	Lost in primary	45%
Virginia				
District 11	Dr. Jay Khim	R	Lost in primary	NA

Source: Asian Week, November 6, 1992, pp. 4-5.

★ 838 ★

California Appointees, Administration of Governor Pete Wilson

Asian American state government officials appointed by Governor Pete Wilson as of March 15, 1993.

Agency or Department	Position	Appointee
Acupuncture Committee	Committee member	David Y.C. Chen
Acupuncture Committee	Committee member	Young D. Park
Advisory Committee on Juvenile Justice and Delinquency	Committee member	Will T. Deguchi
Advisory Committee on Juvenile Justice and Delinquency	Committee member	Roy M. Sumisaki
Agricultural Association, San Francisco	District 5, Association member	Albert C. Chang
Agricultural Association, Santa Cruz	District 14, Association member	Lillian C. Finnerty
Agricultural Association, Monterey	District 7	Frances F. Pabrua
Agricultural Association, San Joaquin	District 2	Ken Yasui
Agricultural Association., Orange	District 32	Gary Y Hayakawa
Agricutural Association, San Francisco (San Mateo)	District 1A	Karen H. Sakai
Alcoholic Beverage Control Appeals Board	Board member	John B. Tsu
Arts Council	Special Assistant to the Director	Anita B. Ahuja
Bay Conservation and Development Commission, San Francisco	Commission member	Henry Chang
Board of Dental Examiners of California	Board member	Stephen S. Yuen
Board of Governors of California Community Colleges	Board member	Larry G.S. Toy
Board of Governors of California Community Colleges	Board members	Julia Li Wu
Board of Registered Nursing	Board member	Kim D. Enomoto
Board of Vocational Nurse and Psychiatric Technician Examiners	Board member	Helen E. Lee
California Community Colleges Board of Governors	Board member	Paul M. Kim
California Environmental Protection Agency	Director of Communications	James J. Lee
California Environmental Protection Agency	Chief Counsel	William F. Soo Hoo
California Exposition and State Fair Board	Board member	George S. Oki
California Exposition and State Fair Board	Public Relations Mgr.	Judy A. Cantorna Tafoya
California Maritime Academy	Member, Board of Governors	Gloria S. Hom
California State Board of Pharmacy	Board member	Darlene F. Fujimoto
CaliforniaExposition and State Fair Board	Member, Board of Directors	Robert P. Cortes
Corrections, Mule Creek State Prison	Warden	Ivalee C.H. Henry
Criminal Justice Planning	Deputy Director, Administration	Eugene L. Balonon
Department of Consumer Affairs	Special Assistant	Lowayne Shieh
Department of Corrections	Construction Project Director	Vicki Lynn Yamamoto
Department of Housing and Community Development	Chief Deputy Director	Joan Kawada Chan
Department of of Rehabilitation,	Chief Deputy Director	Richard R. Bayquen
Department of Trade and Commerce	Executive Assistant to the Director	Ronald Lee
Employment Development Department	Chief Deputy Director	Alfred Ben Lee
Employment Development Department	Communications Specialist	Chiling Tong
Food and Agriculture Department	Liaison for the Department	John Nakamura
Fraud Assessment Commission	Commission member	Kenneth M. Fujino

[Continued]

★ 838 ★

California Appointees, Administration of Governor Pete Wilson (Continued)

Asian American state government officials appointed by Governor Pete Wilson as of March 15, 1993.

Agency or Department	Position	Appointee
Governor's Office	Deputy Director, Community Relations	Gary Lew
Governor's Office	Deputy Appointments Secretary	Ravinder Mehta
Governor's Office of Legislative Affairs		Patricia A. Fong
Governor's Office of Planning and Research		Judy Matsuo Caffrey
Governor's Office of Planning and Research		Victor A. Holanda
Local Government Technical Advisory Committee	Board member	Robert Hung Le
Medical Board of California	Board member	Stewart Hsieh
Medical Board of California	Board member	Mike Mirahmadi
Real Estate Industry	Consumer Liaison	Pablo Wong
Regents of the University of California	Board member	S. Stephen Nakashima
Small Business Development Board	Board member	Elizabeth Szu
Speech Pathology and Audiology Examining Committee	Committee member	Li-Rong L. Cheng
State Athletic Commission	Commission member	H. Andrew Kim
State Board of Barbering and Cosmetology	Board member	Jeanette O. Keaton
State Board of Education	Board member	Irene Chun-I Cheng
State Board of Education		Kyong Hwan P. Kim
State Board of Education	Board member	Dorothy J. Lee
State Board of Equalization	Board member	Matthew Kipling Fong
State Council on Developmental Disabilities	Council member	Thomas Hopkins
Stephen P. Teale Data Center	Director	Chong W. Ha
Student Aid Commission	Commission member	Vishwas D. More

Source: Asian Pacific American Political Education Foundation, San Francisco, CA, March 16, 1993.

★ 839 ★

Minnesota Appointees, Administration of Governor Arne H. Carlson

Appointments in Minnesota under the Administration of Governor Arne H. Carlson, as of March 15, 1993.

Agency or Department	Position	Appointee
Advisory Committee on Genetically Engineered Organisms	Committee member	David Andow
Advisory Council on Wells and Borings	Council member	Thomas Rosga
Alcohol and Drug Abuse Advisory Council	Council member	Nellie Spexet
Board of Abstractors	Board member	Tony N. Leung
Board of Accountancy	Board member	Shu-Ching Ng
Board of Accountancy	Board member	Kenneth Lau
Chemical Abuse Prevention Resource Council	Council member	Beverly Ellis
Children's Trust Fund Advisory Council	Council member	Yvonne Kwok
Children's Trust Fund Advisory Council	Council member	Nkajlo Vangh

[Continued]

★ 839 ★

Minnesota Appointees, Administration of Governor Arne H. Carlson (Continued)

Appointments in Minnesota under the Administration of Governor Arne H. Carlson, as of March 15, 1993.

Agency or Department	Position	Appointee
Council on Asian Pacific Minnesotans	Council members	Jennie Hsiao
		Jinmahn Kim
		Haruo Okazaki
		Renee Pan
		Cherian Puthiyottil
		Lynn Vorasarn
		Pat Siverhus
		Marisi Stromquist
		Tien-Van Tran
		Tong Vang
		Gary Liew
		Ophelia Balcos
Elementary-Secondary-Vocational Computer Council	Council member	Daniel Lai
Export Finance Authority	Member	Johnny Ip
Export Finance Authority	Member	Ching-Meng Chew
Governor's Advisory Committee on Appointments	Committee member	Paul J. Gam
Indian Elder Services Advisory Task Force	Task force member	Wayne Takeshita
Investment Advisory Council	Council member	Han-Chin Liu
Metropolitan Council	Council member	Patrick Leung
Metropolitan Waste Control Commission	Commission member	Roy Taylor
Minnesota Academic Excellence Foundation	Foundation member	Sharon Ming
Minnesota Board of Social Work	Board member	David Yiim
Minnesota Board on Aging	Board member	Mien F. Tchou
Minnesota Higher Education Facilities Authority	Member	Fred Hsiao
Minnesota Humanities Commission	Commission member	Ye Su
Minnesota Indian Scholarship Committee	Committee member	Richard Tanner
Minnesota World Trade Center Corporation	Member	Paul J. Gam
Minority Issues Advisory Committee	Committee member	Marlene Hui
Real Estate Appraiser Advisory Board	Board member	Addie H. Ng
Small Business Procurement Advisory Council	Council member	Hyon T. Kim
State Curriculum Advisory Committee	Committee member	Sumlee Beede
Subcommittee on Children's Mental Health	Subcommittee member	Decorah Mach
Task Force on Education and Employment Transitions	Task force member	Bonnie Rae Lowe

Source: Paul J. Gam, Governor's Advisory Committee on Appointments, Minneapolis, MN, March 18, 1993.

Judicial Officers

★ 840 ★

Federal Judicial Officers by Court and Race/Ethnicity

Number, percent, and percent change from 1986 to 1991 of total federal judicial officers by federal court system and race/ethnicity, as of September 30, 1991[a].

Court/status	Total	Race/Ethnicity				
		Asian	White	Black	Hispanic	American Indian
Total	1,477	9	1,352	71	44	1
Percent		0.6%	91.5%	4.8%	3.0%	0.1%
Circuit Courts[b]	156	1	141	9	5	-
Percent		0.5%	90.4%	5.8%	3.2%	0
District Courts[c]	555	4	490	38	24	1
Percent		0.7%	88.3%	6.5%	4.3%	0.2%
Bankruptcy Judges	294	1	280	9	4	-
Percent		0.3%	95.2%	3.1%	1.4%	0%
U.S. Magistrates						
Full-time	325	2	298	17	8	-
—Percent		0.5%	91.7%	5.2%	2.5%	0%
Part-time	143	1	138	-	3	-
—Percent		0.7%	97.2%	0%	2.1%	0%
Percent change						
1990 to 1991	-0.3%-	-10.0%-	-0.4%	1.4%	2.3%	0
1989 to 1991	1.5%	-18.2%	1.5%	1.4%	7.3%	-50.0%
1988 to 1991	-0.2%	25.0%	-0.1%	0	7.3%	-50.0%
1987 to 1991[d]	3.1%	-25.0%	3.5%	-1.4%	7.3%	-50.0%
1988 to 1991	5.6%	-18.2%	8.2%	-4.1%	12.8%	-50.0%

Source: Legislative and Public Affairs Office, *Annual Report on the Judiciary Equal Employment Opportunity Program* (Washington, DC: Administrative Office of the United States Courts, 1991). Data are for the twelve-month period ended September 30, 1991. Also in source: data on judicial officers by sex and the number of handicapped judicial officers. *Notes:* (a) Excludes judicial officers in senior status. (b) Includes the temporary emergency Court of Appeals. (c) Includes the Territorial Courts; Claims Court; Court of International Trade; Special Court, Regional Rail Reorganization Act of 1973; and Judicial Panel on Multidistrict Litigation. (d) 1987 figures reflect 15-month reporting period.

★ 841 ★

Judicial Officers by State

Judgeships held by Asian/Pacific Americans by state, as of 1990.

State	Asian/Pacific Americans
Arizona	2
Arkansas	2
California	46
Massachusetts	1
New York	2
Washington	4

Source: Selected from Asian Pacific American Municipal Officials (APAMO), *National Directory of Asian/Pacific American Elected and Appointed Officials* (Washington, DC: APAMO and National League of Cities, 1990).

Religion

★ 842 ★

Church Affiliation of Indochinese Refugees in Utah

Reported findings of a study of Indochinese refugee families resettled in Utah between 1975 and 1983.

Religion	In homeland		In United States	
	Number	Percent	Number	Percent
Buddhist	50	52.1%	32	33.7%
Traditional[a]	27	28.1%	18	18.9%
Catholic	7	7.3%	11	11.6%
Protestant	9	9.3%	7	7.3%
Latter Day Saints ("Mormon")	0	0	18	18.9%
None	2	2.1%	8	8.4%
Other	1	1.0%	1	1.0%
(Missing)			(1)	-

Source: Robert E. Lewis, et al., "Religiosity Among Indochinese Refugees in Utah," *Journal for the Scientific Study of Religion* 27, no. 2, p. 276. *Notes:* (a) Includes Confucianism, Taoism, Animism, and Ancestor Worship.

★ 843 ★

Shift in Church Affiliation of Indochinese Refugees

Reported findings of a study of Indochinese refugee families resettled in Utah between 1975 and 1983.

Religion	Gain	Loss	No change
Buddhist	-	17	32
Traditional[a]	1	10	17
Catholic	5	1	6
Latter Day Saints ("Mormon")	3	5	4
Protestant	3	5	4
None	8	2	-
Other	-	-	1
Totals	35	35	60

Source: Robert E. Lewis, et al. "Religiosity Among Indochinese Refugees in Utah," *Journal for the Scientific Study of Religion* 27, no. 2, p. 276. *Notes:* (a) Includes Confucianism, Taoism, Animism, and Ancestor Worship.

★ 844 ★

Presbyterian Congregations in the United States

Numbers of Asian congregations[a] affiliated with the Presbyterian Church (USA) by state and ethnic group, 1993.

Ethnic group	State	Number of congregations
Asian	California	1
Chinese	California	8
	Oregon	1
	New York	1
	Louisiana	1
Filipino	California	5
	Texas	1
	Illinois	1
Japanese	California	13
	Utah	2
	Illinois	1
	Pennsylvania	1
	Washington	1
Korean[a]		
Taiwanese	California	14
	Texas	5
	Michigan	3
	New Jersey	3
	Maryland	2
	Hawaii	1
	Illinois	1
	Kentucky	1
	Missouri	1
	Virginia	1
Vietnamese	California	3
	Illinois	1

Source: Presbyterian Church (USA), *Asian Church Directory* (Louisville, KY: Racial Ethnic Ministry, Presbyterian Church USA, March 1993, preliminary draft). Also in source: minister, address, and telephone number of each congregation. *Note:* (a) Excludes Korean congregations. See separate table, "Presbyterian Korean Congregations in the United States."

★ 845 ★

Presbyterian Korean Congregations in the United States

Numbers of Korean presbyteries and congregations[a] affiliated with the Presbyterian Church (USA) by regional group (synod), 1993.

Synod	States represented	Number of Presbyteries	Number of congregations
Northeast	Connecticut, Massachusetts, New Jersey, New York,	16	45
Trinity	Pennsylvania	5	12
Mid-Atlantic	Delaware, Maryland, North Carolina, Virginia	9	35
South Atlantic	Florida, Georgia, South Carolina	11	27
Living Waters	Alabama, Kentucky, Mississippi, Tennessee	8	14
Covenant	Michigan, Ohio	8	10
Lincoln Trails	Illinois, Indiana	6	21
Lakes and Prairies	Minnesota, Nebraska, North Dakota, Wisconsin	4	5
Mid-America	Kansas, Missouri	4	5
Sun	Louisiana, Oklahoma, Texas	6	20
Southwest	Arizona	2	4
Rocky Mountains	Colorado, Utah, Wyoming	5	7
Alaska/Northwest	Alaska, Washington	6	17
Pacific	California (part), Nevada, Oregon	8	23
Southern California and Hawaii	California (part), Hawaii	7	60

Source: Presbyterian Church (USA), *Korean Presbyternia Church Directory* (Louisville, KY: Racial Ethnic Ministry Unit, Presbyterian Church USA, 1993). Also in source: minister, address, and telephone number of each congregation, information on National Korean Presbyterian Council, National Korean Presbyterian Men, and National Korean Presbyterian Women. *Note:* (a) Excludes other Asian ethnic group congregations. See separate table, "Presbyterian Congregations in the United States."

★ 846 ★

Church Affiliation of Korean Americans, Philadelphia

Religious affiliation of Korean Americans in Philadelphia reported in 1988.

Religion	Number	Percent
Total	145	100%
Christianity	79	55%
Buddhism	1	1%
Other	6	4%
No religion	57	39%
Unknown	2	1%

Source: Jin H Yu, Ph.D., "Black-Korean Relationships in Philadelphia: A Korean Perspective," *The State of Intergroup Harmony - 1988* (Philadelphia, PA: Philadelphia Commission on Human Relations, 1988), p. 30. Primary source: Tong Soo Chung, "Roots and Assimilation," *Philip Jaisohn Memorial Papers No. 11* (Elkins Park, PA: Philip Jaisohn Memorial Foundation, 1981).

★ 847 ★

Church Affiliation of Korean Immigrants to the United States

Reported findings of a 1986 study of Church affiliation of Korean immigrants to the United States.

622 Korean immigrants (334 males and 288 females) were interviewed.

4.2% of the Korean immigrants were Buddhist.

52.6% were affiliated with Christian churches in Korea prior to immigration.

Of those not affiliated with a church in Korea, about half became affiliated with a church in the United States.

Total church affiliation after immigration increased significantly—from 52.6% to 76.8%.

Almost all of the respondents in this study attended Korean ethnic churches of various denominations.

Source: Won Moo Hurh and Kwang Chung Kim, "Religious Participation of Korean Immigrants in the United States," *Journal for the Scientific Study of Religion,* 29 (1), p. 24.

★ 848 ★

Church Denomination Affiliation of Korean Immigrants to the United States

Reported results of a 1986 study of church affiliation in Korea and in the United States by Korean immigrants to the United States.

Affiliation	In Korea		In United States	
	Number	Percent	Number	Percent
Protestants				
Presbyterian	160	48.9%	200	41.9%
Methodist	46	14.1%	65	13.6%
Holiness	15	4.6%	11	2.3%
Baptist	7	2.1%	20	4.2%
Evangelical	8	2.4%	25	5.3%
Seventh Day Adventist	9	2.8%	13	2.8%
Non-Denominational	14	4.3%	64	13.4%
Roman Catholic	66	20.2%	65	13.6%
American Churches	2	0.6%	14	2.9%
Totals	325	100.0%	477	100.0%

Source: Won Moo Hurh and Kwang Chung Kim, "Religious Participation of Korean Immigrants in the United States," *Journal for the Scientific Study of Religion* 29, no. 1 (1990): p. 24.

★ 849 ★

Church Participation of Korean Immigrants to the United States

Reported findings of a 1986 study comparing church participation by immigrants who were affiliated with a church prior to immigration and those who were not church-affiliated.

Participation	Church affiliates in Korea		Non-Church affiliates in Korea	
	Number	Percent	Number	Percent
Currently holding staff position (minister, elder, deacon, etc.)	89	27.9%	21	13.3%
Participating in church activities	113	35.4%	31	19.6%
Attending church at least once a week	266	83.4%	102	64.6%

Source: Won Moo Hurh and Kwang Chung Kim, "Religious Participation of Korean Immigrants in the United States," *Journal for the Scientific Study of Religion* 29, no. 1 (1990): p. 25.

★ 850 ★

Motivation for Church Participation
of Korean Immigrants to the United States

Reported findings of a survey to determine Korean immigrants' reasons for attending church.

Question/response	Percent responding
What are the main reasons for you to attend church? "to worship God, to strengthen faith, for eternal life and salvation, to encourage children's religious faith"	74%
"to see friends and meet with other Koreans"	13%
"personal comfort and peace of mind"	8%

Source: Won Moo Hurh and Kwang Chung Kim, "Religious Participation of Korean Immigrants in the United States," *Journal for the Scientific Study of Religion* 29, no. 1 (1990): p. 25.

Appendix

Terminology and Scope, Current Population Survey, U.S. Bureau of Census

Population coverage. The Current Population Survey of the U.S. Census Bureau includes the civilian noninstitutional population of the United States and approximately 952,000 members of the Armed Forces in the United States living off post or with their families on post, but excludes all other members of the Armed Forces. The poverty data also exclude unrelated individuals under 15 years of age. Poverty rates exclude inmates of institutions, Armed Forces members in barracks, and unrelated individuals under 15 years form the denominator as well as numerator.

Revised survey procedures. During the period from April 1984 through June 1985 the Census Bureau systematically introduced a new sample design for the Current Population Survey. The purposes of this new sample design are to update the sampling frame to the 1980 census base, to improve survey efficiency, and to improve the quality of the survey estimates. About 80% of the geographic areas selected for the new sampling frame were also included in the survey based on the 1970 census base.

Geographic regions. The four major regions of the United States for which data are presented in the Current Population Survey report represents groups of states as follows:

Northeast: Connecticut, Maine, Massachusetts, New Hampshire, New Jersey, New York, Pennsylvania, Rhode Island, and Vermont.

Midwest: Illinois, Indiana, Iowa, Kansas, Michigan, Minnesota, Missouri, Nebraska, North Dakota, Ohio, South Dakota, and Wisconsin.

South: Alabama, Arkansas, Delaware, District of Columbia, Florida, Georgia, Kentucky, Louisiana, Maryland, Mississippi, North Carolina, Oklahoma, South Carolina, Tennessee, Texas, Virginia, and West Virginia.

West: Alaska, Arizona, California, Colorado, Hawaii, Idaho, Montana, Nevada, New Mexico, Oregon, Utah, Washington, and Wyoming.

Metropolitan Areas in the U.S. Bureau of Census Surveys

Metropolitan Statistical Area. The population residing in Metropolitan Statistical Areas (MSAs) constitutes the metropolitan population. MSAs are defined by the U.S. Office of Management and Budget for use in the presentation of statistics by agencies of the federal government. An MSA is a geographic area consisting of a large population nucleus, together with adjacent communities which have a high degree of economic and social integration with that nucleus. The definitions specify a boundary around each large city so as to include most or all of its suburbs. Entire counties form the MSA building blocks, except in New England where cities and towns are used. The former term SMSA was changed to MSA in 1983.

An area qualifies for recognition as an MSA if (1) it includes a city of at least 50,000 population, or (2) it includes a U.S. Census Bureau-defined urbanized area with population of at least 50,000 with a total metropolitan population of at least 100,000 (75,000 in New England). In addition to the county containing the main city or urbanized area, an MSA may include other counties having strong commuting ties to the central county.

CMSA and PMSA. If specified conditions are met, certain large MSAs are designated as Consolidated MSAs (CMSAs) and divided into component Primary MSAs (PMSAs).

SMSA. This acronym for Standard Metropolitan Statistical Area was replaced with MSA (Metropolitan Statistical Area) in 1983.

Change in MSA definitions. In July 1985, the U. S. Census Bureau's Current Population Survey (CPS) began carrying the metropolitan statistical area definitions announced by the Office of Management and Budget on June 30, 1984. Figures published from the CPS in the early 1980s and throughout most of the 1970s referred to metropolitan areas as defined on the basis of the 1970 census. Since there are important differences in the population classified as metropolitan using the 1970 and 1984 definitions, comparisons should be avoided.

The new Current Population Survey metropolitan estimates have consistently been higher than independent estimates of the metropolitan population prepared by the U.S. Census Bureau; correspondingly, the new CPS nonmetropolitan estimates have been lower than the independent estimates. The apparent overestimation of metropolitan and underestimation of nonmetropolitan population in the CPS relative to the Census Bureau's independent estimates should be taken into account when using the data.

Nonmetropolitan areas. The territory outside Metropolitan Statistical Areas (MSAs) is referred to here as nonmetropolitan.

Central cities. The largest city in each MSA is always designated a "central city." There may be additional central cities if specified requirements designed to identify places of central character within the MSA are met. Although the largest central cities are generally included in the title of the MSA, there may be central cities that are not part of the title. The balance of the MSA outside the central city or cities often is regarded as equivalent to "suburbs."

Outside central cities. The territory outside central cities of metropolitan statistical areas but within MSAs is referred to here as "outside central cities."

Demographic Characteristics in the U.S. Bureau of Census Surveys

---

Age. The age classification is based on the age of the person at his last birthday.

Race. The race of individuals was identified by a question that asked for self-identification of the person's race. Respondents were asked to select their race from a flashcard listing racial groups.

The population is divided into three groups on the basis of race: "white," "black," and "other races." The term "other races" refers to that portion of the United States population that is neither white nor black. The "other races" category includes American Indian, Eskimo and Aleut; Asian and Pacific Islander; and any other specified race.

The category "Asian and Pacific Islander" includes persons who identify as either Asian or Pacific Islander. The Asian population includes persons who identify as Chinese, Filipino, Japanese, Asian Indian, Korean, Vietnamese, Cambodian, Hmong, Laotian, Thai, or Other Asians. Pacific Islander includes persons who identify as Hawaiian, Samoan, Guamanian, or Other Pacific Islanders.

Marital status. The marital status classification identifies four major categories: "never married," "married," "widowed," and "divorced." These terms refer to the marital status at the time of the enumeration.

The category "married" is further divided into "married, spouse present," "separated," and "other married, spouse absent." A person was classified as "married, spouse present" if the husband or wife was reported as a member of the household, even though he or she may have been temporarily absent on business or on vacation, visiting, in a hospital, etc., at the time of the enumeration. Persons reported as "separated" included those with legal separations, those living apart with intentions of obtaining a divorce, and other persons permanently or temporarily separated because of marital discord. The group "other married, spouse absent" included married persons living apart because either the husband or wife was employed and living at a considerable distance from home, was serving away from home in the Armed Forces, was residing in an institution, had moved to another area, or had a different place of residence for any other reason except separation as defined above.

Household. A household consists of all the persons who occupy a housing unit. A house, an apartment or other group of rooms, or a single room is regarded as a housing unit when it is occupied or intended for occupancy as separate living quarters; that is, when the occupants do not live and eat with any other persons in the structure and there is direct access from the outside or through a common hall.

A household includes the related family members and all the unrelated persons, if any, such as lodgers, foster children, wards, or employees who share the housing unit. A person living alone in a housing unit, or a group of unrelated persons sharing a housing unit as partners, is also counted as a household. The count of households excludes group quarters.

Head versus householder. Beginning with the 1980 Current Population Survey, the U.S. Census Bureau discontinued the use of the terms "head of household" and "head of family." Instead, the terms "householder" and "family householder" are used. Recent social changes have resulted in greater sharing of household responsibilities among the adult members, and therefore have made the term "head" increasingly inappropriate in the analysis of household and family data. Specifically, the Bureau has discontinued its longtime practice of always classifying the husband as the reference person (head) when he and his wife are living together.

Householder. The householder refers to the person (or one of the persons) in whose name the housing unit is owned or rented (maintained) or, if there is no such person, any adult member, excluding roomers, boarders, or paid employees. If the house if owned or rented jointly by a married couple, the householder may be either the husband or the wife. The person designated as the householder is the "reference person" to whom the relationship of all other household members, if any, is recorded.

Prior to 1980, the husband was always considered the householder in married-couple households. The number of householders is equal to the number of households. Also, the number of family householders is equal to the number of families.

Tenure. A housing unit is "owned" if the owner or co-owner lives in the unit, even if it is mortgaged or not fully paid for. A cooperative or condominium unit is "owned" only if the owner or co-owner lives in it. All other occupied units are classified as "rented," including units rented for cash rent and those occupied without payment of cash rent. Additional information on the housing characteristics of Asian and Pacific Islander households may be found in the American Housing Survey.

Family. A group of two persons or more (one of whom is the householder) related by birth, marriage, or adoption and residing together; all such persons (including related subfamily members) are considered as members of one family. Beginning with the 1980 Current Population Survey, unrelated subfamilies (referred to in the past as "secondary families") are no longer included in the count of families, nor are the members of unrelated subfamilies included in the count of the family members.

Family household. A family household is a household maintained by a family (as defined above), and any unrelated persons (unrelated subfamily members and/or secondary individuals) who may be residing there are included. The number of family households is equal to the number of families. The count of family household members differs from the count of family members, however, in that the family household members include all persons living in the household, whereas family members include only the householder and his/her relatives. See the definition of "family."

Married couple. A married couple, as defined for census purposes, is a husband and wife enumerated as members of the same household. The married couple may or may not have children living with them. The expression "husband-wife" or "married-couple" before the term "household " or "family " indicates that the household or family is maintained by a husband and wife. The number of married couples equals the count of married-couple families plus related and unrelated married-couple subfamilies.

Related children under 18 years of age. In a family, related children under 18 years of age include sons and daughters, including stepchildren and adopted children, of the householder and all other children in the household who are related to the householder by blood, marriage, or adoption.

Years of school completed. Data on years of school completed are derived from the combination of answers to questions concerning the highest grade of school attended by the person and whether or not that grade was finished. The questions of educational attainment apply only to progress in "regular" schools. Such schools included public, private, and parochial elementary and high schools (both junior and senior high), colleges, universities, and professional schools (whether day schools or night schools). Thus, regular schooling is that which may advance a person toward an elementary school certificate, a high school diploma, or a college, university, or professional school degree. Schooling in other than regular schools was counted only if the credits obtained were regarded as transferable to school in the regular school system.

The median years of school completed is defined as the value which divides the distribution into two equal groups, one having completed more schooling and one having completed less schooling than the median. These medians are expressed in terms of a continuous series of numbers representing years of school completed. For example, a median of 9.0 represents the completion of the first year of high school and a median of 13.0 means completion of the first year of college.

Labor force and employment status. The definitions of labor force and employment status relate to the population 15 years old and over.

Employed. Employed persons comprise (1) all civilians who, during the survey week, containing March 12, 1991 and 1990, did any work at all as paid employees or in their own business or profession, or on their own farm, or who worked 15 hours or more as unpaid workers on a farm or in a business operated by a member of the family and (2) all those who were not working but who had jobs or businesses from which they were temporarily absent because of illness, bad weather, vacation, or labor-management dispute, or because they were taking time off for personal reasons, whether or not they were paid by their employers for time off, and whether or not they were seeking other jobs. Excluded from the employed group are persons whose only activity consisted of work around the house (such as own-home housework, and painting or repairing own home) or volunteer work for religious, charitable, and similar organizations.

Unemployed. Unemployed persons are those civilians who, during the survey week containing March 12, 1991 and 1990, had no employment but were available for work and (1) had engaged in any specific job seeking activity within the past 4 weeks, such as registering at a public or private employment office, meeting with prospective employers, checking with friends or relatives, placing or answering advertisements, writing letters of application, or being on a union or professional register; (2) were waiting to be called back to a job from which they had been laid off; or (3) were waiting to report to a new wage or salary job within 30 days.

Labor force. Persons are classified as in the labor force if they were employed as civilians, unemployed, or in the Armed Forces during the survey week. The "civilian labor force" comprises all civilians classified as employed or unemployed.

Not in the labor force. All civilians 15 years and over who are not classified as employed or unemployed are defined as "not in the labor force." This group who are neither employed nor seeking work includes persons engaged only in own-home housework, who were attending school or were unable to work because of long-term physical or mental illness, persons who are retired or too old to work, seasonal workers for who the survey week fell in an off-season, and the voluntarily idle. Persons doing only unpaid family work (less than 15 hours during the specified week) are also classified as "not in the labor force."

Occupation. The data on occupation refer to the civilian job held longest during the income year. The data on occupation of employed persons refer to the civilian job held during the survey week. Persons employed at two or more jobs were reported in the job at which they worked the greatest number of hours during the week.

In 1980, the U.S. Census Bureau revised the Standard Occupational Classification System (SOC) for use in its tabulation program for the 1980 census and subsequent published reports on occupational data. Consequently, the new classification system was incorporated into the Current Population Survey (CPS) tabulation program in January 1983. While the new system provides comparability between the CPS and other data sources, it causes a break in continuity for all CPS series containing occupational data.

Differences between the 1970 and 1980 occupational systems affect classifications at all levels. Such commonly used identifiers as white-collar, blue-collar, professional and technical, craft workers, and operative occupations have been eliminated. These identifiers have been replaced with new categories which represent conceptual as well as language changes. Moreover, many of the components of the former groupings have been shifted to such an extent that they cannot be made to correspond readily to the new categories. For a more complete explanation and description of the changes from the old to new occupational classification system see the February 1983 issue of "Employment and Earnings" by the Bureau of Labor Statistics.

The occupation classification system developed for the 1980 census consists of 503 specific occupation categories arranged into six summary and 13 major occupation groups. The major occupation groups are combined in the Current Population Survey reports into six summary groups as follows:

> Managerial and professional specialty occupations
> Technical, sales, and administrative support occupations
> Service occupations
> Farming, forestry, and fishing occupations
> Precision production, craft, and repair occupations
> Operators, fabricators, and laborers

Year-round, full-time worker. A year round, full-time worker is one who worked primarily at full-time civilian jobs for 50 weeks or more during the preceding calendar year.

> *Class of worker* refers to the subdivision of workers into three groups: "wage and salary workers," "self-employed workers," and "unpaid family workers." The first group refers to persons working for wages, salaries, commissions, tips, pay "in kind," or at piece rate for a private employer or for any government unit. The second group refers to persons working without pay in a business operated by a member of the household to whom they are related by birth or marriage.

Income. For each person 15 years old and over in the sample, questions were asked on the amount of money income received in the preceding calendar year from each of the following sources: (1) money wages or salary; (2) net income from nonfarm self-employment; (3) net income from farm self-employment; (4) Social Security or railroad retirement; (5) Supplemental Security Income (SSI); (6) public assistance or welfare payments; (7) interest (on savings or other investments which pay interest); (8) dividends, income from estates or trusts, or net rental income; (9) veterans' payments or unemployment and worker's compensation; (10) private pensions or government employment pensions; (11) alimony or child support, regular contributions from persons not living in the household, and other periodic income.

It should be noted that although the income statistics refer to receipts during the preceding calendar year, the demographic characteristics, such as age, labor force status, and family or household composition are as of the survey date. The income of the family does not include amounts received by persons who were members of the family during all or part of the income year if these persons no longer resided with the family at the time of the enumeration. However, family income includes amounts reported by related persons who did not reside with the family during the income year but who were members of the family at the time of enumeration.

Data on "consumer income" collected in the Current Population Survey by the U.S. Census Bureau cover money income received (exclusive of certain money receipts such as capital gains) before payments for personal income taxes, Social Security, union dues, Medicare deductions, etc. Therefore, money income does not reflect the fact that some families receive part of their income in the form of noncash benefits such as food stamps, health benefits, and subsidized housing and energy assistance; that some farm families receive noncash benefits in the form of rent-free housing and goods produced and consumed on the farm; or the noncash benefits are also received by some non-farm residents which often take the form of the use of business transportation and facilities, full or partial payments by business for retirement programs, medical and educational expenses, etc. These elements should be considered when comparing income levels. Moreover, readers should be aware that for many different reasons there is a tendency in household surveys for respondents to underreport their income. From an analysis of independently derived income estimates, it has been determined that income earned from wages or salaries is much better reported than other sources of income, and is nearly equal to independent estimates of aggregate income.

Total money income. This is defined as the algebraic sum of money wages and salaries, net income from self-employment, and income other than earnings. The total income of a family is the algebraic sum of the amounts received by all income recipients in the family.

The income tables for families include, in the lowest income group (under $2,500) those who were classified as having no income in the income year and those reporting a loss in net income from farm and nonfarm self-employment or in rental income. Some of these were living on income "in-kind," savings, or gifts, or were newly-constituted families. However, other families or unrelated individuals who reported no income probably had some money income which was not recorded in the survey.

Total money earnings. The algebraic sum of money wages or salary and net income from farm and nonfarm self-employment. For a detailed explanation, see Current Population Reports, Series P-60, No. 174, *Money Income of Households, Families, and Persons in the United States: 1990.*

Number of earners. This includes all persons in the household with one dollar or more in wages and salaries, or one dollar or more (or a loss) in net income from farm or nonfarm self-employment.

Per capita income. Per capita income is the mean income computed for every man, woman, and child in a particular group. It is derived by dividing the total income of a particular group by the total population in that group (excluding patients or inmates in institutional quarters).

Poverty. Families and unrelated individuals are classified as being above or below the poverty level using the poverty index originated at the Social Security Administration in 1964 and revised by Federal Interagency Committees in 1969 and 1980. The poverty index is based solely on money income and does not reflect the fact that many low-income persons receive noncash benefits such as food stamps, Medicaid, and public housing. The index is based on the Department of Agriculture's 1961 Economy Food Plan and reflects the different consumption requirements of families based on their size and composition. It was determined from the Department of Agriculture's 1955 Survey of Food Consumption that families of three or more persons spend approximately one-third of their income on food; the poverty level for these families was, therefore, set at three times the cost of the Economy Food Plan. For smaller families and persons living alone, the cost of the Economy Food Plan was multiplied by factors that were slightly higher in order to compensate for the relatively larger fixed expenses of these smaller households. The poverty thresholds are updated every year to reflect changes in the Consumer Price Index (CPI). The average poverty threshold for a family of four was $13,359 in 1990. For a detailed explanation of the poverty definition, see Current Population Reports, Series P-060, No. 175, *Poverty in the United States: 1990*.

Median. The median is presented in connection with the data on age, years of school completed, earnings, and income. It is the value which divides the distribution into two equal parts, one-half of the cases exceeding this value. The median income for families is based on all families. The median income for persons is based on persons with income.

Bibliography

Asian Americans and Asian Canadians—General

Asians in America: A Selected Annotated Bibliography—Expansion and Revision. Davis: University of California, Asian American Studies, 1983. Annotated bibliography on historical and sociological writings.

Chan, Sucheng. *Asian Americans: An Interpretive History*. Boston: Twayne Publishers, 1991. Comprehensive history of Asian Americans in the United States. Includes list of films about the Asian American experience, a chronology of Asian American history from 1600 to 1989, and a bibliographic essay describing available works for those interested in further research.

Fawcett, James T. and Benjamin V. Carino. *Pacific Bridges: The New Immigration from Asia and the Pacific Islands*. New York: Center for Migration Studies, 1987.

Furtaw, Julia C., ed. *Asian American Information Directory*. Detroit: Gale Research, 1990.

Hsia, Jayjia. *Asian American in Higher Education and at Work*. Hillsdale, NJ: Lawrence Erlbaum Assoc., Publishers, 1988. A 218-page book reporting on education and employment trends in the 1980s. 83 tables, 11 pages of references.

Hune, Shirley. *Pacific Migration to the United States: Trends and Themes in Historical and Sociological Literature*. Washington, DC: Research Institute on Immigration and Ethnic Studies, 1977.

Kim, Hyung-chan, ed. *Dictionary of Asian American History*. Westport, CN: Greenwood Press, 1986. Entries by various authors on a range of topics.

Kim, Hyung-chan, ed. *Asian American Studies: An Annotated Bibliography and Research Guide*. Westport, CN: Greenwood Press, 1989. Bibliography on historical and sociological writings, especially for Asian American studies programs.

Kitano, Harry H. L. and Roger Daniels. *Asian Americans: Emerging Minorities*. Englewood Cliffs, NJ: Prentice Hall, 1988. 195-page book covering Chinese, Japanese, Korean, Filipino, Asian Indians, Southeast Asians, and Pacific Islanders, with appendix of tables of 1980 U.S. census data, and suggestions for further reading.

Knoll, Tricia. *Becoming Americans: Asian Sojourners, Immigrants, and Refugees in the Western United States*. Portland, OR: Coast to Coast Books, 1982.

Lee, Joann Faung Jean. *Asian American Experiences in the United States: Oral Histories of First to Fourth Generation Americans from China, the Philippines, Japan, India, the Pacific Islands, Vietnam, and Cambodia*. Jefferson, NC: McFarland and Co., Inc., Publishers, 1991.

Lieberson, Stanley and Mary C. Waters. *From Many Strands: Ethnic and Racial Groups in Contempo-

rary America. New York: Russell Sage Foundation, 1988. From *The Population of the United States in the 1980s: A Census Monograph Series.* A 268-page book examining trends in ethnic and racial composition in the U.S., based on data from the 1980 Census. 51 tables, bibliography.

Poon, Wei-Chi. *A Guide for Establishing Asian American Core Collections.* Berkeley: University of California Asian American Studies, 1988.

Roy, Patricia E. "'White Canada Forever': Two Generations of Studies." *Canadian Ethnic Studies* XI, no. 2 (1979).

Takaki, Ronald. *Strangers from a Different Shore: A History of Asians Americans.* Boston: Little, Brown and Company, 1989. A 570. book recounting history of Chinese, Japanese, Koreans, Asian Indians, Filipinos, and Southeast Asians, with extensive reference notes and index.

Ward, W. Peter. *White Canada Forever: Popular Attitudes and Public Policy towards Orientals in British Columbia.* Montreal, 1978. Introduction to white response to Asians in Canada through 1941.

Chinese

Chan, Anthony B. *Gold Mountain: The Chinese in the New World.* Vancouver, BC: New Star, 1982. Reports the author's own family experience and focuses on the 1970s.

Chan, Sucheng. *This Bittersweet Soil: The Chinese in California Agriculture, 1860-1910.* Berkeley and Los Angeles: University of California Press, 1986.

Chinn, Thomas W. *Bridging the Pacific: San Francisco's Chinatown and Its People.* San Francisco: Chinese Historical Society of America, 1989.

Con, Harry and Ronald J. Con, et al. *From China to Canada: A History of the Chinese Communities in Canada.* Toronto, 1982.

Daniels, Roger. *Asian America: Chinese and Japanese in the U.S. since 1850.* Seattle: University of Washington Press, 1988.

Glick, Clarence E. *Sojourners and Settlers: Chinese Immigrants in Hawaii.* Honolulu: University of Hawaii Press, 1980.

Great Basin Foundation, ed. *Wong Ho Leun: An American Chinatown.* San Diego: Great Basin Foundation, 1988. This study deals with the Chinese settlement in Riverside, California.

Lai, Him Mark. *A History Reclaimed: An Annotated Bibliography of Chinese Language Materials on the Chinese of America.* Los Angeles, 1986.

Lydon, Sandy. *Chinese Gold: The Chinese in the Monterey Bay Area.* Capitola, CA: Capitola Book Company, 1985.

Lyman, Stanford M. *Chinese Americans.* New York: Random House, 1974.

Mark, Diane Mei Lin. *A Place Called Chinese America.* Dubuque, IA: Kendall/Hunt. A history of Chinese in America prepared under the sponsorship of Organization of Chinese Americans.

Minnick, Sylvia Sun. *Samfow: The San Joaquin Chinese Legacy.* Fresno: Panorama West, 1988.

Posner, Gerald L. *Warlords of Crime: Chinese Secret Societies—The New Mafia.* New York: McGraw-

Hill Book Co., 1988. 261-pages. book on Triads, the Chinese secret societies, with 14 pages. bibliography.

Tan, Jin and Patricia E. Roy. *The Chinese in Canada*. Ottawa: Canadian Historial Society, 1985. A 24-page booklet describing the Chinese population segment in Canada.

Tsai, Shih-san Henry. *The Chinese Experience in America*. Bloomington, IN: Indiana University Press, 1986.

Wong, Bernard. *Patronage, Brokerage, Entrepreneurship and The Chinese Community of New York*. New York: AMS Press, 1988.

Yee, Paul. *Salt Water* City. History of Chinese in Vancouver.

Yung, Judy. *Chinese Women of America: A Pictorial History*. Seattle: University of Washington Press, 1986.

Filipino

Alcantara, Ruben R. *Sakada: Filipino Adaptation in Hawaii*. Washington, DC: University Press of America, 1981.

Bulosan, Carlos. *America Is in the Heart*. Seattle: University of Washington Press, 1973.

Mangiafico, Luciano. *Contemporary American Immigrants: Patterns of Filipino, Korean, and Chinese Settlement in the United States*. New York: Praeger, 1988.

Teodoro, Luis V., Jr., ed.. *Out of This Struggle: The Filipinos in Hawaii*. Honolulu: University of Hawaii Press, 1981.

Asian Indian

Chandrasekhar, S., ed. *From India to America*. La Jolla, CA: Population Institute, 1984.

Gibson, Margaret. *Accommodation without Assimilation: Sikh Immigrants in an American High School,* 1988.

Jensen, Joan M. *Passage from India: Asian Indian Immigrants in North America*. New Haven and London: Yale University Press, 1988. A 350-page. book with extensive notes, selected bibliography, and listing of unpublished sources and court cases.

La Brack, Bruce. *The Sikhs of Northern California, 1904-1975*. New York: AMS Press, 1988.

Leonard, Karen. *Ethnic Choices: California's Punjabi-Mexican Americans, 1910-1980*. Philadelphia: Temple University Press, 1991.

Saran, Parmata. *The Asian Indian Experience in the United States*. Cambridge, MA: Schenkman, 1985.

Singh, Jane. *South Asians in North America: An Annotated and Selected Bibliography*. Berkeley: Center for South and South Asian Studies, 1988.

Japanese

Adachi, Ken. *The Enemy that Never Was: A History of the Japanese Canadians*. Toronto, 1976. Emphasis on the 1940s.

Conroy, Hilary and T. Scott Miyakawa, eds. *East across the Pacific: Historical and Sociological Studies of Japanese Immigration and Assimilation*. Santa Barbara, CA: ABC-Clio Press, 1972.

Daniels, Roger. *Asian America: Chinese and Japanese in the Unites States Since 1850*. Seattle: University of Washington Press, 1988.

Daniels, Roger. *Concentration Camps, North America: Japanese in the United States and Canada During World War II*. Melbourne, FL: Krieger, 1981.

Ichioka, Yuji. *The Issei: The World of the First Generation Japanese Immigrants, 1885-1924*. New York: Free Press, 1989.

Kitano, Harry H. L. *Japanese Americans: The Evolution of a Subculture*. Englewood Cliffs, NJ: Prentice-Hall, 1969.

Kimura, Yukiko. *Issei: Japanese Immigrants in Hawaii*. Honolulu: University of Hawaii Press, 1988.

LaViolette, F.E. *The Canadian Japanese and World War II: A Social and Psychological Account*. Toronto, 1948. Examines the wartime crisis in the Japanese Canadian community.

Lukes, Timothy J. and Gary Y. Okihiro. *Japanese Legacy: Farming and Community Life in California's Santa Clara Valley*. Cupertino: California History Center, 1985.

Niiya, Brian, ed. *Japanese American History: An A-to-Z Reference from 1868 to the Present*. New York: Facts On File, 1993.

Noda, Kesa. *Yamato Colony, 1906-1960: Livingston, California*. Livingston: Japanese American Citizens League, 1981.

Petersen, William. *Japanese Americans: Oppression and Success*. New York: Random House, 1971.

Walls, Thomas K. *The Japanese Texans*. San Antonio: Institute of Texas Cultures, University of Texas, 1987.

Ward, W. Peter. *The Japanese in Canada*. Ottawa: Canada Historical Association, Booklet No. 3, 1982. A 21-page booklet describing the Japanese population in Canada.

Korean

Choy, Bong-youn. *Koreans in America*. Chicago: Nelson-Hall, 1979.

Hurh, Won Moo, et al. *Assimilation Patterns of Immigrants in the United States: A Case Study of Korean Immigrants in the Chicago Area*. Washington, DC: University Press of America, 1978.

Kim, Hyung-chan, ed. *The Korean Diaspora*. Santa Barbara, CA: ABC–Clio Press, 1977.

Yoo, Jay Kun. *The Koreans in Seattle*. Elkins Park, PA: Philip Jaisohn Memorial Foundation, 1979.

Kim, Illsoo. *New Urban Immigrants: The Korean Community in New York*. Princeton, NJ: Princeton University Press, 1981.

Pacific Islanders

Macpherson, Cluny, Bradd Shore, and Robert Franco, eds. *New Neighbors: Islanders in Adaptation.* Santa Cruz, CA: University of California, 1978.

Vietnamese, Cambodian, Laotian, and Hmong

Caplan, Nathan, et al. *The Boat People and Achievement in America: A Study of Family Life, Hard Work, and Cultural Values.* Ann Arbor: University of Michigan Press, 1989.

Criddle, Joan and Teeda Butt Mam. *To Destroy You Is No Loss: The Odyssey of a Cambodian Family.* New York: Atlantic Monthly Press, 1987.

Downing, Bruce T. and Douglas P. Olney, eds. *The Hmong in the West: Observations and Reports.* Minneapolis: University of Minnesota Center for Urban and Regional Affairs, 1982.

Espiritu, Yen Le. *Vietnamese in America: An Annotated Bibliography of Materials in Los Angeles and Orange County Libraries.* Los Angeles: Asian American Studies Center, 1988.

Freeman, James A. *Hearts of Sorrow: Vietnamese-American Lives.* Stanford, CA: Stanford University Press, 1989.

Gim, W. and T. Litwin. *Indochinese Refugees in American: Profiles of Five Communities.* Washington, DC: U.S. State Department, 1980.

Haines, David W. *Refugees as Immigrants: Cambodians, Laotians and Vietnamese in America.* Totowa, NJ: Rowman and Littlefield, 1989.

Hayslip, Le Ly (with Jay Wurts). *When Heaven and Earth Changed Places: A Vietnamese Woman's Journey from War to Peace.* New York: Doubleday, 1989.

Hendricks, Glenn, ed. *The Hmong in Transition.* Staten Island, NY: Center for Migration Studies, 1985.

Kelly, Gail. *From Vietnam to American: A Chronicle of the Vietnamese Immigrants to the United States.* Boulder, CO: Westview Press, 1978.

Loescher, Gil and John A. Scanlan. *Calculated Kindness: Refugees and America's Half-Open Door, 1945 to the Present.* New York: Free Press, 1986.

Liu, William T. *Transition to Nowhere: Vietnamese Refugees in America.* Nashville, TN: Charter House, 1979.

May, Someth. *Cambodian Witness: The Autobiography of Someth May.* New York: Random House, 1986.

Montero, Darrel. *Vietnamese Americans: Patterns of Resettlement and Socioeconomic Adaptation in the Unites States.* Boulder, CO: Westview Press, 1977.

Muir, Karen L. *The Strongest Part of the Family: A Study of Lao Refugee Women in Columbus, Ohio.* New York: AMS Press, 1988.

Ngor, Haing (with Roger Warner). *Haing Ngor: A Cambodian Odyssey.* New York: MacMillan, 1987.

Quincy, Keith H. *Hmong: History of a People.* Cheney: Eastern Washington University Press, 1988.

Strand, Paul J. and Woodrow Jones, Jr. *Indochinese Refugees in America*. Durham, NC: Duke University Press, 1985.

Szymusial, Molyda. *The Stones Cry Out: A Cambodian Childhood, 1975-1980*. New York: Hill & Wang, 1986.

Tepper, Elliot L., ed. *Southeast Asia Exodus: From Transition to Resettlement*. Ottawa, 1980. Provides insights into the refugee crisis and problems of resettlement in Canada.

Wain, Barry. *The Refused: The Agony of the Indochina Refugees*. New York: Simon and Schuster, 1982.

Yathay, Pin. *Stay Alive, My Son*. New York: Free Press, 1987.

Index

A

Page numbers, p. NNN, are followed by table numbers in brackets, [t. NNN].

Page numbers, p. NNN, are followed by table numbers in brackets, [t. NNN].

B

C

Page numbers, p. NNN, are followed by table numbers in brackets, [t. NNN].

Page numbers, p. NNN, are followed by table numbers in brackets, [t. NNN].

Page numbers, p. NNN, are followed by table numbers in brackets, [t. NNN].

Page numbers, p. NNN, are followed by table numbers in brackets, [t. NNN].

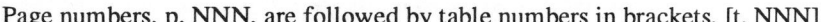

Page numbers, p. NNN, are followed by table numbers in brackets, [t. NNN].

Page numbers, p. NNN, are followed by table numbers in brackets, [t. NNN].

Page numbers, p. NNN, are followed by table numbers in brackets, [t. NNN].

Page numbers, p. NNN, are followed by table numbers in brackets, [t. NNN].

I

Page numbers, p. NNN, are followed by table numbers in brackets, [t. NNN].

Page numbers, p. NNN, are followed by table numbers in brackets, [t. NNN].

K

Page numbers, p. NNN, are followed by table numbers in brackets, [t. NNN].

Page numbers, p. NNN, are followed by table numbers in brackets, [t. NNN].

Page numbers, p. NNN, are followed by table numbers in brackets, [t. NNN].

Page numbers, p. NNN, are followed by table numbers in brackets, [t. NNN].

Page numbers, p. NNN, are followed by table numbers in brackets, [t. NNN].

Page numbers, p. NNN, are followed by table numbers in brackets, [t. NNN].

Index

Page numbers, p. NNN, are followed by table numbers in brackets, [t. NNN].

Page numbers, p. NNN, are followed by table numbers in brackets, [t. NNN].

Page numbers, p. NNN, are followed by table numbers in brackets, [t. NNN].